L
Au

"Lighthearted and sophisticated, informative and fun to read. *[Let's Go]* helps the novice traveler navigate like a knowledgeable old hand."

—Atlanta Journal-Constitution

"The guides are aimed not only at young budget travelers but at the independent traveler, a sort of streetwise cookbook for traveling alone."

—The New York Times

Let's Go writers travel on your budget.

"Retains the spirit of the student-written publication it is: candid, opinionated, resourceful, amusing info for the traveler of limited means but broad curiosity." ***—Mademoiselle***

"The writers seem to have experienced every rooster-packed bus and lunar-surfaced mattress about which they write." ***—The New York Times***

"All the dirt, dirt cheap." ***—People***

Great for independent travelers.

"A world-wise traveling companion—always ready with friendly advice and helpful hints, all sprinkled with a bit of wit." ***—The Philadelphia Inquirer***

"Lots of valuable information for any independent traveler."

—The Chicago Tribune

Let's Go is completely revised each year.

"Unbeatable: good sight-seeing advice; up-to-date info on restaurants, hotels, and inns; a commitment to money-saving travel; and a wry style that brightens nearly every page." ***—The Washington Post***

"Its yearly revision by a new crop of Harvard students makes it as valuable as ever." ***—The New York Times***

All the important information you need.

"Enough information to satisfy even the most demanding of budget travelers...*Let's Go* follows the creed that you don't have to toss your life's savings to the wind to travel—unless you want to."

—The Salt Lake Tribune

"Value-packed, unbeatable, accurate, and comprehensive."

—The Los Angeles Times

Let's Go Publications

Let's Go: Alaska & the Pacific Northwest 1998
Let's Go: Australia 1998 **New title!**
Let's Go: Austria & Switzerland 1998
Let's Go: Britain & Ireland 1998
Let's Go: California 1998
Let's Go: Central America 1998
Let's Go: Eastern Europe 1998
Let's Go: Ecuador & the Galápagos Islands 1998
Let's Go: Europe 1998
Let's Go: France 1998
Let's Go: Germany 1998
Let's Go: Greece & Turkey 1998
Let's Go: India & Nepal 1998
Let's Go: Ireland 1998
Let's Go: Israel & Egypt 1998
Let's Go: Italy 1998
Let's Go: London 1998
Let's Go: Mexico 1998
Let's Go: New York City 1998
Let's Go: New Zealand 1998 **New title!**
Let's Go: Paris 1998
Let's Go: Rome 1998
Let's Go: Southeast Asia 1998
Let's Go: Spain & Portugal 1998
Let's Go: USA 1998
Let's Go: Washington, D.C. 1998

Let's Go Map Guides

Berlin
Boston
Chicago
London
Los Angeles
Madrid
New Orleans
New York City
Paris
Rome
San Francisco
Washington, D.C.

Coming Soon: Amsterdam, Florence

Let's Go Publications

Let's Go Australia 1998

Bentsion R. Harder
Editor

M. Allison Arwady
Associate Editor

Amanda C. Rawls
Associate Editor

St. Martin's Press New York

HELPING LET'S GO

If you want to share your discoveries, suggestions, or corrections, please drop us a line. We read every piece of correspondence, whether a postcard, a 10-page email, or a coconut. Please note that mail received after May 1998 may be too late for the 1999 book, but will be kept for future editions. **Address mail to:**

Let's Go: Australia
67 Mount Auburn Street
Cambridge, MA 02138
USA

Visit Let's Go at **http://www.letsgo.com,** or send email to:

fanmail@letsgo.com
Subject: "Let's Go: Australia"

In addition to the invaluable travel advice our readers share with us, many are kind enough to offer their services as researchers or editors. Unfortunately, our charter enables us to employ only currently enrolled Harvard-Radcliffe students.

Distributed outside the USA and Canada by Macmillan.

ISBN: 0-312-16880-2

First edition
10 9 8 7 6 5 4 3 2 1

Let's Go: Australia is written by Let's Go Publications, 67 Mount Auburn Street, Cambridge, MA 02138, USA.

Printed in the USA on recycled paper with biodegradable soy ink.

ADVERTISING DISCLAIMER

All advertisements appearing in Let's Go publications are sold by an independent agency not affiliated with the production of the guides. Advertisers are never given preferential treatment, and the guides are researched, written, and published independent of advertising. Advertisements do not imply endorsement of products or services by Let's Go. If you are interested in purchasing advertising space in a Let's Go publication, contact: Let's Go Advertising Sales, 67 Mount Auburn St., Cambridge, MA 02138, USA.

Contents

Maps

About Let's Go

THIRTY-EIGHT YEARS OF WISDOM

Back in 1960, a few students at Harvard University banded together to produce a 20-page pamphlet offering a collection of tips on budget travel in Europe. This modest, mimeographed packet, offered as an extra to passengers on student charter flights to Europe, met with instant popularity. The following year, students traveling to Europe researched the first, full-fledged edition of *Let's Go: Europe,* a pocket-sized book featuring honest, irreverent writing and a decidedly youthful outlook on the world. Throughout the 60s, our guides reflected the times; the 1969 guide to America led off by inviting travelers to "dig the scene" at San Francisco's Haight-Ashbury. During the 70s and 80s, we gradually added regional guides and expanded coverage into the Middle East and Central America. With the addition of our in-depth city guides, handy map guides, and extensive coverage of Asia and Australia, the 90s are also proving to be a time of explosive growth for Let's Go, and there's certainly no end in sight. The first editions of *Let's Go: Australia* and *Let's Go: New Zealand* hit the shelves this year, expanding our coverage to six continents, and research for next year's series has already begun.

We've seen a lot in 38 years. *Let's Go: Europe* is now the world's bestselling international guide, translated into seven languages. And our new guides bring Let's Go's total number of titles, with their spirit of adventure and their reputation for honesty, accuracy, and editorial integrity, to 40. But some things never change: our guides are still researched, written, and produced entirely by students who know first-hand how to see the world on the cheap.

HOW WE DO IT

Each guide is completely revised and thoroughly updated every year by a well-traveled set of over 200 students. Every winter, we recruit over 140 researchers and 60 editors to write the books anew. After several months of training, Researcher-Writers hit the road for seven weeks of exploration, from Anchorage to Adelaide, Estonia to El Salvador, Iceland to Indonesia. Hired for their rare combination of budget travel sense, writing ability, stamina, and courage, these adventurous travelers know that train strikes, stolen luggage, food poisoning, and marriage proposals are all part of a day's work. Back at our offices, editors work from spring to fall, massaging copy written on Himalayan bus rides into witty yet informative prose. A student staff of typesetters, cartographers, publicists, and managers keeps our lively team together. In September, the collected efforts of the summer are delivered to our printer, who turns them into books in record time, so that you have the most up-to-date information available for your vacation. And even as you read this, work on next year's editions is well underway.

WHY WE DO IT

We don't think of budget travel as the last recourse of the destitute; we believe that it's the only way to travel. Living cheaply and simply brings you closer to the people and places you've been saving up to visit. Our books will ease your anxieties and answer your questions about the basics—so you can get off the beaten track and explore. Once you learn the ropes, we encourage you to put *Let's Go* down now and then to strike out on your own. As any seasoned traveler will tell you, the best discoveries are often those you make yourself. When you find something worth sharing, drop us a line. We're Let's Go Publications, 67 Mount Auburn St., Cambridge, MA 02138, USA (email: fanmail@letsgo.com).

HAPPY TRAVELS

Acknowledgments

Thanks to: Emily "Prom Postie" Stebbins, Luis "West Island" Campos, Monica "Feed Me" Eav, and Nick "Cap't Climate" Corman. To Anne Chisholm, for her sage advice. To Emily B., Elena, and our many typists. To Julia Palmour for days in the library and in our files. To Derek McKee for help with maps, Cillin Perera for movies, and everyone else who pitched in at the end. To Dave Collins for seeing us through from beginning to end. We wouldn't have had Buckley's chance without you.—**Team Oz**

Allison & Amanda, your judgment and tireless energy guided this to the end. Monica, thanks for taking my hand. Without you, there'd be no *Australia,* and my back would be awfully tight. Thanks: Katie, Carolyn, & Amahl for dancing at Ryles. My far-ranging 'mates Marc, Josh, Dan, & Dave. The *LG* folks (Dave C, Pai, Vivek, Pooja, Nick, & all) for foodfests, Fun Day and four-square. My parents for breath, words, and wanderlust. And Jessica, journey forth with my everlasting love (and a good travel guide).—**BRH**

So many thanks to Ben and Amanda for laughs, dedication, and phone code inspiration. To NZ for bells and whistles. To Vandana for grilled cheese and Sisi. To Kristy for endless postcards and the couch. To Joseph for amazing food and welcome distraction. To Erica for Mondays and terrific summer planning. To Anne for support—last-minute typing and otherwise. To Erika for a friendship without letters and a great Aug. weekend. To Mom, Dad, Meredith, Rand and Abbey for all I do not say.—**MAA**

A huge thanks to Ben for keeping things in perspective, Allison for keeping us laughing and never losing speed. To Monica, my role model. To Mom & Dad for getting me there. To Krzysiu for encouraging me and making tea. To Chris Kohn for the music, and Cherry Collins for a last-hour summary of... everything. Dave, I never would've or could've done it without you. Thanks for the late-night chats, last minute edits, and continual support. Let's go back together some time.—**ACR**

Researcher-Writers

Without precedent or example, this army of seasoned travel-writers marched out in high spirits. Last minute alterations of itineraries, more than a few flat tires, a flipped vehicle, a near miss, and a 'roo or two later, the resolute force finally triumphed, planting the Let's Go flag firmly on the soil of the southern hemisphere. The travel guide industry will never be the same, thanks to them. Thanks to it, nor will they.

Avril Alba *South Australia*

With the eye of an insider-outsider, Avril returned home to stately Adelaide to capture its cafes and parklands with her upbeat wit, scoring early in the bookteam's postcard contest with a convincing reminder not to import fruit. She tried valiantly from the day dot to lead Let's Go into the age of the laptop and saved us some typing, while unknowingly providing invaluable assistance with our 'Strine glossary. Her educational background manifested itself in her writing, lifting our spirits and cheering our souls, and her enthusiasm for her home state carried over into her copy! Avril continued with the job when it would have been tough for others to go on. We admire her strength and thank her for South Australia, and for the Minties.

Rucker Alex *Brisbane, southern Queensland, and northern NSW*

Rucker's enthusiasm and commitment to her job rubbed off on her editors, if not on NSW tourist officials. She charmed her way into photo-ops with Bengal tigers and free rides to national parks several days' walk off her itinerary (we don't doubt she would have walked if she'd had to). Supplementing her copy with from-the-heart essays and photos that broadened our view of "scenery," she numbered the mozzies, introduced us to the locals, and warned us away from red. As we in Cambridge set to work on her voluminous copy, our ears rang with her callsign, "I love Australia!" Not satisfied to call the job done as she boarded her plane, Rucker returned home to hone her copy into prose as beautiful as red raspberries.

Steven Japangardi Berbeco *Tropical and outback Queensland*

Neither incognito nor incommunicado, Steven constantly mystified us with emails and regaled us with tales of cocktails. Dashing through tropical Queensland and its sub-zero outback (hope your toothpaste thaws in time for those custard apples!), Steven found time to discover the most interesting spots to fall out of the sky, while his copy kept us laughing out loud. With a knack for encountering the unusual, Steven braved haunted hostels, aneuploidy toilet facilities, and even a late-night dance lesson with a mother-daughter con team. This paragon of virtue deftly extricated himself from every situation and rumbled on toward the smokestacks of Mount Isa, taking a moment to teach us a little Warlpiri on the side.

Josh Berson *Western Australia*

A flash in the sun as he sped down this highway or that, vociferously denouncing the inefficacious means of traversing the monoclines, Josh paused only long enough to grant interviews to a pastiche of radio stations and newspapers, spreading the Let's Go gospel along his ambit from the penumbral outback to littoral paradises in hot pursuit of our competition. Bearing a nimbus of chivalry, Josh gave lifts to mysterious, bare-footed strangers despite their putative hebephrenia, and had the chutzpah to dispense promises of grape-frosted pop tarts throughout the provinces. Between drives, he paused to toil over a plethora of palimpsests that were entertaining and insightful, never grisaille, and kept our well-worn dictionary close at hand. In a final, irreplaceable contribution to the book, Josh joined us at HQ to type in his own copy and that of his comrades, earning a cachet of distinction and dedication.

Alexander de la Fuente *Tasmania, western Victoria, and outback NSW*
Other R-Ws would have paled before the course set out for Alex. With stoic bravery he crossed the most remote of Australia's states…and the more remote halves of two others! Not flustered by the theft of his car mirror, a crime perpetrated by that well-loved but sorely maladapted marsupial, Alex stared in awe at the starry sky of Broken Hill. If he was the only tourist in Tassie, he was plenty for the state to handle; no sight goes unvisited when Alex is afoot. As if thriving on the isolation, Alex found the inspiration to become an artist on the side: his dazzling artwork and tongue-in-rain-drenched-cheek comments kept his editors in good humor (and educated on plate tectonics), while his excellent copy, even on that flimsy paper, kept multiple typists busy. Alex, like his wombats and their devil-proof rumps, proved adaptable to every challenge Australia could offer—except, perhaps, coin-op showers.

Marc P. Diaz *Melbourne, eastern Victoria, and Kangaroo Island, SA*
Bounding through the antipodean winter in his ill-fated station wagon, this stalwart veteran left his mark on Melbourne. Marc used his Let's Go camera to document the inequity visited upon him by Melbourne metermaids, broke into the car after it swallowed his keys in Albury, and dauntlessly escaped through a window when the orange tank literally turned his itinerary upside-down. And through it all he toted his indestructible bottles of strawberry wine. Ever-thoughtful, Marc flooded our mailbox with postcards; ever-thorough, he swamped our file cabinets with maps, brochures, and voluminous, meticulously researched copy. With determination and enthusiasm that any Top Gun pilot (or look-alike) would aspire to display, Marc topped off his supreme effort by bringing us volunteer coverage of Kangaroo Island.

Gavin Steckler *Northern Territory and the Kimberley, WA*
To his editors, Gavin was an endless source of scatological humor and a disembodied voice (to those to whom he was a voice at all). Nobody knows what he looks like, but he certainly has some pillar! Going beyond the duty of a star travel-writer, Gavin took the time to produce some excellent character-driven works of fiction. He gave the author of *On The Origin* a moralistic bent, the NT tourist board a story behind its symbol, and our emphasis on orientation a whole new meaning. Gavin traveled thousands of kilometers on buses in NT completing his itinerary, and, as if that weren't enough, took a bus from Broome to Sydney. We were pleasantly surprised to find that, in Kakadu, even Gavin could be impressed. Thank Gavin for our stellar NT coverage; thank God for the semicolon.

Michelle C. Sullivan *Sydney, southern and central NSW, and the ACT*
The reliable anchor of the best R-W team ever assembled, Michelle jumped at the opportunity to make one more tour under the banner of Let's Go. From her flawless copy that literally edited itself to her infinite understanding with her ever-changing itinerary, Michelle deserves more praise than we can give. She also volunteered for the responsibility of keeping her editors sane—her animated marginalia and contest-winning stream of postcards kept us chuckling well past midnight. Seemingly unfazed by a harrowing near-descent of Mt. Kaputar, Michelle carried on with a new vehicle and renewed determination. Quoth Michelle: "I came, I saw, I almost fell off the mountain. Nuff said." What she forgot to mention was her conquest of Australia.

Let's Go Picks

Best Accommodations A vacation in itself at **Taggerty Bush Settlement** (p. 466). Bunking in the **Old Castlemaine Gaol B&B** for slumber in the slammer (p. 486). **Gagaju,** in the midst of Cooloola National Park (p. 304). Port Macquarie's **Lindel Backpackers** (p. 156). Bushstyle in the Flinders Ranges at **Andu Backpacker Lodge** (p. 410). The **Pioneer YHA's** outdoor Alice cinema, with a pool beneath the silver screen (p. 252). The swanky brightness of **Excape Backpackers** in Exmouth (p. 557). **On the Wallaby** in the Atherton Tablelands (p. 349).

Best Food, Wineries, and Pubs The Sydney tradition of fish and chips on the Watson's Bay wharf from **Doyle's Take-out** (p. 109). **Betty's Burgers** in Noosa, with burgers from a buck (p. 302). Best vegetarian food in SA at **Vego and Lovin' It,** Adelaide (p. 379). Gooey mud cakes and pots of Earl Gray in **Revely's Cafe** in the Old Perth Boys School (p. 532). Killer seafood at **On the Inlet,** Port Douglas (p. 352). Australian cultural caricature at **Ettamogah Pub** (p. 208). Free semillion and a $1 appetizer plate at **Saltram Wine Estate** in the Barossa Valley, SA (p. 401). Tally-ho and cheers for wine at becastled **All Saints' Estate,** Vic (p. 506). Afternoon glass of chardonay at **Treeton Estate** (p. 539), near Margaret River, WA. The drunken ghost at the outback pub in **Prairie**, between Mount Isa and Townsville (p. 362).

Best Wildlife Crocodiles leaping vertically to snatch hunks of meat on the **Jumping Croc Cruise** (p. 235). **Little penguins** stumbling home in **Penneshaw,** Kangaroo Island (p. 394). Tickling fruit bats, cuddling sea cucumbers, tangoing with kangaroos. Riding **camels** outside Alice Springs (p. 256). **Sea lions** sunning on the beach at Seal Bay Aquatic Reserve (p. 394). Nearly wild Australian native species at the **Healesville Sanctuary** (p. 465). Fossils of **megafauna** at Naracoorte (p. 397). The **Atherton Tablelands,** populated by sheep, cows, and the occasional flock of cockatoos (p. 347). Scuba diving the **Great Barrier Reef** out of Cairns (p. 338)... or anywhere else.

Best Natural Attractions The natural playground of the **Devil's Marbles** (p. 249). **Katherine River Gorge** by canoe (p. 245). **Wildflowers** covering Bluff Knoll in the Stirling Range (p. 543). White sands and beautifully clear water at **Jervis Bay** (p. 191). Royal National Park's **Coastal Walking Track** (p. 122). The **Remarkable Rocks,** in Flinders Chase National Park (p. 395). Tidal flats of the ingloriously named **Pretty Pool** in Port Hedland (p. 559). Rainforests of **Fraser Island** (p. 306). **Ruined Castle** walk, Blue Mountains N.P. (p. 133). **Protestor's Falls** in Nightcap (p. 170). A leisurely drive along **Bells Line of Road** (p. 137) or **Alpine Way** between Cooma and Jindabyne, NSW (p. 196). Bushwalking Tasmania's **Overland Track.** The gorgeous **Whitehaven Beach** in the Whitsunday Islands (p. 325).

Only in Australia **Aboriginal art** at Ubirr in amazing Kakadu National Park (p. 238). The grandeur of Kalgoorlie's **super-pit** (p. 548). **Gulgong Pioneer Museum** near Murwillumbah (p. 149). The walk across **Harbour Bridge** (p. 90) and up the **Southern Pylon Lookout** (p. 111) for views of Sydney. Aboriginal culture at **Kalkadoon Tribal Council Centre** in Mount Isa (p. 365) and **Tjapukai Theatre,** outside Cairns (p. 346). Picnic on top of **Parliament House** in Canberra (p. 80). The **Priscilla Queen of the Imperial** drag show (p. 119) at the Imperial Hotel in Erskineville, NSW.

Unforgettable Moments Sharing meals with strangers before log fires in **New England** highway pubs. A spooky evening tour of the **Old Melbourne Gaol.** Watching a shark writhing in the surf off **Fraser Island.** Frozen toothpaste on outback mornings. Climbing **Ayers Rock.** Cricket at the **MCG.** Hang gliding over **Bent's Lookout** on Mt. Buffalo. Hauling up **Mt. Warning** to find the summit enveloped in thick mist. Sunrise at the windblown **Wilsons Prom** lighthouse. Sprinting to the **FedEx drop.**

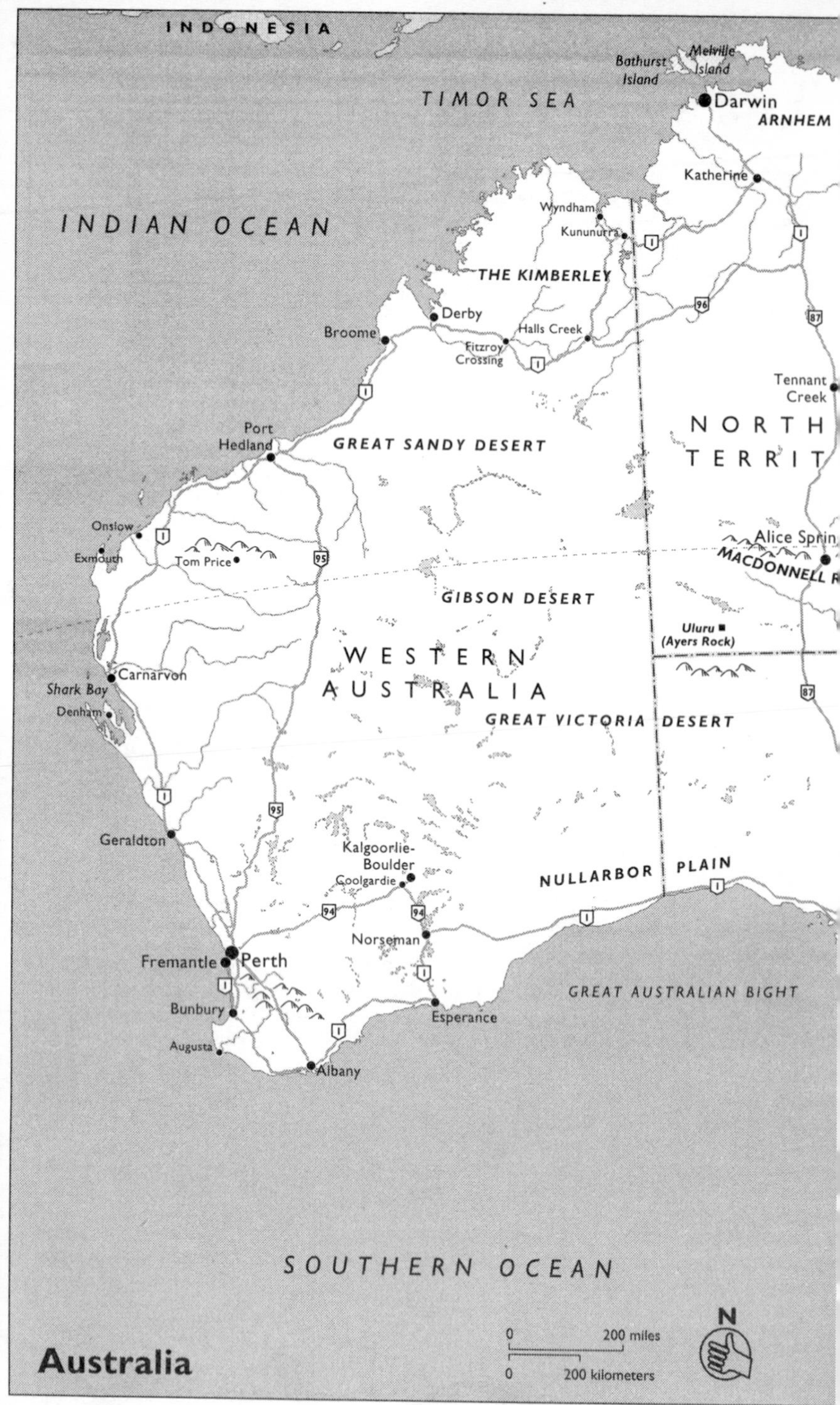

INDONESIA
TIMOR SEA
Bathurst Island
Melville Island
Darwin
ARNHEM
Katherine
INDIAN OCEAN
Wyndham
Kununurra
THE KIMBERLEY
Derby
Broome
Halls Creek
Fitzroy Crossing
Tennant Creek
NORTH
TERRIT
Port Hedland
GREAT SANDY DESERT
Onslow
Exmouth
Tom Price
Alice Sprin
MACDONNELL R
GIBSON DESERT
Uluru (Ayers Rock)
WESTERN AUSTRALIA
Carnarvon
Shark Bay
Denham
GREAT VICTORIA DESERT
Geraldton
Kalgoorlie-Boulder
Coolgardie
NULLARBOR PLAIN
Norseman
Fremantle
Perth
Bunbury
Augusta
Esperance
Albany
GREAT AUSTRALIAN BIGHT
SOUTHERN OCEAN
N
0 200 miles
0 200 kilometers
Australia

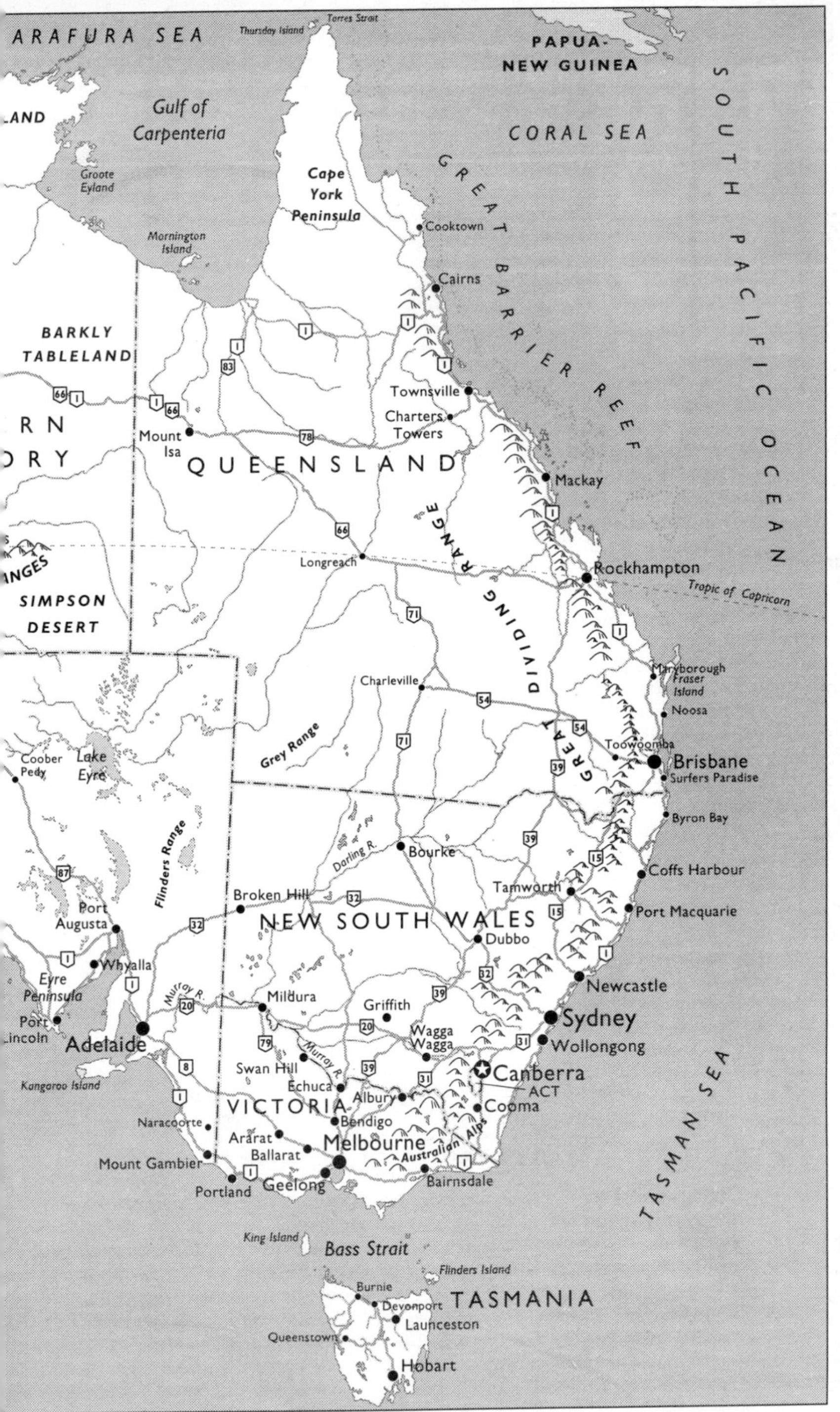

ARAFURA SEA
Thursday Island
Torres Strait
PAPUA-NEW GUINEA
Gulf of Carpenteria
CORAL SEA
SOUTH PACIFIC OCEAN
Groote Eylandt
Cape York Peninsula
GREAT BARRIER REEF
Cooktown
Mornington Island
Cairns
BARKLY TABLELAND
Townsville
Charters Towers
Mount Isa
QUEENSLAND
Mackay
GREAT DIVIDING RANGE
SIMPSON DESERT
Longreach
Rockhampton
Tropic of Capricorn
Maryborough
Fraser Island
Noosa
Charleville
Grey Range
Toowoomba
Brisbane
Surfers Paradise
Coober Pedy
Lake Eyre
Byron Bay
Flinders Range
Darling R.
Bourke
Coffs Harbour
Tamworth
Port Macquarie
Broken Hill
Port Augusta
NEW SOUTH WALES
Dubbo
Whyalla
Eyre Peninsula
Newcastle
Murray R.
Mildura
Griffith
Sydney
Port Lincoln
Adelaide
Wagga Wagga
Wollongong
Swan Hill
Murray R.
Canberra
ACT
Kangaroo Island
Echuca
Albury
VICTORIA
Cooma
Bendigo
Naracoorte
Ararat
Ballarat
Melbourne
Australian Alps
Mount Gambier
Portland
Geelong
Bairnsdale
TASMAN SEA
King Island
Bass Strait
Flinders Island
Burnie
Devonport
TASMANIA
Launceston
Queenstown
Hobart

How to Use This Book

A good travel guide—like the Wizard of Oz—strives to be all things to all people. If a friend were too eager to please, you'd call him shallow, but please, for the love of God, don't judge us so harshly as we travel the country together.

While whimsical jaunts can be the most thrilling, thoughtfully planned journeys are usually the most successful. The beginning **Essentials** section (p. 1) is chock-full of organizations just dying to save you a few dollars or a few hours of trouble on the road. We'll help you figure out the intricacies of visas and customs, sort out exchange rates and currency, and choose between traveler's checks and electronic banking. We offer helpful hints on how to stay safe and healthy, whether you're exploring the outback or diving on the Great Barrier Reef. We also suggest some alternatives to traditional sightseeing, and provide information for travelers with special concerns. This section contains a host of money-saving tips, too; read it *before* you venture out and then relax in informed bliss while on the road.

Of course travel is about more than practicalities. For a digestible introduction to the country, read the **Australia** chapter (p. 53), which is shorter than it sounds and contains brief essays on history, politics, literature, music, wildlife, food, and all things Aussie. While by no means exhaustive, these summaries will help you hold your own in discussions of the nuances of Aussie Rules or the fate of Men at Work.

Our coverage of Australia itself is broken into **eight chapters,** one corresponding to each of the six states and two territories that comprise the land down under. Each chapter opens with its capital city, followed by regional subdivisions. Within each region, cities, parks, and points of interest appear in a geographic order that made sense at the time (generally beginning with those closest to the state capital). After beginning with an impressionistic introduction, each destination has an **orientation** to show you around, important **practical information** (including tourist and travel information, financial services, emergency, medical, and social services, and post and communications), listings of **accommodations** (ranked in order of value) and **food** establishments (also ranked), descriptions of **sights** that shouldn't be missed, venues for **entertainment,** and **activities** we hope you'll try.

Our **maps** guide you through unfamiliar terrain with the sure hand of a savvy companion. The **appendix** fills in the gaps with climatic info so you know how to pack, a primer on the perpetually "transitioning" phone code system, and a glossary on 'strine dialect, so you can shout a stubbie for your new-found chinas. *Let's Go: Australia 1998* ends with a comprehensive **index,** so you find that national park that everyone's raving about at your hostel.

Your bible to budget travel this guide may be, but it is no prophet. We urge you to take your own walkabout, experiment with your itinerary, and discover that out-of-the-way gem. When you find a place that's magic, send us a postcard so we know to check it out next year when we're working on *Let's Go: Australia 1999.* We've put some of our own favorite finds under **Let's Go Picks** on the preceding page. But enough about us; Australia is calling. Let's draw the curtain on the wizard and go....

A NOTE TO OUR READERS

The information for this book was gathered by *Let's Go*'s researchers from May through August. Each listing is derived from the assigned researcher's opinion based upon his or her visit at a particular time. The opinions are expressed in a candid and forthright manner. Other travelers might disagree. Those traveling at a different time may have different experiences since prices, dates, hours, and conditions are always subject to change. You are urged to check beforehand to avoid inconvenience and surprises. Travel always involves a certain degree of risk, especially in low-cost areas. When traveling, especially on a budget, always take particular care to ensure your safety.

ESSENTIALS

PLANNING YOUR TRIP

A vacation is ideally an escape, a spontaneous affair, conceived on a whim and completed without hassle. In today's world, however, escapes are not made without prior planning. Traveling is a complex process, and budget travel is, in many ways, even more difficult—you pay for ease, after all. You can eliminate a lot of surprises by setting aside the time to read through this chapter before you jump into anything. With a little more research you may find better and cheaper ways of doing things. Before you get on the plane, it is a good idea to have at least a tentative itinerary, and to read through *Let's Go*'s listings of those towns. These days, even some hostels require reservations, so you can't always fly by the seat of your pants. Don't be afraid to change your plans, though; just remember: the more knowledge you have, the more prepared you will be to be spontaneous.

When To Go

Australia is big. Really big. When you want to travel depends on what you are planning to do and what part of the country you will be visiting. Because Australia is in the southern hemisphere, the **seasons** are reversed from those in the northern hemisphere. This means that summer lasts from December to February, autumn from March to May, winter from June to August, and spring from September to November. In the northern, tropical part of the country, temperature does not vary nearly as much as precipitation, and the seasons are defined as **"the Wet"** (November to April) and **"the Dry"** (May to October).

As a general rule, tourism peaks when school is out of session. Summer holidays for primary and secondary schools generally include the months of December and January. Universities usually take **summer vacation** from the end of November to the end of February.

In the Australian summer, Western Australia, Northern Territory, and northern Queensland are all quite hot. In the Australian winter, these regions are considerably warmer than the southern areas, and remain fairly tropical throughout the year. In the wet season, some roads in Northern Territory and northern Queensland flood.

January and February are the rainy months on the **Great Barrier Reef;** the water is clearest between April and October. Skiing is possible in New South Wales and Victoria between June and September, and the famous wildflowers of Western Australia are at their peak from September to December.

See the **Appendix,** p. 571, for average temperature and rainfall regional charts.

Useful Information

GOVERNMENT INFORMATION OFFICES

The government-sponsored **Australian Tourist Commission** provides literature and assistance to potential international visitors; it does not distribute any tourist information within Australia. The ATC sponsors helplines as well, with the catchy name "Ask Our Aussie." In addition to general information about Australia, the ATC carries specific books, magazines, and fact sheets for backpackers, younger people, disabled travelers, and others with special interests or concerns. Check out the ATC's fairly comprehensive web page at http://www.aussie.net.au. Requests for literature should be directed to the addresses below.

New Zealand: Level 13, 44-48 Emily Pl., Auckland 1 (tel. (09) 379 9594; fax 307 3117). Helpline: tel. (0800) 650 303 or (09) 527 1629; fax (09) 377 9562.
U.K.: Gemini House, 10-18 Putney Hill, **London** SW156AA (tel. (0181) 780 2227; fax 780 1496). **U.K. & Ireland** (tel. 0990 022000). For brochure orders only in the U.K. & Ireland tel. 0990 56 1434.
U.S./Canada: P.O. Box 7925, Mt. Prospect, IL 60056 (tel. (847) 296-4900 for travel counselor, general information (800) 333-4305; fax (847) 635-3718).

TRAVEL ORGANIZATIONS

American Automobile Association (AAA) Travel Related Services, 1000 AAA Dr. (mail stop 100), Heathrow, FL 32746-5063 (tel. (407) 444-7000; fax 444-7380). AAA membership is reciprocal in Australia; members receive free road maps and travel guides. Offers emergency road services (for members), travel services, and auto insurance. The International Driving Permit (IDP) is available for purchase from local AAA offices. To become a member in the U.S., call (800) 222-4357.

Council on International Educational Exchange (CIEE), 205 East 42nd St., New York, NY 10017-5706 (tel. (888)-COUNCIL (268-6245); fax (212) 822-2699; http://www.ciee.org). A private, not-for-profit organization, Council administers work, volunteer, academic, internship, and professional programs around the world. Council also offers identity cards (including the ISIC and the GO25) and a range of publications, among them the useful magazine *Student Travels* (free). Call or write for further information.

Federation of International Youth Travel Organizations (FIYTO), Bredgade 25H, DK-1260 Copenhagen K, Denmark (tel. 33 33 96 00; fax 33 93 96 76; email mailbox@fiyto.org; http://www.fiyto.org), is an international organization promoting educational, cultural, and social travel for young people. Member organizations include language schools, educational travel companies, national tourist boards, accommodation centers, and other suppliers of travel services to youth and students. FIYTO sponsors the GO25 Card (http://www.go25.org).

International Student Travel Confederation, Herengracht 479, 1017 BS Amsterdam, The Netherlands (tel. (020) 421 2800; fax 421 2810; http://www.istc.org; email istcinfo@istc.org). The ISTC is a nonprofit confederation of student travel organizations whose focus is to develop, promote, and facilitate travel among young people and students. Member organizations include International Student Surface Travel Association (ISSA), Student Air Travel Association (SATA), IASIS Travel Insurance, the International Association for Educational and Work Exchange Programs (IAEWEP), and the International Student Identity Card Association (ISIC).

USEFUL PUBLICATIONS

Hippocrene Books, Inc., 171 Madison Ave., New York, NY 10016 (tel. (212) 685-4371; orders (718) 454-2366; fax 454-1391; email hippocre@ix.netcom.com; http://www.netcom.com/~hippocre). Free catalogue. Publishes travel reference books and guides, including the *Australia Companion Guide* (US$17).

Hunter Publishing, P.O. Box 7816, Edison, NJ 08818 (tel. (908) 225-1900; fax 417-0482; email hunterpub@emi.net; http://www.hunterpublishing.com). Has an extensive catalogue of travel books, maps, and guides, among them *Insider's Guide to Australia* (US$19).

Specialty Travel Index, 305 San Anselmo Ave., #313, San Anselmo, CA 94960 (tel. (415) 459-4900; fax 459-4974; email spectrav@ix.netcom.com; http://www.spectrav.com). Published twice yearly, this is an extensive listing of "off the beaten track" and specialty travel opportunities. One copy US$6, one-year subscription (2 copies) $10. The web site has a directory of Australia-specific special interest tours, from camel safaris to tours of churches.

U.S. Customs Service, P.O. Box 7407, Washington, D.C., 20044 (tel. (202) 927-6724; http://www.customs.ustreas.gov). Publishes 35 books, booklets, leaflets, and flyers on various aspects of customs. *Know Before You Go* tells everything the international traveler needs to know about customs requirements; *Pockets Hints* summarizes the most important data from *KBYG.*

INTERNET RESOURCES

Along with everything else in the 90s, budget travel is moving rapidly into the information age, with the **Internet** as a leading travel resource. On today's net people can make their own airline, hotel, hostel, or car rental reservations and connect personally with others abroad, allowing people to become their own budget travel planners. **NetTravel: How Travelers Use the Internet,** by Michael Shapiro, is a very thorough and informative guide to this process (US$25). The forms of the Internet most useful to net-surfing budget travelers are the World Wide Web and Usenet newsgroups.

Travelers who have the luxury of a laptop can use a **modem** to call an internet service provider. Long-distance phone cards specifically intended for such calls can defray normally high phone charges. Check with your long-distance phone provider to see if it offers this option; otherwise, try a **C.COM Internet PhoneCard** (tel. (888) 464-2266), which offers Internet connection calls for 15¢ per minute with a minimum initial purchase of US$5. Note: a few areas, bypassed by the information superhighway, may require that you dial an international outside line to access the Internet, but this is rapidly changing.

The World Wide Web

Increasingly the Internet forum of choice, the **World Wide Web** provides its users with text, graphics, and sound. **Search engines** (services that search for web pages under specific subjects) can significantly aid the search process. **Lycos** (http://a2z.lycos.com) and **Infoseek** (http://guide.infoseek.com) are two of the most popular. **Yahoo!** is a slightly more organized search engine; check out its travel links at http://www.yahoo.com/Recreation/Travel. Another good way to explore is to find a good site and start "surfing" from there, through links from one web page to another. Check out Let's Go's own page (http://www.letsgo.com) for a list of links.

Let's Go lists relevant web sites throughout different sections of the Essentials chapter, but web sites come and go very rapidly; a good web site one week might disappear the next, and a new one might quickly take its place. Thus, as with normal travel, it is important for you to head out on your own in cyber-travel as well. A few Australia-specific sites to get you started include:

Charles Sturt University's Guide to Australia (http://www.csu.edu.au/education/australia.html) aims to be the ultimate index to Australia-related web sites, and does a pretty good job.

Australian Tourist Commission (http://www.aussie.net.au) is a potentially excellent page, but at the time of this writing it still had a few bugs to work out in accessing links.

Telstra Springboard to Australia (http://springboard.telstra.com.au/australia/index.htm) provides a comprehensive list of links to Australian travel, business, arts, entertainment, and even maps.

City.Net Travel (http://city.net/countries/australia) provides current weather reports in big and mid-size cities, with numerous links to other Australian info sites.

Bushwalking in Australia (http://bushwalking.hightide.net.au) focuses on—yes—bushwalking.

Australia Outdoor Connection (http://flinders.com.au/home.htm) is sponsored by Flinders Camping in Adelaide, and provides camping and environmental information and links.

Australian Yellow Pages and White Pages (http://www.yellowpages.com.au and http://www.whitepages.com.au) are the official Telstra phone book—on-line. You can search by business or private name, state, or type of service. The white pages take into account which country you are calling from and provide access codes, as well as a nifty time converter.

Australian Recipe Collection (http://www.wsnet.com/~ang/recipe) is an excellent private web page which gives ingredients and advice for making scores of Australian recipes. The site's owner will even reply personally if you have pavlova or lamington questions.

Australian Football League (http://www.odyssey.com.au/sports/afl/links.html) offers a list of links for AFL fans.

To keep up with daily events in Oz, read the **Sydney Morning Herald** online at (http://www.smh.com.au) or Melbourne's **The Age** at (http://www.theage.com.au). The official Sydney **Olympics** home page is at (http://www.sydney.olympic.org).

Usenet Newsgroups

Another popular source of information are **newsgroups,** which are forums for discussion of specific topics. One user "posts" a written question or thought, which other users read and respond to in kind. There are thousands of different newsgroups and more crop up every day, so there is information available on almost every imaginable topic. **Usenet,** the name for the family of newsgroups, can be accessed easily from most Internet gateways. In UNIX systems, a good newsreader is "tin" (just type "tin" at the prompt). Most commercial providers offer access to Usenet, and often have their own version of Usenet, limited to the members of the provider, which has similar information.

There are a number of different hierarchies for newsgroups. The "soc" hierarchy deals primary with issues related to society and culture. The "rec" (recreation) hierarchy is especially good for travelers, with newsgroups such as **rec.travel.air** or **rec.travel.australia+nz.** The "alt' (alternative) hierarchy houses a number of different types of discussion. Finally, "Clari-net" posts AP news wires for many different topics. Since the quality of discussion changes so rapidly, and new groups are always appearing, it's worthwhile for a new user to scan through the newsgroups to find appropriate topics.

Documents and Formalities

Having all of your paperwork in order before departing for Australia and upon returning home can make the difference between a smooth transition and a bureaucratic nightmare. If the information listed below does not apply to your individual situation, please contact the nearest Consulate General and make sure you have everything you need. All applications should be filed several weeks or months in advance of your planned departure date. Demand for passports is highest between January and August in most countries, so leave extra time in those months. A backlog in processing can spoil your plans.

When you travel, always carry on your person two or more forms of identification, including at least one photo ID. A passport combined with a driver's license or birth certificate usually serves as adequate proof of your identity and citizenship. Many establishments, especially banks, require several IDs before cashing traveler's checks. Never carry all your forms of ID together, however; you risk being left entirely without ID or funds in case of theft or loss. Also carry several extra passport-size photos that you can attach to the sundry IDs you may eventually acquire. If you plan an extended stay, register your passport with the nearest embassy or consulate.

AUSTRALIAN EMBASSIES AND CONSULATES

Canada: All visa applications should go to Ottawa.

Australian High Commission, 50 O'Connor St. #710, Ottawa, ON KIP 6L2 (tel. (613) 783 7665; fax 236-4376).

Australian Consulate General, 999 Canada Pl., #602, Vancouver, BC V6C 3E1 (tel. (604) 684-1177; fax 684-1856).

Australian Consulate General, 175 Bloor St. East, #314, Toronto, ON M4W 3R8 (tel. (416) 323-1155; fax 323-3910).

Ireland: Fitzwilton House, Wilton Terrace, Dublin 2 (tel. (01) 676 1517; fax 678 5185).

New Zealand: 72-78 Hobson St., Thorndon, Wellington (tel. (04) 473 6411; fax 498 7118). Union House, 32-38 Quay St., Auckland 1 (tel. (09) 303 2429; fax 377 0798).

South Africa: 292 Orient St., Arcadia, Pretoria 0083 (tel. (012) 342 3740; fax 342 4222), also in Cape Town.

United Kingdom: Australia House, The Strand, London WC2B 4LA (tel. (0171) 379 4334; fax 465 8210), also in Edinburgh and Manchester.

United States of America: Some offices are only open in the mornings; call ahead.

Australian Embassy, 1601 Massachusetts Ave. NW, Washington, D.C. 20036-2273 (tel. (202) 797-3000; fax 797-3100).

Australian Consulate General, Level 4, 630 Fifth Ave., New York, NY 10111 (tel. (212) 408-8400; fax 408-8485).

Australian Consulate General, 1 Bush St., #700, San Francisco, CA 94104 (tel. (415) 362-6160; fax 956-9729).

Australian Consulate General, 1000 Bishop St., Penthouse, Honolulu, HI 96813 (tel. (808) 524-5050; fax 531-5142).

Australian Consulate General, Century Plaza Towers, 19th Fl., 2049 Century Park East, Los Angeles, CA 90067 (tel. (310) 229-4800, visa office direct tel. 229-4840; fax 277 5620).

ENTRANCE REQUIREMENTS

Citizens of Canada, Ireland, New Zealand, South Africa, the U.K., and the U.S. all need valid **passports** to enter Australia, and to re-enter their own country. Some countries do not allow entrance if the holder's passport expires in under six months; returning home with an expired passport is illegal, and may result in a fine. **Australia also requires all visitors to carry a visa.** New Zealand nationals will receive a "special category" visa upon arrival in Australia; all other visitors need to procure a visa before arriving. Your home country may require children to carry their own passports, in which case they would also need their own visas. For more information, please see **Visas,** p. 7.

Upon entering a country, you must declare certain items from abroad and must pay a duty on the value of those articles that exceed the allowance established by that country's **customs** service. Keeping receipts for purchases made abroad will help establish values when you return. It is wise to make a list, including serial numbers, of any valuables that you carry with you from home; if you register this list with customs before your departure and have an official stamp it, you will avoid import duty charges and ensure an easy passage upon your return. Be especially careful to document items manufactured abroad.

When you enter Australia, dress neatly and carry **proof of your financial independence,** such as a visa to the next country on your itinerary, an airplane ticket to depart, enough money to cover the cost of your living expenses, etc. Admission as a tourist does not include the right to work, which is authorized only by a work permit. If you are studying in Australia, immigration officers may also want to see proof of acceptance from a school and proof that the course of study will take up most of your time in the country, as well as proof that you can support yourself.

No vaccinations are required to enter the country unless you have been in an area with **yellow fever** within the last six days. No other health certificate is required. If you require vaccinations while in Australia, perhaps before visiting another country, the **Traveller's Medical and Vaccination Centre,** 428 George St., level 7 (tel. (02) 9221 7133), in Sydney, can do the job. The consultation fee is $35; you'll then pay per vaccination (open Mon.-Wed. and Fri. 9am-6pm, Thurs. 9am-8pm, Sat. 9am-1pm).

PASSPORTS

Before you leave, photocopy the page of your passport that contains your photograph, passport number, and other identifying information. Carry one photocopy in a safe place apart from your passport, and leave another copy at home. These measures will help prove your citizenship and facilitate the issuing of a new passport if you lose the original document. Consulates also recommend that you carry an expired passport or an official copy of your birth certificate in a part of your baggage separate from other documents.

If you do lose your passport, immediately notify the local police and the nearest embassy or consulate of your home government. To expedite its replacement, you will need to know all information previously recorded and show identification and proof of citizenship. A replacement may take weeks to process, and it may be valid only for a limited time. Some consulates can issue new passports within 24 hours if you give them proof of citizenship. Any visas stamped in your old passport will be irretrievably lost. In an emergency, ask for immediate temporary traveling papers that will permit you to reenter your home country.

Your passport is a public document belonging to your nation's government. You may have to surrender it to a foreign government official, but if you don't get it back in a reasonable amount of time, inform the nearest mission of your home country.

Canada Application forms in English and French are available at all **passport offices,** Canadian **missions,** many **travel agencies,** and **Northern Stores** in northern communities. Citizens may apply in person at any one of 28 regional Passport Offices across Canada. Travel agents can direct applicants to the nearest location. Canadian citizens residing abroad should contact the nearest Canadian embassy or consulate. Children under 16 may be included on a parent's passport. Processing takes approximately five business days for applications in-person; 10 days if by mail. For additional info, contact the Canadian Passport Office, Department of Foreign Affairs and International Trade, Ottawa, ON, K1A 0G3 (tel. (613) 994-3500; http://www.dfait-maeci.gc.ca/passport). Travelers may also call (800) 567-6868 (24hr.). Refer to the booklet *Bon Voyage, But...* for further help and a list of Canadian embassies and consulates abroad. It is available free at any passport office or by calling InfoCentre at (800) 267-8376.

Ireland Citizens can apply for a passport by mail to either the Department of Foreign Affairs, Passport Office, Setanta Centre, Molesworth St., Dublin 2 (tel. (01) 671 1633), or the Passport Office, Irish Life Building, 1A South Mall, Cork (tel. (021) 272 525). Obtain an application at a local Garda station or request one from a passport office. Passports cost IR£45 and are valid for 10 years. The new **Passport Express** Service, available through post offices, allows citizens to get a passport in 2 weeks for an extra £3. Citizens under 18 or over 65 can request a three-year passport for £10.

New Zealand Application forms for passports are available in New Zealand from travel agents and Department of Internal Affairs Link Centres in the main cities and towns. Applications may also be forwarded to the Passport Office, P.O. Box 10526, Wellington, New Zealand. Standard processing time in New Zealand is 10 working days for correct applications. The fees are adult NZ$80, and child $40. An urgent passport service is also available for an extra $80. Different fees apply at overseas posts. Children's names can no longer be endorsed on a parent's passport—they must apply for their own, which are valid for up to five years. An adult's passport is valid for up to 10 years.

South Africa Citizens can apply for a passport at any **Home Affairs Office** or **South African Mission.** Tourist passports, valid for 10 years, cost R80. Children under 16 must be issued their own passports, valid for five years, which cost R60. If a passport is needed in a hurry, an **emergency passport** may be issued for R50. An application for a permanent passport must accompany the emergency passport application. Time for the completion of an application is normally three months or more from the time of submission. Current passports less than 10 years old (counting from date of issuance) may be **renewed** until December 31, 1999; every citizen whose passport's validity does not extend far beyond this date is urged to renew it as soon as possible to avoid the expected glut of applications as 2000 approaches. Renewal is free, and turnaround time is usually two weeks. For further information, contact the nearest Department of Home Affairs Office.

United Kingdom British citizens, British Dependent Territories citizens, British Nationals (overseas), and British Overseas citizens may apply for a full passport, valid for 10 years (5 years if under 16). Application forms are available at passport offices, main post offices, many travel agents, and branches of Lloyds Bank and Artac World Choice. The fee is UK£18. Children under 16 may be included on a parent's passport. Processing by mail usually takes four to six weeks. The London office offers same-day, walk-in rush service; arrive early. The formerly available British Visitor's Passport (valid in some western European countries and Bermuda only) has been abolished; every traveler over 16 now needs a 10-year, standard passport. The U.K. Passport Agency can be reached by phone at (0990) 21 04 10, and information is available on the Internet at http://www.open.gov.uk/ukpass.

United States Citizens may apply for a passport at any federal or state courthouse or post office authorized to accept passport applications, or at a U.S. Passport Agency. Refer to the "U.S. Government, State Department" section of the telephone directory or the local post office for addresses. Parents must apply in person for children under age 13. Passports are valid for 10 years (5 years if under 18) and cost US$65 (under 18 $40). Passports may be renewed by mail or in person for $55. Processing takes three to four weeks. Rush service is available for a surcharge. Given proof of citizenship, a U.S. embassy or consulate abroad can usually issue a new passport. Report a passport **lost or stolen** in the U.S. in writing to Passport Services, 1425 K St., NW, U.S. Department of State, Washington, D.C. 20524 or to the nearest passport agency. For more info, contact U.S. Passport Information (24hr. tel. (202) 647-0518). Additional information (including publications) about documents, formalities, and travel abroad is available through the Bureau of Consular Affairs homepage at http://travel.state.gov, or through the State Department site at http://www.state.gov.

VISAS

A **visa** is an endorsement that a foreign government stamps into a passport which allows the bearer to stay in that country for a specified purpose and period of time. Australian **tourist visas** are free and allow you to spend three months in the country, within one year from the date of issue. **Work visas** vary according to your plans; contact the Australian embassy or consulate in your home country with questions. **All visitors to Australia need a visa before arriving, with the exception of New Zealand nationals.** Visas can be acquired in person or by mail from the Australian embassies and consulates in your home country (see p. 4), and airlines and travel agents sometimes have copies of the application forms available for their clients. If you have access to the Internet, you can download the visa application from the web at http://www.anzac.com/aust/visa.htm. If you apply in person, tourist visas can generally be issued while you wait; allow at least three weeks if you apply by mail. If you are planning to stay in Australia for longer than three months, or if you need a visa good for multiple visits anytime in a four-year period, then you will have to pay a fee (currently US$21/CDN$28).

For more information, send for Foreign Entry Requirements (US$0.50) from the **Consumer Information Center,** Department 363D, Pueblo, CO 81009 (tel. (719) 948-3334; http://www.pueblo.gsa.gov), or contact the Center for **International Business and Travel (CIBT),** 25 West 43rd St. #1420, New York, NY 10036 (tel. (800) 925-2428 or (212) 575-2811 from NYC), which secures visas for travel to and from all countries for a variable service charge..

CUSTOMS: ENTERING

Australia Because of its isolation as an island nation, Australia has been able to avoid some of the pests and diseases that plague other countries. But with increased tourism, there is an increased risk of contamination from imported goods. Customs is therefore taken extremely seriously. Australia expressly forbids the entry of drugs, steroids, weapons, and articles subject to quarantine. This may include live animals, food, animal products, plants, plant products, and protected wildlife. These articles are not automatically forbidden, but they will undergo a **quarantine inspection.** Don't risk large fines or hassles when entering Australia—throw out questionable items in the big customs bins as you leave the plane and declare anything about which you have the slightest suspicion. The beagles in orange smocks know their stuff, and they WILL find you out. If you are planning to stay for a while and must bring your **pets** with you, contact the **Australian Quarantine and Inspections Service,** GPO Box 858, Canberra, ACT 2601 (tel. (02) 6272 3933; fax 6280 7128) to obtain a permit. Pick up a **Customs Information for Travellers** pamphlet at an Australian consulate or any travel agency for additional helpline numbers and more detailed information. If you wish to enter or leave Australia with more than AUS$5000 or the equivalent in foreign currency, you must first inform the Australian Customs Office. It is a good idea to declare valuables you have brought from home as well.

New Zealand Australia's neighbor to the southeast has similarly strict regulations restricting many food, plant, and animal goods from entering the country; check with the nearest embassy, consulate, or tourist official for more information.

CUSTOMS: GOING HOME

Upon returning home, you must declare all articles you acquired abroad and pay a **duty** on the value of those articles that exceed the allowance established by your country's customs service. Goods and gifts purchased at **duty-free** shops abroad are not exempt from duty or sales tax at your point of return; you must declare these items as well. "Duty-free" merely means that you need not pay a tax in the country of purchase. For country-specific information, contact your national customs office.

Canada: Contact Canadian Customs, 2265 St. Laurent Blvd., Ottawa, ON K1G 4K3 (tel. (613) 993-0534), phone the 24hr. Automated Customs Information Service at (800) 461-9999, or visit Revenue Canada at http://www.revcan.ca.

Ireland: Contact The Revenue Commissioners, Dublin Castle (tel. (01) 679 27 77; fax 671 20 21; email taxes@iol.ie; http://www.revenue.ie) or The Collector of Customs and Excise, The Custom House, Dublin 1.

New Zealand: Contact New Zealand Customs, 50 Anzac Ave., Box 29, Auckland (tel. (09) 377 35 20; fax 309 29 78).

South Africa: Contact the Commissioner for Customs and Excise, Private Bag X47, Pretoria 0001 for the pamphlet *South African Customs Information.* Citizens residing in the U.S. should contact the Embassy of South Africa, 3051 Massachusetts Ave., NW, Washington, D.C. 20008 (tel. (202) 232-4400; fax 244-9417) or the South African Home Annex, 3201 New Mexico Ave. #380, NW, Washington, D.C. 20016 (tel. (202) 966-1650).

United Kingdom: Contact Her Majesty's Customs and Excise, Custom House, Nettleton Road, Heathrow Airport, Hounslow, Middlesex TW6 2LA (tel. (0181) 910-3744; fax 910-3765).

United States: Consult the brochure *Know Before You Go,* available from the U.S. Customs Service, Box 7407, Washington, D.C. 20044 (tel. (202) 927-6724).

YOUTH, STUDENT, & TEACHER IDENTIFICATION

The **International Student Identity Card (ISIC)** is the most widely accepted form of student identification. Flashing this card can procure you discounts ("concessions") for sights, theaters, museums, accommodations, meals, train, ferry, bus, and airplane transportation, and other services. Present the card wherever you go, and ask about discounts even when none are advertised. It also provides insurance benefits, including US$100 per day of in-hospital sickness for a maximum of 60 days, and US$3000 accident-related medical reimbursement for each accident (see **Insurance,** p. 19). In addition, cardholders have access to a toll-free 24-hour ISIC helpline whose multilingual staff can provide assistance in medical, legal, and financial emergencies overseas.

Many student travel agencies around the world issue ISICs, including STA Travel in Australia and New Zealand; Travel CUTS in Canada; USIT in Ireland and Northern Ireland; SASTS in South Africa; Campus Travel and STA Travel in the U.K.; Council Travel, Let's Go Travel, and STA Travel in the U.S.; and any of the other organizations under the auspices of the International Student Travel Confederation (ISTC). When you apply for the card, request a copy of the *International Student Identity Card Handbook,* which lists by country some of the available discounts. You can also write to Council for a copy. The card is valid from September to December of the following year and costs US$19 or CDN$15. Applicants must be at least 12 years old and degree-seeking students of a secondary or post-secondary school. Because of the proliferation of phony ISICs, many airlines and some other services require other proof of student identity, such as a signed letter from the registrar attesting to your student status and stamped with the school seal or your school ID card. The US$20 **International Teacher Identity Card (ITIC)** offers the same insurance coverage and similar but limited discounts. For more information on these cards, consult the organization's web site (http://www.istc.org; email isicinfo@istc.org).

Federation of International Youth Travel Organizations (FIYTO) issues a discount card to travelers who are under 26 but not students. Known as the **GO25 Card,** this one-year card offers many of the same benefits as the ISIC, and most organizations that sell the ISIC also sell the GO25 Card. A brochure that lists discounts is free when you purchase the card. To apply, you will need a passport, valid driver's license, or copy of a birth certificate; and a passport-sized photo with your name printed on the back. The fee is US$19, CDN$15, or UK£5. Information is available on the web at http://www.fiyto.org or http://www.go25.org, or by contacting Travel CUTS in Canada, STA Travel in the U.K., Council Travel in the U.S., or FIYTO headquarters in Denmark (see **Budget Travel,** p. 27).

INTERNATIONAL DRIVING PERMIT

If you plan to drive a car in Australia, you may want an **International Driving Permit (IDP),** though an international traveler may drive with his or her own country's license as long as it remains current. Most car rental agencies don't require the permit, but a very few do and it can serve as an additional piece of identification in a tough situation. An IDP, valid for one year, must be issued in your own country before you depart and must be accompanied by a valid driver's license from your home country. Contact the national automobile association in your home country for details and application information.

Money

CDN$1=AUS$1.01	**AUS$1=CDN$0.99**
IR£1=AUS$2.01	**AUS$1=IR£0.50**
NZ$1=AUS$0.90	**AUS$1=NZ$1.12**
SAR1=AUS$0.30	**AUS$1=SAR3.34**
UK£1=AUS$2.25	**AUS$1=UK£0.44**
US$1=AUS$1.38	**AUS$1=US$0.72**

If you stay in hostels and prepare your own food, expect to spend a minimum of US$20-60 per person per day in Australia, depending on the local cost of living and your needs. Transportation will increase these figures. Don't sacrifice your health or safety for a cheaper tab. No matter how low your budget, if you plan to travel for more than a couple of days, you will need to keep handy a larger amount of cash than usual. Carrying it around with you, even in a money belt, is risky but necessary; personal checks from home are seldom accepted no matter how many forms of identification you have, and even traveler's checks may not be accepted in some locations.

CURRENCY AND EXCHANGE

It is cheaper to buy domestic currency than to buy foreign, so as a rule you should convert money after arriving. However, converting some money before you go will allow you to zip through the airport while others languish in exchange lines. It's a good idea to bring enough foreign currency to last for the first 24-72 hours of a trip, to avoid getting stuck with no money after banking hours or on a holiday. Travelers living in the U.S. can get foreign currency from the comfort of home; contact **Capital Foreign Exchange** on the East Coast (toll-free (888) 842-0880; fax (202) 842-8008), or on the West Coast, **International Currency Express** (toll-free (888) 278-6628; fax (310) 278-6410). These organizations will deliver foreign currency (for over 120 countries) or traveler's checks overnight (US$12) or second-day (US$10) at competitive exchange rates.

Watch out for commission rates and check newspapers to get the standard rate of exchange. Banks generally have the best rates, but this is by no means a hard and fast rule; sometimes tourist offices or exchange kiosks have better deals. A good rule of thumb is to only go to banks or bureaux de change which have only a 5% margin between their buy and sell prices. Anything more, and they are making too much profit. Be sure that both prices are listed. Since you lose money with every transaction, convert in large sums (unless the currency is depreciating rapidly), but don't convert more than you need, because it may be difficult to change it back to your home currency, or to a new one.

If you are using traveler's checks or bills, be sure to carry some in small denominations (US$50 or less), especially for times when you are forced to exchange money at disadvantageous rates. However, it is a good idea to carry a range of denominations since charges may be levied per check cashed, depending on location.

TRAVELER'S CHECKS

Traveler's checks are one of the safest and least troublesome means of carrying funds, as they can be refunded if stolen. Several agencies and many banks sell them, usually for face value plus a small percentage commission. **American Express** and **Visa** are the most widely recognized, though other major checks are sold, exchanged, cashed, and refunded with almost equal ease. Keep in mind that in small towns, traveler's checks are less readily accepted than in cities with large tourist industries. Nonetheless, there will probably be at least one place in every town where you can exchange them for local currency. If you're ordering your checks, do so well in advance, especially if large sums are being requested.

Each agency provides refunds **if your checks are lost or stolen,** and many provide additional services. (Note that you may need a police report verifying the loss or theft.) Inquire about toll-free refund hotlines in Australia, emergency message relay services, and stolen credit card assistance when you purchase your checks. You should expect a fair amount of red tape and delay in the event of theft or loss of traveler's checks. To expedite the refund process, keep your check receipts separate from your checks and store them in a safe place or with a traveling companion, record check numbers when you cash them and leave a list of check numbers with someone at home, and ask for a list of refund centers when you buy your checks. Keep a separate supply of cash or traveler's checks for emergencies. Never countersign your checks until you're prepared to cash them, and always bring your passport with you when you plan to use the checks.

Buying traveler's checks in Australian dollars can either be a wise measure or an exercise in futility. Depending on fluctuations in currency, you may gain or lose money by converting your currency beforehand. Use your best judgement.

American Express: Call 1800 251 902 in Australia; in New Zealand (0800) 44 10 68; in the U.K. (0800) 52 13 13; in the U.S. and Canada (800) 221-7282). Elsewhere, call U.S. collect (801) 964-6665. American Express Traveler's Cheques are now available in 10 currencies including Australian, British, Canadian, U.S., and soon

South African. They are the most widely recognized worldwide and the easiest to replace if lost or stolen. Checks can be purchased for a small fee (1-4%) at American Express Travel Service Offices, banks, and American Automobile Association offices (AAA members can buy the checks commission-free). Cardmembers can also purchase checks from American Express Dispensers at Travel Service Offices at airports and by ordering them via phone (tel. (800) ORDER-TC (673-3782)). American Express offices cash their checks commission-free, although they often offer slightly worse rates than banks. You can also buy *Cheques for Two* which can be signed by either of 2 people traveling together. Request the American Express booklet *Traveler's Companion,* which lists travel office addresses and stolen check hotlines for each European country. Visit their online travel offices at (http://www.aexp.com).

Citicorp: Call (800) 645-6556 in the U.S. and Canada; in Europe, the Middle East, or Africa (0171) 508 7007; from elsewhere call U.S. collect (813) 623-1709. Sells both Citicorp and Citicorp Visa traveler's checks in Australian, Canadian, British, and U.S. currency, among others. Commission is 1-2% on check purchases. Checkholders are automatically enrolled for 45 days in the Travel Assist Program (hotline (800) 250-4377 or collect (202) 296-8728) which provides travelers with English-speaking doctor, lawyer, and interpreter referrals as well as check refund assistance and general travel information. Citicorp's World Courier Service guarantees hand-delivery of traveler's checks when a refund location is not convenient. Call 24hr. per day, 7 days per week.

Thomas Cook MasterCard: For 24hr. cashing or refund assistance, call (800) 223-9920 in the U.S. and Canada; elsewhere call U.S. collect (609) 987-7300; from the U.K. call (0800) 622 101 free or (01733) 502 995 collect or (01733) 318 950 collect. Offers checks in Australian, Canadian, British, South African, and U.S. currencies, and ECUs. Commission 1-2% for purchases. Thomas Cook offices may sell checks for lower commissions and will cash checks commission-free. Thomas Cook Traveler's Checks are also available from **Capital Foreign Exchange** (see **Currency and Exchange,** p. 10) in Canadian, British, and U.S. monies.

Visa: Call (800) 227-6811 in the U.S.; in the U.K. (0800) 895 492; from anywhere else in the world call (01733) 318 949) and reverse the charges. Any of the above numbers can tell you the location of their nearest office. Any type of Visa traveler's checks can be reported lost at the Visa number.

CREDIT CARDS

Credit cards are generally accepted in all but the smallest businesses. Major credit cards like **MasterCard** and **Visa** can be used to extract cash advances from associated banks and teller machines throughout the country. Credit card companies get the wholesale exchange rate, which is generally 5% better than the retail rate used by banks and even better than that used by other currency exchange establishments. However, you will be charged ruinous interest rates if you don't pay off the bill quickly, so be careful when using this service. **American Express** cards also work in some ATMs, as well as at AmEx offices and major airports. All such machines require a **Personal Identification Number (PIN),** which credit cards in the United States do not usually carry. You must ask your credit card company to assign you a PIN before you leave; without it, you will be unable to withdraw cash with your credit card outside the U.S.

Credit cards are also invaluable in an emergency—an unexpected hospital bill or ticket home or the loss of traveler's checks—which may leave you temporarily without other resources. Furthermore, credit cards offer an array of other services, from insurance to emergency assistance, which depend completely on the issuer.

American Express (tel. (800) 843-2273) has a hefty annual fee (US$55) but offers a number of services. Cardholders can cash personal checks at AmEx offices outside the U.S., and U.S. Assist, a 24-hour hotline offering medical and legal assistance in emergencies, is also available (from abroad call U.S. collect (301) 214-8228). The card also offers extensive travel related services, including holding your mail at one of the more than 1700 AmEx offices around the world.

MasterCard (tel. (800) 999-0454) and **Visa** (tel. (800) 336-8472) are issued in cooperation with individual banks and some other organizations; ask the issuer about services which go along with the cards.

CASH CARDS (ATM)

Cash cards—popularly called **ATM** (Automated Teller Machine) cards—are widespread in Australia, and are in all but the smallest of towns. ANZ and National Australia Bank are among the most common banks with these wonderful machines. Depending on which system your bank at home uses, you will probably be able to access your own personal bank account whenever you're in need of funds. Look on the back of your ATM card to see which systems the card can tap into (or call your bank). The two major international money networks are **Cirrus** (U.S. tel. (800) 4-CIR-RUS (424-7787)) and **PLUS** (U.S. tel. (800) 843-7587). Cirrus is the most widespread ATM network in Australia; Plus is almost as good, and Visa is probably third best. Mastercard and American Express are found less often, but are still possibilities. NYCE is not found in Australia. If you are planning travel to northern Western Australia, keep in mind that ATMs are found much less frequently.

Happily, ATMs get the same wholesale exchange rate as credit cards, and are oh-so-easy, since they spit out local currency. Despite these perks, do some research before relying too heavily on automation. There is often a limit on the amount of money you can withdraw per day (usually about US $250-500, depending on the type of card and account), and computer network failures are not uncommon. Be sure to memorize your PIN code in numeral form, since machines in Australia don't always have letters on the keys. Also, if your PIN is longer than four digits, ask your bank whether the first four digits will work, or whether you need a new number. Many ATMs are outdoors; be cautious and aware of your surroundings. Finally, keep all of your receipts—even if a misbehaving ATM won't give you your cash, it may register a withdrawal on your next statement. You will probably be charged US$1-5 each time you withdraw non-domestically, depending on your bank's policy, but the better exchange rate usually makes up the fee.

EFTPOS, which stands for Electronic Funds Transfer at Point Of Sale, is a common way for Australians to pay for goods. ATM cards (from Australian banks only) work like credit cards, except that money is withdrawn directly from the person's bank account. This means that people can carry less cash, without worrying about credit card bills or overextending their capital.

GETTING MONEY FROM HOME

One of the easiest ways to get money from home is to bring an **American Express** card. AmEx allows green-card holders to draw cash from their checking accounts at any of its major offices and many of its representatives' offices, up to US$1000 every 21 days (no service charge, no interest). AmEx also offers Express Cash from ATMs (see **Cash Cards,** p. 12). Green-card holders may withdraw up to US$1000 in a seven-day period. There is a 2% transaction fee for each cash withdrawal, with a US$2.50 minimum/$20 maximum. To enroll in Express Cash, Cardmembers may call (800) CASH NOW (227-4669). Outside the U.S. call collect (904) 565-7875. Unless using the AmEx service, avoid cashing checks in foreign currencies; they usually take weeks and a US$30 fee to clear.

Money can also be wired abroad through international money transfer services operated by **Western Union** tel. (800 325-6000). In the U.S., call Western Union any time at (800) CALL-CASH (225-5227) to cable money to Australia with your Visa, Discover, or MasterCard. The rates for sending cash are generally US$10 more than with a credit card, and the money is available in Australia in 13-15 hours.

Some people also choose to send money abroad in cash via **Federal Express** to avoid transmission fees and taxes. FedEx is reasonably reliable; however, this method may be illegal, it involves an element of risk, and it requires that you remain at a legitimate address for a day or two to wait for the money's arrival. In general, it may be safer to swallow the cost of wire transmission and preserve your peace of mind.

In emergencies, U.S. citizens can have money sent via the State Department's **Overseas Citizens Service, American Citizens Services,** Consular Affairs, Room 4811, U.S. Department of State, Washington, D.C. 20520 (tel. (202) 647-5225, nights, Sundays, and holidays (202) 647-4000; fax (on demand only) (202) 647-3000; http://travel.state.gov). For a fee of US$15, the State Department will forward money within hours to the nearest consular office, which will then disburse it according to instructions. The office serves only Americans in the direst of straits abroad; non-American travelers should contact their embassies or information on wiring cash. The quickest way to have the money sent is to cable the State Department through Western Union depending on the circumstances.

TIPPING AND BARGAINING

Tipping is not required at restaurants or bars, in taxis, or hotels—service workers are fully salaried and do not rely on tips for income. Tips are occasionally left at more expensive restaurants, if you think the service was exceptionally good. In this case, 10% is more than sufficient.

DISCOUNTS

"Concessions" is the Australian catch-all phrase for discounts always given to specific groups, most often students, senior citizens, and youth. However, it may include any combination of these or be limited to holders of specific Australian concession cards. "Pensioners" are Australian senior citizens, and discounts for pensioners may or may not apply to non-Australians who otherwise fit the bill. Student discounts often require that you show an ID, and may only apply to Australian University students, or even to university students within the particular state. Discounts on accommodations are regularly given to VIP, YHA, ISIC, or Nomads card holders. Play it safe and carry a couple forms of ID with you at all times.

OPENING A BANK ACCOUNT

Banks are generally open from 9:30am to 4pm Monday through Thursday, and from 9:30am to 5pm on Friday. Larger cities may mean longer hours. To open an Australian bank account, you need to accrue 100 "points" of identification. A passport, driver's licence, birth certificate, or other major ID will each give you 40 points. Minor IDs (like credit cards) are worth 20 points. So, for example, a passport, driver's license, and credit card in your name will suffice. Visitors who apply within six weeks of arrival to the country, however, need only show a passport. If you open an account, be sure to obtain an Australian Tax File Number, so that your interest is not taxed at the highest rate. This Tax File Number will also let you claim lower deduction rates when you get a job.

Safety and Security

PERSONAL SAFETY

Although Australia is a relatively safe country, it is always important to keep personal safety in mind. Tourists are particularly vulnerable to crime for two reasons: they often carry large amounts of cash and they are not as street savvy as locals. To avoid unwanted attention, try to **blend in** as much as possible. The gawking camera-toter is a more obvious target than the low-profile traveler. Walking directly into a cafe or shop to check a map beats checking it on a street corner. Better yet, look over your map before setting out. Muggings are more often impromptu than planned; nervous, over-the-shoulder glances can be a tip that you have something valuable to protect.

When exploring a new **city,** extra vigilance is wise, but no city should force you to turn precautions into panic. Find out about unsafe areas from tourist information, from the manager of your hotel or hostel, or from a local whom you trust. Especially if you travel alone, be sure that someone at home knows your itinerary. Never say that you're traveling alone. You may want to carry a small **whistle** to scare off attackers or attract attention. Anywhere in Australia, **dial 000 for emergency medical help, police, or fire.**

Whenever possible, *Let's Go* warns of unsafe neighborhoods and areas, but you should exercise your own judgment about the safety of your environs; buildings in disrepair, vacant lots, and unpopulated areas are all bad signs. A district can change character drastically between blocks. Awareness of the flow of people can reveal a great deal about the relative safety of the area; look for children playing, women walking in the open, and other signs of an active community.

There is no sure-fire set of precautions that will protect you from all of the situations you might encounter when you travel. A good self-defense course will give you more concrete ways to react to different types of aggression, but it often carries a steep price tag. **Impact, Prepare,** and **Model Mugging** can refer you to local self-defense courses in the United States (tel. (800) 345-KICK). Course prices vary from $50-400. Women's and men's courses are offered. Community colleges frequently offer inexpensive self-defense courses.

Sleeping in your car is one of the most dangerous (and often illegal) ways to get your rest. If your car breaks down, wait for the police to assist you. Do not wander away from your car looking for assistance—your car is easier to find than you are. If you must sleep in your car, do so as close to a police station or a 24-hour service station as possible. Sleeping out in the open can be even more dangerous—camping is recommended only in official, supervised campsites or in wilderness backcountry.

FINANCIAL SECURITY

Don't put a wallet with money in your back pocket. Never count your money in public and carry as little as possible. If you carry a purse, buy a sturdy one with a secure clasp, and carry it slung across your body, away from the street with the clasp against you. Secure your packs with small combination padlocks which slip through the two zippers. A **money belt** is the best way to carry cash; you can buy one at most camping supply stores. A nylon, zippered pouch with belt that sits inside the waist of your pants or skirt combines convenience and security. A **neck pouch** is equally safe, although far less accessible. Refrain from pulling out your neck pouch in public; if you must, be very discreet. Avoid keeping anything precious in a "fanny-pack" (even if it's worn on your stomach): your valuables will be highly visible and easy to steal. (The word "fanny" refers to female genitalia in Australia and New Zealand, so if you must carry one of these packs, it's best to find a new name for it.)

In city crowds and especially on public transportation, pick-pockets are amazingly deft at their craft. Rush hour is no excuse for strangers to press up against you on the train. If someone stands uncomfortably close, move to another car and hold your bags tightly. Also, be alert in public telephone booths. If you must say your calling-card number, do so very quietly; if you punch it in, make sure no one can look over your shoulder. **Photocopies** of important documents allow you to recover them in case they are lost or filched. Carry one copy separate from the documents and leave another copy at home. Keep some money separate from the rest to use in an emergency or in case of theft. Label every piece of luggage both inside and out.

Be particularly careful on **buses** (for example, carry your backpack in front of you where you can see it), don't check baggage on trains, and don't trust anyone to "watch your bag for a second." *Let's Go* lists locker availability in hostels and train stations, but you'll often need your own padlock. Lockers are useful if you plan on sleeping outdoors or don't want to lug everything with you, but don't store valuables in them. Try never to leave your belongings unattended; crime occurs in even the most demure-looking hostel or hotel. If you feel unsafe, look for places with either a curfew or a night attendant. When possible, keep valuables or anything you couldn't bear to lose at home.

If you travel by **car,** try not to leave valuable possessions—such as radios or luggage—in it while you're off rambling. Radios are especially tempting. If your tape deck or radio is removable, hide it in the trunk or take it with you. If it isn't, at least conceal it under a lot of junk. Similarly, hide baggage in the trunk—although savvy thieves can tell if a car is heavily loaded by the way it sits on its tires.

DRUGS AND ALCOHOL

Australia has fairly strict drug laws, and **illegal drugs** are best avoided altogether. Australia does not differentiate between "hard" drugs and more mainstream ones such as marijuana, all of which are illegal to possess in any quantity. A meek "I didn't know it was illegal" will not suffice. Remember that you are subject to the laws of the country in which you travel, not to those of your home country, and it is your responsibility to familiarize yourself with these laws before leaving. If you carry **prescription drugs** while you travel, it is vital to have a copy of the prescriptions themselves readily accessible at country borders.

Strict drunk-driving laws apply and most states operate random breath-testing. The maximum legal blood-alcohol limit in Australia is .05%. Public bars are generally licensed to serve alcohol between 10am and 10pm, Monday through Saturday. Sunday licensing laws vary by state. Restaurants and clubs usually have longer hours. Although alcohol consumption laws vary slightly by state, you must be 18 years old to purchase or consume alcohol in public.

Health

In the event of a serious illness or emergency, **call 000 from any phone**—this is a free call—to connect to police, ambulance, or the fire department.

Common sense is the simplest prescription for good health while you travel: eat well, drink and sleep enough, and don't overexert yourself. Travelers complain most often about their feet and their gut, so take precautionary measures. Drinking lots of fluids can often prevent dehydration and constipation, and wearing sturdy shoes and clean socks, and using talcum powder can help keep your feet dry. To minimize the effects of jet lag, "reset" your body's clock by adopting the time of your destination immediately upon arrival. Most travelers feel acclimatized to a new time zone after two or three days.

BEFORE YOU GO

Australia is generally a safe and healthy country in which to travel. If you haven't visited a commonly infected country in the past 14 days, no **vaccinations** are necessary to enter Australia. Although no amount of planning can guarantee an accident-free trip, preparation can help minimize the likelihood of contracting a disease and maximize the chances of receiving effective health-care in the event of an emergency. Good medical care is widely available in Australia, but hospitals and doctors may expect immediate cash payment of around $35 for health services. Foreign medical insurance is not always valid abroad (see **Insurance,** p. 19 for details).

Citizens of New Zealand, the United Kingdom, Malta, Sweden, Italy, Finland, and the Netherlands are covered by **Medicare,** Australia's national health insurance plan, while traveling in Australia. Medicare will cover any immediately necessary treatment (but not elective treatments, ambulance service, etc.). Citizens of these countries can register at any Medicare office, but should check with the health insurance plan of their home country before heading to Australia to have the proper documents.

For minor health problems on the road, bring a compact **first-aid kit,** including bandages, aspirin, or other pain killer, antibiotic cream, a thermometer, a Swiss Army knife with tweezers, moleskin, a decongestant for colds, motion sickness remedy, medicine for diarrhea or stomach problems, sunscreen, insect repellent, and burn ointment.

In your passport, write the names of any people you wish to be contacted in case of a medical emergency, and also list any allergies or medical conditions of which you would want doctors to be aware. If you wear glasses or contact lenses, carry an extra prescription and pair of glasses or arrange to have your doctor or a family member send a replacement pair in an emergency. Allergy sufferers should find out if their conditions are likely to be aggravated in the regions they plan to visit, and obtain a full supply of any necessary medication before the trip, since matching a prescription to a foreign equivalent is not always possible. Carry up-to-date, legible prescriptions or a statement from your doctor, especially if you use insulin, a syringe, or a narcotic. While traveling, be sure to keep all medication with you in carry-on luggage. Australian pharmacies, called chemists, can fill most prescriptions, but they need to be written by an Australian doctor.

Those with medical conditions (e.g. diabetes, allergies to antibiotics, epilepsy, heart conditions) may want to obtain a stainless steel **Medic Alert** identification tag (US$35 the first year, and $15 annually thereafter), which identifies the disease and gives a 24-hour collect-call information number. Contact Medic Alert at (800) 825-3785, or write to Medic Alert Foundation, 2323 Colorado Ave., Turlock, CA 95382. Diabetics can contact the **American Diabetes Association,** 1660 Duke St., Alexandria, VA 22314 (tel. (800) 232-3472) to receive copies of the article "Travel and Diabetes" and a diabetic ID card, which carries messages in 18 languages explaining the carrier's diabetic status.

PREVENTING DISEASE

You can minimize the chances of contracting a disease while traveling by taking a few precautionary measures. Australia is officially free of the **rabies** virus, but there have been reports of a rabies-like disease among indigenous bats. If you are bitten, clean your wound thoroughly and seek medical help immediately to find out whether you need treatment.

Dengue Fever is an "urban viral infection" transmitted by Aedes mosquitoes, which bite during the day rather than at night. Dengue has flu-like symptoms and is often indicated by a rash three to four days after the onset of fever. There is no vaccine; the only prevention is to avoid mosquito bites. To treat the symptoms, rest, drink lots of water, and take fever-reducing medication such as acetaminophen (but avoid aspirin). The risk is present but low in the Pacific Islands, and even lower in Northern Queensland and the Torres Strait Islands.

From Carnarvon north in Western Australia, certain species of mosquito can transmit the Ross River and Barmah Forest viruses, as well as encephalitis. See **Mosquito-Borne Diseases** on p. 555 for more specific information. The Health Department of Western Australia recommends wearing long, loose clothing and using topical DEET to fend off bites. Try to avoid long periods outdoors at dawn and at dusk.

Australia sometimes requires that the passenger compartments of incoming aircraft be sprayed with insecticide while passengers are present. Called **disinsection,** this practice is used to prevent the importation of insects such as mosquitoes. The World Health Organization has determined that disinsection is safe, but it may aggravate allergies and other medical conditions. Call the airlines and ask your doctor for more information.

FOOD- AND WATER-BORNE DISEASES

Parasites (tapeworms, etc.) hide in unsafe water and food. *Giardia,* for example, is acquired by drinking untreated water from streams or lakes all over the world, including Australia. It can stay with you for years. Symptoms of parasitic infections in general include swollen glands or lymph nodes, fever, rashes or itchiness, digestive problems, eye problems, and anemia. Boil your water if it comes from a questionable source, wear shoes, avoid bugs, and eat cooked food. See the camping section below for more specific precautions while in the outback.

Hepatitis A (distinct from B and C) is a low risk in Australia. Hepatitis A is a viral infection of the liver acquired primarily through contaminated water, ice, shellfish, or unpeeled fruits and vegetables (as well as from sexual contact). Symptoms include fatigue, fever, loss of appetite, nausea, dark urine, jaundice, vomiting, aches and pains, and light stools. Ask your doctor about a new vaccine called "Harvix," or ask to get an injection of immune globulin (IG; formerly called Gamma Globulin). Risk is highest in rural areas and the countryside, but is also present in urban areas.

DANGEROUS WILDLIFE

When Gondwanaland split up into continents ages ago, Australia ended up with more than her fair share of extremely dangerous animal life. With a few precautions, travelers should be able to avoid the nastiest creatures out there, but hospitals do stock anti-venoms and if you get bitten or stung, it is best to take the offending creature to the hospital with you (if you are not in danger of being bitten or stung again) so that doctors can administer the right anti-venom.

Sea life can be deadly during certain times of year, and warnings to stay out of the water should be strictly observed. The most notorious of these beasts is the **box jellyfish,** which inhabits the waters of northern Australia from November to April. Swimming on beaches north of Rockhampton, Queensland during these months is forbidden. The sting is potentially lethal to adults, and almost certainly lethal to children. Box jellyfish that have washed up on shore are still dangerous, so walking barefoot at the water's edge is discouraged. The **stonefish** and **blue-ringed octopus** also present danger at the beach. Sharks are common to some Australian shores, but lifeguards at heavily visited beaches keep a good look out—don't swim outside the red and yellow flagged areas.

Fresh and saltwater **crocodiles** present another water and water's-edge hazard in north and northwest Australia. "Salties" are the more dangerous of the two. They can be found in fresh and salt water, are hard to see, and attack without provocation. Heed local warning signs, don't swim or paddle in streams, lakes, the ocean, or other natural waterways, and keep kids and dogs away from the waters edge. "Freshies" are found in fresh water and will not attack unless provoked, but they are also hard to see and you may provoke one without knowing it's there.

Several Australian **snakes** are venomous and thus very dangerous. Most snakes attack if threatened or alarmed, so watch where you walk in the bush. Wear boots, socks, and long pants to minimize the danger.

Of the two most dangerous **spiders** in Australia, the funnel-web is found in and around Sydney, and the redback is common throughout Australia. Stinging **insects** abound in Australia, including the bull-ant, wasp, bee, and bush-tick, and although these may hurt a lot, they are not life-threatening. If you know that you are allergic to bee stings or other insect bites, you should carry your own epinephrine kit. After a period of time in the bush, check for lumps on your skin to find and remove bush-ticks. For a friendlier description of Australia's wildlife, see **Biodiversity** (p. 64).

FIRE

Although fire is essential to the reproductive cycle of much of Australia's plant life, it presents a real hazard to people, animals, and plants alike when it rages out of control. Bushfires are more likely during hot, dry weather, and **Total Fire Bans** are often imposed when weather conditions are right (or wrong, as the case may be). Building fires in camping areas is expressly forbidden during Total Fire Ban Days. The bans will be announced by radio, television, and billboards.

HOT AND COLD

It pays to be extra careful regarding sunblock. The ozone's thinner down under, and Australians have the highest rate of **skin cancer** in the world. Be sure to wear the highest SPF level sunblock at all times, a hat, and some form of upper body cover during the hottest times of the day. And drink *lots* of water.

Common sense goes a long way toward preventing **heat exhaustion,** characterized by profuse sweating, flushed skin, dizziness, and nausea. Relax in hot weather, drink lots of non-alcoholic fluids, and lie down out of the sun if you feel awful. Continuous heat stress can eventually lead to **heatstroke,** characterized by rising body temperature, severe headache, and cessation of sweating. Wear a hat, sunglasses, and a lightweight longsleeve shirt to avoid heatstroke. Victims must be cooled off with wet towels and taken to a doctor as soon as possible. Always drink enough liquids to keep your urine clear. Alcoholic beverages and caffeine are dehydrating. If you'll be sweating a lot, be sure to eat enough salty food to prevent electrolyte depletion, which causes severe headaches.

Extreme cold is just as dangerous as heat—overexposure to cold brings the risk of **hypothermia,** a lowering of the body's core temperature that can lead to coma and death. It is caused by exposure to cold (even temperatures around 45°F/7°C) and accelerated by wind, moisture, dehydration, and fatigue, all common in Australia's mountains. It is important to detect the condition at an early stage and to get victims to a doctor as soon as possible. Symptoms include pale skin, shivering, poor coordination, disorientation, and poor judgment. Advanced symptoms include a decrease in shivering, slurred speech, hallucinations, and collapse leading to the big sleep. Before this happens, take action. If hiking, stop immediately and seek shelter from wind and rain. Remove the victim's wet clothing, and get him or her into a sleeping bag if available. Give warm, sweet liquids in moderation. Do not give caffeine or alcohol, which cause dehydration, increase the rate of heat loss, and decrease the body's ability to regulate temperature. To avoid hypothermia, stay hydrated and well-fed, keep dry, and stay out of the wind.

When the temperature is below freezing, dress in layers and watch for **frostbite.** Look for skin that has turned white, waxy, and cold, and if you find frostbite do not rub the skin. Drink warm beverages, get dry, and slowly warm the area with dry fabric or steady body contact. Take serious cases to a doctor as soon as possible; skin that has been frostbitten once is more likely to become so a second time.

WOMEN'S HEALTH

Women traveling in remote areas with unsanitary conditions are vulnerable to urinary tract and bladder infections, common and severely uncomfortable bacterial diseases which cause a burning sensation and painful and sometimes frequent urination. Drink tons of vitamin-C-rich juice, plenty of clean water, and urinate frequently, especially right after intercourse. Untreated, these infections can lead to kidney infections, sterility, and even death. If symptoms persist, see a doctor. If you often develop vaginal yeast infections, take along enough over-the-counter medicine. Women may also be more susceptible to vaginal thrush and cystitis, two treatable but uncomfortable illnesses that are likely to flare up in hot and humid climates. Wearing loosely fitting trousers or a skirt and cotton underwear may help. Refer to the *Handbook for Women Travellers* by Maggie and Gemma Moss (published by Piatkus Books) or to the women's health guide *Our Bodies, Our Selves* (published by the Boston Women's Health Collective) for more extensive information specific to women's health on the road.

BIRTH CONTROL

Reliable contraceptive devices can be difficult to find while traveling. Women on the pill should bring enough to allow for possible loss or extended stays. Bring a copy of your prescription—forms of the pill vary a good deal but with that information you will probably be able to match yours. Women who use a diaphragm should have enough contraceptive jelly on hand. Though condoms are widely available, you might want to stock up on your favorite national brand before you go; availability and quality vary.

Although abortion laws differ by state, abortion is in general not available on request, but only to protect the mental or physical health of the mother. Parental consent is required for minors in some states. For information on contraception, condoms, and abortion in Australia and worldwide, contact the **International Planned Parenthood Federation.** The western hemisphere regional office is in New York (tel. (212) 248-6400). The European regional office is at Regent's College Inner Circle, Regent's Park, London NW1 4NS (tel. (0171) 487 7900; fax 487 7950). The southern hemisphere regional office is in Canberra (tel. (02) 6285 1244; fax 6282 5298; email 100246.3104@compuserve.com). Planned Parenthood is not a referral service.

AIDS, HIV, STDS

Acquired Immune Deficiency Syndrome (AIDS) is a growing problem around the world. The World Health Organization estimates that there are around 13 million people infected with the HIV virus. Well over 90% of adults newly infected with HIV acquired their infection through heterosexual sex; women now represent 50% of all new HIV infections. The easiest mode of HIV transmission is through direct blood to blood contact with an HIV+ person; *never* share intravenous drug, tattooing, or other needles, or have sexual intercourse without using a latex condom lubricated with spermicide (nonoxynol-9). Casual contact (including drinking from the same glass or using the same eating utensils as an infected person) is not believed to pose a risk.

For more information on AIDS, call the **U.S. Center for Disease Control's** 24-hour Hotline at (800) 342-2437. In Europe, write to the **World Health Organization,** attn: Global Program on AIDS, 20 Avenue Appia, 1211 Geneva 27, Switzerland (tel. (022) 791-2111), for statistical material on AIDS internationally. Or write to the **Bureau of Consular Affairs,** #6831, Department of State, Washington, D.C. 20520. Council's brochure, *Travel Safe: AIDS and International Travel,* is available at all Council Travel offices.

Hepatitis B is a viral infection of the liver transmitted by sharing needles, having unprotected sex, or coming into direct contact with an infected person's lesioned skin. If you think you may be sexually active while traveling or if you are working or living in rural areas, you are typically advised to get the vaccination for Hepatitis B. Vaccination should begin six months before traveling.

Sexually transmitted diseases (STDs) such as gonorrhea, chlamydia, genital warts, syphilis, and herpes are a lot easier to catch than HIV, and can also be very serious. Condoms may protect you from certain STDs, but oral or even tactile contact can lead to transmission.

Insurance

Beware of buying unnecessary travel coverage—your regular insurance policies may well extend to many travel-related accidents. **Medical insurance** (especially university policies) often cover costs incurred abroad; check with your provider. **Medicare's** "foreign travel" coverage for U.S. residents is valid only in Canada and Mexico, not in Australia. Canadians are protected by their home province's health insurance plan for up to 90 days after leaving the country. Australia has Reciprocal Health Care Agreements (RHCAs) with Finland, Italy, Malta, the Netherlands, New Zealand, Sweden, and the U.K.,; when traveling in Australia citizens of these nations are entitled to many of the services that they would receive at home, and vice versa. Your **homeowners' insurance** (or your family's coverage) often covers theft during travel. Homeowners are generally covered against loss of travel documents (passport, plane ticket, railpass, etc.) up to US$500.

ISIC and **ITIC** provide basic insurance benefits (see **Youth, Student, and Teacher Identification,** p. 8), and access to a toll-free 24-hour helpline whose multilingual staff can provide assistance in medical, legal, and financial emergencies overseas (tel. (800) 626-2427 in the U.S. and Canada; elsewhere call the U.S. collect (713) 267-2525). **Council** and **STA** offer a range of plans that can supplement your basic insurance coverage, with options covering medical treatment and hospitalization, accidents, baggage loss, and even charter flights missed due to illness. **American Express** cardholders receive automatic travel accident coverage (US$100,000 in life insurance) on flight purchases made with the card; call Customer Service (tel. (800) 528-4800). YHA travel insurance gives a 10% discount on Australian and overseas travel insurance policies.

The Berkely Group/Carefree Travel Insurance, 100 Garden City Plaza, P.O. Box 9366, Garden City, NY 11530-9366 (24hr. tel. (800) 323-3149 or (516) 294-0220; fax 294-1096). Offers 2 comprehensive packages including coverage for trip cancellation/interruption/delay, accident and sickness, medical, baggage loss, accidental death, and dismemberment. Trip cancellation/interruption may be purchased separately at a rate of US$5.50 per $100 of coverage.

Globalcare Travel Insurance, 220 Broadway, Lynnfield, MA 01940 (tel. (800) 821-2488; fax (617) 592-7720); email global@nebc.mv.com; http://www.nebc.mv. com /globalcare). Complete medical, legal, emergency, and travel-related services. On-the-spot payments and special student programs, including benefits for trip cancellation and interruption. Also included at no extra charge is a Worldwide Collision Damage Provision.

Alternatives to Tourism

STUDY

Foreign study programs vary tremendously in expense, academic quality, living conditions, degree of contact with local students, and exposure to local culture and languages. There is a plethora of exchange programs for high school students. Most American undergraduates enroll in programs sponsored by U.S. universities, and many colleges have offices that give advice and information on study abroad. Ask for the names of recent participants in these programs, and get in touch with them in order to judge which program is best for you.

American Field Service (AFS), 198 Madison Ave., 8th Fl., New York, NY 10016 (tel. students (800) AFS-INFO (237-4636), administration (800) 876-2376; fax (503) 241-1653; email afsinfo@afs.org; http://www.afs.org/usa). AFS offers summer, semester, and year-long homestay international exchange programs in Australia and New Zealand for high school students and recent high school graduates. Financial aid available.

American Institute for Foreign Study, College Division, 102 Greenwich Ave., Greenwich, CT 06830 (tel. (800) 727-2437). Organizes programs for high school and college study in universities in Australia. Scholarships available.

Beaver College Center for Education Abroad, 450 S. Easton Rd., Glenside, PA 19038-3295 (tel. (888) BEAVER 9 (232-8379); fax (215) 572-2174; email cea@beaver.edu; http://www.beaver.edu/cea/). Operates study abroad programs in Australia as well as a Peace Studies program. Summer and graduate study programs also available. Applicants must have completed 3 full semesters at an accredited university. Call for brochure.

School for International Training, Kipling Rd., P.O. Box 676, Brattleboro, VT 05302 (tel. (800) 336-1616; fax (802) 258-3500). Offers extensive **College Semester Abroad** programs in Oceania. Programs cost US$9300-11,500, including tuition, room and board, and airfare. Scholarships are available and federal financial aid is usually transferable from home college or university. Write for a brochure. At the same address, the **Experiment in International Living** runs 3-5 week summer programs offering cross-cultural, educational homestays, community service, and ecological adventure in Australia (tel. (800) 345-2929; fax (802) 258-3428; email eil@worldlearning.org; http://www.worldlearning.org). Positions as group leaders are available world-wide if you are over 24, have previous in-country experience, are fluent in the language, and have experience with high school students.

Council on International Education Exchange, 205 E. 42nd St., New York, NY 10017 (tel. (888) COUNCIL (268-6245); fax (212) 822-2699; email info@ciee.org; http://www.ciee.org) sponsors over 40 study abroad programs throughout the world. Contact them for more information.

Institute of International Education (IIE), 809 United Nations Plaza, New York, NY 10017-3580 (tel. (212) 984-5413; fax 984-5358). For book orders: IIE Books, Institute of International Education, P.O. Box 371, Annapolis Junction, MD 20701 (tel. (800) 445-0443; fax (301) 206-9789; email iiebooks@pmds.com). A nonprofit, international and cultural exchange agency, IIE's library of study abroad resources is open to the public Tues.-Thurs. 11am-3:45pm. Publishes *Academic Year Abroad* (US$43, $5 postage) and *Vacation Study Abroad* (US$37, $5 postage). Write for a complete list of publications.

International Association for the Exchange of Students for Technical Experience (IAESTE), 10400 Little Patuxent Pkwy. #250, Columbia, MD 21044-3510 (tel. (410) 997-3068; fax 997-5186; email iaeste@aipt.org; http://www.aipt.org). Operates 8- to 12-week programs in over 50 countries for college students who have completed 2 years of study in a technical field. Non-refundable US$50 application fee; apply by Dec. 10 for summer placement.

Peterson's Guides, P.O. Box 2123, Princeton, NJ 08543-2123 (tel. (800) 338-3282; fax (609) 243-9150; http://www.petersons.com). Their comprehensive *Study Abroad* (US$30) annual guide lists programs in countries all over the world and provides essential information on the study abroad experience in general. Their new *Learning Adventures Around the World* (US$25) annual guide to "learning vacations" lists volunteer, study, and travel programs all over the world. Purchase a copy at your local bookstore or call their toll-free number in the U.S.

Youth For Understanding International Exchange (YFU), 3501 Newark St. NW, Washington, D.C. 20016 (tel. (800) TEENAGE (833-6243) or (202) 966-6800; fax 895-1104; http://www.yfu.org). Places U.S. high school students worldwide for year, semester, summer, and sport homestays.

WORK

There's no better way to immerse yourself in a foreign culture than to become part of its economy. Call the Consulate or Embassy of Australia to get more information about work permits. It is often easier to find work in large cities than smaller towns, and some work, like fruit picking, is necessarily seasonal. Check newspapers under "Situations Vacant," especially on Saturdays and Wednesdays. The **Commonwealth Employment Service's** many offices provide information, and backpacker magazines or hostels usually have info on seasonal work. If you are planning to work for an extended period of time or want to open a bank account in Australia, you should apply for a Tax File Number. These are not required, but without one, tax will be withheld at the highest rate. Contact a local branch of the Australian Taxation Office.

If you are a **U.S. citizen** and a full-time student at a U.S. university, the simplest way to get a job abroad is through work permit programs run by **Council on International Educational Exchange (Council)** and its member organizations. For a US$225 application fee, Council can procure three- to six-month work permits (and a handbook to help you find work and housing) for Australia and New Zealand. Vacation Work Publications publishes *Work Your Way Around the World* (UK£11, £2.50 postage, £1.50 within U.K.) to help you along the way (see below). Riverina Regional Tourism's (tel. (02) 6921 6422 or (02) 6993 2190) brochure *Working Holidays in the Riverina* addresses fruit picking issues in southwest New South Wales, where there's something ripening every month of the year.

The Archaeological Institute of America, 656 Beacon St., Boston, MA 02215-2010 (tel. (617) 353-9361; fax 353-6550; email aia@bu.edu; http://csa.brynmawr.edu/web2/aia.html), puts out the *Archaeological Fieldwork Opportunities Bulletin* (US$11 non-members) which lists over 300 field sites throughout the world. This can be purchased from Kendall/Hunt Publishing, 4050 Westmark Dr., Dubuque, IA 52002 (tel. (800) 228-0810).

Office of Overseas Schools, A/OS Room 245, SA-29, Dept. of State, Washington, D.C. 20522-2902 (tel. (703) 875-7800; http://www.state.gov/www/about_state/schools/). Keeps a list of schools abroad and agencies that arrange placement for Americans to teach abroad.

Useful Publications

Transitions Abroad Publishing, Inc., 18 Hulst Rd., P.O. Box 1300, Amherst, MA 01004-1300 (tel. (800) 293-0373; fax (413) 256-0373; email trabroad@aol.com; http://www.transabroad.com). Publishes *Transitions Abroad*, a bi-monthly magazine listing all kinds of opportunities and printed resources for those seeking to study, work, or travel abroad. They also publish *The Alternative Travel Directory,* a truly exhaustive listing of information for the "active international traveler." For subscriptions (in U.S. US$25 for 6 issues, Canada US$30, other countries US$38), contact them at *Transitions Abroad,* Dept. TRA, Box 3000, Denville, NJ 07834 or call (800) 293-0373.

Vacation Work Publications, 9 Park End St., Oxford OX1 1HJ (tel. (01865) 24 19 78; fax 79 08 85). Publishes a wide variety of guides and directories with job listings and info for the working traveler, including *The Au Pair and Nanny's Guide to Working Abroad* (UK£9, £2.50 and £1.50 postage). Opportunities for summer or full-time work in numerous countries. Write for a catalogue of their publications.

VOLUNTEERING

Volunteer jobs are readily available almost everywhere. You may receive room and board in exchange for your labor, and the work can be fascinating (or stultifying). You can sometimes avoid the high application fees charged by the organizations that arrange placement by contacting the individual workcamps directly; check with the organizations. Listings in Vacation Work Publications's *International Directory of Voluntary Work* (UK£10; postage UK£2.50, £1.50 within the U.K.) can be helpful (see above).

Willing Workers on Organic Farms (WWOOF), Mt. Murrindal Co-op, Gelantipy Rd., Buchan Vic 3885 (tel. (03) 5155 0218; email BuchanNH@b150.aone.net. au). This Australian subset of the world-wide organization distributes a list of names of farmers who offer room and board in exchange for help on the farm. WWOOF has about 200 sites in Australia, mainly in Victoria, New South Wales, and Queensland. To join, send AUS$15 (or AUS$20 from overseas) and you'll get a membership number and booklet listing sites all over the country.

Australian & New Zealand Scientific Exploration Society (ANZSES), P.O. Box 174, Albert Park, Vic 3206 (http://home.vicnet.net.au/~anzses/). Annually conducts a youth expedition (ages 17-25), an all-women's expedition, and an open expedition. Participants collect data for a range of natural science projects to assist resource management bodies such as National Parks and Wildlife Services, universities, state museums, and the Australian Commonwealth Scientific and Industrial Research Organization (CSIRO). Expeditioners pay a fee to cover transport, food, and equipment. As of September 1997, the web site listed above contained an incorrect phone number for the organization.

Australian Trust for Conservation Volunteers (tel. (03) 5333 1483). Does conservation projects including tree planting, track construction, sand dune restoration, and heritage programs. Volunteers pay AUS$20 per day for food and lodging while working on projects throughout the country. Long term packages also available.

Council has a Voluntary Services Dept., 205 E. 42nd St., New York, NY 10017 (tel. (888) COUNCIL (268-6245); fax (212) 822-2699; email info@ciee.org; http://www.ciee.org) which offers 2- to 4-week environmental or community services projects in over 30 countries. Participants must be at least 18 years old. Minimum US$295 placement fee; additional fees may also apply for various countries.

Specific Concerns

WOMEN TRAVELERS

Women exploring on their own inevitably face additional safety concerns, but these warnings and suggestions should not discourage women from traveling alone. Be adventurous, but avoid unnecessary risks. Trust your instincts: if you'd feel better somewhere else, move on. Always carry extra money for a phone call, bus, or taxi. You might consider staying in hostels which offer single rooms that lock from the inside or in religious organizations that offer rooms for women only. Communal showers in some hostels are safer than others; check them before settling in. Stick to centrally-located accommodations and avoid solitary late-night treks or metro rides. **Hitching** is never safe for lone women, or even for two women traveling together.

If you spend time in cities, you may be harassed no matter how you're dressed. Your best answer to verbal harassment is no answer at all (a reaction is what the harasser wants). In crowds, you may be pinched or squeezed by oversexed slimeballs. Wearing a conspicuous **wedding band** may help prevent such incidents. The look on the face is the key to avoiding unwanted attention. Feigned deafness, sitting motionless, and staring at the ground will do a world of good that reactions usually don't achieve. The extremely persistent can sometimes be dissuaded by a firm, loud, and very public "Go away!" If need be, turn to an older woman for help; her stern rebukes will usually be enough to embarrass the most determined jerks.

Don't hesitate to seek out a police officer or a passerby if you are being harassed. *Let's Go* lists emergency numbers (including rape crisis lines) in the Practical Information listings of most cities. See **Safety and Security** for additional tips. The following resources may be helpful if you want more information:

Handbook For Women Travellers by Maggie and Gemma Moss (UK£9). Encyclopedic and well-written. Available from Piatkus Books, 5 Windmill St., London W1P 1HF (tel. (0171) 631 07 10).

Women Travel: Adventures, Advice & Experience by Miranda Davies and Natania Jansz (Penguin, US$13). Info on several foreign countries plus a decent bibliography and resource index. The sequel, *More Women Travel,* costs US$15. Both from Rough Guides, 375 Hudson St. 3rd Fl., New York, NY 10014.

Women Going Places is a women's travel and resource guide geared towards lesbians which emphasizes women-owned enterprises. Advice appropriate for all women. US$15 from Inland Book Company, 1436 W. Randolph St., Chicago, IL 60607 (tel. (800) 243-0138; fax (800) 334-3892), or a local bookstore.

A Foxy Old Woman's Guide to Traveling Alone, by Jay Ben-Lesser (Crossing Press, US$11). Info, informal advice, and a resource list on solo travel on a low-to-medium budget.

OLDER TRAVELERS

Senior citizens are eligible for a wide range of discounts on transportation, museums, movies, theaters, concerts, restaurants, and accommodations. If you don't see a senior citizen (or "pensioner") price listed, ask; you may be delightfully surprised. Agencies for senior group travel include the following.

Elderhostel, 75 Federal St., 3rd Fl., Boston, MA 02110-1941 (tel. (617) 426-7788, fax 426-8351; email Cadyg@elderhostel.org; http://www.elderhostel.org). For those 55 or over (spouse of any age). Programs at colleges, universities, and other learning centers in over 70 countries on varied subjects lasting 1-4 weeks.

Eldertreks, 597 Markham St., Toronto, ON M6G 2L7 (tel. (416) 588-5000; fax 588-9839; email passages@inforamp.net).

No Problem! Worldwise Tips for Mature Adventurers, by Janice Kenyon. Advice and info on insurance, finances, security, health, packing. Useful appendices. US$16 from Orca Book Publishers, P.O. Box 468, Custer, WA 98240-0468.

Unbelievably Good Deals and Great Adventures That You Absolutely Can't Get Unless You're Over 50, by Joan Rattner Heilman. After you finish reading the title page, check inside for some great tips on senior discounts. US$10 from Contemporary Books.

BISEXUAL, GAY, AND LESBIAN TRAVELERS

The profile of bisexual, gay, and lesbian people in Australia has risen in recent years, most notably in the popularity of the **gay and lesbian Mardi Gras** in Sydney each year. The east coast is especially gay friendly—Sydney would probably rank in the top five most gay-friendly cities on earth. The farther into the country you get, the more homophobia you may encounter. Homosexual acts are now legal in all states; Tasmania was the last to drop its anti-homosexuality laws, in the spring of 1997.

The **Australian Gay and Lesbian Tourist Association (AGLTA)** is a nonprofit organization that publishes a Tourism Service Directory which lists over 130 gay-friendly organizations. They can be reached at P.O. Box 208, Darlinghurst NSW 2010 (tel. (02) 9955 6755; fax 9922 6036), or take a look at their web site at (http://aglta.asn.au/index.htm). Listed below are contact organizations and publishers which offer materials addressing gay and lesbian concerns.

Ferrari Guides, P.O. Box 37887, Phoenix, AZ 85069 (tel. (602) 863-2408; fax 439-3952; email ferrari@q-net.com; http://www.q-net.com). Gay and lesbian travel guides: *Ferrari Guides' Gay Travel A to Z* (US$16), *Ferrari Guides' Men's Travel in Your Pocket* (US$16), *Ferrari Guides' Women's Travel in Your Pocket* (US$14), *Ferrari Guides' Inn Places* (US$16). Available in bookstores or by mail order (postage/handling US$4.50 for the first item, $1 for each additional item mailed within the U.S.; overseas, call or write for shipping cost).

International Gay and Lesbian Travel Association, P.O. Box 4974, Key West, FL 33041 (tel. (800) 448-8550; fax (305) 296-6633; email IGTA@aol.com; http://www.rainbow-mall.com/igta). An organization of over 1300 companies serving gay and lesbian travelers worldwide. Call for lists of travel agents, accommodations, and events.

Spartacus International Gay Guides (US$33), published by Bruno Gmunder, Postfach 61 01 04, D-10921 Berlin, Germany (tel. (030) 615 00 3-42; fax 615 91 34). Lists bars, restaurants, hotels, and bookstores around the world catering to gays. Also lists hotlines for gays in various countries and homosexuality laws for each country. Available in bookstores and in the U.S. by mail from Lambda Rising, 1625 Connecticut Ave. NW, Washington, D.C., 20009-1013 (tel. (202) 462-6969).

TRAVELERS WITH DISABILITIES

Hotels and hostels have recently become more accessible to disabled persons, and many attractions are trying to make exploring the outdoors more feasible. Call ahead to restaurants, hotels, parks, and other facilities to find out about the existence of ramps, the widths of doors, the dimensions of elevators, etc. Establishments that are not wheelchair accessible are usually willing to do whatever they can to accommodate special needs. However, public transportation is lagging a bit behind; arrange transportation well in advance to ensure a smooth trip. If you give sufficient notice, some major car rental agencies offer hand-controlled vehicles at select locations. Wheelchair-accessible taxis are available in most large cities.

For information on accessible transport, accommodation, and venues, contact the **National Information Communication Awareness Network (NICAN),** P.O. Box 407, Curtin, ACT 2605 (tel. (02) 6285 3713; fax 6285 3714; email nican@spirit.com.au). The **Australian Association of the Deaf** can provide resources for deaf travelers on services available including telephone relay systems, interpreting services, and specially designed items such as hearing aid batteries, vibrating alarm clocks, or TTYs. Contact Robert Adam at rcrcja@cc.newcastle.edu.au or Alastair McEwin at almcewin@ozemail.com.au for more information on the available state and national resources.

There are a number of general books helpful to travelers with disabilities. The following organizations provide information or publications that might be of assistance.

Mobility International, USA (MIUSA), P.O. Box 10767, Eugene, OR 97440 (tel. (514) 343-1284 voice and TDD; fax 343-6812; email info@miusa.org; http://miusa.org). International Headquarters in Brussels, rue de Manchester 25 Brussels, Belgium, B-1070 (tel. (02) 410-6297; fax 410 6874). Contacts in 30 countries. Information on travel programs, international work camps, accommodations, access guides, and organized tours for those with physical disabilities. Membership US$30 per year. Check out a copy of *A World of Options: A Guide to International Edu-*

cational Exchange, Community Service, and Travel for Persons with Disabilities (US$30, nonmembers $35; organizations $40).

Society for the Advancement of Travel for the Handicapped (SATH), 347 Fifth Ave., #610, New York, NY 10016 (tel. (212) 447-1928; fax 725-8253; email sathtravel@aol.com; http://www.sath.org). Publishes a quarterly color travel magazine *OPEN WORLD,* and publishes a wide range of information sheets on disability travel facilitation and accessible destinations. Annual membership US$45, students and seniors $30.

Directions Unlimited, 720 N. Bedford Rd., Bedford Hills, NY 10507 (tel. (800) 533-5343, in NY (914) 241-1700; fax 241-0243). Specializes in arranging individual and group vacations, tours, and cruises for the physically disabled. Group tours for blind travelers.

MINORITY TRAVELERS

Australia is a generally tolerant and diverse country, but a fear of losing jobs to **Asian** immigrants has inflamed racism. This may well extend to Asian travelers. **Gay and lesbian** travelers will find rural areas, particularly in the north, less tolerant of their lifestyle, but may be surprised by the number of gay-friendly establishments even in notoriously uptight Darwin. Sydney, of course, is a sort of gay mecca, with the world-famous gay **Mardi Gras** celebration. White Australians are often described as racist in their attitudes toward the **Aboriginals,** and this assessment is not unfounded. However, the political-correctness craze has not really struck Australia yet, and the use of labels like "blackfella" and "abo" do not necessarily imply a derogatory attitude. Blacks of African descent are likely to get a few stares in smaller towns, and may encounter some hostility in outback areas, but will probably not be discriminated against in cities. As always, cities tend to be more tolerant than small towns, but don't let this dissuade you from venturing off the beaten track. *Let's Go* asks that its researchers exclude from the guides establishments that discriminate. If in your travels, you encounter discriminatory treatment, you should firmly but calmly state your disapproval, but do not push the matter. Make it clear to the owners on any involved establishment that another hostel or restaurant will be receiving your patronage. Then mail a letter to *Let's Go,* if the establishment is listed in the guide, so we can investigate the matter next year (see **Helping Let's Go,** in the very front of this guide).

TRAVELERS WITH CHILDREN

Family vacations can be extraordinary experiences, if you slow your pace and plan ahead. When deciding where to stay, remember the special needs of young children; if you pick a B&B, call ahead and make sure it's child-friendly. If you rent a car, make sure the rental company provides a car seat for younger children. Consider using a backpack-style device to carry your baby on walking trips. Be sure that your child carries some sort of ID in case of an emergency or in case she gets lost, and arrange a reunion spot in case of separation when sight-seeing (e.g., the 6th gum tree on the left, or the water fountain). The following publications offer tips for adults traveling with children or distractions for the kids themselves.

Backpacking with Babies and Small Children (US$10). Published by Wilderness Press, 2440 Bancroft Way, Berkeley, CA 94704 (tel. (800) 443-7227 or (510) 843-8080; fax 548-1355; email wpress@ix.netcom.com).

Travel with Children by Maureen Wheeler (US$12, postage $1.50). Published by Lonely Planet Publications, Embarcadero West, 155 Filbert St., #251, Oakland, CA 94607 (tel. (800) 275-8555 or (510) 893-8555; fax 893-8563; email info@lonelyplanet.com; http://www.lonelyplanet.com). Also at P.O. Box 617, Hawthorn, Vic 3122.

DIETARY CONCERNS

Vegetarians should have little problem finding suitable cuisine in Australia, despite the prevalence of meat pies. Most restaurants have vegetarian selections on their menus, and some cater specifically to vegetarians. *Let's Go* often notes restaurants with good vegetarian selections in city listings. Small towns may present more of a problem. Travelers who keep **kosher** should contact synagogues in larger cities for information on kosher restaurants. Kosher food is much more difficult to find than vegetarian fare in Australia. If you are strict in your observance, consider preparing your own food on the road. **The Jewish Travel Guide** lists synagogues, kosher restaurants, and Jewish institutions in over 80 countries, including Australia. It is available in the U.K. from Ballantine-Mitchell Publishers, Newbury House 890-900, Eastern Ave., Newbury Park, Ilford, Essex IG2 7HH (tel. (0181) 599 88 66; fax 599 09 84); in the U.S., contact Sepher-Hermon Press, 1265 46th St., Brooklyn, NY 11219 (tel. (718) 972-9010; US$15 plus $2.50 shipping).

Packing

Plan your packing according to the type of travel you'll be doing (multi-city backpacking tour, week-long stay in Sydney, bushwalking in Tasmania) and the area's high and low temperatures (see **Appendix,** p. 571). If you don't pack lightly, your back and wallet will suffer. The more things you have, the more you have to lose. The larger your pack, the more cumbersome it is to store safely. Before you leave, pack your bag, strap it on, and imagine yourself walking uphill on hot asphalt for the next three hours. A good rule is to lay out only what you absolutely need, then take half the clothes and twice the money.

LUGGAGE

Backpack: If you plan to cover most of your itinerary by foot, a sturdy backpack is unbeatable. Many packs are designed specifically for travelers, while others are for hikers; consider how you will use the pack before purchasing one or the other. In any case, get a pack with a strong, padded hip belt to transfer weight from your shoulders to your hips. Be wary of excessively low-end prices, and don't sacrifice quality. Good packs cost anywhere from US$150-$420.

Suitcase or trunk: Fine if you plan to live in 1 or 2 cities and explore from there, but a bad idea if you're going to be moving around a lot.

Daypack, rucksack, or courier bag: Bringing a smaller bag in addition to your pack or suitcase allows you to leave your big bag behind while you go sight-seeing. It can be used as an airplane carry-on to keep essentials with you.

Moneybelt or neck pouch: Guard your money, passport, railpass, and other important articles in either one of these and keep it with you *at all times.* The moneybelt should tuck inside the waist of your pants or skirt; you want to hide your valuables, not announce them with a colorful fanny- or butt-pack. See **Safety and Security,** p. 13, for more information on protecting you and your valuables.

CLOTHING AND FOOTWEAR

Clothing: When choosing your travel wardrobe, aim for versatility and comfort, and avoid fabrics that wrinkle easily (to test a fabric, hold it tightly in your fist for 20 seconds). Solid colors match and mix best. Always bring a jacket or wool sweater.

Walking shoes: Well-cushioned **sneakers** are good for walking, though you may want to consider a good water-proofed pair of **hiking boots.** A double pair of socks—light silk or polypropylene inside and thick wool outside—will cushion feet, keep them dry, and help prevent blisters. Bring a pair of flip-flops for protection in the shower. Talcum powder in your shoes and on your feet can prevent sores, and moleskin is great for blisters. Break in your shoes before you leave.

Rain gear: A waterproof jacket and a backpack cover will take care of you and your stuff at a moment's notice. Gore-Tex® is a miracle fabric that's both waterproof and breathable; it's all but mandatory if you plan on hiking. Avoid cotton as outer-wear, especially if you'll be outdoors a lot, because it's useless and even dangerous when wet.

MISCELLANEOUS

Some valuable items: **sunscreen,** sun hat, sunglasses, **first-aid kit** including moleskin (for blisters), garbage bags (for lining your pack, covering your pack), sealable **plastic bags** (for damp clothes, soap, food, shampoo, and other spillables), alarm clock, waterproof matches, **needle and thread,** safety pins, pocketknife, plastic water bottle, compass, string (makeshift clothesline and lashing material), clothespins, towel, padlock, **flashlight,** whistle, rubber bands, toilet paper, earplugs, **insect repellent,** duct tape (for patching tears), maps, tweezers, and vitamins.

Sleepsacks: If you plan to stay in **youth hostels,** don't pay the linen charge; make the requisite sleepsack yourself. Fold a full size sheet in half the long way, then sew it closed along the open long side and one of the short sides. For those less handy with a needle, sleepsacks can be bought at any HI outlet store. Many hostels will not allow sleeping bags as a substitute.

Contact lenses: Machines that heat-disinfect contact lenses will require a small converter (about US$20) if your home current is not 240V. Consider switching temporarily to a chemical disinfection system, but check with your lens dispenser to see if it's safe to switch. Your preferred brand of contact lens supplies are sometimes rare or expensive; bring enough for your entire vacation, or wear glasses.

Washing clothes: Most hostels and many caravan parks offer laundry facilities, which in Australia often means wash only, and laundromats are easy to track down in town. Sometimes, though, it may be easiest to use a sink. Bring a rubber squash ball to stop up the sink, and a travel clothesline.

Electric current: In Australia, as in most European countries, electricity is 240V AC, enough to fry any 120V North American appliance. Australian outlets are made for 3 pronged plugs with the top 2 prongs angled in. Visit a hardware store for an adapter (which changes the shape of the plug) and a converter (which changes the voltage). Don't make the mistake of using only an adapter (unless appliance instructions explicitly state otherwise), or you'll melt your radio.

Film is expensive just about everywhere. Bring film from home if you know where to get a good deal. If you're not a serious photographer, you might want to consider bringing a **disposable camera** or two rather than an expensive permanent one. Despite disclaimers, airport security X-rays *can* fog film, so either buy a lead-lined pouch, sold at camera stores, or ask the security to hand inspect it. Always pack it in your carry-on, since higher-intensity X-rays are used on checked bags.

GETTING THERE

Budget Travel Agencies

Students and people under 26 ("youth") with proper ID qualify for enticing reduced airfares. These are rarely available from airlines or travel agents, but instead from student travel agencies which negotiate special reduced-rate bulk purchase with the airlines, then resell them to the youth market. Return-date change fees also tend to be low (around US$35 per segment through Council or Let's Go Travel). Most flights are on major airlines, although in peak season some agencies may sell seats on less reliable chartered aircraft. Student travel agencies can also help non-students and people over 26, but probably won't be able to get the same low fares.

Austravel, 51 East 42nd St., Suite 616, New York, New York (http://australia-online.com/austravel.html). Specializes in flights through Los Angeles from the continental U.S. to Sydney. Packages available. To book by phone: (800) 633-3404; in New York call (212) 972-6880.

Campus Travel, 52 Grosvenor Gardens, London SW1W 0AG (http://www.campustravel.co.uk). Forty-six branches in the U.K. Student and youth fares on plane, train, boat, and bus travel. Skytrekker, flexible airline tickets. Discount and ID cards for students and youths, travel insurance for students and those under 35,

and maps and guides. Puts out travel suggestion booklets. Telephone booking service: in Europe call (0171) 730 34 02; in North America call (0171) 730 21 01; worldwide call(0171) 730 81 11; in Manchester call (0161) 273 17 21; in Scotland (0131) 668 33 03.

Council Travel, the travel division of Council, is a full-service travel agency specializing in youth and budget travel. They offer discount airfares on scheduled airlines, railpasses, hosteling cards, low-cost accommodations, guidebooks, budget tours, travel gear, and international student (ISIC), youth (GO 25), and teacher (ITIC) identity cards. In the **U.S.,** call 800-2-COUNCIL (226-8624) for the agency nearest you. The **London** office is located at 28A Poland St. (Oxford Circus), London, W1V 3DB (tel. (0171) 437 77 67). Visit the web site at http://www.ciee.org/cts/ctshome.htm.

Let's Go Travel, Harvard Student Agencies, 17 Holyoke St., Cambridge, MA 02138 (tel. (617) 495-9649; fax 496-8015; email travel@hsa.net; http://hsa.net/travel). Railpasses, HI-AYH memberships, ISICs, ITICs, FIYTO cards, guidebooks, maps, bargain flights, and a complete line of budget travel gear. All items available by mail; call or write for a catalogue (or see the catalogue in the center of this book).

Journeys International, Inc., 4011 Jackson Rd., Ann Arbor, MI 48103 (tel. (800) 255-8735; fax (313) 665-2945; email info@journeys-intl.com; http://www.journeys-intl.com). Offers small-group, guided explorations of 45 different countries in Asia, Africa, the Americas, and the Pacific. Call or email to obtain their free 74-page color catalogue, *The Global Expedition Catalogue.*

STA Travel, 6560 Scottsdale Rd. #F100, Scottsdale, AZ 85253 (tel. (800) 777-0112 nationwide; fax (602) 922-0793; http://sta-travel.com). A student and youth travel organization with over 150 offices worldwide offering discount airfares for young travelers, railpasses, accommodations, tours, insurance, and ISICs. 16 offices in the U.S. Call for the one nearest you. In the U.K., 6 Wrights Ln., **London** W8 6TA (tel. (0171) 938 47 11). In New Zealand, 10 High St., **Auckland** (tel. (09) 309 97 23). In Australia, 222 Faraday St., **Melbourne** Vic 3050 (tel. (03) 9349 6911), and 13-15 Garema Pl., on the corner of CityWalk, **Canberra** ACT (tel. (02) 6247 8633, fast fares 1300 360 960; email traveller@statravelaus.com.au; http://www.statravelaus.com.au/). Specializes in discounted fares and packages for students and young travelers. Open Mon.-Fri. 9am-5pm.

Travel CUTS (Canadian Universities Travel Services Limited), 187 College St., Toronto, ON M5T 1P7 (tel. (416) 979-2406; fax 979-8167; email mail@travelcuts). Canada's national student travel bureau and equivalent of Council, with 40 offices across Canada. Also in the U.K., 295-A Regent St., **London** W1R 7YA (tel. (0171) 637 31 61). Discounted domestic and international airfares open to all; special student fares to all destinations with valid ISIC. Issues ISIC, FIYTO, GO25, and HI hostel cards, as well as railpasses. Offers the free *Student Traveller* magazine, as well as information on the Student Work Abroad Program (SWAP).

Usit Youth and Student Travel, 19-21 Aston Quay, O'Connell Bridge, Dublin 2 (tel. (01) 677 8117; fax 679 8833). In the U.S.: New York Student Center, 895 Amsterdam Ave., New York, NY, 10025 (tel. (212) 663-5435; email usitny@aol.com). Additional offices in Cork, Galway, Limerick, Waterford, Maynooth, Coleraine, Derry, Athlone, Jordanstown, Belfast, and Greece. Specializes in youth and student travel. Offers low-cost tickets and flexible travel arrangements all over the world. Supplies ISIC and FIYTO-GO 25 cards in Ireland only.

By Plane

The privilege of spending up to 24 hours on an airplane doesn't come cheap. Full-price fares to Australia from the eastern United States usually run between US$1300 and $1800, although if you fly from Los Angeles, you may be able to find flights as low as $850. Special deals can knock that price down even more. Flights from the United Kingdom are usually even more expensive, and a London to Sydney link will likely set you back £800-925.

The **airline industry** attempts to squeeze every dollar from customers; finding a cheap airfare will be easier if you understand the airlines' systems. Call every toll-free number and don't be afraid to ask about discounts; if you don't ask, it's unlikely they'll be volunteered. Have knowledgeable **travel agents** guide you; better yet, have an agent who specializes in the region(s) you will be traveling to guide you. An agent whose clients fly mostly to Nassau or Miami will not be the best person to hunt down a bargain flight to Sydney. Travel agents may not want to spend time finding the cheapest fares (for which they receive the lowest commissions), but if you travel often, you should definitely find an agent who will cater to you and your needs, and track down deals in exchange for your frequent business.

Students and others under 26 should never need to pay full price for a ticket. Seniors can also get great deals; many airlines offer senior traveler clubs or airline passes with few restrictions and discounts for their companions as well. Sunday newspapers often have travel sections that list bargain fares from the local airport. The Saturday travel section of the *Sydney Morning Herald* is worth consulting at a library or on-line. Outsmart airline reps with the phone-book-sized *Official Airline Guide* (check your local library; at US$359 per yr., the tome costs as much as some flights), a monthly guide listing nearly every scheduled flight in the world (with fares, US$479) and toll-free phone numbers for all the airlines which allow you to call in reservations directly. More accessible is Michael McColl's *The Worldwide Guide to Cheap Airfare* (US$15), an incredibly useful guide for finding cheap airfare.

To obtain the **cheapest fare,** buy a round-trip ticket and stay over at least one Saturday. Midweek round-trip flights run about US$40-50 cheaper than on weekends; weekend flights, however, are generally less crowded. Traveling from hub to hub (for example, Los Angeles to Sydney) will win a more competitive fare than from smaller cities. Return-date flexibility is usually not an option for the budget traveler; traveling with an "open return" ticket can be pricier than fixing a return date and paying to change it. When dealing with any commercial airline, buying in advance is best. Periodic **price wars** may lower prices in spring and early summer months, but they're unpredictable; don't delay your purchase in hopes of catching one. Most airlines allow children under two to fly free (on the lap of an adult).

It is not wise to buy **frequent flyer tickets** from others—it is standard policy on all commercial airlines to check a photo ID, and you could find yourself paying for a new, full-fare ticket. If you have a frequent flyer account, make sure you're getting credit when you check in. It's many kilometers to Australia, no matter where you're coming from.

Whenever flying internationally, pick up your ticket well in advance of the departure date, have the flight confirmed within 72 hours of departure, and arrive at the airport at least three hours before your flight to ensure you have a seat; airlines often overbook. (Of course, being "bumped" from a flight doesn't spell doom if your travel plans are flexible—you will probably leave on the next flight and receive a free ticket or cash bonus. If you would like to be bumped to win a free ticket, check in early and let the airline officials know.)

Many airlines are now offering ticketing and reservations over the internet, and some award discounts to web reservers. Free worldwide flight schedules are available at http://www.travelocity.com. **TravelHUB** (http://www.travelhub.com) will help you search for travel agencies on the web. The **Air Traveler's Handbook** (http://www.cis.ohio-state.edu/hypertext/faq/usenet/travel/air/handbook/top.html) is an excellent source of general information on air travel. Marc-David Seidel's **Airlines of the Web** (http://www.itn.net/airlines) provides links to pages and 800 numbers for most of the world's airlines. The newsgroup **rec.travel.air** is a good source of tips on current bargains.

The following programs, services, and fares may be helpful for planning a reasonably-priced air trip, but always be wary of deals that seem too good to be true:

COMMERCIAL AIRLINES

The commercial airlines' lowest regular offer is the **Advance Purchase Excursion Fare** (APEX); specials advertised in newspapers may be cheaper, but have more restrictions and fewer available seats. APEX fares provide you with confirmed reservations and allow "open-jaw" tickets (landing in and returning from different cities). Generally, reservations must be made seven to 21 days in advance, with seven- to 14-day minimum and up to 90-day maximum stay limits, and hefty cancellation and change penalties (fees rise in summer). Book APEX fares early during peak seasons. Look into flights to less-popular destinations or on smaller carriers. Even if you pay an airline's lowest published fare, you may waste hundreds of dollars. For the adventurous or the bargain-hungry, there are other, perhaps more inconvenient or time-consuming options, but before shopping around it is a good idea to find out the average commercial price in order to measure just how great a "bargain" you are being offered.

TICKET CONSOLIDATORS

Ticket consolidators resell unsold tickets on commercial and charter airlines at unpublished fares. The consolidator market is by and large international; domestic flights, if they do exist, are typically for cross-country flights. Consolidator flights are the best deals if you are traveling: on short notice (you bypass advance purchase requirements, since you aren't tangled in airline bureaucracy); on a high-priced trip; to an offbeat destination; or in the peak season, when published fares are jacked way up. Fares sold by consolidators are generally much cheaper; a 30-40% price reduction is not uncommon. There are rarely age constraints or stay limitations, but unlike tickets bought through an airline, you won't be able to use your tickets on another flight if you miss yours, and you will have to go back to the consolidator to get a refund, rather than the airline. Keep in mind that these tickets are often for coach seats on connecting (not direct) flights on foreign airlines, and that frequent-flyer miles may not be credited. Decide what you can and can't live with before shopping.

Not all consolidators deal with the general public; many only sell tickets through travel agents. **Bucket shops** are retail agencies that specialize in getting cheap tickets. Although ticket prices are marked up slightly, bucket shops generally have access to a larger market than would be available to the public and can also get tickets from wholesale consolidators. Look for bucket shops' tiny ads in the travel section of weekend papers; in the U.S., the Sunday *New York Times* is a good source. In London, a call to the **Air Travel Advisory Bureau** (tel. (0171) 636 50 00) can provide names of reliable consolidators and discount flight specialists. Kelly Monaghan's *Consolidators: Air Travel's Bargain Basement* (US$7 plus $2 shipping) from the Intrepid Traveler, P.O. Box 438, New York, NY 10034 (email intreptrav@aol.com), is an invaluable source for more information and lists of consolidators by location and destination.

Be a smart shopper; check out the competition. Among the many reputable and trustworthy companies are, unfortunately, some shady wheeler-dealers. Contact the local Better Business Bureau to find out how long the company has been in business and its track record. Although not necessary, it is preferable to deal with consolidators close to home so you can visit in person, if necessary. Ask to receive your tickets as quickly as possible so you have time to fix any problems. Get the company's policy in writing: insist on a **receipt** that gives full details about the tickets, refunds, and restrictions, and record who you talked to and when. It may be worth paying with a credit card (despite the 2-5% fee) so you can stop payment if you never receive your tickets. Beware the "bait and switch" gag: shyster firms will advertise a super-low fare and then tell a caller that it has been sold. Although this is a viable excuse, if they can't offer you a price near the advertised fare on *any* date, it is a scam to lure in customers—report them to the Better Business Bureau. Also ask about accommodations and car rental discounts; some consolidators have fingers in many pies.

For destinations **worldwide,** try **Airfare Busters,** offices in Washington, D.C. (tel. (202) 776-0478), Boca Raton, FL (tel. (561) 994-9590), and Houston, TX (tel. (800) 232-8783); **Pennsylvania Travel,** Paoli, PA (tel. (800) 331-0947); **Cheap Tickets,** offices in Los Angeles, CA, San Francisco, CA, Honolulu, HI, Seattle, WA, and New York, NY (tel. (800) 377-1000); or **Discount Travel International,** New York, NY (tel. (212) 362-3636; fax 362-3236), which has recently begun booking flights to large cities in Australia and New Zealand. **Moment's Notice,** New York, NY (tel. (718) 234-6295; fax 234-6450; http://www.moments-notice.com) offers air tickets, tours, and hotels; US$25 annual fee. **NOW Voyager,** 74 Varick St. #307, New York, NY 10013 (tel. (212) 431-1616; fax 334-5243); email info@nowvoyagertravel.com; http://www.nowvoyagertravel.com), acts as a consolidator and books discounted international flights, mostly from New York, as well as courier flights (see **Courier Companies,** below), for a registration fee of US$50. For a processing fee, depending on the number of travelers and the itinerary, **Travel Avenue,** Chicago, IL (tel. (800) 333-3335; fax (312) 876-1254; http://www.travelavenue.com), will search for the lowest international airfare available, including consolidated prices, and will even give you a rebate on fares over US$300.

Mr. Cheap's Travel, 9123 SE St. Helen's St., #280, Clackamas, OR 97015 (tel. (800) 672-4327 or (503) 557-9101; fax (800) 896-8868; http://www.mrcheaps.com). Additional office in San Diego, CA (tel. (800) 636-3273 or (619) 291-1292).

NOW Voyager, (primarily a courier company; see below), does consolidation with reliability which rivals that of most charter companies (97% of customers get on flights the first time) and prices which are considerably lower. NOW sells tickets over the internet at its web page (http://www.nowvoyagertravel.com).

CHARTER FLIGHTS

Charters are flights a tour operator contracts with an airline (usually one specializing in charters) to fly extra loads of passengers to peak-season destinations. Charters are often cheaper than flights on scheduled airlines, especially during peak seasons, although fare wars, consolidator tickets, and small airlines can beat charter prices. Some charters operate nonstop, and restrictions on minimum advance-purchase and minimum stay are more lenient. However, charter flights fly less frequently than major airlines, make refunds particularly difficult, and are almost always fully booked.

Schedules and itineraries may also change or be cancelled at the last moment (as late as 48hr. before the trip, and without a full refund), and check-in, boarding, and baggage claim are often much slower. As always, pay with a credit card if you can; consider traveler's insurance against trip interruption.

Eleventh-hour **discount clubs** and **fare brokers** offer members savings on Pacific travel, including charter flights and tour packages. Research your options carefully. **Last Minute Travel Club,** 100 Sylvan Rd., Woburn, MA 01801 (tel. (800) 527-8646 or (617) 267-9800); and **Travel Avenue** (tel. (800) 333-3335; see **Ticket Consolidators** above) are both options. Study these organizations' contracts closely; you don't want to end up with an unwanted overnight layover.

COURIER COMPANIES AND FREIGHTERS

Those who travel light should consider flying to Australia as a **courier.** The company hiring you will use your checked luggage space for freight; you're only allowed to bring carry-ons. You are responsible for the safe delivery of the baggage claim slips (given to you by a courier company representative) to the representative waiting for you when you arrive—don't screw up or you will be blacklisted as a courier. You will probably never see the cargo you are transporting—the company handles it all—and airport officials know that couriers are not responsible for the baggage checked for them. Restrictions to watch for: you must be over 21 (18 in some cases), have a valid passport, and procure your own visa (if necessary); most flights are round-trip only with short fixed-length stays (usually two weeks in Australia); only single tickets are issued (but a companion may be able to get a next-day flight); and most Australian flights depart from Los Angeles, although some leave from New York. Many companies charge a one-time registration fee of approximately $50 when you first purchase a ticket.

Air-Tech, Ltd., 588 Broadway #204, New York, NY 10012 (tel. (212) 219-7000; fax 219-0066), offers courier flights to Australia. For approximately US$700 from Los Angeles, you can get a plane ticket good for a two-week stay in Australia. The only other departure point is New York, and although you can stay three months and fly on Qantas, the ticket will likely cost US$1200. Contact the company at least a month in advance for details. Air-Tech also arranges confirmed seats at discount rates.

NOW Voyager, 74 Varick St. #307, New York, NY 10013 (tel. (212) 431-1616; fax 334-5243; email info@nowvoyagertravel.com; http://www.nowvoyagertravel.com), acts as an agent for many courier flights worldwide. Flights to Australia leave from Los Angeles and New York, and prices are similar to Air-Tech prices, although the New York fares may be slightly cheaper. (They also act as a consolidator; see **Ticket Consolidators,** above.) Other agents with flights to Australia are **Halbart Express,** 1000 W. Hillcrest Blvd., Inglewood, CA 90301 (tel. (310) 417-3048; fax 417-9792); and **Discount Travel International** (tel. (212) 362-3636; see **Ticket Consolidators,** above).

For an annual fee of $45, the **International Association of Air Travel Couriers,** 8 South J St., P.O. Box 1349, Lake Worth, FL 33460 (tel. (561) 582-8320), informs travelers (via computer, fax, and mailings) of courier opportunities worldwide. Steve Lantos publishes a monthly update of courier options in **Travel Unlimited** as well as general information on low-budget travel (write P.O. Box 1058A, Allston, MA 02134 for a free sample newsletter; subscription runs US$25 per year). Most flights originate in New York or London and travel to Europe, Asia, or South America, although flights to Australia exist.

For a practical guide to the air courier scene, check out Kelly Monaghan's **Air Courier Bargains** (US$15 plus $3 shipping), available from Upper Access Publishing (UAP), P.O. Box 457, Hinesburg, VT 05461 (tel. (800) 356-9315; fax 242-0036; email upperacces@aol.com), or consult the **Courier Air Travel Handbook** (US$10 plus $3.50 shipping), published by Bookmasters, Inc., P.O. Box 2039, Mansfield, OH 44905 (tel. (800) 507-2665; fax (419) 281-6883).

ESSENTIALS

By Boat

If you really have travel time and cash to spare, **Ford's Travel Guides,** 19448 Londelius St., Northridge, CA 91324 (tel. (818) 701-7414; fax 701-7415), lists **freighter companies** that will take passengers to Australia. Boats depart from many points in the United States, especially along the East Coast, and arrive in Melbourne, Sydney, and Brisbane. Trips cost between US$81-108 per person, per day, and the trip takes between 23 and 42 days one-way. You can also travel from many points in Europe, although be warned: a trip by sea from Italy to Australia takes 81 days. Ask for their *Freighter Travel Guide and Waterways of the World* (US$16, plus $2.50 postage if mailed outside the U.S.).

ONCE THERE

Embassies and Consulates

Canada: The High Commission on Commonwealth Ave., **Canberra** ACT 2600 (tel. (02) 6273 3844; fax 6273 3285). Consulate General at Level 5, Quay West Building, 111 Harrington St., **Sydney** NSW 2000 (tel. (02) 9364 3000; fax 9364 3098). Consulate near **Melbourne** at 123 Camberwell Rd., East Hawthorn, Vic 3123 (tel. (03) 9811 9999; fax 9811 9969). Consulate at 267 St. George's Tce., 3rd Fl., **Perth** WA 6000 (tel. (08) 9322 7930; fax 9261 7700).

Ireland: Embassy in **Canberra** at 20 Arkana St., Yarralumla ACT 2600 (tel. (02) 6273 3022; fax 6273 3741). Honorary Consul General at P.O. Box 20 (Aberdeen St. in the Northbridge district), **Perth** WA 6865 (tel. (08) 9385 8247; fax 9385 8247).

New Zealand: High Commission on Commonwealth Ave., **Canberra** ACT 2600 (tel. (02) 6270 4211; fax 6273 3194). Consulate-General at GPO Box 62 (Watkins Pl. Building, 288 Edward St.), **Brisbane** QLD 4001 (tel. (07) 3221 9933; fax 3229 7495). Consulate-General at 60 Albert Rd., South **Melbourne** Vic 3205 (tel. (03) 9696 0501, immigration tel. 9696 0445; fax 9696 0391). Consulate-General at GPO Box 365 (level 14, Gold Fields Building, 1 Alfred St., Circular Quay), **Sydney** NSW 2000 (tel. (02) 9247 1999, customs police tel. 9247 8567; fax 9247 1754).

South Africa: High Commission in **Canberra** at State Circle, Yarralumla ACT 2600 (tel. (02) 6273 2424).

U.K.: The British High Commission in **Canberra,** Commonwealth Ave., Yarralumla ACT 2600 (tel. (02) 6270 6666, recorded info tel. 0055 63220; fax 6273 3236). Consul-General on level 26, Waterfront Pl., 1 Eagle St., **Brisbane** QLD 4000 (tel. (07) 3236 2575; fax 3236 2576). Consul-General on 17th Fl., 90 Collins St., **Melbourne** Vic 3000 (tel. (03) 9650 3699; fax 9650 2990). Consul-General on level 26, "Allendale Square," 77 St. Georges Tce., **Perth** WA 6000 (tel. (08) 9221 5400; fax 9221 2344). Consul-General on level 16, The Gateway, 1 Macquarie Pl., **Sydney Cove** NSW 2000 (tel. (02) 9247 7521; fax 9251 6201). Consul on level 22, Grenfell Centre, 25 Grenfell St., **Adelaide** SA 5000 (tel. (08) 8212 7280; fax 8212 7282). Honourary Consul on 39 Murray St., **Hobart** Tas 7000 (tel. (03) 6230 4647; fax 6223 2279).

United States: Embassy in **Canberra,** 21 Moonah St., Yarralumla ACT 2600 (tel. (02) 6270 5000; fax 6273 3191). Consulate at Level 59, MLC Centre, 19-29 Martin Pl., **Sydney** NSW 2000 (tel. (02) 9373 9200; fax 9373 9184); Consulate at 553 St. Kilda Rd., P.O. Box 6722, **Melbourne** Vic 3004 (tel. (03) 9526 5900; fax 9510 4646). Consulate on 13th Fl., 16 St. Georges Tce., **Perth** WA 6000 (tel. (08) 9231 9400; fax 9231 9444). The U.S. Consulate in **Brisbane** closed in March, 1996.

Getting Around

BY PLANE

Because Australia is so large, many travelers, even budget travelers, take a domestic flight at some point while touring the country. Those with foreign passports and international flight receipts generally earn 30% off on domestic flights; be sure to have the receipts with you when booking flights. Backpackers may also be able to receive discounts.

Oz Experience and Qantas offer an Air-Bus Pass with which travelers can fly one way, and bus back (or vice versa) around Australia. Passes are available for 6-12 months with unlimited stops. Airbus reservations can be made by calling (02) 9221 4711 in Sydney or 1300 103 359 anywhere else.

Qantas and Ansett Australia are the two major domestic carriers. Both offer varying packages for within-country flights.

Qantas: Reservations tel. 13 13 13; http://www.qantas.con.au. Offers 373 flights per week between Sydney and Brisbane, and 181 each week between Melbourne and Brisbane. On domestic flights, children under three fly free on Qantas.

Ansett Airlines: Reservations tel. 13 13 00. Specializes in domestic routes in Australia and New Zealand, although it also flies internationally to Japan, Hong Kong, and Bali/Indonesia. Major port cities include Adelaide, Cairns, Denpasar (Bali), Hong Kong (China), Melbourne, Osaka (Japan), Perth, Sydney, Canberra, and Darwin.

BY TRAIN

Each state runs its own rail service, and transfers between services may require a bus trip to the next station. The main rail companies are **CountryLink,** based in New South Wales, **V/Line** in Victoria, **Queensland Rail** in Queensland, and **Westrail** in Western Australia. All of them can be reached at the same number (reservations tel. 13 22 32). Wheelchair access on interstate trains is generally poor, since the corridors are too narrow for most wheelchairs. Some of the larger stations provide collapsible wheelchairs, but all do not.

Railpasses are available. The **Austrail Pass** allows eight days of travel over a 60-day period anywhere in the country for AUS$360. Fifteen days of travel over a 90-day period will set you back AUS$475. The **Austrail Flexipass** allows you to purchase 8, 15, 22, or 29 traveling days over a six-month period and is slightly more expensive. Victoria and Queensland also offer state rail passes..

On the Right Track

The history of Australia's rail system is a classic case of colonial confusion. In the 19th century, when the country's original six colonies started building railroad tracks, each individual colony conferred with London instead of its neighbors. The result: by 1901 (the year of Australian federation), the six areas of the country had tracks of six different widths. Australians have been standardizing the system ever since, and travelers can now visit all of the state capitals with the exception of Darwin (and Hobart, of course) on a train. Lines also run up to Cairns and into outback Queensland, and a track runs south to Adelaide from Alice Springs. But track and operator discrepancies linger, and these differences can make rail travel slow, inefficient, and not particularly cheap. It is, however, a comfortable way to see the country, and a good option if you don't have wheels of your own.

BY BUS

People travel by bus (coach) in Australia much more frequently than they travel by train. Buses run regularly to major cities, but journeys off the beaten track may require a wait of a few days.

Major express routes run daily: Sydney-Adelaide (24hr.); Sydney-Canberra (4½hr.); Sydney-Melbourne (14½hr.); Canberra-Melbourne (9½hr.); Melbourne-Adelaide (9½hr.); Adelaide-Alice Springs (20hr.); Adelaide-Perth (35hr.); Adelaide-Brisbane (33½hr.); Darwin-Alice Springs (19hr.); Darwin-Kakadu (3½hr.); Alice Springs-Ayers Rock (6hr.); Cairns-Brisbane (25hr.); Cairns-Darwin (42hr.); Brisbane-Sydney (17hr.); Brisbane-Melbourne (25hr.); and Perth-Darwin (33hr.).

Greyhound Pioneer (tel. 13 20 30) covers the whole country, including Western Australia. Greyhound has dozens of travelpass options. Seven to 21-day passes allow you to travel on any Greyhound route within 30 to 60 days, depending on the length of your pass; days of travel do not have to be consecutive. These passes cost between AUS$499 and $982. The **Aussie Explorer Pass** allows you to predetermine a route and take up to 12 months to get there, while an **Aussie Kilometer Pass** lets you choose a number of kilometers which can be used on any Greyhound route. All of these passes can be used to take one or more of the **Greyhound Pioneer Tours,** which offer combinations of tours for National Parks and scenic spots in Central Australia, Western Australia, and the Top End. If the pass is purchased overseas, a 10-15% discount is available for YHA, VIP, Euro26, ISIC, Nomad, and Discover Card holders.

McCafferty's Coachlines (tel. 13 14 99) runs through most of the country. The buses can't take you into Western Australia, but they can arrange for you to connect to the Indian Pacific train from Adelaide to Perth, and can get you almost anywhere else. **Travel Australia passes** are valid for three to 12 months, and let travelers ride with unlimited stops one-way along any of eight predetermined routes. These passes can be purchased from a local travel agent or at any McCafferty's terminal for AUS$640; discounts for international students, international pensioners, and backpacker cardholders are available when the purchase is made outside of Australia (AUS$540). McCafferty's also offers two kinds of **day passes for international travelers** only; these must be purchased before arrival in Australia. These **Discover Australia** day passes allow unlimited unrestricted travel on the McCafferty's network for a set number of days within a longer period, or for a set number of consecutive days. A seven day pass, good for any seven days of travel within a 30-day period, costs AUS$480. A seven-day consecutive pass costs AUS$316 ($280 for YHA, VIP, or ISIC cardholders). Ten, 15, 21, 30, 60, and 90-day consecutive and within-period passes are all available. For the within-period passes, overnight segments are allowed to equal one day, since a day is defined as a 24-hour period.

Other popular bus companies include **Oz Experience,** 3 Orwell St., Kings Cross, NSW 2011 (tel. (02) 9368 1766; fax 9368 0908; email backpack@world.net; http://www.ozex.com.au/), which offers backpacker tour packages with a lot of flexibility, and drivers who double as tour guides. Oz Experience passes are valid for up to a year. **Wayward Bus** (tel. (08) 8232 6646; fax 8232 1455; email wayward@camtech.com.au; http://www.camtech.com.au/tea/wayward_bus/index.htm), runs similar trips with a natural focus, appealing to backpackers of all ages.

BY CAR

Some regions of Australia are virtually inaccessible without a car, and in many areas, public transportation options are simply inadequate. Because very few travelers arrive in Australia with a car, renting or buying is a popular option.

Renting

Although the cost of renting a car can be prohibitive for long distances, renting for local trips may be reasonable, especially with a group. **Car rental agencies** fall into two categories: national companies with hundreds of branches, and local agencies which serve only one city or region. Budget, Hertz, Avis, and Thrifty are Australia's largest national companies. These complement dozens of smaller local agencies, which usually have lower prices. International travelers may want to contact large companies in their home countries to get the number for a specific Australian city office, and reserve before they go.

Avis (tel. in Sydney (02) 9353 9000, toll-free outside of Sydney (800) 225 533; in Canada (800) 272 5871; in Ireland (021) 28 11 11; in Auckland, New Zealand (09) 525 1982, in the rest of New Zealand (800) 655 111; in South Africa (011) 392 3240; in the U.K. (0990) 90 05 00; in the U.S. (800) 230-4898; http://www.avis.com). YHA members may be able to get a 30% discount in Australia (members should quote No. P081600 when making reservations).

Budget (tel. in Sydney (02) 9669 1467, outside of Sydney (03) 9206 3222; fax (03) 9206 3636; in Canada (800) 268 8900; in Ireland (021) 274 755; in New Zealand (09) 309 6737; in South Africa (011) 394 2905; in the U.K. (0800) 18 11 81; in the U.S. (800) 472 3325; http://budgetrentacar.com). Offers an occasional deal to YHA members, renting small manual cars for 7 days for AUS$59 per day with unlimited kilometers. Call the National Reservations area (tel. 13 38 48) and give the code 113.

Hertz (tel. in Australia 13 30 39 or (03) 9698 2555; fax (03) 9698 2295; in Canada (604) 606 4711; in Ireland (01) 676 7476; in Auckland, New Zealand (09) 303 4924, in the rest of New Zealand (800) 654 321; in South Africa (011) 337 2300; in the U.K. (0990) 996 69; in the U.S. (800) 654 3131; http://www.hertz.com). Renters must be 25, but if a member of AAA (RACV, etc.) can be between 21 and 24.

Thrifty (tel. in Australia, excluding Tasmania, 800 652 008, in Tasmania 800 030 730; in Ireland 61 45 3049; in New Zealand (09) 275 6666; in the U.K. (0990) 168 238; in the U.S. (800) 367-2277; http://www.thrifty.com).

To rent a car from most establishments in Australia, you need to be at least **21 years old**. Some agencies require renters to be 25, and many charge those aged 21-24 an additional insurance fee. Policies and prices vary from agency to agency. Small local operations occasionally rent to people under 21, but be sure to read the fine print.

Rental car prices start at around AUS$45 a day from national companies, $35 from local agencies. Expect to pay more for larger cars and for 4WD. Cars with **automatic transmission** often cost more—sometimes to the tune of $15 a day more—than those with manual transmission, and in Western Australia, Northern Territory and more remote areas of the eastern states, automatic transmission cars are almost non-existent.

Most rental packages offer unlimited kilometers. Quoted rates do not include petrol or tax, so ask for the total cost before handing over the credit card; airport surcharges are another "don't ask, don't tell" possibility. Return the car with a full tank of petrol to avoid high fuel charges at the end. And when dealing with any car rental company, be sure to ask whether the price includes **insurance** against theft and collision. Every registered car automatically carries a green slip that provides no-fault insurance, but not necessarily anything more. Remember that if you are driving on a **dirt road** in a rental car, you are usually not covered by insurance; ask about this before leaving the rental agency. Cars rented on an **American Express** card in Australia do *not* carry the automatic insurance that they would in some other countries.

If you rent, lease, or borrow a car, you will need to get a **green card,** or **International Insurance Certificate,** to prove that you have liability insurance. These can be obtained through the car rental agency; most include coverage in their prices. If you lease a car, you can obtain a green card from the dealer. Even if your auto insurance applies abroad, you will need a green card to certify this to foreign officials.

National chains sometimes allow cars to be picked up in one city and dropped off in another, although **one-way rentals** are not usually allowed into or out of Western Australia or Northern Territory. There is usually a minimum hire period and sometimes an extra charge, so be sure to read the small print.

On the Road

Australians drive on the left side of the road, and a "give way to the right" rule means that in unmarked intersections, a driver must yield to vehicles entering the intersection from his or her right. **Be sure to buckle up**—if your seat has a seatbelt you're required to wear it; risk a fine otherwise. The speed limit in most areas of Australia is 60kph (35mph), while on highways it's 100 or 110kph (62 to 68mph). Speed radar guns are sometimes used to patrol well-traveled roads. **Gasoline (petrol)** costs about 70¢ per liter in cities and 80¢ per liter in outlying areas, but prices can vary widely according to state gasoline taxes.

When traveling in the summer or in the outback bring 20 liters (5 gallons) of **water** per person for drinking and for the radiator. For long outback drives, travelers should register with the police before beginning the trek and again upon arrival at the destination. Check with the local automobile club for details. In the north, **four-wheel-drive (4WD)** is essential for seeing the parks, particularly in the Wet, when dirt roads turn to mud. When traveling in the outback or for long distances, tune up the car before you leave, make sure the tires are in good repair and have enough air, and get good maps. A **compass** and a **car manual** can also be very useful. You should always carry a **spare tire** and **jack, jumper cables, extra oil, flares, a torch (flashlight),** and **blankets** (in case your car breaks down at night or in the winter). If your car does break down, by all means **stay with your car.** Many of the roads in rural Australia are still unpaved, or "unsealed," and conditions can range from smooth, hard-packed sandy earth to an eroded mixture of mud, sand, and stones. Locals are a good source of information on the road conditions in the immediate vicinity. If you're planning longer-range driving, ask at tourist bureaus. Generally the roads are accessible to 2WD cars, although many in the north are passable only by 4WD vehicles after rain. Remember, one can skid on gravel almost as badly as on ice. Be sure to park your vehicle in a garage or well-traveled area. Children under 40 lbs. should ride only in a specially-designed carseat, available for a small fee from most car rental agencies. Study route maps before you hit the road; some roads have poor (or nonexistent) shoulders, few gas stations, and roaming animals. In many regions, road conditions necessitate driving more slowly and more cautiously than you would at home.

The **Australian Automobile Association (AAA)** is the national organization that encompasses all of the local automobile organizations. You won't often see it called the AAA, though; in most states, the local organization is called the **Royal Automobile Club (RAC).** In New South Wales and the ACT, motorists turn to the **National Royal Motorist Association (NRMA).** AAA's services—from breakdown assistance to map provision—are similar to those offered by the United Kingdom's RAC or AA, Germany's ADAC, or the United States' AAA. If you are a member of one of these overseas organizations and bring proof of your membership to Australia, you'll be able to use AAA facilities free of charge, since they all operate on a reciprocal basis within the country.

If you have car trouble, **AAA roadside assistance** can be reached at tel. 13 11 11 in all states and territories except Northern Territory, where you should call (08) 8941 0611. It's possible to join the Australian Automobile Association through any state's organization. *Let's Go* lists the location of the state automobile organization in most large towns. If no local number is listed, try:

ACT/New South Wales: National Royal Motorist Association (NRMA; tel. 13 21 32).
Northern Territory: Automobile Association of the Northern Territory (AANT; tel. (08) 8981 3837).
Queensland: Royal Automobile Club of Queensland (RACQ; tel. (07) 3361 2444).
South Australia: Royal Automobile Association of South Australia (RAA; tel. (08) 8202 4500).
Tasmania: Royal Automobile Club of Tasmania (RACT; tel. (03) 6232 6300).
Victoria: Royal Automobile Club of Victoria (RACV; tel. 13 19 55).
Western Australia: Royal Automobile Club of Western Australia (RACWA; tel. (08) 9421 4444).

Buying and Selling Used Cars

The option of purchasing a used car is especially attractive to those under 25. Automotive independence can be yours for AUS$1600-5000. In addition to the commercial used-car lots, capital cities and large towns often have **used car lots** filled with backpackers and others trying to **buy and sell used cars.** Lot owners charge people trying to sell cars a fixed rate to park their cars and sit by them; buyers stroll around and haggle for deals. Hostel or university bulletin boards are another good bet. In Sydney, check the *Weekly Trading Post* on Thursdays for used car advertisements, and the *Daily Telegraph Mirror* and *Sydney Morning Herald* on Fridays and weekends. It's always easiest to sell a car for the best price when demand is high; consider the high tourist season for the region you're in. Vehicles are also easier to sell if they are registered in the state where they are being sold. This is because new owners need to register the car, and some states don't allow registration transfer by mail. If you buy a car privately, check the registration papers against the license of the person who is selling the car.

Because many people buy (or rent) cars and sleep in them while traveling (definitely not recommended from a safety standpoint), station wagons and campervans are favorites. The **Ford Falcon, Holden Kingswood,** and **Holden Commodore** are among the most popular large cars, while the **Toyota Corolla** and **Mazda 626** have cornered much of the small-car market. Those who buy campervans report having the most luck with **Toyota.** Buying popular automobiles can pay off if you end up needing parts in the middle of nowhere. Holden, Ford, Nissan, Toyota, Mazda, and Mitsubishi are all fairly safe bets. Keep in mind the low resale value of used cars—you probably won't turn a profit or finance your ticket home at the end of your trip.

Before buying a used car, check in with the local branch of the AAA, because states have varying requirements for a transfer of ownership, and local organizations can advise you on how to get your money's worth. For example, the NRMA in New South Wales publishes brochures entitled *International Tourists Car Buying Advice* and *Worry-free Guide to Buying a Car.* In Victoria, all cars are required to carry a Road Worthiness Certificate, and it's probably unwise to purchase a car without one. Local auto clubs also do mechanical inspections (NRMA vehicle inspections tel. 13 21 32).

When considering buying a car, call the **Register of Encumbered Vehicles** to confirm that a vehicle is unencumbered—that it has not been reported as stolen, and has no outstanding traffic warrants. For cars registered in ACT, Qld, or NT, dial (02) 9600 0022 or 1800 424 988. For cars registered in Vic, dial (03) 9348 1222. For cars registered in Tas, dial 13 11 05. For cars registered in SA, dial (08) 8232 0800. For cars registered in WA, dial (08) 9222 0711. You'll need to provide the registration number, engine number, and VIN/chassis numbers of the vehicle. In New South Wales, a car must have a pink inspection certificate to guarantee that it is roadworthy. It is valid for 20 days, and is available at most service stations.

Insurance and Registration

Third-party personal injury insurance, sometimes called a green slip, is automatically included with every registered vehicle. In the event of an accident, this covers any person who may be injured except the driver at fault, but does not cover damage or repairs to any cars or property. Even travelers trying to save money should consider purchasing additional insurance. **Third-party property damage insurance** covers the cost of repair to other people's cars or property if you're responsible for an accident. **Full comprehensive insurance,** which covers damage to all vehicles, including your own, is more expensive, but provides more peace of mind.

Within two weeks after purchase, you'll need to **register** the car in your name at the Motor Vehicle Registry. Although requirements vary from state to state, re-registration costs about AUS$15, and must be completed within about two weeks. Again, turn to the local automobile organization for help in this area.

Another option is to purchase a car from a dealer who guarantees to buy the car back at the end of your trip. Be especially wary of small print when contemplating these **buy-back deals.**

BY BICYCLE

Australia has many **bike tracks** to attract cyclers and few cars to distract them. Much of the country is flat, and road bikers can travel long distances without needing to huff and puff excessively. In theory, bicycles can go on **buses and trains,** but most major bus companies require you to disassemble your bike and pay a flat AUS$15 fee. You may not be allowed to bring your bike into the train compartment with you.

The **Bicycle Federation of Australia (BFA),** a nonprofit bicycle advocacy group, publishes *Australia Cyclist* magazine and has a list of regional bicycling organizations at http://www.ozemail.com.au/~bicycle. Member groups include the **Bicycle Institute of South Australia** (tel. (08) 8271 5824), the **Western Australia Cyclists' Action Group** (tel. (08) 9384 7409), **Bicycle Tasmania** (tel. (03) 6233 6619 or 6229 3811), **Bicycle New South Wales** (tel. (02) 9283 5200; fax 9283 5246), **Bicycle Victoria** (tel. (03) 9328 3000; fax 9328 2000), and the **Bicycle Institute of Queensland** (tel. (07) 3844 1144; fax 3844 1144). Some cyclists say that some of these organizations focus more on resources for daytrips and short excursions than on long-distance riding, but they are definitely the place to begin.

Safe and secure cycling requires a quality helmet and lock. A good **helmet** costs about $40—much cheaper than critical head surgery. Helmets are required in Australia. Cyclists recommend traveling with **maps** from the state Automobile Associations.

BY MOTORCYCLE

Motorcycles (or motorbikes, as they're sometimes known in Australia) remain a popular way to travel the long stretches of highway. You are required by Australian law to have a **license and a helmet.** See the section on renting and buying cars (p. 40), since many of the same suggestions apply. It may be cheaper than car travel, but it takes a tenacious soul to endure a motorcycle tour. If you must carry a load, keep it low and forward where it won't distort the cycle's center of gravity. Fasten it either to the seat or over the rear axle in saddle or tank bags. Of course, **safety** should be your primary concern. Motorcycles are incredibly vulnerable to crosswinds, drunk drivers, the blind spots of cars and trucks, and wandering wildlife. *Always ride defensively.* Dangers skyrocket at night; travel in the daytime. For **trail bike riding** information, contact the **Australian Motorcycle Trail Riders Association** (AMTRA) at P.O. Box 8, Ringwood Vic 3134 (tel. (03) 9434 1039).

BY THUMB

> *Let's Go* strongly urges you to seriously consider the risks before you choose to hitch. We do not recommend hitching as a safe means of transportation and none of the information printed here is intended to do so.

Given the infrequency of public transportation to several popular destinations, travelers often need to find other ways to get where they're going. Hostels frequently have message boards where those seeking rides and those seeking to share the cost of gas can meet up. If you are looking to travel with a stranger, car-less travelers report having a good deal of luck meeting willing drivers in roadhouses or cafes. This arrangement gives them an opportunity to size up potential lifts before accepting a ride. On the east coast, backpacker traffic moves from Sydney to Brisbane, and those who go with the flow are sure to make friends who have wheels.

Standing on the side of the highway with your thumb out is much more dangerous than making a new friend at your hostel. Safety issues are always imperative, even when you're traveling with another person. Hitching means entrusting your life to a random person who happens to stop beside you on the road and risking assault, sexual harassment, and unsafe driving. If you're a woman traveling alone, don't hitch. It's just too dangerous. A man and a woman are a safer combination; two men will have a harder time finding a ride. Avoid getting in the back of a two-door car, and never let go of your backpack. Hitchhiking at night can be particularly dangerous. Don't

accept a ride that you are not entirely comfortable with, or get into a car that you can't get out of again in a hurry. If you ever feel threatened, insist on being let off, but keep in mind that the vast distances between towns on some stretches of highway increase your chance of being left literally in the middle of nowhere, without food, water, or the possibility of another ride for days.

Accommodations

While hotels in large cities are typical of hotels in large cities around the world, **"hotels" in rural Australia,** particularly in Victoria and New South Wales, are actually simple furnished rooms above local pubs. Some smack of fancy Victorian-type lodging with grand back staircases, high tin ceilings, and wrap-around verandas. Others have been converted to long-term worker housing, and are thus less conducive to brief overnight stays. Singles in these hotels usually cost AUS$15-30. This generally includes a towel, a common (shared) bathroom, and a private bedroom (no bunks, usually). A simple breakfast may be included, and there's usually a common kitchen. The pubs are fully functional downstairs, so it's a good idea to choose a quieter one if you're fond of tucking in early. The term **motel** in Australia is reserved for accommodations with parking.

HOSTELS

For tight budgets and those lonesome traveling blues, hostels can't be beat. Hostels are generally dorm-style accommodations, often in single-sex large rooms with bunk beds, although some hostels do offer private rooms for families and couples. They sometimes have kitchens and utensils for your use, bike or moped rentals, storage areas, and laundry facilities. There can be drawbacks: a very few Australian hostels close during certain daytime "lock-out" hours, have a curfew, impose a maximum stay, or, less frequently, require that you do chores. But most, especially in backpacker-heavy coastal Queensland, are so anxious to court budget travelers that they have swimming pools, free local transportation, and even free weekly barbecues. Fees generally range from AUS$10-20 per night and hostels associated with one of the large hostel associations often have lower rates for members. If you have Internet access, check out the **Internet Guide to Hostelling** (http://hostels.com), which includes details on hostels from around the world in addition to oodles of information about hostelling and backpacking worldwide.

Australia's YHA is a member of the international youth hostel federation Hostelling International. Australia's other main hosteling organization is Backpackers Resorts International, which is often abbreviated BRI. Discounts from BRI are usually designated **VIP.** If a hostel gives VIP discounts, it means that guests get AUS$1 off per night. **Nomads Backpackers** is a third major hosteling chain in Australia.

Reservations for over 300 **Hostelling International (HI)** hostels (see listing below) may be made via the International Booking Network (IBN), a computerized system which allows you make hostels reservations months in advance for a nominal fee (U.S. tel. (202) 783-6161). Overseas visitors who join HI in their own countries are able to stay in HI/YHA hostels worldwide (see below). If you do not join before arriving, however, you can buy a one-year Hostelling International Card in Australia. This costs AUS$44 and is available from state membership and travel centers or directly from many hostels. In Sydney, the office to pick up cards is at 422 Kent St. (tel. 9261 1111).

Australian Youth Hostels Association (AYHA), Level 3, 10 Mallett St., Camperdown NSW 2050 (tel. (02) 9565 1699; fax 9565 1325; email YHA@zeta.org.au). Memberships AUS$44, renewal $27; under 18 $13.

Hostelling International-American Youth Hostels (HI-AYH), 733 15th St. NW #840, Washington, D.C. 20005 (tel. (202) 783-6161; fax 783-6171; email hiayhserv@hiayh.org; http://www.hiayh.org). Memberships can be purchased at many travel agencies (p. 27) or at the national office in Washington, D.C. One-year membership US$25, under 18 $10, over 54 $15, family cards $35.

Hostelling International-Canada (HI-C), 400-205 Catherine St., Ottawa, ON K2P 1C3 (tel. (613) 237-7884; fax 237-7868). IBN booking centers in Edmonton, Montreal, Ottawa, and Vancouver; expect CDN$9-22.50 per night. Membership packages: 1yr. under 18 CDN$12; 1yr. over 18 $25; 2yr. over 18 $35; lifetime $175.

An Óige (Irish Youth Hostel Association), 61 Mountjoy St., Dublin 7 (tel. (01) 830 4555; fax 830 5808; anoige@iol.ie). One-year membership is IR£7.50, under 18 £4, family £7.50 for each adult with children under 16 free.

Scottish Youth Hostels Association (SYHA), 7 Glebe Crescent, Stirling FK8 2JA (tel. (01786) 89 14 00; fax 89 13 33; email syha@syha.org.uk; http://www.syha.org.uk). Membership UK£6, under 18 £2.50.

Youth Hostels Association of England and Wales (YHA), Trevelyan House, 8 St. Stephen's Hill, St. Albans, Hertfordshire AL1 2DY (tel. (01727) 85 52 15; fax 844126). Enrollment fees are: UK£9.50; under 18 £3.50; £19 for both parents with children under 18 enrolled free; £9.50 for 1 parent with children under 18 enrolled free; £130 for lifetime membership.

Youth Hostels Association of Northern Ireland (YHANI), 22 Donegall Rd., Belfast BT12 5JN (tel. (01232) 32 47 33 or 31 54 35; fax 43 96 99). Prices range from UK£8-12. Annual memberships £7, under 18 £3, family £14 for up to 6 children.

Youth Hostels Association of New Zealand (YHANZ), P.O. Box 436, 173 Gloucester St., Christchurch 1 (tel. (03) 379 9970; fax 365 4476; email info@yha.org.nz; http://www.yha.org.nz). Annual membership fee NZ$24.

Hostel Association of South Africa, P.O. Box 4402, Cape Town 8000 (tel. (021) 24 2511; fax 24 4119; email hisa@gem.co.za; http://www.gen.com/hisa). Membership SAR45, group 120, family 90, lifetime 250.

BED AND BREAKFASTS

For a cozy alternative to impersonal hotel rooms, B&Bs (private homes with rooms available to travelers) range from the acceptable to the sublime. Hosts will sometimes go out of their way to be accommodating by accepting travelers with pets, giving personalized tours, or offering home-cooked meals. On the other hand, many B&Bs do not provide phones, TVs, or private bathrooms.

Several travel guides and reservation services specialize in B&Bs. *The Complete Guide to Bed and Breakfasts, Inns and Guesthouses in the U.S., Canada, and Worldwide* (US$17) lists over 11,000 B&Bs and inns, and includes Australia locations (available through Lanier Publications, P.O. Box D, Petaluma, CA 94953 (tel. (707) 763-0271; fax 763-5762; email lanier@travelguides.com; http://www.travelguides.com)). If you can stand the name, **Nerd World's Bed and Breakfasts by Region** (http://www.nerdworld.com/users/dstein/nw854.html) offers an excellent listing of international B&Bs, including accommodations in Australia. **Bed and Breakfast Australia,** 666 Pacific Highway, Killara NSW 2071 (tel. (02) 9498 5344; fax 9498 6438), can help groups and individuals plan itineraries and make advance bookings.

UNIVERSITY RESIDENCE HALLS

Many Australian **universities** open their residence halls to travelers when school is not in session. Because they are in student areas, the dormitories are often good sources for information for things to do, places to stay, and possible rides out of town. The typical summer break at the university level is from late November to late February. Easter break lasts for two weeks over Easter, while winter break encompasses the first two weeks of July. The Universities of Canberra, Sydney, and Queensland, as well as Flinders University of South Australia, Melbourne University, and Monash University in Melbourne are among those occasionally offering accommodation. No one policy covers all of these institutions. Contact the universities directly, or request the *Campus Accommodation* **information sheet** from the Australian Tourist Commission (http://www.aussie.net.au). Dorms are popular with many travelers, especially those looking for longer-term lodging, so book ahead. Getting a room may be difficult, but rates tend to be quite low.

HOMESTAYS AND FARMSTAYS

Homestay Associations are usually near public transportation and guests can usually stay anywhere from a few days to six months or more. One week's stay in a single room, with breakfast and dinner every day, ranges from AUS$150-250. The Australian Tourist Commission publishes a *Homestay Information* sheet.

Dele Rule's ECOLE/Homes Across The Sea, 11 Murphy St., Ipswich Qld 4305 (tel. (07) 3812 0211; fax 3812 2188). Over 250 host families throughout Australia, including homes in the outback, the tropics, capital cities, and the coast.

Homechain, 575 Mulgrave Rd., Cairns Qld 4870 (tel. (07) 4054 3250; fax 4054 7708). Organizes many types of homestays including farmstays and outback station placements.

Homestay Network, 5 Locksley St., Killara NSW 2071 (tel. (02) 9498 4400; fax 9498 8324). Over 300 homes on Sydney's north shore and eastern suburbs, which can accommodate stays ranging from a few days to six months or more.

Unique Australian Holidays Pty Ltd., 67 Rathowen Parade, Killarney Heights NSW 2086 (tel. (02) 9975 4550; fax 9975 1655), can help arrange accommodation and study tours around Sydney, the Gold Coast, Perth, and Melbourne.

Agritours Australia, 108 Taylor St., Armidale NSW 2350 (tel. (02) 6772 9230; fax 6772 2244). Arranges farmstays on cattle or sheep stations. Can tailor itineraries to specific group needs. Min. group size of 3 is not strictly enforced.

Australian Farm and Country Tourism Association (AFACT), 6th Fl., 230 Collins St., Melbourne Vic 3000 (tel. (03) 9650 2922; fax 9650 9434). Arranges farm stays on 135 Victorian host farms. Prices for doubles AUS$60-150. Book in advance, particularly during summer and school holidays.

HOME EXCHANGE AND RENTALS

Home exchange offers the traveler with a home the opportunity to live like a native, and to dramatically cut down on accommodation fees—usually only an administration fee is paid to the matching service. Once the introductions are made, the choice is left to the two hopeful partners. Most companies have pictures of member's homes and information about the owners (some will even ask for your photo). A great web site that lists many exchange companies can be found at http://www.aitec.edu.au/~bwechner/Documents/Travel/Lists/HomeExchangeClubs.html. Renting a home may also be a good deal for some: this will depend on the length of stay and the desired level of services.

HomeLink International, P.O. Box 260, Maldon Vic 3463 (tel. (03) 5475 2829; fax 5475 1078). Listing of 11,000 homes worldwide, and 600 homes throughout Australia.

International Travel and Home Exchange, 43 James St., Guildford WA 6055 (tel. (08) 9279 2366; fax 9279 1451). Australian-based organization matches up international home exchanges.

Latitudes Home Exchange, 28 Waverley St., South Perth WA 6151 (tel. (08) 9367 9412; fax 9367 9576). Offers temporary home exchange for 1-24 months. Computerized matching service or directory listings, circulated 3 times per year.

Longer Stays

Be sure that your visa is in order before extending your stay, and that you have a **work visa** if you plan on earning money. If looking for a job, it's likely you'll have better luck in cities or in **fruit-picking** areas. Once you've got yourself a source of funds, **housing** will probably be the most pressing concern. Look around the town of your choice for real estate agencies who may be able to arrange rentals or leases. Check the larger city papers and university campus notice boards for employment and apartment listings. In rural Australia, many hostels and guesthouses cater to seasonal laborers, offering discounted longer-term rates and providing job placement. **Council's** work program will help with job-placement and housing. Renting a room is also a very common housing solution for the ex-pat. For more info on long-term accommodation, see **Home Exchange and Rentals,** above.

Food shopping and the other details of living should not be difficult to arrange. *Let's Go* attempts to list the most significant markets and supermarkets in the towns we visit to give you a good start.

Camping and the Outdoors

If your travels take you to Australia when the weather is agreeable, camping is by far the cheapest way to go. Many hostels have camping facilities or at least allow guests to pitch tents in the yard, and the ubiquitous caravan parks offer sites without power for tent campers. Apart from being a sound financial decision, the flexibility of camping allows you to access the more remote corners of the country's numerous wilderness areas, including any of the 11 World Heritage Sites.

Every World Heritage Site has been determined to have significant ecological or cultural value for the world, and most countries have only a handful. Some of the other World Heritage Sites are the Acropolis, Stonehenge, the Serengeti, and Yellowstone. Australia's include **The Great Barrier Reef** and **Fraser Island** in Queensland; **Kakadu National Park** and **Uluru** (Ayers Rock in Kata-Tjuta National Park) in Northern Territory; **Lord Howe Island** and **Willandra Lakes** in New South Wales; **Shark Bay** in Western Australia; and **Naracoorte Conservation Park** in South Australia, as well as Tasmanian wilderness, fossil sites in Queensland and South Australia, and the wet tropics of Queensland. For more information on World Heritage Sites, check out http://www.cco.caltech.edu/~salmon/world.heritage.html.

USEFUL RESOURCES

Australia is full of government agencies that protect, monitor, and administer national parks and wilderness areas. Many of these can be useful in supplying information or camping permits to prospective bushwalkers, or in providing boating information.

ACT Parks and Conservation Service: P.O. Box 1119, Tuggeranong ACT 2901 (tel. (02) 6207 5111).

National Parks Service: Dept. of Natural Resources and Environment, P.O. Box 41, East Melbourne Vic 3002 (tel. (03) 9412 4011).

National Parks and Wildlife Service Head Office: 43 Bridge St., Hurstville NSW 2220 (tel. (03) 9585 6333). Open Mon.-Fri. 9am-5pm.

State Forests of NSW: Building 2, 423 Pennant Hills Rd., Pennant Hills NSW 2120 (tel. (03) 9980 4296). Open Mon.-Fri. 9am-5pm.

NSW Confederation of Bushwalking Clubs: GPO Box 2090, Sydney NSW 2001 (recorded information tel. (02) 9548 1228).

Yachting Association of NSW: P.O. Box 537, Glebe NSW 2037 (tel. (02) 9660 1266). Open Mon.-Fri. 8:30am-5pm.

NSW Canoe Association: Tel. 9660 4597. Open Mon. and Wed. 9:30am-6pm.

A variety of publishing companies offer hiking guidebooks to meet the educational needs of novice or expert. See the special-interest publications listed above for some options. For **topographical maps of Australia,** contact the Australian Surveying & Land Information Group at (02) 6201 4201. Or write to AUSLIG, Department of Administrative Services, Scrivener Bldg., Fern Hill Park, Bruce ACT 2617. For further information about camping, hiking, and biking, write or call the publishers listed below to receive a free catalogue.

Adventurous Traveler Bookstore, P.O. Box 1468, Williston, VT 05495 (tel. (800) 282-3963; fax (800) 677-1821; email books@atbook.com; http://www.AdventurousTraveler.com). Free 40-page catalogue upon request. Many outdoor adventure travel books, including titles like *100 Walks in Tasmania* (US$12) or *Rivers and Lakes of Victoria* (US$15). Good web site, too.

The Mountaineers Books, 1001 SW Klickitat Way, #201, Seattle, WA 98134 (tel. (800) 553-4453 or (206) 223-6303; fax 223-6306; email mbooks@mountaineers.org). Many titles on hiking (the *100 Hikes* series), biking, mountaineering, natural history, and conservation.

CAMPING AND HIKING EQUIPMENT

Purchase **equipment** before you leave. This way you'll know exactly what you have and how much it weighs. Spend some time examining catalogues and talking to knowledgeable salespeople. Whether buying or renting, finding sturdy, light, and inexpensive equipment is a must.

Sleeping bags: Most good **sleeping bags** are rated by "season," or the lowest outdoor temperature at which they will keep you warm ("summer" means 30-40°F, "3-season" means 20°F, and "4-season" or "winter" means below 0°F). Sleeping bags are made either of down (warmer and lighter, but more expensive, and miserable when wet) or of synthetic material (heavier, more durable, and warmer when wet). Prices vary, but might range from US$65 to $100 for a summer synthetic to US$250-550 for a good down winter bag. **Sleeping bag pads,** including foam pads (US$15 and up) and air mattresses (US$25-50) cushion your back and neck and insulate you from the ground. A good alternative is the **Therm-A-Rest®,** which is part foam and part air-mattress and inflates to full padding when you unroll it.

Tents: The best **tents** are free-standing, with their own frames and suspension systems; they set up quickly and require no staking (except in high winds). Low profile dome tents are the best all-around. When pitched their internal space is almost entirely usable, which means little unnecessary bulk. Tent sizes can be somewhat misleading: 2 people *can* fit in a 2-person tent, but will find life more pleasant in a 4-person. If you're traveling by car, go for the bigger tent; if you're hiking, stick with a smaller tent that weighs no more than 3-4 lb. Good 2-person tents start at US$150, 4-person tents at US$400, but you can sometimes find last year's model for half the price. Seal the seams of your tent with waterproofer, and make sure it has a rain fly.

Backpacks: If you intend to do a lot of hiking, you should have a **frame backpack.** Backpack choice is a personal matter, and you'd do best to try a couple out before making a purchase. **Internal-frame packs** sit closer to your back, keep a lower center of gravity, and can flex adequately to allow you to hike difficult trails that require a lot of bending and maneuvering. **External-frame packs** keep the weight higher and allow more packing options, but they are inconvenient for plane, train, or bus travel. Whichever you choose, make sure your pack has a strong, padded hip belt, which transfers the weight from the shoulders to the hips. Any serious backpacking requires a pack of at least 4000 cubic in. Allow an additional 500 cubic in. for your sleeping bag in internal-frame packs. Sturdy backpacks cost anywhere from US$125-500. This is one area where it doesn't pay to economize—cheaper packs may be less comfortable, and the straps are more likely to fray or rip. Before you buy any pack, try it on and imagine carrying it, full, a few miles up a rocky incline.

Boots: Be sure to wear hiking boots with good **ankle support** which are appropriate for the terrain you are hiking. Your boots should fit snugly and comfortably over one or two wool socks and a thin liner sock. Be sure that the boots are broken in—a bad blister will ruin your hiking for days.

Other necessities: Rain gear should come in 2 pieces, a top and pants, rather than a poncho. **Synthetics,** like polypropylene tops, socks, and long underwear, along with a pile jacket, will keep you warm even when wet. When camping in autumn, winter, or spring, bring along a **"space blanket,"** which helps you to retain your body heat and doubles as a groundcloth (US$5-15). Plastic **canteens** or water bottles keep water cooler than metal ones do, and are virtually shatter- and leak-proof. Large, collapsible **water sacks** will significantly improve your lot in primitive campgrounds and weigh practically nothing when empty. Bring **water-purification tablets** for when you can't boil water. For those places that forbid fires or the gathering of firewood (common in Australian summers and dry seasons), you'll need a **camp stove.** The classic Coleman starts at about US$30. Flammable liquids are not allowed on airplanes; you may want to wait to purchase a stove until arriving in Australia, so that you can determine fuel availability. A **first aid kit, swiss army knife, insect repellent,** and **waterproof matches** are essential camping items, and a **repair kit** with replacement parts for backpack and stove can save you a lot of grief.

The mail-order firms listed below offer lower prices than those you'll find in many stores, but shop around locally first in order to determine what items actually look like and weigh. Keep in mind that camping equipment is generally more expensive in Australia, New Zealand, and the U.K. than it is in North America.

Campmor, P.O. Box 700, Saddle River, NJ 07458-0700 (tel. (800) CAMPMOR (526-4784), outside the U.S. call (201) 825-8300; email customer-service@campmor.com; http://www.campmor.com), has a wide selection of name brand equipment at low prices. One-year guarantee for unused or defective merchandise.

Eastern Mountain Sports (EMS), One Vose Farm Rd., Peterborough, NH 03458 (tel. (603) 924-9591), has stores throughout the U.S. Though slightly higher-priced, they provide excellent service and guaranteed customer satisfaction on most items sold. They don't have a catalogue, and they generally don't take mail or phone orders; call the above number for the branch nearest you.

Recreational Equipment, Inc. (REI), 1700 45th St. E, Sumner, WA 98390 (tel. (800) 426-4840; http://www.rei.com), stocks a wide range of the latest in camping gear and holds great seasonal sales. Many items are guaranteed for life (excluding normal wear and tear).

L.L. Bean, Freeport, ME 04033-0001 (tel. (800) 441-5713 in Canada or the U.S., (0800) 962 954 in the U.K., (207) 552-6878 elsewhere; fax (207) 552-3080; http://www.llbean.com). This monolithic equipment and outdoor clothing supplier guarantees 100% satisfaction on all purchases. Open 24hr. per day.

Mountain Designs, P.O. Box 1472, Fortitude Valley Qld 4006 (tel. (07) 3252 8894; fax 3252 4569) is a leading Australian manufacturer and mail order retailer of camping and climbing gear.

YHA Adventure Shop, 14 Southampton St., London, WC2E 7HA (tel. (01718) 36 85 41). Main branch of one of Britain's largest outdoor equipment suppliers.

CARAVANNING

Many North American campers harbor a suspicion that traveling with a camper or caravan is not "real camping." No such stigma exists in Australia, where caravanning is both popular and common.

Many campgrounds double as caravan parks, consisting of both tent sites and powered sites for caravans. On-site caravans (also called on-site vans) are a frequent feature at caravan parks, and save those on holiday the expense and hassle of renting a caravan by anchoring one permanently to the site and renting it out. "Cabins" at caravan parks are often analogous to an on-site van, with a toilet inside.

There is a distinction to be made between caravans and campervans. The former needs to be pulled as a trailer, while the latter has its own cab. Renting a caravan will always be more expensive than tenting or hosteling, but the costs compare favorably with the price of renting a car and staying in hotels. The convenience of bringing along your own bedroom, bathroom, and kitchen makes it an attractive option for some, especially older travelers and families with small children.

It is not difficult to arrange a campervan rental from overseas, although you will want to begin gathering information several months before your departure. Rates vary widely by region, season (Dec., Jan., and Feb. are the most expensive months), and type of van. It always pays to contact several different companies to compare vehicles and prices. **Avis** (tel. (800) 331-1084) and **Hertz** (tel. (800) 654-3001) are U.S. firms which can arrange caravan rentals overseas. **Maui Rentals** (tel. (09) 275 3013; fax 275 9690) rents campervans in Australia and New Zealand.

WILDERNESS AND SAFETY CONCERNS

Stay warm, stay dry, and **stay hydrated.** The vast majority of life-threatening wilderness problems stem from a failure to follow this advice. On any hike, however brief, you should pack enough equipment to keep you alive should disaster befall. This includes **rain gear, hat** and **mittens,** a **first-aid kit, high energy food,** and **water.** Dress in warm layers of **wool** or **synthetic materials** designed for the outdoors. Pile fleece jackets and Gore-Tex® raingear are excellent choices (see **Camping and Hiking Equipment**). *Never* rely on **cotton** for warmth. This "death cloth" will be absolutely useless should it get wet. When camping, be sure to bring a proper tent with rain-fly and warm sleeping bags.

Check **weather forecasts** and pay attention to the skies when hiking. Weather patterns can change instantly. If on a day hike when the weather turns nasty, turn back. If on an overnight, start looking immediately for shelter. Whenever possible, let someone know when and where you are going hiking, either a friend, your hostel, a park ranger, or a local hiking organization. Do not attempt a hike beyond your ability—you may be endangering your life.

See **Health** (p. 15) for information about environmental dangers, basic medical concerns and first-aid, and outdoor ailments such as giardia, rabies, and insects. A good guide to outdoor survival is *How to Stay Alive in the Woods,* by Bradford Angier (Macmillan, US$8).

ENVIRONMENTALLY RESPONSIBLE TOURISM

While protecting yourself from the elements, take a moment to also consider protecting the wilderness from you. At the very least, a responsible traveler practices **"minimum impact camping"** techniques. Leave no trace of your presence when you leave a site. Don't cut vegetation or clear new campsites. A campstove is the safer (and more efficient) way to cook, but if you must, make small fires using only dead branches or brush. Never do this on a Total Fire Ban Day however; you don't want to be responsible for starting a bushfire. Make sure your campsite is at least 200 ft. from water supplies or bodies of water. If there are no toilet facilities, bury human waste (but not paper) at least 4 in. deep and above the high-water line 200 ft. or more from any water supplies and campsites. Always pack your trash in a plastic bag and carry it with you until you reach the next trash can.

Responsible tourism means more than picking up your litter, however. Growing numbers of "ecotourists" are asking hard questions of resort owners and tour operators about how their policies affect local ecologies and local economies. Some try to give something back to the regions they enjoy by volunteering for environmental organizations at home or abroad. Above all, responsible tourism means being aware of your impact on the places you visit, and taking responsibility for your own actions.

If you want to know more about "ecotourism" or responsible travel in a particular region, contact the **Center for Responsible Tourism,** P.O. Box 827, San Anselmo, CA 94979 (tel. (415) 258-6594), or **Ecotourism Association of Australia,** P.O. Box 3839, Alice Springs NT 0871 (tel. (08) 8952 8308).

ORGANIZED ADVENTURE

Organized adventure tours offer another way of exploring the wild. Activities include hiking, biking, skiing, canoeing, kayaking, rafting, climbing, photo safaris, and archaeological digs, and go *everywhere.* Begin by consulting tourism bureaus, which can suggest parks, trails, and outfitters as well as answer more general questions. The **Specialty Travel Index,** 305 San Anselmo Ave., San Anselmo, CA 94960 (tel. (415) 459-4900; fax 459-4974; http://www.specialtytravel.com) is a directory listing hundreds of tour operators worldwide. **Roadrunner International**, 6762A Centinela Ave., Culver City, CA 90230 (tel. (800) TREK USA (873-5782) in North America; (01892) 51 27 00 in Europe and the U.K.), offers hostel tour packages to Australia and New Zealand, as well as Europe and North and South America.

Keeping In Touch

TIME DIFFERENCES

Calculating time differences is more confusing than it might seem. Hemisphere differences, daylight savings time, and large time differences all combine to create chaos. Australia stretches across three time zones. The three most northern states (WA, NT, and Qld) do not observe daylight savings time, but the other states do. One possible additional complication is that border towns sometimes take the time zone of a neighboring state. There is a comprehensive chart of time conversions by state and season in the **appendix** (p. 574).

MAIL

Sending Mail to Australia

When sending mail to Australia, make sure to include the name, street address or P.O. box, city name or post office of delivery, state or territory abbreviation (ACT, NSW, NT, Qld, SA, Tas, Vic, WA), and postal code. The bottom line should say AUSTRALIA in all capitals. *Let's Go* lists postal codes in the **Practical Information** section for each major city and in most towns. All of Australia's **postal codes** are at http://www.auspost.com.au.

Mail can be sent internationally through *Poste Restante* (the international phrase for Hold Mail) to any city or town; it's well worth using, generally has no surcharges, and is much more reliable than you might think. Mark the envelope "HOLD," add the regular required postage to Australia, and address it with the last name capitalized and underlined followed by the appropriate city, state, and postal code; GPO stands for general post office, and is almost always the best destination choice. For example: Dave COLLINS, Poste Restante, GPO Melbourne, Melbourne Vic 3550, AUSTRALIA. The mail will go to a special desk in the central post office, and Dave Collins can arrive in person, show the clerk his passport, and pick up his package free of charge. *Poste Restante* mail is generally held for only 30 days. If the clerks insist that there is nothing for you, have them check under your first name as well.

American Express travel offices throughout the world will act as a mail service for cardholders if you contact them in advance. Under this free **"Client Letter Service,"** they will hold mail for 30 days, forward upon request, and accept telegrams. Some offices will offer these services to non-cardholders (especially those who have purchased AmEx Travellers' Cheques), but call ahead to make sure. Check the **Practical Information** section of the cities you plan to visit; *Let's Go* lists AmEx office locations for most large cities. A complete list is available free from AmEx (U.S. tel. (800) 528-4800), in the booklet *Traveler's Companion,* or online at http://www.americanexpress.com/shared/cgi-bin/tsoserve.cgi?travel/index.

Sending Mail from Australia

General post offices (GPO) are usually **open** from 9am to 5pm Monday through Friday. Larger branches also open on Saturday mornings. Visa, Mastercard, and American Express are often accepted if the bill is greater than AUS$10.

Air mail to the United States and Canada takes approximately seven to 10 business days. **Economy air mail,** which is slightly cheaper, takes anywhere from two to six weeks. **Sea mail** is by far the cheapest and slowest way to send mail, although letters and postcards can not be sent by sea mail from Australia. It can take up to three months for sea mail packages to cross the ocean—appropriate for sending large quantities of items you won't need to see for a while. It is vital, therefore, to distinguish your air mail from surface mail by explicitly labeling all letters and packages "air mail." If regular airmail is too slow, ask about more expensive options.

Postcards and letters sent within Australia cost 45¢. Postcards to Canada or the USA cost 95¢ air mail or 80¢ economy air mail. Small letters cost $1.05/90¢. Postcards to the U.K., Ireland, South Africa, and Europe cost $1/85¢. Small letters cost $1.20/$1. Postcards to New Zealand cost 70¢/65¢. Small letters cost 75¢/70¢.

Aerograms, printed sheets that fold into envelopes and travel via airmail, are available at post offices and cost 75¢ to any destination worldwide. When ordering books and materials from abroad, always include one or two **International Reply Coupons (IRCs)**—a way of providing the postage to cover delivery. IRCs should be available from your local post office as well as abroad (US$1.05).

TELEPHONES

Public phones are easy to find nearly everywhere you go in Australia. Some phone booths in Australia are coin-operated, some are phone-card operated, and some accept either coins or phone cards. Local calls from phone booths cost 40¢. In addition to phone booths, public phones can sometimes be found in bars and hotels, and local calls on these often cost 50¢. Residential phone services (like in a home or business) do not provide free local calls, which cost 30¢.

Australia has two telecommunications companies: Optus and Telstra. Telstra **prepaid phonecards** are available in AUS$5, $10, $20, and $50 denominations from many newsagents and pharmacies. They are accepted in over 75% of Australia's phones. The time is measured in minutes or "talk units," and the card usually has a toll-free access telephone number and a personal identification number (PIN). Cards that must be inserted into phones are also available. As phone cards have grown in popularity, so have the number of booths accepting cards only. Telstra telephones are often bright orange. Phones in motels and restaurants are sometimes small blue boxes which don't take phone cards. Most phones accept coins only larger than 10¢, and you sometimes can't put in an initial combination of over five coins.

For **directory assistance,** you can call 013 from any public phone at no charge. A table of other directory assistance numbers is in the **appendix** (p. 573). Six digit phone numbers beginning with **13** are information numbers that can be dialed from anywhere in Australia for the price of a local call. Numbers beginning with 1300 operate very similarly. Unfortunately, Phone Away cards can not be used for 13 calls (normal pre-paid phone cards are fine). Phone numbers beginning with **1800** are toll-free.

Nine-digit phone numbers beginning with 018, 019, or similar combinations indicate **mobile phones** and require all nine digits when being dialed. Mobile phones are everywhere in urban Australia; people walk down the street talking on the phone, and some hotel owners routinely ask guests to register their mobile phones when they check in. Usually the caller picks up the charges when calling a mobile phone, and charges run about 80¢ per minute.

Long-distance calls within Australia use STD (Subscriber Trunk Dialing) services. These are calls for which you have to dial a **phone code** before the eight-digit number. You'll get the cheapest long-distance rates if you call between 6pm Saturday and 8am Monday, or at night during the week. Long-distance calls overseas use international direct dialing (IDD) services.

Calling Australia

You can place **international calls** from most telephones. To call direct, dial the universal international access code for the country you're calling from (see the **appendix,** p. 573) followed by the country code (61 for Australia), the state telephone code (two digits—see the beginning of each chapter or the appendix—don't dial the initial zero), and the local number (usually eight digits). 1800 numbers cannot be reached from overseas, but 13 numbers often can be. Wherever possible, use a calling card (see **calling cards,** below) for international phone calls, as the long-distance rates for national phone services are often unpredictable and exorbitant.

Calling Home

To **dial overseas direct,** press 0011, then the country code, the city code, dropping the initial zero (e.g. 171 for London, 212 for New York) and the telephone number.

See the **appendix** (p. 573) for a table of country codes. A Telstra call to Britain or the U.S. **costs** AUS$1.35 per minute ($1.03 off-peak). A call to New Zealand costs AUS$1.09 a minute (72¢ off-peak).

You can usually make direct international calls from **pay phones,** but you may need to drop your coins as quickly as your words if you're not using a phone card or credit card. Be wary of more expensive, private pay phones; look for pay phones in public areas, especially train or bus stations. If private pay phones are to be feared, one should all but flee from the insidious in-room hotel phone call. Although incredibly convenient, these calls invariably include an arbitrary and sky-high surcharge (as much as AUS$10 in some establishments). If you really don't want to leave your hotel, find a pay phone in the lobby.

Operators will place **collect calls** for you. It's cheaper to find a pay phone and deposit just enough money to be able to say "Call me" and give your number (although some pay phones can't receive calls). Some companies, seizing upon this "call-me-back" concept, have created **callback phone services.** Under these plans, you call a specified number, ring once, and hang up. The company's computer calls back and gives you a dial tone. You can then make as many calls as you want, at rates about 20-60% lower than you'd pay using credit cards or pay phones. This option is most economical for loquacious travelers, as services may include a US$10-25 minimum billing per month. For information, call **America Tele-Fone** (tel. (800) 321-5817), **Globaltel** (tel. (770) 449-1295), **International Telephone** (tel. (800) 638-5558), and **Telegroup** (tel. (800) 338-0225).

A **calling card** is probably your best and cheapest bet; your local long-distance service provider will have a number for you to dial while traveling (either toll-free or charged as a local call) to connect instantly to an operator in your home country. The calls (plus a small surcharge) are then billed either collect or to the calling card. See the **appendix** (p. 573) for access numbers from Australia. MCI's WorldPhone also provides access to MCI's **Traveler's Assist,** which gives legal and medical advice, exchange rate information, and translation services. Many other long distance carriers and phone companies provide such travel information; contact your phone service provider.

OTHER COMMUNICATION

If you want to keep in touch with friends or colleagues in a college or research institution, **electronic mail (email)** is an attractive option. With a minimum of computer knowledge and a little planning, you can beam messages anywhere for no per-message charges. One option is to befriend college students as you go and ask if you can use their email accounts. If you're not the finagling type, look for bureaus that offer access to email for sending individual messages. Search through http://www.cyberia-cafe.net/cyberia/guide/ccafe.htm to find a list of **cybercafes** around the world from which you can drink a cup of joe and email him too. Most big cities in Australia have cybercafes; *Let's Go* lists them under individual cities' **practical information** sections.

AUSTRALIA

Oz. It's no place like home.

—Popular tourism slogan

History

Australia Before the Europeans

According to recent estimates, the ancestors of the **Aboriginal** people of Australia inhabited this island continent as long as 60,000 to 100,000 years ago. Fossil records suggest that migration to Australia may have occurred in waves that predated the advent of agriculture in Asia and the Middle East. The Aboriginal people were **foragers,** living in even the driest areas of the country and migrating seasonally in search of native food plants and animals. Although they did not farm, they did increase the land's productivity by burning large tracts each year. Fire replaced necessary nutrients in the soil and allowed the germination of plants with seed pods that open only under intense heat.

Because Aboriginals lived in such interdependence with the land, complex relationships developed among their kinship structures, the land, and its resources. These relationships evolved into a complicated system of joint ownership and stewardship of particular areas of land by members of different family groups. The relationships also formed the basis and focus of Aboriginal **spiritual life** and the land was thus the most important factor in determining a person's spiritual and secular identity. The relationship between people, landscape, and resources was interconnected in a way that Europeans who arrived in Australia never understood.

The Dreaming

The concept of the Dreaming is one of the most famous ideas associated with the Australian Aboriginals. It is not a single story or idea, but one that arose in different forms in various tribes. Once called the Dreamtime, the name was changed in the 1950s to reflect the ever-presentness of the Dreaming within the cyclical Aboriginal understanding of time. It describes the basis of the Aboriginal relationship with the land, which they believe to be a spiritual phenomenon, created by spiritual forces that once emerged from a formless earth. These forces took forms that frequently combined features of humans, animals, plants, and other forces—serpent-women, bush fig-men, wind, and even diarrhea—and moved over the surface of the landscape. As they moved, they and their activities, tracks, and artifacts were transformed into the features of the land and the heavens. The whole of the land was therefore sacred to the Aboriginals, dotted with sites significant to the Dreaming stories and tied to the origins of the people themselves. In one case, the kangaroo-man was the ancestor of one tribe of Aboriginals, and when he sat up to view the country, he became a rocky ridge.

Before the English

Although Australia's history is inextricably linked with England's, the British were not the first outsiders to lay claim to the land. **Chinese** explorers were almost certainly the first non-Aboriginals to arrive, and 15th-century **Portuguese** and **French** sailors knew details about the existence of *Terra Australis* (southern land). On 16th-century maps, a misshapen Australia is labeled New Netherlands, since the western and northernmost coasts had been explored and mapped by the **Dutch,** who concluded that the continent contained very little of value and never established a settlement. **Abel Tasman,** the explorer after whom Tasmania was eventually named, was an early Dutch explorer under the commission of Governor General Anthony van Diemen of the Dutch Indies. Tasmania was called Van Diemen's Land for many years. As early as 1573, occasional English documents suggested exploring the southern hemisphere although few raised the prospect of settling.

English Exploration and Settlement

In 1770, on a scientific mission to observe the transit of Venus across the sun, the English captain **James Cook** explored the eastern coast of what would become Australia. The other sides of the island continent had all been explored and mapped, but the Great Barrier Reef had previously deterred explorers from the east. Cook and his crew of astronomers and scientists discovered and named **Botany Bay,** and returned to England wth stories of strange animals and plants.

When Something Goes Missing

In the late 18th and early 19th centuries, it didn't take much to win a free trip to Australia, as long as you didn't mind traveling aboard a convict ship. Most of the convicts were guilty of petty thievery—and of being poor, ill-connected, and, often, Irish. Many had originally been sentenced to death, with those sentences commuted to "transportation beyond the seas" and seven years' service upon arrival. For example, records show that the disappearance of one coffee pot, one guinea, 28 lb. of hair powder, six live turkeys, five woolen blankets, one piece of yellow canvas, three petticoats, 11 yards of printed cotton, 8 lb. of cheese, or one sheep was enough to send one convict or another to Australia. One man was convicted of destroying 12 cucumber plants, while another "unlawfully cut down one maiden ash timber tree." One woman was convicted of "spoiling, burning, and defacing the garment of a female." Another woman received a sentence of death, commuted to Australian transportation, for stealing two linen aprons. A boy, age 11, was shipped out for stealing one pair of silk stockings.

There is no simple answer to the question of why England settled Australia in 1788. One factor, certainly, was that in the wake of the American Revolution, England could no longer dispose of convicts by transporting them to America to serve their sentences. A doctor who had been on Cook's voyage testified before Parliament that the unclaimed southern lands might serve the purpose. The prisons in London were full, and Australia, by all accounts, was remarkably empty. The land in the southern hemisphere, though unwelcoming, seemed free for the taking, and preparations for a convict settlement began in 1785. But full prisons were not the only justification for such expense. The English government wanted a base for its global navy in the eastern seas and anticipated finding natural resources, particularly timber, for its fleet.

The 11 ships of the **First Fleet** sailed from England with their unwilling cargo on May 13, 1787. **Lord Sydney** (less formally known as Thomas Townshend) was the secretary of state for home affairs and appointed Arthur Phillip commander of the fleet. About 730 convicts—570 men and 160 women—were on board, along with more than 250 guards, officers, wives, and children. Over the course of the eight-month voyage 36 men and four women died, and seven children were born. The fleet arrived at Botany Bay on January 19 or 20, 1788. But when the harbor, soil, and water were all found to be lacking, Commander Phillip headed north to Port Jackson. The English flag was finally planted on **January 26,** and a colony was born in the spot that Sydney stands today.

The Early Years

Upon arrival in Australia, the convicts and their guards faced a country foreign and unyielding. The first years of the colony went even more poorly than many had feared. Half of the potential labor was used up guarding the other half. The livestock escaped into the bush, relations with the Aboriginals rapidly deteriorated, most of the follow-up supply ships wrecked, and the land itself seemed supremely inhospitable. According to plan, the convicts were put to work on **government-sponsored farms,** but since most of them came from the slums of London, they had no agricultural experience. In addition, the English seeds and cuttings that the fleet had so carefully carried across the sea did not thrive in the strange soil and new climate. In the first six months, the First Fleeters managed to build only four huts (for officers); everyone else lived in tents. Captain Phillip's grandiose plans for streets 200 ft. wide in Sydney had to be scrapped, since the colony had **no power source** other than the inhabitants' own labor: no mill or even team of cattle was available for over eight years.

While the convict colony struggled on in Sydney, an English naval officer named **Matthew Flinders** headed an 1801 expedition to circumnavigate and chart the southern land. At the end of three years, he declared it one mass and argued that the name New Holland or New Netherlands should be replaced with a different moniker: Australia. This suggestion sat well with the leaders of the English government, who considered the land England's anyway, but the term "Australia" was not used on a regular basis to describe the continent until 1817.

The End of the Convict Era

In 1809, when **Colonel Lachlan Macquarie** came to power in Australia, he argued that convicts who had served their seven years (but who remained in Australia, unable or unwilling to pay for passage back to the mother country) should be allowed to begin their lives again, and he gave them **full rights** as citizens. Not surprisingly, many streets in Australia today bear his name.

Meanwhile, the responsibility of paying for the upkeep of the convicts became an increasingly onerous economic burden on England, since the colony was not self-supporting. After 1815, as ever more convicts arrived on Australia's shores, the government began to **assign convicts to private employers** to lighten the strain on the Crown's purse. By 1830, a total of about 50,000 male convicts and 8000 female convicts had arrived in Australia, and many had worked on private farms and in private workshops. But after the abolitionist crusades in the 1830s, some Brits began to argue that the Australian practice of assigning convicts to private employers smelled suspiciously of **slavery.** In 1840, the practice was abolished, and suddenly, Australians thought that more convicts seemed like less of a good idea. People in more-populated eastern Australia began to protest against continued convict arrival, and the Crown virtually stopped sending convicts to the eastern regions by 1852. Western Australia and Tasmania continued to receive convicts until January 10, 1868, when the last convict ship arrived in Australia. In all, a total of approximately 160,500 convicts had been sent to Australia (24,700 of whom were women).

Gold and Expansion

In addition to sending convicts, England encouraged free settler migration with **land grants** until 1831 and offered inexpensive passage to women (to try to improve the gender imbalance). In 1833, **young single women** between the ages of 18 and 30 "of good health and character" paid just £6 for passage to Australia and promise of employment upon arrival. **Wool** was Australia's major product for export beginning in the mid-1830s. By 1845, sheep farming was the most profitable business in the country. Despite the land grant incentives and economic improvements, population growth through this period remained stagnant.

The discovery of Australian gold in 1851 accomplished what the promise of land could not. Wealth and immigrants flooded the country.

The discovery of Australian **gold** in 1851 accomplished what the promise of land could not. The precious metal was first unearthed by a man who had failed to find fortune in the California gold rush two years earlier. Wealth and immigrants flooded the country as Australia's own gold rush geared up, and by the end of 1851, non-Aboriginals in Australia numbered around 450,000, eight times the population of a quarter-century earlier. Just a decade after the discovery of gold, 1,150,000 gold-hungry non-Aboriginals lived in Australia. Competition for gold inevitably led to conflict, and the 1854 Eureka Stockade Rebellion marked Australia's closest brush with civil war. Miners in Ballarat, Victoria, formed a collective and built a stockade, in protest of the government's licensing fees for miners. Government forces crushed the uprising in a 15-minute clash that cost about two dozen miners their lives.

The three decades between 1829 and 1859 forms an important period of growth. Four of the six states (Northern Territory is not a state) were formed during this time. The English Parliament first ratified New South Wales's and Victoria's constitutions in 1855—bringing **self-government** to Australia for the first time. Throughout the second half of the 19th century, however, each individual colony had very little formal relation with the other colonies, communicating directly with London and concentrating its attentions on its own capital (see **On the Right Track,** p. 35). The **University of Sydney** was founded in 1850, and the **University of Melbourne** in 1853.

White Australia Policies

A combination of the end of the convict era and the gold rush led to racially influenced immigration policies. Australia's main source of labor dried up in the 1840s when convicts stopped arriving in New South Wales, and Europeans subsequently began importing Chinese laborers. But as more **Chinese immigrants** came to the country, and particularly when they started working the goldfields, many English colonists wanted to keep Asian immigration to a minimum.

Laws were couched in political language. An 1855 "Act to Make Provision for Certain Immigrants" was passed in Victoria. The act put a tax on each Chinese arrival and stipulated that only one Chinese person would be granted entrance for every 10 tons of shipping. In 1879, an Intercolonial Trades Union Congress, one of the first national meetings with representatives from all of the states, published a warning that Chinese immigration "supplanted white labour, and would leave no work or hope for the rising generation, who would fill the jails in consequence." By 1888, the so-called "Chinese question" had begun to make its way onto the political front stage, and a Queensland journal first coined the rallying cry **"White Australia."** As the movement gained power, racism extended to all non-European immigrants. At an 1896 Premiers' Conference colonies extended the anti-Chinese legislation to all non-whites.

In another pointed attempt to exclude Asian immigrants, the new federal government passed the **Immigration Restriction Act of 1901,** which required immigrants to pass, at the discretion of the immigration officer, a 50-word dictation test in a European language. In 1905, responding to complaints from New Zealand, Australia's prime minister ruled that Maori, New Zealand's indigenous people, could have European status.

Federation and Women's Suffrage

By 1901, Australia's non-Aboriginal population had reached 3,370,000, 64.5% of whom had been born in Australia. The Commonwealth of Australia was founded on January 1, 1901, with a formal proclamation in Sydney by the Governor-General, who read a letter from the queen. It was September 3 of that year, however, before the first **Australian flag** flew over the Exhibition Building in Melbourne, the winner in a design contest that had attracted 32,823 entries from all over the world. The blue flag has the Union Jack in the upper left corner, with the star of Australia directly underneath, today with seven points, one for each state or territory in the federation. The Southern Cross star formation is to the right.

In 1902, Australia became only the second country in the world—after New Zealand—to grant federal suffrage to women.

The very next year, in 1902, Australia became only the second country in the world (after New Zealand) to grant federal suffrage to women. (The statute which had barred women was not the only law that seems archaic today. In the same year, police arrested a man at Manly, outside Sydney, for swimming during the day, in direct defiance of the law prohibiting daylight swimming.) In the 1903 federal election, the first in which women could vote, four women ran unsuccessfully for Parliamentary seats. In 1921, **Edith Dircksey Cowan** became the first female in a state parliament when she was elected to the Western Australia legislative assembly.

As the 1900s rolled into the 1910s and the 1910s became the 1920s, the national government gained more power over the states, symbolized by **Canberra's** new national capital status in 1927. In 1922, **Qantas** (Queensland And Northern Territory

Air Service), the government-sponsored outback air-mail service, began regular passenger service between Charleville and Cloncurry, in outback Queensland. An 85-year-old man named Alexander Kennedy was the first passenger, chosen because he had been the first to make the eight-month mail trek by wagon, decades earlier.

The World Wars

When **World War I** gripped the world, Australia's Prime Minister declared that Australia would back the mother country, saying in 1914, "Our duty is quite clear—to gird up our loins and remember that we are Britons." Approximately 330,000 Australians girded up and 60,000 lost their lives. While these figures pale in comparison to the number of casualties from other countries, they become shocking when considered as a percentage of the country's relatively small population. Australia would never again lose that many soldiers in a conflict.

On April 25, 1915, members of the **Australia and New Zealand Army Corps** (ANZAC) landed at Gallipoli, Turkey, as part of the Dardanelles campaign. In the predawn hours, thousands of men stormed cliffs defended by Turkish machine gun batteries, and over 2000 ANZACs were killed on the first day alone. The fighting dragged on for eight months, until December 20, 1915, when 90,000 men were evacuated and Gallipoli was abandoned. Approximately 8500 Australian soldiers died over the course of the campaign and 19,000 were wounded. **Anzac Day** is an Australian national holiday, celebrated every April 25 to remember the heroism of these troops.

"I make it quite clear that Australia looks to America, free from any pangs about our traditional links of friendship to Britain."

A generation later, **World War II** struck even closer to home. After the Japanese attack on the United States' Pearl Harbor (Dec. 7, 1941), Australian citizens became increasingly concerned about the safety of their own shores. In December, 1941, in a poignant counterpoint to what Australia's Prime Minister had said less than three decades earlier, Prime Minister Curtin revealed that his nation would turn to America for future foreign protection when he pronounced, "I make it quite clear that Australia looks to America, free from any pangs about our traditional links of friendship to Britain." The concern was justified—15,000 Australians became prisoners of war when Singapore fell on February 15, 1942. **Darwin,** the capital of the Northern Territory, suffered the first of a series of destructive bombings at the hands of the Japanese just four days later. Over the course of the war, about 30,000 Australian soldiers died while fighting with the Allies.

The Last Half-Century

From 1948, when the Holden, the first domestically manufactured car rolled out of the factory, until 1956, when Australia's first television programs were broadcast, the country enjoyed a time of relative peace and prosperity marked by rapid immigration. In fact, the population nearly doubled in the thirty years following the end of the war, growing from seven million in 1945 to 13.5 million. In the meantime, Australian-American relations were formalized in 1951 with the signing of the **Australia-New Zealand-United States (ANZUS)** pact.

Consequently, when the United States became embroiled in the **Vietnam** conflict, Australians were conscripted to serve, touching off a slowly gathering storm of anti-war protest. Violent protests in Sydney and Melbourne in 1968 led to a call to expel students from university who disobeyed conscription laws. Dissension culminated in 1969, when Australian students stormed the U.S. Consulate in Melbourne.

In 1965, the **White Australia** clauses, added early this century to discourage Asian immigration, were finally erased from the books. In 1967, Australia broke its **currency link** with Britain in deciding not to follow the mother country's lead to devalue the pound sterling. In that same year, **Japan** replaced the United Kingdom as the primary recipient of Australian exports. In 1984, Japan passed the United States as Australia's largest supplier of imports. Australia today is a member of the **Asia Pacific Economic Cooperation (APEC).**

Echoing movements the world over, the 1970s also saw the beginnings of **environmental activism** in Australia. The first case to create a nationwide impact was a disagreement over **Lake Pedder** in Tasmania. Despite environmentalists' protests, a hydroelectric dam was erected in 1973, making Lake Pedder a lake no more. The loss galvanized environmentalists to organize and protest, and eventually to put a "Green" political party in power in Tasmania in 1989.

The Last Three Years

In 1995, after French President Jacques Chirac decided to sponsor **nuclear weapon testing** in the South Pacific, the French consulate in Perth was fire-bombed, and demonstrations were held all over the country. On April 28, 1996, at **Port Arthur, Tasmania,** deranged citizen Martin Bryant shot and killed 35 strangers. This tragedy fueled Australia's gun-control movement, and led to a much-touted plan to ban rapid-fire weapons. In recent years, the government **privatized** several of its large corporations, including its 1992 sale of **Qantas.** In May of 1997, the Australian government funded a $1.3 billion project to clean up the Murray and Darling Rivers, by selling **Telstra,** the previously state-owned telecommunications company.

Pauline Hanson, a Queensland member of federal Parliament, has received a great deal of negative press in recent months for her inflammatory political platform. Hanson, a reactionary conservative, is a leader of the **One Nation Party,** and the most controversial figure in Australian politics today. The One Nation Party supports isolationist policies, charges that Asian interests have corrupted Australian business, and calls for strict limits on immigration. Hanson's views may be hurting Australia's economy: in July of 1997, Chinese investors halted a multi-million dollar industrial project in Ballarat, in response to the anti-Asian racism that Hanson has stirred up. The party also maintains that Aboriginals receive preferential treatment from the government, and challenges the Aboriginal welfare system. Such xenophobic tendencies are a recurring theme in Australia's history, from the first white-Aboriginal contact to the strained relations between English and Chinese gold diggers in the 19th century. The nation's response to the collision of cultures will continue to shape Australia, as debate persists over what exactly defines an Australian—and who has the power to change that definition.

Aboriginal Issues

ABORIGINAL LAND RIGHTS

When the British landed in Australia and claimed the land for the Crown, they did so under a doctrine of *terra nullius,* or empty land. Estimates of the original Aboriginal population of the continent vary widely, from 300,000 to over a million. It has been estimated that there were more than 250 distinct languages with up to 600 dialect groups. *Terra nullius* meant, depending on one's interpretation, either that the previous inhabitants did not use the land in a way that suggested ownership, or that there were no people on the continent, only animals. However rationalized, this doctrine gave the British free rein to take what land they wished, regardless of who lived on it, without the hassle of treaties or agreements. The Northern Territory was set aside as land primarily for the Aboriginal people, but large numbers of Aboriginals were killed and most groups were displaced if not eradicated. The history of Aboriginal and white interaction in Tasmania, where the Aboriginals had remained isolated for over 12,000 years, is particularly horrid; systematic genocide of the Aboriginal population caused their complete extinction within 70 years of first contact.

When the British landed in Australia and claimed the land for the Crown, they did so under a doctrine of "terra nullius," or empty land.

In 1933, the Aboriginal population of Australia hit a low of 73,828. By 1981 this had risen to just over 171,000, and the most recent census (1996) counted 353,000 Aboriginals, making up two percent of the total population. The Australian Bureau of Statistics points to many people's increased willingness to answer "yes" to the Census

The "Big Three" Cases in Aboriginal Land Rights

In 1966, after a strike on a cattle station, the **Gurindji** Aboriginal people from northwest Northern Territory formed the first Aboriginally-owned and operated cattle station, Daguragu. Although it took 20 years, the Gurindji were officially given inalienable freehold (that is, for ever and ever) title to the land in a 1986 court decision. This Aboriginal success led to a claim by Koiki (Eddie) **Mabo,** a Torres Straits Islander who fought for the return of Murray Island to the Mer people (its original inhabitants) through the Australian legal system. The bid was successful in 1992, and the precedent of *terra nullius* was finally struck down. Eddie Mabo himself never heard the ruling: he died of cancer a scant four months before the court handed down its findings. The most recent important case is the **Wik** case, and its complementary "10-Point Plan." The Wik and Thayorre peoples of western Cape York managed to fix a ruling that the granting of pastoral lease by the government (the Crown rents its land to a farmer for a long, long time) does not necessarily mean that the Aboriginals who live on that land have to leave. In fact, both the farmer and the Aboriginal people can claim rights to the same land, and live peacefully within the fabric of Australian law; pastoral leases can co-exist with Native Title, although in case of a conflict, the former takes precedence. The High Court decision in *Wik* was entirely theoretical; Native Title has yet to be applied to the pastoral lands in question. Following this decision, in a setback for Aboriginal land rights, the government developed a **10-point plan on Native Title** that provided for the extinguishment of Native Title in certain circumstances. Aboriginal leaders and their supporters understandably condemn this plan. As each case heard by the High Court sets a new precedent, it is clear that the Aboriginals' struggle for land rights is far from over.

question: "Do you have Aboriginal or Torres Strait Islander origin?" as a partial explanation for the rising numbers. Many Aboriginals live an impoverished existence, often dependent on government social welfare programs. Until recently there was no legal recourse for Aboriginals to make claims on their ancestral lands, but recent High Court decisions have changed this.

These Court rulings have drawn an enormous outcry from Australian farmers, miners, and conservatives who fear that the Aboriginals will claim Native Title to the whole of the continent. However, the Native Title Act of 1993 laid out the guidelines under which claims could be made to ensure that this would not happen, and set out a means of compensating Aboriginals whose Native Title was lost. The Act also levied conditions on future acts which might affect Native Title land and waters, and created a Land Fund to help Aboriginal and Torres Strait Islander peoples acquire and manage land. The issue of Native Title is a new and constantly evolving one. For updated information on Aboriginal political events and Native Title claims, check out the web site of the Aboriginal and Torres Strait Islander Commission at http:\\www.atsic.gov.au, or that of the Australian Institute for Australian and Torres Strait Islander Studies at http:\\www.aiatsis.gov.au.

ABORIGINAL ASSIMILATION: STOLEN CHILDREN

As early as 1837, the **Select Committee on Aborigines in the British Settlements** published a report suggesting that British action toward Aboriginals in Australia had led to the destruction of Aboriginal society. "Europeans have entered [the Aboriginal] borders uninvited," the document read, "and, when there, have not only acted as if they were undoubted lords of the soil, but have punished the natives...They are driven back into the interior as if they were dogs or kangaroos." The report suggested that the way to repair the damage was to invest in more missionaries and pay for additional Christianizing programs. Since the early 1800s, some missionaries had tried to make Aboriginals "employable" by converting them to Christianity and teaching them European skills and customs, often with policies that seem ridiculous today. Some of the program leaders decided that this was impossible if Aboriginal children were raised by Aboriginal parents, and the children were moved out of their homes to live with European families. The **removal of young children from their Aboriginal mothers** became state policy in New South Wales in 1883 and, astonishingly, was not officially discontinued until 1969. Aboriginals refer to these children as "taken" or "stolen," and it is estimated that there may be 100,000 people of Aboriginal descent today who do not know their families or the communities of their birth. Many are still seeking restitution or merely an overdue government apology.

Government

Since federation in 1901, Australia has been a democracy under a federal system, in which power is divided between the federal and state levels. State government is particularly strong and active, and laws can vary widely between states. Australia established universal suffrage for whites in 1902; Aboriginals were given the vote in 1962 and did not gain full citizenship rights until 1967. **Compulsory voting** was introduced in 1925, and since then voter participation has risen to nearly 90%, partly because anyone eligible to vote who does not appear at the polls on election day can be fined. Voting is also **preferential,** meaning that a voter must rank the candidates in order of preference, rather than just voting for his or her first choice.

There are two main political parties, the **Liberal Party** (the conservatives) and the **Labor Party** (more liberal, in the left-wing sense, than the Liberals themselves, but becoming increasingly moderate). Several other strong parties influence the outcome of voting in Parliament. The **Green Party,** the farthest left, began to win Senate seats in the 80s, and became a powerful force in Tasmanian state politics. The **Democrats,** an independent party, have held the balance of power in the Senate in recent years. The **National Party,** formerly the Country Party, usually votes in coalition with the Liberals. Independent candidates can also win seats in Parliament, and those with particularly strong views can often have a significant effect on policy and debate. In the federal government there are two houses of Parliament: the **Senate** and the **House of Representatives.** The **Prime Minister** is not elected directly but rather is the head of the party that holds a parliamentary majority in the House of Representatives. The **Australian Head of State** is the British monarch, currently Her Majesty Queen Elizabeth II. Her representative, the **Governor General,** is the highest authority in Australia. Traditionally, this post has been largely symbolic, and the Governor General has simply approved bills proposed by Parliament and presided over ceremonies of state.

Australians are often stereotyped as uninterested in politics. This may have been the case in the nation's early political history, but was clearly disproven on November 11, 1975, when the Governor General, acting in response to a deadlock over government finances, exercised his right to **dissolve Parliament** in times of crisis. The deadlock had occurred after two states replaced outgoing Labor members of Parliament with Liberals, swaying the Parliamentary balance of power in favor of the Liberals. The Governor General responded by dismissing the Labor Prime Minister, Edward Gough Whitlam, and appointing Malcolm Fraser, a Liberal, to lead a caretaker government. This act shocked the Australian people and raised popular support for **Republicanism,** a movement geared toward gaining full Australian independence from the British Commonwealth. Nevertheless, in the elections that followed a year after the dissolution, the Liberals under Fraser were indeed voted into power and remained there for eight years.

Whitlam's dismissal shocked the Australian people, and raised support for Republicanism, a movement for full independence from Britain.

In 1983, Labor once again took control of Parliament under **Bob Hawke,** who retained power through four terms. He was succeeded by **Paul Keating,** also a member of the Labor Party, who fought for "Mabo" legislation, tried to improve economic relations with Asia, and sought to transform Australia into a republic by the Sydney Olympics in 2000. In 1996, after 13 years of uninterrupted Labor rule, the Liberals regained control of Parliament under **John Howard,** whose platform includes industrial relations reform and privatization. A social conservative and a constitutional monarchist, he has sought to reverse some of the more liberal policies of the previous Labor administration. **Sir William Deane** is the current Governor General.

The People

According to the most recent census (1996), the Commonwealth of Australia is home to **17.9 million people**. The census showed that 22% of the population was **born overseas.** Nearly 1.1 million of these 3.9 million foreign-born people came from the U.K. The next largest source was New Zealand (291,000), then Italy, Vietnam, Greece, China, Germany, the Philippines, and the Netherlands. More than half of the overseas-born lived in Sydney or Melbourne. **English** was the only language spoken at home in 81% of Australian homes.

Just over 70% of Australians (approximately 12.6 million) declared themselves **Christians** in the 1996 census. Roman Catholics made up 38% of the population, while Anglicans accounted for 31%. The census showed that 5% of Australians (about 616,000) belong to **non-Christian** religions, with Buddhism, Islam, Judaism and Hinduism leading the list. Roughly a quarter of all Australians rejected organized religion, and declared an atheistic, agnostic, humanist, or rationalist position.

Australia's population density is 15 people per square kilometer; in comparison, the United States fits 192 people into an average square kilometer and the United Kingdom squeezes 1590 people into the same area. Eighty-five percent of Australians live in urban areas, and the suburbs are still growing. The coasts of Queensland and northern New South Wales boast the fastest-growing populations of Australia.

In 1996, Australians earned a median weekly **income** of $292. Residents of the ACT reported the highest median income, at $430 per week, while residents of Tasmania reported the lowest, at $257. The median **age** was 33 years for men and 34 years for women, and approximately 12% of the population was over 65. Females outnumbered males in every state except Northern Territory.

The Arts

Australia is a very young country, relatively speaking, and Australian arts in the European tradition are just entering an age of maturity. Historically, European arts exerted a strong influence on Australian artists and writers, and the artists responded by seeking to create an Australian identity and to define the Australian experience. Many focused particularly on Australians' relationship with a landscape and climate so different from anything encountered in Europe. Australian artists today are moving into a variety of artistic styles and approaches. At the same time, the most popular national arts are still those that depict traditional themes, sustain an Australian mythology, or explore some facet of the nation's unique heritage.

Many artists have focussed on Australians' relationship with a landscape and climate so different from anything encountered in Europe.

LITERATURE

Australian literature truly got its start with the advent of ***The Bulletin,*** founded in Sydney in 1880. This literary journal, thought to be the most famous and significant of its kind, started a tradition of publishing new and original works with an emphasis on Australian content, encouraging local artists and writers by providing a regular outlet for their work. *The Bulletin*'s contributions to literature continued through the 20th century, but as its politics became increasingly conservative and anachronistic, sales fell. The journal became *The Bulletin with Newsweek* after coming under new ownership, and has made insignificant contributions to Australian literature in the past three decades. However, numerous other literary magazines have risen to take its place, catering to a variety of tastes and genres.

Bush Ballads and Poetry Possibly the first uniquely Australian literature was the **bush ballad,** a form of poetry frequently published in *The Bulletin* that celebrated the workingman and the superiority of life in the bush to urban life. The most famous of these ballads is Banjo Paterson's **Waltzing Matilda,** often thought of as the Australian national anthem. Banjo Patterson also wrote the popular poem *The Man from Snowy River.* Despite the popularity of the ballad, a strong division existed between popular and intellectual **poetry;** many an intellectual poet was seen as maintaining a connection too close to his or her European heritage. This has changed in the last generation, as the sense of writing as an exile in an historical vacuum has subsided. **Judith Wright** has led a movement towards a re-examination of colonial literature, thus establishing a continuity of identity with the poets of the past. A good example of this continuity is **A.D. Hope's** "Australia" which, while expressing his dislike of Australia's insularity, is an affirmation of faith in her future.

Short Stories The **short story** was popularized with stories of life in the bush, as well. **Henry Lawson** and **Barbara Baynton** are two writers who captured the essence of this experience. Many short story writers still strive to define the relationship between person and landscape, and search for cultural identity and historical continuity in their stories. In recent years the prose style of short stories has diversified with increased overseas influences, and the short story has come to explore social issues and to express the realities of urban life.

Novels The Australian **novel** has a complicated history, in part because many of the early novelists spent most of their adult lives outside of Australia. Like artists of other genres, early novelists focused on the search for Australian identity, providing the definitions that allow contemporary writers to branch out with great diversity. Among the better-known early writers is **Miles Franklin,** author of *My Brilliant Career.* Franklin rejected the traditional female role of wife and mother to work as a journalist and feminist in Sydney, bequeathing her estate to establish a prestigious annual literary award in her name. One of the most famous works of Australian literature is *Voss,* by Nobel Prize-winning author **Patrick White.** Focusing on the uniqueness of Australia—the vacancy at the center, life on the perimeter, the obsession with the bush by those who live in the cities—*Voss* has been the basis for a play and an opera of the same name.

"Voss" focusses on Austrlia's vacant center, its life on the perimeter, and the obsession with the bush by those who live in the city.

The strong tradition of mateship and misogyny that was apparent in early bush ballads and short stories provoked a sort of war between male and female writers earlier in this century, but the contribution of female writers has grown steadily, as has the attention given to "ethnic" writing, Aboriginal literature, and song-cycles. Today's names in literature continue to broadly examine the meaning of being Australian, but the meat of their work is increasingly varied. **Peter Carey** is best known as the author of *Bliss,* a humorous exploration of the Australian national character. **Tim Winton,** Western Australian short-story writer and novelist, writes about the everyday lives of the Westralians. **Elizabeth Jolley,** who emigrated to Australia as an adult, explores the lives of refugees and foreigners in her work. **David Malouf's** background as a poet comes through in his fiction, which explores the relationships between past and present on the changing face of Australia.

A growing number of Aboriginal writers are gaining recognition on a national scale. For samplings of contemporary Aboriginal literature, check out *Paperbark,* an anthology of contemporary Aboriginal writing. However, many of these artists continue to encounter racism and difficulties with mainstream acceptance, and most Australians still encounter Aboriginals primarily at staged "Aboriginal Culture Shows," the authenticity of which are often questionable.

POPULAR MUSIC

Australia's early colonial music was the folk music of its British settlers, with lively fiddle and drum reels of Irish immigrants playing for bushdances in cleared-out sheep-shearing sheds. Like the society in general, though, popular music has grown rich with imports from America and Europe in the 50s and 60s, and more recently with Aboriginal sounds. You can now find almost any sound you want in Sydney or Melbourne, all at locally grown prices. Australia's youth radio, **Triple J,** plays a lot of contemporary local music, and is always promoting new acts.

Popular music in Australia began in the late 50s, and was epitomized by rocker **Johnny O'Keefe** whose sound, inspired by the unique musical blend emerging from the American south, took the country by storm. Television hit Australia at the same time as rock and roll, creating a booming youth culture based around shows like Australian Bandstand.

The Beatles rolled into town in the early 60s, before their American tour, shaping the next decade of Australian music and spawning dozens of Beatles-esque bands like the Easybeats who jumped into the British music scene with a single hit and then disappeared. At the same time, a lively folk music scene, heavily influenced by groups like Peter, Paul, and Mary, thrived in the 50s and 60s, but few names gained international recognition. **The Seekers,** a wholesome quartet with hits in England and America, were the great exception.

In the late 70s, **AC/DC** hit the charts with blues-influenced heavy metal grown out of pub culture. But after making it big, the group moved its headquarters to Europe and is no longer considered truly Australian. **The Skyhooks** became extremely popular locally and were heavily promoted on television. Refusing to simply emulate American and English sounds, **Cold Chisel, Goanna,** and **Australian Crawl** gained similar local fame and influence; their Aussie-themed hits are still perennial favorites on rock radio.

The 80s saw the advent of politically aware bands like **Midnight Oil,** another group born out of heavy rock pub culture, became popular for its enthusiastic live shows, and then used the fame and influence to promote social causes. While most popular Australian bands never managed to sell their sound outside of Australia, a few notable exceptions exist. **Men At Work** broke into the American music scene with a couple of huge hits before fading out of the limelight. **INXS** and **Crowded House** followed in their footsteps and are now firmly entrenched international bands.

Today's Australian music is very diverse, influenced by grunge as well as by world music. Aboriginal groups have entered the mainstream music culture, particularly **Yothu Yindi,** a band out of Arnhem Land in the Northern Territory that has combined traditional Aboriginal musical styles and themes with dance music and rock, and continues Midnight Oil's tradition of using the spotlight to further political causes. Other similarly politicized Aboriginal "bush rock" groups are the **Coloured Stones** and the **Warumpi Band. Archie Roach,** a country-influenced Aboriginal musician who sings of his background as a "stolen child" and the problems of Aboriginals in urban Australia has gained recent popularity as well.

Country music is big, with a popularity celebrated at an annual **Country Music Festival** in Tamworth, the "country capital" of Australia. The music takes its cues from its American counterpart, but is strongly influenced by the peculiarities of Australian rural life. **Slim Dusty** is the style's founding father, having sold over three million albums since he began songwriting at age 12.

Archie Roach is a popular Aboriginal musician who sings of his background as a "stolen child" and of the problems of urban Aboriginals.

U.S. soldiers brought big band **jazz** to Australia during WWI, and the American music has found increasingly firm footing. **Don Burrows** and **Graeme Bell** were inspired leaders of big and small groups in the 60s, establishing an Australian jazz scene that gained mainstream attention with the likes of too-hip singer **Vince Jones,** instrumental wizard **James Morrison,** and genius pianist **Paul Gabowsky** in the 80s. Each capital city has a flourishing live scene, nourished by intensively creative jazz programs in the conservatories of Perth and Sydney and the Victorian College of the Arts in Melbourne, all excellent places to look for music and musicians.

VISUAL ARTS

Australian visual art began, like other arts, with a search for Australian identity, creating uniquely Australian symbols and mythology to set the young nation apart from its European ancestors and influences. This trend is seen clearly in the work of early Australian impressionists such as **Tom Roberts** (1856-1931), whose *Break Away* depicts the red, dry, dusty land of the cattle station, and **Frederick McCubbin** (1850-1917), whose *Lost Child* shows the thin forests of smoky green gum trees. Later landscape paintings by artists like **Hans Heysen, Robert Juniper,** and **Russell Drysdale** continue to focus on similar natural features, with a greater variety of style, color, and mood.

The themes and images of Australia have lent themselves particularly well to series painting. Possibly the most famous series of Australian paintings is the **Sidney Nolan** Ned Kelly paintings, which tell of the folk hero's exploits, final capture, and execution. Completed in 1945 and 1954, these pieces appear in Australia's National Galleries today. Nolan has also done series on the Eureka Stockade, Gallipoli, and images of drought, among others. Other prominent contemporary artists include **John Perceval,** the expressionist **Albert Tucjer,** the abstract artist **John Colburn,** and **Arthur Boyd,** who depicts popular figures of Australian legend. Younger Australian painters (**Mandy Martin, Susan Norrie,** and **Neil Taylor**) are flooding the scene, often with difficult-to-categorize images and explorations of post-industrial Australia.

Aboriginal painting is, of course, the nation's original visual art, although its origin was not exclusively artistic, but educational, spiritual, and functional. Because these origins are not conducive to large-scale production of commercial art, the Aboriginal art sold today is generally either fictitious reproductions of traditional themes minus the sacred symbols, or modern Aboriginal art incorporating images, styles, and materials of the constantly changing world. Some Aboriginal artists have also moved into the mainstream, creating landscape paintings and images that do not superficially resemble traditional Aboriginal art, yet share an underlying understanding of the world with these older works.

Biodiversity

The one who stands apart often proves to have something special to offer. Such is the case with Australia's wildlife, which has benefited from millions of years of isolation on a very large island. This sheltered existence has bred one of the world's most distinctive arrays of plants and animals. When the first immigrant species landed on a continent with an abundance of habitats, many found themselves in a nursery for biological variation, nearly devoid of competition. The consequence was a series of adaptive radiations that produced a multiplicity of plants and animals from a limited number of ancestral taxa.

The wildlife has benefitted from millions of years of isolation on a very large island, able to play an entirely altenate evolutionary ballgame.

Much of this variety is currently threatened. Australia's inevitable contact with outside species presented enormous challenges to its biologically unique character. The colonization of the continent by human hunters introduced a new and dangerous predator, and both Aboriginals and Europeans brought species that upset Australia's delicate ecology. In recent years, Australian environmental policy has begun to recognize the importance of protecting the continent's unique and precious biodiversity.

INDIGENOUS FAUNA

Marsupials are the stars of the Australian menagerie. Because marsupials, which bear immature young and nurse them in a pouch, had few mammalian competitors on the continent, they radiated into many different niches. The common names that early naturalists have applied to many of these animals reflect the families of other ecosystems, not any phylogenetic relationship. Thus, the koala is *not* a bear; the marsupial "rat" is not a rat; and the marsupial "cat" and "mole" are more closely related to each other than either is to its respective namesake. Images of **kangaroos** bounding across the landscape are virtually synonymous with Australia. This national icon is overabundant, and kangaroo-culling programs have been enacted to control population numbers (see **Kangaroos!,** below, for more on this furry favorite). The kangaroo's lookalike cousin, the **wallaby,** is another common critter in the outback. Some other distinctive marsupials include **wombats, possums, bandicoots,** and **quolls.**

Kangaroos!

Let no one say that the cover of *Let's Go: Australia* panders to kitschy stereotypes about the region. The fact is, wherever you go in Australia, be it Ayers Rock or the suburbs of Perth, you will see "Kangaroo Crossing" road signs just like the one pictured on our cover. Crows will scatter from their feast of kangaroo sweetbreads as you careen down the highway where some other driver failed to heed those bright yellow signs. Kangaroos travel in groups known as mobs, which can have over 20 members. Several dozen species can be categorized into two groups: red kangaroos are generally larger and a bit more aggressive than grey. Male red kangaroos can grow to be 3m (10 ft.) long, nose to tail, and are capable of propelling themselves nearly 9m (30 ft.) at a single bound. (Their ability to leap tall buildings remains largely contested.) The animals can be seen feeding docilely in many national parks, especially during the morning hours, and tourists may hold a downy-furred joey at a nature preserve.

Kangaroos, like most indigenous Australian mammals, are marsupials; after approximately 33 days of gestation, an embryo emerges from the uterus and follows a trail of saliva, lain by the mother, from her pudenda to her pouch. From the age of two, a female kangaroo is likely to have, at any one time, one offspring in the womb, one living in the pouch, and one making occasional visits to the pouch—this productivity accounts for the female's markedly shorter lifespan. This style of reproduction, combined with the kangaroo's unique ability to suspend embryonic gestation in a state of dormancy for up to two years, ensures survival in harsh desert environments. Kangaroos have thrived on the fringes of human communities since colonization, leading the Australian government to conduct an annual program of kangaroo culling. Contrary to popular myth, kangaroos do not feed marmalade sandwiches to small bears or send their young out to play with tree-dwelling pigs and tail-bouncing tigers.

Neck in neck with the kangaroo in the race to be the most beloved marsupial, the **koala** lives on and among the leaves of certain eucalypt trees. Sleeping, on average, 18 of every 24 hours and existing on a diet made up exclusively of the semi-toxic eucalyptus leaves, the koala hasn't much energy for hunting, gathering, or even moving. Seeing a koala is often just a matter of being patient enough to scan the treetops for a familiar furball or impatient enough to find the nearest zoo or nature preserve.

Still more fantastic, giant marsupials once roamed the landscape of prehistoric Australia. Now extinct, these **megafauna** included towering relatives of kangaroos called diprotodons. The megafauna died off soon after the arrival of humans on the continent, due either to hunting or to climatic changes. The **thylacine,** or Tasmanian tiger, is a more recent loss. Resembling a large wolf with stripes, this predator was driven to the edge of extinction by competition with dingoes, then hunted ruthlessly by white settlers who feared for their livestock. One infamous marsupial carnivore has survived, however. Fierce in temperament, **Tasmanian devils** are primarily nocturnal scavengers. They also hunt small prey and have been known to take helpless livestock with their powerful jaws. (See **Sympathy for the Sarcophilus harrisii,** p. 430, for more information about these much-maligned critters.)

So outrageous did the platypus anatomy seem that early British naturalists refused to consider stuffed specimens real.

Australia's list of peculiar mammals does not end with marsupials. There are just two families of **monotremes,** or egg-laying mammals. **Echidnas** are small ant-eaters that resemble porcupines or hedgehogs with protruding snouts. When threatened, the echidna buries itself in the ground, leaving only long spines exposed. Strangest of all, the **platypus** sports a melange of zoological features: the bill of a duck, the fur of an otter, the tail of a beaver, and webbed claws. So outrageous did this bizarre anatomy seem to European colonists that early British naturalists refused to consider stuffed specimens real.

Outshining Australia's mammalian wildlife in vividness of color, if not in biological singularity, is a tremendous diversity of **birds.** The **emu** is related to other flightless birds such as the African ostrich and the extinct moa of New Zealand. Also flightless, hordes of **little** (or **fairy**) **penguins** can be spotted at sites on the south coast, where they wade ashore each night. Australia's flight-endowed birds include noisy flocks of **galahs,** colorful **rainbow lorikeets,** and unreasonably large **cassowaries** (see p. 334). Songs and poems have immortalized the unmistakable laugh of the **kookaburra.**

The most fearsome of Australia's **reptiles,** saltwater crocodiles (**salties**) actually live in both brine and freshwater and grow to lengths of 7m. They can be dangerous (see **Safety and Security,** p. 13, for tips on how to avoid becoming croc fodder), more so than their less threatening freshwater cousins. For a primer on discriminating between the salty and its less threatening freshwater relative, take a look at **Freshies and Salties,** p. 233. In addition to its crocodiles, Australia's reptiles include aggressive **goannas** and a wide array of **snakes.**

INTRODUCED FAUNA

Humans have been responsible for the introduction of animals to Australia since prehistoric times. The **dingo,** a lithe, wild canine with a bite but no bark, crossed the Timor Sea with ancestors of Aboriginal populations several thousand years ago. The creatures mainly hunt small, wild prey, but may also menace livestock. Although dingoes pose no threat to adult humans, ranchers detest them and kill those they encounter near their flocks. They've even gone so far as to build a "Dingo Fence" over 3300km long to keep the beasts away from cattle and sheep.

More recent arrivals accompanied European colonists. Domesticated **cattle** and **sheep** are of tremendous economic importance in Australia, with stations (ranches) across the continent. These species have had a dramatic impact on the landscape and ecological balance of the nation; vast tracts have been converted to pasture to support the meat industry.

In addition to economically important species, many animals that are considered pests have been introduced, whether intentionally or accidentally. **Rabbits,** purportedly introduced to Australia to provide practice targets for marksman, have become one of Australia's gravest wildlife problems. Accidental introductions such as European **rats** also represent serious threats to native fauna.

The Foxgloves Come Off

"Buy Australian" campaigns are all over Australia at the moment, but food and manufactured goods are not the only imports that are panned. Exotic flora and fauna cause great consternation by outcompeting native species or otherwise disturbing ecological balances established over the course of thousands of years. For example, the growing of pine trees on plantations outside Perth has led to a marked lowering of the area's water table, because the pines consume so much more water than marri, jarrah, or other eucalypts. Foxes, introduced fauna which kill sheep on stations, have become a particular problem. With no natural competitors around (save humans), fox numbers have grown to epidemic levels. Enter Poison 1080 and Operation Foxglove. You'll see signs in parks and along highways featuring red triangles and a warning to keep pets on leashes. Although it may sound like the name of a nightclub, Poison 1080 is a chemical cocktail derived from Australian plants. It is lethal to introduced mammals but harmless to native marsupials. Every year, fox baits laced with 1080 are dropped from airplanes on infested areas. In an interesting aside, the enormous success of Operation Foxglove has sparked controversy over the plight of the dingo. Although they came ashore from Indonesia long before European colonization, dingoes are not truly indigenous and are therefore susceptible to Poison 1080. Australians think of the dingo as an Australian animal, though, and the canines have become well-integrated into the ecosystem, particularly because they hunt rabbits, an overabundant, recent introduction. This unforeseen side-effect of Poison 1080 has produced a dispute over whether or not the dingo should be protected from this threat. For the time being, fox eradication will continue.

MARINE LIFE AND THE GREAT BARRIER REEF

Fur seals, elephant seals, and **sea lions** populate Australia's southern shores during their summer breeding seasons, but it's the **Great Barrier Reef** that makes Australia's sea life particularly unique. The longest coral formation in the world, the reef is actually a series of many reefs that stretches along the eastern coast of Queensland from the Tropic of Capricorn to Papua New Guinea, a distance of more than 2000km. Although adult **coral polyps** are sedentary (fixed in one spot), corals actually belong to the animal kingdom. Thus, the Great Barrier Reef is the only community of animals visible to the eye from space.

Corals rely on sunlight filtering down from the ocean surface and cannot grow at depths greater than 50m. Reef accumulates whenever a coral polyp dies and leaves behind its skeletal legacy of calcium carbonate. This goes on for quite a while (up to 18 million years in the case of the Great Barrier Reef). As layers of **limestone** build, the reef rises toward the surface. Once the coral reaches the top of the waves it's doomed: the surf pounds it to bits, and then smaller bits, and then sand-size bits. Add some more years and the sand-size bits have formed a little mound that sticks out of the water, which is called a **cay.** Birds come along, land on the cay, and ingloriously deposit seeds from the mainland in a cozy bed of fresh fertilizer. Vegetation turns the cay into a fair dinkum island. Sea turtles and birds come to nest, and soon a whole **ecosystem** has literally risen from the water.

Colonies of coral grow by asexual reproduction, but new colonies propagate by **sexual reproduction.** The act is quite a feat for these polyps, fixed as they are to the spot. They've devised a mechanism to synchronize the release of their gametes so as to maximize the chance of fertilization and reduce losses to **hungry fish.** Using the moon to time the process, corals the length of the reef release their sperm and eggs on a single night each October, filling the water with a impenetrable fog of reproductive cells.

Thus, the Great Barrier Reef is the only community of animals visible to the eye from space.

The corals themselves aren't the only animals on the reef happy enough to stay put. Many fish are territorial about a small patch of coral and will never venture more than a few meters from home. Mollusks, some growing to enormous proportions, and echinoderms, like starfish, also dwell in the vast playground.

The coral reef represents a unique marine environment that supports a remarkable array of fishes. From fearsome hammerheads to harmless **white-tipped reef sharks,** from rays and eels to **parrot fish** and milk fish, from predatory lizard-fish to marlins, the reef offers unparalleled marine biodiversity. Many species have devised adaptations for life on the reef. The **anemone-fish,** for example, lives in close association with a single **anemone** for the duration of its adult life, never venturing more than a short distance to feed or mate. The anemone's stinging cells (to which the fish is immune) discourage predators from approaching. The reef's oversized denizens include **grouper** fish, which grow to a length of 3m and weigh more than 250kg, and **giant clams,** which rest impassively on the ocean floor, their shells ajar like gaping blue maws. The ethereal **manta ray** resembles a mythical bird as it slowly beats its 5m-wide fins. These specimens are just a sampling of those that confront divers on the Great Barrier Reef, all in vivid, living color.

FLORA

Dominating Australia's forests virtually from coast to coast, the **eucalypts,** or **gum trees,** demonstrate the extent to which biological taxa can successfully adapt to diverse environments. Despite their common origin, gums have taken on many different shapes and sizes across the continent. The majestic **karri** soars over 50m skyward in ancient stands along well-watered valleys, while the **mallee** gum grows in stunted copses across scrubland such as that of western Victoria. The characteristically bulging trunk and splayed branches of the **boab** mark the horizon of the Kimberley in Western Australia.

Gums grow everywhere, from the Snowy Mountains to the parched Red Centre, but they share their habitats like well-behaved kindergartners. Other regulars appearing in the bush and coastal thickets include **banksias, ti trees,** and **grevillias.** Feathery and almost pine-like in appearance, **casuarinas** also exist in multiple habitats. In temperate, rain-fed stretches of Victoria and Tasmania, valleys of tall, dinosaur-era **tree ferns** are dwarfed by towering **"mountain ash,"** the tallest flowering plant in the natural kingdom (and yet another gum).

Most of Australia's large tree species have trunks that are lighter in color than their leaves, and the leaves themselves usually grow high above the ground. The effect created is quite different than that of European and North American forests. Here bushwalkers find themselves surrounded by white and gray in place of brown and green.

A remarkable feature found along parts of Australia's tropical coasts, the **mangrove** has adapted readily to its unfavorable environment, and stilt-like trunks cling tenaciously to the briny mud of alluvial swamps.

Australia has wide swaths of land that grow nary a tree. The arid outback is dominated by **spinifex** grasses, which grow in dense tufts across the vast interior of the world's flattest continent. Another notably common form of vegetation is the **saltbush,** a hearty shrub that grows in soil too salty for other plants and which has been pivotal in converting harsh habitats to pastures for sheep and cattle.

In more fertile areas, **wildflowers** are abundant. Western Australia is the favorite cruising ground for **swamp bottlebrush, kangaroo paw,** and **Ashby's banksia,** along with nearly 10,000 other species. Expansive fields of yellow and pink **everlastings** cover fields across the country, to the delight of casual wildflower viewers, but rare **spider orchids** hidden in the forests reveal themselves only to the most dogged of investigators. The **Sturt pea** adds a distinctive splash of red and black to the inland deserts of South Australia and WA. Acacia trees also contribute to Australia's floral colors; one common species in the drier areas of the southeast is the **golden wattle.** Elsewhere in the country, **orchids** and **begonias** provide additional visual garnish.

Food and Drink

Australians eat three meals a day: breakfast, lunch, and dinner (usually called "tea"). Aussies hardly ever eat their **"brekkie"** out and most restaurants don't open until noon. Lunch more or less meets international expectations and is smaller than the evening meal. Australians have **tea** (a full meal, not like Devonshire tea) in the evening. In restaurants, beware of ordering only an **"entree,"** which is an appetizer in Australia. A **"cuppa"**—tea or coffee—should tide you over between meals. **Tipping** in Australian restaurants and pubs is rare and never expected.

The infamous Vegemite, a dark, yeasty bi-product of the beer-brewing process, should be scraped thinly rather than spread liberally.

The diet of most Australians is largely shaped by their ethnicity, but tourists will find an abundance of flavors to choose from in the more cosmopolitan cities. Food courts generally present a balance of Asian, fish and chips, and fast food. **Kosher** foods are unknown in much of the country, but **vegetarians** shouldn't go hungry despite Australia's meat-hungry reputation. Trendy urban eateries will frequently cater to special diets, but traditional establishments rarely will. Restaurants may offer to remove meat from dishes, but won't necessarily prepare them separately.

BUSH TUCKER

Coastal Aboriginals have eaten crayfish, **yabbies** (freshwater shrimp), and fish for centuries, and the first English settlers rapidly followed suit. But in the harsh environments of the bush, Aboriginal foragers exploited food resources that early colonists found a little too unorthodox to stomach. **Witchetty grubs** are the most well-known of the bush foods that make first-timers recoil in horror. Yet some bush tucker, particularly indigenous sources of meat, has made it on to hip urban menus. **Kangaroo** steaks are growing in popularity and **crocodile** meat is highly regarded by those in

On Eating a Country's Fauna

Kangaroo has a tangy slam to it, not unlike grilled liver. The meat is tough and demands a thick peanut sauce. Crocodile is indifferent: bleached and as tasteless as virgin sand, it must be regarded from a respectful distance. Buffalo, with its wandering edges of gristle and chewy texture, is sanguine and can only be penetrated under the spell of soy sauce. Emu has a curious flavor that becomes clear to the tongue when presented with pineapple, or better, a more vigorous fruit, like the mango. The meat otherwise lies gray. Barramundi is cream-fish, the mousse you simply could not finish, the last rum ball that would have turned your stomach. A slice of lemon is the only recourse. Save the barramundi for dessert, dodge and play with the emu while you can, and treat the kangaroo with the honor and respect it deserves.

the know. If you want to sample **emu, goanna,** or **ants,** however, you might have to catch dinner yourself or join one of the Red Centre tours that feature bush tucker.

IMPORTED CUISINES

Australia's origin as a humble convict colony didn't exactly endow the country with a subtle palate. Australia still suffers from a reputation of having a notoriously dull national cuisine, but it has been remarkably successful at adding layers of flavor with each wave of immigration. From the **British** come cholesterol-heavy **pub meals,** such as steak and eggs, and the Aussie institution of **fish and chips.** "Chippers" are the quintessential Aussie eating establishment, the equivalent of the American pizzeria. These small eateries may have a few tables, but most specialize in takeaway (takeout). A popular meal for families on Friday nights, the fish is fried, battered, rolled in newspaper, and served with American french fries. **Chook** (chicken) is often substituted for fish to create much-needed variety. **Meat pies** are the epitome of unimaginative Australian fare. Inexplicably popular, these square, doughy shells contain meat of dubious origin and frequently a mushy vegetable filling. Most consumers douse them in **sauce** (a sweet ketchup-like concoction) to disguise the taste. Use Australian condiments sparingly until you are familiar with them; Aussie mustard delivers a horseradishy kick to the unwary, and the infamous **Vegemite,** a dark, yeasty bi-product of the beer-brewing process, should be scraped thinly rather than spread liberally.

Recent European and Middle Eastern arrivals have spiced up Australian menus with **Greek** souvlaki, **Italian** pasta, and **Lebanese** tabouleh. The cheapest way to sample these flavors is at any of numerous takeaway joints. Influxes of immigrants from Asian and Pacific countries have further defined Australian cuisine. This trend began as early as the 1850s, when Australia's gold rush made the continent a magnet for Chinese laborers. **Chinese** dishes first arrived with Chinese gold prospectors in the 1850s and have so infiltrated the menu that even their names have taken a uniquely Australian twist: **"dim sims"** are Australian dim sum. The consistent quality of Chinese food is a boon to travelers who find themselves in unfamiliar places, since Chinese reliably contains a standard array of vegetables and predictable sauces. **Japanese, Thai, Malay,** and **Vietnamese** restaurants also are abundant, particularly in Darwin and cosmopolitan centers in the southeast.

Australia has plentiful pickings when it comes to **fruit;** its tropical north supports fruit industries that other western countries can only fantasize about. Travelers from fruit-deprived regions of the globe will encounter exotic offerings such as custard apples, lychees, passion fruit, star fruit, coconuts, mangoes, and pineapples. Queensland is the main fruit-producing region, although Tasmania ships its apples to the

Keep Your Kiwis Off This Pavlova!

The term "pavlova" is of debatable origin. Rather, its origin has been debated. Let's set the record straight. The delectable dessert came into existence in 1935 when the chef of Perth's Esplanade Hotel, Bert Sachse, decided to create a new dish in honor of their famous Russian guest: the ballerina Anna Pavlova. Ignore hogwash to the contrary propagated by *Let's Go: New Zealand 1998.*

mainland. Of the typical prepared desserts: the ubiquitous **lamington** is a coconut-covered chunk of pound cake dipped in chocolate, and the festive **pavlova** is a chewy meringue covered in whipped cream and fresh fruit.

BEER AND WINE

For many, a close associate exists between Australia and **beer,** and with good reason. Australians produce some of the world's best brew and consume it readily. Darwin in particular claims fame as Australia's thirstiest city. Some Australians display scorn for **Fosters,** which owes its international name-recognition to saturation advertising. Instead, loyalty is expected to the state brew. **Victoria Bitter** (VB), **Toohey's,** and **XXXX** ("four-ex") hail from Victoria, New South Wales, and Queensland, respectively. **Strongbow,** Australia's favorite cider, is quietly gaining popularity in pubs as a potent and tasty alternative, but beer unequivocally prevails. If you're heading to the beach, throw a **slab** (24 containers of beer) in your **Esky** (ice chest). The favorite place to **shout** your mates a coldie, however, is the omnipresent Aussie **pub.** For more beer terminology, consult the **appendix,** p. 578.

Australian **wines** rival those the world over. Overseas export began soon after the first vineyards began to produce wine in the early 1800s. The **Hunter Valley** (in New South Wales), the **Barossa Valley** (in South Australia), the **Swan** and **Margaret Rivers** (in Western Australia), and the **Derwent** and **Tamar Valleys** (in Tasmania), possess some of the best Aussie vineyards. Many cafes and low-end restaurants advertise that they are **BYO,** or "bring your own." Though not licensed to serve alcohol, these establishments permit patrons to furnish their own bottle of wine with the meal and charge only a small **corkage fee,** usually by bottle or by glass. The **cask** of wine, another Australian innovation, is ideal for picnics.

Sport

Australians, spectators and participants alike, take sport very seriously. The 1956 Melbourne Olympics inaugurated national television broadcasting in Australia, and televisions in public places have, more or less, been tuned to sporting events ever since. The national team-sports melodrama extends year-round. In winter, Western Australia, South Australia, and Victoria catch **footy fever** for **Australian Rules Football,** while New South Wales and Queensland traditionally follow **rugby.** In summer, **cricket** is the spectator sport of choice across the nation. Throughout the year, star Aussie Rules football players and top cricketers enjoy hero status similar to that accorded basketball players in the U.S., soccer players in Europe, or badminton players in Taiwan. For good insight into Australian sport culture, tune in to H. G. Nelson and Roy Slaven's Saturday morning Triple-J radio show, *This Sporting Life.*

The 1956 Melbourne Olympics inaugurated national television broadcasting, and TVs have, more or less, been tuned to sports ever since.

CRICKET

Uninitiated Americans may have trouble making sense of a sport where people can "bowl a maiden over of five flippers and a googly," but visitors won't be able to avoid match enthusiasm. In cricket, two teams of 11 players face off in a contest that can last anywhere from an afternoon to five days. At the national level, cricket teams compete throughout the summer for the **Sheffield Shield,** culminating in the March finals.

Each summer, the national Shield competition is supplanted by international cricket. A "Test match" is not a test at all (except that success in the Tests indicates the well-being of the entire national psyche), rather it is the most lengthy and serious form of international cricket. In 1877, Australia's cricket team headed to England for its first international Test against the mother country. Surprisingly, the colonials won. The Australians, as a shocked English reporter wrote, had "taken off with the ashes" of English cricket. Ever since that first match, the England and Australian Test teams have been in noble competition for **"the Ashes"** (the trophy is actually a small, symbolic urn). In the summers when the England team does not come to Australia, a different international team arrives for a **full tour,** which consists of five test matches, one each in Melbourne, Sydney, Perth, Adelaide, and Brisbane. These five-day matches are supplemented by smaller, titillating one-day matches. The tour takes place in December and January; check out any cricket magazine in a newsagency for a summer cricket schedule. When watching a Test, where all players wear white, distinguish Australian players by their **baggy green caps.** Earning the right to wear such a cap is the highest privilege for an Australian cricket player. The international tour is over by February, and the country then turns its attention to national cricket just in time for the Sheffield Shield finals.

AUSTRALIAN RULES FOOTBALL

In Victoria, South Australia, and West Australia in winter, the **Australian Football League (AFL)** teams fill the void that the end of the cricket season might otherwise leave. The game was originally designed to keep cricket players in shape during the winter, and is played on cricket ovals. Aussie Rules is actually a fairly simple game with a few basic rules. Essentially, teams just need to get the red leather ball from one end of the field to the other and kick it through the opposing team's posts to score. Each team of 18 players actually defends three sets of posts for four 20-minute quarters: six points are earned for scoring in the middle goal, and one point for reaching either side goal. The basic move in AFL is the **punt,** used for both passing and scoring, and good players can punt the ball over 70m. The most spectacular move, though, is the **mark.** If a player can catch the ball on the kick before it bounces, he is entitled to unobstructed possession of that ball. Consequently, just after a kick, the players all pack together and run, jump, and soar, on, under, and over each other, in a heroic effort to snatch the ball from the sky.

In the last decade, the Victorian football league expanded to become a national league. Therefore, the AFL is still composed mainly of Victorian teams with a few regional teams thrown in, explaining why teams from huge geographic regions (like West Coast) play teams from obscure Melbourne suburbs. The AFL grand final falls in early September, and is a marvelous spectacle at the home of Australian sport, the **MCG (Melbourne Cricket Ground).**

OTHER SPORT

But all in Australia is not cricket shots or footy marks. On Boxing Day, even as the Melbourne cricket Test gets underway, half of Australia's amateur sailing community fills Sydney Harbour with billowing white sails to begin the **Sydney-to-Hobart yacht race,** the highlight in a full calendar of water and surf sports. Melbourne hosts tennis' grand-slam event, the **Australian Open,** each January. Grassy tennis courts, bowling greens, and golf courses pepper the cities coast-to-coast. Every town also has a race track, and on the first Tuesday in November, the entire country stops to watch jockeys jockey for the prestigious **Melbourne Cup.**

Finally, as Sydney anticipates hosting the **2000 Summer Olympics,** the world's largest celebration of sport, the city is already a blur of preparation and pride. Australia and Greece are the only two countries that have participated in every summer Olympics since 1896, the beginning of the modern games, and the Sydney Olympics will mark the second time Australia has hosted the games. The **Sydney Millennium Olympics** will run from Friday, September 15 to Sunday, October 1, 2000, and the **mascots** will be a platypus named Syd, an echidna named Millie, and a kookaburra named Olly (representing sea, land, and air).

Australia and Greece are the only two countries to have participated in every summer Olympics.

Even if you'll miss the Olympics, cricket seems eternally confusing, or Aussie Rules football is still incomprehensible, just join in the crowds, cheer for whichever team the people around you side with, and remember the old adage that many an Australian sports fan takes to heart: **It's all fun and games until somebody loses an eye—then it's sport.**

Australian Capital Territory

Canberra

ACT

From its inception in 1908, Canberra has had what few modern cities ever get—the opportunity to start from scratch and plan out every step of its development. The site selected to be the capital of the newly federated nation of Australia was not a thriving center for national affairs. Instead, it was a clean compromise located between the rival poles of activity at Sydney and Melbourne. An international competition was conducted to find a design for the new city, and an American named Walter Burley Griffin won the chance to see his vision of a city come to life. Construction began in 1913, and the first Canberra Parliament convened in 1927. Despite sporadic growth during the Great Depression and WWII, the pace picked up in the late 1950s, and by 1960, the city had a population of 50,000.

Today, Canberra supports a metropolitan population of 300,000 and boasts the fastest growth rate of any city in Australia. As Canberra grows into the role foreseen by its founders, the order that remains from the city's original tidy design is remarkable. Testament to the power of a good plan well executed, Canberra is exactly what it was intended to be: a national exhibition and the international face of the political body of Australia. From its unique traffic pattern to its well-rounded roster of national centers and memorials, a sense of purposeful order pervades life in this city. This order, as much as the tangible presence of the national government (or the fact that it's the only Australian city to experience inland winters), gives the city its reputation as dull. But in turn, it gives Canberra physical beauty and the recognizable grace of a place living out its intended purpose. Unlike Sydney and Melbourne, which twist and change in waves of urban energy, Canberra resonates with a refined hum. Big-city excitement may not be easy to come by in Canberra, but budget travelers and museum-seekers can find everything they need.

Phone numbers in the ACT have recently changed. Regional phone codes are now all 02, followed by eight digit numbers. If you have trouble making a call, use the following scheme to get the old number, and try that instead. For more details, see the **Appendix** (p. 574).

New Number:	Old Number:
(02) 62xx xxxx	(06) 2xx xxxx

ARRIVAL AND DEPARTURE

By Plane

Located in Pialligo, 7km east of the city center, the Canberra Airport is an easy target by car. From Commonwealth Ave., take Parkes Way east past the roundabout at Kings Ave. where it becomes Morshead Dr. Morshead Dr. in turn becomes Pialligo Ave. a bit farther on and passes right outside the airport. ACT **Minibuses Airporter Shuttle** (tel. 6280 0000 or 018 625 719; fax 6280 0990) makes the trip for $5 ($8 for 2) in either direction. Notice of at least one hour is required.

Getting out of Australia from Canberra requires a stop in nearby Sydney, as Canberra's airport handles only domestic flights. Both **Qantas** (tel. 6250 8211 or 13 13 13) and **Ansett** (tel. 6249 7641 or 13 13 00) connect Canberra to Sydney (30min., $158), Melbourne (1hr., $222), Brisbane (90min., $321), and Adelaide (90min., $327) and offer discounts for advance reservations.

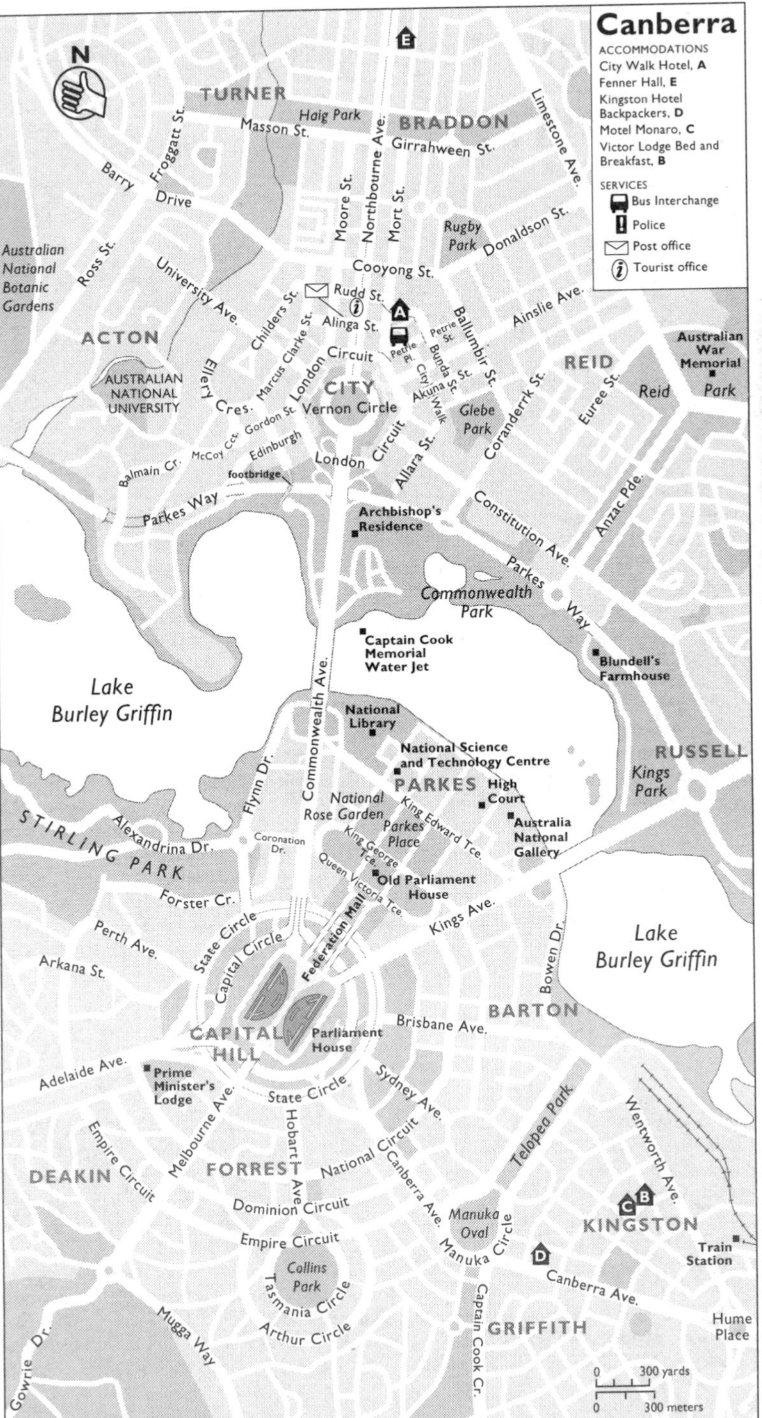
Canberra
ACCOMMODATIONS
City Walk Hotel, A
Fenner Hall, E
Kingston Hotel Backpackers, D
Motel Monaro, C
Victor Lodge Bed and Breakfast, B
SERVICES
Bus Interchange
Police
Post office
Tourist office
N
TURNER
Haig Park
BRADDON
Masson St.
Froggatt St.
Northbourne Ave.
Girrahween St.
Limestone Ave.
Barry Drive
Moore St.
Mort St.
Rugby Park
Donaldson St.
Australian National Botanic Gardens
Ross St.
University Ave.
Cooyong St.
Rudd St.
Childers St.
Marcus Clarke St.
Alinga St.
Petrie St.
Ballumbir St.
Ainslie Ave.
ACTON
London Circuit
Petrie Pl.
Bunda St.
Akuna St.
City Walk
REID
Euree St.
Reid
Australian War Memorial
Park
AUSTRALIAN NATIONAL UNIVERSITY
Ellery Cres.
CITY
Vernon Circle
Glebe Park
Corranderrk St.
Gordon St.
Edinburgh
McCoy Cct.
Balmain Cr.
London
Circuit
Allara St.
footbridge
Parkes Way
Anzac Pde.
Archbishop's Residence
Constitution Ave.
Parkes Way
Commonwealth Park
Captain Cook Memorial Water Jet
Blundell's Farmhouse
Lake Burley Griffin
Commonwealth Ave.
National Library
National Science and Technology Centre
RUSSELL
Kings Park
Flynn Dr.
PARKES
High Court
National Rose Garden
King Edward Tce.
Australia National Gallery
STIRLING PARK
Alexandrina Dr.
Coronation Dr.
Parkes Place
King George Tce.
Queen Victoria Tce.
Old Parliament House
Forster Cr.
State Circle
Capital Circle
Federation Mall
Kings Ave.
Perth Ave.
Arkana St.
Lake Burley Griffin
Bowen Dr.
BARTON
CAPITAL HILL
Parliament House
Brisbane Ave.
Adelaide Ave.
Prime Minister's Lodge
State Circle
Sydney Ave.
Melbourne Ave.
Hobart Ave.
Empire Circuit
DEAKIN
FORREST
National Circuit
Canberra Ave.
Telopea Park
Wentworth Ave.
Dominion Circuit
Manuka Oval
Manuka Circle
KINGSTON
Train Station
Empire Circuit
Collins Park
Tasmania Circle
Canberra Ave.
Arthur Circle
Mugga Way
Captain Cook Cr.
GRIFFITH
Hume Place
Gowrie Dr.
0 300 yards
0 300 meters

ACT

By Bus

Intercity buses through Canberra are based at **Jolimont Tourist Centre,** 67 Northbourne Ave., just north of Alinga St. in Civic. (Center open in summer daily 6am-8:30pm; in winter 5:30am-7:30pm. Public showers available. Lockers $4 per day, overnight storage available by prior arrangement.) Several bus companies, both major domestic airlines, and Countrylink (open Mon.-Fri. 7am-5:30pm) have desks in the building.

Greyhound Pioneer (tel. 13 20 30) provides frequent service to Sydney (6-8 per day, 4-5hr., $32), Melbourne (2 per day, 8½-10hr., $52), Adelaide (4 per day, 15-20hr., $99), Goulburn (3 per day, 1hr., $18), and the New South Wales Snowfields (June-Oct., $38). **Murray's** (tel. 13 22 51) runs buses to Sydney with a little less frequency and a little less expense (3-4 per day, 4hr., $28). Extensive coverage of New South Wales' southern coast is their specialty (to Bateman's Bay 1-2 per day, 2½hr., $21.75). During school holidays, **Sid Fogg's** (tel. 1800 045 952) sends three buses per week to Newcastle (Mon., Wed., and Fri. 7:30am, 6½hr., $45). **Transborder Express** (tel. 6241 0033) makes the trip to Yass (5 per day, 1hr., $10). Always ask about student and senior discounts when buying bus tickets.

By Train

The **Canberra Railway Station,** on Wentworth Ave. in Kingston, 4km from the city center, is on ACTION bus route #313 (station open daily 5am-11:30pm). Driving from Civic, follow Commonwealth Ave. south to State Circle and exit on Brisbane Ave. Wentworth Ave. continues southeast where Brisbane Ave. ends, four blocks from State Circle. The station houses little more than a **Countrylink office** (tel. 6239 7039 or 13 22 32; open Mon.-Sat. 6:20am-5:30pm, Sun. 10:30am-5:30pm). Trains leave for Sydney (3 per day, 4hr., $41), Melbourne (1 per day, 8½hr., $77), Brisbane (1 per day, 23hr., $109), and Adelaide (1 per day, 23hr., $129). Students, seniors, and ages 4-16 receive a 50% discount.

By Car

The **Canberra Visitors Centre** (see below) has great free maps of Canberra. The **NRMA automobile club,** 92 Northbourne Ave. (tel. 6240 4620), is the place to turn for road service or car problems (open Mon.-Fri. 8:30am-5pm). For 24-hr. **emergency road service,** call 13 21 32. **Budget** (tel. 13 27 27; open Mon.-Fri. 8am-5pm, Sat. 8-11am), on the corner of Mort St. and Girrahween St., **Avis,** 17 Lawnsdale St. (tel. 6249 6088 or 1800 225 411; open Mon.-Fri. 8am-6pm, Sat. 8-11am), **Hertz,** 33 Mort St. (tel. 6257 4877; open Mon.-Fri. 8am-6pm, Sat. 8am-noon), and **Thrifty,** 29 Lawnsdale St. (tel. 6247 7422 or 1800 652 008; open Mon.-Fri. 8am-5:30pm, Sat.-Sun. 8am-5pm), all have offices in Braddon and at the airport. Local outfits **Value Rent-a-Car** (tel. 6295 6155; open Mon.-Fri. 8am-6pm, Sat. 8am-noon), in the Regis Capital Hill Hotel at Canberra Ave. and National Circuit, and **Oz Drive,** 13 Yallourn St. (tel. 6239 2639; call ahead to book Mon.-Fri. 9am-6pm), both charge about $40 per day with rates decreasing over longer rentals. No surcharges applied for ages 21-25, just a higher deductible. **Rent a Dent,** 41 Whyalla St. (tel. 6257 5947), in Fyshwick, rents used cars for $25 per day or $155 per week (open Mon.-Fri. 8:30am-5pm, Sat. 9am-noon).

ORIENTATION

Lake Burley Griffin, a man-made lake formed by the damming of the Molonglo River, splits Canberra in two. The area known as the Parliamentary Triangle spans the lake with one point at **Capital Hill** on the south shore. From Capital Circle, running around Capital Hill, **Commonwealth Ave.** stretches north to **Vernon Circle,** the city's center, and **King's Ave.** crosses the lake heading northeast to the government offices in Russell and ending at the Australian-American Memorial. **Parkes Way** connects the two avenues on the north shore. These boundaries encircle most of the city's museums and government-related attractions. The area around Vernon Cir., known as **Civic,** contains necessary service centers such as the bus station (3 blocks north on Northbourne Ave.), the GPO (2 blocks north on Alinga St.), and a series of shopping centers organized around **City Walk,** where you'll find travel agencies, currency exchange offices, and City Market. **Northbourne Ave.,** leading north from Vernon Circle, is the major axis for navigating the city's northern half.

There are two distinct features that help one understand the Canberra city plan. To avoid the unpleasant appearance of sprawling suburbs creeping up the hills, construction in the city is restricted to the valleys; it must not extend above a certain altitude. Street signs therefore often direct one to a valley rather than to a specific street. The city, based on a system of roundabouts surrounded by concentrically ringed streets and wheel-spoke off-shoots, makes perfect sense to people who live here. For the part of the world's population raised in gridded environments, it's completely counter-intuitive. The easiest way to approach the city's traffic pattern is to travel by bus and avoid the issue. If you do decide to drive, a good map will be invaluable. The Canberra Visitors Centre distributes a free street map covering most areas of interest. Take time to familiarize yourself with the general locations of the city's named districts. Canberra's roundabouts are well-marked but often only specify districts, not the streets you'll encounter down the road. **Kingston,** southeast of Capital Hill, is home to the railway station and several budget accommodations. The embassies populate **Yarralumla,** just west of Capital Hill. **Dickson,** northeast of Civic via Northbourne Ave. and Antill St., and **Manuka** (ma-NIK-uh), southeast of Capital Hill, both include clusters of reasonably-priced restaurants. And these are just a few. If you find you've taken the wrong spoke at any time, stop and refer to the map. All too often, people assume that turning onto a side street will lead directly to their intended route, as it might in a gridded city, only to find that a hill, a park, or a serpentine tangle of little streets stands between them and their goal. It is often easiest to go back to the original roundabout and start again. Thanks to an excellent system of bicycle paths, the capital's relatively long distances can also be covered easily on a bicycle.

GETTING AROUND

Public transportation in Canberra consists of the **ACTION (ACT Internal Omnibus Network)** (tel. 6207 7600, route and fare information tel. 6207 7611; TTY 6207 7689; http://www.netinfo.com.au/action), which centers on the city bus interchange, on East Row at Alinga St., one block south of the Jolimont Tourist Centre. Buses cover all of Canberra and the inner suburbs with connections to the greater ACTION network for travel to the entire populated area of the ACT. The *Bus Book* ($2), available at the bus interchange, at the Canberra Visitors Centre, and from newsagents, contains maps and timetables for all of the ACTION routes and is an excellent resource for anyone planning to get around Canberra by bus for more than a couple of days. Route maps are posted at the city bus interchange as well. Bus service operates roughly Monday through Friday from 6:30am to 11:30pm, Saturday from 7:30am to 11pm, and Sunday from 8:30am to 6pm, although any given route may run more limited hours. All ACTION buses accommodate wheelchairs and guide dogs.

Bus fare for any regular route is $2; students, seniors, and children ages 5-15 pay $1. FareGo Tickets are available for four rides ($7.20, $2.80) or 10 rides ($17, $7). Daily ($6.70, $2.70), weekly ($29, $12) and monthly ($109, $45) tickets provide for unlimited travel over the allotted period of time. For weekday travel beginning after 9am, or any weekend travel, the off-peak daily ticket (valid Mon.-Fri. 9am-4:30pm and after 6pm, Sat.-Sun. all day; $4, seniors $1) may be the best bargain. Commuter Express Services (the 700 series buses) cost two times the regular fare, and routes #901 and 904, the sight-seeing buses, require daily tickets ($6.70) for any amount of use. The special "replica tram buses" which travel the two city center rings just outside Vernon Cir. (route #301), provide free transport Monday through Friday from 11am to 2:40pm.

Murray's Canberra Explorer (tel. 6295 3611) makes 19 stops over a 25km route, and allows passengers to get on and off as many times as they like. (Tickets $18, seniors $16, ages 3-14 $8; discounted tickets available at YHA and Victor Lodge $10). Buses set off each hour from Jolimont Centre (daily 10:15am and 4:15pm). A one-hour, no-stop pass gives you a look at the city for $7 (seniors $6, ages 3-14 $5).

Aerial Taxi Cab (tel. 6285 9222) covers the city and suburbs. (24hr. Base fare $2.60. Mon.-Fri. 92¢ per km, Sat.-Sun. $1.05 per km. Pick-up fee 60¢.) For **bike rental,** try **Mr. Spokes Bike Hire and Cafe** (tel. 6257 1188), on Barrine Dr. in Acton Park, near the Ferry Terminal. (Bikes $8 for the 1st hr., each additional hr. $7. Child's bike $7, $6. Adult bike with child seat $9, $8. Tandem bike $16, $14. Helmets included. Open in summer daily 9am-6pm; in winter 9am-5pm.) Another option is **Dial-a-Bicycle** (tel. 6286 5463; $25 per day, 2 days $40; delivery, pick-up, helmet, and lock included; calls taken daily 8am-6pm).

PRACTICAL INFORMATION

Tourist and Travel Information

Tourist Office: Canberra Visitors Centre (tel. 6205 0044; 24hr. information tel. 1800 026 166; fax 6205 0776; http://www.canberratourism.com.au), on Northbourne Ave., about 2km north of Vernon Cir. Take bus #431, 437, 439, or 469. Excellent free map available. Handy but imperfect pocket-sized *Canberra Visitors' Map* and the ever-useful *Bus Book* for sale, $2 each. Free accommodations booking. Wheelchair-accessible. Open daily 8am-6pm. **ACT Tourism Booth** (tel. 6247 5611), inside Canberra Centre Mall, 2 blocks from the city bus interchange on City Walk, has a somewhat smaller selection. Open Mon.-Fri. 9am-5:30pm, Sat. 9am-5pm, Sun. 10am-4pm.

Budget Travel Office: STA Travel, 13-15 Garema Place (tel. 6247 8633; Fast Fares tel. 1300 360 960; email traveller@statravelaus.com.au; http://www.statravelaus.com.au), on the corner of City Walk. Specializing in discounted fares and packages for students and young travelers. Open Mon.-Fri. 9am-5pm.

Financial Services

Currency Exchange: The **Advance Bank branch** on City Walk (tel. 6243 5827; fax 6243 5886) at the corner of Petrie Plaza stays open Mon.-Thurs. 9am-5pm, Fri. 9am-7:30pm, Sat. 9:30am-2pm. **Thomas Cook** (tel. 6257 2222), in Canberra Centre shopping mall on Bunda St. at the corner of Petrie Plaza, operates Mon.-Fri. 9am-5pm, Sat. 9:30am-12:30pm. Many banks close at 4pm Mon.-Thurs.

American Express: Shop 1, Centrepoint, 185 City Walk (tel. 6247 2333), on the corner of Petrie Plaza. Cardholders and Traveller's Cheque users can have mail held for 3 weeks at no charge. Send mail ATTN: Client Mail, P.O. Box 153, Canberra ACT 2601. No fee for Traveller's Cheque transactions, changing or cashing. Currency exchange incurs a 1% fee, $3 minimum. Open Mon.-Fri. 8:30am-5:30pm, Sat. 9am-noon.

Local Business Hours and Holidays: Most businesses maintain the conventional Mon.-Fri. 9am-5pm schedule, but shopping centers stay open until 9pm on Fri. In addition, stores are generally open Sat. 9am-4pm and Sun. 10am-4pm.

Embassies and Consulates

Britain (tel. 6270 6666, visas 6257 1982, passports 6257 5857; fax 6257 5857), on Commonwealth Ave. Yarralumla. Open Mon.-Fri. 9am-4:30pm. Phone inquiries taken Mon.-Fri. 10am-4:30pm. **Canada** (tel. 6273 3844; fax 6270 4060), on Commonwealth Ave., south of the lake. Open for consular services Mon.-Fri. 8:30am-12:30pm and 1-4:30pm. **France,** 6 Perth Ave. (tel. 6216 0100), Yarralumla. For personal passport or visa matters, contact the consulate in Sydney. **Germany,** 119 Empire Circuit (tel. 6270 1911; fax 6270 1951), Yarrulumla. Open Mon. and Wed.-Thurs. 8am-noon, Tues. 2-4pm, Fri. noon-2pm. **Indonesia,** 8 Darwin Ave. (tel. 6250 8600; fax 6273 3545), Yarralumla. Open Mon.-Fri. 9am-12:30pm and 1:30-5pm. **Ireland,** 20 Arkana St. (tel. 6273 3022; fax 6373 3741), Yarralumla. Open Mon.-Fri. 9:30am-12:45pm and 2-5pm. **Japan,** 112 Empire Circuit (tel. 6273 3244; fax 6273 1848), Yarralumla. Open Mon.-Fri. 9am-12:30pm and 2-4pm. **New Zealand** (tel. 62704211; fax 6273 3194), on Commonwealth Ave., south of the lake. For consular services, contact the consulate in Sydney. **South Africa** (tel. 6273 2424; fax 6373 4994), on the corner of State Cir. and Rhodes Pl., Yarralumla. Open Mon.-Fri. 8:30am-2pm. **Switzerland,** 7 Melbourne Ave. (tel. 6273 3977), in Forrest. Passport and visa matters handled in Sydney. **Thailand,** 111 Empire Circuit (tel. 6273 1149;

fax 6273 1518), Yarralumla. Open Mon.-Fri. 9am-12:30pm. **USA,** Moonah Pl. (tel. 6270 5000), in, you guessed it, Yarralumla. Open Mon.-Fri. 8:30-10:30am. Calls taken Mon.-Fri. 2-4 pm.

Emergency, Health, and Social Services

Public Markets: Locals recommend the **Gorman House Markets** (tel. 6249 7377), on Ainslie Ave., between Currong and Doonkuma St. (Sat. 7am-2pm), the **Hall Markets** (tel. 6282 4411), at the Hall Showground (Feb.-Dec. 1st Sun. of the month 10am-3pm) and the **Old Bus Depot Markets,** 49 Wentworth Ave. (tel. 6292 8391; Sun. 10am-4pm).

Library: ACT Library Service (tel. 6207 5155), inside the Civic shopfront, on East Row, between Alinga St. and London Circuit. Regular library resources plus free Internet access. Open Mon.-Thurs. 10am-5pm, Fri. 10am-7pm, Sat. 9:30am-4pm.

Bookstores: Travelers Maps and Guides (tel. 6249 6006), inside the Jolimont Tourist Centre. Open Mon.-Thurs. 8am-6pm, Fri. 8am-7pm, Sat. 9am-5pm. **Beaky's Books** (tel. 014 685 507), in City Markets, sells, purchases, and exchanges paperbacks. Open Mon.-Thurs. 9am-5:30pm, Fri. 9am-9pm, Sat. 9am-4pm.

Ticket Agencies: Ticketek (tel. 6248 7666; http://www.com.au/ticketek), on Bunda St., in Canberra Centre, makes entertainment bookings. Open Mon.-Fri. 9am-5pm, Sat. 9am-noon.

Late-Night Pharmacy: Day and Night Chemist, 7 Sargood St. (tel. 6248 7050 or 6249 1919), in the O'Connor Shopping Centre. Open daily 9am-11pm. **Urgent Prescription Service** (tel. 6249 1919) operates after 11pm for emergencies.

Hotlines: Lifeline, 24hr. tel. 6257 1111. **Drug and Alcohol Crisis Line,** 24hr. tel. 6205 4545. **Poison Information Centre,** 24hr. tel. 13 11 26. **Lesbian Line,** tel. 6247 2726; Mon.-Fri. 6-10pm. **Women's Information and Referral Service,** tel. 6205 1075; Mon.-Fri. 9am-5pm.

Hospital/Medical Services: Canberra Hospital (tel. 6244 2222; 24hr. emergency line 6244 2324), on Yamba Dr., Garren. Follow the signs to Woden heading southwest from Capital Hill. **Travelers Medical and Vaccination Centre** (tel. 6257 7165), inside City Walk Arcade on the second level. Advice and vaccinations for a full range of tropical diseases. Consultations $35-52. Open Mon.-Fri. 9am-5pm.

Police: (tel. 6256 7777), on London Circuit opposite University Ave.

Emergency: Dial 000.

Post and Communications

Telegrams: Telstra (tel. 13 12 91) sends telegrams overseas. Open Mon.-Fri. 9am-5pm.

Internet Access: The ACT Library Service (listed above) and the National Library (see **Sights,** below) allow visitors to sign up for free 30min. blocks of Internet time. **Jolimont Tourist Centre** charges $2 per 8min.

Post Office: General Post Office (GPO), 53-73 Alinga St. (tel. 6201 7070). Open Mon.-Fri. 8:30am-5:30pm. For stamps and counter service, the Australia Post office at Civic Square, outside Canberra Centre mall, is open Mon.-Fri. 8:30am-5:30pm, Sat. 9am–noon. **Postal code:** 2601.

Phone Code: 02.

ACCOMMODATIONS AND CAMPING

Hostels and Dorms

Victor Lodge Bed and Breakfast, 29 Dawes St. (tel. 6295 7777; fax 6295 7777), 7km south of the city center in Kingston. Free pick-up in Civic daily 7am-8pm. Bus #265 from London Circuit stops 2 blocks away on Eyre St. This place is so clean and accommodating that the staff actually washes up after hostelers in the common kitchen. Room fees include linen, and a breakfast of cereal, fruit, and yogurt. Tea and coffee are available all day long, so curl up by the TV and relax. Reception open daily 7:30am-10pm. Check-out 10am. Dorms $17; singles $35; doubles $44. Weekly: singles $175; doubles $280. VIP. Discounted Canberra Explorer passes $10. Laundry $2.40 to wash, $1.60 to dry. Key deposit $10.

Canberra YHA Hostel (YHA), 191 Dryandra St. (tel. 6248 9155; fax 6249 1731; email yha@yhansw.com.au), 5km northwest of the city center in O'Connor. Take bus #304 (weekends and evenings #366) from the city interchange, and follow the signs from the stop at the corner of Miller and Scrivener St. To reach the hostel by car, follow Northbourne Ave. north from Vernon Cir. Take a left on MacArthur, go 2km, and turn right on Dryandra. YHA's capital city hostel inhabits a clean, modern building with big windows and leafy views. Travel desk, bike rental (half day $11, full day $16), off-street parking, small store for necessities, and fully equipped kitchen (open daily 7am-10:30pm), common room with TV, and laundry facilities. Reception open daily 7am-10:30pm. Check-out 10am. 4-bed dorms $16, under 18 $8; twins $20-22, $11. Discounted Canberra Explorer tickets $10. Linen $2. Key deposit $10.

Kingston Hotel Backpackers, 73 Canberra Ave. (tel. 6295 0123; fax 6295 7871), in Kingston, about 7km from Civic. Take bus #238 or 265. Canberra's least expensive rooms are situated over the popular bar and restaurant combo affectionately known as "the Kingo." The rooms tend to be a little dark, and much of the kitchen equipment seems to have gone walkabout. Still, it's friendly and spacious, and you'll never have to call a cab from the pub. Rooms have sinks but share baths. Check-out 8-10am. 1- to 4-bed rooms $12 per person. Linen $4. Key deposit $10.

ACT

City Walk Hotel, 2 Mort St. (tel. 6257 0124; fax 6257 0116; email citywalk@ozemail.com.au), visible from the city bus interchange. The only budget accommodation in the city center, City Walk Hotel rents tidy 8-bed dorms and rooms with shared or private baths. Kitchen, common room with TV, laundry facilities, and an elevator (operational daily 7:30am-10pm, after-hour access by stairs). Reception open Mon.-Sat. 7:30am-10pm, Sun. 7:30am-7pm. Check-out 10am. Wheelchair accessible. Dorms $16; singles $36, with bath $50; doubles $42, with bath $55. Weekly: 7th night free. Linen included. Key deposit $10.

Australian National University (tel. 6249 3454 for housing) offers casual accommodation in several of its residence halls, depending on student need. **Toad Hall** (tel. 6297 49999), on Kingsley St. on campus, 3 blocks west of Northbourne Ave. via Barry Dr., is the only residence offering term-time lodging for travelers. Singles $15, students $13. Office open Mon.-Fri. 9am-5pm. **Fenner Hall,** 210 Northbourne Ave. (tel. 6279 9101; open Mon.-Fri. 8:30am-12:30pm and 1:30-5pm; after-hours duty warden 6279 9017), and **Burton and Garran Hall** (tel. 6267 4350) can lodge temporary visitors only during university holidays, but enthusiastically welcome travelers during the early Dec. to late Feb. summer break. Single rooms in the more recently refurbished Fenner $31, students $18. Rooms in Burton and Garran $30, students $22. All three halls have ample kitchens and shared baths.

Camping

Canberra Motor Village (tel. 6247 5466 or 1800 026 199; fax 6249 6138), 5km northwest of the City Center, on Kunzea St., O'Connor. Take Bus #304 (366 on weekends and evenings) to Miller and Macarthur St. Take a left on Macarthur and go 2km to Dryandra. Take a right and then turn left almost immediately on to Kunzea. By car, follow Northbourne Ave. north from Civic. Tent sites, on-site caravans, and cabins are surrounded by trees and actually feel like they're in the wilderness in some spots. With the abundance of nearby facilities, toilets, hot showers, and laundry facilities seem almost passé. Tennis courts, BBQ area, pool, store, restaurant, playground. Reception open daily 7am-10:30pm. Check-out 10am. Sites with power for 1 person $10; for 2 $15; for a family of 2 adults and any number of children $20. With electricity and water $16; $20; $25. Each additional person $5. Wheelchair accessible facilities available.

Canberra Carotel (tel. 6241 1377; fax 6241 6674), 6km north of the city center, on Federal Hwy. in Watson. Buses #305 and 364 stop behind the camping area. Follow Northbourne Ave. out of town until it becomes Federal Hwy. Then take a right at the sign. The huge, grassy area set aside for tents makes this a particularly popular place with the young people who come to town for the Street Machine Summernats (auto show) at the nearby Exhibition Centre. The rest of the year, tents look across an empty field of grass toward the treeline or the motel. Bar, restaurant, store, swimming pool, playground, and BBQ area complement the usual toilets, showers, and laundry facilities. Reception open Mon.-Fri. 7:30am-9pm, Sat.-Sun.

7:30am-8pm. Check-out 10am. Tent sites for 2 people $10, with power $12; each additional person $2. On-site caravans with cooking facilities for 1 person $30; each additional person up to 4 $3. Cabins for 2 people (no cooking facilities) $45; cabins with cooking facilities for up to 5 people (wheelchair accessible) $70.

Motels and Guest Houses

Northbourne Lodge, 522 Northbourne Ave. (tel. 6257 2599), Downer, 4km north of the city center. Bus #500 passes out front. Canberra's next step up from hostel lodging is a big one. Newly decorated rooms come with TVs, refrigerators, tea-and-coffee-making facilities, and a full cooked breakfast. Breakfast served daily 7:30-9am. Check-out 10:30am. Reception open daily 7:30am-noon and 3pm-early evening. Owner always reachable via courtesy phone. Singles $50-60, with bath $65; doubles $55-60, with bath $70. Skip breakfast and all prices drop around $10. Weekly rates available.

Blue and White Lodge, 524 Northbourne Ave., and **Blue Sky Lodge,** 528 Northbourne Ave. (tel. for both 6248 0498; fax 6248 8277). Located next to the Northbourne Lodge, these 2 guest houses offer similar-sized rooms at similar prices. The green and brown color scheme is a bit dated. Rooms have TVs, fridges, and kettles, and there's a comfortable TV lounge downstairs at the Blue and White Lodge. Full cooked breakfast served daily 7:30am. Reception open daily 10am-4pm. Check-out 10am. Singles $50, with bath $60; doubles $60, with bath $75.

Motel Monaro, 27 Dawes St. (tel. 6295 2111; fax 6295 2466), in Kingston, 7km from Civic. A Best Western joint, the Motel Monaro is a standard 80s style motel. Upmarket enough to have overpriced snacks tempting guests from baskets in every room. You can use the TV, fridge, toaster, hair dryer, and other electrical goodies at no charge. Family units are a good deal with the per-person pricing system. Reception open Mon.-Thurs. and Sun. 24 hr., Fri.-Sat. 8am-9:30pm. Check-out 10am. Rooms for 1 person $62; each additional person $10. Laundry $5.

ACT

FOOD

In a city populated by government officials, cheap food is never easy to find. Canberra's restaurant scene supports this rule with a large number of establishments in the moderate $15-per-main range but very few with plates closer to $10. Cafes in the city center and the food court at Canberra Centre provide welcome exceptions. For a slightly unusual twist on groceries, visit **City Market,** on Bunda St. across from Canberra Centre. Along with the **Supabarn** supermarket (tel. 6257 4055; open Mon.-Thurs. 8am-9pm, Fri. 8am-10pm, Sat.-Sun. 8am-7pm), the complex packs in fruit stands, butcher shops, and prepared food stalls in a variety of flavors and prices. The **Woolworths** locations most convenient to the city center and budget accommodations are in Dickson, opposite a great string of restaurants on Woolley St. at 1 Dickson Pl. (tel. 6249 6809; on bus routes #304 and 367), and in Manuka (tel. 6295 0738), on Flinders Way, on bus route #311 (both stores open daily 7am-midnight).

Sizzle City (tel. 6248 5399), on Bunda St. at the entrance to the City Market. A Japanese hole-in-the-wall serving tasty, fresh sushi at great prices. Construct your own combination from individual pieces or take a ready-made bento lunch ($5.20-6.80). Vegetarian lunch $5.20. Open Sun.-Thurs. 9:30am-5:30pm, Fri. 9:30am-8:30pm.

Fisho Cafe, 48 Giles St. (tel. 6295 3153), across from Tench St. Take bus #238 or 265. Surrounded by the bustle of the Kingston Shops, this cafe quietly earns rave reviews for fresh fish and elegant preparation. It's a bit of a splurge with daily specials averaging $15-20, but it won't be wasted. Mussels Marinara $9.80. Selection of pastas $11.80 and risottos $12.80. Licensed and BYO, bottles only. Corkage $3.50 per bottle. Open Mon.-Sat. 10am-10pm.

Belluci's Trattoria (tel. 6257 7788), on the corner of Woolley St., Dickson. Take bus #304 or 367. Surprisingly, Belluci's columns, wine racks, and faux grape arbor create the feeling of a vineyard, without spilling over into camp. The best deal in the house is the pasta platter, which allows you to select 3 of the original pasta dishes, such as Spirali Calcutta (combining Italian flavors with a lightly curried chicken), for 1 pasta feast ($14 per person, 2-person min.). Licensed and BYO, bottled wine only. Corkage $2 per person. Open Mon.-Fri. noon-3pm and 6-10:30pm, Sat.-Sun. 6-10:30pm.

Ali Baba Take Away (tel. 6295 2207), on Furneaux St., Manuka. Take bus #311, 360, or 361. Next door to the restaurant of the same name, this little sandwich counter serves generous portions of fresh, cheap Lebanese food. Sit outside to avoid the fast-food-joint decor. Super vegetarian falafel sandwich $3.80. Plates $8-9. Open Sun.-Thurs. 9am-10pm, Fri.-Sat. 9am-11pm.

Tutu Tango, 124 Bunda St. (tel. 6257 7100), between Petrie Plaza and Garema Pl., fills a niche often ignored in Australia's restaurant market, specializing in Southwestern cuisine (a.k.a. Tex Mex) with a gourmet twist. Outdoor seating. Licensed and BYO, bottled wine only. Corkage $4 per bottle. Open daily 10am-late.

SIGHTS

Lookouts

Considering the difficulty of orienting oneself in Canberra, a stop at one of the city's lookouts is an appropriate start to a sight-seeing tour of the capital. From a hill in Commonwealth Park, at Regatta Point on the north shore of Lake Burley Griffin, the **National Capital Exhibition** (tel. 6257 1068; fax 6247 1875) surveys the capital in more than just the usual sense. The exhibition focuses on the planning, construction, and growth of Canberra, providing visitors with a ready grasp of the city that surrounds them. Photographs, audio-visual presentations, and an excellent light-up model of the city illuminate both the process behind the capital's creation and the city which has grown to fulfill Walter Burley Griffin's vision. (Open in summer daily 9am-6pm; in winter 9am-5pm. Free. Wheelchair accessible.) Farther back from the city's center, Mt. Ainslie and Black Mountain offer broader views of the city. Located north of Lake Burley Griffin and east of the city center, Mt. Ainslie rises to a height of 843m to overlook the lake, the Parliamentary Triangle, and the Australian War Memorial. To reach the summit by car, take Fairbairn Ave. east from the end of Anzac Pde. to Mt. Ainslie Dr. Trails lead to the top from behind the War Memorial. The two lookout points on Black Mountain look down on the city in different directions. The first lookout on Black Mountain Dr., accessible by taking Barry St. to Clunies Ross St. and heading southwest, faces southeast and takes in the Parliamentary Triangle and Lake Burley Griffin. The second viewpoint is oriented to the north, and takes in the surrounding countryside and the Australian Institute of Sport. Sight-seeing bus #904 stops at the summit, and walking tracks to the top start from Frith Rd., Belconnen Way, and Caswell Dr. From the peak of Black Mountain, **Telstra Tower** (tel. 6248 1911 or 1800 806 718; fax 6257 6600) climbs an additional 195m to ensure an unobstructed view in every direction. Exhibits in the tower treat the history of Australian telecommunications, and, as every observation tower should, Telstra Tower contains a revolving restaurant. (Tower open daily 9am-10pm. Admission $3, seniors and ages 4-15 $1, under 4 free.)

Parliamentary Triangle

A showpiece of grand architecture and cultural attractions, Canberra's Parliamentary Triangle is the center of Walter Burley Griffin's plan for the capital. **Parliament House** (tel. 6277 5399; fax 62775068), the focal point of the triangle, takes the ideal of unifying architecture with the landscape to a new level. The building is actually built into Capital Hill so that it seems to spill out of the sides of the hill, leaving the grassed-over hilltop on its roof undisturbed. The effect is something like an inverted football stadium with the Senate to the west, and the House of Representatives to the east, both curving away from the center of the hill. The building itself is magnificent in both design and decoration, and the free guided tours, conducted every half hour, give a good overview of both the unique features of the building and the workings of the government housed inside. (Open daily 9am-5pm. Free. Wheelchair accessible.) Visitors can also observe both houses of Parliament from galleries above the chambers. The House of Representatives, which fills up more often then the Senate, allows people to book seats in advance by calling ahead (tel. 6277 4890). The lawn above Parliament House remains open for public use 24 hours a day. **Old Parliament House** (tel. 6270 8222; fax 6270 8111) served as Australia's seat of government from

1927 until 1988, when the current Parliament House was completed. The building sits in a direct line with the front of Parliament House, but 500m closer to the lake. Its original purpose now usurped, Old Parliament House houses the **National Portrait Gallery** (tel. 6273 4723; fax 6273 4493) and stages temporary exhibitions from the wayward Australian Museum (see **Northwest,** below). Admission to Old Parliament House covers the National Portrait Gallery and any current exhibits (open daily 9am-4pm; $2, students, seniors, and ages 4-16 $1, families $5; wheelchair accessible).

The third tier of the Parliamentary Triangle is comprised of the four large modern building on Parkes Pl., just off King Edward Tce. On the southeastern end, nearest Kings Ave., the **National Gallery of Australia** (tel. 6240 6411; fax 6240 6529) displays an extensive collection of works by Aboriginal artists and Australian artists of European descent. Traveling shows from around Australia and the world supplement the gallery's standing collection. A worthwhile stop for any art-lover, the gallery is particularly satisfying for those with an interest in Aboriginal art. (Open daily 10am-5pm. Free 1hr. guided tours daily 11am and 2pm. Admission $3, students and ages 4-16 free; separate fees apply for special exhibits. Wheelchair accessible.) The surrounding sculpture garden is free and open 24 hours. Next door, the **High Court of Australia** (tel. 6270 6811 or 6270 6850; fax 6273 3025) presents a seven-story wall of glass and steel on the outside of its grand public hall. When the court is in session, visitors may watch the proceedings in Australia's highest court from public galleries in the three court rooms. (Open daily 9:45am-4:30pm. Free. Wheelchair accessible.) The **National Science and Technology Centre,** also known as **Questacon** (tel. 6270 2800; fax 6270 2888) inhabits the buildings on the court's northwest side. Inside, interactive devices mete out hands-on science lessons to kids of all ages. Exhibits attempt to explain the science behind everyday occurrences such as cooking. Anyone with an interest in science can expect to spend several hours. Free displays at the entrance let you decide if it's for you before you pay. (Open daily 10am-5pm. Admission $8, students and seniors $5, ages 5-16 $4, under 5 free. Wheelchair accessible.) The final stop on Parkes Pl., the **National Library of Australia** (tel. 6262 1111; fax 6273 5483) is open for research and for casual visitation. The nation's largest library (7 million books) not only mounts exhibitions from its literary and pictorial collections, but also holds free movie screenings occasionally (call 6262 1156 for program) and provides free Internet access through its Cybercafe. (Open Mon.-Thurs. 9am-9pm, Fri. 9am-5pm, Sat.-Sun.1:30-5pm. Wheelchair accessible.)

The last two attractions in the Parliamentary Triangle are actually located *in* Lake Burley Griffin. The **Captain Cook Memorial Jet** blows a six-ton column of water to heights of up to 147m to commemorate Captain James Cook's arrival at the east coast of Australia. Hey, why not? Australian monarch Queen Elizabeth II dedicated the jet on the bicentennial of Cook's landing in 1970. The bell tower of the **National Carillon** (tel. 6254 9694) is located on Aspen Island at the other end of Lake Burley Griffin's central basin. A gift from Britain on Canberra's 50th birthday in 1963, the Carillon is played several times per week for 45-minute concerts (spring, summer, and fall Mon.-Fri. 12:30pm, Sat.-Sun. 2:45pm; in summer also Thurs. 5:45pm; in winter Wed. 12:45pm, Sat.-Sun. 2:45pm).

Northeast

Anzac Pde. extends northeast from Parkes Way, continuing the line formed by the old and new Parliament Houses across the lake toward the **Australian War Memorial** (tel. 6243 4211), on bus routes #302, 303, and 362 from Civic. The galleries, displaying war-related artifacts, photographs, and documents, as well as a collection of art by major Australian artists depicting life in wartime, make the Memorial a moving and unexpected favorite among visitors to the city. The Hall of Memory holds the tomb of an unknown Australian soldier transported to his final resting place from a WWI battlefield in France in 1993. (Open daily 10am-5pm. Tours daily 10, 10:30, 11am, 1:30, and 2pm. Free. Wheelchair accessible.) The nearby **St. John the Baptist Church** (tel. 6248 8399; fax 6247 5481), on the corner of Anzac Pde. and Constitution Ave., has been in service since 1845, long before the current city rose up around it. The church's former school house is now a museum recording some aspects of pioneer life in Canberra (open daily 9am-5pm; free). This visit to historic Canberra continues at **Blundell's Cottage** (tel. 6273 2667), on Wendouree Dr. off Constitution Ave., an 1860 house built as lodging for farm workers who once worked the land where Lake Burley Griffin is today (open Tues.-Sun. 10am-4pm, last entry 3:30pm; admission $2, students, seniors, and ages 5-14 $1, families $5). From this area, the 79m-tall **Australian-American Memorial,** a column topped by an eagle to commemorate Australian and American Cooperation in WWII, is hard to miss. The base of the monument stems from the eastern end of Kings Ave. **The Canberra Planetarium and Observatory** (tel. 6249 7817), in the Downer Club on Hawdon Place, off Antill St. in Dickson, shares its telescopes and the expertise of an astronomer with the general public every evening. Observatory time comes in 30-minute blocks from 8:30 to 10pm (in fall and winter 7:30-10pm; $7.50, ages 5-12 $2). The planetarium has four shows daily ($7.50, ages 5-12 $4).

Northwest

One of Canberra's least-sung and most enjoyable tourist attractions, the **National Film and Sound Archive** (tel. 6209 3111; fax 6209 3165), on McCoy Circuit, in Acton, is a bonanza of sight and sound relics dating from the 1800s to today. Interactive exhibits, movie memorabilia, and continuous screenings provide several ways of delving into the history of radio, film, television, and recorded sound in Australia. (Open daily 9am-5pm. Admission $6.50, students, seniors, and ages 4-16 $4.50, families $20. Wheelchair accessible.) The archive's back side abuts the **Australian National University** (tel. 6249 0794; fax 6249 5568), and both are best reached by bus #433 or 434 to Liversedge St. from the city bus interchange. Contemporary art exhibitions at the university's **Drill Hall Gallery** (tel. 6249 5832), on Kingsley St., are some of the best reasons to stop in for a tour of the campus. The **Australian National Botanic Gardens** (tel. 6250 9540; fax 6250 9599) run along the northwestern border of the campus on Clunies Ross St. at the foot of Black Mountain. Though only sightseeing bus #904 goes to the entrance to the gardens, buses #433 and 434 stop nearby on Daly Rd. Billed as "the world's finest collection of Australian native plants," the gardens contain cultivated collections of fauna from several climate zones, including a rainforest that's well outside the norm for the middle of Canberra. Saturday evenings in January, the sound of free jazz concerts wafts through the eucalypt grove where the gardens are situated (open daily 9am-5pm; free; wheelchairs available).

From Parkes Way, heading out of the city to the west, Lady Denman Dr. branches south toward the **National Aquarium and Australian Wildlife Sanctuary** (tel. 6287 1211; fax 6288 0477) at Scrivener Dam. The combination of an aquarium, including diving tanks and an underwater tunnel exhibit, with a wildlife sanctuary, covering nearly 7 hectares with native Australian fauna, makes the trip out of the city center worthwhile. (Open daily 9am-5:30pm. Admission $10, students, seniors, and ages 4-16 $6, under 4 free, families $32. Wheelchair accessible.) The **Yarramundi Visitor Centre** (tel. 6256 1126; fax 6256 1233) is located on Lady Denman Dr. 2km before the National Aquarium and Australian Wildlife Sanctuary at the future site of the **National Museum of Australia.** Until the museum is completed, sometime after 2000, the center will continue to present bits and pieces of the museum's collection and to conduct programs relating to the themes of the planned museum (open daily 10am-4pm; free). Sight-seeing bus #904 runs the closest to these sights.

The **Australian Institute of Sport (AIS)** (tel. 6252 1444 or 6252 1010; fax 6252 1932; http://www.ausport.gov.au/aistours.html), on Leverrier Cr. just northwest of O'Connor, was established in 1981 as a training facility for the nation's top athletes. Tours led by athletes working at the institute take regular humans through the world of the aerobically, nutritionally, and electronically conditioned, for a glimpse at the latest in sports technology. If the atmosphere inspires you to put in a workout, ask about public use of the pool and tennis courts. (Reservations tel. 6252 1281. Pool use $3.50. Inside courts $12 per hr. Outside courts $8 per hr. Admission with 1½hr. tour $7.50, students and seniors $5.50, ages 5-15 $3.50, families $15.) Take bus #431 from Civic to reach AIS.

Southwest

West of Capital Hill on the south side of the lake, **Yarralumla** is peppered with the **embassies** of over 70 nations, many of which have been built in architectural styles representative of the county's traditions. A drive through the area includes views of everything from Siamese temple architecture at the Thailand Embassy to colonial American architecture at the U.S. Embassy. Traveling west on Adelaide Ave. from the back of Capital Hill, you'll pass the **Lodge,** the official residence of the Australian Prime Minister. Because the building is closed to the public, all you can really do is pass this semi-sight. Farther out Adelaide Ave., the **Royal Australian Mint** (tel. 6202 6999 or 6202 6819; fax 6285 1443; email ramint@netinfo.com.au), on Denison St. in Deakin encourages tourists to stop in and watch the minting process in action. The mint produces all of Australia's coins and some used by other countries as well, and has a collection of rare coins on display. (Open Mon.-Fri. 9am-4pm, Sat.-Sun. 10am-3pm; coin production Mon.-Fri. 9am-noon and 12:40-4pm. Free. Wheelchair accessible.) For a look at **Government House,** the home of the Governor-General (the British/Australian monarchy's representative in Australia), follow Adelaide Ave., bear right on Cotter Rd., then turn onto Lady Denman Dr. Approaching Scrivener Dam from the south, the house occupies the last point of land before the dam shuts the lid on Lake Burley Griffin. The house is not open for visitation.

ACT

NIGHTLIFE AND ENTERTAINMENT

Due to the city's political focus, Canberra's nightlife often goes unnoticed. The student population, however, keeps a good number of establishments open throughout the week, while relaxed licensing means they stay open through the night. Most bars and nightclubs claim to close "late," meaning 11pm on slow nights and as late as people feel like raising a glass on the nights when things get rolling. Canberra has fewer pub-style watering holes than most Australian cities, tending instead toward dance clubs and sleeker bars. The Thursday *Good Times* supplement in the *Canberra Times* has a full roster of the capital's entertainment options.

The Phoenix, 21 East Row (tel. 6247 1606), keeps the pub tradition going by providing Guinness by the pint ($4.70) or schooner ($3.50) to happy people who like their drinks in a semi-Irish setting (open Mon.-Tues. 11am-11pm, Wed. 11am-midnight, Thurs. 11am-12:30am, Fri.-Sat. 11am-1am, Sun. 4pm-midnight). The sprawling **Kingston Hotel,** 73 Canberra Ave. (tel. 6295 6844), in Kingston on bus routes #238 and 265, appeals to a mixed clientele with a noticeable backpacker contingent brought in by the accommodation above (schooners of Toohey's New $2.40; open Sun.-Mon. 8am-10pm, Tues.-Wed. 8am-midnight, Thurs. 8am-1am, Fri.-Sat. 8am-3am). **La Grange Boutique Bar and Brasserie** (tel. 6295 8866), on Franklin St. in Manuka, on bus routes #311, 360, and 361, nurtures a mellow bar scene during the week, spilling over from dinner into the late hours. It earns its reputation as a dance club Thursday through Saturday when a DJ comes in to help Canberra's twenty-somethings unwind. (DJ Thurs.-Sat. 11pm-4am. Cover Sat. $5. Open Mon.-Wed. 4pm-late, Thurs.-Sun. 11am-late.) On Bunda St., right in the center of Canberra's shopping and eating district, **Heaven Nite Club** (tel. 6257 6180) entertains a largely gay male crowd with techno beats so persistent they sometimes outlast the dark hours (open Tues.-Fri. 9pm-late, Sat. 10pm-Sun. 7am). The nearby **Gypsy Bar and Brasserie,** 9 East Row (tel. 6247 7300), has live music (Tues.-Sat.) ranging from jazz to Indie rock (no cover for Tues. jazz, $10 for traveling acts; open Mon.-Fri. noon-late, Sat. 6pm-late). **Casino Canberra,** 21 Binara St. (tel. 6257 7074), and the nightclub **Deja Vu** inside are quite popular with Canberra's over-40 population.

In addition to the usual assortment of first-run cineplex theaters, Canberra gives movie-goers a few alternatives. **Electric Shadows** (tel. 6247 5060), on Akuna St. near City Walk, screens art-house fare every day of the week (tickets $12, students $8). The **National Gallery** (tel. 6240 6411) offers free Friday matinee showings (12:45pm) of videos and films on art and artists. The Gallery calendar has details on the Friday programs and on occasional evening features (evening tickets around $7).

Housing several venues in varying shapes and sizes, the **Canberra Theatre** (tel 6257 1077 or 1800 041 041) is the best place to start looking for live entertainment The center presents local and traveling productions year-round and hosts the National Festival of Australian Theatre every October. For information on the theater and other presentations at the **Australian National University** call *What's On Next Week* at 6249 0742.

Canberra's calendar is packed with minor **festivals,** but there are two annual events that temporarily change the flow of daily life in the city. For 10 days in March (March 7-16 in 1998), **Canberra Festival** brings the nation's capital to life with musical productions, a hot-air balloon show, and street parties. The last day of the festival, the third Monday in March, is a public holiday known as Canberra Day. Each September and October (Sept. 19-Oct. 18 in 1998), the **Advance Bank Floriade** (tel. 1800 020 141) paints the shores of Lake Burley Griffin with thousands of springtime blooms.

ACT

South of Canberra

Bushland pushes in on Canberra's borders to offer a constant reminder of the city's youth and an easy retreat from its refinement. Most notably, **Tidbinbilla Nature Reserve** and **Namadgi National Park,** south of the city, together cover nearly half of the entire area of the ACT. The **Tidbinbilla Visitor Centre** (tel. 6237 5120 or 6205 1233), off Paddy's River Rd., a 40-minute drive southwest of Civic, has information on bushwalks and ranger-led activities throughout the 500-hectare park (open Mon.-Fri. 9am-6pm, Sat.-Sun. 10am-6pm). Dedicated to preserving the natural gum forest habitat of the kangaroos, wallabies, koalas, emus, and other animals who roam the area, the reserve loosely encloses its residents to better your chances of encountering them. Bushwalking trails in the park range from 30-minute strolls to day-long outings. The walk to Gibraltar rock (3hr. round-trip) rewards easy hiking or not-so-easy rock climbing with stupendous views. (Park open daily 9am-6pm. Admission $8 per car. Wheelchair access at visitor center and on enclosed area paths throughout the park.) **Namadgi National Park** forms the western border of Tidbinbilla Nature Reserve and fills almost all of the southern arm of the ACT with preserved alpine wilderness for bushwalkers of all levels of expertise. Traversed by only one major road, Naas/Bobayan Rd., the park is noted for its untrammeled recesses accessible only to more serious hikers. The Yankee Hat Trail (3hr. round-trip), signposted from the Bobayan Rd. in the southern part of the park, is an excellent moderate hike which leads to an Aboriginal art site. The **Namadgi Visitor Centre** (tel. 6207 2900), on the Naas/Bobayan Rd. 3km south of **Tharwa,** distributes topographical maps and information on Aboriginal rock painting and camping in the park (open Mon.-Fri. 9am-4pm, Sat.-Sun. 9am-4:30pm). Campsites at the Orroral River and at Mt. Clear, located only 20m from car parking in both areas, have firewood and toilets but little else ($2 per person). The water at the sites should be boiled before drinking.

Between Canberra and the parks, two attractions direct visitors' attention skyward. Off Cotter Rd., midway between Canberra and Cotter Dam, the **Mt. Stromlo Exploratory** (tel. 6249 0276), the visitors center for **Mt. Stromlo Observatory,** gives visitors a look at the work of professional astronomers through hands-on exhibits. Its daylight-only hours preclude actual stargazing, however (open daily 9am-4:30pm; admission $5, students, seniors, and ages 5-15 $3). One of the three most powerful antenna centers in the world, **Canberra Deep Space Communications Complex,** off Paddy's River Rd., is for serious space junkies. The 70m radio dish at the site tracks and records signals from orbiting spacecraft, and the visitors information center, known as the **Canberra Space Centre** (tel. 6201 7800) has displays on the history of space exploration (open in summer daily 9am-8pm; in winter 9am-5pm).

Built in several stages over the course of the 1800s, the buildings at **Lanyon Homestead** (tel. 62375136; fax 6291 9912), on Tharwa Rd. 30km south of the city, comprise a survey of Canberra's European history from the days of convict labor to turn-of-the-century colonial elegance. Meanwhile, Aboriginal campsites and a canoe tree on the grounds give evidence of earlier habitation at the same site. The homestead, considered a living museum, buzzes with colonial-era activities, such as butter-churning, to complete the view of times gone by. Lanyon's greatest draw may be the gallery of **Sir Sidney Nolan paintings** (tel. 6237 5192; fax 6237 5202), located on the grounds. The works at the gallery, donated to the people of Australia by Nolan himself, include several of Nolan's paintings of bushranger Ned Kelly. (Open Tues.-Sun. 10am-4pm; grounds open until 5pm. Admission to homestead buildings $3, students, seniors, and ages 5-15 $1.50, families $7.50. Gallery admission $1.20, 60¢, $3. Wheelchair accessible.)

North of Canberra

The village of **Gold Creek,** just off the Barton Hwy., 15km northwest of Canberra's center, features three popular attractions. The privately-owned **National Dinosaur Museum** (tel. 6230 2655; fax 6230 2357), on the Barton Hwy., at the corner of Gold Creek Rd., seems to poke fun at Canberra's endless list of "national" sights, but it gains some legitimacy as the first museum in all of Australia to be devoted exclusively to prehistoric animals. The collection of artifacts includes 10 full-sized dinosaur skeletons and three reconstructions which show Australian dinosaurs as they would have looked skin, teeth, and all. (Open daily 10am-5pm. Admission $8, students and seniors $6, ages 5-14 $5, families $23.) Also at Gold Creek Rd. and Barton Hwy., **Ginninderra Village** (tel. 6230 2995), is a complex of arts and crafts shops organized around an historic 1883 schoolhouse (open daily 10am-5pm; free for browsing). Just beyond the Village, **Cockington Green** (tel. 6230 2276 or 1 800 627273; fax 6230 2490) transports travelers to diminutive lands oh-so-far-away with miniature reproductions of buildings from Britain and, more recently, the rest of the world, set among winding garden paths and sculptured bushes. The expansion of the collection helps to diffuse the thick cloud of Anglophilia about the place, but the concept is still more precious than many travelers enjoy. (Open daily 9:30am-4:30pm. Admission $8.50, seniors $6.50, children $4.25, families $22.) **Murray's** (tel. 13 22 51) runs a daily tour to Cokington Green which covers travel and admission, and allows for approximately two hours there ($18, seniors $13, children $5; departs Jolimont Centre daily 10am).

Just over the New South Wales border on the Murrumbidgee River, **Ginninderra Falls** sits at the center of a park bearing the same name (tel. 6254 9637). The falls themselves spill down the 200m Ginninderra Ravine and provide spectacular views from several bushwalking trails. The park is also known for its rock climbing faces. (Open daily 10am-5:30pm. Admission $5, students and seniors $2, children $1.)

New South Wales

As the site of Captain Cook's landing and the area first populated by colonial settlers, New South Wales has played a leading role in Australia's history as a nation. It was here that British convicts lived through the first bitter years of colonization, dreaming of what might lie beyond the impassable Blue Mountains, and here that explorers first broke through the Great Dividing Range, opening the interior of the country for settlement and ensuring the stability of the colony. In the central plains and on the rich land of the Riverina, Merino wool and agricultural success provided the state with its first glimpses of prosperity. Then, in 1851, prospectors struck gold just west of the mountains, and Australia's history changed forever. No longer the desolate prison of exiled convicts, New South Wales became a place that promised new life and a chance to strike it rich. Over the next decade, the state was divided to create Victoria and Queensland. Although it no longer included all of the known continent, New South Wales remained and remains Australia's most populous state and a widely diversified land.

The country's most prominent city, Sydney sits on the central coast as the state capital and the urban center of the nation. North and south of the city, sandy beaches string together in an almost unbroken scenic strip from the cool, untouristed fishing towns by the Victoria border to the lively, tropical resorts of the far north coast. Many of New South Wales' beaches are great for surfing and swimming, and, thanks to the state's extensive roster of national parks, much of this area is set aside for public enjoyment and conservation.

Directly west of Sydney's suburban reaches and just 100km inland, the Blue Mountains of the Great Dividing Range separate the coastal strip and its hinterlands from the expansive Central West and outback regions. Once an insurmountable obstacle, the mountains now encompass some of the state's, and the nation's, favorite getaways. Year-round bushwalking, rock-climbing, and cave exploration are premier attractions of the mountains. The New England Plateau, along the Great Dividing Range north of the wineries of the Hunter Valley, achieves an unusually lush and high-altitude setting for a cosy collection of small Australian towns.

Just below the carved-out enclave of the Australian Capital Territory, the Snowy Mountains offer winter skiing and superb summer hiking. Sandwiched between these unplowable peaks and the barren outback beyond, the fertile plains of the Central West and the Riverina provide the state's agricultural base. Life slows to a standstill as the last drops of moisture disappear from the air and landscape "Back of Bourke" unfolds desert-like toward the South Australian border.

The attractions of New South Wales are as varied as the terrain. Whether in the cosmopolitan fun of Sydney, the laid-back surf culture of coastal towns such as Byron Bay, the challenging bushwalks of the Blue Mountains, or the post-apocalyptic simplicity of the outback, most visitors find something to write home about.

Phone numbers in New South Wales have recently changed. Regional phone codes are now **almost all** 02, followed by eight-digit numbers The last two digits of the old area code have become the first two digits of the new number. If you have trouble making a call, use the following scheme to get the old number, and try that instead. For more details, see the **appendix** (p. 574). Towns close to the Queensland or South Australia borders may take those state's new area codes.

New number:	Old number:
(02) 43xx xxxx	(043) xx xxxx
*(08) 80xx xxxx	*(080) xx xxxx (Broken Hill)
*(07) 45xx xxxx	*(075) xx xxxx (Tweed Heads)

Sydney

Australia's oldest and largest city, Sydney (pop. 3,775,000, approximately 20% of the national total) has descended from the first British settlement of Port Jackson, now more commonly known as Sydney Harbour, which remains the city's centerpiece. In 1788, this stupendous natural harbor drew the first ships of the British colonists and convicts north from their intended settlement site at Botany Bay. Today, the iconic Harbour Bridge and Sydney Opera House occupy the foreshores of Sydney Cove and ensure that every visitor to the city spends at least a few photo-framing moments recognizing the importance of the harbor in the life of New South Wales's capital. On sunny days, when sailboats skim across the water and the sidewalk cafes buzz with a hundred conversations, those few moments easily become hours.

After deplaning in Sydney, many travelers head west immediately, in search of the stark, natural beauty which drew them to Australia. Others stop for several weeks to take advantage of the easy market for casual work and to save for their cross-continental adventures. The remainder fail prey to the city's charms and sing the praises of its beautiful harbor and ocean beaches, its never-ending nightlife, and its world-class cultural attractions. The pace of life in Sydney may seem fast to most Australians, but compared to cultural capitals elsewhere in the world, the hustle and bustle is kept to an exciting but manageable hum.

Unlike most other cities in Australia, Sydney has had time to grow into a vibrant urban center. Long past its first violent, hungry years as a penal colony and its many decades in the shadow of the British empire, Sydney has emerged as an energetic city of international prominence. Content to expand westward into endless suburbs until the 1950s, the city has seen only a few decades of truly urban growth. Today, skyscrapers tower gracefully over the central business district, testament to the city's passage into an era of self-reliance. With a vocal and growing Asian community, and over 200 years of European settlement, Sydney's international presence is both Eastern and Western. In September 2000, the Olympic Games will give the city a chance to show off its ever-mounting skyline and revel in its new-found confidence. As the Games approach, Sydney is abuzz with construction and beautification projects, and spirits are high.

Arrival and Departure

BY PLANE

Sydney's **Kingsford-Smith Airport** (tel. 9667 6058), 10km southwest of the central business district, serves most major international carriers. **Qantas** (tel. 13 13 13) and **Ansett** (13 13 00) cover most domestic destinations. **Luggage** lockers are $4 per day. Larger items can stay in a storage room for $6 per day. **New South Wales Tourism Centre** (tel. 9667 6050), in the international terminal, offers brochures, a complete booking service, and free calls to all of the area's youth hostels (open daily 5:30am-10:30pm).

Local bus #100 goes from the airport to the city center, but officials discourage use of the bus by travelers with luggage (every 30min., Mon.-Fri. 6:30am-6:30pm, $2.50). Instead, **Airport Express** (tel. 13 15 00) runs from the airport to stops throughout the city center (#300) or Kings Cross (#350). The green and yellow buses stop at matching stations outside both the domestic and international terminals. (Service daily 5am-11pm. $5.50, ages 4-14 $3.50, under 4 free. Return good for 2 months $9.) **Kingsford Smith Transport** (tel. 9667 3221) takes travelers to or from any accommodation in the city or the inner suburbs for only slightly more (every 20min., daily 5am-11pm, $6). From international arrivals proceed outside Gate B to bus bay 1 or 2. Most hostels offer free pick-up with a one- or two- night booking, so it's worth stopping to make arrangements for accommodation at the New South Wales Tourism Centre. A **taxi** to the city center costs approximately $16 from the domestic terminal or about $20 from the international area. Driving to the city's center from the airport takes about 10 minutes.

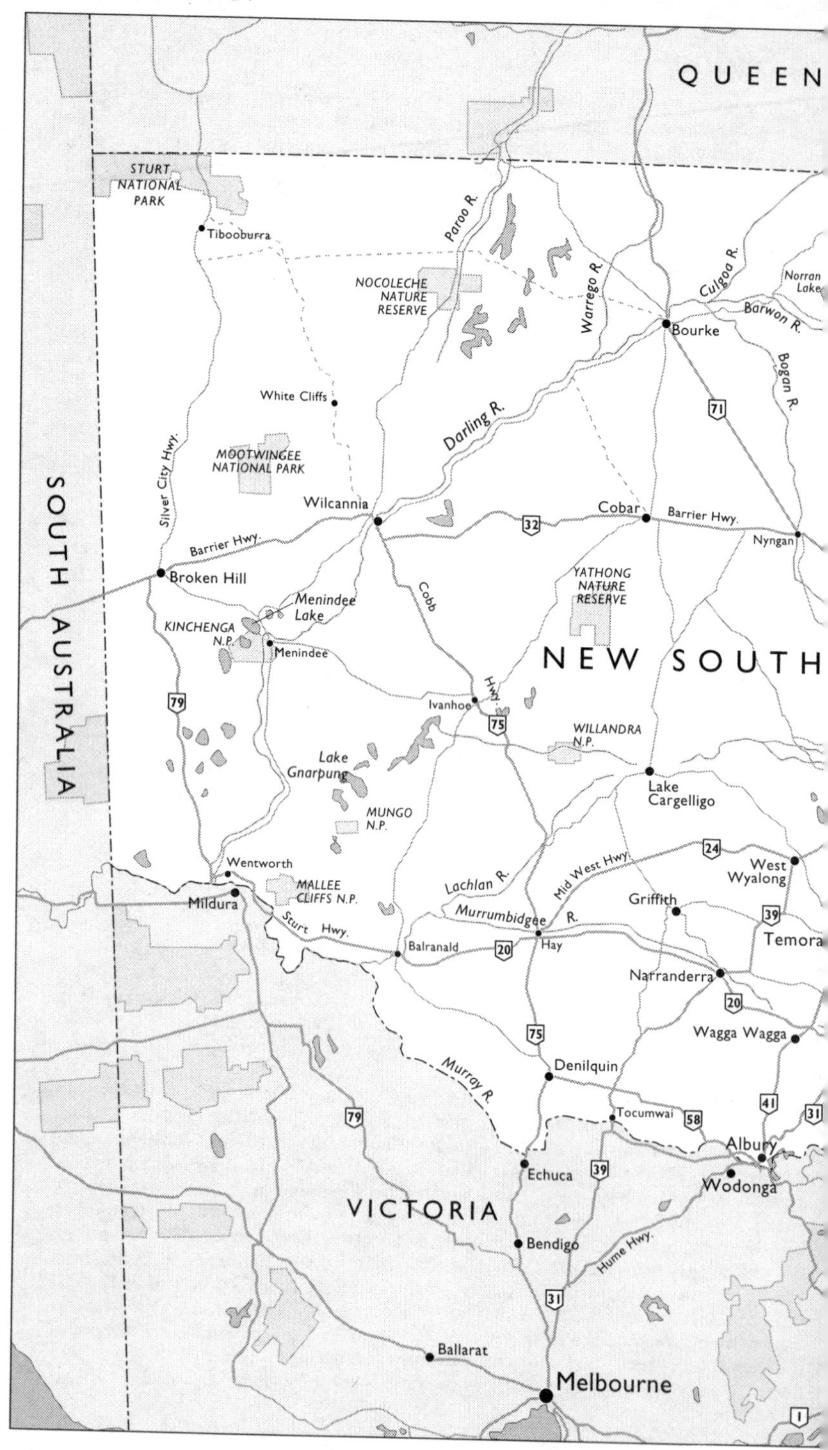
QUEEN
STURT NATIONAL PARK
Tibooburra
Paroo R.
NOCOLECHE NATURE RESERVE
Warrego R.
Culgoa R.
Norran Lake
Barwon R.
Bourke
Bogan R.
71
White Cliffs
Darling R.
MOOTWINGEE NATIONAL PARK
Silver City Hwy.
SOUTH AUSTRALIA
Wilcannia
Cobar
Barrier Hwy.
32
Nyngan
Barrier Hwy.
Broken Hill
Menindee Lake
Cobb
YATHONG NATURE RESERVE
KINCHENGA N.P.
Menindee
NEW SOUTH
Hwy.
79
Ivanhoe
75
WILLANDRA N.P.
Lake Gnarpung
Lake Cargelligo
MUNGO N.P.
Wentworth
Mid West Hwy.
24
West Wyalong
Lachlan R.
Mildura
MALLEE CLIFFS N.P.
Griffith
Murrumbidgee R.
39
Sturt Hwy.
Hay
Temora
Balranald
20
Narranderra
20
75
Wagga Wagga
Murray R.
Denilquin
79
41
31
Tocumwal
58
Albury
Echuca
39
Wodonga
VICTORIA
Bendigo
Hume Hwy.
31
Ballarat
Melbourne
1

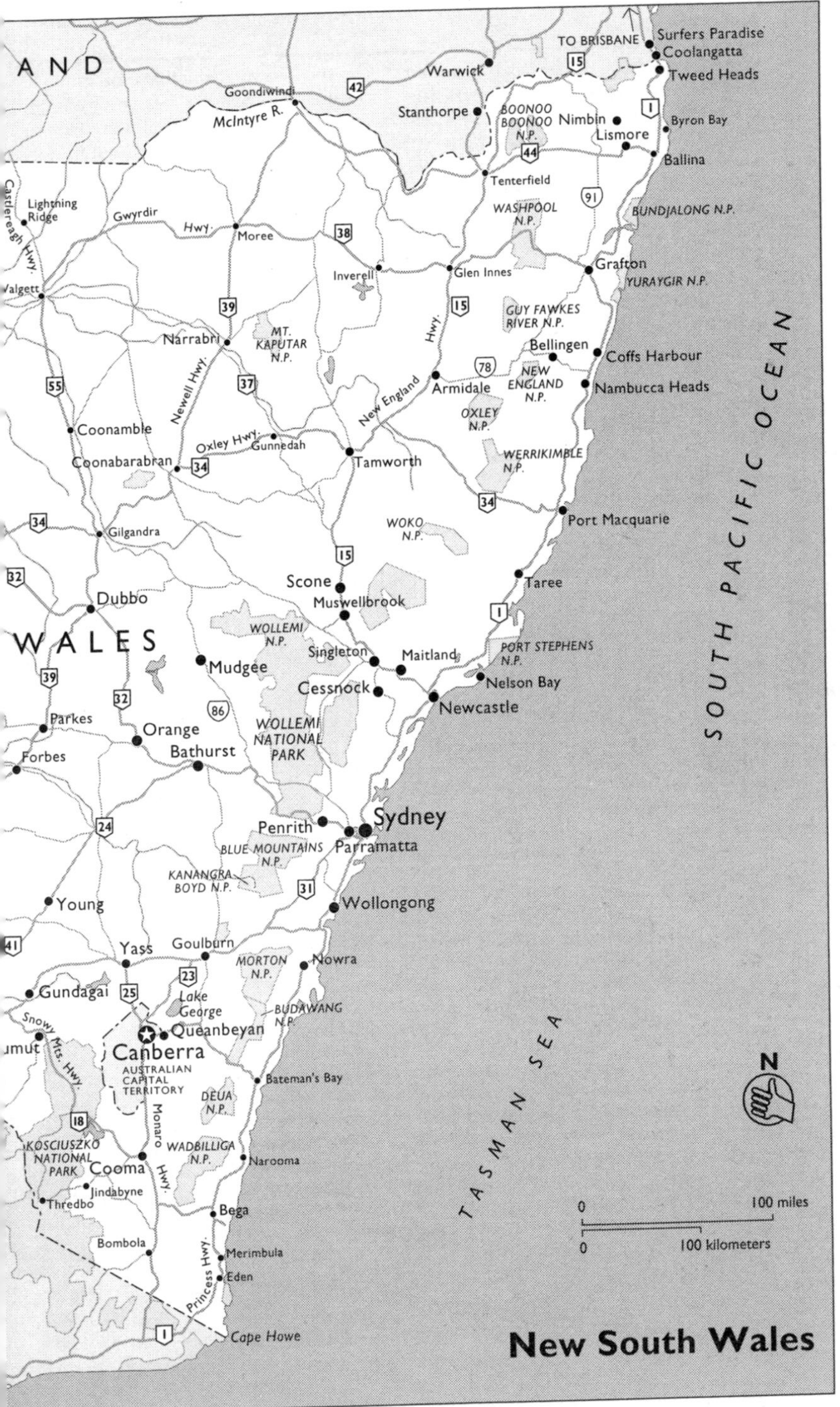
New South Wales
SOUTH PACIFIC OCEAN
TASMAN SEA
WALES
AND
TO BRISBANE
Surfers Paradise
Coolangatta
Tweed Heads
Warwick
Goondiwindi
McIntyre R.
Stanthorpe
BOONOO BOONOO N.P.
Nimbin
Lismore
Byron Bay
Ballina
Tenterfield
WASHPOOL N.P.
BUNDJALONG N.P.
Lightning Ridge
Castlereagh Hwy.
Gwyrdir Hwy.
Moree
Inverell
Glen Innes
Grafton
YURAYGIR N.P.
Walgett
GUY FAWKES RIVER N.P.
Narrabri
MT. KAPUTAR N.P.
Bellingen
Coffs Harbour
Nambucca Heads
Armidale
NEW ENGLAND N.P.
OXLEY N.P.
New England Hwy.
Newell Hwy.
Coonamble
Oxley Hwy.
Gunnedah
Tamworth
WERRIKIMBLE N.P.
Coonabarabran
Port Macquarie
Gilgandra
WOKO N.P.
Scone
Taree
Muswellbrook
Dubbo
WOLLEMI N.P.
Singleton
Maitland
PORT STEPHENS N.P.
Nelson Bay
Mudgee
Cessnock
Newcastle
Parkes
Orange
WOLLEMI NATIONAL PARK
Forbes
Bathurst
Sydney
Penrith
Parramatta
BLUE MOUNTAINS N.P.
KANANGRA BOYD N.P.
Young
Wollongong
Yass
Goulburn
MORTON N.P.
Nowra
Gundagai
Lake George
BUDAWANG N.P.
Snowy Mts. Hwy.
Tumut
Queanbeyan
Canberra
AUSTRALIAN CAPITAL TERRITORY
Bateman's Bay
DEUA N.P.
Monaro Hwy.
KOSCIUSZKO NATIONAL PARK
Cooma
WADBILLIGA N.P.
Narooma
Jindabyne
Thredbo
Bega
Bombola
Princess Hwy.
Merimbula
Eden
Cape Howe
0 100 miles
0 100 kilometers
N
15
42
1
44
91
38
39
15
78
55
37
34
34
34
32
15
1
39
32
86
24
31
41
23
25
18
1

BY TRAIN

Countrylink (tel. 13 22 32) has its main office in the Central Railway Station on Eddy Ave. Offices at Town Hall Station, in the Countrylink New South Wales Travel Centre next door to Wynyard Station, on Alfred St. at Circular Quay, and in Bondi Junction Station also sell tickets, but all trains embark from Central Station. Trains run to Adelaide (2 per week, 26hr., $148), Canberra (3 per day, 4hr., $40), Melbourne (2 per day, 10½hr., $90), Newcastle (many per day, 3¼hr., $20), and Brisbane (2 per day, 13½-15½hr., $90), via Coffs Harbour (8½hr., $65), Byron Bay (12½-13½hr., $79), and Surfer's Paradise (13-15hr., $85). Trains go less frequently to Perth, Cairns, Mount Isa, and Alice Springs. Many Countrylink itineraries include bus connections. Students, seniors, and ages 4-16 pay half-price on trips within NSW and slightly less discounted rates on interstate travel; children under 4 ride free in NSW and at a discount on interstate trips. See **By Bus,** below, for luggage storage information.

BY BUS

Fifteen bus companies operate from the **Sydney Coach Terminal,** Central Station (tel. 9281 9366), on Eddy Ave. at Pitt St. **Luggage lockers** cost $4 or $6 depending on size. Payment of the first day's fee must be made to secure the locker; the rest is paid upon retrieving your stuff. Because special rates and concessions vary from time to time and route to route, it is always wise to consult a travel agent for the lowest rate on any given itinerary at a given time. The two major national companies, **McCafferty's** (tel. 13 14 99; email infomcc@mccaffertys.com.au; http://www.mccaffertys.com.au) and **Greyhound Pioneer** (tel. 13 20 30), generally offer more frequent trips to major destinations than do the smaller regional carriers, but their rates are not always the best. **McCafferty's** to Adelaide (1 per day, 22hr., $96), Brisbane (4-5 per day, 15-17hr., $69), Byron Bay (1 per day, 13½hr., $67), Canberra (2 per day, 4½-5hr., $28), Coffs Harbour (2 per day, 11hr., $55), Melbourne (2 per day, 13½hr., $50), and Surfers Paradise (2-3 per day, 13½-16hr., $69). International students receive a 10% discount. Australian students, seniors, and ages 4-14 receive a 20% discount. Children under 4 free with two adults, half price with one adult. **Greyhound Pioneer** to Adelaide (3 per day, 20-23½hr., $99), Brisbane (3 per day, 15-16hr., $75), Byron Bay (3 per day, 12½-13½hr., $73), Canberra (9-12 per day, 4-5hr., $32), Coffs Harbour (3 per day, 9-10hr., $61), Melbourne (6 per day, 12-20hr., $66), and Surfers Paradise (3 per day, 13½-15hr., $75). Students, seniors, and ages 4-12 receive a 20% discount. Children under 4 travel for half price.

■ Orientation

In its broadest definition, the Sydney metropolitan area is huge and contained only by the force of nature, with Ku-Ring-Gai Chase National Park in the north, the Blue Mountains to the west, Royal National Park in the south, and the Pacific Ocean and Sydney Harbour on the east. Much of this area, however, is covered by the largely residential outer suburbs which few travelers feel a need to visit.

SYDNEY COVE AND THE CITY CENTER

Sydney's most famous sights lie on the harbor at **Sydney Cove,** directly north of the city center. On the west, the southern end of the **Sydney Harbour Bridge** is anchored in **The Rocks,** where tourists' dollars and developers' dreams have made it hard to imagine how a rowdy, run-down neighborhood could have existed before the boutiques. Drivers entering the southern half of the city from the north have two options, the Harbour Bridge and the **Harbour Tunnel** (southbound toll for either $2). Though less scenic, the tunnel is a more convenient route for anyone heading into the eastern suburbs. On the other side of the cove, **Sydney Opera House** occupies the most distant reach of Bennelong Point, with the Royal Botanic Gardens and a park called **the Domain** at its back. Ferries embark from the **Circular Quay** (pronounced key) wharves.

NEW SOUTH WALES

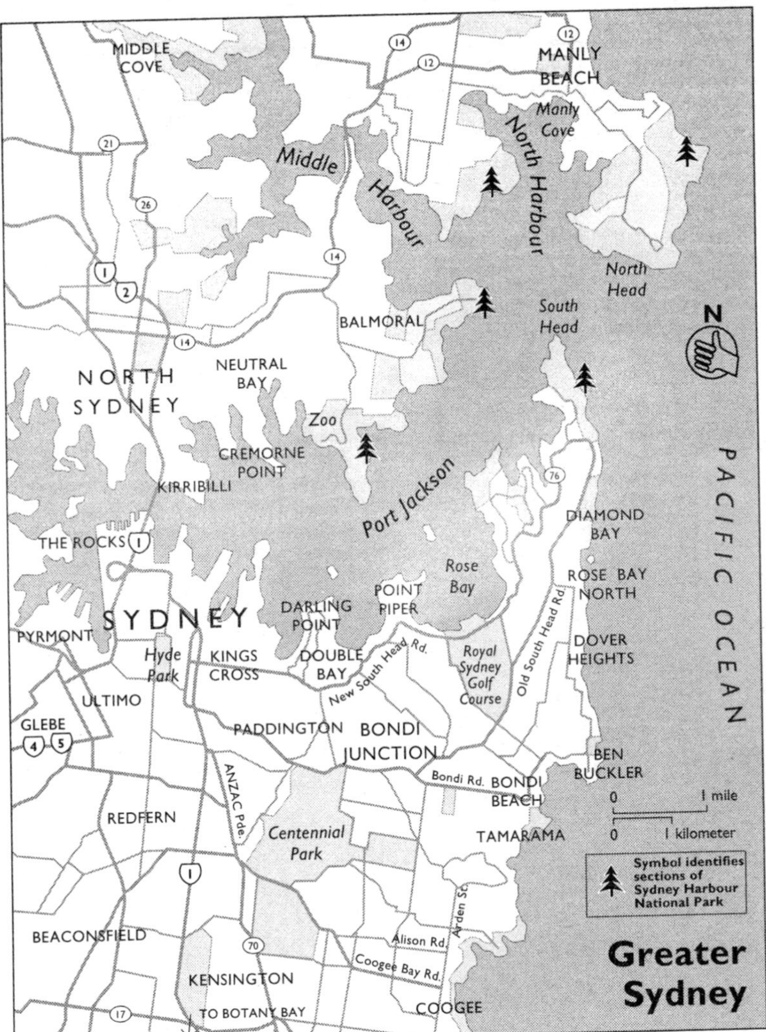

The city's attractions and most tourist services remain clustered in the area extending only about 5km south from Sydney Harbour between Johnstons Bay and Rushcutters Bay. Sydney proper, or the **city center,** is situated between **Circular Quay** in the north and **Central Station** in the south, and bounded roughly by Darling Harbour on the west and the **Royal Botanic Gardens** and **Hyde Park** on the east. The **central business district** centers on Martin Place, a pedestrian mall spanning the five blocks between George and Macquarie St. Moving south, the next major center of activity is **Town Hall,** located on Druitt St. between George and Kent St.

The city's one-stop travel hub, **Central Station,** on Eddy Ave. between Pitt and Chalmers St., is the arrival and departure point for regional buses and trains and a major stop for local public transportation. Convenient to most of the city's attractions by foot, bus, or subway, the area around Central Station supports several back-

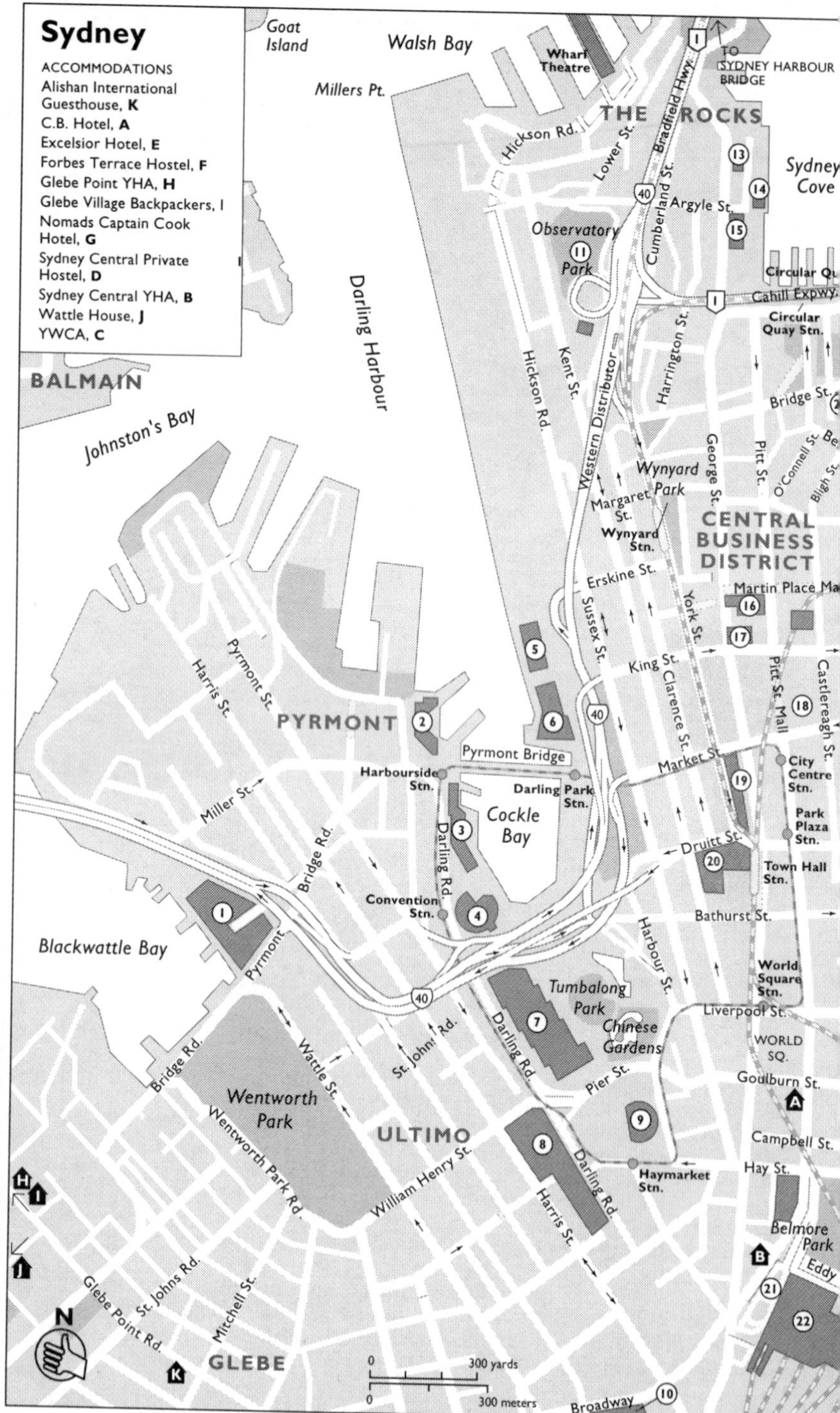
Sydney
ACCOMMODATIONS
Alishan International Guesthouse, K
C.B. Hotel, A
Excelsior Hotel, E
Forbes Terrace Hostel, F
Glebe Point YHA, H
Glebe Village Backpackers, I
Nomads Captain Cook Hotel, G
Sydney Central Private Hostel, D
Sydney Central YHA, B
Wattle House, J
YWCA, C
Goat Island
Walsh Bay
Millers Pt.
Wharf Theatre
TO SYDNEY HARBOUR BRIDGE
THE ROCKS
Hickson Rd.
Lower St.
Bradfield Hwy.
Cumberland St.
Argyle St.
Sydney Cove
Observatory Park
Circular Quay
Cahill Expwy.
Circular Quay Stn.
Darling Harbour
BALMAIN
Johnston's Bay
Hickson Rd.
Kent St.
Western Distributor
Harrington St.
Bridge St.
George St.
Pitt St.
O'Connell St.
Bligh St.
Wynyard Park
Margaret St.
Wynyard Stn.
CENTRAL BUSINESS DISTRICT
Erskine St.
Martin Place
York St.
Sussex St.
King St.
Clarence St.
Pitt St. Mall
Castlereagh St.
Pyrmont St.
Harris St.
PYRMONT
Pyrmont Bridge
Market St.
City Centre Stn.
Harbourside Stn.
Darling Park Stn.
Cockle Bay
Park Plaza Stn.
Miller St.
Darling Rd.
Druitt St.
Town Hall Stn.
Bridge Rd.
Convention Stn.
Bathurst St.
Blackwattle Bay
Pyrmont
Harbour St.
World Square Stn.
Tumbalong Park
Chinese Gardens
Liverpool St.
WORLD SQ.
Wattle St.
St. John's Rd.
Darling Rd.
Pier St.
Goulburn St.
Bridge Rd.
Wentworth Park
ULTIMO
Campbell St.
Wentworth Park Rd.
William Henry St.
Darling Rd.
Haymarket Stn.
Hay St.
Harris St.
Belmore Park
Eddy
Glebe Point Rd.
St. Johns Rd.
Mitchell St.
N
GLEBE
0
300 yards
300 meters
Broadway

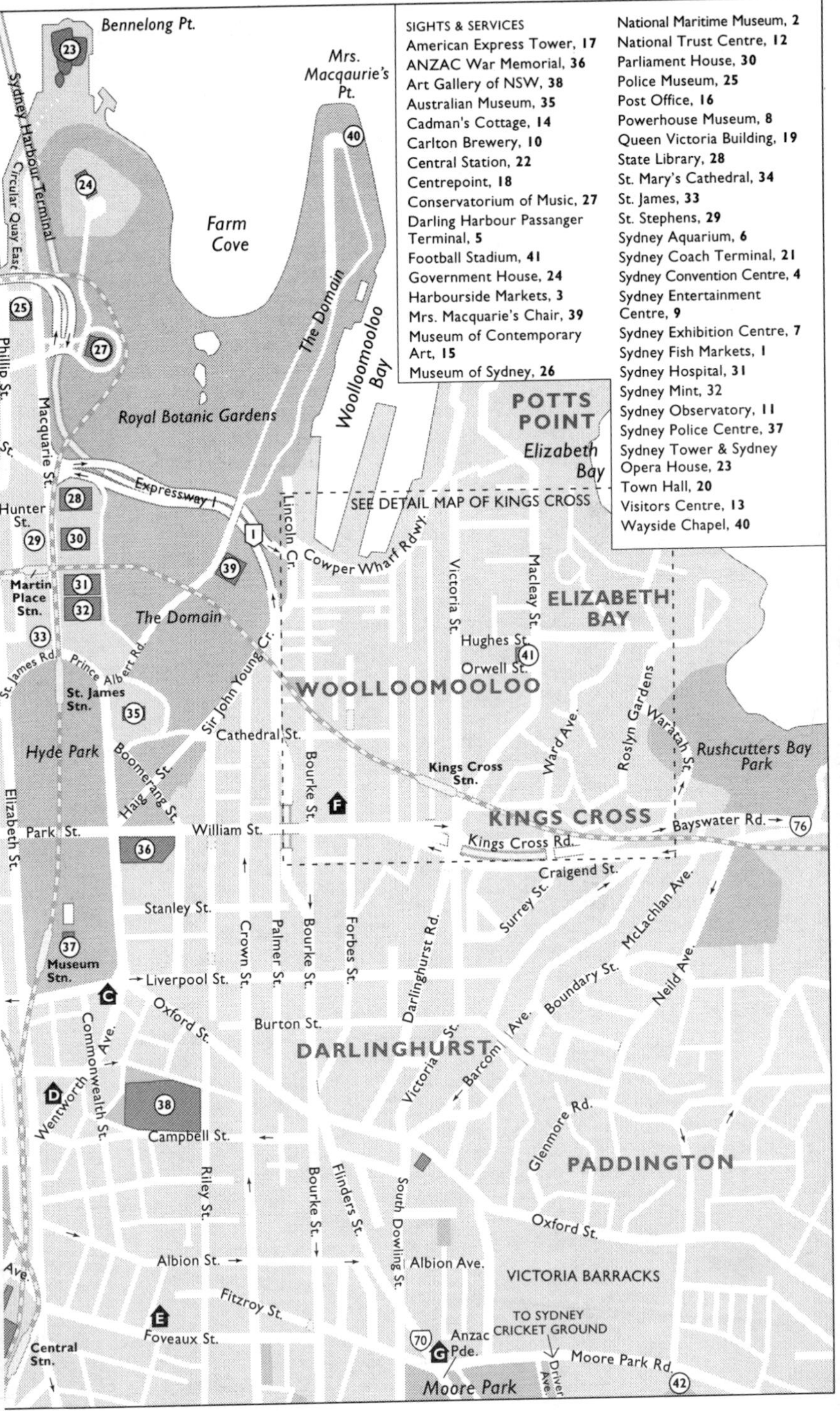
SIGHTS & SERVICES
American Express Tower, 17
ANZAC War Memorial, 36
Art Gallery of NSW, 38
Australian Museum, 35
Cadman's Cottage, 14
Carlton Brewery, 10
Central Station, 22
Centrepoint, 18
Conservatorium of Music, 27
Darling Harbour Passanger Terminal, 5
Football Stadium, 41
Government House, 24
Harbourside Markets, 3
Mrs. Macquarie's Chair, 39
Museum of Contemporary Art, 15
Museum of Sydney, 26
National Maritime Museum, 2
National Trust Centre, 12
Parliament House, 30
Police Museum, 25
Post Office, 16
Powerhouse Museum, 8
Queen Victoria Building, 19
State Library, 28
St. Mary's Cathedral, 34
St. James, 33
St. Stephens, 29
Sydney Aquarium, 6
Sydney Coach Terminal, 21
Sydney Convention Centre, 4
Sydney Entertainment Centre, 9
Sydney Exhibition Centre, 7
Sydney Fish Markets, 1
Sydney Hospital, 31
Sydney Mint, 32
Sydney Observatory, 11
Sydney Police Centre, 37
Sydney Tower & Sydney Opera House, 23
Town Hall, 20
Visitors Centre, 13
Wayside Chapel, 40
Bennelong Pt.
Mrs. Macqaurie's Pt.
Farm Cove
Sydney Harbour Terminal
Circular Quay East
Phillip St.
Macquarie St.
Royal Botanic Gardens
The Domain
Woolloomooloo Bay
POTTS POINT
Elizabeth Bay
Expressway 1
SEE DETAIL MAP OF KINGS CROSS
Lincoln Cr.
Cowper Wharf Rdwy.
Victoria St.
Macleay St.
ELIZABETH BAY
Hunter St.
Martin Place Stn.
Hughes St.
Orwell St.
St. James Rd.
Prince Albert Rd.
St. James Stn.
Sir John Young Cr.
WOOLLOOMOOLOO
Roslyn Gardens
Waratah St.
Rushcutters Bay Park
Ward Ave.
Hyde Park
Boomerang St.
Haig St.
Cathedral St.
Bourke St.
Kings Cross Stn.
KINGS CROSS
Bayswater Rd.
Elizabeth St.
Park St.
William St.
Kings Cross Rd.
Craigend St.
Surrey St.
McLachlan Ave.
Stanley St.
Crown St.
Palmer St.
Forbes St.
Darlinghurst Rd.
Museum Stn.
Liverpool St.
Boundary St.
Neild Ave.
Oxford St.
Burton St.
Commonwealth Ave.
DARLINGHURST
Victoria St.
Barcom Ave.
Wentworth Ave.
Commonwealth St.
Campbell St.
Glenmore Rd.
PADDINGTON
Riley St.
Flinders St.
South Dowling St.
Albion St.
Albion Ave.
VICTORIA BARRACKS
Fitzroy St.
TO SYDNEY CRICKET GROUND
Foveaux St.
Anzac Pde.
Moore Park Rd.
Central Stn.
Moore Park
Driver Ave.

packer accommodations and a good number of cheap restaurants. Sydney's growing **Chinatown** can be found just northwest of the station, radiating from the intersection of Hay, Sussex, and George St.

INNER SUBURBS

Many tiny municipalities known as the **inner suburbs** populate the rest of Sydney's central urban area. Despite their proximity, the suburbs do maintain distinct characters and special attractions. The only confusing part of the system is that many areas overlap and some are known by more than one name. West of the city center, **Pyrmont** covers the point of land between Darling Harbour and Blackwattle Bay. This area, the waterside part of which is also called **Darling Harbour,** contains several of the city's major museums and presents itself as something of an up-market tourist park. South of Pyrmont, **Ultimo** approaches the west side of Central Station and reaches up to the area around Hay St. which is both recognized as Chinatown and referred to as **Haymarket. Glebe,** southwest of Ultimo and just north of the University of Sydney, benefits from the presence of students in all of the usual ways: casual cafes, cheap food, fun pubs, and good bookstores. Glebe Point Rd. is the center of activity in this district. **Newtown,** on the southern side of the uni, feels the student influence, but manages to stay a little rougher around the edges. Body-piercing is more than a fad in the cafes on King St.

The inner suburb of **Kings Cross,** east of the city center at the far end of William St., reigns as the undisputed center of Sydney backpacker culture. Lively, crowded hostels and cafes line Victoria St. north of William St., while car rental agencies light up William St. into the evening. As the XXX theaters on Darlinghurst Rd. suggest, however, the neighborhood has a reputation for vice. Travelers should watch all belongings in the Cross and take caution walking alone at night.

North of Kings Cross, **Woolloomooloo** gets down to the business of shipping while Potts Point and Elizabeth Bay house and feed some of Sydney's wealthier denizens. Here again, suburban borders get fuzzy; a Potts Point address may be across the street from your Kings Cross hostel. To the south of Kings Cross, **Victoria St.** goes chic with some of the city's coolest cafes lining the way to **Darlinghurst.** Along with **Surry Hills** to the south and **Paddington** to the east, Darlinghurst provides fashionable housing for young, creative types. The shops and eateries on **Oxford St.,** the main road through Darlinghurst, Paddington, and Woollahra, to the east, offer a tempting slice of this life to anyone who has the time to browse. **Moore Park,** just south of the army's stately Victoria Barracks, and **Centennial Park** on the eastern side of Moore Park form the city's largest swath of greenery. Here you'll find Sydney's major **athletic facilities,** including Sydney Football Stadium, Sydney Cricket Ground, and the Royal Agriculture Society Showgrounds. **Redfern,** southeast of Surry Hills and directly south of Central Station, is a low-income neighborhood considered unsavory and possibly unsafe by many Sydney-siders.

FAR EAST AND SOUTHERN BEACHES

Outside of these central areas, the surroundings get significantly less urban. Just east of Paddington, Woollahra's terrace houses provide a nice change of scenery from the city center highrises. Double Bay and Rose Bay dip into the shore north of Woolahra, lending their names to some of Sydney's most expensive residential areas. **Bondi Junction,** south of Woolahra, is the last train stop on the eastern end of the subway system. Here, travelers looking for the shore catch the bus that will take them 10 minutes east to Sydney's famous **Bondi** (BOND-eye) **Beach,** the scene after which many a surf movie has been modeled. Farther south, the beaches of Tamarama, Clovelly, and **Coogee,** also accessible by bus, offer low-key alternatives for families and quieter sunbathers.

NORTH SHORE

The second half of Sydney's professional district fronts the **north shore** of Sydney Harbour at the other end of Harbour Bridge. Tourist attractions on the north shore are essentially limited to **Taronga Park Zoo** in Mosman and the beach community of **Manly.** The ferry ride is enough to justify a trip across, though, and Manly works hard to make itself inviting by complementing natural beauty with galleries and other attractions.

■ Getting Around

Sydney is nothing if not navigable. The standard city map, with its many boldfaced suburban labels, creates the impression that Sydney's central area is far larger than it actually is. In truth, the areas that Sydney-siders call suburbs most other people would call neighborhoods, and small ones at that. The walk from Central Station to Circular Quay along Pitt St. takes less than 30 minutes. From Kings Cross, one can walk to Town Hall in 15 minutes.

Comprised of **Sydney Buses, CityRail** trains, and **Sydney Ferries,** the **Sydney Transit Authority (STA)** network stops just about anywhere one might want to go, from the city center to the farthest suburbs. For **information** or route advice on any part of the STA system, call 13 15 00 (TTY 1800 637 500; calls taken daily 6am-10pm). Although the STA does not distribute maps, the free brochure *Sydney: The Official Book of Maps,* available from all CountryLink offices and most tourist information outlets, contains detailed maps of all train and ferry routes and an overview of the suburban bus system. The network divides Sydney into several travel zones, and assigns different fees for travel between particular zones. If you plan to be in Sydney for more than a couple of days, it may be worthwhile to figure out the range of exploration you plan to undertake and to purchase one of the many passes which allows passengers to combine two or three types of transportation within a given area. The one-week **TravelPass** for the four center-most zones includes unlimited seven-day access to buses, trains, and ferries for just $21. An additional $6 expands the range of travel to include the ferry to Manly and more suburban buses.

BY BUS

Because several bus routes pass many Sydney bus stops, passengers must be prepared to hail the correct bus like a taxi when it comes down the road. Drivers may not stop for a pick-up unless someone at the bus stand is signaling. A bus ticket may cost as little as $1.20 for travel within the city center and as much as $4.60 for more distant suburban destinations (students and ages 4-16 pay half-price, seniors buy special $1-3 tickets). Most trips within the areas which are of primary interest to travelers run about $2. Payment is expected upon boarding the bus, but drivers will give change. Color-coded **TravelTen** passes cover 10 bus trips at a significant discount. Price varies with the distance to be traveled; a Blue TravelTen accounts for trips within the city center and in most inner suburbs ($8.40), while a Red TravelTen allows for a wider range of options ($16.40). The **Bus Tripper** ($7.80) covers one day of unlimited bus travel. Most buses circulate between 5am and 11:30pm, but there is 24-hour service between the city center, Kings Cross, and other central locales. If you are concerned about being out too late to catch a bus, call the STA info line (tel. 13 15 00) before setting out.

In addition to local commuter bus service, the STA operates two sight-seeing buses, the **Sydney Explorer** and the **Bondi & Bay Explorer,** which allow passengers to get on and off at major tourist attractions along their designated routes. The Explorer service is expensive, at $22 for a one-day pass for either route (ages 4-16 $16, 2-parent families with any number of kids $60), but it can be an excellent way to do concentrated touring. The Sydney Explorer takes in sights between the harbor and Central Station, moving as far east as Woolloomooloo Bay and as far west as Darling Harbour, at 15- minute intervals from 8:40am to 6:50pm. Bondi & Bay Explorer service visits the eastern bays and southern beaches, down to Coogee, from 9:15am to 5:55pm every 25 minutes. Start early if you want to get your money's worth.

The granddaddy of all Sydney Transit passes, the **Sydney Pass** includes unlimited bus, train, and ferry use within the basic TravelPass zone, round-trip Airport Express service, access to both Explorer Buses, and passage on Sydney Harbour cruises and the higher-speed ferries to Manly and Parramatta. The Sydney Pass can be purchased for use on three, five, or seven days within any seven-day period (3-day pass $66, ages 4-16 $55, families $187; 5-day pass $88, $77, and $253; 7-day pass $99, $88, and $286), and constitutes a serious financial commitment to hard-core sight-seeing.

BY TRAIN

Sydney's **CityRail** subway system rumbles under the city from Bondi Junction in the east to the most distant corners of the suburban sprawl in the north, west, and south. Service is fast, frequent, and easy to navigate. CityRail's lowest fare is $1.60, but most trips cost a bit more. During peak hours (before 9am on weekdays) return fares are double the one-way price. At all other times, purchase of a round-trip "off-peak return" ticket gets you a sizable discount. The combined service TravelPass detailed above generally works out to a bargain for regular subway users. CityRail trains hug the rails daily from 5am to 11:30pm.

BY FERRY

An inexpensive way to get an excellent view of the harbor, a ferry ride can be seen as both transport and entertainment. Aimless cruising is highly recommended. Ferries embark from the **Circular Quay** wharves between the Opera House and the Harbour Bridge. Short trips in the harbor cost $2.80 one-way; a **FerryTen** pass for the same area, much like the TravelTen bus pass described above, has a price tag of $16.60. The fare for high-speed JetCat cruises to Manly is $3.80, and the corresponding FerryTen pass goes for $26.60. The STA's fastest, longest, and most expensive commuter ferry service is the RiverCat to Parramatta ($4.60 one-way; FerryTen $31). For $12, **DayPass** affords you unlimited use of the full range of Sydney Ferries and local buses for one day. Ferries set out daily 5am to 11:30pm.

Always thinking of the tourist's travel needs, STA administers several daily **Sydney Ferries Harbour Cruises,** the one-hour Morning Cruise ($12, ages 4-16 $8, families $32), the two-and-a-half hour Afternoon Cruise ($16, $12, $44) and the 90-minute after-dark Harbour Lights Cruise ($14, $10, $38). The Sydney Ferries information line (tel. 9207 3166) has departure times and route descriptions for all of these trips. Quayside Booking Centre (see **Practical Information,** below) has brochures for private companies which offer more deluxe ferry cruise services.

BY CAR

National Roads and Motorists Association (NRMA), 151 Clarence St. (tel. 13 11 22 or 9892 0355; open Mon.-Fri. 9am-5pm, Sat. 9am-noon), in the block between King and Barrack St., publishes good maps of Sydney and New South Wales. Mechanical inspections $105, or $125 for nonmembers. Members, and members of affiliated national auto clubs (see **Essentials,** p. 37), can also call for roadside assistance. Membership costs $84 for the first year, $44 for each additional year.

All major international **rental** companies have desks in Kingsford-Smith Airport, and most appear again on William St. near Kings Cross. The big names include **Avis,** 214 William St. (tel. 9353 9000), **Budget,** 76 Anzac Parade (tel. 13 27 27), **Hertz** (tel. 13 30 39), on the corner of William and Riley St., and **Thrifty,** 78 William St. (tel. 9380 5399). Budget cuts a little lower than the others with small, manual transmission cars for $55 per day (with 100km free), and automatic transmission cars for $59 per day. Deductibles (called "excess" in Australia) are $2500, or $900 with a $12 per day fee. (25¢ per extra km. Ages 21-24 pay $18 per day surcharge. Open daily 7:30am-6pm.) Younger drivers should try Thrifty, but those under 21 will have trouble tracking down a car at any major operation. Thrifty cars start at $61 per day, with unlimited kilometers, plus an $8 per day surcharge for ages 21 to 24. The deductible is $1500, or $250 with a $10 per day fee (open daily 8am-6pm).

In general, local or regional companies offer much better deals than the big companies. **Delta Car Rentals,** 77 William St. (tel. 9380 6288), has small, manual cars for $29 per day with a rental of at least one week. Automatics cost $52 per day, with 50km included (deductible $1500, ages 21-24 $5000; open Mon.-Fri. 7:30am-6pm). **Ascot,** 113 William St. (tel. 9317 2111), drops to $29 per day for manual transmission cars on rentals of one month or more, while automatics go for $35 per day. By the week, manual cars cost $49 per day, and automatics $56 per day. All rentals include 100km per day. (Extra km 15¢, ages 21-24 pay a $7 surcharge per day. Deductible $1000, ages 25-28 $1500, ages 21-24 $2500. Open daily 7am-7pm.) All companies offer reduced rates for rentals over longer periods, and most offer free pick-up from the airport or Central Station.

Hostel noticeboards overflow with fliers for privately-owned cars, campers, and motorcycles **selling** for as little as several hundred dollars. See **Essentials,** p. 37, for more information on car sales. **Kings Cross Car Market** (tel. 9358 5000 or 1800 808 188; fax 9358 5102), on the second level of the Kings Cross Car Park on the corner of Ward Ave. and Elizabeth Bay Rd., brings buyers and cars together daily from 9am to 5pm. **Travellers Auto Barn,** 177 William St. (tel. 9360 1500; fax 9360 1977), caters to the need for certainty with guaranteed buy-back agreements on cars from $3000. Minimum buy-back rates range from 40% to 50% of purchase price depending on the length of time you take the car. (Free NRMA Service membership; open Mon.-Sat. 9am-6pm, Sun. 10:30am-4pm.) **Boomerang Car Market,** 30 Ewan St. (tel. 9700 8595), in the southern suburb of Mascot, guarantees buy-back at 40% on cars from $2000 (call ahead for free pick-up; open daily 9am-5pm). Both outfit cars with camping gear and provide full auto maintenance before you go. When it comes time to sell, try the car market or other private means before collecting on your guaranteed buy-back price. People often lose less than they expected to.

BY TAXI

Finding a ride on most corners in the city center and inner suburbs is as easy as stepping off the curb. Taxis charge an initial fare of $3 plus $1.07 per kilometer of travel. An additional charge of $1 is applied for call-in pick-up service. The city's major cab providers include **Legion Cabs** (tel. 13 14 51), **RSL Taxis** (tel. 9581 1111), and **Taxis Combined** (tel. 9332 8888). All three conduct business 24 hours.

BY BICYCLE

Bicycle rental shops are less common than you might expect in a backpacker-friendly city like Sydney, although several "hire" shops are located south of Centennial Park, on Clovelly Rd. (bus #339 from Central Station). **Australian Cycle Company,** 28 Clovelly Rd. (tel. 9399 3475), across from the bus stop on Earl St., has 18-speed mountain bikes for $8 per hour (2hr. $12, full day $25; open daily 9am-5pm). Closer to the center of town, **Inner City Cycles,** 31 Glebe Point Rd. (tel. 9660 6605), 50m from the Broadway St. end of the road on the right, rents similar bikes for $30 per day ($150 per week; open Mon.-Wed. and Fri. 9am-6pm, Thurs. 9am-8pm, Sat. 9am-4pm, Sun. 11am-4pm). For a coastal ride, visit **Manly Cycle Centre,** 36 Pittwater Rd. (tel. 9977 1189), at Denison St. in Manly. (1hr. $10, each additional hr. $5, full day $25, week $60. Open Mon.-Wed. and Fri. 9am-6pm, Thurs. 9am-7pm, Sat. 9am-4:30pm, Sun. 11am-3pm.) All of these shops require a credit card or a prohibitive cash deposit.

■ Practical Information

TOURIST AND TRAVEL INFORMATION

Tourist Office: Country Link New South Wales Travel Centre, 1-31 York St. (tel. 9224 4744), at Margaret St. in the city center (Train: Wynyard Station), functions as both a tourist information center and a travel agency. Lots of brochures, free maps—including the otherwise hard to find local subway and bus maps—and Australia-wide plane, train, bus, and accommodation reservation service. Open Mon.-Fri. 8:30am-5pm. **Sydney Visitors Information Kiosk** (tel. 9235 2424), on top of Martin Place subway station, between Castlereagh and Elizabeth St. Open Mon.-Fri. 9am-5pm. **Quayside Booking Centre,** Jetty 6, Circular Quay (24hr. tel. 9555 2700; fax 9555 2701), on the waterfront, is open daily 8am-6pm.

Travel Offices: Student Uni Travel, 92 Pitt St., on level 8 (tel. 9232 8444; email unitrav@world.ne; http://www.ozomail.com.au/~gotravel), across from the GPO on Martin Place. Free email and internet access. Mail forwarding. Open Mon.-Fri. 8:30am-6pm, Sat. 10am-2pm. **Travellers Contact Point,** 428 George St., level 7 (tel. 9221 8744; fax 9221 3746; email tcp@travellers-contact.com.au), between King and Market St. Internet access $5 per 30min. Word processing $5 per hr. Mail forwarding and holding in Australia $40 per year. Open Mon.-Fri. 9am-6pm, Sat. 10am-4pm. **YHA Membership and Travel Center,** 422 Kent St. (tel. 9261 1111), behind Town Hall, between Market and Druitt St. Domestic ($2) and international ($5) hostel reservations available. Open Mon.-Fri. 9am-5pm, Sat. 10am-2pm.

Consulates: Canada, 111 Harrington St., level 5 (tel. 9364 3000). Open Mon.-Fri. 8:30am-4:30pm. **France,** 31 Market St. (tel. 9261 5779). Open Mon.-Fri. 9am-1pm. **Germany,** 13 Trelawney St. (tel. 9328 7733), off Ocean St. in Woollahra. Open Mon.-Fri. 9am-noon, Wed. 2-3pm. **New Zealand,** 1 Alfred St., level 14 (tel. 9247 1999), on the corner of George St. at Circular Quay. Passport office open Mon.-Fri. 9am-4pm, no phone service 1-2pm. Visa office open Mon.-Tues. and Fri. 10am-4pm, Wed.-Thurs. 10am-noon and 2-4pm, no phone service Mon.-Fri. noon-2pm. **Switzerland,** 500 Oxford St., level 23 (tel. 9369 4244), in Bondi Junction over the Westfield Shopping Centre. Open Mon.-Fri. 9am-2pm. **U.K.,** 1 Macquarie Pl., level 16 (tel. 9247 7521). Open Mon.-Fri. 10am-4:30pm. **U.S.,** 19-29 Martin Pl., #59 (tel. 9373 9200), in the MLC Centre. Open Mon.-Fri. 8am-12:30pm.

FINANCIAL SERVICES

Banks and exchange offices which will change money and traveler's checks during regular business hours (roughly Mon.-Fri. 9am-5pm) are scattered liberally throughout the central business district, the harborside, and Kings Cross. Abundant ATMs are affiliated mostly with the Plus and Visa networks. Cirrus machines are less common.

Thomas Cook has several locations in the international terminal of Kingsford-Smith Airport. Service charge 3%; minimum of $4. Open daily 5:30am-10:30pm.

Singapore Money Exchange, 67 Darlinghurst Rd. (tel. 9368 0972), in Kings Cross, exchanges at competitive rates with no commissions or service charges for currency or traveler's checks. The exception: 4% service charge to cash traveler's checks in Australian dollars. Other offices at 304-308 George St. (tel. 9223 6361), opposite Wynyard Station; in Chinatown, 401 Sussex St. (tel. 9212 7124); and on the Castlereagh St. level of Centrepoint Tower (tel. 9223 9222). All offices open Mon.-Sat. 9am-6pm, Sun. 9am-5pm.

Money Change, on the pedestrian mall at Darlinghurst Rd. and Springfield Ave. in Kings Cross, keeps the best hours in town, but the commission goes as high as 5% for traveler's checks. Open Sun.-Fri. 8am-11pm, Sat. 8am-1am.

American Express Office, 92 Pitt St. (tel. 9239 0666; fax 9236 9240), around the corner from Martin Pl., next door to the ANZ Bank. Traveller's Cheques cashed and currency exchanged for a 1% commission. Mail held for up to a month; $1 charge for those who use neither an AmEx card nor their Traveller's Cheques. Open Mon.-Fri. 8:30am-5:30pm, Sat. 9am-noon.

EMERGENCY AND SOCIAL SERVICES

Library: Sydney City Library, Town Hall House (tel. 9265 9470; 24hr. recorded information 9265 9053), on the corner of Kent and Druitt St. From Town Hall Station, walk through the arcade and enter off of Sydney Square. Open Mon.-Fri. 8am-7pm, Sat. 9am-noon. Another location at 744 George St. (tel. 9281 9491). Open Mon.-Fri. 8:30am-6pm, Sat. 10am-1pm.

Bookstores: Dymocks Booksellers, 424-430 George St. (tel. 9235 0155). For the traveler collecting superlatives, the southern hemisphere's largest bookshop.

Open Mon.-Wed. and Fri. 9am-6pm, Thurs. 9am-9pm, Sat. 9am-5pm, Sun. 10am-5pm. **Abbey's Bookshops,** 131 York St. (tel. 9264 3111), next to the Queen Victoria Building. Open Mon.-Fri. 8:30am-6pm, Sat. 9am-5pm, Sun. 10am-5pm. **Berkelouw Books,** 19 Oxford St. (tel. 9360 3200). Open daily 10am-midnight. Both are local favorites for selection, atmosphere, and pricing. **Gleebooks,** 49 Glebe Point Rd. (tel. 9660 2333; new books), just off Parramatta Rd., keeps its huge collection of used books and children's literature at 191 Glebe Point Rd. (tel. 9552 2526), just north of St. John's Rd. Both locations open daily 8am-9pm.

Ticket Agencies: Ticketek (tel. 9266 4800; http://www.com.au/ticketek) and **Halftix** operate out of the same kiosk as Sydney Visitors Information, at Martin Place, between Castlereagh and Elizabeth St. Ticketek handles full-price advance booking for music, theater, sports, and selected museums in the Sydney area. Ticketek open Mon.-Fri. 9am-5:30pm, Sat. 10:30am-5pm. Halftix sells half-priced same-day tickets for a less extensive slate of events and discounted admission to the city's major museums. The daily roster of available tickets is posted on the kiosk at noon and can be accessed by phone from 11am. Halftix open Mon.-Fri. noon-5:30pm, Sat. 10:30am-5pm. **First Call** (24hr. tel. 9320 9000) handles ticketing for many of the city's theatrical venues, both large and small, sometimes overlapping the Ticketek offerings.

Weather: For conditions 24hr., dial 1196.

Hotlines: Wayside Chapel Crisis Centre, 29 Hughes St. (tel. 9228 2111), off MacLeay St. in Potts Point, just north of Kings Cross. Calls taken daily 7am-11pm, 11pm-7am when staffing permits. **Alcohol and Drug Information Service:** tel. 9361 2111. Crisis counseling 24hr. **Rape Crisis Centre:** 24hr. tel. 9819 6565. **HIV/AIDS Information Line:** tel. 9332 4000 or 24hr. 9332 1090.

Late-Night Pharmacy (Chemist): Wu's Pharmacy, 629 George St. (tel. 9211 1805), near Hay St. in Chinatown. Open Mon.-Sat. 9am-9pm, Sun. 9am-7pm. **Chemist Emergency Prescription Service:** 24hr. tel. 9235 0333.

Medical Services: Sydney Hospital (tel. 9382 7111; vaccinations 9361 2685), on Macquarie St. opposite the Martin Pl. station. **Traveller's Medical and Vaccination Centre,** 428 George St., level 7 (tel. 9221 7133). Consultation fee $35. Open Mon.-Wed. and Fri. 9am-6pm, Thurs. 9am-8pm, Sat. 9am-1pm. **Kings Cross Travellers' Clinic,** 13 Springfield Ave. (tel. 9358 3066). Consultation fee $30. Open Mon.-Fri. 9:30am-6pm, Sat. 10am-noon. A full complement of vaccinations for traveling in tropical regions will cost about $150 at either place. **Contraceptive Services,** 195 Macquarie St., level 13 (tel. 9221 1933), specializes in contraception and sexual diseases. Open Mon.-Fri. 8:30am-4:30pm.

Police: Sydney Police Centre, 151 Riley St. (24hr. tel. 9265 4144), on Goulburn St., in Surry Hills.

Emergency: Dial 000.

POST AND COMMUNICATIONS

Internet Access: Coin-operated internet terminals are popping up throughout the city, and several Kings Cross hostels will feature this perk by 1998. **Student Uni Travel** and **Travellers Contact Point** (see **Travel Offices,** p. 98) currently offer free access. **Jolly Swagman Backpackers,** 27 Orwell St. (tel. 9358 6400), and **Kings Cross Hotel,** at the intersection of Victoria St., Darlinghurst Rd., and William St., across from the giant Coke sign, both offer 10min. for $2 at convenient locations in Kings Cross. The Internet Cafe at **Hotel Sweeney,** 236 Clarence St. (tel. 9261 5666), has 9 terminals charging $2 per 10min. Open Mon.-Fri. 9am-9pm, Sat. noon-6pm.

Post Office: Sydney General Post Office (GPO), 159-171 Pitt St. (tel. 13 13 17), on Martin Pl., is currently being renovated. Stamps, boxes, and other postal supplies can be purchased across the street at 130 Pitt St. Open Mon.-Fri. 8:15am-5:30pm, Sat. 9am-1pm. *Poste Restante* awaits at 310 George St., inside Hunter Connection across from Wynyard Station. Enter under the "Through to Pitt Street" sign. Computer terminals allow you to check whether or not anything has arrived for you before you bother the person at the counter. Open Mon.-Fri. 8:15am-5:30pm. **Postal code:** 2000 for city center, 2001 for *Poste Restante.*

Phone Code: 02.

■ Accommodations

As most travelers' gateway to Australia, Sydney supports a thriving hostel and budget hotel market with little seasonal variation in pricing. Dorm beds in the city generally cost only $2 more than the listed price during the high season of November through February. The beach areas see the largest rate hikes, with prices rising as much as 40% during these months.

The first question most travelers must answer when finding a bed in Sydney is whether or not to stay in Kings Cross. Well-located, traveler-friendly, and party-ready, Kings Cross has a well-known reputation among backpackers, and the high concentration of hostels ensures that beds are almost always available. However, the presence of prostitutes and the profusion of go-go bars make many travelers uncomfortable. In addition, stories of regular theft are rampant. If you do opt to stay in the Cross, be sure you feel comfortable with your hostel's security measures before letting your valuables out of your sight. Because the seediness of Darlinghurst Rd. tends toward the 24-hour-neon-induced variety, matters of personal safety usually feel less pressing than questions of property security.

Sydney's **camping** areas have been banished to the outskirts of the metropolitan area by haphazard urban growth. The three listed (see p. 106) are all accessible by public transportation, but the cost of repeated bus and train trips makes most sites less economical than hostel beds in the city center.

Unless stated otherwise, hostels accept major credit cards, and have a common room with a TV, hall bathrooms, 24-hour access, a $10 key deposit, and free pick-up from airport, bus, and train stations. They have no chores, no parking, and no wheelchair access. Laundry, when facilities are present, is $2 per wash or dry.

KINGS CROSS AND AROUND

Jolly Swagman Backpackers, 144 Victoria St. (tel./fax 9357 4733; http://www.ozemail.com.au/~bacpac); 16 Orwell St. (tel. 9358 6600), under the Sydney Central Backpackers sign; and 27 Orwell St. (tel. 9358 6400). Among its 3 locations, the Jolly Swagman offers just about every service a traveler could need: a travel agency and roof-top dining on Victoria St., a cafe and internet access ($2 per 10min.) at 27 Orwell St., and a respite from the relative craziness of the Cross at 16 Orwell St. All 3 focus first on providing clean, bright rooms and some of Sydney's most engaging hostel atmospheres. The common rooms and kitchens are ample and lively, and group activities such as videos and pub crawls fill the calendar. Fridges, lockers, and sinks in the rooms. Coin-op laundry at the Orwell St. locations. Reception open daily 8am-8pm; 24hr. at 27 Orwell St. Check-out 9am. 4-bed dorms $16; doubles $35. Weekly: $93; $240. Linen included. Key deposit $20.

The Pink House, 6-8 Barncleuth Sq. (tel. 9358 1689), off Ward Ave. Unlike the other Kings Cross hostels, the Pink House feels like a house—a big, fun, and very pink house. Rooms and common spaces have big windows that look out into the surrounding foliage. Brick kitchen opens onto garden terrace. Planned events include weekly trivia nights and happy hours. Laundry facilities. Free email and word-processing at another location. Internet $7 per hr. Up to 6-bed dorms $17; doubles and twins $38; garden flats $20. Weekly: $100; $220; $120. VIP, YHA. Deposit $15-30, depending on whether you just borrow the key or add on linens and kitchen supplies. Often full, so reserve in advance.

Eva's Backpackers, 6-8 Orwell St. (tel. 9358 2158; fax 9358 3259). Primary colors may remind you of a child's bedroom, but the homecoming is a happy one. Eva's is popular for its tidy rooms, agreeable management, and homey community feel. Roof-top garden, laundry facilities, and plentiful common space add to its charm. Safe for valuables. 28-day max. stay. Reception open daily 8am-1pm and 5:30-8:30pm. Check-out 10am. Bunks in 4- to 10-bed dorms, with or without bath, $17; doubles and twins $38. 7th night free. One-time fee for linen $1. Key deposit $5. Book ahead.

Potts Point House, 154 Victoria St. (tel. 9368 0733; fax 9358 0733). Newly renovated, this is the most elegant hostel in the Cross. Spacious dorms have both bunk beds and single beds, the kitchen features light wood and matching dishes, and the

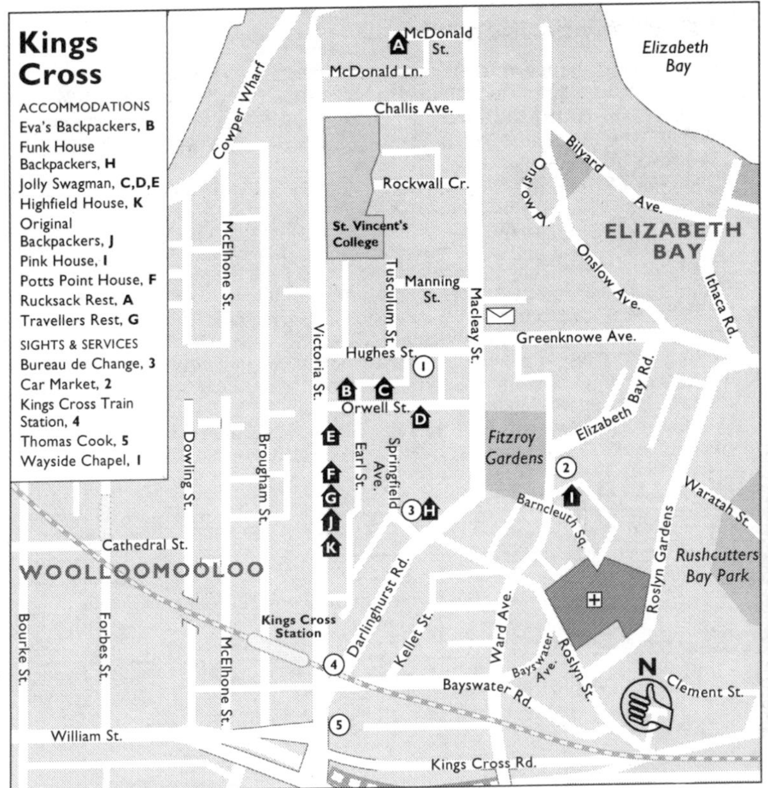

bathroom porcelain is an unblemished white. TVs and fans in the rooms. Laundry facilities. Reception open daily 8am-noon and 4-7pm. Check-out 10am. Dorms $18; doubles and twins $45, $36 per night for 2-6 nights; triples $50, $40 per night for 2-6 nights. Weekly: $110; $220; $250. Linen included.

Travellers Rest, 156 Victoria St. (tel. 9358 4606). Less lively than the bigger Kings Cross hostels, Travellers Rest caters to working travelers, and provides a good balance of quiet and camaraderie. Rooms all feature TVs, phones, fridges, basins, and kettles. Small kitchen and dining area open daily 6am-10:30pm. Laundry facilities. Reception open daily 8am-noon and 4:30-6pm. Check-out 9am. 4-bed dorms $17; singles $35; twins $36, with private bath $40. Weekly: $99; $155; $210, $230. Linen included.

Highfield House, 166 Victoria St. (tel. 9326 9539; fax 9358 1552). Fresh pastel paint and a security-coded lock make Highfield House downright serene for Kings Cross. The kitchen and TV room are small, and guests keep to themselves. Safe for valuables. Reception open Mon.-Fri. 7:30am-7pm, Sat.-Sun. 8am-noon and 5-7pm. Check-out 10am. 3-bed dorms $15; doubles $32 or $45. Weekly: $95; $200 or $250. Linen $2.50.

Funk House Backpackers, 23 Darlinghurst Rd. (tel. 9358 6455 or 1800 247 600; fax 9358 3506), above Hungry Jack's. Enter beyond Hungry Jack's, through the colorful doorway on the first left-hand alleyway. Murals brighten nearly every flat surface inside the Funk House—look for Aboriginal designs, rock and roll icons, and general psychedelia on the way to your cozy 3- to 4-bed dorm. Rooftop area is good for sun but not so great for scenery. Laundry facilities. Reception open daily 6:30am-9 or 10pm. Check-out 10am. Dorms $16; twins $36; doubles $38. Weekly: $96; $216; $228. VIP.

Original Backpackers, 160-162 Victoria St. (tel. 9356 3232; fax 9368 1435). Located in 2 old Victorian houses, this hostel's 4- to 6-bed dorms are graced with high ceilings and wood floors; 1 room even comes with a full-sized front porch. The kitchen and indoor/outdoor patio dining area comprise the most spacious hostel common area in Kings Cross. Laundry facilities. Reception open daily 7am-8pm. Dorm bunks $16; doubles $38. Weekly: $99; $230. Blankets $2 plus refundable deposit of $8.

Rucksack Rest, 9 MacDonald St. (tel. 9358 2348), off MacLeay St., a few blocks north of Kings Cross proper, in Potts Point. Rucksack Rest gives travelers a nearby option to the Cross with most of the convenience and none of the hubbub. The owner lives on site, and the house rides the line between hostel and home. Fridge and sink in room. Fully-equipped kitchen. Check-out is casual, around 11am. Call ahead to make sure the owner will be there when you arrive. Dorm beds $16; twins $34. 7th night free. Linen included. No key deposit. Foreign travelers only.

Forbes Terrace / G'day Backpackers, 152 Forbes St. (tel. 9358 4327; fax 9357 3652), off William St., a few blocks west of Darlinghurst Rd. Hidden behind the unassuming green facade is a very clean hostel with roomy apartment-style dorms and a cozy cafe-style dining area. Each room has a TV and sitting area, a fridge, and a teapot. Security is excellent. Laundry facilities. Reception open daily 8am-10pm. 6-bed dorms $16; singles $45. Weekly: $84-$105; $270. Linen included.

NEAR CENTRAL STATION AND SOUTH

Sydney Central YHA (tel. 9281 9111; fax 9281 9199), on the corner of Pitt St. and Rawson Pl., visible from the Pitt St. exit of Central station. The mothership has landed. The world's largest hostel with 532 beds, Sydney Central has every facility and service one could think to include in a hostel: pool (open daily 7:30am-10:30pm), game room, staffed employment desk, travel desk, projection TV video room, internet access ($2 per 10min.), parking ($7 per night), multiple kitchens, and on and on. It's both amazing and a little alienating, but it should be your top choice if you're collecting strange hostel stories from around the globe (or if you're really a hotel person at heart). Recently expanded calendar of outings and activities is making things more personal. Laundry facilities. 14-day max. stay. Reception open 24hr. Check-out 10am. Check-in noon. 4-bed dorms $21, 6-bed dorms $18, 8-bed dorms $17; twins $32, with bath $56. Under 18 half-price. Non-members pay $3 more on all rooms. Fully wheelchair accessible. Linen $2, towels $1, lockers $3.

Alfred Park Private Hotel, 207 Cleveland St. (tel. 9319 4031; fax 9318 1306), behind the railyard end of Central Station. The former home of a family with 14 children, Alfred Park Hotel has an intimate homey feel, spotless dorms, and a large common kitchen with terraced dining space. Rooms feature TVs, fridges, fans, and armoirs. Laundry facilities. Reception open daily 8am-10pm. Check-out 10am. 4-bed dorms $16, with bath $18. Weekly: $84, $112. Linen included.

Excelsior Hotel / City-Side Backpackers (VIP Backpackers), 64 Foveaux St. (tel. 9211 4945). Exit Central Station on Chalmers St. Foveaux St. intersects Chalmers at the north corner of the station. A clean, friendly place made brighter by good windows, it's situated over a lively pub. Carpet and furnishings are somewhat worn, but add to the atmosphere. Laundry facilities. Reception open daily 6:30am-midnight. Check-out 10am. Dorm beds $16. Weekly $95. VIP. Linen included.

Y on the Park (YWCA), 5-11 Wentworth Ave. (tel. 9264 2451; fax 9285 6288). 4 blocks north of Central Station, the Y is a shorter walk from Museum Station. Renovation of the bedrooms was being carried out as this book was being written, and work will begin on the ground floor facilities in 1998. The location will continue to be excellent, at the southeast corner of Hyde Park, and barring construction chaos, the facilities should be new, clean, and ample. No kitchen. Reception open 24hr. Check-out 10am. Check-in 1pm. 4-bed dorms $24, under age 12 $18; singles $52, with bath $70; twins $70, with bath $95; triples $85, with bath $100. Discount for YWCA members 10%. Laundry $1 per wash or dry.

Nomads Captain Cook Hotel, 162 Flinders St. (tel 9331 6487 or 1800 655 536; fax 9331 7746). A 20min. walk from Central Station down Foveaux St., past where it ends and Fitzroy St. continues, and another block beyond South Dowling St. Call for free pick-up or take bus #373, 374, or 377 from Wynyard or #339, 391, or 393 from Central Station. Perched atop a pub and eatery, hostel decoration seems to be second on Captain Cook's list of priorities. The small kitchen gets crowded at times. Mail holding. Free lockers. Free tea and coffee. Laundry facilities. Reception open daily 7am-midnight. Check-out 9:30am. Dorms $15-16. Singles with double beds, doubles, and twins $40. Weekly: $7 less. Nomads cardholders get $1 off per night. Linen and key deposit $15.

Sydney Central Private Hotel, 75 Wentworth Ave. (tel. 9212 1005). Exit Central Station on Chalmers St., walk 4 blocks north, and turn right on Wentworth Ave. It's a cinderblock box with uninspired, institutional rooms, but the hotel affords its guests inexpensive privacy with maximum convenience. TV room, kitchen, laundry facilities, shared baths, and excellent security. Reception open 24hr. Check-out 10am. Singles $30; doubles and twins $50; doubles with bath $65. Weekly: $120; $200; $260. Key deposit $20.

George Street Private Hotel, 700A George St. (tel./fax 9211 1800). Exit Central Station on Pitt St. and take Rawson Pl. from the north corner of the station to George St. The hotel gives the strange impression that everything inside is the same gray-blue color as the walls. It's not bad, but it's not eye candy. Rooms are narrow and simple with small windows. Guests have use of a common TV room and a very basic kitchen area. Reception open daily 6am-11:30pm. Check-out 10am. Singles $32; doubles $48, with bath and TV $70; triples $60; quads $70; quints $80. 7th night free. Linen included.

C. B. Hotel, 417 Pitt St. (tel. 9211 5115 or 9281 0202; fax 9281 9605), a 5min. walk from Central Station. Unadorned rooms in this large, quiet hotel make guests wish more of the ample common space had been allotted to the rooms. The decor dates from a bland day in the 1950s, but the staff does its best to keep things tidy. Free airport pick-up, laundry facilities, TV lounge, shared baths, safe for valuables, and luggage storage for afternoon departures from the city. Reception open 24hr. Check-out 10am. Singles $32; doubles and twins $52; triples $62; quads $70. Weekly: $150; $300; $372; $490.

GLEBE

To get to Glebe Point Rd., take bus #431 or 434 from George St. outside Town Hall.

Wattle House, 44 Hereford St. (tel. 9552 4997), a 5min. walk from Glebe Point Rd. Wattle House is the sort of place usually reserved for people who stay in B&Bs. The country home decor includes lace curtains, a brick kitchen, and a manicured backyard garden. Plush bean bags fill the small TV room, where guests get acquainted over long-term stays. Laundry facilities. 29 beds. Reception open Mon.-Fri. 9am-noon and 6-7pm, Sat. 10-11am. 3- to 4-bed dorms $19; doubles $50. Weekly: $115; $322-350. A $20 deposit covers key, linen, and kitchen needs.

Glebe Village Backpackers, 256 Glebe Point Rd. (tel. 9660 8133 or 1800 801 983; fax 9552 3707; email bacpac@iaccess.com.au). The already-appealing accommodation was going through considerable renovations at the time this book was written. But it is unlikely that the hostel's shaded, leafy surroundings or its packed calendar of outings and activities will be traded in during the change. Daily sight-seeing tours; Sun. table tennis competitions. Laundry facilities. A dearth of shared baths. Kitchen and common room close at 1am. Internet access $2 per 10min. Reception open daily 8am-9pm. Check-out 9:30am. Dorms with 4-10 beds $16-18. Weekly: $85-105. VIP. Work exchanges for rent possible on longer stays. Linen included.

Glebe Point YHA, 262 Glebe Point Rd. (tel. 9692 8418; fax 9660 0431). With long narrow halls and boxy rooms, the hostel feels like a college dorm with cleaner bathrooms. Guests are encouraged to hang out on the roof. Dorm rooms and the subterranean kitchen and common area get a little cold on winter mornings. Sinks in rooms, a pool table, a common big screen TV, and regular pub outings make life better. 120 beds. Internet access $2 per 10min. Reception open daily 7am-11pm. Laundry open 7am-10pm. 4-bed dorms $20; 5-bed dorms $18; twins $48; doubles $50. Non-members pay $3 more. Linen $2. Towel $1.

Alishan International Guest House, 100 Glebe Point Rd. (tel. 9566 4048; fax 9525 4686; e-mail alishan@mpx.com.au). This lovely yellow Victorian houses new rooms with TVs and refrigerators, while the dorm decor has had just a little more time to age. The bathroom tiles glisten, and rooms on the front of the house come with terrace access. Reception open daily 8am-11pm. 4-bed dorms $20; singles with bath $75; doubles with bath $85. Weekly: $126; $455; $560. Family room with bath $95. Wheelchair-accessible room available. Linen included.

BONDI BEACH

Indy's Bondi Beach Backpackers, 35A Hall St. (tel. 9365 4900), just beyond the Commonwealth Bank, set back from the street, 2½ blocks inland from Campbell Pde. Bondi's newest hostel goes the extra mile to attract visitors with free breakfast, tea, and coffee, an open video library, and scuba and surfing lessons. Guests also get use of bikes, surf and boogie boards, and in-line skates ($4 charge). Reception open Mon.-Sat. 7:30-11am and 4-8pm, Sun. 8-11am. Check-out 10:30am. Large dorms $18, in winter $14 for the first night and $16 thereafter. Winter weekly rate $95. Dorm partitions available for improvised privacy.

Lamrock Lodge, 19 Lamrock Ave. (tel. 9130 5063 or 1800 625 063), at the corner of Consett Ave., 2 blocks inland from the beach. Although Lamrock Lodge was being renovated when this book was being written, its previous style suggests that this will continue to be the Bondi hostel most likely to fulfill your surf movie beach house fantasies. Big windows and comfy common spaces keep the atmosphere mellow. Common room with TV (open until 1am nightly), kitchen (open until midnight nightly), fans in bedrooms. Reception open 24hr. Check-out 10am. Dorm beds $20 with 3-night min. stay. Weekly: $100. Singles $300 per week with 1-week min. stay, $120 per week in winter. Off-street parking $5 per night. Key and linen deposit $100 or credit card.

Bondi Lodge, 63 Fletcher St. (tel. 9365 2088 or 9130 3685; fax 9365 2177). Take Sandridge St. from the south end of Campbell Pde. and turn west on Fletcher St. From the international flags adorning the pink roofline to the light wood and pastel room decor, Bondi Lodge is the most appealing wedding cake of a budget hostel in the Sydney area. Room rates include buffet-style cooked breakfasts and 3-course dinners to make up for the lack of a common kitchen. Fans and fridges in rooms. Rooftop sundeck with spa. Laundry facilities. 4-bed dorms $30, space in a 2-bed dorm $40; singles $50. Weekly: $140; $210; $280. TV rental $5 per night, $15 per week. Linen included. Key deposit $50.

Bondi Beach Guest House, 11 Consett Ave. (tel. 9389 8309), off Hall St., 2 blocks from Campbell Pde. Furnishings and facilities show their age, but the overall effect is comfortable. Kitchen and large patio area make the place more friendly. Reception open 24hr. Check-out 9:30am. Dorms $15; doubles $35. Weekly: $90; $210. Linen included. Key deposit $20.

COOGEE BEACH

Original Coogee Beach Backpackers, 94 Beach St. (tel. 9315 8000 or 9665 7735; fax 9664 1258), high atop the steep hill at the north end of the beach. Standing sentinel over the surf, this hostel completes your beach experience with the feel of a surfy beach cottage and a view that's worth the hike. Common room with TV, 2 kitchens, big windows, and good vibes. Laundry facilities. Reception open daily 8am-noon and 5-8pm. Check-out 9:30am. 10-bed dorms $16; 3-bed dorms $18; doubles and twins $38-40. Weekly: $95; $95; $230-240. Key deposit $20.

Surfside Backpackers, 186 Arden St. (tel. 9315 7888; fax 9315 7892), above the McDonald's, overlooking the beach. The least expensive place in Coogee, Surfside proves you don't have to pay to par-tay. The narrow halls lead to sunny rooms facing the beach or the athletic fields next door. Long balconies connect the rooms, making things that much more open for socializing. The common TV room may have seen a few too many parties, but it's not that important when the beach is so close. Internet access $2 per 10min. Laundry facilities. Reception open daily 8:30am-12:30pm and 5-8pm. Check-out 9:30am. Dorms $16-17; doubles $38. Weekly: $85-95; $105. VIP. Key, kitchen, and linen deposit $20.

Aegean Backpackers, 40 Coogee Bay Rd. (tel. 9314 5324), 3 blocks inland from the beach. With sparkling white walls and multiple balconies, the Aegean really does hold a shadowy resemblance to a Greek island bungalow. The Aegean, however, has traded its open spaces for plentiful amenities which fill every spare inch of the building: pool, sauna, TV room, 6 kitchens (open daily 8am-10pm), and dorms with lofted bunks. Despite the closeness of things, or perhaps because of it, the hostel has a relaxed communal feel. Free airport pick-up comes with a required 2-night stay. Reception open in summer daily 8am-10pm, in winter 8am-noon and 5-10pm. Check-out 10am. 4-bed dorms $18, in winter $16; weekly $105, in winter $90. Twin rooms with bunks $40. Linen $2 in summer. Key deposit $20. Luggage storage $10 per week.

Indy's Coogee Beach Backpackers, 302 Arden St. (tel. 9315 7644), a 5min. walk south from the central beach area. Indy's maintains a quieter atmosphere than most of the hostels near the beach by catering to long-term travelers, many of whom work during the days and kick back in the evenings. The house is left feeling like a well-used home, with a comfortable common room and a busy kitchen. Free cereal, tea, coffee, and use of bikes, boards, and blades. Laundry included. Reception open daily 7:30-11:30am and 4:30-7pm. Check-out 10:30am but casual. 6-bed dorms $18, in winter $14 for the 1st night and $16 thereafter. Weekly in winter $94.50. Key and linen deposit $20.

Metro Coogee Beach Budget Accommodation, 171 Arden St. (tel. 9665 1162; fax 9665 0365), a 5min. walk north from the central beach area. This quiet, private establishment is far brighter and more comfortable than many of its kind. Straddling the line between hotel and hostel has its perks. There's a fully-equipped kitchen, and breakfast (daily 8-9am), linen, and bedroom TVs are included. Free monthly BBQs. Reception open Mon.-Thurs. 7:30am-12:30pm and 2:30-6:30pm, Fri. 7:30am-12:30pm and 1:30-6:30pm, Sat. 7:30am-12:30pm and 4-6:30pm, Sun. 8:30am-12:30pm and 4-6:30pm. Check-out 10am. 2- to 6-bed dorms $20; singles $40; doubles $50. 7th night free. Key and sheet deposit $20. Towel deposit $10.

NEW SOUTH WALES

NORTH SYDNEY

Kirribilli Court Private Hotel, 45 Carabella St. (tel. 9955 4344), in Kirribilli. Unlike Sydney's other hostels, Kirribilli Court nestles in a residential neighborhood with little noise and many trees. The big white house would benefit from a little more indoor upkeep, but the facilities are ample and quite spacious. Big, messy dorm rooms have wood floors and 2-4 beds. 3 kitchens and laundry facilities. Reception open 24hr. Dorm beds $12; singles $25; doubles $30. Weekly: $80; $140; $160. Linen included.

MANLY

Manly Backpackers Beachside, 28 Raglan St. (tel. 9977 3411; fax 9977 4379), closer to the corner of Pitt St. than its name suggests. Despite the blank, narrow hallways, the hostel manages to have an open, friendly atmosphere and clean, cozy dorms. Surf pictures liven up the walls in the bedrooms, although the beach is actually 2 blocks distant. Picnic tables bring guests together over meals in the kitchen and on the patio dining area. Free use of body boards. Laundry facilities. Reception open Mon.-Fri. 9am-1pm and 4-8pm, Sat.-Sun. 9am-1pm and 4-7pm, holidays 9am-noon only. Check-out 9:30am. 4- to 6-bed dorms $15; 3-bed dorms or larger rooms with a balcony $16. Weekly: $102; $105. Winter weekly rate for all dorms $85. Doubles and twins $42, with bath $48. VIP. Linen and blankets included.

Manly Astra Backpackers, 68-70 Pittwater Rd. (tel. 9977 2092). These 2 small, white houses overcome their strangely surfaced appearance (tile in the front yard, concrete in the back, plastic flooring in the hallways) through friendly management, sunny bedrooms, comfortable common space, and pleasing cleanliness. The rooms on the enclosed porches at the front of the houses get especially good light. Reception open daily 9am-noon and 6-7pm, but the live-in manager often answers the bell outside these hours. Check-out 9:30am. Kitchen open daily 5am-9:30pm. Dorms $15; twins $34. Weekly: $90; $190. VIP. $20 deposit covers key, linen, colorful Mexican blankets, and dishes.

Manly Beach Resort, 6 Carlton St. (tel. 9977 4188 or 1800 252 343; fax 9977 0524), at the corner of Pittwater Rd. Manly Beach Resort expends no extra energy brightening up the barren dorms and cafeteria-style common room in the house attached to the main motel. Rooms include 4 beds, a bathroom, and no more. Laundry facilities. Reception open 24hr. Check-out 9:30am. Dorms $15, $98 per week. VIP. Required fee for linen $2. Blankets not provided. Key deposit $20.

Manly Cottage Inn, 25 Pittwater Rd. (tel. 0419 022 250), between Raglan and Denison St. The red-tinted glass in the front door windows is the first tip-off that things aren't quite as cute inside the cottage as they are outside. Rooms, space, and facilities are adequate but none-too-charming. Bedrooms have bright, colored walls and more breathing room than the common areas or bathrooms. Reception open 24hr. Check-out 10am. 4-bed dorms $15, $100 per week; twins $40. Linen and blankets included. Key deposit $30.

Steyne Hotel (tel. 9977 4977), on Steyne St., at the end of the Corso. Rooms at the Steyne far outclass average pub accommodation. Rooms are nicely furnished, shared bathrooms are vigorously scrubbed, and floors creak with the attitude of a slightly upscale old beachfront hotel. Linen and hot breakfast included. Check-in daily 11am-late. Check-out 10am. 4-bed dorms $25. Singles $49; doubles with shared bath $74. Weekly: $280; $385. Key deposit $100 or signed credit card slip.

CAMPING

Sheralee Tourist Caravan Park, 88 Bryant St. (tel. 9567 7161), in Rockdale. Take CityRail to Rockdale, and walk down Bryant St. toward the water (15min.). None-too-scenic tent camping in an open grassy patch comes with toilets, hot showers, a kitchen area, and a TV room. Laundry facilities. Reception open Thurs.-Tues. 9-10am and 5-6pm, Wed. 9-10am and 5-5:30pm, but arrivals are welcome any time. Sites for 1-2 people $12, with power $18. Each additional person $4.

Lakeside Van Park (tel. 9913 7845), on Lake Park Rd., in Narrabeen. Take bus #190 from Wynyard Station toward Palm Beach, and ask for the 3rd stop after Narrabeen Lake. Although the general caravan park setting is uninspiring, the tent camping area lies closest to the adjacent beach and has both the wind and the view to show for it. Toilets, showers, and common kitchen area on-site. Reception open daily 8am-6pm. Sites for 2 people $17, with power $19. Each additional person $4. Deposit for gate card $25.

Lane Cove River Van Village (tel. 9805 0500), on Plassey Rd., in North Ryde. Take CityRail to Chatswood, then catch bus #550 or 551. At the outer edge of Lane Cove National Park, the tent camping area features the most trees you'll find in a caravan park near Sydney. The Lane Cove River and shoreline walking tracks are an easy walk away. Toilets, showers, laundry facilities. Reception open daily 8am-9:30pm. Sites for 2 $18, with power $19. Each additional person $6, under 16 $3. Deposit for campers with cars $10.

■ Food

Sydney's streets overflow with eateries of every flavor for any budget. Asian options, most notably Thai cuisine, rank highly among the international selections, and the quality clearly benefits from the competition. The Central Business District, the northern half of Sydney proper, is rife with quick lunch stops for the masses still dreaming of three-martini lunch status. Sandwiches, meat pies, and focaccias run $2.50 to $6 at sandwich counters throughout these blocks. The glassed-in atrium dining area at **Sky Gardens Food Court,** on the Pitt St. Mall, raises the inexpensive food court concept to a more attractive level.

Slightly south, the feeding frenzy of Chinatown lurks west of Central Station around Hay, Little Hay St., and the Dixon St. Plaza. Just east of center, the Oxford St. social artery runs between Surry Hills, in the south (where many of the city's best Thai kitchens line up on Crown St.), and the (very) Little Italy on Stanley St., between Crown and Riley St., in Darlinghurst. Cafes in the latter area serve excellent coffee and hearty hot sandwiches. Continuing east through Darlinghurst, the strip of restaurants on Oxford St. near St. Vincent's Hospital is known for good quality and a variety of Asian and European flavors. Victoria St. runs north from Oxford at the hospital into the land of high cappuccino chic before depositing the last of its cafe class amidst the hostels of Kings Cross. Darlinghurst and Bayswater Rd. offer fare similar to the neighborhood's atmosphere: late-night cheap bites, fast food chains, and little else.

As usual, a large, nearby student population means good, cheap cafes and restaurants on both Glebe Point Rd. in Glebe and Kings St. in Newtown. Blues Point Rd. on McMahons Point and Fitzroy St. in Kirribilli lead the north shore's attempts at affordability with appeal, featuring several cafes well-loved by the locals. Breakfast is big on the beachfront drives of Manly, Bondi, and Coogee. At most coastal cafes $6 to $7 buys a large cooked breakfast and an excuse to stop and appreciate the view over a morning paper. Manly offers even less expensive carnival-style food counters along the Corso.

CHINATOWN

Dixon House Food Court, downstairs on the corner of Little Hay St. For filling East Asian meals from several nations, you can do no better than the photo-lined walls of the Dixon House food stalls. Dishes are consistently more appetizing than their bland-though-helpful pictorial representations. Meals average $6-10. Be ready for the bell at the counter where you ordered; meals don't always know to wait for their proper owner. Open daily 10:30am-8:30pm.

B.B.Q. King, 18-20 Goulburn St. (tel. 9267 2433; fax 9267 2001). Spare, dingy decor and plastic dishes from your childhood tea set leave only the food to plead this restaurant's case. After a meal of fresh, crispy, well-prepared Chinese vegetables and perfectly cooked meats, the royal moniker makes a lot more sense. Braised chicken with cashew nuts $9. Spring rolls $3.50 for 4. BYO corkage $2 per person. Open daily 11:30am-2am.

Hingara, 82 Dixon St. (tel. 9212 2169). The setting is rather old and quite casual with simple Chinese accents. Hingara's food, consistently tasty but not groundbreaking, is its showpiece, and in the chaos of Chinatown, that's enough to make it an institution. Crispy spring rolls $4 for 4. Main dishes $8-14. BYO wine only. Corkage $2.50 per person. Open Sun.-Thurs. 9:30am-3pm and 5-9:30pm, Fri.-Sat. 10am-3pm and 5-10:30pm.

NEWTOWN

Kilimanjaro African Eatery, 280 King St. (tel. 9557 4565). Unusual among the European and Asian offerings lining King St., Kilimanjaro re-creates the flavors of several African nations, including Mali, Senegal, Algeria, and Tunisia with dishes cooked in glazed clay pots and served in a simple dark-wood setting. Couscous replaces the usual noodles or rice under main dishes that make filling meals at just $7.50. Entrees and sides $4.50. BYO, no corkage. Open Sun.-Thurs. 6-10pm, Fri.-Sat. 6-11pm.

Sleaze, 341 King St. (tel. 9519 8659), near the train station, just south of where Enmore Rd. branches off King St. The sweet peach interior of this cafe contrasts nicely with the name, and the smiling staff dispels any last doubts you may have about the establishment's wholesomeness. Breakfast is served until 4pm daily, with cooked meals for around $6.50. Coffee ($2) and dessert here may be your best meal of the day. Fudgy, rich chocolate cake $6 and worth it. Lemon tart with cream $3.50. BYO wine only. Corkage $1 per glass. Open Mon. 11am-6pm, Tues.-Thurs. 11am-11pm, Fri. 11am-midnight, Sat. 9:30-midnight, Sun. 9:30am-11pm.

Old Saigon, 107 King St. (tel. 9519 5931). The tiny dining room hides behind a painted bamboo curtain and features aluminum can helicopters and lights shaded by conical straw hats. Despite the decor, Old Saigon serves some of Sydney's most beloved Chinese, Thai, Indonesian, and Vietnamese food. The Kan Keow Wan, Thai-style green curry chicken ($13), earns repeat visits from locals. Mains cost $10-17. Lychees with ice cream are fresh, fruity, and $5. Licensed and BYO corkage $1 per person. Open Tues. and Sat.-Sun. 6-10pm, Wed.-Fri. noon-2pm and 6-10pm.

SURRY HILLS

Prasits Northside Thai Take Away, 395 Crown St. (tel. 9332 1792), several blocks south of Oxford St. Prasit has made a name for himself in the tight Sydney Thai market by serving hot, fresh, hot, creative, hot dishes for sit-down dining or takeaway. His third location, the Northside Take Away, offers all of the taste and a little less of the tariff. Unusual, tasty spring rolls have corn inside ($1.50 each). The green peppercorn stir-fry might be used to melt iron if it weren't so yummy ($10.50). Limited seating available. BYO. Open Tues.-Sun. noon-3:30pm and 5:30-10pm.

Mehrey Da Dhaba Indian Street Restaurant, 466 Cleveland St. (tel. 9319 6260). Named for the roadside foodstalls of north India, the Dhaba brings a tradition of hearty, inexpensive, and filling food across the ocean without losing any of the flavor. The clean, simple decor is a welcome improvement on the unhygienic carts of the homeland. Whole tandoori chicken $8. Vegetarian meals $6-8. Meat dishes $8-11. Naan or roti 90¢. BYO. Open Mon.-Tues. 5:30-11pm, Wed.-Thurs. and Sun. noon-3pm and 5:30-11pm, Fri.-Sat. noon-3pm and 5:30pm-midnight.

DARLINGHURST

Burgerman, 116 Surry St. (tel. 9361 0268), just off Victoria St. It's the result of combining London techno-hip style with an American burger joint menu, and cooking everything up in the land of beet root salad. The black, orange, and silver decor goes as well with the electronic soundtrack as the french fries ($2-3.50, and yes, Burgerman calls them "fries," not "chips") go with the squeezy tomato-shaped ketchup bottles. Scrumptious vegetarian burger $7.20. Open daily noon-10:30pm. Licensed and BYO corkage $1 per person or $4 for the bottle.

Green Chillies, 113-115 Oxford St. (tel. 9361 3717). Despite the address, the entrance is around the corner on Crown St. This elegant little restaurant serves traditional Thai dishes with far more style than you pay for. Dishes are flavored liberally with chili, lime, mint, and coriander for a distinctive Thai taste. Spicy beef larb $10. Dainty spring rolls $5.80 for 4. Delicious Pad Hokkien Mee $9. Takeaway lunch specials Mon.-Fri. 11:30am-3:30pm $7. BYO wine only. Corkage $2 per person. Open daily 6-11pm, plus Tues.-Fri. 11:30am-3:30pm.

Metro Cafe, 26 Burton St. (tel. 9361 5356). A favorite of Sydney vegetarians and anyone who doesn't need to have meat at *every* meal, Metro lurks quiet, cool, and out-of-the-way, near the west end of Burton St. The wooden booths and fan-shaped wall mirrors lend a low art-deco European flair, and add to the feeling that diners have all uncovered the same little secret. Stuffed peppers with potatoes and cheese have a tasty, nutty twist ($8.50). Main dishes $8.50. Half meals $6.50. Entrees $5.50. BYO, no corkage. Open daily 6-10:30pm, sometimes later.

KINGS CROSS

Harry's Cafe de Wheels, on Cowper Wharf Rdwy., in Wooloomooloo, northeast of Kings Cross proper. Although it's not actually in Kings Cross, Harry's is close enough to be an easy late-night wander down Brougham St. for a post-party pie. The pie cart, which has been around since 1945, faced possible closure at the end of its lease in Nov., 1997, but grass-roots support may have saved this institution. The house special, pie and peas (beef pie $2.50, chicken pie $2.80), clearly reflects more than 50 years of pie-making expertise. Open Sun.-Thurs. 7am-2am, Fri.-Sat. 7am-4am.

Hampton Court Hotel, 9 Bayswater Rd. (tel. 9357 2711). The Fri. and Sat. night dinner deal may be the best bargain in Kings Cross: fried fish, pasta, or cook-it-yourself steak with bread, salad, and a beer sets you back just $4.50 on weekend evenings. Backpackers fill the place, making it easy to make a friend or 2 at the grill before heading out to the pubs. Live bands play (mostly) covers in the evenings. Throughout the week, breakfast is either continental ($6) or cooked ($9). Sun. evening roast $5. Open for food service Mon.-Thurs. 6:30-10:30am, Fri.-Sun. 6:30-10:30am and 5-9pm. Bar open Fri.-Sun. 5pm-midnight.

Roys Famous, 176 Victoria St. (tel. 9357 3579). The coppery glow of Roy's walls attracts the stalwarts of urban chic for coffee and lunch. Nestled in the middle of Kings Cross's hostel strip, the combination of body piercing and backpacking makes other diners as interesting as the food. Lunch from $7.50. Tandoori chicken pizzetta with fruit chutney and feta cheese $11. Breakfast all day from $2.50. Yogurt, fruit, and muesli $5. Licensed for alcohol with meals. BYO wine only. Corkage $3 per bottle. Open daily 9am-midnight. Service stops at 11pm.

William's on William (tel. 9358 6680), on William St. around the corner from the Kings Cross Hotel. Just when you think it's impossible to get a cooked meal in Sydney for under $5, or maybe at the moment you mourn the demise of neighborhood greasy spoon lunch counters, it's time to venture out to the end of William St. William's breakfast deal is as cheap as it gets: eggs, sausage, toast, and home fries for $4. Meals of the blue plate variety $8-9. Spring for the special ($10) and you get 2 courses, plus soup. Licensed. Open daily 7am-11:30pm.

INNER EAST AND WATSON'S BAY

Spice Market, 340 New South Head Rd. (tel. 9328 7499), in Double Bay. Primarily a takeaway counter, Spice Market regularly fills the few wooden tables in its simple yet attractive space. Dishes range from sweet to spicy with delightful flavor on both ends of the spectrum. Spring rolls have a bit of peppery kick ($1.50 each). The pumpkin and tofu stir-fry is an absolute masterpiece ($7.50). Meals with rice feed 2 people easily. Lunch specials Mon.-Fri. noon-4pm $5.50. BYO, no corkage. Open Mon.-Fri. noon-4pm and 5-10pm, Sat.-Sun. 5-10pm.

Doyle's Take-out (tel. 9337 1572), on the wharf, at Marine Pde., in Watsons Bay. Take bus #324 or 325. A Sydney institution, Doyle's has taken over the wharf at Watsons Bay with 3 restaurants within a stone's throw of the water. The take-out counter, located closest to the Wharf Restaurant, allows those of us who can't afford to sit and be served a taste of Sydney's best fish and chips (huge portions $8). If your arteries just can't take it, try the sushi ($6). Open daily 10:30am-5pm.

Tak's Thai, 462 Oxford St. (tel. 9332 1380), in Paddington, at the Centennial Park end of Oxford St. Sydney-siders would walk a mile for the snappy Thai style and black-and-white tile as the chefs compile food that make them smile. (Rhyming is so puerile!) The staff suggests the spicy coconut milk laksa ($6). Heaping chicken Thai noodles $5.80. Main dishes $6-11. BYO. Open Sun.-Fri. 6pm-midnight, Sat. 12:30pm-midnight.

BONDI AND COOGEE BEACHES

Beechwood, 100 Campbell Pde. (tel. 9365 5986), directly across from the beach's center. Yellow walls, light wood, and terra-cotta accents frame the prototypical beachside cafe. The brunch special—2 eggs any style, bacon, sausage, mushrooms, hashbrowns, tomatoes, and toast ($6.50)—stays on the menu all day long. Muesli, fruit, yogurt, and juice $6. At dinner, pasta dishes cost $9 or $13. Fully licensed and BYO wine only. Corkage $1.50 per person. Open Mon.-Fri. 9am-midnight, Sat.-Sun. 8am-midnight.

Barlovento, 32a Fletcher St. (tel. 9365 0201), hidden from the beach and the crowds. Follow Sandridge St. to reach Fletcher from the south end of Campbell Pde. This neighborhood hole-in-the-wall sports the bohemian decor of an upscale cafe with none of the attitude. Specializes in breakfast combos. The date bars are divine ($2.50). Pizzettas and focaccias $5-7. Open daily 7am-6pm.

Barzura (tel. 9665 5546), on the end of Karr St., at the south end of the beach. Coogee's answer to the beach and breakfast combo, with lots of outdoor seating and a prime location near the local Surf Lifesaving Club. Berry flapjacks $6.50. Meals with eggs and toast $7. Fully licensed and BYO wine only. Corkage $2 per person. Open daily 7am-7pm.

NORTH SHORE

Billi's Cafe, 31a Fitzroy St. (tel. 9955 7211), in Kirribilli, just east of Harbour Bridge. This simple cafe provides North Shore residents with a quiet breakfast refuge near their homes and workplaces. Fresh baked goods, quiche ($9.50), and coffee ($2.20) are house staples. Grab the paper, sit down outside, and relax, knowing that the hidden skyscrapers have no claim on your time. Eggs Benedict $9. BYO, corkage $1 per bottle. Open Mon.-Fri. 7am-10:30pm, Sat. 8am-10:30pm.

Blues Point Cafe, 135 Blues Point Rd. (tel. 9922 2064), on McMahon's Point. When lunches turn into 4hr. events, locals can't blame the fast, friendly service. Fault must lie somewhere in the herb omelettes ($6), or maybe in the strong coffee (flat white $2), or even in the lamb fillets (with Caesar salad at dinner $8.50), but certainly not in the light, upbeat atmosphere or the patio dining area. Dinner specials $8.50. Breakfast specials $5. Both make ample full meals. Licensed and BYO, no corkage. Open Mon.-Fri. 7am-11pm, Sat.-Sun. 8am-11pm.

Witham's Coffee Shop, 97 Bay Rd. (tel. 9955 4762), in Waverton. Discerning coffee drinkers say that Witham's daily brew, roasted on-site and served piping hot, is Sydney's best cup of joe. Decide for yourself—*Let's Go* has no desire to make definitive claims on such important issues, knowing the ire of caffeinated connoisseurs who may not agree with our pro-Witham's stance. The much-hailed flat white is $2.20. Lunches range from the huge leg of ham sandwich ($5.50) to the toasted bagel laden with salmon, cream cheese, and capers ($8). Open daily 8am-6pm.

MANLY

Green's Eatery, 103 Sydney Rd. (tel. 9977 1904), on the pedestrian stretch of Sydney Rd. near the Corso. This sunny little vegetarian cafe serves amazingly hearty meals with rice and any number of interesting vegetable combos for $3-6. A medium serving ($5) makes a fine full dinner. Try the chick pea casserole or the sauteed vegetables with tofu. Baseball-sized tuna rissoles $2.80. BYO, no corkage. Open daily 8am-6:30pm.

Bluewater Cafe, 28 South Steyne St., shop 2 (tel. 9976 2051), on the water between Wentworth St. and the Corso. A beautiful setting for breakfast with a surf-gone-stylish feel. Outdoor seating is as close to the beach as Manly eateries get. Big bowl of fruit, yogurt, muesli, and milk $6.50. Later in the day, mains go for $9-15. Specials include the Camenbert and walnut torte ($8.50). Fully licensed and BYO wine allowed. Corkage $1.50 per person. Open daily 7:30am-late.

■ Sights

Sydney's sights range from architectural landmarks to beaches, from museum tours to neighborhood strolls. Because of the city center's diminutive size, many of the cultural attractions can be seen in a couple of days of serious sight-seeing. Exploring the tasty cafes, interesting stores, and little nooks and crannies of the suburbs will take much longer.

THE HARBOR

Sydney Harbour National Park (tel. 9337 5511; office open Mon.-Fri. 8:30am-5pm) preserves four harbor islands, several south shore beaches, and a few green patches on the northern headlands, insuring that the harbor exceeds its calling as a seaport by providing numerous outlets for recreational urges (see **Water Activities,** p. 116). Visits to the harbor islands must be arranged in advance through the **National Park Information Centre,** 110 George St. (tel. 9247 5033), in Cadman's Cottage, in the Rocks. The early colony's most troublesome convicts were once isolated on Pinchgut Island, off Mrs. Macquarie's Point. Now called **Fort Denison,** the island supports a fort built to protect the city from a feared Russian invasion. West of the city center, not far from the shore at Balmain, the sandstone gunpowder station and barracks of **Goat Island** were the site of cruel punishments for the convicts who built them. National Park tours departing from Cadman's Cottage offer the only opportunities to stop on either island. (Fort Denison tours Mon.-Fri. noon and 2pm, Sat.-Sun. 10am, noon, and 2pm; $9, students, seniors, ages 5-15 $6.50. Goat Island tours Sat. 11am and 1pm, Sun. 11:30am and 1:30pm; $11, $7.50. Both tours last approximately 2hr. Reservations required.)

Shark Island and **Clark Island,** also administered by the park, are accessible only by privately owned boats or discouragingly expensive water taxis. People must notify the park, nonetheless, of plans to visit these islands. **Harbour Taxis** (tel. 9922 425[illegible]) charges $35 for the trip to either island, plus $5 for each passenger after the first.

The park's south shore beaches, **Nielson Park, Camp Cove,** and the nude, gay beach called **Lady Bay,** are situated on Vaucluse Bay and Watsons Bay, reaching out toward the harbor's outermost southern headland, South Head. All three beaches lie near bus routes #324 and 325 to Watsons Bay. Popular north shore harbor beaches include **Balmoral Beach,** on the north side of Middle Head, a 15-minute walk from Military Rd. (bus #178, 180, or 182), **Chinaman's Beach,** north of Balmoral, a seven-minute walk from Spit Rd. (bus #178, 180, or 182), and **Manly Cove,** surrounding the ferry port at Manly Wharf.

THE ROCKS AND CIRCULAR QUAY

The arching steel latticework of **Harbour Bridge** spans the harbor from the northern tip of Dawes Pt. to the southern tip of Milson's Point. Opened in 1932, the bridge has long been a visual symbol of the city and is still the best place to get a look at the harbor and the surrounding cityscape. Pedestrians can enter the bridge walkway from a set of stairs on Cumberland St., just south of Argyle St., in the Rocks. The bridge's southern pylon has an entry on the walkway leading to a 200-step stairway and spectacular views. The **Harbour Bridge Museum** (tel. 9247 3408 or 9831 0911), inside the pylon, tells the story of the bridge's construction (open daily 10am-5pm; admission to lookout and museum $2, seniors and ages 4-15 $1).

At the base of the bridge, the Rocks is the site of the original Sydney Town settlement. Built during the lean years of the colony's founding, the area remained quite rough well into this century. In the 1970s, when plans to finally raze the slums were developed, a movement to restore the area to its historic potential began. Today The Rocks bustles with tourists wandering from historic cafe to historic storefront. Despite the gentrification, the area really is a lovely place for strolling and browsing and the only place to begin a search for Sydney's history. The **Rocks Visitors Centre** (tel. 9255 1788; open daily 9am-6pm) and the **Rocks Walking Co.** (tel. 9247 6678) share the white, three-story Sailor's Home at 106 George St. The former has brochures on local attractions and displays detailing the history of the Rocks, and the latter conducts informative walking tours of the neighborhood (Mon.-Fri. 10:30am, 12:30, and 2:30pm, Sat.-Sun. 11:30am and 2pm; 80min.; $11, ages 10-16 $7.50, under 10 free). Built in 1816, **Cadman's Cottage,** 110 George St., next door to the Sailor's Home, is the oldest standing house in Sydney and the current home of the Sydney Harbour National Park Information Centre.

The huge, sandstone **Sydney Observatory** (tel. 9217 0485; fax 9217 0489; email obs@phm.gov.au; http://www.phm.gov.au), on Watson Rd., at the top of Observatory Hill, allows star-gazers to see the southern skies through telescopes both high-tech and low-tech, including Australia's oldest working lens telescope. The Observatory is on Miller's Point, a quick walk west of George St. via Argyle St. Guided tours of the heavens (that is, through telescopes) take place six nights per week by prior arrangement (open Thurs.-Tues.; $6, students, seniors, ages 5-15 $3, families $15). In the daytime, the observatory functions as a museum of astronomy with displays, films, talks, and simulated skyscapes (open Mon.-Fri. 2-5pm, Sat.-Sun. and school holidays 10am-5pm; free). Also on Observatory Hill, the **National Trust Centre and S.H. Ervin Gallery** (tel. 9258 0150) has information on Sydney's historical sights and changing shows of both recent and historic Australian art (open Tues.-Fri. 11am-5pm, Sat.-Sun. noon-5pm; admission $5). The building is a former military hospital.

The **Museum of Contemporary Art,** 140 George St. (tel. 9252 4033; recorded info 9241 5892; fax 9252 4361; http://www.mca.com.au), injects a little life into an area largely concerned with what has come and gone. Devoted to displaying works created in the last 25 years, the museum puts on approximately 20 exhibitions per year (about 5 at a time) and leaves none of its collection on permanent display. Exhibits showcasing the museum's extensive collection of Aboriginal work are consistently worthwhile, but taken as a whole, the museum is a bit too small to justify the full admission price (open daily 10am-6pm; $9, students, seniors, YHA members, backpackers, and under 16 $6, families $16).

On Bennelong Point, opposite the base of Harbour Bridge, the striking **Sydney Opera House** (tel. 9250 7250) stands like a fleet of sailboats beating into the wind (or, perhaps, like the monster clams of a Godzilla-era Japanese horror film). Designed by Danish architect Jørn Utzon, Sydney's pride and joy took 14 years to produce. A saga of bureaucracy and broken budgets (planned at $7 million, the building cost $102 million by the time it was finished) surrounded the construction and eventually led the architect to divorce himself from the project prior to its completion. In 1973, the queen of England opened the building, despite strong winds, a false fire alarm, and 1400 spectator seats initially set up facing the wrong way. In 1998, the 25th anniversary of the building's opening, it is difficult to imagine that any such misfortune could taint the much-beloved structure. In addition to starring in thousands of tourist photographs every day, the Opera House stages operas, ballets, classical concerts, plays, and films throughout the year (see **Entertainment,** below, for box office information). Tours of the building take place daily between 9:15am and 4pm (Wed. 9:15am-noon because of matinees). Although there's no firm schedule, tours depart roughly every half hour ($9, students $6).

Inland from the Opera House, the plants, flowers, and trees of the **Royal Botanic Gardens** fill the area around Farm Cove. Daily guided walks begin at the Visitors Centre (tel. 9231 8125; open daily 9:30am-4:30pm), located in the southeast corner of the park near Art Gallery Rd. (walks 10:30am; 1½-2hr.; free). Within the gardens, attractions such as the Aboriginal plant trail and the formal rose garden are free, but the **Tropical House,** a pair of shapely glass greenhouses housing plants from Australia and around the South Pacific, charges admission (open daily 10am-4pm; $5, students, seniors, and under 11 $2). **Government House** (tel. 9913 5222), in the northeast corner of the Botanic Gardens, served as the home of the governor of New South Wales as recently as 1996. With the governor now living in his own home, the dignified house and grounds are open for touring (grounds open daily 10am-4pm, house open Fri.-Sun. 10am-3pm; free). On the eastern headland of Farm Cove, the Royal Botanic Gardens end at Mrs. Macquarie's chair. The chair, carved from the stone at the end of the point, was fashioned for the wife of Governor Lachlan Macquarie, so that she could sit and look out over the harbor in comfort. Another classic spot for Sydney pictures, the chair maintains an excellent view, although one quite different than Mrs. Macquarie likely ever imagined.

Circular Quay, between Dawes Point and Bennelong Point, is the departure point for both the city ferry system and numerous private cruise companies, as well as the site of the northernmost south shore CityRail station. An important center for commuters during the week, the wharves become a lively hub of tourist activity on the weekends with street performers, souvenir shops, and easy access to many of the city's major sights. Directly inland from the southeastern corner of Circular Quay, the **Justice and Police Museum** (tel. 9252 1144), at the corner of Albert and Phillip St., indulges Sydney's outlaw past. Displays detail some of the city's more infamous historical events, along with the investigations that brought the perpetrators to justice (open Jan. Sun.-Thurs.10am-5pm; Feb.-Dec. Sun. 10am-5pm; admission $5, students, seniors, and ages 5-18 $3, families $12). The recently built and stylish **Museum of Sydney** (tel. 9251 5988), on the corner of Phillip and Bridge St., celebrates the history of the city through films and high-tech exhibitions. Although the period covered by the museum begins in 1788 with the founding of Sydney Town, attention is given to both European and Aboriginal involvement in the city's history (open daily 10am-5pm; admission $6, students, seniors, and ages 5-18 $4, families $15).

CITY CENTER AND THE DOMAIN

Sydney's age insures that architecture in the center of town is far from being uniformly modern. The French Renaissance **Town Hall** (tel. 9265 9233) fronts George St. between Park and Bathurst St. Built during the prosperity of the late 1800s, the building's outrageous excess merits at least a passing look. The wood-lined concert hall boasts an 8000-pipe organ which was once the world's largest (Town Hall open Mon.-Fri. 8am-6pm). The imposing statue of Queen Victoria, visible from the north corner of Town Hall, guards the entrance to the lavish **Queen Victoria Building,** 455 George St. The Byzantine edifice was constructed in 1898 as a home for the city markets, but recent renovations have brought in more familiar shopping venues. Though the shops inside are distinctly upmarket, a stroll through the shopping center's fantastic wood and brass interior doesn't cost a cent.

Around the corner at the end of the Pitt St. pedestrian mall, the **Sydney Centrepoint Tower,** 100 Market St. (tel. 9229 7444), rises 325m above sea level for a stunning, panoramic view of the city and the surrounding areas. The 40-second ride to the top is steep in grade and price, so don't waste a trip on a cloudy day. When the sky is clear, views extend as far as the Blue Mountains to the west, the New South

Wales central coast to the north, and Wollongong to the south. (Open Sun.-Fri. 9:30am-9:30pm, Sat. 9:30am-11:30pm; admission $10, ages 5-16 $4.50, families $22.)

Set aside in 1810 by Governor Lachlan Macquarie, **Hyde Park,** between Elizabeth and College St. at the eastern edge of the city center, is Sydney's most structured public green space, complete with fountains and stately trees. A buzzing urban oasis during the day, the park warrants some caution when walking through at night. In the southern half of the park, below Park St., the **ANZAC Memorial** (tel. 9267 7668) commemorates the service of the Australia and New Zealand Army Corps in WWI, as well as that of the Australians who have fought in the nation's nine overseas conflicts. An exhibit inside the memorial traces the history of Australian involvement in international conflict (open daily 9am-5pm; free tours daily 11:30am and 1:30pm). The **Australian Museum** (tel. 9320 6000; recorded information 0055 29408), on the corner of College and William St., at the east side of Hyde Park, achieves an interesting mix of natural and cultural history in its exhibits. Stuffed re-creations of prehistoric Australian megafauna cast shadows over popular Aussie animals such as the koala and kangaroo. Although some of the exhibits devoted to scientific matters are aimed at children and hold little interest for older people, the museum's treatment of the cultures of indigenous Australian peoples, both as historic groups and as parts of Australian society today, is superb and engaging. (Open daily 9:30am-5pm; admission $5, students $3, ages 5-12 $2, seniors and under 5 free, families $12.)

Macquarie St., named for Governor Macquarie (in office 1809-1821), runs from the north end of Hyde Park to Circular Quay, and defines the eastern edge of the central business district. Macquarie was the first leader to consider Sydney more than a colonial outpost, and his vision gave rise to several of the city's first architectural landmarks. The first of these treasures, **Sydney Hospital** (1814) faces Macquarie St. at the end of Martin Pl. Denied crown funding for his grandiose schemes, Macquarie financed the sandstone hospital with monies earned by granting certain traders a monopoly on rum trade from the colony. The central section of the building carries on the tradition of the original "Rum Hospital" as Sydney's main medical facility. The **NSW Parliament House** (tel. 9230 2111) occupies the former north wing. Visitors are welcome in the building, which has both daily free tours and open access to public viewing galleries during parliamentary sessions (open Mon.-Fri. 9:30am-4pm; tours Mon.-Fri. 10, 11am, and 2pm, during parliamentary session Tues. only). In 1854, with new wealth coming in from the recent gold rush, Sydney Hospital's south wing became a branch of the Royal Mint. The building's current **Old Mint Museum** (tel. 9217 0311) mounts displays on stamps, coins, and the history of the Australian gold rush (open Thurs.-Tues. 10am-5pm, Wed. 10am-noon; admission $5, students, seniors, and children $2, 1st Sat. of the month free). Next door to the Mint Museum at Queens Sq., the 1819 **Hyde Park Barracks** (tel. 9223 8922), designed by former convict and bargain-basement architect Francis Greenway, stands as another of Macquarie's innovative methods for getting around British penny pinching. The barracks, originally used to house convicts, now houses a museum devoted to the daily lives of those who once inhabited the building. Temporary exhibitions give broader views of Australian history. (Open daily 10am-5pm; admission $5, students, seniors, and ages 5-18 $3, families $12.) Greenway is also responsible for **St. James Church** (completed in 1824) across the plaza from Hyde Park Barracks. Beside the north end of the former hospital complex, the **State Library of New South Wales** (tel. 9273 1414) houses galleries and research facilities (open Mon.-Fri. 9am-9pm, Sat.-Sun. 11am-5pm).

Behind the buildings on Macquarie St., the unmanicured, grassy expanse of **the Domain** stretches east along the south edge of the Royal Botanic Gardens. Concerts fill the open area during January's **Sydney Festival** (see p. 120). During the rest of the year, the park is most popular for weekday lunch breaks from downtown offices and for Sunday-morning rabble-rousing at Speakers' Corner. Located in the northeast corner of the park, the **Art Gallery of New South Wales** (tel. 9225 1744; recorded info 9225 1790; http://www.agnsw.gov.au), on Art Gallery Rd., is Sydney's major metropolitan art museum. The gallery houses displays of Australian art from both indigenous and European artists, a collection of international painting, and a photography gallery. The collection's strength lies in its modern Australian paintings and extensive collection of Aboriginal work (open daily 10am-5pm; free, except special exhibits).

DARLING HARBOUR

Darling Harbour, on the west side of the city center, is developed enough to be both upmarket and tacky. Still, the concentration of tourist attractions in this small area makes it a perfect outing for afternoon sight-seeing and a popular spot for families. On foot, Darling Harbour lies only 10 minutes from Town Hall Station. (Follow George St. north to Market St. and Market St. west to Pyrmont Bridge.) Bus #456 approaches Darling Harbour from Circular Quay by way of Town Hall, and ferries run from Circular Quay to the Aquarium steps. For transportation as tourist-oriented as the destination, hop on the monorail from Pitt St., at Park or Market St., in the city center ($2.50, seniors $1.80, under 6 free; day pass $7, family day pass $19).

Fish from Australia's many aquatic regions inhabit the tanks at **Sydney Aquarium** (tel. 9262 2300; fax 9290 3553), on the pier at Darling Harbour's east shore. If you need more evidence that Australia has the weirdest fauna on earth, stop at the mudskipper containment. These freaks of the fish world display their ability to live out of water by absorbing moisture from the air. More conventional attractions are the seal pool and a small touching pool. The underwater Oceanarium, a plexiglass walking tunnel through a huge fish enclosure, makes the pricey admission less bothersome. (Open daily 9:30am-9pm. Admission $15, students $10, seniors $11, ages 3-15 $7, under 3 free; families $20.90-34.90, depending on number of adults and children. Aquariumpass covers admission and round-trip ferry transport from Circular Quay: $18, ages 3-15 $9, families $47. Wheelchair accessible.)

The massive Soviet submarine docked opposite the aquarium belongs to the **National Maritime Museum** (tel. 9552 7777; recorded info 0055 62002). The short walk across Pyrmont Bridge takes visitors from a look at fish in their natural habitat to a look at humans in fishes' natural habitat. Australia's ever-present involvement with the ocean makes the museum particularly interesting, not only as an isolated look at seafaring but as a survey of Australian history from the times of early Aboriginal trading to the present. Standing exhibitions are less war-oriented than the special exhibits. (Open daily 9:30am-5pm. Admission including one special exhibit $7, students, seniors, and ages 5-15 $4.50, families $18. Museum and all special exhibits $15, $9, $59; special exhibits only $13, $8, $34. Wheelchair accessible.)

Australia's largest museum, the **Powerhouse Museum,** 500 Harris St. (tel. 9217 0111; recorded info 9217 0444; fax 9217 0333), just south of Darling Harbour between Ultimo and Haymarket, explores the breadth of human enterprise and ingenuity through exhibits, interactive displays, and demos. With subject matter ranging from decorative arts to space exploration, the museum's astounding variety gives it endless room for the fun and innovative projects that make it popular with visitors of all ages. (Open daily 10am-5pm. Admission $8, students $3, ages 5-15 $2, seniors and under 5 free, families $18. Wheelchair accessible.)

The serene **Chinese Garden** (tel. 9286 0111; fax 9281 1052), at the corner of Harbour and Pier St., was a bicentennial gift to New South Wales from her sister province in China, Guangdong. Executed in traditional southern Chinese style, the delicately manicured garden provides a breathtaking and refreshing experience within the context of a city. (Open daily 9:30am-5:30pm. Admission $3, students, seniors, and children $1.50, families $6, wheelchair-bound persons free.)

INNER EAST

The suburbs just east of the city center are some of Sydney's most vibrant areas for shopping, eating, and meandering. Although Kings Cross tends to be a bit seedy, the neighborhood is not without a certain charm, particularly for travelers with an interest in nightlife or in meeting other travelers. Oxford St. slides through Surry Hills, Darlinghurst, and Paddington in an endless string of cafes, clothing shops, and hip homewares outlets. Sydney's large, outgoing gay community calls this strip home for much of its length. **Victoria Barracks** (tel. 9339 3000), on Oxford St., in Paddington, has housed members of the Australian Army since its opening in 1841. Free guided tours allow outsiders into this oh-so-sprawling-and-exclusive residence, and a small museum tells tales of army history. (Open for tours Thurs. 10am-3pm; museum open Sun. 10am-4pm; both free.) South of the Barracks, **Moore Park** contains **Sydney Football Stadium** and the city's professional cricket oval. For a tour of the two facilities and a small museum of Australian sports history, call **Sportspace** (tel. 9380 0383; tours Mon.-Sat. 10am, 1, and 3pm; admission $18, seniors and under 19 $12, families $48). Until this year, Moore Park was also the home of the Royal Agricultural Society's Easter Show. Now that the RAS has moved their event to the Homebush Bay Olympic Site, the park stands poised to take on a new carnival, a 20th Century Fox studio, and an entertainment center slated to open in 1999. **Centennial Park,** the city's largest park, abuts Moore Park's east side and stretches north to meet Oxford St. between Paddington and Woolahra. The park includes eight small lakes, a bird sanctuary, athletic fields, and tracks set aside for walking, cycling, and horseback riding. Buses #378, 380, and 382 run the length of Oxford St. from the city center and provide easy connections to all of the inner eastern suburbs.

NORTH SHORE

Often forgotten in the rush to see the south shore sights, Sydney Harbour's north shore supports several worthwhile sights and many beautiful harbor views. At the north base of Sydney Harbour Bridge, the cotton-candy-colored Ferris wheel of **Luna Park** (tel. 9922 6644) beckons grown-up children back to days gone by. The unfortunate truth, at least for the time being, is that those days cannot be recaptured. The tantalizing little park at the bottom of the bridge is closed indefinitely due to a combination of financial problems and neighbors' noise complaints. Milson's Point and the quiet park still command picturesque views of the harbor well worth a quick stop for travelers with wheels.

Kirribilli fills the point of land extending eastward from the bridge's northern pylon. The two grand residences at the end of Kirribilli Point belong to the Australian Governor-general and Prime Minister. The Governor-general's house, known as **Admiralty House,** is the larger abode directly across from the Opera House. Although both figures split their time between these residences and houses in Canberra, they are more often in Sydney, and neither house is open for public inspection.

Koalas, kangaroos, and tigers live with million-dollar harbor views in the **Taronga Park Zoo** (tel. 9969 2777; recorded info 0055 20218), at the end of Bradley's Head Rd., in Mosman. To reach the zoo, you'll need to take a 12-minute ferry ride from Circular Quay then a short jaunt on a bus. The zoo's impressive collection includes animals from all over Australia and the world, but some visitors come away disappointed by the amount of space given each of the animals. The cable car is widely considered the best part of the visit. (Open daily 9am-5pm; admission $15, students, seniors $9, ages 4-15 $7.50, under 4 free. Zoopass covers admission, ferry and bus transport, and the cable car ride inside the zoo: $21, ages 4-15 $10.50.)

Coastal amusements at the northern beach resort at **Manly** emanate a Coney Island boardwalk feel unusual for an Australian beach. The funfair atmosphere on the wharf and along the Corso means that most visitors find Manly either charming or repellent. The **Manly Visitors Bureau** (tel. 9977 1088), on South Steyne St. at the ocean end of the Corso, has brochures on a small collection of sights to occupy visitors who need to get out of the sun on occasion (open daily 10am-4pm). **Ocean World** (tel. 9949 2644; fax 9949 7950), on the West Esplanade at Manly Cove, earns rave reviews for the many strange and rare specimens in its large tropical fish collection. Unlike the staff at Sydney Aquarium, the people at Ocean World have no qualms about letting animals perform or showing off their feeding techniques. Experienced divers should ask about swimming with sharks in the gigantic tank that surrounds the underwater tunnel view area. (Open daily 10am-5:30pm; admission $13.50, students, seniors, and kids $7, families $34.)

Sydney 2000: The Olympics Are Coming

The September 2000 Olympic Summer Games aren't here quite yet. But the energy in the city is palpable as Sydney-siders spruce up key areas of the harborfront and get ready for their city to come to life in the eyes of the world. Construction of the Homebush Bay Olympic Site, 12km west of the city center on the Parramatta River, is well under way. The two largest projects are the Olympic Stadium, an 80,000-seat venue for track and field events and the football finals, and the Olympic Village, a community to accommodate 15,000 athletes during the games and 6000 suburban settlers after the games. A new ferry terminal and train station make the site easily accessible, but the trip will continue to be something of a disappointment until the area gets close to completion. If you are interested in visiting the Homebush Site or any of the completed venues, call the Olympic Coordination Authority's **Information Centre,** 1 Australia Ave. (tel. 9735 4344; open daily 9am-5pm), in Homebush Bay. Tours of the site depart from the center six days per week (Mon.-Fri. 10:30, 11:30am, and 12:30pm, Sat. 11:30am and 12:30pm; $5, students, seniors, and children $2). Housed within the information center, a walk-through exhibit on the site's plans and progress leads to a vantage point to survey the surrounding construction (free).

■ Activities and Entertainment

Let the Games begin! But until they do, you've got a few options.

SPECTATOR SPORTS

Sailboat races in the harbor provide a picturesque and sporting distraction on winter Sundays and summer Saturdays. Views from the bridge give a good perspective on most of the course. In Moore Park, the **Sydney Football Stadium** (tel. 9360 6601) draws crowds for rugby league action as the site of the Wynfield Cup finals in September. The **Sydney Cricket Ground** (tel. 9360 6601), also in Moore Park, fields a number of matches and tests throughout the year including the one-day World Series matches. Since their appearance in the Grand Finals in 1995, the **Sydney Swans,** the local Australian Football League side, have begun to generate huge turn-outs at home games on the cricket ground.

WATER ACTIVITIES

Sydney's most popular pastimes take advantage of the harbor and coastline's natural playgrounds. On any sunny day, white sails can be seen clipping across the waters. **Sydney by Sail** (tel. 9371 6228) conducts 90-minute hands-on introductory sailing lessons from the National Maritime Museum ($39 per person; trips daily depending on weather and demand; 6-person max.; call ahead to book). **Elizabeth Bay Marina,** 1 Ithaca Rd. (tel. 9358 2977), in Elizabeth Bay, allows you to test the waters for yourself with rental boats (17-foot launches for up to 6 people $65 for a half day, full day $110, deposit $50; open daily 8:30am-4:30pm). The Marina is a short walk from Kings Cross. Follow MacLeay St. to Greenknowe St., take a right, and then take the second left at Ithaca Rd. **East Sail Sailing School** (tel. 9327 1166) caters to those who don't yet know their way around a sailboat and provides advanced instruction for more experienced mariners (beginning sailing course $345; trial lesson $80, groups $280).

Sydney's rocky shores include several worthwhile spots for both shore diving and boat diving. **ProDive,** with locations in the city center, 428 George St. (tel. 9264 6177; open Mon.-Wed. and Fri. 9am-5:30pm, Thurs. 9am-8:30pm, Sat. 9am-5pm, Sun. 11am-4pm) and at Coogee, 27 Afreda St. (tel. 9665 6333; open Mon.-Fri. 8:30am-7pm, Sat.-Sun. 7:30am-6pm), has excellent advice on local diving spots and all the gear you'll ever need (boats and gear for a full day of diving $60-100, depending on day, season, and specials; gear alone Mon.-Fri. $25, Sat.-Sun. $50).

Surfing at Bondi Beach makes all of the postcards, but Sydney has other surfing beaches with equally appealing waves. On the south ocean shore, try Bondi, Tamarama, and Coogee. Heading north, the hot spots are Manly, Curl Curl, Dee Why, North Narrabeen, Newport Reef, and Palm Beach. **Bondi Surf Co.,** 72 Campbell Pde. (tel. 9369 0870), rents boards with wetsuits included for $30 per day (3hr. $20; credit card or passport required; open daily 9:30am-6pm). At Manly, try **Aloha Surf,** 44 Pittwater Rd. (tel. 9977 3777; full day $25, half-day $15, wetsuit included; open Mon.-Wed. and Fri.-Sat. 9am-7pm, Thurs. 9am-9pm, Sun. 9am-6pm). The beach communities also see a fair number of people exploring the seaside strips on in-line skates. For rentals, visit **Bondi Boards and Blades,** 148 Curlewis St. (tel. 9365 6555; open daily 10am-6pm) in Bondi, or **Manly Blades,** 49 North Steyne St. (tel. 9976 3833), in Manly. Both rent skates and pads for $10 for the first hour and $5 per hour thereafter.

To explore the area's considerable inland waterways or to get a more in-depth look at the harbor coast, paddlers call **Balmoral Marine** (tel. 9969 6006), on Awaba St. at Balmoral Beach. (Canoes $10 per hr.; kayaks $15 per hr., half-day $50, full day $80. sea kayaks $20 per hr., half-day $60, full day $100; open daily 8am-5pm.) Take bus #244 or 247 toward Mosman from Wynyard Station.

PERFORMING ARTS

Sydney's prized **Opera House** (box office tel. 9250 7777; open Mon.-Sat. 9am-8:30pm and before Sun. shows) has four auditoriums and a wide variety of cultural endeavors. Reserved opera seats start at $70 and often sell out quickly. Restricted view seats vary in quality, and mean that you'll see 25-75% of the stage (in advance $35; from 9am on the performance day $20, limit of 2 tickets per person). Tickets for standing room go on sale at 9am the morning of a performance ($20, limit 2 per person). Any tickets left unsold 30 minutes prior to a performance are sold at student rush rates ($25). People often line up before tickets become available, so it is wise to get to the Opera House before the 30-minute window. The resident theater company, **Drama Theatre,** presents works from well outside the canon, and tickets tend to be both less expensive and less sought-after than those for opera.

The **Sydney Symphony Orchestra** (24hr. tel. 9334 4600) performs at the Sydney Opera House and at **Eugene Goosens Hall,** 700 Harris St. (tel. 9333 1500; calls taken Mon.-Fri. 9am-5pm), in Ultimo, from February through November. Ticketing is handled by the Symphony and, for Opera House performances only, by the Sydney Opera House box office. Student rush tickets, when available, must be purchased on the day of the concert at that evening's venue ($12). Concerts in Sydney's **Town Hall Auditorium** (tel. 9265 9333) are booked by Ticketek (see **Practical Information,** p. 98). The **Sydney Conservatorium of Music** (tel. 9230 1263), in the Royal Botanic Gardens, stages free concerts during school terms, which range from jazz to classical (Wed. and Fri. 1:10pm).

The **Sydney Theatre Company** and the **Sydney Dance Company,** the city's premier performance groups in their respective fields, perform at the **Wharf Theatre** (tel. 9250 1777; open Mon.-Sat. 9am-8:30pm), at Pier 4, on Walsh Bay. For tickets to performances of either company's work, call the theater box office or First Call (see **Practical Information,** p. 98). Other First Call theater venues include the **Capitol Theatre** (tel. 9230 9122), at George and Campbell St., just north of Central Station, the **Theatre Royal** (tel. 9320 9122), on King St., in the MLC Center, and the fabulously ornate and ostentatious **State Theatre,** 49 Market St. (tel. 9373 6655), between George and Pitt St. These are the city's three main stages for touring shows and splashy musical productions. For more unusual theatrical fare, try the **Belvoir St. Theatre,** 25 Belvoir St. (tel. 9699 3444), in Surry Hills.

Dendy Cinema, 624 George St. (tel. 9264 1577), near the neon of the first-run Greater Union Cinema, and **Academy Twin Cinema,** 3a Oxford St. (tel. 9361 4453), in Paddington, both screen art-house flicks at mainstream prices (tickets $12, students $9, seniors and under 15 $7.50). At the other end of the cinematic spectrum, **Panasonic Imax Theatre** (tel. 13 34 62), on the Southern Promenade at Darling Harbour, blasts viewers with a screen 10 times the size of one in a normal movie house (tickets $14, students and seniors $11, children $10).

■ Nightlife

When the weather is fine, many Sydney-siders go out for drinks or dancing as many as four or five nights per week. Different neighborhoods have distinctly different scenes, and little mixing occurs. Bars in Kings Cross attract a large, straight male crowd which quickly spills over from the strip joints into the pubs and dance clubs. Backpackers round out the mix in this neighborhood, giving several venues an unexpectedly international feel. Outside Kings Cross, travelers generally congregate in pubs to avoid the high cover charges and inflated drink prices of Sydney's high-profile dance venues. **Gay Sydney** struts its stuff on Oxford St. in Darlinghurst and Paddington, where many establishments are specifically gay or lesbian and others are open, mixed, and comfortable. Because the gay clubs provide most of the city's best dance music, flocks of young, beautiful club scenesters fill any extra space on Oxford St.'s vibrant, vampy dance floors. Taylor Sq., at the intersection of Oxford, Flinders, and Bourke St., is the heart of this district. Suits clog the bars in the Central Business District, and night spots in the Rocks tend toward the expensive. For more casual pub crawling, wander on Bourke and Flinders St. in Surry Hills.

Aside from the major concerts in the **Sydney Entertainment Centre** (tel. 1900 957 333; box office open Mon.-Fri. 9am-5pm, Sat. 10am-1pm), on Harbour St. in Haymarket, the **Hordern Pavillion** (tel. 9331 9263), at the RAS Show Ground in Moore Park, or the **Enmore Theatre,** 130 Enmore Rd. (tel. 9550 3666), in Newtown, Sydney's live music scene consists largely of local bands casting their pearls before pub crowds. The *Metro* section of the Friday *Sydney Morning Herald* and free weeklies such as *Beat* and *Sydney City Hub* contain listings for upcoming shows, along with info on art showings, movies, theater offerings, and DJ appearances city-wide. *Capital Q Weekly* (free) focuses on the gay community with commentary, news, and local listings. *Drum Media* covers music almost exclusively with listings, news, and reviews.

PUBS

Dirty Nelly's, 9-11 Glenmore Rd. (tel. 9360 4467), in Paddington, just off Oxford St. at Gipps St. Sydney's most authentic Irish bar does its best to carry on the tradition of its namesake in Ireland's County Clare. Even when it's packed, a common phenomenon on weekend nights, the dark wood decor coupled with Guinness (schooners $3.20) creates a relaxing refuge from the Oxford St. melee around the corner. Popular with folks under and over 40. Open daily 11am-midnight.

Scruffy Murphy's, 43 Goulburn St. (tel. 9211 2002 or 9281 5296), in the city center, on the corner of George St. Nightly live music, $5 jug nights, and frequent specials for the nearby Sydney Central YHA, rank Scruffy Murphy's high on the list of Sydney backpacker haunts. On some nights the young clientele is largely travelers and British ex-pats. Schooner of VB $2.40. Open Sun.-Thurs. 11am-2am, Fri.-Sat. 11am-4am.

O'Malley's Hotel, 228 William St. (tel. 9357 2211), in Kings Cross, at the corner of Brougham St. O'Malley's achieves a good mix of upscale style and casual pub atmosphere. The low lighting and shiny wood could easily make it a suit bar. Instead, the eclectic crowd shows that backpackers, business-types, and more casual locals can indeed mix well. Quite possibly the most appealing spot for a couple of quiet beers anywhere in Kings Cross. Schooners of Toohey's New $3. Mixed drinks with house spirits $4. Open daily 11am-2:30am.

Hopetoun Hotel (tel. 9361 5257), in Surry Hills, at the corner of Bourke and Fitzroy St. Yet another pub-style corner bar with Irish flair. This time though, the Surry Hills setting makes things a little more funky. An excellent stop on a crawl through Surry Hills. Live nightly music ranges from acoustic ensembles to rock. Occasional cover about $5. Schooners of draft $3 in the daytime, $3.30 at night. Open Mon.-Sat. noon-midnight, Sun. noon-10pm.

Taxi Club, 40 Flinders St. (tel. 9331 4256), in Darlinghurst. Waves of rumor and intrigue emanate from one of Sydney's most notorious alternative bars. From transvestites to muscle-bound bouncers, the Taxi Club guarantees a wild time with a mixed crowd. It's as close to 24hr. as a Sydney bar gets without craps tables (closed only Tues.-Thurs. 5:45am-9am; dance club open Fri.-Sun. evenings). Check it out post-party for one last, cheap drink, but be careful on the oh-so-steep stairs. Cover in the dance club $10.

Orient Hotel (tel. 9251 1255), in the Rocks, at the corner of Argyle and George St. The pubs of the Rocks can be a bit more expensive than their counterparts in other parts of town. The Orient softens the blow with free live entertainment every night. Drink 10 beers from around the world, preferably in a weekend, and they'll throw in a free T-shirt. Schooners from $3. Open Mon.-Thurs. 10am-2am, Fri.-Sat. 10am-3am, Sun. 10am-midnight.

Coogee Bay Hotel (tel. 9665 0000), on Campbell Pde. at Coogee Beach. The large, swanky Coogee Bay Hotel supplies the juice for Coogee's nightlife scene year-round. Drinks are cheap every night (schooners of draft $2.70-3; house spirits $3.50), but things go plum loco on Tues. and Thurs. when prices drop to $1. Holy backpackers, Batman! Selina's Entertainment Center, in the hotel, is one of Sydney's more popular concert venues and sometimes gets international acts. Three bars open Mon.-Thurs. 9am-3am, Fri.-Sat. 9am-5am, Sun. 9am-midnight.

DANCE CLUBS

Ministry of Dance, 54 Darlinghurst Rd. (tel. 9357 3800), in Kings Cross. Two floors of dancing and enough drink specials to make cirrhosis affordable. Wed. ($2 beer 8-10pm, $1 vodka 8-11pm) and Thurs. ($1 house spirits and schooners 8-10pm, $2 after 10pm) draw travelers like Catholic school boys to confession. The downstairs bar makes little connection with the supposed theme, but gothic archways and backlit stained-glass crosses get the point across on the 2nd level. Full-priced drinks and $15 cover during the Sat.-Sun. overnight. Open Mon.-Fri. 9am-4am, Sat. 9am-8pm and 10pm-Sun. 6pm.

Rhino Bar, 24 Bayswater Rd. (tel. 9357 7700), in Kings Cross. The subdued African safari lodge theme makes weekend DJ'd dance parties a little incongruous, but that's the last thing on anyone's mind. Live entertainment and give-aways bring in backpackers on Tues. DJs work their magic Thurs.-Sat. Jugs $8 (usually $5 on Thurs.). Drinks $2 all day, Fri.-Sat. 9pm-midnight. Cover Fri.-Sat. $5. Open Mon.-Thurs. 3pm-late, Fri.-Sat. 3pm-6am.

Midnight Shift, 85 Oxford St. (tel. 9360 4319), in Darlinghurst. The boy toy pictures downstairs come to life on the video screens up above, where DJs spin hot dance tunes for an almost exclusively gay male audience. The showy, sexual atmosphere, enhanced by a catwalk and dancing stands, gets deeper and dirtier on Friday's candle-lit Black Out Night (cover $5). Wed. is Transformers Night with a drag show and a $5 cover. Sat. cover $10. Draft beers $2.40-3.20. Open Mon.-Fri. noon-3am or later, Sat. 6am-Sun. noon, Sun. 2pm-midnight.

Kinsela's, 383 Bourke St. (tel. 9331 2699), in Darlinghurst. A Sydney standby for funk, R&B, and acid jazz. Each of the 3 floors has its own agenda, so there's always something groovy going on. The ground floor features live or DJ'd funk and popular appearances by the band Professor Groove. The middle bar tends to stick closer to R&B with DJs in control. The top floor varies with theme nights, multiple-band lineups, and other big events (Sat. cover $5 until midnight, $10 after midnight). Everybody is welcome, and gay, lesbian, and straight folks all show up in large numbers. Drinks hover around $4-5. Sun. nights are "The Other Side" for lesbians. Open Mon.-Sat. 8pm-3am, Sun. 8pm-midnight.

Imperial Hotel, 35 Erskineville Rd. (tel. 9519 9899), in Erskineville. Take a train to Erskineville, take a taxi, make the hike. The costumes and wigs at the outrageously fabulous weekend drag shows make it worthwhile. The "Priscilla Queen of the Imperial" show adds one more layer to the wall of parody and homage surrounding Swedish super-group Abba. Get there early; the crowd is gay, lesbian, straight, and huge by showtime. Schooners of VB $2.50-3. No cover. Shows Fri.-Sat. 11:30pm (Priscilla) and 2:15am (changing themes, always topical). Open Mon. 11am-10pm, Tues. 11am-2am, Wed.-Fri. 11am-5am, Sat. 2pm-5am, Sun. 2pm-midnight.

Albury Hotel, 6 Oxford St. (tel. 9361 6555), in Paddington. Two large rooms provide separation between the drag show entertainment and dancing and the less-energized bar scene. Differences aside, both halves are part of a pretty scammy whole. Gay men and straight females place bets on which of the bartenders will go shirtless next. Shows change all the time; check the movie-style posters outside for the current line-up. Schooners of draft $3.20. Liberal shots of Jack Daniels $5.50. Open daily 2pm-2am.

DCM, 33 Oxford St. (tel. 9267 7380), in Darlinghurst, near the west end of Oxford. You can't miss it; the glowing rainbow rings and huge glittery letters can be seen for blocks. The dancing is fast, hard, and showy and the crowd young and beautiful. Avoid Sat. nights unless you have time to waste standing on the sidewalk. Otherwise, it's great, sweaty fun for all. Drinks average $5.50. Cover Thurs. $5, Fri. and Sun. $10, Sat. $20 with invite. Open Thurs.-Sun. 11pm-early morning.

■ Markets and Festivals

Sydney has numerous year-round weekend markets, all of which tend more toward arts, crafts, and gifts than toward fresh produce. Still, the scene is fun, the food is reasonably priced, and there's generally at least one cart selling fresh fruit. **Paddington Market,** 395 Oxford St., in Paddington, is perhaps Sydney's best known and most lively market (open Sat. 10am-4pm). **Balmain Market,** at St. Andrew's Church, on the corner of Darling St. and Curtis Rd., and **Glebe Markets,** at Glebe Public School, on the corner of Glebe Point Rd., and Derby Pl., also operate on pleasant Saturdays from 10am to 4pm. **Paddy's Markets,** on Ultimo Rd. at Hay St., is enclosed and a bit more commercial. It's also the only market in Sydney to feature a wide array of produce (open Sat.-Sun. 9am-4:30pm, rain or shine). **The Rocks Market** (tel. 9255 1717), at the north end of George St. under the bridge, takes the market concept up-market with a fair number of booths devoted to antiques, jewelry, and collectibles (open Sat.-Sun. 10am-5pm, rain or shine).

Sydney Festival kicks off the year's calendar with arts and entertainment events throughout the month of January (Jan. 3-26 in 1998). Check the newspaper for details on free concerts in the Domain, street theater in the Rocks, and fireworks in Darling Harbour. In February, the gay community does it up in **Mardi Gras** fashion. Festivities climax on the last Saturday of the month (Feb. 28 in 1998) with a parade, attended annually by over half a million people, and a gala party at the RAS Show Ground in Moore Park. Though the party is restricted and the guest list fills up long before the night of the event, gay and lesbian international travelers can get their names included by contacting the organizing committee (tel. 9557 4332) and becoming "International Members of Mardi Gras" well in advance ($20 per person).

Beginning in 1998, the **Royal Agricultural Society's Easter Show** (RAS tel. 9331 9111) will be held at the Homebush Olympic Site (April 4-18 in 1998). The carnival atmosphere surrounding the show makes it fun for everyone, not just those with an interest in farming. The ornate State Theatre, 49 Market St., between George and Pitt St., comes alive with the **Sydney Film Festival** (tel. 9373 9050; recorded info 9660 3844) each June. The 14-day festival showcases new works and classics from around the world. Falling on even years, the **Sydney Biennale** (tel. 9368 1411) will reappear in 1998, and bring special showings of international art to the Art Gallery of New South Wales, the Powerhouse Museum, and other gallery spaces citywide from August through October. The **City to Surf Run** (tel. 9633 1211), held on the second Sunday in August (Aug. 9 in 1998), draws over 30,000 contestants for a semi-serious trot from Park St. to the beach at Bondi. Entries are accepted up to the day of the race for a fee of $18 (under 18 $12).

Spring festivals include the **Manly Jazz Festival** over Labor Day weekend (Oct. 3-5 in 1998) and the **Kings Cross Carnival** at the end of October. At **Christmas,** Bondi sets the pace for debauchery up and down the coast as travelers from around the world gather for one foot-stomping beach party. The Boxing Day **Sydney to Hobart Yacht Race** brings the city's attention back to civilized entertainment for a brief interlude before end-of-the-year festivities reclaim the harbor on **New Year's Eve.**

AROUND SYDNEY

Botany Bay National Park

The two sections of Botany Bay National Park, located on the outermost reaches of land surrounding Botany Bay, have been preserved for their historical significance rather than for their scenic beauty. The two sites, designated together as a National Park in 1988, memorialize the voyages of English Captain James Cook and French explorer Jean-Françoise de Galaup, Count de Laperouse. Cook's landing at Kurnell on the southern headland of the bay resulted in the colony which has become the nation of Australia. The Laperouse expedition, to which the northern half of the park is dedicated, ended less successfully with the mysterious disappearance of two ships and scores of men. Despite popular impressions of Botany Bay as either sleepy and suburban or ugly and industrial, visitors often remember best the ocean views and beaches.

The arrival of the English ship *Endeavour* on April 29, 1770, is Botany Bay's first claim to fame. James Cook and his crew spent eight days in the area collecting plant specimens and exploring. During this time the Europeans made unsuccessful attempts to communicate with the local Guyeagal people and then, despite orders to act only with "consent of the natives," established a land claim. The **Discovery Centre** (tel. 9668 9923), 450m beyond the toll gate inside the park's southern section, has a fine exhibit on the three-year voyage of the *Endeavour.* Exhibits are also devoted to the Guyeagal people and their reaction to Cook's arrival. (Open Mon.-Fri. 11am-3pm, Sat.-Sun. 10am-4pm.) Nearby, a short walking trail passes several monuments and historical markers related to Cook's landing. Most of the park's ocean-front shoreline is considered dangerous for water activities, but **swimming, fishing,** and **diving** are possible on the Botany Bay shore near the Discovery Center. Surfers should move down the beach to Cronulla. (Gates open daily 7am-7:30pm. Park entry $7.50 per car, collected only Sat.-Sun. and holidays. Pedestrians free.) To access the park's southern section from Sydney, take the Cronulla train from Town Hall or Central Station to Cronulla ($3.20, off-peak return $3.80). Kurnell Bus Company (tel. 9524 8977) has regular service from Cronulla Railway Station to the park on Hwy. 987 (Mon.-Fri. 11 per day, Sat. 8 per day, Sun. 3 per day; $2.80, students, seniors, and ages 4-18 $1.40). By car, follow the Princes Hwy. south and branch left at Taren Point Rd. Turn left on Captain Cook Dr., which heads directly to the park.

The northern half of the Botany Bay National Park charges no entrance fee. Here, the **Laperouse Museum** (tel. 9311 3379), at the end of Anzac Pde., recounts the tale of Laperouse and his mysterious last voyage. The mystery's not huge—the poor guy sank—but the museum does an excellent job of building suspense. (Open Wed.-Sun. 10am-4:30pm. Admission $2, students, seniors, and under 15 $1.) The French govern-

It Might've Been "L'Australie"

On January 26, 1788, members of the British First Fleet were surprised to see two ships approach the shore at Botany Bay. The French Laperouse expedition arrived just six days after the British brought the first load of convicts to the planned penal colony. Three years into an around-the-world exploratory mission, the French crew needed time to rest and make repairs to their vessels. The British Captain Phillip moved north to Port Jackson, later renamed Sydney, while Laperouse stayed at Botany Bay for six weeks. Despite national rivalry, the two groups interacted regularly and were on friendly terms throughout the stay of the French. On March 10, Laperouse and his party set sail and cruised into the South Pacific, never to be seen again. The French government sent out its first search party in 1791, and Louis XVI's last request (in 1793) was "any news of Monsieur de Laperouse?" But 30 years passed before any trace of his wreck was found.

ment's **monument** to Laperouse, erected in 1828, stands near the current museum. Across a short footbridge, **Bare Island Fort** once guarded Sydney's southern approach from the none-too-likely threat of attack. Today the fort is accessible only on guided tours (Sat.-Sun. 12:45, 1:30, 2:30, and 3:30pm; 40min.; $5, students, seniors, and under 15 $3; call the Laperouse Museum for bookings). The **Boatshed Cafe** (tel. 9661 9315), on the water near the Laperouse Museum, is a convenient spot to grab lunch and watch the windsurfers or the ships on Botany Bay (fish, grilled or fried, and chips $6, hamburger $3.50; open Tues.-Fri. 10am-5pm, Sat.-Sun. 10am-6pm, longer in summer). The surrounding rocks are perfect for an impromptu take-away picnic. When you're tired of watching, rent a boat or windsurf board from **First Fleet Marine** (tel. 9661 9315), inside the Boatshed Cafe Building (motor boats $20 for the first hr., $15 each additional hr.; paddle boats $10 per hr.; pedal boats $10 per ½hr.; windsurf boards available spring and summer only). Fisherfolk will find bait and tackle for sale ($2-4), but there's no equipment to rent. The beach below the cafe is clean, sandy, and suitable for swimming. Sydney bus #393 from Railway Square and #394 from Circular Quay make the trip to this end of Botany Bay regularly. Drivers need only take Anzac Pde. until it ends at the Laperouse Museum.

Royal National Park

Just 30km south of Sydney's city center, **Royal National Park** is an easy and glorious escape from city life. The park, Australia's oldest and the world's second-oldest (after the United States' Yellowstone), covers 14,969 hectares of beach, heath, rainforest, swamp, and woodland. The range of activities available in the park is as broad as the diversity of habitat would suggest. Bushwalkers, birdwatchers, swimmers, and surfers all find favorite getaways in different corners of the park, while an extensive network of trails and driving routes allows everyone to spread out during the busy summer weekends. Across the Princes Hwy. on the west side of the park, the smaller, often-forgotten **Heathcote National Park** contributes another 2000 hectares of heathland to the cause of travelers and Sydney-siders trying to lose themselves in the green.

Getting There **CityRail trains** from Sydney come to Loftus in the northwest ($2.80, off-peak return $3.40), Waterfall in the west ($3.80; $4.40 round-trip), or Otford at the park's southern point ($4.40; $5.20). From Waterfall or Otford, walk east to enter the park. To approach the northeast corner, take CityRail to Cronulla ($3.20; 3.80 from Central Station) and then catch a **Cronulla National Park Ferries** (tel. 9523 2990) boat to Bundeena, home of **Bonnie Vale campground** and the **Coastal Track** trailhead. (To Bundeena Mon.-Fri. 5:30am-6:30pm, hourly on the half hr., Sat.-Sun. 8:30am-5:30pm; no 12:30pm departure. To Cronulla Mon.-Fri. 6am-7pm hourly on the hr., Sat.-Sun. 9am-6pm; no 1pm departure. $2.40, ages 4-15 and seniors $1.20.) By car, the Princes Hwy. provides easy access to the park from Sydney. Follow the signs to head east on Farnell Ave. south of Loftus.

Practical Information **The Audley Visitor Centre** (tel. 9542 0648, open daily 8:30am-1pm and 2pm-4:30pm), 2km inside the park's entrance and 4km south of Loftus, distributes information on walking trails, ranger-led activities, and camping in the park. The main park road, running from the northwest entrance to Otford, stays open 24 hours, but turn-offs have locked gates from 7:30pm to 7am. Toilet kiosks are located at Dudley (wheelchair accessible), Wattamella, and Garie Beach. Entrance to the park costs $7.50 per car (pedestrians and cyclists free).

Camping and Accommodations The National Parks and Wildlife Service (NPWS) administers one car-accessible serviced camping area in Royal National Park, **Bonnie Vale,** just inside the park at Bundeena. From Dudley, take the main park road to Bundeena Rd. and follow the signs to Bonnie Vale. Sites have access to parking, toilets, showers, water, laundry facilities, pay phones, and trash bins and cost $10 for the first two people (each additional person $2, children under 6 free; no electrical hook-ups or individual water supplies). No open fires are permitted anywhere in the park. The gates on Bundeena Rd. close from 6am to 9:30pm, but keys may be borrowed from the Audley Visitors Centre or from the camp manager (deposit $25). The NPWS also oversees 150 free, **primitive campsites** in six locations throughout Royal National Park and at the popular Kingfisher Pool camping area in nearby Heathcote National Park. Required permits for any of these areas can be obtained at the Audley Visitors Centre or by mail. For bushcamping permits or to put in an application for a Bonnie Vale lottery periods (conducted for sites during school holidays), write to NPWS South Metropolitan District, P.O. Box 44, Sutherland NSW 2232.

Royal National Park's only public accommodation with a roof is the **Garie Beach YHA Hostel,** an unstaffed and very basic (read: no electricity, phone, or plumbing) three-room house overlooking Garie Beach. In the right mood, it's idyllic. In the wrong mood, the mice under the house and the holes in the floor could be annoying. Either way, the view is fabulous (12 beds; $6, under 18 $3). Reservations and key pick-up must be arranged in advance through the YHA Travel and Membership Centre, 422 Kent St., Sydney (tel. 9261 1111), or at either of the Sydney YHA hostels.

Sights and Activities The breathtaking 26km **Coastal Track** tops Royal National Park's list of bushwalking trails. Running along the sandstone cliff line between Bundeena and Otford, the trail is generally approached as a two-day affair, allowing time to enjoy the wildflowers of the heath, the depths of the coastal caves, and the sheer expanse of the ocean views. Hikers with less time often hike a piece of the trail from one of the park roads and then return to their starting point. The park's only **wheelchair-accessible trail** runs up to Bungoona Lookout from the Audley Visitors Centre (1km round-trip). The short **Aboriginal rock engravings** walk begins at Jibbon Beach, on Port Hacking, east of Bundeena. The engravings, believed to be between 800 and 5000 years old, depict animals that were important to the local tribe's diet. Although Aboriginal carvings appear on rocks throughout the park, officials only direct tourists to the Jibbon site. Defacement at the site makes their reasoning obvious. From Otford Lookout, at the park's southern tip, the 1km **Werrong (Hellhole) Track** leads to the only **nude swimming beach** in Royal National Park. When the wind is right, Werrong is also an excellent surf spot (wetsuit recommended). The park visitors' center has maps and directions to other walking trails, many of which lead to swimming holes, waterfalls, or secluded beaches.

Most **surfers** favor the beaches at Wattamolla, Garie, North and South Era, or the secluded Burning Palms area. Surf Life Saving Clubs overlook the beaches at both Garie and Burning Palms. Although visitors are prohibited from touching animals inside the park, **fishing** off the shore is quite all right, and Jibbon Point, Wattamolla, Garie, and Burning Palms are all popular spots for casting a line. The **Audley Boatshed** (tel. 9545 4967), off Farnell Ave., about 500m beyond the Audley Visitors Centre, rents rowboats, canoes, kayaks (1hr. $10, 2hr. $16, half-day $16-18, full day $20), **mountain bikes** (1hr. $6, full day $22), **tandem bicycles** (1hr.$12, full day $44), and **aqua bikes** ($8 per half hr.). All rentals require a $10 deposit. (Open daily 8:30am-before sundown, roughly 7pm in summer and 4:30pm in winter.)

The water off of Bonnie Vale, Jibbon Beach, Wattamolla, and Little Marley is safe for **swimming.** Marley Beach, just north of Little Marley, is considered unsafe. Inland, freshwater swimming holes, such as Deer Pool, near Marley Beach, and the Kangaroo Creek, southwest of Audley, offer more placid and secluded settings for a dip.

Ku-Ring-Gai Chase National Park

Seven years old when the Australian colonies federated in 1901, the country's second-oldest national park, Ku-Ring-Gai Chase, came close to gaining a far more central role in the new nation's development as the site of the capital city. However, the proposal to build the city on the park land in medieval English style—as a moated fortress capital to be called Pacivica—was eventually passed over in favor of the plan which led to the creation of Canberra. The park, located just 24km from downtown Sydney, has remained the preserve it was intended to be from the outset and has since grown to include over 14,000 hectares and to cover most of the southern headlands of Broken Bay.

The volunteer-run **Kalkari Visitors Centre** (tel. 9457 9853), on Ku-Ring-Gai Chase Rd., 4km inside the park gates, has brochures on this and other Sydney-area national parks and distributes free hiking maps. Volunteers from the center run a program of mostly free **guided walks** highlighting Aboriginal engraving sites and the park's scenic gems (open daily 9am-5pm). **Bobbin Head Information Centre** (tel. 9457 1049), inside the Wilderness Shop, at the bottom of the hill at Bobbin Head, is the official National Parks and Wildlife Service information outlet for the park (open daily 9am-4pm). Four roads provide vehicle access to the park: Ku-Ring-Gai Chase Rd. from the Pacific Hwy. and Bobbin Head Rd. from Turramurra, both in the southwest corner of the park, and Booralie Rd. and Pittwater Rd., which branch from Mona Vale Rd. to enter the southeast section of the park (park fee $7.50 per car). Ferries come into the park from **Palm Beach Ferry Service** (tel. 9918 2747 or 9974 5235), stopping at the Basin (5-11 per day, $3.50), Bobbin Head (daily at 11am, $14), and Patonga (daily at 9, 11am, and 3pm, $6). Sydney Bus #190 goes from Wynyard Station to Palm Beach near the wharf from which the ferries set out. Public transportation for other destinations within the park is explained below.

NEW SOUTH WALES

The park's **camping area** and **hostel** can be approached by car from the east side of the park, but each requires that you leave the car behind somewhere along the way. The campground at the Basin (recorded info tel. 9451 8124) is accessible by ferry from Palm Beach or by a 2.5km hike on the Basin track from West Head Rd. The site has cold showers, toilets, wood BBQs, and a public phone, but all supplies must be carried in. (Sites for 2 $10, each additional person up to 6 $2; during school holidays $15, $3; children under 5 free.) Required bookings must be arranged through the NPWS office at **Garigal National Park** (tel. 9972 7378; open Mon.-Fri. 9am-4pm), but payment can be made at the site.

Possibly the most refreshingly remote hostel in the greater Sydney area, the **Pittwater YHA Hostel** (tel. 9999 2196 or 015 214 511; fax 9997 4296), accessible by ferry from Church Point (round-trip $6), enjoys lush green scenery from its lofty perch over Pittwater. Take bus #155 from Manly or bus #186 from Wynyard or follow Pittwater Rd. to reach the Church Point wharf. The open, outdoorsy hostel provides a retreat without the distraction of TV or radio. Hosts encourage guests to get out and use any of the 16 walking trails which start in the immediate area or to partake of a summer swim in the nearby bioluminescent bay. (Canoe rental $6 for length of stay. Reception open daily 8-11am and 5-9pm. Dorms $15, under 18 $8; twins $38. Sat. $20, $10; $24; YHA non-members pay $3 more. Linen $2-3. Bookings required.)

Ku-Ring-Gai Chase National Park has a good number of quality bushwalking trails for walkers of any level of expertise. The 20-minute **discovery walk** just outside the Kalkari Visitors Centre is a quick, easy way to see the local animal life and experience the varied habitats contained within the park (wheelchair accessible). The circuit created by linking the Bobbin Head Track and the Sphinx Track, between the Bobbin Head Rd. entrance to the park and Bobbin Head, covers almost 10km, passing through mangroves, along a creek, and near an Aboriginal engraving site and numerous middens. Take **Shorelink Tours** (tel. 9457 8888) bus #577 from Turramurra Railway Station (from Central Station $2.80, off-peak return $3.40) to the park entrance gates (Mon.-Sat. every 30min., limited service on Sun.). There are no patrolled swimming beaches in the park, but the protected coves of Pittwater along West Head, in particular at the Basin, are less turbulent than the open waters of Broken Bay. **Halvorsen Boats** (tel. 9457 9011), at Bobbin Head near the Wilderness Shop, rents motorboats (1st hr. $30, each additional hr. $6; deposit $30) and rowboats ($10, $4, $10). Sundays are often quite busy, but reservations are not accepted; call ahead to check availability, and get there early (open Mon.-Fri. 8:30am-4pm, Sat.-Sun. 8:30am-4:30pm).

Parramatta to Penrith

In April 1788, Governor Phillip of the Sydney colony led an expedition west to see what lay up the river from the new town settlement. Australia's second town was established as a result of that exploratory mission in November of the same year. Then called Rose Hill, the settlement grew into the present-day town of Parramatta, a 20-minute drive from Sydney along Parramatta Rd. Before reaching Parramatta, the road becomes the M4 Tollway, at Strathfield, the most direct route to the Blue Mountains (toll $1.50).

PARRAMATTA

The village whose fertile farmland once fed the starving Sydney colony is now a suburban extension of the nearby city. Parramatta does, however, maintain several buildings from the early days of colonization which rank high on many history-minded tourists' must-see lists. The most notable of these buildings is **Old Government House** (tel. 9635 8149; fax 9891 4102), in Parramatta Park at the west end of town. Originally a plaster cottage built by Governor Phillip in 1790, the house grew into its current Georgian grandeur through renovations made by Governor Lachlan Macquarie between 1815 and 1816. The National Trust now owns the house, which finished its service as a governor's residence after the completion of Sydney's Government House in 1855, and offers tours of the buildings and the colonial furniture collection housed within. (Open Tues.-Fri. 10am-4pm, Sat.-Sun. 11am-4:15pm, last admission 30min. before closing; admission $5, students, seniors, and under 16 $3, families of 4 $12; 1½hr.; tours happen whenever people gather; combined admission ticket with Experiment Farm Cottage $8, concessions $6.)

Elizabeth Farm, 70 Alice St. (tel. 9635 9488; fax 9891 3740), in Rosehill, east of the town center, was the home of John and Elizabeth Macarthur, founders of the Australian Merino wool industry. A bungalow-style home exemplary of early Australian architecture, the farm house features furnishings in the style of the late 1700s and early 1800s and a large number of historical replicas made to fit descriptions of pieces owned by the MacArthurs. (Open daily 10am-5pm; admission $5, students, seniors, and ages 5-15 $3, under 5 free, families of 5 $12.)

John Macarthur built **Hambleton Cottage** (tel. 9635 6924), on the corner of Hassall St. and Gregory Pl., in 1824 as a home for his son Edward. (Open Wed.-Thurs. and Sat.-Sun. 11am-4pm; admission $2.50, seniors $2, ages 5-12 $1.) In 1790, the colonial government made its first land grant in the Australian colony to James Ruse at the site of **Experiment Farm Cottage** (tel. 9635 5655; open Tues.-Thurs. 10am-4pm, Sun. 11am-4pm; admission $5, students, seniors, and under 15 $3; combined admission ticket with Old Government House $8, $6).

The **Parramatta Visitors Centre** (tel. 9630 3703), on the corner of Church and Market St., distributes information on these and other historical sights in the Parramatta area (open Mon.-Fri. 1am-4pm, Sat. 9am-1pm, Sun. 10:30am-3pm). From Sydney, trains (from Central Station $2.80, off-peak return $3.40) and ferries both make the trip to Parramatta. The ferry ride ($4.80), a 70-minute cruise on a sleek, new RiverCat pontoon boat, is far preferable to the 30-minute train ride.

West of Parramatta, in Doonside, **Featherdale Wildlife Park,** 217 Kildare Rd. (tel. 9622 1644; recorded info 9671 4984; fax 9671 4140), provides interactive animal fun, allowing visitors to feed kangaroos and interact with members of the country's largest collection of native Australian animals (open daily 9am-5pm; admission $10.50, students $9.50, seniors $7, ages 4-14 $5.50, families of 4 $26). Forty minutes from Sydney by car, the park is also accessible by bus #725 from the Blacktown train station (from Central Station $3.20, off-peak return $5.80). Attractions at **Australia's Wonderland** (tel. 9830 9100 or 1800 252 198; recorded info 9830 1777; fax 9675 2002) run the gamut from wombats to waterslides. (Open April-Nov. daily 10am-5pm; Dec.-March Sun.-Fri. 10am-5pm, Sat. 10am-10pm; admission $32, seniors and ages 4-12 $22, under 4 free.) To reach this carnival paradise, take the Wallgrove Rd. exit from the M4, or catch **Busways** bus #738 (round-trip $4.20) from the Rooty Hill train station (from Central Station $3.80, off-peak return $4.60).

PENRITH

The town of **Penrith,** 35km west of Parramatta along the Great Western Hwy., hovers at the edge of Sydney's sphere of suburban influence, at the base of the Blue Mountains. Running through the west half of town, the **Nepean River** is one of Penrith's best features, a wide, placid corridor perfect for paddling. Though the Olympic Coordination Authority has recognized the potential of the Nepean by designating it the venue for canoe sprints and rowing events in the 2000 Olympics, no one in town rents boats for casual use. The closest travelers can get to the river is a cruise on the **Nepean Belle** (tel. 4733 1274 or 4733 1888), a paddlewheel riverboat which makes leisurely trips to the dramatic Nepean Gorge in Blue Mountains National Park. The double-decker boat departs Tench Reserve Park, off Tench Ave., on an irregular schedule; call ahead (cruise 90min.; $12, ages 3-11 $6).

Closer to the center of town, the **Museum of Fire** (tel. 4731 3000), on Castlereagh Rd. one block north of the Great Western Hwy., educates and amuses with entertaining films and more serious displays on the history of fire and fire-fighting in New South Wales. The exhibit on bushfire and the simulation of a home fire are important additions to what might otherwise be primarily a collection of historical fire-fighting gadgetry. (Open Mon.-Sat. 10am-3pm, Sun. 10am-5pm; admission $5, students, and seniors $3, ages 2-16 $2.50, families of 5 $12.50.) Devoted to the development of modernism in Australian art, the **Penrith Regional Gallery and the Lewers Bequest,** 86 River Rd. (tel. 4735 1100; fax 4735 5663), west of town in Emu Plains, mounts changing exhibitions, to augment the modest standing collection, in a riverside house surrounded by a sculpture garden. (Open Tues.-Sun. 11am-5pm; admission $2, students, seniors, ages 7-15 $1, under 7 free.)

The **Penrith Visitors Centre** (tel. 4732 7671), on Mulgoa Rd., inside the Panther's World Entertainment Complex, covers Penrith and carries additional information on the Blue Mountains. The **Nepean River Caravan Park** (tel. 4735 4425) provides excellent, inexpensive sleeping arrangements. Tent sites lie at the bottom of a steep hill, secluded from the rest of the park and surrounded by trees. (Reception open daily 8am-6pm. Sites $10; with power $17.50; cabins for 2 $39, each additional person up to 6 $7. Amenities key and gate card deposit $10. Laundry facilities). **CityRail** trains to Penrith and Emu Plains, the end of the suburban line, take approximately one hour from Central Station (to either station $5.20, off-peak return $6.20).

The Upper Hawkesbury

The fertile farmland of the Upper Hawkesbury has been cultivated since the first decade of Australian colonial inhabitance, but it was not until 1810 that towns were established in the area. Governor Lachlan Macquarie selected sites for five towns, naming them **Windsor, Richmond, Wilberforce, Castlereagh,** and **Pitt Town.** Today, these towns, collectively known as the Macquarie Towns, lie at the east end of Bells Line of Road (see p. 137), a scenic alternative to the freeway between the outskirts of Sydney and the Blue Mountains. **Tourism Hawkesbury** (tel. 4588 5895; fax 4588 5896), on Richmond Rd. between Windsor and Richmond, has information on the entire area, including the helpful booklet *Richmond and Windsor Walks* ($1; office open daily 9am-5pm).

Clifton Cottage, 22 Richmond Rd. (tel. 4587 7135), just outside Windsor, offers bed and breakfast in an antique-laden garden setting for reasonable rates. (Reception open daily 8am-8pm. Check-out 10am. Singles $45; doubles $65.) The town of Windsor is particularly well-preserved, and the refurbished center at Thompson Square features several historical buildings. On the square, the Daniel O'Connell Inn houses the **Hawkesbury Museum of Local History** (tel. 4577 2310) and a small tourist information office (both open daily 10am-4pm; museum admission $2.50, students, concessions, and ages 5-15 $1.50, under 5 free). The 1815 **Macquarie Arms Hotel,** next to the Daniel O'Connell Inn, shares the claim of being "the oldest pub in Australia" with several others, but it is nonetheless an interesting historical edifice. A plaque on the building's front wall marks the height of the flood of 1867, the greatest of many floods which have plagued the Hawkesbury region. **St. Matthew's Anglican Church** (tel. 4577 3193), built between 1817 and 1822, on the corner of Tebbutt and Little Church St., is considered to be one of the greatest achievements of ex-convict architect Francis Greenway (open Fri.-Sun. dawn-dusk). The church cemetery contains stones dating from 1810.

Windsor River Cruises (tel. 9831 6630) conducts informative cruises up the Hawkesbury River with coffee and commentary. Trips depart Windsor Wharf Wednesdays at 10:30am and Sundays at 1:30pm barring weather difficulties (2½hr., $15, ages 5-15 $7.50, families of 4 $35). Sights along the route include the 1809 **Ebenezer Church** (tel. 4579 9350), 10km outside Wilberforce on Coromandel Rd., Australia's oldest church still used for public worship. The grounds of the sandstone country church, which seats only 25 people, include a cemetery with the graves of several of the areas earliest European inhabitants (open daily 10am-3:30pm). **Hawkesbury Heritage Farm** (tel. 4575 1457; fax 4575 1383), on Rose St. in Wilberforce, 6km northeast of Windsor off Putty Rd., re-creates early colonial life in a collection of historical buildings and reproductions (open Thurs.-Sun. 10am-5pm; admission $6, students, seniors, and ages 5-15 $6, under 5 free, families of 5 $25). Richmond, 10km northwest of Windsor via Richmond Rd., has a nice collection of 1800s homes and churches, as well as a **National Parks and Wildlife Service** office (tel. 4588 5247; open Mon.-Fri. 9:30am-12:30pm and 1:30-5pm). CityRail trains from Sydney's Central Station reach both Windsor ($4.60, off-peak return $5.60) and Richmond ($5.20, $6.20).

BLUE MOUNTAINS

For the first 25 years of British colonization the unscalable walls of the Blue Mountains, just 100km from the coast, contained the growth of the new colony and the exploration of Australia. Numerous expeditions approached the mountains only to come away stumped. Because the so-called mountains are actually a series of canyons separated by several high plateaus, the explorers found cliffs at the edges of the valleys instead of hills. It was not until 1813, when Blaxland, Lawson, and Wentworth, assisted by local Aboriginal know-how, attempted to cross the mountains along a ridge that a successful route was found. Today, the mountains are the first stop on most trips west from Sydney and an easy year-round getaway for Sydney-siders. The short drive inland, just an hour and a half from the city center, grants summertime visitors from the city a reprieve from the oppressive heat that hangs over the coast. In winter, crisp and sunny days, occasional snowfalls, and the festive Yuletide celebrations at inns throughout the area continue to draw travelers by the busload.

Although a variety of adventure activities, such as rappelling (locally known as abseiling) and canyoning have become popular in recent years, the Blue Mountains' major drawcards remain their excellent hiking trails and lookouts. Govett's Leap in Blackheath, which looks onto the Grose Valley, and Echo Point in Katoomba, which takes in the Three Sisters and the Jamison Valley, are two of the more famous and most arresting of the Blue Mountains' viewpoints. Overlooking a carpet of blue eucalypt forest, each serves as the trailhead for several walking tracks of varied difficulty. Sunlight filtering through eucalyptus oil suspended in the air gives the forest its tint. From the lookout points, the earth falls away into an endless sea of blue foliage speckled with white bark and bordered by distant sandstone cliffs.

Three national parks divide the wild stretches of the region. **Blue Mountains National Park,** the largest and most accessible of the three, covers most of the Jamison Valley (south of the Great Western Hwy. between Glenbrook and Katoomba), as well as the Megalong Valley (south of the Great Western Hwy. west of Katoomba) and the Grose Valley (north of the Great Western Hwy. and east of Blackheath). The Grose and Jamison Valleys appeal primarily to hikers, while horseback riders favor the Megalong Valley (see **Blackheath,** below, for more information on horse-riding).

Kanangra-Boyd National Park, tucked between two sections of Blue Mountains National Park in the southwest reaches of the mountains, is reserved for serious bush-walkers. The park, accessible by partially paved roads from Oberon and from Jenolan Caves, has only one 2WD road. The state's largest preserved wilderness area, **Wollemi National Park,** is a place so unspoiled and untrafficked that a species of pine tree only before seen in fossil form was found here, alive and well, in 1994. Access to the park, the south edge of which abuts the north side of **Bells Line of Road,** is possible at Bilpin and at several points north of the central Blue Mountains.

Thanks to a broad selection of accommodations and food, a stay in the Blue Mountains falls well within any traveler's budget. Still, despite the popularity of the mountains, the sheer expanse of the area's canyons, gorges, and plateaus, and the wide variety of hiking trails ensure that every hiker can have at least one long moment alone at the edge of a breathtaking rocky outcropping secure in the knowledge that no one else will be coming down the path for a while.

GETTING THERE AND AROUND

The Blue Mountains are an easy 90-minute drive west of Sydney. Take Parramatta Rd. west from the city to the Western Motor Tollway (toll $1.50) at Strathfield. The tollway passes through Penrith to become the Great Western Hwy., the main route through the mountains. The area's major service centers and scenic attractions lie on or near this path. Alternatively, the northern route across the mountains, Bells Line of Road, stretches west from Windsor, northeast of Parramatta, providing a more beautiful and less developed passage.

CityRail makes stops throughout the Blue Mountains at most of the towns along the Great Western Hwy., offering the least expensive option for travelers who are willing to walk from rail stations and bus stops to trailheads. Within the towns, most distances are walkable, and local bus companies cover those that aren't. (See **Katoomba,** below, for more info on local buses.) Public transportation does not provide access to areas such as Jenolan Caves, Kanangra-Boyd National Park, or Wollemi National Park.

Several companies run tours to the mountains from Sydney. A common one-day package includes stops at Katoomba's Echo Point, the Scenic Railway and Skyway, and at Govett's Leap in Blackheath, plus visits to the Edge Maxvision Cinema in Katoomba and the Australian Wildlife Park at Australia's Wonderland. (Trips daily; $74, students and seniors $67, under 15 $37. Does not include Scenic Railway and Skyway tickets.) Another trip focuses on bushwalking with 45-minute stops at Echo Point, the Wentworth Falls Conservation Hut, and Govett's Leap (trips made Mon., Wed., Fri., and Sat.; $69, $62, $35). **AAT Kings** (tel. 9252 2788), at Sydney's Circular Quay, **Australian Pacific Tours** (tel. 9252 2988), and **Great Sights South Pacific** (tel. 9241 2294) all have offices in Sydney that can book these tours (calls accepted 24hr.). AAT Kings also offers a third package which includes transportation to Jenolan Caves by way of Echo Point, a cave tour, and an optional stop at the Edge Maxvision Cinema ($83, $74, $42; with Edge tickets $92, $46, $80).

Glenbrook to Leura

Glenbrook Located on the Great Western Hwy. outside the easternmost section of Blue Mountains National Park, the **Blue Mountains Tourist Authority,** Glenbrook office (tel. 4739 6266) serves as the gateway to the Blue Mountains for travelers coming from Sydney. The helpful staff has extensive information on accommodations and attractions and good advice on hiking in the region (open Mon.-Sat. 8:30am-5pm, Sun. 8:30am-4:30pm). The **National Parks and Wildlife Service Glenbrook Visitors Centre** (tel. 4739 2950), south of Glenbrook on Bruce Rd., marks the nearest entrance to the park (open Sat.-Sun. and daily during school holidays 11am-4pm). An entrance fee is collected at the gate here when the visitors center is open ($7.50 per car, cyclists and pedestrians free). From the highway, take Ross or Green St. to Euroka St. Bruce Rd. proceeds east and then south from the end of Euroka St.

Inside the park, 4km beyond the Bruce Rd. entrance over partially unpaved roads lies the **Euroka Clearing Campground.** The site has pit toilets, but no water or cooking facilities. Wallabies congregate close by in the cool fall and winter months. Call the NPWS in Glenbrook or Richmond (tel. 4588 5247) to arrange permits in advance (fees for 1-2 people $5 per night plus park entrance, for 3 people $7 per night plus park entrance). The **Red Hands Cave trail** from the Glenbrook Visitors Centre runs an easy 8km circuit through patches of rainforest to an Aboriginal rock engraving site. Taking the trail in a counterclockwise direction, it's possible to branch off toward Euroka Clearing on the return. CityRail runs from Sydney's Central Station to Glenbrook ($6, off-peak return $7.20).

Blaxland At Blaxland, less than 1km west of Glenbrook, Layton Ave. turns off the highway toward **Lennox Bridge.** The sandstone bridge, constructed between 1832 and 1833, is the oldest bridge on the Australian mainland and a pretty 2km detour. The National Trust-owned **Norman Lindsay Gallery,** 14 Lindsay Cr. (tel. 4751 1067), in **Faulconbridge,** houses a large collection of work by the artist who once inhabited the house. Lindsay's projects ranged from oil paintings and watercolors to fiction writing, and space is devoted to each of his pursuits (open Wed.-Mon. 10am-4pm; admission $6, students and seniors $4, under 17 $2). The turn-off for the gallery, Grose Rd., is east of Faulconbridge in Springwood. A second **NPWS campsite** can be found at **Murphy's Glen,** 10km south of the Great Western Hwy. outside of Woodford. Take Park Rd. from the highway to Railway Pde., then head south along Bedford Rd. The road is unpaved for most of the way, and the campground, located in a thick eucalypt forest, has only pit toilets (free camping; no permits required). CityRail trains stop in Blaxland ($6, $7.20), Springwood ($6.80, $8.20), Faulconbridge ($6.80, $8.20), and Woodford ($7.60, $9.20).

NEW SOUTH WALES

Wentworth Falls The next center of activity on this stretch, Wentworth Falls, hugs the highway 2km beyond Woodford. At the east edge of town, **Yester Grange** (tel. 4757 1110; fax 4757 3528), on Yester Rd. just off the highway via Tableland Rd., commands a spectacular panoramic view of the central mountains. The house, built in 1888, contains beautifully restored rooms filled with period furniture and paintings, as suitable a setting for Devonshire tea ($7) as the mountains have to offer. An incongruous downstairs gallery displays and sells work by local artists with occasional forays into the truly bizarre. (Open Mon.-Fri. 10am-4pm, Sat.-Sun. 10am-5pm; admission to house and gallery $5, students and seniors $4, high school students $2.50, under 12 $1.)

The national park's **Ingar Campground** is a 13km drive farther southeast along Tableland Rd. and the unpaved and sometimes steep Queen Elizabeth Dr. The campground has pit toilets, no water, and no cooking facilities (free; no permits required). Falls Rd. leads south from the highway through the center of Wentworth Falls to the trailhead for the short walk to **Princes Rock Lookout.** At the lookout, the eastward view centers on Wentworth Falls. On the west end of town, the **National Park Conservation Hut** (tel. 4757 3827) perches on a cliff for a majestic view of Jamison Valley. The hut, which serves primarily as a tea room (tea or coffee $2.50), distributes limited information on tourist facilities and walking tracks in the Blue Mountains (open daily 10am-4pm). Several excellent trails split off from the trailhead at the hut. The **Valley of the Waters walk,** a 4km circuit of medium difficulty (3hr.) provides stunning views of several nearby waterfalls and connects to the longer, more difficult **National Pass circuit** (6km; 4½hr.), a gorgeous walk hewn into the side of the cliff line. The return trail has some of the best possible views of Wentworth Falls. The CityRail train from Sydney to Wentworth costs $8 (off-peak return $9.60).

Leura The likeable town of Leura, 3km west of Wentworth Falls, offers quaint shops, cafes, and galleries along its central street, Leura Mall. Situated next to the Great Western Hwy., at the north end of the Mall, **Leura Village Caravan Park** (tel. 4784 1552) has campsites, on-site vans, an indoor heated pool, and toilets and showers with nary an unpaved road in sight (laundry facilities; reception open daily 8am-9pm; check-out 11am; sites for 2 $16, with power $18, each additional person over 15 $5, under 15 $2). **Everglades Gardens,** 37 Everglades Ave. (tel. 4784 5190), is a lush example of the floral cultivation for which the town is known (open Sept.-Feb. 10am-5pm; March-Aug. 10am-4pm; admission $5, students and seniors $3, ages 6-12 $1, under 6 free). Nearby, Fitzroy St. leads east to Watson's Rd. which soon turns into Sublime Point Rd. and ends at the breathtaking overlook at **Sublime Point.** For travelers continuing west, the 8km **Cliff Drive,** beginning at Gordon Rd., near the south end of Leura Mall, provides a scenic escape from the highway. The loop skirts the south edge of Katoomba passing many lookouts and a handful of trailheads. The views from Leura Cascades and Katoomba's Echo Point (see below) are stand-outs.

Katoomba

The golden towers of the Three Sisters are the image most widely associated with the Blue Mountains throughout the world, and Katoomba is the place to see them. Popularity bred of physical beauty, excellent hiking, and convenience swells the town's ranks with backpackers and other lay-mountaineers on weekends. During the week, however, the town goes quiet and reveals its own slightly crunchy small-town flavor. Katoomba's charm lies in this ability to cater to the needs of its many visitors without becoming a service center devoid of character. Being positioned on the northwest rim of the Jamison Valley doesn't hurt either.

ORIENTATION AND PRACTICAL INFORMATION

Katoomba sits south of the Great Western Hwy. 2km west of Leura and 109km from Sydney. The town's main street, **Katoomba St.,** runs south from the **Katoomba Railway Station** through town toward Echo Point. Echo Point Rd. finishes the trip, bringing visitors to the Blue Mountains' most famous view, the Three Sisters. In the downtown area, Katoomba St. is flanked by Lurline St. to the east and Parke St. to the west. Pioneer Pl. occupies the area between Katoomba and Parke St., and can be reached via narrow alleys off either street. At the north end of town **Main St.** runs parallel to the Great Western Hwy. becoming Gang Gang St. east of the railway station and Bathurst St. to the west.

Tourist Office: Blue Mountains Tourism Authority (tel. 4739 6266), on Echo Point at the end of Echo Point Rd. Take Lurline St. south from the middle of town and veer left onto Echo Rd. when Lurline St. ends. In addition to all the brochures and souvenirs a traveler could hope for, the center has an amazing clifftop view through a wall of plate glass windows. Starting point for many hikes, including the Three Sisters. Open daily 9am-5pm. Available here, the *R.A. Broadbent Blue Mountains Tourist Map* ($5) has a good mix of road and trail coverage.

Budget Travel Office: Fantastic Aussie Tours, 283 Main St. (24hr. tel. 4782 1866; fax 4782 1860), next to the railway station. Books all of the bus tours listed below and distributes info on area attractions. Open Mon.-Fri. 9am-5pm.

Trains: Katoomba Railway Station, on Main St., at the north end of Katoomba St., is part of the **CityRail** network. Trains between Lithgow and Sydney stop at least hourly every day of the week. To Sydney's Central Station (2hr.; $9.40), Glenbrook ($3.80, off-peak return $4.60), Blackheath ($2, $2.40), and Lithgow ($4.60, $5.80).

Buses: Greyhound Pioneer (tel. 13 20 30) stops on the Great Western Hwy., opposite the Gearins Hotel, once daily on the way from Sydney to Adelaide. To: Bathurst (2hr., $22), Dubbo (4½hr., $39), and Broken Hill (13½hr., $99). For casual day-touring at your own pace, the **Blue Mountains Explorer Bus** (24hr. tel. 4782 1866) runs an 18-stop circuit around the Katoomba area and allows passengers to get on and off as often as they choose. Stops include Echo Point, the Scenic Railway and Scenic Skyway, Leura Cascades, Gordon Falls, Everglades Gardens, and the Edge Maxvision Cinema. Buses run Sat.-Sun. and public holidays hourly 9:30am-4:30pm. $15, seniors $14, ages 5-15 $8, family of 4 $40.

Local Public Transportation: Blue Mountains Bus Company (tel. 4782 4213), runs between Katoomba and Woodford with stops at Katoomba Station, near Echo

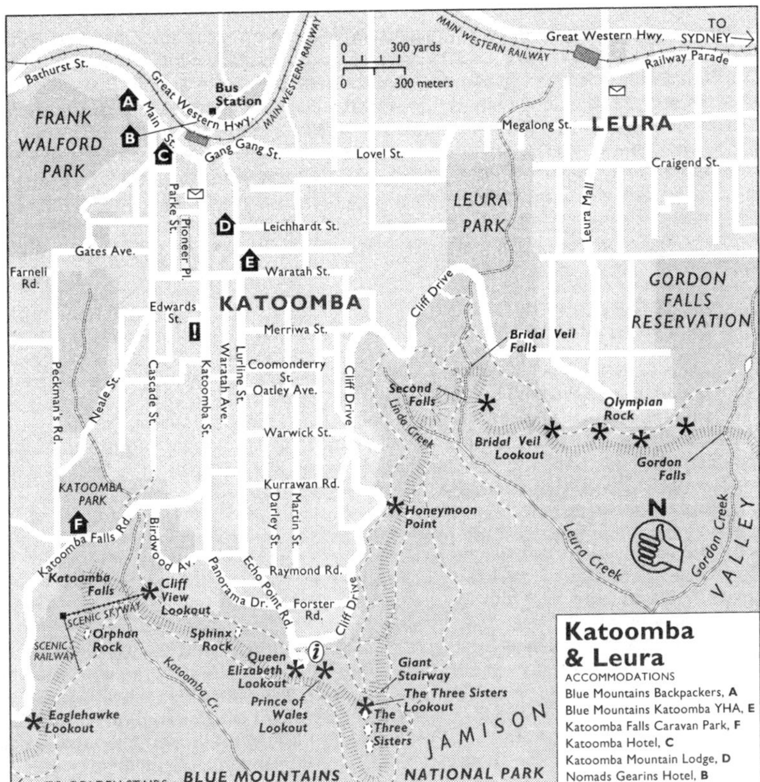

Point, at the Edge Cinema, on Leura Mall, at the Valley of the Waters trailhead, and in Wentworth Falls. Fares $1.60-3, students and ages 5-18 half off. Regular service approximately 7:30am-6pm. **Mountainlink** (tel. 4732 3333) covers Katoomba and the region, including the sights of Leura, Blackheath, and Mt. Victoria. Fares from $1.20, students, seniors, and ages 5-15 half off. Katoomba to Blackheath $4. Service times vary by route. Timetables for both services are available at the Blue Mountains Tourism Authority center on Echo Point.

Taxis: Katoomba Leura Radio Cars (tel. 4782 1311) picks up anywhere between Wentworth Falls and Mt. Victoria 24hr. ($1). Initial fare $4, plus $1.07 per km.

Car Rental: Cales Car Rentals, 136 Bathurst Rd. (tel. 4782 2917), has cars from $55 per day including insurance and 250km. Must be 21. Deductible $500. Lower rates for longer rentals. Open Mon.-Sat. 8:30am-5pm, Sun. 8-9am and 5-6pm.

Automobile Clubs: NRMA (tel. 13 21 32; road service 13 11 11).

Bike Rental: Cycletech, 3 Gang Gang St. (tel. 4782 2800; fax 4782 4550), across from the railway station, rents bikes with helmets, locks, and repair kits included. On-road $10 for half-day, full day $20, 2 days $35. Off-road $5 extra. Credit card, passport, or cash deposit required. 10% off for YHA members and backpackers. Open Mon.-Fri. 8:30am-5:30pm, Sat. 8:30am-4pm, Sun. 10am-4pm.

Hotlines: Lifeline (24hr. tel. 13 11 14); **Poison Information Centre** (24hr. tel. 13 11 11); **Rape Crisis Centre** (24hr. tel. 1800 551 800).

Hospital: Blue Mountains District Anzac Memorial Hospital (tel. 4782 2111), on the Great Western Hwy., 1km east of the railway station.

Emergency: Dial 000.

Post office: Shops 4-5, Pioneer Pl. (tel. 13 13 18). *Poste Restante* care of Post Office, Katoomba, NSW. Open Mon.-Fri. 9am-5pm. **Postal code:** 2780.

Phone Code: 02.

ACCOMMODATIONS AND CAMPING

Blue Mountains Backpackers, 190 Bathurst Rd. (tel. 4782 4226), a 10min. walk west of the railway station. Clean, fun, friendly accommodation in a house staffed by young people. Sleeping arrangements range from mattresses on the floor to doubles, insuring that anyone can afford a Blue Mountain getaway. Small kitchen and dining area, common room with VCR, rides to trailheads, safe for valuables. Reception open daily 9am-noon and 6-9pm. Check-out 10am. Larger dorms $15; 4-bed dorms $18; mattresses on the floor $14; doubles or twins $40; tent sites $10. Weekly: $84; $98; $84; $210; $63. VIP, YHA discount $1-2. Bike rentals $20 per day. Abseiling (from $59) and rafting (from $69) trips. Linen $1. Key deposit $10 on doubles only.

Blue Mountains Katoomba YHA (tel. 4782 1416), on the corner of Lurline and Waratah St. A big old guesthouse with tons of common space, clean facilities, and ample dorms. It rides the line between convenient and institutional, but remains comfortable. Kitchen open 7am-9:30pm. Common room with VCR, game room, free lockers (locks $3), and excellent security. Check-out 10am, late fee $5. Reception open daily 7am-10pm. 8- to 14-bed dorms $12, with bath $14; 6-bed dorms with bath $15; 4-bed dorms $14, with bath $16; family room with bath $62.50; doubles and twins $50. YHA non-members pay $3 more. Key deposit $10. Linen $2, blankets provided. Bike rental $20 per day.

Nomads Gearins Hotel, 273 Great Western Hwy. (tel. 4782 6028), directly behind the train station. The Gearins provides weary wanderers with a tidy dorm-share set-up over Katoomba's most diverse pub. Free linen, lockers, and thick blankets and comforters for cold mountain nights. Common room with TV, but no kitchen. Reception open daily 8am-6pm. Check-out 10am. 4- to 6-bed dorms $15; singles $25; doubles $50. Key deposit is often forgotten.

Katoomba Mountain Lodge, 31 Lurline St. (tel. 4782 3933). An old guest house with unexciting dorms, the Mountain Lodge would benefit from a bit more attention to the bathrooms and a layer of carpet in the bedrooms. The fire in the common room is a nice touch, but it doesn't make up for the frosty mornings. Kitchen open daily during meal times. Blankets provided, but no linen. Reception open daily 8:30am-6:30pm. Check-out 10am, or risk forfeiture of key deposit. Dorms $11-15. VIP. Singles and doubles Sun.-Thurs. $23 per person, with light breakfast $28, Package deals include single or double Fri.-Sat. $60 per person. Ages 3-12 half-price if sharing a room with 2 adults. Key and cutlery deposit $10.

Katoomba Falls Caravan Park (tel. 4782 1835), on Katoomba Falls Rd., south of town via Katoomba St., well-positioned for several bushwalks and the Scenic Skyway and Scenic Railway. The sterile, uniform rows of on-site vans sit quite close to the small, treeless tent-camping area, removing any hint of wilderness. Toilets, hot showers, indoor BBQ area. On-site caravans and cabins require guests to bring their own linens and blankets. Reception open daily 8am-6pm. Check-out 10am. Sites $7 per person, families of 4 $18; with power $10, families $25; additional person $5. Cabins with bath for 2 people $51; each additional person $10. On-site caravans for 1 person $31, each additional person up to 7 $5—a great deal for groups. Key deposit $5 for campers, $10 for caravan or cabin occupants.

FOOD AND ENTERTAINMENT

Katoomba's two largest grocery stores stand to either side of the K-Mart on Pioneer Pl. The **Jewel Food Barn** (tel. 4782 1819) has discount groceries (open Mon.-Fri. 8:30am-9pm, Sat. 8:15am-6pm, Sun. 10am-4pm), and **Coles** (tel. 4782 6133) has unbeatable hours for midnight munchies (open Mon. 7am to Sat. 10pm, Sun. 8am-8pm). The **Katoomba Village Fruit Market,** 170 Bathurst Rd. (tel. 4782 4972), a seven-minute walk west of the train station, carries a warehouse full of high-quality produce at great prices (open Mon.-Fri. 8am-6pm, Sat.-Sun. 8am-5pm).

When you're ready for someone else to do the cooking, wander down Katoomba St. Cafes and restaurants along this strip offer a variety of cuisines at consistently reasonable rates. **Diana's Sandwich and Takeaway Bar,** 123 Katoomba St. (tel. 4782 4307), stands out among the pie shops for plump, fresh pies with tasty fillings ($2.60). The sandwiches are healthy and veggie-oriented (burgers, veggie burgers, tofu burgers $3.20; open Mon.-Fri. 8:30am-4:30pm, Sat. 8:30am-3pm). At the south end of the street, **Pins and Noodles,** 189 Katoomba St. (tel. 4782 3445), earns accolades for steaming soups with udon noodles made fresh each day. The clean, simple dining room fills up on weekends, so call ahead. (Miso soup $1.50, pasta or rice dishes $6-$9; BYO with no corkage fee; open Mon.-Sat. 11am-2:30pm and 5:30-8:30pm except Wed. lunch only; no credit cards.) Ornate gilded mirrors decorate the wood-paneled walls of **Siam Cuisine,** 172 Katoomba St. (tel. 4782 5671), for an effect somewhat less appealing than the menu. Don't be put off; the food is spicy and delicious. (Lunch specials $6, dinner mains $8.50-14.50, spring rolls 4 for $5; BYO with no corkage; open Tues.-Sun. 11:30am-2:30pm and 5:30-10pm.)

Katoomba's nightlife revolves around the two main downtown pubs. The **Katoomba Hotel** (tel. 4782 1106), at the corner of Main and Parke St., offers the usual beer and pokies until everyone heads home (schooners $2.60; open daily 10am-midnight or later). The **Gearins Hotel,** 273 Great Western Hwy. (tel. 4782 6028), keeps the same hours and mixes things up a bit with sometimes-rowdy Jam Nights on Wednesdays and mixed crowds gathering on Saturdays (schooners of VB $2.70).

The **Edge Maxvision Cinema,** 225 Great Western Hwy. (tel. 4782 8928; fax 4782 4002), projects a 38-minute film on the Blue Mountains, called The Edge, onto a six-story screen for the closest possible cinematic approximation of actual exploration. Just in case the draw of a seat more comfortable than an abseiling harness doesn't grab you, the movie goes to several places in the mountains which cannot be accessed by visitors, including the secret grove where the recently-discovered Wollemi pine grows (6 shows daily between 10am and 5:15pm; tickets $12, students and seniors $10, ages 3-15 $8). In addition to other giant-format films shown occasionally throughout the day, the Edge Cinema screens recent feature films every evening (tickets $9.50, $8.50, $7.50; call for programs and showtimes).

SIGHTS AND ACTIVITIES

The Blue Mountains' most famous snapshot view, the romantic **Three Sisters,** stands just south of Katoomba off Echo Point. Between dusk and 11pm each night, the view of the three rocky dames takes on a new brilliance under the slow glow of strategically placed floodlights. The easy half-hour return walk to Three Sisters Lookout is one of only two wheelchair-accessible trails in Blue Mountains National Park. From the lookout, the **Giant Stairway** makes a steep descent to the floor of the Jamison Valley to meet the **Federal Pass trail.** Walkers generally prefer the west-bound leg of the pass, winding around the base of the Three Sisters and along the cliff-bottom to **Orphan Rock.** There are two options for getting back up to civilization level near Orphan Rock, the **Furber Steps** (a moderate climb, 30min.) or the **Scenic Railway** (tel. 4782 2699; $3, ages 3-13 $1, packs $1; total trip from Giant Stairway using Scenic Railway 5km, 2½hr. circuit). Many bus tours and individual travelers approach the steep scenic railway from Katoomba Falls Rd. and take the short trip just for kicks (10min. round-trip; $5), but for hikers coming from either the Federal Pass or the Ruined Castle Track (see below), the ride is a restful way to cover the last 250 vertical meters after a long day's walk. The **Scenic Skyway** (tel. 4782 2699; fax 4782 5675), is a cable gondola which departs from the Scenic Railway station for a quick trip out over Katoomba Falls Gorge and back (7min.; $5, ages 3-13 $3). As tourist attractions, both rides run a little too short to justify the fares, but they do allow travelers without the time or the interest in hiking to see some of the area's more astonishing views. (Both open daily 9am-5pm, last rides 4:50pm.) On the west side of town, the easy walk along **Narrow Neck Plateau** beyond the gate on Glenraphael Dr. leads to fabulous views of the Megalong and Jamison Valleys on either side of the clifftop trail. Before the gate, about 1km out onto the plateau from the Cliff Dr., the **Golden Stairs** run down the cliff face to the Ruined Castle Track. The walk to **Ruined Castle,** a distinctive rock formation reminiscent of crumbling turrets, makes a difficult five-hour round-trip via the Golden Stairs. Because of the stairs' taxing grade, many walkers tack on an extra hour and walk east to the Furber Steps or the Scenic Railway on the return trip.

Several companies in Katoomba organize adventure activity trips throughout the Blue Mountains region. The **Australian School of Mountaineering,** 166b Katoomba St. (tel. 4782 2014; fax 4782 5787; email asm@pnc.com.au), inside the Paddy Pallin outdoor shop, conducts introductory rappelling ($79 per day) and rock-climbing courses ($90 per day). Book a day ahead (open daily 8:15am-5:30pm; YHA, Nomads, VIP members and student travelers receive a $10 discount). **Blue Mountains Adventure Company,** 190 Katoomba St. (tel. 4782 1271), inside the Mountain Design Shop, has similar packages for both rappelling ($89, YHA and VIP $75) and rock-climbing ($110 per day; open Mon.-Fri. 9:30am-5:30pm). Both companies run rappelling trips daily year-round depending on demand, but rock-climbing outings are scaled back to two or three per week in winter. Groups can count on getting discount rates.

The **Blue Mountains Highlights tour** (24hr. tel. 4782 1866), covers the area's star attractions in three hours, thrice daily ($29, VIP or YHA $18, seniors $26, ages 5-15 $15, families of 4 $70). Tours to the Jenolan Caves (24hr. tel. 4782 1866) include stops at Echo Point and Govett's Leap and about three hours to explore the caves or the surrounding area ($49, $40, $42, $24, $125). Overnight return trips to the caves, not including accommodation or cave tours cost $32 each way (seniors $30, ages 5-15 $16, families of 4 $79). A one-way ticket combined with two to three days of walking and camping on the Six Foot Track, a 42km trail from Nellies Glen Rd., off the Great Western Hwy. at the west end of town, to Jenolan Caves, makes an affordable and adventurous outing for serious walkers.

Blackheath

The Great Western Hwy. snakes 11km west and north from Katoomba to the town of Blackheath on the way to Mount Victoria. The Upper Mountains section of Blue Mountains National Park extends east and north from this plateau-top town into the Grose Valley, encompassing some of the mountains' best lookouts and several good trails. The Megalong Valley, to the south of the town, is a farmland area popular for horseback riding. Given its prime position between these two areas and its easy accessibility, Blackheath is a natural choice as a Blue Mountains base. The only factors to detract from its appeal are the small selection of inexpensive sleeping spaces and the relative lack of services when compared with Katoomba. Whether you decide to stay in town or not, Blackheath's natural attractions easily fill a day's visit.

Practical Information The **Blue Mountains Heritage Centre** (tel. 4787 8877), on Govett's Leap Rd., just inside the national park, is the main NPWS visitors center for the Blue Mountains and carries detailed trail guidebooks (50¢-$4). A small exhibit inside the center presents the history of Aboriginal and European peoples in the mountains and also explains the geology of the region (open daily 9am-4:30pm). **Mountainlink** (tel. 4782 3333) runs buses from Katoomba to Mount Victoria by way of Blackheath, coming as close as possible to the town's major trailheads (fares from $1.20, students, seniors, and ages 5-15 from 60¢; from Blackheath Railway Station to Blue Mountains Heritage Centre $1.60; service Mon.-Fri. 7:30am-6pm, Sat. 6:30am-4:30pm). **CityRail** runs to Blackheath from Sydney's Central Station via Katoomba ($10.60, off-peak return $12.80).

Accommodations and Food The clean, almost frilly rooms in the Art Deco **Gardner's Inn Hotel,** 255 Great Western Hwy. (tel. 4787 8347), set a high standard for pub accommodation (lounge with piano, no kitchen; reception at the bar open daily 11am-late; check-out 10:30am; singles, doubles, and twins Mon.-Thurs. $20 per person, Fri.-Sun. $25). The tent camping area at **Blackheath Caravan Park** (tel. 4787 8101), on Prince Edward St., off Govett's Leap Rd., lies in a tree-covered grove secluded from the rest of the park by a steep hill. Though the privacy is nice, tree coverage means the sites get little sun and can become quite cold. The area also gets boggy after rainstorms, but when there's room, the managers let campers sleep among the powered sites up the hill. (Toilets, showers, BBQs. Reception open daily

8am-6pm. Check-out 10am. Sites $7 per person, families of 4 $18; sites with power for 2 $10, each additional person $5, families $25. Key deposit $5.)

The nearest **free national park camping areas** can be found at Perry's Lookdown, on the sometimes paved Hat Hill Rd., 8km from the Great Western Hwy., and at Acacia Flat, on the floor of the Grose Valley, a two-hour hike from Govett's Leap. Both sites have pit toilets and no other facilities. Water from Govett's Creek is available at Acacia Flat, but it must be treated before use. Blackheath's food and services line the Great Western Hwy. and the first few blocks of Govett's Leap Rd. leading away from the highway, to form a tiny town center. Among the small eateries, the **Wattle Cafe,** 240 Great Western Hwy. (tel. 4787 8153), is a particularly cozy place for a sandwich (burgers $3, breakfast served all day; open daily 7:30am-7pm).

Lookouts, Walks, and Rides Walks in the Blackheath area vary widely in length and level of difficulty. The Fairfax Heritage Walk is a one-hour (2km), wheelchair-ready alternative to the 350m drive between the Blue Mountains Heritage Centre and **Govett's Leap,** truly one of the most spectacular lookouts in the national park. The moderate walk from Govett's Leap to the lookout at **Pulpit Rock** (2.5km) follows the cliffline for an almost non-stop display of breathtaking views out over the Grose Valley. Following the cliffs in the other direction leads to **Evans Lookout** (3km), at the end of Evans Lookout Rd. from the south end of town. One of two possible trailheads for the popular hike through Grand Canyon, Evans Lookout gives way to a manageable descent to the canyon floor. The trail then runs alongside Greaves Creek through the wet, forested clime of the narrow canyon and up again at **Neates Glen,** the other possible entry point. A short walk on the unpaved portion of Evans Lookout Rd. completes the four-hour circuit back to Evans Lookout. From the Great Western Hwy., Hat Hill Rd. leads north of town to **Perry's Lookdown,** then branches off to the superb lookout at **Anvil Rock** nearby. From Perry's Lookdown, a trail leads into the valley to the beautiful **Blue Gum Forest** (2hr.). Returning along the same route makes the trip to the forest a difficult five-hour trek. The other option is to turn toward Govett's Leap and make a full day of walking through the forest along Govett's Creek (circuit using cliff-top track and Hat Hill Rd.; 10hr., difficult).

The **scenic drive** into the Megalong Valley begins on Shipley Rd., across the Great Western Hwy. from Govett's Leap Rd. Megalong Rd., a left from Shipley Rd. just after Centennial Glen Rd., leads down into the valley, a picturesque farmland area which contrasts nicely with the wilderness of its surroundings. In the valley, several outfitters conduct guided trail rides or supply horses for hourly use. **Werriberri Trail Rides** (tel. 4787 9171), on Megalong Rd. near Werriberri Lodge, offers rides from 15-minute walks ($15) to three-hour outings with more opportunities to get up some speed ($48; open for reservation calls daily 7:30am-8:30pm; 1st ride 9am, last ride 3:30pm). The **Megalong Australian Heritage Centre** (tel. 4787 8188; fax 4787 9116), a bit farther south on Megalong Rd., has longer guided rides and allows riders to make unguided outings. (Full day ride with lunch $95; 3hr. ride with lunch $65; horses alone $20 for 1st hr., each additional hr. $18; rides daily 10am-4pm; office open daily 8:30am-6pm.) Unguided rides from the **Packsaddlers** (tel. 4787 9150), at Green Gulley, farther south on Megalong Rd., are slightly cheaper (1hr. $20, 2hr. $35, 3hr. $50, full day 9:30am-4:30pm $65; office open daily 9am-5pm).

NEW SOUTH WALES

Mount Victoria and Hartley

The westernmost of the mountain towns, **Mount Victoria** is a quiet village 18km beyond Katoomba on the Great Western Hwy. The town has long been considered a getaway destination, and several old hotels and holiday homes number among Mount Victoria's historic buildings. Converted servants' quarters house pricey dorm accommodation amidst the sumptuous Victorian grandeur of the **Hotel Imperial** (tel. 4787 1233; fax 4787 1461), on the Great Western Hwy. at Station St., allowing the hoi polloi to continue the tradition of living simply in the presence of great elegance. Private rooms in the hotel are prohibitively expensive, but mid-week discounts bring prices down significantly. (Reception open daily 8am-late. Check-out 11am. Dorms $27.50; private rooms with shared bathrooms Sun.-Thurs. $49, Fri.-Sat. $74; cancel the included breakfast and all prices drop $8.) The **Victoria and Albert Guesthouse,** 19 Station St. (tel. 4787 1241; fax 4787 1588), has slightly lower prices on private rooms, but, unlike the lavish lobby, the rooms are a bit less charming than those at the Imperial. (Pool, spa, sauna, tea and coffee lounge. Reception open daily 24hr. with advance call. Check-out 10am. Bed and breakfast with shared bathrooms Sun.-Thurs. $45 per person, Fri.-Sat. $60). The **Bay Tree Tea Shop** (tel. 4787 1275), on Station St. at the head of Harley Ave., supplies a culinary experience as quaint as its surroundings. The tiny cottage has only two to three tables per room and a roaring fire when the temperature drops. (Tea or coffee $2; Devonshire tea $5.50. Open Thurs.-Mon. 10:30am-5pm, during school holidays daily 10:30am-5pm.)

High points in a tour of Mount Victoria's historical buildings include **Westwood Lodge** (built 1876), on Montgomery St., the former summer home of John Fairfax, and the **Toll Keeper's Cottage** (1849), 1km east of town off the Great Western Hwy., a remnant of the days when passage over the mountains was restricted to those who could pay for it. The small museum in the **Mount Victoria Railway Station** (tel. 4787 8534) sheds light on the history of the town and its older buildings (open Sat.-Sun. and public and school holidays 2-5pm; admission $2, ages 5-15 50¢). For an entertaining mix of new and old, take in a recent blockbuster or an offbeat art-house offering at **Mount Vic Flicks** (tel. 4787 1577) on Harley Ave., the teacup-sized cinema located in the town's old Public Hall (tickets $7, students, seniors, and under 12 $5).

An administrative center for the growing farm settlements west of the mountains from the 1830s, the town of **Hartley** went into hibernation when bypassed by the railway in 1887. The town, now administered by the National Parks and Wildlife Service as an historical site, contains 17 buildings left standing from its heyday, including the sandstone courthouse built in 1837 and a lovely old Catholic church. The **NPWS office** (tel. 6355 2117), in the old Farmer's Inn, sells antique-style gifts, and rangers lead excellent, personalized tours of the public buildings whenever two or more paying adults congregate. Tours cater to the interests of those involved ranging in subject from convict life in colonial Australia to preservation techniques used by the park service ($3 per building, prices likely to change by Jan. 1998; open daily 10am-1pm and 2-5pm). Maps from the NPWS and plaques mounted outside each building make it possible to have an informative unguided tour as well.

NEW SOUTH WALES

Jenolan Caves

The amazing limestone and crystal formations of Jenolan Caves, on Jenolan Caves Rd., 52km south of the Great Western Hwy. from Hartley, have beguiled visitors since they were discovered in 1838. One can reach the caves by bus from Katoomba (see p. 130). The cave system, overseen by the **Jenolan Caves Reserve Trust** (tel. 6359 3311; fax 6359 3307), contains nine open caves, accessible through the trust's extensive program of **guided tours,** and many more unexplored recesses (10-25 tours per day; 1-2hr.; $12-20, seniors and ages 5-15 $6-20, families of 4 $30-50; ticket office open daily 9am-5pm). Because it displays a broad range of the features seen throughout the caves, **Lucas Cave** is generally presented as the place to start (1½hr. tour, $12, $6, $30). Large group sizes detract from the experience, however. **Orient Cave** and **Imperial Cave** both have a more tolerable flow of visitors as well as several noteworthy rock formations. (Orient 1½hr.; $16, $8, $40. Imperial 1-1½hr.; $12, $6, $30.) A recent addition to the tour program, **adventure tours** take small groups (limited to 8-12) through some of the cave system's wilder areas—the hard way. These tours, organized primarily for bus touring companies, involve moderate to strenuous climbing, some crawling, and a good bit of darkness. Individual travelers interested in joining an adventure tour should inquire at the ticket office about any open spaces (2-6hr., from $25). Three arches are open for unguided viewing as well; ask for a map of the area from the tour ticket office.

Kanangra-Boyd National Park

Kanangra-Boyd National Park comprises 68,000 hectares of stark wilderness punctuated by uncontaminated rivers and creeks, undeveloped caves, and the dramatic sandstone cliffs which mark the edges of the Boyd Plateau. The park's remote location and rugged cliff-and-gorge terrain attract serious bushwalkers with a hankering to be alone, very alone, for days at a time. The park is nonetheless worthwhile for the more casual visitors who follow its only 2WD road across the Boyd Plateau to the famous lookouts at Kanangra Walls.

Sandwiched between sections of Blue Mountains National Park to the east and south, Kanangra-Boyd National Park extends one small arm north to nearly surround Jenolan Caves. A dirt road continues from the end of Jenolan Caves Rd. and enters the park only 3km past the caves. This path, through Jenolan Caves from the Great Western Hwy., is the only car-accessible eastern approach to the park. From the west, one road, also called Jenolan Caves Rd. and paved for only half its length, comes in from the town of Oberon. These roads meet at the edge of the park to become Kanangra Walls Rd., the direct 26km route to the cliff-top lookout of the same name. The **National Parks and Wildlife Service** office, 38 Ross St. (tel. 63336 1972), in Oberon, has details on the park's longer tracks. People hoping to do cave exploration must register here for the necessary permits at least four weeks in advance (open Mon.-Fri. 8:30am-4:30pm).

The **Boyd River Campground,** on Kanangra Walls Rd. 5km before Kanangra Walls, has the park's only car-accessible camping. In addition to toilets and potable water from the Boyd River, the camping area has fireplaces, but park authorities encourage campers to bring in wood or fuel stores to cut down on disturbances to the park's natural dead-wood recycling process. Camping in the rest of the park is free and carries only two rules: stay 500m from any major path and always minimize your impact.

Three **scenic walks** begin at the **Kanangra Walls** car park. **Lookout Walk** (10min. one-way, easy) is a wheelchair-friendly path leading first to the lookout over the Kanagra Creek gorge and then to the view over the eight-tiered 400m **Kanangra Falls.** The **Waterfall Walk** (20min. one-way with steep return) leads from the second lookout to the pool at the bottom of the cascading **Kalang Falls.** The **Plateau Walk,** which branches from the Lookout Walk between the parking lot and the first lookout, descends briefly from the plateau before ascending to Kanangra Tops for views of Kanangra Walls. Along the way, **Dance Floor Cave** contains signs of old-time recreation in the park. A water container placed in the cave in 1940 catches pure, drinkable water which drips from the cave ceiling (2hr. return plus breaks, moderate). Longer walks, such as the overnight trip to **Batsch Camp** (pit toilets, no water), on the park's southern border, should be planned in advance with help of the Oberon NPWS office.

Bells Line of Road

The difference between taking the Great Western Hwy. and taking Bells Line of Road through the Blue Mountains is similar to the difference between setting out to get drunk with a tumbler of straight gin and doing so with a bottle of fine wine. You end up in the same place, but one route is a little slower and a lot more pleasant. This 87km drive between Windsor and Lithgow provides rambling, scenic passage through the mountains, perfect for anyone with a car and a little extra time.

At the top of Kurrajong Heights, 16km west of Richmond, the **Kurrajong Heights Grass Ski Park** (tel. 4567 7184 or 4567 7260) rents "grass karts" and skis for thrill-riding fun on the mountainside regardless of the weather or season. An uphill lift ensures visitors get the most out of their time. (Must be 130cm tall; 1st hr. $9, each additional hr. $6; open Sat.-Sun. and public holidays 9am-5pm.)

The town of **Bilpin,** 5km west of Kurrajong Heights, has several active **orchards,** and roadside fruit stands here sell fresh-picked produce most of the year. The **Pines Orchard** (tel. 4567 1195) allows travelers to pick their own fruit, in season, at the

NEW SOUTH WALES

going rate with no additional bag charges (peaches, plums, and nectarines late Dec. to late Feb., apples late Jan. to mid-June; open daily 8am-5pm).

A couple kilometers west of Berambing, **Mt. Tomah Botanic Garden** (tel. 4567 2154; fax 4567 2037) is the cool-climate and high-altitude plant collection of the Royal Botanic Garden in Sydney. The plants, most from the southern hemisphere, grow in naturalistic arrangements with the exception of the herbs and roses in the formal terrace garden. The garden's best moments are in spring, when the large collection of rhododendrons and other flowers bloom (Sept.-Nov.), and in fall, when the deciduous forest areas change their colors (March-May). Volunteers conduct free guided tours each day from the visitors center. (Entrance fee $5 per car, $2 per pedestrian or cyclist. Open March-Sept. daily 10am-4pm; Oct.-Feb. 10am-5pm.)

The formal gardens of the town of **Mt. Wilson,** 8km north of Bells Line of Road between Mt. Tomah and Bell, seem all the more remarkable in the context of the surrounding patch of rainforest. In spring and fall, many gardens around town open their gates as tourists climb the mountain to see the flowers or the foliage. Three gardens stay open throughout the year: **Sefton Cottage** (tel. 4756 2034), on Church Ln. (open daily 10am-6pm; admission $2, under 15 free), **Merry Garth** (tel. 4756 2121), on Davies Ln. 500m from Mt. Irvine Rd. (open daily 9am-6pm; admission $3, under 15 free), and **Lindfield Park** (tel. 4756 2148), on Mt. Irvine Rd., 6km northeast of Mt. Wilson (open daily 10am-6pm; admission $3, under 14 free). The **Cathedral of Ferns,** on Mt. Irvine Rd. 1.5km from Mt. Wilson, is a small rainforest area traversed by a 20-minute circular walk.

The **Zig Zag Railway** (tel. 6353 1795; recorded info 6351 4826; fax 6353 1801), at Clarence, 10km east of Lithgow, is a piece of the 1869 track which first made regular travel down into the Lithgow Valley possible. The line's Z-shaped formation was hailed as an innovation. Service continued until 1907, when new tunnels and trains were introduced to increase the flow of traffic through the area. Trains make the 1½-hour trip to the bottom and back three to four times per day. (All tickets round-trip: $12, students and seniors $10, ages 5-18 $6.) **CityRail** trains from Sydney's Central Station stop near the bottom of the track ($12.40, off-peak return $14.80).

Wollemi National Park

Wollemi (WO-lem-eye) National Park, New South Wales's largest wilderness area at 487,500 hectares, sprawls from the Blue Mountains in the south to the Hunter and Goulburn River valleys in the north. With limited vehicle access and a largely undeveloped interior, the park is a wild place with pockets that remain unscrutinized to this day. One such area yielded an amazing find in 1994, when scientists recognized a pine tree whose closest relatives had only previously been seen in fossil form. Although the location of the **Wollemi Pine** is a secret guarded by a small cache of scientists and rangers, most visitors find the park's deep forests, sandstone gorges, and mountain rainforests sufficiently unique and awe-inspiring. Entrance to Wollemi National Park is free, but a small charge for camping in the few designated camping areas has been collected since the spring of 1997. Bushcamping throughout the park is free.

The park's southernmost entrance point is at Bilpin on Bells Line of Road. In this corner of the park, also accessible from Putty Rd. north of Windsor, The **Colo River** slices through the landscape along the 30km Colo Gorge. The car-accessible **camping area** at **Wheeny Creek** lies near a handful of good walking tracks, a clean creek, and recommended swimming holes. The nearest **National Parks and Wildlife Service office,** 370 Windsor Rd. (tel. 4588 5247), in Richmond, has information on camping and walking in the southeast corner of the park (open Mon.-Fri. 9:30am-12:30pm and 1:30-5pm).

Farther west, roads from Lithgow and Wallerawang enter the park at Newnes, where a one-time industrial village now lies in neglect since its desertion in the 1940s. The **Newnes Historic Ruins Track** (5km, medium difficulty) tours the remains of the village along the banks of the Wolgan River. The large, unserviced camping area and the striking rocky faces which surround the Wolgan Valley make Newnes one of Wollemi's more popular stops. Ten kilometers south of town, an abandoned railway tunnel is inhabited by hundreds of tiny **bioluminescent worms** who happily provide hours of free semi-psychedelic entertainment every evening. **Glow Worm Tunnel** can be reached by following a walking track from Newnes or by a half-hour walk from a carpark on the road from Lithgow. Maps of the area and of the path to Glow Worm Tunnel are available at the **Lithgow Visitors Centre,** 1 Cooerwull Rd. (tel. 6353 1859), off the Great Western Hwy. in Lithgow (open daily 9am-5pm).

The **Mudgee NPWS office,** 79 Church St. (tel. 6372 3122), administers the central section of the park, including the campground at **Dunn's Swamp,** and distributes trail maps for the area (open Mon.-Fri. 8:30am-5pm). Known for its canoeing and bushwalking, Dunn's Swamp, 90 minutes from Mudgee by way of Rylstone, is also an excellent place to look for Aboriginal engravings and paintings. The area's sandstone pagodas provide beautiful views of the surrounding wilderness.

From Mudgee, a series of sometimes paved roads makes an arc along the park's north edge to Bulga in the northeast. Along the way, roads dip into the park, providing access to breathtaking views in the **Widden Valley** and to the creeks which lace the region. These routes often pass through private property, however, so it is advisable to inquire at the **Bulga NPWS office** (tel. 6574 5275), on Putty Rd., before venturing into this part of the park (open Tues.-Thurs. 8:30am-4pm). There are no marked trails in the northern section of Wollemi National Park; bushwalkers should be certain to carry a compass and a small-scale topographic map, available at the Bulga NPWS office. South of Bulga, Putty Rd. traces the west edge of the park with 4WD access to the wilderness at several points along the way.

CENTRAL WEST

The agricultural cities and towns of the Central West lie between the rugged plateaus of the Blue Mountains and the stark dryness of outback New South Wales. The major route into the region from the east is the Great Western Hwy., which crosses through the Blue Mountains to Lithgow and Bathurst. From Bathurst, the Mitchell Hwy. heads northwest to Dubbo, Bourke, and beyond, and the Mid Western Hwy. runs southwest to Cowra, and, eventually, Hay. Both of these roads intersect the Newell Hwy., the major route between Melbourne and Brisbane, which cuts a long path across the Central West. Most of the major and minor centers of the Central West are regarded as waystations between grander destinations, and several have enough interesting sights to fill an afternoon between buses. To get to know this area, however, takes a longer stay with time to get beyond the desire for tourist-style attractions, and to appreciate the individual towns' agricultural or industrial significance.

Lithgow

The Great Western Hwy. and Bells Line of Road meet on the west side of the Blue Mountains at Lithgow, a medium-sized industrial city a two-hour drive from Sydney. As the end of the CityRail train line, Lithgow is a natural stopping point. The small downtown area, organized around Main St., provides all the necessary service for a short stay. A one-time center for steel production and still largely supported by coal mining, Lithgow has little inherent charm above and beyond its utility as a base for exploring nearby wilderness areas such as **Wollemi National Park** to the north and **Jenolan Caves** and **Kanangra-Boyd National Park** to the south.

Practical Information Lithgow lies 40km west of Katoomba and 61km east of Bathurst on the Great Western Hwy. The **Greater Lithgow Visitors Centre** (tel. 6353 1859; fax 6353 1851) occupies the old Bowenfels Railway Station, off the Great Western Hwy. on the Bathurst end of town. Their free map is extremely helpful (open daily 9am-5pm). The **Lithgow Souvenir and Tourist Information Centre,** 285 Main

St. (tel. 6351 2307), has somewhat less information but keeps it in a location closer to town. Trains run through the center of town letting passengers off either on Main St. or on Railway Pde., one block north (**CityRail** from Sydney's Central Station $14.20). **CountryLink** (tel. 13 22 32) coach service sets out from Lithgow to Bathurst (2-6 per day, 1hr., $9) and Mudgee (1-2 per day, 2-2½hr., $18). **Greyhound Pioneer** buses (tel. 13 20 30) between Adelaide and Sydney stop at the McDonald's on the Great Western Hwy. West-bound service includes a stop at Broken Hill (1 per day, 13hr., $99). Lithgow's **post office** (tel. 6351 3562), on Main St. across from the train station, is brought to you by the postal code 2790 (open Mon.-Fri. 9am-5pm).

Accommodations, Camping, and Food The **Grand Central Hotel,** 69 Main St. (tel. 6351 3050), has well-maintained singles with appealing hall baths for $18. (Reception at the bar daily 10am-midnight or later. Check-out 11am. Doubles $30. Linen included.) The popular downstairs bistro serves full dinners with meat and vegetables for $7.50 (open daily 11:45am-2pm and 6-8pm). For camping space, visit the friendly folks at **Lithgow Caravan Park,** 58 Cooerwull Rd. (tel. 6351 4350). The park includes big, clean bathrooms and showers, laundry facilities, and an open area for tent camping. (Reception open daily 8:30am-9:30pm. Check-out 10am. Sites $8, powered sites for 2 $14, each additional person $2.) The Lithgow outpost of **Coles** grocery stores (tel. 6352 1966) can be found on Hassan St. Go one block south from Main to Mort St. on Naomi St. Take a right then the first left onto Hassan St. (open Mon. 6am-Sat. 10:30pm, Sun. 8am-8pm). Just outside the Lithgow Railway Station, the **Blue Bird Cafe,** 175 Main St. (tel. 6353 1250), prepares huge omelets covered in melted cheese and your choice of other toppings ($6.50; open daily 8am-3pm).

Sights Tourist attractions in Lithgow glorify the city's industrial history. For those with an interest in small-town development and industrial evolution, the small collection of museums provides a full afternoon's entertainment. Others will choose to move on to outlying areas more quickly. (See **Bells Line of Road,** above, for information on the Zig Zag Railway and **Wollemi National Park,** below, for coverage of the Glow Worm tunnel at Newnes.)

Eskbank House (tel. 6351 3557), on Bennett St., off Inch St., a sandstone home built in 1842, is Lithgow's local museum and a beautifully-preserved example of 19th-century upper crust living. Four rooms remain decorated in their original fashion, replete with rich fabrics and fine wood furniture. The back of the house and the outlying buildings contain displays on local history. Exhibits on mining, iron smelting, and railway transport begin Lithgow's roster of industrial history attractions. (Open Thurs.-Mon. 10am-4pm. Tours conducted on request. Admission $2. Morning or afternoon tea $4.) Nearby, the imposing ruins of **Blast Furnace Park** mark the site of Australia's first blast furnace, an integral part of the country's first steelworks. The original furnace, built in 1907, and a second furnace at the site, built in 1913, fell into disuse in 1928 when the steel industry relocated to Port Kembla to take advantage of its coastal location. The remaining, crumbling structures at Lithgow are a striking reminder of the transience of prosperity.

Still in its initial stages, the **State Mine Railway Heritage Park** (tel. 6353 1513; fax 6353 1185), on Mine Gully Rd., northeast of the town center, will one day be developed into the third piece of a Lithgow industrial history trinity. At present, the museum feels noticeably incomplete with only a small collection of mining artifacts, one room dedicated to explaining the mining process, and several spooky, life-sized miner statues. The old train cars in the surrounding sheds and trainyards are more interesting. (Open in 1998: March 29-Oct. 3 10am-4pm; Oct. 4-March 28 9am-5pm. Admission $2, students and seniors $1, ages 5-15 50¢; free guided tours.) One final museum captures the spirit of another Lithgow industry less often praised: small arms manufacturing. **Lithgow Small Arms Museum** (tel. 6351 4452), on Methuen St. at the head of Ordnance Ave., houses one small room of non-violent devices made at the factory during times of peace and one large room of guns, guns, and guns from all over the world. (Open Sat.-Sun. and public holidays 10am-4pm. Admission $4, seniors $3, ages 6-14 $2, under 6 free, families of 4 $10. Wheelchair-accessible.)

■ Near Lithgow: Mt. Piper

Pacific Power's newest power station at Mt. Piper proves that an industrial site doesn't have to be old to be educational. The **Mt. Piper Energy Expo** (tel. 6354 8155), at the plant 20km northwest of Lithgow, stands 8km past the Wallerawang Power Station on the road to Mudgee. A high-tech, fully interactive exhibit reveals the wonders of electricity and the methods by which it is produced. Using videos, talking phones, and computerized information displays, the expo comes off as a bit too shiny and promotional at times. Still, the exhibit is well-designed and quite interesting, especially for children (open daily 9am-4pm; tours 9:30, 11am, 1:30, and 3pm; free).

Bathurst

Declared a settlement by Lachlan Macquarie in 1815, Bathurst is Australia's oldest inland city and a growing regional center. The city's wide avenues and large, ornate lampposts suggest that Bathurst was always slated for greatness, but it is an unadorned route on the southwest corner of town which has brought the city notoriety. Originally built as a scenic drive in 1938, the 6km circular road up Mt. Panorama and back down does double duty as both a public road and the track for the annual **Bathurst 1000 touring car race,** held the first weekend in October. The race draws over 40,000 people into the city each year, making it either the place to be or a place to avoid depending on your interests. The rest of the year, Bathurst is a quiet place with the feel of a small town, working hard to maintain its history while adjusting to its continued growth.

Practical Information Bathurst is located 101km west of Katoomba at the end of the Great Western Hwy. From Bathurst, the Mid Western Hwy. heads to Cowra (109km) and beyond, and the Mitchell Hwy. branches slightly north to Orange (56km) then more sharply north to Dubbo (206km). The **Bathurst Visitors Centre,** 28 William St. (tel. 6332 1444; fax 6332 2333), has brochures and free maps for Bathurst and towns throughout the Central West (open daily 9am-5pm). **Bathurst Railway Station** receives trains and buses at the end of Keppel St., three blocks from the town center. The **CountryLink** office (tel. 6332 4844 or 13 22 32; open Mon.-Thurs. 8am-5:30pm, Fri. 7:30am-5:30pm, Sat. 8:45am-12:15pm and 1:15-5:15pm) books buses to Lithgow (2-6 per day, 1hr., $9), Orange (2-6 per day, 45min.-1½hr., $8), Cowra (6 per week, 1½hr., $15), and Dubbo (1 per day, 3½hr., $42). **Greyhound Pioneer** (tel. 13 20 30) passes through on its runs between Sydney and Adelaide (1 per day in each direction). The Bathurst **post office,** 230 Howick St. (tel. 6331 3133), is open Monday to Friday 9am to 5pm. The local postal code is 2795.

Accommodations, Camping, and Food Bathurst has a large number of pubs with accommodation in its downtown area. The **Victoria Hotel** (tel. 6331 5777), on the corner of Keppel St. and Havannah St. directly across from the train station, charges decent rates for clean rooms with bedwarmers. The bathrooms cry out for a fix-up. (Free tea and coffee. Reception at the bar open Mon.-Sat. 10am-late, Sun. 11am-10:30pm. Check-out 10am. Singles $20; twins $27. Light breakfast $3.50.) Bathurst's only year-round camping area, **East's Bathurst Holiday Park** (tel. 6331 8236), on Sydney Rd. (also known as the Great Western Hwy.), 5km east of the town center, provides a hilly, tree-strewn tent camping area more appealing than most. (BBQ, toilets, showers, laundry facilities, games, and TV room. Reception open daily 8am-8pm. Check-out 10am. Sites $6 per person; with power for 2 $14, each additional person $6.)

You can stock up on provisions at **Coles** grocery store, 41 William St. (tel. 6331 1500; open Mon. 7am-Sat. 10pm, Sun. 8am-10pm), or wander past the cafes and restaurants on William St. at mealtime. The **Acropole,** 68 William St. (tel. 6331 1310), serves hearty lunch specials with dessert included ($7; open Sun.-Wed. 9am-10pm, Thurs.-Sat. 9am-10:30pm).

Sights To drive the **Mount Panorama circuit** head southwest on William St. until it becomes Panorama Ave. From there, the large banners and overpasses make it quite obvious where the track begins. The **Mount Panorama Motor Racing Hall of Fame** (tel. 6332 1872), on the track at Murray's Corner, just beyond the starting line, keeps the thrill of the race alive year-round with photos, trophies, and other memorabilia, as well as a number of the cars that have graced the track over the years. (Open Wed.-Mon. 9am-4:30pm. Admission $5, ages 15-17 and seniors $3, ages 5-15 $1.50, families of 4 $12.) The **Bathurst Goldfields** (tel. 6332 2022), at the end of the Conrod Straight, remembers the city's gold rush days through exhibits and antique equipment. Tours include a chance to pan for a little of the good stuff. (Admission through tours only $7, families of 5 $20. Call the Bathurst Visitors Centre for tour days and times.) Also at the track, **Sir Joseph Banks Nature Park** (tel. 6333 6286), on the far corner from the starting line, keeps koalas, wombats, dingoes, and other Aussie animals in a 41-hectare enclosure. Several walking trails circle through the park for views of the animals and the scenic countryside. (Open daily 9am-4:15pm. Admission by donation.)

Bathurst's **courthouse,** on Russell St., was considered so grand when it was built in 1880 that residents of the town thought there must have been a mistake in building the structure in Bathurst. Rumors proposed that the building was meant either for a more prominent colonial outpost in India or for a location in Africa where the massive railings encircling the building might have been necessary for keeping out elephants. The courthouse, registered with the National Trust, remains quite a sight inside and out with its Neoclassical columns and Renaissance dome (open Mon.-Fri. 9am-1pm and 2-4pm). The east wing houses a lovely historical museum. (Open Tues.-Wed. and Sun. 10am-4pm, Sat. 9:30am-4:30pm. Admission $1, ages 5-18 50¢, under 5 free.) The family who lives in **Abercrombie House** (tel. 6331 4929; fax 6331 9723), 8km northeast of downtown on the Ophir Rd., opens the Gothic mansion to the public for tours many Sunday afternoons and on select other days throughout the year. Tours begin at 3pm, and anyone not at the gates for admittance by 3:15pm will not be granted entry. Call for tour days, or pick up a schedule from the Bathurst Visitors Centre (admission $4, under 15 $3). Recent addition to the house's tour program are the special exhibits, such as the **Museum and Archive of Australian Monarchy** (MA'AM) after the tours ($2; $1 in addition to the tour fee).

■ Around Bathurst

The area surrounding Bathurst is peppered with preserved historic towns, many of which came into being during the gold rush years of the 1850s. **Rockley,** 32km south via College Rd. through Perthville, is one such town. Registered with the National Trust, the town has about a dozen interesting historical buildings. The **Rockley Mill Museum** (tel. 6337 9624), on Budden St., takes on the history of the town and of milling, and houses an exquisite collection of antique clothing (open Sun. and public holidays 11:30am-4:30pm; admission $1.50, under 12 20¢).

Sofala, 44km north of Bathurst on the road through Peel, is the oldest existing gold town in Australia. Little more than a village now, the town was home to over 10,000 people during its gold boom. The **post office** and **courthouse,** typical structures of the 1870s, stand among nearly 20 remaining historical buildings. The **Sofala Souvenir Shop** (tel. 6337 7075; open daily 9am-5:30pm), on Denison St., distributes tourist information in Sofala, and the Bathurst Visitors Centre has driving and walking tour sheets to help you get there and around.

The mining town of **Hill End,** 70km northwest of Bathurst and 38km west of Sofala, has been declared a National Historical Site, but extensive restoration has kept the town from becoming merely a museum. People live and work in many of the buildings built during the town's short boom (1871-1873). The **NP&WS Visitors Centre,** on Hospital Ln., is the starting point for tours of Hill End.

Abercrombie Caves (tel. 6368 8603; fax 6363 8634), 72km south of Bathurst beyond Rockley, features the largest natural limestone bridge in the southern hemisphere, the **Archway.** (Office open for reservations daily 9am-4pm. Self-guided tours of the Archway $10, seniors and ages 5-15 $5, families of 4 $25; guided tours Mon.-Fri. 2 per day, Sat.-Sun. 5 per day; 1hr.; $12, $6, $30; Cathedral Cave $12 per person.)

Orange

Orange is a pleasant, attractive town, the type of place where people raise children knowing their children will be able to raise children there as well. At the heart of a prosperous agricultural district which produces fruits, grains, and livestock, the town is a well-equipped service center and a fine place to spend a day strolling the wide clean streets and thinking of simpler times.

Orange's most famous native son is **Andrew Boyle "Banjo" Paterson,** the poet and journalist who penned the lyrics to *Waltzing Matilda.* Paterson was born February 17, 1864, at Narrambla, a relative's home that formerly stood at the location of **Banjo Paterson Park,** on the Ophir Rd. at the northeast corner of town. The park consists solely of a simple monument at the side of the road overlooking sloping hills speckled with trees and farms, but the site is worth a stop. The **local history museum** (tel. 6362 8905), on McNamara St. has more information on the local boy done good (open Sun. and public holidays 2-4pm; admission $2, ages 5-16 $1, families of 4 $5).

Approaching from the east, Orange is 55km beyond Bathurst on the Mitchell Hwy., and Dubbo lies 150km farther down the road. Smaller roads lead directly to the smaller regional hubs at Cowra, Forbes, and Parkes. **Orange District Tourism** (tel. 6361 5226), on Byng St., has all the necessary information for in-town exploration and a good free map to boot (open daily 9am-5pm). To get to Orange or away again, you have several options. **Hazleton Airlines** (tel. 13 17 13) flies in from Sydney (3-5 per day, 45min., $150.50). **CountryLink** (tel. 6361 9500 or 13 22 32), on Peisley St. at the railway station, goes to Sydney (2-5 per day, 5hr., $38) and places in between (office open Mon.-Fri. 8am-5pm, Sat. 8:30am-noon). For cheaper daily coach service within the region, call **Rendell's** (tel. 1800 023 328; to: Dubbo 2hr., $30; Sydney 4½hr., $30; Bathurst 1hr., $20; Canberra 4hr., $35; and Cowra 1½hr., $25). **Orange Coaches** (tel. 6362 3197; open Mon.-Fri. 8:30am-5pm) handles local transportation (service Mon.-Fri. roughly 7:30am-6pm, Sat. 9am-2pm; fares $1.20-3). **Australia Post,** 222 Summer St. (tel. 6362 3088), carries postal code 2800 (open Mon.-Fri. 9am-5pm).

Pub accommodation in Orange is uncommonly nice, and the prices explain the quality. The **Metropolitan Hotel** (tel. 6362 1353), on the corner of Byng and Anson St., has excellent rooms, a TV lounge, a simple kitchen area, and a free light breakfast. (Inquire at the bar Mon.-Sat. 10am-2am, Sun. 10am-10pm. Check-out 10am. Singles $35; twins $50.) When it's not filled with miners, **Great Western Hotel** (tel. 6362 4055), directly across Peisley St. from Orange Railway Station, may have more basic beds for $15 per person (reception at the bar open daily 10am-midnight or later). The more central of Orange's two caravan parks, the **Colour City Showground Caravan Park,** on Margaret St., at the end of McLachlan St., about 2km from the town center, is an unexciting sort of a place, but how exciting is a caravan park ever? It has all the necessary amenities and no hidden fees, which is as much as anyone can expect. (Toilets, hot showers, laundry. Live-in owner around most of the time. Sites for 2 $7.50, with power $11; each additional person $2. Wheelchair-accessible.)

Both **Coles** (tel. 6362 4922; open Mon. 6am-Sat. midnight, Sun. 8am-10pm), inside MetroPlaza, and **Woolworths,** 197 Anson St. (tel. 6362 4655; open Mon.-Sat. 7am-10pm, Sun. 8am-6pm), have large grocery stores in downtown Orange, and there are a number of pleasant cafes on Summer St. or within a block of this strip. **Cafe 48,** 48 Sale St. (tel. 6361 7748), fosters a chic but comfortable atmosphere for international cuisine with a leafy outdoor dining area (licensed; hot drinks $2-2.50; meals $7.50-$14; open Sun.-Mon. 10:30am-4pm, Wed.-Sat. 10:30am-10pm or later).

Cowra

On August 5, 1944, over 1000 Japanese soldiers staged a daring escape attempt at the Prisoner of War camp in Cowra. The prisoners split into several groups, some running directly into fire from the machine gun towers at the camp's periphery and others escaping into the fields around the stronghold. In the nine days that followed, 231 Japanese men perished as the escapees were rounded up and returned to camp. Many fell victim to the violence of the outbreak, while those who could not go along committed suicide at the camp. Today, three monuments commemorate the **Cowra Outbreak** and bring an international focus to what would otherwise be a charming but isolated country town.

Cowra sits in the Lachlan Valley 109km southwest of Bathurst on the banks of the Lachlan River. The Mid Western Hwy. cuts through town toward Grenfell and parts west, while Rte. 81 heads north to meet the Mitchell Hwy. For free maps, brochures, and good advice, see the people at **Cowra Tourism** (tel. 6342 4333), on the corner of Boorowa Rd. and the Mid Western Hwy. (open daily 9am-5pm). Transportation arrangements for Sydney-bound **CountryLink** (tel. 13 22 32) and **Greyhound Pioneer** (tel. 13 20 30) buses through Cowra can be made at **Harvey World Travel** (tel. 6342 1288; open Mon.-Fri. 8:30am-5:30pm). Greyhound Pioneer is the only company to go to Forbes (1 per day, 1½hr., $39). **Rendell's** (tel. 1800 023 328) makes stops in Orange (2 per week, 1½hr., $25) and Canberra (2 per week, 3hr., $30).

Each of the three hotels on Cowra's main street, Kendal St., has its strong point. The **Lachlan Hotel,** 66 Kendal St. (tel. 6342 2355), rents good, clean pub rooms with decent bathrooms and throws in a light breakfast for the lowest price in town (reception at the bar open Sun.-Thurs. 10am-10pm, Fri.-Sat. 10am-2am; $20 per person). Rooms at the **Imperial Hotel,** 15-18 Kendal St. (tel. 6341 2588), have been recently refurbished to motel quality. (Light breakfast included. Reception at the bar open daily 10am-midnight. Singles $25; doubles $35.) The **Cowra Hotel,** 2 Kendal St. (tel. 6342 1925), is a bit dodgier, but there's a TV room with a refrigerator (see the bartender after 10am; singles $25; doubles $35). Just under the Kendal St. bridge over the Lachlan River, on the town center side of the river, **Cowra Van Park** (tel. 6342 1058), on Lachlan St., provides riverside camping right in the center of town. (Toilets, showers, laundry. Wheelchair-accessible bathrooms. Reception open daily 8am-10pm. Check-out 10am. Sites for 2 $11; with power $15, each additional person $4.) The local **Woolworths** (tel. 6342 2255) is hidden one block south of Kendal St. on Railway Ln. (open Mon.-Sat. 7am-9pm, Sun. 10am-4pm).

The first of Cowra's memorials is a **monument at the site of the outbreak,** on Sakura Ave. at the corner of Farm St. The foundations of the POW camp's buildings still divide the field into barracks and lanes, and a photograph shows how the camp looked in 1944. Two kilometers north of the actual memorial, the adjoining **Japanese and Australian War Cemeteries,** on Doncaster Dr., recognize the unity these countries have experienced in death and make a powerful statement of common mourning. The **Japanese Gardens and Cultural Centre** (tel. 6341 2233; fax 6341 1875), on Scenic Dr., a continuation of Brisbane St. just north of the downtown area, was opened in 1979 as a statement of peace and friendship between Australia and Japan. The serene gardens, designed in traditional Japanese style, are punctuated by ponds, streams, and low benches for quiet contemplation. (Open daily 8:30am-5pm; admission $6.50, students and seniors $6, ages 5-18 $4.50, families $16.) In recognition of the way in which Cowra has participated in Japanese sorrow over the escape attempt and turned the event into a starting point for understanding, the town was selected to house the **Australian Peace Bell,** a replica of the World Peace Bell which hangs outside the United Nations headquarters in New York City. The bell can be seen in Civic Square, on Darling St. just north of Kendal St.

Near Cowra

The town of **Canowindra,** 28km north of Cowra from Redfern St. on the way to Orange bills itself as the **"Hot Air Balloon Capital of Australia."** In addition to

The MCI Card with WorldPhone Service... The easy way to call when traveling worldwide.

For more information or to apply for a Card call: 1-800-444-1616

Outside the U.S., call MCI collect (reverse charge) at: 1-916-567-5151

Please cut out and save this reference guide for convenient U.S. and worldwide calling with the MCI Card with WorldPhone Service.

COUNTRY		WORLDPHONE TOLL-FREE ACCESS #
#American Samoa		633-2MCI (633-2624)
#Antigua	(Available from public card phones only)	#2
#Argentina (CC)		0800-5-1002
#Aruba ✣		800-888-8
#Australia (CC) ◆	To call using OPTUS ■	1-800-551-111
	To call using TELSTRA ■	1-800-881-100
#Austria (CC) ◆		022-903-012
#Bahamas		1-800-888-8000
#Bahrain		800-002
#Barbados		1-800-888-8000
#Belarus (CC)	From Brest, Vitebsk, Grodno, Minsk	8-800-103
	From Gomel and Mogilev regions	8-10-800-103
#Belgium (CC) ◆		0800-10012
#Belize	From Hotels	557
	From Payphones	815
#Bermuda ✣		1-800-888-8000
#Bolivia ◆		0-800-2222
#Brazil (CC)		000-8012
#British Virgin Islands ✣		1-800-888-8000
#Brunei		800-011
#Bulgaria		00800-0001
#Canada (CC)		1-800-888-8000
#Cayman Islands		1-800-888-8000
#Chile (CC)	To call using CTC ■	800-207-300
	To call using ENTEL ■	800-360-180
#China ❖	(Available from most major cities)	108-12
	For a Mandarin-speaking Operator	108-17
#Colombia (CC) ◆		980-16-0001
	Colombia IIIC Access in Spanish	980-16-1000
#Costa Rica ◆		0800-012-2222
#Cote D'Ivoire		1001
#Croatia (CC) ★		0800-22-0112
#Cyprus ◆		080-90000
#Czech Republic (CC) ◆		00-42-000112
#Denmark (CC) ◆		8001-0022
#Dominica		1-800-888-8000
#Dominican Republic (CC) ✣		1-800-888-8000
	Dominican Republic IIIC Access in Spanish	1121
#Ecuador (CC) ✣		999-170
#Egypt ◆	(Outside of Cairo, dial 02 first)	355-5770
El Salvador ◆		800-1767
#Federated States of Micronesia		624

FOLD

COUNTRY		WORLDPHONE TOLL-FREE ACCESS #
#Fiji		004-890-1002
#Finland (CC) ◆		08001-102-80
#France (CC) ◆		0800-99-0019
#French Antilles (CC)	(includes Martinique, Guadeloupe)	0800-99-0019
French Guiana (CC)		0-800-99-0019
#Gabon		00-005
#Gambia ◆		00-1-99
#Germany (CC)		0130-0012
#Greece (CC) ◆		00-800-1211
#Grenada ✣		1-800-888-8000
#Guam (CC)		950-1022
Guatemala (CC) ◆		99-99-189
#Guyana		177
#Haiti ✣		193
	Haiti IIIC Access in French/Creole	190
Honduras ✣		122
#Hong Kong (CC)		800-96-1121
#Hungary (CC) ◆		00▼800-01411
#Iceland (CC) ◆		800-9002
#India (CC) ❖	(Available from most major cities)	000-127
#Indonesia (CC) ◆		001-801-11
Iran ✣		(SPECIAL PHONES ONLY)
#Ireland (CC)		1-800-55-1001
#Israel (CC)		177-150-2727
#Italy (CC) ◆		172-1022
#Jamaica ✣		1-800-888-8000
	(From Special Hotels only)	873
	Jamaica IIIC Access	#2-from public phones
#Japan (CC) ◆	To call using KDD ■	0039-121▶
	To call using IDC ■	0066-55-121
	To call using ITJ ■	0044-11-121
#Jordan		18-800-001
#Kazakhstan (CC)		8-800-131-4321
#Kenya ❖	(Available from most major cities)	080011
#Korea (CC)	To call using KT ■	009-14
	To call using DACOM ■	00309-12
	Phone Booths✣	Press red button, 03, then ∗
	Military Bases	550-2255
#Kuwait		800-MCI (800-624)
Lebanon ✣		600-MCI (600-624)
#Liechtenstein (CC) ◆		0800-89-0222
#Luxembourg		0800-0112

FOLD

COUNTRY		WORLDPHONE TOLL-FREE ACCESS #
#Macao		0800-131
#Macedonia (CC) ◆		99800-4266
#Malaysia (CC) ◆		800-0012
#Malta		0800-89-0120
#Marshall Islands		1-800-888-8000
#Mexico	Avantel (CC)	91-800-021-8000
	Telmex ▲	95-800-674-7000
	Mexico IIIC Access	91-800-021-1000
#Micronesia		624
#Monaco (CC) ◆		800-99-019
#Montserrat		1-800-888-8000
#Morocco		00-211-0012
#Netherlands (CC) ◆		0800-022-9122
#Netherlands Antilles (CC) ✣		001-800-888-8000
#New Zealand (CC)		000-912
Nicaragua (CC)	(Outside of Managua, dial 02 first)	166
Nicaragua IIIC Access in Spanish	*2 from any public payphone	
#Norway (CC) ◆		800-19912
#Pakistan		00-800-12-001
#Panama		108
	Military Bases	2810-108
#Papua New Guinea (CC)		05-07-19140
#Paraguay ✣		008-112-800
#Peru		0-800-500-10
#Philippines (CC) ◆	To call using PLDT ■	105-14
	To call using PHILCOM ■	1026-14
	Philippines IIIC via PLDT in Tagalog	105-15
	Philippines IIIC via PhilCom in Tagalog	1026-12
#Poland (CC) ✣		00-800-111-21-22
#Portugal (CC) ✣		05-017-1234
#Puerto Rico (CC)		1-800-888-8000
#Qatar ★		0800-012-77
Romania (CC) ✣		01-800-1800
#Russia (CC) ◆ ✣	To call using ROSTELCOM ■	747-3322
	(For Russian speaking operator)	747-3320
	To call using SOVINTEL ■	960-2222
#Saipan (CC) ✣		950-1022
#San Marino (CC) ◆		172-1022
#Saudi Arabia (CC)		1-800-11
#Singapore		8000-112-112
#Slovak Republic (CC)		00421-00112
#Slovenia		080-8808

Marti's Balloon Fiesta, which attracts balloonists from around the world each April, the town supports several companies that offer casual balloon outings. **Balloon Aloft,** 199 Rodd St. (tel. 6344 1797 or 1800 028 568), takes to the sky each morning at dawn, weather permitting. The production lasts several hours, including an earth-bound champagne breakfast to celebrate your trip ($175, ages 8-12 $130, standby booking $150). **Aussie Balloontrek** (tel. 6364 0211 or 018 114 239), has a similar service for slightly less ($160, under 12 $100).

The huge man-made lake created by the damming of the Lachlan River at **Wyangala Dam,** 40km east of Cowra, is a veritable treasure-trove of outdoor fun. **Wyangala Waters State Park** (tel. 6345 0877; fax 6345 0897) includes the lake and the surrounding bush (open 24hr.; free). The **BP Service Station** (tel. 6345 0801), just outside the park entrance, rents aluminum boats with outboard motors (2hr. $25, full day $60; cash deposit $100; open in summer daily 7:30am-8:30pm; in winter 8:30am-5:30pm).

Forbes

The former stomping grounds of famed bushranger **Ben Hall,** Forbes today shows little evidence of its checkered past. The compact town center contains few compelling sights, but an overall feeling of timelessness and a handful of good pubs more than compensate for its lack of cultural attractions.

The Newell Hwy. runs through Forbes, with Dubbo (153km) to the northeast and West Wyalong (on the Mid Western Hwy., 105km) to the southwest. There are also reasonably direct routes east to Orange (93km) and southeast to Cowra (70km). The downtown area nestles in a curve on the north bank of the Lachlan River. The old railway station on Union St. has been converted into the **Forbes Railway Arts and Tourist Centre** (tel. 6852 4155), now that passenger trains no longer service the town (open daily 9am-5pm). **Harvey World Travel,** 6 Templar St. (tel. 6852 2344; fax 6852 4401), sells tickets for all inter-city buses from Forbes (open Mon.-Fri. 9am-5pm, Sat. 9am-noon). **CountryLink** (tel. 13 22 32) runs to Orange (6 per week, 2hr., $13) and Parkes (6 per week, ½hr., $4), from the railway station, and **Greyhound Pioneer** (tel. 13 20 30) handles service to Cowra (1 per day, 1hr., $39) from the Cal-Tex 24 Roadhouse, 1km north of town on the Newell Hwy.

Pubs in Forbes offer excellent quality rooms for standard prices. The **Albion Hotel,** 135 Lachlan St. (tel. 6351 1881), makes $15 per person feel like the deal of the week with big, clean rooms, free tea and coffee to go with the in-room kettle and toaster, and a couple of complimentary cookies to make it a proper cuppa. The TV lounge

Ben Hall: Scourge of the Central West

From the place and date of his birth to the manner in which he met his death, the story of the notorious bushranger Ben Hall is a hotly contested page in Australian history. Legend has it that Hall, the son of convict parents, was a hardened criminal raised into a career of willing crime. Sympathizers, many of whom can be found in the town of Forbes, contend that Hall strove to rise above his background. They maintain that he turned to crime only when forced to do so by the local police force who wrongly accused him on several occasions and eventually destroyed the life he had worked to build. There is no question, however, that by the age of 25 Ben Hall was living a life of crime full-time, nor that he spent the two years between 1863 and his death in 1865 terrorizing the towns of the Central West with a gang of other bushrangers. Hall's gang robbed banks and private citizens and left a trail of violence wherever they went. (Whether or not Hall committed any of the violence himself is one of the points of debate.) The final, incontrovertible fact of Hall's life is his death, which took place on May 5, 1865, when a group of policemen and one Aboriginal tracker caught up with Hall and shot him just outside of the town of Forbes. The site of Hall's demise and his simple grave can both be seen in Forbes.

has a fridge for groceries as well. (Reception at the bar open Mon.-Sat. 10am-midnight or later, Sun. noon-10pm.) On the corner of Court St., the **Vandenberg Hotel** (tel. 6852 2015), has flower-fresh bathrooms, peachy country-style bedrooms, with toasters, kettles, and mini-fridges, and a comfortable TV lounge (inquire at the bar daily 10am-late; singles $20, doubles $32).

Forbes Country Club Caravan Park (tel. 6852 1957), on Sam St. off the Newell Hwy., just north of the railway station, is conveniently located (toilets, showers; reception daily 7am-9pm; check-out 10am; sites for 2 $7, with power $13, $1 per additional person; laundry $1.40 per wash, $1 to dry), but the lovely riverbank location of the **Apex Caravan Park,** 86 Reymond St. (tel. 6852 1929), 2km south of the town center via Bridge St. and Flint St., is well worth the drive for anyone with a car. (Toilets, showers, laundry facilities, small pool, store on premises. Live-in owners will receive visitors anytime. Sites for 2 $9; with power $12, $4 per additional person.) Groceries can be found at **Woolworths** (tel. 6852 2421), on Rankin St. (open Mon.-Sat. 7am-9pm, Sun. 9am-6pm).

The **Forbes Museum** (tel. 6852 2635), on Cross St., has a small collection of local artifacts and displays on the town's most notorious resident, Ben Hall (open Oct.-May daily 2-4pm, June-Sept. 3-5pm; admission $2, ages 5-15 $1). The **place where Hall was shot** is now part of the **Lachlan Vintage Village** (tel. 6852 2655), on the Newell Hwy., 1km south of the town center. The village encompasses some 50 historic buildings, many built during the gold rush years, and admission includes the opportunity to pan for gold in the town stream. (Open daily 8am-5pm; admission $8, seniors $6, ages 5-18 $4, under 5 free.) Ben Hall's grave is in **Forbes Cemetery,** 1km outside of downtown on Bogan Rd. **Ned Kelly's sister Kate** is buried here as well.

■ Near Forbes: Parkes Radio Telescope

The **64m dish** visible from the Newell Hwy. 55km northeast of Forbes belongs to the **Parkes Radio Telescope.** A major contributor to our international understanding of astronomy since its opening in 1961, the Parkes Telescope has participated in such high-profile projects as the televising of the first moon walks and the rescue of NASA's Apollo 13 voyage. More recently, the telescope is turning heads in astronomical circles for the information it is generating toward a possible explanation for the mysterious **dark matter** which populates the cosmos. The **Visitors Discovery Centre** (tel. 6361 1777; fax 6861 1730) is a surprisingly low-tech facility housing displays on the telescope and its accomplishments. The knowledgeable and talkative staff and a 30-minute film make the whole thing quite accessible and interesting even for non-scientists. (Center open daily 8:30am-4:30pm; free. Film runs whenever viewers gather; $3, seniors, students, and ages 5-18 $2.)

Dubbo

The hub of the Central West, Dubbo sits at the intersection of the Newell Hwy. between Melbourne and Brisbane, and the Mitchell Hwy., leading from Bathurst to parts west. It is common for travelers to spend only one night in Dubbo, breaking the monotony of a long journey along either of these major routes. Headlined by the Western Plains Zoo, Dubbo's roster of attractions is a perfect size for such a stop. Travelers with more time and less of a hankering for tourist-oriented entertainment may learn to see Dubbo as more than a travel hub, but making this leap requires a willingness to appreciate the place for its settled pace and its agricultural significance.

Practical Information The Newell Hwy., which runs between Melbourne and Brisbane, and the Mitchell Hwy., which travels west from Sydney to Broken Hill and beyond, meet at Dubbo. The city, located 150km north of both Forbes and Orange and 420km northeast of Sydney, is the jumping-off point for many forays into the northwest and the outback. The **Dubbo Visitors Centre** (tel. 6884 1422), at the corner of Erskine and Brisbane St., is at the northwest corner of the small downtown area (open daily 9am-5pm). **CountryLink** trains run daily to Sydney ($55) from the railway station on Talbragar St. The **Inter-city Coach Terminal,** on Erskine St. between Carrington Ave. and Darling St., is serviced by **CountryLink** (tel. 13 22 32) and **Rendell Coaches** (tel. 6884 2411). CountryLink coaches make daily connections to Orange (2hr., $18), Bathurst (3½hr., $28), and Lithgow (4¼hr., $35), and three per week to Canberra (Tues., Thurs., and Sun., 8hr., $47). Rendell's buses move only south and east from Dubbo, but service to Sydney (1 per day, 6½hr., $45), Canberra (Mon. and Fri., 6hr., $45), and points in between is generally less expensive than on CountryLink. Flights from Sydney (3-7 per day, 1hr., $15) come to **Dubbo Airport,** northwest of town off the Mitchell Hwy., on **Hazelton Airlines** (tel. 13 17 13). **Dubbo Coaches** (tel. 6882 2900; office open Mon.-Fri. 8:30am-5pm) conducts limited coach service between the city center and suburban residential areas (fares $1.20-2.60), but renting a bike from **Wheelers Cycles** (tel. 6882 9899) is probably a more sensible and convenient mode of transportation ($10 per day; open Mon.-Fri. 8:30am-5:30pm, Sat. 8:30am-1pm). Dubbo's **post office** (tel. 6882 2022), on Talbragar St. between Macquarie and Brisbane St. (open Mon.-Fri. 9am-5pm), answers to the postal code 2830.

Accommodations and Camping Hotels can be found in the city center, with several on Talbragar St. All charge $20 or more for singles, but a couple include breakfast. The least expensive beds in Dubbo are at the **Dubbo YHA Hostel,** 87 Brisbane St. (tel. 6882 0922), off Erskine St. between the bus station and downtown, a homey place with exotic birds, a fireplace, and a relaxing porch off the bedrooms. Guests can rent bikes ($6 per day) or arrange a ride with the owners for zoo outings or trips to the local stockyards (Mon., Thurs., and Fri.), one of the owners' favorite ways of acquainting travelers with life in Dubbo. (Kitchen, common room with TV and games, linen and blankets included. Reception open daily 8:30am-evening, call if you'll be late and make yourself at home if no one's around. 4-bed dorms $14, twins and doubles $28.) A few doors down the block, **Hub of the West,** 79 Brisbane St. (tel. 6882 5004), caters to long-term guests with substantial weekly discounts. The rooms are clean but plain and come with access to a small kitchen and two TV rooms. (Reception open daily 8am-noon and 1-6pm. Singles $25; doubles $45. Weekly: $75; $125.) **Christina's Catering Service and Accommodation House,** 68 Bultjie St. (tel. 6884 1828; fax 6884 5311), is basically a boarding house that welcomes short-term visitors. Rooms (singles only) have TVs and refrigerators, and use of the laundry machines is free. (Reception open daily 8:30am-5pm, but you can reach the proprietor at home by phone later in the evening. Singles $20, weekly $85.) The excellent **Dubbo City Caravan Park** (tel. 6882 4820; fax 6884 2062), on Whylandra St., just before it becomes the Newell Hwy. southwest of the city center, has a shady landscaped tent camping area and a view of the Macquarie River. (Toilets, showers, on-site store. Reception open daily 8am-7pm. Check-out 11am. Sites for 2 $11; with power $14-18, each additional person $4, under 14 $2).

Food Sandwich shops and bakeries are plentiful on Macquarie St., Brisbane St., and Talbragar St. in the city center, and both **Coles** and **Woolworths** have huge grocery stores inside the plazas off Macquarie St. The **Dubbo Markets** (tel. 6882 6699), on the corner of Darling and Erskine St., offers a more local grocery selection with fresh fruits, vegetables, meats, and breads all under one roof. (Open Mon.-Wed. 8:30am-6pm, Thurs. 8:30am-8pm, Fri. 8:30am-6:30pm, Sat.-Sun. 8:30am-4pm.) The casual comfort of the **Grapevine Cafe,** 144 Brisbane St. (tel. 6884 7354), is enhanced by a cozy couch and a fireplace. The eclectic menu includes a good number of vegetarian options. (Vegetarian breakfast with eggs $8.50; vegetable curry with Basmati rice at lunchtime $9.80; dinner $10-14. Open Mon.-Sat. 8am-10:30pm, Sun. 8am-6pm.) The **Bus Stop Cafe** (tel. 6884 4677), in the Inter-city Coach Terminal on Erskine St., proves that bus stop food isn't always an afterthought. For sandwiches and meals, the cafe is clean, friendly, and inexpensive without the slightest hint of greasy spoon chaos (hamburgers $3.50, steak sandwiches $4.95, full breakfast $6.95; open 24hr.).

Sights Dubbo's premier tourist attraction is the **Western Plains Zoo** (tel. 6882 5888; fax 6884 1722), on Obley Rd. off the Newell Hwy. south of the city center, a 300-hectare park split into loose enclosures with many animals wandering completely unrestrained. In addition to Australian native species, the zoo houses Bengal tigers, black rhinoceri (including a calf born in the park), and Australia's only African elephants. Although the sealed road is suitable for cars, those who walk or cycle the park's 6km circuit get to spend more time out in the open with the animals. (Open daily 9am-5pm, no entry after 3:30pm. Admission $15, students $10.50, seniors $9, ages 4-16 $7.50, under 4 free, families of 5 $38, each additional child $6.40. Bike rental $8 for 4hr., deposit $10. Keeper-led zoo walks Sun. and Wed., Sat. during school holidays 6:45am, $2.50 per person plus admission, under 4 free.) Two kilometers beyond the zoo on Obley Rd., **Dundullimal Homestead** (tel. 6884 9984) is a National Trust-registered slab house dating from the 1830s. A saddlery workshop, petting zoo, and picnic area complement the historical homestead which remains furnished in traditional style (open daily 9am-5pm; admission $5, students $3, seniors $4, under 17 $2). On Macquarie St., two attractions highlight the city's more recent history. The dough-faced animatronic models of **Old Dubbo Gaol** (tel. 6882 8122; fax 6882 2422) tell the sometimes sad and macabre stories of Dubbo's bygone criminals in a way that proves any subject can be funny when you add enough goofy talking mannequins. (Open daily 9am-5pm, last entry 4:30pm. Admission $5, students, and seniors $3.50, ages 5-16 $1, under 5 free.) Down the street, the **Dubbo Museum** (tel. 6882 5359) manages to keep a straighter face on local history. (Open daily 9am-4:30pm. Admission $5, students, and seniors $3.50, ages 5-16 $1, under 5 free, families of 4 $11.)

Mudgee

Cradled by the foothills of the Dividing Range, Mudgee lives up to its Aboriginal name meaning "nest in the hills." The picturesque valley locale seems particularly suitable for the center of an area known for its **wines** and **honeys.** With over 20 wineries peppering the hills around the town, Mudgee is a less touristed, if less hailed, alternative to the Hunter Valley.

Though only a 3½-hour drive from Sydney, Mudgee, situated on Hwy. 86 between Lithgow (159km) and Dubbo (109km), feels pleasantly remote. Armed with maps and good advice, the **Mudgee Visitors Centre,** 84 Market St. (tel. 6372 5875), is a fine first stop and one of two spots where **CountryLink** coaches (tel. 13 22 32) pause on the way through town. Buses between Sydney (5hr., $38) and Coonabarabaran (3hr., $64) come through once or twice a day in each direction stopping in Lithgow (2½hr., $18) and Gulgong (30min., $5) as well. The **NPWS office,** 79 Church St. (tel. 6372 3122), administers the central section of Wollemi National Park (see p. 138).

There's one inexpensive hotel near each of the two inter-city bus stops. The **Woolpack Hotel,** 67 Market St. (tel. 6372 5875), near the visitors center, is slightly less expensive (free tea and coffee, fridge; reception open daily 8:30am-midnight or later; check-out 10am; $15 per person), but the **Federal Hotel** (tel. 6372 1908), on Inglis St., near the old train station, has a couple more perks (free tea and coffee in rooms, bedwarmers; reception open daily 10am-11pm or midnight; check-out 10am; $17 per person). The slightly dreary **Mudgee Riverside Caravan and Tourist Park,** 22 Short St. (tel. 6372 2531), is just behind the visitors center near the Cugewong River (toilets, showers, laundry facilities; reception open daily 8am-10pm; check-out 10am; sites for 2 $10, with power $13, each additional person $4). The unusually light and open setting in the **Lawson Park Hotel Bistro,** 1 Church St. (tel. 6372 2183), is a great spot for good grub (steak dinner $9.50, local wine by the glass from $3.50, by the bottle from $9; open Sun.-Thurs. noon-2:30pm and 6-9pm, Fri.-Sat. noon-2:30pm and 6-9:30pm). The bar stays active a bit later (schooner of Toohey's $3; open Sun.-Thurs. 10am-midnight, Fri.-Sat. 10am-3am).

A full tour of Mudgee's **wineries and vineyards** would take quite a lot of time and a healthy tolerance for alcohol. Because there are so many small vineyards in the area, many share their wine-making facilities. Thus, tours of the larger wineries, such as **Craigmoor Winery** (tel. 6372 2208; fax 6372 4464; open Mon.-Sat. 10am-4:30pm, Sun. 10am-4pm), on Craigmoor Rd., **Montrose Winery** (tel. 6373 3883; fax 6373 3795; open daily 10am-4:30pm), on Henry Lawson Dr., and **Huntington Estate Wines** (tel. 6373 3825; open Mon.-Fri. 9am-5pm, Sat. 10am-5pm, Sun. 10am-3pm), on Cassilis Rd., tend to be most interesting. **Botobolar,** 89 Botobolar Rd. (tel. 6373 3840; fax 6373 3789), is Mudgee's only **organic winery,** and the 40-minute self-guided tour leads out into the vineyards, an unusual feature for most tours (open Mon.-Sat. 10am-5pm, Sun. 10am-3pm). The historic Fairview winery has recently been reopened by **Platt's Wines** (tel. 6372 7041; fax 6372 7043), on Cassilis Rd. at Henry Lawson Dr. With a resident sculptor and a reasonably-priced cafe on the premises of the old winery, Platt's makes a nice longer stop among the tours (open daily 9am-3pm; cafe open Wed.-Sun.). Travelers stopping in Mudgee in September (Sept. 5-27, 1998) will find the streets alive with the music and the wine tastings of the **Mudgee Wine Festival.**

■ Near Mudgee: Gulgong

The narrow streets and wooden buildings of Gulgong, 30km northwest of Mudgee, off the road from Dubbo, harken to the days of the frontier, when the discovery of gold at Red Hill made the town a bustling center. The **Gulgong Pioneers Museum,** 73 Herbert St. (tel. 6374 1513), keeps that time alive through an amazing collection of pictures, personal items, furniture, buildings, vehicles, and music from times gone by. The volunteer-run museum is expertly organized and interesting enough to suck up a whole day (open daily 9am-5pm; admission $4, seniors $3, students, and ages 5-15 $2). The **Henry Lawson Centre,** 147 Mayne St. (tel. 6374 1665), celebrates the life and achievements of the famous writer who grew up in nearby Eurunderee. From photographs and drawings of Lawson to books and clippings of his work, the center does a fine job of preserving Henry Lawson's wit and style. (Open Sun.-Fri. 10am-noon, Sat. 10am-3pm. Admission $2, seniors $1, ages 5-15 50¢.)

The **Gulgong Tourist Information Centre,** 109 Herbert St. (tel. 6374 1202), has information on other area sights (open Mon.-Fri. 8am-4:30pm, Sat. 9am-3pm, Sun. 9:30am-2pm). The bus from Mudgee arrives and departs from the **post office,** on Herbert St. (1-2 per day, 30min., $5). For lodging, try the **Commercial Hotel,** on Mayne St. (free tea and coffee, bedwarmers; reception at the bar Mon.-Sat. 10am-midnight, Sun. 10am-10pm; check-out 10am; beds $20). The **Red Hill Field Studies Centre** (tel. 6374 2558; fax 6374 2560), on Tom Saunders Ave. off White St., is an educational center for primary school children but welcomes travelers whenever there are free beds (no linen or pillows; office open Mon.-Fri. 8:30am-3:30pm; $10 per person).

NORTH COAST OF NEW SOUTH WALES

Dream of surfing beaches and environmentally conscious residents, and you dream of the north coast of New South Wales. Often called the Holiday Coast by Sydney-siders, this sand-strewn fantasyland caters equally to leisurely backpackers, die-hard surfers, and hordes of families. Newcastle and Port Macquarie, with urban shores only a day from Sydney, draw holiday-makers itching to sunbathe, water-ski, or wet their surfboards. At the other end of the spectrum, inland eco-activist centers like Lismore and Bellingen thrive on highly productive agricultural land punctuated by scenic national parks and fast-flowing rivers.

With virtual cult status, Byron Bay synthesizes these two distinct flavors. Whether they've come for water sports or didgeridoo lessons, most travelers find that their itineraries slow to at least a temporary halt to hear the siren song of Byron Bay. Yet its lighthouse, which marks the easternmost point in Australia, unerringly guides wayfarers on toward the Queensland border and the clutch of beaches beyond. For coverage of Tweed Heads, see **Tweed Heads and Coolangatta,** p. 291.

Newcastle

Newcastle (pop. 265,000) is trying hard to shake its reputation as a smokestack industry metropolis. It's New South Wales' second largest city, but a building code which limits construction to eight stories keeps man's work from overwhelming nature's. Newcastle is still the world's largest coal exporter, shipping out one million tons each week aboard long, lean cargo ships which dot the bay and glide through the harbor. But since the recent shutdown of the major steelworks, Broken Hill Proprietor (known as BHP), Newcastle has concentrated on developing another side of its natural resources: those which attract tourists. It's long been a mecca for surfers eager to spy on and share a wave with the likes of world champion Mark Richards, and is gathering broader attention every year. With a solid commercial base, sunny surfing beaches, gorgeous parks for flying kites and riding bikes, nearby wilderness and wetlands reserves, and easy access to the Hunter Valley wineries, Newcastle has what it takes; tourism may have just needed a jump-start.

ORIENTATION

Newcastle's commercial district is on **Hunter St.,** which runs parallel through the city to both the waterfront (Wharf Rd.) and King St. Hunter St. becomes Scott St. at Newcastle Station as the land stretches east in a long, thin strip. At the tip of Nobby's Head is Nobby's Lighthouse, surrounded by **Nobby's Beach,** a terrific surfing spot. Also on the peninsula is **Fort Scratchley,** high on the hill, and the **Harbour Foreshore Park. Queen's Wharf** begins with the **Tourist Centre** at 92 Scott St., across the street from the park and opposite the railway station and long-distance bus depot. The tall **Queen's Wharf Tower,** open for 360° views of the city and harbor, stands in the center of a group of harbor-side cafes and upscale pubs. A passenger **ferry** runs across Newcastle Harbor to Stockton, a mostly residential suburb with a history of fatal shipwrecks, the remains of which can be seen along its shores.

Newcastle's shore is lined with white sand beaches, tidal pools, and green parks. Walking clockwise around the peninsula from Nobby's Beach leads to a large, free ocean bath, a surf pavilion, Bogey Hole, a historic convict-created ocean Bath at the edge of the lovely King Edward Park, a cliff walk which leads to the Susan Gilmore nude beach, and, farther south, the large Bar Beach, popular with surfers.

To the east, Hunter St. becomes the highway to Hexham, where the Pacific and New England Hwy. fork; the former heads north up the coast and the latter branches west to the Hunter Valley wineries and the New England region.

PRACTICAL INFORMATION

Tourist Office: 92 Scott St. (tel. 4929 9299), in the Old Stationmaster's Cottage opposite the railway station. Open Mon.-Fri. 9am-5pm, Sat.-Sun. 10am-3:30pm.

Currency Exchange: The Mall has several **banks** (open Mon.-Thurs. 9:30am-4pm, Fri. 9:30am-5pm), with **ATMs** open 24hr.

Trains: Newcastle Railway Station information line (tel. 13 15 00; open daily 6am-10pm). **CityRail** travels locally throughout Newcastle and to the Hunter Valley region; trains to Maitland ($3.20) and Sydney ($14.20) leave several times daily from the station. Luggage storage available.

Buses run along Hunter St. every 15min. during the day, less frequently at night. Tickets allow unlimited travel for a specified length of time; a 1hr. ticket costs $2. **Rover Motors** (tel. 4990 1699) operates a service between Newcastle and Cessnock. Mon.-Fri. 6 per day, Sat. 3 per day. Coaches start at Newcastle's Watt St. terminal and go to Cessnock's Vincent St. ($8).

Ferries: A passenger ferry (tel. 4929 2106) leaves from in front of the tower every 30min. or less (Mon.-Sat. 5:15am-midnight, Sun. 8:30am-10pm), and crosses Newcastle Harbor to Stockton. The **Cruise Cat ferry** (tel. 4927 8555 or 018 685 544) leaves from Queen's Wharf Thurs.-Sun. and public holidays ($12, children $8).

Taxis: Newcastle Taxi Services (tel. 4962 2622 or 4969 6333) provides local taxi service, airport shuttles, and private sight-seeing tours of Newcastle.

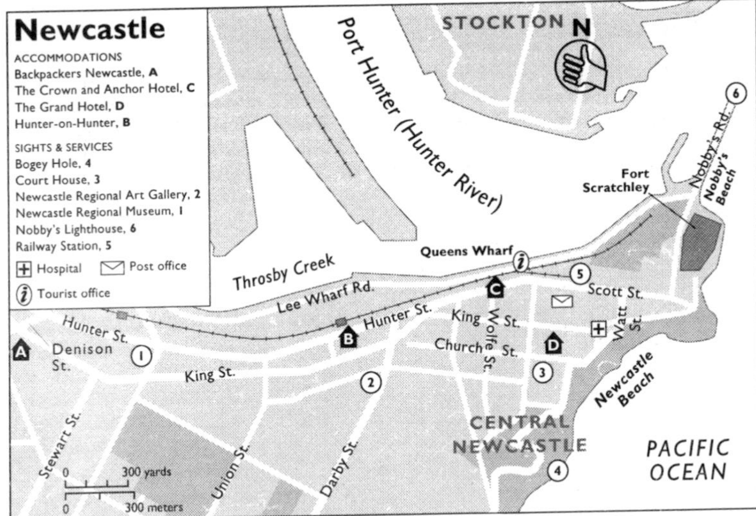

Car Rental: ARA, 86 Lawson St. (tel. 4962 2488), in Hamilton, rents 4-door sedans from $49 and 2-door hatches from $39. **Thrifty** (tel. 4942 2266) is on Parry St.

Bicycles: The Bicycle Center (tel. 4929 6933), at the corner of King and Darby St. 1st day $35; additional days $15. **Trike Hires** (tel. 4958 7582), on the foreshore, rents tricycles built for 3. Open Sat.-Sun., and public holidays 11am-4:30pm. $6 per 30min. If bikes and trikes just won't cut it, **Harley Davidson Motorcycle Rentals** (tel. 4962 2488) start at $120 for 8hr.

Post office: 96 Hunter St., in the Hunter Street Mall. Open Mon.-Fri. 9am-5pm.

ACCOMMODATIONS

Backpackers Newcastle, 42-44 Denison St., Hamilton (tel. 4969 3436), has free pick-up from town. It's a good 25min. walk to the city center, but buses run often along Hunter St. The owner keeps guests informed about events and activities. Communal kitchen, TV area, and laundry facilities. Linen and plates are provided. Dorms $15; doubles $34. The building at 44 Denison St. (same prices) is much more elegant, with its own kitchen and sitting area.

Hunter-on-Hunter, 417 Hunter St. (tel. 4929 3152), is a pub motel converted into a backpackers. Washing machine and kitchen area with a burner, frying pan, toaster, and cooler. Reception usually open daily 8-10pm. Large dorms $10; 6-bed dorms $15; 3-bed dorms $20. Linen $5.

The Grand Hotel (tel. 4929 3489) is an upmarket pub on the corner of Church and Bolton St. Large double or single rooms for $40, with bath $50.

The Crown and Anchor Hotel, 189 Hunter St. (tel. 4929 1027), is the cheapest hotel accommodation in the city. Singles $25; doubles $34.

Stockton Beach Caravan and Tourist Park (tel. 4928 1393), across the harbor, has campsites ($5) and on-site caravans ($13).

FOOD

For the cheapest eats, search out the huge and ultra-cheap **Bi-Co** supermarket (tel. 4926 4494) in Newcastle West at the West End Marketown. **Coles,** 202 Union St. (tel. 4969 3899), is in the city center.

Hunter Street has many hot bread shops, hot food takeaways, and small ethnic restaurants, most with $5-6 lunch specials. Many cafes throughout the city specialize in super-cheap meals in the early part of the week. Hamilton's **Beaumont Street,** a 25-minute walk from the city, is filled with good, cheap Italian restaurants. Two tasty non-Italian choices are **Yianni's Taverna** (tel. 4969 3233), Newcastle's only Greek restaurant, and **Marrakech Express** (tel. 4969 3833), which serves $5 African-style pasta on Mondays and Tuesdays. Perhaps the best deal in Hamilton is the student TAFE restaurant (tel. 4969 9411), on Parry St., with mains for $3.50 and salads for $1 (open Mon.-Fri. noon-1:15pm, plus Thurs. 6-7:15pm); call ahead to confirm hours.

Darby St. welcomes you with **Benvenuti Restaurant,** 88 Darby St. (tel. 4926 4798), and the **Black and White Cafe,** 150 Darby St. (tel. 4925 2151), both with $5 pastas Monday to Wednesday. **Emilio's Pizzeria,** 127 Darby St. (tel. 4929 4710), has $5 pastas and $5 large takeaway pizzas on Tuesdays and Wednesdays from 6 to 7:30pm. **Mucho's Mexican Restaurant,** 52 Glebe Rd. (tel. 4969 2060), in the Junction, serves up $7 dinners on Mondays. **Arrivederci Restaurant,** 53 Glebe Rd. (tel. 4963 1036), lets you select from 10 pastas (Mon.-Tues. $5), and sends folks away full.

Queen's Wharf has many waterfront cafes, but you can't beat the combination of views and prices at **Scratchley's** (tel. 4929 1111), right on the water. Award-winning main courses, including seafood, cost $7-15. The cafe is BYO but a local store will deliver alcohol for those who request it within 10 minutes (open Mon.-Sat. 11:30am-3pm and 5:30-9pm, Sun. 10:30am-9pm; make reservations on weekends).

Alcron, 116 Church St. (tel. 4929 2423), is the oldest licensed restaurant in Australia. Set in a gorgeous old Queenslander high on a cliff overlooking the harbor, it's a bit pricey but worth it if you're partial to chandeliers, antiques, and white linen. Dinner entrees are $13-15 and mains are $18-25, but our researcher was told that a cheaper lunch menu was in the works. Live classic guitar strums through the week, and a pianist takes over the corner spot on Thursdays, Fridays, and Saturdays (open Tues.-Sat. 12:30-2:30pm and 6:30-9:30pm; weekend reservations essential; BYO).

SIGHTS

Even in days long gone, Newcastle suffered from image problems: the city was established in 1804 as a convict settlement, and was originally referred to as "Sydney's Siberia." Many of its gorgeous **heritage buildings** were built by unwilling convicts, and 80% of the structures survived until the disastrous 1989 earthquake. Many have since be reconstructed. A delightful and informative overview of the city and these buildings is offered through **Newcastle's Famous Tram** (tel. 4929 1822). The 45-minute tours leave the Newcastle Railway Station daily on the hour from 10am to 3pm; excellent weekday tours focus more on the architecture of sights, while the weekend tours specialize in history. Toby, the weekday tour guide, is especially enthusiastic. (Tours $8, $10 with unlimited stops, children $5, concessions $7, families of 4 $20.)

Fort Scratchley is a must-see attraction. It has one of the area's best views of the city and harbor, two museums, and an important history. The fort was originally constructed during the 1880s as a strategic defense against the Russians, but it rose to dubious glory as the only fort used against the Japanese during WWII. The skirmish was a comical failure. The Japanese fired 27 shells in an effort to blow up BHP Steelworks and missed every time. The Australians returned six shells and managed only to blow off a roof in nearby Stockton. The fort has been an inactive military site since 1972, but now houses the **Military Museum** (open Sat.-Sun. and public holidays noon-4pm; free). Next door, at the **Maritime Museum** (tel. 4929 2588), you'll get a descriptive pamphlet on the fort's history and the opportunity to explore the underground tunnel system (open Tues.-Sun. noon-4pm; tunnels open Sat.-Sun. only; admission $1.50).

Third Time's the Charm

The windmill on Nobby's Point was built in 1820 as a landmark for the many ships which were turning into nearby Lake Macquarie, thinking it was Newcastle Harbor. The 1989 earthquake ruined the landmark, and it took 47 men four months and ten days to repair it. Ten days later, lightning struck the new structure and catapulted it 3m into the air.

The **Newcastle Regional Museum,** 787 Hunter St., Newcastle West (tel. 4962 2001), is a wonderful three-level collection of hands-on science exhibits and heritage displays, including a reconstruction of a coal mine (open Tues.-Sun. 10am-5pm; free). The **Newcastle Region Art Gallery** (tel. 4929 3263), on Laman St., off Darby St. and behind Civic Park, contains almost exclusively Australian art (open Tues.-Sun. 10am-5pm; free). **Grandpa's Gallery,** 23 Mitchell St. (tel. 4920 1720), in Stockton, features a collection of recycled arts and crafts. Even more off-beat and morbidly fascinating is the small **Newcastle Police Station Museum,** 90 Hunter St. (tel. 4925 2265), located in the original police station. Exhibits include a hand-stitched padded leather cell streaked with fingernail scratches, among other treasures (open Mon.-Fri. 9am-1pm, Sat.-Sun. 11am-4pm; admission $1).

The **Blackbutt Reserve** (tel. 4952 1449) is a lovely 200-acre tree sanctuary with walking trails, small caves, and many animals. There's a koala enclosure and kangaroo and emu reserves (open daily 9am-5pm; free). Bring your own food for a picnic or BBQ; no food is available at the reserves. Bus #216 from the city center goes to the Blackbutt Shops; a 10-minute walk from the reserve. The 20-minute bus ride costs $2.

The **Wetlands Centre** (tel. 4951 6466) offers sanctuary to birds, reptiles, and humans, with walking and cycling paths and a creek and swamp for canoeing. The center rents canoes and sponsors a monthly "Breakfast with the Birds" as well as twilight guided walks each Sunday. Take the CityTrain to Sandgate, in the suburb of Shortland, and then walk 10 minutes to the Wetlands Centre (open daily 9am-5pm; donation $2).

ENTERTAINMENT

The *Newcastle Herald* publishes an entertainment guide with Thursday's paper. Extra copies are available at the information center and in most motels. The **Civic Theatre,** 375 Hunter St. (tel. 4929 1501, for tickets 4929 1977), has excellent productions of shows such as *HMS Pinafore.* The **Lyrique Theatre** (tel. 4929 5019), on Wolfe St. off the Hunter St. Mall, specializes in foreign and art films. More mainstream screenings are offered down the street at the **Greater Union Tower Cinemas,** 183 King St. (tel. 4926 2233). On Tuesdays, movie theaters charge $6. The last weekend in August, the **Newcastle Jazz Festival** (info tel. 4982 1264), brings musical talent from around the country into the city.

The nearby university keeps Newcastle's night scene rocking. Most students stick with the following clubs and travel between them during the night. **The Castle** nightclub is loud, large, and lively, and popular on Wednesday and Thursday evenings; **STs,** on Beaumont St., is another good rock venue, particularly on Thursdays. **Jack,** on King St., has $2 drinks on Friday from 8 to 10pm. The **Northern Star Hotel** and the **Kent Hotel,** both on Beaumont St., are good for jazz. For more upscale and refined fun, try **The Brewery,** on Queen's Wharf, a pub that brews its own.

■ Near Newcastle

Fifteen minutes south of Newcastle is **Lake Macquarie,** Australia's largest coastal saltwater lake (four times the size of Sydney Harbour), and a holiday-tourist development. The coastline is popular with surfers and families alike, with great waves, caverns to explore at Caves Beach, and an old mining village at Catherine Hill Bay. The district has many caravan parks and motels; it's also convenient to stay in Belmont or Charlestown, close suburbs of Newcastle. The **Lake Macquarie information center** (tel. 4972 1172) is at 72 Pacific Hwy. in the Blacksmiths (open Mon.-Fri. 9am-5pm, Sat.-Sun. 9am-4pm).

Tree-covered mountains, home to the **Watagan State Forests,** separate Lake Macquarie from the Hunter River. An hour's drive from Newcastle and the Hunter Valley, they're ideal for day hikes, picnics, or camping. There are six campsites in the forests, most with firewood, BBQ facilities, toilets, and tap water. Call the State Forests of NSW office (tel. 4973 3733) for more information.

Port Stephens

North of Newcastle, Port Stephens is a lovely bay and collection of townships surrounded by clear blue water and the Tomaree National Park. During the summer, surfing beaches and luxury resorts draw backpackers and families alike, clogging central shopping areas with traffic. The port is home to 80 bottlenose dolphins, and whale-watching season runs from the end of May through July and September through October; many ships offer inexpensive cruises. On the coastal edge of the national park, visit abandoned forts left over from WWII training camps for Australian and American soldiers.

GETTING THERE AND ORIENTATION

From Newcastle, Nelson Bay Rd. forks off into Gan Gan Rd., which leads to Anna Bay, the first of four residential townships on the spit of land south of the port. Gan Gan Rd. then continues up to Nelson Bay, the largest of the townships, and finally to Shoal and Fingal Bays. The **tourist office** (tel. 4981 1579), marina, shopping center, and cafes are located on Victoria's Pde. in Nelson Bay. Shoal Bay is surrounded by beaches and the **Tomaree National Park,** and Fingal Bay is quite rural and out of the way.

Port Stephens Buses (tel. 4981 1207) runs from Sydney and Newcastle to the four townships. A trip from Newcastle to Port Stephens costs $8 (Mon.-Fri. 10 per day, Sat. 4 per day, Sun. and holidays 3 per day, 1½hr.). The bus from Sydney to Port Stephens leaves at 2pm and costs $22 (return $36, 2¾hr. each way). The bus runs about once an hour locally, connecting the bay townships. **S&A Countrylink** (tel. 13 22 32) also travels from Newcastle. The **Myall Lady and Ferry** (tel. 018 682 117) makes occasional trips to Tea Garden, one of two towns (along with Hawks Nest) just across the water from Nelson's Bay (frequency depends on season, so call for details).

NEW SOUTH WALES

ACCOMMODATIONS

Port Stephens, like most resort areas, has many lodgings, but beds go quickly and prices shoot up in the summer and during holidays. If you can, book early. All of the following are on the Port Stephens bus route.

Samurai Beach Bungalows (tel. 4982 1921), on Frost Rd., just off Nelson Bay Rd. and right outside Anna Bay. It's a truly wonderful find for the ecotourist, or for anyone eager to escape typical hostel housing. Small cabins with porches are circled around an open green. The sheltered and equipped communal kitchen is next to a campfire; at night many guests while away time telling stories, stargazing, and playing on the owner's drum. The owner is an amateur horticulturist, and clusters of trees and potted plants are scattered about. There's a shed with a TV, a pool table, and free bikes, surfboards, and boogie boards. Many beaches are within walking distance, and a courtesy van drives the 5min. into Nelson Bay. Dorms $15, weekly $90; twins and doubles $40-60. Linen included.

Seabreeze Hotel (tel. 4981 1511), on Stockton St., a block up the hill from the tourist center in the heart of Nelson Bay. It has a large lounge area with a TV. Clean 8-bed and triple rooms $20, $15 with proof of being an international backpacker; doubles with private bath and TV $50, $60 in peak season. Linen included.

Shoal Bay YHA (tel. 4984 2315), in the Shoal Bay Motel, directly across from the beach and a 15min. walk from the Tomaree National Park. The rooms are clean and well-lit and have heat and A/C. There's also a communal kitchen, comfortable TV lounge, and a turkish spa in the courtyard. Dorms with bath $13, YHA non-members $15.

Shoal Bay Holiday Park (tel. 4981 1427), just up the street from the YHA. The park boasts tent and caravan sites and cabins, but prices vary widely depending on season. Powered tent and caravan sites $17 (May-Sept. $15; during Christmas and Easter $21-22; 7th night free). Cabins with bath $38-53. Book ahead in summer.

ACTIVITIES

Dolphin and whale-watching **cruises** usually depart twice daily in the summer and once daily in the winter. The cheapest of the lot is on the large *Tamboi Queen* (tel. 4982 0707), which offers a two-hour cruise for $9. The *M.S. Waywind* (tel. 4982 2777) is a small, beautiful, no-motor sailing vessel with a boom net. It offers a variety of cruises, and prices run about $16 for two hours.

There are several **sports rental** stores in the area. **Nelson Bay Sports,** 77 Victoria Pde. (tel. 4981 2333), opposite the tourist office, rents cycles ($10 for 2hr., $20 per day), snorkeling gear ($10 for 4hr., $15 per day), body boards ($10 for 4hr., $20 per day), roller blades ($12 for 2hr., $25 per day), and fishing gear ($10 per day; open daily 8:30am-5pm). **Shoal Bay Bike Hire,** 63 Shoal Bay Rd. (tel. 4981 4360), near the YHA, also rents out bikes and accessories for similar prices. **Sunseeker Sailboards** (tel. 4981 4360), at Sandy Point, rents catamarans, sailboards, and surfskis.

Sahara Trails (tel. 4981 9077) offers two-hour horse rides on the Blue Lagoon Trail for $30 and spectacular two-hour coastal dune and beach rides for $40 (open Sat.-Sun. and school holidays, Mon.-Fri. by appointment only). **Toboggan Hill Park** (tel. 4984 1022), at Salamander Way on Nelson Bay, is a big theme park with a 700m downhill toboggan run, a 19-hole mini golf course, and indoor rock climbing.

Port Macquarie

Port Macquarie (pop. 30,500) is an easily accessible coastal town, and a popular stopover on a trip up the coast from Sydney. The town usually feels quiet, although it comes alive during the summer, when its river, beaches, water sports, small theme parks, and nearby nature reserves lure hoards of families and surfers. Port Macquarie was founded as a remote lock-up of sorts for Sydney's worst offenders; guard dogs stationed at Port Stephens, near Newcastle, prevented escapees from swimming to freedom. Many of the town's historic buildings, including the St. Thomas Church, were built by convicts. The town was opened to free settlers in 1840.

ORIENTATION AND PRACTICAL INFORMATION

Port Macquarie's town center is bordered on the north by the Hastings River and on the west by a small bridged creek. **Horton St.,** parallel to **Hay St.,** is the main commercial street with banks and retail outlets, and the streets in the surrounding one- to two-block radius comprise the central business district. To the northwest, across the bridge, is **Settlement City,** an upmarket residential district with its own shopping center. The marina from which cruises depart is opposite the tourist office; parks and picnic tables run parallel to this section of the bay.

The **Visitor Information Centre** (tel. 6583 1077, bookings 1800 025 935) hands out brochures at the corner of Clarence and Hay St. (open Mon.-Fri. 8:30am-5pm, Sat.-Sun. and public holidays 9am-4pm). The nearby town of **Wauchope,** pronounced "WAR-hope," is the closest **trains** run to Port Macquarie. **McCafferty's** and **Greyhound buses** both run through Port Macquarie daily. **Port Macquarie Bus Service** (tel. 6583 2161) provides local transportation. The **depot** is at Ritz Corner, across from the tourist office. Local buses run to Wauchope (3-5 per day, $7) and Kempsey (Mon.-Fri. except holidays, 3 per day). **Sonters Travelways** (tel. 6559 8989) travels between Dunbogan, Laurieton, and Port Macquarie (Mon.-Fri. 5 per day, Sat. 2 per day). If you have the means, the easiest way to get there is by car. **Budget** (tel. 6583 5144, reservations 13 27 27), at the corner of Gordon and Hollingsworth St., **Hertz,** 102 Gordon St. (24 hr. tel. 6583 6599), and **Thrifty** (tel. 6584 2122), at the corner of Horton and Hayward St., all compete for customers. The **post office** is at the corner of Horton and Clarence St. (open Mon.-Fri. 9am-5pm; postal code 2444).

ACCOMMODATIONS

Given its billing as a holiday destination, Port Macquarie has a wide range of accommodation options. The hostels all have free pick-up and complimentary tea and coffee. Motels and some caravan parks jack up their prices by as much as 100% during summer months, Christmas, and Easter; book far in advance for these times.

Lindel Port Macquarie (tel. 6583 1791), at the corner of Hastings River Dr. and Gordon St., is 5-10min. from the town center. Inside this lovely Heritage-listed house, the facilities are modern and most rooms are painted a tasteful dark green. A TV room, small bookshelf, and sunny kitchen give Lindel a wonderfully relaxed, social feel. Outdoors, guests enjoy a small pool, BBQ facilities, and a picnic table. Super-friendly owners organize not-to-be-missed 10km morning beach walks. Free use of bikes and boogie boards. Quiet time at 11pm. Dorms $16; twins $38. VIP, YHA. 7th night free. Linen included.

Beachside Backpackers, 40 Church St. (tel. 6583 5512), is the Port Macquarie YHA. It's the closest hostel to the beaches and a 5-10min. walk from the town center. The hostel is clean and quiet, almost stiflingly so, and has a large kitchen area and TV lounge. Most bathrooms are in a separate building directly behind the hostel. The owner takes daily swimming/surfing trips to the beach at 7:30am; you're welcome to join him. Free use of surfboards, bikes, boogie boards, and fishing rods. 11pm lights-out in common area is *strictly* enforced. Dorms $13, YHA non-members $16. Twins currently under construction. Linen provided.

Backpackers on the Water (tel. 6583 3381), Shoreline Dr., is in a house on a lake, nearly 10km from the town center. Free pick-up and drop-off, but it's hard to get into town without your own transportation. Dorms $10.

Sundowner Brenkwill Tourist Park, 1 Munster St. (tel. 6583 2755), is an enormous waterfront caravan park near Town Beach. It has a large pool, BBQ facilities, and even a mini-convenience store. Check-in 2pm. Tent sites $15, during Easter and Christmas $24. Caravans $37, during school holidays $53, and during Easter and Christmas $69. 7th night free. Each additional person $5. Book far in advance in summer. No pets allowed.

Hotel Macquarie (tel. 6583 1011), at the corner of Horton and Clarence St., is the cheapest and most centrally located above-pub accommodation. Rooms are very basic, but all have a wardrobe. Singles $25, with bath $30; doubles $40, with bath $45. Breakfast included. 7th night free. The motel next door has triples for $80; quads $90.

Central Views Motel (tel. 6583 1171), at the corner of Clarence and School St., has a pool and excellent views of the water from the deck. Rooms are clean and well-furnished. Twins $100 during summer holidays, $45 off-peak. Doubles $110, $50.

FOOD

The best bet for fresh seafood takeout is **Macquarie Seafood** (tel. 6583 8476), at the corner of Clarence and Short St. (fish and chips $4.20; open daily 11am-9pm). **Cafe Margo** (tel. 6583 5145), on Clarence St., is a local favorite and has an outside eating area (main courses $6-13.50; open daily for breakfast, lunch, and dinner). If you plan to cook it yourself, visit the **Fisherman's Co-op,** at the marina on the bottom of Clarence St., where cheap seafood comes straight off the boat.

SIGHTS

The National Parks and Wildlife Service (NPWS; tel. 6584 2203) sponsors tours to the otherwise unrecognizable **Lunes ruins,** the badly neglected site of a colonial mansion. Guided tours are given on the first and second Sundays of the month (9am-noon; $10; bookings essential). One of the historical monuments to Port Macquarie's past is the beautiful **St. Thomas Church,** built by convicts between 1824 and 1828. The former superintendent of the jail is buried under one of the pews. As the story goes, he feared that his body would have been exhumed by vengeful convicts had he

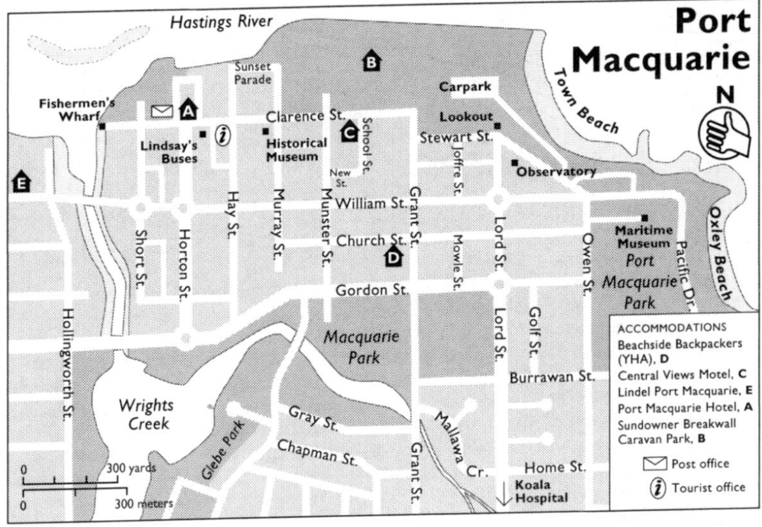

been buried in the church cemetery. (Church open for public inspection Mon.-Fri. 9:30am-noon and 2-4pm. Admission $2, children $1.)

The **Historical Museum,** 22 Clarence St. (tel. 6583 1108), has a huge and well-catalogued collection of photos, clothing, military weapons, and other Port Macquarie paraphernalia. (Open Mon.-Sat. 9:30am-4:30pm. Admission $4, children $1.) On clear starry nights, consider heading to the small **Observatory** (tel. 6583 1933), at the top of Clarence St. in Rotary Park. You'll get a quick lesson on telescopes and astronomy that will teach you to pick out the Southern Cross. (Open in summer Wed. and Sun. 8:15-9:30pm; in winter Wed. and Sun. 7:30-9pm. Admission $2, children $1.)

In neighboring Wauchope is **Timbertown,** a much praised historical recreation of an Australian country town 100 years ago. Costumed men and women act out the daily routines of school teachers, blacksmiths, and bakers. A steam train runs around the village, which becomes increasingly crowded as the day wears on. (Open daily 9:30am-3:30pm. Admission $16, students $12, children $8, families $42.)

You're in luck if you like koalas. One of Australia's few **Koala Hospitals** (tel. 6584 1522) is located a 20-minute walk out of the town center on Lord St. There are usually between five and ten injured or sick koalas on site (more during summer's breeding time), which volunteers nurse back to health. You can visit daily (9am-4:30pm), but it's best to go during feeding times (7:30am, winter afternoons 3pm, summer afternoons 3:30pm). There's a small gift shop with koala paraphernalia. Admission is free, but a $2 donation is requested. The Koala Hospital is behind **Roto House,** an historic homestead open to the public (daily 9am-4pm).

Koalas thrive at the **Billabong Koala Breeding Centre,** 61 Billabong Dr. (tel. 6585 1060), on the way to Kempsey, where you can touch many other species of Aussie wildlife, including wallabies, kangaroos, and wombats (admission $7, children $4).

Over 70 hectares of the last subtropical rainforest on the coast is preserved at **Sea Acres Rainforest Centre** (tel. 6582 3355), a few minutes out of town at Miner's Beach. A 1.3km boardwalk circles through the forest. (Open daily 9am-4:30pm. Admission $8.50, children $4.50.)

Unbelievably tacky but surprisingly entertaining is **The Big Bull** (tel. 6585 2044), a theme park based on dairy farming 15 minutes from Port Macquarie off the Oxley Hwy. The main feature at the park is an eyesore: the **world's largest fiberglass bull.** Be sure to take the hayride, and revel in the farmer's wacky commentary. There's also a farm animal nursery and tours of a working dairy farm (open daily 9am-5pm; admission $5, children $4).

ACTIVITIES

Port Macquarie specializes in beaches (it has 9) and nature walks. During the summer, the beaches nearest to town can be quite crowded, but walks down the sand are pleasant year-round. A lovely walk begins at the **Lighthouse Beach** lookout (Lindel Backpackers will drop you here). Head down Lighthouse Beach Rd. (5-10min.) until you get to the **"Miner's Beach"** sign on the right; an entrance by a subtropical forest path leads to the beach. The 10km beachwalk winds through the sand and up through sometimes hard-to-locate cliff paths. Three kilometers down is **Shelly's Beach,** said by some to be Port Macquarie's best. It has BBQ and toilet facilities, but is, more importantly, also the place to meet Harry, the Port's living legend. He's been living in a small caravan on the beach since 1960, keeps an autograph and souvenir book, and is a delight to talk to. His two major contributions to the area are a "thong tree" and a more respected and spectacular railed footpath up to **Harry's Lookout**—which offers a view so gorgeous that it's been the site of more than 100 weddings.

Nobby's Bend, the next beach to the north, is easily identified by the adjacent Nobby's Headland. The obelisk on the headland stands in memory of people who have died while swimming in the dangerous blowhole in the headland's base. Continuing north, **Flynn's Beach** is most popular with surfers. The southern end of **Town Beach** is good for swimming and sunbathing, and provides showers, toilets, and fast food. The area next to the caravan park attracts a parade of tourists and locals who fish from the colorful and entertaining graffiti-covered rocks. At the end of Horton St. is the entrance to the peaceful **Kooloonburg Creek Nature Park,** where several kilometers of footpaths wind through mangroves and rainforest.

A short trip across the bay leads to **Point Plomer and Limeburner Creek Nature Reserve,** the site of Aboriginal artifacts and the Big Hill walking track. From Settlement Point, a vehicular ferry runs across the river. The 16km coastal road to Point Plomer is unsealed and rough, but bikeable. There are campsites at Barries Bay and Point Plomer; book ahead in summer (tel. 6583 8805). The tourist office has a list of nearby national parks and nature reserves.

For beach adventures, there are a few surf shops in and around town. **Hydro Surf,** 53 Pacific Dr. (tel. 6584 1777), opposite Flynn's Beach, rents surfboards ($15 for 4hr., $25 per day), and wetsuits ($10 for 4hr., $15 per day). They usually have a blue trailer set up at Town Beach. **Gypsy Boat Hire,** 52 Settlement Point Rd. (tel. 6583 2353), rents fishing boats ($16 for 2hr., $30 for 4hr.) and cabin cruisers ($30 for 2hr., $50 for 4hr.). **Settlement Point Boatshed** (tel. 6583 6300), on the river next to Settlement Point Ferry, rents fishing boats ($20 for 2hr., $35 for 4hr.) and canopy runabouts ($25 for 2hr., $40 for 4hr.). They also rent picnic and BBQ boats, which hold 10 to 12 people, and start at $35 ($50 for 2hr.). For canoes, try **Lilybrook Canoe Hire** (tel. 6585 1600), on Oxley Hwy.

Many companies offer boat cruises up the Hastings River and to the Everglades. **M.V. Port Venture** has the largest boat, and Thursday through Tuesday runs two-hour Devonshire tea and dolphin spotting cruises for $15 (children $5.50, families $35). Every Wednesday at 10am is a five-hour BBQ cruise to a private park (cruise $28, children $13, families $65). **Sunshine Jet** (tel. 6585 1168) is a small, very mobile jet boat capable of traveling sideways quickly. Rides are guaranteed to get you wet ($25 for 30min., $35 for 1hr.). **Port Macquarie Camel Safaris** (tel. 6583 7650) offers even more unusual jaunts at Lighthouse Beach ($12 for 20min., $22 for 1hr.).

Nambucca Heads

If your idea of beauty includes an endless horizon of blue water, your idea of recreation includes water activities, and your idea of art includes roadside sculptures of sea monsters made out of tea cups, Nambucca Heads (pop. 6000) is your kind of place. With more days of sunshine per year than any other town in New South Wales, Nambucca ("nam-BUH-kuh") is a place to relax and recuperate. Surfing, fishing, and strolling along strips of isolated beach are all favorite pastimes. Even in the summer, when parents bring their families back to this vacation spot they enjoyed as children, sunny Nambucca retains its slow-paced, unpretentious feel.

ORIENTATION AND PRACTICAL INFORMATION

The tiny **Nambucca Valley Visitor Information Centre** (tel. 6568 6954; open daily 9am-5pm) and nearby **long-distance bus terminal** are on the Pacific Hwy., a good 2km south of the town center. Behind the bus terminal is a shopping center with a supermarket and a movie theater. Riverside Dr. splits right off the Pacific Hwy. just past the information center, and cuts through town, becoming first Fraser, then Bowra, then Mann St. The **post office** is on Mann St., and a **bank** (open Mon.-Fri. 9am-5pm) and chemist are in the town center. The Nambucca Heads **Railway Station** is just out of town: from Mann St., bear right at the roundabout to Railway Rd. To get to Coffs Harbour, take Riverside Dr. to the Pacific Hwy. and turn right.

Newman's Coaches (tel. 6568 1296) has service between Nambucca Heads, Bowraville, Macksville, and Coffs Harbour (Mon.-Fri. 4 per day, less frequently during school holidays). A trip from Nambucca to Coffs costs $6. **Pell's** (tel. 6568 6106) connects Nambucca Heads, Macksville, and Valla Beach (Mon.-Fri. 6 per day, during school holidays 4 per day, no service on public holidays). **Joyce's** (tel. 6655 6330) links Urunga, Bellingen, and Nambucca (Mon.-Fri. 4 per day, during school holidays 3 per day). One day of unlimited travel costs $10, or $8 for backpackers. Both **Greyhound** (13 20 30) and **McCafferty's** (13 14 99) serve Nambucca Heads daily on their Sydney-Brisbane route (to Brisbane $50, students $40; Sydney $58, $47). **Radio Cabs** (tel. 6568 6855) has 24-hour service.

A 16km beach separates Nambucca Heads and **Scotts Head,** an excellent surfing beach and small residential town to the south. **Bowraville,** 25 minutes west, and Macksville, 20 minutes southwest along the Pacific Hwy., are both small residential townships with limited accommodations. **Taylors Arm,** home of the misleadingly-named **Pub With No Beer** (tel. 6564 2101), is a 40-minute drive from Nambucca Heads, and west of Macksville. The tavern stars in the hit country song by Slim Dusty.

ACCOMMODATIONS AND FOOD

Nambucca and the surrounding townships of Bowraville, Scotts Heads, and Valla Beach are chock-full of places to sleep. To be safe, though, book ahead for summer holidays. There are few lodgings in the town center, but a solid mass around the beaches, and a full line of cheap motels along the Pacific Hwy. near the tourist office.

Nomads Golden Sands Backpackers (tel./fax 6568 6000), at the corner of Back and Bowra St. Nomads is located on the basement floor of the Golden Sands Motel, 2min. down the hill from the post office. Clean rooms with baths have coffee and tea, large lockers, color TV, small fridge, and bedside lamps. Guests have use of the upstairs kitchen. There's no common area, but upstairs is a lively pub and good-value, swanky bistro. Free courtesy pick-up. 4-bed dorms $12; doubles and twins $32; triples $42. Weekly: $1 less per night. Linen and towels included.

Nambucca Heads Backpackers, 3 Newman St. (tel. 6568 6360). From Bowra St., bear right at the intersection with Mann St., continue 2 long blocks to Newman St., and turn right. The 2 adjoining houses hold around 30 beds in basic bedrooms. The common area has a TV and some books. The owners are helpful but the rules are strict: check-out is 10am, $3 fee if you stay later. 24hr. courtesy pick-up, meaning they'll pay for your cab fare at night. Dorms $15, off-peak 3-night special $39 (with VIP $36); doubles $32. Linen included.

White Albatross Holiday Resort (tel. 6568 6468; fax 6568 7067), at the far end of Wellington Dr. This glorified caravan park has a gorgeous setting near a swimming lagoon and facing the mouth of the Nambucca River. There are picnic and BBQ areas, a convenience store, and a takeaway cafe. All prices based on 2 people per site. Tent and caravan sites $15; on-site caravans $25; 1-bedroom flat $45. Weekly: $77; $120; $270. Extra adult $5, child $4. Weekly: $25, $20. Easter and Sept.-Oct. school holidays, tent and caravan sites $21, weekly $126; mid-Dec. to late Jan. tent and caravan sites $22, weekly $154. Book well in advance for summer.

Scott's Guesthouse, 4 Wellington Dr. (tel. 6568 6386), at the town end of Wellington Dr. Built in the 1880s, this B&B is one of the area's oldest buildings, and worth a splurge. It is beautifully restored and has all of the thoughtful details one could dream of in a small-town beach resort, including comfy bedrooms with TV, fridge, and private balcony. The breakfast room downstairs has lace-covered tables. Covered parking (no lace). A short walk to 2 good restaurants. Doubles $60, with water view $80; extra person $10, $20.

Bikeotel (tel. 6564 7041), on Bowra St. in Bowraville, caters to cyclists. The owner will show guests good cycling paths. Bed for 1 night $15, 2 nights $20.

Bowra St. has an assortment of quick, cheap food. **Midnight Express,** across from the Golden Sands Motel on Back St., has great burgers ($3.40) and is open late. The **RSL Club** at the bottom of Back St. is newly renovated and has a gorgeous view of the river (meals $6-10). The **V-Wall Tavern** (tel. 6568 6344), at the mouth of the Nambucca River on Wellington Dr., also has unbeatable views. The **Bluewater Brasserie,** the tavern's restaurant, is pricier ($7.50-17.50), but worth it.

SIGHTS AND ACTIVITIES

Nambucca has some delightful and spontaneous artwork. Don't miss the **mosaic wall** in front of the police station on Bowra St. A talented local artist, armed with teacups, broken tile, shiny mirrors, and paint, transformed a once-drab concrete wall into a glittering, 3-dimensional, 60m-long sea **serpent scene.** Many of the town's lampposts are painted with colorful underwater scenes, and hundreds of rocks along the breakwater wall are spray-painted in rainbows of color and inscribed with dates and rhyming ditties from seasons of tourists. Strolling along the boardwalk is like sifting through layers of an archaeological dig. The tradition began with Nambuccan honeymooners; occasionally, you'll spot a rock revisited and reinscribed by couples on their anniversary.

The **Headland Historical Museum** (tel. 6568 6380), beside the Headland parking area at the Main Beach off Liston St., gives a history of the area and a depiction of early Australian life (open Wed. and Sat.-Sun. 2-4pm and by appointment; admission $1, children 50¢). The **Nambucca Heads Island Golf Club** (tel. 6569 4111) is an 18-hole course on Stuart Island, connected to Riverside Dr. by a bridge. The club also has squash courts, BBQ facilities, picnic tables, and a restaurant.

Shelly Beach and **Beilby's Beach** are to the east of town. Ridge St. forks as it leaves town. Liston St., to the left, leads to the Headland and Main Beach. Parkes St., to the right, leads to Shelly Beach. The **Nambucca Boatshed,** 1 Wellington Dr., (tel. 6568 5550), has a good selection of fishing gear and boats for hire. (Boat rentals start at $15 for 1hr., $31 for 3hr. Canoes, kayaks, and fishing rods $7 per hr. Open daily 7am-5pm, 5:30-8pm.) **Beachcomber Marine** (tel. 6568 6432), on Riverside Dr., also rents boats and fishing gear. **Nambucca Dive Centre,** 3 Bowra St. (tel. 6569 4422), in the Mobil Service Station at the intersection with Wellington Dr., rents equipment and conducts diving courses.

Bellingen

Bellingen (pop. 2350) is a calm, scenic town between Coffs Harbour and Nambucca Heads, 30 minutes from Dorrigo National Park. Although its heyday was 50 years ago, when it was the financial and commercial center for the Coffs Harbour region, Bellingen has recently earned a reputation as an artsy community. Craft shops and organic whole food cafes abound, and the annual jazz festival draws many visitors.

Orientation and Practical Information **Hyde St.** forms the city center, and leads in one direction to Urunga (20min. away), Coffs Harbour, and the ocean. Dorrigo and Armidale are in the other direction. The **tourist office** is currently in **Bellingen Travel** (tel. 6655 2055), on Hyde St. **Joyce's Valley Link** (tel. 6655 6330) provides **bus** service through Bellingen, Nambucca Heads, and Urunga (Mon.-Fri. 4 per day, Sat.-Sun. and school holidays 3 per day). A trip from Bellingen to Nambucca costs $5. The nearest train station is in Urunga. If you need a lift to a place the buses don't run, call **Bellingen Valley Taxi** at 018 653 535. The **post office** is across the street from the tourist office (open Mon.-Fri. 9am-5pm; postal code 2454).

Accommodations and Food **Bellingen Backpackers,** 2 Short St. (tel. 6655 1116), is in a gorgeous two-story house a block and a half off Hyde St. The owners' family lives upstairs. The floors are polished wood and the peacefully TV-less downstairs lounge/kitchen has oversized floor pillows, complimentary tea and coffee, and a big wicker basket of magazines. Hand-drawn pictures of possible day activities decorate the walls. Owners provide courtesy pick-up from the Urunga train or bus stations (return $5), and will arrange group trips to Dorrigo National Park ($10 per person). Most weeks, you'll be treated to fresh eggs from the resident hens and seasonal fresh fruit (6-bed dorms $15, weekly $95; doubles or twins $32). Across Bellingen River on Dowle St. is **Bellingen Caravan Park** (tel. 6655 1338), a small area which fronts the entrance to Bellingen Island. (Toilets, showers, and laundry facilities provided. Tent sites $10, with power $14; on-site caravans $25. Holiday surcharge of $2 per site.)

For cheap eats, small organic supermarkets can be found on Hyde St. Off Hyde St., Church St. has a row of cafes, eateries, and coffee shops, some with outdoor seating. **The Carriageway Cafe** (tel. 6655 1672), on Hyde St., is classy and cheap. Sandwiches ($4), cake slices ($4.50), and a range of vegetarian options are served on a sheltered terrace out back. The **Old Butter Factory Cafe** (tel. 6655 2150), opposite the high school playing fields on Hyde St., has outdoor seating and lovely snacks and meals, including scones with jam and cream ($3.30).

Sights, Activities, and Events The **Historic Museum** on Hyde St. has a collection of Bellingen Valley history, including newspaper clippings of the famous Sara quadruplets (open Mon.-Fri. 2-4pm, plus Wed. 10am-noon, Sat. 11am-3pm; admission $1). The **Old Butter Factory** (tel. 6655 1750), on Hyde St., is a complex of shops and craft galleries that feature locally made wind chimes, soaps, pottery, and art. Two blocks up Hyde St., **The Yellow Shed** (tel. 6655 1189) is devoted exclusively to regionally produced crafts and native rainforest plants.

Behind the Bellingen Caravan Park, across the river, is the entrance to **Bellingen Island,** summer home to an active colony of "flying foxes," or fruit bats. A walking trail loops through the subtropical rainforest around the peninsular "island." **Bellingen Canoe Hire** (tel. 6655 8510) rents canoes ($30 per half-day, $45 per day).

The **Promised Land** and the **Never Never River,** lovely spots with BBQ facilities and excellent swimming holes, are easier to reach than their names might imply. Both are an easy 10-15km bike ride from town. Cross the Bellingen Bridge and take a left at the first rotary. Continue straight until you see a sign for Glennifer; bear right at this sign and continue for 6km. The river is behind the church. Cross the bridge and take the first right turn to the Promised Land. Platypuses live in the river; it's possible to see them in the early morning or late afternoon.

On the Wallaby (tel. 6655 2171) provides 4WD tours through the valley and Dorrigo Plateau ($25 per half-day). Half-day tours of local sites with an Aboriginal guide are offered through **Gambaarri Tours** (tel. 6655 4195; tours Sat.-Sun. and school holidays; $45, children $25). In mid-August, Bellingen sponsors its **Jazz Festival,** with both ticketed performances and street performers. For more information, call 6655 9345, or email belljazz@midcoast.com.au.

■ Near Bellingen: Dorrigo National Park

Dorrigo (DOOR-uh-go) National Park is a World Heritage-listed rainforest area 30 minutes north of Bellingen and 60km west of Coffs Harbour, accessible off the Dorrigo-Bellingen Rd., 2km east of Dorrigo. It's one of the most popular and beautiful parks in the area. The **Dorrigo Rainforest Centre** has an historical exhibit on environmental politics, and a 15-minute video (open daily 9am-5pm). Behind the Centre, a rainforest skywalk allows visitors to walk over the forest canopy. There are a few easy, well-trod trails through the forest. The longest is the **Woupa Walk,** a 5.8km loop which leads past Tristania Falls and the spectacular Crystal Shower Falls. Other walks include the 200m **Walk With the Birds** boardwalk, which provides a good opportunity to see some of the park's 120 bird species. For more information, call the Dorrigo NPWS at 6657 2309.

Coffs Harbour

A water sports haven in a sub-tropical climate, Coffs Harbour basks in its own natural beauty. It's a regularly functioning town of 58,000, which just happens to be situated along a gorgeous coastline, backed by hills covered in lush banana plantations, and located a boat ride away from a nationally recognized marine reserve. Coffs Harbour was discovered by and named after Captain Korff, a cedar-towing seaman who used the harbor as a safe resting point on his way to Bellingen. A misspelling in the official gazette gave the town its name, and the construction of a jetty turned the natural harbor into a busy shipping port for timber and produce. A good portion of the town's tourism industry today aims to please adrenaline-seekers with cash to spare.

ORIENTATION AND PRACTICAL INFORMATION

The **Pacific Highway** is Coffs Harbour's main street and roughly divides the town in two; the majority of the commercial buildings and lodgings lie along the highway or to the east. The highway is called Grafton St. as it passes through the center of town, and then becomes **Woolgoolga Rd.** north of the showgrounds. **High St.** is the main east-west thoroughfare. Interrupted by the pedestrian **City Centre Mall,** it continues east past the Botanic Gardens and all the way to the **jetty.** The jetty itself is a narrow strip of land with fish stores, markets, and a marina. **Muttonbird Island Nature Reserve** is accessible by walking down the marina boardwalk.

Tourist Office: Visitor Information Centre (tel. 6652 1522; bookings tel. 1800 025 650), to the right just off Woolgoolga Rd., at the corner of Rose Ave. and Marcia St. Open daily 9am-5pm.

Currency Exchange: ANZ bank is on the corner of Moonee and High St.; other banks are in the City Mall and on Grafton St.

Airport: South of the city off Hogbin Dr. Serviced by **Ansett Express** (tel. 6652 6666) and **Eastern Airlines** (tel. 6651 1966).

Trains: The **railway station** is at the end of Angus McLeod St. by the jetty. From High St., turn right on Camperdown St. and take your first left.

Buses: Both **McCafferty's** and **Greyhound** stop at least 3 times per day in Coffs. The long distance bus stop is at 34 Moonee St., near the corner of High and Grafton St; hostel owners meet nearly all arrivals and tout their establishments forcefully. **Pioneer Motor Service** (tel. 1300 368 100) travels through Coffs on its Sydney-Brisbane run (3 per day; to Sydney $46, Byron Bay $35). **Jessup's** (tel. 6653 4552) operates between Coffs, Urunga, and Bellingen (3 per day Mon.-Fri., $4.50). **Countrylink** (tel. 6651 2757) passes through Coffs several times daily.

Car Rental: Coffs Harbour Rent-A-Car (tel. 6652 5022), at the Shell Roadhouse, corner of Pacific Hwy. and Marcia St., is open daily and rents cars from $43. Free pick-up within 15km. **Budget** (tel. 13 27 27) has free delivery and rents from $44; **Hertz,** 45 Grafton St. (tel. 6651 1899), rents from $48 for a minimum of 3 days, free delivery within 10km; **Thrifty,** at the corner of the Pacific Hwy. and Marcia St. (tel. 6652 8622), rents from $49 for a minimum of 4 days; **A Little Car and Truck Hire,** 32 Alison St. (tel. 6651 3004), rents cars and 4WD vehicles from $29.

Police can be reached at 6652 0299. In an **emergency,** dial 000.

Internet Access: Happy Planet, 84 City Centre Mall, 2nd Fl. (tel. 6651 7520; email hpcafe@nor.com.au), has internet access for $2 per 10min. and $10 per hr., along with Italian coffee and cake. Open Mon.-Fri. 9am-5pm and Sat. 9am-2pm. **Wallis's**

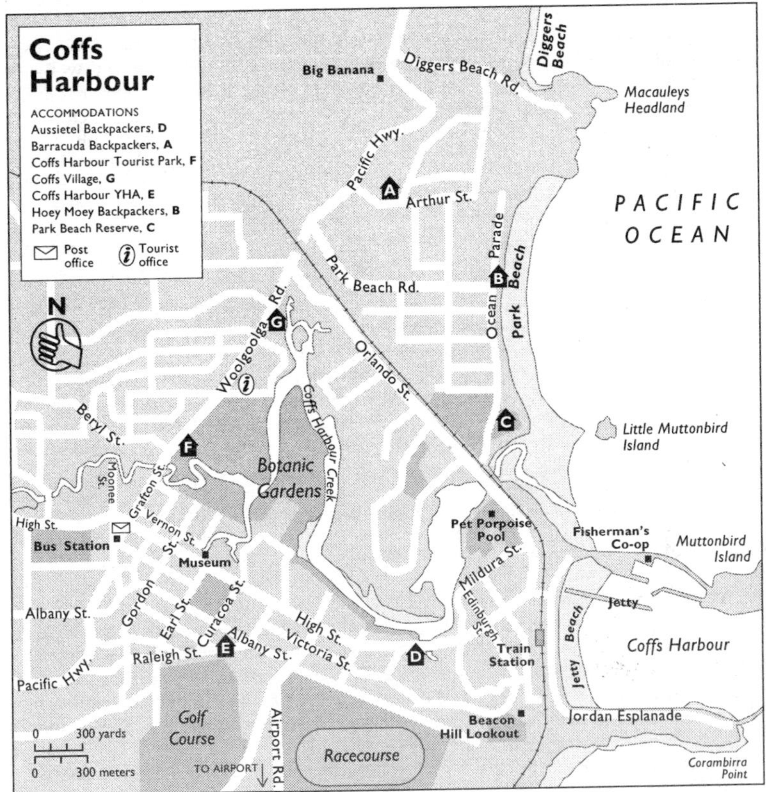

Web, 321 High St.(tel. 6651 7707; email webby@cofs.net.au), on Coff's Promenade near the Jetty, has the same rates. Open Mon.-Fri. 9am-5pm, Sat. 10am-4pm.

Post Office: (tel. 6652 2022) in the Palm Centre. From the tourist office, go south along the hwy. and the center will be on your left at the second set of traffic lights. Open Mon.-Fri. 8:30am-5pm. **Postal code:** 2450.

Phone Code: 02.

ACCOMMODATIONS AND FOOD

All four hostels in Coffs Harbour are quite good and offer 24-hour courtesy pick-up, winter discounts, and good laundry and kitchen facilities. Dozens of motels are clustered along the highway just outside of town, along Grafton St. and Woolgoolga Rd., and along Park Beach Rd. Coffs has three central caravan parks.

Barracuda Backpackers, 19 Arthur St. (tel. 6651 3514), near the corner of Arthur St. and the Pacific Hwy. and opposite the Park Beach Plaza parking lot. Barracuda is the newest of Coff's hostels, and it's the "child" of a young, excited couple. The hostel is small and immaculate, and the common room has comfy leather couches. Each 4-bunk bedroom is neat and well-cared for, with colorful linen, lockers, and a fridge. Guests have use of a BBQ, pool, and jacuzzi in the front yard. Kitchen facilities, laundry room, free weights, bikes, boogie boards, and surfboards. 5-10min. walk to the beach. Dorms $13, weekly $78; doubles $28.

Aussitel Backpackers, 312 High St. (tel. 6651 1871), 25min. walk down High St. from the town center, 10min. to the jetty's marinas, and across the street from the Coffs Promenade. Social, clean, and wholesome; it's family-run and determined to be known as a "small and friendly hostel." People constantly mill about the kitchen/eating/common area, or hop on the bus for one of the hostel-sponsored activities. Outdoor heated pool, creek across the street, surfboards, boogie boards, bikes, and canoes available for guest use. Discounts on activities like diving, surfing, and whitewater rafting. 6-bed dorms $15; doubles $32. Weekly: $84; $192. Off-season special: 3 nights for $33, weekly $65. VIP, YHA, ISIC discounts.

Coffs Harbour YHA, 110 Albany St. (tel. 6652 6462), 15min. walk from the town center down High St., then right on Curacoa St. to Albany St. The YHA is the closest hostel to town. The staff is friendly and can offer more tips on great deals in Coffs than you'll have time for. Perhaps because of the age spread of guests, the YHA is quite mellow—most nights find people sitting on couches watching videos. Everything is clean but has a 1970s feel. Outdoor pool and BBQ. 6-bed dorms $14, weekly $84; twins and doubles $32. Winter special: 3 nights for $35.

Hoey Moey Backpackers, Ocean Pde. (tel. 6651 7966 or 1800 683 322), 3km from the city center at the end of Park Beach Rd. The Hoey Moey is 50m from the beach and is connected to an animated pub with weekly live entertainment and a beer garden. The "Booze Cruizer" courtesy bus runs twice daily to town. Rooms are functional with bath and fridge, but could use refurbishing to save them from motel-style 70s-dom. Small kitchen, picnic tables, BBQ, and a bedroom converted to a common room. Free bikes, surfboards, and boogie boards. 4-bed dorms $14; doubles $32. Weekly: $84, $192.

Camping: Coffs Harbour Tourist Park (tel. 6652 1694) and **Coffs Village** are on Woolgoolga Rd. near the tourist office; **Park Beach Reserve** (tel. 6652 3204), near the Surf Club on Ocean Pde., a 5min. walk to the beach. Tent sites $11, $3 per additional person; caravan sites $13.50; on-site caravans $26. Off-season: 7th night free.

The **Fisherman's Co-op** (tel. 6625 2811) at the end of the jetty is popular year-round for its fresh, delicious seafood—so popular that it can take 30 minutes to get fish and chips in the summer. The fresh fish and sushi counters are open daily 8:30am to 5pm; the cooked counter is open daily 10am to 7pm. For another jetty seafood option, try **Cafe Reggae** (tel. 6652 5725), at the Yacht Club on Marina Dr. The restaurant has a pub and outdoor deck with a somewhat obscured view of the bay. Lunch specials (noon-3pm) are $5.50; dinner specials (from 6pm) are $8.

SIGHTS

The Coffs Harbour **jetty** was built in 1890 and was the center of a busy marine industry in the first years of this century. Nowadays, pleasure boats and charter boats predominate, and the jetty has taken on more historic significance. At the end of the marina is **Muttonbird Island,** a high-elevation nature reserve, which is home to several species of birds and is a terrific lookout for spotting whales. The jetty foreshore has BBQ facilities and is an easy walk from **Jetty Beach,** popular with families.

The **Botanic Gardens** (info centre tel. 6648 4188; open Mon.-Fri. 10am-2pm, Sat.-Sun. 9am-5pm) are about 1km east down High St. from the City Centre Mall; the parking area is at the end of Hardacre St. The lovely 20-hectare gardens make for great self-guided walks through mangroves, plants used by the Aborigines and early settlers, and an herb garden. The two-hour Creek walk leads from the city center to the harbor. It officially begins in Rotary Park at Coff St. From there, it's 5.4km out past the marina to Muttonbird Island. (Open daily 9am-5pm. Admission by donation.)

On Orlando St. by the bank of Coffs Creek, water animals star at the **Pet Porpoise Pool** (tel. 6652 2164), also known as the Oceanarium. Dolphins and seals perform tricks daily at 10:30am and 2:15pm. You can also pet dolphins, talk to cockatoos, watch kangaroos and their joeys, and see peacocks strut their stuff. (Open daily 9am-4:30pm. Admission $10, backpackers $9, students $8, children $5, families $32.)

The **Coffs Harbour Historical Museum,** 191 High St. (tel. 6652 5794), documents the history of the area with a model banana plantation and other displays (open Tues.-Thurs. and Sun. 1:30-4pm). Others may prefer the **Bunker Cartoon Gallery** (tel. 6651 7343), at the corner of Hogbin Dr. and Albany St., near the airport. It's Australia's first and only collection of contemporary and original cartoons. (Open daily 10am-4pm; school holidays 9am-5pm. Admission $2, concessions $1.)

Eighty species of mammals live at the **Coffs Zoo** (tel. 6656 1330), just past Moonee Beach, 12km north of Coffs. The zoo has a talk on rainforest birds at 10am, koala shows at 11am and 3pm, and a reptile presentation at 1:15pm. (Open daily 8:30am-5pm. Admission $12, students $9, children $6, families $30.) The **Big Banana** (tel. 6652 4355), on the Pacific Hwy., is quintessential kitsch. Zoom around the plantation on a space shuttle-like monorail and learn more than you need to know about banana cultivation methods. (Open daily 9am-4pm. Free admission, monorail tour $9.50, children $5.50.)

In Bonville, 14km from Coffs, the **Kiwi Down Under Farm** (tel. 6653 4449), a commercial organic fruit farm, conducts tours and allows visitors to feed the animals (feedings Sat.-Sun. and holidays 2, 3, and 4pm). The farm also runs a retail store which sells organic produce (open Wed.-Sun. and public holidays noon-5pm). The why-would-you-want-to-go-there prize is awarded to the **Big Fat Worm Farm** (tel. 6669 5297), 45km south of Coffs Harbour on Valla Rd. You can pick, pack, and race the worms, or just passively watch them at work in their factories. (Open daily 10am-4pm; guided tours on the hr. Admission $5, families $12.)

ACTIVITIES

There's no shortage of things to do in Coffs. Hostels can offer good rates on diving courses and skydiving lessons, but don't hesitate to call companies directly and ask about commission-free fun.

Diving

Now that Coffs Harbour's **Solitary Islands** have been declared a national marine park, they are becoming increasingly respected as a top diving spot; some even prefer Coffs' reef, with both tropical and cold-water fish, to the Great Barrier Reef. It's possible to swim with harmless gray nurse sharks year-round. Coffs has three diving centers, all of which rent equipment and conduct lessons and trips to the Solitary Islands Marine Park.

Divers Depot (tel. 6652 2033) offers discounts for backpackers staying at Coffs Harbour hostels. A double dive (day or night), with gear supplied, costs $75; a PADI course is $250. During the winter, PADI certification using offshore dives start at $150. The minimum class size is four.

The Jetty, 398 High St. (tel. 6651 1611), has weekend dive packages, with four dives and two nights accommodation for $160. The PADI course is $245; double dives with gear start at $90, snorkel double dive charters at $45.

Pacific Blue Dive Center, 321 High St. (tel. 6652 2759), in the Coffs promenade, is the newest dive shop and has two sister schools in Japan. Their dive equipment is new, though limited. They offer pick-up and will copy a tape of your dive. Double dives with gear are $65, and PADI courses are $250.

Water Sports and Adrenaline Activities

The region's rivers offer some of the best whitewater rafting in New South Wales. Most tour companies pick-up from both Coffs and Byron, but the drive from Byron can be three times as long. The **Nymbodia River,** about an hour west of Coffs, is the most popular. The rapids are mainly grade 3 to 4 (on a scale where grade 6 is "waterfall"), with sections of grade 5, and pass through dense rainforest. The **Gwydir River** flows only November through February; the release of cotton irrigation water from the Coperton Dam creates a nearly constant grade 4 to 5 river which runs through granite country. The **Goolang River** is actually a man-made concrete kayaking course at a steady grade 3. Full-day trips offer superior value to half-day specials.

A few tour companies offer trips with courtesy shuttles from Coffs and big lunches included. **Rapid Rafting** (tel. 6652 1741) has full day ($110), half day ($70), and one-hour ($40, transportation not provided) trips on the Nymbodia or Goolang River. They have backpacker discounts on Tuesdays and Thursdays.

Whitewater Rafting Professionals (tel. 6654 4066) does a one-day kayaking trip to the Goolang River for $115, and a 12-hour trip with tea, lunch, a BBQ dinner, and a break for rope swinging for $135; a two-day trip is $285. Backpackers get $5 discounts. **Wildwater Adventures** (tel. 6653 4469) conducts daytrips for $125 and two-day trips for $265 (Sat.-Sun. $280). The two-day Gwydir River trip includes accommodation and leaves from Inverell. **Endless Summer Adventures** (tel. 6658 0590) runs three-hour sea kayaking trips from Charlesworth Bay to Park Beach. The $29 cost includes breakfast.

The best **surfing beaches** are at Digger's Beach, north of Macauleys Headland and accessible off the Pacific Hwy. by Diggers Beach Rd., opposite the Big Banana. **Coopers Surf Centres,** 380 High St. (tel. 6652 1782), at the Coffs Harbour jetty, rents surfboards by the day. (Malibus $25, surfboards $15, bodyboards $10. Open Mon.-Wed. and Fri. 9am-5:30pm, Thurs. 9am-8pm, Sat. 9am-2:30pm, Sun. 9am-2pm.) **East Coast Surf School** (tel. 6651 5515) has two-hour lessons ($25) and private one-hour lessons ($35). Although there's no guarantee you'll be standing by the end, the instructors do a great job teaching the basics. They also have classes for more advanced surfers.

Absolute Adrenaline, 396B High St., at Coffs Harbour jetty, is a private bookings center that has good displays, including videos, of selected "action activites." **Soaring Adventures** (tel. 6653 6331) conducts 20-minute glider flights from 3000ft. (900m) over Coffs and the region for $75; 10-15 minute flights are $65. **Coffs City Skydivers** (tel. 6651 1167) offers tandem skydiving from 10,000 ft. (3000m). A 40-second free fall followed by about five minutes of parachuting costs $270. Backpackers get a special deal on Tuesdays and Thursdays: $250 for a jump, including a video which records your six-minute defiance of nature.

Bikes, Horses, and Rocks

Mud, Sweat and Gears (tel. 6653 4577), in Valery, 13km from Coffs, has mountain bike tours of the Bellingen Valley ($25 for 2hr., half-day $45). **Bob Wallis Bicycle Centre** (tel. 6652 5102), at the corner of Collingwood and Orlando St. at Coffs Harbour jetty, rents mountain bikes, locks, and helmets ($15 per day, $50 deposit; open Mon.-Fri. 8:30am-5pm, Sat. 8:30am-1pm). **Valery Trails** (tel. 6653 4301), in Valery, offers two-hour horseback rides with tea (Sat.-Thurs. 10am and 2pm, school holidays daily; $30), but no transport to Valery. A good rainy day activity is **Coffs Rock** indoor rock climbing (tel. 6651 6688), at GDT Seccombe, off Orland St. (Open Tues. 4-8pm, Wed.-Fri. noon-8pm, Sat.-Sun. 10am-6pm, holidays 10am-8pm. $8 per hr., $10 for 4hr., $16 per day.)

Tours

The double-decker **Coffs Explorer bus** (tel. 6653 7115) has full-day trips to area sights during the week, lunch and tea included, for $30. Trips are also offered to the Bellingen Market and Dorrigo National Park, but the bus doesn't run during school vacation weeks. **Coffs Harbour Mountain Trails 4WD Tours** (tel. 6658 3333) has full day tours through rainforests and past waterfalls for $72 (occasionally $58 off-peak).

Phil and Margaret's Motorcycle Tours (tel. 6653 7725) is run by a couple who practically grew up on Harleys. A 30-minute city circuit tour costs $30, or try a one-hour coastal and country circuit tour for $50. **Coffs Classic Cruisers** (tel. 015 256 016) also has Harley tours with free pick-up and photos. Prices start at $30.

Whales swim by Coffs from June to July and again (in the other direction) from September to November. Many chartered boats convert to whale-watching cruisers during these times. **Warrendi** (tel. 6652 4433), a 50-ft. vessel, leaves from Coffs Harbour Marina ($40). The **Laura E** (tel. 6651 1434) has two-hour cruises for $25. The most adventurous can try "parawhaling," or parasailing 100m above the ocean off of a chartered boat. The parasailing cruise is $58; book through the Marina Booking office.

ENTERTAINMENT

Coffs' nightclubs are mainly along Grafton St. and the Pacific Hwy., and hostels usually organize trips to the clubs on weekends. The *Coffs Harbour Advocate* publishes an entertainment guide each Thursday. You'll find some of the cheapest drinks at the

Ex-Services Club, although you'll need a passport to get in. The Hoey Moey Backpackers has live entertainment a few nights a week, usually hard rock.

The **RSL Club,** on the corner of Vernon St. and Pacific Hwy., has cheap meals and cheaper drinks; be sure to bring a photo ID. Across the street is the **Plantation Hotel,** with live rock music on Thursdays, Fridays, and Saturdays (no cover before 11pm). The **Coffs Harbour Hotel** and the **Fitzroy Hotel** also have live music on weekends; the Fitzroy has a 24-hour license, and often waits to close until the last person leaves.

Ballina

Ballina is a peaceful port, quiet beach town and thriving retirement community three hours north of Coffs Harbour, known to backpackers primarily as a transportation hub for trips north to Lennox Head or west to Lismore. Pre-planned activities are few and far-between, but this may come as a welcome respite from the usual tourist traps. If you're interested in a guided tour and are willing to pay, **Forgotten Country** (tel. 6687 7845) can take you to nearby rainforests and waterfalls, gold panning, or fishing (each tour departs daily at 7:30am and returns at 6:30pm; $95). To explore a bit on your own, **Jack Rauson Cycles,** 16 Cherry St. (tel. 6686 3485), rents bikes by the day, half-day, or week.

The main drag is the Pacific Hwy., known as **River St.** in the town center. The well-organized **Information Centre** (tel. 6686 3484; open daily 9am-5pm) is located at the corner of River St. and Las Balsa Plaza, toward the far end of the town if you arrive at the Transit Centre. The center's maps show good **dolphin viewing** spots and cycling and walking tracks.

McCafferty's and **Greyhound** stop in Ballina on their Sydney-Brisbane runs. **Kirkland's** (tel. 6686 7124) also runs between Sydney and Brisbane twice daily. **Blanch's Coaches** (tel. 6686 2144) leaves Ballina's River St. stop, outside of Jetset Travel, for Lennox Head ($3.60) and Byron Bay ($6.20; Mon.-Fri. 6 per day, Sat. 5 per day, Sun. and holidays 3 per day to both destinations). The **Transit Centre** is a good 5km from the center, located in a large building complex known affectionately as **"The Big Prawn"** for the enormous pink shrimp nailed to the roof. The only way to get to town from here is by taxi; the **Ballina Taxi Service** (tel. 6686 9999) will get you there for $8. For a bit more mobility, **North Coast Rent-A-Car** (tel. 6681 1707) rents from $35 per day; as does **Earth Car Rentals** (tel. 6685 7472).

Ballina Travelers Lodge, 36-38 Tamar St. (tel. 6686 6737), two blocks from the tourist office, is a motel and YHA hostel. The owners are friendly and intent on keeping their lodge quiet and meticulously clean. The YHA half has a large communal kitchen and lots of showers. Larger motel rooms come with baths and TVs. There's a small pool, free bikes and surfboards, and courtesy pick-up from the Transit Centre. (4-bed dorms $14, YHA non-members $16; doubles $32, $36. Linen included. Motel singles $45; doubles $46, up to $85 at Christmas.)

The government-owned **Shaws Bay Caravan Park** (tel. 6686 2326) is on the Richmond River 1km east of the post office, near Missingham Bridge. (Sites $11, with power $13; peak-season sites $14, with power $16. Weekly: $66, $78; $85, $100.)

If you're in Ballina on a clear day, try **Shelly's on the Beach** (tel. 6686 9844), next to the Surf Club between Shelly and Lighthouse Beach, for breakfast ($4-9) or lunch ($4-15) in front of a spectacular view (open daily from 7:30am).

Near Ballina: Lennox Head

Lennox Head (pop. 2300) lies between Ballina and Byron Bay. It's renowned for its excellent surf, and is home to **Grumfest,** a national surfing competition for under-16s, in early July. Lennox is also good for beachside dolphin spotting, especially along **Seven Mile Beach.** The main road skirts Lennox Head, and the easiest way to get to the center is to go north onto Ballina St. at the roundabout. After passing one block of establishments (which qualifies as the town center, for lack of competition), the road curves and becomes Pacific Pde., which runs along Seven Mile Beach. **Lake**

Ainsworth is at the north end of Pacific Pde., about 2km from the town center. Two kilometers in the opposite direction along the beach is **Lennox Point,** an excellent but crowded surf area. The **Surf Club** (tel. 6667 7380) is on Pacific Pde. **Lennox Cycle Hire** (tel. 6687 7210) rents bikes ($12 per half-day, $18 per day).

Although McCafferty's and Greyhound once stopped in Lennox Head regularly, both are phasing out their service. You may still be able to use it on a request-only basis. **Blanch's Coaches** still runs through Lennox Head. The northbound stop (to head toward Byron) is on Ballina St. outside the medical center, and the southbound stop (to head toward Ballina) is near the town center, opposite the Service Center.

The **Lennox Head Beach House** (tel. 6687 7636) is at 3 Ross St., 100m from Seven Mile Beach and a short walk from Lake Ainsworth. The hostel's owners are zealous in their efforts to make guests happy. There's free use of surfboards, boogie-boards, bicycles, and fishing rods, while unlimited use of windsurfers and catamarans will set you back just $5. The owner even gives catamaran-sailing or windsurfing lessons. Aspiring gourmets can help themselves to the herb garden, prepare a meal in the communal kitchen, and dine in the open courtyard. One night a week, enjoy a free massage from their "natural healing center." Bedrooms are small but tidy (dorms $15; doubles $35). **Lake Ainsworth Caravan Park** (tel. 6687 7249) has tent sites ($11) and cabins ($33) next to the lake.

Lismore

Lismore (pop. 45,500) is a large yet restrained industrial town. Emphasis on environmental protection follows naturally from its surroundings: three world heritage rainforests, volcanic remains, and a disproportionately high number of rainbows (due to the position of valleys). The students at nearby Southern Cross University inject palpable activist energy, and a thumping social conscience and help to sustain Lismore's cultural venues.

ORIENTATION AND PRACTICAL INFORMATION

In the hinterlands west of Ballina, Lismore lies off the Bruxner Hwy., called **Ballina St.** in town, just east of the **Wilson** (or **Richmond**) **River.** Approaching the river from the east, Ballina St. crosses **Dawson, Keen,** and **Molesworth St.** At the corner of Molesworth and Ballina St., the **tourist office** (tel. 6622 0122; fax 6622 0193; email tourism@nor.com.au; http://www.liscity.nsw.gov.au) is a sight to see. The center has a small indoor tropical rainforest with some real vegetation (admission $1), lots of pretty rock crystals, a mini-museum with a pictorial history of the area, and a handy topographical map of the national parks (open daily 9am-4:30pm). Past the tourist office, Ballina St. crosses the river. Further north, several blocks down Molesworth St., **Woodlark St.** also crosses the river. **Magellan St.** runs parallel to Woodlark but ends at the east bank.

Greyhound Pioneer buses stop at the **Ampol Roadhouse,** 136 Woodlark St. (open 24hr.). Greyhound includes Lismore on its coastal Brisbane-Sydney service (1 per day to Brisbane $29, students $24; Sydney $67, $54). The **Kirklands** buses terminal (tel. 6622 1499) is at the end of Magellan St., just past Molesworth St. Kirklands runs to Byron Bay ($10.50), Brisbane (several times per day, $27.50), Surfers Paradise ($25), Tweed Heads ($17.40), Lennox Head ($10), and Ballina ($8.70); backpackers and YHA members pay 30% less. Kirklands also stops in some of Lismore's nearby villages, although the best way to get around might be to rent a car. **Hertz,** 4-9 Dawson St. (tel. 6621 8855), is open daily. **Countrylink** has several services daily through Lismore. The railway station is on Union St., right across the river.

ACCOMMODATIONS

More like a home than a hostel, **Currendina Lodge,** 14 Ewing St. (tel. 6621 6118), offers clean rooms, accessible by an outside set of stairs, all with bureaus and small tables. From the information center, take a left on Ballina, cross Molesworth and

Keen St., and turn left on Dawson St. Ewing is halfway down Dawson St. The well-equipped kitchen has complimentary tea and coffee and opens to a sunny eating area, and guests enjoy a comfy TV lounge and laundry facilities. The backyard has a compost pile and a worm bin. (4-bed dorms $15; singles $17-25; doubles $40-50. Weekly: $90; $105-140; $180-240. Additional person $10. VIP, YHA, ISIC discounts.)

Gollan Hotel (tel. 6621 2295), on the corner of Keen and Magellan St., is an above-the-pub option. From the information center, go up Molesworth St. and take a right on Magellan St.; Keen is 2 blocks ahead. Rooms down the hall from **Tribes** restaurant are surprisingly nice and freshly painted. (Singles $20; doubles $25; either with a big bathroom $35. Weekly: $90; $90; $120.)

FOOD

Lismore's students' demand for vegetarian cheap eats has turned out some terrifically funky, yummy cafes. Shop for yourself at the cheapest grocery in town, **Woolworths** on Keen St. (back entrance on Carrington St.; open Mon.-Sat. 7am-10pm, Sun. 10am-4pm). **Fundamental Foods,** 140 Keen St. (tel. 6622 2199), is a moderately priced supermarket specializing in organic food, vegetables, and vitamins (open Mon.-Fri. 9am-5:30pm, Thurs. 9am-7pm, Sat. 8:30am-noon).

Dr. Juice Bar (tel. 6622 4440), on Keen St., is a student haunt. This vegetarian eatery has a few long wooden booths and a wall plastered with community notices. The Doctor prescribes marvelous smoothies ($3), vegetarian burgers ($4), and a wildly popular apricot tofu cheesecake ($2.80). Open Mon.-Fri. 9am-6pm, Sat. 9am-1pm.

Caddies Coffee, 20 Carrington St. (tel. 6621 7709), tees off with an indoor split-level deck, an outdoor patio, and beautiful stained glass. Fresh sandwiches, bagels, and foccacia ($3.50-9.50). Open Mon.-Fri. 8am-6pm, Sat. 8am-2pm.

Northern Rivers Hotel (tel. 6621 5797), at the corner of Bridges and Terina St. Follow Woodlark St. to the bridge, cross it, and turn left on Bridges St. The best deal in town is a choice of about 10 dishes, including lasagna, steak, and roast chicken with vegetables or salad for lunch ($2) or dinner ($3). You can also cook your own T-bone for $7, and there's a leafy courtyard to eat in.

20,000 Cows, 58 Bridge St. (tel. 6622 2517), is across from the hotel. This ironically named 100% vegetarian restaurant has mismatched, wildly patterned tablecloths pinned down with tall candlesticks and a delightful assortment of chairs that look like they're straight off the Salvation Army clearance floor. Unbelievably fresh pasta and Middle Eastern food ($6-11). Open Tues.-Sun. from 6pm.

Red Cross Tea Room, 132 Keen St. (tel. 6622 5476). Elderly volunteers operate this trusty eatery, smoothing out the lace tablecloths and fussing over guests with pots of tea and cake ($1.50). Sandwiches $2. Open Mon.-Fri. 9am-2pm.

The Left Bank, 133 Molesworth St., next to the Art Gallery, has all vegetarian and vegan dishes ($8.50-10). It's more upmarket, but classically casual tables spill out onto the sidewalk for great people-watching.

SIGHTS, NATURE, AND FESTIVALS

Almost two blocks up Molesworth St. from Ballina St. is the **Lismore Regional Art Museum,** 131 Molesworth St. (tel. 6622 2209), the third oldest regional gallery in New South Wales. It houses a two-floor collection of paintings, sculpture, and photographs. Visiting exhibitions make it especially worth a look (open Tues.-Sat. 10am-4pm; donation requested).

Farther along the street is the fabulous **Richmond River Historical Society,** 165 Molesworth St. (tel. 6622 9993), in the Municipal Building. The collection is organized roughly by theme. There's a pioneer room, a shipping room with musical instruments and lifesaving trophies, a natural history room with preserved baby crocs and mummified tropical birds, and a hallway with Aboriginal boomerangs and tools. Not inspired yet? Strange as it sounds, the best part is the timber panel collection, the life work of a very dedicated Australian who's collected well over 100 species of rare and common woods and sanded and polished them with loving care. The museum has a genealogical research room down the hall, frequented by frail, bonneted, and determined ladies (open Mon.-Fri. 10am-4pm; admission $2).

For a breath of fresh air, there are many parks nearby. Behind the visitor's center on Molesworth St. is **Rotary Park,** six hectares of hoop pine and giant fig tree rainforest equipped with an easy boardwalk. The **Boatharbour Nature Reserve,** 6km northeast of Lismore on Bangalow Rd., sports 17 hectares of rainforest trees, the remnants of the "Big Scrub Forest." The original 75,000 hectares of lowland forest throughout northern New South Wales has been almost completely deforested. The **Tucki Tucki Nature Reserve,** which doubles as a koala sanctuary, is 15 minutes from Lismore on Wyrallah Rd. Lismore's water supply comes from the **Rocky Creek Dam,** home to a waterside boardwalk and a platypus lagoon.

Lismore comes alive during the **Northern Rivers Folk Festival** (festival office tel. 6621 7537) held the first weekend in October. In late May, a **Lantern Festival** brings saints and sinners together for a peaceful solstice celebration. Participants craft hundreds of colorful paper lanterns and parade around the city streets at twilight, filling the rising darkness with tranquil flickering.

■ Around Lismore: The Villages

Each of the 10 small villages within the Lismore region, boasts some unique feature to draw visitors, if only for an afternoon. **Bexhill's** main attraction is an open-air cathedral and periodic organ recitals. **Dunoon,** near the Whian Whian State Forest, has rows of macadamia nut factories, some with free samples. Pastoral roads leading to **Rosebank** end in a scenic town, particularly lovely in late October, when the jacarandas are in bloom.

The Channon, 20 minutes from Lismore, is home every second Sunday to the Channon Markets, the largest in the region, with their spectacular displays of music, homemade food, and nuts. The Channon is also the closest village to the lovely **Protester's Falls,** named by a group of activists who, in 1979, were determined to prevent logging of the Terania Creek Forests. Their efforts paid off: the tall, elegant stands of intertwined limbs were declared a national park in 1983, and the powerful chutes of water still empty into a shaded swimming hole.

Nimbin

At the climax of Nimbin's 1995 Mardi Grass Festival (organized as a protest by HEMP: Help End Marijuana Prohibition), 200 participants rolled joints, blazed up, headed to the police station, and demanded to be arrested. Marijuana use is a criminal offense in Nimbin, as it is throughout New South Wales, but the police were helpless, as they had only enough cells to arrest two people. This kind of event epitomizes the psychedelic-striving side of Nimbin. The prevalence of dredlocks, drugs, and long layered skirts encourage the town's dubious hippies-gone-bad image. The hills near Nimbin are littered with those who prefer to remain more faithful to the ideals of the 60s. This area has more than 350 communes, some of which are open to visitors.

Practical Information Nimbin's commercial district stretches on Cecil St. between the police station and the corner hotel. You'll know you're there by the murals with vivid color schemes, wild store-front displays, and thin shrouds of smoke. Nimbin has no tourist center, just a self-appointed tourist official hell-bent on promoting Nimbin's "straight" side. He works in **The Nimbin Connection** (tel. 6689 1764; also a transportation booking agency) at the end of Cecil St. The **Nimbin Shuttle Bus** (tel. 6687 2007) departs daily to Nimbin from Byron Bay at 10am, returning at 1:30pm ($12). For visitors who just want a glimpse of this spectacle, Byron-based tours to nearby national parks often stop in town for an hour or two. **Jim's Alternative Tours** (tel. 6685 7720) and **Bay to Bush** (tel. 6685 6889) have $25 full-day tours of the region leaving from Byron Bay. The **Nimbin Explorer Eco-Tours** (tel. 6689

1557) runs daily two-hour tours of the sacred rocks, Permaculture Education Center, and Rainbow Power Company ($12).

Accommodations and Food **Granny's Farm (YHA)** (tel. 6689 1333) is a five- to 10-minute walk from the town center down Cecil St. to Cullen St. The creek-side lodge has two pools, showers, a kitchen, and laundry facilities (dorms $13; tent sites $6-8; train car lodging $13). **The Rainbow Retreat,** 75 Thorburn St. (tel. 6689 1262), is 10 minutes from the town center. **The Nimbin Caravan Park** (tel. 6689 1402) is on Sibley St., next to the turnoff for the Rainbow Power Company. The **community pool,** closed in the winter, is on site. There are laundry and BBQ facilities but no kitchen. (2-person tent sites $12; caravan sites $15. Weekly: $60; $70.)

Many of the area communes are part of WWOOF (tel. (03) 5155 0218), where Willing Workers exchange their labor for homestays On Organic Farms (see p. 20). The Nimbin Connection sells directories for $25. Nimbin has a few good eateries, all on Cecil St. **Rick's Cafe** makes terrific big veggie burgers ($4). Close by, the **Rainbow Cafe** has wide, wooden tables, a porch deck out back, and vegetarian meals from $4.

Sights and Activities The mural-covered **Nimbin Museum,** on Cecil St., redefines creativity and historical interpretation. Party vans burst through the front facade, and the 3D tangle of cobwebs, wire mesh, clocks, psychedelic fans, live tree branches, and kitchen appliances lend credence to Einstein's quote, found in the second room: "Imagination is more important than knowledge." Perhaps so: the rooms are a progression of regional history according to the museum's founders. The first room is for Aboriginals, the second for European settlers, and the next five for the hippies. This last group of social and environmental activists is illustrated by dollhouses mixed with fluorescent-lit cave rooms, melted skeletons (presumably illustrating nuclear meltdown), and still more marijuana legalization propaganda ($2 donation requested).

In 1973, the Australian Union of Students brought a proposal for a festival before the Lismore City Council. The Aquarius Festival, with 5000 participants, was born as a forum for creating a new future. The most direct outcome of the festival, and a major employer in Nimbin, is the **Rainbow Power Company** (tel. 6689 1430), a 10-minute walk from the city center down Cecil St. to Alternative Way, on the right. The building, made of mud bricks, has a rainforest inside and solar panels on the roof. It's a remarkable achievement in energy production; they even sell their excess generated power back to the electricity grid for general consumption. One-hour factory tours are available for $1-4, depending on group size (min. 4) and need advance booking (open Mon.-Fri. 9am-5pm, Sat. 9-noon).

Byron Bay

Here, locals in beaten leather sandals mix with couples in Gucci suits, and yoga gurus hold babies with body pierces. Here, dredlocked backpackers in bikinis sign up for drumming lessons, didgeridoo tutorials, and diving trips. Here, things move at an easy pace; two-day stopovers morph into week-long relaxation sessions and 10-minute beach walks become three-hour strolls. Here is Byron Bay, with its famously "alternative" attitude. Byron may boast palm reading, massage classes, and bead shops, yet the town is more than commercialized karma. That wouldn't be enough to make locals stay, bring tourists back, and position the town as one of the most popular stops on the Sydney-to-Cairns route. Byron's lighthouse, the first in Australia to see the sunrise, seems a beacon for travelers the world over. Thousands of them come for Byron's excellent surfing beaches, or because they are drawn to its active environmental movement and vocal arts community. As herds of surfers in singlets march past shopkeepers in hemp overalls, it becomes clear that, in a strange twist, Byron Bay's pleasantly alternative atmosphere is itself the town's commercial appeal.

ORIENTATION

Back in the 1970s, when Byron had one restaurant, the town center was 3 or 4km south of its current position along **Bangalow Rd.** Since then, the center has crept closer to the beach, and most of the shops and offices now lie along **Jonson St.** on the six blocks leading north to **Main Beach.** From Main Beach, it's possible to see "the Wreck," the unspectacular remnants of a shipwreck and now a popular surfing site. Left of Main Beach is Belongil Beach. The **Tourist Information Centre** is in the old stationmaster's cottage, directly behind the long-distance bus stop and in front of the railway station. Toward the beach from the station, Jonson St. passes Byron St. and comes to the Lawson St. rotary and Bay St. beyond. Away from the beach, Jonson passes Marvell, Carlyle, and Kingsley St.

PRACTICAL INFORMATION

Tourist Office: Tourist Information Centre (tel. 6685 8050), next to the railway station on Jonson St. It currently shares the space with, and is operated by, the environmental center, so don't expect many pamphlet handouts or a necessarily pro-tourist staff. Luggage storage $2 per day. Open daily 10am-4pm.

Budget Travel: Byron Bus and Backpacker Centre (tel. 6685 5517), behind the long-distance bus stop, is a booking agency ($3 per-call charge) for transportation, tours, and accommodation (backpack storage $3 per day; open daily 7am-7pm).

Currency and Exchange: ANZ (tel. 6685 6502), 57 Jonson St.; **National** (tel. 6613 2265), 33 Jonson St.; **Westpac** (tel. 6685 7407), 73 Jonson St. All open Mon.-Thurs. 9am-4pm, Fri. 9am-5pm.

Buses: Greyhound and **McCafferty's** pass through once or twice daily on their Sydney-Brisbane route (to Sydney 12½hr., to Brisbane 3¼hr.). **Kirklands** stops in Byron between Brisbane and Lismore (each way Mon.-Fri. 5 per day, Sat.-Sun. 2 per day). **Blanches Coaches** runs between Byron, Ballina, and Lennox.

Car Rental: Earth Car Rentals (tel. 6685 7472) and **JetSet Travel** (tel. 6685 6554) have the cheapest car rentals in the area, from $35 per day, and Earth delivers cars to your accommodation.

Taxis: Byron Bay Taxis (tel. 6685 6290) operates 24 hours.

Hospital: Byron District Hospital (24hr. tel. 6685 6200) on Wordsworth St.

Emergency: Dial 000.

Police: 24hr. tel. 6685 6300.

Internet Access: Koo's Cafe (tel. 6685 5711), on Marvell St., calls itself Byron's **internet cafe,** though they only have 1 computer ($4 for 15min., $11 per hr.). Open Mon.-Fri. 7:30am-5pm, Sat. 7:30am-3pm.

Post Office: Located diagonally across from the bus zone toward the beach and next to the community center. Open Mon.-Fri. 9am-5pm. **Postal code:** 2481.

Phone Code: 02.

ACCOMMODATIONS

Byron currently has 11 hostels, and rumor has it that one more is coming. Winter visitors reap the benefits of their nasty price wars, but in summer, especially around Christmas, Byron floods with thousands of tourists; hostels, motels, apartments, and camping grounds are packed, and some prices go up 150-200%. Many unlucky would-be Byron dwellers make do with accommodation in Ballina or Lennox Head. The best advice is to book early for summer stays. *Let's Go* has listed summer prices as quoted; be aware that these change week to week. Many of the hostels have strict 11pm lights-out in the common room, and all have 10am check-outs.

Aquarius Backpackers Resort, 16 Lawson St. (tel. 6685 7663; fax 6685 7439; email aquarius@om.com.au), corner of Lawson and Middleton St., 2 blocks off Jonson St. A converted resort, and it's easy to tell: the 230 large rooms have beautiful rosewood beds, many with sliding glass doors, porches, sinks, and fridges. Outdoor heated pool, small kitchen. 8-bed dorms $18; doubles $45, with bath $65. Winter: $16; $40, $55. The separate "round room"—a beautiful circular double

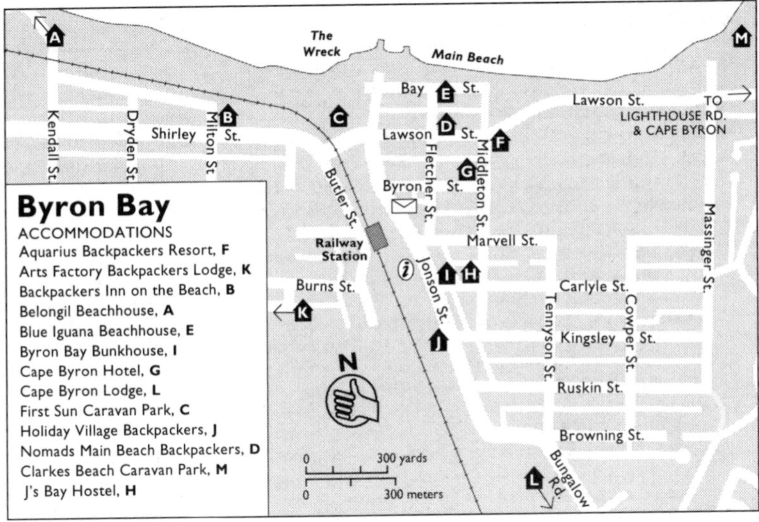

with bath—runs $80 and up; $60 in winter. Next to the Aquarius Cafe, open 24hr. in summer, with meals from $4.

Nomads Main Beach Backpackers (tel. 6685 8695; fax 6685 8609), on the corner of Lawson and Fletcher St. Take a right on Lawson from the beach end of Jonson St. Nomads is a true beauty, with high ceilings and wooden accents. Logs burn in the fireplace in winter, and the fine rooftop deck is the place to chill in warmer weather. The hostel is friendly but surfer-centric and quiet, except for the music blasting through the kitchen. There's a patio, saltwater pool, and a BBQ in back, and a comfortable common room with TV and pool table. Bedrooms are clean and have individual lockers. 16-bed dorms $15; 4-bed dorms $20; doubles $45, with bath $60. Winter: $10; $15; $35, $45.

Arts Factory Backpackers Lodge, Skinners Shoot Rd. (tel. 6685 7709; fax 6685 8534; email artsfact@om.com.au). Cross the railroad tracks behind the bus stop and take a right on Burns St. to Skinners Shoot Rd. The Arts Factory's motto is "relax, rejuvenate, recycle," and guests do all 3 with weirdly wonderful sleeping options from teepees to island bungalows in the 5 acres of woods. Daily activities include didgeridoo making, yoga, and drumming workshops. Mon. night 70s theme and talent show, Wed. night BBQ party ($6.50). Free use of bikes and body boards; volleyball courts, pool, spa, and outside deck. Dorms $16. Covered wagon, teepee, or women-only pentagon tent $13. Doubles on island or in bungalows $34. Twins or doubles in wooden log room $40. Weekly: $105; $85; $215; $270. Camping is allowed with separate facilities for $9. Weekly $50. Discounts for 4-night stays, YHA, VIP, students, and in the off season.

The Blue Iguana Beachouse, 14 Bay St. (tel. 6685 5298), opposite the Surf Club on the corner of Bay and Fletcher St. With 18 beds, this smallest of Byron's hostels is set in a lovely, brightly colored house with a sundeck, across from the beach. The front porch is screened and has wide couches and a TV. Kitchen. Dorms with bath $18; doubles $60-100. Winter: $16; $50. 7th night free.

J's Bay Hostel (YHA), 7 Carlyle St. (tel. 6685 8853 or 1800 678 195), across from the Woolworths on Jonson St. Clean, colorful, and so quiet that guests feel compelled to whisper. Common areas include outdoor picnic tables and a well-lit glass-enclosed room with wooden tables, a TV, and stereo system. Large kitchen and outdoor heated pool. Game room, free use of bikes and boogie boards. Dorms $14.

Holiday Village Backpackers, 116 Jonson St. (tel. 6685 8888; fax 6685 8777), 2 blocks from the tourist center. Family-owned hostel set up motel style with a large open air courtyard and picnic tables. Solar heated pool and spa in back. TV and video room. Self-contained apartment units next door, for the same price as hostel rooms. Free use of bikes, surfboards, and boogie boards. 8-bed dorms $14; 4- to 6-

bed dorms $16; doubles $45, with bath $47. Winter: $11; $14; $32, $42. Weekly: $7 off. VIP; YHA discount in winter. All you can eat BBQ Mon. and Fri. nights $8.

Byron Bay Bunkhouse, 1 Carlyle St. (tel. 6685 8311 or 1800 241 600; fax 6685 8258), across from the Jonson St. Woolworths. Crowded and loud, but sets the standard for cheap quality deals. Music pumps constantly over the stereo system, and people hang out on the couches in the mural-covered main room. The hostel is better suited for half of its current capacity (100 beds), creating lines for the 6 showers and literally too many cooks in the kitchen around dinner time. Live entertainment on weekends, cafe. Free bikes and surfboards. 6- and 8-bed dorms $10. Dinner $1.50-2 most nights. Free breakfast cereal on your first morning.

Belongil Beachhouse, Childe Rd. (tel. 6685 7868; fax 6685 7445). A 15min. walk down the beach to Belongil Beach, or a 25min. walk from the town center. Cross the railroad tracks to Shirley St. and take a right on Kendall St. Belongil is past the Epicentre Club. Gorgeous high-ceilinged wooden lodges, with an earthy, therapeutic feel created by the incense-filled walkways from the dimly lit residential massage center. The fantastic Belongil Cafe is right next door, and the beach, which sometimes goes nude, is across the street. Dorm rooms are with bath, but there are 10 beds to each toilet, with extra facilities near the common area. Free bikes, boogie boards, and volleyball. Courtesy bus to town center 5-6 times daily. 5-bed dorms $16-17; doubles $38-48. Motel-style rooms with kitchenette $60-90. Small, beautiful cottages with 2 double beds $75-125. VIP, YHA. Large lockers $1 per day or $5 per week.

Cape Byron Hostel (YHA) (tel. 6685 8788 or 1800 652 627; fax 6685 8814), at the corner of Middleton and Byron St. From the tourist office, go 2 blocks down Marvell St. and take a right on Middleton St. Large loft kitchen above common areas with wicker chairs, wooden tables, TV, VCR, and stereo. Picnic tables outside near a large heated pool. Free bikes and boogie boards. 10-bed dorms $16; 5-bed dorms $18; doubles $46. Winter: $15; $17; $44. Weekly dorm discount $7. YHA discount. Linen $1.

Cape Byron Lodge, 78 Bangalow Rd. (tel. 6685 6445 or 1800 247 070). 15-20min. from the town center down Jonson St., then another 10min. to the quiet Tallow Beach. This hostel's claim to fame is the free pancake breakfast the first morning; it also has free bikes, surfboards, and boogie boards. Several courtesy buses per day run to town, and the hostel has its own nightlife in the summer. Decor is quirky and jungle-themed, with a leafy green printed foyer accented by a purple lizard. Bathrooms, especially sinks, are small. Common area has a pool table and ancient TV, and opens to a courtyard. 8-bed dorms $16 (winter: $10); 4-bed dorms $12; doubles $30. 7th night free.

Backpackers Inn on the Beach, 29 Shirley St. (tel. 6685 8231; fax 6685 5708), corner of Shirley and Milton St. Follow Jonson St., veer left onto Lawson St., cross the railroad tracks and continue on Shirley St. for a long block. This is the only beachfront backpackers; it's 50m across the backyard to the sand. It's large (180 beds), functional, and geared toward socializing, with an outdoor pool, BBQ area, and pool table. Free bikes and boogie boards. Rooms have ceiling fans and a storage space. Dorms $17; doubles $40. Winter: $14; $35. Weekly party and BBQ, sometimes with $5 all-you-can-quaff sangria. A small on-site cafe sells food for under $4.

First Sun Caravan Park, Lawson St. (tel. 6685 6544), near the railroad tracks. On the main beach and popular with backpackers. All prices are seasonal. Tent sites for 2 $13-22. Weekly: $78-154. Additional person $4-5.50. Cabins $38-50, with bath $50-75. Weekly $230-350, $300-525. Linen and TV rental available. $40 non-refundable deposit for bookings.

Clarkes Beach Caravan Park (tel. 6685 6496), off Lighthouse Rd., on Clarkes Beach. Pretty, well-kept sites. Book 12 months ahead for peak holidays. Prices seasonal. Tent sites for 2 $14-20 (additional person $5.50-6); cabins with bath $48-77. Weekly: $84-140; $288-540. $40 non-refundable deposit for bookings.

Byron Central Apartments (tel. 6685 8800; fax 6685 8802), on Byron St. One of the best non-hostel accommodation deals in town. Small, spotless rooms with bath, TV, kitchenettes, closets, and tables surround a courtyard pool. Split-level apartments for 4 or studio apartments for 2. Prices vary widely depending on season. Daily $65-145, weekly $365-950. Weekends with 2 night min. stay $75. Winter weekends $65. Subject to availability and minimum stays. Wheelchair accessible.

FOOD

Belongil Cafe, next to Belongil Beachhouse, is a lovely eatery. The atmosphere is trendy, high-brow, and literary, and the cafe runs nightly specials ($6-11) and super-cheap, great-tasting "backpacker specials" ($4.50-7). Guests can sit inside at graceful wooden tables or out on the patio. Live entertainment most Sun. nights. Open daily 8am-late.

Supernatural Foods (tel. 6685 5833), at the Arts Factory, says it has vegetarian "karma-free" food, a reference to the fact that their meals are meticulously prepared in what used to be a pig slaughterhouse. Presumably, the gods have forgiven them, for the Hare Krishna staff makes fabulously popular dinners ($4-11). Candles and lights hang from ropes suspended from the lofty ceiling. Long wooden tables and booths are surrounded by stone statues, sculptures, and a splashing waterfall.

Bay Kebabs (tel. 6685 5596), at the corner of Jonson and Lawson St., serves up delicious takeaway foot-long toasted kebabs for $4.80. Lamb, barbecued chicken, and falafel from this unassuming restaurant are all tasty. Open daily 10am-late.

Cafe Carpark (tel. 6685 5880), located in the Woolworths parking lot next to the Carpark nightclub, has great cafeteria-style deals on vegetarian food. There are at least a dozen hot dishes and 7-8 fresh, healthy salads; fish is served on weekends. The laid-back owners play Irish music and encourage you to heap your plate high. A small plate costs $4, a large plate is $6, and $10 gets you all you can eat. They also make smoothies and freshly-squeezed juice for $3. Open daily noon-late, but go at mealtimes to get the hot food while it's fresh.

Ringo's Cafe (tel. 6685 6433) Jonson St., is plastered with posters and funky memorabilia. Byron's trendy, intellectual spot has a small secondhand bookshop at the rear. At night, the lights go dim, the music's turned up, and candles appear on the tables. Burgers ($4.50-$8), nachos ($9.50). Breakfast ($3-9.50). Open daily 8:30am-9pm.

The Services Club (tel. 6685 6878) at the southern end of Johnson St., has $3 lunches daily from noon to 2pm. You can choose among 6 meals, including fish and chips and roast. Tues. and Thurs. feature $7 roast dinners from 6-8:30pm. Wed. nights mean 2-for-1 specials. The bar also has fairly cheap drinks and some of the cheapest six-packs in town ($7).

The Pass Cafe (tel. 6685 6074), Brooke Dr. on the Cape Byron Walking Track. This eatery overlooks the beach and is a perfect stop along the track, although it's a little expensive ($7-13 for lunch, $14-17 for dinner). Open in summer Sun.-Thurs. 8am-3pm, Fri.-Sat. 8am-9:30pm; in winter daily 9am-3pm.

Earth 'n' Sea, 11 Lawson St. (tel. 6685 5011), is one of Byron's most popular cheap sit-down restaurants. It serves exclusively pizza and pasta, but the food incarnations are as varied as the clientele. There are 2 dozen kinds of pizza alone, including the seafood *Cruel Sea,* banana, prawn, and pineapple *Beethoven,* and spinach, feta, and olive *Greenpizza.* Small pizzas are big enough for 2 ($11.50); large are $19, and giants, at $24, can easily fill 4 stomachs. Licensed and BYO.

SIGHTS AND ACTIVITIES

The **Byron Bay Lighthouse** is Cape Byron's crowning glory. A steadily rotating beam pierces through 40km of darkness every night, as it has since first constructed in 1901. The interior is of red cedar, cut by Byron's original settlers, while the outside shell is constructed from molded concrete blocks. The last lighthouse keeper left in 1988, long after the lighthouse become fully automated. The keepers' cottages are still standing, however. One is a small museum and the other is available for private holiday rental. The site is at the end of Lighthouse Rd., which starts at the east end of Lawson Rd. It can also be reached via a boardwalk that leads to the right along Main Beach to Clarks Beach and the **Captain Cook Lookout.** From here, a walking circuit follows the beach to The Pass, and winds up a steep gradient past Wategos Beach to the **Headland Lookout,** the easternmost point in Australia and an excellent place for spotting dolphins and whales. From here, the lighthouse is just a short distance along the track which leads through forest and back to Captain Cook Lookout. Tours of the lighthouse and its own lookout are run only during school holidays (grounds open daily year-round 8am-5:30pm).

West of the town is the **Arts and Industrial Estate,** off Ewingsdale Rd. (the western part of Shirley Rd). Galleries and studios, with paintings, sculptures, and other crafts, complement great bargains on shoes. Colin Heaney's famous **glassblowing studio,** 6 Acacia St. (tel. 6685 7044), is open daily, as is the **Brooklet House Gallery,** 1 Tasman Way (tel. 6685 7654; open Mon.-Fri. 9am-5pm, Sat. 10am-4pm, Sun. 11am-4pm).

On the Water: Mostly Surfing

Byron Bay is a surfer's mecca; it's not uncommon to see herds of boys and the occasional girl, boards slung over their shoulders, trudging dutifully toward the beach at sunrise. To entice novices, two major surf schools and a number of independent operators provide all equipment and often solicit through hostels. **Byron Surf School** (tel. 6685 7536 or 1800 707 274) is in the Byron Surf Shop at the corner of Lawson and Middleton St. The school has three-hour daily group lessons at 10am and 2pm (1st lesson $20, 2nd $18), and rents surf boards ($12 half-day, $20 full day) and wetsuits ($5 per day). The **East Coast Surf School** (tel. 6685 5989) has group lessons (2½hr., $20) while its agent, **Bay Action,** 14 Jonson St. (tel. 6685 7819), also rents surfboards, boogie boards, flippers, and wetsuits. (Surfboards $5 per hr., $20 per day, $60 per week. Wetsuits $3 per hr., $10 per day, $40 per week.)

Byron is famous for its excellent surfing spots, located around the bay so that there are good waves no matter what the wind conditions. A crowded spot off Main Beach, **The Wreck** is known for fast waves that break close to the beach. Working down the beach toward the lighthouse, **The Pass** is great for long, challenging rides, but dangerous because of overcrowding, sharp rocks, and boats. The water off **Wategos Beach,** close to The Pass, is best for longer surfboards since the waves are slow and rolling. Again, though, the rocks can be dangerous. **Cosy Corner,** on the other side of the headland from Wategos, is great for northern-wind surfing. On the other side of Main Beach, southern winds bring **Broken Head** and **Belongil Beach** alive.

Ocean kayaking is a great way to see the dolphins, and **Ocean Kayaking Byron Bay** (tel. 6685 7651) runs half-day trips past the wrecks and reefs to a snorkeling site ($20 if booked directly, pick-up and return included). **Byron Bay Sea Kayaks** (tel. 6685 5830) offers $30 trips which include breakfast.

Underwater: Scuba Diving

Byron has three dive shops, all with similar prices. Check around to see which suits you best. Most diving is done at Julian Rocks, 2.5km off Main Beach, widely considered one of the 10 best dive sites in Australia. Julian Rocks has both warm and cold currents and is home to 400 species of fish, including the occasional grey nurse shark. Required medical clearances are $35-50. The dive certification courses go up by $70-100 or more during the summer.

Sundive (tel. 6685 7555), on Middleton St. opposite the Court House, has an on-site pool and offers five-day PADI certification courses for $395, in the winter $280 (plus medical check $40). Courses usually start on Mondays, but weekend certification courses are sometimes offered (introductory dives $95; snorkeling $35). **Byron Bay Dive Center** (tel. 6685 7149), 9 Lawson St., but moving to Jonson St., has four-day SSI certification courses for $280-350 (medical check $35). The "deluxe" five-day course includes five dives at the marine reserve, four nights "on-site" accommodation, the medical check, a mask and snorkel set, and a BBQ presentation for $450, in the winter $390. Both courses give an additional free dive upon completion (introductory dive $95; snorkeling $40). Smaller **Bayside Scuba** (tel. 6685 8333), at the corner of Lawson and Fletcher St., offers a four-day SSI certification course for $280 (medical check $40; introductory dives $95; snorkeling $35).

Indoors, Outdoors, and Falling Out of the Sky

Samadhi Flotation Centre (tel. 6685 5876), opposite Woolworths on Jonson St., has cheap, great-value massage classes (1hr. float, 1hr. massage) and a backpacker special for $45 (regularly $60). Introductory massage classes ($30) are held every Saturday and on demand from 10am-6pm. These include hands-on training, a manual, a certificate, and morning and afternoon tea. Shiatsu classes ($30) are held Mondays from 10am to 6pm. Book three to five days ahead in the summer (open daily 9am-6pm). The other major massage center, **Relax Haven** (tel. 6685 8304), at the rear of Belongil Beachhouse, 2km from town, is much smaller. A one-hour float and one-hour massage is $40, which includes tea.

Cabin fever victims might enjoy the small but wildly-colored **Wave Rock** (tel. 6680 8777) on Centennial Circuit at the Arts and Industrial Estate. It's a well-plotted indoor rock climbing room with over 50 different climbs. The long-limbed staff are enthusiastic, but they scurry up difficult paths so quickly that they can't help but make the beginner feel clumsy. ($10 for 2hr. or $15 for the day, including harness. Boot rental $5. Open daily 10am-10pm.)

There are two horseback riding companies in the area. **Spirit of Equus** (tel. 6684 7499), in Tyagarah, 10 minutes from Byron, has daily two-hour rides on isolated beaches for $40, pick-up included. **Pegasus Park Equestrian Centre** (tel. 6687 1446), about 15 minutes west of Byron, leads rides along Byron Creek for $30-35; three-hour sunset rides are $45. In late July, Byron holds a huge **kite festival** on its beaches. Amateurs can try kite-flying at any time of the year; **Byron Kite and Juggle Shop** (tel. 6685 5299), in the Byron St. arcade, sells one-string kites ($8-17) and two-string stunt kites ($30-80).

Tandem hang-gliding affords a unique perspective of the lighthouse, bay, and town. **Tandem Flights** (tel. 015 257 699) has flights from the cliffs west of the lighthouse (30min., $75), as does **Flight Zone** (tel. 6685 8768). **Skylimit** (tel. 6684 3711) offers hang-gliding and motorized ultralight tours from $55. For tandem skydiving, **Skydive** (tel. 6684 1323) has daily 3050m (10,000 ft.) drops for $275 (pay cash $260).

NEW SOUTH WALES

Tours

Two companies offer good-value tours of neighboring areas. **Jim's Alternative Tours** (tel. 6685 7720) runs a great trip through Minyon Falls, Nimbin, Protester's Falls, and the half-crazy but entirely delightful **Fruit Spirit botanical gardens.** The gardens have been cultivated for over 20 years by Dr. Paul Recher, a New York City "environmental refugee" and a first-class character. He walks visitors through his estate (9½hr., $25) and slices open some of his hundreds of fruit species for sampling, all the while explaining the importance of energy conservation for our future. The day is expertly synchronized to CD music selections by Jim, who also throws in interesting, witty commentary. **Bay to Bush** (tel. 6685 6889) has similar $25 day tours through Nimbin, Minyon Falls, and the rainforest, that include a stop at a swimming hole and tea. Both companies also provide shuttle service to the **Channon** ($10 return) and **Bangalow** ($5 return) markets. **Dreamtime Journey Tours** (tel. 6680 8212) has Aboriginal culture tours (6hr., $25). The tours focus on Aboriginal history and take you to the rainforest and to sacred Aboriginal sites. Guides even tell Dreaming stories and provide a kangaroo meat BBQ lunch.

ENTERTAINMENT

The **Railway Friendly Bar** (tel. 6685 7662), next to the railway station on Jonson St., has meals and live music nightly. It's usually packed with eager, loud backpackers. The **Northern Rivers Hotel** on the beach end of Jonson St. generally has nightly entertainment, too, although it draws a marginally more mellow crowd. At the end of Jonson St. by the beach is the **Beach Hotel,** frequented by older drinkers and music lovers. Families have meals here during the Sunday afternoon live entertainment. For dancing, the **Carpark** nightclub in the Woolworths parking lot is hot, sweaty, loud, and heavy on techno. Wednesdays are $1.50 sangria nights. **Cocomangas,** 23 Jonson St. (tel. 6685 8493), has theme nights, including 70s night on Mondays, backpacker parties on Tuesdays, and live bongo music on Wednesdays. On the way to the **Arts and Industrial Estate,** the enormous **Epicentre** studio complex is home to many a wild no-alcohol rave; it's also used as a concert venue. Ask around to see if anything's going on during your stay.

Pighouse Flicks (tel. 6685 5833 after 4:30pm) at the Piggery on Skinners Shoot Rd., next to the Arts Factory, shows art and foreign films three times nightly ($7.50). The theater features a black-lit foyer, large, comfy seats, and room to stretch out in the first couple of rows. You can take off your shoes, so BYO socks. There's a movie/dinner deal (dinner from $11.50) at the nearby vegetarian restaurant.

Murwillumbah

Twenty-two million years ago, the Mt. Warning shield volcano began oozing soft lava, which was then covered by harder, more viscous lava, over an area of 4000 square kilometers. Eventually, cracks in the cooled, hard lava allowed water to seep in, and caused the soft lava to erode; 10 million years ago, the unsupported hard lava collapsed, creating hills, valleys, and rocky terrain. What remains today is Mt. Warning (which is now half of its original size), the surrounding Tweed Valley, and a circular volcanic rim now encompassing several national parks. The rim stretches north to Beenleigh, south to Coraki, west to Kyogle, and east to Pacific Ocean reefs. There are four national parks near Murwillumbah: Nightcap (30km southwest), Border Ranges, Lamington, and Mt. Cougal.

Murwillumbah (more-WOOL-um-bah) is a small country town whose name has several suggested meanings, including "place of high mountain which catches sun" and "place of many possums and people." The residents have seized on part one of the second definition and has begun to paint possum murals on their Art Deco public buildings in an attempt to create a cohesive, if strange, motif.

ORIENTATION AND PRACTICAL INFORMATION

Murwillumbah is halfway between Byron Bay and Tweed Heads. The **Tweed River** runs through the east side of town, and the Pacific Hwy. and the **railway station** are on the east bank. The stop for **Greyhound** and **McCafferty's** is opposite the railway station. In Budd Park at the corner of the highway and Alma St., the **World Heritage Rainforest Centre** (tel. 6672 1340; fax 6672 5948) acts as the **tourist information center** for the region.

The town is centered on the west bank of the Tweed River, which is crossed by the **Alma St. bridge,** behind Tweed Tavern. Alma St. crosses Commercial St. and becomes **Wollumbin St.** (also known as Main St.), which has several cheap eateries and a shopping center with a 24-hour **Coles supermarket** at the end of the block on the left. The cross street is **Brisbane St.,** which goes one block to the right to **Murwillumbah St.** The **post office** (postal code 2484) is at the corner of Brisbane and Murwillumbah St. The **Pioneer Motor Services** and **Kirkland's bus** depot is on Murwillumbah St., across from the **National Bank.**

ACCOMMODATIONS AND FOOD

The **Mt. Warning/Murwillumbah YHA,** 1 Tumbulgum Rd. (tel. 6672 3763), is the second oldest YHA in NSW, and a well-kept, informative, family-oriented lodge. From the railway station, cross the Alma St. bridge, turn right on Commercial St. and follow the riverbank to the YHA. Set right on the Tweed River, the YHA offers free use of rowboats, canoes, surfskis, fishing gear, and, in the summer, inner tubes for lazing in the river. Every night at 8pm the owner dishes out free ice cream at the long wooden dining table. A small courtyard in front is good for eating dinner or talking to the resident parakeets (dorms $13; twins $32; doubles $30). The porch out back overlooks the river and spots Mt. Warning 17km distant (accessible by bike, $5 per day).

Commercial Rd. has several inexpensive ethnic restaurants. At the corner of Wollumbin St. and Commercial Rd., **South of the Border** serves up Mexican cuisine (open for dinner Wed.-Sun. and lunch on Fri.). The **Austral Cafe,** 88 Main St., has been around for more than 75 years, and it's beginning to show its age (lunches $3-5; open Mon.-Fri. 7:30am-5pm, Sat. 7:30am-1pm). Across the street is **Govinda's Natural Foods,** a buffet-style vegetarian restaurant run by Hare Krishnas (meals $4-7; open Mon.-Fri. 10am-4pm).

SIGHTS

The area's main attraction is the splendid **Mt. Warning,** the extinct volcano, now covered in tall tree rainforest, that sparked the creation of many of the area's national parks. The view from the summit encompasses the entire perimeter of the volcanic rim and nearby national parks. The 8.8km trail is well-maintained and not terribly strenuous, though it becomes extremely steep and rocky near the summit, where there's a chain to help hikers keep their balance. Don't attempt to climb to the top after noon during the winter; the round-trip hike takes four to five hours, and darkness falls quickly. Those going for sunrise should bring flashlights, and all hikers should carry extra layers of clothing and plenty of water, as no drinking water is available on or near the mountain.

There is a debate as to the meaning of the word Wollumbin, the Aboriginal name for the mountain. One of the possibilities, "cloud catcher," is particularly apt. Plan on enjoying the hike for its own sake, not necessarily for the view at the summit, since two and a half hours of sweat may reward you with heavy fog. Mt. Warning is fairly easy to reach from Murwillumbah. A **taxi** (tel. 6672 1344; Mon.-Fri. $40 return, Sat.-Sun. $45) may work out economically for small groups. **Tailor Made Cars** (tel. 6672 5454) rents vehicles for trips to Mt. Warning at $35, and 24-hour rentals, permitting time for a jaunt to Natural Arch, are $45. The **school bus,** which leaves from Knox Park at 7:10am and returns at 4:40pm ($2 one-way), goes past the turnoff for the Mt. Warning National Park, a 6km walk from the mountain's parking lot.

If hiking's not your thing, the small **Art Gallery** (tel. 6672 0409), which happens to award the world's biggest art prize ($100,000 for portraiture), is down Tumbulgum Rd. (open Wed.-Sun. 10am-5pm). The **historical museum,** off Murwillumbah St. on Queensland Rd., five minutes from the town center, has a collection of different kinds of radios (open Wed. and Fri. 11am-4pm, market days 9am-noon; admission $2). Murwillumbah holds two **markets,** one on the second Sunday of the month near the Coles, and a larger market on the fourth Sunday of the month in the showgrounds, off Queensland Rd.

Chillingham Trail Rides (tel. 6679 1369), 20 minutes from Murwillumbah, conducts horse rides twice per day through the Chillingham Valley ($40). The **Permaculture Institute** (tel. 6679 3442), 30 minutes west of Murwillumbah in Tyalgum, devotes itself to creating sustainable agricultural products (2hr. tours Mon. and Thurs. at 10am; tours $10).

HUNTER VALLEY

The Hunter Valley is home to 77 wineries, many of which have an international reputation for producing high quality wines at reasonable prices. The region specializes in *shiraz,* a spicy, peppery wine, and *semillon,* a dry wine. Most of the wineries are in the lower Hunter Valley, clustered northwest of Cessnock; seven are in the upper Hunter area, centered in Denman, one hour north.

From Newcastle, the closest town is **Cessnock,** about 10-15 minutes away from the vineyards. The **Cessnock Visitors Centre** (tel. 4990 4477), 1.2km off Vincent St. on Abeudare Rd., has information on the wineries and weekly specials on accommodations and meals (open Mon.-Fri. 9am-5pm, Sat. 9:30am-5pm, Sun. 9:30am-3:30pm). Pokolbin, in the middle of the wineries northwest of Cessnock, is a geographically convenient up-market tourist center with many pricey B&Bs, inns, and restaurants nestled between the vineyards.

Maitland is 30 minutes east of Cessnock along the Hunter River. A heritage city, it once rivaled Sydney as a potential state capital. Its 150-year-old buildings continue to earn it architectural praise, and are the stars of the town's Heritage Walk. Artistic, cultural, and vintage train exhibitions are among the main objects of attention during Maitland's Heritage Month Celebrations every April. The **Visitor's Information Centre** (tel. 4933 2611) is in Ministers Park (open daily 9am-5pm).The **Imperial Hotel** (tel. 4933 6566) on High St. offers singles for $30 with breakfast.

Morpeth is a five-minute drive directly to the north of Maitland. It has many tearooms, art collections, and antique shops, as well as a "weird and wonderful teapot exhibition" each August. Perhaps the biggest event, though, is the two-day Jazz Festival held in May. For more information call 4933 6240.

Scone Well northwest of Cessnock, in the upper Hunter Valley, Scone (pop. 9375) is a small but pretty town which prides itself on being the horse capital of Australia. The distinction is owed to the annual week-long **Scone Horse Festival** in mid-May, which includes an air show featuring WWII fighter jets. The week culminates in three days of thoroughbred racing for the Scone Cup. The racecourse is five minutes from the town center. Large thoroughbred stud farms sprawl alongside the New England Hwy. near the town, and many are open for tours. The **tourist information center** (tel. 6545 1526) is at the corner of Kelly and Susan St., across from Elizabeth Park. The **Scone YHA** (tel. 6545 2072) on Segenhoe Rd. is 8km off the highway in a converted country school building near horse stud farms. It has a kitchen, BBQ facilities, and campfires (dorms $13; doubles $28). The **Highway Caravan Park,** 248 New England Hwy. (tel. 6545 1078), offers a place to pitch a tent. **The Station Cafe** (tel. 065 45 2144), at the railroad station, makes tomato soup to die for.

TOURS IN THE HUNTER VALLEY

Most wineries are open daily for free tastings and occasional tours from 10am to 5pm, although some are only open on weekends. If you're able, the best time to tour is during the week, since the wineries can become very crowded on weekends, when you'll receive less time and attention. Of the 77 wineries, the largest are McGuigans (which also has a cheese outlet with free tastings), McWilliams, Mt. Pleasant, Lindemans, Tyrrells, and Rothbury Estate. The smaller ones are not as glitzy, but are generally more relaxed.

Unless you have a car, you'll need to arrange some kind of tour to see the wineries. The **Vineyard Shuttle Service** (tel. 4991 3655, mobile tel. 019 327 193) makes pick-ups at accommodations and shuttles folks to designated wineries for $12 (every 20min.) One-day with unlimited stops and an evening restaurant shuttle costs $20; full weekend passes run $24. **Hunter Vineyard Tours** (tel. 4991 1659, mobile tel. 018 497 451) has pick-ups from Newcastle and Maitland for $34, with lunch $50. Pick-ups from Cessnock and the vineyards are $29, with lunch $45. **Jump Up Creek Vineyard Tours** (tel. 6574 7252, mobile tel. 019 453 674) specializes in the smaller wineries and offers small, personalized tours, with pick-ups from Cessnock, Maitland, Singleton, and the vineyards ($27.50; Sat. $30). **Grapemobile** (tel. 4991 2339, mobile tel. 018 404 039) has day bicycle tours, including lunch, for $98. Bicycle rental is available from the Hermitage Lodge in Pokolbin (tel. 4998 7639). If you'd like a running start on wine tasting, **Hunter Cellars School of Wine** (tel. 4998 7466) has daily lessons from 10am to 12:30pm ($20).

Springtime brings additional entertainment to the wineries. **Opera in the Vineyards** is an evening of opera, wine and cheese tastings, and fireworks held in mid-October on Wyndham Estate. (Fri. and Sat. nights, Sun. afternoon). Picnic-style tickets are $34. For more information, call 9299 6488. The following Saturday in October is **Jazz in the Vines,** a full-day music extravaganza held at Tyrrell's Long Flat Paddock (a winery) in Pokolbin. Call 4938 1345 for more information (tickets $17-20).

ACCOMMODATIONS

Most Hunter Valley accommodations raise their prices from 10 to 100% on Friday and Saturday; some require that you take two-night B&B packages. **Cessnock Caravan Park** (tel. 4990 5819) on the corner of Allandale and Branxton Rd., 2km north of town, has campsites ($6 per person, with power $14 for 2 people), on-site caravans (Sun.-Thurs. $30, Fri.-Sat. $40), and cabins ($48, $65). Discounts are offered for extended stays. There is no public transportation to the park on the weekends; taxis from town cost $6-8. The **Royal Oak Hotel** (tel. 4990 2366), at the corner of Vincent St. and Aberdare Rd. about 500m from the bus station, has large bedrooms, a TV lounge, and a modern, fully equipped kitchen. (Sun.-Thurs. singles $25, Fri.-Sat. $30; doubles $40, $45; discounts for extended stays; light breakfast included.) Across Vincent St. is the **Black Opal Hotel** (tel. 4990 1070), a surprisingly nice lodging with an outside beer garden (4-bed dorms $15; singles $25; doubles $40). The **Chardonnay Sky Motel** (tel. 4991 4812) is about a 10-minute drive out of town, on Allandale Rd., but it has backpacker accommodation with private baths for $20.

NEW ENGLAND

A lovely, scenic alternative to the coast, with rustic beauty and relatively cooler year-round climates, the New England Highway begins in Sydney, continues along Hwy. 15 to Brisbane, and is serviced by most major bus lines. Most of this 380km stretch of highway is dotted with inviting country towns. The highway traverses the **Hunter Valley** (see p. 179), undergoing a subtle but sure change of scenery from Newcastle's industrial machines and coal ships, along Maitland's vineyards, past Singleton's army base and mines, and through Muswellbrook's coal mines and Scone's horse stud farms to the rather dramatic climb up the Dividing Range from Tamworth to Armidale, in New England proper.

Greyhound and **McCafferty's** make runs along the New England Highway at least once daily. **Crisps Bus Service,** part of Suncoast Pacific (tel. 7681 2299), runs daily buses from Brisbane to Warwick ($22.20) and Tenterfield ($34.70), leaving at 9am and 3:30pm. **Eastern Australian Airlines,** a subsidiary of Qantas (tel. 13 13 13) has daily flights from Sydney to Newcastle ($97 one-way; $64 with 7-day advance purchase), Port Macquarie ($185; $123), and Tamworth ($181; $120).

The **national parks** in the New England region (clustered in southern Queensland and northern New South Wales) are worth re-routing an itinerary for. There are absolutely no entrance fees, and almost all of the parks have picnic areas, camping sites, toilets, fireplaces, and spectacular views. Unfortunately, most are accessible only by vehicle (some only by 4WD), although there are companies attempting to start cheap shuttle service; call the Armidale Visitors Centre (below) for an update.

Tamworth

Tamworth (pop. 50,000) calls itself the country music capital of Australia, and the hugely popular Country Music Festival brings famous crooners to town each January. Cheesy tourist attractions seeking to capitalize on this reputation include a giant golden guitar that redefines tackiness and a concrete slab with handprints of country artists. Up until the mid-1980s, Tamworth was a big dairy and egg-producing region, but when the government-regulated industry collapsed, many farmers started to plant olive trees instead, hoping to tap into a ripe domestic market. The tourist office, however, prefers to embrace Tamworth's musical side, and is itself fashioned in the shape of a guitar—an olive would have been too easy.

ORIENTATION AND PRACTICAL INFORMATION

Tamworth is 380km north of Sydney on the New England Hwy., and is a convenient rest stop on a journey to Brisbane. The heart of the commercial district lies along eight blocks of **Peel St.,** between Kable St. and Bicentennial Park, on the bank of the Peel River. The bus depot and information center are on the southeast end of Peel St., while the Macquarie St. rotary and Viaduct Park are on the northwest side. Marius St., which houses the **railway station** between Bourke and Brisbane St., runs parallel to Peel St. Brisbane St. continues west across the Peel River and becomes Bridge St. in West Tamworth.

The **information center** (tel. 6766 9422 or 1800 803 561) is at the corner of Peel and Murray St. (open Mon.-Fri. 8:45am-4:35pm). Several **banks** are in the center of Peel St., and the **post office** is on Fitzroy St., a block south of Brisbane St. A **24-hour supermarket** is in the shopping center on the bus depot end of Peel St.

ACCOMMODATIONS AND FOOD

Most rooms for January's Country Music festival are gone by the previous March, but throughout the rest of the year, beds are plentiful and easy to come by. The centrally located hotels (most within a 2-block radius of Peel and Brisbane St.) are a better option than the more expensive motels.

Country Backpackers, 169 Marius St. (tel. 6761 2600), opposite the railway station, is guiding hostels into a new era. Brand-new and impeccably clean, with towels, good coffee, and friendly country folk willing to fix you a cuppa, Country Backpackers' only fault is that the stairwell is narrow. Its best feature, and one that deserves to be added to the tourist map, is the **art gallery** painted along the second floor hallway walls: a talented guest reproduced such great masterpieces as Rodin's *The Thinker* and Munch's *The Scream,* and renamed them after great Australian country music stars. Dorms $15-20. Breakfast in the sunny eating area included.

Minbalup Hostel (tel. 6766 9295), 45km northwest of Tamworth, is perched 1000m above sea level on 28 square km of land around Altunga Creek. Dorms $15 1st night, $13 following nights. Wheelchair accessible.

Tamworth Hotel, 147 Mapilus St. (tel. 6766 2923), opposite the railway station, is the most upscale pub of the lot. Rooms are tiny, although they include a bureau, sink, and dresser. Singles $25; doubles $36. Weekly: $95; $180.

Tattersall's Hotel (tel. 6766 2114) is at the east end of Peel St., a good 10 to 15-min. walk from the city center. Rooms are large and nicely furnished. But the real reason to stay at Tattersall's is the **Noses of Fame** (a spoof on Tamworth's Hands of Fame), which ingloriously line a small patch of pavement out back. Singles $20; twins $30.

Paradise Caravan Park (tel. 6766 3120) is next to the information center, bordering the creek. The park has a laundry, BBQ facilities, and a playground. Tent sites $11.50 for 2 people, with power $14. Weekly: $69, $83. Cabins for 2 with bath $50; on-site caravans $31. Additional person charge: $5 per night, $30 per week. Surcharge of 25% on long weekends and during the music festival.

Austin Caravan Park is farther west at 581 Armidale Rd. (tel. 6766 6275), with laundry, BBQ facilities, a playground, and a pool.

Tamworth's **internet cafe** is also located in one of its best coffee shops, **The Coffee Bean** (tel. 6766 3422; email thebean@mpx.com.au), in the Tamworth Arcade. It costs $2 to check and send email (internet $6 for 30min., $11 for 1hr.). Cheap, lower tech fare can be found in pub bistros. Lunch runs from noon to 2pm and costs about $5. Dinners usually start at 6pm and cost $6-12. **Brumby's Homestead Cafe** (tel. 6766 4512) in the Shearer Arcade on the bottom of Fitzroy St. serves good lunches for around $7.

SIGHTS AND ENTERTAINMENT

Tamworth does its best to live up to its billing as Australia's country music capital. The turn-off for **The Country Collection** (tel. 6765 2688) is marked on the New England Hwy. by a gaudy 12m Golden Guitar. The complex features a wax "Gallery of Stars" museum and a gem and mineral display (open daily 9am-5pm; admission $4, children $2). The **Andale Flag Inn** on the New England Hwy. has a guitar-shaped swimming pool with an Aussie flag painted on the bottom. The popular **Hands of Fame Cornerstone** is on the corner of the New England Hwy. and Kable Ave. (Tattersall's Hotel's Noses of Fame is a great counterpart.)

Parallel to Peel St. is **Bicentennial Park,** a quiet, reclusive stretch of greenery and ponds. In 1988, Tamworth used a grant from the government to commission a delightful bit of masonry on the rocks in the park. If you look closely, you'll find more than a dozen reliefs of animals including frogs and platypuses jutting off the stones near the water fountain. A 90-minute, 4.7km **Heritage Walk** loops through the town. The tourist office has copies of the guide. If you'd like a more rigorous walk, try the

Kamilaroi Walking Track, a three-hour scenic tour beginning at Oxley Scenic Lookout. The track passes by **Endeavor Drive Marsupial Park,** at the top of Brisbane St. The park has picnic areas for lunches (open daily 8am-4:45pm). For a bird's eye view of the city and surrounds, the **Oxley Scenic Lookout** at the top of White St. is definitely worth visiting. The **Tamworth City Gallery** (tel. 6768 4459) shares a building on Marius St. with the library. It has 700 Australian and European paintings, a fiber collection, and an extensive exhibition on textile practices (open Mon.-Fri. 10am-5pm, Sat. 9-11:30am, Sun. 1-4pm). The **Tamworth Powerstation Museum** (tel. 6766 1999) is at the Macquarie St. end of Peel St. (open Tues.-Fri. 9am-1pm). **Phil's Adventure Tours** (tel. 6767 0200) provides activities like paragliding in Manilla ($65), tandem skydiving ($250), and gliding ($30).

Be the cowgirl you always knew you could be at one of the **"Jackaroo and Jillaroo schools"** in the Tamworth area. These crash courses in station-hand life teach students how to ride horses, pen sheep, train dogs, milk cows, lasso, and operate farm equipment. Upon completion, students receive certificates and are often offered help finding jobs. **Leconfield** (tel. 6769 4230) has highly recommended 11-day camps for $495 with free pick-up and drop-off from Tamworth. Get a taste for $60 per day, with a minimum of three days. **Echo Hills Station** (tel. 6769 4217 or 1800 810 242) offers a six-day course for $349 ($10 discount for VIP, YHA), breakfast included. **Oakey Creek** (tel. 6766 1698 or 1300 300 043) offers a same length program, price, and meal plan. They offer a 10% discount for YHA, YIP, and students. An additional week costs $229; the 10% discount applies to the second week, too. Oakey Creek has early Sunday morning pick-ups.

Outside of the January festival, don't expect to find much country music inspiration here. The **RSL Club** (tel. 6766 4661) behind Peel St. on Kable Ave. is the only club venue which regularly serves it up. On weekends, they have live entertainment. On the third Saturday of each month, the **Tamworth Country Theater** (tel. 1800 803 561) hosts a lively evening of country singing (tickets $15). Most pubs cater to a non-country clientele. The **Imperial** draws a younger crowd, and even a few celebrities in October, during its month-long outdoor beach-theme party (live rock music Thurs.-Sat. nights).

Armidale

Armidale is, at heart, a lovely small country town laced with creeklands and hilly side-streets, as comfortable as cocoa and Sesame Street on Saturday mornings. The town (pop. 22,000) was only granted city status because of its two cathedrals, which complement the many historical and architecturally significant buildings decorating its streets. The University of New England's campus is 5km from Armidale's center, but the annual infusion of students doesn't overpower the city. Residents in surrounding towns joke about Armidale's chilly winter weather, brisk because the city is perched near the top of the Great Dividing Range. But it's one of the few towns in the state with four distinct seasons, and July's chill can be cut with log fireplaces and patchwork quilts as easily as January's dry heat can be assuaged with swimming holes. Perfectly positioned at the beginning of "waterfall way," Armidale is convenient for exploring the many surrounding national parks.

Orientation and Practical Information Armidale's main drag is **Marsh St.** The **Visitors Centre** (tel. 6772 4655 or 1800 627 736; fax 6771 4486; email armvisit@northnet.com.au; http://www.com.au/neiss/armitour) and **bus terminal** are at 82 Marsh St., behind the Pizza Hut. (Visitors Center open Mon.-Fri. 9am-5pm, Sat. 9am-4pm, Sun. 10am-4pm. Luggage storage $1 per day.) One block up Marsh St. is the start of the **Beardy St. Mall,** Armidale's cluster of upscale shops and cafes. A supermarket, Kmart complex, and Woolworths are at the far end of the Mall, and **banks** and the **post office** are at the center.

Accommodations, Food, and Entertainment All accommodations can be booked through the visitors center. In addition to the listings below, rooms over pubs run $20-30, and for a splurge there are some lovely B&Bs near the city center. The **Wicklow Hotel** (tel. 6772 2421) is directly opposite the tourist office on the corner of Marsh and Dumaresq St. Referred to as the "pink pub" for its unusual facade, it's friendly and family-oriented (singles $20; doubles $30; showers $2).

A bit farther down the street is the **St. Kilda Hotel** (tel. 6772 4459), on the corner of Marsh and Rusden St. The rooms have wooden wardrobes and dressers (singles $22; doubles or twins $32; family rooms $40). The **Royal Hotel** (tel. 6772 2259) on the corner of Marsh and Beardy St. has singles for $30 and triples for $60, breakfast included. Two kilometers east of town on Grafton Rd., past the racecourse, is the **Pembroke Caravan Park** (tel. 6772 6470). The adjoining **YHA hostel** is packed with bunks. The grounds have a swimming pool, tennis courts, and a gorgeous hilly backdrop. (Dorms $14, tent sites $12, caravan sites $14.50. Cabins and on-site caravans available; price depends on season.)

Many of the pubs have bistros with cheap or all-you-can-eat meals. The **Wicklow's** $10 dinners are delicious; they also have $2 cappuccino and freshly squeezed orange juice. In the winter, you can eat in front of a log fire. The historic **New England Hotel,** on the corner of Faulkner and Beardy St., has great steak dinners and has been serving beer since it opened in 1857. Both **Rumors** and **Cafe Midale** on the Mall are wildly popular, have outside seating, and serve $4-8 sandwiches. For a cup of coffee with a country feel, nothing beats the **Walnut Tree** at 130 Marsh St. Housed in a Hansel and Gretel-like cottage, it has mobiles hanging from the rafters and small pottery bowls on each table (open daily).

Students hang out at the campus bistro, and also frequent pubs in town. **Sevens,** on the east mall, is a popular student night spot. **Tattersall's Hotel** brings in live entertainment on the weekends, also catering to students. The **New England Hotel** and the **ex-Serviceman's Club** are popular for their cheap drinks. The **Belgrave Twin Cinema** (tel. 6772 2856) screens recent releases and art films daily. Armidale's biggest festival is the annual **Wool Expo,** a one-week event in early May.

Sights and Entertainment The visitors center has guides for the 3km or 6.2km **Heritage Walking Tours,** covering 35 National Trust buildings in the city, and the two-hour **Heritage Drive,** a 25km tour of many of the same buildings, and more. Following Marsh St. south and up the hill leads to the intersection with Kentucky St., and the front entrance of the much-praised **New England Regional Art Museum** (tel. 6772 5255). The museum has over 3000 paintings, but limited display space, so exhibits rotate every six weeks. The largest collection is by Howard Hinton, a huge benefactor and the main reason the museum was built. In the early part of the century, Hinton shipped crates of paintings to the Armidale Teachers' College, across the street from the museum's current site. Over a period of 50 years, the College's walls became clothed in paintings, literally hung floor to ceiling for lack of space. The **Coventry collection** has more contemporary Australian paintings. (Museum open Mon.-Sat. 10am-5pm, Sun. 1-5pm. Admission $5, concessions $2.) As you come out of the art museum, on your right is the **Aboriginal Cultural Centre and Keeping Place** (tel. 6771 1249; open Mon.-Fri. 9am-5pm, Sat.-Sun. 2-5pm; admission $3, concessions $1.50). The **Folk Museum** on the corner of Faulkner and Rusden St. stores a small collection of cultural and architectural objects and souvenirs, including a reproduction of a colonial house and a room devoted to Aboriginal art (open daily 1-4pm; free).

Horseback riding tours can be arranged through **Harlow Park** (tel. 6778 4631) or **Beambolong** (tel. 6771 2019). **Wilderness Rides** (tel. 6778 4631) offers tours for experienced riders through the New England Blue Mountain Gorge. The visitors center has information and maps on New England fishing; **Fly Fish New England** (tel. 6772 5085) or **Matts Sport Safari** (tel. 6772 8689) offer tours.

A 5.7km cycleway runs along Dumaresq Creek to the University. Some of the National Park sites can be reached by daytrips along the side of main roads. **Armidale**

Bicycle Center (tel. 6772 3718) and the **University Sports Union** (tel. 6773 2316) rent bikes for about $10 per day.

National Parks near Armidale

If you have a car, consider taking the route along **Waterfall Way,** the road from Armidale to the coast. Starting from Armidale, you'll pass a hydroelectric dam at the **Oxley River National Park;** drive through **Hillgrove,** now a nearly abandoned mining town; go past **Long Point,** with accessible and spectacular dry rainforests and views of gorges; see **Wollomombi Gorge,** with the highest waterfalls in NSW; pass the ancient granite boulders of **Cathedral Rock;** and finish at **Ebor Falls** in Guy Fawkes National Park, 79km from Armidale. Call the Armidale National Parks and Wildlife Service (NPWS) district office (tel. 6773 7120) for more information.

Over 90,000 hectares make up **Oxley Wild Rivers National Park,** whose starring attractions are deep gorges and over 750 plant species. **Gara Gorge** is 16km from Armidale on Castledoyle Rd. and makes for a great day's bike ride, punctuated by a dive into the Blue Hole swimming area. This site of Australia's first large hydroelectric project has picnic and BBQ areas, plus marked walking tracks. **Long Point** has 1.5km and 5km walks through unique dry rainforest. **Wollomombi Gorge,** 90km from Armidale on the Grafton Rd., has, at 220m, the highest waterfalls in NSW. **Dangars Gorge,** another spectacular waterfall, splashes down 21km southeast of Armidale. The area has three easy and worthwhile walks leading from the parking lot. Other points of interest in the park are Budds Mare, Apsley Gorge, and Tia Gorge. Call the Armidale office (tel. 6773 7211) for more information.

Cathedral Rock National Park, 70km east of Armidale off the Armidale-Grafton Rd., is best known for its granite boulders, wildflowers, and eucalypt forests. Park residents include grey kangaroos, wallabies, cockatoos, and wedge-tailed eagles. Three walking tracks range from 1km to 10.4km. Picnic and camping facilities are available at Barokee and Native Dog Creek Rest Areas. Contact the Dorrigo Park ranger at 6657 2309.

The nearly 30,000-hectare **New England National Park** encompasses the New England Plateau and its nearly vertical cliffs, which make up the Great Dividing Range. Banksia Point, Wrights Lookout, and Point Lookout have spectacular views; on a clear day, you can see the coast from Point Lookout. Easy walks range from 15 minutes to three and a half hours. The park contains nearly 500 species of plants living in swamp and heath. Lower areas of the park forest are sub-tropical and listed with World Heritage; the ridgetops are covered with eucalypt forest. Wildlife include platypus, echidna, and over 100 species of birds. **Camping** is permitted in the Thungutti camping area; there are also three spiffy fully self-contained cabins; contact the Dorrigo ranger for details at 6657 2309. The park is accessible on the Armidale-Grafton Rd., 85km east of Armidale.

Northern New England

The New England Highway continues north from Armidale to the Queensland border. On the far side, the town of **Stanthorpe** lies in the Southern Downs (see p. 295).

Glen Innes With street signs in both Gaelic and English, Glen Innes (pop. 6500), two-and-a-half hours north of Tamworth off the New England Hwy., bills itself as **Australia's Celtic Capital.** Hey, everybody's gotta be something. The tradition is celebrated each year with the Celtic Festival, held the first weekend in May. People come from as far off as Sydney to mix with the descendants of the first Scottish settlers, sing, dance, and celebrate all things Celtic. The **tourist office** (tel. 6732 2397) is on the New England Hwy., called Church St. in town. **Amron Bed and Breakfast,** 35 Lindsay Ave. (tel. 6732 2170), boasts a pretty sunroom and a central location (singles $35; doubles $60). Farther out of town on Bullock Mountain Rd., **Boolabinda Homestead** (tel. 6732 2215), is an activity-oriented accommodation with a campground (bunks $10; cabins $20).

Tenterfield In 1889, Sir Henry Parkes spoke at the Tenterfield School of Arts, explaining his vision of Australia as "one nation." This speech, some argue, was the spark for the eventual Federation of Australian States, established in 1901. Today, Tenterfield (pop. 3500) preserves its history through its buildings. One such structure is the Saddlery, immortalized in a song by the late Peter Allen. Bald Rock and Boonoo Boonoo National Parks are a short car ride away, and the Queensland border (see **Stanthorpe,** p. 295) lies farther north on the New England Hwy. The Tenterfield **tourist office,** 157 Rouse St. (tel. 6736 1082), is open daily 9:30am to 5pm. Near the old railway station, the YHA-affiliated **Tenterfield Lodge** (tel. 6736 1477), shows off its National Trust building listing (dorms $15; doubles $35). On Manners St., 1km west of the post office, is the **Tenterfield Lodge Caravan Park** (tel. 6736 1477; tent sites $10, on-site caravans $22).

Bald Rock National Park is just north of Tenterfield (take Logan St.) and becomes Girraween National Park as it crosses the Queensland border to the west. In the northwest corner of the park, along the access road, travelers who can't visit Uluru make do with **Bald Rock,** the largest exposed granite rock in Australia. A two-hour, 2km walking trek leads to the summit. South Bald Rock, a smaller version of the rock, is roughly 6km southwest along the border road. Short term camping is permitted at the rest area below Bald Rock.

Boonoo Boonoo National Park (pronounced, inexplicably, "Bunner Bernoo") is 22km north of Tenterfield and immediately north of Bald Rock off Woodenbong Rd. The Boonoo Boonoo River, once mined for gold, winds through a 210m deep gorge. During rainy seasons, the waterfall down the gorge is spectacular, and can be viewed from a nearby platform. The park has grey kangaroos, open forest, and, in the spring, wildflowers. Picnic areas are provided and camping is allowed. For camping or other information on either Bald Rock or Boonoo Boonoo Park, contact the ranger in Glen Innes (tel. 6732 5133).

SOUTH COAST OF NEW SOUTH WALES

The coastal towns south of Sydney, strung together by the Princes Hwy., are far less touristed than their northern counterparts. As a result, many towns remain focused on industry. Between the industrial factories of the Wollongong area, the oyster beds of Bateman's Bay, and the famous Bega cheese factory, however, surfing beaches and scenic drives provide ample escapist distraction. Cool winters cause the area to be particularly deserted between June and August, but the windy coastline does retain a certain charm.

Wollongong

Wollongong (pronounced woolen-gong) suffers from the same city-versus-town identity crisis that plagues many mid-sized cities. New South Wales's third largest metropolitan area, Wollongong has a city center small enough to be walkable yet urban enough to be unattractive. The mall at the center of town is anything but quaint. A well-deserved reputation for industry, based on the proximity of Port Kembla's steel, copper, coal, electricity, and grain plants compounds Wollongong's image problems. Still, Wollongong's location between the green peaks of the Illawarra Escarpment and the foamy blue of the Pacific Ocean creates diversions enough to fill a short stay with pre-industrial outdoor entertainment.

ORIENTATION AND PRACTICAL INFORMATION

The Princes Hwy. leads directly into Wollongong, becoming Flinders St. just north of the city center. When Flinders St. ends by merging into Keira St., you've reached downtown. The north-south streets to remember in this area are **Keira St., Church St., Kembla St.,** and **Corrimal St.,** moving from west to east. The cross streets

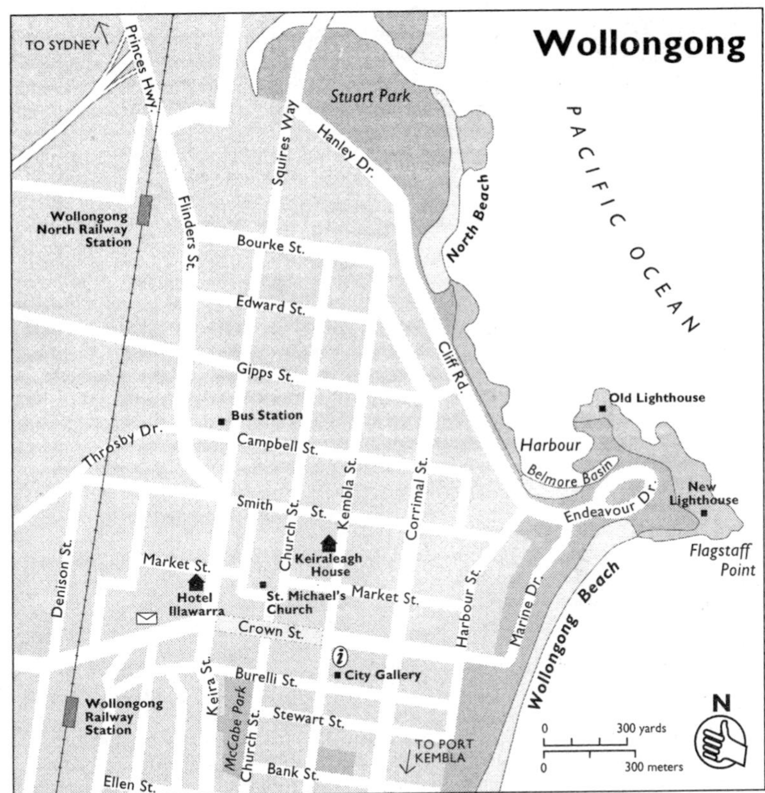

Campbell St., Smith St., Market St., Crown St., and **Burelli St.,** progressing southward, form a fairly neat grid. The **pedestrian shopping mall** on Crown St., between Keira and Kembla St., is the city's commercial heart. **Buses** arrive at the Wollongong City Coach Terminus (tel. 4226 1022; fax 4228 9090), on the corner of Keira and Campbell St. (open Mon.-Fri. 7:30am-5:30pm, Sat. 7:30am-2:30pm; Sun. buses meet passengers outside the station). **Pioneer Motor Service** (tel. 1300 368 100) conducts daily buses north to Sydney (2-3 per day, 2hr., $11) and south to Nowra (2-3 per day, 1¼hr., $11), while **Greyhound Pioneer** (tel. 13 20 30) sends one more expensive bus to Sydney daily ($18) except Sunday and another to Nowra daily ($18) except Saturday. **Murray's** (tel. 13 22 51) covers the road to Canberra (1 per day, 3½hr., $28). **CityRail trains** stop at Wollongong City Station on Station St., and continue on to stops at Port Kembla ($1.80, off-peak return $2.20), Berry ($5.20, $6.20), and Bombaderry, the closest stop to Nowra ($5.80, $6.80). Heading north, stops include Fairy Meadow ($1.60, $1.80), Corrimal ($1.80, $2.20), Bulli ($2, $2.40), Thirroul ($2, $2.40), Coal Cliff ($2.80, $3.40), and, finally, Sydney's Central Station ($6.60, $7.80). Check the City Rail information line (tel. 13 15 00) for train times before setting out; trains come to these more distant stops only every one to two hours.

The corner of Keira and Burelli St., at the south end of the Gateway Shopping Center, figures in to most **local bus routes.** Two companies, **Rutty's** (tel. 4271 1322; open Mon.-Fri. 7:30am-5pm) and **John J. Hill** (tel. 4229 4911), split the local area, so there's no central information line or standard fare for Wollongong buses. Timetables for both companies' services are displayed at the Gateway stop and can be picked up at Tourism Wollongong.

The staff at **Tourism Wollongong,** 93 Crown St. (tel. 4227 5545; fax 4228 0344), on the corner of Kembla St., offer good advice for travelers with varied interests (open Mon.-Fri. 9am-5pm, Sat. 9am-4pm, Sun. 10am-4pm). To pick up mail, visit the **post office** (tel. 4228 9322), in the Gateway Shopping Center, on Keira St. between Crown and Burelli St. (open Mon.-Fri. 9am-5pm).

ACCOMMODATIONS AND CAMPING

The growing backpacker market has not significantly impacted Wollongong's accommodation selection, leaving pub/hotels as the standard budget option. Both pub lodgings listed here have sinks in every room, baths in the hallways, and noise in the evenings.

Keiraleagh House, 60 Kembla St. (tel. 4228 6765 or 018 163 368), between Market and Smith St., is the least expensive and most friendly option. The big green house shows its age, but there's a kitchen, dining area, TV lounge, and friendly curly-coated retriever. Laundry facilities. Live-in owners can be reached on their mobile phones if not around the house. Check out 10am. 3-bed dorms $15; singles $20. Cereal, toast, coffee, and tea included. Key deposit $10.

Hotel Illawarra (tel. 4229 5411), on the corner of Market and Keira St. Rooms are less swanky than the bar downstairs, but they're spacious and tidy. The bartender can direct you to the reception. Check-out 9am. Singles $25; doubles $40. Laundry $2 per wash or dry. Key deposit $20.

Dicey Riley's, 333 Crown St. (tel. 4229 1952), also lets rooms above the pub. Ask at the bar Sun.-Tues. 10am-10pm, Wed. 10am-11pm, Thurs. 10am-midnight, Fri.-Sat. 10am-1am. Singles $25; doubles $40. Key deposit $10. Free laundry.

Wollongong Surf Leisure Resort, on Pioneer Rd. in Fairy Meadow (tel. 4283 6999; fax 4285 1620), is located 4.5km north of downtown Wollongong, and brings camping as close to Wollongong as it gets. Travelers with cars should follow the Princes Hwy. north to Elliot's Rd., take a right, and then go left on Pioneer Rd. after crossing the bridge. It's a 10min. walk from the Fairy Meadow CityRail. With a convenience store, pool, spa, and steam room, the park can't really be called natural. Tent sites are grassy patches with easy beach access. Office, store, pool area, and game room open Mon.-Sat. 8am-9pm, Sun. 8am-6pm. Tent sites for 2 people vary seasonally $15-26, with electric hook-up $18-30. Each additional person $5 per night. Hot water 10¢ per 5min. Laundry $2 per wash or dry. Bicycle rental $4 per hr. Wheelchair-accessible sites and rest rooms available. Key deposit for toilet and shower blocks $10.

Wollongong City Caravan Parks operates 3 less expensive and less proximal camping areas: **Corrimal Beach** (tel. 4285 5688 or 018 426 828), on Lake Parade, in Corrimal, about 6km north of Wollongong; **Bulli Beach,** 1 Farrell Rd. (tel. 4285 5677 or 018 426 829), in Bulli, another 5km north; **Windang Beach** (tel. 4297 3166 or 018 426 827), on Fern Rd., in Windang, about 15km south of Wollongong. Each is located just off a patrolled ocean beach, and the Windang area abuts Lake Illawarra on its other side. Tent sites for 2 people $15, in winter $12; with electrical hook-up $19, $15. Each additional person over 5 years old $5.

FOOD AND NIGHTLIFE

Eating cheaply in Wollongong is made easy by the large selection of downtown cafes and sandwich shops. **Woolworths,** on the corner of Kembla and Burelli St., provides the grocery option and some of the city's most convenient serving hours (open Mon.-Fri. 7:30am-midnight, Sat. 7:30am-9pm, Sun. 9am-6pm). The restaurants lining Keira St. north of Market St. cover a wide variety of cuisines with main dishes averaging $9-12. The most affordable stop on these blocks, **Food World Gourmet Cafe,** 148 Keira St. (tel. 4225 9655), serves healthy platefuls of tasty Chinese and Vietnamese dishes for $5.50-7.50 (open daily 11am-8pm). Further north, **Benny's Place,** 108 Keira St. (tel. 4227 3755), has a nicer decor and a chicken in lemon and ginger wine sauce ($8.80) that's worth the extra dollars (open daily 11am-11pm). **Tannous,** 52 Crown St. (tel. 4228 3213), on the corner of Corrimal St., gives you as much tabouli as you can safely wrap a pita around for the great low price of $2.50 (tabouli plate with hummus, red cabbage, and a basket of bread, $4.50). The bougag (80¢) makes an excellent after-dinner gift to yourself or a loved one (BYO; open daily 8:30am-late). For a picnic lunch at North Beach, stop in at **North Beach Coffee Cove** (tel. 4229 7876), on Bourke St. half a block from the beach, and pick up sandwiches ($2.50-4.50), potato wedges ($2), or fruit salad ($2-5; open daily 7:30am-5pm). **Seaview Fish Market** (tel. 4228 8515), at the shore end of Belmore Basin on Wollongong Harbour, has all the fixings for a do-it-yourself fish feast including lemon, lime, batter, and tartar sauce (open daily 7:30am-5pm).

The **Illawara Hotel** and **Dicey Riley's** (see **Accommodations and Camping,** above) both draw crowds throughout the week. Illawara Hotel, centrally located and recently redecorated, takes a more urban approach with interesting cocktails and loud dance music. The Irish theme at Dicey Riley's is enlivened by trivia, pool competitions, cover bands, and occasional Irish performers. The earthy **Plant Room Cafe** (tel. 4227 3030), on Crown St., just east of Denison St., has acoustic performers and buffet dinners on Wednesdays ($15 for dinner and the show). Fridays are reserved for jazz jams. (BYO. Vegetarian and vegan selections. Open Mon.-Fri. noon-2pm and 6-10pm. Entertainment starts around 7:30 or 8pm.) Up-and-coming rock bands play at **Oxford Tavern,** 47 Crown St. (tel. 4228 3892; fax 4226 9755), every Thursday through Saturday (open Mon.-Sat. 10am-3am, Sun. 10am-10pm).

SIGHTS AND ACTIVITIES

In 1988, some well-paid public relations geniuses and a team of landscapers set out to turn the industrial complex in Port Kembla, 3km south of Wollongong, into a tourist attraction. This sleight of hand resulted in **Australia's Industry World,** a renamed industrial complex with popular and informative weekly tours. Call Tourism Wollongong for details on the free Friday morning tour, or pick up the self-guided driving tour map at the tourist office. By displaying the work of regional visual artists in changing exhibits, the **Wollongong City Gallery** (tel. 4228 7500; fax 4226 5530), on the corner of Kembla and Burelli St., gives visitors a more conventional view of the creative force (open Tues.-Fri. 10am-5pm, Sat.-Sun. noon-4pm; free). The **Illawarra Museum,** 11 Market St. (tel. 4228 7770, 4228 0158, or 4229 8225), east of Corrimal St., covers the history of Wollongong and the surrounding area with exhibits and period room recreations from the late 1800s (open Thurs. noon-3pm, Sat.-Sun. 1-4pm; admission $2, students $1, children 50¢).

Wollongong's **harbor** is quite possibly its nicest feature. The small, sandy cove shelters both sailboats and the fishing fleet that docks in Belmore Basin. The old lighthouse, visible from the beach, adds an air of old-time nautical charm that's absent from the rest of the city. Just north, **surfers** wait for waves at **North Beach. Stuart Park,** at the end of Cliff Rd., inland from North Beach, has picnic areas, a cricket oval, and plenty of open space. **North Beach Bicycle Hire** (tel. 018 040 722), on Stuart Park, outside the Novotel on Cliff Road, rents bikes on weekends and holidays ($6 per hr., 6hr. $30; weekday bookings available for groups only).

South of Port Kembla, **Lake Illawarra** draws crowds from Wollongong when the weather is good. Most of the lake beaches are suitable for swimming, and the area around the mouth of the lake is especially good for children. **Windang Boat Shed,** 1 Judbooley Pde. (tel. 4296 2015), on the lake in Windang, has motor boats and rowboats for use by the day or by the hour (open Mon.-Fri. 7am-sunset, Sat.-Sun. 8:30am-sunset). Train service gets you to the Port Kembla CityRail Station ($1.80, off-peak return $2.20), just a short walk from the lake. Otherwise, John J. Hill buses #50 and 51 run from the Wollongong City Station or the Gateway Shopping Center to Windang Bridge (fare approximately $3), also a short walk to the lake. From Port Kembla Station, the **ocean beaches** of Port Beach (patrolled at least Oct.-April) and MM Beach are also nearby.

■ Near Wollongong

The **Bulli Pass** takes the Princes Hwy. inland to the Southern Freeway, 12km north of Wollongong, and provides an excellent view of the area from its crest. Down at sea level, **Bulli Point,** also know as Sandon Point, and **Austinmer Beach** have some of the area's best **surfing** (take CityRail to Bulli or Thirroul; from Wollongong $2, off-peak return $2.40). **Thirroul,** between Bulli and Austinmer, was the temporary home of English writer D.H. Lawrence for several months in 1922. During this time, Lawrence wrote most of *Kangaroo,* and his house (at 3 Craig St.) and the shore behind it are recognizably featured in the novel. Because the home is privately owned, it is inaccessible to the public, but the beach is open for strolling and fine for literary speculation. Lawrence Hargrave Dr., along the coast north of Bulli Pass, winds past several breathtaking views before reaching the lookout at **Bald Hill,** north of Stanwell Park, perhaps the best of all the views on this stretch of coast. It was here that Lawrence Hargrave contributed to the development of aviation by experimenting with box kites. Today, the hill continues its service as an aeronautical jumping-off point in the employ of area **hang gliders.**

The Illawarra Escarpment defines Wollongong's inland border. The nearest peak, **Mt. Keira,** is a short drive from town on Mt. Keira Rd., but cannot be reached by bus or train (taxi fare $7-8 from city center). At the top, bushwalking trails and a panoramic overlook await.

In the southern suburb of Berkeley, on the north shore of Lake Illawarra, the largest Buddhist Temple in the southern hemisphere, **Nan Tien Temple** (tel. 4272 0600), on Berkeley Rd., welcomes visitors (wheelchair accessible; call for visiting hours). Rutty's bus #34 goes right to the temple from the Gateway Shopping Center ($1.80).

Kiama and Around

Under the right conditions, when the wind is high and the seas are running from the southeast, water washing into a rock cave in Kiama is forced upward through a hole in the rocks to heights of 20-35m. The awesome spray at Kiama's Blowhole draws visitors for miles around. But even if the wind doesn't comply, Kiama and the surrounding area remain good places to stop. Forty kilometers south of Wollongong via the Princes Hwy. or the F6 Freeway, Kiama and the nearby beaches at Gerringong and Gerroa lie conveniently within Sydney's CityRail daytrip territory.

Practical Information The center of tourist life in Kiama is Blowhole Point, where you'll find both the natural oddity of the same name and the **Kiama Visitors Center** (tel. 4232 3322 or 1800 803 892; open daily 9am-5pm). The **CityRail station** is located near the base of Blowhole Point off of Bong Bong St. (to Sydney $10.60, off-peak return $12.80; Wollongong $3.80, $4.60; Gerringong $1.80, $2.20; Bombaderry $3.20, $3.80). Daily **Pioneer Motor Service** (tel. 1300 368 100) buses depart for Sydney via Wollongong from the Kiama Leagues Club, on the corner of Terralong and Gipps St. (to Sydney 2-3 per day, 3¼hr., $16; Wollongong 2-3 per day, 30min., $11). The **post office** (tel. 4232 1389), on the corner of Terralong and Manning St. bears the postal code 2533.

Accommodations and Food The **Kiama Backpackers Hostel,** 31 Bong Bong St. (tel. 4233 1881), right outside the CityRail Station, looks like a kindergarten building with beds. (Kitchen, TV, parking, free use of bikes, fishing poles, and surfboards. Wheelchair accessible. Reception open daily 8am-late evening. Dorms $15; doubles and twins $35; singles $20. Private rooms cost a few dollars more in summer. Weekly: 7th night free. Key deposit $10.) Six kilometers south, a short walk from Werri Beach, in Gerringong, the **Nestor House YHA Hostel** (tel. 4234 1249), on Fern St., occupies a building on the grounds of a Uniting Church. The rooms are clean and comfortable but spare. (Big new kitchen. No TV. Linen available. Reception open daily 5-8pm. No check-ins after 10pm without prior agreement. 4-6 bed dorms $13, under 18 $6.50.)

Behind the visitors center on Blowhole Point, the **Kiama Coast Holiday Park** (tel. 4232 2707) rents tent or caravan sites perched over the ocean and is perfect for an Aussie Christmas party. (Summer rates $16 for 2, with electricity $18. Each additional person $4. Winter rates $9.50 for 1, $12.50 for 2, with electricity $14.50; seniors $8.50, with electricity $10.50. A/C or electric heater $5. Hot showers 10¢. Key deposit $10.) Other Kiama Coast Holiday Parks operating with the same fees and services include **Surf Beach** (tel. 4232 1791), on Bourroul St. near Kendalls Point, **Kendalls Beach** (tel. 4232 1790; wheelchair-accessible sites and restrooms available), on Bonaira St., **Werri Beach** (tel. 4232 1285; wheelchair accessible), on Bridges Rd. in Gerringong, and **Seven Mile Beach** (tel. 4232 1340), on Crooked River Rd. in Gerroa. For a tasty coastal treat, locals name the fish and chips at **Kiama Harbour Take Away** as the best on the point (in the beige building nearest the mainland as you head onto Blowhole Point; fish and chips $5, pelican food $2; open daily 10am-5pm).

Sights Every visitor to Kiama should give the **Blowhole** a chance to do its trick. But if it just won't blow, there are plenty of other places to go. The **natural rock pool** at the neck of Blowhole Point is a good swimming spot for both children and adults. A second rock pool, across Kiama Harbour from the north shore of Blowhole Point, is deeper and more suitable for serious swimmers. On the other side of Pheasant Point, experienced surfers brave the rip tides at Bombo Beach. The protected area inside the next headland to the north goes by two names. Sightseers interested in the striking rock formations which mark the spot call it **Cathedral Rock.** Surfers know it as the **Boneyard,** and, despite the menacing nickname, it's a popular spot for catching waves. To the south, surfers and swimmers frequent the patrolled Surf Beach at Kendalls Point. **Little Blowhole,** on Marsden Head at the end of Tingira Crescent, may be the redemption of disappointed Blowhole-watchers. Set off by waves from the northeast, Little Blowhole erupts more regularly than its neighbor. The next major stop on a surfer's tour of the Kiama area comes 5km south at **Werri Beach** in Gerringong. Seven Mile Beach, stretching long and sandy south from Gerroa, was the starting point for Charles Kingsford-Smith's 1933 flight to New Zealand, the first commercial flight between the two countries.

The **Saddleback Mountain Lookout** offers travelers with cars views that extend from Wollongong toJervis Bay on clear days. From Manning St., turn west on Bonaira St., which becomes Saddleback Mountain Rd. at the edge of town. Be careful not to get on the Princes Hwy. A sign 2km outside of town will direct you to turn south onto the road which goes up the mountain. Farther west, accessible by Jamberoo Mountain Rd. by way of Hwy. 48 through Jamberoo, the **Barren Ground Nature Reserve** contains several moderate hiking trails ranging in length from 2km to 19km. The area is known for the presence of several species of rare birds. Turning off Jamberoo Mountain Rd. about 1km from the highway will lead you to **Minnamurra Rainforest** (tel. 4236 0469), in Budderoo National Park, and more bushwalking options (park open daily 9am-5pm, rainforest access until 4pm; entrance $7.50 per car).

Shoalhaven

The area known as the City of Shoalhaven stretches from Berry in the north to Durras North in the south and includes inland areas extending through **Morton National Park.** Encompassing both the unusual white beaches of Jervis Bay and the renowned bushwalking trail at Pigeon House Mountain, Shoalhaven provides outdoor travelers with a variety of options only two hours from Sydney or Canberra.

Berry On the Princes Hwy. 15km south of Gerringong, Berry is a quiet, historic village known for its antiques and craft shops. Pub accommodation at the **Hotel Berry** (tel. 4464 1011), on the Princes Hwy. in the middle of town, rises above the average with comfortable rooms, floral couches, and a patio overlooking the shops on the main street. (Tea and coffee facilities, shared baths. Singles $55, Mon.-Fri. $45; doubles $60, $50. Inquire at the bar daily from 10am.) **CityRail** trains from Sydney

($12.40, off-peak return $14.60; from Wollongong $5.20, $6.20) stop just outside of town on Station St. Take Alexandria St. into the center of town for a browse.

Kangaroo Valley The steep and winding drive to Kangaroo Valley is lovely and scenic but sometimes rough, making the town even less populous than Berry. If you go, be sure to continue through to the northwest end of town, where the sandstone **Hampden Bridge** spans the Kangaroo River. The bridge, built in 1898, is Australia's oldest suspension bridge. Located at the south side of the bridge, **Kangaroo Valley Safaris** (tel. 018 22 1169; after hours 4465 1502; fax 4465 1636), on the corner of Jenanter Dr., organizes canoe camping trips on the river and rents canoes, kayaks, and camping gear for personalized excursions. Kangaroo Valley is, first and foremost, the land of the B&B, but **Glenmack Caravan Park and Camping** (tel. 4465 1372), on the main road just west of town, deigns to provide a less expensive option. (Toilets, showers. Reception open daily 9am-early evening. Tent sites on an open, grassy area $9 per person, in winter $6. Cabins for 2 people $35 in winter. Each additional person $6.) Eighteen kilometers beyond Kangaroo Valley on Moss Vale Rd., **Fitzroy Falls** is a spectacular sight and one of the few places where Morton National Park can be entered on its eastern side. The **Fitzroy Falls Visitor Centre** (tel. 4887 7270) has maps for local and regional bushwalking trails (open daily 8:30am-5pm).

Nowra and Bombaderry The population centers of the Shoalhaven area sit on the Princes Hwy. on opposite shores of the Shoalhaven River. Bombaderry, in the north, is home to the **Shoalhaven Tourist Centre,** 245 Princes Hwy. (tel. 4421 0778 or 1800 024 261; open daily 9am-5pm). The **National Parks and Wildlife Service (NPWS),** 55 Graham St. (tel. 4423 9800), has an office in Nowra, on the south shore, with information on parks throughout the Shoalhaven (open Mon.-Fri. 8:30am-5pm). Because it is close to both Berry and Kangaroo Valley in the north and the Jervis Bay area to the south, many people choose to stay in Nowra when exploring the area. **M&M's Guesthouse,** 1a Scenic Drive (tel. 4422 8006; fax 4422 8006), on the grounds of the Riverhaven Motel, off to the right just across the bridge from Bombaderry, offers shared or private rooms with shared bathrooms and a light breakfast for $20 per person. (TV, pool table, fireplace, laundry. No kitchen. Reception open daily 8am-evening.) Overlooking the Shoalhaven River, tent camping sites at the **Nowra Animal Park** (tel. 4421 3949), on Rockhill Rd., are the area's cheapest and most scenic. (Toilets, hot showers, picnic tables. Reception open daily 7:30am-5pm. Sites for 2 $19, in winter $13. Each additional person $3. Rock climbers pay $4.50 per person year-round.) Take a right on Illaroo Rd., just before the bridge to Nowra. Follow McMahon's Rd. from the roundabout, and take a left on Rockhill Rd. The park itself is worth a look, especially for overseas travelers who haven't seen the unusual Australian fauna in a natural setting yet (open daily 7:30am-8pm; admission $6, seniors $5, children $3; campers pay once and get unlimited access). The owner can direct you to local **rock climbing** areas. **CityRail** stops in Bombaderry on Railway St., a 15-minute walk from the tourist center by way of Bunberra St. (To Sydney $12.40, off-peak return $14.60; Wollongong $5.80, $6.80.) Heading south from Nowra, the **Australian Naval Aviation Museum** (tel. 4421 1920), 8km southeast of Nowra on Albatross Rd., makes an interesting stop for flight enthusiasts and history buffs (requested donation $2; open daily 10am-4pm).

Jervis Bay Almost entirely enclosed by its northern headland, the Beecroft Peninsula, Jervis Bay is a serene body of water surrounded by strikingly white beaches. For a secluded escape, stop at any of the towns along the shore and wander down the sand until the scenery suits your taste. Hyams Beach claims to have the world's whitest sand. **Huskisson,** 24km southeast of Nowra, is a good base for a stay. For tourist information, visit the **Huskisson Trading Post** (tel. 4441 5241), on the corner of Owen and Dent St. **Leisure Haven Caravan Park** (tel. 4441 5046), 1km outside of town on Woollamia Rd., charges $10 for two-person tent sites in a wooded area on Currambene Creek (laundry facilities; reception open daily 8am-evening; sites with electricity $12; each additional person $3; key deposit $20). The **Husky Pub** (tel. 4441 5001), on Owen St. overlooking the Bay, is the town's social center and the source of an excellent all-you-can-eat lunch-time salad bar ($4; burger with fries $5; open for lunch Mon.-Sat. noon-2pm, Sun. noon-2:30pm; bar open daily 10am-late). Too quiet for surfing, Huskisson gains its notoriety among fishermen who troll the Currambene Creek. **Husky Hire-a-Boat** (tel. 4441 6200) will rent you a boat, deliver it to a local boat ramp, and lend you a rod if you want to try your luck ($15 per hr., 2hr. min.; calls taken daily 9am-5pm). On the southern end of the bay, **Booderee National Park,** formerly Jervis Bay National Park, has three **camping** areas: Greenpatch and Bristol Point on Jervis Bay, and Cave Beach on Wreck Bay to the south. (toilets, water, cold showers; no electricity; tent sites for up to 5 people $10, in winter $8). The **Visitors Centre** (tel. 4443 0977; fax 4443 8302), just beyond the park entry gates, accepts campsite bookings and inquiries Monday through Friday between 10am and 4pm. (Visitors Centre open daily 9am-4pm. Park entrance fee $5 per car.) The park's recent change of name stems from a shift of management from the Commonwealth Government to the Wreck Bay Aboriginal community. The traditional Aboriginal name for the area means "bay of plenty" and will be applied to the **Botanic Gardens** (tel. 4442 1122) inside the park as well (open Mon.-Fri. 8am-4pm, Sun. 10am-5pm; free).

Ulladulla The next major service center moving south through the Shoalhaven is at Ulladulla. There's a **Shoalhaven Tourist Information Centre** (tel. 4455 1269 or 1800 024 261), on the Princes Hwy. in the Civic Centre (open Mon.-Fri. 10am-5pm, Sat.-Sun. 9am-5pm). **Pioneer Motor Service** (tel. 1300 368 100) buses stop at the Marlin Hotel on the way south to Bateman's Bay (2-3 per day, 45min., $9) and Bega (3-4hr., $25). Northbound buses to Nowra (2-3 per day, 1hr., $12) and Sydney (4½hr., $24) pause at the Traveland Travel Agency. **Greyhound Pioneer** (tel. 13 20 30) runs the same routes once per day for more money.

The local hostel, **South Coast Backpackers,** 63 Princes Hwy. (tel. 4454 0500), between Narrawallee and North St., was closed for minor renovations when this book was being written. Check it out and decide for yourself. (Kitchen, TV, sundeck, laundry, off-street parking. Reception open daily 7:30am-9:30pm. Call for rates.) At the end of South St., **Holiday Haven Tourist Park** (tel./fax 4455 2457) reserves ample oceanfront space for tent camping. Extras include hot showers, toilets, gas BBQs (20¢), laundry facilities, a pool, and access to a secluded beach nearby. (Reception open daily 8am-9pm. Check-out 10am. Sites for 2 $21, with electricity $24; in winter $13, $16. Each additional person over 4 years old $5.)

The people at the **Ulladulla Dive Shop,** 10 Wason St. (tel. 4455 5303), can give advice on diving in the area or take you out themselves. (Gear rental $50 per day. Trips with gear $60 for 1 dive, $90 for 2. Open daily 7am-7pm; in winter Mon.-Fri. 9am-5pm, Sat.-Sun. 8am-5pm.) Bushwalkers generally stop in Ulladulla on the way south to the **Pigeon House Walk.** Turn off the Princes Hwy. onto Wheelbarrow Rd. 3km south of Burrill Lake. The trailhead is located at a picnic area 26km farther on. The walk, which involves some ladder climbing to reach the summit, is a strenuous 5km round-trip affair, but the view at the top is a knock-out. The nearby lakes, Burill and Conjola, have nice swimming beaches, and Mollymook Beach, just north of town, is good for surfing.

Murramarang National Park The last piece of Shoalhaven coastline is located within Murramarang National Park, tucked away from the Princes Hwy. at the far end of a 30-minute drive over mostly unpaved roads. An unserviced campground is located at **Pebbly Beach** (tel. 4478 6006 to book for summer use; in winter first-come, first-served), and there are caravan parks and cabin accommodations at several other locations in the park. Tent camping is cheapest at the Pebbly Beach camping area (sites for 2 $10; each additional person up to 6 people $2; plus a park use fee of $7.50) or at **Moore's Pioneer Caravan Park** (tel. 4478 6010), at Depot Beach (sites $4, plus $3 per person; hot showers 20¢ per 3min; office open daily 9am-9pm). At the southernmost point in the Shoalhaven half of Murramarang Park, **Durras North** looks onto Durras Lake and a beautiful windswept ocean beach. At dawn and dusk each day, kangaroos gather here to frolic in the sand. **Durras Lake North Caravan Park** (tel. 4478 6072), the first of several caravan parks at the end of Durras Rd., is clean and just meters from the kangaroo gathering place. (Hot showers 20¢. Tent sites $7. Caravan for 1-3 $14. Store and reception open daily 8:30am-5pm, but you can check in until 11pm.)

Bateman's Bay to Bega

Bateman's Bay, about 10km south of Durras Lake on the Princes Hwy., marks a change in the NSW coast. Traveling out of the City of Shoalhaven, the towns feel a little more industrial and less tourist-oriented. You'll still find beautiful beaches, good surf, and all of the necessary travel services, but the economic focus in this region is on fishing or, further south, on dairy farming, rather than on crafts or souvenirs.

Bateman's Bay Where the Kings Hwy. from Canberra (152km inland) meets the Princes Hwy. at the coast, **Bateman's Bay** begins. The town, situated just south of this junction at the mouth of the Clyde River, caters to upmarket tourists on holiday from the capital, but has enough amenities to make it suitable for budget travelers too. The staff at the **Bateman's Bay Tourist Information Centre** (tel. 4472 6900 or 1800 802 528), on the Princes Hwy. at Beach Rd., can outfit you with brochures and give good advice about local beaches for swimming or surfing (open Mon.-Sat. 9am-5pm, Sun. 9am-4pm). For award-winning hostel accommodation, stay with Peter and Moira Miller at the **Bateman's Bay Backpackers (YHA)** (tel. 4472 4972), on the corner of Old Princes Hwy. and South St., just off the new Princes Hwy. The Millers run daily trips to Pebbly Beach ($8) and Mogo ($3), rent bikes and surfboards ($10 per day for either), and keep things cozy, clean, and friendly. (TV, VCR, stereo, fully equipped kitchen, laundry. Free pick-up. Reception open daily 8-10am and 4-6pm. Check-out 10am. 6-bed dorms $17, in winter $15; doubles and twins $38. 7th night free. Non-members pay $3 more on all rooms year-round. Linen included.)

Buses come and go from Bateman's Bay outside the St. George Bank on Orient St. **Pioneer Motor Service** (tel. 1300 368 100) goes north to Wollongong (2-3 per day, 3½hr., $28) and on to Sydney (5½hr., $30). Canberra (1-2 per day, 2½hr., $21.75) is **Murray's** territory (tel. 13 20 30). **Greyhound Pioneer** makes trips to Melbourne (1 per day, 12hr., $66) or Bega (1 per day, 2hr., $30).

Traveling south on the coastal road, you'll find good **surf** at Surf Beach, Malua Bay, and Broulee. The inland route leads to **Mogo,** 10km south of Bateman's Bay, an 1850s gold rush town currently riding the craft craze. **Old Mogo Town** re-creates the gold rush days and offers visitors the chance to try their hands at the pans.

Narooma With a **National Parks and Wildlife Service** office (tel. 4476 2888; open Mon.-Fri. 9am-5pm), on the Princes Hwy. at Field St., and several free parks within an hour's drive, the town of **Narooma** provides an excellent base for outdoor exploration. Just 9km off-shore, the **Montague Island Nature Reserve** is home to Australian and New Zealand fur seals, crested terns, and some 10,000 pairs of Fairy Penguins. The reserve, administered by the NPWS, is accessible only on official tours (1 per day, depending on weather and demand; 3½hr.; $50, under 15 $35), for which most people say the thrill outweighs the cost. Tours can be booked at the **Narooma Visitors Centre** (tel. 4476 2881), one block beyond the NPWS office, on the Princes Hwy. (open daily 9am-5pm).

Bluewater Lodge (YHA), 11-13 Riverside Dr. (tel. 4476 4440), signposted from just across the Wagonga Inlet Bridge, is a great deal. The house has hardwood floors, heat, laundry, a view of the Wagonga Inlet, and free use of bikes and canoes. (Reception open daily early morning-9pm. Check-out 10am. Dorm beds $15, second night $10. Nonmembers pay $2 more per night. Linen included.) Right between the Narooma Golf Course and Narooma Beach, **Surf Beach Caravan Park** (tel. 4476

2275), on Ballingala St., has open tent sites with amazing ocean views and beach access. (Reception open daily 9am-5pm, later in summer. Sites for 2 $19, with power $22. Weekly: $122.50, $133. Winter rates $14, with power $16. Weekly: $81, $96. Senior discounts in winter. Each additional person over 16 $3, ages 5-16 $2.)

At the other end of the golf course, on Wagonga Head, ocean waves and coastal winds have left one rock, known as **Australia Rock,** with a familiar marking: a hole in the shape of Australia. Some find the resemblance more striking than others do, but the area is pretty whether you appreciate the rock or not. **Glasshouse Rocks,** another locally famous rock formation, lies at the south end of Narooma Beach. **Pioneer Motor Service** (tel. 1300 368 100) stops in Narooma, outside the St. George Bank (northbound) and the Westpac Bank (southbound), and runs to Sydney (2-3 per day, 6½-7½hr., $40) and Bega (2-3 per day, 1½hr., $13). **Murray's** (tel. 13 22 51) travels from Narooma Plaza to Canberra (1-2 per day, 4½hr., $33).

The historic town of **Central Tilba** sits 15km south of Narooma off the Princes Hwy. Built in the 1890s and partially rebuilt in the 1980s, the town's turn-of-the-century appearance is complete enough to make it well worth a short detour. **Mount Dromedary,** named by Captain Cook for its resemblance to that hump-backed animal, overlooks Central Tilba and Tilba Tilba (the neighboring village with an 11km round-trip trail up the mountain).

Bermagui Famous for its game fishing, in particular that of writer Zane Grey, **Bermagui** is located on the coast southeast of Tilba Tilba, 30 minutes from the Princes Hwy. Hidden from the flow of traffic, the town remains a fishing port first and a sport fisherman's paradise second. For tourist information, stop at the **BP Automotive Centre** (tel. 6493 4174; open daily 7am-7pm), on Coluga St. just before town. **Blue Pacific Flats,** 73 Murrah St. (tel. 6493 4921), opens its pleasant cabins, laundry, kitchens, and all, to backpackers on demand (single beds $15; double beds $17 per person). Closer to the center of town, the bunkhouse at the **Horseshoe Bay Hotel,** 10 Lamont St. (tel. 6493 4206), is a more basic option, with motel style rooms and a no-frills dorm. (Ask at the bottle shop daily 10am-11pm. Dorms $20; singles $40; doubles $50.) You can sample the town's pride and joy at the **Bermagui Fish Co-op** (tel. 6493 4239), on the waterfront where Bridge St. becomes Cutajo St. (Fish and chips $7.60. Dozen open oysters $7. Open Mon. 9am-4pm, Tues.-Thurs. 9am-6pm, Fri.-Sat. 9am-6:45pm, Sun. 9am-6:30pm.) Those who prefer **swimming** to fishing cluster at Horseshoe Bay between Bermagui Point and Shelly Beach or at the natural rock pool known as Blue Pool on Scenic Dr.

Bega If you've been to the dairy department of an Australian grocery store, you've heard of **Bega** (BEE-ga). In the heart of dairy country, about 50km south of Cobargo, where the road from Bermagui rejoins the Princes Hwy., Bega is the town that produces Bega Cheese. The **Bega Tourist Information Centre,** 91 Gipps St. (tel. 6492 2045), is one block off Carp St. on the corner of Zingel Pl. (open Mon.-Fri. 8:45am-5pm). Arriving in Bega from the Princes Hwy., it's impossible to miss the **Bega YHA Hostel (YHA)** (tel. 6492 3103), on Kirkland Crescent, just off Kirkland St. Under the roof with the huge lettering you'll find a modern mud-brick building with clean dorms, large wheelchair-accessible bathrooms, and a pool table. (TV, kitchen with supplies, laundry facilities. Reception open daily 8-10am and 5-10pm. Check-out 10am. Dorms $13, under 18 $7; doubles $34. Non-members pay $2 more. Day fee $4. Linen $2.)

The Bega Co-Operative Creamery Co. has been making cheese in Bega since 1899, and the **Bega Cheese Factory and Heritage Centre,** off the Princes Hwy. northwest of town, offers visitors a look at the cheese-making process used today and the company's growth over the century. Cheese tasting and free admission make it interesting for folks who aren't so fascinated by dairy (open daily 9am-5pm).

Several bus companies pass through Bega making stops outside the tourist information office on Gipps St. **Pioneer Motor Service** (tel. 1300 368 100) heads to Sydney (2-3 per day, 8hr., $48). **Bega Valley Coaches** (tel. 6492 2418) runs between Bega and Bermagui (Mon.-Fri. 5 per day, 1hr., $12.10). To get to Canberra (1 per day, 3½hr., $28) call **Countrylink** (tel. 13 23 32). **Greyhound Pioneer** (tel. 13 20 30) covers Melbourne (1 per day, 9½ hr., $62, concessions $50).

Twenty-two gravel-paved kilometers northeast of Bega, **Mimosa Rocks National Park** contains over 5000 hectares of coastal land and lagoon. In addition to several short walking tracks and three picnic areas, the park has land set aside for primitive tent camping. The **camping areas,** at Aragunnu and Picnic Point, in the section of the park north of Wapengo Lake and at Middle Beach (trail access only) and Gillards Beach in the area closer to Bega, have no facilities or drinking water (sites for 2 $5, each additional person $2; pay collector at site).

SNOWY MOUNTAINS

Australia's highest mountains, the Snowies are a winter wonderland for skiers and snowboarders. Too low to maintain year-round snow, the mountains attract hikers in the warm months, and towns in the region are becoming more and more equipped to serve summer visitors. Kosciuszko National Park, home of Mt. Kosciuszko (2228m; Australia's highest peak) and nine other mountains reaching over 2100m, covers much of the area. Car entrance fees for the park are a steep $12 per day (motorcycles $3.50) due to limited parking space; plan ahead for the expense, or take advantage, when possible, of frequent winter bus service. The Snowy Mountains Hwy. and the Alpine Way, major routes through the area, feature rambling, boulder-strewn countryside and clear passage for most of the year.

Cooma

The friendly town of Cooma sits at the eastern edge of the Snowy Mountains region, 113km from Canberra on the Monaro Hwy. Although it's a one-hour drive from the slopes, Cooma fills up during ski season (early June to early October) with snow-seekers looking for bargain accommodations. In the spring, summer, and fall, the town attracts a number of backpackers who find work harvesting fruit and vegetables in the surrounding area.

Practical Information The **Cooma Visitors Centre,** 199 Sharp St. (tel. 6450 1742 or 1800 636 525; fax 6450 1798), in the center of the village, can direct you to accommodations and services in town (free accommodation booking service; open mid-Oct. to May daily 9am-5pm; early June to early Oct. 7:30am-6pm). **Impulse Airlines** (tel. 13 13 81) flies into town from Sydney (in summer 2 per day, more in winter, 1hr., $185). **Buses** come through frequently during ski season, but service is severely curtailed the rest of the year. **Greyhound Pioneer** (tel. 13 20 30) covers Jindabyne (2 per day, 1hr., $32) and Thredbo (2 per day, 2hr., $38) during winter and Sydney (2 per day, 6hr., $45) and Canberra (2 per day, 2½hr., $16) year-round. **Countrylink** (tel. 13 22 32) and **Murray's** (tel. 13 22 51) work on similar schedules and come in slightly cheaper for trips to Sydney and Canberra. See the staff at **Harvey World Travel,** 114 Sharp St. (tel. 6452 4677; fax 6452 1121), across the street from the visitors center, for reservations or further information on any of these services (open Mon.-Fri. 9am-5pm, Sat. 9am-noon). Staff here will also know whether someone has decided to pick up summer transportation to the mountains where the major services have left off. **Harvest Helpers** (tel. 6452 2172; fax 6452 5536) arranges placement in specific jobs with accommodation, transportation, and gear for harvest-related work in New South Wales and Victoria throughout much of the year. Based in town, the company has a special focus on work in the Cooma area during the summer and fall (one-time consulting fee $50).

Accommodations and Food The **Cooma Bunkhouse Motel,** 28-30 Soho St. (tel. 6452 2983), on the corner of Commissioner St., has great year-round hostel accommodation with bathrooms, kitchens, and TVs in each of the small dorms. (Central heat, free linen and blankets. Reception open daily 6:30am-10pm, call ahead for later arrivals. Check-out 10am, but arrangements can be made for afternoon bus departures. Dorms $15, discounts available for longer stays.) The neat and homey **Alpine Country Guest House** (VIP), 32 Massie St. (tel. 6452 1414), acts as a B&B during the ski season, and turns into a hostel specializing in housing temporary workers between December and June. (Central heat, kitchen, TV in rooms, baths in most rooms. Reception open daily 8-9am and 4-6pm. Check-in noon. Check-out 10am. Dec.-June dorms $15. VIP. Weekly: $70 with min. 6-week stay. Doubles and twins $30-40. July-Nov. singles, doubles, and twins Sun.-Thurs. $40, Fri.-Sat. $60; family rooms $70, $100.) Backpackers often choose **Dodd's Hotel** (tel. 6452 2011), on Commissioner St., when it comes down to staying in a pub, but the fact that everyone drinks here can make it a less than restful arrangement. (Heaters, electric blankets, common room with TV and books. Reception at the bar daily 11am-late. Singles and doubles $20 per person.) On the Snowy Mountains Hwy. 6km west of Cooma, **Mountain View Caravan Park** (tel. 6452 4513), provides a semi-equipped campers' kitchen along with its basic campsites. (Toilets, showers; laundry facilities. Reception open daily 7am-10pm. Check-out 10am. Sites $10, with power $15.)

Cooma's pubs are the favorite for hot lunches. For creative dinners, pasta specials, vegetarian options, and a lively social atmosphere, many frequent **Cafe Upstairs,** 21 Sharp St. (tel. 6452 4488), next to the visitors center. (Lunch $5-9, dinner $9-14. Fully licensed. Open daily 10am-midnight or later.) The local **Woolworths** (tel. 6452 3638) is on Vale St. at Massie St. (open Mon.-Sat. 7am-10pm, Sun. 7am-6pm).

Skiing and Sights Ski and snowboard rental shops clutter the village streets, evidence of the area's most popular pastimes. Rates are comparable to those closer to the mountains, so the only advantage to renting in Cooma may be availability. Discounts given for bringing in advertisements may make rentals slightly more economical, but you can generally expect to pay $30 for the first day and $5-10 for each day thereafter. The **Snowy Mountains Hydro-Electric Scheme,** carried out between 1949 and 1974, is Cooma's original claim to fame. The project, responsible for nearly every body of standing water in the Snowy Mountains, included the construction of 16 large dams and involved workers from over 30 countries. The **Snowy Mountains Hydro-Electric Authority Visitors Centre** (tel. 6453 2004), on the Monaro Hwy. just north of town, has models, brochures, and a 15-minute film explaining the grand plan which supplies water from the Murray and Murrumbidgee Rivers to the dry regions west of the mountains and, almost as an afterthought, creates energy for the entire southeast corner of Australia. Though the film feels a tad self-promotional and glosses over the possibly ruinous effects of such large-scale tampering with the environment, the project is truly colossal enough to make a short visit to the center quite interesting (open Mon.-Fri. 8am-5pm, Sat.-Sun. and holidays 8am-1pm; free).

Jindabyne

On the scenic shores of man-made **Lake Jindabyne,** the mountain town of Jindabyne is a logical stopping point for those who can't afford to sleep at the foot of the Thredbo chairlifts. The **Snowy Region Visitors Centre** (tel. 6456 2444), on the Alpine Way at the east end of town, combines an office of the National Parks and Wildlife Service and a local tourist information center for one-stop planning. Entrance passes for off-hour trips into **National Park** can be purchased here as well ($12 per car per 24hr., motorcycles $3.50; open mid-Oct. to May daily 8am-6pm; early June-early Oct. Mon.-Fri. 8am-6pm, Sat.-Sun. 7am-7pm). Both **Deane's Buslines** (tel. 6299 3722; fax 6299 3828) and **Jindabyne Coaches** (tel. 041 927 9552) run shuttles from Jindabyne to Thredbo ($12) and to the Skitube train station for Perisher Blue ($6) between early June and early October, the full ski season. The Snowy Region Visitors

Centre has timetables. Transportation in and out of Jindabyne from the northeast passes through Cooma (see above) and operates only during the ski season.

Accommodations and Food Even in the height of ski madness, affordable accommodation in Jindabyne does exist, but availability may be a problem; be sure to book well in advance. **Lazy Harry's Lodge,** 18 Clyde St. (tel. 6456 1957; fax 6456 2057), has dorms with bathrooms, a large, well-equipped kitchen, and a cozy fireplace. (Reception open mid-Oct. to May daily 7:30am-9:30pm; early June-early Oct. 6:30am-11pm. Check-out 10am. Dorms $15, June-Oct. $25; doubles $40, $70; family rooms $50, $90.) Down the street, **Kookaburra Lodge,** 10 Clyde St. (tel. 6456 2897; fax 6456 2747), suffers from a bad case of *faux* wood paneling, but rents otherwise palatable singles for reasonable rates that include a hot breakfast. (Reception open Mon.-Thurs. 7am-8pm, Fri. 6:30am-late, Sat.-Sun. 6:30am-8:30pm. Check-out 10am. Singles $30, with bath $55.) **Jindabyne Holiday Park** (tel. 6456 2249; fax 6456 2302), in the center of town on a choice stretch of Lake Jindabyne shoreline, provides easy access to the town shopping area and plentiful space for lakeside camping. When this book went to press, a campers' kitchen was planned for completion by early 1998. (Toilets, showers, laundry facilities. Reception open Mon.-Thurs. 7:30am-7pm, Fri. 7:30am-late, Sat.-Sun. 7am-7pm. Check-out 10am. Unpowered sites for 1 $10, each additional person $3; June and Sept. to early Oct. $11.50, $3.50; July-Aug. $17, $4. Powered sites $14, $3; June and Sept. to early Oct. $16.50, $3.50. July-Aug. $17, $4. Key deposit $20.) Jindabyne has a gaggle of agencies which charge small fees for arranging lodge or apartment rentals, one of the cheapest ways for groups to stay in town. **Kosciusko Accommodation** (tel. 6456 2022) and **Raine and Horne** (tel. 6456 2999 or 1800 802 315) rank high among the recommended companies.

Activities In the winter, skiing and snowboarding top the list of activities in Jindabyne, but the development of summer adventure activities in the area has made the town a fun place to go year-round. **Snowy Mountain Magic** (tel. 6456 1199 or 018 483 756; fax 6456 1219) organizes abseiling outings (half-day $50, ages 7-15 $30; full day $80, $55) and Murray River rafting trips ($110 per person per day) and rents canoes and kayaks for individual paddling trips. (Lake-use canoes for 2 people $10 per hr., 3hr. $25; kayaks $10, $20. River-use canoes for 2 people, half-day $30, full day $60; kayaks $25, $40.) **Paddy Pallin** (tel. 6456 2922 or 1800 623 459; fax 6456 2836) has a full selection of similar services for prices a shade higher, but also rents mountain bikes ($10 per hr., half-day $24, full day $35). In the evenings, people relax at the **Lake Jindabyne Hotel** (tel. 6456 2203), on Kosciuszko Rd., in the center of town, where entertainment ranges from good-old-fashioned drinking to concerts by top-notch rock bands (schooners of VB $3.10, basic mixed drinks $4; open daily 10am-2am or later).

Kosciuszko National Park

Named after the heroic Polish nationalist, but horribly mispronounced, "Kah-zee-AH-sko" National Park marches along the New South Wales and Victoria border. Within the park, Australia's highest peaks loom over some of the country's largest power and irrigation projects. Skiers and hikers traipse about the mountaintops oblivious to the hydroelectric activity under their feet. Selwyn's super-cheap skiing and the beautiful Yarrangobilly Caves are just two of the park's prime natural attractions.

THREDBO

Home of the country's longest ski runs, Thredbo has long been considered *the* place to go for Australian snow, and, with a busy schedule of summer events and activities, the resort is gaining a year-round reputation for outdoor entertainment. The **Kosciuszko National Park** entry fee of $12 per car per day (motorcycles $3.50) applies to all vehicles heading into Thredbo, whether from Khancoban (82km north-west) or Jindabyne (34km northeast). From early June to early October, the entire ski

The Thredbo Landslide

Shortly before midnight on Wednesday, July 30, 1997, the tiny community at Australia's premier ski resort awoke in shock as a landslide loosed the foundations of two Thredbo ski lodges and sent them tumbling down the mountainside in the middle of the village. Over the next week, rescue volunteers worked almost without pause to move piece by piece the pile of concrete, glass, steel, and personal belongings that remained of the lodges in search of the 19 people trapped inside. Two days into the ordeal, a voice called out from the wreckage in response to workers' shouts, and the miraculous rescue of ski instructor Stuart Diver began. The disaster's only survivor, Mr. Diver was carried free of the rubble some 12 hours later. He had lain in a concrete pocket for a total of 56 hours and suffered only frostbite and minor lacerations. The Thredbo landslide claimed the lives of 18 people, almost all employees of the resort and members of the village's tiny year-round population. Though the rest of the lodges in Thredbo have been judged structurally sound, aside from the one nearest the landslide area which has been evacuated, the tragedy has caused widespread reconsideration of the level of development which is safe and sustainable in such precarious locales. Understandably, it has also profoundly affected the people who live and work here.

season, two companies, **Deane's Buslines** (tel. 6299 3722; fax 6299 3828) and **Jindabyne Coaches** (tel. 041 927 9552) conduct shuttles between Thredbo and Jindabyne ($12). During these months, **Greyhound Pioneer** (tel. 13 20 30) runs regular bus service from Cooma (see above) as well.

Accommodations at most lodges can be booked through the **Thredbo Resort Centre** (tel. 6457 6360 or 1800 020 589). People at the center will know which of the lodges is least expensive at any given time. The **Thredbo YHA Lodge,** 8 Jack Adams Path (tel. 6457 6376; fax 6457 6043), keeps lodging prices down to a manageable level during ski season and comes in far cheaper than anywhere else in town the rest of the year. Though less luxurious than its neighbors, the lodge is quite comfortable and features ample common spaces, a big kitchen, and a balcony that looks out onto the slopes. (Reception open daily 7-10am and 4:30-9pm. Check-out 10am, early June to early Oct. Mon.-Fri. 10am, Sat. 9am, Sun. 4pm. Dorm beds $15, under 18 $7.50; early June to early Oct. $25-75, $17-50, Sun.-Fri. 6-night packages $105-220, $70-127.) Reservations for the ski season are made by lottery in late April. Applications must be submitted through the YHA Travel Centre, 422 Kent St. (tel. 9261 1111), in Sydney; call the travel center for details. For visits with less preparation, contact the manager at the lodge about single night openings resulting from cancellations.

During the 1997 ski season, **lift tickets** cost $60 per day (under 15 $34), and group ski lessons went for $32. Charges for ski and snowboard rentals at **Thredbo Sports** (tel. 6459 4100 or 6459 4175), at the east end of the village, were a bit higher than in Jindabyne or Cooma, so it may make sense to rent equipment before getting to Thredbo. For the use of hikers and ganderers, the **Crackenback Gondola Chairlift** runs year-round (early Oct. to early June $16.50 per day). Several excellent walks depart from the top of the mountain for sweeping views of Kosciuszko National Park. At the village level, spring opens the way for mountain biking as well as walking. Free maps of all of the local trails are available throughout the village. For indoor athletics, stop in at the Thredbo **Alpine Training Centre** (tel. 6459 4294; fax 6457 6470), a complex of training facilities open for use by both elite athletes and health-conscious visitors. (Swimming pool use $6, under 15 $3; squash court rental $12 per hr. Open daily 10am-9pm.) Thredbo's annual **Blues Festival** (Jan. 16-18 in 1998) and **Jazz Festival** (April 30-May 3 in 1998) bring the hills alive in the summer and fall.

YARRANGOBILLY CAVES

Nestled in the northern edge of the Kosciusko National Park, 77km south of Tumut and 109km northwest of Cooma, the Yarrangobilly Caves attract curious visitors and hard-core spelunkers alike. Located just off the Snowy Mountains Hwy. (Hwy. 18), the **Yarrangobilly River** runs through a 12km-long stretch of limestone, riddled with caves. Marked walking trails help tourists better understand the beauty of the caves and the surrounding canopies. The **visitors center** (tel. 6454 9597) at the caves is an essential first stop. In addition to stocking maps and information about the caves and the park, the office offers guided tours—the only way you can see the most impressive caves (Mon.-Fri. 1pm, Sat.-Sun. 11am, 1, and 3pm). With advance notice, tours can be scheduled at virtually any time.

The **Jillabenan Cave** is the smallest and shortest (1hr.) of the guided tour caves. Uniquely wheelchair accessible (with ramps and tracks built in), its array of fascinating stalactite and stalagmite formations amid pools and crystal-lined nooks is spectacular. The slightly longer **Jersey Caves** tour requires about an hour and a half to see equally stellar sights, while the **Castle Cave** involves a 4km return walk and one hour in the cave. (Entrance and tours of the Jersey or Jillabenan Caves $10, children $7.) The **Glory Hole Cave** and **North Glory Cave** are accessible from the carpark, and entry is free and self-guided. After wandering around the caves, take a load off and relax in the 27°C thermal pools. Plants cover the pool floor, and there's a small kiddie pool too.

The park is 6.5km from the highway and open daily from 9am to 5pm. Fill up your tank before you leave. The nearest petrol stations are 43km north in Talbingo or 47km south in Cabramurra. No camping is permitted in the Yarrangobilly Caves area, and food is unavailable, so plan ahead.

NEW SOUTH WALES

MT. SELWYN

Along the Snowy River Highway between Cooma and Tumut, and less than 100 km from either, the **Selwyn Snowfields** (tel. 6454 9488; fax 6454 9482; http://selwynsnow.com.au) offer beginner budget skiing steals. Promoted as a family resort, beginner runs predominate (only 12% of the runs are considered "most difficult"). Elevation at the base is 1492m; the summit is 122m higher. Selwyn advertises 12 **lifts,** but only one of these is a standard double chairlift: the others include T-bars, ropetows, and even a toboggan lift. **Lift tickets** are inexpensive: a one-day ticket costs $28 (under 15 $16; valid 8:30am-4:30pm). **Half-day passes** are also available ($21, under 15 $13; valid 8:30am-12:45pm or 12:45-4:30pm). People over 65, and children under six ski free. Forty-five marked trails make **cross-country skiing** another attractive option. A shelter, toilets, and a carpark are located at the entrance to the cross-country trails.

Ski hire for alpine or cross-country skis costs $23 for a full day and $16 for a half-day, and (under 15 $18; $13). **Ski pants and parkas** can also be hired, if you're traveling without bulky winter clothes (day hire for pants or parka $14; half-day hire $10). **Snowboard hire** costs $30 for a full day and $20 for a half-day. **Toboggans** are also available ($7 for the day). Or try out a **lift and lesson** package (1½hr. lesson with a day-long lift ticket; $45; under 15 $33). A credit card or deposit with identification is necessary to hire any equipment.

To save money on accommodations, spend the night in Tumut or Cooma and commute by car for the day. Because the Kosciuszko region is Australia's highest, use tire chains and exercise caution on the often icy roads. **Lever Coachlines** (tel. 6297 3133) also offers a daytrip skiing package from Canberra (round-trip bus, park entry, lift ticket, lesson, and ski hire $65).

HUME CORRIDOR

As the major route between Australia's two largest cities, the Hume Highway provides fast travel without too much in the way of scenery. Upgrades are slowly making the road into a divided freeway for the entire route, but, at present, stretches are still two-lane and heavily trafficked. Scenic detours and stretches where the Old Hume

Hwy. departs from the new make it possible to cover most of the distance near, but not quite on, the Hume route. It takes nine to ten hours to cover the 872km between Sydney and Melbourne along the highway; for coverage of towns in the Hume Corridor in Victoria, please see p. 501.

Sydney to Goulburn

As the state capital recedes in the rearview mirror, the Hume Hwy. leads into an area known as the Cow-pasture, a name given for its use as grazing land outside the young colony at Sydney. Now divided into the towns of **Liverpool, Campbelltown, Camden,** and **Narellan,** this area was the site of some of Australia's first colonial land grants, including the 1805 grant to John Macarthur, popularly considered the starting point of the nation's wealth. The Macarthur family's involvement in the development of the Merino wool industry is well-known, but the family was also among the first to plant grapevines in Australia, beginning in the 1820s. The **Quondong Visitors Centre** (tel. 4645 8922; fax 4645 8920), on Art Gallery Rd., in Campbelltown, 55km from Sydney's center, has information on area history and attractions and walking tour brochures for Campbelltown and the surrounding towns (open Mon.-Fri. 8:30am-4:30pm, Sat.-Sun. 10am-5pm). Housed at **Mt. Annan Botanic Garden** (tel. 4648 2477), off the F5 freeway between Campbelltown and Camden, the native plants collection of Sydney's Royal Botanic Garden includes specimens collected throughout Australia (open April-Sept. daily 10am-4pm; Oct.-March 10am-6pm; entrance $5 per car, $2 per cyclist or pedestrian, seniors pay half-price; wheelchair access and free entrance for wheelchair-bound visitors). For an action-packed day of Australiana, **Gledswood** (tel. 2606 5111; fax 2606 5897), on Camden Valley Way closer to Camden, entertains visitors through a variety of Aussie farm-style activities from sheep-shearing to boomerang-throwing to wine tasting (open daily 10am-4pm; admission $16, seniors $12.50, ages 5-12 $9; wheelchair accessible). **Busways** (tel. 4655 7501) buses #896 and 899 go to Gledswood from Campbelltown station every day at 9:50am (fare $2.80; CityRail fare from Sydney's Central Station to Campbelltown $4.60, off-peak round-trip $5.60).

Mittagong and Bowral The town of **Mittagong** lies along the Hume Hwy., 40 minutes south of Campbelltown. The helpful staff at the fragrant **Southern Highlands Regional Visitors Centre** (tel. 4871 2888; open daily 8am-5:30pm), on the Hume Hwy. at the north end of Mittagong, can direct you to nearby bushwalking trails at Mt. Alexandria and to resources in town. Only 100m north of the visitors center, **Mittagong Caravan Park** (tel. 4871 1574) devotes a shaded, grassy area to tent camping. The location isn't too scenic, but it's possible to settle in among the trees and get some privacy. (Toilets, showers, store, live-in owners. Laundry facilities. Reception in service station open daily 7am-7pm. Sites for 2 $9, with power $12. Each additional person $2.) The **Lion Rampart Hotel** (tel. 4871 1090; fax 4871 1990) rents clean, comfortable pub rooms with electric blankets and new wallpaper for reasonable rates (singles $25, doubles $35; inquire at the bar daily 10am-11pm). Australia's famous cricketer, **Sir Donald Bradman,** grew up in **Bowral,** 3km south of Mittagong. The **Bradman Museum** (tel. 4862 1247; fax 4861 2536), on Saint Jude St. next to the Bradman Oval, documents the history of Australian cricket in sporting club luxury. Dedicated to Bradman, the museum covers his feats and the accomplishments of other players through the use of game videos, old newsreels, and a large collection of memorabilia (open daily 10am-4pm; admission $5, ages 5-15 $2.50, families of 4 $13). For a more personal look at the Don's years in Bowral, stop by his former home at 52 Shepherd St., but don't expect to get inside—the house is closed to sightseers. **CityRail** service from Sydney reaches both Mittagong ($7.60, off-peak return $9.20) and Bowral ($10.60, $12.80). Between the two towns, a westward turn-off from the Hume Hwy. leads to **Wombeyan Caves** (tel. 4843 5976; fax 4843 5988), a series of five caves open for public exploration. The trip to Wombeyan (65km from the Hume Hwy.) takes about 90 minutes, but the depth and beauty of the caves easily makes up for the detour. (Open daily 8:30am-5pm, last tour 4:30pm. Admission $10, ages 5-15 $5, families $25; with guided tour $12, $6, $30.)

Berrima Fifteen kilometers south of Mittagong, the Hume Hwy. passes through the historic town of Berrima, which was frozen in time in the 1860s when the nearby railway passed it by. Formerly slated to be a regional administrative center, Berrima proudly sports both a jail and a courthouse built in the 1830s. **Berrima Court House** (tel. 4877 1505), on Argyle St., at Wilshire St., acts as both an historical site with trial displays and life-sized models, and a tourist information office (open daily 10am-4pm; admission $3, students, seniors, and ages 5-15 $2). The collection at the **Berrima Historical Museum** (tel. 4871 2297), on Market Pl. across from the public park, consists largely of the personal effects of former residents of Berrima. For visitors who have the time to stop and chat, the staff's knowledge fleshes out the story told by the clothing, household wares, and furniture and helps explain the town's growth, disappearance, and rediscovery over the last 160 years. (Open Sat.-Sun. and public and school holidays 10am-4pm. Admission $1, ages 5-15 20¢.) **Berrima Coaches** (tel. 4871 3211; fax 4871 3225; open Mon.-Fri. 8:30am-5pm) handles transportation between Bowral and Berrima (bus #812; Mon.-Sat. 4-5 per day, 30min., $5, concessions $2.50).

Bundanoon On the edge of **Morton National Park,** off the Hume Hwy. by way of the Bundanoon/Exeter exit 15km south of Berrima, Bundanoon serves as the park's easiest base town. The area, covered by thick forests that stretch toward the sandstone cliffs of the park's interior, harbors excellent walking trails and a superb hostel. Located in a spacious old guesthouse, **Bundanoon YHA Hostel** (tel. 4883 6010), on Railway Ave. on the north end of town, combines warm management and top-notch facilities for a great hostel experience. Theme dinners such as Saturday night Christmas in July celebrations (every Sat. in July) liven things up on occasion, and Xavier always has tons of good suggestions for bushwalks. (Fully-equipped kitchen, common room with games, no TV. Lots of blankets but no heat in bedrooms. Reception open daily 8-10am and 5-10pm. Dorm beds $14, under 18 $7; twins $33; doubles $35; family rooms $39. YHA non-members pay $3 more. Laundry facilities. Bike rentals $10 per day.) From the hostel, a short walking trail leads to the bioluminescent bliss of the **Glow Worm Glen** (1hr. round-trip). Trails from the glen cross into **Morton National Park,** providing opportunities to circle back toward the hostel on hikes of four hours or longer. The nearest park information center is at Fitzroy Falls (see **Kangaroo Valley,** p. 192) a 20-minute drive from Bundanoon, but the hiking maps available at the hostel cover the entire area. Regular CityRail trains from Sydney's Central Station stop at Bundanoon's railway station daily ($5.20, off-peak return $6.20).

Goulburn

Settled in the early 1830s, Goulburn was proclaimed a city by order of Queen Victoria in March 1863, and was the last city in the British empire to come into being in this manner. As an agricultural and judicial center connected to Sydney first by coach, then, in 1869, by rail, the city has grown over the last century and a half to a population of 26,000. Goulburn, today the regional hub of the Merino wool industry, maintains a large number of public and private buildings which date from the 1800s and are still in use. This day-to-day connection with its history gives Goulburn a feeling of continuity unusual among the historical towns of New South Wales.

Orientation and Practical Information Situated on the Hume Hwy. between Yass (87km) and Sydney (195km), Goulburn is just 10km east of the junction of the Federal and Hume Hwy. **Countrylink** trains (tel. 4827 1485) traveling between Sydney (3 per day, 2¾hr., $28) and Canberra (3 per day, 1½hr., $11) stop at **Goulburn Railway Station,** on Sloane St. **CityRail** (tel. 13 15 00) trains also run toward Sydney from the station (to Bundanoon $5.20, off-peak return $6.20; Mittagong $7.60, $9.20; Sydney $22, $23). **Fearnes Coaches** (tel. 1800 029 918) travels the Hume Hwy. to Sydney (1 per day, 3hr., $25) with stops in between. **Greyhound Pioneer** (tel. 13 20 30) has more expensive service to Sydney and to points west by way of Canberra. **McCafferty's** (tel. 13 14 99) does the Canberra leg of the journey for lower fare (1 per day, 1hr., $17).

Olympicycle, 474 Auburn St. (tel. 4822 3780; fax 4822 3790), on the corner of Citizen St., handles in-town transportation with bike rentals (1hr. $7, $3 per additional hr.; day-long hire on application; pick-up and delivery $10; deposit required; open daily 10am-5:30pm). Across from Belmore Park, the **Goulburn Visitors Centre,** 2 Montague St. (tel. 4823 0492; open daily 9am-5pm), distributes heaps of good advice and brochures, include the free *Historic Two Foot Tour* guide to the city's historic buildings. A Victorian-era Italianate building which houses the Town Clock, the **post office,** 105 Auburn St. (tel. 4821 1422), not only holds *Poste Restante* mail (postal code 2580), but also happens to be the second stop on the local historic walking tour (open Mon.-Fri. 8:30am-5pm).

Accommodations The owners of the **Goulburn Gateway Service Station** (tel. 4821 9811; fax 4821 2055), at the corner of Common St. and the Hume Hwy., at the north end of town, have converted the defunct bus depot behind their gas station, store, and restaurant complex into two small **dormitories.** The location is somewhat off-putting, but the bedrooms are clean, well-lit, and livable. (Bathrooms, showers, no kitchen, no blankets. Reception open 24hr. at gas station counter. Beds $13. Linen $3.) At the opposite end of town, **Goulburn South Caravan Park** (tel. 4821 3233), on Hume St., as you enter town on the Hume Hwy. from the southwest, rents basic camping space near the highway. (Toilets, showers, cooking facilities. Reception open daily 8am-8pm. Park gates open daily 8am-9pm. Sites $9, for 2 $11; with power $14. Laundry $2 to wash. Use of stove 20¢.)

Sights and Activities An enduring, if tacky, monument to the city's livelihood, the **Big Merino** (tel. 4821 8800), a three-story sheep, stands next to the Hume Hwy. at the southwest end of town. Climb up into his head and look out over Goulburn through the eyes of the Big Merino; enlightenment will come. Postcards to commemorate the moment can be purchased downstairs in the gift shop (open daily 8am-7pm; free admission).

The high points of the historic walking tour lie on Montague St. in the center of town. On one end, near Sloan St., across from Belmore Park, the dome of the **1887 Court House** (tel. 4821 9522) towers over stately grounds and a magnificent interior (open Mon.-Fri. 9:30am-4pm; free). Two blocks up the street, **St. Saviour's Cathedral** (tel. 4821 2206) interrupts Montagne St. The white sandstone church, built between 1874 and 1884, was designed by Edmund Blackett. The bell tower was a 1988 bicentennial addition (open Mon.-Sat. 10am-4pm; small donation requested with guided tour). The **Goulburn Brewery** (tel. 4821 6071), on Bungonia Rd., southeast of the city center, doesn't appear on the walking tour but deserves a stop nonetheless. The buildings, designed by Francis Greenway and built in the 1830s, stopped being used as a brewery in 1929 when Tooth's Brewery Co., the original owners, went out of business. After a hiatus of nearly 70 years, the brewery was acquired by Father Michael O'Halloran, who reopened the establishment in 1996, producing three tasty ales from the original recipes and using traditional brewing techniques. The buildings are open daily for visitation, but guided tours and tastings happen only on Sundays. The restaurant and bar on the premises serve tea, lunch, dinner, and, of course, beer. (Buildings and restaurant open Mon.-Thurs. 11am-7pm, Fri.-Sat. 11am-7pm or later, Sun. 11am-5pm. Tours Sun. 11am and 3pm, 40min., $5, under 18 free.)

Yass

The former home of famous Australian explorer Hamilton Hume, Yass lies one hour northwest of Canberra, just west of the Barton Hwy.'s junction with the Hume Hwy., and one hour west of Goulburn. **Transborder Express** (tel. 6241 0033) connects the town to Canberra (5 per day, 1hr., $10), and **Greyhound Pioneer** (tel. 13 20 30) passes through on its way from Sydney to Adelaide (5 per week, 2¼hr., $29). **Fearnes Coaches** (tel. 1800 029 918) has service to Sydney (1 per day, 5hr., $25). The **Yass Tourist Information Centre** (tel. 6226 2557), at Coronation Park, on Comur St., serves as the stopping point for these services (open daily 9am-5pm).

Next door to the information center, the **Hamilton Hume Museum** (tel. 6226 2557) houses a small collection of artifacts from Hume's life and expeditions (open Sat.-Sun., holidays, most Fri., and weekdays when volunteers are available 10am-4pm; admission $2, concessions $1, ages 5-15 50¢). East of town, between Yass and the Barton Hwy. on Yass Valley Way, **Cooma Cottage** (tel. 6226 1470) is the home in which Hamilton Hume lived out his days. Born in Parramatta in 1796, Hume was unique among the early colonial explorers of Australia for being Australian-born. His use of bush methods learned from Aboriginal friends made him an exceptional explorer from the time of his earliest expeditions as a teenager. By the time he was 25, Hume had seen more of the Australian continent than almost any European in the colonies and was considered a successful explorer. Indeed, it was Yass that stole his heart, and where he returned when he settled permanently nearly 20 years later. Cooma Cottage, now owned by the National Trust, has become an interesting museum on Hume and an exquisite example of the simple elegance characteristic of country homes in Australia in the mid-1800s. (Open Wed.-Mon. 10am-4pm; admission $4, students, seniors, and ages 5-15 $2, families of 4 $10.) For travelers with cars, **Carey's Caves** (tel. 6227 9622), at Wee Jasper, 42km southwest of Yass, make an excellent detour from the highway. Open only for guided tours, the caves contain seven main chambers of limestone and crystal formations. (Tours Mon. and Fri. noon, 1, and 2pm, Sat.-Sun. noon, 1, 2 and 3pm; admission $8, ages 5-15 $4.)

Gundagai

Tucked between the Murrumbidgee River and the Hume Hwy., Gundagai's (GUN-dah-GUY) idiosyncratic appeal breaks the monotonous efficiency of a Hume commute. The **Gundagai Tourist and Travel Centre** (tel. 6944 1341) on **Sheridan St.** east of the Hume Hwy. provides tourist information, and operates transportation from Gundagai via **V/Line, McCafferty's,** and **Greyhound.** More uniquely, the office houses a stunning tribute to craftwork and neurosis: **Frank Rusconi's Marble Masterpiece,** a miniature marble cathedral composed of 20,948 pieces of handcrafted marble and constructed between 1910 and 1938 (office open daily 9am-5pm; admission to the marble masterpiece $1, children 50¢). Also of interest are Gundagai's **Historic Bridges,** just south of Sheridan St.'s eastern end. Gaze across the Prince Alfred Bridge Viaduct's impressive wooden structure and admire the second-oldest metal truss bridge in Australia. South of Sheridan, the **Gundagai Historical Museum** on Homer St. houses an hodgepodge of old machinery, refurbished farm equipment, and even a Model T (admission $3, children $1). The bridges and surrounding areas offer numerous striking vistas. A final sight to catch is the **Dog on the Tuckerbox** (tel. 6944 1450), immortalized in poetry and song and mercilessly milked by the surrounding tourist complex 9km north of Gundagai.

The **Criterion Hotel** (tel. 6944 1048), on the corner of Sheridan and Byron St., provides an excellent above-the-pub lodging with complementary continental brekky. The solid Art Deco building is thoroughly clean, with practical amenities (singles $20; doubles $30). Restaurants are scarce, with pub grub filling all food groups. The **Foodtown market** is open Monday through Friday 8am-6pm and Saturday 8am-12:30pm.

Tumut

The small town of Tumut (ti-MUUT) in the heart of the Tumut Valley offers only its scenery, but with scenery like this, nobody's complaining. Hilly, deciduous forests rim the valley and provide fine walking trails and scenic drives. The town's tourism efforts are geared toward outdoor recreation, and bushwalkers should enjoy the beautiful sloping terrain. A gateway to the northern reaches of Kosciuszko National Park, Tumut is also near the massive Snowy Mountains Scheme, which includes the dams and hydroelectric power generators for the region.

Accessible from the Hume Hwy. via a tourist drive which circles back to the highway, Tumut also connects to Kosciusko via the Snowy Mountains Hwy. The Snowy Mountains Hwy. (Hwy. 18) runs to Cooma. **Buses** to nearby Cootamundra (1½hr., $6; via Gundagai) depart from the corner of Wynward and Russell St. Like most places along the nearby Hume Hwy., the town is probably not worth the stop if you're tied to public transportation.

For information on surrounding bushwalks such as the **Hume and Hovell Trail,** visit the **Tumut Visitors Centre** (tel. 6947 1849). Located on Fitzroy St. (Snowy Mountains Hwy.) and open daily 9am to 5pm, it's two blocks south of Tumut's main street, **Wynward St.** Wynward is also where to find the **post office** (open Mon.-Fri. 9am-5pm, postal code 2720) and **Festival Supermarket** (open Mon.-Fri. 8:30am-7pm, Sat. 8:30am-6pm, Sun. 10am-4pm). There are no ATMs in town.

The best budget accommodation available is the **Oriental Hotel** (tel. 6947 1174), on the corner of Wynward and Fitzroy St. Although the rooms are a bit dim and the beds have seen better days, the hotel is clean and adequate, with a small TV lounge and amicable staff (singles $20, doubles $30; breakfast available).

Holbrook

Situated halfway between Sydney and Melbourne along the Hume Hwy., Holbrook is a good place to stretch your legs if you're intent on quickly commuting from one big city to the other. The Hume Hwy. bisects the city (as Albury St.), running north-south. On the Sydney-bound (west) side, a gargantuan **black submarine** lurks beside the road. This nautical behemoth was inaugurated in June 1997 by Mrs. Gundula Holbrook, widow of the town's namesake, Submarine Commander Lt. Norman Holbrook. This valiant Brit torpedoed a Turkish battleship in WWI and inspired residents to replace the town's then-loathed name, "Germantown." Read more of the story in the appropriately titled official tourist brochure *Where the Hell is Holbrook?* Also worth checking out is the **Woolpack Inn Museum** (tel. 6036 2131), on the west side of Albury St. Its turn-of-the-century wool shearing implements provide a brief glimpse into the past (open daily 9:30am-4:30pm; admission $3, children $1). Next door is the **Holbrook Information Centre** (tel. 6036 2131). An Ampol service station beckons northbound drivers to fill up their tanks, while a Shell station does the same for southbound travelers (both accept V, MC, and AmEx).

A few coffee shops dot Albury St., while **Mackies Budget Rite** offers market fare. Albury, just 64km south, provides a greater variety of accommodations, but if you must bed down in Holbrook, the **Riverina Hotel** (tel. 6036 2523) on the west side of Albury St. near the south of town will do. The old brick structure houses bare rooms with hand basins and clean shared bathrooms. There's a pub downstairs (singles $18; doubles $25).

Albury-Wodonga

Spanning the westward-flowing Murray River, the border between New South Wales and Victoria, the Albury-Wodonga metropolitan area (pop. 90,000) belongs to both states. Right on the Hume Hwy., it breaks the transit between Sydney and Melbourne and provides a convenient base for daytrips into the neighboring Riverina, Murray country, wineries, and alpine retreats.

New South Wales' Albury dominates its sibling with superior attractions and accommodations, casting a shadow over more residential Wodonga. Albury's newly refurbished main street, Dean St., showcases an eclectic array of buildings and serves as the lively shopping and idling boulevard. Albury serves as the Murray's finest cultural base, with high-quality museums, galleries, and theaters, but doesn't neglect the Hume Hwy.'s trucking industry.

Wodonga presents a more discreet facade, with modern storefronts lining High St. and predominantly residential neighborhoods. The military has modeled much of Wodonga's contemporary identity, beginning with the formation of a base here in 1943. Following WWII, Wodonga became a new home for many displaced persons and refugees from war-torn Europe. This international presence contributes a cosmopolitan edge to Albury-Wodonga.

ORIENTATION

The **Hume Hwy.** (Hwy. 31) winds through Albury, generally heading south and east before turning west to bypass Wodonga. The **Murray Valley Hwy.** (Hwy. 16) runs along the Victorian side and enters Wodonga from the southeast, where it runs through town before uniting with the Hume Hwy. Running along the Murray River on the New South Wales side, the **Riverina Hwy.** (Hwy. 58) goes from Corowa east towards Khancoban, where it joins the Murray Valley Hwy.

In Albury, **Dean St.** forms the central east-west artery, beginning at the railroad tracks and crossed by **Young St.** (Hume Hwy.), Macauley, David, Olive, Kiewa, and Townsend St. heading west through the city center, toward the hilltop monument. **Smollett St.** runs parallel to Dean St. one block south. In Wodonga, **High St.** defines the city center, crossed by Laurence St. to the south and Stanley and Elgin to the north, before crossing the railroad tracks.

PRACTICAL INFORMATION

Tourist Office: Gateway Tourist Information Centre (tel. 6041 3875 or 1800 800 743; fax 6021 0322) in the Gateway Village no-man's land between Albury and Wodonga on the east (Melbourne-bound) side of the Hume Hwy. (open daily 9am-5pm). Tune in to 88 FM for tourist information.

American Express Office: 574 Dean St. (tel. 6041 3333, 24hr. tel. 0419 244 989; fax 6021 1139), in Albury Travel. No mail-holding service. Provides currency exchange, Travellers' Cheques, and travel services for cardholders. Wheelchair-accessible. Open Mon.-Fri. 9am-5:30pm, Sat. 9am-noon.

ATMs: Along Dean St. The ANZ machine on the corner of Kiewa and Dean St. accepts MC, Visa, Cirrus, and Plus.

Trains and Buses: Albury Travel Centre (tel. 6041 9555) on Railway St. north of a turn in the Hume Hwy., 1 block east of Dean St. offers **CountryLink** train service and **McCafferty's, Greyhound Pioneer, Firefly,** and **V/Line** coach service to Sydney (by train, 11:36am and 11:10pm, 7½hr., $70), Melbourne (6 per day, 4am-4pm, 3hr., $37.80), Echuca (Tues., Thurs., and Sat., 3:15am, $30), Mildura (Tues., Thurs., and Sat., 7:20am, $54), Adelaide (daily 4:25am, $54), and Canberra (by train 11:30am, $42; by bus 3:40pm, $25). Open for bookings Mon.-Fri. 8:30am-5pm, Sat.-Sun. 9:30am-4:30pm.

Airport: Northeast of the city center in the direction of Lake Hume. Signs from Hume Hwy. point the way. Hazleton and Ansett fly from Albury to Sydney (about $110) and to Melbourne (about $81). Prices fluctuate seasonally.

Supermarket: Coles, at Kiewa and Smollett St. Open daily 7am-midnight.

Laundromat: On the corner of Smollett and David St. (tel. 6041 4050), across from Albury Backpackers.

Police: (tel. 6023 9299), on Olive St. near Dean St.

Emergency: Dial 000.

Post Office: At the corner of Dean and Kiewa St. (tel. 6021 1755). Open Mon.-Fri. 9am-5pm with *Poste Restante* service. **Postal code:** 2644. Branch in the **Big W Shopping Centre,** North Albury (tel. 6025 1264), open Mon.-Wed. and Fri. 9am-5:30pm, Thurs. 9am-7pm, Sat. 9am-noon.

Phone code: 02.

ACCOMMODATIONS

Albury offers pub hotels and excellent budget accommodations. Stay in Wodonga and you'll have to commute to get to the heart of dining and happenings. But you won't have to worry about fruit flies (see signs along river for explanation).

Albury Backpackers, 459 David St. (tel. 6041 1822), on the corner of Smollett St. A quintessential backpackers, this 38-bed dorm-style arrangement in the city center is a comfy, spirited place to meet fellow travelers. Free bicycle use, a tidy, well-serviced kitchen, canoe hire, local tours and trips, and free pick-up from the railway station. Within easy walking distance of the station. No smoking. Laundromat, pub, and supermarket a stone's throw away. With fans in the summer, free tea and coffee, and a good stash of stuff for breakfast, Albury's a steal. Dorms $14, weekly $70; doubles and twins $30. Subsequent nights $1 off. VIP.

Albury Motor Village, 372 Wagga Rd. (Hume Hwy.) (tel. 6040 2999; fax 6040 3160), on the northern extreme of Albury across from the KFC and Cal-Tex. The pristine YHA hostel is newly-renovated, with shiny metal bunks and large windows. Downstairs, ample bathroom facilities glisten. A kitchenette and TV lounge in an adjacent pavillion provide a perfect place to unwind next to the swimming pool. Laundry and parking make this facility even better. Despite its out-of-the-way location, a Big W shopping mall and 24hr. diner sit across the street. Dorms $14, YHA non-members $17. Powered sites $16 for 2 people. Cabins for 2 range from $43-76. All but deluxe cabins are BYO linens and towels. Book in advance during the summer. V, MC, AmEx.

Commercial Hotel, 430 Smollett St. (tel. 6021 3111), just west of the Hume Hwy., 1½ blocks from the railway station. Location's the key in this best of the pub hotels, the city's closest accommodation to the railway station. Basic rooms with A/C, electric blankets, hand basins, and clean bathroom facilities. Singles $20; doubles $35. V, MC.

NEW SOUTH WALES

FOOD

Dean St. proffers a fine collection of international cuisine ranging from Thai and Indian to Mexican and Lebanese. **Restaurant 2000,** 639 Dean St. (tel. 6041 2330), between Wodonga and Townsend, serves an all-you-can-eat smorgasbord lunch and dinner. A rich variety of vegetables, fruit, and desserts fills the table, and the entrees and soups are warm and tasty. (Lunch served noon-2:30pm; $7.90, children $4.90. Dinner served 5:30-9:30pm nightly; Mon.-Thurs. $12.50, Fri. and Sun. $13.50, Sat. $14.50. V, MC, AmEx.) For a funky change of pace, try **Cafe Gryphon,** 468 Dean St., with a Formica-meets-mismatched-dinette-set decor and a fun, lively mood. You can wolf down $5 foccacias or $7-12 dinner entrees, but some swear by the luscious mud cake (open 10:30am-late).

SIGHTS AND ACTIVITIES

The **Albury Regional Art Centre,** 546 Dean St. (tel. 6023 8187; fax 6041 2482), presents an array of contemporary art exhibitions, and organizes concerts, readings, dance performances, and theatrical productions in the adjacent **Albury Community Theatre** (open Mon.-Fri. 10:30am-5pm, Sat.-Sun. 10:30am-4pm; gallery free). On the Hume Hwy., as you enter Albury from Wodonga, you'll find the **Albury Regional Museum,** Wodonga Pl. (tel. 6041 3416), adjacent to the large park. The museum assembles exhibitions on topics of regional significance ranging from science and history to craft and culture (open daily 10:30am-4:30pm; free). Just north of the museum on Wodonga Pl. between Smollett and Dean St., the **Albury Botanic Gardens** (tel. 6023 8241) rest in green splendor. The four-hectare site displays a diverse collection of trees, some dating back to 1877. The gardens are a wonderful picnic spot, or just a great place to relax. Admission is free, and group tours can be arranged with advance notice. To take in a sweeping view of the region, climb to the top of the **Monument Hill Parklands** and gaze out on Albury-Wodonga from the Deco obelisk Albury War Memorial. You can walk directly uphill from Dean St., or drive up and around the back of the hill.

Departing from Norieul Park on the Murray River, the steamboat **P.S. Cumberoone** (tel. 6021 1113; fax 6041 6388) paddles along the river during spring, summer, and autumn. (1hr. cruises $8, children $4.50; 1½hr. $9.50, children $4.50. Cruises depart Wed., Sat., and Sun. 10am, noon, and 2pm; Thurs.-Fri. 2pm.) On the Riverina Hwy. 14km east of Albury, the **Hume Weir Trout Farm** (tel. 6026 4334) raises Rainbow Trout for commercial and recreational purposes. You can pet trout, catch trout (rods $1, free bait, fish cost $8.50/kg, cleaning 20¢ per fish), ogle at rare golden and albino trout, and eat smoked trout and trout *pâté.* You can also tour the fowl-filled grounds and admire the gushing waterfalls (open daily 9am-dusk; admission $5, students $4, children $2). Nearby, massive **Lake Hume** offers fishing, boating, and waterfront picnic areas.

Wodonga claims the **Albury/Wodonga Military Museum** (tel. 6055 2525), just east of Wodonga off the Murray Valley Hwy. A large collection of memorabilia and machinery is on display (open Mon.-Fri. 10am-3pm, Sat.-Sun. 10am-4pm).

■ Near Albury-Wodonga: Ettamogah Pub

Just 15km north of Albury along the Hume Hwy., the Ettamogah Pub explodes in goofy fun as it caters to gawking tourists and satirizes and stereotypes all things Aussie. Based on the work of cartoonist **Ken Maynard,** this Disneyesque village is composed of eye-popping, off-kilter buildings decorated with a running stream of witticisms. The centerpiece is the hilariously constructed Ettamogah Pub, capped with a vintage Fosters beer truck and filled with business-card-slathered walls. Other sites include a hollowed-out tree ensconced in bars and dubbed Lock Out, a police "offise" covered in corny cop punnery, a real pottery studio, and Dodgie Bros. Auto Repairs and Fire Brigade, which houses vintage autos. There's even a T-Rex Hall, which displays Australia's only real Tyrannosaurus rex skeleton and a collection of other fossils (admission: "Groanups" $4, "Ankle Biters" $2). The **Ettamogah Winery** at the rear of the complex has free tastings and wine sales (daily 10am-4pm). There's no admission to tour the site, and signs will clearly direct you from the highway.

RIVERINA

Dry, brown, and flat, much of the Riverina's natural terrain does not look like a land suited for farming. But heavy irrigation has in fact has turned the soil into fertile plains. Although not a prime sight-seeing destination, the Riverina is deal for budget travelers seeking seasonal farm or fruit-picking labor. Wagga Wagga is the state's largest non-coastal city, and the unofficial capital of the region. The designation "Riverina" generally refers to towns scattered about the Murray River drainage area, and the large towns listed here sit more specifically along the Murrumbidgee River. The Murrumbidgee starts as a trickle in the Snowy Mountains and then widens to a major waterway that runs parallel to the Sturt Hwy. before feeding the Murrumbidgee Irrigation Area (MIA) around Griffith and finally joining the Murray River.

Wagga Wagga

New South Wales' largest inland city, sprawling greater Wagga Wagga (population 55,600) actually begins 56km from the city center. Wagga (mercifully abbreviated, and pronounced WAU-guh) is surrounded by a suburban and rural expanse and is more of a commercial and residential center than a tourist destination. The Sturt Hwy., which runs from Adelaide to Sydney, passes through town.

Orientation and Practical Information Visitors focus on Wagga's downtown, 32km west of the Hume Hwy., bounded by the train station one block south of **Edwards St.** (the Sturt Hwy.) on **Baylis St.** and continuing north as Baylis slants into Fitzmaurice St. Wagga's **tourist information center** (tel. 6923 5402; open daily 9am-5pm), on Tarcutta and Morrow St. can be reached by turning north near the overpass that crosses Sturt Hwy., or by going two blocks east of Baylis St. along Morrow St. (right before the Murrumbidgee River). The elegantly restored **train station,** haughtily entitled the Wagga Wagga Travel Centre (tel. 6939 5488), runs **Countrylink** service once per day to Sydney (12:20pm, 7hr., $62), Melbourne (2:15pm, 16hr., $62),

Griffith (2:40pm, 2½hr., $17), Mildura (2:40pm, 12hr., $74), and Canberra (12:45pm, 4hr., $25). Fares are discounted up to 40% with advance booking. The **post office** occupies a store in the **Wagga Wagga Marketplace** mall on Baylis St. between Forsyth and Morgan St. (open Mon.-Fri. 8:30am-5pm, Thurs. 8:30am-7pm, Sat. 9am-noon; postal code 2650).

Accommodations and Food Baylis St. pub hotels dominate the budget accommodations market. A clean, inexpensive choice is the **Tourist Hotel,** 97 Fitzmaurice St. (tel. 6921 2264), north of the river. Although the rooms are a bit old and worn, the doona, linens, and electric blanket work well and look attractive. With a hand basin in each room and decent bathroom facilities, the hotel serves its namesake well (singles $20; doubles $30; V, MC). For a more upscale pub hotel, **Romano's Hotel and Cafe** (tel. 6921 2013) provides razzmatazz renovations with a Victorian decor. Beautifully-patterned linens adorn beds in spacious rooms with extra perks like bed lamps, alarm clocks, hand basins, coffee and tea service, and sheepskin-covered chairs. Shared bathrooms glisten, and a convenient carpark and award-winning cafe restaurant wait below. In a town where other pub hotels fail to reach a pleasant plateau, Romano's is worth the little extra. (Singles $30; twins $38; doubles $38, with showers $45, with private bath $65. Discounts on extended stays. V, MC. Wheelchair accessible.) The **Wagga Wagga Tourist Caravan Park,** 2 Johnston St. (tel. 6921 2540), is two blocks east of Baylis St. on the river. A great location for warm weather fun, the park offers tent sites ($10 for 2 people), powered caravan sites ($14 per twin), and fully-furnished caravans and cabins from $35-50. They even rent two- and three-bedroom apartments off-site for $60 per night. BBQ, playground, laundry, TV room, and beach are all on-site. Visa and MC are accepted.

A fine selection of international cuisine lines Baylis St., with a few Middle Eastern offerings on the north end, Italian restaurants clustered near the Sturt Hwy., and a large number of fast food, pizza parlor, and tea room offerings in between. A **Coles supermarket** on Baylis and Forsyth is open 24 hours.

Sights Several attractions in Wagga are worth a visit. The **Wagga Wagga City Art Gallery,** 40 Gurwood St. (tel. 6923 5419), just east of Fitzmaurice St. by the lagoon, houses the **National Art Glass Collection** and the **Carnegie Print Collection.** The print collection showcases innovative printmakers' work which dates from 1940 to 1976, as well as coordinating temporary exhibits of regional and national artists and artisans. (Open Tues.-Fri. 11am-5pm, Sat. 10am-5pm, Sun. and public holidays 2-5pm. Free. Wheelchair accessible.) South of the city (in the direction of the big hill) is the **Wagga Wagga Botanic Gardens** and the neighboring **Wagga Wagga Historical Museum** (tel. 6925 2934). To reach them, go west from Baylis St. to Best St., cross the railroad tracks and head south to Urana St., and then go east on Urana as it becomes Lord Baden Powell Dr. The museum displays 19th-century tools, clothes, and community relics, and even includes a hollowed-tree canoe constructed by the Wiradjuri Aboriginals (open Tues.-Wed., Sat.-Sun., and public holidays 2-5pm). Next door, an attractive and diverse botanical garden is arranged across nearly nine hectares. A beautiful **aviary** envelops visitors in native birdlife, and pleasant pathways wind among the brooks and trees. There's also a kidsville and a native-animal **petting zoo** (park open daily from dawn to dusk).

Narrandera

Narrandera blends convenience with a peppering of unique attractions and merits at least a quick road stop along the Newell Hwy. The town attracts travelers with a koala sanctuary, a water park, heritage buildings, and an interesting local history. But the town doesn't trip over itself to nab tourists and has kept its small-town intimacy. Situated about halfway between Adelaide and Sydney, the town provides excellent budget accommodations for commuters. It is also about a day's drive from Melbourne en route to Brisbane.

Orientation and Practical Information Narrandera's sprawling streets are usually shaded by large, leafy canopies and are beautiful to drive and stroll along. The town's main road, **East St.,** runs north-south one block east of Cadell St. Most accommodations, restaurants, and services lie along East St. The **Narrandera Tourist Information Centre** (tel. 6959 1766), located on Cadell St. next to the large park, one block west of East St., provides excellent maps and accommodation and restaurant listings. It also houses the **world's largest playable guitar.** In addition, the tourist center operates the **Tiger Moth Memorial** next door. This building houses a vintage WWII aircraft and serves as a reminder of Narrandera's role as a training site for the Royal Australian Air Force (both the tourist office and the Tiger Moth open Mon.-Fri. 9am-5pm, Sat.-Sun. 10am-4pm). Two blocks east of East St.'s northern end is the **railway station** (tel. 6959 3424), which is really only a snack shop for departing and arriving motor coach passengers. The **post office** is located on the corner of Twynam and East St. (open Mon.-Fri. 9am-5pm; postal code 2700).

Accommodations and Food Across from the railway station, the **Star Lodge** (tel. 6959 1768; fax 6959 4164) provides bed and breakfast as well as YHA hostel accommodations. Registered with the National Trust, the well-maintained guest house preserves elegant high ceilings, archways, stained-glass, and ample verandas in their early 20th-century flavor. Dorms sleep four; bed and breakfast rooms are a tad fancier and have sinks. All rooms include heating, evaporative cooling, and linens. Bathrooms are single sex and immaculate. Downstairs, a TV lounge, sitting room with fireplace, dining room, laundry facility, and guest kitchen provide additional conveniences. (Dorms for YHA members $14; singles $30; doubles $55. Breakfast included. V, MC, AmEx.) For even cheaper lodging, try the **Royal Mail Hotel** (tel. 6959 2007), with reasonable rooms and a carpeted, inconspicuous gray and peach decor. With a Chinese restaurant and pub downstairs and a main street location, the Royal Mail's not a bad deal for the price (singles $10; doubles $20).

For good Chinese food, sample an item from the extensive menu of **Hing Wah** (tel. 6959 2069), downtown on East St. The large dining room is bedecked in Chinese lanterns and has a strange orange painting of sunset over Hong Kong. (Open nightly 5pm-9pm, also Tues.-Fri. noon-2pm. Takeaway available. V, MC.) For staples, hit **Tuckerbag's Supermarket** on East St. (open Mon.-Wed. 8am-6:30pm, Thurs.-Fri. 8am-7pm, Sat. 8am-3pm, Sun. 9am-2pm).

Sights and Activities While in Narrandera, drive south to Lake Dr. and cross the canal bridge to enter the **Narrandera Nature Reserve.** After driving east along the main dirt road for 3.4km, you'll arrive at the **Koala Regeneration Reserve** where a disease-free colony of koalas is steadily growing (open daily from dawn to dusk). The animals can be best spotted during the twilight hours, or during the daytime by searching tree bases for droppings. For warm weather fun, two **beaches** are marked off the main dirt road. These sandy spots on the Murrumbidgee River are great places for summer relaxation. Also enjoyable for sunny fun is the **Lake Talbot Holiday Complex** on Broad St., which borders the creek just past the Narrandera Nature Reserve bridge. Entrance to the **pool** complex costs $2, $1 for children, and has a steep **water slide** (30¢ per ride) and a winding water flume (20¢ per ride).

■ Near Narrandera: Leeton

Tired of wine? Leeton puts a new spin on the free tasting idea, with free rice tasting. The town considers itself Australia's rice capital and produces a large array of agricultural products. It's an ideal spot if you've always wondered how fruits and veggies get to market, or if you're interested in harvesting to earn a bit of money. The **Leeton Visitors Centre** (tel. 6953 2832, but may be switching numbers) on Kurrajong Ave. provides more agricultural information than you'd ever want to pick through (open Mon.-Fri. 9am-5pm, Sat. 9am-3pm, Sun. 9am-2pm). An excellent guide available here and throughout the Riverina is *Working Holidays in the Riverina,* a booklet which details the harvesting seasons for towns throughout the region. Oh, and for the free rice, head to **Sunrice Country Visitors Centre** (tel. 6953 0596) on Calrose St.

Griffith

Griffith (pop. 22,000) positively bustles as a residential and commercial center, at least when compared to the farmland around it. It is the cultural locus of the region, and also a home base for many fruit pickers, with the accompanying budget lodgings. An Italian influence on the town's food and drink means that dining cheaply doesn't just mean choosing between fish and chips shops.

Orientation and Practical Information Designed by Walter Burley Griffin (of Canberra fame), broad boulevards radiate out from the town's hub. The main street, **Banna Ave.,** which runs east-west, is lined with strip-mall-style shops and inexpensive lodgings. The **Griffith Visitors Information Centre** (tel. 6962 4145), located on the corner of Jondary and Banna Ave., sits beneath a WWII vintage airplane (open Mon.-Fri. 9am-5pm, Sat. 9am-3pm, Sun. 9am-2pm). The **post office** is at 245-263 Banna Ave. (open Mon.-Fri. 9am-5pm, postal code 2680).

On Barra Ave., inside the Mobil service station, **Griffith Travel & Transit** (tel. 6962 7199) operates bus service with **McCafferty's, Greyhound Pioneer,** and **Countrylink** (tickets sold Mon.-Fri. 9am-6pm, Sat. 9am-12:30pm, Sun. 1:30-2:30pm). Griffith is a stop on most major inter-city bus routes, though often in the middle of the night. There is service to Sydney (3 per day, 11hr., $35-40), Canberra (3 per day, 6hr., $21-32), Melbourne (1 per day, 6hr., $24), Adelaide (2 per day, 11hr., $60-73), and Mildura (3 per day, 6hr., $29-36).

Accommodations and Food For backpackers or fruit harvesters seeking unique and inexpensive accommodation, the **Griffith Pioneer Park** has **shearer's quarters** with dorm-style triples, a communal kitchen, and bathroom facilities ($10; weekly $60). Contact the Pioneer Park Museum for booking information. Downtown on Banna Ave., the **Area Hotel** (tel. 6962 3122) offers above-the-pub lodging in a recently decorated modern facility (singles $30, with breakfast $35; V, MC). The **Griffith Tourism Caravan Park** (tel. 6964 2144), four blocks south of the information center on Jondaryan St., provides a wide range of accommodations. Unpowered tent sites cost $13, weekly $65. Worker caravans, furnished with sleeping quarters and kitchenettes, are rented weekly (singles $90, doubles $125, plus gas and electric bills; V, MC). Clean cinderblock ablutions are close by, and a barbecue and tennis court are available for guests' use. For flavorful cuisine, try any of the Italian restaurants or cafes along Banna Ave.

Sights and Activities Griffith's attractions are clustered around the **bush reserve,** located on the town's northern bluffs. The **Griffith Pioneer Park Museum** (tel. 6962 4196), on the corner of Rembrance Driveway and Scenic Dr., displays 40 buildings which chronicle Griffith's development within the Murrumbidgee Irrigation Area. Two hours is plenty of time to see the buildings and admire the preening peacocks (open daily 9am-5pm; admission $5, children $2; V, MC; wheelchair accessible). Traveling east from Pioneer Park along **Scenic Drive,** travelers can scope out the surrounding area from two lookouts. **Rotary Lookout** offers panoramas from a metal platform, while farther east, **Sir Dudley DeChair's Lookout** overlooks a suburban development and citrus groves. Prowl around the rocks here and explore **Hermits Cave,** where Valerio Recitti tried to find privacy.

Back in town, the **Griffith Regional Theatre** (tel. 6962 7466) shows productions suitable for all audiences. The handcrafted stage curtain was created by over 300 locals and displays a panorama of Griffith (box office open Mon.-Fri. 10am-5pm, Sat. 9am-noon). East on Banna Ave., an eye-catching pastel building houses the **Griffith Regional Art Gallery** (tel. 6962 5991; temporary exhibitions Tues.-Sat. 10:30am-4:30pm).

NORTHWEST AND BACK O' BOURKE

The empty stretches of northwest and far west New South Wales couldn't be more antithetical to the state's urbane capital—further evidence, were it necessary, of Australia's manifold personalities. Although it encompasses the watershed of the Murray and Darling Rivers, the continent's largest river system, the region's arid climate has discouraged widespread settlement. So remote is the image Bourke (pronounced "Burke") evokes in the minds of Sydney-siders, that dubbing the state's outback as "back o' Bourke" is tantamount to declaring it the end of the earth. Cotton agriculture supports a modest economy, bolstered by the lead- and silver-mines at Broken Hill. Sprinkled across this lesser-known half of New South Wales are some of Australia's most remote national parks, including Lake Mungo, which has yielded evidence of human occupation in Australia dating to many tens of thousands of years ago.

Coonabarabran

The town of Coonabarabran, 159km northeast of Dubbo on the Newell Hwy., serves as a base town for nearby **Warrumbungle National Park** and capitalizes on the area's clear skies as a center for astronomical observation. The **Coonabarabran Visitors Centre** (tel. 6842 1441), on John St., at the east end of town, has tourist information and a surprising display on **Australian megafauna** which includes the skeleton of a giant Diprotodon, the largest marsupial ever to roam the earth (open daily 9am-5pm; free). **Countrylink** (tel. 13 22 32) carries passengers between Sydney and Coonabarabran (6 per week, 8hr., $64), stopping at the visitors center. **Greyhound Pioneer** (tel. 13 20 30) makes trips to Narrabri (1 per day, 1½hr., $48) and Dubbo (1 per day, 2hr., $38), as does **McCafferty's** (tel. 13 14 99). Each is less expensive and more convenient at times, so it makes sense to call both before making a reservation. **Harvey World Travel,** 35A Dalgarno St. (tel. 6842 1566; fax 6842 1936) can book seats on any of these buses (open Mon.-Fri. 9am-5pm), but no bus company in town can help you get closer to Warrumbungle National Park. Coonabarabran's main street is John St., and there are several **ATMs** and a **post office** (tel. 6842 1193; open Mon.-Fri. 9am-5pm) along this strip. The postal code for Coonabarabran is 2357.

Beds in Coonabarabran fill up during school holidays, so be sure to call ahead for visits during those weeks. At the time this book was being written, the **Imperial Hotel** (tel. 6842 1023), on John St. at Dalgarno St., was slated to become affiliated with YHA. Whether the plan went through or not, the hotel is a great place to stay with clean, heated bedrooms, spotless bathrooms, a kitchen, TV room, and a sunny porch. (Reception open daily 8am-midnight. Check-out 10am. Dorm beds $14; singles $20; doubles and twins $28. Linen included). On-site caravans at the **John Oxley Caravan Park** (tel. 6842 1635), on Chappell Ave., just before the Newell Hwy. heads north from town, provide the best accommodation deal in town for groups of three or more (reception open daily 8am-noon and 2-9pm; check-out 10am; sites $7.50, for 2 $9.50, each additional person $2.50; with power $11, $12, $3; caravans $22, $25, $3; caravans for 1 or 2 $28.30, for 3 $32.50, for 4 $36.50).

The **IGA Festival** (tel. 6842 1179), on Dalgarno St., attends to all your self-catering needs (open Mon.-Fri. 8:30am-6pm, Sat. 8:30am-4pm, Sun. noon-2pm), while the selection of lunch counters on John St. belies the fact that this one-horse town feeds as many tourists as residents on many occasions. For basic cafe fare and vegetarian selections, the **Jolly Cauli Coffee Shop,** 30 John St. (tel. 6842 2021), is a fine choice (pasties $2, Devonshire tea $4; open Mon.-Fri. 9am-5:30pm, Sat. 9:30am-2pm).

Australia's largest optical telescope resides at **Siding Spring Observatory** (tel. 6842 6211; fax 6842 6226), 28km from Coonabarabran on the road to Warrumbungle National Park. The observatory's visitors center offers an interactive, multimedia window onto the work of the resident astronomers (open daily 9:30am-4pm; admission $5, children $3, families of 4 $13). Because the facility is occupied with scientific research in the evenings, Siding Spring does not allow visitors to look through the telescope after hours.

The nearby **Skywatch Night and Day Observatory** (tel. 6842 2506; fax 6842 2978), on the road to Warrumbungle National Park and 2km from Coonabarabran, however, gladly obliges, with guided nighttime viewing sessions and a planetarium. The hands-on exhibits, open during both day and night hours, are designed for tourists and tend to be a bit more fun than those at Siding Spring. Still, the Skywatch observatory lacks the extra kick that comes from knowing the telescopes are engaged in ground-breaking research. (Open daily 2-5pm and 6:30-9pm; 1hr. viewing sessions at 7 and 8pm. Admission $10, ages 5-16 $5, families of 4 $26.)

Between the two observatories, **Shea's Miniland Dinosaur Theme Park** (tel. 6842 1164 or 1800 649 339) is dedicated to good old-fashioned fun with no pretense of educational value. The small-time amusement park cashes in on dino-mania with concrete dinosaurs scattered among attractions including a miniature railway, miniature cars, paddle boats, and a waterslide. (Open daily 9am-5:30pm. Admission $10, under 2 free, families of 5 $45, each additional child $5.)

Warrumbungle National Park

The jagged spires and rambling peaks of the Warrumbungle Mountains are the result of volcanic activity which took place millions of years ago. As the softer sandstone has worn away under the hardened lava rock, unusual shapes have been left to slice into the sky above the forested hills. Botanically, the mountains sit at the juncture of two climates and habitats, the lush, moist east and the barren, dry west. Warrumbungle National Park sets aside this singular mix of terrain and plant life for the kangaroos and wallabies who have long called the area home, as well for the hikers, rock-climbers, and campers who have more recently discovered the splendor of the mountains.

A 75km **scenic drive** branches off from the Newell Hwy. 39km north of Gilgandra and runs through the park, circling back to the Newell Hwy. at Coonabarabran. The road is paved between Coonabarabran and the park's western edge. Drivers hoping to avoid gravel roads should proceed to Coonabarabran on the Newell Hwy. and approach the park from the east. The park entry fee of $7.50 per car (motorcycles $3, cyclists and pedestrians free) should be paid at the **Warrumbungle National Park Visitors Centre** (tel. 6825 4364), on the park road 33km west of Coonabarabran. In return, the center provides detailed information on resources and walking tracks in the park and distributes the permits necessary for rock-climbing (free) and bush camping ($2 per night; students, seniors, and ages 6-15 $1, under 6 free). A light-up map inside this edifice of edification gives a great overview of the park, highlighting some of the more unusual rock formations (open daily 8:30am-4pm).

Of the park's serviced camping acres, only four are open to individual travelers. **Camp Blackman** has toilets, water, showers, a public payphone, and car-accessible sites (for 2 $10, each additional person $2; with power $15, $3; wheelchair-accessible). The unpowered sites at **Camp Pincham** lie a short walk from the nearest car park, while those at **Burbie Camp** require a 4km hike from the park road (both areas feature toilets, showers; sites for 2 $10, each additional person $2). **Gunneemooroo** can be reached by a much longer hike from Burbie Camp or by car over the unpaved road from **Tooraweenah** (toilets, water; sites for 2 $10, each additional person $2).

The **Gurianawa Track** runs in an easy circle around the visitors center (15min.) and gives a quick introduction to the park environment, including views of the Siding Spring Observatory and the area's extinct volcanoes. Be sure to look for kangaroos on the flats below the trail. The short walk to **Whitegum Lookout** (1km round-trip), at the east end of the park, 27km from Coonabarabran, provides striking views of the surrounding mountains without too much effort. Both of these trails are surfaced and graded for wheelchairs. The most popular of the park's longer walks, the hike to **Grand High Tops** starts at a parking area situated 1km south of the main park road and 500m west of the turn-off for the visitors center. The steep walk makes a 12.5km circuit through the southern half of the park, passing stunning views of **Breadknife,** an imposing 90m stone tower, and turn-offs for most of the park's other major sights. The walk back via West Spiney adds 2km to the route and affords walkers a chance to see the eagles which often fly around **Bluff Mountain.** Allow five to six hours for the entire trip and an additional two hours if you plan to climb Bluff Mountain (2.4km). The *Park Guide* brochure available at the park visitors center or at the Coonabarabran Shire Visitors Centre in Coonabarabran has further details on long walks.

Narrabri

Equidistant from Sydney and Brisbane (560km), the prosperous cotton-growing center of Narrabri has two major attractions: the six-dish **Australia Telescope** complex and the beautifully rugged scenery of **Mount Kaputar National Park.** The town itself, 118km northeast of Coonabarabran on the Newell Hwy., is a friendly place, small enough that neighbors know each other and people look after one another.

A cotton gin and a telescope dish, clear symbols of the community's strengths, mark the **Narrabri Visitors Centre** (tel. 6792 3583), on Tibbereena St., on the banks of Narrabri Creek (open daily 8:30am-5pm). **Greyhound Pioneer** (tel. 13 20 30) buses stop in Narrabri on the way between Melbourne (1 per day, 16hr., $123) and Brisbane (1 per day, 7½hr., $56), with service to Coonabarabran on the southern leg (1 per day, 1½hr., $48). A full complement of services line Maitland St., parallel to Tibbereena St. one block from the creek. These include an office of the **National Parks and Wildlife Service,** 100 Maitland St., level 1 (tel. 6799 1740; open Mon.-Fri. 8:30am-4:30pm). All seven pubs along the central three-block stretch offer accommodation.

One of Narrabri's quieter watering holes, **Tattersall's Hotel** (tel. 6792 2007) is a particularly good deal because of the basic kitchen area and comfortable TV room (reception at the bar daily 10am-midnight; rooms $20, weekly $65). **Campers** should head out of town to Mt. Kaputar National Park (see below) or stop for the shady sights and clean amenities of the **Highway Caravan Park,** 86 Cooma Rd. (tel. 6792 1438), where the Newell Hwy. leaves town for Coonabarabran (laundry facilities; live-in owners receive guests anytime; check-out 10am; sites for 2 $11, with power $14, each additional person $3.50). For food, several lunch counters and bakeries on Maitland St. will happily do the cooking for you. **Woolworths,** between Maitland St. and Tibbereena St. at Lloyd St., has all the fixin's for homemade feasts (open Mon.-Fri. 8am-9pm, Sat.-Sun. 8am-5pm).

Signs on the Newell Hwy. heading toward Coonabarabran lead the way to the **Australia Telescope,** 20km west of Narrabri, a set of six large radio dishes which comprise the largest, most powerful telescope array in the southern hemisphere. Working together, the telescopes achieve the accuracy of a dish 6km across. When that's just not good enough, the Narrabri dishes can be operated in conjunction with telescopes at Parkes and Coonabarabran to act as one telescope over 300km in diameter. The **Australia Telescope Visitors Centre** (tel. 6790 4070; fax 6790 4090) employs the ultimate interactive exhibit, a fully-informed staff, to explain these and other astronomical wonders Monday through Friday. On the weekends, videos and displays take over (open daily 8am-4pm, staffed Mon.-Fri; free). East of Narrabri, the peaks of the **Nandewar Range** beckon travelers to leave the paved road behind and scale the summit of Mt. Kaputar for a grand view that takes in one-tenth of New South Wales. The entrance to the central section of Mount Kaputar National Park, where you'll find both of the park's serviced camping areas (**Bark Hut Camping Area,** 14km inside the park, and **Dawsons Spring Camping Area,** 21km inside, near the Mt. Kaputar summit) lies 31km east of Narrabri via Maitland St. and Old Gunnedah Rd. Both campsites have hot showers, toilets, drinking water, electricity, and barbecues, but neither is equipped for caravans. (No reservations, payment made to honesty boxes. Sites $15 regardless of occupancy.) The park's most famous scenic attraction is undoubtedly the amazing basalt rock formation know as **Sawn Rocks,** located in the park's northern section, accessible from the Newell Hwy. north of Narrabri. The perfect rock pleats tower over the easy walking track which leads from the nearby **Sawn Rocks Picnic Area.** Detailed descriptions of this walk and others throughout the park can be found in the excellent *Park Guide* pamphlet available from the NPWS office in Narrabri ($3). A copy of this brochure is posted at the Dawson Spring ranger's cabin for free reference.

Broken Hill

In 1883, Charles Rasp, a German-born boundary rider employed on the lonesome Mt. Gipps sheep station, discovered that the misshapen hill known locally as the "hog's back" was in fact one of the biggest lodes of silver-lead ore in the world. Rasp and his associates became fabulously wealthy; mines opened by their Broken Hill Proprietary (BHP) company obtained thousands of tons of lead, silver, and other valuable metals and attracted thousands of people, transforming worthless scrubland into a booming, wealthy city almost overnight. Conditions in the mines were harsh, and the BHP was in a position to exploit its workers. The Amalgamated Miners' Association, one of the earliest unions in Australia, was formed in 1886, and a series of highly charged strikes gradually won more equitable treatment for the miners. Mining continues to this day, on the same giant lode discovered by Rasp. Known reserves of ore are projected to run out in less than 20 years, and the town is expected to lose half of its population when the mines close, since there is little else to hold people in this harsh land. Broken Hillers though, are proud of their isolation, and have of necessity developed an independent streak. Perched on the edge of the back o' beyond, Broken Hill is a stronghold of old-time Aussie perseverance.

ORIENTATION

Rather than use arbitrary points of the compass, Broken Hill's streets are aligned with the line of lode that is the city's lifeblood. Most streets have names taken from the periodic table, and they form a relatively regular grid. Shops and services congregate in the rectangle bounded by Iodide, Bromide, Crystal, and Mica St., and the city is quite manageable on foot. The railway station lies on **Crystal Street.** A short mall connects to **Argent Street,** which becomes the **Barrier Hwy.** at its northeast end and strikes eastward across 1157km of wasteland to Sydney. Parallel to Argent, 1km to the northwest, **Williams Street** is also called the Barrier Hwy. as it runs out of town toward Adelaide, 512km distant. Several outlying attractions require motorized transport (particularly Silverton, Mungo National Park, and the Living Desert), but rental cars are extremely expensive. Organized tours are a reasonable option for seeing all of the sights if you don't drive into town.

PRACTICAL INFORMATION

Tourist Office: Broken Hill Tourist Centre (tel. 8087 6077; fax 8088 5209) on the corner of Blende and Bromide St. From the railway station, turn left onto Crystal and walk 2 blocks west, then turn right onto Bromide; the office is 2 blocks down on the left. Local tours can be booked. Public **showers** $3. Open daily 8:30am-5pm.

National Parks Information: New South Wales National Parks and Wildlife Service, 5 Oxide St. (tel. 8088 5933).

Bank: ANZ, 357 Argent St. (tel. 8088 4288), open Mon.-Thurs. 9:30am-4pm, Fri. 9:30am-5pm. There are many **ATMs** on Argent St.

Airport: (tel. 8087 1969 or 8087 4128), 7km southeast of town, serves Ansett, Qantas, and Hazleton. One-way flights to Sydney ($350) and Adelaide ($173) are cheaper if booked in advance. Tickets to Melbourne cost about $227.

Trains: The **train station** (tel. 8087 1400, after hours 13 22 32; fax 8087 0442) is on Crystal St. near the intersection with Chloride St. The **Indian-Pacific** runs to Sydney (Wed. and Sun., 3:20pm, 18hr., $98) and to Adelaide (Tues. and Fri., 9am, 7hr., $50) continuing to Perth (22hr., $280). **Countrylink** trains to Sydney (daily 4am and Thurs. 7:30pm, 16¾hr., $99) and to Melbourne (Wed. and Fri., 3:45pm, 15hr., $89), stopping in Mildura (4¼hr., $37), Ballarat (13hr., $83), and Geelong (14hr., $87).

Buses: The **bus depot** (tel. 8087 2735 or 8088 4040; for 24hr. info. 13 20 30) is in the same building as the visitor center at the corner of Blende and Bromide St. . Daily **Greyhound** buses to Adelaide (7hr., $56, $51 for YHA members), Dubbo (8½hr., $84, $76 for YHA), and Sydney (overnight, $99, $90 for YHA). Buses to Mildura (Wed. and Fri., 3hr., $37, no discount).

Car Rental: Thrifty, 190 Argent St. (tel. 8088 1928), $75 per day, plus 25¢ per km over 100. 21- to 23-year-olds pay an $8 per day surcharge. **Holmes,** at 475 Argent St. (tel. 8087 2210), charges $50 per day, plus 20¢ per km over 100. Renters must be at least 25.

Bike Rental: Johnny Windham, 195B Argent St. (tel. 8087 3707). $5 per day, $25 per month; deposit $50. Open Mon.-Fri. 9am-5pm.

Library: Charles Rasp Memorial Library, Blende St. (tel. 8080 2229; fax 8087 8055). **Internet access** $3 per hr. Open Mon.-Wed. 10am-8pm, Thurs.-Fri. 10am-6pm, Sat. 10am-1pm, Sun. 1-5pm.

Road Conditions: (tel. 8091 5155 or 8087 0660).

Police: (tel. 8087 02999), on the corner of Comstock and Patton St.

Emergency: Dial 000.

Post Office: 260 Argent St. (tel./fax 8088 1991). Open Mon.-Fri. 9am-5pm. **Postal code:** 2880.

Phone Code: 08. Although Broken Hill is in New South Wales, it has adopted the phone code and time zone of South Australia.

ACCOMMODATIONS AND FOOD

Nomads Astra Backpackers, 393 Argent St. (tel. 8087 7788), right in the city center. A long-established, well-run facility in an old hotel. The lofty lounge is fairly unfinished, but comfortable enough, with a cheery woodstove. The dining room boasts a pool table and an extremely loud pinball machine. Well-equipped kitchen, heavily used by the families and couples who frequent this hostel. Dorms $13. Key deposit $5. The manager can assist with tours and bookings.

West Darling Hotel, 400 Argent St. (tel. 8087 2691). One of the many old hotels on Argent St., the West Darling provides plain, neat shared rooms that look out on a spacious veranda. The veranda is perched above Argent St. and is equipped with BBQ for balmy summer evenings. Each room has a washbasin, and the aging, tiled bathrooms are clean enough. Beds $18. No real kitchens, but the downstairs pub has the best counter fare in town, usually under $10. Meals served noon-2pm and 6pm-7:30pm. Massive breakfast $5.

The Tourist Lodge, 100 Argent St. (tel 8088 2086; fax 8087 9511). Broken Hill's YHA hostel is designed for groups: there is an industrial kitchen, the dining room boasts a dozen large wooden tables, and there are more rooms than you can shake a stick at. Nevertheless, the place often fills completely, especially during school holidays. Most rooms are twin share and all are equipped with a ceiling fan to beat the desert heat. The tourist center and bus depot are right at the back door. Rental bikes are available, and the courtyard features a heated salt swimming pool. Twin share rooms $14 per person; singles $18; guest house rooms $22.

There are numerous takeaway joints along Argent St. **Schinella's Food and Liquor,** on Argent St. across from the YHA hostel, sells groceries and hootch, both in good variety. The **Pussy Cat Restaurant,** 425 Argent St. (tel. 8087 4354), serves a wide variety of grilled flesh, Broken Hill's dietary mainstay. Most dishes cost about $10 (BYO-licensed; open Mon.-Sat. 5:30-9:30pm, Sun. 5:30-9pm). **Brumby's Hot Bread and Pastries,** 413 Argent St. (tel. 8088 5533), bakes a marvelous loaf, and the sweets aren't bad either (open Mon.-Fri. 7am-6pm, Sat. 7am-5pm, Sun. 7am-3pm; ask for something fresh from the oven). **Ruby's Coffee Lounge** (tel. 8087 1188), also on Argent St., provides much-needed vegetables, as all meals are served with salad. Sandwiches, grills, and several vegetarian options under $6 (breakfast from 8am).

SIGHTS AND ENTERTAINMENT

Mining is Broken Hill, and Broken Hill is mining. Gain insight into this relationship with a tour of the original **Broken Hill Proprietary Mine** (tel. 8088 1604, after- hours 8087 4905) through Delprat's Mine Tours. The two-hour trip features demonstrations of (fairly) modern mining equipment and a thorough explanation of the modern mining labor system, all 200m underground. Tours leave at 10:30am and 2pm from the BHP mine site on top of the Broken Hill ($23; call to book). The **Albert Kersten Geo-Centre** (tel. 8080 2222; fax 8088 1702), on the corner of Bromide and Crystal St., offers a more scientific look at mining, concentrating on the geological history of the region and the metallurgical techniques used in Broken Hill. There is also an extensive display of mineral specimens (open Mon.-Fri. 10am-5pm, Sat.-Sun. 1-5pm; admission $3, concessions and ages 5-15 $2, under 5 free).

Diagonally across from the tourist center, on the corner of Blende and Bromide St., the **Sulphide Street Station Railway, Mineral, and Train Museum** is housed in the old narrow-gauge tramway building that serviced a privately-owned rail link to Cockburn in South Australia between 1888 and 1970. The museum preserves relics from the tramway's years of operation (open 10am-3pm; admission $2).

Broken Hill is on the western frontier of Australia's populated east, and therefore serves as a hub for the surrounding outback. The **School of the Air** provides educational programs for distant schoolchildren. Visitors can observe the proceedings (Mon.-Fri.) but must book at the tourist office the day before and be seated by 8:30am (demerits for tardiness). The **Royal Flying Doctor Service** (tel. 8088 0777), at the Broken Hill Airport, provides health care to outback residents. A museum and brief film detail the history and workings of this noble institution (open Mon.-Fri. 10am-noon and 3-5pm, Sat.-Sun. 10am-noon).

The **Broken Hill City Art Gallery,** on the corner of Blende and Chloride St. (tel. 8088 5491; fax 8087 1411), has an interesting variety of excellent local work and an especially strong collection of 20th-century Australian painting. Works of note include the *Silver Tree,* a delicately wrought arboreal centerpiece commissioned by Charles Rasp, and a mural donated by the Communist Party of Australia (open Mon.-Fri. 9am-4pm; admission $2, concessions $1). Broken Hill is also home to numerous private commercial galleries, most specializing in expansive landscapes, a natural consequence of the local terrain. Art of a different sort has been set up north of town in the Living Desert Reserve. In 1993, the **Broken Hill Sculpture Symposium** commissioned a group of sculptors to create works that harmonized with the stark beauty of the outback; the results can be seen by walking a few minutes north on Kaolin St. If you must drive, a gate key can be obtained from the tourist office for a fee, but the walk is more fun and is absolutely free.

Walking tours of Broken Hill leave from the tourist center daily at 10am, and the fee is actually a donation to charity. Many private-sector tour operators offer trips into the outback, to the sights near Broken Hill, or to one or many of the area's national parks. Details and bookings can be pursued at the Visitor Information Centre. Few of them are particularly cheap, but the sights are truly memorable. **Entertainment** in Broken Hill centers around the clubs and hotels. Argent St. is lined with fine pubs, and the clubs are welcoming to visitors. Be warned that pokies (gambling machines) play a large part in the nightlife.

■ Near Broken Hill: Silverton

Silverton came to be as a result of the silver-zinc-lead ore discovered at Thackaringa in 1876. Prospectors arrived in numbers, and the population peaked at around 3000 in 1885. Unfortunately for Silverton, most of the ore was gone by this point, just as the Line of Lode discovered by Charles Rasp in Broken Hill was revealing its precious potential. This combination of circumstances rendered Silverton a ghost town, today home to fewer than 100 hermits. Silverton revels in its emptiness and has been used in numerous bleak films and television spots (including the classic *Mad Max*). But don't let concern over post-nuclear desert mutants keep you away from Silverton; it is an experience like no other.

Silverton's handful of buildings includes a selection of galleries worth a look. Entry is generally by donation. Also of interest is the **Silverton Gaol Museum,** erected in 1889. The Gaol was used infrequently after the evaporation of Silverton's population and was converted to a boys' reformatory in the 1930s. The buildings were closed in 1943 and then reopened as a museum in 1968 (open Mon.-Fri. 9:30am-4:30pm; admission $2, concessions $1, children 50¢). Outback country is thirsty country, making the legendary **Silverton Hotel** the most important building in town. Filled to the rafters with memorabilia and humorous junk, the hotel serves simple food and drink until 9 or 10 in the evening. Don't leave before taking "The Test."

During the last Ice Age, glaciers scraped the plains west of Silverton until they were as level as a freshly-zambonied ice rink. If you still doubt that the world is a sphere, drive 6km west to **Mundi Mundi Scenic Lookout.** The curvature of the planet is clearly visible. Let's Go does not recommend the Mundi Mundi plain to agoraphobics.

National Parks of the Far West

MUNGO NATIONAL PARK

During the last Ice Age, Lake Mungo was one of many lakes in the Willandra system. The area has been continually inhabited for 40,000 years and provides a record of Aboriginal culture through 1600 generations. The archaeological information is invaluable, and the entire **Willandra Lakes** region has been declared a World Heritage Site. Today the lakes are dry, and Mungo has undergone some spectacular weathering. Piles of sand have been swept across the lake bed and sculpted into strange, otherworldly landforms by the tireless westerly wind. These Walls of China have revealed countless fossils and artifacts as the sands have shifted from place to place.

Mungo is 110km northeast of Mildura on the Acumpo-Ivanhoe Rd. Roads within and around the park are unsealed but accessible for 2WD vehicles in good weather. Road conditions can be checked with the NP&WS (tel. 8091 5155 or 8087 0660). There is an excellent, 60km driving tour that encompasses all of the best features of the park. The visitor center near the park entrance provides information on the natural and cultural history of the area (and collects entry fees). Decent **bunk accommodation** ($15) is available near the center, and camping is allowed near the Arump Rd. entrance and at Belah Camp on the driving tour. Visitors must bring drinking water and firewood. (Park day use fee $7.50 per vehicle; **campsites** for 2 $5, each additional person $2.) All fees operate on an honor system, so be honorable.

Cenozoic Megafauna

Evidence collected at many places in Australia strongly suggests that the early Aboriginals shared the continent with some fearsome beasts: giant mammals now termed megafauna. Overgrown versions of modern animals such as possums and kangaroos are frequently unearthed, but stranger still are the novel species, such as *Zygomaturus trilobus.* This buffalo-sized creature was built much like a wombat but possessed either a horn similar to a rhinoceros's or a short, flexible trunk. Long-dead marsupial carnivores have been found, perhaps ancestors of the almost extinct Tasmanian Tiger. Strangest of all is *Procoptodon goliah,* a kangaroo twice as big as the largest red 'roos, but with eerily human facial features. The skull was flattened and the eyes were set forward in the head, just like ours. Unlike regular kangaroos, goliah's arms and shoulders allowed it to manipulate objects and even reach overhead, much like the ancestors of human beings. If primates hadn't beaten out marsupials in the race toward sentience as we define it, we might all be hopping today.

KINCHEGA NATIONAL PARK

Kinchega, 85km southeast of Broken Hill on the road to Menindee, lacks any remarkable landmarks but is an extremely pleasant place for a drive or a stroll. Sunsets over Menindee Lake are gorgeous, and the lake itself is perfect for boating. The area has a long pastoral history, and the old **shearers' quarters** still provide accommodation. Bunk beds ($15) must be booked ahead (tel. 8088 5933) and are equipped with showers and a communal kitchen. **Camping** is available along the Darling River or at Emu Lake when the water is high. Sites (2 people $5, each additional $2) are equipped with BBQ and tables, and the showers at the shearers' quarters are available on a donation basis. Bring your own firewood.

MOOTWINGEE NATIONAL PARK

Located 130km northeast of Broken Hill, Mootwingee is famous for its Aboriginal paintings and rock engravings. An area of deep, twisting gorges lined with river redgums, Mootwingee harbors abundant animal life. The Aboriginal cultural artifacts are spiritually significant to the modern Aboriginal community, and are therefore closed to the general public. They can be viewed through organized guided tours, given at regular intervals by knowledgeable park staff. In addition to these relics, several scenic walks and drives allow for further exploration. The unsealed tracks become impassable after a rain. **Campsites** are available ($10 per site and $2 for each person after the first 2). They are equipped with tables, toilets, and barbecues. All users are required to pay $7.50 per vehicle. Call 8088 5933 for more information.

Northern Territory

Once upon a time, the people of the Northern Territory gathered together to agree upon a Territorian symbol. A bloke from the capital city of Darwin piped up, "The fierce, mighty saltwater crocodile!" "Look," replied a woman from the Red Centre town of Alice Springs, "Darwin may have nearly half of our 180,000 people, but you know those salties of yours don't venture far from the tropical forests of the Top End. On my side of the Tropic of Capricorn," she continued, "it's the kangaroo that..." "Kanga-!@#*@%$-roo!" blurted a drunk fella in the back of the room. "Don't give me that! Our puerile obsession with that marsupial makes a mockery of our country!" The crowd stared in confusion. "I say *bee-uh!*" the man shouted, holding his tinny of beer aloft. A roar of relief and understanding filled the room.

"But our drinking has its dangers, too," pointed out a thoughtful 29-year-old tourist bureau official (who had the median age of a Territorian). "We'd do better to stress our efforts to control it, if anything." There were grunts of sober agreement. "I've got it!" announced the driver of an enormous multi-trailer truck aptly called a road train. "The Stuart Highway carries the name of the pioneer whose exploration of our outback encouraged South Australia to annex it in 1863. Now thousands of kilometers of smooth bitumen connect Darwin and Alice to Adelaide and the world beyond. The Stuart is the backbone of our Territory!" "True," concurred a ranger from Kakadu National Park, "but think how many of our 1,346,000 square kilometers are not accessible from that road. We might as well recognize the telegraph, for giving investors a reason for surveying that path in the first place." A black man, quiet all this time, finally spoke up. "Mates, the Territory is full of us Aboriginals. We're one in four people, a higher proportion than in any other state in Australia. What's more, tourists are enchanted by the sound of our native wind instrument, the didgeridoo. Let's make *that* our symbol." "Tyranny of the minority!" screamed a notorious member of Parliament, putting an end to that line of discussion.

"A boomerang?" someone ventured cautiously. "Too obvious." "Ayers Rock?" "Worse." Then, as if on cue, a ripple of consensus ran through the room. "Our spirit! Our proud, rugged, no-worries spirit! Let's make that our symbol! It's our mentality that really sets us apart from other Australians!" Shouts of rowdy approval. When the excitement died down, someone queried "But how do we represent our spirit with a logo?" "I know," the median-aged tourist official beamed with inspiration. "A lithe, graceful bird flying before a sunset of red and yellow!" And so it is.

Phone numbers in Northern Territory have recently changed. Regional phone codes are now all 08, followed by eight digit numbers. If you have trouble making a call, use the following scheme to get the old number, and try that instead. For more details, see the **appendix** (p. 574).

New Number:	**Old Number:**
(08) 89xx xxxx	(089) xx xxxx

THE TOP END

A lush tropical crown atop a vast interior desert, the winterless Top End enjoys perpetually warm weather; seasons here are divided only into the Wet and the Dry. During the May-to-October dry season, backpack-toting pilgrims descend on the city of Darwin to worship its twin deities: a cloudless sky and a shirtless culture. While enjoying the budding metropolis itself, travelers also use this oasis of civilization as a base from which to explore the region's prime natural wonder—Kakadu National Park. A spectacular rainforest reserve crawling with exotic antipodean wildlife, Kakadu is Australia's largest national park and is best explored in the dry season, when the roads are more likely to be

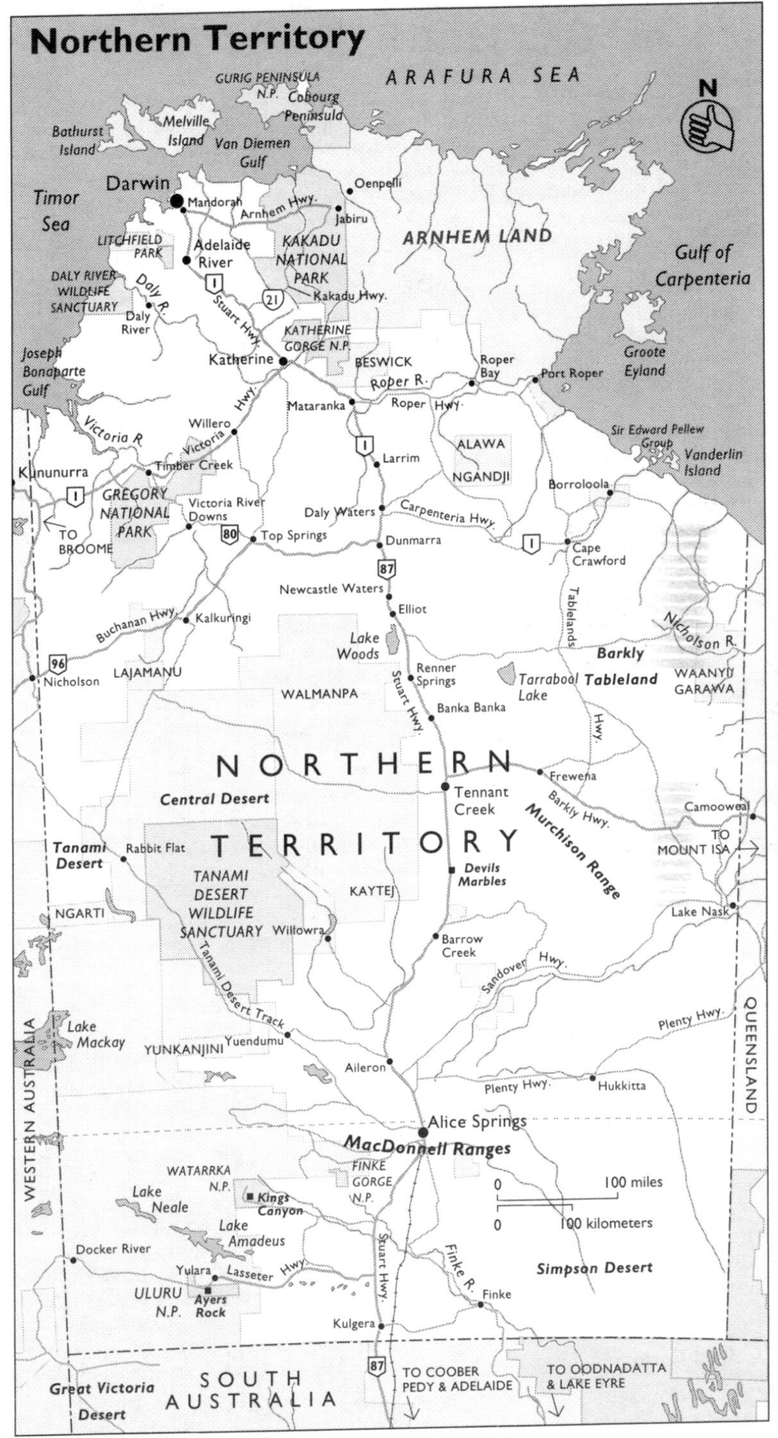
Northern Territory
ARAFURA SEA
GURIG PENINSULA N.P.
Cobourg Peninsula
Melville Island
Bathurst Island
Van Diemen Gulf
Timor Sea
Darwin
Mandorah
Arnhem Hwy.
Oenpelli
Jabiru
ARNHEM LAND
Gulf of Carpenteria
LITCHFIELD PARK
Adelaide River
KAKADU NATIONAL PARK
Kakadu Hwy.
DALY RIVER WILDLIFE SANCTUARY
Daly R.
Daly River
Stuart Hwy.
KATHERINE GORGE N.P.
Joseph Bonaparte Gulf
Katherine
BESWICK
Roper R.
Roper Bay
Port Roper
Groote Eyland
Mataranka
Roper Hwy.
Victoria R.
Willero
Victoria Hwy.
Larrim
ALAWA
NGANDJI
Sir Edward Pellew Group
Vanderlin Island
Kununurra
Timber Creek
GREGORY NATIONAL PARK
Victoria River Downs
Daly Waters
Carpenteria Hwy.
Borroloola
TO BROOME
Top Springs
Dunmarra
Cape Crawford
Newcastle Waters
Elliot
Buchanan Hwy.
Kalkuringi
Lake Woods
Tablelands Hwy.
Nicholson R.
Barkly Tableland
Nicholson
LAJAMANU
WALMANPA
Renner Springs
Tarrabool Lake
WAANYI/GARAWA
Banka Banka
NORTHERN TERRITORY
Frewena
Central Desert
Tennant Creek
Barkly Hwy.
Murchison Range
Camooweal
TO MOUNT ISA
Tanami Desert
Rabbit Flat
Devils Marbles
TANAMI DESERT WILDLIFE SANCTUARY
KAYTEJ
NGARTI
Willowra
Lake Nash
Barrow Creek
Sandover Hwy.
Tanami Desert Track
Plenty Hwy.
QUEENSLAND
Lake Mackay
YUNKANJINI
Yuendumu
Aileron
Hukkitta
WESTERN AUSTRALIA
Alice Springs
MacDonnell Ranges
WATARRKA N.P.
FINKE GORGE N.P.
Kings Canyon
Lake Neale
Lake Amadeus
0 100 miles
0 100 kilometers
Docker River
Finke R.
Yulara
Lasseter Hwy.
Simpson Desert
ULURU N.P.
Ayers Rock
Finke
Kulgera
SOUTH AUSTRALIA
Great Victoria Desert
TO COOBER PEDY & ADELAIDE
TO OODNADATTA & LAKE EYRE
NORTHERN TERRITORY

intact. The wetlands teem with the saltwater crocodiles that have captured the popular imagination. Crocodile Dundee's nemesis may become convincing reality on a tour of the park or a visit to a croc farm.

From November to April, the monsoonal Wet drenches parched hills and stony escarpments. Awesome thunderstorms dump over a meter of rain in unbelievably thick sheets. The Wet can be cruelly restrictive, as riverbeds fill like the Red Sea and roads become impassable torrents, yet the seasonal pulse of the monsoon is the heartbeat which sustains the Top End's luxuriant array of life.

Darwin

With barely 80,000 permanent residents, remote Darwin is Australia's smallest capital (and not, technically speaking, a state capital at all). Once the homeland of the Larrakia Aborigines, the site of the current settlement was called Port Darwin and Palmerston at different points in its colonial history. The Overland Telegraph Line from Adelaide connected here to an underwater cable to Europe via Indonesia. Construction of the telegraph and later a railway, accompanied by a gold rush and a long-standing pearling industry, established a trend of immigration which persists today.

Particularly rapid growth in recent years has produced one of the nation's newest and most eclectic cities. Asian immigrants mix with Greeks and Italians, complementing Darwin's large Aboriginal community and earning it the title, "the front door to Australia." As the moniker implies, Darwin isn't a final destination for many. Backpackers aren't the city's only transient population; many young Aussies come to Darwin for a time to "give it a go." Consequently, Darwin enjoys a youthful and cosmopolitan flavor known equally for its thirst for beer and its sense of adventure.

Yet isolated Darwin epitomizes Territorian resilience, maintaining an easy-going personality despite the catastrophes and tribulations which pockmark its history. Australia's hardest-hit WWII target, Darwin suffered nearly two years of intense Japanese bombing beginning February 19, 1942. Extensive destruction and high casualties elicited sympathy from the rest of the country, powering rapid post-war reconstruction. But fate hadn't finished its work. On Christmas Day, 1974, Cyclone Tracy flattened Darwin as it swept through with winds in excess of 200kph. Once again, assistance from Canberra was crucial in rebuilding the devastated outpost into the architecturally and technologically modern city that it now is.

A prosperous mining industry and booming tourist trade contribute to Darwin's current fortune. Parks landscaped to a tee lie just beyond a conveniently compact city center, rendering a vision of coastal paradise strikingly different from the untamed expanse of the Northern Territory. A refreshing outdoor mall, scores of new hostels, and well-developed transportation services augment the city's appeal to backpackers. No longer a mere tropical outpost, Darwin today links two continents and provides a point of entry to the natural wonders of the Northern Territory. Here, the spirit of the Australian frontier remains alive and well.

Who's Fittest Now?

Charles Darwin was not aboard the HMS Beagle in 1839 when it sailed into the harbor that now bears his name. The site was dubbed Port Darwin by shipmates who had accompanied him on an earlier trip to the Galápagos Islands in 1835. On that same voyage in 1836, Darwin himself disembarked near modern-day Sydney. His tour of Australia consisted of a trip to the Blue Mountains in New South Wales, which he described as having a "desolate and untidy appearance." In his journal he wrote of the continent, "Nothing but rather sharp necessity should compel me to emigrate." The biologist might find Australia a different species today.

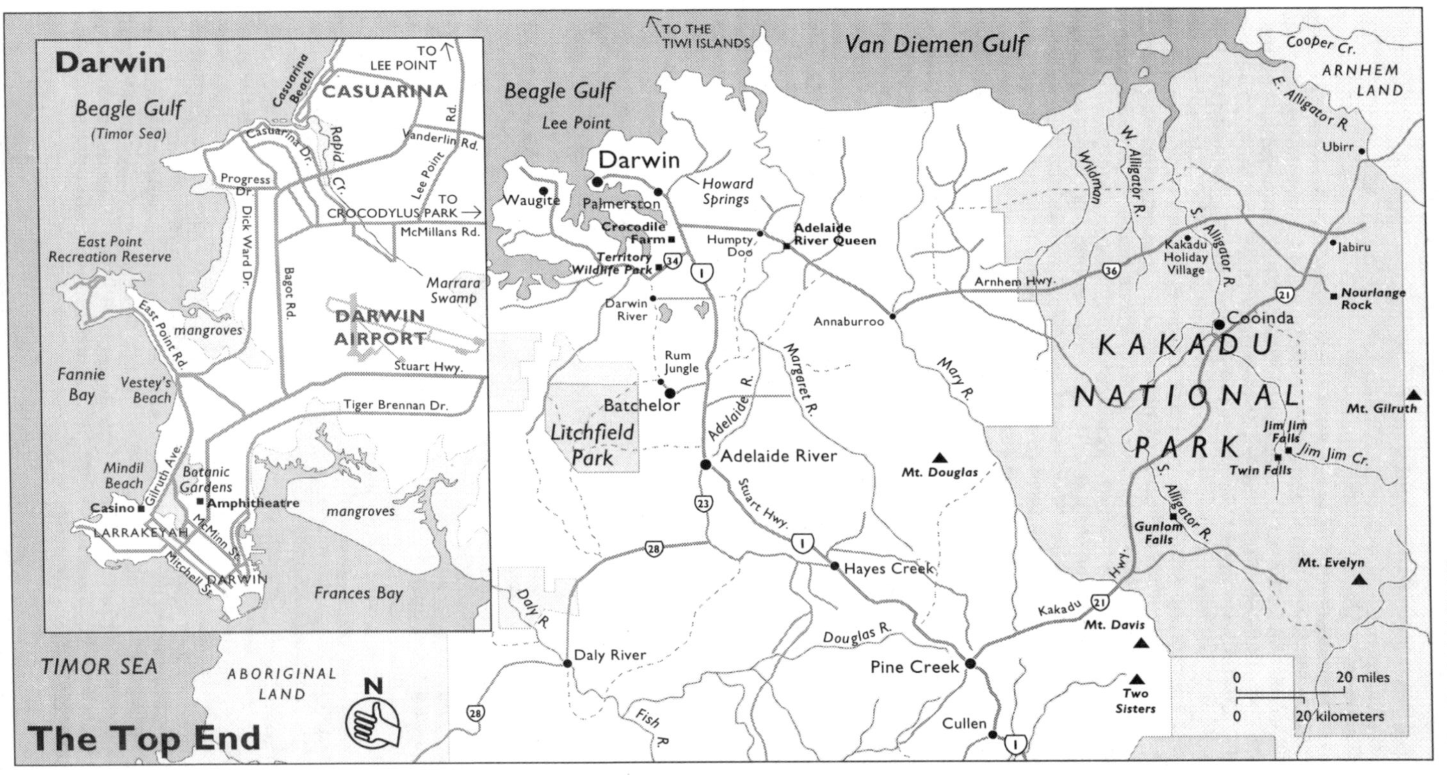
Darwin
Beagle Gulf
(Timor Sea)
TO LEE POINT
CASUARINA
Casuarina Beach
Casuarina Dr.
Rapid Cr.
Vanderlin Rd.
Lee Point Rd.
Progress Dr.
TO CROCODYLUS PARK
McMillans Rd.
East Point Recreation Reserve
Dick Ward Dr.
Bagot Rd.
Marrara Swamp
DARWIN AIRPORT
East Point Rd.
mangroves
Stuart Hwy.
Fannie Bay
Vestey's Beach
Tiger Brennan Dr.
Mindil Beach
Gilruth Ave.
Botanic Gardens
Amphitheatre
Casino
mangroves
LARRAKEYAH
McMinn St.
Mitchell St.
DARWIN
Frances Bay
TO THE TIWI ISLANDS
Van Diemen Gulf
Beagle Gulf
Lee Point
Darwin
Waugite
Palmerston
Howard Springs
Crocodile Farm
Humpty Doo
Adelaide River Queen
Territory Wildlife Park
Darwin River
Rum Jungle
Batchelor
Litchfield Park
Adelaide R.
Margaret R.
Adelaide River
Annaburroo
Mary R.
Mt. Douglas
Stuart Hwy.
Hayes Creek
Daly R.
Daly River
Douglas R.
Pine Creek
Fish R.
Cullen
Arnhem Hwy.
Wildman
W. Alligator R.
S. Alligator R.
Kakadu Holiday Village
Cooper Cr.
ARNHEM LAND
E. Alligator R.
Ubirr
Jabiru
Nourlange Rock
Cooinda
KAKADU NATIONAL PARK
Mt. Gilruth
Jim Jim Falls
Jim Jim Cr.
Twin Falls
Gunlom Falls
Mt. Evelyn
Kakadu Hwy.
Mt. Davis
Two Sisters
0 20 miles
0 20 kilometers
TIMOR SEA
ABORIGINAL LAND
N
The Top End

ARRIVAL AND DEPARTURE

By Plane

Darwin International Airport (tel. 8920 1850), is about 10km northeast of the city center on McMillans Rd. (take Bagot Rd. off the Stuart Hwy.). Many hostels offer free airport pick-up for arrivals. Options from the city to the airport include airport shuttles (tel. 8981 5066 or 1800 358 945; $6) and taxis (tel. 8981 2222 or 13 21 18; $13-15). **Qantas** and **Ansett** have domestic service to: Adelaide (about $410); Alice Springs ($267); Ayers Rock-Yulara ($363); Broome (about $260, less than one per day); Cairns (about $320), Melbourne ($482); Sydney (about $485); and Perth (about $470). All above prices include standard backpackers' discounts (30% with Qantas). Numerous airlines offer international service to Southeast Asian and trans-oceanic destinations. Currency exchange, lockers, and public showers are all available.

Airline offices include **Ansett Australia** (19 the Mall; tel. 8941 3666), **Qantas** (16 Bennett St.; tel. 8982 3316), **Singapore Airlines** (in the Mall above the plaza; tel. 8941 1799), and **Garuda Indonesia** (9 Cavanagh St.; tel. 8981 6422). **Airnorth** (tel. 8945 2866) is a local carrier with an office at the airport.

By Bus

The **Transit Centre** at 69 Mitchell St. is the locus of all bus travel to and from Darwin. **Greyhound Pioneer** (24hr. reservations: tel. 13 20 30; transit center counter staffed 6am-6pm; all fares assume 10% discount for YHA or VIP cards; ISIC receives 20% off) runs daily service to Alice Springs (10am, 1pm, 19-20hr., $133) via Katherine (7:45am, 10am, 1pm, 4hr., $38) and Tennant Creek (10am, 1pm, 12½hr., $91). Passes for regional travel or a fixed number of kilometers (in multiples of 1000) offer substantial savings. **McCafferty's,** 71 Smith St. (tel. 8941 0911; reservations tel. 13 14 99; open Mon.-Fri. 8am-6pm, Sat.-Sun. 9am-6pm), also runs daily service to Alice Springs (9am, 20¼hr., $145), Katherine (9am, 4:30pm, 4¼hr., $39), and Tennant Creek (9am, 13¾, $101) with a 10% discount for YHA and VIP. Inquire about passes, which will reduce the expense of your trip.

By Car

The **Auto Association of the Northern Territory (AANT),** 79/81 Smith St. (tel. 8981 3837; open Mon.-Fri. 8am-5pm) honors all foreign motor club memberships and provides members with free advice and maps. Non-members must pay for maps.

Cars are a popular way to see the sights of the Top End, but vast distances and (seasonally) wet climate make depreciation high, resulting in higher rates. Rent with several people if possible. **Territory Rent-a-Car** (tel. 8924 0000) has locations all over NT, including Darwin airport (open 4:30am-10:30pm) and 64 Stuart Hwy., a 25-minute walk from Mitchell St. (open 8am-6pm). Their cars start at about $45 per day with the first 100km free, although 4WD vehicles are substantially dearer. **Nifty,** 89 Mitchell St. (tel. 8981 2999; fax 8941 0662), is also a good budget choice and offers a one-day special rate of $89 with 400km free, ideal for touring Litchfield Park. **Rent-a-Rocket,** 7 McLachlan St. (tel. 8941 3733), is another local option. **Avis,** 145 Stuart Hwy. (tel. 8981 9922) and at the airport (tel. 8981 9800), and **Hertz,** Smith and Daly St. (tel. 13 30 39), are reliable, if more expensive. **Brits,** at 44/46 Stuart Hwy. (tel. 8981 2081) and **Backpacker Campervans,** located more conveniently at the corner of Cavenagh and Edmunds St. (tel. 8941 1811; open Mon.-Sat. 8am-4:30pm) both offer campervans with unlimited kilometers for around $65 per day. Most agencies require that drivers be over 21 for insurance purposes.

If you are looking to **purchase a car,** or sell one off, you'll have company in Darwin. Check out the **Backpackers Car Market** at Peel and Mitchell St. Sellers pay $30 per week to cram into the lot, but buyers browse for free. Cars sell fastest between May and October. Otherwise, check out bulletin boards in hostels. Newly purchased cars must be registered at the **Motor Vehicle Registry** (tel. 899 3145) on Goyder Rd. (turn off the Stuart Hwy. at Tom's Tyres). Transferring registration costs $12 and must be done within 14 days of purchase.

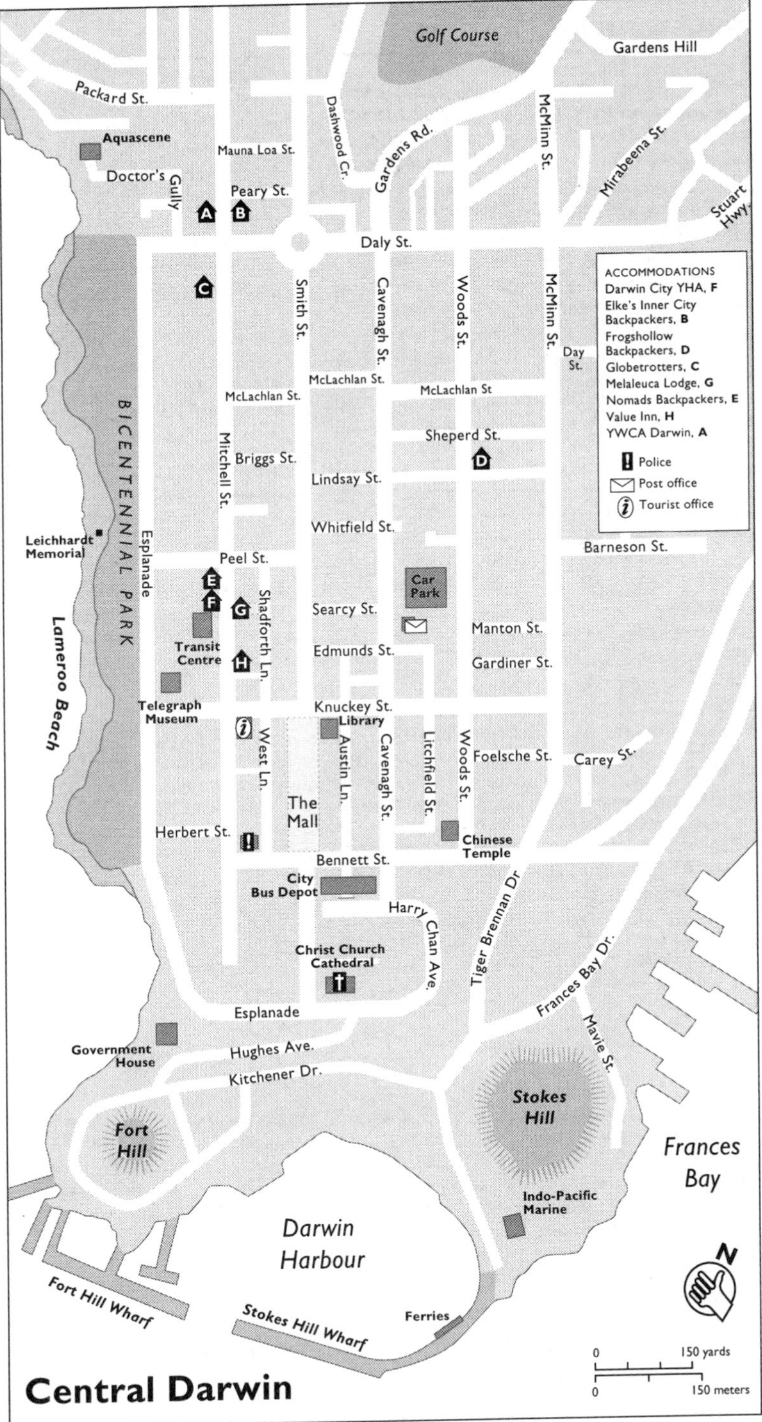
Golf Course
Gardens Hill
Packard St.
Aquascene
Mauna Loa St.
Dashwood Cr.
Gardens Rd.
McMinn St.
Mirabeena St.
Doctor's Gully
Peary St.
Stuart Hwy.
Daly St.
Smith St.
Cavenagh St.
Woods St.
McMinn St.
Day St.
ACCOMMODATIONS
Darwin City YHA, F
Elke's Inner City Backpackers, B
Frogshollow Backpackers, D
Globetrotters, C
Melaleuca Lodge, G
Nomads Backpackers, E
Value Inn, H
YWCA Darwin, A
Police
Post office
Tourist office
McLachlan St.
McLachlan St.
McLachlan St
Sheperd St.
BICENTENNIAL PARK
Mitchell St.
Briggs St.
Lindsay St.
Whitfield St.
Barneson St.
Leichhardt Memorial
Esplanade
Peel St.
Car Park
Shadforth Ln.
Searcy St.
Manton St.
Lameroo Beach
Transit Centre
Edmunds St.
Gardiner St.
Telegraph Museum
Knuckey St.
Library
West Ln.
Austin Ln.
Cavenagh St.
Litchfield St.
Woods St.
Foelsche St.
Carey St.
The Mall
Herbert St.
Chinese Temple
Bennett St.
City Bus Depot
Harry Chan Ave.
Tiger Brennan Dr
Christ Church Cathedral
Frances Bay Dr.
Esplanade
Mavie St.
Government House
Hughes Ave.
Kitchener Dr.
Stokes Hill
Fort Hill
Frances Bay
Indo-Pacific Marine
Darwin Harbour
N
Fort Hill Wharf
Stokes Hill Wharf
Ferries
0
150 yards
0
150 meters
Central Darwin

ORIENTATION

Darwin has a conveniently small city center. The **transit center,** where intercity buses stop, is on **Mitchell St.** To the right, Mitchell continues across **Knuckey** and **Bennett St.** To the left, it crosses **Peel** and **Daly St.** and ends 500m away at **Lambell Terrace.** Most points of interest lie in the grid of blocks between the parallel Daly and Bennett St. and the perpendicular cross streets. A block behind the transit center is the **Esplanade,** which runs along the grassy harborside area. A block past Mitchell away from the harbor is **Smith St. The Mall** occupies the block of Smith between Knuckey and Bennett St., which is closed to traffic. Beyond Smith St. is **Cavenagh St.**

Facing the harbor, turn left and follow the Esplanade to the Government House, where it curves around to meet Smith St. Here a wooded slope conceals **Stokes Hill Wharf,** a prime entertainment location.

In the other direction, Daly St. becomes the **Stuart Hwy.** on its way northeast out of town. It then curves south toward the **Darwin International Airport.** Lambell Tce., which continues to hug the coast after crossing Mitchell St., becomes Gilruth Ave. and then East Point Rd. on its way to the **MGM casino, Mindil Beach,** and **Vestey Beach.** The road ends at the **East Point Reserve,** 6km from the city center.

GETTING AROUND

Local buses covering Darwin's suburban sprawl depart from the **bus terminal** (tel. 8924 7666) between Bennett St. and Harry Chan Ave. Fares are $1. Destinations not on the bus routes can be reached by **taxi** (tel. 8981 8777 or 13 10 08). If you'd rather get around by yourself, **Freedom Cycles,** 89 Mitchell St. (tel. 8981 9995, mobile phone 0411 873 6997), can put you on a moped for the day ($25, unlimited distance; open daily 8am-5pm). **Bicycles** can be rented from many hostels or from **Frogshollow,** 27 Lindsay St. (tel. 88941 2600; $3 per hr. or $15 per day).

NORTHERN TERRITORY

PRACTICAL INFORMATION

Tourist Office: Darwin Region Tourism Association (DRTA), in Beagle House Bldg. at Mitchell and Knuckey St., ground floor (tel. 8981 4300; fax 8981 0653). Leaving the transit center, walk a block to the right on Mitchell to Knuckey St. Representatives speak French, Japanese, and German. Wheelchair accessible. Open Mon.-Fri. 8:30am-6pm, Sat. 9am-3pm, Sun. 10am-2pm, and public holidays 10am-3pm. The airport also has a DRTA kiosk.

Travel Office: STA, in Galleria, Smith St. Mall (tel. 8941 2955; fax 8941 2386). From the transit center take Mitchell St. to the right. Turn left on Knuckey and right on Smith St., then right at the second indoor court. Sells ISIC cards ($10) and VIP cards ($25). Wheelchair accessible. Open Mon.-Fri. 9am-5pm.

Consulates: France, 47 Knuckey St. (tel. 8981 3411); **Germany,** P.O. Box 38995, Winnellie (tel. 8984 3770); **Indonesia,** 18 Harry Chan Ave. (tel. 8941 0048); **Japan,** P.O. Box 1616 (tel. 8981 8722); **Philippines** (tel. 8984 4411).

Currency exchange: ANZ Bank (tel. 13 13 14), on Knuckey St. by the entrance to the Smith St. Mall, processes bank cards and traveler's checks. Open Mon.-Thurs. 9:30am-4pm, Fri. 9:30am-5pm. **Interforex** (tel. 8981 0511), further down the mall, is open daily 8am-7:30pm.

American Express: Travelers World, 18 Knuckey St., (tel. 8981 4699; fax 8981 1462). Holds mail addressed: ATTN: Client Mail, GPO Box 3728, Darwin NT 0800. Held for 30 days, longer by request. Open Mon.-Fri. 8:30am-5pm, Sat. 9am-noon.

Backpacking supplies: NT General Store, 42 Cavenagh St. (tel. 8981 8242; fax 8981 6737). A full selection of travel and camping equipment.

Bookstores: Planet Oz, Transit Centre, 69 Mitchell St. (tel. 8981 0690), carries fiction and travel guides. Open daily 10am-10pm. **Angus & Robertson Bookshop,** across from STA in the Galleria at Smith St. (tel. 8941 3489) has a larger selection. Open Mon.-Fri. 9am-5:30pm, Sat. 9am-3pm (also Sun. 10am-3pm in the dry).

Library: Northern Territory Library (tel. 8999 7177), at the corner of Mitchell and Bennett St., inside the Parliament building. Open Mon.-Sat. 10am-6pm.

Pharmacy: Darwin Pharmacy, store 46 in the Smith St. Mall (tel. 8981 9202). Entering the mall from Knuckey St. look to the left. Wheelchair access. Open Mon.-Sat. 9am-8pm, Sun. 9am-5pm.

Medical: Royal Darwin Hospital (tel. 13 11 26) is located in the suburb of Tiwi 9km from the city center. More centrally located, family physician and travel health consultant **Dr. Tony Colebath** (tel. 8981 7862; mobile tel. 0412 336 924) runs a clinic at 153 Mitchell St. (consulting hours Mon.-Fri. 2-7pm, Sat. 9-11am, and Sun. by appointment only). For **vaccinations,** visit the **Australian Government Health Service,** 43 Cavenagh, first floor of Cavenagh Ctr. Bldg. (tel. 8981 7492). Appointments recommended. Open Mon.-Fri. 8:30am-noon, 1:30-3:30pm.

Emergency: Dial 000.

Police: Dial 8922 3344 (24hr.). Station is on Mitchell near Bennett St. Open Mon.-Fri. 8am-5pm.

Post Office: General Post Office Darwin, 48 Cavenagh (tel. 8980 8226). Mail held *Poste Restante* for 30 days. A computerized listing tells you if mail is waiting. **Postal code:** 0801.

Phone Code: 08.

ACCOMMODATIONS

To meet demand, Darwin has sprouted hostels like mushrooms in recent years. Hostels often fill up during the dry season (from May to October), so call ahead if you're arriving late in the day. When the stream of travelers slows to a trickle in the wet season, most accommodations lower their prices to sustain business. Many hostels are concentrated near the transit center on Mitchell St., but others lie along Mitchell toward Daly St. Those past Daly are less convenient to the city center, but tend to be quieter. Laundry at most hostels is $2 each for wash and dry. Standard check-out time is 10am.

Darwin City YHA, 69 Mitchell St. (tel. 8981 3995; fax 8981 6674), in the same building as transit center. Friendly, clean, and efficient, this YHA has a game room and inexpensive luggage storage. "Slip, slop, slap" on the sunscreen and relax on the sundeck, or enjoy open-air self-catered dining. Dorm beds $18, $15 with YHA. Key deposit $10. Reservations recommended.

Melaleuca Lodge, 50 Mitchell St. (tel. 8941 1395; fax 8941 1368), across the street from the transit center. The landscaping artists of this lodge have created a peaceful garden in the busiest part of town. A formidable number of rooms coil around a shady patio and a pool to beat the heat. Conscientious management maintains high standards for cleanliness given the capacity of 267. Rooms female, male, or coed, all with A/C and lockers. Laundry room and kitchen facilities. Dorm beds $15, $14 in wet season; doubles (with TV and fridge) $44. Free pancake breakfast. Airport shuttle free. Wheelchair accessible. Key deposit $10.

Nomads Backpackers, 69A Mitchell St. (tel. 8941 9722), adjacent to transit center. As a chain, Nomads shows up on the scene with high quality furniture, carpeted rooms, and swanky facilities (kitchen, pool, and spa). All rooms have A/C and sink. Dorm $15. VIP, YHA. Twins and doubles $36, with bath $44. Make reservations; people frequently book ahead from other Nomads locations.

Elke's Inner City Backpackers, 112 Mitchell St. (tel. 8981 8399 or 1800 808 365), just past Daly St., 10min. from the transit center. Elke's friendly management has taken advantage of the quiet neighborhood by planting a stand of trees to create a shady canopy. Pool, spa, 2 kitchens, TV room, and free evening meals with drink purchase. Staff speaks German and French. Check-out 9am, but as long as you're out of the room you can hang around. 4-bed dorms with fridge and A/C $14.50, lower during the wet. Singles $30; doubles or twins $33. Laundry. Free breakfast and luggage storage. 24hr. pick-up at airport or transit center.

Frogshollow Backpackers, 27 Lindsay St. (tel. 1800 068 686, 24hr. 8941 2600; fax 8941 0758). Calm, spacious, and relaxed, Frogshollow lies nestled in the woods 10min. from the transit center. Balconies, spas, picnic tables, and a pool take advantage of the arcadian setting. Cramped dorms with A/C $14. VIP. Doubles $33, with A/C $38, with bath $44. Laundry. Linen and a breakfast of toast and coffee included. Free pick-up at transit center or airport.

Gecko Lodge, 146 Mitchell St. (tel. 8981 5569; for bookings only 1800 811 250). A small, conscientious outfit 20min. walk from the transit center. Courtesy buses from airport or transit center, or reimbursement for cost of shuttle. The undergrowth isn't the only thing vegetating at this chilled-out hostel. Kitchen, TV room, and cozy pool. All rooms have A/C, fridges and supplied linens. Dorms $14, $13 in the wet; doubles $45, $35 in the wet. Pancake breakfast included. Free luggage storage. Laundry. Key deposit $20.

YWCA Darwin—"Banyan View Lodge," 119 Mitchell St. (tel. 8981 8644; fax 8981 6104), just past Daly St., across from Elke's. Accepts men, although designed specifically to be female-friendly. Large kitchen and spa. Dorms $15; singles with fan $28, with A/C $30; twins with fan $40, with A/C $45. All rooms with shared bath. Key deposit equal to one night's stay.

Value Inn, 50 Mitchell St. (tel. 8981 4733), across the street and 50m down from the transit center. True motel style: you're paying for quiet, long hallways, and your own bathroom, TV, and fridge. A/C. Pool. Reception staffed 10am-11pm. All rooms ($64 in high season) sport a queen-sized and a single bed, allowing three to share.

Globetrotters, 97 Mitchell St. (tel. 8981 5385 or 1800 800 798; fax 8981 9096), a 5min. walk from the transit center, just before Daly St. Globetrotters' significant popularity stems from the feast it provides nightly for an army of Darwin's backpackers, not from its hominess. The bar and pool hall are the scenes to be seen in, but some guests complain that the concrete-walled rooms are dank. Dorms $14. VIP. Doubles and twins $44, both with TV. Laundry. Bedding and breakfast included. 24hr. pick-up from airport. Key deposit $20.

Camping options leave something to be desired. With unfriendly weather half the year and no campgrounds in central Darwin, die-hard campers will need to head out of town on the Stuart Hwy. to pitch their tents. **Lee Point Resort** (tel. 8945 0535) is on Lee Point Rd., off MacMillans Rd., itself off Stuart Hwy. (Tent sites $14; campervan sites $18. Weekly: $75, $80.) **Shady Glen** (tel. 8984 3330) is just off the highway about 10km from central Darwin. Tents are $8 per person, campervan sites $19 per night. Call ahead for conditions and availability. A few kilometers on, **Overlander Park,** also visible from the highway, has tent and campervan sites for $14.

FOOD

Darwin may not be the land of fine dining, but quality budget eateries abound. Hostels may serve a light breakfast (often nothing more than toast), but plenty of cafes step up to the challenge. An extremely popular dinner option is the mass serving line at the **Globetrotters** pool, which you can join by buying a drink at the bar. **Elke's** has a similar service. Both always offer a vegetarian dish. Try the trusty international fast food joints all over the city center as a fallback.

The food stalls that crowd inside the transit center and lurk across the street offer hot, relatively cheap, and mostly Asian cuisine ($5-6) throughout the day. **Mental Lentil** (tel. 8981 1377) specializes in creative vegetarian options. Food counters in the alcoves off the **Smith Street Mall** also reflect Darwin's heterogenous ethnic makeup. The town's favorite meal is the sunset food festival each dry season Thursday at the **Mindil Beach Market,** where different Asian and European cuisines compete for the favor of Darwin's palate (a full meal is usually $5-6).

Coyotes Cantina, 69 Mitchell St. (tel. 8941 3676), in the transit center. An excellent open-air Mexican restaurant popular with travelers, particularly at night. Piñatas decorate the bar and (sometimes live) music transports patrons to the other side of the globe. The $15 fajitas and $9 burritos may be a bit expensive, but Santa Ana himself would not be disappointed. Open 11:30am-2am.

Crepe Expectations, on Mitchell St. across from the transit center. Crepes made on the spot for breakfast, lunch, and dinner, with fresh ingredients of your choice. All crepes and breakfast specials $6. Open Mon.-Sat. 9am-2pm and 6pm-midnight, Sun. 10am-2pm and 6-10pm.

Oasis Cafe, 50 Mitchell St. (tel. 8941 3152), in the Melaleuca Lodge complex across from the transit center. A 24hr. snack bar in the same convenient area as Crepe Expectations. Muffins, yogurt, and soft drinks. Burgers and other meals run $3-6.

Salvatore's Extraordinary Coffee, intersection of Knuckey and Smith St. (tel. 8941 9823). This bright modern cafe's outdoor seating and wide street-facing windows make it ideal for people-watching. Have coffee ($2) with breakfast ($5-8), or enjoy pasta ($7.50) later in the day. Open daily 7am-midnight.

Cafe Capri, 37 Knuckey St. (tel. 8981 0010; fax 89page 24181 4942), between Smith and Cavenagh St. "Your Mediterranean Oasis in Darwin" is a bit more elegant than many of Darwin's restaurants. A wide range of pastas for $10 (the vegetarian dishes are heartily recommended); other entrees more expensive. Open Sun.-Thurs. 10am-11:30pm, Fri.-Sat. 10am-midnight.

Sizzler, at the corner of Briggs and Mitchell St. (tel. 8941 2225), just a few minutes from the transit center. The world-famous steakhouse delivers exactly what put it on the map: a gluttonous, miles-long, piled-on, gorge-yourself-till-your-pants-split soup, salad, pasta, fruit, and dessert bar. Come early, since the same food costs $7 a head before 4pm and $11 after 4pm. Open Sun.-Thurs. 10am-9:30pm, Fri.-Sat. 11am-10pm.

SIGHTS

There is no shortage of tourist literature in Darwin. For the tourism officials' latest recommendations, pick up a copy of *Darwin and the Top End Today* or the white pamphlet titled *Touring and Attractions* at any hostel or the tourist office. The former has a guide to an *Historical Stroll Around Darwin*. Many of the sights are clustered in the city center, and some backpackers never leave this district. One semi-affordable way to get to more distant sights is aboard the inanely-named **Tour Tub** (tel. 8981 5233; fax 8981 8228). The Tub is an open trolley that rounds up passengers at major accommodations and then runs hourly to 10 popular sights from Stokes Hill Wharf to the East Point Reserve. A $16 pass allows you to ride the Tub between the sights you want from 9am to 5pm. (April-Oct. runs daily; Nov.-March Tues.-Fri. 10am-2pm, Sat.-Sun. 10am-4pm).

In addition to home-grown attractions, Darwin is the gateway for Kakadu National Park (p. 233). Daytrips and longer tours operate from the city; see page page 241 for more details.

Central Darwin and Stokes Hill Wharf

Aquascene (tel. 8981 7837; fax 8941 8844), at the end of Doctors Gully Rd., is probably the most unusual sight in Darwin. With the waterfront on your left, walk up the Esplanade to Daly St. Take a right and then a quick left on Doctors Gully Rd. Past the YMCA and around the corner, you'll arrive at the scene of this daily fish feeding frenzy. Each high tide, families and backpackers gather here to continue a 30-year tradition of hand-feeding a large quantity of bread to an enormous horde of fish. Milkfish, mullet, catfish, bream, and batfish (but no hammerheads, sorry) dart around their feeders' legs, jostling their kin for morsels. Call ahead for the feeding schedule, as Aquascene is only open a few hours each day. Admission is $4 (under 15 $2.50).

Another nearby landmark is the historic **Lyons Cottage,** at the corner of Knuckey St. and the Esplanade. This survivor of Japanese bombs and tropical cyclones was the 1925 headquarters for the construction of the BAT, the telegraph cable between Australia and Britain. Lyons was a politician who later resided in the cozy cottage. Its photo history of Darwin probably wouldn't be worth the visit if it weren't free (open daily 10am-5pm).

At the southeast end of Smith St. past the ruins of the **Old Town Hall,** Hughes Ave. descends to the right and intersects Kitchener Dr. Take a sharp left on this drive and pass the **WWII storage tunnels** (open for self-guided tours April-Oct. daily 9am-5pm; Nov.-March Tues.-Sun. 10am-2pm) along Darwin Harbour. The drive then curves to the right on to **Stokes Hill Wharf.** The Wharf is a pylon-supported strip of concrete that curves out into the harbor and ends in the **Wharf Arcade,** a corrugated-metal building containing restaurants and shops. The Arcade is a popular sunset dining spot

Ruling Passion

The rugged, independent, macho reputation of Australia's Northern Territory doesn't exactly lend itself to a homosexual presence... or does it? Dino Hodge's study *Did You Meet Any Malagas?* uses oral and written sources to out over a century of Top End culture, starting with Aboriginal communities. It was here that Europeans did a double-take at the young boys tagging along with elder tribesmen for a little bit of lovin'. When asked about the arrangement, the boys only smiled matter-of-factly, although after several generations of white homophobia living next door, the stigma gradually set into Aboriginal communities. European households were not devoid of their own open-mindedness: with 172 males and 29 females in the NT in 1871, the land was not the only thing the pioneersmen were exploring. One woman wrote in her diary about George, a handsome, tidy stockman who "shared his hut with a 'chum,' his own special friend... [both] alike in their love of the ruling passion of their lives—horses, and the wild, roving bushman's existence." During WWII, homosexual surveillance on NT bases was heavy, but behind closed doors men would be men. Even after the war ended some of the beat (or "cruising") areas from that era retained their earlier function. Nevertheless, it was 1970 before gay liberation hit Darwin, and homosexuality was only decriminalized in the NT by the **Criminal Code Act** in the late 1970s.

where parents dine at tables by the water and children feed unwanted vegetables to the fish (food served until 9:30pm). The Wharf also supports the **Indo Pacific Marine** (tel. 8981 1294), an aquarium simulating the ecosystems of Northern Territory coral reefs. (Open Tues.-Sun. Nov.-March 10am-5pm; April-Oct. 9am-5pm. Admission $10, children $4.) Nearby, the **Australian Pearling Exhibition** (tel. 8941 2177) reveals the danger involved in this romantic industry (open Mon.-Fri. 10am-4:30pm, Sat.-Sun. 10am-5:30pm).

East Point Road and Beyond

Mindil Beach and **Vestey's Beach,** off Gilruth Ave., are two of Darwin's favorite places to soak in sun (or rain in the wet season). Walk north on Smith St. past Daly and turn right on Gilruth Ave. at the traffic circle. Mindil Beach is on the left behind the Casino, and Vestey's Beach is a few hundred meters on. Shuttles to and from the city center ($1.50 each way) will save you a half-hour walk. The former hosts the gem of Darwin's markets, the **Mindil Beach Sunset Market,** a shopping and eating experience like few others. Beneath the setting sun, musicians serenade a throng of craftsmakers and foodsellers. Make a dinner of dim sims, fresh-squeezed juice, and ice cream for about $6. Activity lasts from around 5 to 10pm on Thursdays and Sundays (though on a smaller scale) during the dry season.

Just past Mindil Beach, on the opposite side of Gilruth Ave., are the **Darwin Botanic Gardens** (tel. 8989 5535; another entrance on Geranium St. off the Stuart Hwy.). Shaded walkways wind through a spacious landscape of tropical plants. The gardens are old enough to have survived cyclones in 1897, 1937, and 1974 (though Tracy, the most recent, stripped 80% of the trees and shrubs). Although regrown, this peaceful park is not heavily visited (open daily 7am-7pm; free).

The Museum and Art Gallery of the Northern Territory (tel. 8999 8201) is situated along the shore heading toward Vestey's Beach. Pass the high school on Gilruth Ave. and turn left on Conacher St. to the museum. If you only have time to visit one Darwin museum, this should be the one. The seaside building contains comprehensive exhibits of Aboriginal artwork and Territorial wildlife, including "Sweetheart," a 5m croc famous for sinking fishing boats. Past his menacing pose is the Cyclone Tracy room, with a video and before-and-after photos capturing the devastation. A maritime annex to the museum includes a boatyard and the partial skeleton of a 20m blue whale. (Open Mon.-Fri. 9am-5pm, Sat.-Sun. 10am-5pm. Free. Wheelchair accessible.)

Also part of the museum, the **Fannie Bay Gaol** (tel. 8999 8201) opened in 1883 and served as Darwin's main jail for nearly a century, closing only in 1979. At first glance, it appears to be nothing more than a jumble of one-story buildings. Follow the marked self-tour, however, and you'll find yourself in eerie, empty rooms where prisoners once slept and died. The Infirmary, built in 1887, was the site of a pair of executions in 1952. Guards and prisoners now claim the building to be haunted. You can visit this uplifting place for free (open daily 10am-5pm).

To the north of the Gaol, East Point Rd. enters the beautiful peninsular park called **East Point Reserve.** The Reserve itself has picnic areas and predator-free swimming in Lake Alexander. Groups of wallabies can often be spotted in the reserve, especially in the evening (free). East Point Rd. becomes Alec Fong Lim Dr., which leads to the **East Point Military Museum** (tel. 8981 9702). This exhibition is located at the site of a WWII anti-aircraft station built to fend off Japanese attacks. The huge 9.2 in. diameter guns attest to Darwin's efforts, but photos and a video inside reveal the decimation wrought upon the city despite these measures. The museum is 40 minutes by bike from downtown (open daily 9:30am-5pm; admission $6, children $3).

Several inland sights are scattered farther from central Darwin. These outliers include **Crocodylus Park** (tel. 8947 2510), one of several crocodile theme parks in the Top End. Catch the local #5 bus from the bus depot on Bennett St. It stops 10 minutes' walk from the park. Crocodylus doubles as an "educational adventure" and a research center dedicated to the study of crocodiles and alligators. Educational adventure apparently means letting tourists hold baby crocs and look on as the adults devour hunks of meat (open daily 9am-5pm, feeding and tour 11am and 2pm; admission $12, under 16 $6). Crocodylus overlooks **Holmes Jungle Nature Reserve.** Also removed from the city center is the **Australian Aviation Heritage Centre** (tel. 8947 2145) on the Stuart Hwy. in the suburb of Winnellie. The highlight of this exhibition is an old American B-52 bomber (open daily 8:30am-5pm; admission $8, children $4).

RECREATION

The seasonality of the Top End cuts deeply into Darwin's outdoor recreation. The wet season casts clouds, figuratively and literally, over the drenched city. Those who like getting wet rent out **scuba diving** equipment to explore sunken vessels in the harbor. But coastal waters are unsafe for swimming in large portions of the year: deadly box jellyfish cruise the ocean during the wet season, and saltwater crocs refuse to share their habitat with humans at all. See **Dangerous Wildlife** on p. 17 for more details. Always check with the locals before taking a dip. The Esplanade is replete with popular **picnicking and sunning** spots. More private locations lie along Mindil and Vestey's Beaches and in the East Point Reserve.

The sunny days of the dry season are celebrated by the Darwinians with a variety of **special events.** The **Darwin Beer Can Regatta** is held off Mindil Beach in early August. Teams of devout beer-chuggers use their empties to construct vessels fit for America's Cup competition and race them across the harbor. In May of every other year, the **Arafura Sports Festival** comes to town. It's a tournament of athletic competitions in 26 different sports, with competitors haling from all over the Pacific Rim. The annual **Cannonball Run** is a 4000km road race from Darwin to Ayers Rock and back. The Greek population of Darwin stages the **Glenti Festival,** a musical and culinary event, on the second Sunday of June on the Esplanade. Inquire at the tourist office about catching a match of **Aussie Rules football;** several important competitions are held in March.

ENTERTAINMENT AND NIGHTLIFE

Territorian ockers and rowdy backpackers encourage Darwin's lively pub scene. For a more family-oriented affair, check out the night market at the intersection of Mitchell and Peel St. each evening from 5 to 11pm. The shops along the **Smith Street Mall** sell merchandise of Aboriginal design and are a good place to spend any money you haven't managed to lose at the **MGM Grand Casino** (at the top of Mindil Beach).

The **Darwin Cinema Centre,** 76 Mitchell St. (tel. 8981 3111), screens recent mainstream flicks from 10:30am to 9:30pm daily (tickets $11.50, students $8.50, Tues. special rate $7.50). The less conventional **Deckchair Cinema** (tel. 8981 0700) shows off-beat, artsy films (many foreign) under the stars in a sunken amphitheater. Heading away from Darwin Harbor on Bennett St., turn right on McMinn and left on Frances Bay Dr. The driveway to the cinema is 100m down on the right. Walking takes 20 minutes. Showings (Wed.-Sun. 7:30pm, additional shows Fri.-Sat. at 10pm) are $10.

Darwin has several venues for **theater.** The **Darwin Entertainment Center,** the imposing coral facade on Mitchell St. halfway between Peel and Daly St., tends to host the noteworthy events. The **Botanic Gardens Amphitheatre** presents open-air theater in the midst of the lush gardens. **Brown's Mart,** on Smith St. near Bennett St., features local productions in one of Darwin's oldest buildings. For the buzz on all this biz, flip through the *NT News* (80¢-$1), the free bi-monthly paper *Pulse,* or Darwin's monthly calendar of events, *The Daily Plan-It.*

The **nightlife** scene caters both to locals and the backpacker set. Clubs are required by law to charge a cover of $5 after midnight on Friday and Saturday nights. Few exceed that or charge a cover on any other night. **Rattle 'n' Hum,** 65 The Esplanade (tel. 8981 4011), between Knuckey and Herbert St., is the best publicized of the clubs. The Hum draws a crowd with its nightly table-dancing bar scene. From 6pm until 9:30pm the wooden tables are used for dinner and the music is kept low; when the food is taken away, the DJ rocks (and rattles) the house. (Drinks $3-4, $2 on Sun. Free barbecue on Mon. and Wed. starting at 7:30pm.) **Beachcombers** (tel. 8981 6511), at Mitchell and Daly St., is a dance-oriented pub that opens nightly and draws a youngish crowd. (Draft beers $2.50. Open 8pm-4am. Casual dress but no sandals.) If you want a bar and disco combined with some history, the **Victoria Hotel** (tel. 8981 4011) in the Smith St. Mall is for you. The pub occupies the bottom floor, while the dance hall and pool tables entice patrons upstairs. At the Victoria, a handful of travelers attempt to elbow their way into a dense crowd of Territorians—don't be surprised if you're left waiting outside. (Open 10am-4am, $2 meals served 7-9pm.) Establishments like **Moose's Place** in the Don Hotel at Cavenagh and Bennett St., the **Grasshouse** on Mitchell at Herbert St., and the **Time** on Edmunds St. behind Woolworths operate in the same vein. For a snazzier feel, the MGM Grand's **Sweethearts** headlines live music Thursday through Sunday (open 8pm-4am, beer $3.80).

Darwin is more **gay-friendly** than most Northern Territory settlements. **Pandora's,** at Cavenagh and Bennett St. in the Don Hotel, turns into a gay dance club Thursday through Saturday (Sat. drag performances). Find a more relaxed atmosphere at the **Railcar Bar** (tel. 8981 3358) on Gardiner St. Follow Knuckey St. to a left on Woods St., then take the first right on to Gardiner and look to the right at the end of the block. Next to the gay restaurant Mississippi Queen, the Railcar Bar is a sociable gay pub after 10pm. Patrons here are somewhat older than at those at Pandora's.

■ Off the Coast of Darwin: The Tiwi Islands

Eighty kilometers north of Darwin, the Tiwi Islands—**Melville** and **Bathurst**—sit relatively undisturbed, as they have for centuries. Melville, the larger, ranks behind only Tasmania as the largest isle off Australian shores. Together, the Tiwis represent 8000 square kilometers of tropical land. With so much area in such pleasing weather (ignoring the cyclones), it's a bit of a surprise that the Tiwi are off the beaten track, and yet they always have been. The ancestors of the resident Tiwi Aboriginals hardly interacted with mainland peoples until a century ago. The main attractions of present-day Bathurst and Melville Islands are the contemporary Aboriginal communities, the relaxing beaches, and a remoteness which lets visitors forget the daily trials of mainland life. Visiting the Tiwis is only allowed in an organized tour. Contact **Tiwi Tours** at 1800 811 633 for further information, or phone the Darwin Region Tourism Association (tel. 8981 4300).

Freshies and Salties

The Top End has two different kinds of crocodiles. The freshwater crocodile, *Crocodylus johnstoni,* lives only in fresh water, while the saltwater crocodile, *Crocodylus porosus,* lives in fresh or salt water. It is easiest to learn the difference between "freshies" and "salties" through association. When you see a sign about freshies, it will probably refer to minimum risk and warn you merely to be cautious, since freshies nip only when provoked. When you see a sign about salties, it will most likely refer to death or danger and tell you to stay out. This is because salties eat humans. Freshies have to mind this distinction themselves, because salties eat freshies, too. That's why many areas inhabited by salties don't have freshies. Or swimmers.

■ The Stuart Highway out of Darwin

The Stuart Highway swings east and south out of Darwin through the town of **Palmerston,** which has been titled the "fastest growing city in Australia." Palmerston's crown: at least one set of golden arches. The highway connects Darwin to Adelaide and divides the continent in two. The first important junction is that with the **Arnhem Highway,** 33km south of Darwin. From here, the Arnhem Hwy. heads east into some of the wildest, most memorable wetlands in Australia (see **Kakadu,** below). The Stuart Hwy. continues south, "down the track" toward the towns of **Adelaide River** and Katherine, and the outback beyond.

The **Darwin Crocodile Farm** (tel. 8988 1450) is 40km south of Darwin on the right side of the Stuart Hwy., soon after the Arnhem Hwy. junction, but on the road to Litchfield. Crocodiles are indeed farmed here, raised for giftshop wallets, belts and snack bar croc burgers. But this does not undermine the staff's respect for the fierce, formidable creatures, who are fed "spent layer hens" in a dramatic fashion. (Feedings daily 2pm, additional feedings Sat.-Sun. and public holidays at noon. Admission $9.50, children $5. Open daily 10am-4pm.) **Darwin Day Tours** (tel. 8941 3844) provides trips to the Croc Farm for the transport-impaired.

Further south, it is possible to take a right off the Stuart Hwy. onto **Cox Peninsula Rd.,** which eventually leads to **Litchfield National Park** (see p. 242). En route, the road passes another attraction of enormous acclaim, **Territory Wildlife Park** (tel. 8988 7200; fax 8988 7201). This wildlife complex, 60km out of Darwin, encompasses 400 hectares of Top End bush. Acquaint yourself with all sorts of marsupials, or feast your eyes on the enclosed tunnel aquarium and its 180° view of barramundi and stingrays. There's the requisite reptile pavilion, a house for nocturnal critters, birds of prey, and plenty more. The park recommends four hours for a visit (admission $12, students $6; open daily 8:30am-4pm). Next door, the **Berry Springs Nature Park** provides a lot of shade and a natural spring for soaking (open daily 8am-6:30pm; free). About 15km past these sights, a gravel road turns off to the left. This is the northern approach to Litchfield. In the Wet, the Finniss River can cover this unsealed track with 1m of water. The total distance from Darwin to Litchfield by this route is 115km.

Kakadu National Park

The world, the nation, and *Let's Go* all agree that Kakadu National Park in the Top End of Australia demands a lot of attention. The largest of the continent's national parks, Kakadu covers a whopping 19,804 square kilometers—comparable in size to Israel or Wales—and contains an entire multi-branched river system, from source to mouth. The land varies from prairie-like woodland to rainforest to bog to dramatic escarpments, and is believed to contain some of the oldest geological formations in the world. The weather cycles in a crazy pattern from crackling dry to raging wet. The Aboriginal communities in the region have an estimated history of some 50,000 years; the rock art their ancestors have left behind is the largest, and perhaps the oldest, collection in the world. Somewhat impressed by these specs, the United Nations Education, Scientific and Cultural Organisation (UNESCO) proclaimed Kakadu one of a handful of international World Heritage sites a little more than a decade after the park was founded in 1979. The award is given for either cultural or natural value; Kakadu snagged both.

The name Kakadu comes from "Gagudju," the primary Aboriginal language spoken here a century ago. About 300 Aboriginal people live in Kakadu today, most "traditional owners" and descendants of the 2000 or so inhabitants prior to colonization. About 50% of the land officially belongs to the traditional owners and is leased to the Australian National Parks and Wildlife Service (ANPWS) for operation. The other half is in the hands of the national government.

The Land One hundred forty million years ago, Kakadu was shallow sea floor. The **Arnhem Land Plateau,** now bordering the park to the east, was flat earth jutting out of a great ocean. Gradually, silt from the plateau built up the ocean floor, and aided by the receding oceans, the Kakadu region broke to the surface. Rivers carved through the muddy earth as they drained into the ebbing sea to the north.

Kakadu is the result of the course of these millions of years of natural processes. What once was a cliff overhanging the sea has become the looming eastern boundary of Kakadu, a gray massif which now commands a vast ocean of trees. This **escarpment country** runs along the East Alligator River, varying from echeloned slopes to sheer faces that are adorned with waterfalls during the Wet. Isolated buttes called "outliers" are freaks of elemental nature, standing many kilometers west of the Arnhem plateau. More accessible are the **lowlands,** the woodlands that cover more than half of Kakadu and are a familiar sight around the Top End. The roads, especially highways, usually stick to these solid surfaces, which make a better foundation than the notorious **floodplains.** Even so, many roads are forced to close during the Wet.

In the dry season, water in Kakadu is confined primarily to the **Alligator River System.** Named by an explorer who had had a little too much of the Americas (there are no alligators in Australia), this system is distinctive because it exists entirely within the borders of Kakadu, with the headwaters in the southern hills and basins of the park. In the wet season, the Alligator tributaries swell and inundate many miles of floodplain. Woodland areas and mudflats become lakes, near-stagnant **billabongs** (watering holes) turn into gushing waterways, and all life formerly confined within the river banks (fish, aquatic plants, crocs) flows out onto the land. The floodplain is a phenomenon as well as a habitat; nourished by annual deposits of rich soil, the wetlands are some of the most fertile areas of the planet.

Along the coast where the rivers meet the sea, a different sort of ecosystem thrives. The brackish estuaries and tidal flats are affected by both the increased volume of the wet season and the year-round movement of the tides. Mangroves, adapted as they are to the oxygen-deficient saline mud, are the characteristic residents of these parts.

The People The story the Aboriginals tell of their history in Kakadu is closely related to the story they tell of the land (see **Kakadu in the Dreaming**). It is different from the whitefella's tale, which suggests that between 120,000 and 60,000 years ago, long after Kakadu emerged from the ocean, fickle ice-age glaciers repeatedly advanced and retreated, causing sea level to fluctuate. When the ice caps were mostly frozen and the sea was at its lowest—possibly as early as 110,000 years ago—ancestors of the Aboriginals sailed the 60-100km strait between Indonesia and New Guinea and walked the rest of the way to Australia. A dry period lasted until about 8000 years ago, when the oceans rose again and rivers flooded. This **estuarine period** ushered in a rich new ecosystem and contributed to the Aboriginal diet, adding barramundi, crocodile, shellfish, and catfish. Between 4000 and 1500 years ago, **freshwater** replaced brackish estuaries, further enriching the land with turtles, lilies, and lots of aquatic birds. This abundance of food in the Kakadu region allowed Aboriginals to give up their nomadic existence and settle into communities of about 2000 people by the time the first Europeans arrived.

Kakadu in the Dreaming

Aboriginals believe that Kakadu, like the rest of the world, was created during the Dreaming, the spiritual time when the acts and deeds of powerful ancestral beings shaped the land. A triangular rock at Nourlangie, for instance, is the stolen feather of a powerful spirit, and another slanted slate atop a mountain near Ubirr is the ill-fated raft of a bushwoman who challenged the Rainbow Serpent, one of many ancestors important in the formation of Kakadu. Because the features of the land are linked to the ancestors, the land is not an inherited possession, but a sacred site. Aboriginals discriminate between three classes: ceremonial sites, djang, and djang andjamun. The ceremonial sites are presently used for burials, rites of passage, and other such events. At djang sites, a creator passed through, took shape, or entered or exited the Earth, but is now gone, leaving the site safe to visit. At djang andjamun sites, however, the ancestor still lingers, and the sites are considered spiritual hazard zones. Laws prohibit entry to the last group of sites, perhaps to appease the Aboriginals, perhaps to avoid the catastrophes that would occur if mortals interfered with the Dreaming.

The Seasons Tour guides say they have a hard time describing wet Kakadu to dry season visitors, and vice versa. When's the best time to visit? **The Dry,** from April to October, is hands-down the most convenient and comfortable, and offers the most expansive view of the park. Dry season highs average 30°C (86°), lows 17°C (59°F), and the humidity is low. It can get cold at night, so bring an extra layer, and some repellant to poison commando mosquitoes. All roads are open whether paved or unpaved, and all camping, accommodations, and attractions are also operating.

The most encouraging description of Kakadu in **the Wet** is "dynamic;" the most frank: "hell on earth." From October to April, expect oppressive humidity and 35°C (95°F) highs and 25°C (77°F) lows. Bring mosquito protection and rain gear. Some camping areas and most unpaved roads are closed. The famous falls, particularly Jim Jim and Twin, are at their most powerful but can only be seen from the air. One plus—boat cruises are up and running, as the Ubirr drive becomes a river.

The Aboriginals, more acquainted with the climatic patterns, break the year into six seasons of dramatic change. **Gunumeleng,** from mid-October to late December, is the "whisper of the wet," which comes in the form of drenching afternoon thundershowers punctuated by the greatest frequency of lightning strikes on the planet (an average 10,000 per month Nov.-Jan.). Landscape burned brown by the dry months turns green again, amid high temperatures and oppressive humidity. From January to March, the "real" wet season—**Gudjewg**—brings monsoon rains to Kakadu. Enormous amounts of water pour down, humidity hits its peak, the land is green and overflowing, and the waterfalls gush. While the ubiquitous spear grass shoots up 3m, the animals that live on the ground can get trapped in the swollen waterways. April comes, and with it **Banggerreng,** the first glimpse of sunny skies. A handful of storms late in the month interrupt the clear weather, flattening the towering spear grass. The beginning of dry times is the cool **Yegge,** May to mid-June, when the wetlands begin to recede, leaving fields of waterlilies in their wake. The coldest weather comes in **Wurrgeng,** from mid-June to mid-August. With no rains to replenish the floodplains, the land dries out and turns brown. This season slips into **Gunung,** a time of dry heat and very little water, whose end is signaled in October by the return of the thunderclouds of Gunumeleng.

THE ROAD TO KAKADU

From its junction with the Stuart Hwy. (see p. 233), the **Arnhem Highway** proceeds east toward Kakadu. One of the first rivers it crosses is the Adelaide. Here, 64km from Darwin, you can embark on one of the Top End's classic tourist experiences, the **Adelaide River Queen Jumping Crocodile Cruise** (tel. 8988 8144). As patrons enjoy either the air-conditioned lower deck or the exposed viewing deck, attendants guide the boat down the waterway and pause to dangle large hunks of meat several meters above the water, provoking voracious crocs to breach the still surface and devour the tucker offered them. (Cruises May-Aug. daily 9, 11am, 1, 3pm; Sept.-April 9, 11am, and 2:30pm; 1½hr.; $26, children $15.) For transport, **AAT King's** (tel. 8941 3844) and **Darwin Day Tours** (tel. 8981 8696) run buses to the cruise site from Darwin. The **Window on the Wetlands Visitor Centre,** 3km before the croc cruise on Beatrice Hill, provides an education about the floodplain region, complete with a view.

About 50km farther down the Arnhem Hwy., the **Mary River Wetlands** surround the road. It's best to explore this recreational wilderness on solid ground or by boat, as the wetlands are home to lots of salties. In fact, the **Shady Camp Billabong,** 25km down an access road from the highway, has the world's highest concentration of saltwater crocodiles. Two good bases for exploring the Mary River region are the **Annaburoo Lodge** and the **Bark Hut Inn,** located across from each other on the highway. You can stop for fuel and a snack; from here, it's only 19km to Kakadu.

ORIENTATION

Kakadu National Park has a roughly rectangular shape, the straightest side being the eastern border along the Arnhem escarpment. There are only two ways to drive into the park: the **Arnhem Hwy.** in the north and the **Kakadu Hwy.** in the south. These two roads are paved for their entire length and eventually converge in the park's northeastern interior, near the township of **Jabiru.** They remain open year-round, except during the most severe (usually cyclonic) flooding conditions.

Kakadu's north gate is on the Arnhem Hwy., 120km from its junction with the Stuart Hwy. The Arnhem runs eastward through the **South Alligator Region,** which sprawls around the mighty South Alligator River and includes the **Kakadu Holiday Village.** After 81km, the highway enters the **East Alligator Region,** and arrives at **Ubirr Rd.,** the turn-off to the rock art sight and lookout of Ubirr Rock, 39km to the north. Ubirr is the only paved road in the park that is routinely closed in the wet season, when it becomes a virtual river-crossing. The junction of the Arnhem and Kakadu Hwy. is about 1km past Ubirr Rd., in the **Jabiru Region.** Located just 2km from the junction, Jabiru is the primary town in Kakadu Park, with a post office, bank, medical center, pharmacy, supermarket, and police. The Arnhem Hwy. ends 5km past Jabiru, and a secondary road goes 1km farther to the **Jabiru Airport.**

Many of the park's tourist hotspots are situated off the Kakadu Hwy. Starting from the junction with the Arnhem, the **Bowali Visitor Centre** is just 2km down the Kakadu Hwy. on the right. The turn-off for the **Nourlangie rock art site** and **Nourlangie Region** is 19km farther, on the left. The **Nourlangie Rd.** itself is 12km long, paved, and generally open in any season. Continuing on another 19km, the **Jim Jim/Twin Falls Road** makes a gravelly left toward the waterfalls of the same names. This 4WD-only route (impassable in the Wet) runs 60km to the Jim Jim camping area and 10km more to Twin. Its opening day in the dry season, eagerly awaited by tourists and tour guides alike, can be frustratingly uncertain. Nine kilometers past the Jim Jim/Twin Falls Road, the road to Cooinda/Yellow Water (paved 500m) turns off to the right of the Kakadu Hwy. The **Yellow Water and Jim Jim Region** surrounds the Cooinda area and the two waterfalls. It is 99km farther on the Kakadu Hwy. through the **Mary River Region** to the south gate of Kakadu, and an additional 59km to **Pine Creek** on the Stuart Hwy. The total length of the loop from the Arnhem Hwy. to the Stuart Hwy. along the Kakadu Hwy. is 207km, and comes out at Pine Creek, 90km north of Katherine. The best distance map is in the **Kakadu Air/Kakadu Parklink** brochure, available in most of the lodges in the park.

PRACTICAL INFORMATION

Entrance Fee: National Park admission $15, under 16 free, good for 14 days. Ticket may be requested at any time to prove you've paid.

Tourist Information: The Bowali Visitor Centre (tel. 8938 1121; 8938 1115) disperses huge amounts of park knowledge and presents a welcome from the Gukburlerri Aboriginals. A new facility with displays, cafe, and phones. Wheelchair accessible. Open daily 8am-5pm. The park manager is at Jabiru, P.O. Box 71, NT 0886. Outside of the park, contact Parks Australia North (tel. 8946 4300; fax 8981 3497), at GPO Box 1260, Darwin, NT 0801.

Travel Agency: Jabiru Tourist Centre (tel. 8979 2548) in Jabiru plaza.

Money: Westpac Bank in Jabiru, open Mon.-Thurs. 9:30am-4pm, Fri. 9:30am-5pm, has **ATMs.** ATM also at reception of Cooinda Lodge.

Potable water: At Bowali, Jabiru, Cooinda, Kakadu Holiday Village, and Merl and Gunlom camping areas.

Wheelchair access: At Bowali Visitor Center, and at the Merl, Mardugal, Muirella Park, and Gunlom camping areas. Also along the Ubirr and Nourlangie walking tracks, plus the path from Cooinda to the **Warradjan Cultural Centre.**

Airport: The Jabiru Airport, 6.5km east of Jabiru, is the base for aerial tours of Kakadu. Shuttle buses run by **Kakadu Parklink** depart Jabiru for the airport at 7:45, 9:45, 10:45am, 12:45, and 3:45pm, and leave the airport for Jabiru at 8:30am, noon, 3, and 4:30pm ($5 one-way). **Kakadu Air** offers $60 half-hr. flights and $100 hr. flights above the park. Airport, Kakadu Parklink, and Kakadu Air can all be reached at 1800 089 113 or 8979 2411; fax 8979 2302.

Car Rental: There is a car rental office in Jabiru. Your task is to find it.

Automobile Services: Diesel and unleaded **fuel stations** are to be found at the Kakadu Holiday Village (on the Arnhem, 42km east of the north entrance), Jabiru, Cooinda, the Border Store near Ubirr, and the Mary River Roadhouse at the south entrance. Jabiru has **car servicing facilities,** if unfortunately necessary. For-up-to-date **road conditions,** call the Bowali Visitors Centre (tel. 8938 1120).

Emergency: The Jabiru Police (tel. 8979 23122) and **Jabiru Health Clinic** (tel. 8979 2018) handle all emergencies. Ranger stations can relay information to these facilities from more remote areas, but aren't always open.

Hitchhiking: Kakadu has some extremely desolate roads, so hitching often becomes walking, and is strongly discouraged.

Ranger Stations: South Alligator Ranger Station (tel. 8979 0194), 40km west of Bowali Center near Kakadu Holiday Village; **East Alligator Ranger Station** (tel. 8979 2291), 40km north of Bowali Center toward Ubirr; **Jim Jim Ranger Station** (tel. 8979 2038), down a 2.5km road that turns off the Kakadu Hwy. 45km south of Bowali; **Mary River Ranger Station** (tel. 8975 4578), 1km from the south entry station. **Entry stations: south** (tel. 8975 4859) and **north** (tel. 8979 0100).

Post Office: Licensed Post Office in Jabiru News Agency, in plaza. Open Mon.-Tues. 9am-5pm, Wed.-Fri. 9am-5pm and 6-7pm.

ACCOMMODATIONS

The cheapest, most convenient way of sleeping in Kakadu is to camp, but do consider the sweltering heat of the wet season. There are four large, park-run campgrounds. All cost $5 per person (payable to an on-site manager or at the Bowali Visitor Centre), and include toilets and solar heated showers. **Merl Camping Area** is a short walk south of Ubirr Rock, near the supply-stocked Border Store. Sunsets from Ubirr are said to be spectacular, but, like the operating of this campground, are dependent on the season. **Muirella Park Camping Area,** 32km south of Bowali, is on a revegetated airstrip near the Kakadu Hwy. Flooding can shut down parts of it in the Wet. The **Mardugal Camping Area,** near Yellow Water, is named after the Aboriginal name for the billabong. Near the south end of the park, 42km east of the south entry station, the **Gunlom Camping Area** stands 200m from a waterfall and pool and is 2WD accessible. For info on Kakadu camping, call 8938 1100.

Private campgrounds are more expensive than park-operated ones. The **Frontier Kakadu Lodge** in Jabiru offers sites at $7.50 per person, with power $20 for the first two people, $7.50 for each additional person. **Gagudju Lodge Cooinda** charges $7 per person, with power $8. At **Kakadu Hostel Village,** sites go for $7 for two people, $3.50 per additional person, with power $10, $5 per additional person. All of these have shared ablution blocks with flush toilets and showers, and shared cooking facilities.

The park also contains free camping areas, with the most basic facilities or none at all. (In the **South Alligator area:** Two Mile Hole, Four Mile Hole, West Alligator Head,

Red Lily Billabong, and Alligator Billabong. In the **Nourlangie area:** Malabanjbandju, Burdulba, and Sandy Billabong. In the **Jim Jim/Cooinda area:** Black Jungle Spring, Jim Jim Falls, Jim Jim Billabong, and Magule. In the **Mary River area:** Kabolgie.) Of course, there are also more expensive options with four walls and real beds.

Kakadu Hostel (tel. 8979 2232), 2km south of Ubirr Rock on Ubirr Rd. Next to the Border Store, this dingy hostel's value is its location in an area that has no indoor alternatives. Above-ground pool, shared bath. Entrance just north of the border store. Check-out 10am. 2- to 10-bed dorms $15. Reservations recommended.

Gagudju Lodge Cooinda (tel. 8979 0145). This Cooinda complex has pricey motel rooms ($135 plus tax), campgrounds (see above), and budget rooms in a cul-de-sac of trailers. The rooms are compact but spotless 2-bed arrangements with good A/C. Shared bath, fridge, and coin-operated BBQ facility. Reception open daily 6am-, 11pm. Check-in for budget rooms by noon. Check-out 10am. Budget beds $15, YHA non-members $19. Linen included. Reservations required.

Frontier Kakadu Lodge (tel. 8979 2422), in Jabiru. In an operation that caters to the cheaper side of Jabiru, Frontier has dorm beds ($25), 4-bed rooms ($95), and self-contained cabins (each with a double bed and 3 singles, private bath, and kitchen; $150). All rooms have A/C, linen, towels, and aside from the cabins, shared bath and coin-operated BBQ. Swimming pool, laundry facilities. 2 cabins wheelchair accessible. Reservations recommended.

FOOD

Save some money by **bringing your own food** into Kakadu. Because of the long haul required to supply shelves and kitchens, food in the park is very expensive. Still, shopping for food in the park is a whole lot cheaper than eating at a restaurant there. The biggest selection is at the supermarket in the plaza at Jabiru. The **Border Store** near Ubirr and the **Gagudju Lodge Cooinda** also sell the simplest groceries, like bread, yogurt, and canned foods. The former is open 8:30am-5:30pm, the latter 6am-7:30pm.

Generally, food is found where accommodations are found, and snack stands are the most economical ready-made food option. The Border Store sells $3 sandwiches and burgers, or $4 specialty burgers made from buffalo, croc, or barramundi. The snack bar at the Cooinda lodge may serve up a ham sandwich for $3.50, but a burger will cost you $11.50. Food stores always sell abundant liquids, as staying hydrated is critical in this hot, often dry, environment.

The only restaurants are within the lodges, and the more expensive the rooms, the finer the dining. **Mimi's Restaurant** at the Cooinda Lodge has mouth-watering meals such as the pasta del giorno ($11) and the platter of bush tucker ($24; open daily noon-2:30pm and 6:30-9:30pm).

SIGHTS AND ACTIVITIES

A plethora of sites, walks, and experiences awaits in the remote stretches of Kakadu. The walking paths in the park are generally very well-marked. **Carry water** wherever you go, and ask before swimming anywhere—salties don't like sharing their jacuzzis.

South Alligator Region

Mamukala Wetlands, 8km east of the South Alligator River crossing, is a floodplain and bird viewing area off the Arnhem Hwy. There's a bird hide 600m from the parking lot, and a 3km circular walk that trails the edge of the wetlands and takes about two hours. Starting 150m from the Kakadu Holiday Village, the **Gungarre Monsoon Rainforest Walk** is an easy 3.6km circular path that weaves through monsoonal rainforest, and is generally open all year.

East Alligator Region

Because of the flooding of the Magela Creek, this remarkable area becomes restricted in the wet season. Visit during the Dry. **Ubirr** is the gem of East Alligator: a collection of sandstone outliers on which Aboriginal ancestors have left their art. Of the 80% of *Crocodile Dundee* shot in Australia, 60% was filmed here. A wheelchair-accessible 1km circuit passes many of the significant art sites, including the **Namarrgarn Sisters** and the enormous **Main Gallery.** Then there's the slightly steep 250m climb to the fantastic lookout over the **Nardab floodplain,** where Dundee pointed to a stagnant billabong in the distance and claimed it was the river where a croc attacked him. Sunsets here are amazing, whether or not you can bask in the satisfaction of pinning a saltie. Ubirr is open daily during the Dry (8:30am-sunset) and conditionally during the Wet (2pm-sunset).

There are several walks along the East Alligator River nearby. The **Manngarre Monsoon Rainforest Walk** departs from the downstream boat ramp for a primarily flat 1.6km circular walk (1hr.). The trail comes close to the river banks here and there, and crocs can be spotted at low tide. The highlights of the **Bardedjilidji Sandstone Walk,** which begins at the upstream boat ramp and circuits 2.5km in about two hours, are the weathered sandstone pillars, arches, and caves. The **Cahills Crossing** spans the river and is the only road access from Kakadu into **Arnhem Land** (see p. 241). There's a safely raised platform for viewing the crocs and other animals that hang out along the river.

The popular **Guyluyjambi Aboriginal Culture Cruise** (tel. 1800 089 113) journeys down the river and into some interesting aspects of Aboriginal life. The tour (part of **Kakadu Parklink**) runs from the upstream boat ramp (May-Oct. daily 9, 11am, 1, and 3pm; 1¾hr.; $25). A free shuttle connects to the Border Store and Merl Camping Area. Call for wet season tour times and bookings.

Jabiru Region

The **Bowali Visitor Centre** is a good place to start a tour of the park, but in this, the most developed region of Kakadu, it's no surprise that most sights are man-made. The curious can check out the **Gagudju Crocodile Hotel,** but its quirky, croc-shaped design is best appreciated from the air. Far to the east, past the airport, the **Ranger uranium mine** is the most active such mine on Kakadu land. Tours explore this operation daily, leaving from the Jabiru Airport at 10:30am and 1:30pm (May-Oct.), or by sufficient demand. Reservations (tel. 1800 089 113) are essential.

Nourlangie Region

The principle pull of this part of the park is **Nourlangie** itself, a huge rock outlier used as a shelter and an art studio by earlier Aboriginals. A 1.5km walking track takes about 45 minutes to pass the Main Gallery. Part of the track is wheelchair-accessible. Many mystical images are painted on the walls of Nourlangie, including Nabulwinj-bulwinj, a dangerous spirit who eats females after striking them with a yam. The farthest point on the loop is **Gunwarrdehwarrde Lookout,** a craggy climb that affords a surreal view of the distant escarpment, where Aboriginals believe Lightning Man Namarrgon lives. He is painted on Nourlangie too, in the Main Gallery.

The serene **Anbangbang Billabong,** close to Nourlangie Rock, has picnic tables, BBQs, and an easy 2.5km walk circling the water (about 1hr.), but is only open in the dry season. **Nawurlandja,** a rock outlier next to Nourlangie, is accessible by a road that branches off the Nourlangie Rd. The hike to the rock is a steep 600m loop (30min.). A 4km trek goes to **Nanguluwur,** a large art site on the western face of Nourlangie (about 2hr.). There are lots of other hikes in the region, such as the **Mirrai Lookout** (1.8km, 1hr.), **Bubba Wetlands** (5km, 2hr.), and the challenging **Barrk Sandstone Walk** (6-8km, full day, open year-round), which scales the sandstone landscape and goes past Nanguluwur.

Yellow Water and Jim Jim Region

Yellow Water, part of Jim Jim Creek, is the most popular billabong in Kakadu—not to swim in, but to cruise past meters-long crocodiles, sunning themselves on the banks or floating ominously on the surface of the water. Yellow Water is also famous for its abundant birdlife, visible on a 1.5km circular walk. There's also a wheelchair-accessi-

The Writing on the Wall

Over 5000 sites of Aboriginal rock art have been noted in Kakadu, most on the escarpment wall, and an estimated 10,000 sites remain undiscovered. The age of the art is difficult to determine, partly because pictures dating back thousands of years sit side-by-side with paintings done in the 1980s. Certain works have been "repainted" by descendants who are familiar enough with the old stories to "retell" them by the brush. Some recovered painting materials date to 50,000 years ago, some depicting extinct animals. Corresponding to the climatic changes that affected prehistoric Aboriginals, there are three general styles identified in the rock art. The pre-estuarine period (50,000-8000 BC) corresponds to a wooded Kakadu with an overall uniform style suggesting a small regional population. The estuarine period (8000-2000 BC), during the bountiful hunting era when the ocean was rising, shows previously unknown animals in an "x-ray" art style, which depicts the insides as well as outlines of animals. Booming wildlife meant growing communities, reflected in a rise in artistic diversity. In the freshwater period (2000 BC-present), Aboriginals captured an even greater variety of species with more complex x-ray images, eventually adding their own renditions of first contact with the white colonists. Aboriginals look to the rock art as a window into the past, and as a written history, some of which was painted in the Dreaming.

ble platform to view the billabong. But the most popular way to do Yellow Water—sort of a Kakadu rite—is on a **Yellow Water Cruise.** These narrated pontoon voyages last either an hour and a half ($22.50) or two hours ($26.50). The shorter ones leave daily at 11:15am, 1, and 2:45pm, the longer ones at 6:45, 9am, and 4:30pm (sunset). The cruise can be booked at Gagudju Lodge Cooinda (tel. 8979 0145) where a courtesy shuttle bus picks up passengers 20 minutes before departure. Also near the Cooinda lodge, the **Warradjan Aboriginal Cultural Centre** shows visitors the culture of Kakadu and complements Bowali's focus on wildlife. Videos and other media explore both traditional and contemporary Aboriginal life.

Jim Jim and **Twin Falls** are gushing cascades in the Wet, visible only from the air. In the Dry, the water in the road shrinks significantly, but so do the falls. Only accessible by 4WD, the Jim Jim cascade crashes 150m into a pool and can be viewed via a 1.8km hike (1hr.) from the gravel road. Another hike, the Barrk Malam Walk, takes a 6km (4hr.) route to the top of the plateau above Jim Jim and back. Jim Jim trickles off by the middle-to-end of the dry season, but Twin Falls, the spring-fed cascade 10km down the road, lasts year-round. From the parking lot it's a 400m trek and a 1km swim or boat ride down a narrow gorge. Maguk, or **Barramundi Falls,** is a smaller cascade in the region. It flows during both seasons, and has a 2km hike (1½hr.) through monsoon forest.

Mary River Region

This is the land where the rivers begin. In the headwaters of the South Alligator River, a series of falls called **Gunlom** flow rapidly from December to May, but cease almost completely in the Dry. A wheelchair-accessible footbridge leads to the plunge pool, and a steep 2km circuit walk travels to the top of the falls and back for a view of the South Alligator valley (about 1hr.). Gunlom, on the 2WD-accessible Gunlom Rd., is the only escarpment cascade that conventional vehicles can reach in the dry season.

Remember those djang andjamun areas that bring catastrophic consequences if entered? **Jarrangbarnmi** is such a site. This series of pools on **Koolpin Creek** is home to **Bula** and **Bolung,** two creation ancestors. No one can enter the area without a permit. **Yurmikmik,** however, the land between the Marrawal Plateau and the South Alligator River, is a popular hiking area. Paths head off in various directions from the parking lot off the Gunlom access road. They lead through the hilly southern landscape, where, in the wet season, several waterfalls plunge from the plateau.

Tours of Kakadu National Park

With a park map and a thorough guidebook, it's easily possible to do Kakadu in your own vehicle. Remember that many areas of the park are open only to 4WD vehicles, and some may not be open at all. Posted signs will fill in most of the gaps. One popular way of visiting the park without a vehicle is by two-day tour from Darwin with **Greyhound Pioneer;** expandable to three or more days by adding nights in the park. This is an especially economical option for those with a **Greyhound kilometer pass.** The conductor doubles as a knowledgeable, witty tour guide, and although the visit compresses the main sights, it does give a memorable dose of Kakadu.

If you're looking for a more rugged experience and have some extra time and money, a tour company package may be the better way to go. Almost all 4WD operations work out of Darwin. Some rely on lodge accommodations, others camp under the stars, but all encourage more than two or three days to *really* see the park. **Wilderness 4WD Adventures** (tel. 1800 808 288) is a highly recommended company that specializes in four- and five-day tours geared toward nature lovers who will truly appreciate the biology-trained tour guides. **Backpacking Australia Tours** (tel. 1800 652 628) caters three-day tours to budget travelers. Their guides may not be biologists, but they do have three years of experience. **Gondwana Kakadu Plus** (tel. 1800 658 378) gets kudos for making a side trip to the Shady Camp Billabong just outside the park, where you can ride motorized dinghies past crocodiles that dwarf the boats. These tours are for fit travelers who don't mind a lot of hiking and hot sun.

Arnhem Land

Arnhem Land isn't often heard in the same breath as Kakadu. Nor, in many ways, should it be. Kakadu is a national park that happens to be Aboriginal-owned. Adjacent to it, Arnhem Land is an Aboriginal *homeland,* and one roughly the size of Victoria at that! Nearly 20,000 Aboriginal people live in the region, speaking among them some 40 languages. The name of the land they live on is probably Dutch, after a ship that skimmed past the coast in 1623. The inland borders of the Arnhem are cut straight and square, but the expansive coastline takes a wild, jagged path from the **Cobourg Peninsula** in the west (location of **Gurig National Park**) to the Gove Peninsula in the east. Arnhem also includes the Goote and Elcho islands offshore.

By law, Arnhem Land is off limits to non-Aboriginals, except by permit issued by the **Northern Land Council.** Exceptions are made for the **bauxite mine** on the **Gove Peninsula,** and the urban outpost of **Nhulunbuy,** 15km away (pop. 3500; hospital, bank, and shopping facilities). These areas are formally leased from the Aboriginal owners of the land. Apart from Nhulunbuy, little is commonly known about Arnhem Land. Travelers venture into Arnhem with hopes of dispelling the mystery that surrounds daily Aboriginal life and obtaining a cultural education. **Aboriginal tour businesses** based in Darwin, Katherine, and Kakadu ensure them both, running trips within Arnhem's borders for a couple of days, a week, or longer.

To obtain **permits** to Arnhem Land, contact the Northern Land Council. The Darwin office is at P.O. Box 42921, Casuarina, NT 0811 (tel. 8920 5100; fax 8945 2633; open weekdays 8am-5pm). There's also a West Arnhem office in Jabiru at P.O. Box 18 Fabiu, NT 0886 (tel. 8979 2410; fax 8979 2650). Allow two to four weeks for processing by mail. **Vehicle entrances** to Arnhem Land are at either **Cahills Crossing** in the East Alligator Region of Kakadu ($15 entrance fee), or about 60km south of Katherine on a road that travels 700km east to Nhulunbuy. This road has camping and fuel (last fuel stop at Bulman) along the way, but can close during the Wet. The Katherine police (tel. 8972 0111) give a **road conditions** report.

For those just interested in the fishing, diving, and mining in Nhulunbuy, an airport 10km from town has daily flights to and from Darwin and Cairns. This allows you to skip the long drive, and the permit business as well, as long as you don't plan to leave the township or mine lease areas.

Litchfield National Park

Splendid bushland plateaus and dramatic waterfalls produce the relaxing natural beauty of Litchfield National Park. Established in 1986, these 146,000 hectares of parkland tempt visitors to swim, hike, and take pictures. Litchfield can be done comfortably in a day's swing down from Darwin, but camping is permitted for those who want a more extended stay.

The most memorable sights of Litchfield are its waterfalls. **Wangi Falls,** at the end of the main road, is the most popular because the way to it is paved. A pair of towering cascades feed a croc-free swimming area. Goannas and kookaburras have been attracted to the area by tourist hand-outs, but feeding the wildlife is discouraged. Wangi is wheelchair-accessible and has an info booth, a snack bar, and an emergency call device. Closer to the Batchelor entrance and with paved access as well are **Florence Falls** and **Buley Rockhole.** Florence is wheelchair accessible up to an intimidating but stable look-out deck over the falls; past the deck there's a stairway descending a steep cliff to the swimming hole at the base. Buley Rockhole's smaller, more relaxing set of cascades is not wheelchair accessible. There are campgrounds at all three of these sites, and Wangi has unpowered caravan sites. **Tolmer Falls,** off the main road, can also be reached by 2WD. It is wheelchair accessible, but the walkway from the parking lot to the lookout is a 400m tread. Swimming is prohibited because of the endangered orange horseshoe bat that lives in caves just above the pool. Only travelers with 4WD can access the **Tjayner (Sandy Creek) Falls** or the sandstone rock formations nicknamed the **Lost City.** These drivers can reach the park's **Campgrounds Tjaynera;** a second set of campgrounds sits below the falls at Florence. Camping fees are paid on an honor system. The **Parks and Wildlife Commission** (tel. 8999 4411) handles camping fees and information. Entrance to the park is free.

Like the entire Top End, Litchfield is thrashed by the Wet (Oct.-April). Flooding can shut down certain swimming areas, and the sealed main road, **Litchfield Park Rd.,** from Batchelor to Wangi Falls, can be closed due to flooding for several days at a time. When dry, a network of 4WD gravel roads access other areas in the park and create several potential entrance points (see p. 233). Call 8922 3394 for road conditions.

En route to Litchfield: Batchelor

The paved access to Litchfield National Park is from the east. From Darwin, continue south on the Stuart Hwy. (see p. 233) past Cox Peninsula Rd. and the **Manton Dam Recreation Area.** Turn off to the right on **Batchelor Rd.,** 90km out of Darwin. This way takes you past the town of **Batchelor** (pop. 350), which is proud home to three things: the **Litchfield Parks and Wildlife Office** (ranger station), Batchelor College,

Living Rocks

On the way in to Litchfield from Batchelor, hulking stone-like mounds of various sizes and shapes rise up out of the bush. These termite mounds, full of eggs and nutrients, can be anywhere from 50 to 100 years old. The ones with lumpy columnal structures are called cathedral mounds. These mounds are usually built in wooded areas and are among the largest in the world, reaching up to 6m in height. Shorter, flatter mounds are called magnetic mounds because of the miraculous way they're aligned along a north-south axis, like the needle of a compass. The termites aren't aware of the earth's magnetic fields; they instinctively build the faces of their mounds to face the rising and setting sun. This way, the mound is warmed by the softer rays of the morning and afternoon, but appears as a mere hyphen to the glaring mid-day sun at the top of the sky. Like anyone without air-conditioning living in Northern Territory, the termites have got to mind their temperature. A short boardwalk off the Litchfield Park Road lets you stare across a "graveyard" of these magnetic mounds without damaging the fragile ground around them.

and **Karlstein Castle.** The 6m-high replica of a 600-year-old Bohemian castle was built by a European resident of Batchelor in the 1970s. The town also contains a pub, service station, post office, bank, supermarket, and **Caravillage Camping Park.** The **Rum Jungle Motor Inn** (tel. 8976 0123) is a wonderful stop just north of Batchelor where a uranium mine was dug in the 1950s. The mine is now a 220m-deep lake which filled up just two wet seasons after the mine closed in the 70s. The peaceful scene overlooks some submerged tractors. The **Banyan Tree Caravan Park** (tel. 8976 0330), also in this area, sells food and drinks. Continue west on the Batchelor Rd. to reach Litchfield National Park.

DOWN THE TRACK

Between the tropical Top End and the arid Red Centre, the Stuart Highway traverses a climatic gradient from the hilly, dense vegetation of the north to the flat, crispy desert of central Australia. The "track" was once proclaimed "the most sing-on-able road in the world." There isn't much else to do. From Katherine to Tennant Creek, the Stuart Hwy. passes through some of the emptiest and most uninspiring stretches in the outback. The people here consider their land "the Never Never," referring to the tendency residents have to never, never leave. But chances are ten to one that after canoeing down the Katherine River, bathing in the hot springs of Mataranka, or taking in the Devil's Marbles and some mining history near Tennant Creek, you *will* leave—and quite contentedly—singing "Waltzing Matilda" as you head down the Stuart Hwy. in search of more blessedly populated ground.

Katherine

A few blocks of storefronts along the Stuart Hwy. cling to the frontier of the Top End's thick, green bush as if in fear of the remote stretches of desert that await to the south. Katherine (pop. 10,700) lies 345km south of Darwin, and is the largest settlement between there and Alice Springs. This provincial highway town subsists on agriculture, cattle husbandry, and mining. Katherine's Aboriginal communities, primarily Jawoyn and Dagoman, are among the most visible in the Northern Territory. As in any self-respecting frontier town, a rough-and-tumble atmosphere pervades this junction of the Top End, the Red Centre, and the Kimberley of WA. After a brief water-break on the banks of the Katherine River and a peek in the nearby gorges, most travelers are ready to journey onward to one of these more alluring destinations.

ORIENTATION

Lonely Katherine lies 700km north of Tennant Creek and 510km east of Kununurra, WA. The Stuart Hwy. goes under the guise of **Katherine Terrace** as it rumbles through town. The main blocks of this strip lie between the **transit center,** at Lindsay St., and the **Victoria Hwy.,** which heads toward Western Australia. A few hundred meters south of the center, Giles St. heads left toward Katherine Gorge. Parallel to Katherine Tce., First through Fourth St. house various tourist accommodations.

PRACTICAL INFORMATION

Tourist Office: Katherine Region Tourist Association (tel. 8972 2650; fax 8972 2969), at Lindsay St. south of the transit center and across the street. The visitors center here (open Mon.-Fri. 8:45am-5pm, Sat. 10am-4pm, Sun. 10am-3pm) is more impartial than the travel desk in the transit center.

Budget Travel: Traveland, 15 Katherine Tce. (tel. 8972 1344; fax 8972 2763), near Giles St. Open Mon.-Thurs. 9am-5pm, Fri. 9am-7pm, Sat. 9am-noon. Harvey World Travel, in the transit center, is *not* the only licensed outfitter of reservations for Katherine Gorge.

Currency Exchange: Westpac, Commonwealth, and **ANZ** all maintain banks and ATMs on Katherine Tce. All open Mon.-Thurs. 9:30am-4pm, Fri. 9:30am-5pm.

Airport: Tindal Airport, 20km south of Katherine, is connected to an RAAF base. **Airnorth** (tel. 8971 7277) serves Darwin (2 per day, in wet season 1 per day, $114) and Alice Springs (1 per day, $369).

Buses: Greyhound and **McCafferty's** bus counters don't open until 20min. prior to departure. Book through **Harvey World Travel** (tel. 8972 1044) in the transit center. **Greyhound Pioneer** runs to: Darwin (4:45am, 1, and 6:15pm, 3½hr., $38), Alice Springs (2:25 and 6pm, 15hr., $125) via Tennant Creek (8-8¾hr., $61), Broome (12:20pm, 19hr., $154) via Kununurra (4½hr., $49). **McCafferty's** runs to: Darwin (7:30am and 12:30pm, 4¼hr., $35), Townsville ($170), and Alice Springs (2:05pm, 15¼hr., $133) via Tennant Creek (8½hr., $61).

Car Rentals: Territory (tel. 8972 3183) is in the transit center. **Hertz** (tel. 8971 1111), **Avis** (tel. 8971 0520), and **Budget** (tel. 8971 1333) also have offices.

Bookstore: Pom's Odds and Sods, 34 Katherine Tce. (tel. 8971 1195), is a musty secondhand exchange. Open Mon.-Fri. 9am-6pm, Sat. 9am-2pm, Sun. 10am-2pm.

Pharmacy: Amcal (tel. 8972 1229 or 1800 621 229) in Woolworths Shopping Centre across from the transit center. Open Mon.-Fri. 8:30am-6pm, Sat.-Sun. 9am-5pm.

Hospital: (tel. 8973 9294) on Giles St. (Gorge Rd.), 3km from Katherine Tce.

Police: (tel. 8972 0111), 2km south of the tourist office on the Stuart Hwy.

Post Office: On the corner of Katherine Tce. and Giles St. Open Mon.-Fri. 9am-5pm. **Postal code:** 0851.

Phone Code: 08.

ACCOMMODATIONS

All three hostels in town have A/C, fans, a pool, and a 10am check-out time. The high season for tourism coincides with the dry season, roughly March to October.

Kookaburra Backpackers, corner of Lindsay and Third St. (tel. 8971 0257 or 1800 808 211), 3 blocks from the transit center. Every group of 8 guests shares a clean bathroom and a kitchenette overflowing with pots and pans. Relaxed social atmosphere centers around the picnic tables and the pool. Laundry facilities, free transport to and from transit center. Reception open daily 7:30am-7:30pm. With YHA or VIP card dorms $12; twins $35. Key deposit $10. Book ahead in the high season.

Victoria Lodge, 21 Victoria Hwy. (tel. 8972 3464; fax 8971 1738), a 10min. walk from Katherine Tce. Somewhat isolated, this lodge is laid out in a cluster pattern similar to Kookaburra, each with bathroom, spacious kitchenette, and color TV. Fuzzy thin carpet, fuzzy sweet owners. BBQ. Free transport to and from buses. Dorms $13, weekly $85; twins and doubles $40. Book ahead.

Palm Court Backpackers, corner of Third and Giles St. (tel. 8972 2722 or 1800 089 103; fax 8971 1443), just a block from Kookaburra. The amusingly zany management has given each room its own TV, fridge, and bath, but the bunks sag, and the kitchen crawls with clicking, unwanted visitors. Plates and cutlery provided (leave ID as collateral). Laundry facilities. Reception open daily 7am-9pm. Sardine-package dorms $12-14; doubles $45. VIP, YHA. Key deposit $10.

Camping: South of town, **Frontier Katherine** (tel. 8972 1744; fax 8972 2790), near the Stuart Hwy. on Cyprus St., has unpowered campsites for $8 per person, with power and shower $20. **Red Gum Caravan Park,** 42 Victoria Hwy. (tel. 8972 2239; fax 8972 2385), has sites for $7 per person, with power for 2 people $17, each additional person $7. **Knotts Crossing** (tel. 8972 2511; fax 8972 2628) is toward the gorge on the corner of Giles and Cameron St. before the hospital. Unpowered sites $7.50 per person or $16 max.

FOOD

Ever the cheapest place to fill your stomach, **Woolworths** stands across from the transit center (open Mon.-Sat. 7am-9pm, Sun. 9am-7pm).

Mekhong Thai Cafe, at the junction of Stuart and Victoria Hwy. (tel. 8972 3170). A simple, fluorescent-lit interior is decorated with little more than tables and a beverage freezer. The food is excellent, reasonably authentic, and vegetarian friendly. Stir-fried scallops with basil ($14.50), beef fried with ginger ($10.50), mixed vegetable curry ($12). Open Mon.-Fri. 5-10pm, Sat.-Sun. 6-10pm.

Popeye's Gourmet Food, on Katherine Tce. near Giles St. The main event of this sailor-themed joint is the all-you-can-eat pizza buffet (nightly 5-9pm, $6). The tomato pies will stave off scurvy, and the spacious seating is pleasant. Pies are served with salad ($6). Open Mon.-Fri. 9am-10pm, Sat.-Sun. 11am-10pm.

Terrace Cafe (tel. 8972 2728), in the Woolworths shopping center. A worthy little place for breakfast or standard greasy, meaty, Australian tucker. Scrambled eggs on toast $6. Open Mon.-Fri. 7:30am-5pm, Sat. 8:30am-1:30pm, Sun. 9:30am-1pm.

SIGHTS

Katherine Museum (tel. 8972 3945) is off Giles Rd. 3km from Katherine Tce., across from the hospital. This local heritage display's gears are turned by the Historical Society (open March-Oct. Mon.-Fri. 10am-4pm, Sun. 2-5pm; Nov.-Feb. Mon.-Fri. 10am-4pm). Nearby, the **Katherine School of the Air,** on Giles St. about 2km from Katherine Tce., broadcasts lessons to rural schoolchildren and mistakenly identifies itself as the largest classroom in the world; that distinction belongs to the Alice Springs school (see p. 255). Still, 80 million hectares is a long way to throw a spitball. During school hours you can observe these primary school DJs (open April-Oct. Mon.-Fri. daytime; admission $4, children $2).

The **Katherine Orchid Nursery,** 12 Stutterd St. (tel. 8972 1905; fax 8972 1906), across the highway from the Victoria Backpackers Lodge, waters a proud collection of 25,000 blossoms. Down the road, 3km along the Victoria Hwy. from the Stuart Hwy., local **hot springs** bubble up on the bank of the **Katherine River.** Although not quite Mataranka, these springs provide safe swimming, toilets, and wheelchair access along Croker St. There are many **art galleries** in town detailing the Aboriginal cultures of the Katherine region; the visitors center has a publication called the *Katherine Arts and Crafts Trail* to help navigate this anthropological journey.

A little farther from Katherine, **NT Rare Rocks** (tel. 8971 0889) has an array spanning the geologic composition of the Territory. To reach this display of rocks, head north on the Stuart Hwy. and turn left on Zimin Dr. **Springvale Homestead,** the oldest homestead in the Northern Territory, is farther down Zimin Dr., after a left at Shadforth. This livestock lair was established by Albert Giles in 1878; today it offers a window to the region's early days, and a departure point for wildlife and cultural tours.

Edith Falls are at the end off a 20km paved access road that begins 42km north of Katherine on the Stuart Hwy. Officially part of **Nitmiluk National Park,** these permanent falls originate from the Arnhem Land escarpment. Activities include swimming, hiking, and camping (tel. 8975 4869; access to toilets, showers, BBQ, picnic area).

■ Katherine Gorge (Nitmiluk National Park)

The 292,008 hectares of Nitmiluk cover the region northeast of Katherine. Since 1989 the park has been owned by the local Jawoyn Aboriginals, who manage it jointly with the Parks and Wildlife Commission. The park's star attraction is Katherine Gorge, actually a series of 13 gorges on the Katherine River, broken by small cascades. The rocky cliffs on either side vary from sloped and vegetated to vertical and cavernous to set-in-relief-behind-sandy-beaches. In the wet season (Oct.-April) the individual cascades are subsumed by a single gushing current that restricts access to the gorge.

Katherine Gorge is 30km out of Katherine on Giles St., later called Gorge Rd. **Travel North** (tel. 8972 1044; fax 8972 3989) runs buses from the hostels in Katherine several times per day (one-way $8, return $15, children half-price; book ahead). The tourist area next to the gorge has picnic tables, toilets, and trailheads. There is a car park at the new **Nitmiluk Centre.** The center contains a grocery store, museum, park information desk, and a veranda that overlooks the awesome gorge (open dry season daily 7am-8pm; wet season 7:30am-5:30pm). A winding concrete path connects the center with another car park and the **boathouse.** Contact the **Parks and Wildlife Commission** (tel. 8972 1886; fax 8971 0702) in Katherine for more info on Katherine Gorge. Although some drink water straight from the river, visitors are beseeched to bring their own water and to baste themselves in sunblock.

On the Katherine River

From May to September, quieter waters create a picturesque setting for canoeing, boating, and walking. **Canoeing** justifiably takes the cake in popularity, allowing boaters to glide up to intriguing spots for closer inspection, or approach freshwater crocodiles without the drone of an engine. Paddling on the water is also more comfortable than hiking, since temperatures here are sizzling, even in the winter. No more than 75 canoes are permitted in the gorge at a time. **Nitmiluk Canoes** (tel. 8972 3604 or 8972 3150) does most of the hiring, although other agents do consolidated booking through them. Single-handed canoes (full-day 8am-5pm $33, half-day 8am-noon or noon-5pm $24; deposit $20) and double-handed canoes (full-day $49, half-day $36; deposit $20) are both available, and all canoes come with a waterproof safe. It's easy to team up at the river if you come alone. But paddling is only half the fun; the portage from one gorge to the next requires hauling the canoe over rocky trails.

Another popular aquatic activity is **swimming,** but keep in mind that you may be sharing the space with freshwater crocs (most canoeists spot at least one). Many people like to swim near the boathouse. Travel North runs **boat tours** up and down the gorge (book through Nitmiluk Canoes). A series of flat, shaded motor vessels zoom along the gorges—at the end of one gorge, passengers hike over to a new boat on the next. The crowded arrangement makes it hard to enjoy the natural solitude of the area (peak season 4hr., 3 per day, $41, children $19; off season 2hr., 4 per day, $27, children $12). You can also take an eight-hour "safari" cruise or a helicopter flight.

On Terra Firma

Walking tracks in the national park range in length from 400m to 66km. The excellent scenery provides a totally different view from canoeing, but the sun can be brutal. Bring lots of water and a wide-brimmed hat. Register at the Nitmiluk Centre for extended bushwalks, such as the one from the gorge to Edith Falls (5 days). The *Guide to Nitmiluk National Park* has a topographical map and spares no detail about the trails (available at the center; $5). Most hikes begin at the gorge access area.

Overnight camping in the depths of the park is permitted ($3 per person per night, $20 deposit; register at the center). Bush-style camping areas are located along the walking tracks and at the fifth, sixth, and ninth gorges. They're graced with toilets and, usually, a water source. Fires are permitted at the walking track sites but not along the gorges. There are also trim, permanent campgrounds next to the Nitmiluk Centre and at Edith Falls. These can take on both tents and caravans, but only the Gorge boasts powered sites. The **Gorge Caravan Park** has tent sites ($7 per person, with power for 2 people $18; toilets, showers; more facilities than at the Falls).

■ Stuart Highway from Katherine to Tennant Creek

A desolate strip of bitumen proceeds south from Katherine toward the center of Australia. **Cutta Cutta Caves Nature Park,** 27km south of Katherine, is an unsung gem. Two caverns, the Cutta Cutta and the Tindall, expand spaciously 15m underground, but you must be on a tour to enter this underworld. (Tours daily 9, 10am, 1, 2, and 3pm. Admission for 1 cave $7.50, for both $13, children half price.)

Mataranka Homestead Lured by soothing 34°C waters rising from cracks in the earth, bathers make this stop 106km south of Katherine on the Stuart Hwy. The **Mataranka Thermal Pools,** several kilometers down a well-marked access road from the highway, are part of **Elsey National Park.** They flow all year from the Rainbow Springs at a steady rate of 30.5 million liters per day. Bedecked naturally in *Livinstona rigida* palms, the pools provide a rewarding tropical relaxation spot. Mataranka is the center of the original **Never Never,** and the birthplace of this prideful title that would come to describe the entire region.

Greyhound and **McCafferty's** routes between Katherine and Tennant Creek all stop at the **Mataranka Homestead Tourist Resort** (tel. 8975 4544; fax 8975 4580), located next to the pools. The YHA here doesn't face much competition (dorms $13, twins and doubles $26; non-members $15, $30). Its campground has hot showers, laundry, tent sites ($7 per person), and powered sites ($18 for 2 people, $7 each additional person). Canoeing, fishing, and horseback riding can round off an onerous day of soaking in the clear aqua springs.

Three Ways An unassuming junction 26km north of Tennant Creek, Three Ways is where the Barkly Hwy. branches eastward from the Stuart Hwy. toward Townsville, Queensland. Mount Isa, the first substantial town over the Queensland border, is 640km distant. Alice Springs is 532km south on the Stuart Hwy., with Adelaide beyond. The Stuart's northern terminus, Darwin, is a whopping 981km away.

Tennant Creek

Tennant Creek began as a glimmer in the eyes of NT settlers. Gold discovered here in 1930 made Tennant Creek and the Barkly region around it the NT's prima donnas of gold mining. Located 506km south of Darwin on the Stuart Hwy., the town rises as a rare blip of urban development amid desolate desert and vast Aboriginal land. The name was coined in 1860 in tribute to a South Australian chap called John Tennant. It took a while for the town to get up to speed, but since the 1960s, the Tennant Creek area has mined about $4 billion worth of gold.

Although there are still active mines in the area, today's outpost of 3500 people is as much a highway town as a mining center. It occupies a convenient stop-over point just south of the Three Ways junction. Yet, between its mining history, the living legacy of the native Warumungu Aboriginals, and the fascinating valley containing the Devil's Marbles 104km south, there's more to do in Tennant Creek than change buses or crash for the night.

ORIENTATION

This desert creature is a compact little fellow. **Paterson St.,** otherwise known as the Stuart Hwy., runs from north to south to form its backbone. Cross streets form ribs, if you will. Moving south, there's **Stuart St.** (not to be confused with the erstwhile highway) and **Davidson St.,** then a scoliated rib called **Peko Rd.** on the east side of Paterson, and gnarled **Windley St.** on the west. Continuing south we find **Memorial Dr.,** a truncated rib only occurring west of Paterson. As you may expect, this creature has horrible back problems.

PRACTICAL INFORMATION

Tourist Office: Tennant Creek Battery Hill Regional Centre (tel. 8962 3388; fax 8962 2509). This new center provides informational brochures and tours, many of Battery Hill itself (see **Sights,** below). Open Mon.-Fri. 9am-5pm, Sat. 9am-noon, and Sun. for tours. The center does a shuttle run to accommodations at 9am every day to spare you the hike—tell the hostel owner if you're interested.

Currency Exchange: ANZ Bank (tel. 8962 2002), just a few doors south of the transit center on Paterson St. **ATMs.** Open Mon.-Thurs. 9:30am-4pm, Fri. 9:30am-5pm. **Westpac Bank,** at Paterson St. and Peko Rd., has similar exchange facilities and the same hours.

Buses: The **transit center,** on the west side of Paterson St., has phones, a snack bar, and public showers. Greyhound to: Alice Springs (3:15am and 11:25pm, 5½-6hr., $72), Darwin (3:30am and 8:40pm, 12-13hr., $94), via Katherine (8-9½hr., $38), Townsville (11:15pm, 20¼hr., $138). **McCafferty's** to: Alice Springs (10:40pm, 6½hr., $70), Darwin (3am, 13¾hr., $91) via Katherine (8½hr., $61), and Townsville (11pm, 20hr., $135).

Auto Club: AANT (tel. 8962 2468, after hours tel. 8962 3126).
Bicycle Rental: Bridgestone Tyre (tel. 8962 2361), on the corner of Paterson and Davidson St. Bikes $10 per day.
Market: Tennant Creek News Agency, a few doors south of ANZ, is an impressive store with anything from magazines to groceries and camping gear. Open Mon.-Fri. 8:30am-6pm, Sat. 8:30am-12:30pm and 5-6pm, Sun. 9am-noon and 5-6pm.
Police: (tel. 8962 4444), on Paterson St. south of Peko.
Hospital: Tennant Creek Hospital (tel. 8962 4399, after hours tel. 8962 1900) is on Schmidt St., a left turn at the end of Memorial Dr.
Emergency: Dial 000.
Post Office: (tel. 8962 2196), at the corner of Paterson St. and Memorial Dr., is open Mon.-Fri. 9am-5pm. **Postal code:** 0860.
Phone Code: 08.

ACCOMMODATIONS

Safari Backpackers (tel. 8962 2207; fax 8962 3188) on Davidson St. From the transit center, just stroll to the end of the block and take a right on Davidson. The 30 dorm beds are sort of an "annex" to the motel of the same name; reception for both is in the motel building. Shared bath, kitchen, and lounge. Dorms $12; triples $39; twins and singles $34. To use the facilities after 10am $5 per day. Book in advance.

Tourist's Rest Hostel (tel. 8962 2719; fax 8962 2718), concentrates on giving backpackers a basic night's rest. Friendly staff make up for the less-than-sparkling rooms. Walk south on Paterson St. to Windley St., turn right and follow it to Leichardt St. (15min.). Shared bath, kitchen, pool, TV room. Check-out 11am. Uncarpeted twins, doubles, and triples, $12 per person. Linen included. VIP, YHA. Day use policy lenient. Free pick-up and drop-off at the terminal.

Outback Caravan Park (tel. 8962 2459; fax 8962 1278), on the left side of Peko Rd., 200m from Paterson St. Office open 7:30am-noon, and 2-6:30pm. The park has a grocery, shared bath, kitchen, and BBQ. Tent sites $6 per person, $9 with power; powered caravan sites $16 for 2 people.

NORTHERN TERRITORY

FOOD

Near the transit center, **Paterson St.** is lined with takeaway snack bars, from fried chicken to Chinese to Italian. The owner of **Rocky's** (tel. 8962 2049) boasts about his tomato pies and offers two large pizzas, two garlic breads, and two liters of soda for $20 (open daily 4-11pm). The takeaway counter at the **Margo Miles Steakhouse and Italian Restaurant** (tel. 8962 2227), across the street from the terminal, serves up a tub of fettucine alfredo ($6), and other pastas (open daily 5-10pm). The Margo Miles Steakhouse itself features more stylish dishes in an intimate sit-down atmosphere. (Chicken florentine $14, kangaroo filet $14.50. Open daily noon-2pm and 6pm-late.) One sit-down restaurant of note is the **Dolly Pot Inn** (tel. 8962 2824), past the Safari Backpackers on Davidson St. The atmosphere is relaxed (with a rather strange view into 3 plexiglass squash courts) and the menu is mostly seafood, pasta, and steak. (Veal parmigiana $16.50, vegan salad $9.50; open noon-2pm, 6pm-late.) **The Tennant Food Barn** (tel. 8962 2296), at Paterson St. opposite Memorial Dr., offers the cheapest groceries.

The best opportunity to feast and drink with locals is at the **Tennant Creek Memorial Club** (tel. 8962 2474), a jovial war veteran's lodge at the end of Memorial Dr. on Schmidt St. It's a members-only affair, but the regulars welcome travelers as their guests—just dress nicely and follow the custom of removing your hat in the clubhouse. Rest your bones on a bar stool, at a table in front of the TV, or in the food window area. Meals are moderately priced (grilled chicken $10, seafood basket $9) but not exactly vegetarian, and the club has the cheapest beer prices in town (lunch served noon-2pm, dinner 6-8:30pm).

SIGHTS

The **Battery Hill Regional Centre** (tel. 8962 3388) doubles as the tourist office and as an historical site itself. The location was used from 1939 as a gold stamp battery, where ore was crushed and flakes of gold extracted. Expeditions into the battery (daily 9:30am and 5pm, 1½hr.) are heavy on history and the mechanics of ore processing (admission $8, under 14 $4). A replica of a mine has been newly constructed in the depths of the hill at the center, complete with authentic machinery and sound effects. A tour into the mine runs daily at 11am. The center has a few free mining-lore displays as well.

The tours at Battery Hill are led by **Norm's Gold and Scenic Tours** (tel. 9062 3388, mobile tel. 0418 891 711), a company that visits other big gold strike sights in the area. The owners, Jill and Norm, will run any of their tours for just one person. **Ten Ant Tours** (tel. 8962 2168 or 8962 2358) features a night descent into **The Dot,** one of the Creek's oldest mines.

The **Parks and Wildlife Commission** (tel. 8962 4599) manages two outdoor areas near Tennant Creek—the **Tennant Creek Telegraph Station Historical Reserve** and the **Davenport Range National Park**—but the best sights of NT's outback lie farther down the track.

■ Near Tennant Creek: Devil's Marbles

Next to the Stuart Hwy., 104km south of Tennant Creek, there is a sight spectacular enough to grace the front cover of the 1997-98 NT Phone Book and to warrant at least a momentary visit (if not a stop of a few hours or an overnight). It is the Devil's Marbles, a heap of spherical boulders spread out in an expanse of field surrounded by hills. The relatively recent name, according to one local, comes from the tendency of Australians to attach the prefix "Devil's" to anything they don't understand. Science's hypothesis of 1.6 billion years of "granite wind erosion" is hardly a satisfying explanation for why, in this one spot, 7m-thick boulders stack like smooth globes atop each other, in piles too numerous for the eye to see at once. In many places you can see where rocks split apart, or where some fell from others, and mentally try to "put the puzzle back together." Even without understanding, the Devil's Marbles is a confounding, impressive, and very photogenic wonder of nature.

The closest town to the 1827-hectare reserve is **Wauchope,** 9km south. The bus stops there, or may drop you at the Marbles themselves, if you beg sufficiently. The campground at the reserve is a spartan gravel lot, with pit toilets but no running water (bring your own firewood; $2.50 per person in the box). Alternatively, day tours make the lap from Tennant Creek. **Norm's Tours** (tel. 8962 3388; mobile tel. 0418 891 711) does an afternoon/evening loop that leaves at 2:30pm and returns to the Creek at 6pm for a sunset BBQ at Battery Hill, included in the $40 price. No worries—the tour will still go even if you're the only one signed on.

THE RED CENTRE

The dry, desolate outback at the center of Australia takes its name from the color of the oxidized dust that stretches to the horizon. To many travelers, the Red Centre represents the essence of Australia. Flat lands bake perpetually under a burning sun which is rarely obscured by rain clouds. The gnarled vegetation is weedy and sparse, and the wildlife is locked in a constant struggle for survival with the unforgiving climate and the unbearable bush flies. Out of this stark landscape, at the geographic center of the continent, rises Uluru (Ayers Rock), a celebrated symbol of the land down under.

Alice Springs is the region's unofficial capital and the gateway to the natural wonders beyond. The most impressive works of nature include the MacDonnell Ranges, Kings Canyon, Ayers Rock, and its companion range, the Olgas, all of which do their best to penetrate the reddish monotony of central Australia. These monuments have magnetic appeal, and tourists flock to the remote Red Centre as if to an eighth wonder.

Alice Springs

Alice Springs is the only significant human beat in the heart of Australia. As if in deference to neighboring constructions of nature, architects have refrained from giving "the Alice" an obtrusive skyline. A desert outpost connected to the rest of the world only by long mirage-filled highways, Alice's closest significant neighbor is a rock that seems stolen from the background of a Dali painting. Alice is nestled in a break in the MacDonnell Ranges carved by the Todd River. The so-called "river" that passes through the town is usually a dry, overgrown trench of grass and sand. A spring 3km east of town, discovered in 1871 by telegraph workers, was named after Alice Todd, the wife of the foreman, and became the town's namesake.

Alice had just 40 residents in 1927. Rapid growth began when the Old Ghan railway reached Alice from Adelaide in 1929, and was perpetuated by the sealing of the Stuart Hwy. to Darwin during WWII. Today, Alice's population is a respectable 27,000, making it the largest city in central Australia. Tourism recently eclipsed the cattle and mining industries, and the burden of 250,000 annual visitors is beginning to stress the local ecology. If the spring that is Alice's lifeline continues to fall 3m per year, residents and visitors alike may need to look elsewhere for water in another 30 years. Although tourism is inescapably woven into the city's identity, the streets of this oasis are often as silent in the evenings as the desert which surrounds them.

ORIENTATION

The **Stuart Highway** runs through Alice Springs on its way from Darwin (1490km distant) to Adelaide. Seen from the north, the MacDonnell Ranges form a backdrop for Alice. A break in the ranges called **Heavitree Gap** permits both the highway and the **Todd River** to pass south. Although usually dry, the river is an important landmark, as it borders the east side of the town center. The southern outskirts of town lie beyond the Gap, as does the airport (20km south).

A compact grid of streets along the west bank of the riverbed contains central Alice Springs. Todd St. runs parallel to the river, with a pedestrian mall at the north end. **Todd Mall** covers two blocks between Gregory Tce. and Wills Tce. Parsons St. is the block in between, and intersects Todd Mall at the **Alice Plaza,** a large indoor arcade. Another major landmark on Todd St. is the **Melanka Lodge Complex,** a block and a half south of the Gregory Tce. end of Todd Mall, which houses the **Greyhound-Pioneer** depot. Further south, Todd St. becomes Gap Rd. and runs toward the mountains, eventually joining the Stuart Hwy. at a traffic circle. **McCafferty's** is on Gregory Tce., a few doors down from the end of the Todd Mall. The major routes to the outskirts of Alice Springs are the Stuart Hwy. north and south and **Larapinta Drive,** the extension of Stott Tce. **Anzac Hill,** a rocky rise next to Wills Tce., is the best vantage point in town.

PRACTICAL INFORMATION

Tourist Office: Central Australian Tourism Industry Association (tel. 8952 5800), at the corner of Hartley St. and Gregory Tce. From the south end of Todd Mall, take Gregory Tce. 1 block to Hartley. Open Mon.-Fri. 9am-6pm, Sat.-Sun. 9am-4pm.

Budget Travel: Traveland (tel. 8952 7186), on Gregory Tce. at the end of Todd Mall. Open Mon.-Fri. 8:30am-5pm, Sat. 9am-noon. Most hostels have a tour desk.

Money: Banks with **currency exchange** and **ATMs** cluster in Todd Mall. **National Australia** (tel. 8952 1611) and **ANZ** (tel. 8952 1144), are both open Mon.-Thurs. 9:30am-4pm, Fri. 9:30am-5pm. **Interforex** (tel. 8953 0220), on Gregory Tce. near the beginning of Todd Mall, is open daily 8am-8pm.

Airport: Alice Springs Airport (tel. 8951 1211), 20km south of the city on the Stuart Hwy., provides domestic service only, but has tourist information, currency exchange, and car rental agencies. A **shuttle bus** (tel. 8953 0310) greets all incoming flights and sees off all departures. Runs to central Alice: one-way $9, return $15 (guests of many hostels get free transport into the city). **Qantas** (tel. 8950 5211)

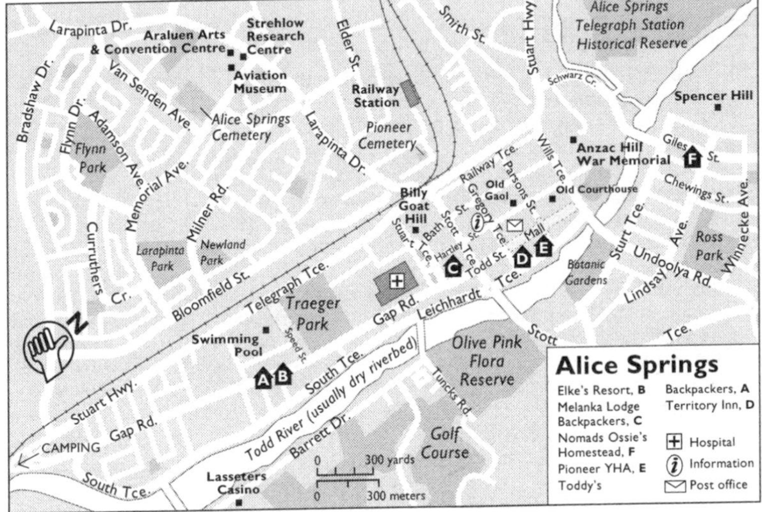

has offices in the airport and in Todd Mall (open Mon.-Fri. 8:30am-5pm, Sat. 8:30am-noon). Timetables shift with daylight savings. To: Darwin (daily 12:20 and 6pm, 2hr., $381); Yulara/Ayer's Rock Resort (daily 9:25am and 12:35pm, 1hr., $182); Cairns (daily 6:05pm, 2¾hr., $420); Sydney (daily 12:10pm, 3¼hr., $563); Adelaide (daily 5:35pm, 2hr., $402); Perth (daily 9:35am, 2¼hr., $539); Broome (Sun. 12:05pm, 1hr., $357). Backpackers holding passports and international tickets receive a 30% discount. **Ansett** (tel. 8950 4118 or 13 13 00) also has offices in the airport and in Todd Mall (open Mon.-Fri. 8:45am-5pm, Sat. 8:30am-noon). Discounted fares to: Darwin (daily 11:55am, 2hr., $267); Cairns (daily 2:40pm, 3hr., $296); Sydney (daily 2:10pm, 3¼hr., $395); Adelaide (daily 4:50pm, 2hr., $281); Perth (Tues., Thurs., Sat. and Sun. 6pm, 3hr., $377); Broome (Sat. 4:10pm, Sun. 12:45pm, 45min., $263). **Airnorth** (tel. 8952 6666) flies to destinations within NT.

Trains: Alice Railway Station (tel. 8951 6161 for arrivals and departures) is a 20min. walk from central Alice. Take Stott Tce. across the Stuart Hwy. Stott becomes Larapinta Dr. The station is at the end of George Tce., the first right. No trains run to Darwin. To Adelaide (Tues. and Fri. 2pm, $150 full fare, $105 present special). Open Tues. and Fri. 8am-2:30pm. Traveland makes reservations.

Buses: Greyhound Pioneer (tel. 8952 7888 or 13 20 30) operates from the Melanka Lodge complex. To: Darwin (2:30 and 8:30pm, 18-20hr., $133); Katherine (14-15hr., $123); Tennant Creek (5½hr., $72); Yulara (8:30am, 5½hr., $76); Adelaide (11;15am and 3pm, 19-20hr., $133). A 3-day tour of Uluru and Kings Canyon is $175. Open daily 4:45am-8:30pm. **McCafferty's** (tel. 8952 3952) is on Gregory Tce., half a block toward the river from the Todd Mall. To: Darwin (9pm, 20¼hr., $145), Katherine (9pm, 15hr., $133), Tennant Creek (4:30 and 9pm, 6hr., $78), Townsville (4:30pm, 26hr. $206), Yulara (11:30am, 6hr., $55) and Adelaide (11:30am, 20hr., $135). 10% discount with YHA, VIP, or ISIC. Open 5am-8:30pm.

Taxis: Alice Springs Taxis (tel. 8952 1877) line up on Gregory Tce. in front of Todd Mall.

Car Rental: Thrifty (tel. 8952 2400) in the Melanka complex at 94 Todd St., has a deal Thurs.-Mon. from $65 per day, including 250km. Open daily 8am-5pm. **Territory** (tel. 8952 9999), at the corner of Hartley St. and Stott Tce., has seasonal rates, often with cheap relocation deals. One-way one-day special to Ayers Rock $99 plus 500km free. **Hertz,** 76 Hartley St. (tel. 8952 2644 or 1800 891 112), across the street, is open Mon.-Fri. 7:30am-5:30pm, Sat.-Sun. 7:30am-5pm. **Avis** (tel. 8953 5533), at the corner of Hartley and Gregory St., is open Mon.-Fri. 8am-5:30pm, Sat.-Sun. 8:30am-4:30pm. All companies have counters in the airport.

Roadside Assistance: AANT (24hr. tel. 8952 1087).

Bike Rental: At various hostels. Pioneer YHA charges $8 per half-day, $12 per day.

Library: The public library (tel. 8950 0544), by the park at the corner of Gregory and Leichardt St. Open Mon.-Fri. 9am-6pm, Sat. 9am-1pm, Sun. 1-5pm.
Bookstore: Bookworm, 76 Todd St. (tel. 8952 5843), in an arcade outside the mall. Buys, sells, and trades used books. Open Mon.-Fri. 9am-5:30pm, Sat. 9am-1pm.
Hotlines: Crisis (tel. 1800 019 116). **Gayline** (tel. 8953 2844) has info for gays and lesbians in Alice and throughout NT. Leave a number; your call will be returned.
Pharmacy: Amcal Chemist (tel. 8953 0089) in Alice Plaza, by Parsons St. in the Todd Mall. Open daily 8:30am-8:30pm.
Hospital: Alice Springs Hospital (tel. 8951 7777, emergency 8951 7529), on Gap Rd., the continuation of Todd St. south of Melanka's.
Emergency: Dial 000.
Police: (Tel. 8951 8888), at Parsons and Bath St., 2 blocks from Todd Mall.
Internet Access: Affordable Home Computing in the Coles shopping center on Gregory St. between Bath and Railway Tce. Access costs $4 per 20min., $10 per hr. Open Mon.-Fri. 9am-5pm, Sat. 9am-1pm.
Post Office: GPO (tel. 8952 1020; fax 8953 4049) on Hartley St., a block off the Todd Mall down Parsons St. **Postal code:** 0870. Open Mon.-Fri. 8:15am-5pm.
Phone Code: 08.

ACCOMMODATIONS

The hostels of Alice are concentrated in the city center, but several quieter digs lie across the river. All listings have air-conditioned rooms.

Melanka Lodge Backpackers, 94 Todd St. (tel. 8952 4744 or 1800 896 110), adjacent to the Greyhound depot and just a block and a half from Todd Mall. Free transport from the airport; $3 to the airport. Melanka's is a huge operation, taking up a solid city block (half of which is the cleaner and more fragrant Motel Melanka). The complex lures tourists with a snack bar, sofa-strewn TV room, and nightclub. The long multi-story hallways are strikingly reminiscent of a university dorm, complete with the party atmosphere. Pool, beach volleyball court, free safe and luggage storage. Reception open daily 5am-8:30pm (or check-in at the Desert Waterhole in the same building). 6- to 8-bed dorms $12, 3- to 4-bed dorms $14; singles $30; twins and doubles $32. VIP and just-off-the-bus discounts. Key deposit $10.

Pioneer YHA (tel. 8952 8855), on the corner of Parsons and Leichardt St., less than a block off Todd Mall from Alice Plaza entrance. Originally a deckchair cinema, this landmark was rescued from demolition a decade ago. Some of the deckchairs remain in the courtyard where the audience once sat, and guests quietly relax around the pool. Spacious heated dorms, scrubbed showers, and tidy kitchen. Laundry facilities, free safe and luggage storage. Reception open daily 6:30am-7:30pm. Check-out 10am. 4 to 6-bed dorms $14, YHA non-members $17; doubles and twins $36 and $42, respectively. Linen $2. Key deposit $10. Book in advance.

Elke's Resort, 39 Gap Rd. (tel. 8952 8134; fax 8952 8143), 1km south of the Greyhound office (turn right on Todd St.). Elke's compensates for its distance from town by providing transport to and from the airport and bus station. The kind folks here have converted a motel into the classiest hostel in town. Each dorm room has its own bath, kitchenette, TV, and balcony. Pool. Reception open daily 8am-8pm. Check-out 10am. 6- to 8-bed dorms $13, with VIP, YHA, or ISIC $12; doubles and twins $40, with YHA $35, with VIP $33. Key deposit $10. Free breakfast 6-9am, dinner at Scotty's Tavern $4 with voucher.

Nomads Ossie's Homestead, at Lindsay Ave. and Warburton St. (tel. 8952 2308 or 1800 628 211). At the north end of Todd Mall, take Wills Tce. to the right over the causeway which crosses the Todd River. Lindsay Ave. is several blocks east on Undoolya Rd. Turn left on Lindsay and the hostel is on the left. An intimate (40-bed) suburban hostel, Ossie's is a genuine hide-away. Small kitchen, clean bath. Free luggage storage and sporadic pick-up at the airport and bus station. 12-bed dorms $12, 4-bed dorms $14. VIP, YHA. Singles $30. Key deposit $20. Breakfast, all linens, and kitchen utensils included.

Toddy's Backpackers, 41 Gap Rd. (tel. 8952 1322; fax 8952 1767), 1km from Greyhound next to Elke's. The cheapest beds in town. Two buildings flank a pool and contain the spartan budget annex. Courtesy bus tries to meet most flights and buses. Reception 6am-8:30pm. Check-out 10am. 8-bed dorms $8; 6-bed dorms $10, with bath $12; Singles, doubles, and twins with sink and fridge $34. VIP. Key deposit $10. Free breakfast 6-8:30am; all-you-can-eat dinner ($7) starts at 7pm.

Territory Inn, Leichardt Tce. (tel. 8952 2066; fax 8952 7829), in the middle of Todd Mall near Parsons St. Enter this "Inn" from Leichardt and you've entered a shampoo-included world of marble bathrooms and sport-coated receptionists. The Territory regales its guests with minibar fridges, TVs, radios, in-room phones, and daily housekeeping. Hotel-style rooms are arranged around a porticoed atrium with BBQ facilities and a view of Todd Mall. Check-out 10am. A room with a double bed, a single bed, and a bathroom costs $80.

Camping

Campsites begin just outside the town along the major thoroughfares. The **Heavitree Gap Outback Resort** (tel. 8952 4866 or 1800 896 119; fax 8952 9394) is just 3km from central Alice. Follow the Stuart Hwy. south, take a left on Palm Circuit, and the resort is on the left. The estate has a motel, bistro, and ranging wallabies. Sites are $6 per person, with power $15 (1 or 2 people). **G'Day Mate Tourist Park** (tel. 8952 9589; fax 8952 2612) and **MacDonnell Range Holiday Park** (tel. 8952 6111) are right down the road on Palm Cct. In the other direction on the Stuart Hwy., **Stuart Caravan Park** (tel. 8952 2547), 1km north of the city center and on the right, has sites for $6.50 per person, with power $16 (1 or 2 people; $6.50 per additional person).

FOOD

As a desert oasis, Alice spoils its visitors with a heap of attractive, ethnically diverse restaurants, from Chinese to Mexican to "Swiss and Indian." These are tasty but not always budget. There are several **supermarkets** near Todd Mall. **Woolworths,** the biggest and cheapest, is in the Yeperenye Plaza on Hartley St. between Gregory and Parsons St. (open Mon.-Sat. 7am-midnight, Sun. 7am-10pm). **Coles,** one block toward Bath St., is open 24 hours.

La Casalinga (tel. 8952 4508), Gregory Tce. near the beginning of Todd Mall. Lots for little at this pizza bar. Large specialty pizzas ($13), lasagna ($7.50), and plenty of other pasta dishes, in a sit-down, Pizza-Hut-like restaurant without the packaged feel or the stupid roof. Open daily 5pm-1am.

Chopsticks Restaurant (tel. 8952 3873), on Hartley St. across from the post office and a block from Todd Mall along Parsons St. Cantonese and Northern Chinese dining with a sizeable vegetarian list. Dinner mains begin at $8.50, and include lemon chicken ($15.50) and sweet and sour vegetables ($11.50). Open for lunch (Mon.-Fri. noon-2pm) and dinner (daily 5:30-11pm).

Bar Doppios, inside the Fan Arcade at the Gregory Tce. end of Todd Mall (tel. 8952 6525). This trendy Mediterranean-style cafe is squeezed against a long glass facade. Patrons look out on the arcade and watch fresh salads, fruit drinks, and affordable main courses being prepared. Thai chicken and coconut curry ($11.50), lentil burgers ($6), and marinated tofu with stir-fried vegetables ($9). Open daily 9am-8:30pm.

Swingers (tel. 8952 9291), just around the corner from Bar Doppios on Gregory St., pumps good alternative vibes in a spacious, colorful setting. A nice place for coffee if you're not in the mood for a meal. Open Mon.-Tues. 7:30am-6pm, Wed.-Sat. 7:30am-11pm.

Red Ochre Grill (tel. 8952 2066), on Todd Mall, near the Territory Inn. The scintillating outback cuisine delves so deeply into regional ingredients that the menu literally needs its own glossary. Aboriginal artwork and didgeridoo music round out the atmosphere for an elegant, memorable meal. A fantastic array of dishes suits the vegetarian and spoils the meat-eater. Kangaroo filet with chili glaze $16; the steamed vegetable appetizer ($6) is a nearly meal itself. Open daily 6:30am-9pm.

SIGHTS

Town Centre

Most of the sights within the town center are near the Todd Mall. The **Museum of Central Australia** (tel. 8951 5335), in fact, looms directly above the Mall in the Alice Plaza. Go up to the second floor and follow the signs. Browsing here is a comfortable, educational experience. Primarily a natural history exhibition, the museum contains dinosaur casts and lots of stuffed animals, including a baby croc that's vertically cross-sectioned (open Mon.-Fri. 9am-5pm, Sat.-Sun. 10am-5pm; admission $2).

A handful of quick-see historical buildings are down Parsons St. The **Old Courthouse** (tel. 8952 9006) and the **Residency** sit across from each other at the corner of Parsons and Hartley St. The former houses the **National Pioneer Women's Hall of Fame** (open daily 10am-2pm; donation requested). The latter was a home to government officials as early as 1928, and was restored as a heritage site in 1973 (open Mon.-Fri. 9am-4pm, Sat.-Sun. 10am-4pm). The **Stuart Town Gaol,** a block farther down Parsons St. on the left, is the oldest remaining building in Alice, completed in 1909 (open Mon.-Fri. 10am-12:30pm, Sat. 9:30am-noon).

One attraction worthy of a visit is **Panorama Guth,** 65 Hartley St. (tel. 8952 2013). Take Gregory Tce. a block up to Hartley from the south end of the Mall, turn left, and the Guth will be halfway down the block on the left. Henk Guth is the Dutch artist who arranged this museum of Aboriginal artifacts, Aboriginal watercolors, and watercolors of his own. (Open Mon.-Sat. 9am-5pm, Sun. (March-Nov. only) 12-5pm. Admission $3, concessions $1.50.)

The famous **Royal Flying Doctor Service** (tel. 8952 1129) is two blocks farther down Hartley, just past Stuart Tce. and to the right on a small service lane. This building dates back to 1939 and houses a gallery of medicine, transportation, and communications. (Open Mon.-Sat. 9am-4pm, Sun. 1-4pm; admission free; tours $3.)

The **Flynn Memorial Church,** dedicated to John Flynn on May 5, 1956, stands next to the Lions Club sign in Todd Mall. Flynn is one of the heroes of Alice Springs. A pioneer in outback medicine, he was responsible for getting the Royal Flying Doctor Service off the ground, and for ordering construction of the first hospital in central Australia. The hospital is now the **Adelaide House John Flynn Museum,** which stands near the church, and houses relics of the Flying Doctor's early days. The museum dates back to 1926. (Open Mon.-Thurs. 10am-4pm, Fri.-Sat. 10am-noon. Admission $3, concessions $2).

The best place to take in a postcard sunset in Alice is atop **Anzac Hill.** On foot, walk to Wills Tce. between Bath and Hartley St. Here, a metal arch marks the start of the "Lions Walk" from the base of the hill to the obelisk at its top (an easy 10min. climb). The hill is named in memory of the Australian and New Zealand Army Corps soldiers who died in WWI. To the Aboriginals it is *Untyeyetweleye,* part of the "Corkwood Story," which explains how this landscape formed. To the tourists it is a great site for snapping pictures of Alice Springs and the MacDonnell Ranges. Vehicle access is around the corner on the Stuart Hwy.

Outskirts

Covering Alice's more distant sights is difficult without a vehicle, and you won't be allowed to test drive the cars in the transportation museum. The **Alice Wanderer** (tel. 8952 2111) shuttle service circles past 13 sights in the Alice area throughout the day (9am-4pm). It departs first from the Gregory Tce. end of the Todd Mall (day ticket $18, start early so you can linger at sights you like).

Olive Pink Botanic Garden (tel. 8952 2154), nestled on the opposite bank of the Todd River, is 2km from Todd Mall. Head south on Leichardt Tce. with the river on your left, pass the traffic circle at Stott Tce., and cross the river at the next left. This is **Tuncks Rd.,** and the Garden is ahead on the left. It may be hard to picture a "garden" in this desert vegetation, but Olive Pink displays and labels any green that survives. (Gardens open daily 10am-6pm, visitor center 10am-4pm; admission by donation.)

The Largest Classroom in the World

It's Monday morning, and 140 children between the ages of 4 and 13 are standing thousands of kilometers apart, yet singing their national anthem together. They are able to hear the familiar sound of their morning assembly by tuning to a certain 5 kHz frequency on short-wave radios. This is the School of the Air, central Australia's educational answer to its vast geography and isolated families spread out on remote cattle stations, roadhouses, and Aboriginal lands. The School of the Air, stationed in Alice and in a dozen other outback towns, uses two-wave radio to bring the children of these families in contact with each other and their Alice-based teachers for three to four hours each week. Their makeshift classrooms are sheds, trailers, or rooms in their homes. A parent or appointed instructor supplements their education with an additional five to six hours of weekly schooling. The closest student to Alice is 80km away; the farthest is 1000km. First begun in 1951, the Alice School is the oldest of its kind, though Australia now has 16 such institutions. It covers 1.3 million square kilometers of land, and has thus been dubbed "the largest classroom in the world." This distinction has attracted prestigious guest lecturers; Prince Charles is among the celebrities who have stopped by to chat with the kids.

The **Alice Springs Telegraph Station,** one of the town's most popular parks, is 4.5km north of town on the Stuart Hwy., and has a marked turn-off. This original location of the Alice Springs township rests among rolling hills. Today, actors play out a period scene around the original 19th-century buildings (open Nov.-March daily 8am-9pm, April-Oct. 8am-7pm). Before the turn-off to the telegraph station, a sign on the Stuart Hwy. points down Head St. to the **School of the Air** (tel. 8951 6834; fax 8951 6835). The school was started in 1951 to educate children in remote areas of central Australia via CB radio. The broadcast location—which has no students—doubles as a visitors center, where guests can learn about the pioneering program, enjoy the colorful kiddie artwork on the walls, and, when school's in session, watch through soundproof glass as teachers conduct class with students spread far and wide across the NT outback. Gift shop purchases help subsidize program improvements (school open Mon.-Sat. 8:30am-4:30pm, Sun. 1:30-4:30pm; admission $3).

Another cluster of attractions awaits on Larapinta Dr. From Todd St., take Stott Tce. past the Stuart Hwy. (Stott becomes Larapinta), and after a traffic circle look for Memorial Dr. on the left. This intersection has three sites of interest. The most impressive is the **Strehlow Research Centre** (tel. 8951 8000; fax 8951 8050). The center is named after the professor who spent much of his life in local Aboriginal communities. Its contemporary white and packed-earth brown walls (the largest packed-earth wall in the southern hemisphere) are a metaphor for the mixture of computerized electronic technology and natural, often spiritual subject matter they enclose. The $4 admission fee ($2.50 for backpackers) is a pittance to pay for the slide presentation on the earth wall, the richly designed walkways, and the 30-minute environs cycle that imitates the passing of an outback day with lights and sound. This is a working research center as well as a tourist attraction (open daily 10am-5pm; wheelchair accessible). Next door is the **Araluen Arts and Convention Centre** (tel. 8952 5022), which is a prime entertainment venue and also includes two painting galleries, one featuring the work of a famous Aboriginal painter **Albert Namatjira** (open daily 10am-5pm; admission $2). On the other side of the Strehlow is the **Aviation Museum** (tel. 8951 5686), a free historical site composed of nothing more than a small hangar of aircraft and a nearby shed telling the story and displaying the remains of the *Kookaburra,* a plane that crashed in the Tanami (hangar open daily 10am-5pm). Next door on Memorial Dr. is a **cemetery** that contains the resting places of notable Alice residents, including Albert Namatjira.

The Stuart Hwy. follows the Todd River south through the **Heavitree Gap.** After the Gap, the first left is Palm Circuit. **Pitchi Richi** ("break in the mountains") is an Aboriginal cultural attraction on the right side, 300m from the turn and 4km from

Workin' on the Railroad

Railroad transport has never quite worked out in central Australia. Back in the days of Afghan cameleers, residents dreamed of a transcontinental track from Adelaide to distant Darwin. Construction of the dream began in 1878, 15 years after South Australia gained possession of the giant Northern Territory. Tracks were laid north from Port Augusta, and south from Darwin, but various depressions, wars, and budget problems kept the construction sporadic. The tracks never met in the middle, and the project—known as the *Old Ghan,* in a nostalgic nod to the Afghan cameleers —was abandoned in 1929. Even the completed sections were rendered obsolete by an oversight: all of the states, eager to get their choo-choos chooing, had used different-sized gauges in their designs. When tracks eventually met at border towns, all cargo and people had to be transferred to a new car at the beginning of the next line. The *Old Ghan*'s narrow gauge (1067mm), already known to wash away easily in rains, was eclipsed by the newly coordinated standard gauge (1435mm) in 1971. The *Ghan* line that now runs from Alice to Adelaide is west of the *Old Ghan* tracks. The Territory government and Korean business interests have contemplated extending the line to Darwin but, as yet, the dream remains unattained.

Alice. This sanctuary (tel. 8952 1931) charges an exorbitant $15, especially considering how little money seems to go into upkeep. A dilapidated trail passes the often-vandalized clay sculptures of the late William Rickets, the white creator of Pitchi Richi. Easy-going guides offer tea, delicious damper bread, and an explanation of some implements of local Arrente heritage (open daily 9am-2pm).

The **Mecca Date Gardens** (tel. 892 2425), 300m farther down Palm Circuit on the right, is Australia's oldest date plantation. There's not much to see, but plenty to buy: date muffins, date ice cream, date this, date that. You could even try to pick up a hot date (open Mon.-Fri. 9am-5pm, Sat. 9am-1pm). Beyond, Palm Circuit crosses a traffic circle and emerges as the Ross Hwy. The land is quite empty east of here, so it's easy to spot the **Alice Springs Ostrich Farm** (tel. 8955 5559) on the right. It was the first one in the NT (open Mon.-Sun. 10am-4pm; admission $4). Moving on, 3km down the road (for a total of 8km from the town center), is the **Frontier Camel Farm** (tel. 8953 0444 or 1800 806 499). Alice Springs considers itself the camel capital of Australia, and the **Camel Museum** (open daily 9am-5pm) keeps the claim alive by offering tours ($10, students $8) which include a camel ride. For more wildlife, visit the adjacent **Arid Australia Reptile House** (admission $5).

Instead of turning on Palm Circuit, keep south on the Stuart Hwy. to reach the **Transport Heritage Area** (tel. 8955 5047), one of Alice's defining sights (also about the farthest at 10km from the city). The access road is Norris Bell Ave., but you might see the restored steam locomotive in an empty field first. Alice has transportation in her blood, as the two parts of the Heritage Area show. The **Old Ghan Museum** highlights the trials and tribulations of the enormous locomotive project to link Adelaide and Darwin via Alice Springs. *Old Ghan* refers to both the original narrow gauge train tracks which ran from Adelaide to Alice (and from Darwin to Larrimah), and to the train itself, currently being restored in the big gray building at the back of the lot. The **Road Transport Hall of Fame** is a spacious warehouse with a collection of vehicles from memory lane, including a 1923 Rolls Royce and a 1911 Ford Model T. Here, where only long highways connect people to civilization, road transport gets the respect it deserves. (Each museum open daily 9am-5pm; admission to each $4.).

ENTERTAINMENT

The *Centralian Advocate* has an entertainment section for upcoming events. The 500-seat **Araluen Theatre** (box office tel. 8953 3111, open daily 10am-5pm), on Larapinta Dr., presents arthouse flicks every Sunday and live events. The popular **Sounds of Starlight Theatre** (tel. 8952 8861) runs regularly a few doors down from Parsons St. on the Todd Mall. This intense, didgeridoo-led performance—part outback education, part Pink Floyd laser light show—is accompanied by striking slides of Red Centre landscape (April-Nov. Tues.-Sat. 7pm; admission $15). The **Alice Springs Cinema** (tel. 8952 4999), at the end of the Todd Mall nearest Anzac Hill, runs Hollywood movies from 10am to 9pm. (Admission $10.50, students $8; Tues. admission $7.50. Melanka Lodge guests get 2 tickets for 1.)

For a unique evening of entertainment, head for **Lasseters Casino,** across the Todd River on Barrett Dr., and a 45-minute walk or $5 taxi ride from the city center. The setting of the climax of *Priscilla, Queen of the Desert,* the casino has tinted black doors and no windows at all, so that patrons can forget the time of day and concentrate on what really matters: the cherries and aces in the slot machines. This is your chance to win that didgeridoo you've had your eye on—or to lose your airfare home (open Mon.-Tues. 10am-10pm, Wed.-Sun. 10am-3pm).

It seems that half of the shopping in town is directed toward tourists. Nowhere is this truer than in **Todd Mall,** where the heart of Alice beats with the sounds of didgeridoo music coming from dozens of stores. The other major shopping area is the **Yeperenye,** an indoor mall which starts roughly across from the post office on Hartley St. and continues through to Bath St.

The **Desert Waterhole** at the Melanka Lodge is a casual night spot, with pool tables, a dance floor, and a DJ after 10pm (open nightly 5pm-2am). **Scotty's Tavern,** in Todd Mall, has a stronger pub feel, with a permanent cloud of smoke, live music almost every night, and rowdy ockers to sustain the din (open Sun.-Thurs. 11am-midnight, Fri.-Sat. 11am-1am). But the slickest, biggest, best-known night spot is **Legends** (tel. 8953 3033), overlooking the Todd Mall from the second floor of Alice Plaza. This sprawling disco has a purple interior that belongs on a cruise ship. There's live music nightly, but the $2 drinks on Fridays are the big draw. Tuesday is under-19 night (open Tues.-Sat. 10pm-4am; Fri. cover $6). Despite the legacy of a world-renowned gay flick, Alice is no ongoing drag show. The lesbian-owned **Swingers** is a popular gay social place. Ask about the location of the **"warehouse dance,"** on the first Friday of every month.

FESTIVALS

September or October brings the definitive Alice Springs festival, the **Henley-on-Todd Regatta.** A good-natured mockery of the dry river, the race is in bottomless "boats" propelled Flinstones-style—by foot. The race is subject to cancellation: the river flowed in 1993. The **Honda Masters Games,** also in these months, is a friendly biennial 30-sport competition for elderly athletes, and the **Country Music Festival** is a weekend of twanging and bellowing Aussie-style. The **Corkwood Festival** in November is a folk event featuring craft booths in the day and energetic bush dancing at night. January has the interesting **Lasseters Indoor Challenge,** at the casino, which is a card and board games tournament with high stakes. The scheduled 1998 event, January 4-10, promises over $30,000 in prizes. **Heritage Week** is an historical NT celebration usually held in April. The horses head out of the gates at Pioneer Race Park on Stuart Hwy. on the first Monday in May for the lavish **Alice Springs Cup Racing Carnival,** and on the same day the **Bangtail Muster** brings a parade and other entertainment to Alice's streets. The 7.8km walking race **King of the Mountain** sends tourists and locals to the top of Mt. Gillen (off Larapinta, west of town), also in May. On the **Queen's Birthday Weekend** in early June, the plucky cars of the **Finke Desert Race** traverse 240km of roadless dusty desert from Alice to the town of Finke in the south. The traditional **Alice Springs Show** and not-so-traditional **Lions Club Camel Cup** race occur in June and July. The **Alice Springs Rodeo** and the **Alice Marathon** are both held in August.

■ Off the Stuart Highway

The highways stretch out from Alice toward all four points of the compass, like songlines snaking across the Dreaming landscape. You can't make the wrong choice: each road leads to places worthy of a visit.

North of Alice Springs along the Stuart Hwy., a few sights break up the monotony of the long drive to or from Darwin. A grand landmark pinpoints the place where the **Tropic of Capricorn** slices through the outback 29km north of Alice on the Stuart Hwy. Stand on the line, and you'll be simultaneously tropical and subtropical. Farther north, 69km from Alice, the **Plenty Hwy.** branches to the right. Plenty of what? The answer lies 70km down the road at the **Gemtree** (tel. 8956 9855; fax 8956 9860), a private gemfield for your fossicking pleasure. Gems for sale, gems for study, and at rather steep prices, gems for hunting. The road is sealed and the site offers campsites and indoor rooms.

South of Alice, the Stuart Hwy. passes Heavitree Gap and Palm Circuit. Near the road to the airport, the **Old South Road** veers left on its way to a couple of impressive sights in the **Simpson Desert.** Charles Stuart first explored this part of the Simpson in 1845. The first tourist-worthy spot along this road, 39km south of Alice, is the **Ewaninga Rock Carvings,** which were etched into sandstone by ancient Aboriginals. Maryvale Station, 62km farther, marks the turn-off to **Chambers' Pillar.** No one remembers who Chambers was, but he certainly had some pillar. This sandstone formation served early travelers as a rather conspicuous landmark 155km south of Alice Springs, and the drive is recommended for high-clearance 4WD only. Camping en route is $2.50 per person. **Rainbow Valley,** another photogenic Simpson desert spot, is a jagged, U-shaped ridge standing in the desert like a Hollywood backdrop. The valley lies 21km east of Stuart Hwy., on a sandy track that begins 81km south of Alice (4WD necessary; camping $2.50 per person). Another 51km down the Stuart, the unpaved **Ernest Giles Road** veers west; the **Henbury Meteorite Craters** are on the right. This circular ridge of mountains is all that's left of a prehistoric meteorite impact.

■ The MacDonnell Ranges

Alongside Ayers Rock, the Olgas, and Kings Canyon, the 460km-long MacDonnell Ranges round out the Red Centre's cast of impressive geological formations. The MacDonnells, to the east and west of Alice Springs, were formed by fault shifts that began some 600 million years ago, and once towered as high as the Himalayas. Erosion has broken the single chain of mountains into a series of ridges and valleys, which is 120km across at its widest point, and nature's work has sculpted the ranges into many interesting formations.

WEST MACDONNELLS

More often visited than their eastern counterparts, the gorges and waterholes of the West MacDonnells are rich in natural beauty and recreational opportunities.

Larapinta Drive

Heading westward on Larapinta Dr. from Alice Springs, the first attraction is actually a man-made one: **Alice Springs Desert Park** (tel. 8951 8788; fax 8951 8720) is a showcase of the plants and wildlife in the desert environment. Opened in March 1997, this quasi-zoo boasts the largest exhibit of nocturnal animals in Australia as well as several smaller habitat displays, but the highlight of the park is the beautiful film on the evolution of the outback landscape. The park is 6km out of Alice (open daily 7:30am-6pm; admission $12, students $6). For a lift, call the shuttle (tel. 8952 4667, one-way $4).

The **John Flynn Memorial Grave** rests 1km farther west on Larapinta Dr. The massive boulder resting on the grave was taken from the Devil's Marbles formation near

Tennant Creek. **Mt. Gillen,** named after one of Alice's first postmasters, serves as a backdrop for the grave. Cross the street to find the trailhead for the popular 17km bike path through the bush to **Simpson's Gap.** Erosion from millions of years of prehistoric floods created this striking opening in the mountain ridges. By road, Simpson's Gap is 11km farther west on Larapinta Dr., and 7km up an access road. The 2km walk from the parking lot to the gap itself might give you a glimpse of wallabies. One kilometer west of the Simpson's Gap turnoff along Larapinta Dr. is a sight you may have seen before: the **twin ghost gums** of Albert Namatjira's watercolor (still hanging in Alice's Panorama Guth). Visitors and vandals have taken their toll, however, and the gums (which stand on the left side of the road), appear withered when compared to the famous painting.

Standley Chasm (tel. 8956 7440) is 21km farther on. The 80m-high fissure through the MacDonnells was named after the first white woman (Alice Springs' first schoolteacher) to walk through it. Aboriginals own the land and collect $4 at the end of the 9km access road. It took 100 million years to form, but half an hour is sufficient to traverse the rocky path, see the big crack, and return. When the sun shines directly into the crevasse at midday, the walls glow orange (entry permitted 7:30am-6pm).

Namatjira Drive

Larapinta Dr. forks 46km west of Alice Springs, and the right-hand path, Namatjira Dr., follows a more northerly route (see below for the westward continuation of Larapinta Dr.). **Ellery Creek Bighole** is 42km down Namatjira and another 2km down an access road. The 18m-deep pool in a creek through a gap in the mountains serves as a swimming hole when the weather's nice, and hasn't gone dry in recorded history. A 200m path connects the parking lot to the pool. Camping is $2.50 per person. Next stop is **Serpentine Gorge,** which slithers through the mountains 11km later. The **Ochre Pits,** 12km after that, is a place just next to the highway where Aboriginals once mined paint supplies.

Another 17km brings you to sparkling **Ormiston Gorge**. With a 14m-deep permanent waterhole, a small visitors center, and popular camping facilities ($5 per person), Ormiston is a veritable MacDonnells happy meal. The gorge was named by explorer Peter Warburton, who thought that the area looked a lot like his own Glen Ormiston back in Scotland. He's right, except for the gorge's dry vegetation, sand dunes, and steep orange cliffs. A 10-minute walk goes from parking lot to gorge, or a 7km circuit hike sneaks around the gorge through the hillside. Across the highway a few kilometers, the **Glen Helen Gorge** breaks through the range on behalf of the **Finke River,** as it winds its way south to the Simpson Desert. The **Glen Helen Lodge** (tel. 8956 7489) provides an oasis of restaurants, motel rooms, and camping. An unsealed Namatjira (the road, not the artist) continues past Glen Helen 25km to **Redbank Gorge,** where a narrow slit in the mountains shades a perennially chilly pool from the warming rays of the sun. One way to see the Namatjira Dr. part of the MacDonnells is to take the **Larapinta Trail,** an enormous, nearly-complete hiking trail which starts at the Telegraph Station in Alice and will extend 220km west to **Mt. Razorback.** The trail is usually hiked in pieces, from one gorge to another.

Larapinta Drive Revisited

For the hardy, Larapinta Dr. continues west from its intersection with Namatjira Dr. The left turn 48km ahead leads an additional 18km to **Wallace Rockhole Community** (tel. 8956 7415), an Aboriginal settlement next to a natural water hole. Residents welcome tourists here, offering campgrounds (no permit required) and tours (April-Sept. daily 9:30am and 1pm). Larapinta Dr. turns gravel 26km west of the Wallace Rockhole turnoff. Only a 4WD vehicle can negotiate the last 10km to **Finke Gorge National Park.** This 46,000 hectare park contains the Finke River, reputedly the oldest river on the planet; some stretches date back 350 million years. The park includes Palm Valley, whose lush palm stands are among the least expected sights in central Australia. Camping is $5 per person. Near the turnoff to Finke Gorge is the **Hermannsburg Historical Precinct** (tel. 8956 7402; fuel available). Birthplace of the

Aboriginal artist Albert Namatjira, Hermannsburg confers insight into the early days of mission settlement. Namatjira's legacy lives on at a painting school.

EAST MACDONNELLS

Just beyond Heavitree Gap south of Alice, Palm Circuit branches off the Stuart Hwy. and heads east. After a few kilometers, Palm Cct. becomes the **Ross Hwy.,** which plunges into the East MacDonnells. The East Macs are less thrilling geologically than their western counterparts, but have been populated longer and have some sights of historical interest. The **Emily and Jessie Gaps,** popular picnic sights, carve through the range in the first 10km of the Ross. An additional 35km drive to the east brings travelers to **Corroboree Rock Conservation Reserve,** where local Aboriginals perform ceremonies near a rock outcropping. **Trephina Gorge Nature Park,** another 23km east (plus 9km of access road), has a double gorge with quartzite cliffs and five walking tracks. Campsites cost $5 per person.

The road continues east toward the **Ross River Homestead** (tel. 8956 9711), but the last 9km of road to this historic settlement is unpaved. Try hands-on outback activities such as camel riding, bushwalking, and boomerang throwing. Located a total of 88km east of Alice, Homestead is one of the most popular destinations in the East MacDonnells. **N'Dhala Gorge,** the site of an estimated 6000 Aboriginal carvings, is an 8km drive down a 4WD track. A left fork before the Homestead traverses 36km of unsealed road to the **Arltunga Historic Reserve,** the remains of central Australia's first official town. Some of the buildings of this mining outpost have been restored. Vehicles with 4WD can push on 39km to the remote **Ruby Gap,** which produced garnets but never rubies.

■ Kings Canyon (Watarrka National Park)

Watarrka National Park contains oft-visited Kings Canyon, which cuts deep grooves in a section of the **George Gill Mountains,** forming sheer concave walls beneath a precariously suspended rim. A long natural history of erosion is visible across the canyon, especially in the eccentric domes atop both sides of the precipice. The weathered surfaces of these humps appear to be natural, giant-sized stairs to the fantastic views atop. The scatter of layered domes on the flat canyon roof creates an intimidating maze which has been dubbed **Lost City.** Thankfully, the park has two well-marked paths. An easy 1km walk follows **Kings Creek** into the bottom of the canyon and then out. A more challenging 6km hike scales the rocky semi-steep slope, winds around the top of the canyon, and traces through much of the Lost City and along the exhilarating rail-less edge. The longer walk also descends into the **Garden of Eden,** a waterhole shaded by palm trees and the narrow walls of the canyon.

Water and tough hiking **footwear** are essential at Kings Canyon. There's an outhouse and an information display at the parking lot, but no other facilities in the park. The long canyon walk does have three emergency call boxes. The **ranger station** is 22km east of the canyon.

There are three different ways to get to Kings Canyon from Alice Springs. The fully-paved route runs south from Alice Springs to the crossroads settlement of **Erldunda,** 202km down the Stuart Hwy. at its junction with the Lasseter Hwy. Travelers changing buses here may end up spending the night. To book a room or campsite at the **roadhouse,** call 8956 0984. From the junction, take the Lasseter Hwy. west 112km and turn right on Luritja Rd., which goes north 168km to the Kings Canyon park entrance. Vehicles with 4WD can take a shortcut along Ernest Giles Rd., a 98km stretch of unpaved road that begins 132km south of Alice. Ernest Giles meets Luritja Rd. 100km south of the park entrance. It's also possible to reach Kings Canyon via Hermannsburg in the West MacDonnells by taking Larapinta Dr. and the scenic **Mereenie Loop Road** (4WD vehicle and permit required).

The **Kings Canyon Resort** (tel. 8956 7442; fax 8956 7410), several kilometers up the road from the canyon, is the beginning and the end of civilization in Watarrka.

The Path of Priscilla

If you want to trace the route of the *Priscilla, Queen of the Desert* drag queen caravan, you'll need a car, a feathered boa, and lots of sequins. First the drag queens went west from Sydney (p. 87), probably on Hwy. 32, to the town of Broken Hill (p. 215), where Bernadette triumphed over the pub shrew. Continuing west, they decided to hop on an unsealed back road instead of going to Port Augusta (although their left turn would not actually have put them on a northwest course toward Alice Springs). They broke down somewhere in the vast desert of South Australia, crashed the Aboriginal Corroboree, and eventually received a lift to an outback town somewhere east of Coober Pedy (p. 412). With Bob on board, Priscilla pushed on to Coober Pedy, where Felicia narrowly escaped a group of rough miners. Finally they covered the last stretch north along the Stuart Hwy. to Alice Springs (p. 250). Mitzie's reunion with his wife and their glorious drag show gig was filmed on location in Lasseters Casino, in Alice Springs (p. 257). The final scene occurs atop Kings Canyon in the Northern Territory (p. 260). For more film references, see **You, the Australian Cinema Stalker** (p. 292).

The compact village's major drawback is its unkindness to travelers' budgets. (4-bed dorms with A/C, heat, TV, and fridge $33 per person, $106 for 4. Utensils deposit $20. Shared bath and kitchen.) Dorm beds are held for Greyhound passengers; otherwise book ahead. Comfortable grassy **campsites** with flush toilets, showers, and pool are $10 per person, with power $25. Reception for all of these is open 6:30am-9:30pm, and check-out is 10am. The resort has a **grocery store** and **fuel station** (open 7am-7pm), and a somewhat low-end restaurant, the **Desert Oaks Cafe** (burgers $5; open 5:30am-9pm). The **medical center** (tel. 8956 7807, after hours 8956 7997) can summon a Flying Doctor in an hour if necessary. In an emergency, dial reception at 8956 7442.

NORTHERN TERRITORY

Uluru-Kata Tjuta National Park

Dusk approachs. Pilgrims from the corners of the earth have assembled quietly, staring east as the sun descends at their backs. Before them unfolds a spectacle so awesome and humbling that it could occur only once—and yet it has repeated itself each day for 600 million years. Captivated spectators look on in hushed awe as the rock before them turns a brilliant, glowing red. A ripple of sighs and a burst of camera flashes moves through the throng. Here, at the junction of desert and sky, of day and night, is Ayers Rock.

At the core of Australia in every sense, **Ayers Rock** (known as Uluru in the language of the Anangu) is the largest single rock in the world. Oxidation of iron in the sandstone gives the rock its uniquely orange color, which turns a fiery red at sunrise and sunset. Just as old and taller still, **the Olgas** are a cluster of similar-hued domes that might have weathered from one great "superdome," many times larger than Uluru.

Together, these formations in the red dust are the defining landmarks of Uluru-Kata Tjuta National Park, a 132,500 hectare protected area 461km southwest of Alice Springs, at the very heart of the continent. Since 1985, the park has been co-managed by the National Parks Service and its traditional Anangu residents. The Anangu have occupied the desert dunes around Uluru for 22,000 years, and the rock is a landmark on the dreaming trails of their mythical ancestors. Europeans have only known of it since 1872, when the explorer Ernest Giles came upon it. William Gosse reached the summit in 1873 and dubbed it Ayers Rock, after the governor of South Australia. He named Mt. Olga after the Queen of Spain.

GETTING THERE AND PRACTICAL INFORMATION

To get from Alice Springs to Uluru-Kata Tjuta by road, travel south on the Stuart Hwy. 202km to Erldunda (see p. 260), then 254km west on the Lasseter Hwy. Long before reaching Uluru, you'll see **Mt. Connor,** a big mesa in the distance. This tricky imitation, often mistaken for Ayers Rock, has its own viewing area. The Uluru-Kata Tjuta National Park entrance station lies 5km past the Yulara resort village. Uluru (Ayers Rock) is 14km ahead, with a turnoff 4km up that leads 42km west to Kata Tjuta (the Olgas). These roads are all paved.

The **Cultural Centre** (tel. 8956 3138; fax 8956 3139), 1km from Uluru, is an effort by the Anangu to enlighten tourists about the natural and cultural history surrounding the rock (open Nov.-March daily 7am-6pm; April-Oct. 7am-5:30pm). For more information, call the **information officer** at the Cultural Centre or contact the **Australian Nature Conservatory Agency** (P.O. Box 119, Yulara, NT 0872). As in the rest of the Red Centre, the **bush flies** can be unbearable in the late summer and fall. Bring mesh netting to cover your face. To avoid tour crowds, consider spending the morning at Kata Tjuta (the Olgas) and the afternoon and evening at Uluru.

The park is open daily (Dec.-Feb. 5am-9pm; March 5:30am-8:30pm; April 6am-8pm; May 6am-7:30pm; June-July 6:30am-7:30pm; Aug. 6am-7:30pm; Sept. 5:30am-7:30pm; Oct. 5am-8pm; Nov. 5am-8:30pm). The entrance passes ($15 per person) grant access for five consecutive days. **No camping** is permitted within the park.

ULURU (AYERS ROCK)

If the Sydney Opera House is the icon of cosmopolitan Australia, Uluru is the essence of its untamed outback. The hype is big, but Ayers Rock is bigger: 348m in height, 3.1km in length, 1.9km in width, and 9.4km around. Two-thirds of the sandstone block is actually buried, and the mass may reach an additional 3km down and 10km across. Eons of geological activity have tilted and eroded once-horizontal sedimentary layers into vertical grooves on the surface of the rock. Up close, these "grooves" become meters-long gorges, and the seemingly smooth rock walls dissolve into a rough, scaly exterior.

The strategically situated **Sunset Viewing Area,** 5km from the rock, is the place to hear the nightly oohs and aahs of awestruck travelers, punctuated by the clicking shutters of hundreds of cameras. Closer to the rock is the **Park Headquarters Visitors Centre,** and the **paved loop** around the rock. The **main car park** and toilets are just to the left along the loop. A **Sunrise Viewing Area** lies on the opposite side of the rock, halfway around the loop.

Although the Anangu attach spiritual importance to the path up Ayers Rock, and prefer that tourists abstain from mounting the summit, hundreds of tourists nonetheless undertake the **climb** each day. A steady stream of would-be Sir Hillarys traversing the 1.6km return hike resembles a column of ants. A chain makes the first, and steepest part of the hike more accessible, but this is no easy jaunt; plaques memorialize people who have died (mostly of heart attacks) while climbing Ayers Rock. Avoid climbing in the middle of the day and allow two hours. Wear **rugged footwear,** bring plenty of **water,** secure your hat against the wind, and plan to take rests along the way. The climb is not recommended for people with medical conditions or loosely attached hairpieces. The summit affords a panorama of the Red Centre's flat, barren expanse, broken by the Olgas and Mt. Connor in the distance.

The Anangu appeal to visitors to enjoy Uluru from more humble and humbling vantage-points around the base. An ambitious 10km **circuit walk** traces the base of the impressive rock (allow 4hr.). Signs indicate which areas are closed to non-Aboriginals. The **Mala Walk** is a 1km segment of this walk which begins at the main parking lot and leads past magnificent walls to **Kantju Gorge.** A smaller parking lot to the right from the loop entrance serves the 1km **Mutitjulu Walk,** which leads to the waterhole home of the serpent **Kuniya.** Both are wheelchair accessible. The educational **Liru Track** runs from the visitors center to the main car park via 2km of bush. Liru Track walks are led by an Anangu guide.

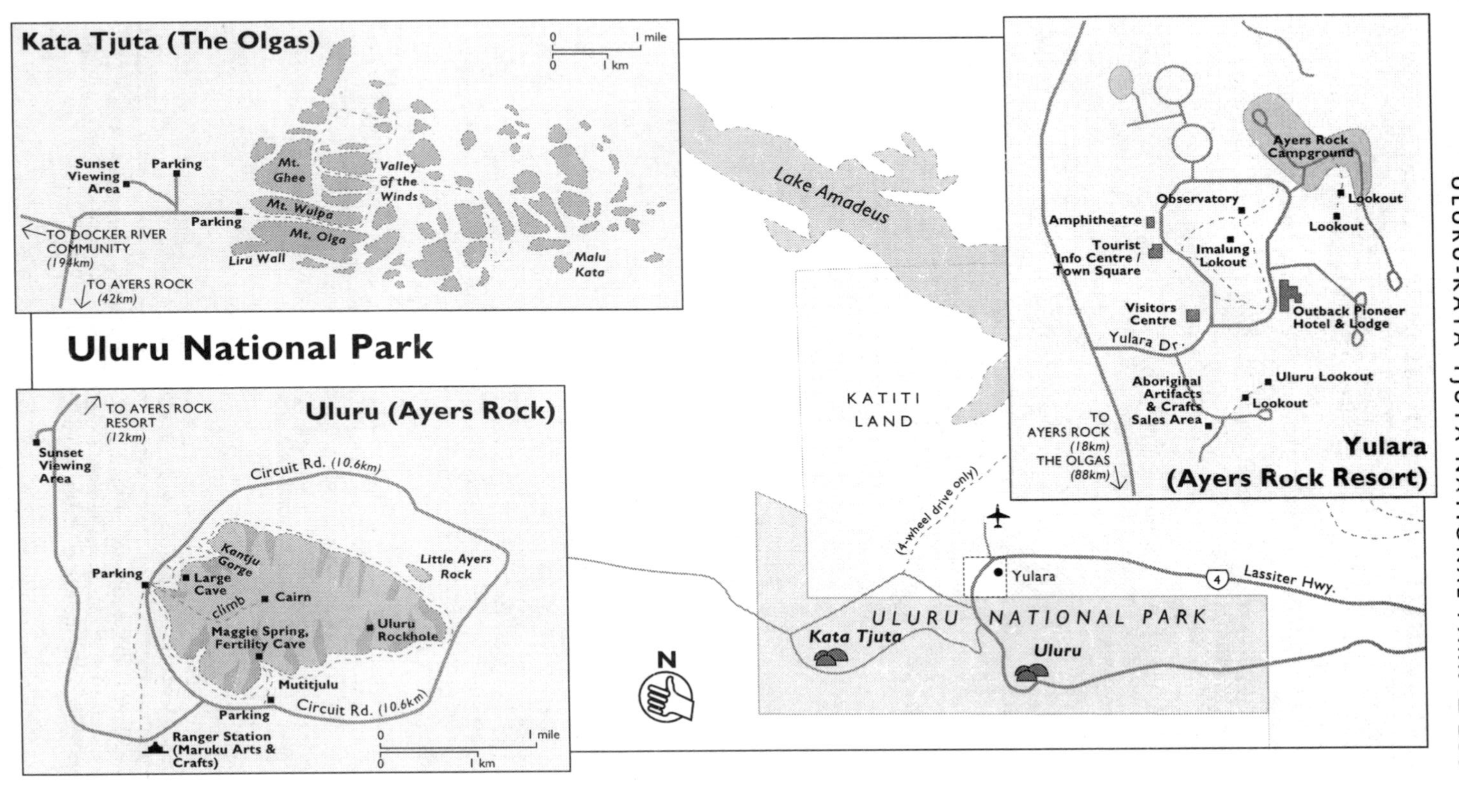

NORTHERN TERRITORY

KATA TJUTA (THE OLGAS)

Perhaps more beautiful, if less awe-inspiring, are the 36 smooth domes scattered over an area several times the size of Uluru. Kata Tjuta ("many heads") is the second conspicuous rock formation in the Red Centre. The road passes south of the formation and curves around to the western side. The **sunset viewing area** (toilets available) is just short of the starting points for two walks. The **Olga Gorge walk** is an easy 1km path between a pair of the most daunting domes. The dome on the right upon entering is the 546m Mt. Olga, the highest peak in the range. It takes an hour to walk to the end of the path, scan the western horizon, and return to the car park. The majestic **Valley of the Winds walk** traces an eerie 7km circuit through the outer wall of domes, into the inner sanctuary, and along the winding exit path. There are plenty of shady spots and an emergency water source at the halfway point. Bring lots of water and allow four hours.

Yulara (Ayers Rock Resort)

Between the Rock and a dry place stands a well-sculpted community. Yulara is a municipal name that shelters employees of Ayers Rock Resort from the embarrassing fact that they live on a tourist farm resembling a child's gameboard. The road that loops around Yulara curves in an effort to avoid looking pre-planned, and the town's facilities are carefully landscaped in a futile effort to blend into the outback. Yulara's monopoly on the tourist market, however, is not as disguised; be prepared to pay hefty mark-ups on goods transported into the village, and more than a bit extra for prime real estate just 19km down the street from the world's largest monolith.

PRACTICAL INFORMATION

The so-called **Visitors Centre** (tel. 8957 7377), with a grand set of stairs rising from the road near the entrance to the village, is actually little more than a gift shop and outdated museum (open daily 8:30am-5pm). The preferred office for tourist services is the **Tourist Information Centre** (tel. 8956 2240), in the main town square shopping area, farther down on the left. This office has a keen general information counter, a list of daily conditions (temperature, sun, etc.) and desks for **Territory Rent-a-Car** (tel. 8956 2030), **Hertz** (tel. 8956 2244), **Avis** (tel. 8956 2266), and several tour agencies. (Center open daily 8:30am-8:30pm; service desks maintain shorter, variable hours.) **Connellan Airport,** to the north of town, serves **Qantas** (to Alice $182, continuing to Darwin $516, to Cairns $501, to Sydney $542; 30% discount for international backpackers), **Ansett** (to Alice $145, continuing to Darwin $412, to Cairns $372, to Sydney $400), and **Airnorth,** and has offices for the car rental agencies. A free **airport shuttle** run by AAT Kings meets all incoming flights, and also picks up from all accommodations 90 minutes before departures. **Greyhound Pioneer** departs for Alice Springs daily at 1:45pm (5½hr., $76).

Ayers Rock Resort runs a free **village shuttle** around the Resort loop (every 15min., daily 10:30am-2:30pm and 6:30pm-12:30am). This takes you past the **police** (tel. 8956 2166; **emergency** tel. 000), a 24hr. **medical center** (tel. 8956 2286; clinic open Mon.-Fri. 9am-noon and 2-5pm, Sat.-Sun. 10-11am), as well as all accommodations and the **town square.** Many facilities are located in the town square, including an **ANZ bank** (open Mon.-Thurs. 9:30am-4pm, Fri. 9:30am-5pm; 24hr. ATM). Next door is the **post office** (tel. 8956 2288, postal code 0872, open Mon.-Fri. 9am-6:30pm, Sat.-Sun. 10am-2pm) and a pricey **supermarket** (open daily 8:30am-9pm) beyond. The **Mobil** station rents **bicycles.**

ACCOMMODATIONS AND FOOD

The resort offers little choice when it comes to accommodations within a given price range. For all reservations call 8956 2737 or fax 8956 2270 (from Sydney, tel. 9360 9099). The **Outback Pioneer Hotel** has a rather impersonal YHA hostel. Reception is open from 4am to 11pm. Check out by 10am. Dorm beds in barracks-like 20-bed rooms go for $17 (YHA non-members $19). (Daytime luggage storage $1. Locker key and linen each require a $10 deposit. Reservations essential.) The dorms themselves do not lock. Deposits can only be recovered by showing your receipt upon check-out. **Ayers Rock Campground** corners the market on camping, since it is not allowed elsewhere in the national park. Campers have access to a swimming pool, communal kitchen, laundry, hot showers, and free gas BBQ. (Grassy tent sites $10 per person, ages 6-14 $5; powered sites for 1 $16, each additional person $10.)

The **Outback Pioneer** has a run-of-the-mill snack bar with burgers and salad, as well as a self-cook BBQ, open to the whole village every night. This dinner is the best deal available in Yulara, apart from fixing your own meals. There's also a **Takeaway Food** counter in the town square which has an excellent sandwich bar (all sandwiches $5; open 9am-8pm). The restaurants listed on the back of the Resort map have Uluru-sized prices.

SIGHTS AND ENTERTAINMENT

Entertainment within the resort is contrived and aimed at high-budget tourists. The **Inmapiti Amphitheatre** next to the town square sets the stage every night for **Nukanaya Dreaming,** a powered-up musical and dance display of Aboriginal culture (Sept.-April 9pm; May-Aug. 8pm; admission $15, under 12 $7). The auditorium behind the Visitors Centre shows recent films (Fri. 8:30pm, Sat. 7:30pm, Sun. 6 and 11pm; admission $6, children $3).

The main sight, of course, is the red monolith that protrudes from the desert south of the resort. A handful of walks around town lead to lookout points. To get to the rock, you'll need a vehicle. **Sunworth Shuttles** (tel. 8956 2152) offers the most flexible transportation to the Rock (starting at $20 return) and the Olgas (starting at $35 return). Among the private tour companies, **Anangu Tours** (phone the Cultural Centre) is the only one owned by Aboriginals. The **Greyhound Pioneer tour** grants an excellent sunset viewing and a good chance to climb the Rock, but only skims the Olgas and lacks play time near the Rock or in Yulara. Often combined with Kings Canyon, it's a compact, rushed way to see the best parts of the Red Centre.

Queensland

If Queensland could be distilled into a strong cocktail, the drink would be overwhelmingly warming. The blend of Brisbane's pragmatic body and the salty whip of a Whitsunday breeze produces as long an aftertaste as the narrow-gauge railway that traces the coastline from Fraser Island to the murky Daintree. An unmistakable fruity quality embodies the balmy sweetness of sugar cane fields and the smooth taste of custard apples, while a pungent aroma emanates from the expanse of rainforest that heaves its breath around Cape Tribulation. But the flavor that rises above the others is an intoxicating swirl as vivid as the hues of the Great Barrier Reef. Travelers raise their glasses to Cairns, Queen of the Land atop her northern throne, who surveys her subjects down the coast and inspects the jewels of her coral crown.

The state's true gems are buried beneath its outback, but the attractions that bring droves of tourists to Queensland lie offshore: the Great Barrier Reef beneath the waves and a chain of backpacker-friendly islands above. The well-trod path up the coast leads multitudes from the glitzy beaches and riverside capital of the south to the scuba mecca of Cairns. Along the way, adventure activities satisfy those in search of adrenaline, and forays into the teeming bush enchant naturalists. Over 300 national parks contain variegated species of trees and wildlife, while rich, tropical fruits and cash crops grow on the lush lowlands. West of the Great Dividing Range, spinifex-covered plains support beef cattle and sheep stations. Miners of gold and precious stones extract a living from the vast and arid outback that bred both Qantas and the Flying Doctors.

The capital of Brisbane is temperate in every sense of the word, but tropical Queensland can be hard to swallow in the heat summer. Casual labor is plentiful for those with working holiday permits and the patience and stamina to last through days of fruit-picking. Along the central coast, hostels arrange work for guests year-round, except in the sweltering months from January to March, when the only thing growing is the thermometer's mercury and the only thing to do is hide in a air-conditioned room or bathe in the turquoise water off one island or another. The summer also brings rain. An unwieldly amount falls at points along the coast, roads in the far north get washed out, and some creek crossings become roaring rivers which can swallow cars. These torrents drain through magnificent mangrove swamps and into the Coral Sea, where they drift over the curtain of coral that nearly spans the length of the state. From the Tropic of Capricorn to the virginal tip of the Cape York Peninsula, the Great Barrier Reef beckons. Don a snorkel mask or scuba gear and drift through this living gallery to witness the myriad colors of Queensland's famous, watery netherworld.

Phone numbers in Queensland have recently changed. Regional phone codes are now all 07, followed by eight-digit numbers. If you have trouble making a call, use the following scheme to get the old number, and try that instead. For more details, see the **appendix** (p. 574).

New Number:	Old Number:	New Number:	Old Number:
(07) 3xxx xxxx	(07) xxx xxxx	(07) 55xx xxxx	(075) xx xxxx
(07) 40xx xxxx	(070) xx xxxx	(07) 46xx xxxx	(076) xx xxxx
(07) 41xx xxxx	(071) xx xxxx	(07) 47xx xxxx	(077) xx xxxx
(07) 54xx xxxx	(074) xx xxxx	(07) 49xx xxxx	(079) xx xxxx

Brisbane

If it weren't for Brisbane's tall office buildings and sleek commuter ferries, visitors might almost expect to see cows grazing on the city's carefully manicured lawns or wooden produce stands teetering outside its elegant houses. Although Brisbane (pop. 800,000) is the capital of Queensland and Australia's third largest city, its recent

Queensland
Detail Map of Sunshine Coast and Gold Coast
Nambour
Maroochydore
Caloundra
Kilcoy
Caboolture
Esk
Bribie Island
Moreton Island
Redcliffe
Brisbane
North Stradbroke Island
Ipswich
Beenleigh
QUEENSLAND
Southport
Surfers Paradise
Coolangatta
Tweed Heads
Murwillumbah
NEW SOUTH WALES
Byron Bay
Lismore
Casino
Ballina
Sunshine Coast
Gold Coast
Torres Strait
Torres Strait Islands
Thursday Island
Bamaga
JARDINE RIVER NATIONAL PARK
Cape York
Peninsula
Gulf of Carpenteria
Weipa
ARCHER BEND NATIONAL PARK
ROKEBY N.P.
CAPE MELVILLE NATIONAL PARK
Coen
LAKEFIELD NATIONAL PARK
Cooktown
Laura
Daintree
DAINTREE N.P.
Port Douglas
Mossman
Cairns
Mareeba
Atherton
Atherton Tablelands
Innisfail
Mornington Island
STAATEN RIVER NATIONAL PARK
Karumba
Burketown
Normanton
Mount Surprise
Georgetown
Hinchinbrook Island
Ingham
Magnetic Island
Townsville
GREAT BARRIER REEF MARINE PARK
(MARINE PARK BOUNDARY)
0 200 miles
0 200 kilometers
N
Camooweal
PORCUPINE GORGE NATIONAL PARK
Charters Towers
Bowen
Whitsunday Islands
Airlie Beach
Proserpine
Mount Isa
Cloncurry
Flinders Hwy.
Richmond
Prairie
Hughendon
EUNGELLA NATIONAL PARK
Mackay
Sarina
Landsborough Hwy.
QUEENSLAND
GREAT DIVIDING RANGE
Winton
Muttaburra
Clermont
Boulia
BLADENSBURG NATIONAL PARK
Yeppoon
Great Keppel Island
Barcaldine
Emerald
Tropic of Capricorn
Longreach
Capricorn Hwy.
Rockhampton
FRASER ISLAND N.P.
Gladstone
Blackall
SIMPSON DESERT NATIONAL PARK
Windorah
CARNARVON NATIONAL PARK
Bundaberg
Hervey Bay
Childers
Fraser Island
ROBINSON GORGE N.P.
Maryborough
Birdsville
Rainbow Beach
Noosa
Mitchell Hwy.
Charleville
Roma
Miles
Chinchilla
Maroochy
Nambour
Dalby
Toowoomba
Cunnamulla
St. George
Brisbane
Warwick
Goondiwindi
SOUTH AUSTRALIA
Surfers Paradise
Lightning Ridge
NEW SOUTH WALES
1
54
15
62
83
66
78
55
71
17
39
49
42

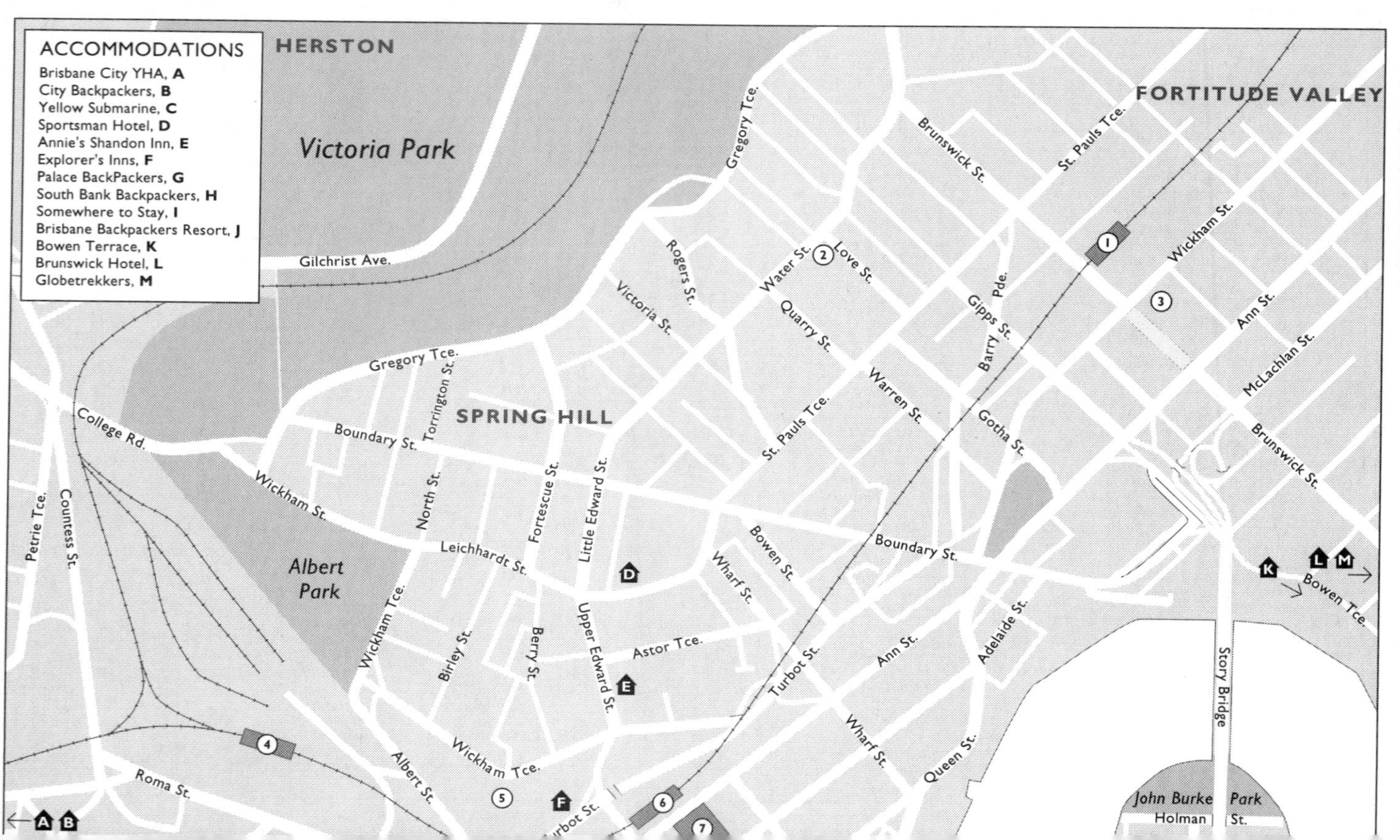
ACCOMMODATIONS
Brisbane City YHA, A
City Backpackers, B
Yellow Submarine, C
Sportsman Hotel, D
Annie's Shandon Inn, E
Explorer's Inns, F
Palace BackPackers, G
South Bank Backpackers, H
Somewhere to Stay, I
Brisbane Backpackers Resort, J
Bowen Terrace, K
Brunswick Hotel, L
Globetrekkers, M
HERSTON
Victoria Park
FORTITUDE VALLEY
SPRING HILL
Albert Park
John Burke Park
Gilchrist Ave.
Gregory Tce.
Brunswick St.
St. Pauls Tce.
Wickham St.
Ann St.
McLachlan St.
Rogers St.
Water St.
Love St.
Victoria St.
Quarry St.
Gipps St.
Barry Pde.
Warren St.
Gotha St.
Torrington St.
College Rd.
Boundary St.
North St.
Fortescue St.
Little Edward St.
Wickham St.
Leichhardt St.
Bowen St.
Wharf St.
Petrie Tce.
Countess St.
Wickham Tce.
Birley St.
Berry St.
Upper Edward St.
Astor Tce.
Turbot St.
Ann St.
Adelaide St.
Bowen Tce.
Story Bridge
Wharf St.
Queen St.
Albert St.
Roma St.
Holman St.

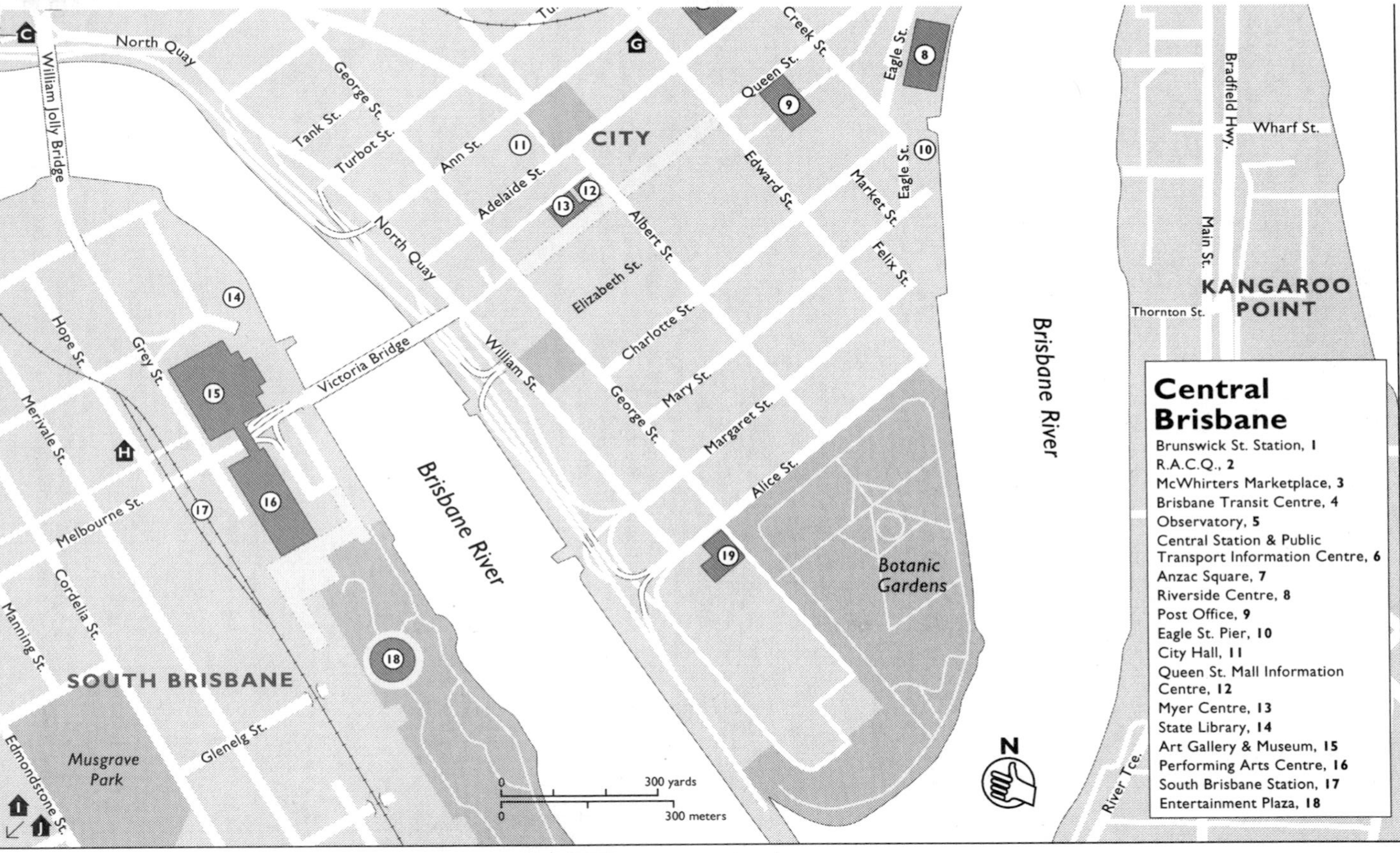
Central Brisbane
Brunswick St. Station, 1
R.A.C.Q., 2
McWhirters Marketplace, 3
Brisbane Transit Centre, 4
Observatory, 5
Central Station & Public Transport Information Centre, 6
Anzac Square, 7
Riverside Centre, 8
Post Office, 9
Eagle St. Pier, 10
City Hall, 11
Queen St. Mall Information Centre, 12
Myer Centre, 13
State Library, 14
Art Gallery & Museum, 15
Performing Arts Centre, 16
South Brisbane Station, 17
Entertainment Plaza, 18
North Quay
William Jolly Bridge
George St.
Tank St.
Turbot St.
Ann St.
CITY
Adelaide St.
Creek St.
Queen St.
Eagle St.
Edward St.
Market St.
Albert St.
Felix St.
Elizabeth St.
Charlotte St.
Mary St.
Margaret St.
Alice St.
George St.
William St.
Victoria Bridge
Brisbane River
Botanic Gardens
Bradfield Hwy.
Wharf St.
Main St.
KANGAROO POINT
Thornton St.
River Tce.
N
Hope St.
Grey St.
Merivale St.
Melbourne St.
Cordelia St.
Manning St.
SOUTH BRISBANE
Glenelg St.
Edmondstone St.
Musgrave Park
300 yards
300 meters

growth has not obliterated its deliciously relaxed country town feel, and the city seems like a ruddy-cheeked farmboy who's suddenly outgrown his britches. Originally founded as a penal colony for second-time convicts, it's not glamorous or proudly industrial, but it is practical, clean, and brimming with energy.

Always a good bet for temporary employment, Brisbane earned a reputation as a tourist and holiday destination only recently, after hosting the 1988 World Expo and the 1992 Commonwealth Games. The sunny, warm climate has attracted artistic emigres, eager to shed winter jumpers and rev up the city's cultural institutions. Thanks to them, travelers visit Brisbane for more than the weather. They come for its gorgeous, modern Cultural Centre, 19th-century historic buildings, corner cafes, rocking nightclubs, extensive parklands, and water.

The Brisbane River lends an easygoing grace to the metropolis it bisects. Riverine transportation is simple and enjoyable, with hulking ferries and slim kayaks riding tandem between Chinatown and the South Bank Parklands, and between the investment banks and the trendy West End. The city of Brisbane lets nature flow freely: it understands that concrete and glass are less intimidating when cushioned with water and that hard urban edges can be softened with indoor pools in art galleries and ebullient fountains in the middle of shopping centers.

ARRIVAL AND DEPARTURE

By Plane

Brisbane International Airport, 17km northwest of the city center, is packed with restaurants, duty-free stores, showers, currency exchange, and luggage storage ($4-10 per day). The three-year-old facility is served by 23 international airlines, including **Qantas** (domestic office: 247 Adelaide St; international office: 241 Adelaide St.; tel. 13 13 13) and **Ansett** (corner of George and Queen St.; tel. 13 13 00). Shuttles run regularly from the international terminal to the domestic terminal. Ask about concessions and special deals; international travelers can qualify for 30% off full-price economy tickets. The round-trip fare from Brisbane to Ayers Rock is about $597, to Cairns about $333, to Melbourne about $391, and to Sydney about $233.

The **Travellers Information Service** (tel. 3406 3190), in the international terminal, can answer general queries. The desk opens with the first incoming flight and closes with the last. The **Roma Street Transit Centre** (tel. 3236 2020) has an information desk on level two and an accommodations booking service on level three (open Mon.-Fri. 7am-6pm, Sat.-Sun. 8am-5pm).

CoachTrans (tel. 3236 1000), on level three of the Transit Centre, runs a daily **shuttle bus** between the airport and Transit Centre (5am-8:30pm, every 30min., one-way $6.50, return $12). A trip to one of the major hotels costs $7.50 (hotel to airport trips must be booked in advance by calling 5588 8777). A **taxi** ride between the airport and downtown costs $17-20.

By Train

The Roma Street Transit Centre, 500m west of the city's center, is Brisbane's main intercity bus and train terminal, with all major bus offices. **Lockers** ($3 per 6hr.; $4 per 24hr.) are on level three, and showers are on level two. **Queensland Rail** (tel. 3235 2222; bookings tel. 13 22 32) has 10 services that run throughout Queensland, each with a different name. The *Queenslander* and *Sunlander* run to Cairns; the *Spirit of Capricorn* to Rockhampton; the *Inlander* to Mt. Isa; and the *Spirit of Outback* to Longreach. One-way fares include travel to: Cairns ($135, 32hr.), Longreach ($118, 24hr.), Melbourne ($145), Rockhampton ($67, 9hr.), Sydney ($90, 14hr.), and Townsville ($119).

For longer travel intineraries, Queensland Rail's **Sunshine Rail Pass** is good for six months from date of issue and valid for travel anywhere in Queensland. It's sold by the number of travel days available for use. (Economy class: 14-day $267; 21-day $309; 30-day $388). Australian students and children qualify for half-price concessions. First class tickets include individual berths in the sleeper car, but are 50% more expensive. Tickets must be purchased at the Queensland Rail booth at Roma Street Transit Centre or Central Station. All travel must be booked in advance. Many trains have dining services and showers. **Countrylink** combines bus and train travel from Brisbane to Sydney. Trains leave daily at 7:30am ($90 economy, $125 first class, 16hr.).

By Bus

Greyhound Pioneer (tel. 3258 1670; 24hr. reservations tel. 13 20 30) and **McCafferty's** (tel. 3236 3035; reservations tel. 13 14 99; open daily 6:30am-8pm) offer very similar fares to destinations throughout Australia, although McCafferty's is sometimes a bit cheaper. Major cities served include Airlie Beach ($111, concessions $100), Stanthorpe (1 per day, 6:30pm), Byron Bay ($22, $20), Cairns ($148, $134), Melbourne ($134, $121), and Sydney ($75, $68). **Pioneer Motor Services** (tel. 3236 444; 24hr. tel. 1300 368 100) leaves southbound for Sydney six times per day, permitting several stops along the way (backpackers $50 with 1 stopover, $56 with 2, $67 with 3; 30% concession for children, students, and pensioners). **Kirkland's Coaches** (tel. 3236 5222) leaves a few times every day for the Gold Coast, Byron Bay, Lismore, and Ballina, among other destinations (concessions for students 20%, pensioners 50%, children 50%). For travel within Queensland, **CoachTrans** (tel. 5588 8777) leaves for the Gold Coast about six times per day ($29, round-trip $50, 75min.). **Suncoast Pacific** (tel. 3236 1901) has regular direct trips to the Sunshine Coast ($19.80; concessions with VIP or YHA card).

By Car

The **Royal Automobile Club of Queensland (RACQ),** is at 300 St. Paul's Terrace, Fortitude Valley (tel. 3361 2444; fax 3220 0029). Affiliated with major clubs throughout the world, RACQ provides excellent maps, car buying or selling information, and technical services for cars and motorcycles. (Branch office 261 Queen St. Both open Mon.-Fri. 8:30am-5:30pm. 1-yr. membership fee $65.)

Most **car rental** agencies require renters to be at least 21 years old with a valid driver's license. Many offer free car delivery. Expect to pay $25-$39 per day. **Ideal Rental Cars,** 63 Esker St. in Pinkenba near the airport off Eagle Farm Rd. (tel. 3260 2307 or 1800 065 172; fax 3260 1392) has 24-hour service and rents from $25 per day (free pick-up and delivery). **Compass Car Rentals,** 683 Main St. at Kangaroo Point (tel. 3891 2614), rents new vehicles from $29 per day. **Allcar Rentals,** 925 Ann St. in Fortitude Valley (tel. 3852 3334), arranges one-way rentals between its offices in Brisbane, Cairns, Port Douglas, and Sydney from $39 per day. **Shoe Strings,** 360 Nudges Rd., Hendra (tel. 3268 3334), rents air-conditioned vehicles, some with car phones, from $32.20 per day. **Allterrain,** corner of Ann and Jones St., Fortitude Valley (tel. 3257 1101), rents 4x4 jeeps and trucks and has Fraser Island accommodation packages. **Budget,** 105 Mary St. (tel. 13 27 27 or 3220 0699, airport tel. 3860 4466), rents from $29 per day.

ORIENTATION

The Brisbane River hems the city and creates easily identifiable landmarks; the city's heart is cradled in the bottom of a sideways S-curve, connected to South Bank by the Victoria Bridge. The **Transit Centre** is on Roma St.; a left turn out of the building and a five-minute walk down Roma St. leads to the corner of Albert and Ann St. and the grassy King George Square (a front lawn for the grand City Hall). Adelaide St. runs along the opposite side of the square, and a block beyond is the **Queen Street Mall,** a popular, open-air pedestrian thoroughfare lined on both sides with shops and cafes. Underneath the Mall and the adjoining Myer Centre shopping complex is the **Queen Street Bus Station.** Seven clearly marked entrances are spread throughout the Mall. The **city center's** streets are organized by the gender of famous English figures. From Queen St. moving toward the river lie Elizabeth, Charlotte, Mary, Margaret, and Alice St.; from the river moving inland lie William, George, Albert, and Edward.

Brisbane's neighborhoods radiate out from the city center. A right turn out of the transit center leads to **Petrie Terrace** and **Paddington,** both most easily reached by passing under the bridge and taking the first left up the hill. North of **Boundary St.** is **Spring Hill,** bordered to the west by Victoria Park and 10-15 minutes from the Queen Street Mall up the steep Edward St. **Fortitude Valley** is farther east of Spring Hill and is home to Chinatown. It is only a 20-minute walk down Ann St. to **Brunswick St.** and Chinatown's ornate entrance gate. Although the nightclub-heavy Fortitude Valley is now considered alternative enough to be acceptably trendy, it shares its space with the red light district, whose establishments are spread thick on the far north end of Ann St. Solo pedestrians should be wary at night. A right on Brunswick St. leads to **New Farm,** farther from the city center than the Valley; it officially begins at the intersection of Brunswick and Hardcourt St.

South of the river, the Victoria Bridge footpath turns into Melbourne St. and heads into **South Brisbane,** crossing Boundary St. six blocks later. **South Bank** is to the left of the southern end of the bridge; the intersection of Boundary and Vulture St., further on, is considered the heart of the **West End.**

GETTING AROUND

By Train

Citytrain, Queensland Rail's intercity train network, has three major stations. The main transit center is at Roma St., while Central Station is at Ann and Edward St., and the final station is at Brunswick St. One-zone journeys in the city area are $1.20. One-day unlimited travel after 9am Monday to Friday is $8.50. (Trains run Mon.-Thurs. 5am-11:30pm, Fri. 5am-1am, Sat. 6am-1am, Sun. 6am-11pm. All one-way and round-trip tickets half-price Sat.-Sun.)

By Bus

Citybus is the "all-stops" major service. Most buses depart from the **Queen Street Bus Station,** a huge underground terminal beneath the Myer Center and Queen St. Mall. Platforms have been given animal names—your bus might leave from Koala, Kangaroo, Crocodile, or Platypus. Stops spread throughout the inner city are sorted by color. Schedules organized by suburb and bus number are posted throughout the city, particularly in the Queen St. Mall. For example, "West End" is serviced by bus #177 (Brown 2) and 29 (Orange 6). Suburban bus route schedules vary; call **TransInfo** (tel. 13 12 30) or stop by the Queen St. Bus Station Information Center. Fares depend on the distance traveled and range from $1.20 to $2.80 (children half-price). The **City Circle** bus #333 runs a loop around the central business district (70¢; Mon.-Fri. 7am-5:30pm). **Cityxpress** buses, white with blue and yellow stripes, run directly from the suburbs to the city every 30 minutes. During peak hours, **Rockets** go from selected suburban stops express to the city. The **Great Circle Line,** #598 or 599, connects to major suburban shopping centers.

QUEENSLAND

By Ferry

Brisbane has an excellent ferry system which makes good use of the Brisbane River, providing both "practical" transport and cheap sight-seeing tours at sunset. The **City Ferry** and the newer, sleeker, **City Cat** ferry run from the University of Queensland to Bretts Wharf. The City Cat is wheelchair accessible, allows free bike transport, and has toilets and public phones. (Runs daily 6am-10:30pm every 30min. or less. Schedules posted at every dock and stop. Cost depends on distance; 1-sector fare $1.40, 2-sector fare $2.)

By Taxi

Brisbane Cabs (tel. 3360 0000), **Yellow Cab Company** (tel. 3391 0190), and **Black and White** (tel. 13 10 08) operate 24 hours per day.

By Bike or In-line Skates

Bicycles are a great way to see Brisbane. Local public transportation carries them free of charge, and within Brisbane City alone there are 350km of cycling paths. It's also possible to bike to nearby sights, like Mt. Coot-tha and Stradbroke Island. The Brisbane City Council publishes a pamphlet called *Brisbane Bicycle Maps.* **Backpackers Mountain Bike Hire** (tel. 3256 0155) rents bikes for $16 per day, including maps and a helmet (free delivery and pick-up of bikes; phone by 8pm the previous day to book). **Brisbane Bicycle,** 87 Albert St. (tel. 3229 2433), carries a wide range of bikes ($9 per hr. or $20 per day; open daily and late on Fri.). **Skatebiz** (tel. 3220 0157) on the corner of Mary and Albert St., rents in-line skates and pads.

PRACTICAL INFORMATION

Tourist Office: Tourism Brisbane in City Hall (tel. 3221 8411) is open Mon.-Fri. 9am-5pm. There is also an information booth in the middle of the Queen St. Mall (tel. 3229 5918; open Mon.-Thurs. 8:30am-5pm, Fri. 8:30am-8:30pm, Sat.-Sun. 9am-4pm). Helpful resources include the *Brisbane Tourism* guide, available at many tourist booths, and **InfoBrisbane,** a touch-screen computer info system available in several locations around town.

Travelers with Disabilities: Guides and brochures include *Access Brisbane, Accessible Brisbane Parks, Brisbane Mobility Map,* and *Brisbane Braille Trail,* all available from the Brisbane City Council customer service centers, public libraries, or the Disability Services Unit (tel. 3403 5796). The Disability Information Awareness Line (DIAL) can answer questions (tel. 3224 8444 or 1800 177 120; email dial@fsaia.qld.gov.au), as can the Queensland Deaf Society (tel. 3356 8255; TTY 3856 4237).

Budget Travel Offices: Flight Centre has 8 offices and guarantees to beat any quoted current price (tel. 13 16 00; 24hr. tel. 13 31 33). **STA Travel,** 111 Adelaide St. (tel. 3221 3722; fax 3229 8435), has agents specializing in backpackers (open Mon.-Fri. 9am-5pm, Sat. 9am-3pm). **Dial-A-Coach,** room 12, balcony level of the Brisbane Arcade on Queen St. (tel. 3221 2225), specializes in cheap bus fares (open Mon.-Fri. 9:30am-5pm, Sat. 9am-noon). For budget travel packages, try **Adventure Travel Australia** (tel. 3844 0206; fax 3844 9295; email BrisbaneBackpackers@6022.aone.net.au), located in the lobby of the Brisbane Backpackers Resort at 110 Vulture St. in the West End.

Currency Exchange: Banks are clustered in the Queen St. Mall area and along Boundary St. in the West End. Banking hours are generally Mon.-Thurs. 9:30am-4pm, Fri. 9:30am-5pm. Most banks don't charge to exchange cash but have a fee of around $5 for cashing traveler's checks. **American Express,** 131 Elizabeth St. (tel. 3229 2729). Open Mon.-Fri. 8:30am-5:30pm, Sat. 9am-noon.

ATMs: Throughout the city, particularly in the Queen St. Mall area, the transit center, and shopping centers. Most accept Australian bank cards, credit cards, and Cirrus.

Bookstores: The Queen St. Mall area has a huge selection of bookstores. **Dymocks** has 2 branches in the city, at 239 Albert Street (tel. 3229 4266) and 250 Edward Street (tel. 3220 0146). **Angus and Robertson** (tel. 3229 8899) has a branch located right in the mall.

Libraries: The **State Library** (tel. 3840 7666) is in the Cultural Centre, next to the Museum and Art Gallery. For free **internet access** call 3840 7785.

Public Markets: South Bank Markets (see **Sights,** p. 279); **Brunswick Markets,** held on Brunswick St. in Fortitude Valley Sat. mornings; **Riverside Markets,** held in the city on Eagle St. all day on Sun.

Hotlines: Brisbane Crisis Line (tel. 3252 1111); Rape Crisis Line (tel. 3844 4008); Domestic Violence (tel. 1800 811 811; TTY 800 812 225).

Hospital: The Royal Brisbane Hospital, Herston Rd., Herston (tel. 3221 8083), supplies travel medicine and vaccinations.

Emergency: Dial 000.

Police: tel. 3367 6464.

Telephones: Public telephones are located throughout the city. Local calls cost 40¢; phonecards are available in denominations of $5-50 from many retail outlets.

Information numbers: Weather (tel. 1196); time (tel. 1194); tourist infoline (tel. 11654); tide times (tel. 3224 2616); marine report (tel. 1182).

Directory Assistance: The **Hello Yellow** Service allows you to receive a list of category-specific businesses over the phone. Call 3404 1111; available daily 7am-11pm. Local directory assistance: 013; Australia: 0175; International: 0103.

General Post Office (GPO): at 261 Queen St. (tel. 3405 1435; fax 3405 1428), half a block from the end of the mall. *Poste Restante* questions can be directed to tel. 3405 1465; check a computer to make sure you have mail before requesting collection. *Poste Restante* forwarding $5. $6 surcharge for international money orders. Open Mon.-Fri. 7am-6pm. **Postal code:** 4000; GPO code: 4001.

Phone Code: 07.

ACCOMMODATIONS

Brisbane is blessed with plenty of high-quality, low-price hostels, most with TVs, videos, in-house bars, free tours of local sights, and courtesy pick-up service from the Roma Street Transit Centre. Accommodations are clustered in four main areas of the city. The city center, with middle-range motels and B&Bs, is where to find the action; South Brisbane and West End are near the cultural sights; Fortitude Valley and New Farm are trendy and alternative but not the safest areas at night; Petrie Terrace and Paddington are close to the transit center and Caxton St. Unless otherwise noted, check-out time is 10am and key deposits are $10. Most hostels and all motels provide linen, but some require a deposit for sheets, blankets, and crockery.

City Center

Palace BackPackers, at the corner of Ann and Edward St. (tel. 3211 2433, bookings tel. 1800 676 340; fax 3211 2466), is a 2min. walk from the Queen St. Mall. The former Salvation Army headquarters, this 5-story building retains an older-era elegance despite its party-central reputation. Access to the roof and 3-story verandah. Enormous basement kitchen and rocking basement pub. Rooms have lockers and either A/C or ceiling fans. 6 and 7-bed dorms $15; 4 and 5-bed dorms $16; 3-bed dorms $17; doubles $38; singles $24. VIP. Wheelchair accessible.

South Brisbane and the West End

Brisbane Backpackers Resort, 110 Vulture St. (tel. 3844 9956, bookings tel. 1800 626 452; fax 3844 9295). Near the intersection of Vulture and Boundary St., the Resort has large rooms with fridge, balcony, and lockers. Each floor shares a small kitchen. Tennis court, swimming pool, sauna, and nightly movies. Travel agency in lobby. All rooms with bath. Reception open 24hr. 6-bed dorms $15; doubles $40. Weekly: $90; $250.

Somewhere to Stay, 45 Brighton St. (tel. 3846 2858, bookings tel. 1800 812 398; fax 3846 4584) at the corner of Franklin St., sits atop a quiet hill surrounded by vegetation. Large rooms with wooden bedframes; those in the front have a gorgeous view of the city. 4-bed dorms $12, with bath $13, with TV and fridge $14; doubles $30, $35, $45.

South Bank Backpackers, at the corner of Melbourne and Hope St. in the Sly Fox Hotel (tel. 3844 0022, bookings tel. 1800 061 522), is an easy 5min. walk from the Cultural Centre at South Bank. The converted luxury hotel has seen better days (hallway furniture consists of ripped-out car seats covered with sheets). Access to a large roof, sprinkled with plastic lawn chairs and tables; guests bring beers and guitars up at night to watch the sun set and see the city lights. Small kitchen, free Sat. night BBQs. 4-bed dorms $10, with shower $12; twins $30. VIP.

Fortitude Valley and New Farm

Brisbane's Homestead, 57 Annie St. (tel. 3358 3538). Fairly quiet, 2-floor house. Bedrooms are pink with high ceilings and wooden bunks. Small swimming pool, kitchen, ping-pong and pool tables. Monday Madness drinking races. 8-bed dorms $13; twins $32, with bath $56. Weekly: $75; $175. VIP, YHA.

Brunswick Hotel (Red Hot Chili Packers), 569 Brunswick St. (tel. 3392 0137, bookings tel. 1800 686 650; fax 3844 8192). Located above the Brunswick Hotel and bar, this hostel is another converted luxury hotel. The hallway floors are lined with what looks like the original red carpet, now well-worn. Kitchen, pool tables, small courtyard, and job club. Reception 24hr. Dorms $12. $5 discount for 2nd night.

Globetrekkers, 35 Balfour St. (tel. 3358 1251; email bidlake@gil.com.au). In a small, 100-year-old house between Brunswick St. and Bowen Tce., this is a quiet artist's enclave, with pictures on the wall and half-finished sculptures on the porch. Resident dog Spock jumps over railings, fetches keys, and performs other tricks to entertain guests. Small kitchen; rooms are orderly and clean. 5-bed dorms $13; doubles $30, with bath $34. Weekly: $77; $196, $210. Call ahead for booking.

Bowen Terrace, 365 Bowen Tce., off Brunswick St. (tel. 3254 1575). Warm and welcoming colonial house. Home to international student boarders most of the year, but worth trying to secure a room. Basement has an informal lounge and small kitchen. Outside wooden deck strung with white Christmas lights. Bedrooms are small but equipped with desks. Singles $15; doubles (with TV and fridge) $35. Weekly: $95; $210. Book ahead, as space is limited.

Petrie Terrace/Paddington

Brisbane City YHA, 392 Upper Roma St. (tel. 3236 1004; fax 3236 1947). Clean, friendly, low-key, and private. Although a new brightly colored building with modern facilities was recently added, the old building remains inexplicably popular. Kitchen and wonderful reading loft. 4- to 6-bed dorms $16; 3-bed dorms $17; doubles $20, with bath $25. Wheelchair accessible.

City Backpackers, 380 Upper Roma St. (tel. 3211 3221, bookings tel. 1800 062 572). Friendly, knowledgeable staff, large rooms, and kitchen. Emphasis on "in-house" activity nights. Reception open daily 7am-7:30pm. 4- to 6-bed dorms $14. Weekly: $195. Wheelchair accessible. YHA, VIP.

Yellow Submarine, 66 Quay St. (tel. 3211 3424). A little house with lots of character and a shrine to Beatle-mania. Formerly the home of a governor, now most rooms are painted yellow, an "Octopus' Garden" is outside, and the basement walls are covered with graffiti and murals from past travelers. Table tennis, free BBQ on Sun. 6-bed dorms $12; doubles $28. Book ahead, as rooms fill quickly.

Motels and B&Bs

Although Brisbane's hostels are high quality and offer motel-like amenities at $12-15 a night, motels and B&Bs often have more privacy and conveniences the hostels don't usually provide, like towels. The first three listed are clustered on the border of Brisbane City, a short walk from the Queen St. Mall.

Annie's Shandon Inn, 405 Upper Edward St., Spring Hill (tel. 3831 8684; fax 3831 3073). Staying here is like being back in grandma's house. The inn has been in the family for 100 years; family pictures and photocopies of birth and marriage certificates line the front hall, while miniature dolls grace the front porch step. Singles $40, with bath $50; doubles or twins $50, with bath $60; $5 each additional child, $10 each additional adult. Breakfast included. 10% discount for 7-day stay.

Explorer's Inns, 63 Turbot St., near the Transit Centre (tel. 3211 3488, reservations tel. 1800 623 288), has a modern look and facilities but feels a bit too compact. Rooms are clean and have full length mirrors, phones, mini bars, small TVs, coffee makers and mugs, clock radios, and A/C. Wheelchair accessible units available. Non-smoking. Singles, doubles, twins $64, with bath $84. 4-person family rooms $84. Licensed restaurant in the basement with light meals from $5-8.

Edward Lodge, 75 Sydney St., New Farm (tel. 3254 1078). Gorgeous, modern rooms exclusively for gays and lesbians. Quiet neighborhood. Breakfast included and served in a high-ceilinged, bright room with a Michaelangelo-esque angel mosaic painted on the ceiling (but there's something different about those angels...). New, large jacuzzi and twin open shower. All rooms with bath. Singles $65; doubles $75. Laundry $5. Book early, especially for Mardi Gras.

Sportsman Hotel, 130 Leichhardt St., Spring Hill (tel. 3831 2892; fax 3831 2106), also exclusively for gays and lesbians. Located directly above Sportsman's Bar. Dark, smoky hallways, but clean rooms and bathrooms. Free coffee, tea. Singles $25; doubles $40. Reservations required 6 months in advance.

FOOD

Restaurants and cafes are roughly clustered by type and atmosphere. The West End has small, trendy sidewalk cafes and ethnic restaurants, particularly along Boundary St. and Hargrove Rd. Chinatown in Fortitude Valley has many small, cheap Chinese and Asian food establishments, while New Farm has recently sprouted more trendy and expensive eateries. The city center has a range of options.

City Center

Govinda's Vegetarian Restaurant, upstairs at 99 Elizabeth St. (tel. 3210 0225), is run by Hare Krishnas and only serves one meal, but it's hearty, all-you-can-eat, and only $6. Open Sun. 5-7pm, Mon.-Sat. 1:30-2:30pm, Fri. also 5:30-8:30pm. Sun. $3 feast and "cultural celebration" with music.

Caffe Libri, at the American Bookstore, 173 Elizabeth St. (tel. 3229 7559), is a down-home eatery surrounded by bookshelves. The selection is small but savory: coffee, bagels, enormous Caesar and smoked chicken salads, fresh homemade cakes and tortes, and, a perennial favorite, big bowls of homemade pumpkin soup in the winter ($5). Call ahead to reserve a bowl—they go fast. Open Mon.-Thurs. 8am-5:30pm, Fri. 8am-6pm, Sat. 9am-4pm.

Parrots, 93 Elizabeth St. (tel. 3229 0187), serves up 15 varieties of thick, juicy gourmet hamburgers ($8-11) guaranteed to satisfy the most voracious carnivore. The decorating is quirkily elegant, with framed paintings of parrots hanging on green walls and tropical vegetation guarding the corners and lining the windowsills. A modest selection of sandwiches complements the burgers. Licensed. Open Tues.-Thurs. 11:30am-10:30pm, Fri.-Sat. 11:30am-11pm, Sun. 11:30am-9:30pm.

West End

Three Monkeys, 53 Mallison St., on the West End rotary off Boundary St. (tel. 3844 6045). Popular with Queensland Performing Arts Centre audiences. Posters of theater productions hang on the wall next to African and Indian artwork, woven baskets, and statuettes. The atmosphere is reluctantly casual; despite the dim lighting and sophisticated jazz in the background, the menu is varied and reasonably priced. Quiche ($6), nachos ($6.50), spanakopita ($8), and a delectable choice of 15-20 cakes and cookies are among the menu items. The terrace out back is filled with leafy plants. Open daily 9:30am-late.

Cafe Babylon, 142 Boundary St. (tel. 3846 4505). Walls of burning incense mingle with the rich smell of Middle Eastern food while patrons order everything from coffee to 4-course meals. Sit outside on the terrace or relax around a small table in a wicker chair. You'll savor every bite of the rich, middle-eastern inspired concoctions. Two appetizers (about $4-5 each) can make a meal, or try an array of dips, spreads, breads, and other samples for $10. Open Tues.-Sun. for lunch and dinner.

Caravanserai, 1 Dornock Tce. at the corner of Hargrove Rd. (tel. 3217 2617). Middle Eastern, Mediterranean, and Turkish food served on a veranda. Not only do you get the views from the porch, but you also get to see live belly dancing. Main dishes $8.50-10.50. Open daily for lunch and dinner.

New Farm

Getties, at the corner of Brunswick and Baker St. (tel. 3358 5088). Loud Latin and jazz music pump through the narrow interior of this cornerside cafe, but it doesn't stop the trendy yuppies from squeezing in, sipping wine, chatting, and soaking up the atmosphere. Lemon peppered calamari with citrus mango for $7 from the bar Open Mon.-Sat. 11:30am-midnight, Sun. 9am-late.

Rosati's at the Park, 938 Brunswick St. (tel. 3358 1422). Large, contemporary dining room with classy silver metal chairs and a gorgeous display of wine bottles over the bar. More upscale and out of the way, but worth it if you like well-prepared Italian dishes. Mains range from $12-14, but many people come for coffee and dessert. Open daily 11:30am-10:30pm; Sun. breakfast from 7am.

Moray Cafe, at the corner of Moray and Merthyr Rd. (tel. 3254 1342), sits in a quiet location off Brunswick, across the street from the river. Bright colors, loud music, and a display case full of goodies make this hip, half-inside, half-outside cafe popular with hungry locals. A selection of international dishes, including vegetarian. Famous for their Caesar salad ($10.50). Licensed. Open daily 8am-midnight.

Fortitude Valley

Lucky's Trattoria, 683 Ann St., seems to have achieved cult status with younger members of the Valley community. Pasta dishes and vegetarian food ($8-16).

Cafe Europe, 360 Brunswick St., is a popular French eatery ($11 and up for main dishes), partly because it catches hungry tourists and weary shoppers at the top of the Brunswick St. Mall.

Mellino's, on the Brunswick St. Mall, is a favorite with famished clubbers for a late-night re-energizer or an early morning pick-me-up; the cheap eatery serves breakfasts, pizzas and pastas and is open 24hr.

Garuva, 174 Wickham St., may have a bit of a wait for a table (a bar helps to pass the time), but soon enough you'll be whisked to the eating area, which is filled with incense, beads, mirrors, and tables so low to the ground you'll end up sitting on the floor.

South Bank

Sirocco (tel. 3846 1803), north South Bank Parklands. Popular, loud, and packed with couples and families on Sun., this Mediterranean restaurant has funky lighting and outdoor seating. On the weekends they bring in a band and diners dance 'til midnight. Entrees $8-13. Licensed. Book ahead for the weekend. Open daily for lunch from noon-3pm, dinner 6-10pm.

Cafe San Marco (tel. 3846 4334), South Bank Parklands, claims to have one of the best views of Brisbane in the city, and it's probably right. The outside terrace is strategically arched to give a view of the Captain Cook Bridge and the Brisbane skyline. The inside bar is long and cushioned with customers for the 5-6pm $5 cocktail happy hour. Although main courses run $8-14, you're welcome to order coffee and a muffin from the counter and revel outside in the river breeze. Open Sun.-Thurs. 8am-11pm, Fri.-Sat. 8am-midnight.

Chez Laila (tel. 3846 3402), South Bank Parklands, has an outdoor deck overlooking the river and city skyline and a cordoned-off living room area with couches, soft chairs, and coffee tables—perfect for nursing a cappuccino ($2.50). Shish kebab $11.50, vegetarian falafel plate $11. Open daily 8am-midnight.

SIGHTS AND MUSEUMS

On the south side of Victoria Bridge, the **Queensland Cultural Centre** (tel. 3840 7190) contains many of Brisbane's major artistic venues, including the art gallery, museum, performing arts complex, state library, and theater company.

Inside, the **Queensland Art Gallery** (tel. 3840 7303; 35¢ per min. infoline tel. 0055 39373) has over 10,000 works spread over two levels. Although it displays international and contemporary collections, the focus is on Australian art. Shallow pools of water cover the ground floor, and light bulbs within the pools lend a liquid, mesmerizing feel to surrounding paintings. The gallery's licensed cafe serves coffee, cakes, and sandwiches on a terrace facing the sculpture court. (Free admission to the permanent collections; special exhibitions charge fees. Open daily 10am-5pm. Guided 1hr. tours Mon.-Fri. 11am, 1, and 2pm; Sat.-Sun. 11am, 2, and 3pm.)

The **Queensland Museum** (tel. 3840 7555), spacious and brightly lit, houses dinosaur skeletons, whale models, and exhibits emphasizing cultural heritage and the environment. (Open 10am-5pm. Free admission to regular collection; special exhibitions admission $6, concessions $4, children $2.)

The Queensland Office of Arts and Cultural Development (tel. 3224 4248) publishes a pamphlet, *Brisbane Inner City Galleries,* which lists names, phone numbers, and addresses of all galleries within a 15-minute walk of the city center.

The collection in the **City Hall Art Gallery and Museum** in King George Square dates back to 1859, but currently focuses on Brisbane's young artists (open daily 10am-5pm; free admission). The **Institute of Modern Art** (tel. 3252 5750), on the corner of Ann and Gibbs St. in Fortitude Valley, is devoted to experimental Australian and contemporary international art (open Tues.-Fri. 11am-5pm, Sat. 11am-4pm).

Queensland Aboriginal Creations, 135 George St. (tel. 3224 4741), showcases Aboriginal prints, photography, printings, and sculpture (open Mon.-Fri. 8:30am-4:30pm).

The **Queensland State Library** (tel. 3840 7810) holds large collections of books, journals, newspapers, photographs, and music. The John Oxley Library (tel. 3840 7881), located on level four, is devoted to Queensland research and history, and holds historical exhibitions throughout the year. Technologically advanced, the State Library allows free public access to the Internet (bookings essential; call 3840 7785). Bags must be stored in lockers on level one (library open Mon.-Thurs. 10am-8pm, Fri.-Sun. 10am-5pm).

The **Sciencentre** (tel. 3220 0166), at 110 George St. (next to the Conrad International Hotel), has over 200 hands-on exhibits on three floors. (Open daily 10am-5pm. Admission $7, backpackers $6.30, children $5, families $24.)

City Tours

One of the best deals for a city tour is **City Sights,** offered through Brisbane Transport. An open tram-style bus covers 19 cultural and historical attractions during the 80-minute loop; passengers can get on and off at their leisure, but may want to take the loop through once and then begin to explore on foot. Tickets can be purchased on the bus, from any customer service center, or at most tourist info centers. The ticket allows unlimited access to all Council bus and ferry networks, including the City Cat ferry, for the day. (Tickets $15, children $10, families of up to 6 $30. Tours leave at 40min. intervals daily 9am-4:20pm.)

Earlystreet Village (tel. 3398 6866) is a five-acre area holding a collection of Queensland heritage buildings, including preserved houses from as early as 1865, re-created colonial stables, blacksmith's shops, cottages, and manicured gardens. Devonshire tea on lace tablecloths is served daily in the Gothic Garden; bookings are essential for lunch. Take bus #125, 145, 155, or 255 to stop 28A. Buses leave from the Ann St. side of King George Sq. (open Mon.-Sat. 10am-4:30pm, Sun. 11am-4:30pm). The City Council publishes a series of *Heritage Trail* brochures which detail self-guided walks through Brisbane's districts. For more information, call 3403 5232.

The City Hall was officially opened in 1930 and quickly earned the epithet "Million Pound Town Hall" for its outrageous building cost. The clock tower stands 92m high, and an **observation deck** with a nearly 360-degree view of the city is free and accessible to all. Take the City Hall elevator to the third floor (deck open Mon.-Fri. 8:30am-3:30pm, Sat. 10:30am-1pm). **City Hall** has 45-minute guided tours (tel. 3403 6586; Mon.-Fri. at 10am, noon, and 2pm; $4, concessions $3, under 13 free).

For a tour of the Brisbane River, the large **Kookaburra Queen** (tel. 3221 1300) paddlewheel boat departs daily from the Eagle St. Pier. A 90-minute tea cruise leaves at 10am ($20); the lunch cruise leaves at 12:45pm ($20-45, depending on menu); a Sunday afternoon tea cruise ($20) departs at 3:30pm; and nightly dinner cruises ($40 or $55) leave at 6:30pm. Book ahead.

Queensland's **XXXX** beer is brewed close to Brisbane, and it's common for hostels to organize free trips to tour the **Castlemaine Brewery** (free 40min. tours Mon.-Wed. 11am, 1:30, 4:30, and 7pm). Tours are followed by 30 minutes of free product sampling. The **Carlton Brewhouse** (tel. 3826 5858) in Yatala, producers of Victoria Bitter, Foster's, and Carlton beers, is 30 minutes south of Brisbane. CoachTrans stops in Yatala on the way to the Gold Coast and buses leave daily from the Transit Centre at 9:15am, 11:15am, and 1:15pm. Carlton's tours, too, are followed by a complimentary tasting session.

PARKS, GARDENS, AND OUTDOOR ACTIVITIES

Brisbane's **Botanic Gardens** (tel. 3403 7913) are a 15-minute walk from the city center. City Circle bus #333 stops at Albert or George St., near the entrance on Alice St. The gardens were begun in 1928 to supply fruit and vegetables to the penal colony at Moreton Bay, and seeds were later distributed to settlers for cultivation throughout Queensland. Today, visitors can take a pleasant stroll past the lily ponds, and through palm groves and camellia gardens. Free guided tours (tel. 3229 1554) leave from the rotunda near the Albert St. entrance (Tues.-Sun. at 11am and 1pm).

Brisbane's other botanic garden is **Mt. Coot-tha Park** (tel. 3403 2533), 7km from the city center. The park has a tropical dome (open daily 9:30am-4:30pm; free), a Japanese Garden, and a bamboo grove, among other attractions. Although organized tours and transportation tours are offered through private companies, the cheapest way to see the park is to take public bus #39A, or 598 and 599. A 30-minute walk from the gardens leads to the Mt. Coot-tha summit, which affords a spectacular view of greater Brisbane. The casual **Kuta Cafe** (licensed) and the more formal **Mt. Coot-tha Summit Restaurant** both have breathtaking views.

City Heights is a two-hour tour that leaves from the City Hall City Sights bus stop at 2pm and travels to the Mt. Coot-tha lookout and the Botanical Gardens (tickets $7, concessions $5, groups $15). The **City Nights** tour leaves the City Hall City Sights bus stop at 6pm, heads to Mt. Coot-tha, and then travels to South Bank and the Story Bridge (tickets $15, concessions $10, groups $30).

It took four years to transform the South Brisbane riverbank, site of the 1988 World Expo, into the 1.25km long **South Bank Parklands,** but the sights and activities now offered prove it was well worth the wait. Some choose to explore the three paid attractions: **Gondwana Rainforest Sanctuary, Butterfly House,** and the **South Ship Ferry** (see listings under **Wildlife,** below), but there's plenty to do for free. During the day, people swim in the man-made lagoon, bike along the designated pathway, check out the "Opal World" jewelry store, and hang from jungle gyms. On the weekends, the park center (behind the swimming lagoon) becomes home to crowded **craft markets** (held Fri. 5pm-10pm by lantern-light, Sat. 11am-5pm, Sun. 9am-5pm). The parklands are located just across the river to the left of the Victoria Bridge, and can be reached on foot, by bus (the orange B stop on Grey St.), CityTrain (South Brisbane or Vulture St. Stations), or by ferry (terminal stop South Bank). The **Visitor Information Centre** (tel. 3867 2051, 24hr. entertainment infoline 3867 2020) is toward the Victoria Bridge end of the park; maps, guides, and advice are all free (center open Sun.-Thurs. 8am-6pm, Fri.-Sat. 8am-8pm). The Parklands also has phones, toilet facilities, an ATM, a volleyball court, and, for good measure and a hint of mystery, a Nepalese Pagoda. Although there are no official gates, South Bank is "open" 5am to midnight (lifeguard on duty summer 5am-midnight; winter 7am-6pm).

Twenty minutes from the city, **Brisbane Forest Park** (tel. 3300 4855) covers 28,500 hectares. It's possible to picnic, camp, hike, birdwatch, cycle, and even ride horses. The *Information Guide* describes more than a dozen short and half-day walks, including the 1.7km Bellbird Grove's Turrbal Circuit Trail (with signs describing the life-style of Aboriginal dwellers), the Golden Boulder Track (which leads past abandoned gold digs), and the 1.5km Egernia Circuit Track (which cuts through a wet eucalypt forest).

Brisbane has many waterways that are perfect for **canoeing.** Maps and guides to the popular trails Oxely Creek and Boondsill Wetlands are available from libraries or tourist offices (for more information, call 3403 6757 or **Queensland Canoeing, Inc.,** at 3278 1033). Several companies rent canoes, including **Wild Adventure Sports,** Edward St. (tel. 3221 5747), and **Goodtime Surf and Sail,** 29 Ipswich Rd., Woolloongabba (tel. 3391 8588).

WILDLIFE

The South Bank Parklands shelter Brisbane's animal populations. The **Gondwana Wildlife Sanctuary** (tel. 3846 4155, info line 3846 2691), situated in a carefully reproduced rainforest, contains 700 native Australian animals and plants, many freed from cages and glass walls (the snakes and crocodiles, of course, are out of harm's way). Have your picture taken with a wombat, call back to kookaburras, and come nearly face to face with grandma turtles and baby crocs in the underwater crocodile lagoon. (Open daily 8am-5pm. Admission $12, concessions $9.50, children $7.50, family $32.)

The world's largest collection of Australian butterfly species flutters about in the humidity of the **South Bank Butterfly House** (tel. 3844 1112). If the captive butterflies don't hold your attention, watch the daily butterfly release or check out the creepy-crawly insects on the lower level. (Open daily 8:30am-5pm. Admission $7, with VIP $6.30, children and concessions $4.50, families $20. Guided tours $5 extra.)

A ticket on the **South Ship Ferry** buys unlimited one-day travel on a guided 30-minute ferry tour of the South Bank waterways (ferry tickets $5, children $5, families $13). The Visitor Centre sells discounted "Discovery" tickets for all three attractions on the South Bank.

Koala addicts can make plans to visit the world's largest sanctuary of its kind, the **Lone Pine Koala Sanctuary** (tel. 3378 1366; fax 3878 1770), in operation since 1927. The grounds teem with more than 80 species of Australian fauna, including the infamous tasmanian devils, emus, wombats, dingoes, reptiles, birds, kangaroos, and of course, koalas. Kids love it. Bus #581 departs from the underground Queen St. platform "Koala N" almost hourly; **Mirimax** boat cruises (tel. 3221 0300) depart daily from North Quay in the city center. (Open daily 8am-5pm. Admission $12.50, ages 3-13 $6.50, students $9, concessions $7.)

The **Alma Park Zoo** (tel. 3204 6566), 30 minutes north of Brisbane, is another sanctuary that allows hands-on contact with some of its animals. The zoo has walk-through kangaroo and deer enclosures, koalas, tropical monkeys, camels, and water buffalo. Twenty acres of gardens and barbecue facilities make it an ideal spot for a picnic (open daily 9am-5pm; admission $15, children and concessions $8).

The **Australian Woolshed** (tel. 3351 5366; fax 3351 5575) is all about sheep. The Ram Show gives a shearing demonstration, there's a wool spinning display, and you can even make a farm visit to koalas, wallabies, kangaroos, and cows—some of which you can touch and feed (admission $12, concessions $8, children $5.50). The Woolshed is located 800m from the Ferny Grove railway station in Ferny Hills, and has its own restaurant. The popular Bush Dance and Dinner (Fri. and Sat. nights, minimum age of 18) is in the restaurant.

ENTERTAINMENT

Brisbane is full of enough theaters to satisfy any culture-craving traveler. Call the Queensland Cultural Centre (tel. 3840 7190) for a current schedule and info on discounts. The **Performing Arts Complex,** located in the center on the south side of the river, is composed of three theaters; the **Concert Hall** hosts symphony and chamber orchestras; the 2000 seat **Lyric Theatre** sponsors performances like the Pirates of Penzance and the Bolshoi Ballet; and the 315-seat **Cremora Theater** stages more intimate productions. Whether or not you see action on stage, the theaters are gorgeous. Free guided tours of the complex leave weekdays at noon from the tour desk at the ticket sales foyer.

The **Queensland Conservatorium** (tel. 3875 6241, concert inquiries tel. 3875 6222) presents university staff, student, and fellows concerts for free or very low price admission. **Opera Queensland** (tel. 3875 3030) produces three extravagant productions a year. For contemporary Australian theater, **La Boite** (tel. 3369 1622) offers six plays annually. The **Queensland Ballet** (tel. 3846 5266), the oldest dance group in the country, is world renowned for its neo-classical style.

In the former state treasury building at the corner of Queen, Elizabeth, and George St., see a different kind of show at the Conrad International Treasury **Casino** (tel. 3306 8888). The ridiculously glitzy casino has four restaurants, over 100 gaming tables, and more than 1000 gaming machines, some which take as little as 5¢ a game to play (open 24hr.).

The **Entertainment Centre** (tel. 3265 8111, event info line 1902 241 131), on Melaleuca Dr. in Boondall, is Brisbane's largest indoor complex for sports, concerts, and special events. By Citytrain, take the Shorncliffe line to Boondall Station. The **"Gabba"** (tel. 3891 5464), at Vulture and Stanley St. in Woolloongabba, is Queensland's major cricket and football stadium, home of the Brisbane Lions AFL team. Take the bus to the station on the corner of Main and Stanley St.

Festivals in Brisbane include the **Queensland Winter Racing Carnival,** held each May and June, the **Biennial International Music Festival,** held in May and June of even years, and the **International Film Festival,** held each August.

NIGHTLIFE

Nights roll by with sweaty nightclubs, noisy pubs, and smoky jazz clubs. For a weekly rundown of what's happening, check out the Wednesday or Saturday edition of the *Courier-Mail.* Other entertainment guides are *Rave, Time Off, Scene,* and *Brother Sister* (a guide to gay and lesbian entertainment and clubs), all available at the record store **Rocking Horse,** 101 Adelaide St. (tel. 3229 5360), and at many local nightclubs.

For **after-hours transportation,** Brisbane Transport operates **Night Rider,** a late-night bus service on Friday and Saturday which loops between Brisbane's most popular inner city nightclubs. The route passes through Caxton St., Fortitude Valley, Riverside Centre, and city spots like the casino. Buses begin at 8pm and run every 15 minutes until 3am (fare $2). Call TransInfo (tel. 13 12 30) for more information.

Nightclubs

Brisbane's **mainstream** night scene is centered on Caxton St. in Petrie Terrace. People refer to the area as "the Triangle" because the four nightclubs—the **Underground, Casablanca's, Hotel LA,** and the **Caxton Street Hotel**—are in close proximity to each other. The first two are particularly attractive to backpackers.

The **alternative** scene is concentrated mainly in Fortitude Valley. Particularly lively clubs are the **Beat,** 677 Ann St. (tel. 3253 2543), and, on the other side of the Brunswick St. Mall, **The Tube** at 210 Wickham St. The Beat is wildly popular, plays loud techno music, and is gay-oriented; the Tube, especially in the summer, plays equally loud funk, and sponsors occasional raves (open nightly 9pm-5am; $5 cover after 11pm). Two blocks down from The Tube is **Hotel Wickham,** 308 Wickham St. (tel. 3852 1301). During the day this is a friendly, relaxed, gay-and lesbian-focused bar. At night it brings in a DJ, pumps up the dance music, and holds wild drag parties (open daily noon-5am). Upstairs at the Empire Hotel, at the corner of Ann and Brunswick St., is **Super Deluxe,** an alternative dance club packed to capacity with backpackers and twenty-somethings looking for loud music and cheap beer (9-11pm stubbies and spirits $2; open Fri.-Sat. 9pm-5am).

The gay-oriented **Out,** 25 Warner St. (tel. 33257 0619), parallel to the Brunswick St. Mall, has disco balls, purple walls, green marble poles, a laser lighting show, and UK/Detroit techno on Saturdays; every Sunday night is "Go Girl," a female-only night (cover $8; open 9pm-5am). The **Sportsman Hotel and Bar,** 130 Leichhardt St. in Spring Hill (tel. 3831 2892), is dark and smoky and has drag shows Friday and Saturday nights (open daily 1pm-3am). Down the street from the Sportsman is **Options** (tel. 3831 4214), at the corner of Leichhardt and Little Edward St., another popular night club center of the hip gay scene (open Wed.-Sun. 8:30pm-5am).

City Powers at the trendy Eagle St. Pier is up-market and crowded with suited business-types drinking martinis in the early evening hours, but as the night wears on, the suits disappear. *Vogue* magazine's idea of a singles bar, the jazz and blues bar **Travelodge,** is on the ground floor of the Roma St. Travelodge (tel. 3238 2222). It hosts a mostly business crowd on Friday afternoons, but at night becomes mixed and very, very friendly. Friday and Saturday nights are devoted to acid funk (open Mon.-Fri. 4:30pm-late, Sat.-Sun. 6pm-late).

Backpacker Nights

Backpackers tread a well-known and religiously-followed path of pubs through the week. Monday nights are spent at the **Story Bridge Hotel,** 200 Main St., Kangaroo Point (tel. 3391 2266). Wednesdays are at the **Sly Fox Hotel,** 73 Melbourne St., South Brisbane, where $5 gets you a meal and jug of beer. **Rosie's,** on Edward St. in the city center, is a new competitor, serving free drinks from 7 to 9pm. On Friday and Saturday nights, young partiers lured by cheap drinks and table dancing descend on the **Down Under Bar** at the Palace, at the corner of Ann and Edward St. in the city center. The **Brunswick Hotel,** 569 Brunswick St., New Farm (tel. 3358 1181), still attracts crowds on Fridays with meals from $3.50, sumo wrestling, and pool competitions. **Hogie's,** on Mary St. in the city center, has $1 drinks until midnight and $2 drinks afterwards every night. The more mellow crowd plays pool upstairs while the rowdier backpacker-types congregate downstairs at the nightclub.

MORETON BAY

The forest of masts on the tranquil marina in Manly promises smooth sailing on the crystal-clear waters of Moreton Bay. Here, at the mouth of the Brisbane River, thrives a comfortable culture in perpetual slow-motion. Across the bay, North Stradbroke Island offers wonderful snorkeling, diving, and swimming. Although the area as a whole doesn't have much pre-packaged fun, its out-of-the-way location contributes to a refreshingly quiet atmosphere. Stroll in solitude along Manly's peaceful boardwalk to Wynnum's mangrove sanctuary or whack your way through North Stradbroke Island's bush. If you've had your fill of crowds, surf, and high-rises, Moreton Bay offers a pleasant place to unwind in relative seclusion.

Manly

Manly is a rightfully content harborside village on Moreton Bay. To enter it is to forget the sight of a skyscraper, the sound of a raucous party, and the exhaustion of the rat race. The main shopping street leads to a picturesque harbor filled with unmasted ships, and provided you have your own equipment or book on a tour, you can fish, sail, or scuba dive. But many looking for a slower pace just walk for hours along the Esplanade, a foot and bike path that runs along the bay for miles and is bordered by strings of green parks. Manly is also an alternate accommodation base for exploring Brisbane (25-30min. away by train) or many of the nearby islands.

ORIENTATION AND PRACTICAL INFORMATION

Manly is easily accessible by public transportation. From Brisbane, $4 buys a round-trip Citytrain ticket on the Cleveland line; the ride takes 30 minutes from Central Station. To reach Manly's **commercial district** and the **harbor,** exit the station grounds and walk out of the parking lot, straight past the small rotary, and left onto **Cambridge Parade.** Bear right so the small park is on your left, and continue to the far end of Cambridge Pde. Shops include a **supermarket, bank, post office,** bakery, seafood store, and butcher shop, all open daily, and several small cafes and restaurants. The **tourist office** is in the **Nautical Gift Shop** (tel. 3839 1936), next door to Nomad's Moreton Bay Lodge. A brisk 30-minute walk from the harbor (facing the harbor, turn left) brings you to the center of **Wynnum by the Bay,** a nearby town.

ACCOMMODATIONS AND FOOD

Nomads Moreton Bay Lodge, 45 Cambridge Pde. (tel. 3396 3020), is the best bet for backpacker-style lodging. It has impeccably clean, spacious rooms with fresh linen, a TV lounge area, a functional kitchen, and spotless bathrooms. Nomads also offers trips to Peel Island ($85) and Moreton Island ($245), which include two nights at the lodge. (6-bed dorms $14; singles $30, with bath $35; doubles $40, $50; triples $50, $60; suite $60, $70. Weekly: dorms $91. Key deposit $20.) A neat symmetry divides the hostel from the casual but lovely **Bay Window Cafe and Bar** (tel. 3396 3020), which has gorgeous harbor-view windows and serves coffee and thick slices of cake for $4.50 (meals $7-15).

Manly Hotel (tel. 3396 8188), across the street, is a newly remodeled favorite of businessmen paying by company check. Wood paneling, thick patterned rugs, and leather chairs adorn the newer, small-sized rooms (doubles $90). The older section has more simply furnished rooms (singles $35, with bath and A/C $45; doubles $45, with bath and A/C $55). **Pelican's Inn,** 143 the Esplanade, Wynnum (tel. 3396 3214), has two-bedroom units with bath, kitchen, dining area, and living room for $280 per week (each additional person $5). Across the street from the Inn is a huge saltwater wading pool, parks, and a pier extending to the bay.

Taking full advantage of its seaside locale, Moreton Bay eateries tend to serve fish, fish, exotic Australian animals, and fish. **Pelican's Nest,** next door to the Pelican's Inn in Wynnum, is a clean, sharp version of the typical streetside fish and chips shop; it's run by Mike O'Shea, a community linchpin, and the ceiling is covered with real hang-gliders. Offerings include salad ($8), freshly breaded and grilled fish ($1.50-4.50), and a popular fish smorgasbord ($15.80). The **Fish Cafe** (tel. 3893 0195) at the corner of Cambridge Pde. and the Esplanade in Manly, is an idyllic three-in-one eatery. The take-away menu includes huge kangaroo and crocodile burgers ($4-6), fish and chips ($1.50-5), and large milkshakes ($2). The cafe terrace has lighter fare. The indulgent venture into the front room of the restaurant, where floor-to-ceiling picture windows showcase the excellent harbor view. **William's Fish Cafe** is at the corner of St. Catherine's Tce. and Cusack Pde., halfway to Manly from the Pelican's Nest. William's opened before WWII, and, in its own idiosyncratic way, is still going strong. It's open Thursday through Sunday from noon and closes without warning on school holidays, but residents patiently wait and obediently return to its lime green countertops when it reopens.

SIGHTS AND ENTERTAINMENT

What Manly-Wynnum lacks in nightlife it makes up for in natural beauty. An hour's stroll along the Esplanade (through Wynnum, past the end of the harborwalk, through the soccer fields) leads to the **Wynnum Mangrove Boardwalk,** a 500m walk guided by informative signs. The mangroves grow in dense concentration and it's possible to see clearly their *pneumatophores,* specialized "breathing roots," protruding through the mud in small clumps. For the history buff, the Brisbane City Council's *Heritage Trail: Wynnum-Manly* booklet outlines a fascinating daytrip in the region.

Across the street from the Pelican's Nest is the huge **Wynnum tidal pool.** Because the muddy bay is unsuitable, people swim here instead. In the afternoons, some race model sailboats across the length. Parks with colorful changing rooms and toilet facilities run along the Esplanade, and there are plenty of barbecues.The Wynnum **public pool,** on the Esplanade, is open September to April from 8am to 7pm (admission $2, children $1.60). If sailing floats your boat, book a trip on **Solo** (tel. 3893 1936), a famous Australian ocean racing yacht (Thurs.-Sun.). A daytrip ($48) includes snorkeling, swimming, sand tobogganing on Moreton Island, and water tobogganing. For free sailing, show up at noon on Wednesdays at The **Royal Queensland Sailing Club** (tel. 3396 8666). Yacht owners are always looking for temporary crew; if you are a beginner, they may teach you. **Alibi Charters** (tel. 3893 1936) operates daily offshore reef fishing trips.

Near Moreton Bay is **St. Helena Island,** currently a boulevard-filled national park but once a jail for Queensland's toughest criminals. A 30-minute cruise from Manly aboard the **Cat-o'-Nine-Tails** and a guided island tour on a horse-drawn carriage will set you back $28 (concessions $23, children $15; call 3396 3994 to book). The Cat-o'-Nine-Tails visits several tourist destinations, including Peel Island and the Tangalooma Wrecks, a scuba diving haven.

The whale-watching vessel **Satrya Express** cruises daily during whale season (mid-May to early Nov. 9:30am-3pm; tickets $75, children $40). Queensland National Parks and Wildlife Service publishes a helpful pamphlet on the history and features of the **world's second largest sand island,** Moreton Island, located near Moreton Bay. The island is completely uninhabited. Camping is allowed, but permits from QNP&WS are required. Call the ranger station at 3408 2710 for more information. Several boats go to the island, including the **Moreton Venture** barge from Whyte Island (tel. 3895 1000; departs daily except Tues.), the **Combie Trader** from Scarborough Harbor (tel. 3203 6299), and the **M.V. Sirenia** from Redland Bay (tel. 3829 0600; departs Fri.-Sun.).

North Stradbroke Island

A fierce cyclone in 1896 cleanly severed what was once Stradbroke Island, creating distinct northern and southern land masses. While South Stradbroke has remained relatively uninhabited, its northern neighbor is now home to 3500 people, mainly miners and their families. Many residents claim that North Stradbroke Island is Australia's best-kept and best-protected secret, and they have a valid case. Miles of white beaches with great surf and famously blue inland lakes make for ideal swimming. Some boast that the nearby dive sites compete with those at the Great Barrier Reef. They're certainly popular with manta rays, trumpet fish, turtles, dolphins, whales, gray nurse sharks, tuskfish, moorish idols, and sea urchins. Point Lookout is the easternmost point in all of Australia, which makes it an ideal land-based lookout for the annual whale migration from the Antarctic between late May and early November.

ORIENTATION AND PRACTICAL INFORMATION

North Stradbroke Island has three distinct townships: **Dunwich,** the ferry drop-off point and home to many mining families; **Amity Point,** north of Dunwich and near great surfing beaches; and **Point Lookout,** 22km northeast of Dunwich, with two hostels. The southern end of the island is mostly lakes, swamps, national park land, and habitat reserves.

Despite its sense of isolation, North Stradbroke can be easily reached from Brisbane by public transportation. Take Citytrain to the Cleveland stop; the courtesy bus **Stradbroke Flyer** (tel. 3821 3821) regularly delivers passengers to the ferry depot, 2km away, and then has a water taxi service to the island. The **Stradbroke Water Taxi** (tel. 3286 2666) departs Cleveland 10 times per day from 7am (Sat.-Sun. 8am) to 6pm (Fri. 7pm). Round-trip tickets are $40, and the trip takes about 30 minutes each way. The **Vehicular Ferry** (tel. 3286 2666) also operates several times per day (starts running Mon.-Sat. 5am, Sun. 6:45am; 1hr.). Passengers can sit up on deck (round-trip car transport $67, passengers $8).

The **North Stradbroke Island Bus Service** (tel. 3211 2501) runs from Brisbane to Point Lookout and includes ferry service (departs the Roma Street BCC stop #1 Mon.-Fri. 8, 9am, 12:30, 4, and 5pm). The service also runs between Point Lookout, Amity, and Dunwich 10 times per day; the tourist office carries schedules. During the day the **Stradbroke Island Taxi** (tel. 3409 9124) usually waits at the top of the hill, across from the bakery. Most, if not all, **car rental** companies on the mainland will not rent vehicles to Stradbroke Island travelers because of problems with salt corrosion. If you want to see the island by car, **Stradbroke Island Tours** (tel. 3409 8051) offers half and full-day 4WD tours ($25, $50). Private cars need to buy beach access permits from the tourist office. Local Aboriginal guides lead 90-minute walking tours of Dunwich, pointing out and explaining bush tucker, bush medicine, and Aboriginal artifacts (Mon. and Fri. $12; call the tourist office to book).

The **tourist office** (tel. 3409 9555) is the yellow building to the left and at the base of the Dunwich green. The *What's on Where* guide is helpful. (Open Mon.-Fri. 8:30am-4pm, Sat.-Sun. 8:30am-3:30pm. Beach access permits $5 for 48hr., $10 per week.) Although there's no bank on the island, the three post office branches serve as Commonwealth bank agents and several shops have EFTPOS. Point Lookout has small general stores, but since most close by 6pm and are expensive, it's best to bring your own supply of food.

ACCOMMODATIONS, FOOD, AND PUBS

The tourist office has brochures for several of the island's resorts, hotels, campgrounds, and hostels. The island has two good hostels, both in Point Lookout. **Stradbroke Island Guesthouse** (tel. 3409 8888; fax 3409 8715) is on the left at the entrance to the Point Lookout area and sits close to Home Beach. The rooms are functional and tidy, with a huge shared kitchen and a lounge area with games tables (6-bed dorms $15; doubles and triples $35). A courtesy bus ($7) departs Monday,

Wednesday, and Friday at 2:30pm from the Abbey Hotel, across from the Roma St. Transit Center in Brisbane; book ahead.

The Stradbroke Island Hostel, 79 Mooloomba Rd. (affectionately known as "Straddie Hostel," tel. 3409 8679) is halfway between the Guesthouse and the end of Point Lookout. Relaxed and much more communal than the Guesthouse, it also has one of the most colorful common area lounges in the region; the walls seem supported by decorated surf boards, the hat rack is a sturdy tree branch, and a bed draped with colorful fabric serves as the TV couch. Purple-walled bedrooms have ceiling fans and there's a small, oldish kitchen (6-bed dorms $12; sectioned-off doubles $28).

Stradbroke Tourist Park (tel. 3409 8127) has a range of accommodations, including cabins with bath, A/C, and TV (1 person $38; weekly $239), tent sites (2 adults $10; weekly $57), and a backpackers' cabin ($10). The island also has six ranger-operated campsites, most of which have powered sites, toilets, showers, and caravan sites. Rates range from $10 per night to $50 per week.

Up the hill from the ferry landing at Dunwich is a small row of shops, including a bakery and a take-out. Most food is in Point Lookout, which has several eateries clustered in the Lookout Shopping Village and Centre Point Shopping Centre, both along two main roads. The Straddie Hotel on East Coast Road operates the **Waves Brasserie** (tel. 3409 8188; meals $5-15; open daily for lunch noon-2pm, dinner 5-8pm). There's live entertainment on weekends, with blues on Friday nights, rock on Saturday nights, and Sunday afternoon jazz. The adjoining **Straddie Hotel Pub** is the main watering hole for locals, and is packed on the weekends. The owner of the **Blue Water Bistro** (tel. 3409 8300), Centre Point Shopping Village, is one of Queensland's top chefs and spends his days fishing and his nights frying the day's catch for appreciative diners. Finally, the **Laughing Buddha Cafe** (tel. 3409 8549), on the end of Mooloomba Rd., serves up some of the best coffee and cake on the island.

SIGHTS AND ACTIVITIES

The easiest and cheapest thing to do on North Stradbroke Island is walk—miles of unspoiled beaches, dirt roads, and seemingly unexplored bush will keep a spirited traveler busy for days. Heading toward the end of Point Lookout on the left is a "Beach Access" sign for Frenchman's Beach, a convenient starting point for any beach walk. Further up and near the RSL Club, find the entrance to the **Gorge Walk,** a 15-minute stroll along sea cliffs, famous for dolphin-spotting. The Gorge Walk also passes "The Blowhole," so named because crashing waves are channeled up a narrow gorge and transformed into fountains of dolphin-like spray. A swimming lagoon 4.5km along the beach, past the RSL Club, makes a lovely day hike, swimming, or picnic spot. On hot summer days, **Myora Springs** is a refreshing way to cool off.

The island is perhaps most famous for its scuba diving, and $35 buys an introductory lesson and equipment rental from The **Stradbroke Island Scuba Center** (tel. 3409 8715; fax 3409 8588), located below the Guesthouse. Daily boat trips to the island's 15 dive sites leave at 9, 11:30am, and 2pm; there's a scuba tank in the back for beginners to practice. Snorkeling is $39 for the boat trip and gear.

For alternative adventures, **Island Boat Mine** (tel. 3409 8896) rents boats, and **Straddie Kites** (tel. 3409 8145) rents kites. The island's breezes make either a great choice. The **Eagle's Nest Ropes Course** costs $49 per half-day (Sun.-Tues. 9am and 1pm). The folks at **Sea Kayaks** (tel. 3409 8082, 3409 8696) offer daily three-hour trips at 8:30am and 2pm; they can also take you sandboarding for two hours ($25).

GOLD COAST

With gorgeous beaches, thumping nightclubs, excellent theme parks, and plenty of accommodations, the Gold Coast is justifiably known as Australia's premier holiday destination. The region's population quadruples to 1.2 million every summer as Australian and foreign tourists alike flock to the sun, sand, and party. The term "Gold

Coast" has a few possible origins, each of which addresses the Coast's lure. Tourist officials say it's for the stretches of golden sand beaches; cynics point to high rises and tacky tinsel glitter; realists note the high concentration of visitors in their golden years. The seniors linger longer in Tweed Heads-Coolangatta, with its lower expenses and fewer high-rises, than they do in Surfers Paradise, although both have near-perfect beaches. For the younger set, the combination of New York City skyline and Bahamas surf seems irresistible, yet the more ambitious may find an extended stay culturally dulling. The glitz and noise and tanning opportunities that comprise the Coast's siren song ensure that passing travelers will succumb, if only briefly, to the well-hyped thrill.

Surfers Paradise

Surfers, at the heart of the Gold Coast, makes no pretense about its function: to house and entertain scores of thousands of eager annual visitors. Hotel towers stand high and close together, blocking out unlucky neighbors' sunlight and creating an oddly sci-fi atmosphere of extremes. Miles of gorgeous beach are literally a block from the lightbulb-framed storefronts packed in along the main drags and side alleys. This long, narrow strip of faux-Las Vegas hugs the beach. A huge Australian family resort and an enormous draw for Japanese tourists, Surfers also appears on nearly every backpacker's itinerary for two reasons: the stuporous days at the beach and the intoxicating possibilities for nightlife. If days here are hot, nights are hotter, as clubs throb with techno and 5am closing times often just transfer the parties into the street. Although Surfers is neither quiet nor natural, nearby national parks such as Lamington National Park and sights like Tamborine Mountain and the Natural Arch swimming hole provide opportunities for a day or two of outdoor exploration. But for those content to sink into the hedonism of neon-streaked nightclubs or dazzling Pacific waters, Surfers is a self-contained Paradise.

ORIENTATION AND PRACTICAL INFORMATION

Maps of Surfers Paradise are long and narrow and reflect that the entire culture is squeezed into a strip only blocks wide between the Pacific Ocean and the **Nerang River** and then stretch for many kilometers. The **Gold Coast Hwy.** and the **Esplanade** are the main thoroughfares, which run parallel to the coast and cross dozens of smaller streets at not-quite-perpendicular angles.

Central Surfers is most easily distinguished by the **Paradise Centre** pedestrian shopping mall, enclosed by the Esplanade and the highway, **Cavill Mall** to the north and Hanlan St. to the south. Consider employing the pink-and-turquoise hotel skyscrapers as landmarks for determining your latitudinal position.

The Esplanade runs north along the beachfront from Surfers, past Main Beach to the Marina and **the Spit,** the end of a peninsula of land just past Seaworld. To the south is **Broadbeach,** home to the enormous Conrad Hotel Jupiter Casino and directly across Hooker Blvd. from the monolithic **Pacific Fair Shopping Centre.**

Tourist Office: Gold Coast Tourism Bureau (tel. 5538 4419; fax 5570 3259) has two centers: an outside kiosk on Hanlon St. and an kiosk inside the Cavill Mall. Both sell bus schedules for 20¢.

Buses: Surfers Paradise Bus Station, or the Transit Centre, services the major bus companies from the corner of Beach Rd. and Remembrance Dr., 1 block west of Paradise Centre. There's a **backpackers accommodation desk** (tel. 5592 2911), where the staff will gladly call for courtesy pick-up to area hostels (open daily 8:30am-6pm).

Public Transportation: Surfside (tel. 5536 7666), the local 24hr. bus company, runs every 10min. from the back of the Pacific Fair mall to Surfers for $1.70.

Taxis: If a bus won't get you where you need to go, try **Regent Taxis** (tel. 13 10 08).

Car Rental: Kangaroo Car Hire, 18-20 Orchid Ave. (tel. 5592 1788), has old car rentals for $19 per day and new cars from $29, with free pick-up and delivery.

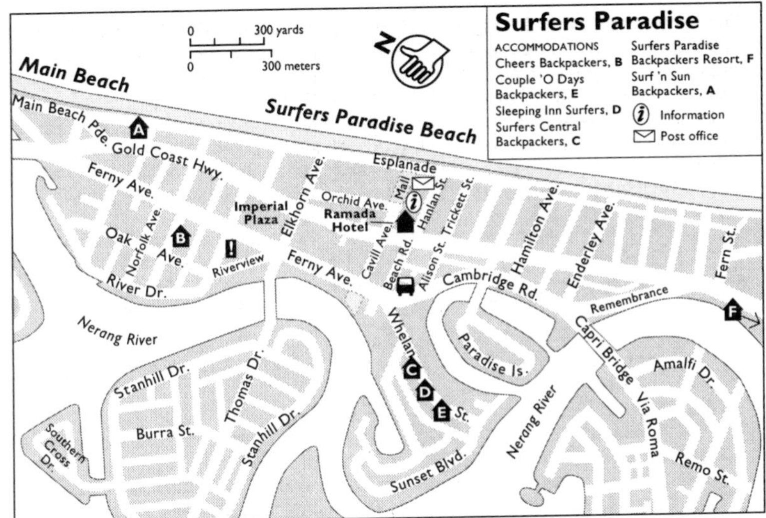

Under-21s rent from $35 per day (tel. 5570 1300). Moped rental for 2hr. $35. **Thrifty** (tel. 5538 6591) rents from $29 per day, and **Surfers Rent-A-Car** (tel. 5572 0600) rents small cars from $15 per day and gives every 8th day free.

Emergency: Dial 000.

Medical Services: The medical center (tel. 5539 8044) is on Trickett St. The Gold Coast **hospital** can be reached at 5571 8211.

Police: At 68 Ferny Ave. (tel. 5570 7888), opposite the Cypress Ave. carpark.

Post Office: Main post office is inside the Cavill Mall. Open Mon.-Fri. 8:30am-5:30pm, Sat. 9am-noon. **Postal code:** 4217.

Phone Code: 07.

ACCOMMODATIONS

Most people come to Surfers to party, and the backpacker hostels keep that well in mind when creating their atmosphere. Quieter accommodations may be found at highway strip motels, which may have doubles as low as $30. Of the hostels described below, only five are in the city center. The other four, although arguably nicer, are a good 30- to 50-minute walk north in **Southport.** All have kitchens, laundry, pools, courtesy pick-up from the Transit Centre, and near-nightly trips to the pubs and nightclubs. Because of the tough competition, prices are subject to change.

Cheers, 8 Pine Ave. (tel. 5531 6539 or 1800 636 539; fax 5575 6750), 5 blocks down Ferny Ave. toward Southport; take a left on Pine Ave. Friendly, large, and loud, Cheers delivers a bar with a 3am license, a huge video screen that plays rock videos and movies, weekly theme nights, cheap meals, and lots of music. The rooms aren't in the best shape, but they're sufficient and three-quarters of the beds are waterbeds. Self-contained apartments owned by Cheers are across the street. Dorms $14-15, weekly $85; doubles $28-32.

Sleeping Inn Surfers, 26 Whelan St. (tel. 5592 4455). This immaculate hostel has self-contained dorm units. Decidedly not a party hostel, this mellow place keeps its theme nights low-key. Palm trees line the grounds, and there's a covered outdoor common area with a pool table and BBQ. Units have central kitchens, small living rooms with TVs, and 5 beds in 2 bedrooms. Staff speaks Japanese. Dorms $16, weekly $98; doubles $40. VIP, YHA, ISIC.

Surf 'n' Sun, 3323 Gold Coast Hwy. (tel. 5592 2363), 4 blocks toward Southport, the hostel is on the corner with Ocean Ave. Recently renovated and a block from the beach, diminutive Surf 'n' Sun lazes around the pool out front and maintains a comfortable—though deliberately party-oriented—atmosphere. Unrefurbished dorm rooms have bathrooms, a sink, TV, and fridge. Dorms $15-16, weekly $95; doubles $36. VIP, YHA. Meals ($4) offered 3 times per week.

Trekkers, 22 White St. (tel. 5591 5616), is near Southport's "Australia Fair" shopping complex. Walk north from Surfers for 45min. or pay $1 for the bus. 10-15min. from Main Beach. The small house sometimes feels cramped, particularly the downstairs kitchen, but there's another upstairs next to a common space with couches, a piano, and board games. The mellow, friendly staff tend spotless rooms with private baths. Reception open daily 7am-noon and 5-7:30pm. Dorms $15; doubles $32. Weekly: $85; $190. VIP, YHA.

Surfers Paradise Backpackers Resort, 2837 Gold Coast Hwy. (tel. 5592 4677), a good 30min. walk south along the highway to the corner of Wharf Rd., in front of the Parkroyal Hotel. The newer hostel building surrounds a half-court for tennis and volleyball, and older self-contained apartments with decks are next door. The big kitchen and TV room are kept as tidy as the clean dorm rooms (with private bath). The games room has a new nautilus weight machine, a pool table, and a sauna ($4 for 45min). Max. stay 2 weeks. 5-bed dorms $15; doubles $36. Weekly: $93; $120. VIP. Book 1-2 weeks in advance in summer.

British Arms International Backpackers Resort, 70 Seaworld Dr. (tel. 5571 1776 or 1800 680 269; fax 5571 1747), 30min. north of Surfers on the way to Seaworld. British Arms is a new YHA affiliate on the water at Fisherman's Wharf. Rooms are clean and bare. An outdoor wraparound porch deck with chairs and picnic tables acts as the walkway between the dorms and a functional indoor common room/TV area/kitchen. 6-bed dorms $14, weekly $85; doubles $32. VIP, YHA. The hostel is directly across from the British Arms pub, which gives daily happy hour drinks and $3 discounts on meals to guests.

Surfers Central Backpackers, 40 Whelan St. (tel. 5538 4344), 2 blocks down Whelan St. off Ferny Ave. Although it's the closest hostel to the city center, Surfers Central is a little low on atmosphere. Staff's helpful, kitchen's large, pool's big, but the centerpiece is a carpark. Complimentary tea and coffee, squash court, and TV lounge. 8 and 4-bed dorms with bath $16, weekly $100; doubles $40.

Couple O' Days Backpackers, 18 Whelan St. (tel. 5592 4200 or 1800 646 586). A little worn around the edges but with a quiet, focused atmosphere. Small kitchen, TV lounge. 6-bed dorms $12; doubles $28. Weekly: $70; $168.

Gold Coast Backpacker Resort, 44 Queen St. (tel. 5531 2004), at the corner of Queen St. and S. Scarborough St. in Southport, 45min. from the city center. The silent hostel keeps fairly clean but feels empty on atmosphere and little in the way of homey decorations. 3-to 4-bed dorms $14, weekly $84; doubles $28.

FOOD

Surfers has dozens of inexpensive cafes and bistros and offers good deals on hotel buffet meals. Right in the middle of things, **Sweethearts Wholefoods** (tel. 5538 6299), on Orchid Ave., has big healthy sandwiches, burgers, salads, and vegetarian meals for $4-7 (open daily 8am-5:30pm). For Asian fare, the **Cavill Ave. Mall** has two all-you-can-eat Chinese restaurants with $7 lunches and dinners. A block over on Hanlan St., **Sushi Train** circulates plates of sushi ($2-6) on little engines that run on wide circular tracks (open daily noon-2:30pm and 5:30-9:30pm).

A couple of good seafood takeaways near the Spit on Seaworld Dr. warrant a visit if you're in the area and like fresh fish. **Peter's Fisherman's Markets** (tel. 5591 7747) sells fresh and cooked fish from the wharf; a fish and chips takeaway is $5 (open Mon.-Fri. 9am-8pm, Sat.-Sun. 8am-8pm; cooked fish available noon-8pm). Across from the British Arms hotel, brightly colored **Frenchy's Seafood Restaurant** (tel. 5531 3030) sits right on the water. Takeaway fish and chips for $6 or sit down to a slightly more expensive meal (open Mon.-Sat. noon-3pm and 5:30-9pm, Sun. noon-9pm).

The Hospitality Training Company Australia operates **Ghekko's** (tel. 5538 3786), on the Gold Coast Hwy., a couple of blocks past the Cavill Mall toward Broadbeach. The small, meticulously tidy tables contribute to the cozy atmosphere. Nicely prepared mains range $8-11 and a set menu meal is $15 (open in summer Tues.-Sat. 8am-9pm; in winter Tues.-Sat. 5-9pm).

SIGHTS AND ACTIVITIES

A typical day at Surfers is spent lazing on the beach, visiting one of the nearby huge theme parks, or shopping in the enormous mall complexes. Tours visit scenery away from the coast, and a couple of museums entertain visitors on the odd rainy day or when beach burn-out strikes suddenly.

Beaches, Surfing, and Water Sports

The beach stretches, unbroken, from the quiet **Main Beach** on the Spit peninsula to Duranbah. The most popular beach is **Surfers North,** near the end of Staghorn Ave. and just north of **Surfers Paradise,** the most central hangout off the Paradise Centre Mall and the recipient of blaring music from the local radio station during the summer. Farther south is **Broadbeach,** then **Kurrawa,** near the Pacific Fair Shopping Center. **Burleigh Heads** has a popular surfing area, though it can get very crowded.

For equipment rental, the **Surfers Beach Hut** kiosk (tel. 5526 7077), on the beach end of the Cavill Mall, rents long boards at $25 per day, and short boards, in-line skates, and mountain bikes at $20 per day (open daily 9am-4pm). **Dial-A-Sports** (tel. 018 764 170) has slightly cheaper prices and free delivery and pick-up (open daily 7:30am-8:30pm). Both companies also rent flippers and wetsuits. **Coast to Coast Surfing School** (tel. 5536 9881) has daily learn-to-surf classes.

Theme Parks

Dreamworld (tel. 5573 3300 or 1800 073 300), in Coomera, 25 minutes from Surfers, mirrors Disney World—with a down-under twist. Water rides, koala and kangaroo petting, a "tiger island" with five trained Bengal tigers, and a six-story IMAX screen theater rank among the park's highlights. "The Tower of Terror," the world's tallest, fastest ride, drops passengers 38 stories in seven seconds, producing speeds up to 160kph and impressive rushes of adrenaline. (Park open daily 10am-5pm. Admission $39, concessions and ages 4-13 $22; return pass valid for 14 days $10.)

Movieworld (tel. 5573 8485), 20 minutes north of Surfers, shows off a Warner Brothers theme focusing on Hollywood characters. There's a Police Academy stunt show, adrenaline-injecting rides such as the Lethal Weapon, studio tours, music and special effects talks, and a grand illusion/Wild West show. (Open daily 10am-5pm. Admission $39, concessions and ages 4-13 $34.)

The closest theme park to Surfers, **Seaworld,** near the Spit north of Surfers on Seaworld Dr., has sharks, dolphins, seals, and a water park with thrill rides. (Open daily 9:30am-5pm. Admission $39, ages 4-13 $24.)

On hot summer days the white water flumes of **Wet 'n' Wild** water park (tel. 5573 2277) will cool you down. Other attractions include dry courts for volleyball and soccer, a giant 60kph speed slide, and on summer nights, a movie screen above a wave pool with new release screenings. (Open daily from 10am; closing times vary. Admission $21, children $15.)

Several companies offer transportation to and from the Gold Coast theme parks. The cheapest option is **Surfside** (tel. 13 12 30); return transport is free if you buy the ticket on the bus. **Coachtrans** (tel. 5588 8788) runs between Dreamworld, Movieworld, Wet 'n' Wild, Cable Sports World, and Currumbin Sanctuary for $12 return (children $6, families $28); travel to Seaworld is half-price. Service is door-to-door and requires advance booking. **Activetours** (tel. 5597 0344) and the **Gold Coast Tourist Shuttle** (tel. 5592 4166) also have transfers to theme parks for $12 (children $6).

Museums

The **Ripley's Believe It or Not** museum (tel. 5592 0040), in the Cavill Mall, has the usual optical illusions, magic tricks, and tales of the gross and macabre. (Open daily 9am-11pm. Admission $10, children $6; family discount 10% if you ask for it.)

The **Wax Museum,** 3049 Gold Coast Hwy. (tel. 5538 3975), between Hanlan and Trickett St., has a decent collection of "famous people," fantasy figures, and, for a separate admission fee, a "chamber of horrors" which documents historical methods of torture (open daily 10am-10pm; admission $8.50, children $5.50, families $15).

More traditional art, including art films and a free **art gallery** (tel. 5581 6520), can be found at the **Gold Coast Arts Centre,** 135 Bundall Rd. (tel. 5581 6800), about 3km from the city center (open Mon.-Fri. 10am-5pm, Sat.-Sun. 1-5pm).

Tours

The **Carlton Brewery** (tel. 3826 5858), in Yatala, 35 minutes north of Surfers, has tours, interactive exhibits, and free tastings. CoachTrans departs Surfers at 9am and 1:40pm for the brewery.

If you don't have a car, the easiest way to see the "green behind the gold" is by tour. **Mountain Coach Company** (tel. 5524 4249) has a bus tour of Lamington National Park, Mt. Tamborine, the botanic gardens, and famous O'Reilly's Guesthouse. Tours leave Coolangatta, Burleigh, and Surfers ($35, children $17). **Scenic Hinterland Bus Tours** (tel. 5545 2030) provides a similar tour ($29, pick-up included) to Lamington, O'Reilly's Guesthouse, and Mt. Tamborine. Bushwalking tours to Lamington and the Natural Arch are particularly popular with the summer backpacker crowd. Ample opportunities for swimming complement 5km of walking trails. Tours include a BBQ lunch with lots of wine ($23, free pick-up from hostels). Book through your hostel.

Shopping

The massive commercial centers of Surfers Paradise elevate shopping beyond the practical. Surfers Central has many international shops, especially duty-free stores geared toward Japanese tourists. The enormous **Pacific Fair Mall** (tel. 5539 8766), on the corner of the highway and Hooker Blvd., in Broadbeach, houses over 260 stores. Some hostels, like the Resort, hand out discount vouchers which can be used for 10% off at many of the stores. Southport's **Australia Fair** is a bit smaller, yet still intimidatingly large. Many stores have sales in July, at the end of their financial year.

ENTERTAINMENT

Surfers Paradise is a partier's paradise as well, as its many clubs readily demonstrate. Most hostels arrange nightly excursions, giving free drink passes and tickets for $4 meals, like the famed feast at the **Bourbon Bar** on Cavill. Most nightclubs have 5am licenses and locations in the city center near the Cavill Ave. Mall; a good portion are on Orchid Ave. You'll need your passport to get into the clubs, as many don't accept other forms of ID. The big **backpacker nights** here are Tuesday and Thursday, when a select few clubs cater exclusively to happy drinkers in their 20s. Most hostels have impressively large 70s wardrobes, which they lend to their guests on Tuesdays, who don the garish, often gender-crossing clothes in hopes of winning money and cranking up the ABBA at **Cocktails and Dreams.** This same establishment hosts "Monday Monster Madness," a series of games and fun competitions between hostels. Thursdays bring the famously degrading Man-o-Man competition to **The Party** (tel. 5538 2848), in which one male and one female from each hostel compete against each other for the title.

Shooters (tel. 5592 1144), above **The Party** in both location and class, has cheap meals ($4) and free Sunday dinners. The bulls' heads and American West paraphernalia tacked on the walls allow it to bill itself as an American-style saloon. While you're actually not likely to catch the Sundance Kid bluffing a flush here, many consider it one of the more lively places to play pool and dance to pop.

The **Rose and Crown** (tel. 5531 5425), at Raptis Plaza at the Cavill Mall, has happy hour drinks nightly until 10pm and live music, usually grunge, on Wednesdays and Fridays through Sundays. It's a little slow to start, but the small dance floor can fill quickly and the bar offers good deals on drinks. **Melba's,** 46 Cavill Ave. (tel. 5538 7411), one of the more upmarket nightclubs, grooves to mainstream and techno dance music on Friday and Saturday nights (dressy, 21+). For blues, try the **Doghouse Blues Bar & Grill** (tel. 5526 9000), in Broadbeach. Although a restaurant, it features live entertainment most nights.

High rollers bring their lucky vibes to **Conrad Jupiters Casino** (tel. 5592 8303 or 1800 074 144), one of Australia's largest gaming houses and a definite landmark in Broadbeach. Over 1000 gaming machines echo with the clicks of coins and chips 24 hours per day. The theater at Conrad Jupiters is featuring a magic show called *Illusions* through 1998. Tickets are $40 (children $20, families $90; shows Mon.-Tues. and Thurs.-Fri. 8pm, Wed. 12:30 and 8pm, Sat. 5 and 8pm).

Tweed Heads and Coolangatta

The "twin towns" of Tweed Heads and Coolangatta—separated only by the invisible New South Wales-Queensland border—mark the southern end of the Gold Coast. Years ago, when Queensland was super-conservative, the boundary line was bold: New South Wales' Tweed Heads was home to the area's sleazier entertainment, like strip joints and adult book shops, while Coolangatta had purer, more family-friendly attractions. Both towns have moved toward the middle, though you can still find remnants of Tweed Heads' infamous past on Wharf St. Today the Tweed-Coolangatta border is only really marked by discrepancies in daylight savings time, most notably at New Year's Eve, when eager partygoers and champagne lovers run across the street and ring in the new year twice.

ORIENTATION AND PRACTICAL INFORMATION

The state border divides the settlement down the length of **Dixon St.,** which bends right into **Boundary St.** out on the rounded peninsula. At the end of the peninsula is the infamous **Point Danger,** whose cliffs were responsible for the wreck of Captain Cook's ship. Some great beaches line the perimeter of Tweed Heads-Coolangatta, including the safe and sheltered **Rainbow Bay** to the north and **Flagstaff** and **Duranbah Beaches** to the southeast, the latter famous for its surfing. The main swimming beaches run along Marine Pde., Coolangatta's waterfront strip.

At the enormous, pink spaceship-like Twin Towns Service Club, Boundary St. turns into Griffith St., which passes the **Coolangatta Transit Center** (tel. 5536 1700) at the corner of Griffith and Warner St. Turn left at the club onto Tweed Heads' main drag, **Wharf St.,** and walk two blocks to reach the **Tweed Heads Tourist Information Centre,** 4 Wharf St. (tel. 5536 4244; open Mon.-Fri. 9am-5pm, Sat. 9am-3pm, Sun. 10am-3pm). Pick up a copy of the indispensible *Tweed-Coolangatta Visitors Guide.*

Surfside buslines (tel. 13 12 30) operates daily 24 hours between Tweed-Coolangatta and beaches further north on the Gold Coast, Southport, and Surfers Paradise. A one-day unlimited travel pass is $10, though you can buy sector tickets. The phone number for Tweed-Coolangatta **taxi** is 5536 1144. **Tweed Auto Rentals** (tel. 5536 8000 or 1800 819 051), next to the tourist center, rents cars from $30 per day. **Happy Day Car Rental,** 35 McLean St. (tel. 5536 8388), opposite the Coolangatta **post office,** rents cars for $20-50 per day.

Greyhound, McCafferty's, and **Pioneer Motor Services** stop at the Coolangatta Coach Station on Sydney-Brisbane service. Greyhound and McCafferty's don't serve the Coolangatta-Surfers sector; either take Surfside or affiliated **Coach Trans** (tel. 5588 8777; for schedule info 13 12 30) which operate daily from Tweed Heads to Brisbane. A McCafferty's pass covers the Coach Trans sector, but you need to catch the bus in Tweed Heads at the corner of Wharf and Bay St.; the bus will not pick you up in Coolangatta if your destination is Surfers Paradise.

ACCOMMODATIONS, FOOD, AND CLUBS

As would be expected in a heavily touristed area, there are plenty of beds in the twin towns. The cheapest are along the highway, particularly along Wharf St., where motels charge $30 for a double.

Sunset Strip Budget Resort, 199 Boundary St. (tel. 5599 5517). This friendly motel-style establishment sports an enormous kitchen, outside pool, and huge, clean, nightclub-style lounge rooms. No dorms; if you're traveling alone you must rent a single. Reception open daily 7am-10pm. Singles $30; twins or doubles $40; triples $60; quads $70. Weekly: $150; $210; $270; $360.

Coolangatta YHA, 130 Coolangatta Rd. (tel. 5536 7644), in Billinga. Walk 3km north from Coolangatta on a busy road to reach this clean, presentable establishment by the airport. Large kitchen, laundry facilities, pool, TV lounge. No alcohol allowed. Courtesy pick-up from bus stop with advance notice. 6- to 8-bed dorms $14, in summer $15; twins $16-17; families $42-44. 7th night free. YHA non-members $3 extra.

Coolangatta Sands Hotel (tel. 5536 3066), at the corner of Griffith and McLean St., has decent above-pub rooms, a kitchen, and a nice porch—though it overlooks noisy, bustling McLean St. 8-bed dorm $14; singles $20; doubles $32.

Griffith St. has a number of takeaways, including the popular **Coolangatta Pie Shop** (tel. 5536 1980; open Sun.-Thurs. 5am-late, Fri.-Sat. 24hr.). Live evening entertainment is restricted to casino games and cheap bistro food in the area's big clubs which include the **Twin Towns Service Club** (tel. 5536 2277), the **Bowls Club** in both Tweed Heads (tel. 5536 3800) and South Tweed (tel. 5524 3655), and **Seagulls Rugby League Football Club** (tel. 5536 3433), on Gellan Dr. in Tweed Heads West. All of these clubs (except Bowls) dispatch large roving shuttle buses for courtesy pick-up; call them for times and schedules.

You, the Australian Cinema Stalker

Strike up the ABBA, put on your chunkiest heels, and dance your way through one of Australia's most popular movies. Fans of Australian cinema can relive the making of *Muriel's Wedding,* the 1994 Cannes Film Festival award-winner about a family living in Porpoise Spit and their eldest daughter's coming of age. Porpoise Spit is actually Coolangatta, in Queensland. The Heslops are really a family from Coolangatta, and the movie's mall, motel, Chinese restaurant, and green skyscrapers are all real landmarks in the area. Landmarks they may be; it's up to us to make them tourist destinations.

Pines Mall, K.P. McGrath Dr. off the Pacific Hwy., is the place to begin your whirlwind stalkfest. Although a quick glance at the mall in the final scene might lead you to the South Tweed Mall on Griffith St., the facade is dissimilar upon inspection. Judicious use of your VCR's freeze-frame button proves that Pines is the mall appearing in the film. Run inside for a look, but don't bother asking the bookstore for a copy of the screenplay; they sold out long ago.

On the Beach Motel, 188 Marine Pde. on Greenmount Beach, was brilliantly featured in the poignant honeymoon suite scene. True devotees will be devastated to learn that the last *Official Guest of Muriel's Wedding* t-shirt was recently sold, but the owners are eager to share in *Muriel* fanaticism. Scrutiny of the decor and swinging doors, however, reveals that the inside shots must have been filmed in a studio.

Rickshaw Room was the site of many an encounter between the family and the father's mistress ("Deirde Chambers! What a coincidence!"). Intrepid investigation, though, uncovers a complicated chain of events: those scenes were actually filmed in the Oceanview Restaurant, on Griffith St., which has since been sold and converted into the Rang Mahal Indian restaurant. This fine eatery is not to be confused with the Rosegarden Chinese restaurant, next door.

The Super-Duper Bonus: As unbelievable as it sounds, you may have the opportunity to meet the father on whom the movie is loosely based (director/producer P.J. Hogan's dad), a friendly bloke and a former Coolangatta councilman. You may find him enjoying an afternoon beer at the South Tweed Rugby Club, and, if you pretend to be an obsessed tourist (as if!) and profess that you came to Coolangatta to touch his lapel and converse with him, he might agree to meet you. Spiffy attire, please (no wedding dress required)—it's not every day that you get to meet Mr. Heslop.

SIGHTS AND ACTIVITIES

Two companies operate cruises along the Tweed River. **Tweed Adventure Cruises** (tel. 018 757 748) specializes in small (max. 8 people) environmentally focused tours (90 min. cruise $20; half-day $34). **Tweed Endeavor Cruises** (tel. 5536 8800) is on a 150-person double-decker vessel which leads river and rainforest cruises with BBQ lunch (90 min. cruise $22; 4hr. $38).

The **Minjungbal Aboriginal Cultural Centre** (tel. 5524 2109), 5km south of the border in South Tweed Heads, has guided tours of the Aboriginal resource museum which houses historic photographs, weapons, and crafts. Enjoy a picnic or barbecue outside or watch a Minjungbal dance performance. (Center open daily 9am-4pm; museum admission $6, concessions $3. Performances $3 extra, held Tues. and Thurs. 10am or 11am Daylight Savings Time.) A lovely 1.6km loop bushwalk out back circles past mangrove sanctuaries and along the river. The path leads to the **Bora Ring,** a preserved sacred ceremonial site last used in 1908.

The ever-famous **Tropical Fruit World** (tel. 6677 7222), formerly Avocadoland, 10-15 minutes south of the border, offers free samples of fruits and fabulous ice cream. The owners changed the name when they realized touring through gardens with Chocolate Pudding Fruit and Chewing Gum Trees would be more attractive than inspecting avocadoes (open daily 10am-5pm; admission $16, children $8, families $40).

North of Coolangatta 7km along the Pacific Hwy., **Currumbin Sanctuary** (tel. 5534 1266) maintains a reputation for wildlife so tame that birds frequently perch on visitors' arms and heads and smile for photo-ops. You can touch kangaroos and wallabies and see many other native Australian species in the open-air zoo. Take your "breakfast with the birds" (lorikeet feedings at 8am and 4pm). Other animal presentations occur at 30-minute intervals during the day (open 8am-5pm; admission $16, children $9, families $40).

■ Natural Attractions near Coolangatta

The national parks nearby are worth a visit, and several companies provide tours of the valley area. **O'Reilly's** (tel. 5524 4249) goes to Tamborine Mountain and Lamington National Park, among other destinations (tours $35, pick-up and lunch included). **Beach Farm** (tel. 6674 1201) has tours of the natural arch and rainforest (Mon.) and of Mt. Warning (Thurs.), to name a few, for $25. For travelers visiting these sights with their own transportation, **Murwillumbah** (see p. 178) provides better access.

Natural Arch **Springbrook National Park's** most popular attraction is the Natural Arch, 3km north of the border with New South Wales. The arch, also called Natural Bridge, is a gorgeous cavern with a waterfall created by the force of heavy boulders and constantly flowing water breaking through the hardened lava. Swimmers used to dive off the rocks into the swimming hole below, but a storm a couple of years back sent boulders into the pit, which made it dangerous to jump in; fence-posts and signs now strongly discourage jumping. At night, the cavern comes alive with bats and glow-worms. The cavern is about 1km from the parking lot; you'll pass a wonderful old strangled fig tree, a web of branches around a hollow core, on the way. The phone number for the Springbrook **ranger office** is 5533 5147. Lodging and food can be found in Springbrook village, about 35km east of the arch.

Lamington National Park The 200 sq. km of Lamington National Park comprise one of the region's most accessible rainforest parks. It's fairly easy to get to from Coolangatta or Murwillumbah, NSW, and the well-trod paths lead to spectacular 150m waterfalls, clear springs, and subtropical rainforest. The ranger can be contacted at 5553 3584.

SOUTHERN DOWNS

West of the Great Dividing Range lie the hills and vales of the Southern Downs, and the towns of Toowoomba, Warwick, and Stanthorpe. Travelers are likely to pass through Toowoomba only to change buses, but Warwick and Stanthorpe are located in the most fertile agricultural region of the state and are therefore popular with backpackers looking for seasonal work. Fruit-picking is available essentially year-round, and broke backpackers work 40 hours a week at $9.80 an hour (current going rate), anywhere from two weeks to two months. Work permits are theoretically required, but laborers have confessed that they are not essential. A handy guidebook called *A Book on Fruit Picking Around Australia* will tell you what's in season where. (Stanthorpe: Jan.-Feb. peaches, nectarines, and tomatoes; Feb.-March apples; Jan.-April lettuce. Warwick: July-Oct. strawberries.) For those coming to the Downs with time to spare, Giraween and Sundown National Parks please visitors with their wildflower displays (seasonal, of course), granite outcroppings, and spectacular views. Stanthorpe is also the center of Queensland's only wine region, the Granite Belt wineries, and free tastings are easy to find. The highway transects the region and crosses the border south into the New England region (see p. 181) of New South Wales.

Cold Enough to Freeze the Balls Off a Brass Monkey

In June, July, and August, the Southern Downs area flaunts its refreshingly chilly climate with the **Brass Monkey** season. The annual celebration has a colorful history: sailing ships used to have a brass rack, called a "monkey," to hold cannon balls. During winter, the rainwater collected in the monkey would freeze and expand, forcing the balls off the rack. Hence the expression, "cold enough to freeze the balls off a brass monkey."

Toowoomba Queensland's largest inland city, 90 minutes from Brisbane, Toowoomba (pop. 90,000) is a major transportation hub and home to the McCafferty's bus line headquarters. Their coaches head to Brisbane (departs 9pm) and toward Sydney via Warwick and Stanthorpe (5:25am). The city itself has excellent views, since it's perched on the edge of the Great Dividing Range, 700m above sea level. The **Cobb and Co. Museum** and **Royal Bulls Head Inn** are National Trust buildings and popular tourist attractions. Toowoomba is the only city with a lighted thoroughbred racing track, the **Turf Club's Clifford Park.** Call the **information center** (tel. 7632 1988) for details.

Warwick Warwick's rosebush-lined wide streets were built for horses and carts, and the town's historic sandstone buildings lend the relaxed, colonial feel that one would expect this, the second oldest town in Queensland (pop. 25,000), to have. But the streets become nearly unnavigable during the last weekend in October when the annual **rodeo,** Australia's most famous, comes to town. It's the culminating event in the month's **Rose and Rodeo Festival,** and really brings in the crowds. Call the Warwick **tourist information office,** 49 Albion St. (tel. 4661 3122), for more information (open Mon.-Fri. 9am-5pm, Sat. 10am-3pm). The **Pringle Cottage and Museum,** 81 Dragon St. (tel. 4661 2445), displays furniture and household items from the late 19th century (open Wed.-Mon.; admission $3.50, children 50¢). The **Rose City Caravan Park** (tel. 4661 1662) is 2km north of the city center and has tent sites (1 person $8, 2 people $10), powered sites ($10), on-site vans ($25), and cabins for 2 people ($30, with bath 36). The lovely **Oasis Caravan Park** (tel. 4661 2874), 1km south of Warwick on the New England Hwy., has tent sites, on-site caravans, and cabins, all ranging from $10 to $40.

Stanthorpe

Easily missed on the New England Highway, Stanthorpe (pop. 10,000) is a small, rustic town on what was once a summer hunting ground for the Kambu Wal Aboriginals. A short-lived 1860s tin mining industry gave the town its name: *stannum* means "tin," and *thorpe* means "village." Now, its cool, crisp climate has made it a year-round destination for many Brisbane residents, who are eager to descend on Queensland's best wine region. Italian immigrants after WWI first established vineyards here, and the wineries now ferment world-famous products. The town is also an ideal base for exploring the granite formations and wildflowers of the surrounding national parks, Sundown and Girraween.

ORIENTATION AND PRACTICAL INFORMATION

Coming in from Warwick off the New England Hwy., you will drive down Stanthorpe's main street, **High St.,** which turns into **Maryland St.** as it bends south in the center of town. At the bridge over the Quart Pot Creek, two blocks later, the same road becomes **Wallangarra Rd.,** which merges back into the New England Hwy. The bus station is at the corner of Maryland and Folkestone St.

The über-organized and super-helpful **tourist office** (tel. 4681 2057) is located in the Civic Center at the corner of Lock and Marsh St., just off High St. at the bend in the road (open Mon.-Fri. 8:45am-5pm, Sat. 10am-1pm). At the bend on Maryland St. you'll find **ATMs** at the National and Commonwealth **banks** (open Mon.-Thurs. 9:30am-4pm, Fri. 9:30am-5pm). Across the street from the banks sits the large **post office** (tel. 4681 2181; open Mon.-Fri. 9am-5pm).

Stanthorpe has three major festivals, all with themes of wine and winter weather. The largest is the biennial **Apple and Grape Harvest Festival,** an extravaganza with a gala ball, rodeo, wine fiesta, and museum exhibition, which will be held in late February or early March of 1998. The Granite Belt **Spring Wine Festival** is held during the first two weekends in October. The winter months are devoted to the **Brass Monkey** celebration.

ACCOMMODATIONS AND FOOD

Stanthorpe has many motels, a caravan park, and over a dozen more expensive B&Bs and inns. The cheapest ($15-30 per person) and most central accommodation options are in "hotels," which are actually simple rooms over pubs, clustered on Maryland St. Most of the beds are like hammocks (no springs attached), but the rooms are clean and have sinks; most also have a small TV lounge upstairs and a fireplace room downstairs. The **Central Hotel** (tel. 4681 2044) has friendly management and caters to backpackers. It offers singles for $20 and doubles for $30, and provides cereal or toast in the shared kitchen. Special longer-term deals for seasonal fruit-pickers are also available. **O'Maras Hotel** (tel. 4681 1044) has a verandah, but it doubles as the walkway to the bathrooms (singles $15; doubles $30). **Top of the Town Caravan Park,** 10 High St. (tel. 4681 2030), a 15-minute walk from the town center, has campsites for $7 per person ($12 for 2 people), and hostel beds at $13 ($70 weekly). They, like the Thulimbah **Summit Lodge Backpackers** (tel. 4681 2599), 12km north on the New England Hwy., arrange fruit and vegetable picking work; Top of the Town also offers transport to the farms. The cheapest motel is the **Boulevard Motel,** 76 Maryland St. (tel. 4681 1171), on the edge of town next to Quart Pot Creek. Most rooms have a TV, VCR, toaster, and fridge. Singles start at $37; doubles are $42. The motel also has five-person family rooms for $67.

Alternative accommodations can be found on "host farms," which are actually small cattle stations, but you'll need a car to get there. There are a number of these outside Stanthorpe. Most will set you back $30-40 per person, but **Callemondah** (tel. 4685 6162), 58km from Stanthorpe on Texas Rd., charges just $15 per night (linen $5) to stay on the sheep and cattle station (bookings essential).

Stanthorpe has many coffee and lunch shops on its main road. The **Catholic Women's Association** on Victoria St. serves $2-3 sandwiches Monday through Friday from 11am to 2pm. For dinner, **Il Cavallino,** next to the Central Hotel, serves Italian dishes for $8-12; stick with their (fairly) famous pizza. The hotels all have bars and bistros on the ground floor with inexpensive fare. Restaurants and wineries seize on the tourism potential by holding popular Christmas dinners for Northern Hemisphere residents in July, luring customers in with log fires and homey meals.

SIGHTS AND ACTIVITIES

Stanthorpe is famous for its **wineries,** most of which offer free tours. The tourist office has contact information and lists of wineries. Unfortunately, wineries can't be reached by public transportation or on foot. **Maxi Tours** (tel. 4681 3969) offers day tours for $30; **Murray Gardens** (tel. 4681 4121) has tours for $35. **South West Safaris** (tel. 4681 3685) offers several types of 4WD tours, including a "winery to wilderness" full-day tour with pick-up from Granite Belt accommodations for $55. Another option is to hop on a horse: **Red Gum Ridge** (tel. 4683 7169) gives lessons and day rides to local wineries. Several farms grow berries, and may be open for **berry picking** between October and April. Raspberries are in season from December to April, boysenberries in December, and strawberries from October to April. **The Bramble Patch** (tel. 4683 4205), a commercial berry farm on Townsend Rd., 4km from the New England Hwy., is open year-round for picnicking, strolling, and wine tasting.

Stanthorpe's gem is the fascinating **Historical Museum.** It's near the showgrounds and a 15-minute walk up High St. from the town center. The museum is a delightful cornucopia of historical oddities, like something out of a dusty fantasy novel. Every square centimeter inside the buildings is crammed with relics of years past: fruit fly catchers, ancient heating devices, bellow-operated vacuum cleaners, thousands of blue ribbons for flower shows (all won by one impressive lady), miniature organs, and even a hand-made TV. The wonderful stories of the curators should satisfy every curious amateur historian. Although the museum is officially open Tuesday through Friday from 11am to 4pm and Sunday from 2 to 4pm, it's well-advised to call the museum's president (tel. 4681 1450 or 018 063 662) to request an appointment (suggested donation $3). The more sedate **Stanthorpe Regional Art Gallery** (tel. 4681 1874) is behind the tourist office on Lock St., and usually has small well-presented wood and ceramics exhibitions from Sydney and Melbourne artists (open Mon.-Fri. 10am-4pm, Sat.-Sun. 1-4pm; free).

The 1872 discovery of tin in Quart Pot Creek marked the beginning of years of mining in and around Stanthorpe. Most of the stones in the area are topaz, quartz, citrine, tourmaline, and amethysts; rarer finds include silver, sapphires, diamonds, and gold. Today, amateurs can try their hand at **fossicking,** but they'll need to obtain a fossicker's license first. **Top of the Town Caravan Park** supplies licenses and arranges beginner tours (2 people, 3hr., $35; families $36; guide and equipment supplied). **Blue Topaz Caravan Park** (tel. 4683 5279), in Severnlea, 7km south of Stanthorpe, charges $2.50 per person or $5 per family to fossick on the Severn River. Both parks waive fees for overnight guests.

The second Sunday of every month is reserved for Stanthorpe's hugely popular **Market in the Mountains** (tel. 4681 1912 or 4681 2969), an arts, crafts, and goodies sale held at the Stanthorpe Civic Center. Stargazers who would like a better perspective on night lights can arrange a trip to the **Sundown Observatory** (tel. 4684 1192), on Sundown Rd. in Ballandean. The observatory is at 710m elevation and has 18in. diameter telescopes and a display area with satellite models (admission $5). Stanthorpe's **Recreation Club** (tel. 4681 1276) has large golf and croquet grounds just out of town, where players share fields with over 200 kangaroos and quacking ducks.

In late January, the annual **Jazz in the Vineyard** dinner is held in the Ballandean Estate Winery (tel. 4684 1226). The same winery sponsors the **Opera at Sunset,** a large fund-raiser for cancer patients, on the first Sunday in May. It's a lovely buffet dinner and concert in the Sundown Valley Vineyard, but bookings are required a couple of months in advance (tel. 4684 1226).

■ National Parks near Stanthorpe

The two national parks in the Stanthorpe area both have camping grounds ($3.50 per person). Contact the rangers to arrange for permits. **Girraween National Park,** in Wybera via Ballandean, is a popular destination for bushwalkers, birdwatchers, campers, and picnickers. Just over the border from New South Wales, the park has an average elevation of 900m. Granite boulders, some balanced on top of each other, coexist with eucalypt forests and lyre birds. In the spring, wildflowers sprout from the bases of rocks; *girraween* means "place of flowers." There is a picnic area on the southern end of Bold Rock Creek, next to the **visitors center** (open Mon.-Fri. 2-4pm), as well as rock climbing, swimming, and BBQ areas. Camping is available in designated areas (with hot showers, toilets, and fireplaces), and in more remote areas. Permits are required; contact the ranger (tel. 4684 5157, daily 3-4pm). There is a coin-operated phone in the visitors center parking lot.

Sundown National Park, 75km southwest of Stanthorpe via Texas Rd., has rugged terrain and panoramic views. Most of the 16,000 hectare park is 600-800m above sea level, and has very different geology than neighboring parks, with a mix of sedimentary and igneous rocks that has produced sharp ridges. The Severn River cuts the park in two. Although people in the past attempted to both farm and mine the land, both industries failed, and Sundown remains largely a rustic wilderness area. Only 4WD vehicles can reach the campsites along the river; hikers can park their cars at the entrance to the park. Campsites have pit toilets, fireplaces, and BBQ facilities. From May to September, the nights are cold but the days are warm and clear. To book campsites, contact the ranger at Glenlyon Dam Rd. (tel. (067) 37 5235, daily 1-9pm).

Two New South Wales national parks, Bald Rock and Boonoo Boonoo, are easily accessible from Stanthorpe as well. Full listings for these parks are found in the New South Wales chapter (see p. 186).

SUNSHINE AND FRASER COASTS

The pastel yellow that permeates the Sunshine Coast contrasts sharply with the Gold Coast's pulsating neon. The Sunshine Coast, in many ways, is a kinder, gentler version of vacationland. The crowds are fewer, but expert surfers still dot the waves. Beaches still envelop well-established towns, and waters still greet those eager to partake in aquatic pleasures. Accessible national parks, like Noosa and Cooloola, replace the more artificial theme parks down the coast, and travelers content to relax are more likely to see koalas in the wild.

The largest of the islands that dot Queensland's coastal waters, sandy Fraser Island reclines under a cover of rainforest. Wild horses wander through the bush like fantastical unicorns, pausing to drink from the island's freshwater lakes, and dingoes hunt for wallabies but are happy to take off with shoes instead. On the mainland, Bundaberg is hailed as a particularly lucrative base for casual labor, and a bevy of workers' hostels have sprung up to meet the demand.

Maroochy

Maroochy is the general name for an area of coast encompassing the towns of Maroochydore, Alexandra Heads, and Mooloolaba. Die-hard surfers fill the beaches, and their stereotypically laid-back attitudes permeate even the most urban of Maroochy's districts. **Maroochydore** is the urban center, heavily oriented toward small industry, and is located where the Maroochy River flows into the ocean. It's the main tourist accommodation area, and is also the place to shop. **Alexandra Heads** is best known for its great surfing spots. Its strip of small shops and cheap coffee places overlooks a safe, popular family beach. **Mooloolaba's** largest claim to fame is its oceanarium, Underwater World; it's also known for its beachside nightclubs and is considered the up-and-coming nightlife area.

ORIENTATION AND PRACTICAL INFORMATION

The main commercial strip in Maroochydore, **Sixth Avenue** runs past the huge **Sunshine Plaza** super-mall and beaches. Aerodrome Rd. connects Maroochydore and Mooloolaba. Maroochy's **tourist office** (tel. 5479 1566) is located at the corner of Aerodrome Rd. and South Ave. The free "Maroochy Guide" should answer most of your questions, although it's aimed more at new residents than budget travelers. The local blue-painted **Sunbus** #1 and 1A connect these areas fairly effectively. A 15-minute ride from Maroochydore's Sunshine Plaza to Mooloolaba costs $1.90 and runs every hour—Alexandra Heads and Cotton Tree are on the route. Suncoast Pacific, Greyhound, and McCafferty's all stop in Maroochydore as well.

ACCOMMODATIONS AND FOOD

The majority of Maroochy's motels line Sixth Ave. in Maroochydore. Backpackers and the more budget-conscious can rejoice in two quiet community-oriented hostels. **Suncoast Backpackers Lodge,** 50 Parker St., parallel to Aerodrome Drive, is a small, friendly, and clean, with a generous communal space and kitchen. The owners offer discounts galore for trips and local service and a $5 all-you-can-eat barbecue on Tuesday nights. (Dorm bunks $14, including locker; singles $25; doubles $16 per person; triples $15 per person; YHA, VIP discounts.) The **Cotton Tree Beachhouse,** 15 The Esplanade in Maroochydore (tel. 5443 1755), is directly across the street from the river. The cozy two-story house vibrates with the sound of a magnificent video collection emanating from two TVs and guests' soft talking from couches and comfy chairs. Although the bathroom facilities are tiny and unkempt, Cotton Tree feels like a worn-in home (dorms $13). Don't leave without trying the delicious homemade carrot cake. There is also a **Maroochydore YHA** (tel. 5443 3151), located about 40 minutes from the Cotton Tree. Call ahead for pick-up from the bus station.

Maroochy has cheap, family-oriented food. At **Friday's on the Wharf,** patrons who arrive between 5:30pm and 6pm on Tuesday and Thursday get 50% off any meal except seafood. **Nok's Thai** (tel. 5443 7484), on the corner of Second Ave. and Aerodrome Rd. in Maroochydore, serves up enough food for two for $5.50-10.50. Show a VIP card and receive 10% off. For health food, **Cotton Tree Health and Living,** 17 Cotton Wood Plaza, Maroochydore (tel. 5443 4700) makes four different types of burgers for $4.30. *Let's Go* readers receive a 10% discount on vitamins and minerals. The **Surf Club** at the far end of The Esplanade in Mooloolaba is worth visiting for the $9.50 all-you-can-eat Sunday breakfast. Ask nicely for a seat by the window and you'll be rewarded with floor-to-ceiling glass windows practically on the beach, framing one of Mooloolaba's more gorgeous views. (Live entertainment Fri.-Sun. afternoons. Open Sun.-Thurs.10am-10pm, Fri. 10am-midnight, Sat. 10am-11pm.)

SIGHTS AND ENTERTAINMENT

Being in Maroochy means spending time near the water. There are many surf shops, but **Bad Company,** 6-8 Aerodrome Rd. (tel. 5443 2457; call for current water conditions), is across the street from a good strip of beach and rents boards for $4 per hour or $10 per half-day. If surfing's not your thing, strap on a pair of skates and cruise alongside the river. **Maroochy Skate Biz,** 174 Alexandra Parade (tel. 5443 6111), offers free instruction and a wide range of in-line skates and bikes. Kids and grown-ups alike will enjoy Mooloolaba's **Underwater World** (tel. 5444 2255), Australia's largest tropical oceanarium. Open daily, the oceanarium's seal presentations and interactive exhibits are great, but nothing beats the basement attraction: a moving circular walk guides you through a wrap-around clear aquarium. (Admission $16.50, students and seniors $11, children $9.50, family passes $47.) The **Mooloolaba Yacht Club** (tel. 5444 1355) offers free sailing on Wednesdays and Sundays. Rumor has it that people looking for work on sailing ships will do well to go to the Yacht Club and ask around for jobs, as many owners will exchange board for labor.

Rock On, 89 The Esplanade, Mooloolaba, is one of the busiest nightclubs with 13 TV screens, three bars, a DJ, and a dance floor (open Wed. and Fri.-Sat. 8:30pm-3am, and Tues., Thurs., and Sun. 9pm-3am). **Friday's on the Wharf,** Mooloolaba, "'is more upscale with pool tables and a $6 cover on Friday and Saturday after 9:30pm. For more down-home entertainment, join in the "American Pie" sing-along on Friday and Saturday nights at **Bullockies** steakhouse, 80 Sixth Ave., Maroochydore.

Noosa

Those who think of Noosa (pop. 33,000) as nothing more than a jumping-off point for Fraser Island are in danger of missing one of the Sunshine Coast's loveliest and most versatile spots. Upper-class sophisticates, vacationing Australian families, and backpackers all come to Noosa in roughly equal numbers to mingle at the gorgeous beaches and glitzy shopping areas. Some criticize Noosa for catering to upscale vacationers with carefully crafted trendiness, but the area manages to draw backpackers in droves anyway, which leads to high quality and low prices for budget travelers. Weary, sunburnt backpackers may find welcome relief from the foam and tinsel of the Gold Coast, while the bush is just around the corner. The Noosa area boasts activities to suit every carefree whim: surfing, shopping, cappuccino sipping, koala sighting, and camel riding, while Cooloola National Park, just north of Noosa, is a wilderness ripe for hiking, canoeing, and camping. Noosa also serves as a base for forays to the Everglades River, Eumundi Market, and the Hinterlands.

ORIENTATION

The Noosa area can be a bit confusing to navigate because its distinguishing features all have irritatingly similar names. The three main communities are Noosa Heads, Noosa Junction, and Noosaville, while Noosa National Park is a prime attraction. These areas are connected by Noosa Drive and Noosa Parade, and are located along the Noosa River, which runs into Noosa Sound and Noosa Inlet. Seriously. **Noosa Heads** is the main tourist area, and activity revolves around the sidewalk-chic **Hastings St.,** located one block north of the **Noosa Parade Bus Interchange.** Many trendy shops and upscale hotels line the street, as do roughly one-third of Noosa's restaurants. The entrance to **Noosa National Park** and its carpark are at the end of Hastings St. closest to the bus interchange.

A 15-minute stroll over the hill along the wooden sidewalk ramp leads to the heart of **Noosa Junction,** Noosa's business center. The post office, supermarket, and string of banks all lie within five minutes of each other. **Noosaville** is 3km southwest of Noosa Heads, and is the departure point for most cruises to Fraser Island. The **Sunshine Beach** area is 3km east of Noosa Junction. The cluster of beachfront hostels here are best reached by car, by bus, or by foot along the beach, since the walk along the busy David Low Way takes 40 minutes. Both Sunshine Beach and nearby Sunrise Beach are popular spots, but the total 40km stretch of sand leaves ample room for bathers to spread out.

PRACTICAL INFORMATION

Tourist Office: Noosa Visitors Centre (tel. 5474 8400; fax 5474 8222), directly across from the Noosa Heads bus interchange. Carries the usual brochures on tours and accommodations. Organizes tours of Aboriginal art, and tours for handicapped and gay/lesbian travelers. Bike rental $9 per day, motorcycles $15 per hr. Dutch, German, French, and Greek spoken. Wheelchair accessible. Open daily 8am-6pm; Dec. 26-Jan. 26 and Easter week, 8am-9pm. **Tourism Noosa Information Centre** (tel. 5447 4988; fax 5474 9494; email noosat@squirrel.com.au) on Hastings St., Noosa Heads. From the ceiling-to-floor walls of brochures, *Noosa: the Guide* and *Hello Noosa* are good introductions to the town. Wheelchair accessible. Open Mon.-Sat. 9am-5pm.

Currency Exchange: Westpac Bank, 40 Hastings St., Noosa Heads (tel. 5446 4488). Advance on all major credit cards (with passport). Cashing less than $500 in foreign traveler's checks costs $7; over $500 is free. Wheelchair accessible. **National, Commonwealth,** and **ANZ** banks are clustered in Noosa Junction, most on Sunshine Beach Rd. All open Mon.-Thurs. 9:30am-4pm, Fri. 9:30am-5pm.

Airport: Noosa Flying Services (tel. 5475 0187) operates out of a private airport 5km from town. For a larger regional airport, try Maroochydore or Brisbane.

Buses: Sunbus (tel. 5449 7422) provides frequent hail-and-ride service throughout Noosa and to and from Maroochydore, Mooloolaba, and Caloundra. 15min. service through Tewantin, Hastings St., and Noosa Junction; 30min. service through Noosa Heads, Sunshine Beach, Maroochydore, and Caloundra. Transit maps and timetables available on buses and at the tourist information centers. Fares $1-5; buses run 7am-8pm. **Greyhound Pioneer** (tel. 13 20 30), **McCafferty's** (tel. 3236 3033), and **Suncoast Pacific** (tel. 3236 1901) all run from Noosa south to Brisbane and north toward Rockhampton.

Taxis: Suncoast Cabs (tel. 13 10 08) provide 24-hr. service.

Car Rental: Budget (tel. 5447 4588; fax 5447 2337) on Hastings St., Bay Village, guarantees the lowest price on medium to long-term rentals. Open daily 8am-5:30pm. **Virgin** (tel. 5475 5777 or 1800 659 299), at the corner of Sunshine Beach Rd. and Berrima Row in Noosa Junction, offers airport and hotel courtesy pick-up and rentals from $29 per day. Bookings 7am-7pm. **Thrifty** (tel. 5447 2299) is in Noosa Junction. **Avis** (tel. 5447 4933) is on Hastings St.

Sports Equipment: Sierra Mountain Bike, Hastings St. (tel. 5474 8277). Bikes $12 per day. **Noosa Visitors Centre,** Hastings St. (tel. 5474 8400). Bikes $9 per day. **Inline Skates,** 249 Gympie Tce. (tel. 5442 4344). Bikes $10 per day, skates $7 per hr.

Bookstores: Mary Ryan's, Hastings St., Bay Village (tel. 5474 5275) provides for all your beach-reading needs. Open daily 9am-5:30pm.

Public Toilets: Located in the carpark at the entrance to Noosa National Park, off Hastings St.

Medical Services: Noosa After Hours Medical Centre, 197 Weyba Rd., Noosaville (tel. 5442 4444). Open Mon.-Fri. 6pm-8am and Sat. noon-Mon. 8am. **Nambour Base Hospital** (tel. 5441 9600) is the closest regional hospital.

Police: on Langura St., Noosa Junction (tel. 5447 5888).

Emergency: Dial 000.

Internet Access: If you're tired of surfing Noosa's waves, try the net at **La Sabbia,** 6 Hastings St., Noosa Heads (tel. 5474 5770; http://www.noosanetcafe.com.au).

Post Office: Noosa Post Office, 79-80 Cooroy-Noosa Rd., Noosa Junction (tel. 5447 3280; fax 5447 5160). Poste Restante, **fax,** and electronic post. American Express orders for $6. Open Mon.-Fri. 9am-5pm. **Postal code:** 4567.

Phone Code: 07.

ACCOMMODATIONS

Lodging in Noosa comes in three general categories: hostels, motels or hotels, and "holiday units," which include private homes. Intense competition for budget travelers keep hostel prices low and perks such as courtesy shuttle service, surfboards, on-site bars, pool tables, and free tour bookings standard. Motel and hotel rooms can top $200 on Hastings St., but if you're willing to do without a beachfront view you'll be able to find decently priced accommodations. Families and groups may find it cheaper and more convenient to rent units or homes; many agencies offer discounted weekly rates. It's wise to book ahead for busy times, especially during Christmas and school vacation weeks, when the influx of visitors can double nightly rates. The check-out time for lodgings is generally 10am. Almost without exception, hostels provide courtesy pick-up from the bus station. There are also several places to **camp** in the area (see **Cooloola National Park,** p. 303).

Noosa Heads

Lodging here puts you on or near busy Hastings St., just a short walk from the National Park.

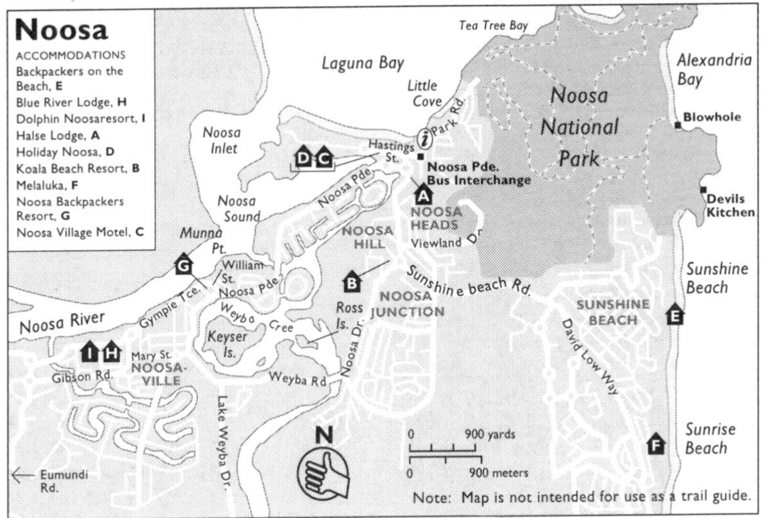

Halse Lodge (tel. 5447 3377), directly opposite the Noosa Parade Bus Interchange. Perched on a small hill, this stately 115-year-old house feels relaxed and removed from Noosa's hustle, but is only 2min. from Hastings St. and the entrance to Noosa National Park. Common areas have long wooden tables, comfortable lounge chairs, and 2 stories of lovely wraparound porches. Attracts a more subdued crowd. Bunks in shared cottage $15; double and twin rooms $50. Breakfast included.

Koala Beach Resort, 44 Noosa Dr. (tel. 5447 3355 or 1 800 357 457), a 10-15min. walk from the bus interchange. Popular with surfers and die-hard partiers. Laundry facilities, pool, and volleyball court, but the focus is on the adjoining **Koala Bar,** which blares loud music, serves meals for $6, and attracts young locals and guests for beer and dancing. Friendly staff encourages group bonding and daytrips. 5-bed dorms $14; doubles $34. VIP.

Noosa Village Motel, 10 Hastings St. (tel. 5447 5800; fax 5474 9282). Clean, modest rooms right on Hastings come with small fridge, TV, and toaster. Doubles $70-$120, depending on season. Triples and units for 5 also available.

Holiday Noosa, 12 Hastings St. (tel. 5447 4011; fax 5447 3410). The Jacaranda complex includes sparsely finished studio rooms which have 2 twin beds and a small TV ($70-$105, depending on season). Suites overlook a lake and sleep 4-5 ($90-$150). Also rents expensive apartments. Discounts for weekly rentals.

Sunshine Beach

Hostels here, though generally more worn than the ones in Noosa Heads, are practically on the beach, but a good 20-minute walk from the Junction.

Backpackers on the Beach, 26 Stevens St. (tel. 5447 4739), across the street from Sunshine Beach. Boogie boards, pool, and surfboard rental. 4-bed dorms $14; twin or double $32. Shared kitchen and bathroom. The self-contained units sleep 5 (minimum $50) and are much nicer. VIP.

Melaluka, 7 Selene St. (tel. 5447 3663). Moderately clean but gloomy self-contained units have common kitchen area, laundry, and TV. The outside paint is chipping and the inside could use an overhaul, but it is just 1min. to the beach. Doubles $32. YHA. Free courtesy van to town, 5-10min. by car.

Noosaville

Most of the travelers who stay in this less glamourous part of town prefer the serenity of the river to the beaches, which are a 30-minute walk away.

Noosa Backpackers Resort, 9-13 Williams St. (tel. 5449 8151). A quiet, low-key hostel driven largely by the energy and friendliness of its owners. Located on a shady side street 2min. from the river, a 30min. walk to the National Park. Free courtesy van, weekly movie nights, and theme dinners, use of pool table and kayaks. Attractive central courtyard and small, decent rooms. 4-bed dorms $14; doubles $32. VIP and weekly discounts.

Blue River Lodge, 181 Gympie Tce. (tel. 5449 7564), directly across the street from Noosa River. Spotless units with 2 bedrooms, kitchen area, and TV $45. Reservations recommended.

Dolphin Noosaresort, 137 Gympie Tce. (tel. 5449 7318). Clean rooms with small kitchens attached. Low-key atmosphere. Hourly trips to national park and beach. Pool, surfboards, weight machines. Dorms $10. VIP, YHA.

FOOD AND ENTERTAINMENT

Many of the restaurants on Hastings St. are expensive, but with over 100 eateries in Noosa, you're bound to find great, cheap food somewhere. Most restaurants have alcohol licenses, while many smaller eateries and cafes invite you to bring your own beverages. There are liquor stores (bottle shops) next to Angello's on Hastings St. in Noosa Heads and also in Noosa Junction. Restaurants frequently offer entertainment, particularly on weekend nights and Sunday afternoons. Cheaper is **Coles Supermarket** (tel. 5447 4000) off Sunshine Beach Rd. on Lanyana Way, Noosa Junction (open Mon.-Fri. 8am-9pm, Sat. 9am-5:30pm, Sun. 10:30am-4pm.)

Betty's Burgers, Hastings St., Noosa Heads (tel. 5447 5639) in the Tingirana Arcade. Tucked down an alley off Hastings St., this 20-year-old establishment is one of the best deals in all Australia. Burgers served up by Betty herself start at a buck and make customers feel like thieves. Complimentary coffee and tea. Thirty kinds of burgers, including 9 vegetarian patties. Open daily 9am-6pm.

Topopo's, 73 Noosa Dr., Noosa Junction (tel. 5447 3700). One of the best deals in town. Generous servings of toned-down Mexican food. Weekly special ($6.50), delicious Mexican pizza ($9.50). Dine in the open air or eat in the colorfully decorated interior. Licensed.

Cafe Le Monde, Hastings St., Noosa Heads (tel. 5449 2366). Most locals agree that the action is here. Classy and comfortable, it's also a morning gathering place for local surfer celebrities. Good for coffee, leisurely breakfasts, or casual dinners. Vegetarian friendly. Musical entertainment 5 nights per week. Try the nachos ($8.50) or one of their 61 wines.

Noosa Reef, Noosa Dr. (tel. 5447 4477), on the hill. Modern and airy, Noosa Reef attracts couples and families more than backpackers. Anyone can take advantage of the cafe deck, though, which offers wonderful views of the town below. Parents can send their kids to the adjoining video/play room for a $7 meal while they enjoy pizza wraps, steaks, and fish and chips for $9-17. Open for breakfast, too.

Saltwater, 8 Hastings St., Noosa Heads (tel. 5447 2234). Sells freshly caught Noosa seafood and operates a lovely upstairs open-air restaurant, where you can sip wine under a white awning (main course $13-20). But the best bet is the $6 melt-in-your-mouth calamari, available through the take-out. Opens at 11:30am.

Bay Village Food Court, off Hastings St., has several small eateries and vendors.

Noosa's hottest night spot, **Rolling Rock,** on Hastings St., Noosa Head (tel. 5447 2255), is packed with the tragically hip. Thumpin' techno rocks the house on Thursday nights, while Sundays feature live local bands. Beverages start around $3 (cover $6 after 10pm Wed.-Sun; open 9pm-3am every night, but doors close at 1:30am). **Mocca Jam,** on Noosa Dr. below the Noosa Reef Restaurant, features pool tables, live bands on Sundays and grunge band nights (open May-Aug Wed.-Sun. 9am-3pm). The **Noosa 5 Cinema,** Cinema Centre, Noosa Junction (program info: tel. 5447 5300; general inquires: tel. 5447 5130) features current releases, art, and foreign films. (Admission $10.50, students and seniors $7.50, children $6.50. Matinee $8, students, seniors and children $6.50.)

SIGHTS AND ACTIVITIES

Noosa National Park (tel. 5447 3243) is a 454-hectare area of tropical vegetation, coastal walking paths, and rare wildlife which bills itself as the second-most visited park in Australia. Follow signs from the Noosa information booth on Hastings St. to the car park and park entrance (1km). The park is ideal for walking and jogging, and the tourist office provides maps of five interconnected walking circuits, ranging from 1 to 4.2km. The coastal track at sunrise (in winter around 6:30 or 7am, in summer a shocking 4:30am) is gorgeous; heat-sensitive strollers should take refuge in the inner rainforest. Be sure to bring water, particularly in the hot summer months. The beaches (some nude, some gay) are on Alexandria Bay on the eastern side of the park. (Picnic area, water, and toilets. Camping and dogs are prohibited, but swimming and surfing are permitted. Wheelchair accessible, with ramps and trails.)

Noosa is crawling with tour companies offering options for guided entertainment. For $59 you can romp with the dolphins, courtesy of **Just Dolphins** (tel. 014 665 183). **Camel Safaris** (tel. 5442 4402) offers two-hour camel trips down the beach for $30. **Clip Clop** horse riding (tel. 5449 1254) lets you splash for two hours through the shallow parts of Lake Weyba saddleback for $30. Thirty dollars will also get you a 100% guaranteed surfing lesson from **Learn to Surf** (tel. 5474 9076); they'll refund your money if you're not upright in two hours. Those itching for non-surf adventure can call **Total Adventure** (tel. 5471 0177) for abseiling, mountain biking, and sea kayaking equipment and trips.

One of Noosa's main attractions is the river. **Everglades Water Bus Company** (tel. 1800 688 045) offers a four-hour tour up the Noosa River for $43. **Everglades Cruises** has an open top deck and a full-day barbecue lunch special for $50. Call the tourist office for more info, or try renting a canoe from any of the shops in Noosaville.

By far the cheapest Fraser Island trip is through **Fraser Explorer** (tel. 5449 8647). Since the company owns its own vans and the ferry, it can offer discounted full-day trips for as low as $70.

■ Near Noosa

COOLOOLA NATIONAL PARK

Extending 50km north of Noosa up to Rainbow Beach is a sandy white coast and 64,000 hectares of forest known as the Cooloola National Park. Intrepid explorers and Sunday strollers alike will enjoy this wilderness area. The beaches are generally less populated than those in Noosa, but in summer months and holidays one can expect to find a thick blanket of tents and picnickers on the sands. From Noosa, take bus #10A to Riverlands and ride the Noosa River ferry across (ferry runs Sun.-Thurs. 6am-10pm, Fri.-Sat. 6am-midnight; free, cars $4). Many people rent 4WD vehicles and drive along the coast to Rainbow Beach or the Fraser Island ferry. Drive only at low tide and during the day.

Part of Queensland's Great Sandy Region Park, the Cooloola National Park forests hold many natural wonders: rainforests developed on pure sand, winding waterways shaded by mangroves, and characteristic Aussie critters like kangaroos, koalas, and ground parrots. Even the plants are unusual: endangered *boroniakeysii* (pink-flowered shrubs) mingle with thin, stubborn stalks of blackbutt, while melaeluka "tea trees" dye the river a deep black. One of the best ways to enjoy the park is to strap on a lifejacket and canoe up to the Everglades, where the dark water creates mirror images of the riverbank.

As in any wilderness area, keep **safety** in mind and watch out for the wildlife. Sharks in the river system occasionally approach the shore. Bullrats, which are little fish with big barbs that give a nasty sting, swim alongside the stingrays, catfish, and jellyfish in the ocean. Don't swim in Lake Kinaba and use caution elsewhere.

The **National Park Information Centre** (tel. 5449 7364) is at the Elanda Point Headquarters, 5km north of Boreen Point. Staff there can answer general questions and provide national park maps, suggestions for guided walks, information on camping sites, safety guidelines, and minimal impact advice.

Accommodations in Cooloola begin with **Gagaju** (tel. 5474 3522). This unique campground 25 minutes from Noosaville borders the Cooloola National Park and Noosa River ($6 per person campsite). Gagaju has an impressive recycled-wood shelter ($10 per bed) and a graffiti-decorated main tent, which holds the kitchen and "lounge" area. Lanterns, candles, and bonfires make up for the lack of electricity. (Running water, laundry facilities, and friendly management. Super-cheap canoeing, kayaking, and bushwalking tours and rentals available.) Many tourists choose the **Lake Cooroibah Holiday Park** (tel. 5447 1706; fax 5442 4452), located 1.2km from the beach with cabins, motel units, on-site tents, and campsites. Take Sunbus #10A to Riverlands, cross the river on the ferry and walk 2km up Maxmillian Rd. from the ferry. (Showers 20¢, laundry facilities, BBQ, horse rides; no pets, no linen supplied. Camping $4-5 per person; on-site tents $20 for 2 or 3 people.)

Fig Tree Point, Harry's Hut, and the privately owned **Elanda Point** grounds are family-oriented campgrounds that provide toilets and firewood. Elanda also has electricity. The other 15 national park sites are available for individual use by booking ahead through the park headquarters. The higher the site number, the more remote the site; sites 4 and up have no facilities and are only accessible by canoe. Camping permits for all sites are $3.50 per person and are payable at the self-registration stations throughout the park and at campgrounds. At the northern-most tip of the park, **Rainbow Beach** (tel. 5486 3160) is another family-oriented campground with a trailer park, shops, and, for the truly desperate, a pub. **Freshwater** camping ground (tel. 5449 7959; reservations required) on the coast has a public phone and is a good place for bass fishing.

THE HINTERLAND

The so-called Hinterland contains several attractions that draw travelers away from the coast. Locals and tourists alike flock to the bustling **Eumundi Market,** a refreshing cornucopia of fresh fruits, jams, antique linen, and arts and crafts (Sat. 6:30am-12:30pm; 40min. from Noosa Heads on bus #12). The village of **Montville** cultivates citrus groves, and nearby towns contain several kitchsy tourist traps, including the **Big Pineapple** plantation (tel. 5442 1333; free; open daily 9am-5pm), and the **Queensland Reptile and Fauna Park** (tel. 5494 1134; open daily 8:30am-4pm). Unfortunately, the Hinterland is inaccessible via public transportation; either rent a car or go with a tour company. **Noosa Hinterland Tours** offers moderately priced trips (tel. 5475 3366; open daily 7am-8pm). Parents can enjoy a day alone with **Kids Day Out** (tel. 0414 769 305); they offer several trips daily.

Bundaberg

Bundaberg and its outlying areas are not high on the list of Australia's choice idling spots; most visitors get a coffee at the bus terminal, stretch their legs, and hop back on board. To its credit, Bundaberg is one of Queensland's hottest spots to put in a few hours on the fruit-picking circuit, and the number of hostels in town reflect this draw. The season is almost year-round (except Dec.-Jan.), and hourly wages hover around $9-12. But Bundy is also home to Australia's finest rum and has convinced many workers that their earnings should never leave and that they themselves have no reason to hurry north. Those who choose to go light on nightlife, at least, quickly replenish their savings for the next leg of travel toward the Tropic of Capricorn.

PRACTICAL INFORMATION

Tourist Office: Tourist Information Centre (tel. 4152 2333). Follow Bourbong St. south from town about 2km toward Childers. Masses of brochures on the few attractions around the city, and an actual-size replica of Hinkler's famous aeroplane. Open 9am-5pm.

Parks Office: (tel. 4153 8620) near the bridge into town, on Quay St., on the ground floor of the "Government Office" building. Open Mon.-Fri. 9am-5pm.

Trains: Train station at the corner of Bourbong and MacLean St. Ticket office open Mon.-Fri. 9am-4:30pm, Sat. 9:30am-1:45pm and 3:30-4:30pm, Sun. 8:45am-1:45pm.

Buses: Coach's In terminal is on Targo St. To get to town, turn right out of the station and walk past the roundabout and McDonald's to Bourbong St. Open 7am-12:30am. **S&S Travel** (tel. 4152 9700) is located in the terminal building, open Mon.-Fri. 8am-5pm, Sat 8:30-11:30am.

Hospital: (24hr. tel. 4152 1222), at the corner of Bourbong St. and Tallon Bridge.

Emergency: Dial 000.

Police: (tel. 4153 9111) on Bourbong St.

Post Office: (tel. 4153 2700; fax 4151 6708) at the corner of Bourbong and Barolin St. Open Mon.-Fri. 8:30am-5pm, Sat. 8:30am-11:45pm. **Postal code:** 4670.

Phone code: 07.

ACCOMMODATIONS

The town's hostels slope quickly and seriously in quality, with the lowest-end places drawing in backpackers with promises of work that often fail to materialize: after paying for a week up front (to the tune of $100), only a couple of days of work are actually offered. A way to prevent the swindle is to ask guests at the hostel whether they have had luck finding work. If the managers object, it's perfectly O.K. to walk out. *Never* give your camera or passport to a hostel's management as bond, on the promise that work is forthcoming.

Bundaberg Backpackers (tel. 4152 2080; fax 4151 3355), across from the bus terminal at the corner of Targo and Crofton St. The optimum in comfortable workers' hostels. Laundry facilities. All bedrooms have A/C. Call for a pick-up at the train station. Dorms $15; doubles $30. Weekly: $100; $190. VIP, YHA. Key deposit $15, linen included.

City Centre Backpackers, at the Gosvenor Hotel, 216 Bourbong St. (tel. 4151 3501; fax 4153 5756). From the train station, walk straight across the parking lot; the hostel is on the right. From the bus terminal, call for a ride. A massive maze of rooms, halls, and common areas with plenty of space to stretch out after a long day of picking. The hostel is often booked solid, a sign of the quality and cleanliness in spite of the presence of a clientele of mud-soaked backpackers. Reception open daily 5am-8pm. Dorms $15, if you're just passing through $12. Weekly: $90. VIP, YHA. Key deposit $10. For a room with bath and TV, add $1. Blanket $1, linen $1.

Federal Guest House at the Federal Hotel, 221 Bourbong St. (tel. 4153 3711). From the train station, walk across the parking lot, and the hostel is in front of you. From the bus terminal, call for a pick-up. Located across from a tombstone engraver, the Federal is a no-frills workers' hostel, a place to kick the mud off your boots. Reception open daily 8am-8pm. Large dorms $14; 4-bed dorms $15. Weekly: $90; $95. Key deposit $15, linen included.

Finemore Caravan Park (tel. 4151 3663; fax 4151 6399), turn off Bourgong St. and onto Burrum St. at the train station. Make a left turn just up past the park. Open 7am-7pm. Campsites $8 (with vehicle $10); covered sites $14. On-site tents for 1 $12, for 2 $16. Cabin for 2 with bath $38, each additional person $4.

If the hostels in Bundy are booked to the gills, consider dropping south one coach stop to the town of **Childers.** The **Palace Backpackers Hostel,** 72 Churchill St. (tel. 4126 2244), is big and beautiful, though the town itself (population 4000) is a bit boring. The owner Jack (pronounced "jock") is happy to arrange work for guests. (Laundry facilities. Dorms $14, weekly $90. Key deposit $10, linen included, blankets $2.)

ACTIVITIES

Diving in Bundaberg is rock-bottom cheap. A carefully timed dive with **Bundaberg Aqua Scuba** (tel. 4153 576), across from the bus terminal, will see you stepping off an incoming coach, down for a dive ($25), back for a shower at the bus terminal ($2,

$5 deposit, key available at the travel agent), and on the next out-going coach. **Salty's,** 208 Bourbong St. (tel. 1800 625 476; fax 4152 6707) offers a PADI course ($149; Mon. and Thurs.). Two off-shore dives with gear cost $40 (2 reef dives $165; open Mon.-Fri. 8am-5pm, Sat. 8am-noon, Sun. 8-10am). The entertainment-strapped Bundy is famous for its **rum;** tours of the distillery (tel. 4152 4077; tours daily 10am-3pm; $5) are popular. Hostels have regular trips out to the distillery for interested guests, or ask at the information center for driving directions.

Fraser Island

Fraser Island was once called K'gari by the indigenous Butchulla people, who rescued the shipwrecked Eliza Fraser and were shortly thereafter moved off the island and into missions. The island remains one of the least tamed, yet most visited, islands off the Queensland coast. The sand dunes, sandblows, beaches, and cliffs are held in place by well-rooted rain forests. Where the vegetation has been removed, the wind moves the sand, inch by inch, until places like Lake Wabby are swallowed whole by advancing dunes. The island changes its entire body decade after decade, as the hills and valleys are swept down and built up again.

If the island's topography is in constant flux, its hourglass moves one grain at a time. The trunks of the King Ferns (*Angiopteris evecta*) on Wanggoolba Creek grow 25mm in diameter every century. Botanists are still waiting for a specimen to spore, but the plants (which have been around since the birth of Mohammed) are taking their time. Hugging a tree in the hidden Valley of Giants is like trying to put your lips around a watermelon—the trees have grown up to 3m in diameter. Dingoes and wild horses (brumbies) roam the island, sharing the land with Bearded Dragons and the Stinkhorn Fungus. Reef sharks patrol the coast, occasionally picking off an unlucky whale on its annual migration between August and November.

GETTING THERE AND AROUND

There are three basic options in getting to Fraser Island. Getting onto the island without a car is either cheap or easy, depending on your point of departure, but doing the trip by vehicle has its drawbacks

Ferries and Barges

Kingfisher Bay Barge (tel. 4125 5511) charges pedestrians $6 (vehicle passengers $4) on runs between Riverheads and Kingfisher Bay on the island (departs daily 7:15, 11:15am, and 2:30pm). Getting out to Riverheads (30min. by car from Hervey Bay) can be tricky. Alternatively, the **Kingfisher Bay Fastcat** (tel. 4125 5511) will pick up in Hervey Bay for free, but charges between Urangan Boat Harbour (just out of town) and Kingfisher Bay (departs daily 8:30am, noon, 4, and 6:30 or 7pm, plus Fri.-Sat. 10:30pm; one-way $15). Their free shuttle will also drop off returning passengers.

If you're going over in a car, you'll need to get a vehicle permit ($30) from the QNPWS or of its agents. **Hervey Bay City Council,** on Tavistock St. (tel. 4125 0222; open Mon.-Fri. 9am-5pm), and **Riverheads General Store,** just shy of the Riverheads barge landing (tel. 4125 7133, open 6:30am-6pm daily) are both agents. Camping permits ($3.50) are also sold in these places, as well as in the convenience stores on the island. The permits are good for all campgrounds except the privately run Cathedral Beach Resort and Dilli Village, both on the east shore.

Barge tickets for automobiles are another heavy expense (unless covered in a package). The barge from **Riverheads to Kingfisher Bay** (bookings tel. 4125 5511) charges $30 per car each way, plus $4 per passenger (motorcycles $7.50). Barges depart at 7:15, 11:15am, and 2:30pm. Getting from **Riverheads to Wanggoolba Creek** costs $30 each way, $5 per passenger, and departs at 9, 10:15am, and 3:30pm (booking tel. 4125 4444). **Urango Boat Harbor to Moon Point** is the same price, departing at 8:30am and 3:30pm, but Moon Point is dangerously close to the perilous swamps of the northwest coast. The barge on the southern tip, **Rainbow Beach to Hook Point** is $25 plus $1 per passenger (runs on demand 7am-4:30pm).

Tours

A more elaborate way to get to the island is with **Fraser Venture Tours** (tel. 4125 4444; fax 4125 4000). The least expensive tour ($30) is a daytrip to the most popular sights, but this is usually pitched to the older set. The next-most expensive tour hovers around $60, depending on the season, and allows you to stop off along the way and catch the next bus the following day (if space is available). The net result is a slow but dependable touring taxi service.

Stepping up the price ladder, almost every hostel in Hervey Bay offers a $95 per day three-day special on a 4WD truck, including almost all necessary gear; they book both guests and non-guests. The particulars change often, so it's worth asking a few questions at several hostels: Are sleeping bags included? What is the maximum number of people in the car? Is there an offer of free accommodations thrown into the bargain? A $500 bond is standard across the board, but you may find one or two that are willing to forego it with a little cajoling. The clear benefit of this option is that it's dead-on easiest.

Vehicle Rental and Driving on Fraser Island

For folks who want the thrill of hurtling down a beach, without the crunch of seven or eight people to a truck, several companies hire old army 4WDs at $75 to 85 per day. Camping kits cost an additional $10 to 30 per day depending on how many goodies you want or need. Some good operators in town include **Safari** (tel. 1800 689 819; fax 4124 6614), **Aussie Trax** (tel. 1800 062 275; fax 4124 4965), and **Hervey Bay Landrover Rentals** (tel. 4124 6177). All of these companies will do local pick-ups. There are several other operators; it's worth asking whether a rental agency (or person) belongs to the **Fraser Coast 4WD Hire Association,** the local self-monitoring watchdog organization.

Driving on Fraser gives you maximal flexibility but is only possible in a 4WD vehicle or a well-equipped motorcycle. Inland roads, usually pot-hole-covered single lane trails, wind through the close forests. Along the edges of the island, the beach acts as a nearly lawless eight-lane highway, where it's perfectly normal to swerve madly to one side to try to avoid a breaking wave or oblivious tern. In any case, you're tempting fate by driving on the beaches south of Dilli Village and Ungowa, or north of the Ngkala Rocks. The west side of the island north of Moon Point is easily mistaken for an automobile-eating swamp.

Etiquette for beach driving dictates that oncoming traffic should indicate with the turn signal which side of the road is preferred (it's almost impossible to hear oncoming traffic over the roar of the waves), but north-going automobiles usually hang surf-side. The most serious danger of beach driving lies in the tiny freshwater creeks which trickle from the hills. Even a shallow creek cuts into the sand enough to send vehicles flying off a mini-cliff—at 80kph that's an easy way to break an axle, bend a pin, or give everyone in the car whiplash.

Driving at night should be avoided since it's difficult to see the creeks that endanger vehicles. As none of the national parks' campgrounds have illuminated signs, it is nearly impossible to find an entrance in the dark. During the day, be certain to **check the low tides** at a ranger's office, convenience store, or on the free Hervey Bay tourist brochure available all over the mainland city. It's generally safe to drive three hours of either side of the low tide (which is a half-hour earlier than on the east coast, which is what's published for Hervey Bay). North of Indian Head this narrows to two hours on either side of low tide.

ACCOMMODATIONS AND SIGHTS

It is assumed that visitors to the island will camp, as the island hotels are prohibitively pricey, and even the beach-side huts are aimed at an upscale market.

Inland

Don't be fooled by the pleasant beige shade of Sunmap's island map; although the inland is made of sand, it is covered by rainforest and scrubby gum forest. Walking tracks zigzag around the island, connecting Central Station to Lake McKenzie (2hr.), Lake Birrabeen (1½hr.) and the closer Basin Lake (30min.), to name a few. If you can manage to get as far as **Lake McKenzie** without a car, it's possible to see most of the southern sights by following the hiking trails to Central Station (6km), Lake Birrabeen (5km), Lake Boomanjin (10km), and Dilli Village (7km). There are national park campsites at Lake McKenzie, and Lake Boomanjin. As there are snakes on the island; it's wisest to tread loudly and carry a big stick.

Lake McKenzie is the most popular of the fresh-water lakes, with white sands and shady pine trees. **Lake Wabby** (3½hr. by foot) is much the same, except that a towering sandblow is slowly devouring the lake as it moves along. (Some visitors enjoy sliding down the dunes into the lake. Not only is this disastrous for the dune's structural integrity, but spinal injuries can result from diving into the lake.) The southernmost lake, **Boomanjin,** is lined with fallen leaves. It's the largest of the lakes, and the largest of its kind in the world. Some of the lakes have tea-colored (but not flavored) water, caused by the overhanging swamp paperbarks and teatrees.

The Eastern Beach

There is a *lot* of beach on Fraser Island, and most of it looks the same, bordered by raging surf, and low-lying trees announce the tentative start of island vegetation. Heading north from Eurong, patches of rocks decorate the beach. There are short bypasses at **Poyungan Rocks** and **Yidney Rocks** and a longer route around the **Indian Head** promontory. Almost at the top of passable beachland, the **Champagne Pools** (or **The Aquarium**), a collection of shallow tide pools, make prime swimming holes at low tide. There's even a "changing nook" under the overhang that swimmers climb down to reach the pools. Be careful of the tides; not only is there a danger of being stranded by high tide, but incoming waves can crash up and over the pools, causing serious injury.

The **Kingfisher Bay Resort** offers a series of guided tours. The free walks are worth a look, especially the bush tucker walk, and are run on demand. Half-day tours ($42.50) are the best way to get to some of the more inaccessible (or impossible-to-find) places, including the Valley of the Giants. The resort also runs a catamaran out to Platypus Bay for whale-watching (Aug.-Oct., $42.50 per person). These trips are geared toward the older set, but don't discriminate; book at the **ranger station** (tel. 4120 3350; fax 4120 3413) in Kingfisher Bay Resort's Day Visitor Pavilion (open daily 8am-4:45pm). Free showers are in the resort; go to the Day Visitor Pavilion and turn right at the snack bar.

Hervey Bay

A dead give-away that someone is fresh into Hervey Bay is that the unwitting soul pronounces the city's name as it's spelled. In the same way that Paris is "Paree" and Krakow is "Krakov," Hervey Bay is actually "HAR-vee" Bay. The city itself is little more than a stepping-off point to Fraser Island, and visitors rarely feel quite like invited guests. The road in winds through one-pub towns, and the closest train station is in Maryborough (although there is a shuttle bus). The whale-watching season, between August and October, draws crowds of enthusiasts. Other than that, however, the local backpacker economy exists to serve visitors who arrive, depart for the island, and return to catch their bus onward. The city lacks a real beach of its own, and "night life" means resting up for the following day's trip.

ORIENTATION AND PRACTICAL INFORMATION

Hervey Bay is actually a clump of suburbs, named from west to east the Pialba, Scarness, Torquay, and Urangan. Most of the action is along The Esplanade at the water's edge. The harbor extends all the way down the Esplanade and then around to Pulgul St., and is a superb place to pick up cheap seafood fresh from the trawlers.

Tourist Office: (tel. 4128 2603), on the main road into town. Open Mon.-Fri. 9am-5pm.

Currency Exchange: National Bank, 415 the Esplanade (tel. 4125 2244). Commission to change traveler's checks $5, except Thomas Cook free; cash $5. Open Mon.-Thurs. 9:30am-4pm; Fri. 9:30am-5pm. The **ATM** accepts V, MC, Cirrus, Plus.

Trains: The station is outside the neighboring town of Maryborough, and a shuttle bus runs from there to Hervey Bay. There is a local bus to Hervey Bay (tel. 4123 1733; Mon.-Fri. 5:40am-5:25pm; Sat. 7:30am, 12:15, and 4pm; $4). When returning to the Maryborough rail station, keep in mind that the shuttle bus leaves town 30min. before scheduled train departure times.

Buses: McCafferty's and Greyhound are both handled by the same agent at the **Bay Bus Terminal** (tel. 4124 4000). No lockers. Most hostels send free courtesy buses to meet incoming coaches. Open Mon.-Fri. 7am-5pm, Sat.-Sun. 7am-1pm.

Public Transportation: Maryborough and Hervey Bay Coaches (tel. 4121 3719) run a circuit along the Esplanade, Boat Harbour Rd., and out to the Urangan Boat Harbour. The service is hail-and-ride, with a sliding rate scale depending on how far you're going. Service every hour Mon.-Fri. 6am-6pm, Sat. around 8am, 1, and 5pm. Schedules are found in tourist offices and most hostels.

Internet: Cyberlink Technologies, on the corner of Liuzzi St. and Old Maryborough Rd. (tel. 4124 7776; fax 4124 7733; email john@cyberlink.com.au). $10 per hr. Open Mon.-Fri. 8:30am-6pm, Sat. 9am-4pm.

Scooter Rental: Hervey Bay Scooter Hire (tel. 015 628 359). $15 first hour, $10 per hour thereafter, $35 per day.

Diving: Divers Mecca, 472 the Esplanade (tel. 4125 1626; fax 4125 1833). One dive uncertified for $80, PADI course $330.

Supermarket: Foodstore, 349 Esplanade (tel. 4124 6288). Open daily 6am-10pm.

Hospital: (tel. 4128 1444), on Long Street Pt. in the suburb of Vernon.

Emergency: Dial 000.

Police: (24hr. tel. 4128 5333), on the corner of Queens Rd. and Torquay Rd.

Post Office: 3 Bryant St. (tel. 4128 1047; fax 4128 2376). Head down Torquay Rd. with the bay to the right. Bryant St. is a 10-15min. walk from the hostels. Open Mon.-Fri. 8:30am-5pm, Sat. 8:30-11:30am. **Postal code:** 4655.

Phone Code: 07

QUEENSLAND

ACCOMMODATIONS AND FOOD

The sheer quantity of hostels in Hervey Bay point to its recent rise as a top backpacker destination. Most are on or next to the Esplanade, and all (except Friendly) pick up at the coach terminal.

Olympus Backpackers, 184 Torquay Rd. (tel. 4124 5331). A spacious re-vamped motel. Every unit has its own kitchen and facilities. Pool with a view of the bay. Reception daily open 6am-9:30pm. Dorms $13; twins and doubles $30. Linen included. VIP, YHA. Tent sites $5. Key deposit $10.

Colonial Backpackers (tel. 1800 818 280) corner of Boat Harbor Dr. and Pulgul St. in Urangan. Rustic, relaxing, and removed from the center of town, the hostel sports a pond, tennis, volleyball and basketball courts, and a pool. Rooms are clean and basic, and the common room ($10 video deposit) is next to an open kitchen—a great social scene. Laundry facilities. Courtesy bus into town 7 times per day, and access to local bus service. Reception open 6:45am-7pm and 8:30-9:30pm. 3-bed dorms $13; twins and doubles $30. Log cabin for 2 $50. Tent sites $6. Linen included. Key deposit $10. Cutlery deposit $5. Dinner $6. Bikes $2 per hr.

Fraser Magic Backpackers, 369 the Esplanade (tel. 4124 3488; fax 4142 5404). A casual and friendly atmosphere with a touch of the eccentric. Some of the dorm rooms are wallpapered with an antique car design. Reception open 7:30-11am and 2-7pm. Dorms $12; twins and doubles $30. Linen included. Laundry, $1 per wash.

Friendly Hostel, 182 Torquay Rd. (tel. 4124 4107). The owners are, indeed, friendly, and their grandparent-like demeanor indicates that guests are expected to behave as proper grandchildren. There are no double beds, but the place feels more like a B&B without the breakfast. Tours can be booked here, but the proprietors generally avoid competing with booking agents. 3-bed dorms $12; twins $24. No key deposit. Linen included.

Boomerang Backpackers Beachhouse, 335 the Esplanade (tel. 4124 3970; fax 4124 6911). An unremarkable motel reincarnated as a hostel, with laundry facilities, pool, and hot tub. Reception open 7:30am-6:30pm. Sliding dorm rates ($10-13) depending on the time of year; twins and doubles $30. $1 discount for VIP, YHA, ITC, or NOMAD. Key deposit $5. Linen included.

Koala Backpackers, 408 the Esplanade (tel. 1800 354 535). A full-on party hostel that looks like it's been through a few too many full-on parties. Daily happy hour at the pub 4:30-7pm. Laundry facilities and pool. Reception open daily 7am-7pm. Dorms $15. Pick up a voucher from the Noosa or Airlie Beach Koala Hostel (discount $3). Deposits for key $5, linen $5, cutlery $5. Dinner from $5.

Scarness Beachfront Caravan Park, on the Esplanade near the corner of Queens Rd. (tel. 4128 1274). Minimum security municipal campground right on the water. Laundry facilities, showers, BBQ. Open 24hr. Tent sites for 2 $12; with power $14; each additional person $3.70.

Hervey Bay has the usual spread of fast food chippies, with a handful of prohibitively expensive restaurants. For Japanese on a budget, try **The Black Dog Cafe,** on the Esplanade. (California roll $4, chicken teriyaki $8, green tea $2. Open 10am-3pm and 5-10pm. Closed Tues.) As the name tantalizingly hints, **O'Riley's Pancake and Pizza Parlor,** 446 the Esplanade (tel. 4125 3100), serves pancakes ($4-6) and pizza ($15-20). Weekend breakfast served 7:30 to 10:30am (Open Sun.-Thurs. 5-9:30pm, Fri. 5-10:30pm). The **Hervey Bay Bakery,** 432 the Esplanade (tel. 4125 1801), offers loaves ($2-3), custard tarts ($1.60), and a sublime cherry ripe slice ($1; bakery open Mon.-Fri. 6:30am-5pm, Sat.-Sun. 6:30am-2pm). **Curried Away** (tel. 4124 1577) makes free delivery of Sri Lankan and Indian yummies such as pumpkin curry ($7.50), Colombo lamb ($8), and samosas (4 for $3; V, MC; open late daily).

CAPRICORN AND WHITSUNDAY COASTS

From the Tropic of Capricorn, the Bruce Highway worms its way north through sugar cane fields and along a tropical coast that parallels the world's longest coral reef. Between Rockhampton and Townsville, some ocenside towns have morphed into backpacker havens like the unstoppable Airlie Beach, while others, such as Mackay, still grimace at the sight of sandals and an unwashed t-shirt. But if the working towns and cities tend to feel like roadside depots, they eagerly point inland to raw national parks and out toward irresistible islands and the Great Barrier Reef.

The isolated Eungella National Park, within easy reach of Mackay, rewards its few intrepid visitors with tumbling waterfalls, elusory platypuses, and graceful, creek-skimming fruit bats. The offshore islands vary in size and flavor, each with its own beaches and maze-like walking trails. Great Keppel Island, almost within sight of Rockhampton's shore, lacks roads entirely; the ferry lets passengers off on the beach. Much farther north off Airlie Beach, the Whitsundays are a blizzard of islands with rare, non-figurative Aboriginal art and the astoundingly pure Whitehaven Beach.

Rockhampton

Australia's "beef capital," Rocky sits on the Tropic of Capricorn, within easy reach of the beach escape of Great Keppel Island. It tries to be a seriously conservative town, with its share of hair salons and saddle shops. The wide streets lined with over 50 National Trust buildings are a tribute to the town's prosperity, which began over 100 years ago. Yet a few anomalies bubble up from the nondescript mass, testaments to a liberal spirit and refuges for the wayward traveler.

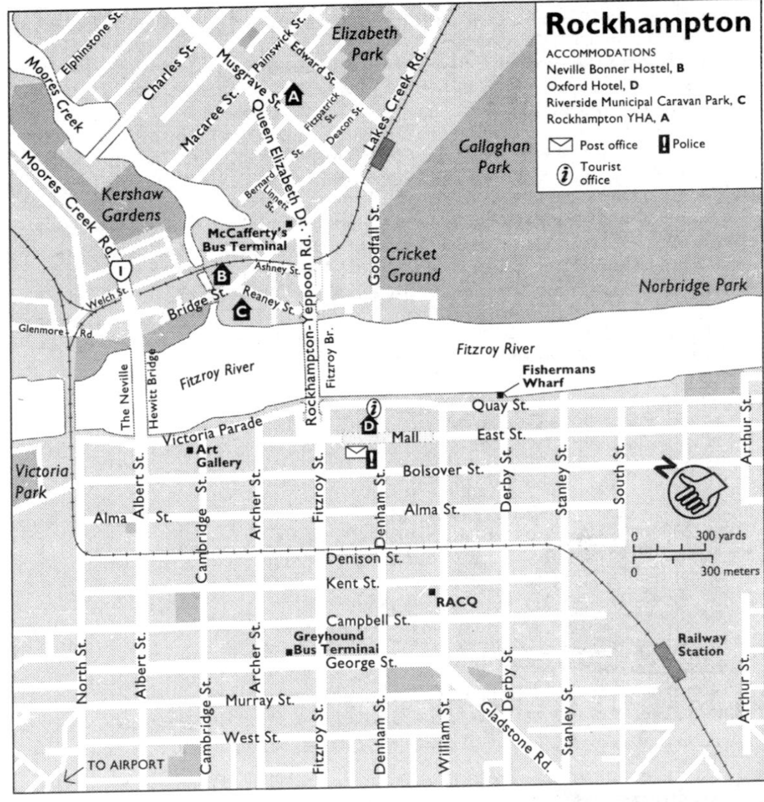

ORIENTATION

Travelers arriving in Rockhampton from either direction are met with a bronze statue of a cow, representing the city's patron livestock. These cows face away from the city, welcoming the visitors, and Rockhampton itself sits between the bovines' buttocks. On the south side of the **Fitzroy River,** the city is sliced into an easy grid design, with most of the action near the river's edge along **Quay St. Denham St.** cuts through Quay (pronounced "key") and sprints all the way out to the airport; along the way, trees make unexpected cameo appearances in the middle of the road, rising magically from the asphalt.

PRACTICAL INFORMATION

Tourist Office: Riverside Information Centre, at the corner of Quay and Denham St., on the riverbank (tel. 1800 805 865). Friendly volunteer staff trip over themselves to sell their city. Accommodation listings are updated regularly. Bus schedules (local and transfers to Yeppoon and the ferry terminal to Great Keppel Island). A free walking map of the city's historic sights. Open Mon.-Fri. 8:30am-4:30pm, Sat.-Sun. 9am-4pm.

Currency Exchange: Commonwealth Bank (tel. 4922 1733), in the mall. Traveler's checks $5 fee, no fee for cash exchange. Visa checks can be cashed with no fee at **ANZ,** 214 Bolsover St. (tel. 4931 7764), between Williams and Denham St. Most banks have **ATMs: National Bank** (corner of East and Denham St., in the mall) accepts V, MC, Cirrus, and Plus; **Commonwealth** (in the mall) and **Westpac** (corner of Quay and Denham) also accept Cirrus.

QUEENSLAND

American Express: Corner of Bolsover and Denham St. (tel. 4927 6288). Open Mon.-Fri. 8:30am-5pm, Sat. 9-11:30am.

Airport: 6km from town, up Denham St. and follow the signs. Carriers include **Qantas** (tel. 4922 1033) and **Ansett** (tel. 13 13 55). Taxis available curb-side. No local bus service but the YHA will provide free pick-ups.

Trains: At the end of Murry St. From the city center go south (away from the river) on any street, then turn left on Murry. The **Queensland Travel Centre** (tel. 4932 0234; fax 4932 0627) handles bookings at the station. Open Mon.-Tues. 7:15am-5pm, Wed. 6-8pm, Thurs.-Fri. 7:15am-8:15pm, Sat. 6-8:25am, Sun. 6:15-8:25am and 6:30-8:15pm. Lockers $2. Taxi into town about $9. Station open daily 6am-8pm.

Buses: McCafferty's terminal (tel. 4927 2844) is just short of the bridge in the city center, off Musgrave St. (which becomes Fitzroy St. on the other side of the bridge). Lockers $2. Open 24hr. **Greyhound's** terminal (tel. 4921 1890) is on the south side of Rockhampton, on George St. between Fitzroy and Archer St. Open daily 8:30am-5pm.

Public Transportation: Sunbus (tel. 4936 1002; fax 4936 2588) covers most corners in the city, with a sliding fare scale (usually $1.50-2). Bus schedules can be found in the Riverside Information Centre, and in most travel agencies.

Taxis: Rockhampton Cab Company (tel. 4922 7111).

Automobile Club: RACQ: Menzies Auto Service/Ampol (24hr. tel. 4926 1022), corner of Dean and Stewart St.

Library: (tel. 4931 1265), at the corner of Williams and Alma St. Travelers can not borrow books, but there is an **internet** terminal with free email access. Bookings for 30min. sessions are possible; ring ahead to get a good time.

Hospital: Rockhampton Base Hospital, on Canning St. between North and Cambridge St. (tel. 4931 6211, emergency room tel. 4931 6270); bus #4A south from city center will get you there in about 5min.

Police: Corner of Denham and Bolsover St. (tel. 4936 1500, open 24hr.).

Emergency: Dial 000.

Internet Access: Free at the library or $4 per hr. at **Magoo's** (in the Heritage Tavern, corner of Quay and Williams St.), open Mon.-Fri. 11am-6pm, Wed.-Sat. 8pm-4am.

Post Office: 150 East St., between William and Derby St. (tel. 4927 6566; fax 4927 6802). Fax services. **Postal code:** 4700. Open Mon.-Fri. 8:30am-5:30pm.

Phone Code: 07.

QUEENSLAND

ACCOMMODATIONS

Rockhampton Youth Hostel (YHA), 60 MacFarlane St. (tel. 4927 5288; fax 4922 6040), across the street and down a block to the left from the McCafferty's terminal. Or take bus #4A north from the corner of Denham and George St., and get off just after the bridge. Alternatively, you can call during office hours to arrange a free pick-up. The blocky brick building is in fine shape despite occasional wafts of gym sock smell from some of the rooms. TV room heated by a pot-bellied wood-burner. The hostel also puts together a package ($75) that includes a night in Rocky, two on Great Keppel at Captain Cook's Camp YHA, and return ferry ticket, including courtesy bus to and from the ferry. Reception open daily 7am-noon and 5-10pm. Dorms $15, YHA non-members $18; twins $32. Linen included. Key deposit $5. Sun. BBQ $5. Bike hire $12.

Downtown Backpackers (Oxford Hotel) (tel. 4922 1837), corner of Denham and East St. From McCafferty's, walk over the bridge, turn left onto East St. and walk halfway through the mall; from Greyhound it's a good bit down Denham St., at the mall. Trading night-time quiet for convenience, the hostel is smack in the middle of the city, right on top of a pub. The thick carpet in the TV room almost makes up for it; the stuff's so plush that it's enough to curl up on it with a good "M*A*S*H" rerun. The kitchen is less inviting. Laundry facilities. Dorms $13.50; doubles $25.

Neville Bonner Hostel, 5 Bridge St. (tel. 4927 3656). From the McCafferty's bus terminal, turn right toward the bridge, then right before the bridge onto Bridge St. From Greyhound, it's a long hike down Fitzroy St., over the bridge and then your first left, or take bus #4A north from the corner of Denham and George St., and ask to be let out at Bridge St. Unusually large motel-style rooms with private bath; linen included. By request, *Let's Go* has not published rates, but they are in line with the competition and include 3 meals per day, plus morning and afternoon tea. Aboriginally owned and operated, Aboriginal and Torres Strait Islander guests take priority for rooms.

The Riverside Municipal Caravan Park (tel. 4922 3779) is just off Bridge St., north of the river (and city center). The only campground in the area, it's extraordinarily popular and only slightly inconvenient. Reception open 24hr. Tent sites $11 for 2 people, $3 each additional person; powered caravan sites $13, $3 for the third or fourth person. Key deposit $5 for showers and toilets.

FOOD

Cafe Neon (ΚαφεΝειοΝ), on Denham St. between Bolsover and Alma St. (tel. 4922 5100). The coziest cafe this side of Brisbane, with plush couches, teddy bears, and a trickling fountain filled with gaping carp. Upstairs is more of the same, although the floors turn hardwood and the afternoon sun seeps in. Gay-friendly. Meals are cheap for the environs, generally $6-8, and cappuccinos go on special daily 5-6pm at $1 a mug. Open daily 9:30am-midnight. Ring ahead to reserve your favorite sofa.

Gnomes Vegi-Tarry-In, 104 Williams St. (tel. 4927 4713), near the intersection with Denison and over the train tracks. The ultimate in vegetarian hide-aways, Gnomes has a roaring fireplace (winters only), wide wicker chairs, a small waterfall out back, and 2 dozen varieties of tea ($2.50-3 a pot). Everything on the menu is vegetarian; a full meal is always $9.50. Live classical guitar music Sat. nights. Open Mon.-Thurs. 10am-10pm, Fri. 10am-11pm, Sat. 11am-11pm.

The Wild Parrot, 66 Denham St. (tel. 4921 4099), up past the railroad tracks. The Parrot, with its classic Caribbean motif, is a bit of a walk for the nighttime crowd, but easy on the wallet (meals $7-10). Open Tues.-Fri. 11am-late, Sat. 6am-late, Sun. 1am-6pm.

Rockhampton Viet Thai, 42 William St. (tel. 4922 1255), corner of William and Bolsover St. Over 80 delectable Thai and Vietnamese dishes, most around $10, with vegetarian dishes mostly $5-8. 10% discount on takeaway orders. Open daily 5-10:30pm and Tues.-Sun. noon-2:30pm.

SIGHTS AND ACTIVITIES

Rockhampton's highlights are the free **zoo** (tel. 4922 1654; open daily 8am-5pm) and **botanic gardens** (tel. 4922 1654; open daily 6am-6pm), next to each other on the south side of town. The zoo has the usual collection of kangaroos, crocs, cassowaries, and koalas (feedings 3pm), as well as a humongous geodesic domed aviary (open daily 8am-4pm) and even a pair of chimpanzees. The gardens are vast and include a fernery and a tranquil Japanese garden. They are a 10-minute ride from the city center with Sunbus on route #4A; catch it on the Denham St. side of the mall (about $6 return). On the other side of town are the **Kerfew Gardens,** another sprawling floral wonder open 24 hours a day (though toilets and the car park gates lock at 6pm). There's a waterfall BBQ area for lazy picnics.

For more culture (or an air-conditioned refuge from the heat of summer), try the **Rockhampton Art Gallery** (tel. 4931 1248; fax 4921 1738; open Tues.-Fri. 10am-4pm, Sat.-Sun. 11am-4pm). It has a permanent collection upstairs and space for touring exhibitions on the ground floor. Among the prints, oils, and acrylics is the unearthly *Burke in Central Australia* by Sidney Nolan (famous for his Ned Kelly series): the painting captures the burning dizziness of the Red Centre. Admission is usually free; touring exhibits may cost a few dollars.

Tucked away in the back corner of a warehouse, the **Rocky Climbing Centre,** 203 East St. (tel. 4922 7800), in the Walter Reid Building next to Schwimmer's Homeopathy, is an indoor climbing club open to the public. The walls are well-studded with funky handholds, and the atmosphere lends itself to a good afternoon's fun. Casual climbing (with a harness) costs $10. If you're traveling with sandals or thongs, real shoes can be hired for $6 (open Tues.-Fri. 1-8:30pm, Sat.-Sun. 10am-6pm; call ahead).

Fifteen minutes north of Rockhampton by car is the **Dreamtime Cultural Centre** (tel. 4936 1655; fax 4936 1671), a humble but at times elegant perspective on the indigenous peoples of Australia and the Torres Strait Islands. The center is set in a park with a meandering trail highlighting different medicinal and gastronomical plants of the area. At one point the tour gets a bit goofy, with an exhibit on Torres Straight Islanders' history set in the belly of a giant dugong, but the serious tone of the Sandstone Belt caves keeps the balance. (Open daily 9am-9:30pm, tours regularly from 10:30am. Admission $11.) **Get-about Tours** (tel. 015 156 069) has a daytrip that includes the botanic gardens and admission to the Dreamtime Centre (Tues. and Sat. departing 8:30am, $28). A less convenient but much cheaper alternative is the local Sunbus line. Route #10 north runs to the university (every 30min., return $6).

Olsen's Capricorn Caverns (tel. 4934 2883; fax 4934 2936) is another popular spot outside of Rocky, just up the road from the Dreamtime Centre. There's a day tour Mondays, Wednesdays, and Fridays (departing 9:30am) that takes visitors up to the caves for $25. Included in the price is an opportunity to take a self-guided tour through a "dry rainforest," not the most compelling attraction of the area. Regular admission for self-drivers is $10 (students $9), and includes a guided tour through the caverns. No public buses run to the site. The best time to hit the caves is during the three weeks on either side of December 22, when the summer solstice does some neat tricks with the cracks in the ceiling (best tour 11am). The caverns are open daily from 9am to 4pm.

NIGHTLIFE AND ENTERTAINMENT

The nightlife in Rocky is seriously lacking, but the university students in town can give it a kick-start when nothing's happening at the student union (university parties are closed to the public). Although every pub throws some music on the jukebox at night, nothing quite compares to **Magoo's** (tel. 4927 6996) at the Heritage Tavern, on the corner of Quay and Williams St. (Thurs.-Sun. live music. Happy hour 8-10pm, Fri. 5-9pm. Open Mon-Fri. 11am-6pm and Wed.-Sat. 8pm-4am. No cover.) Next door is **Flamingo,** widely accepted as the hippest nightclub in town, with multi-media sparkles. Cover is $5 after 9pm (free earlier), but the party doesn't really get started until about midnight. Up Quay St. next to the bridge is **The Criterion Hotel** (tel. 4922 1225), a great place to drink in the history of a gorgeous period hotel with a proper beer garden out back. There's never a cover charge, live music is played Wednesday through Sunday (rock, blues, or jazz), and happy hour is limited to Wednesdays and Thursdays (5:30-6:30pm). For the local **gay scene,** give the **Sports Bar** at Winsalls Hotel (tel. 4922 1836) a try. It's on the corner of Denham and Alma St. ($1 pots daily 5-8pm).

Rockhampton's arts venue, the elegant **Pilbeam Theatre** (tel. 4927 4111), at the corner of Victoria Promenade and Archer St., offers the occasional taste of music or theater, sometimes with student discounts (ticket office open Mon.-Fri. 9am-5pm, Sat. 9:30am-12:30pm). Rush tickets are usually available an hour before the curtain rises. Look for a *Spotlight* event guide at the information center, or get one at the ticket office. **Rockhampton 3 Cinemas** (tel. 4922 1511), at the corner of Denham and Alma St., has Tuesday specials ($7.50; other days $9; nights and Fri.-Sat. $10.60).

Great Keppel Island

A trip to Great Keppel is an instant vacation, the type of high-flying resort escape that suddenly falls within your budget. The butterfly-bespeckled island is mostly tracks and beaches, with fine snorkeling right off shore. The real coup is the pair of resorts (which *are* out of budget) that don't mind the odd backpacker sipping a cappuccino in style, or taking a catamaran out for a lazy afternoon.

GETTING THERE AND ORIENTATION

From the terminal in Rockhampton, **Keppel Tourist Services** (tel. 4933 6744) runs a ferry to the island (daily 9:15, 11:30am, and 3:30pm; tickets $27 return; terminal open daily 7:45am-5:15pm). This is the only ferry company that plies the waters year-round; in summer others may or may not surface, depending on local economics.

Getting to the ferry can be a bit of a problem, unless you're staying at Keppel Kamp-Out, which has a courtesy bus from the Rockhampton hostels and bus and train stations. The YHA throws a courtesy bus in with their two-night package. **Young's Bus Service** (tel. 4922 3813; $12.60 return) runs to the ferry from the corner of Denham and Bolsover St. (Mon.-Fri. 7 per day, Sat.-Sun. 3 per day). **Rothery's Bus Service** (tel. 4922 4320; $14 return) offers toughly the same service. Buy tickets from the driver. Timetables are available at the Riverside Information Centre. Parking is available for free in the dusty carpark outside the ferry terminal. At the roundabout off the main road, take the second left to the underground parking lot. Follow the road down and to the left, until the ferry terminal sign blazes in front of you.

The ferry lets passengers out on a patch of sand called **The Spit.** The main road in town is difficult to miss; there's only one road. In fact, there's just a **sidewalk** that connects one edge of the populated strip to the other end, a five minute stroll. There's a rumor that it's called Guenivere Boulevard, but frankly no one would know for sure.

ACCOMMODATIONS AND FOOD

It is possible to count the number of budget lodgings on one hand. Limiting the survey to accommodations with reasonable facilities, the list narrows to two. There is no camping allowed on the island, except for the hulking green permanent tents set up to handle the shuffle of backpacker traffic.

Captain Cook's Camp (YHA), book through the Rockhampton YHA (tel. 4927 5288) or by fax directly with the Great Keppel hostel (fax 4938 3392). Courtesy bus from Rockhampton to the ferry. A no-frills hostel which offers only what is necessary for a base for trips around the island. Reception open 8am-5pm, closed 12:30-1:30pm for lunch. Dorms $16, YHA non-members $19. Linen included. MC.

Keppel Haven (tel. 4933 6744). Hulking green "safari tents" are seriously overpriced considering there are 6 toilets and 6 showers for the 180 beds in the camp. Laundry facilities. Reception open 7:50am-5pm. Singles $20; doubles $22. Linen $5 per person, $30 deposit. Cutlery deposit $20.

Keppel Kamp-Out (tel. 4939 5799). This all-inclusive, super-vacation package is a borderline "excessive splurge" for the budget-conscious. Accommodation is in those familiar big green tents. Max. 60 people staying in the camp at once, but they're free to use the resort's unmotorized water toys. Laundry facilities. Courtesy bus to the ferry from Rockhampton. V, MC; no traveler's checks. $49 per night ($69 if you book ahead) includes 3 meals, all with fruit, hot drinks, and wine.

Unless you're going to Keppel Kamp-out, you'd do well to bring your own food. A generally overlooked deal is the **Rosslyn Bay Fisherman's Co-op** (tel. 4933 6105; open Mon.-Fri. 9am-5pm, Sat.-Sun. 8:30am-5pm), on the mainland. If you have a few minutes before the ferry takes off, check out the fresh-from-the-water offerings. From the ferry terminal, take a left down the side-street, and it's a two-minute walk. Half the stuff they sell is already cooked (crabs, bugs, prawns) and makes an easy dinner.

Great Keppel itself has limited offerings. At **The Shell House** (tel. 4939 1004), there are approximately one gazillion shells in the front room, where Derek cheerily serves up coffee ($1), tea ($1 a pot), and Devonshire tea ($5). Open daily, from "about early" to "not *too* late." **Island Pizza** (tel. 4939 4699) serves large pizza ($16-20) and garlic bread ($3; open Tues. 6pm-late, Wed.-Sun. 12:30-2pm and 6-9pm).

SNORKELING AND DIVING

Monkey Beach is generally accepted as the best place to go snorkeling off the beach, a mere half-hour jaunt south from the hostels. The hike up to the **Old Homestead** and back takes an afternoon, and a trip to the **lighthouse** at Bald Rock Point takes the better part of a day. Keppel Haven's *Track Map* is ideal for bush walks; it's free at the ferry terminal on the mainland, or 50¢ on the island. A larger, prettier, but less detailed map is also widely sold on the island ($1).

For those desiring a little sport in their island adventures, the **Beach Shed** (tel. 4939 2050) has windsurfers ($8 per 30min.), jet skis ($30 per 15min.), and the old stand-by snorkel and fins ($10 per day). The **Dive Shop** (tel. 4939 5022) right next door offers dives for the certified ($40) and the uninitiated ($80). YHA members making two dives get a 20% discount. For many visitors, however, it's enough to curl up on any one of the beaches, listen to the gentle lap of clear blue waters, and take it easy.

Mackay

There are some excellent places to visit outside of Mackay ("muck-Eye"), and some worthwhile ways of getting out of Mackay, but an extended stay in the city would be overwhelmingly dull to the senses. The downtown area feels as though it simply halted in the 1950s. Pubs are in bright Art Deco style, gentlemen have conservative short-clipped hair, and shopkeepers act reserved and perhaps a little guarded at the sight of newcomers. There is an "underground" of teens and twenty-somethings that has been trying to carve a niche for itself in town, but without much success. Possibly symbolic of Mackay's alter ego, the central section of Victoria St. has wiggling sidewalk mosaics of wildlife scenes, and even the occasional bronze raccoon peeking over the side of a bench.

ORIENTATION AND PRACTICAL INFORMATION

The city proper sits south of the **Pioneer River.** Parallel to the river is **Victoria St.,** the main road and landmark for most of what Mackay has to offer. The Bruce Hwy. comes into the west side of town, and the exit leads to **Gordon St.,** parallel to Victoria. The beach on the east side is phenomenal at low tide, since the water sometimes pulls out as far as one of the outlying islands.

Tourist Office: Mackay Tourism Office, 4km south of town on the Bruce Hwy. (tel. 4952 2677; fax 4952 2034). Open Mon.-Fri. 8:30am-5pm, Sat.-Sun. 9am-4pm.

Budget Travel Office: Flight Centre (tel. 4957 4844; fax 4957 4749) in the Caneland Shopping Centre, near Big W. Open Mon.-Fri. 9am-5:30pm, Thurs. 9am-9pm, Sat. 9am-3pm.

Currency Exchange: Commonwealth Bank, 126 Victoria St. (tel. 4953 5559; fax 4951 5592). Traveler's checks $5 fee, cash no fee. Visa checks can be cashed for free at **ANZ,** corner of Sydney and Victoria St. (tel. 4951 2755; fax 4957 3572). Both have **ATMs** which accept V, MC, and Cirrus, as does **Westpac,** at Victoria and Woods St. Only **National Bank,** at the corner of Victoria and Sydney St., accepts Plus, as well as V, MC, and Cirrus.

American Express Office: 166 Victoria St. (tel. 4953 5210; fax 4953 5727). Holds mail free for 1 month for cardholders, but does not exchange traveler's checks. Open Mon.-Fri. 8:30am-5pm, Sat. 8:30am-noon.

Airport: (tel. 4957 0220), about 5km from town. No public transport, but hostels offer free pick-ups and a taxi costs about $10. **Qantas** (tel. 4953 5999) and **Ansett** (tel. 4957 1574) are the major carriers. Open 24hr.

Trains: The train station is about 5km from town. No public transport (but hostels offer free pick-ups) and a taxi costs about $10. There is no ticket counter at the station; tickets must be purchased in town at any travel agent. **Queensland Rail** bookings (tel. 13 22 32). Lockers $2. Open 24hr.

Buses: The main entrance to the bus terminal (tel. 4951 3088; fax 4951 1009) is on the corner of Milton and Gordon St. Booking desk handles bus, train, and air ticketing. V, MC. Ticket counter open daily 7:30am-7:30pm. Terminal open 24hr. Call hostels for free pick-up.

Taxis: Mackay Taxi (tel. 13 10 08). The **Taxi Transit** program (tel. 1800 815 559) hires taxis for trips as far as the northern beaches (Eimeo Beach $3.50), but not the rail station, airport, or harbor. Open Mon.-Fri. 7am-6:30pm, Thurs. 7am-9:30pm, Sat. 7am-3:30pm. Book at least 1hr. in advance; taxis leave from the Caneland Shopping mall every hr. on the half-hour.

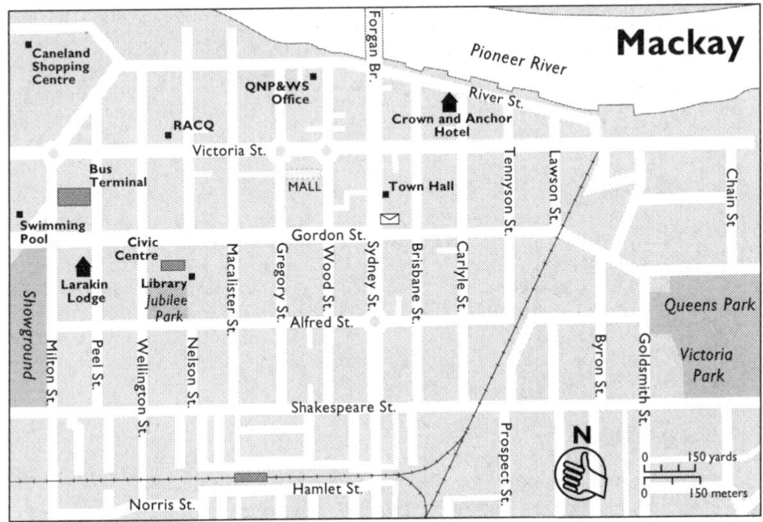

Car Rental: Thrifty (tel. 4957 3677) and **Budget** (tel. 4925 2344) are neck-and-neck for cheapest hires, typically $40 per day with 50km. **Hertz** (tel. 4957 2662) can go as low as $40 per day with 100km, depending on availability.

Automobile Club: RACQ, 35 Evans Ave. (24hr. tel. 4957 3555). Auto repair and towing services.

Camping Supplies: Camping World, corner of Gregory and Alfred St. (tel. 1800 808 783; fax 4953 1966). Maps, cooking supplies (butane canister $3.50), tents (from $70), bush hats ($20-30). Open Mon.-Fri. 8am-5pm, Sat. 8:30am-12:30pm.

National Parks Office: at the corner of River and Wood St. (tel. 4951 8788). Does not take camping bookings. Videos on 'roos and reef. Open Mon.-Fri. 8:30am-5pm.

Hospital: Mackay Base Hospital (tel. 4951 5211). Follow Gordon St. west to the Bruce Hwy. (south), turn right at Bridge St., and it's on the left before the bridge.

Hotlines: Victims of Crime (24hr. tel. 1800 689 339).

Police: On Sydney St., between Victoria and Gordon St. (24hr. tel. 4968 3444).

Emergency: Dial 000.

Post Office: On Sydney St., between Victoria and Gordon St. (tel. 4957 7333; fax 4951 3394). Fax services. **Postal code:** 4740.

Phone Code: 07.

ACCOMMODATIONS

The local YHA hostel, **Larrikin Lodge,** 32 Peel St. (tel. 4951 3728; fax 4957 2978), represents the better half of Mackay's budget hostels. The Lodge is a wide Queensland timber house with sloping ceilings and a covered porch out back, and is just three minutes from the bus terminal (calling for a pick-up is fine, though). There's a dinky little pool out back, one and a half hammocks, BBQ, and laundry. Videos are often playing on the VCR. Reception open daily 7-10am and 5-10pm. If you ring the bell at any other time, you're apt to get a cross manager. (Dorms $14, YHA non-members $16. No doubles. Linen free for YHA members, or $2 for the first night.)

The **Crown and Anchor Hotel,** at the corner of Brisbane and River St. (tel. 4953 1545), offers dorms ($15) stacked in old-style pub rooms with lots of charm and little buffer from the jukebox one floor below. (Linen included. Laundry (no dryer), BBQ, daily lunch and dinner specials $2.) Guests are invited to a free BBQ on Sundays. Camping in the backyard is free, but with no guarantees for your personal safety.

FOOD

Since Mackay is a booming industrial town, pubs try to draw in crowds with $2-3 lunch and dinner specials, expecting (but not requiring) the thirsty workmen to buy a schooner or two. Have a wander down Victoria and River St. to see what's on. For basic shopping needs, there's a **Woolworths** (tel. 4951 2288) in the **Caneland Shopping Centre** (open Mon.-Fri. 8am-9pm, Sat. 8am-5pm; V, MC, and traveler's checks accepted).

The cheapest deal in town for non-fried morsels is the **Tropical Salad Bar** (tel. 4957 3116) at the corner of Victoria and Sydney St., specializing in salad sandwiches ($2-3), homemade soup with bread ($2), and generous fresh fruit salad ($3). The coffee ($1.90 a mug), however, can be weak and watery (open Mon.-Fri. 7am-4pm, Sat.-Sun. 7am-noon). Just as good and a few dollars more are the lunch specials at **The Meeting House,** 53 Sydney St. (tel. 4953 5835), next to the police station. Oversized portions of Indonesian, Chinese, and Korean pan dishes are $5, if you can fight your way in for a seat (open Mon.-Fri. noon-2pm and 6:30-9pm, Sat. 6:30-9pm; reservations accepted). The decor of **Capitol Cafe** (tel. 4957 3913), on Sydney St. between Victoria and River St., carries the spirit of Mackay well. This American 50s-style diner has era memorabilia and the requisite Elvis tunes on the jukebox (open Mon.-Sat. 7am-5:30pm, Fri. 7am-4pm, Sun. 7am-2pm).

Several upscale restaurants offer a fair amount of food below the $10 mark. **The Spotted Dick,** at the corner of River and Sydney St. (tel. 4957 2368), is totally out of place in the conservative city of Mackay; within is a funky Mediterranean decor, with bulbous corners and wacky seating. Good meals can be had for $7-10, and most of the wood-oven pizzas are just under $10. There's a happy hour on weekdays from 5 to 7pm, and live music (no cover charge) on the weekends (open Mon.-Sat. 10am-midnight, Sun. 11am-midnight). **Ban-Na,** at the corner of Victoria and Wellington St. (tel. 4951 3939),is an excellent Thai restaurant best experienced as a takeaway. A big pot of Pad Thai is $7.50, and more exquisite dishes go for about $10. Call ahead for takeaway (open Mon.-Fri. 11:30am-2:30pm and daily 6-10:30pm).

Brumby's Hot Bread (tel. 4957 5722), on Sydney St. next to the post office, is an excellent little bakery, with croissants ($1), bagels (90¢), and a massive variety of breads and $2 sandwiches. On the far end of River St., right on the river, find **Sea Fresh Seafood** (tel. 4951 3888). This small retail store has dozens of types of shellfish and gilled wonders for a couple of dollars under market price, including some ready-made dinners (open Mon.-Fri. 8:30am-5:30pm, Sat. 8:30am-12:30pm).

SIGHTS AND ENTERTAINMENT

The **Queen's Gardens,** on the way to the beach, is where you'll find the lovely **Orchid Gardens** (open Mon.-Fri. 10:30-11am and 2-2:30pm, Sun. 2-5pm). Be careful walking through the park after nightfall. **Roylen Cruises** (tel. 4955 3066) shuttles between Mackay Harbor and **Brampton Island.** A daytrip ($50) includes an obligatory lunch at the resort on Brampton, but you might be able to sweet-talk a lower fare (without the lunch) if you wait to buy your ticket at the pier (departs daily at 9am). From Brampton it's possible to walk across to **Carlisle Island National Park** at low tide, but be certain to check the tides to prevent being stranded.

A **public swimming pool** is at the corner of Gordon and Milton St. (admission $2, towel hire $1. Open June-Aug. daily 9am-5:45pm; Sept. Mon.-Sat. 6am-5:45pm, Sun. 9am-5:45pm; Oct.-April Mon.-Sat. 6am-5:15pm, Mon-Tues. and Thurs.-Fri. until 8pm, Sun. 8am-5:45pm.) For a rainy day, the **Mackay 5 Cinema,** at the corner of Gordon and Sydney St. (tel. 4953 4700), offers movies for $9-10, with weekly budget specials. **Paper Chain,** 8 Sydney St. (tel. 4953 1331), has a wide assortment of second-hand paperbacks, travel guides, and foreign titles, and exchanges are welcome (open Mon.-Fri. 8:45am-5pm, Sat. 8:45am-12:30pm, Sun. 9am-12:30pm).

Occasional word-of-mouth parties pop up at the otherwise dead nightclubs; the best way to find the crowd is by hitting the favorite dive at just the right time. **Coffee**

Club, corner of Victoria and Wood St. (tel. 4957 8294; open Sun.-Thurs. 6:30am-midnight, Fri.-Sat. 6:30am-2am), is that dive. During the third week of June, the **Mackay Show** comes to the fairgrounds on the corner of Gordon and Milton St.

■ Near Mackay

Twenty minutes north of Mackay along the Bruce Hwy. is **The Leap,** a small town named in commemoration of an Aboriginal woman who, with her baby daughter in her arms, leapt from a mountaintop to her death. The details of the story are disputed. Around Mackay, the plot includes a harmless game of "chase the Aboriginal"; the woman took it too seriously and ran for her life. But at The Leap's **pub** (tel. 4954 0993; open Mon.-Sat. 10am-10pm, Sun. 10am-7pm), there's a different slant, according to a display put up by a local historian. The woman, Koweha, was chased up the mountain together with a party of Aboriginals who had raided a white settlement. The pursuers, Native Police collected from distant (and therefore unrelated) tribes, were relentless, and Koweha (unarmed) jumped amid gunfire. Her daughter survived and was adopted and baptized a year later by a white family.

A little farther up the Bruce Hwy. is the exit to **Cape Hillsborough,** a national park with wide beaches and a handful of walking trails. The ranger's office (tel. 4959 0410; open daily 7:30am-4pm) is where to get camping permits for (and directions to) the **Smalley's Beach campsite** (toilets, water, no showers). Advance bookings are essential. Mackay City Council charges $8 per night to camp at **Cape Hillsborough** (toilets, water, showers). A councilman comes around in the morning to collect fees. Powered sites ($15) are available at the neighboring **Cape Hillsborough Holiday Resort** (tel. 4959 0152; reception open daily 8am-7pm).

Eungella National Park

Eungella National Park, 84km west of Mackay, is all about mountains. Much of the 49,610-hectare park, the largest in central Queensland, is inaccessible to the average tourist because the rainforest-covered slopes are too steep and the misty valleys too deep. The mountains trap clouds, resulting in high precipitation, and serve as natural barriers between this park and other swaths of rainforest in Queensland. The combination of lots of water and genetic isolation has resulted in at least six species of plants and animals in Eungella (YOUNG-guh-la) that exist nowhere else on the planet. Herpetologists consider the park a hotspot for frog diversity, in particular, and are concerned about the unexplained probable extinction of more than half a dozen frog species, including the Torent Frog, in the park's area. Still around but endangered is the Eungella Gastric Breeding (also called Platypus) Frog, *Rheobatrachus vitellinus.* This species of frog lays its eggs, swallows them, incubates them in its stomach, and spits out live tadpoles. More common but just as lovely, red cedars, palms, and giant ferns coat many slopes, and platypuses splash in the rushing water at the bottom of some ravines.

MACKAY TO EUNGELLA

The road to Eungella is off the south side of Mackay, along the Bruce Hwy. If you're coming from the north, there's a short-cut down the sugar cane lanes; turn right at the Marian sign, just north of The Leap, and turn right (west) when you hit the main road in Marian. The road passes through a couple of sugar cane towns with looming roadside refineries.

Along the way is the recently relocated **Illawong Sanctuary** in Mirani (tel. 4959 1777; fax 4959 1888), a well-maintained wildlife sanctuary sparsely populated by the usual suspects: koalas, kangaroos, crocs, and kookaburras. The place looks like a miniature golf green, complete with a barbed wire perimeter fence. The thrill of seeing a pineapple bush in the bush is mitigated by the pathside signs warning visitors not to stray from the well-clipped trail, as this is Taipan snake country. (Open daily 9:30am-5pm. Tours and feedings daily at 3:30pm. Admission $10. Return bus to Mackay and ticket combo $40.)

Farther along as you come from Mackay is the **Finch Hatton Gorge.** Its walking trail may or may not yet be repaired; contact the ranger (tel. 4958 4552) for the latest. Walking trail maps are available for free at the QNP&WS office in Mackay, or at the **Palmco Kiosk** (tel. 4958 3285; open daily 9am-5pm), on the road to the gorge. The kiosk is a remarkably cheery shopfront in the middle of a rainforest. Equally improbable are its specialties, including mango cheesecake ($4.50), croissant sandwiches ($4-5), and fresh coffee ($2.50 a mug). The sign out front explains the peculiar economics of a cafe in the middle of nowhere: "Eat here or we'll all starve!"

Also on the dirt road to Finch Hatton Gorge and over one creek is one of the few reasons to go out of one's way and visit the Mackay region: the **Platypus Bush Camp** (tel. 4958 3204 to check availability). It's rough living, no doubt about it, but this **hostel is in the thick of the rainforest,** bordered on one side by a clear creek that is filled with platypus families every 20m. The two shared huts, built on stilts for the summer floods, are also open-sided watchtowers to the surrounding wildlife; beds ($15) are no more than a mattress and pillow, so bring your own linen. To get to a third hut, the double ($40), one must cross a brook, wander a short distance from the base camp, and climb on up. The real winner is the view. Looking down at the creek, you'll be able to watch (with luck) the platypus frolic, the fireflies swarm, and the fruit bats dip for a sip of water. The kitchen area is open-air (bring your own food); there's a gently rocking porch swing in the common area hut, and the toilets and hot showers are rustic but personable. Camping is $5 a head, and free pick-ups in Mackay are possible with a minimum of four people.

THE PARK

The last stretch of road before the park officially begins looks as though it will smack right into a mountain face, but curves at the last moment and then winds up the side of the mountain. At the summit is the **Eungella Chalet** (tel. 4984 8509; open daily 9am-10pm). The cafe provides a panoramic view, and is a great place to sip a cup of coffee ($1.50, free refills) and contemplate life. Around the corner down the road to Broken River is the **Sky Window Church,** a 200m wheelchair-accessible trail with great views, a picnic ground, and toilets.

Broken River is the main draw of the park. It's actually a section of river with excellent platypus-spotting, a picnic area and campground (with toilets and hot showers), and an immensely knowledgeable QNP&WS ranger with narrow office hours (tel. 4958 4552; fax 4958 4501; open daily 7-8am, 11am-noon, and 3-3:30pm, unless he's out fighting a forest fire). Camping permits are $3.50 per person per night. From Broken River there are nine walking trails (10min.-5hr. in length).

Reeforest (tel. 4953 1000) runs tours from Mackay Tuesday through Sunday and includes a BBQ lunch ($45, students $40.50). **Brigitte's Tropical Tours** (tel. 4951 1999, after-hours 015 632 521; fax 4954 8765) generally has smaller groups and doesn't include lunch (Wed. and Sat.; $40). Brigitte comes along for the bush walks, explaining things (in English or German) as the group goes along.

Airlie Beach

Imagine an unspoiled bay with a big grassy spot off the main road where backpackers slow down to sunbathe and to watch the tides roll in and out. The islands blaze in photogenic fury at sunset, and the mountaintops of the Whitsunday Islands rise out of water tinted a strikingly aqua color usually reserved for postcards. Airlie (AY-er-lee) has become something of a port town for seafarers and island-bound divers. Like any small port town, it has an inherent degree of innocent vice. The sunbathers eye each other furtively, couples form at the nightclubs and dissolve again over breakfast, and crowds of men cheer together over afternoon TV sports matches.

ORIENTATION AND PRACTICAL INFORMATION

Airlie Beach's layout is simple enough: one main street, **Shute Harbour Rd.,** gently slopes downward and to the east, with Airlie Bay to the north. Most of the hostels and restaurants are on this stretch, but a series of picnic tables and benches line the parallel Beach Walk. Sunbathers entrench themselves along **Airlie Esplanade,** which turns left toward the bay off Shute Harbour Rd. and heads into the recreation reserve.

Travel Office: One on every street corner, but **Destination Whitsundays** (tel. 1800 644 563; fax 4649 5008), on the corner of Shute Harbour Rd. and the Esplanade, has the most helpful staff. **Internet access** ($10 per hr.). Accommodations and tour booking. Cheap camping gear hire. Open daily 7:30am-6:30pm.
Currency Exchange: Commonwealth Bank, across from the bridge (tel. 4946 7433; fax 4946 7710), cashes most traveler's checks with a $5 commission. No fee for cash exchange. Open Mon.-Thurs. 9:30am-4pm, Fri. 9:30am-5pm.
ATMs: ANZ, next to the post office, accepts V, MC, AmEx, Cirrus, and Plus.
Buses: Greyhound (tel. 13 20 30) and **McCafferty's** (tel. 13 14 99) drop off in the center of town within walking distance of most hostels; accommodations on the outskirts of town send courtesy buses to meet every incoming coach. Almost every travel office and most hostel desks can book transport. **Sampson's Bus** (tel. 4945 2377) picks up (every 30min., $11) at the **rail station** in **Proserpine,** the turn-off for Airlie Beach on the Brisbane-Cairns route.
Local Transportation: Sampson's (tel. 4945 2377) runs between Cannonvale and Shute Harbour, daily 6am-6pm, and stops in front of the post office. Fares depend on distance. Otherwise, call **Whitsunday Taxi** (tel. 1800 811 388), or rent from **Airlie Beach Car and Motor Scooter Rentals** (tel. 4746 6110), on Waterson Rd., off Shute Harbour Rd. $35 half-day, $45 a full day, unlimited kilometers.
Market: Airlie Beach Community Market, along the beach walk. Sat. 8am-noon.
Medical Services: Whitsunday Medical Centre (24hr. tel. 4946 6275). Open Mon.-Fri. 9am-6pm, Sat. 9am-6pm, Sun. 11am-6pm.
Emergency: Dial 000.
Police: (tel. 4946 6445), Shute Harbour Rd., across from Bush Village Backpackers.
Post Office: Up the hill along Shute Harbour Rd. (tel. 4946 6515; fax 4946 6515). Fax. Open Mon.-Fri. 9am-5pm, Sat. 9am-11:30am. **Postal code:** 4802.
Phone Code: 07.

ACCOMMODATIONS

Airlie Beach was an upscale tourist resort until the Pilot Strike of the 1980s, when Queensland's tourism industry ground to a devastating halt for a year and a half. The resorts went backpacker in a bid for survival (as this demographic will sit on a bus for 10 hours to come to town), and most haven't bothered to switch back. As a result, the hostels are generous to luxurious (bathrooms and kitchenettes in-room). Doubles can be difficult to find at times, so booking ahead is recommended. Linen included and $10 deposit expected for key, unless otherwise indicated.

Be forewarned that nearby nightclubs tend to make up in volume what they lack in style, an important consideration when choosing a hostel for a good night's sleep.

Whitsunday Backpackers, also known as Club 13 Begley Street (tel. 4946 7376), is tops, both in room quality (some have tubs) and location (up a steep hill with killer views from the kitchen terraces). There's a pueblo feel to the place, entirely unlike anything else in Airlie Beach. Courtesy bus meets all incoming buses. Pool. Reception open daily 7am-6pm. Dorms $14; doubles (only 2 in the hostel) $34. VIP, YHA. Hot breakfast included.
Koala, Shute Harbour Rd. (tel. 4946 6001; fax 4946 6761), is closer to the beachfront and has a Polynesian flavor, with individual dorm huts set back from the road. One of 2 places in town with camping ($8, $12 for 2 people). Pool, satellite TV in each room, hot tub, laundry. Overwhelmingly aqua reception open daily 7:30am-7:30pm. Dorms $14; twins and doubles $36. VIP. Cutlery $5. Top sheet $5. Blanket $20. Bar dinners from $5.

Club Whitsunday, 346 Shute Harbour Rd. (tel. 4946 6182; fax 4946 6890). The free hot breakfast is the main draw, with the funky rooms coming a close second. Reception open 7:30am-7:30pm daily. Dorms $15; doubles or twins $30-35.

Reef Oceania, 141 Shute Harbour Rd. in Cannonvale (tel. 4946 6137; fax 4946 6846). Far from town (3km), but with free hourly bus service (10am-midnight) back to the clubs and marina. Sprawls across 15 hectares of land including a lengthy stretch of private beach. Courtesy bus pick-ups meet incoming coaches. Laundry, pool. The spacious but potentially noisy bunkhouse ($8) is the only choice with separate bathroom facilities, aside from camping ($5 per person). A bed in the shingle-sided huts is $10; smaller plywood huts run $12.50. Doubles $35. Sun. afternoon all-you-can-eat seafood BBQ $6. Free luggage storage. Book a dive course with Kelly Dive and get 2 nights free.

Backpackers by the Bay, 12 Hermitage Dr. (tel./fax 4946 7267), is a short walk from town with a view of the bay's scintillating waves at high tide and sloppy mud flats at low. The rooms are proper bunk-only style, and the atmosphere is loose and relaxed. Pool, laundry. Courtesy bus meets incoming coaches; a shuttle runs to town 8 times per day. Reception open daily 7am-7:30pm. Dorms $14; twins or doubles $32. VIP. Bikes $14 per day. Top sheet and blanket 50¢ per stay.

Club Habitat (YHA), 394 Shute Harbour Rd. (tel. 4946 6312; fax 4946 7053), is a large white-brick building. Some rooms have TV and air-conditioning. Laundry, pool. Reception open daily 7am-8pm. Dorms $15; doubles and twins $35. Non-members pay $3 extra.

Whitsunday Bunkhouse (tel. 1800 683 566) is the no-frills approach to backpacking. Bare-bones lodging in the middle of town. No pool, no laundry, no pick-ups, no problem. Dorms $12; doubles or twins $30.

An accommodation choice which ensures great privacy at minimal cost is to simply head out and plunk yourself down on an island for a day or three. With 74 islands, most of them uninhabited, it's just you, a tent, and a whole lot of stars at night. **Island Camping Connection** (tel. 4946 5255) takes a minimum of two people to almost any island for $35 return per person, not including national parks camping permits ($3.50, available at the QNPW&S office down Shute Harbour Rd.). Camping kits are available for a small charge, otherwise try renting at the Destination Whitsundays travel office.

QUEENSLAND

FOOD AND ENTERTAINMENT

Mixed in with the expensive restaurants are a handful of solid meals at budget prices. Both **Magnum's** and **Beaches** offer $5-6 dinners, with a free glass of beer, wine, or soda if you show up early (5pm) and pick up a voucher on the street. The restaurants pump music, and seating is generally at long, wooden tables. **Reef Oceania** (tel. 4946 6137) has a Sunday night all-you-can-eat seafood BBQ (with few vegetarian options) for $6. Call for the courtesy hostel bus schedule. **Backpackers by the Bay** (tel. 4746 7267) also has a massive BBQ every Wednesday and Friday for $5.50, with no vegetarian options.

Outside the hostel circuit but still well within the price range, **Chatz** (tel. 4946 7223; next to Club Habitat) has a serious steakburger and chips platter—with a free beer—for $5, lunchtime only. The interior design takes a while to digest, especially the parachute billowing from the ceiling (open daily 11am-11pm). On the breakfast side of things, **Sidewalk Cafe** (tel. 4946 6425) serves French toast, pancakes, or poached eggs ($4 each) all day (open Mon. and Wed.-Sun. 8am-8pm, Tues. 8am-3pm). They're located on the Esplanade, right next to **Jessie's on the Beach** (tel. 4946 6311), which serves greasier breakfasts for even less ($3-4) throughout the day (open Tues.-Fri. 7:30am-9pm, Sat.-Mon. 7am-9pm). Finally, **Tequila Willie's** (tel. 4946 6644) is next to the bridge but set back a bit from the street. A good plate of Tex-Mex runs $6.50-7.50 (open Mon.-Sat. 11:30am-late, Sun. 4:30pm-late).

When prowling for nightlife, it pays to wander along the strip and follow whatever music suits your fancy. Restaurants sometimes have one-night gigs, and a pot of beer costs about the same ($1.80-2.50) no matter which bar you belly up to. **Tricks,** across from the post office, whips up a decent-sized party most nights, with occasional contests and specials (usually no cover charge). **Magnum's** throws the next-biggest blast, offering specials on beer for early arrivals as well as a weekly Mr. Whitsunday competition. **Beaches,** next door, is more of a place to see and be seen. The steakhouse, **KC's,** next to Commonwealth Bank, is geared more toward the older set, but the live music brings varied audiences.

ACTIVITIES

Airlie Beach is not terribly exciting during the day, as there's almost nothing to do (besides the beach scene, of course). The only museum in town is **Vic Hislop's Shark & Whale Expo** (tel. 4946 6928), up Waterson Rd. from the main drag, an air-conditioned shrine to Vic's work to expose the "conspiracy" propagated by the "pretend conservationists," who try to save the worst denizens of the deep, the Tiger and Great White sharks. Newspaper clipping after magazine article monitors Vic's thankless battle to rid the coastal waters of the menaces, and dozens of photographs show Vic alongside sharks he's caught. A real shark sits frozen in a block of ice for your viewing pleasure. Feel the edge of a plastic container that was gnawed by a shark and...you get the idea (open daily 9am-6pm; admission $14, students $4).

To tempt the sharks yourself, rent a catamaran or waterbike from **Water Sports** (tel. 019 070 318; open daily 9am-5pm), on the beach behind Hog's Breath Cafe. They have bikes, too. **Whitsunday Watersports** on the other end of the beach (tel. 4946 7077; open daily 9am-9pm) rents catamarans ($25 per hr.), water bikes ($10 per 30min.), tube ride ($20 per 10min.), jet skis ($35 per 15min.).

Back on the relative safety of the mainland, **Fawlty Tours** (tel. 4946 6848) offers a day tour to a local patch of rain forest for $38 including lunch. If you're not heading much farther north it's definitely worth a look, but if Cape Tribulation is on your itinerary, don't bother. There's also a 60m, $49 bungy jump site at **Barrier Reef Bungy** (tel. 4946 1540; free hostel pick-ups). **Brady Creek Trail Rides** (tel. 4946 6665) offers two half-day rides per day, a good deal at $37.

The most economical way to get into the mainland woodlands is by taking a public bus out to **Conway National Park,** a few kilometers east of Airlie Beach. There's a self-guided walk that lasts a little over an hour and passes wrinkled fig trees, mucky mangrove swamps, and one or two of the rare Bottle Trees. The QNP&WS office (on the way to the park; tel. 4746 7022; open Mon.-Fri. 8am-5pm, Sat. 9am-1pm) has a detailed leaflet on the walk.

If your outdoor plans are rained out, there is **toad racing** twice a week (Tues. and Thurs. nights) at the **Airlie Beach Hotel/Motel,** on the Esplanade (tel. 4946 6233). $3 gets you a toad and a free stubbie of VB. Complimentary toad tickets at the hotel reception are subject to availability.

DIVING

The SCUBA experience is hot stuff in the Whitsunday area, with good value on dive courses and daytrips to the Whitsundays a tempting addition to most courses. Pre-dive medical exams ($40-50) usually aren't included in the price.

Among PADI certification courses, **Island Divers** (tel. 1800 065 755; fax 4946 4367) promises small class size and a two-day trip for $250. **True Blue** (tel. 1800 635 889; fax 4946 6105) offers two-day trips for $275. **Oceania Dive** (tel. 1800 076 035) has an island daytrip as well as a reef trip for $250. **Kelly Dive** (tel. 1800 063 454; fax 4946 4368) has a wide range of options: basic tuition and two-day trip costs $245. The best value for certified divers is an overnight or a two-night Whitsunday trip.

Whitsunday Islands

The Whitsundays are a collection of 74 islands just off the coast of Queensland, some rising majestically from the sea, wooded and christened with creeks and waterfalls, others barely poking a tip above water. The two most important islands from a backpacker's perspective are **Whitsunday Island** itself, home to the impossibly beautiful Whitehaven Beach, and **Hook Island,** with choice snorkeling spots, a handful of caves, and 3000-year-old Aboriginal cave paintings. The names of the islands rapidly lose their staid, predictable nature, and include Dead Dog Island and Plum Pudding Island. All of the islands (and interesting waterways) belong to national parks, so the sights are genuinely, naturally beautiful and visits are kept low-impact by law. Resorts on Hayman and Hamilton Islands are the only eyesores, with guests often arriving on public beachlands by helicopter or seaplane. The water in the Whitsunday channel is usually a dazzling blue. It's not uncommon to see a sea turtle flapping for air in between the waves.

Navigating the Islands, Campsites, and Cruises Short of swimming over (not recommended), there are three basic means of getting to the islands, each with its own merits. In every instance you'll be paying a Reef Tax of $2 per person per day. The least expensive option is an **island transfer** by boat (return ticket $22-25). When setting up a transfer, which can be done through any travel agent, be sure to have written assurance from the company to come and pick up you up on a certain day, lest the skipper decide not to make the run for lack of outgoing passengers and strand you for a day or longer.

Camping in one of the close to 20 different campgrounds run by the QNP&WS will cost you $3.50 per person. Facilities at the campgrounds vary from site to site. **Dugong Beach,** at Cid Harbour on Whitsunday Island, is relatively posh with toilets, sheltered picnic grounds, and drinking water (max. 40 people). At the other end of the scale is **Sea Eagle Beach** (Thomas Island) with just a couple of picnic tables and a maximum capacity of four people. **Whitehaven Beach** (Whitsunday Island) is tremendously popular: with toilets, picnic grounds, and the 6km beach a stone's throw away, it's a virtual paradise limited to 20 lucky souls. Open fires are prohibited on all of these campsites. Bush camping sites, for the more rugged and crowd-shy backpackers, have no toilets, no picnic tables, and **no drinking water**—be sure to bring enough to last well beyond the day you're supposed to leave, in case inclement weather delays your pick-up. **Olden Island,** just off the mainland, has a four-person cap, as does the isolated **Planton Island. Western Beach,** on South Repulse Island, comes with a view of Conway National Park's mountains (max. 18 people). Booking well ahead for the campsites is crucial. The QNP&WS office is outside of Airlie Beach on the way to Shute Harbor, and the local bus runs there every 30 minutes.

The next step up is the **day cruise** and **overnight** circuit, which accommodates passengers in berths on board the vessel. These tend to be less rewarding, since it takes a while to get out and back from the islands, and you'll have less time to romp in the coral. Still, if you're pressed for time, it's not such a bad option. Boats generally leave from Shute Harbour. **Reef Express** (tel. 1800 819 366) zips out and back daily, departing at 9am. It basically includes hanging out on Whitehaven Beach and a quick snorkel off Hook Island for $55 ($90 with a pre-booked dive). **Baby J** (tel. 1800 644 563) is similar to Reef Express: the beach, the snorkel, the $55. **Ocean Rafting** (tel. 1800 644 563) does the same trip at the same price, but whips along in a big yellow raft. The serious downside, however, is your increased exposure to the ruthless, 65 kph wind. **Maxi Ragamuffin** (tel. 4946 7777) is a racing yacht with a slimmer schedule and heftier price tag, but lunch and style to show for it. Trips to Blue Pearl Bay for snorkeling depart Monday, Wednesday, and Saturday, and Whitehaven Beach trips go out Tuesday, Thursday, and Sunday (each trip $63, students $56; both trips $99, students $94).

The **two-nighters** get plenty expensive ($180-275 including shipboard accommodations) and are generally huge floating parties (they're all BYO). At last count there were 24 major operators in the game, most of them booked solid every time they set sail. In choosing a ship, be picky. There are three classes of boats at play: the motor-powered, which chug along and aren't very inspiring (this includes boats that have sails but nonetheless motor everywhere); the tallships with all the rigging from yesteryear; and the proper racing yachts called "maxis," which are generally more expensive, and always sexier. Travel agents may try to push the maxis (which give higher commissions), saying that the faster boats will make it to more island spots. This is hogwash. Given the amount of time available once the boat is in the Whitsunday Islands, everything evens out.

To sort out the maxis, which dominate the market, try asking a few questions. Does the "free snorkel" include fins? How many passengers can the boat take? Does the ship's spinnaker (forward-most sail) ever make an appearance? Are the bunks separate from the common space? Is there an opportunity to dive? What time (morning/afternoon) does the ship depart and return? These are suggestions to help clarify the picture of the trip before you've left shore. Besides permitting BYO, boats generally don't supply snacks or soft drinks. If they do, they're at a mark-up; consider bringing these along. Finally, keep in mind that it can get chilly out on the waves.

Whitsunday Island The principle draw of the Whitsunday Islands is the famed **Whitehaven Beach,** a long slip of white that resembles the foam on a cappuccino. Sand flows deliciously between the towns, as pure as talcum powder. Behind the beach, a forest clings tenuously to the sand. Across the bay is another beach with the bonus of soft coral framed dramatically by the oh-so-white sand, right offshore. Whitehaven Beach is 6km long, with enough space to sunbathe in some privacy. The scene is idyllic if you can ignore the occasional helicopter that bears down, laden with grinning tourists.

On the other side of the island is **Cid Harbour,** a common mooring site for the two-night boat trips. The waves lap up against **Dugong Beach,** wholly unremarkable except as a starting point for the inland walking trail to Sawmill Beach. Whitsunday Island is the largest of the islands, and has bits of rainforest tucked into its far edges.

Hook Island The beaches on Hook have beautiful stretches of coral just offshore, literally a stone's throw away at **Chalkies Beach** and **Blue Pearl Bay.** (Stonehaven Beach, it should be noted, is currently going through a period of "regeneration.") The chief problem with a beautiful stretch of coral, though, is that chunks of it are broken off in storms (or by careless snorkelers), and wash up on shore, creating a "coral beach" which is pretty enough to look at but dastardly painful to walk on.

On the south side of the island is **Nara Inlet,** a popular spot for overnight boat trips. Visitors are greeted by a graffiti-ridden rock outcrop, desecrated by vandals (or "people with underdeveloped frontal lobes," as the local mariners' guidebook explains). Five minutes up the path is a cave shelter used by the sea-faring Ngalandji Aboriginals, bordered on either side by middens, or piles of shells. The rare abstract paintings inside date back to 1000 BC and may have given rise to the popular Australian myth that a boatload of exiled Egyptians washed ashore ages ago, and left hieroglyphic-like traces in various corners of Queensland. Although the story goes unsubstantiated, it is true that at least one glyph in the cave is a good match for "king" in Hieroglyphic Luwian, spoken in ancient Troy. Leave it for those with overdeveloped frontal lobes to figure out.

NORTH COAST OF QUEENSLAND

Townsville sits at the junction of the alluring far north, the rugged frontier of the outback, and the civilized cities of the southern coastline. The coast from here north to Cairns features a constellation of sun-soaked paradises, but the appeal of northern Queensland lies just offshore, in the pounding surf of Mission Beach and the glowing beauty of the Great Barrier Reef. Between the reef and mainland, reserves such as Magnetic Island have beach enough to go around, yet the sand also encircles protected forests where koalas lazily munch leaves in the treetops.

The miles inland can be densely tropical and often hide swaths of rainforest populated by birds, bugs, and bouncing 'roos of every description. A solitary strip of pavement runs west from Townsville toward Charters Towers and the arid center of the continent. The civilization that clings to the coast has wrested its existence from the unrelenting wild. The land north of Townsville, shrouded in intrigue, seems only tenuously possessed by humans, as if rainforest or reef could swallow it at any moment. Cultivators, employing many backpackers among their number, work year-round to keep the rich soil under yoke. Even so, agriculture must choose its battles here, and many pockets of land have been surrendered to the devices of nature.

Townsville

Townsville and Cairns must be twins separated at birth. Each has about the same population now, but where Cairns has grown up to a noble stature, Townsville has grown out, rolling into neighboring fields. As a result, Townsville has a small, focused center surrounded by satellite suburbs of shopping malls and the odd cinema or go-cart track. There's little tourism in town, the real attraction being a quick and easy ferry ride to Magnetic Island. But fine weather is never a strike against a place, and Townsville's annual average of 320 sunny days has attracted 130,000 residents, making it Queensland's second largest city.

ORIENTATION

Central **Townsville** and **South Townsville** are divided by **Ross Creek** which is spanned by three bridges. Most sights and shops are north of the creek, while the majority of hostels are on **Palmer St.** on the south bank, a five-minute walk over the bridge to town. **Flinders Mall** begins at the lip of the **Dean St.** bridge. **Flinders St. East** runs downstream with the creek to the right. A left on Wickham St. leads to the Anzac Memorial Park and **The Strand,** which runs along the waterfront of **Cleveland Bay.** From the other end of the mall, **Stanley St.** heads away from the creek toward the monstrous (but castle-less) **Castle Hill,** and **Flinders St.** continues southwest along the creek and past the **rail station.**

PRACTICAL INFORMATION

Tourist office: Visitor Information Centre (tel. 4721 3660), in the Flinders Mall. From the rail station, Flinders St. heads to the right straight into the mall. From the bus terminal, turn right onto Plume St., left onto Palmer St., cross over the bridge, and the second left is Flinders Mall. Wheelchair accessible. Open Mon.-Sat. 9am-5pm, Sun. 9am-1pm.

Budget Travel: mb travel (tel. 4721 5444), in the bus terminal and in Flinders Mall. Both offices wheelchair accessible and open daily 8am-5:30pm.

Currency Exchange: Bank of Queensland, Stokes St. (tel. 4772 1799) up from Flinders Mall on the left, often has the best rates with the shortest lines. $5 commission on traveler's checks, no commission on cash. Visa traveler's checks are exchanged for no commission at **ANZ,** 121 Sturt St. (tel. 4722 3222) between Stokes and Stanley St. Open Mon.-Thurs. 9:30am-4pm, Fri. 9:30am-5pm.

American Express Office: In the Spotlight Mall off Flinders Mall, behind Suncorp (tel. 4772 4488; fax 4772 5325). Address mail: c/o Northern Australian Travel Agency, P.O. Box 2017, Townsville Queensland 4810. American Express Traveller's Cheques cashed for free; non-AmEx checks have a $5 fee; no fee for exchanging cash. Open Mon.-Fri. 9am-5pm, Sat. 9am-noon.

ATMs: Cirrus is accepted only at Commonwealth Bank (tel. 4721 1290) in Flinders Mall, and at National Bank (tel. 4772 3600) at the corner of Stanley and Sturt St.; **Plus** is accepted only at National Bank and Northern Savings (tel. 4771 5693) in Flinders Mall. V, MC are accepted almost everywhere.

Airport: Domestic and international terminals west of town. An **airport shuttle bus** (tel. 4775 5544) runs to town daily 7am-7pm. Driving, take Bundock St. to Warburton, to Eyre St. From Eyre, Denham St. goes to the town center.

Trains: Rail station at the corner of Flinders and Blackwood St. (tel. 4772 8288). No luggage storage. The **Queensland Rail Travel Centre** (tel. 4772 8358, 24hr. info

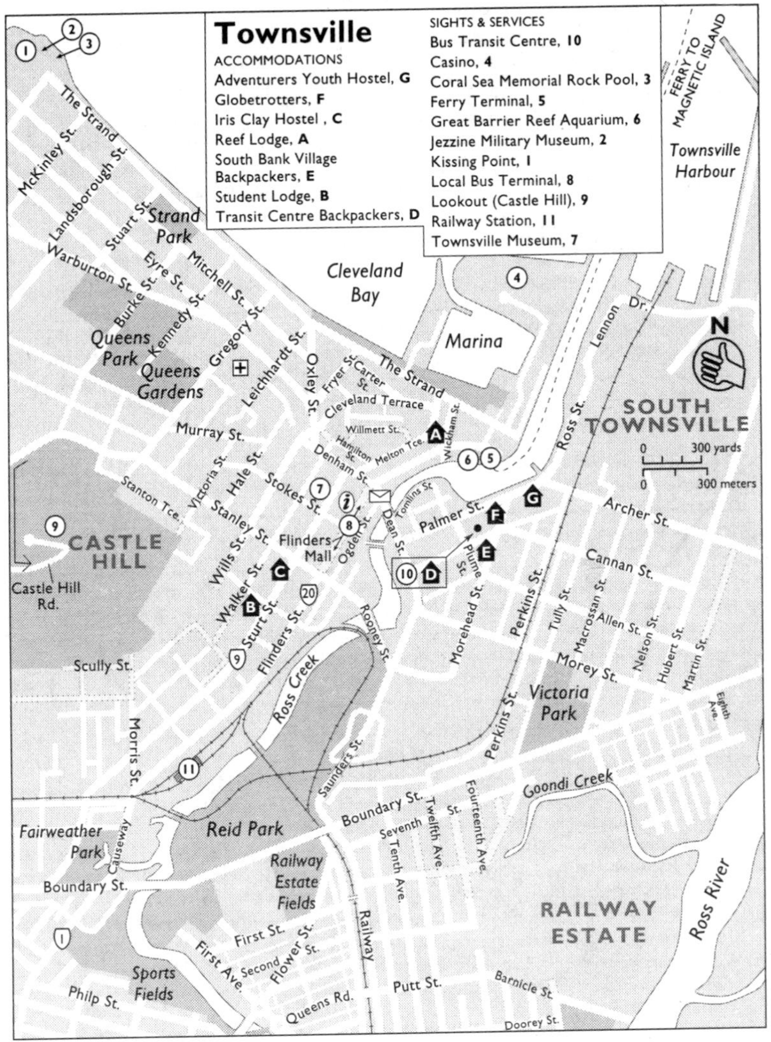

13 22 32) is to the right of the station. Open Mon.-Tues. and Thurs.-Fri. 8:30am-5pm, Wed. 8:30am-6pm, Sat. 12:45pm-4pm, Sun. 8:45am-12:15pm.

Buses: Arrive and depart from the Transit Centre in South Townsville, 5min. from the city center. **McCafferty's** (tel. 4772 5100) open daily 5:30am-4pm. **Greyhound** open Mon.-Sat. 7am-5pm, Sun. 10am-4pm. Lockers $2.

Public Transportation: Sunbus (tel. 4774 8255) has its main terminal in the middle of Flinders Mall.

Taxis: Taxi Townsville (tel. 4713 1008). 24hr. service.

Car Rental: Townsville Car Rentals, 12 Palmer St. (tel. 4772 1093; fax 4721 3678), $45 per day and 100km, scooters $25 per day. **Can Do Rentals,** 194 Flinders St. E. (tel. 4721 4766), $47 per day and 100km. Also: **Budget** (tel. 4725 2344), **Thrifty** (tel. 4772 4600), **National** (tel. 4772 5133), **Avis** (tel. 4721 2688), **Hertz** (tel. 4779 2022). Check around for short-time deals with local companies.

Automobile Club: RACQ, City Vehicle Services, 635 Sturt St. (tel. 4721 2360).

Supermarket: Woolworths (tel. 4772 3200), on Sturt St. between Stanley and Stoke St. Open Mon.-Fri. 8am-9pm, Sat. 8am-5pm, Sun. 8:30am-1pm.
Market: Cotter's Markets, on Sundays outside in the Flinders Mall. Farmers from the area come in to hawk the freshest produce around.
Hospital/Health Services: Townsville General Hospital, on Eyre St. (tel. 4781 9211, emergency room tel. 4781 9753). **Queensland AIDS Council** (tel. 4721 1384), in the old T&G building at the corner of Flinders and Stanley St., 2nd floor. Open Mon.-Fri. 9am-3pm. **Women's Community Health Centre,** 35 Sturt St. (tel. 4771 6867), between Denham and Stokes St. Open Mon.-Fri. 9am-3pm.
Emergency: Dial 000.
Police: Station at the corner of Sturt and Stanley St. (24hr. tel. 4760 7777; mobile tel. 0419 706 529). Open Mon.-Sat. 9am-5pm, Sun. 8am-4pm. Also in Flinders Mall, behind the Visitor Information Centre.
Internet Access: Townzone Arcade, 201 Flinders St. E. (tel. 4771 5780, http://www. townzone.com). $1 per 5min., $10 per hr. Open Sun.-Wed. 9am-10pm., Thurs.-Sat. 9am-2am. Available 24hr. at the **Transit Centre** for $2 per 10min. Also at **Mary Who? Bookshop,** 155 Stanley St. (tel. 4471 3824), on Flinders St. The Townsville Library, near the Dunham St. entrance to Flinders Mall, offers 45min. free internet access (no email). Open Mon.-Fri. 9:30am-5pm, Sat.-Sun. 9am-noon.
Post Office: General Post Office (tel. 4771 6133; fax 4721 1219). At the Denham St. entrance to Flinders Mall. Open Mon.-Fri. 9am-5pm. Fax. **Postal code:** 4810.
Phone Code: 07.

ACCOMMODATIONS

As Townsville is more of a transportation hub for backpackers than a tourist destination, hostels focus on moving people quickly in and out instead of on providing luxurious amenities to keep them around. Most accommodations are located around the transit center. Linen is included in room price unless marked; expect to pay a $10 key deposit.

Globetrotters, 45 Palmer St. (tel. 4771 3242). Turn right out of the bus terminal, right again at the first intersection; the hostel is a few houses further on the right. The owners offer good deals on Magnetic Island ferry-and-hostel packages. Laundry, pool, luggage storage, internet access, BBQ, TV. Gorgeous dorms $13; twins $32. VIP. Linen $1 for dorms, free for twins.
South Bank Village Backpackers, 35 McIlwraith St. (tel. 4771 5849), is the best deal near the bus terminal. Turn left out of the terminal and walk through the BP studio petrol station—it's right across the street. A laid-back collection of Queensland stilt houses with laundry, pool, and TV. Reception open 7:30am-9:30pm. Dorms $10; singles $13; doubles $24.
Iris Clay Hostel, 261 Sturt St. (tel. 4772 3649), between Blackwood and Stanley St., is the only hostel in the city center. Aboriginally-owned and operated, the hostel is part of a national chain which gives preferential housing to Aboriginals and Torres Strait Islanders, but any vacant room can go to backpackers at competitive hostel prices. Laundry, TV room. Reception open 7am-9pm. By request, *Let's Go* has not published rates, but they are highly competitive. Linen and all meals included.
Transit Centre Backpackers, right in the bus terminal (tel. 4721 2322 or 1800 628 836). This is like sleeping on the moon: nice place, no atmosphere. But convenient location and killer views from some of the rooms compensate for the slightly higher rates. Laundry, TV room with a view, weight room, internet access. Wheelchair accessible. Reception open 5:30am-9pm. Dorms $14; singles $26; twins $30; doubles $32. Bikes $2 per hr., $8 per day. Cutlery deposit $5.
Reef Lodge, 4 Wickham St. (tel. 4721 1112; fax 4721 1405), across from the ferry terminal. Decent value given the low price. Laundry, BBQ, and a courtesy bus and rail pick-ups. Guests recommend locking up your valuables. Dorms $12; singles $28; twins $28; doubles $32.
Student Lodge, at the corner of Sturt and Blackwood St. (tel. 4771 6875). The hostel is near the city center and offers low weekly rates. TV room. Reception open Mon.-Fri. 9am-4pm, Sat.-Sun. 9am-noon. Super-clean singles $66 per week, with

bath $73. Private fridges $7 per week. Washing machine is free (no dryer). Tenants pay an up-front $10 "cleaning" charge to mop and shine after they check out.

Adventurers Youth Hostel (YHA), 79 Palmer St. (tel. 4721 1522) is far from anything useful, and for non-YHA members, overpriced. The amenities are generous, though: a complete game room, pool, laundry, and BBQ. Courtesy bus to the ferry terminal twice a day, and a well-equipped tour desk. Rooms have fridges and ceiling fans. Reception open 7-10:45am and 12:15-10pm. Dorms $14; singles $24; doubles and twins $32. Non-members pay $3 extra per person. Next door, **Snapper's Bistro,** 69 Palmer St. (tel. 4771 6657) has $4.50 lunch specials daily noon-2pm.

FOOD

Hidden among Townsville's panoply of steak houses, fish and chips shacks, and upscale dining extravaganzas are enough low-key budget eateries to keep a stomach happy every day of the week. Tuesday is $5 all-you-can-eat chili night at **Cracker Jack's,** 21 Palmer St. (tel. 4721 1478), between the bridge and the bus terminal (food served 5-9pm, happy hour 5-7pm. Wednesday is $2 steak tips and chips night at the **Republic Hotel,** 31 McIlwraith St. (tel. 4771 4316), diagonally across from the petrol station at the bus terminal. Early 80s music and homey local culture complement $1.80 Ned Kelly brew pots. On Thursdays, the **Heritage Cafe and Bar,** 137 Flinders St. E. (tel. 4771 2799), throws a prawn party, offering a half kilo (cooked and served) plus a glass of beer or wine for $7.50, starting at 6pm. On Friday nights there's live music and famously good food at the **Thai Exchange Restaurant,** 151 Flinders St. E. (tel. 4771 3335). Generous bowls of soup ($6) and main courses ($8.50-12) include many vegetarian options. Serving starts at 6pm. On Saturdays, the best bet is **Ghekko's** (tel. 4772 5271), on the Palmer St. corner of the bus terminal. It's a fairly fancy restaurant run by a hospitality training school in town, so meals are super-cheap (all under $10) to make up for any imperfections in the presentation (open Wed.-Sat. 6-10pm). Sunday is Thai again, this time at **Bountiful Thai,** 243 Flinders St. E. (tel. 4771 6338), a small, friendly establishment that serves vegetarian dinners for $7.50-9.50 (open Mon-Fri. 11:30am-2pm and 6pm-late, Sat.-Sun. 6pm-late). Soothe Monday morning hangovers at the **Boiling Billy,** 18 Stokes St. (tel. 4771 4184), a fountain-festooned cafe with 20 varieties of coffee beans. Walk up the hill from the middle of Flinders Mall and it's on the left. Try the Coffee Game, where your $2 cuppa is free if you can guess the bean of the day (open Mon.-Fri. 7am-5pm, Sat.-Sun. 8:30am-2pm).

SIGHTS AND ACTIVITIES

There's easily enough in Townsville to convince travelers to put off a trip to Magnetic Island for a few days. The primo thing to see in Townsville is the **Great Barrier Reef Aquarium,** in the ferry terminal (tel. Mon.-Fri. 4750 0800, Sat.-Sun. 4750 0891). The aquarium starts at the beginning—with coral polyps that create the reef structure—and gives a full perspective on the Great Barrier Reef. There's a "venomous animals" tour, a touch pool, and an opportunity to dive in the shark tank ($65 plus $40 gear hire, call for booking), as well as incredibly-colored fish, underwater cameras that visitors can twist, swivel, and zoom, and a tank full of fluorescent coral (admission $13, students $11; open daily 9am-5pm).

Across the ferry terminal from the aquarium is the **Museum of Tropical Queensland** (tel. 4721 1662; fax 4721 2093), an inexpensive dinosaur fix. In one large room, a life-size plesiosaur with splayed teeth and leering eyes stands near a couple of real sauropod bones, along with detailed displays about other Cretaceous-period Queensland denizens. A third of the exhibits are dedicated to the artifacts of Aboriginal and Torres Strait Islanders, while the remainder feature cleverly designed dioramas of local fauna (admission $4, students $3.50; open daily 9am-5pm).

The quiet and rarely-visited **Townsville Museum,** on the corner of Sturt and Stokes St. (tel. 4772 5725), is one of the best values in town. The museum is a single room crammed with trinkets from the past century, including a fairly complete schoolroom and kitchen. A model, circa 1888, of Flinders St. East proves that The Bank nightclub has always been a local landmark (admission $1, students 50¢). The **Perc Tucker**

Regional Gallery, at the Denham St. entrance to the Flinders Mall (tel. 4722 0289) rotates exhibits throughout the year, with two or three running at a time (free; open Tues., Thurs., and Sat. 10am-5pm, Fri. 2-9pm, Sun. 10am-1pm).

The Great Barrier Reef Marine Park Authority in the ferry terminal maintains an incredible **marine life library,** that includes reference books, journals, CD-ROMs, (free; open Mon.-Tues. and Thurs.-Fri. 10am-noon and 2-4pm).

With the Kelso Reef 10km out, the **diving** scene is alive and kicking in Townsville. **Mike Ball Dive Expeditions,** 252 Walker St. (tel. 4772 3022; fax 4721 2152), offers a five-day PADI certification course, including accommodation, for $480, or a course with fewer dives for $395. **Pro-Dive,** in the ferry terminal (tel. 4721 1760; fax 4721 1791) also has a certification course ($450). **Pure Pleasure Cruises** (tel. 4721 3555) offers five nights' accommodation in Townsville or on Magnetic Island with a one-day reef dive for $155. If you do the math, that's about an $85 dive, quite a bargain for south of Cairns. Always check out the options before deciding on a company; dive shops come and go and prices bob up and down.

A few kilometers south of Townsville on the Bruce Hwy., kangaroos wander at the **Billabong Sanctuary** (tel. 4778 8344; fax 4780 4569; open 8am-5pm daily), a sprawling wildlife sanctuary with a giant pond smack in the middle (complete with a bird blind). The animal talks are particularly informative; call ahead to see if Phoebe (originally from midwestern U.S.A.) is doing her hilarious snake talk, "Indiana Phoebe and the Pythons of Doom." The only way out from town is with the Detours tour company, bookable at any travel desk (tickets $18, students $14).

ENTERTAINMENT

For movies there's the **Townsville 5 Cinemas,** (tel. 4721 1166) at the corner of Sturt and Blackwood St., offers a bargain on Monday nights with $6 flicks; otherwise tickets are $8.50 (students $8) during the day, $10.80 (students $8) at night. V, MC. **Coral Sea Skydivers** (tel. 4725 6780), has the usual 2400 ft. tandem skydive ($197) that's popular up the coast, as well as a 3000 ft. jump ($247) that doubles the free-fall time. There are several pubs in town, and the most inviting nightclubs lie along Flinders St. E.

A multi-media wonder, **The Bank,** 169 Flinders St. E., prices drinks at $2.50 until midnight; free for women on Tuesday nights. Smart dress (jeans and a collared shirt) is the order and cover is $5. On Wednesdays there's no cover charge and your first drink is free if you show a card from your hostel. **Mad Cow,** 129 Flinders St. E., is less drinking and more chewing cud; there's live music upstairs on the weekends, and never a dress code. A few pool tables here and there contribute to the calm-as-a-cow atmosphere. For a mix of music, the **James Cook Tavern,** 237 Flinders St. E. (tel. 4721 5552), offers live music every night. Call ahead to make sure you're not stuck with acid jazz when you're in a funky blues mood (cover free-$2). **PJ's Night Club,** at Mansfield Hotel on the corner of Flinders and Knapp St., is the center of Townsville gay scene. Guys' night at the club on the second and fourth Thursdays of every month; gals' night the first and third Thursday nights. Every Sunday, the club hosts a BBQ at 5pm.

■ Around Townsville

Many attractions near Townsville are inaccessible without a car. However, **Detour Coaches** (tel. 4721 5977) enables travelers to, well, take a detour. Best bets include a visit to the **Billabong Sanctuary** ($29), a trip to dusty old Charters Towers ($67), or the super-tour of downtown Townsville, plus Palmetum and a view from Castle Hill ($22). There is also an all-inclusive package to **Hinchinbrook Island** ($87, a sweet deal considering that the ferry alone costs $66 return). The access point for the island is the town of **Cardwell** (see below), half an hour up the Bruce Hwy. from Townsville. For certified divers, the famous **Yongala wreck,** supposedly one of the world's top wreck dives, is easily explored. **Sun City Watersports** (tel. 4771 6527) sails out to the site daily for $160. The best deal, though, is probably with **Coral Cat Cruises** (tel. 014 444 243), who will bring a group of six or seven (pull the people together before calling) to the wreck site for as little as $75 per person, tanks and weights included.

Magnetic Island

"Maggie Island?" Townsville natives will say with a shrug of the shoulders. "That's just a suburb of Townsville." But, if pressed, the source of their contempt will often emerge: envy. After all, it's almost always sunny on Magnetic Island. The beaches are wide and inviting, and pockets of eucalyptus trees are dotted with live-in-the-wild koalas. Most of the island is national park, so six-hour hikes around Mount Cook are a snap—transportation plans include rolling out of bed and heading into the nearest forest. On the less crowded beaches (or when young children aren't around) people bathe in the buff. Understandably, backpackers flock here in huge numbers, yet even in the peak season with the Australian school holiday crowd mixed in, there still seems to be plenty of room to stretch out in solitude.

GETTING THERE

The quickest way to Magnetic Island is with **Magnetic Island Ferries** (tel. 4772 7122; fax 4771 4052) at the ferry terminal (also called the Great Barrier Reef Wonderland). The trip takes 20 minutes and costs $19 round-trip. Combine this with an all-day unlimited use bus pass for the island for an additional $7; it costs the same on the island. The ferry departs six times daily between 8:30am and 5pm, with an additional 6:15pm trip on Saturdays and Sundays. (Bookings at the Information Centre in the ferry terminal. Open Mon.-Fri. 7:45am-5:15pm, Sat.-Sun. 7:45am-6:15pm.)

A slower but less expensive option is the Capricorn Barge Company's **Magnetic Island Car Ferry** (tel. 4772 5422; fax 4721 3576), located all the way down Palmer St. You'll get an hour chug each way for $12. Bikes ($17), motorcycles ($31), and cars ($96) are also ferried; price includes the passengers. Buy tickets at the terminal; call ahead to book a vehicle. Luggage can be left at no charge. (Departures between 7:30am-3pm, Mon.-Fri. 4 per day, Sat.-Sun. 3 per day. V, MC, AmEx.) A courtesy bus from the ferry company shuttles people off; ask at the information center for details. If you need to get on or off Magnetic Island in a hurry, **Coral Cat Cruises** (tel. 014 444 243) runs a private shuttle at any time for a minimum of $100.

ORIENTATION

The island is shaped like an apple turnover, with one corner facing straight south. Almost all of the accommodations are located among a series of bays along the east coast. The main road on the island runs from the rugged northwest corner (cleverly named West Point), south to the tip (intriguingly named **Nobby Head**), and back up the east side to the north-facing horseshoe-shaped bay (mysteriously named **Horseshoe Bay**). There aren't more than 20km of paved road, and the public bus does a good job of covering most of them. **Picnic Bay,** near Nobby Head, is the island's main settlement and the landing point for most ferries. Horseshoe Bay is also populated (by island standards), as are **Nelly Bay** and **Arcadia,** on the road to Horseshoe Bay.

PRACTICAL INFORMATION

Tourist Office: Information Centre, next to the water taxi pier on Picnic Bay, (tel. 4778 5155; fax 4778 5158). Tour and transit bookings. Wheelchair accessible. Open Mon.-Fri. 7:15am-4:25pm, Sat.-Sun. 8am-2:40pm. Luggage storage 50¢ per hr.

Travel Office: Magnetic Travel in the shopping plaza at Nelly Bay (tel. 4778 5343; fax 4778 5348). Open Mon.-Fri. 8:30am-5:30pm, Sat. 8:30am-12:30pm.

Currency Exchange: There are **no banks** or **ATMs** on Magnetic Island. The supermarket in Nelly Bay's shopping plaza (**Cut-Price,** tel. 4778 5722, open Mon.-Fri. 8:30am-7pm, Sat. 8:30am-5:30pm, Sun. 9am-2pm) will do credit card cash withdrawals (V, MC, AmEx) for $1, or free if you buy at least $10 worth of stuff first.

Ferries: See **Getting There,** above.

Public Transportation: Magnetic Island Bus Service (tel. 4778 5130; fax 4778 5380) runs roughly every hour 6:35am-11:20pm. Stops are marked by blue signs. Tickets can be bought on the bus ($1.40-3.60), but the better deal is a 1-day ($9) or 2-day ($10) unlimited pass, available from any hostel or directly from the bus company. Wheelchair accessible.

Taxis: Magnetic Island Taxis (tel. 4772 1555).

Car rental: Hiring out a "Moke" (an open-air, no-doors, no-frills, looks-like-a-golf-cart automobile) is super-popular. $30 per day and 30¢ per km with **Moke Magnetic** (tel. 4778 5377; $60 per day deposit) and **Holiday Moke Hire** (tel. 4778 5703; $70-90 per day deposit), both at the Picnic Bay ferry pier.

Medical Center: Magnetic Island Health Service Centre, in Nelly Bay (tel. 4778 5107). Open Mon.-Fri. 9am-11am, Sat.-Sun. 9am-2pm.

Police: (24hr. tel. 4778 5270), on the road out of Picnic Bay, heading to Arcadia. Open Wed. and Fri. 8:30am-2pm.

Emergency: dial 000.

Post office: (tel. 4778 5118; fax 4778 5944), in Picnic Bay. Fax services. Open Mon.-Fri. 8:30am-5pm, Sat. 9am-noon, Sun. 10am-noon. **Postal code:** 4819.

Phone Code: 07.

ACCOMMODATIONS

With a staggering number of places to stay, Magnetic Island offers something for everyone. Camping is prohibited in the national park, and only two hostels (Geoff's and Coconuts) have campgrounds with facilities. Most backpackers buy a ferry-and-hostel combination package, usually a good deal. The two "resorts" don't have free pick-up, but other hostels do. Room prices usually include linen. Standard key deposit is $10.

Coconuts, Magnetic Beach (tel. 4778 5777 or 1800 065 696; fax 4778 5507). Flush up against the ocean with kayaks and catamarans ($6 per hr.) and a pool for guests. Welcomes international citizens only, so foreigners flock here to party. Reception open daily 7am-7pm. Meals served 5-9pm. Guests stay in white plastic cocoons ($10) or larger wooden huts ($14). Doubles available in decidedly run-down plastic tents ($28). Camping in the furthest corner from the bathrooms ($6). VIP.

Centaur Guest House, Geoffrey Bay (tel. 4778 5668), is rough on the edges, but has a streak of honest hospitality rare in Queensland's hostels. The owners pride themselves on a sound safety record (no thefts in 9 years) and refuse accommodation to scruffy-looking guests. The homey hostel is within earshot of the ocean and features hardwood floors, books, board games, and a trampoline out back next to the hammocks. The full spice cabinet is at your disposal. Dorms $14; doubles and twins $34. VIP, YHA.

Hideway Budget Resort, Picnic Bay (tel. 4778 5110). Another pleasant base for bushwalkers, this concrete block building with the most enticing swimming pool on the island. Climbing to a room upstairs can feel like going up and down a jungle gym, yet the pool below seductively slopes up to the deck chairs' feet. Laundry, TV, electric organ. Reception open daily 8am-7:30pm. Dorms $14; twins $28; doubles $32. VIP.

Tropical Resort, Nelly Bay on Yates St. (tel. 4778 5955; fax 4778 5601), is a beautiful upscale hotel with spacious and clean rooms. There's not much nightlife, since most guests have brought along families, but it's a sweet place to wake up in the morning (if a fair distance from the beach). Pool, hot tub, laundry; daily Rainbow Lorikeet feeding. Clean dorms ($16) are in the same giant huts as at Geoff's Place, but they have in-hut bathrooms. Doubles $45. Special packages include a ferry ticket with 1 night ($29) or 5 nights ($59). Cutlery $10. Key deposit $5. V, MC.

Arcadia Holiday Resort, down in Geoffrey Bay (tel. 4778 5177), has laundry, pool, hot tub, TV in each room. Reception open Mon.-Fri. 8am-5pm, Sat.-Sun. 8am-4pm. Dorms $15; doubles $35; discounts for longer stays. Linen included except top sheet ($1) and blanket (not available).

Geoff's Place, Horseshoe Bay (tel. 4778 5577; fax 4778 5781), has traditionally been the hot place to stay on the island, but has cooled off recently because of a neighborhood-enforced 11pm curfew on the dancing and loud music. The hostel is a collection of not-quite-stylish, not-quite-clean giant wooden huts 5min. from the beach. Laundry, pool, tour desk. Reception open daily 8am-8pm, excepting lunch and dinner breaks. Dorms $14; doubles $34; campsites $6, with power $16. Meals served (dinner $6.50-8.50). Blankets $2. Cutlery $5.

FOOD

The center of gastronomical gravity is certainly **Picnic Bay,** where cafes, restaurants, and dives elbow each other next to the ferry pier. The **Green Frog Cafe** (tel. 4778 5833; open daily 8:30am-5pm) has absolutely no fried food, just good old-fashioned sandwiches made to order ($3.50-4). Funky **C-Shells** (tel. 4778 5959; open daily 8am-8pm) tries to dish out the healthiest vegetarian pasta ($6), while delving into goodies like hamburgers ($4.50-5) and the devilish "hot and spicy chicken chips" ($2.50). For dinner there's **Max's** (tel. 4778 5911; open daily 11am-late), an open-air wicker chair restaurant with a prohibitively expensive view—but also a $6.50 dinner special for the budget-minded (V, MC, AmEx). The high end of the low-cost dining options is **Andy's Chinese Restaurant** (tel. 4778 5706; open daily 11am-1:30pm and 5:30pm-9pm), with the usual stock of Polynesian plates (about $9).

Nelly's Bay has more than its share of tempting vittles, most notably **Possum's Cafe** in the shopping plaza (tel. 4778 5409; open Mon.-Fri. 8:30am-7pm, Sat. 8am-8pm, Sun. 8am-3:30pm). Besides a brow-raising assortment of delectable sandwiches ($4-5), Possum's offers a hearty warm breakfast for $5. Next to Possum's is a **Cut-Price supermarket,** the largest on the island (tel. 4778 5722; open Mon.-Fri. 8:30am-7pm, Sat. 8:30am-5:30pm, Sun. 9am-2pm). Accepts bank card or credit card (V, MC, AmEx, 3% fee and a minimum $20 charge).

One of the best-kept secrets of Magnetic Island's culinary delights is **Banister's Seafood** (tel. 4778 5700; open daily 8:30am-8:30pm) in **Geoffrey Bay.** In this local haunt, fish and chips ($3.50) can take as long 20 minutes on busy Friday nights. The menu lists six varieties of fish and chips, along with some savory alternatives (honey ginger prawns $9). To get there, turn off the main road on to Bright Ave. (next to Centaur Guest House), follow the short string of stores around to the right, pass the pay phone and go a little further. It'll be on your right, next to the bakery. Other cheap pickings are slim in this bay, although **Alla Capri** (tel. 4778 5448; open Tues.-Sun. 6pm-late) has a Tuesday night all-you-can-eat pasta special for $7.50.

ACTIVITIES AND ENTERTAINMENT

Diving, ever the favorite enterprise of the Queensland coast, is nearly cheap on Magnetic Island. A PADI certification course with **Pleasure Drives Magnetic Island,** at Arcadia Resort, Geoffrey Bay (tel. 4778 5788), is a bargain at $199. Look around for other deals, of course; the market changes rapidly, and today's extravagance can become tomorrow's special. To splash about on the surface, try **Horseshoe Bay Watersports** (tel. 4758 1336; open daily 8:30am-4:30pm, weather permitting), which offers tube rides ($10 per 10min.), water-skiing ($25 per 15min.), paraflying ($50), catamaran ($20 per hr.), and peddle crafts ($8 per 30min.).

To play the young wanderlust type from the movies, ride bare-back on horses as they sprint down the beach and through the crashing waves. **Bluey's Horseshoe Ranch** (tel. 4778 5109), in Horseshoe Bay, has built a solid reputation of making such dream come true. A two-hour beach ride (daily at 9am and 3pm) costs $40; a more intense half-day ride is only $20 more. Another way to whip through the waves quickly is on a jet ski, with **Magnetic Jet** (tel. 4778 5533), in Horseshoe Bay. A tour around the island on a two-seater ($99; $89 with flyer from any hostel) takes a half day, and includes lunch and snorkel rental.

On the pocket-money budget, **Magnetic Island Mini-Golf** (tel. 4758 1066) has table tennis ($4 per hr.) air hockey ($1 per game), and, of course, mini-golf ($4 per game).

It's at Nelly Bay; ask the bus driver to let you off right in front. Keep an eye out for the house special, an all-day play with all the toys for just $5 per person (open Mon.-Fri. 9am-6pm, Sat.-Sun. 9am-10pm, open later on demand).

Like its sleeping namesake, the island's nightlife stands on a leg at **Flamingos,** in the Picnic Bay Hotel. Courtesy buses round up hostel guests at 11pm on Friday nights. Think pink velvet walls. Think hotel lounge room. Think Saturday Night fever soundtrack and liberal use of a fog machine. You're getting closer now. Gay couples should be discreet. No cover.

North of Townsville

The Bruce Highway snakes north from Townsville toward Cairns. On the way, it passes the agricultural town of Cardwell, the point of access to Hinchinbrook Island, and Tully, which marks the turn-off for Mission Beach.

Cardwell If you're reading this sentence while passing through Cardwell on a bus, you've just missed the town entirely. Nevertheless, this small village between Mission Beach and Townsville brushes up against an appealing beach which tempts wayfarers to pause and admire the surf. The town is in the middle of several large farming communities, and the two workers' hostels on the north side of town make it an ideal place to put in a few weeks and juice up the wallet.

Pacific Palms Backpackers, located right on the highway (tel. 4066 8671; fax 4066 8985), offers privacy and a pool, with BBQ, laundry, and linen included. (Dorms $10; twins $12. Key deposit $5.) Across the street and behind the giant mudcrab (which mystified us, too) is **Cardwell Backpackers** (tel. 4066 8014), with laundry facilities, a BBQ, free use of bikes, and A/C but only marginal privacy (dorms $12; twins $28). Both hostels arrange **work** ($10-13 per hr.) year-round; Errol, who works at Cardwell's, drives workers from either hostel for $1 per trip. **Kookaburra Caravan Park (YHA),** on the Bruce Hwy. (tel. 4766 8648; fax 4766 8910), makes free pick-ups from the coach stop. The park loans out bikes, fishing gear, and crab nets. (Tent sites $7 per person, with power $14. Dorms $14, with YHA $13; doubles $30.)

Hinchinbrook Island Cardwell is the access point for **Hinchinbrook Island** and the untrammeled wilderness of its national park, where granite peaks loom above mangrove swamps and quiet beaches. Excellent bushwalks cover the island; the 32km Thorsborne Trail crosses the length of the island. Only 40 people are allowed on the island at a time, so contact **QNP&WS** in Cardwell (tel. 4066 8601), Townsville, or Cairns well in advance. With a permit ($3.50 per person) in hand, getting a ferry isn't hard: **Hinchinbrook Island Ferries** (tel. 1800 682 702), out of Cardwell, makes the trip daily (9am, 1hr., return $66).

Tully Wedged between Mission Beach and Cardwell, Tully is soppy and sweet: soppy for the heavy annual rainfall—up to an astonishing 4m—and sweet for the **Tully Sugar Mill Tours** (tel. 4068 2288; tours Mon.-Fri. 10, 11am, 1, and 3pm; $7), which depart from the Tully Information Centre on the Bruce Hwy. The town is also host to an annual sugar fiesta, the **Tully Show,** on the last weekend in July.

Mission Beach

Rapidly gaining momentum as a major backpacker destination, this nearly continuous stretch of beach is exceedingly long, yet perhaps a bit too slender for its crowd at high tide. Mission Beach the town is, of course, the center of the strip, but the beach stretches 14km from northern Bingil Bay down to Wongaling and South Mission Beach. If you've had enough of the strip, there's always more to do on the beach on Dunk Island, looming just offshore.

ORIENTATION AND PRACTICAL INFORMATION

The town of **Tully** lies on the Bruce Hwy. north of **Cardwell** and south of **Innisfail** (see p. 336). The Mission Beach area is east of Tully, along a waterfront running almost perfectly north-to-south. **Seaview St.** heads inland from Mission Beach, in the center of the coastal strip. Not quite 200m from the beach, **Alexander Dr.** heads north toward Bingil Bay Beach and Garners Beach. Farther down Seaview, **Cassowary Dr.** turns off to the south toward **Wongaling** and South Mission Beach.

The **tourist office** (tel. 4068 7099) is on Alexander St. just north of the Mission Beach town center (open Mon.-Sat. 9am-5pm, Sun. 10am-2pm). Coming into Mission Beach by bus is a soft landing, since all of the hostels have courtesy buses waiting to pick up incoming backpackers. **McCafferty's** drops off in Mission Beach (the central area of the Mission Beach beach) and **Greyhound** calls at Wongaling Beach (next to South Mission Beach) at the **unreasonably large cassowary.**

Harvey's World Travel, in the middle of Mission Beach (tel. 4068 7187; fax 4068 2172) is a Greyhound and McCafferty ticket agent (open Mon.-Fri. 8:30am-5pm, Sat. 9am-noon; V, MC, AmEx). The only bank in town is **ANZ** (tel. 4068 7333; fax 4068 7431) across from Harvey's World Travel, which cashes traveler's checks ($6.50 commission, Visa free) exchanges currency ($5 commission), and accepts Visa and MC (open Mon.-Thurs. 9:30am-4pm, Fri. 9:30am-5pm). The **medical centre** is on Cassowary Dr. between Mission and Wongaling beaches (24hr. tel. 4068 8174; open Mon.-Fri. 8am-6pm). The **post office** is also near Harvey's World Travel across from ANZ (tel./fax 4068 7200; postal code 4582; open Mon.-Fri. 9am-5pm).

ACCOMMODATIONS

The Treehouse (tel. 4068 7137; fax 4068 7028), is perched on a hill, but not in a tree, overlooking Bingil Bay. Sooty, the live-in burro, presides over the house, whose doors are made of interlaced bamboo. The beach is a bit of a trek (2.5km), but a free hostel courtesy bus runs the route (every 2hr.). Pool, laundry, and ultra-comfy reading space with massive pillows and newspapers from around the world. Rooms have no locks. Dorms $16; doubles $40. Linen included. Camping out back is $10, but discouraged. V, MC.

Mission Beach Backpackers Lodge (tel. 4068 8317; fax 4068 8616), south of Mission Beach, past Wongaling Beach. Coming from either direction, turn onto Wongaling Beach Rd. at the very big cassowary; the hostel is on your left. Clean 2-story house with pool, laundry facilities, and a volleyball net out front. Dorms $15; twins $31; doubles $32. With A/C add $3. VIP. Linen included. Dinners served nearly every night ($3-5). Key deposit $5. Accepts V, MC. Mission Beach Resort, across the street, has Tues. $2 dinner specials.

Scotty's Mission Beach House (tel. 4068 8676; fax 4068 8520), farthest south and closest to the beach (follow signs for South Mission Beach), starts the evening festivities early with a free glass of spiked lemonade at 5:30pm. Guests gather on the veranda, sipping and mingling next to the pool and its "topless bathing is permitted" sign with a red cross through a pair of bikini-ed breasts. Backpackers sleep in standard temporary housing units reminiscent of pubs. Laundry facilities, TV room, and shared noisy plumbing. Dorms $15 (4 available for $10 on a first-come basis), with bath $17; twins and doubles $32.

Hibiscus Caravan Park (tel. 4068 8138; fax 4068 8778), on Cassowary Dr. between Mission and Wongaling Beaches, is close to the beach and managed by a zippy family. From the Greyhound stop, walk away from the plaza toward the curve in the road; it's ahead 100m. From the McCafferty's stop, catch a southbound Hail & Ride ($2). Pool, BBQ, and a shopping plaza practically next door. Tent sites $10; with power $13; on-site caravan for 2 $28.

FOOD

Cut-Price in Mission Beach (open daily 8am-7pm) and the slyly named **Foodstore** in Wongaling Beach behind the cassowary (open daily 8am-7pm; V, MC) vend staples. Some cheap eats and great finds hide within Mission Beach's little shopping plazas (take a Hail & Ride bus from your hostel, $2 one-way).

Mission Beach Gourmet Deli (tel. 4068 7660) sits behind Friends Restaurant at the sign of the flying pig. Deli sandwiches of all varieties $3.50; a full picnic basket for 2 $25 (call ahead). Open Mon.-Fri. 9am-5:30pm, Sat. 9am-1pm. V, MC.

That'll Do (tel. 4068 7300), on the cheaper, greasier end of the scale, whips up burgers ($3.50), fish and chips ($4.50), and decent-sized ice creams ($1.50). Open daily 10:30am-8pm.

Ma Donovan's Bakers, in the Wongaling Beach area, to the right of the large cassowary (tel. 4068 8944), sells generously sized foccacia pizzas ($2.80), loaves of fresh bread ($2), and tempting "vanilla slices" ($1.20). Gluten- and yeast-free bread made to order; ring ahead. Open Mon.-Fri. 6am-6pm, Sat.-Sun. 6am-2pm.

SIGHTS AND ACTIVITIES

There's gobs to keep you busy in Mission Beach, as if the rolling surf weren't enough. **Mission Beach Adventure Tours** (tel. 4068 7877) does calm-water canoeing trips ($65), **Mission Beach Trail Rides** sets up horseback riding ($30 per 2hr.), and **Mission Beach Rainforest Treks** (tel. 4068 7137) leads morning ($25) and night ($15) rainforest walks. **Raging Thunder** (tel. 4030 7990) and **R 'n' R** (tel. 1800 079 039) have whitewater rafting packages ($118), and Raging Thunder also offers tamer whitewater kayaking on the Tully River ($90). Any of the hostels can book these trips, often with a 10% YHA discount. Tandem skydiving is a popular leap; try **Jump the Beach** ($198). The ubiquitous dive boats are also in Mission Beach: a PADI certification course is $299 with **Mission Beach SCUBA School,** or $499 with **Mission Beach Dive Charters** (tel. 4068 7294), which also takes divers out to a 100-year-old shipwreck ($139). The *M.V. Friendship* (tel. 4068 7262) handles most of the reef trips ($59; plus $35 to dive if certified, $50 if not).

The local Girramay Aboriginals living in Jumbun have a day-long tour of the rainforest and waterfalls, operated through Mission Beach Adventure Tours. The **Girramay Walkabout** gets you out in the bush, throwing boomerangs and eating grubs (when in season). The tour ($50) includes a BBQ lunch.

In the same complex as the tourist office is the **4C,** or **Community for Coastal and Cassowary Conservation** (tel. 4068 7197), a free quasi-museum and mini-theater of the Mission Beach area wildlife. Giant dioramas of area forests and computers equipped with CD-ROMs explain what you'd see and hear on a bush walk, and a continually-running series of videos discusses cassowary and butterfly biology. The conservation group (entirely volunteer) also has a seedling nursery in the back: members bring in seed-rich cassowary droppings, set them in soil until it becomes clear what sort of plant is developing, and then replant the seedling as part of a massive reforestation program.

A haunt for beachcombers, birds, and butterflies, **Dunk Island** and the other Family Islands stand not far off the shore of Mission Beach. While most of the resorts on the island are rather upscale, it's possible to reserve campsites on Dunk, enabling hikers to explore the steep, lushly overgrown trails between sandy beaches. **Dunk Island Express Water Taxi** (tel. 4068 8310) offers seven 10-minute trips per day from Wongaling Beach ($18). **Dunk Island Ferry** (tel. 4068 7211) is the slow boat (45min.) with two trips per day ($22, $18 if booking through Scotty's hostel). Both offer free pick-up at hostels and campgrounds.

■ North of Mission Beach

A little north of Mission Beach is the totally unexpected **Paronella Park** (tel. 4065 3225), a Moorish castle in the middle of sugar cane fields. Once a visitor gets over the giddy excitement of such a preposterous site a little west of nowhere, the setting sinks in: fountains from the Alhambra, long, winding staircases from El Escorial, and a bamboo forest that dizzies the viewer with its height. This park gushes with romance and intrigue, but it's a pain in the butt to get to, and practically inaccessible by public transportation. Between Innisfail and Mission Beach, look for signs for Paronella (in tiny Mena Creek); the South Johnstone exit is the fastest. Umbrellas available at the entrance for mystical, rainy afternoon visits (open daily 9am-5pm; admission $8).

Innisfail North of Mission Beach on the route to Cairns is a town with little tourist appeal except for its funky day-glo Art Deco architecture along Edith St., the downtown strip. There's an **information center** (tel. 4061 6448; open daily 9am-5pm) along the south stretch of highway out of town and a **post office** (tel. 4061 1077) on the corner of Rankin and Edith St. (open Mon.-Fri. 8:30am-5pm). Just north of Innisfail, the road to the **Atherton Tablelands** (see p. 347) branches off inland toward Millaa Millaa.

Innisfail's main attraction, though, is the year-round casual labor market. The folks at **Endeavour Hostel,** 31 Glady St. (tel. 4061 6610; fax 4061 3773), arrange for work on neighboring farms. From the rail station, follow the Bruce Hwy. toward town until you reach Glady St., then turn right and the hostel's on the left. The bus stop is between Lady and Ernest St.; follow Glady down away from the park, and the hostel will be on your left. Employment listings are posted daily, and work usually fetches an hourly wage of $10. (Pool, laundry facilities, and free shuttle to work. Dorms $12, weekly $65. Key deposit $10. Linen and cutlery deposit $5.) **Backpackers Paradise,** 73 Rankin St. (tel. 4061 2284), was anything *but* paradise before the new management took over with plans to bring it up to speed. Soiled mattresses and moldy fridges are now being replaced. A shuttle runs out to the neighboring farms for $1 per trip. (Pool and laundry. Dorms $11; doubles $24. VIP. Linen included. TV $1 per night or—gotta love this mathematical wizardry—$10 per week. Key deposit $10. Bikes $5 per day plus $10 deposit.) **Susie's,** on Edith St. between Owen and Rankin St., has an all-you-can-eat Saturday breakfast buffet ($5.50).

A mere 8km south of Innisfail along the Bruce Hwy. is the **Sugar Museum** (tel. 4063 2306), actually a huge warehouse divided by partitions that hide a steam engine and a windmill. An ancient IBM mainframe, used to process sugarcane, sits with lights still blinking (open Mon.-Fri. 9am-5pm, Sat.-Sun. 9am-4pm; admission $4).

FAR NORTH QUEENSLAND

The Great Barrier Reef snakes closer to shore at Cairns, Cape Tribulation, and Cooktown than at any other point along its length. For divers, this spells shorter boat trips and longer visits to the spectacular corals of the reef. Boats operate from Cairns and other oceanside towns, usually out to cays where the water is calm and fish weave curiously around divers. Yet the region has as much biological diversity above sea level as below, and manta rays and sea cucumbers must share the far north with tree kangaroos and frog-mouth birds.

As if converging on the reef, the Great Dividing Range advances eastward, pressing the rainforest against the Coral Sea. Abundant natural life flourishes along the creeks, rivers, and rainstorms that feed the sea. The tropical paradise along the coast may have shed all hints of the mining frontier it once was, but the allure of elemental riches first brought outsiders to this land. A steady stream of tin-cup gold miners advanced through Townsville to the then-tiny villages of Cairns and Port Douglas. In the wake of WWII, scuba divers replaced gold prospectors just as the prospectors once displaced native Aboriginals.

The Cook Highway runs north from Cairns, venturing forth as bravely as its storm-tossed namesake. Craggy mountains inch closer to the coast and the rainforest becomes almost impenetrably dense around Cape Tribulation. The legacy of the gold rush lives on in Cooktown, Queensland's northernmost outpost. Beyond lies the Cape York Peninsula, a wild, untamed frontier of hungry crocs and flat tires.

Cairns

In ancient times, travelers made a habit of piling stones by the roadside. These stacks of rocks, or cairns, served as landmarks along frequently traversed routes. Aptly named, the city of Cairns is a metaphorical rock in many travelers' whirlwind tours of Australia. But Cairns appears on many itineraries precisely because it is not all rock: this tropical city is the premier gateway for snorkeling and scuba diving on the Great Barrier Reef, with its exotic sea life and vivid hues. On shore, palm-lined avenues and lush gardens blossom in equally impressive displays of color. The graceful stretch of the Esplanade divides land from water, although tidal mudflats make traditional beach activities impossible.

Cairns (pronounced as in, beer "cans") has two travel markets, one suited to the luxury tourist and the other to the backpacker. The southern end of the city is the bastion of luxury, with opal stores, opulent restaurants, and shop signs in both English and Japanese. North of City Place is the neutral ground, where ritzy hotels and reasonable hostels mix cautiously. The backpackers' ghetto is along the Esplanade. Hostels stand shoulder-to-shoulder, cheap eats await just outside the door, and the strip of green across the street encourages travelers to stop a while, trade a campervan, swap a story, or just watch the gulls and goliath pelicans swoop and twirl.

ORIENTATION

Cairns is tucked between undulating hills to the west and the harbor to the east, while mangrove swamps sandwich the city on the north and the south. **The Esplanade,** with its many hostels, runs along the waterfront. At its southern end is the **tourist office** and **The Pier,** which supports the Pier Marketplace. Farther south, the Esplanade becomes Wharf St. and runs past the **Trinity Wharf** and **Transit Centre.**

Shields St. heads away from the Pier to **City Place,** a pedestrian mall and the destination of most intercity buses. From this intersection, **Lake St.** runs parallel to the Esplanade. Continuing west, Shields St. intersects first Grafton St. then **Sheridan St.** (called Cook Hwy. north of the city). Half a block south of Shields, Grafton and Sheridan St. border **Rusty's Bazaar.** The **Cairns Railway Station** is on McLeod St. at Shields' terminus. The **Bruce Hwy.** begins two blocks to the north.

Scuba Diving on the Great Barrier Reef

The coral of the Great Barrier Reef comes in hundreds of shapes and shades, each produced by the life and death of miniscule colonies of coral polyps. Equally variegated in size and hue, a thousand fish dart about the limestone structure. Brilliantly colored parrot fish gnaw away at living polyps, crunching the coral with their bird-like beaks: the attentive diver can hear the munching from a good distance off. The diver wears a Self-Contained Underwater Breathing Apparatus (SCUBA), a device invented by Jacques Costeau. Put on a tank, vest, weights, and flippers, and you're no longer restrained by such petty things as buoyance. Hover just beneath the ocean's surface for a shark's-eye view of the reef below, then head straight down to an interesting patch of coral. Drift across the bottom, past the odd white-tipped reef shark that rises from the sand and swishes harmlessly away. Fly through the crowds of fish: the dainty and dashing angels, the heavy and petulant grouper, and the noble and sleek rays. The reef shelves are populated with starfish, urchins, and giant "man-eating" (actually plankton-eating) clams. The seafloor is covered with scavengers of all sorts, as well as the deadly stone fish, which sits still on the bottom all day, waiting for something to poison. Sea cucumbers are soft to the touch and fun to tickle—until they get scared and spit out their innards at you. Tiny hills and holes along the floor attest to the presence of crabs and shrimp. There's plenty more, but we're running out of ink. See **Biodiversity** (p. 64), for more on the reef.

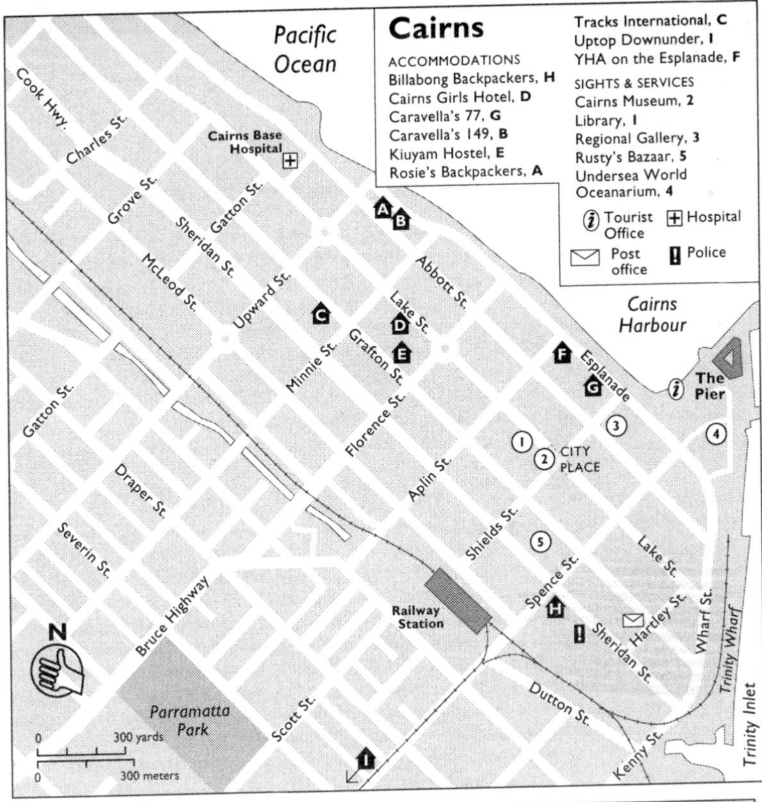

Where and When To Dive

Diving, or at least snorkeling, on the Great Barrier Reef is virtually a mandate for visitors of coastal Queensland. But with 2300km of reef to choose from, the decision about where and when to dive is not always simple. Cairns is the most popular town to dive from, since it has the most diving boat operators and the reef is closest to shore, but diving tends to be cheaper in Airlie Beach, and cheapest of all in Bundaberg. In Bundaberg, however, you're a long way from the reef itself. It can be a good, inexpensive place to earn a certification card, and then take it to dive somewhere else. Townsville tends to be a more expensive base to dive from than Cairns.

The water takes about a day to clear after a storm, and about a month after a cyclone: if you go when the weather's been bad, the coral's vibrant colors will be obscured in a swirling mass of brown dirt, and you usually won't get a refund. Generally, in all weather, the water is clearer the farther out you go, but the life you'll see is not radically different whether you're 20km offshore or 30km (on the so-called "outer reef"). There are three types of reef structure. Fringing reef hugs the coastline and some islands, and is usually soft coral, without the beauty and structure of other reef types. Platform or mid-shelf reef is actually the tops of old undersea mountains, while ribbon reefs are actually the edge of the continental shelf. Platform and ribbon reefs start off the coast of Bundaberg and wind north, almost kissing the coast at Cairns, and fading off the tip of Cape York. It doesn't matter so much which section you see; as long as the weather's been good, you won't go wrong with any piece.

PRACTICAL INFORMATION

Tourist Office: Visitor Information Centre (tel. 4051 3588; fax 4051 0127), on the Esplanade just when it hikes a left to The Pier. From the train station, take a right onto Spence St., then turn left (away from the mountains) and walk to the end of the street. Take a left and you'll see it less than 100m on your right. From the bus station, head right on to Wharf St., which will curve and become the Esplanade. The office is on your right, between Spence and Shields St. Open Mon.-Fri. 9:30am-5:30pm, Sat.-Sun. 9:30am-1:30pm.

Travel Office: Flight Centre, 24 Spence St. (tel. 4052 1077, 24hr. info 13 31 33; fax 4051 9972), guarantees to beat any quoted price. Open Mon.-Fri 9am-5pm, Sat. 9am-noon. **STA Travel,** 43 Lake St. (tel. 4031 4199; fax 4031 6384), open Mon.-Fri. 9am-5pm, Sat. 10am-2pm; *Let's Go* books at a 10% discount.

Money: The best **currency exchange** rates ($3 or 1% commission) are found at the **American Express Office,** 58-70 Lake St., 2nd fl. (tel. 4031 2871; fax 4031 5262), at the Orchid Plaza. Mail held for 30 days with no charge to card members or traveler's check holders. Wheelchair accessible. Open Mon.-Fri. 8:30am-5pm, Sat. 9am-noon. **ATM** machines at virtually every bank accept V, MC, Cirrus.

Airport: 8km north of Cairns on Captain Cook Hwy. (Sheridan St. turns into Captain Cook Hwy. outside of town.) Signs point directly to the airport (tel. 4052 3888; fax 4052 1493). International carriers: Air New Zealand (tel. 1800 061 253), Cathay Pacific (tel. 13 17 47), Garuda Indonesia (tel. 008 800 873), Japan Airlines (tel. 4031 2700), Malaysia Airlines (tel. 4031 0000), Qantas (tel. 1800 177 767), and Singapore Airlines (tel. 4031 7538). Domestic carriers: Qantas (tel. 13 13 13), Flight West Airlines (tel. 13 23 92), and Trans Pacific Air (tel. 4035 9611). Most hostels run a free shuttle bus pick-up service; just call from the terminal. Buses also run to town ($4.50 one-way) from just outside the terminal. Taxis to town are about $10.

Trains: The **rail station** is wedged between Bunda St. and the new shopping mall on McLeod St. From the Esplanade, walk up Spence St. and you'll find it on your right. Travel Centre Office (tel. 13 22 32) sells tickets. 10% discount with YHA card. V, MC. Open Mon.-Fri. 9am-5pm, Sat. 9am-noon. Luggage lockers. Wheelchair accessible. The East Coast Discover Pass ($199) covers rail from Cairns to Sydney.

Buses: Terminal (open daily 6:15am-1am) at Trinity Wharf, on Wharf St. From the station, walk to the right along Wharf St. toward The Pier. Here, the Esplanade begins. Leave luggage at the gift shop. **McCafferty's** (tel. 4051 5899, 24hr. tel. 13 14 99) runs buses southbound toward Brisbane (1, 6:45, 9:30am, 2, and 6:15pm seasonally, 30hr.). V, MC. Student ID discounts. **Greyhound** (24hr. tel. 13 20 30) also runs southbound (1, 8:45am, and 3pm). VIP, YHA, and student ID discounts.

Public Transportation: Sunbus depot on Lake St. in City Place. Fares $1-4; unlimited day pass $9. Routes posted at all information kiosks.

Ferries: Quicksilver runs daily to **Port Douglas** (8am, return departure 5:15pm, 1½hr., one-way $20, return $30, 10% off with YHA card). Departs from The Pier, to the left at the end of the Esplanade. The launch is inside near the back.

Taxis: Black and White (tel. 13 10 08), **Taxis Australia** (tel. 13 22 27), and **Taxi AAA** (tel. 13 10 08) serve Cairns. A fare to the airport should run near $10.

Car Rental: Local companies renting only between Cooktown and Townsville include **Cairns Tropical,** 140 Grafton St. (24hr. tel. 4031 3995; fax 4031 4284 140; open daily 7:30am-6pm), and **Cairns Leisure Wheels,** 196 Sheridan St. (tel. 4051 8988; fax 4051 5656). Larger companies which will rent for trips farther afield are **National,** 143 Abbott St. (tel. 4051 4600), and **Budget,** 153 Lake St. (tel. 4051 9222; fax 4052 1158). 4WD is advisable for trips up to Cape Tribulation.

Maps: Absell's Map Centre, 55 Lake St. (tel. 4041 2699), Andrejic's Arcade. Entrance is by Absell's News, opposite Orchid Plaza. Open Mon.-Sat. 8:30am-6pm.

Automobile Club: Royal Automobile Club of Queensland (RACQ), 138 McLeod St. (24hr. tel. 4051 6543), inside Coral Motors.

National Parks Office: The Queensland National Parks and Wildlife Service (QNPWS), 10 McLeod St. Open Mon.-Fri. 8:30am-4:30pm. Pick up one of 4 **Discover National Parks** mini-books ($3.50 each), or the whole bundle and a camping guide ($17.50). The guide is an indispensable tool for those headed into the bush. Camping permits ($3.50 per person).

Internet: Access at **Parkview Backpackers,** 174 Grafton St. (tel. 4051 3700), daily 7am-9pm; and at **Community Information Service Cairns** in the Tropical Arcade, at the corner of Abbott and Shields St., daily 9am-10pm. Most services $6 for 30min.
Groceries: Woolworths (tel. 4051 2015), on Lake St. next to City Place. Mon.-Fri. 8am-9pm, Sat. 8am-5:30pm, Sun. 1pm-8pm.
Hotlines: Queensland AIDS Council (tel. 4051 1028). Free confidential HIV testing.
Hospital: Cairns Base Hospital (tel. 4050 6333), on the Esplanade past the last trio of hostels (Bel-Air, Rosie's, Caravellers).
Emergency: Dial 000.
Police: (tel. 4030 7000; fax 4030 7144) on Sheridan St., between Spence and Hartley St. Open 24hr. **Police Beat** (tel. 4041 1178; fax 4041 1044), next to the Visitors Information Centre near the corner of Shields St. and the Esplanade. Open Mon. and Thurs.-Sun. 24hr.; Tues.-Wed. 6am-midnight.
Post Office: Cairns General Post Office (GPO) (tel. 4031 4303; fax 4051 3871) at corner of Hartley and Grafton St. *Poste Restante.* All services open Mon.-Fri. 9am-5pm. Another office, on the 2nd floor of the Orchid Plaza, open Mon.-Fri. 9am-6pm, Sat. 9am-12:30pm. **Postal code:** 4870.
Phone Code: 07.

ACCOMMODATIONS

Though small, Cairns is second only to Sydney as a backpacker's destination and is consequently studded with dozens of budget hostels. Most are clustered along the Esplanade, and the more popular are booked year-round. Except where noted, all have a pool, a key deposit of $10, and no curfew. Hostels generally offer coin-operated laundry, free pick-up from the bus and rail stations or the airport, and free dinner at a local pub.

Caravella's 77 Backpacker Resort, 77-81 Esplanade (tel. 4051 2159 or 4051 2326; fax 4031 6329), between Alpin and Shields St., 2min. from the bus station. Smack in the middle of all the action, Caravella's 77 offers choice amenities for the wayward traveler. The kitchens and rooms are clean and colorful (though you'll need to provide your own linen). The front desk staff is tight with all the rental and reef folks in town, and can serve as your own private booking agents. A/C dorms $16; twins and doubles $32; luxury doubles with bath $40. VIP. Flash your *Let's Go* and ask about a discount on your first night's stay.

Cairns Girls Hostel, 147a Lake St. (tel. 4051 2767; fax 4051 2016), between Florence and Minnie St. A true gem (or lifeboat, as the case may be) in the morass of accommodations in Cairns, this women-only hostel has provided a safe haven for travelers for over 30 years. Gentlemen are requested to wait at the front door, and a sizeable Doberman (who likes to gnaw on a stuffed bunny) helps keep order. No nunnery, though, this friendly 16-room family has no curfew and no checkout restrictions. Large twin rooms are cooled by ceiling fans and lit by frosted glass windows. Rates on a sliding scale: $15 for the first night, $12 by the fifth. Weekly: $80 for the first, $75 thereafter.

Kuiyam Hostel, 162 Grafton St. (tel. 4051 6466; fax 4051 6469), across from Munroe Martin Park, between Minnie and Florence St. Short of living with your parents, you will never find a better deal than at Kuiyam Hostel, a member of a nationwide chain of Aboriginal-operated, government-subsidized hostels. The facilities are new and flawless, with a playground for the children and a rec room with a pool table for the adults. No tour desk. No key deposit. Singles, doubles, and family rooms are available. By request, *Let's Go* has not published rates, but they are well below the competition and include 3 meals per day. Getting a room is difficult, since priority goes to Aboriginal and Torres Strait Islanders.

Free Spirit Travellers Accommodation, 72 Grafton St. (tel. 4051 7620). Recently refurbished and smack in the middle of town, with high ceilings and good vibes all around. TV room, kitchen, and small gym. No pool, but cheap, clean beds. Reception open daily 7am-10pm. Dorms $13; doubles $30. No key deposit.

Uptop Downunder Backpackers Resort, 164 Spence St. (tel. 4051 3636; fax 4052 1211). 15-min. walk from town; at night it's safer to take the hourly shuttle bus outside Woolworth's on Lake St. Though an inconvenient distance from downtown, Uptop delivers in service and style. Spotless rooms are equipped with fridges. Trading library, BBQ, and mini-cinema with nightly flicks. Check-out 9:30am. Dorms $15; singles $28; doubles and twins $32. VIP, YHA, student discounts.

Billabong Backpackers, 69 Spence St. (tel. 4051 6946; fax 4051 6022), at the corner of Sheridan St., within spitting distance of the train station. Located diagonally across from Rusty's Bar, the locals' drinking hole of choice, Billabong was recently renovated by a gay-friendly staff. 2-week max. stay. Check-in 7:30pm. Check-out 10:30am. Dorms $14 (with A/C a little more); singles $14; doubles and twins $30. Linen provided, but meals are not. V, MC.

Tracks International Youth Hostel, 149 Grafton St. (tel. 4031 1474 or 1800 065 464; fax 4031 1474), between Minnie and Upward St. To make up for the walk and for unimpressive rooms, Tracks lavishes freebies on its guests, like a glass of wine every night, dinner, trips to Trinity Beach and the Botanical Gardens, weekly BBQs (on a boat when weather permits), and a night cruise once a fortnight. Dorms $14, with A/C $15; singles $20; doubles and twins $28. VIP, YHA. Accepts V, MC.

Caravella's 149, 149 Esplanade (tel. 4031 5680; fax 4051 4097), past the children's playground. Most rooms have A/C and beautiful hardwood floors tread by heavy backpacker volume. Dorms for women $14, for men $16; doubles and twins $32.

Rosie's Backpackers, 155 Esplanade (tel. 4051 0235; fax 4051 5191), just past Caravella's 149 at the far end of the Esplanade; a bit of a walk after a few beers. Sleep off hangovers in the hot tub. Billiards and table tennis. Dorms $15.

YHA on the Esplanade, 93 Esplanade (tel. 4031 1919; fax 4031 4381), on the corner of Alpin St. All rooms have A/C and bath. Dorms $16; doubles and twins $36. Nonmembers of YHA pay $3 extra. No pick-up from the airport or bus station.

FOOD

Cairns is just bubbling with good eats, from all-night kebab and pizza stalls on the Esplanade to upscale restaurants that specialize in frying up local fauna. Coffee shops usually offer a filling **breakfast** (called "morning tea" or "Devonshire tea") for $5-6. An exceptional value is **Le Cake,** in Rusty's Bazaar, Grafton St. side, which is run by a Parisian couple who insist on presenting a proper breakfast: a homemade croissant ($1) and fresh-pressed coffee ($2) to warm the soul (open Wed.-Fri. 7am-5pm, Sat. 5am-1pm, Sun. 6am-1pm). **Coffee Cafe,** 87 Lake St., is within earshot of the open-air concert hall and offers scones, jam, and a pot o' tea for $5 (open daily 6am-10pm). Near the center of town, the **Cairns Bakehouse,** 115 Abbott St., has over 30 types of breads and a mouth-watering panoply of pastries ($2.50): apple brown Betty, macadamia nut tart, mango cheesecake, and a wild, untamed fruit tartlet. The coffee ($3), unfortunately, can be weak and watery (open Mon.-Sun. 6:30am-8pm).

Most of the smaller restaurants have a **lunch** special, but few go as cheap as the **Mouth Trap,** 9 Sheridan St. opposite Rusty's Pub (open Mon.-Fri. 5am-5pm, Sat. 5am-noon). **Tiny's Juice Bar,** at the corner of Grafton and Spence St., offers a variety of juices that is anything but tiny. Some 50 selections, plus half a dozen smoothies ($3-4), stand by to complement your sandwich (open Mon.-Sat. 7:30am-5pm).

No visit to Cairns would be complete without a **dinner** at **Gypsy Dee's,** 41 Shields St. (tel. 4051 5530), near the corner of Sheridan St. The atmosphere is thick with sultry lighting, wide wicker chairs, and strings of shells hanging as chandeliers. As if the stylized gypsy wagon just left of center stage weren't enough, this hot spot has live music every night, generous dinner portions ($8-12), and almost a dozen vegetarian entrees. In an incredible feat of engineering, the entire front of the restaurant (which otherwise looks boarded-up) folds down onto the sidewalk, providing a terrace complete with fig trees (open 6pm-2am). On the top end of things, the **Red Ochre Grill,** 43 Shields St. (tel. 4051 0100), by the corner of Sheridan, combines art-deco surroundings with good Aussie cooking. Entrees, like a kangaroo sirloin or emu and river mint curry, run up to $20 per plate, and can be washed down with anise seed tea ($3) (open Mon.-Sun. 10am-midnight; V, MC). **Dundee's,** 29 Spence St., offers a variety of Australia's tastier fauna: kangaroo soup ($5.50), crocodile sausages ($11.50), and camel balls ($12.50) liven up the menu. Put it all on one plate with the Aussie Sampler ($27.50), served daily 5:30 to 10:30pm.

NIGHTLIFE AND ENTERTAINMENT

Despite its widespread and well-deserved reputation as a haven for backpackers, the nightclub scene here is still a few paces behind that of other cities. An understated friction between locals and tourists has divided the bars and clubs. Some cater directly to the hostel crowd, running shuttle buses to pick up party-goers; others may turn away backpackers at the door. Cairns makes up for quantity with quality, and visitors aren't likely to complain that there isn't enough to do at night. For the latest local word, pick up a copy of *Son of Barfly* (free) at any of the cafes around town. The *Pink Guide to Cairns,* available at Walker's Book Shop, 96 Lake St., details **gay-friendly** nightlife and accommodations.

The Woolshed, 24 Shields St. (tel. 4031 6304 for free shuttle bus), near the City Center. Modelled after its namesake with corrugated aluminum walls and rough-cut tables, the Woolshed offers a low-key environment for meeting backpackers. There are 2 floors, a couple of pool tables, and a small dance floor. Free dinners for guests of Uptop Downunder, U2, and JJ's hostels. Happy hour (7:30-8:30pm, $5 pitchers). Open nightly 6pm-5am.

The Beach (tel. 4031 3944 for free shuttle bus), at the corner of Abbott and Aplin St., hosts most of the hostels' free dinner offers and also wins top billing for nightlife. The warehouse-sized club fills 2 stories with pool tables, 3 bars, a dance floor, and a giant stage set up to look like a pirate ship. Nightly themes include: Mr. Backpacker, Miss Backpacker, Miss Lovely Legs, and the infamous "foam party," which culminates in knots of half-naked backpackers frolicking waist-deep in bubbles. Partiers rave all night, every night, 7pm-5am.

Samuel's (tel. 4051 8211 for shuttle bus), at the corner of Hartley and Lake St., is wedged between a pair of establishments that aren't particularly welcoming to backpackers. From the glassed-in pub room you have a good view of the adjacent club's dance floor, but most backpackers are better off dancing on the tables at Samuel's than attempting to mix with the locals next door. Open nightly 6pm-5am.

Club Trix, 53 Spence St. (tel. 4051 8223), between Grafton and McLeod St., just past Turkish Michael's Cafe. A gay bar and dance club with no dress code. Open Mon.-Sat. 9pm-late. The best shows are Fri.-Sat., but they charge a cover.

Johnno's Blues Bar, at the corner of the Esplanade and Shields St. (tel. 4031 5008). Red hot and cool jazz and blues 7 days a week. Wed.-Sun. $5-6 cover, depending on the band that's in. Happy hour 9-11pm for jugs and pots; Tuesday it's $5 jugs all night long. Open 9pm-late.

If you'd prefer popcorn to beer, check out the famous **Palace Independent Cinema,** 86 Lake St. (tel. 4051 6966), tucked in a corner just south of City Place. It's a one-screen, 470-seat wonder, heavy on the air-conditioning. The projectors run both mainstream and art-house flicks (admission $8.50, with ISIC $6.50). Keep an eye out for the *Rocky Horror Picture Show,* a wild romp that comes to town about four times per year.

SIGHTS AND ACTIVITIES

To the backpacker, Cairns is not so much a final destination as an excellent hub from which to explore the region. There are, however, a handful of worthwhile sites for the odd afternoon. Perhaps the best retreat on a broiling day is the **Cairns City Public Library,** 117 Lake St. (tel. 4050 2404). There is a $50 refundable library fee for non-residents who want to check out materials, but you can enjoy the air-conditioning for free, and internet access should be installed soon (library open Mon. 10am-6pm, Tues.-Fri. 10am-7pm, Sat. 10am-4pm). Almost a library itself, **Walker's Book Shop,** 96 Lake St. (tel. 4051 2410), has a large section on Aboriginal history and lore, as well as bilingual children's titles, a gay literature section, and an assortment of free local papers. (Student discount 10%. Open Mon.-Thurs. 8:30am-5:30pm, Fri. 8:30am-8pm, Sat. 8:30am-4pm, Sun. noon-6pm.)

The volunteer-run **Cairns Museum** (tel. 4051 5586), in City Place, is a low-budget masterpiece. Here you'll find bits of Cairns history; memorabilia of the colonial days surround two spreads of Aboriginal weaponry. There's a small exhibit on Chinese immigrants, and a collection of heavy tools used to clear rainforest (open Mon.-Sat. 10am-4pm; admission $3). When the weather turns sour and obscures the reef with silt, stroll over to the **Undersea World Oceanarium** (tel. 4041 1777) out in the Pier Marketplace, near the wharves. Fish feedings (10:30am, noon, 1:30, and 3pm) are interactive, since the diver is outfitted with a two-way intercom (open daily 8am-8pm; admission $10, children $6). If you've had enough exposure to sea life, stop by the **Cairns Regional Art Gallery** (tel. 4031 6865) at the corner of Abbott and Shields St., with its rotating exhibits of local artists' work (admission $5, concessions $2).

The **Flecker Botanic Gardens** are good for a morning's lazy wander. The grounds include fern and orchid houses, a garden presenting the ways Aboriginals have traditionally used plants, and a meandering boardwalk and walking trail that crosses fresh and saltwater lakes. You can pick up a self-guide booklet ($2) or cassette player ($4) at the **office** (tel. 4050 2454) next to the restaurant; the office also books guided walks ($4.50) on demand, and has a small library of dusty tomes for any nagging questions (office open Mon.-Fri. 8:30am-5:30pm). To get to the gardens, hop the Sunbus from City Place, #1B (one-way $2.30); or drive north on Sheridan St. until you can take a left onto Collins Ave. If the weather is fair and you're in shape, walk the 10km from town (open Mon.-Fri. 7:30am-5:30pm, Sat.-Sun. 8:30am-5:30pm; free).

From the Gardens, it's only a kilometer down Collins Ave. (follow the signs after the traffic circle) to the **Royal Flying Doctor Service Visitors Centre** (tel. 4053 5687; fax 4032 1776). This is the main base for Queensland, and serves an area roughly the size of Japan. There's a movie, information sheets in seven languages, and lots of old radio machinery and medical equipment on display. Best of all though, is the fully-outfitted air ambulance out back, decommissioned only five years ago. Even the flaps still flap when visitors turn the steering column (open Mon.-Fri. 8:30am-5pm, Sat.-Sun. 9am-4:30pm; admission $5).

Another option from the Botanic Gardens is to walk 100m up Collins Ave. toward the Bruce Hwy., to the entrance of **Mount Whitfield Environmental Park,** the last bits of rainforest in the Cairns area. The shorter Red Arrow circuit (marked by, of all things, a series of red arrows) takes about an hour, while the more rugged Blue Arrow circuit is a five-hour trek up and around Mount Whitfield. The area is frequented by cassowaries and brush turkeys, and the very careful observer might find a Papuan Frogmouth bird in the brush. The Botanic Gardens office has a self-guide booklet ($3) that explains some of the Yirrganydji Aboriginal history along the trail.

Getting high is easy enough in Cairns: take a hot-air balloon ride ($105) over the Atherton Tablelands with **Raging Thunder Adventures,** 97 Hartley St. (tel. 4030 7990; fax 4030 7911). Coming back down is a snap with **Paul's Parachuting** (tel. 4035 9666; fax 4035 9966), located in Cairns airport. Tandem jumps are about $200 and drop you in Mission Beach safely distant from incoming air traffic. Retired bombardiers will rejoice at the opportunity to air-drop mail over Cape York. If you don't trust your aim, tag along with **Cape York Air** (tel. 4035 9399) in Cairns airport. Pilots will let passengers accompany them on their daily runs for $120-300. Shorter flights are cheaper and roundly preferred; one can only appreciate so much dense rainforest canopy at a time.

Despite its proximity to arguably the best diving spot in the world, Cairns lacks a beach of its own. At low tide the bay rolls back to reveal a wide expanse of mud flats, but sunbathers must make do with grassy spots in the parks or pool-side lawn chairs, and surfers will find themselves docked. Sigh. For the sand-hungry, a few beaches lie north of Cairns; Sunbus #1 and 1A run to Trinity Beach, the favorite, from the depot in City Place (Mon.-Fri. every 30min., Sat.-Sun. every hr.).

Box jellyfish are serious business—a single jellyfish may have enough poison to kill three adults, and its sting usually proves deadly. They're out and about between October and May in coastal waters north of approximately Great Keppel Island. Always, always ask locals about them before swimming. Some beaches install jellyfish-proof nets, and some diving establishments sell jellyfish-proof wetsuits, but stay out of the water if you are at all concerned about your safety.

While bushwalking, don't walk in wild mangroves, since **saltwater crocodiles** hide out there. The crocs can also be found in northern coastal and inland waters.

DIVING AND SNORKELING

Diving the **Great Barrier Reef,** or at least snorkeling it, is the reason thousands of travelers visit Cairns each year. About a dozen boats leave from Trinity Wharf every day, and competition for a spot on their passenger lists is as cutthroat as the Darwinian struggle for life itself. Hostels will gladly book you on one of these reef-bound vessels (and gladly pocket their 25% commission). Three small fry operators are worth a closer look. **Ocean Free,** 8 Bradford St. (tel. 4031 6601; fax 4031 4361), runs a day tour out to the reef in a double-master schooner, complete with a stopover on Green Island. The price is about standard: $50 for the trip, another $30-45 to dive, depending on certification. **Passions of Paradise** (tel. 4050 0676; fax 4051 9505) runs a similar trip for a few dollars more. Their gussied-up catamaran stops over at Upolu Cay, a hump of sand in the middle of the reef. **The Falla,** 8 Bradford St. (tel. 4031 3488; fax 4035 2585), gets top billing for its swank pearl lugger boat and tight crew; this is decidedly a well-run ship. Lunch is included in the trip ($55), and certified dives are $40 each. The dive masters specialize to the point of zealousness in helping novice divers take their first plunge ($35, second dive $25).

Travelers interested in more than just a one-day shot at the reef may want to consider getting certified to dive independently. There are four major players in the market for diving certification. **Cairns Dive Centre,** 121 Abbott St. (tel. 4051 0294; fax 4051 7531; email divecdc@ozemail.com.au; http://www.ozemail.com.au/~divecdc), is generally the least expensive, with a "floating hotel" catamaran for its flagship. **Down Under Dive,** 155 Sheridan St. (tel. 4031 1288; fax 4031 1373; email dudive@ozemail.com.au; http://www.ozemail.com.au/~dudive), has a nifty two-masted clipper ship with an on-board hot tub. Courses are a touch more expensive at **Pro-Dive,** 116 Spence St. (tel. 4031 5255; fax 4051 9955; email prodive@internet-north.com.au; http://www.prodive-cairns.com.au). **Deep Sea Divers Den,** 319 Draper St. (tel. 4031 2223; fax 4031 1210; email diveden@ozemail.com.au; http://www.ozemail.com.au/~diveden), is in the same price range. Check all four options before enrolling, since prices fluctuate frequently.

The best way—short of writing a marine biology thesis—to prep yourself for a reef trip is to attend the slide-show lecture called **Reef Teach** (tel. 4051 6882), 14 Spence St. (talk given Mon.-Sat. 6:15pm; admission $10, includes tea and biscuits).

SHOPPING

In a city that hides a glitzy, high-priced shopping mall in every city block, finding cheap supplies can drive you batty. The malls all sell the same selection of bush hats, t-shirts, and commercially produced Aboriginal handicrafts. **Rusty's Bazaar,** wedged between Sheridan and Grafton St. just south of Shields St., is hands-down the best shopping experience Cairns has to offer. Fruit, honey, orchids, water pipes, and camera equipment are just some of the options. Show up early before the good stuff sells out (open Fri. 9am-7pm, Sat.-Sun. 6:30am-1pm). On the side of the bazaar, at 81 Grafton St., sits the unassuming **Kaotica Secondhand** (tel. 4051 9386), a Cairns standard for 15 years. Backpackers unload excess belongings and pick up jeans ($15) or dresses ($10-15). Just north of City Place is **City Place Disposals** (tel. 4051 6040), at the corner of Shields and Grafton St. Take a peek at their fine assortment of swags, buck knives, and camping gear (open Mon.-Fri. 8am-5:30pm, Sat. 8am-1pm).

When it comes to **Aboriginal crafts,** be cautious of purchasing boomerangs and spears that are advertised as "made by true Aboriginals." In many cases, Aboriginals surrender their culture to commercialization only grudgingly, and the white middleman takes most of the profit. The handful of Aboriginal-owned businesses that sell such artifacts are the best to patronize. **Firefly,** in the Night Markets off the Esplanade (open daily 5-11pm), and **Bunna Nappi Nappe** in the Tropical Arcade are both 100% Aboriginal enterprises. **Is Aboriginal,** 44 Spruce St. (tel. 4031 2912), allows customers to strip, sand, and make their own didgeridoo under the instruction of the Aboriginal staff. At $100 each ($30 more to paint), you're paying considerably less than you would in the shopping plaza (open Mon.-Sat. 9am-7pm, Sun. 10am-7pm).

■ Around Cairns

Before you go blind staring at the sunlight glinting off the Pacific, remind yourself that there are some inland attractions around Cairns, too. The **Atherton Tablelands** rise above the tropical forest to the southwest of Cairns, and offer a very different appeal than do the offshore reefs. The closest town in the Tablelands is **Kuranda** (see p. 347). On the road to Kuranda are a couple of slick, family-oriented tourist joints. **Rainforestation,** on the Kennedy Hwy. (tel. 4093 9033; fax 4093 7578; open daily 8am-4pm), is the usual bundle of Aboriginal dancers, vicious crocs, and domesticated kangaroos. A full day's package has a hefty price tag ($29), but the rainforest tour (in an amphibious vehicle) might be worth the $11.50. Coach service from Cairns is available (departing 8:30am, 12:30pm) but costs more than the rainforest tour ($18 return). **Adventure in Paradise** (tel. 4093 7264; fax 4093 7267), off the Kennedy Hwy., takes visitors down a track lined with animated animals, many of them having nothing to do with Australia (lions, monkeys, gorillas, a Tyrannosaurus Rex), to a cafeteria in the bottom of a valley (tour $10). The well-designed **mini-golf** course ($3 for 9 holes) is doubtlessly the only such course in the greater Cairns area (complex open daily 9am-5:30pm).

Just north of Cairns and off the Cook Hwy. in neighboring Smithfield is the national coup of Aboriginal cultural parks: **Tjapukai** (tel. 4042 9999; fax 4042 9988; http://www.tjapukai.com.au). Pronounced "JAB-a-guy," this is the most wholly rewarding, intelligently presented, and culturally fair presentation of Aboriginal myth, customs, and history in all of Queensland. Give this experience at least half a day. First see the History Theatre, a slide show presenting the history of European and Aboriginal contact since Cook's landing, then the Creation Theatre, a hologram and laser light show presenting the Tjapukai's creation myth in the Tjapukai language (headsets can be tuned to any of 7 foreign languages). Next, head over a bridge and to the award-winning Tjapukai Dance Theatre, a clever mix of authentic dance, clear narrative and audience participation. The "camp" behind the dance theater has on-going demonstrations of didgeridoos, fire-making, bush tucker and medicine, and boomerang- and spear-throwing. The Tjapukai community has a 51% stake in the $9 million production and most of the staff is Aboriginal. This is an excellent opportunity to experience part of the culture, with some bells and whistles added for show. The park is open

Oolana's Sacrifice

South of Cairns about 40km is the sugar village of Babinda, and the turn-off to Babinda Boulders, a picnic ground with a creepy story. As the story goes, there once lived a stunningly beautiful Aboriginal woman named Oolana who was slated to wed one of the elders, Waroonoo. Instead, she eloped with Dyga, a dashing young fellow from a clan that was passing through. When the lovers were caught and dragged back, Oolana leapt into the gorge rather than marry another. Supposedly, all of the loose boulders crashed down after her. Backpackers who have camped near the water's edge swear that they have heard a woman's voice calling out, as well as a didgeridoo droning through the night. More importantly, the swimming hole has a reputation for drowning men (and the occasional woman), as Oolana reaches out from the depths for her lost love.

daily 9am to 5pm (admission $24). **Sunbus** (tel. 4098 2600) leaves Cairns for Tjapukai every hour on the hour (round-trip $12).

A gem for those on working holiday, the **Palm Beach Resort** (tel. 4055 3630) off the Cook Hwy. 25km north of Cairns, is near the understaffed upscale resorts in **Palm Cove.** While you're hunting for work, explore the rainforest in the backyard. The four-bed rooms are clean and beautifully furnished in wood, linen is provided, and there is no key deposit (dorms $10, weekly $60). A daily shuttle bus goes into Cairns during the week.

Farther along the Cook Hwy. heading north, a pair of complementary roadside attractions exist under one ownership and one system of Linnean classification. **Wild World** (tel. 4055 3669; fax 4059 1160), in Palm Cove along the Cook Hwy., 20 minutes north of Cairns, lets you get up close and personal with kangaroos and koalas (open daily 8:30am-5pm; admission $16). **Hartley's Creek Crocodile Farm** (tel. 4055 3576; fax 4059 1017), just 15 minutes south, is worth a look only for the 3pm "crocodile attack show," where keepers taunt a croc until it eats a hand-fed chicken. At 4pm you can pet a real freshwater crocodile, jaws taped shut, at Hartley's (open daily 8am-5pm; admission $13). Both places offer a wide variety of other animals to ooh and aah at from a safe distance. **Coral Coaches** (tel. 4031 7577 in Cairns, tel. 4099 5351 in Port Douglas) has regular service to the parks (5 per day).

For those who want to sample the scene at **Cape Tribulation** (see p. 354) but lack the patience to piece together an itinerary from public coaches and a series of hostels, **KCT Connections** (tel. 4031 2990) leaps to the rescue. This small-time operation packs it all in, with prices well below the competition. A two-day trip, including a nightly stay at either Crocodylus (YHA) in Cow Bay or PK's Jungle Village in Cape Trib, comes to $78; along the way it's possible to stop a while in Port Douglas and Mossman Gorge, and they even throw in a Daintree River cruise. Add an additional night at either stop for $11 more (departs Cairns about 6pm).

Atherton Tablelands

On a high plateau inland from Cairns, the Tablelands is a rarely visited paradise of rolling creeks, lush vales, and undisturbed glens. Although much of what was once dense jungle has been cleared for agricultural purposes and cattle husbandry, pockets of national parkland remain for hiking or spotting rare wildlife. With a bit of patience, you'll see a platypus playing at creek's edge, or hear the peculiar call of the eastern whipbird. The activity encircles Lake Tinaroo, three-quarters the volume of Sydney Harbour, and the forests, which contain more species of trees than Europe and North America combined. At an elevation of nearly 1000m, the tablelands can be a little chilly during the winter; bring either a jumper or a sweater, depending on how far you've journeyed to get here.

KURANDA

Kuranda is perched above the coast on the mountainous edge of the Atherton Tablelands. Its famous markets, which run Wednesday through Sunday, cause Kuranda to swell from a cozy village of less than a thousand to a bazaar brimming with daytrippers from Cairns. Masses of slow-moving tourists pop in and out of fairly interchangeable arts, crafts, and clothing stores.

Most arrive from Cairns (see p. 338) via the **Kuranda Scenic Railway** (tel. 4013 2232), which pulls in next to the Travel Centre Office in Kuranda's railway station. The torturous journey on this rickety antique, pulled by an ancient diesel engine, comes with torturous commentary regarding the track's 15 tunnels, its 98 caves, and the difficulties workmen had in quelling the restless Aboriginal natives whose land the rail company was slicing up. (Daily from Cairns 8:30 and 10am; to Cairns 2 and 3:40pm. One-way: $25, children $13, students $15; return: $25, $21, $26.)

The principal draw of Kuranda is the famed **Kuranda Markets** (Wed.-Sun.), where you can buy just the same knick-knacks and "authentic Aboriginal" toys as in Cairns, sometimes from the same vendors. There are a few odd additions, like a Harley joyride booth ($20 a pop), but these don't look like they'll last. Across the street, at the bottom of the **Heritage Markets,** sits the **Juanna** Aboriginal dance troupe. The children who comprise this 16-member act sport crude body paint and wield broken boomerangs as they stomp about noisily for the benefit of the camera-toting happy bus culture crowd. With sagging red rag loincloths drooping off their hips, the group looks more like a snapshot from *Lord of the Flies* than the genuine representation of Aboriginal culture it is meant to be. (Shows daily 10:45, 11:30am, 12:15, and 1pm. Admission $12, children $8.)

Birdworld (tel. 4093 9188), in the Heritage Markets, has a collection of 50 Australian squawkers, as well as 25 "exotic species," including the elusive canary and parakeet (open daily 9am-4pm; admission $7, children $3). The **Australian Butterfly Sanctuary** (tel. 4093 7575), at the park all the way down Coondoo St. from the train station, considers itself the world's largest butterfly farm. Visitors are invited to walk among the grazing beauties, and it's normal for a butterfly to land on a brightly-colored shirt and try to feed off its nectar. The insects are more active on sunny days (open daily 10am-3pm; admission $10.50, children $5; guided tours every 15min.; combination ticket for the birds and butterflies $13, children $5).

LAKE TINAROO AND DANBULLA FOREST

Saturated with crater lakes and sprinkled with waterfalls, the volcanic soil of the central Tablelands sprouts massive, bizarre, strangler fig trees and other mixed forest along the shores of **Lakes Tinaroo, Barrine,** and **Eacham.** The **Danbulla Forest Drive** circumscribes Lake Tinaroo, which has been dammed for hydroelectric purposes. Both Lake Eacham and Lake Barrine have walking paths for spotting birds and small, fuzzy animals. The heart of the Tablelands lies some 50km southwest of Cairns, but is only accessible by one of two circuitous routes. From Kuranda, north of Cairns, the Kennedy Hwy. strikes southwest to the town of **Mareeba.** This crossroads settlement straddles the Peninsula Development Rd., which runs north to Cooktown via Mount Carbine (see p. 356) and south to Atherton. The Burke Development Rd. heads west from Mareeba past plump termite mounds to Chillagoe and its nearby caves. Alternatively, one can reach the central Tablelands from Cairns via the Gillies Hwy., which leaves Hwy. 1 just south of Gordonvale. **Atherton** is the largest town in the region, although **Yungaburra** may make a more convenient base for exploration.

Camping in the thick of the forests is definitely the best way to get up close and personal with the Tablelands, though it can get pretty darn chilly on winter nights. There are no fewer than five state forest campgrounds around Lake Tinaroo (self-registration $2 per night; toilets but no showers or firewood). The locations of the campground are depicted on the widely distributed free guide *Danbulla Forest Drive;* ring the **Department of Natural Resources,** 83 Main St. (tel. 4091 1844), in Atherton with any questions. Take care when driving along the Danbulla circuit, since most of the roads are unsealed and the dirt turns to mud when it rains.

ATHERTON

This run-of-the-mill Australian town offers little of interest to the wandering traveler, except that the farms just outside of Atherton usually hire such folk for short-term fruit-picking (Aug.-May). **Atherton Backpackers** (tel. 4091 3552) acts as a go-between for the seasonal workers, offering decent lodging for those in town for a short spell. Approaching from Mareeba, follow the Cook St. exit off the main roundabout in town, then take a right at the Rotaract Park. Take another right just before the Atherton Bowls Club, and a final right onto Alice St. at the fire station. Rooms are well-looked after, and there's a wide veranda on the second floor and an open fireplace for the cold nights. (Laundry facilities. Reception open daily 9am-5pm. Dorms $12-14; singles $17; doubles $29. Bikes $5 per day.) The owners will pick up from Cairns if at least two people want to come.

YUNGABURRA

Yungaburra is tiny by Australian standards—it only has one pub. But it's clean as a whistle, having proudly won a Tidy Town competition in Eacham Shire three of the past four years. The village is smack in the middle of all the good stuff: Lake Tinaroo and the Danbulla forest to the north, waterfalls to the south, Lakes Eacham and Barrine to the east, and the Seven Sisters hills to the west. From Atherton, follow the Cook St. sign at the main roundabout, then keep an eye out for Yungaburra signs for the next 25km. From Cairns, get on the Gillies Hwy. and head west for about 60km.

Accommodations Yungaburra's youth hostel, **On the Wallaby** (tel. 4095 2031), is utterly superb. The common area feels like a mountain hut with rough-edged wood furnishings and a wood-burning stove, the bathrooms and showers are sided with stone and wood, and the bedrooms are clean and fresh. There's a BBQ, laundry facilities, and a self-serve kitchen with a tree frog couple (Trevor and Naomi) that hang out by the fridges. (Dorms $15; twins and doubles $35; camping $8. Transport to or from Cairns $15 one-way.) Overnight tour packages from Cairns ($55) include transport and lodging, a canoe trip, platypus spotting (free nightly anyway), bike hire, and a waterfalls tour.

Up the Gillies Hwy. by Lake Eacham is the **Lake Eacham Caravan Park** (tel. 4095 3730). Avail yourself of their showers, laundry facilities, and questionable cooking surfaces. (Reception open daily 2-7pm. Tent and caravan sites $9; with power $12.) The fee includes admission to a garden and a petting zoo, featuring Pepe the Burro. Yungaburra's limited shops and services include the **Gem Gallery and Coffee Shop** (tel. 4095 3455), which has breakfast for under $2, free didgeridoo lessons after 3pm, and opal-cutting demonstrations throughout the day (open daily 8am-8pm). **Cut-Price** (tel. 4095 2177) is the local supermarket (open daily 7am-7pm).

Sights Just off the west side of Yungaburra (over the bridge) is a sign pointing to the **Curtain Fig Tree,** a monstrous strangler fig with hundreds of shoots forming an eerie curtain in the middle of the rainforest. The other big strangler fig in the Tablelands is the **Cathedral Fig Tree** on the last (east) stretch of the Danbulla Forest Drive before the pavement runs out. The Curtain Fig is a twig compared to the 45m-tall Cathedral Fig, which germinated around the time Columbus arrived in the Americas.

The second-best place for **platypus-spotting** is at the creek under the bridge into Yungaburra. There's a viewing station set up with blinders, so large groups can watch the shy critters at nightfall. The best place to see them, though, is off Picnic Crossing Rd. (heading north), between Saylee's Strawberries and the Barron River bridge. Up past the demonic cattle crossing sign, the road dips to an Atherton Council Pump Station, creekside. There's a concrete picnic table for a late-afternoon snack, and about seven platypus families near that bend in the river.

MALANDA AND THE SOUTHERN TABLELANDS

Undoubtedly the dairy capital of these parts, **Malanda** produces milk consumed as far away as the Northern Territory. Not surprisingly, the town has cows, cows, and more cows, but not much else. A collection of other wildlife can be found 6km east of the town center at the rambling **Platypus Forest Hostel** (tel. 4096 5926), a little-known refuge for nature-buffs who don't mind seeing critters both in the rough and potentially in their soft beds at night. Pademelons (mini-kangaroos) wander in and out of the living room and curl up in visitors' laps, platypuses hang out in the creek, possums show up in the kitchen for some sweet potato, and the swath of rainforest behind the hostel is populated by a colony of tree kangaroos. If you're driving yourself, call ahead for directions and to let them know they should fire up the hot tub and sauna for you. The hostel does pick-ups in Cairns as part of a one-night deal that includes a tour of the sights around Lake Tinaroo, as well as dinner and breakfast ($45 per person). Additional nights are $15 per person (doubles $35), linen included, and $5 per meal.

The **Peeramon Hotel** (tel. 4096 5873), in **Peeramon** between Yungaburra and Malanda, is the oldest hotel in the Tablelands, with a real ghost to prove it. The old (*very* old) lady still floats about the place: you can see a picture of her on display in the bar, mid-air and luminescent in a group picture taken on the hotel's front steps. From Atherton, take the first paved road on the right after leaving Yungaburra; from Cairns it's the first paved left after the Lake Eacham exit off the Gillies Hwy. Rooms upstairs are inexpensive and beautiful in that old Queensland high-ceilings-and-veranda way. (Live music Sat. night and Sun. afternoon. Reception open daily 10am-midnight. Singles $15; doubles $20; camping $10. Breakfast included.)

About 25km south of Malanda and just beyond the town of Millaa Millaa, the **waterfall circuit** leads past a series of spectacular swimming holes that are best visited when it's raining (fewer tourists; more water coming over the falls). From the north a sign just out of Millaa Millaa points to the falls: follow the road from waterfall to waterfall and you'll pop out on the Palmerston Hwy. again. Catch the loop from the south by looking for the "Tourist Drive" sign. **Millaa Millaa Falls** is an example of the perfect waterfall: a straight, even curtain with rocks at the bottom and a bit of green on either side. **Zillie Falls** starts off a sedate creek at the top of the falls; a path down the side follows the roaring drop, and the cascading **Ellinjaa Falls** look like liquid fireworks. Millaa Millaa is the only site with toilets, but all three provide natural showers for wading and frolicking.

Port Douglas

Traveling north from Cairns, the vice of tourism gradually sheds a skin and leaves its hurried pace behind. Here there are no traffic lights. Here the police station closes at two for lack of crime. Here restaurant patrons ask across tables how each others' dinners were. Welcome to Port Douglas, where there's little more to do than relax on the beach all day long.

ORIENTATION AND PRACTICAL INFORMATION

Port Douglas is 80km north of Cairns off the Captain Cook Highway (Hwy. 1). The main drag in town is **Macrossan St.,** a left turn at the end of the long, palm-lined Port Douglas Road that comes into town from the highway. On the east end of Macrossan is **Four Mile Beach,** on the west the **Marina Mirage.**

Tourist Office: The **Visitors Bureau,** 12 Grant St. (tel. 4099 4644; fax 4099 4645; open Mon.-Fri. 9am-5pm), off Macrossan St., has a less biased opinion than the privately owned information storefronts found on almost every corner.

Currency: All banks are open Mon.-Thurs. 9:30am-4pm, Fri. 9:30am-5pm. **ANZ,** 36 Macrossan St. (tel. 4099 5700; fax 4099 5679), exchanges cash for $5 commission. The ANZ **ATM** takes Visa, MC, Plus, and Cirrus. **Commonwealth Bank,** 2nd floor at the corner of Grant and Macrossan St. (tel. 4099 5233), grants Visa cash advances and exchanges traveler's checks ($5 per check) and cash (no commission). The ATM takes MC and Cirrus. **Westpac,** 43 Macrossan St. (tel. 4099 5411; fax 4099 5047), grants Visa and MC cash advances. Exchanges traveler's checks ($7 if exchange is under $500, free otherwise) and cash (no commission). If headed north, keep in mind that there are **no ATMs** north of the Daintree River.

Buses: Coral Coaches, on the corner of Grant and Werner St. (tel. 4099 5351; fax 4099 4235), at the water's edge near the intersection of Wharf and Werner St. Runs to Cairns daily (almost hourly until 7pm, $16, return $30) and to Mossman (9 per day 7am-9pm, $6, return $10).

Ferries: Quicksilver (tel. 4099 5500) leaves Port Douglas daily at 5:15pm for Cairns. Return fare is $30, one-way $20 (10% discount with a YHA card). Catch it at the Marina Mirage, down Wharf St.

Taxis: Port Douglas Limousines (tel. 4099 5950; fax 4099 5955). To airport or Cairns $25 per person.

Car Rental: Crocodile Car Rentals, 50 Macrossan St. (tel. 4099 5555; fax 4099 4114), specializes in 4WD cars (from $69 per day). **Network Rentals,** 5 Warner St. (tel. 4099 5111; fax 4099 4423), and **Allcar Rentals,** 21 Warner St. (tel. 4099 4123; fax 4099 4436), rent vehicles from $45 per day, as does **Port Douglas Moke Hire,** 13 Warner St. in Mobil Station (tel. 4099 5550). All rentals include 200km.

Bike Rental: Port Douglas Bike Hire, 42 Macrossan (tel. 4099 5799). Open daily 8:30am-5pm. Half-day $7; full day (24hr.) $10; week $45.

Public Toilets: On Warner St., next to the beach entrance; and on Wharf St., near the intersection with Macrossan. 24hr.

Book Store: Book Exchange, 12 Macrossan St., behind Star of Siam. Open Mon.-Fri. 10am-5pm, Sat.-Sun. 10am-4pm. **Jungle Books,** 46 Museum St. (tel. 4099 4203). Travel guides in several languages. Open Mon.-Sat. 9:30am-6pm.

Road Report: Tel. 4051 6711.

Pharmacy: Marina Pharmacy (tel. 4099 5223) on Marina Mirage.

Medical Services: Medical Centre, in the Mirage Marina on the left side of the parking lot (24hr. tel. 4099 5043; fax 4099 4216). Office open Mon.-Fri. 8am-6pm, Sat.-Sun. 9am-noon. Port Douglas uses Mossman's **hospital** (tel. 4098 2444).

Emergency: Dial 000.

Police: The **police station** (24hr. tel. 4099 5220), at the corner of Macrossan and Wharf St., is open Mon.-Thurs. 8am-2pm.

Post Office: (tel. 4099 5210; fax 4099 4584) on Owen St. From Macrossan St., head up the hill on the left. Open Mon.-Fri. 9am-5pm, Sat. 9am-noon. Fax service. *Post Restante.* **Postal code:** 4871.

Phone Code: 07.

ACCOMMODATIONS

Word has spread far and wide that **Port o' Call** (tel. 4099 5422; fax 4099 5495), is the fairest YHA of them all. On Port St., left off of Port Douglas Rd. as you come in to town, this impeccable hostel is in the most beautiful of surroundings. The hostel has a free shuttle bus to Cairns (departs Mon., Wed., and Sat. 8:30am; call for a 10am lift north from Cairns). Sink into the pool after a long day of strutting the beaches. Reception, open daily 7:30am to 7:30pm, dispenses tour brochures and advice. (Laundry facilities. 4-bed dorms with bath $17 ($18 YHA non-members). A/C $5 more. Bikes $7 half-day, $10 full day.) The hostel's bistro is open for dinner every night (6-9pm, meals $7.50-10) and swings during happy hour (5-7pm; beer $2, mixed drinks $3).

Smack in the center of town upstairs from a small shopping plaza, **Port Douglas Backpackers,** 8 Macrossan St. (tel. 4099 4883; fax 4099 4827), is clean and groomed for the backpacker crowd. The place feels like an office-turned-dormitory, with fluorescent lighting and carpet tiles. The benefits of location are leveled by the peculiar ability of the hostel's structure to echo sound from a multitude of sources. Showers are blessed with great water pressure, but with only four stalls (2 of which hide behind the laundry) for 50 beds, you're not likely to have much time to sample it. There's always a movie on in the kitchen, but utensils are in short supply. Dorms ($15) are air-conditioned and include linens.

If you're not into hostels, try **Coconut Grove Motel** (tel. 4099 5124; fax 4099 5144), at the corner of Davidson (Port Douglas Rd.) and Macrossan St., two minutes from the beach. (Pool, TV, laundry. Singles with bath $25; doubles with bath $55, with A/C $65. Restaurant serves vegetarian dinners for $7. V, MC, AmEx, DC.) Alternatively, pitch a tent and take a hot shower at **Glengarry Van Park** (tel. 4098 5922; fax 4099 3158), about 10km south of Port Douglas along the Cook Hwy. (Reception open Mon.-Sat. 7am-6pm, Sun. 8am-1pm and 3:30-6pm. Sites $14; with power $17.)

If you've come to the far north to get away from it all and don't mind a bit of a splurge, the **Marae** (tel. 4098 4900; fax 4098 4099), 15 minutes north of Port Douglas by car, presents a peaceful, romantic escape. Having chosen a bush site with mountain views and lots of wildlife around, the owner and designer of this tropical B&B encourages guests to relax in the salt-water pool, chat with the pet cockatoo, or just be. (Doubles from $80; bookings essential.)

FOOD AND ENTERTAINMENT

The cheapest food is found at **Foodtown Supermarket,** 6 Macrossan St. (open daily 7am-9pm; V, MC). **Port Produce Fruit and Veg Mart,** 9 Warner St. (tel. 4099 4989; fax 4099 4080), has a vast selection of fruits and vegetables available at wholesale prices. Recommended tropical delights include custard apples ($3 per kilo) and ross sapote ($3.50 per kilo; mart open Mon.-Fri. 7am-3pm, Sat.-Sun. 8am-noon). For the freshest produce, head down the Cook Hwy. to **Scomazzon's Horticultural Farm,** 5km north of Mossman. Purveyors sell fine fruit, including the local white grapefruit (4 for $1; farm open daily 7am-6pm).

EJ's Seamarkets and Take-Away, 23 Macrossan St., serves hot breakfast with bottomless coffee ($4.50) and lunch sandwiches ($2.50-4.50) daily 7am to 9pm. **On the Inlet** (tel. 4099 5255; fax 4099 5939) is behind the Marina Mirage—take the side street to the right. It's a perfect spot for a sunset beer ($2.80) or generous dinner of fresh seafood right off the trawler ($7.50-10; open 11am-11pm). For a quick bite, stop by **Mocha's Pies,** 16 Macrossan St. (tel. 4099 5295), for a steak and kidney or cheese savory pasty ($2.60). Pies are sold daily until 3pm (or until sold out).

Ironbar Restaurant, 5 Macrossan St., is just across from Port Douglas Backpackers. The restaurant sponsors cane toad races every Tuesday at 9pm, but it's most popular on Saturday nights, when it serves as a venue for Port Douglas's best live music (open daily 8am-2am). The **Court House Hotel** (tel. 4099 5181; fax 4099 4249), at the corner of Macrossan and Wharf St., has live music in the pub (Thurs.-Sun. nights, no cover, stubbies $3, counter meals $5). Texan owner Michael Gabour knows how to throw a party, particularly on the 4th of July, when he goes whole hog. The first 600 people into the beer garden are fed pork and venison for free and encouraged to groove to good times. The gala concludes with a fireworks display unmatched this side of the Pacific.

SIGHTS AND ACTIVITIES

Ben Cropp's Shipwreck Museum (tel. 4099 5858), on Prince's Wharf near the corner of Wharf and Macrossan St., features an incredible collection of displays on major shipwrecks. The exhibit culminates in a re-creation of the legendary Yolanga Tomb (admission $5, students $4). The nearby **Lower Isles Preservation Society** (tel. 4099 4573) grants camping permits for the Lower Isles ($3.50) and hands out general information on the marine park. Ask at the marina (to the left of the Marina Mirage) for a lift to the islands.

Four Mile Beach, at the east end of Macrossan St., is as hard to miss as its name implies. Keep an eye out for the flags near the edge of the water: green means all safe, yellow means use caution, and do *not* swim when there is a red flag up (lifeguard on duty Mon.-Sat. 9am-5pm). If the deeper surf calls, drop by **Port Douglas Water Sports** (tel. 019 340 335), near the beach's Warner St. entrance. Mick gives 20% discounts to backpackers—just mention that you read about him in *Let's Go*—and basic instruction is thrown in free of charge. (Catamaran rental $25 per hr., windsurfer $20 per hr., boogie board $5 per hr. Deposit $20. Open daily Nov.-March 9am-5pm.)

Blue Lagoon Cruise (tel. 4099 4650) sails on what must be the single most beautiful boat that plies the reefs, a sampan with batwing sails and teak detail work. Snorkeling trips are on the high side of the market ($79, including lunch; departs daily at 10am from Berth C2 of the Marina Mirage).

Sail Away-Low Isles, 23 Macrossan St. (tel. 4099 5070, reservations 24hr. tel. 4099 5599; fax 4099 5510), departs daily at 9:30am from berth C17, Marina Mirage (7hr., $85, with YHA $76.50). Catch their free shuttle from Cairns (7:15am) or Port Douglas (8:45am). **Haba Dive,** Shop 3, Marina Mirage (tel. 4099 5254; fax 4099 5385), departs daily at 8:30am with free pick-up and lunch. (Snorkeling $95. Diving with certification $135, without certification $145, 2 dives $175. Max. 40 people.) **Poseidon,** at the end of C Jetty, Marina Mirage (tel. 4099 5599; fax 4099 5070), has somewhat cheaper versions, also with free pick-up and lunch. (Snorkeling $90; certified diving $130 for 2 dives; without certification $145 for 1 dive, $175 for 2. Max. 30 people.) **Wavelength,** 20 Solander Blvd. (tel. 4099 5031; fax 4099 3259), departs daily at

8:30am from the Port Douglas Slipway, to the right of the Marina Mirage. Their sweet deal is snorkeling on the outer reef (8hr., $90 includes lunch), although half-days in the Lower Isles are just $50 (no diving; max. 20 people). **Aussie Dive,** Berth D4, Marina Mirage (tel. 4099 4334 or 1800 646 548), picks up free in Port Douglas. (Snorkeling trip with BBQ lunch $65; 2 dives for certified divers $115, uncertified divers $125. PADI certification course $350.)

The Rainforest Habitat (tel. 4099 3235; fax 4099 3100) has two acres, three enclosures, and over 1000 animals without cages or any discernible fear of people. The entry fee ($16, with ISIC $14.40) might be a bit steep, but where else can you tickle a fruit bat's tummy or scratch a wallaroo behind the ears? Cockatoos and parrots mingle in the cafe (coffee $2), but prefer snacking on blueberry muffins from the kiosk ($1.50). (Open daily 8am-4:30pm, guided tours every 30min. Wheelchair accessible. Coral Coach leaves from the Port Douglas depot hourly from 8am, return $2.20.)

■ Near Port Douglas: Mossman Gorge

Just outside Port Douglas, a few minutes up Cook Hwy., is the entirely unremarkable town of **Mossman,** and its entirely remarkable natural attraction. Disgorge yourself from the idleness of quiet Port Douglas life and bushwhack through the rainforest, dodging vines along the banks of creeks, until you reach gorgeous **Mossman Gorge.** There are no crocs in the gorge, but signs warn of strong currents.

The best spot to get your feet wet is not at the public park site. **Silky Oaks** (tel. 4098 1666) is a posh hunting resort downstream, located on the pristine Norwood Billabong. The good folks at Oaks allow the public to swim, provided one makes a purchase at the restaurant upstairs—perhaps a cappuccino ($3), sipped quietly on the canopy-height Jungle Perch Porch.

Although there's a clear and well-maintained path near the gorge, you may feel more enlightened after spending an hour with an Aboriginal guide from **Kuuku-Yalanji Dreamtime Tours** (tel. 4098 1305), on the road to the gorge. The tour covers authentic medicines and bush tucker, and includes tea and damper at the end (tours Mon.-Fri. at 10, 11:30am, and 2:30pm; $15, students $13.50). The Aboriginal-owned operation should soon have a regular shuttle to Port Douglas for pick-ups. Until then, **Coral Coaches** (tel. 4099 5351) run to Mossman from Port Douglas (8 per day 9:15am-6pm, $10, round-trip $18). If driving, follow Hwy. 1 north from the junction to Port Douglas. Turn left at the Slippery Oaks sign (beside the roadside cemetery) and drive about 5km to the carpark on the right.

FROM MOSSMAN TO DAINTREE

The unwavering Cook Hwy., which slices its way straight north through sugar cane fields, veers right, sharply and suddenly, as if in awe of a smaller-than-small town called **Miallo.** The town, rarely marked on tourist maps, sits in the Whyanbeer Valley, which is nearly impossible to find on any map. In the far corner of Miallo, down the last dirt road in town is **Karnak** (tel. 4098 8144 or 4098 8194; fax 4098 8191), a playhouse that hosts international theater groups. A recent production of *Macbeth* starred a Danish diva who delivered the Lady's lines in Danish amidst an otherwise English-speaking cast. Karnak also hosts a weekly laser-light show, featuring an Aboriginal creation myth. The magnanimous owners are eager to get backpackers into the arts scene up north and will gladly pick up at Mossman or Port Douglas for a night's show ($20, students with Australian ID $10) or laser-light production ($25, $14). Call well in advance to hear what's on.

If you make it as far as Karnak, consider dropping in on Ron Berry, wizard of fruit and proprietor of **High Fall Farms** (tel. 4098 8148). The orchard hides at the end of a kilometer-long unpaved road signposted from the Miallo turn-off. The farm is open daily from 8am to 5:30pm, but try to hit it in the afternoon, after the tour buses from Cairns have cleared out. If Ron has an extra minute, he'll take you on an ambling tour ($3) of the scores of species in the yard: the hulking jackfruit, the sensual araca, the dangling avocados, and the more familiar curry, clove, cacao, and pepper.

Daintree

The sullen Daintree River ripples and gurgles, not from the lethargic currents, but from the teaming mass of estuarine crocodiles. The people of Daintree see the fearsome predator as the town's greatest economic asset. Boatloads of camera-toting croc-hunters skim the river's course each day and keep half a dozen operators in business. The exit off Coast Hwy. dips and turns into town, and can get flooded out. Call one of the restaurants in town to get conditions before setting out.

There are only a handful of places to stay in town. The most comfortable (and not prohibitively expensive) is the **Red Mill House** (tel. 4098 6169) in the middle of town, with singles $25 and doubles $60, including breakfast. **Daintree River View Caravan Park** (tel. 4098 6119), also smack in the middle of town, rents tent sites ($9 for 1 person, $12 for 2; caravans can park for $35; hot showers and BBQ). Competition is not fierce between the restaurants in Daintree. On one side of the street is the **Daintree Village Coffee Shop and Restaurant** (tel. 4098 6173; open daily 9am-5pm). On the other sits the more touristy **Big Barramundi** (tel. 4098 6166; same hours).

Aside from the option of visiting on an all-inclusive tour package from Port Douglas or Cairns, there are several way to set out on the river. The **Daintree Rainforest River Train** (tel. 4090 7676; fax 4090 7660) boards at the ferry crossing along the Cook Hwy. (1hr. cruise 9:15am and 4pm, $12; 1½hr. cruise 10:30am and 1:30pm, $70). At the same price and from the same place, **Daintree Connections** runs hour-long cruises (8:15, 9:30, 10:30am, 1:30, 2:30, and 3:30pm). They all depart hourly on the half-hour (9:30am-3:30pm, then again at 4pm) from the Daintree Original's storefront in town. Both tours offer a package for $95 with pick-up in Cairns or Port Douglas. **Daintree Wildlife Safari** (tel. 4098 6125; fax 4098 6192) has a longer two-hour, wheelchair accessible tour at $20. The cheapest by far is the **Daintree River and Reef Cruise Centre** (tel. 4098 6115) on the road into Daintree (1hr. cruise $9, 1½hr. $14; binoculars included). **Chris Dahlberg** (tel. 4098 6169), owner of the Red Mill House and bird enthusiast, runs morning bird-spotting tours (2hr., $25 per person with limited seating). **James Beitzel** (tel. 4098 6138) also takes folks out for morning bird-watching (2½hr., $25; max. 5 to a boat).

CROSSING THE DAINTREE RIVER

On the approach to the ferry crossing, large wooden signs inform that the roadway over the river is rough, wild, and potentially dangerous. They don't lie; the easy, paved roads of the Cook Hwy. become dirt and eventually crushed stones and roots as the sunny savannah is lost in the shade of the rainforest canopy. Approach the crossing with caution and keep an eye out for saltwater crocs. Never feed the wildlife. And never camp by the river in this region; salties can move without a trace in knee-deep water.

On the south side of the Daintree River, passengers board the **ferry** and are shuttled across the swirling, black, hypnotic waters toward Cape Tribulation (runs daily 6am-midnight; pay the ferryman: walk-on passengers $1, motorcycles $3, cars $6).

From the far shore, a thin road snakes through rainforest. Trees seem to lean in and leer at passing automobiles, dropping sinister vines across their roofs like cold, skeletal fingers brushing one's arm in the night.

Cape Tribulation National Park

The road between Daintree and Cape Tribulation is utterly fantastic. The rainforest comes crashing down to the ocean surf, and every inch of it is filled with living things. The amalgam picture is as vast and impossible to grasp as the fact that at any moment somewhere on the planet a child is being conceived. The rainforest drinks rainwater, eats seeds that have dropped, and grows and decays with the passing seasons. The rainforest is alive; it breathes out oxygen, regulates itself, and metabolizes the flora and fauna that are spawned, fly, swim, float, attract, procreate, hide, hunt, and are consumed at every moment.

The ideal park visitor is neither seen nor heard, treads lightly and unobtrusively, and makes no demands on the surroundings. **Crocodylus Village** (tel. 4098 9166; fax 4098 9131), in the rainforest, has managed to become as unobtrusive and undemanding a visitor as is possible. The hostel is maintained as if it were a garden, with thin gravel paths between the elevated cabins (that feel like spacious tree houses) and a meticulously clean, canopied common area. Superb meals are served three times a day from one kitchen while another is open for self-catering. The amenities (pool, laundry, full bar, free bus to beach twice daily) are presented as secondary to the surroundings: a Strangler Fig Tree, a caged Stinging Plant, and the constant rustle and song from the treetops. Enjoy horseback riding ($39), a sunrise paddle trek ($35), or a guided bushwalk (3hr., $16). (Reception open daily 7:30am-11:30pm. Cabin rooms $15, with YHA $14. Hut for 2 with bath $50, additional guests $10. Linen included. Book ahead.)

The **Rainforest Camp** (tel. 4098 9015) offers an alternative for the camping sort. Located between Cape Tribulation and Crocodylus Village, the camp (laundry facilities, hot showers, powered sites) offers sites for $5 per person whether in a tent or campervan. **Noah Beach Campground,** 7km south of Cape Tribulation, allows tent camping ($3.50 per person; showers and toilets; no open fires). Obtain a permit from the ranger or the QNP&WS in Cairns. Swimming on Noah Beach is allowed, but watch for crocodile warning placards. Noahs themselves are not a threat.

PK's Jungle Village (tel. 4098 0040; fax 4098 0006), about 500km after the "Welcome to the Cape Tribulation" sign, is more appropriately called "PK's Jungle Party." A classic example of ecotourism turned sour, nightly dance parties pale in light of the weekly theme parties, usually four-keggers. There are two happy hours—in case you miss the first one. Activities and rentals include volleyball, horseback riding, guided bushwalking, and bike hire (half-day $10, full day $15). Reception is open daily 7:30am to 7pm; late arrivals should present themselves at the bar. (Dorms $17, with VIP $16; doubles $50. V, MC, AmEx.)

Coral Coaches (tel. 4031 7577 in Cairns; tel. 4099 5351 in Port Douglas) stops twice daily in Cow Bay (departs: Cairns 7am and 3:30pm; Port Douglas 8:30am and 5:15pm).

Routes to Cooktown

BLOOMFIELD TRACK

The road that beats through the bush between Cape Tribulation and Cooktown is cruel on automobiles as it swerves and dips, hugging the sides of precipitously steep mountains and wading through creeks and small rivers. The surface of the road is a mess of stones and roots with the odd fallen branch or sudden pothole. Driving this route, the **Bloomfield Track,** is about as much fun as one can (legally) have in a 4WD vehicle, but is it ever hard on the hiney! The southern section of the Track, with its impossibly steep climbs and drops, goes soft at **Wujal Wujal,** an Aboriginal community. The town's four businesses close on the weekends: the **convenience store** is otherwise open 8am-4:30pm, and you can catch the **service station** 8am to 5pm. Off the highway are the **Bloomfield Falls,** a terrific place to relax after the hard ride.

Between Wujal Wujal and Cooktown there's a dirt road, and the scenery turns to dry savannah as the mountains pull back from the coast. Along the way are small-town hotels and general stores. **The Bloomfield Inn** (tel. 4060 8174) has gas and food, but no lodging (open daily 8am-9pm; meals are about $4; no credit cards). Fifteen minutes north, the **Ayton General Store** (tel. 4060 8125) has all the basics. (Open Tues.-Fri. 8:30am-5:30pm, Sat.-Sun. 8:30am-4pm; $2.50 fee for credit cards; **pay phone** out front.) Just a few meters up the road, **Viv's Takeaway** (tel. 4060 8266) cooks up some tasty sandwiches ($4-5; open daily 8am-6pm).

The most up-market accommodations along the stretch of road is the roomy **Bloomfield Beach Camping** (tel. 4060 8207; fax 4060 8187). There are bathroom and laundry facilities, a track to the beach during the dry season, and two of the planets goofiest dogs, Gus and Eric, for entertainment (furnished tents $15 per person; plain old grassy campsite $6). **Home Rule** (tel. 4060 3925; fax 4060 3902), in Rossville, must be one of the most inaccessible hostels in Queensland. The turn-off from the highway leads 3km down a narrow, buckled road; for those coming on Coral Coach, ask the driver to stop at the general store and ring Hal, the owner, from the payphone out front. The hostel is on 105 acres of land that abut the national park, so there's lots of room to roam (dorms $15, linen included; camping $6, hot showers included). Meals are available (breakfast $7, dinner $10), and there's a self-serve kitchen. Visa, MC accepted. Rossville also has Saturday markets (tel. 4060 3042) every other week.

The final road before Cooktown leads to the **Lion's Den Hotel** (tel. 4060 3911), which sternly warns of its favoritism in clientele: "Keep your dogs outa the bar, and I'll keep my bullets outa your dog." (Open daily 10am-midnight, or whenever the party simmers down; beer $3.20 a heavy, $3 a light). Rooms are pleasant enough (singles $18; doubles $25; campsites $4 per person; no cooking facilities; pub grub runs $10 a plate).

INLAND TO COOKTOWN

The direct, mostly paved inland route to Cooktown is nowhere near as exciting as the coastal track, despite tour companies' hype about the "real outback" and all the cattle stations. Passing a cattle station is about as interesting as sitting by the front gate of a cattle station as a bus passes. Still, if time (or your automobile) demands a less demanding road to Cooktown, there are a handful of interesting stop-offs.

Mount Carbine Mount Carbine once enjoyed the dubious distinction of being a world supplier of the metal wolframite. The collapse of the wolframite market in 1919 nearly erased the town from the map. Had erasure been complete, all that we know about wolframite (or can learn here) would have been lost to the obscurity of time. The **Mount Carbine Village and Caravan Park** (tel. 4094 3160; office open 8am-8:30pm) is an excellent place to base a quick exploration of Mount Carbine's old mining plant, which was auctioned off in 1993, and the mining village, which was also sold off at the same time. The caravan park has laundry facilities, BBQ, and an untreated water supply, as well as dorm rooms ($15 for a soiled mattress), tent sites ($10), and powered sites ($12). The more sublime **Mount Carbine Hotel** (tel. 4094 3108) has a bar that sports a 4m-long didgeridoo and a couple of beer-can biplanes poised to defend the scarce wolframite that remains. Singles ($25) and doubles ($40) have TVs and the usual facilities (open Mon.-Sat. 10am-midnight, Sun. 10am-7pm).

Roadhouses north of Mount Carbine An hour north, along a gently winding, hypnotically bland road, the **Palmer River Roadhouse** appears (tel. 4060 2152). The roadhouse is worth a stop, if only to swoon over the faux rock interior and various frescoes depicting the area's gold mining history. The largest fresco depicts the Aboriginals' massacre of the Chinese and the subsequent massacre of the Aboriginals by whites. Also featured in the mural are a handful of Cooktown's more beloved ladies of ill repute, who are as much a part of the history as anything or anyone else. The roadhouse offers hot showers and camping, so long as you pay in cash (tent sites $2; caravan sites with or without power $10; open daily 7am-11pm).

Closer to the top of the inland route's great arc, the **Lakeland Downs Hotel** (tel. 4060 2142) marks the end of the paved road and the last pit stop before Cooktown, 80km away. A cheap-o room by the pool is $25; to get your own shower is rather pricey (singles $38; doubles $55), but it's not like there's buckets of competition out here. Lunch goes for $4-5; a good dinner is $8 (no self-serve kitchen).

Laura A branch off the Cooktown Development Rd. bumps and coughs its way 62km northwest—except for 10km in the middle which has been paved recently—

toward this tiny Aboriginal community. Laura (population 82 or 83, depending on whether the cafe has a backpacker working) suffers from dusty dehydration most of the year. Laura is the site of the biennial (odd-numbered years) **Aboriginal Dance and Cultural Festival** in June, a humongous series of concerts and workshops sponsored by the local Ang-Gnarra Aboriginals (tel. 4094 1512; fax 4094 1276; email ang-gnarra@internetnorth.com.au). Student price tickets for the 1997 festival were only $5 at the gate.

On the way in to Laura is **Split Rock,** a series of ancient Aboriginal art sites that are open to the public. There's a self-pay tin can at the entrance: if you're only there to see Split Rock pay $3; if you're doing the three-hour trek up and around the rocks to see Guugu Yalangi, that's $10. Call the Ang-gnarra Aboriginal Corporation in Laura (tel. 4060 3214) with any questions.

An unusual alternative to the usual fruit-picking working holiday, **Laura Cafe** (tel. 4060 3230; open daily 7am-10pm) hires backpackers for a minimum of one week to help out around the shop. This is hard-core, small-town Australia, with heaps of good bush walks and some serious peace and quiet. Give Patricia (the owner) a call for pick-ups in Cairns or Lakeland.

The **Quicken Pub** (tel. 4060 3255; open daily 10am-midnight) is the local watering hole for stationhands, who sit on stalls in a semi-circle around the beefy publican, the Master of Ceremonies (and Provider of Stubbies and Crisps). Prevailing politics aren't so eco-friendly: a sign out front urges voters to "say NO to World Heritage Listing—save Cape York from Canberra." Beds ($20) are spartan but clean, and the backyard is the only (legal) place to camp for miles around—at $5 a tent. Next door is the **post office** (open Mon.-Fri. 9am-5pm, lunch at noon; postal code 4871) and a payphone, across the street is a **police** outpost and **medical center** (tel. 4060 3320).

The local Aboriginals open their **Jowalbinna Bush Camp** (tel. 4060 3236) between April and September for camping ($5 per night) and guided tours of rock art sites, like Yam Dreaming and Giant Wallaroo. The camp is an hour southwest of Laura (4WD only); pick up a map at the Laura Cafe before setting out.

Cooktown

A quick trip to Cooktown is utterly disappointing. One feels tricked into visiting a town that feels somehow hollow. The wide, empty streets could easily be mistaken for deserted if it weren't for the occasional buzz of a local ute. To find the subtle beauty of the city requires a degree of patience and an eye for the unusual.

Begin with a sunrise climb up Grassy Hill at the mouth of the Endeavour River. This is where Captain James Cook first touched *Terra Australis.* His ship, the *Endeavour,* brushed too close to the reef and lost more than barnacles. While awaiting repairs, Cook mounted Grassy Hill and surveyed the area, naming the tallest mountain Mount Cook (because, after all, he could). The sparkling bays below encouraged his crew to stay on a month; one might say that their R&R here in the balmy Queensland winter made Cooktown Australia's first tourist destination.

Their departure ushered in a century of solitude at the site, although local Aboriginals remained. The discovery of gold in the late 1800s turned a sleepy village into a port metropolis. Chinese immigrants arrived by the boat-load, and tens of thousands of prospectors filled fields outside of town. Fierce conflict developed between the new arrivals and Aboriginals, climaxing in a massacre at Battle Camp, where spear-throwing Aboriginals futilely resisted rifle-bearing Europeans. Then the gold ran out. The city faded into a town, then a village. A series of fires burned away parts of the village that were never rebuilt. Businesses folded and closed; a cyclone in 1949 wiped away the last traces. The train ceased to run and was finally dismantled in the 1960s.

Yet Cooktown refuses to die and is currently going through the twitches of a town that wants another chance. The place is divided between those intent on survival (many business owners are eager to point out *every single attraction* in the area), and those who would prefer not to recognize the significance of tourist dollars. Cooktown is not for the idle tourist, but holds something profound and meaningful for those willing to look beneath its skin.

ORIENTATION AND PRACTICAL INFORMATION

The Cooktown Development Rd. becomes **Hope St.** as it runs north toward **Grassy Hill.** Two blocks to the west, **Charlotte St.** contains the bulk of Cooktown's shops and services and is crossed as it runs north by Boundary, Howard, Hogg, and Walker St. Just north of Walker is **Furneaux St.,** at a slight angle to the rest of the grid, and Green St. Beyond Green St., Charlotte becomes **Webber Esplanade** and curves along the riverside and wharf around Grassy Hill. A **lighthouse** stands atop the hill, overlooking the river to the north.

Tourist Office: None, but Barbara at **Endeavour Farms Trading Post** (see **Food,** below) is fiercely insistent on helping anyone who comes to town.

Budget Travel Office: Cooktown Travel Centre (tel. 4069 5446; fax 4069 6023), on Charlotte St. next to the Anzac Park. Offers a $90 return airplane ticket to Cairns (one-way $71), flying twice daily on Transtate Air, with a 3-day advance purchase. Open Mon.-Fri. 8am-6pm, Sat. 8am-1pm, Sun. 3-5pm.

Currency Exchange: Westpac (tel. 4069 5477), on Charlotte St., between Green and Furneaux St., takes no commission for exchanging traveler's checks or cash. Permits V, MC withdrawals. Open Mon.-Thurs. 9:30am-4pm, Fri. 9:30am-5pm.

Buses: Coral Coach has service between Cooktown and Cairns. **Endeavour Farms Trading Post** (see **Food,** below) acts as the local ticketing agent. To Cairns, by coastal route (via Cape Tribulation, Tues., Thurs., and Sat., 11:30am, $52), by inland route (via Mount Carbine, Wed., Fri., and Sun., 2:30pm, $47).

Taxis: Cooktown Taxis (tel. 4069 5387).

Automobile Club: RACQ, Cape York Tyres (tel. 4069 5233), at the corner of Charlotte and Furneaux St. Open Mon.-Fri. 7am-7pm, Sat. 7:30am-7pm, Sun. 7:30am-6pm.

Public Toilets and Shower: At the wharf, across from the Wharf cafe.

Library: Cooktown Library (tel. 4069 5009), at the corner of Walker and Helen St. Open Mon.-Fri. 10am-4:30pm, Sat. 9am-12:30pm. Closed for lunch around 1-2pm.

Medical Center: Cooktown Hospital (tel. 4069 5433), corner of Ida St. and the Cooktown Developmental Rd., on the way out of town heading south.

Emergency: Dial 000.

Police: (Tel. 4030 7000) across from the wharf on Charlotte St. Staffed Mon.-Fri. 8am-noon and 1-4pm.

Post Office: (Tel. 4069 5347), on Charlotte St. across from the Sovereign Hotel. Open Mon.-Fri. 9am-5pm. **Postal code:** 4871.

Phone Code: 07.

ACCOMMODATIONS AND FOOD

There is just one hostel in Cooktown, but the energy and wit of its owner, Scott, makes it a place unlike any other. **Pam's Place** (tel. 4069 5166; fax 4069 5964), at the corner of Charlotte and Boundary St., is a hub of Cooktown. Sit down to dinner with the local carpenter/philosopher or a team of mountain trailblazers, or rent a bike and hit the trails yourself. Perks include a kitchen, laundry facilities, a bar with a pool table, and a swimming pool. Scott offers pick-up at the bus station or airport and is a fount of historical knowledge. (Dorms $15; singles $29; doubles $40. Linen included. Key deposit $5. V, MC, $1 surcharge.)

If Pam's is filled, **Hillcrest Guest House** (tel. 4069 5305), on Hope St. at the base of Grassy Hill, has some unusual amenities. In addition to comfortable singles ($30) and doubles ($40), Hillcrest also maintains Cooktown's only aviary and butterfly garden, both free regardless of where you're staying. There is also a pool, laundry facilities, TV, tea room, and picnic hampers for two ($10) to take to the beach.

The hot spot for a quick bite is the **Endeavour Farms Trading Post** (tel. 4069 5723), on Charlotte St. between Hogg and Howard St. At least stop in to chat with Barbara, one of the owners. Barbara insists on helping travelers find their way, having found Cooktown "rough as bags" herself when she first arrived. The fish and chips ($4.50) are generous and the coffee ($1.50) isn't half bad either (open daily 7:30am-7:30pm). The main competition comes from the **Reef Cafe** (tel. 4069 5361), just down Charlotte St. next to Anzac Park. Reef cooks a mean hamburger ($5), and stocks the hearty Bundaberg Ginger Ale at only 80¢ a bottle.

The coffee shack at the wharf is a super place to hang out. The locals each have their own mug, hanging from numbered pegs. Coffee ($2) comes with free refills and can be iced ($2.50) when the mercury gets too high. Toasted sandwiches ($2-3) are tiny but scrumptious (open daily 8am-5pm), and there's always the possibility of running into interesting American ex-pats. For staples, try the **Cooktown Supermarket,** on the corner of Hogg and Helen St. (open daily 8am-5pm).

SIGHTS AND ENTERTAINMENT

The best place to start in Cooktown is the **James Cook Historical Museum** on Helen St., between Walker and Furneaux St. Each room has another small collection of instruments or documents. Take it slowly; like walking into a dark room, one's eyes—and mind—need time to adjust. Fall back in time and sit in the dentist's chair, or toss the Chinese coin in the air. The first room on the right is the old nunnery's chapel—the ticket attendant will put on an informative taped narrative if asked. The rest of the first floor is filled with odds and ends, and the room full of Aboriginal weapons is *not* the museum's high point.

Down the hill and to the right, along Charlotte St., is the curiously names **Jackey-Jackey Store,** across from the Endeavour Lion's Park. Although the store itself has long since disappeared (it's now used as a residence), the front windows still display photographs from yesteryear. The old station, a majestic building that used to stand next to Anzac Park, features prominently in several of them.

The **Botanic Gardens,** off Walker St., were planted and well-maintained during the gold rush, but then left to decay when the town began to clear out. Twenty years ago, in a spirit of renewed energy, the city brought the Gardens back to life; although they're far from breathtaking, there are now over 150 acres of wattle in which to wander. There's a walking path out to **Finch Bay** (which can otherwise be reached by following Walker St. to its end), and the trail to secluded **Cherry Tree Bay** branches out from that. Halfway to Cherry Tree Bay is **Margo's Lookout,** a boulder promontory with a superb panoramic view. The **Cooktown Cemetery,** heading west out of town along the McIvor River-Cooktown Rd., has separate sections for Cooktown's Chinese and Jewish immigrants.

■ Around Cooktown

Black Mountain National Park looks like a couple of burned-out hills when surveyed from the lookout off the north-south Cooktown Developmental Road about 25km south of Cooktown. As you draw nearer, it becomes apparent in an eerie, stomach-turning way that these are just giant piles of black-as-night boulders, placed in an otherwise lush environment. The rocks aren't actually black; lichen colors the stone. According to the local Kuku bidiji Aboriginals, there was a fight here between two Rock Wallaby brothers, Ka-Iruji and Taja-Iruji, both vying for the same Rock Python woman. The brothers threw boulders at each other, but a sudden cyclone shattered both men's pile of stones, killing them; legend has it that one can still hear the Rock Python woman crying for her lovers. Camping isn't allowed, and wandering about is strongly discouraged, as there are Aboriginal taboo areas and 50m chasms among the boulders. The wildlife has adapted to life in the hot, strange climate. This is one of the few habitats in the world to support the carnivorous Ghost Bat.

Lizard Island National Park, about 30km from the mainland, boasts eyefuls of dunes, bays, reef, and beaches. There's plenty of room for everyone because only 20 people are allowed on the island at a time. **Marine Air Seaplanes** (tel. 4069 5915) in Cooktown can fly campers out to the island for $190 per seat, or $150 each if there are at least four people.

OUTBACK QUEENSLAND

Queensland's interior has little of the charm of South Australia's and Northern Territory's outback, but it is, in many ways, more authentic. The land is unforgiving out here, water is scarce, and constant threats such as rabbits and locusts have hardened farmers. There are no "cowboys": the correct title for a greenhorn is "jackeroo" (or "jilleroo" as the case may be, since short-handed stations have no time or need for sexism). From the third year, workers are called stationhands, and thereafter it becomes a hard strike against pride to call one a "jackeroo." While outback towns can be unkind to outsiders, the people living here maintain an ethic of trust. Deceit in the small communities is met with isolation and quietly dispensed local justice. Outback folk look you in the eye, and if they don't like what they see, you'll know it.

The gold rush that started in Cooktown has settled for a time now near the outback towns of Charters Towers and Emerald. Outside of Emerald, it's possible to find hard-core fossickers, bent double from their work and living in tin shacks; some things in Queensland haven't changed at all in the past century. And up by the Gulf of Carpentaria, where buildings were originally made of cement to befuddle the termites, the fishing is excellent, the roads are treacherous, and a single train engine shuttles between isolated Normanton and more isolated Croydon once a week, more out of habit than demand.

The road from Townsville to Mount Isa, and back down to Rockhampton, is just two lanes, streaked by tire tracks where automobiles have tried (with limited success) to keep from hitting kangaroos. Packs of roving emus are more street-savvy and jaunt off the road at the first sign of trouble, while wedge-tailed eagles rise slowly from roadkill at the approach of a car, before circling back to finish the meal. The puffing smelters of Mount Isa loom like sentinels on the horizon. Most travelers just pass through outback Queensland on their way to or from Northern Territory, watching day fade into night and blaze into day again on 40-hour bus rides. Those that stop off are rewarded with—or haunted by—otherworldly sights.

Top 10 Ways to Get into Trouble in an Outback Pub

10. Walk in wearing a cowboy hat.
9. Sing along to Johnny Cash.
8. Call the guy next to you a jackeroo to his face.
7. Show fear.
6. Ask for the vegetarian menu.
5. Ask for a lemon wedge in your Diet Coke.
4. Strike up a conversation about Aboriginal land rights.
3. Strike up a conversation.
2. Order a beer loudly, in Japanese.
1. BYO.

Charters Towers

South of the green Atherton Tablelands, the land dries out and old outback towns pick up. Charters Towers is a gold rush village that's still experiencing its rush. The result is an old-country town with sweeping architecture that shows off the area's wealth, all wrapped up in a down-home attitude. Charters Towers was once the hub of Queensland, nicknamed "The World" for its 1880s cosmopolitan flair, and home to Australia's first stock market. Today, the nickname is reserved for the city's theater, an elegant complex of two cinemas and a 640-seat live theater, where the manager still comes to work every day in a vest and bow tie. The theater and cinemas are each named after one of the gold mines near town, as if to display evidence of the town's vast, hidden wealth.

ORIENTATION AND PRACTICAL INFORMATION

A 90-minute drive from Townsville, Charters Towers lies over the threshold and within the clutches of Queensland's vast, enveloping interior. The town's layout seems like it was devised to befuddle any newcomer; streets curve and wrap back on themselves and seem to run at impossible angles to each other. In any case, follow the signs to the Historic City Centre and keep your eyes open for the twisting directions. The city center itself is a simple T-intersection: government offices and the Cor Mundi, or "The World" theater, run along Mosman St. at top, while most of the shops, restaurants, and banks are on the descending bar, Gill St.

Tourist Office: At the corner of Gill and Mosman St. (tel. 4752 0314). Maps and brochures galore, and a wall chart of the population 1877-1931, showing the rise and fall of the city's empire. Open daily 9am-5pm.
Currency Exchange: Both on Gill St., **Commonwealth Bank** (tel. 4787 1611) cashes traveler's checks for $5, and **Westpac Bank** (tel. 4787 1844) exchanges cash for no fee. Both have ATMs. Open Mon.-Thurs. 9:30am-4pm, Fri. 9:30am-5pm.
Trains: Queensland Rail Station (tel. 4787 0201) is 1 block north of Gill St. To Townsville on Queensland Rail $20, book through Traveland, below.
Buses: Greyhound and McCafferty's pull into the middle of town. Book at **Traveland** on Hill St. (tel. 4787 2622; fax 4787 7570). One-way fares to Townsville: **McCafferty's** $14, **Greyhound** $17, **Douglas Coaches** (the only coach with morning departures) $17. Open Mon.-Fri. 8am-5pm, Sat. 9am-noon.
RACQ: Gold City Wreckers (24hr. tel. 4787 2000), 21 Dundee Lane.
Library: Books and free **internet access** on Gill St., in the Old Bank of New South Wales building (tel. 4752 0338). Open Mon.-Fri. 1:45-4:45pm, plus Mon., Wed., and Fri. 10am-1pm, Sat. 9:20am-noon.
Hospital: On Gill St. (tel. 4787 1099).
Emergency: Dial 000.
Police: On Gill St. (tel. 4787 1333). Station open Mon.-Fri. 8am-4pm.
Post Office: On Gill St. (tel. 4787 1047; fax 4787 4013). Open Mon.-Fri. 9am-5pm. **Postal code:** 4820.
Phone Code: 07.

ACCOMMODATION AND FOOD

Scotty's Outback Inn (tel. 4787 1028) is the only hostel in town. Once upon a time, Scotty's had grand and stately rooms for extremely low prices. But the state of the economy forced the inn to pull its finer rooms out of the backpacker market and pitch them as $60 bed-and-breakfast rooms. The hostel part of the enterprise is now consigned to units in the backyard, although hostel guests can still use the eucalypt-shaped pool. Pick-ups at the coach and rail terminals are free; if you're driving in, find your way to Gill St., turn down the street past the burned-out Sovereign Hotel, and follow the small signs to the inn. (Dorms $14; twins and doubles $38, linen included.)

If you're keen to stay in the middle of town, the **Courthouse Hotel** (tel. 4787 1187), on Gill St., is over a century old, and still has some original woodwork. The pub room brims with rodeo pictures and wild west gear, and locals fill the place most evenings to hear the latest country-western tunes (singles $20; doubles $30; twins $35). The **Mexican Caravan Park** (tel. 4787 1161), at the corner of Towers and Church St., offers unpowered sites for $9 and powered sites for $13.

The old stock exchange building still stands next to the tourist information office on Mosman St., and its once-hallowed halls are now occupied by a **cafe** (tel. 4787 7954) that serves a big bush breakfast all day for just $6 (open Mon.-Sat. 8:30am-5pm, Sun. 9:30-lunchtime). Otherwise, pub grub is—surprise—not hard to find.

SIGHTS AND ENTERTAINMENT

The big attraction in town is, of course, the **gold mine,** the largest in all of Queensland. Tours, however, are squeezed in only once a week (Thurs. mornings; $12), and should be booked through Scotty's Outback Inn. Charters Towers is not a good place for individual gold fossicking; claims are protected tooth and nail, and poking around where you shouldn't poke around is an excellent way to get into heaps of trouble.

Two full-day bush safaris leave from Charters Towers. **Gold City Bush Safaris** (tel. 4787 2118; $35-55) is a sight-seeing trip in an air-conditioned land cruiser, while **Gold Fields Bush Safari** (tel. 4787 1028; $40) is a no-frills deal run by Larry Dulhunty, one of the last of the great traveling showmen. You'll need to book ahead, but trips run on, more or less, a moment's notice.

More locally, there's an **historical walking tour** ($5) that leaves daily at 3pm from the old stock exchange next to the tourist office. The stock exchange contains an unarresting **mining museum** (tel. 4787 2374; open Mon.-Fri. 8:30am-4:30pm, Sat.-Sun. 9am-3pm, closed for lunch; admission $1). A block down Mosman St. is the **Zara Clark Museum,** a collection of local memorabilia which includes the **flying fox money system** introduced by the city instead of the usual pounds and pence (open daily 10am-3pm; free).

Nightlife in Charters Towers is confined to a single nightclub, **Regent Club 96 Bar** on Gill St. (tel. 4787 2600; no cover; rocking nightly until 3am), although there's no shortage of culturally-enriching evening options. The **World Theatre** (also known as Cor Mundi) has regular offerings of ballets, operas, and plays, most with student discounts. (Information tel. 4787 4337; bookings tel. 4787 4344; fax 4787 4158. Ticket office open Mon.-Fri. 10am-1pm, Sat.-Sun. 10am-noon.) The **cinema** is located in the same building, but you'll have to cut around the right side of **Lawson's Restaurant** to get in (shows on Wed.-Sun. nights; tickets $8, students $6, Wed. $5). On the east side of Charters Towers is the staple of every country town, a **drive-in cinema** with second-run films (open Wed.-Sun.; tickets Fri.-Sun. $7, Wed.-Thurs. $5, or $10 per carload).

From Charters Towers to Mount Isa

It's difficult to cast an exciting glow on a drive through the outback. For the casual motorist, the panorama is a series of near-featureless plains with scrub here and stubby trees there. Towns become little more than a lower speed limit, a pub, and a general store with a fuel pump. West of Prairie, Hughendon, and Richmond lies **Cloncurry** (see p. 363).

Prairie After a few hours, the road runs through a town with a pub worth a stretch and a coffee. **The Prairie Hotel** (tel. 4741 5121) was built in the same year that the typewriter was invented (1867), and both seem equally rickety and old-fashioned today. These days, there's a jukebox to enliven the nightlife, but there's still only one room in the hotel (a twin-share, $15 per bed). Camping behind the hotel is another alternative (tent sites $5, unpowered campervan $10, powered campervan $12), but you'll miss out on the spirit of the place, namely, the **ghost** returning to claim a gold sovereign owed him (30¢ for the story from the barmaid, but it's free to see a photograph of the spook). Meals are the usual pub-grub at $8-11 per plate.

Hughendon Hughendon (HYU-endon) marks the eastern edge of the **Dinosaur Highway,** which stretches a few towns west and as far south as Winton's Lark Quarry. The town itself is very, very quiet, which makes it all the more shocking to discover a **completely reconstructed Muttaburrasaurus skeleton** in the back room of the Visitor Information Centre (tel. 4741 1021; open Mon.-Fri. 9am-5pm). If you roll into town on the weekend, just walk around back and take a peek through the glass door. Hughendon will also host a **Dinofest** in August (and again in 2000; ring the info center for details). Reasonable accommodation in town is limited to the ambitiously-named **Grand Hotel** (tel. 4741 1588; singles $20; twins or doubles $30; dinner specials $7-10) and the **Allen Terry Caravan Park** (tel. 4741 1190), across from the rail station. The caravan park makes 24-hour pick-ups from the coach or rail terminals, and a staff that never tires of explaining who Allen Terry was. (Pool and laundry facilities. Reception open Mon.-Fri. 7am-9pm. Tent sites $6, for 2 $9; powered $10, for 2 $13. Wed. sausage sizzle dinner $2.)

The locals in Hughendon play on the beauty and the beast motif when selling their sights: the beast is the Muttaburrasaurus, of course, and the beauty is nearby **Porcupine Gorge,** 60km north of town. The gorge offers a bit of an oasis along the dusty trail, and a clear creek which cuts its way through stiff chasm walls. **Adventure Wildlife and Bush Treks** (tel. 4788 11 26, or book at the caravan park) has full-day trips on demand ($55, if you drive yourself $25).

Richmond West of Hughendon along the Flinders Hwy. is Richmond, another very quiet town that packs an impressive paleological punch. The **Marine Fossil Museum** (tel. 4741 3429; fax 4741 3802) has real bones of cretaceous-era marine reptiles (97-130 million years old). The presentation is well-informed, easy to follow, and diverse in its offerings, and the staff of volunteers is thoroughly committed to explaining the displays in minute detail (open daily 8am-5pm; admission $3). The **caravan park** up the street (tel. 4741 8772; reception open 8:30am-"bedtime" for Mick, the caretaker) is an exceptional value. A bed in the brand-new dongas ($15) includes linen and air-conditioning. The common kitchen is new, as well. (Tent sites $7, with power $10.)

Cloncurry As you approach Mt. Isa from the east, you'll cross a few small mountains that provide a pleasant change from the monotonous plains of the outback. Mt. Isa's nearest "suburb," Cloncurry (2hr. away), isn't particularly inspiring, but it does make a good rest stop. The town has a small **Royal Flying Doctor Service Museum,** which is more of a shrine to John Flynn, its founder, than an informative exhibit. The pleasant **Cloncurry Caravan Park** (tel. 4742 1313), with a pool and barbecue, will do if you can't hack the last leg to the Isa (tent sites for 1 person $7, for 2 $10; powered sites $12, $14). For those who travel tent-less, follow the signs for the public phones to the **Post Office Hotel** (tel. 4742 1411; fax 4742 23 56). The hotel is luxurious by Queensland pub hotel standards, with a TV in each room (singles $25; twins or doubles $34).

One of the more interesting phenomena of the Queensland outback is that of the Cloncurry Min-Min. **Min-Min** is an Aboriginal name for a mysterious dancing light or will-o'-the-wisp that is periodically spotted moving about on the plains outside Cloncurry. Some say it is caused by luminous gases or luminous insects, but the Aboriginals believe it is an apparition of evil spirits. Nobody knows for sure, since no one has ever caught up with a Min-Min.

Mount Isa

When the subject of Mount Isa comes up, backpackers' conversations sober up and casual laughter dwindles. This is the city where hitchhikers coming in from Northern Territory break down and buy a bus ticket. Honeymooning couples have been known to sell their campervans in the Isa and head to the airport. The city itself has the feel of an intergalactic spaceport; walking down the street, it's possible to tick off dozens of languages in overheard chitchat. Two- and three-trailer road trains crowd the outskirts of town, and the careful ear will pick up sounds of the 4am underground mining blasts, part and parcel of the copper mines' 12-hour shifts. There is a certain inconsolable malaise to the city: it's a long way coming in, it's a long way getting out again, and the only company to keep is the twin smokestacks that overshadow the city, constantly billowing like chain-smoking bullies.

ORIENTATION

On the east side of the **Leichhardt River,** the center of town rises slightly near the middle. The outlying area is a mess of awkwardly-angled streets, but the city center is a more manageable four-by-four grid. The **Barkly Hwy.** enters from Northern Territory and runs parallel to the river until the bridge at **Miles End,** and then turns left over the water into the city center on **Grace St.** From Cloncurry in the east, the Barkly Hwy. becomes Grace St. as it comes into town and passes by the **Riversleigh Interpretive Centre,** a major landmark. Across from the Riversleigh Centre and up the hill is a prime lookout spot for panoramic views of Mount Isa.

PRACTICAL INFORMATION

Tourist Information: The info center at the **Riversleigh Interpretive Centre** handles most inquiries (tel. 4749 1555; fax 4743 6296). Open Mon.-Fri. 8:30am-4:30pm, Sat.-Sun. 9am-3pm.

Budget Travel Office: Travelland (tel. 4743 3399), next to the McCafferty's terminal, has occasional specials that include a flight with **National Jet** to Darwin or Townsville for $160, departing Mon. and Fri. Open Mon.-Sat. 9am-noon.

Currency/Exchange: Commonwealth Bank, 23 Miles St. (tel. 4743 5033). Traveler's checks or cash $5. V, MC. Open Mon.-Thurs. 9:30am-4pm, Fri. 9:30am-5pm. **ATM** takes Cirrus. **ANZ,** 16 Miles St., takes V, MC, Cirrus, and Plus.

Trains: Train Station (tel. 4744 1201) on Railway Ave. near Miles End, a $5 taxi ride to town or $8 to the caravan parks.

Buses: McCafferty's (tel. 4743 2006; fax 4743 3399) pulls into the west side of town, over the river. Runs to Townsville ($81), Rockhampton ($154), Darwin ($156), Alice Springs ($135). **Greyhound** (tel. 4743 6655) shares its terminal with the Riversleigh Interpretive Centre. Fares to Townsville ($88), Cairns ($117), Darwin ($182). Open Mon.-Fri. 6:30am-4pm, Sat.-Sun. 6:30-11am.

Taxis: United Cab (tel. 13 10 08).

Automobile Club: RACQ, Power Automobile, 13 Simpson St. (tel. 4743 4300, 24hr. tel. 4743 2542).

Library: on Miles St. (tel. 4744 4266). 3 floors of holdings. Open Mon.-Fri. 10am-6pm, Wed. 10am-8pm, Sat. 9am-noon.

Laundromat: (tel. 018 121 240) at the Riversleigh Interpretive Centre. Open Mon.-Fri. 8:30am-5pm, Sat.-Sun. 9:30am-2pm.

Hospital: (tel. 4744 4444), 30 Camooweal St.

Emergency: Dial 000.

Police: (tel. 4743 2222), on Isa St. Open 24hr.

Post Office: (tel. 4743 2454), at the corner of Camooweal and Isa St. From the hostel, walk downhill on Pamela St., following the road as it swivels to the right. The post office is up on the left. *Post Restante* open Mon.-Fri. 8:30am-5:30pm. Post office open Mon.-Fri. 9am-5pm. **Postal code:** 4825.

Phone Code: 07.

ACCOMMODATIONS AND FOOD

Traveller's Haven (tel. 4743 0313; fax 4743 4007), at the corner of Pamela and Spencer St., is the only hostel in town since the YHA closed its door in January 1997. From either direction on the highway, drive through town following the information signs. At the Riversleigh Interpretive Centre, drive around the left of the building and follow the road for two blocks. The hostel will be on your right. The management has a soft heart and will throw extra mattresses in the rooms rather than send away backpackers to the $80-per-night motels. They'll arrange free pick-ups from the coach terminals and train station. (Reception open daily 6:30am-1pm and 5-7pm. Dorms $13; singles $26; twins and doubles $30. VIP. Key deposit $5. Linen $2.)

If you're prepared to camp, try **Sunset Van Park,** 14 Sunset Dr. (tel. 4743 7668). From the city, drive around the left side of the lookout and Mount Isa water tower. Eventually the road will become Sunset Dr., and the caravan park is on the left before you pass over the creek bed. (Reception open Mon.-Fri. 7:30am-10pm. Tent sites for 1 $7, for 2 $12; powered sites $10, $15. Key deposit $10.)

The **Buffalo Club** (tel. 4743 2365), corner of Grace and Simpson St., offers cheap lunch and dinner ($5-6) and rocking good chips ($3) if you can dig up something reasonable to wear: collared shirt yay, thongs or sandals nay (open daily noon-2pm and after 6pm). **Flamenco Coffee Shop** (tel. 4743 4569), at the top of Marion St., is a local hang-out for miners, school kids, and local business people, and a great place to rub shoulders with folks of random nationalities (open Mon.-Fri. 9:30am-6pm, Sat. 9:30am-5pm, Sun. 9am-5pm).

SIGHTS

Mount Isa offers a tour like none other in Australia—an opportunity to dive into the belly of the beast on a mine tour. Put on the suit, put on the hat, and ride the elevator shaft down into Mount Isa's heart of darkness, a winding labyrinth of tunnels as long as the Great Barrier Reef. Bookings (essential) can be made via the Riversleigh Centre (tel. 4749 1555) or through the hostel. The three-hour tour ($25) leaves twice a day in the morning (Mon.-Fri.) and just...plain...rocks.

The other two pseudo-mine experiences don't really cut the mustard. The **John Middlin Mining Display,** over the bridge and to the left, is a shrine to Mount Isa mining, and a low-budget one at that. Perhaps the museum's highlight is not the much-touted and massively-hokey simulator, but rather the opening film in the theaterette with many, many action shots of Mount Isa, the city (open daily 9am-4pm, admission $2). On the other end of town, between the city center and the Riversleigh Centre, is the **Frank Aston Underground Museum** (tel. 4743 0610), a large collection of brightly-painted machinery without any explanatory notes. Inside the hill, a series of poorly-lit dioramas depict mining life, with certain panels revealing aspects of local (and not-so-local) Aboriginal life. To its credit, the museum has recently received the Museum of Northwestern Queensland's excellent mineral display (open 9am-4pm daily; admission $5).

A better display of local Kalkadoon **Aboriginal artifacts** (with not-so local Northern Territory groups mixed in) is the **Kalkadoon Tribal Centre** (tel. 4749 1435; fax 4749 1001), the vividly colored building next to the Riversleigh Centre. The exhibits aren't much more than a series of posterboards and a few artifacts sitting on a table, but the real gems are the Aboriginal folks who sit by the front door, and wander in and out. If you can catch someone in a chatty mood, you might hear a recipe for spinifex wax or directions to a local art site: take the Lake Moondarra road northeast from Mount Isa, turn right where the telephone lines cross the road (about 3km), and continue down the unsealed road (another 7km). There's a small library of books and videos at the Tribal Centre, too, mostly about recent land rights developments (open Mon.-Fri. 9am-5pm; admission $1).

Next door to the Kalkadoon Centre is the **Riversleigh Fossils Interpretive Centre** (tel. 4749 1555; fax 4743 6296), which houses a collection of animatronic models of early Australian mammals and a display on how to sift through dirt for things of the past (open Mon.-Fri. 8:30am-4:30pm, Sat.-Sun. 9am-3pm; admission $5).

Not everyone in Mt. Isa is entirely supportive of Aboriginal culture or presence in the area. On the road out to coastal Queensland facing Mt. Isa stands a memorial with the plaque: "You who pass by are now entering the ancient tribal lands of the Mitakoodi dispossessed by the European—Honor their name—Be Brother and sister to their descendants." The side facing east has been defaced with a single, thin swastika.

Emerald

The bleak landscape stretching west along the Tropic of Capricorn holds a few precious secrets. The pioneers who've settled here to eke out a living must wrest these treasures from the earth one at a time. The gemfields of Emerald and the surrounding townships have produced sapphires, rubies, gold, and copper, among other valued minerals. Coal, too, is part of the local economy. The region doesn't have much to offer the casual visitor, but Emerald is a convenient waystation on the trip across Queensland's vast—and rarely visited—interior.

Comet This is one of several one-horse towns you'll whizz past on the way inland from Rockhampton to Emerald. The town was named for the Comet River. Or maybe the river was named for the town. In either case, Comet's single attraction is a replica of a tree beneath which Leichhardt (on his second expedition of the area in 1847) buried notes of where his party was headed. The tree is marked "DIG" with an arrow pointing down, a sublime testament to the linguistic genius of the early explorers.

Practical Information Emerald itself isn't much more than a stepping-off point to the gemfields and goldwash. Getting to the town isn't difficult as **McCafferty's** (tel. 4982 2755) stops in on its Mt. Isa-Rockhampton route—but it's a long walk to regional fossicking towns if you lack wheels. Emerald has **internet access** for $5 per hour at the public **library,** 44 Borilla St. (tel. 4982 8347; open Mon.-Thurs. 10am-5:30pm, Fri. 10am-5pm, Sat. 9am-noon). The **hospital** is on Hospital Rd. (tel. 4983 8500). The **police station** is on Egerton St. (tel. 4982 1000). For camping permits, the **QNPWS** office (tel. 4982 4555; fax 4982 2568; open Mon.-Fri. 9am-4pm) is located next to the Emerald Hostel in the Government Offices building.

Accommodations The **Emerald Hostel** (tel. 4982 4188) is reasonably clean, at least in the private rooms, and decidedly inexpensive (laundry facilities; reception open Mon.-Thurs. 5am-6pm). A single with A/C costs $15; a soiled bed in the dorm is $12 (weekly $50; linen and cutlery not included; key deposit $5). Dress code dictates no hats, please. To get to the hostel from the main highway, turn onto Borilla St. across from the train station, then left onto Egerton St., which becomes Hospital Rd. Turn left after the Rotary Park, and then an immediate right. It's up 100m on your left.

Willows Gemfields Caravan Park (tel. 4985 8128) in Willows Gemfields, hires fossicking equipment for free with a four-night minimum stay and offers laundry facilities and a pool (tent sites $10, powered sites $11; weekly: $53, $62). **Gem Air Village** (tel. 4985 8124) is the only competition in town. (Tent sites $10; powered sites $12. Weekly: $50; $62.) Fossicking sets can be hired for $9 per day (weekly $35).

Fossicking in the Emerald area Fossicking, or picking through dirt for pretty stones, is the main draw of the area. The Forestry Department (tel. 4982 8872), on Hospital Rd. next to the Emerald Hostel, in the Government Offices building, handles permits to pan for gold on state forest land, but you can only apply on Fridays from 8:30am to 5pm. Gemstone claims can be made at the **Department of Minerals and Energy office** (tel. 4982 4011; fax 4982 4230; open Mon.-Fri. 8:30am-4:30pm) on the highway road next to the ANZ bank. A **fossicker's license** costs $5.10 per month, and camping at the site is an additional $2 per night or $12.30 per week. Local hardware stores sell the right kits ($100 and up).

Alternatively, you can just drop by one of the working fossicking parks west of town. **Anakie** (pronounced "Anarchy" with a broad Australian accent) is a little more than 40km from town, and has an **information center** (tel. 4985 4525) which can point you toward a good field in Sapphire (about 10km north) or **Rubyvale** (8km north of Sapphire). **S 'n' S Mine** in Rubyvale (tel. 4985 4307) has an underground mine that visitors can take a crack at, but it's a bit pricey ($60 per half-day, $95 per day); bring rubber-soled, enclosed footwear. Old hands should go directly to the town of **Willows Gemfields,** 25km west of Anakie.

If you're feeling down on your luck and in need of some divine intervention, head an hour south of Emerald to **Springsure,** a tiny town that boasts the Virgin Rock, where early settlers had a vision of the lady herself. There's also a **caravan park** (tel. 4984 1418) on the far side of town, at the BP station. (Tent sites $5, with power $8; hot meals in the petrol station $7-10 until about 8pm.) The station itself is open from 6:30am to 9pm. From Springsure, it's another two to three hours to **Carnarvon** (can-AIR-van) **National Park;** turn right at Rolliston and get ready for a bumpy ride (4WD only). You can pick up a camping permit ($3.50 per night) and handfuls of free maps at the QNPWS office in Emerald.

Barcaldine

The outpost of Barcaldine (bar-CALLED-in) is the most authentic outback town in Queensland that can easily be reached by bus (McCafferty's), train (en route to Longreach), or car. Most of the tourists who come through are the long caravans of pensioners making their way up the Matilda Hwy., and they usually hang out in the caravan parks. The outlying population manages to keep six pubs afloat: one for every day of the week except Sunday, when everyone rolls into church.

ORIENTATION AND PRACTICAL INFORMATION

Keep your trees straight in Barcaldine—all the streets bear the names of tree species. Oak St., for example, is the main drag. You can purchase an aerial photograph of the city, with all streets labelled, from the information center ($5 for this truly unique souvenir).

Tourist Office: On the main highway (tel. 4651 1724; fax 4651 2243). Open daily 9am-12:30pm and 1:30-5pm.
Currency Exchange: Commonwealth Bank, corner of Ash and Beech St. (tel. 4651 1600). Commission of traveler's checks $5, on cash $5. Open Mon.-Thurs. 9:30am-4pm, Fri. 9:30am-5pm. **ATM** accepts V, MC, Cirrus, Maestro.
Trains: Ticket office at the station (open Mon.-Fri. 9am-5pm) prefers that tickets be booked through the central reservations desk (tel. 13 22 32).
Buses: McCafferty's drops off at the BP station (tel. 4651 1333; open daily 6:30am-9pm) on the west side of town, at the corner of Oak and Box St.
Automobile Club: RACQ, at Barcaldine Engineering Works on Oak St. (tel. 4651 1337; after hours tel. 4651 1544).
Hospital: (tel. 4651 1311), on Oak St.
Emergency: Dial 000.
Police: (tel. 4651 1322), on Ash St.
Post Office: Corner of Ash and Beech St. (tel. 4651 1147; fax 4651 1120). Fax services. Open Mon.-Fri. 9am-5pm, Sat. 9-11am. **Postal code:** 4725.
Phone Code: 07.

ACCOMMODATIONS

Between six hotels and two campgrounds, there's almost always an empty bed in town. Hotel rooms are basic and fairly clean, without much difference in quality as you go up and down Oak St.

Artesian Hotel, 13 Oak St. (tel. 4651 1691). Mostly iron-bar poster-beds. Singles $10; twins $15; one double with a window that compromises occupants' privacy $15. Home-cooked meals (as in, whatever the proprietor is having) $5.
Shakespeare Hotel, on Oak St. (tel. 4651 1610), across from the tourist office. Bathroom has a tub. Beer garden is shared with a hulking A/C unit. Singles $15; twins and doubles $25.
Railway Hotel (tel. 4651 1188). The ping-pong table here is the main attraction. Singles $15; twins and doubles $30.
Homestead Caravan Park (tel. 4651 1308), on Box St. Your basic caravan park. Laundry facilities. Tent site for 1 person $7, for 2 $10; powered site for 1 $10, for 2 $13; cabin $30, for 2 $35. Free tea and damper, hot dinners $5-7 every night.
Showgrounds Council Caravan Park, on the east side of town. Lash down your bedding; the winds can get mighty fierce at night. Laundry facilities. The caretaker collects fees every morning: tent sites $2, powered sites $10.

SIGHTS

For a tiny town, there's surprisingly much to do. The main draw is the **Australian Workers Heritage Centre** (tel. 4651 2422), a glowing tribute to Australia's civil servants, marked by a giant circus tent in the middle of town. The exhibits are sectioned off into little houses—policemen here, doctors and nurses there, even re-creations of a one-room school and a legislative assembly (complete with a voice-over of incessant argumentation). The real meat of the center is the exhaustive history of Australia's Labor Party, which got its start under the now sepulchrous ghost gum, the **Tree of Knowledge,** in the middle of town (center open daily 9am-5pm; admission for 1 week $7, students $5; wheelchair accessible).

Out at the end of Pine St. (turn off the main road, between the hospital and the cleverly-named Cafe Cafe) sits **Mad Mick's Beta Farm Outback Heritage and Wildlife** (tel. 4651 1172). Mick is indeed slightly off-center as he leads folks around his restored slab hut homestead, hanging out with Ned the emu and viewing a shockingly large 1000-doll collection. Best to book ahead at the information center. (Farm open April-Sept. 9:30am-noon most days, depending on Mick's whim. Admission $7, includes tea, damper, and BBQ lunch.)

Artesian Country Tours (tel. 4651 2211; fax 4651 2499) has an on-demand daytrip to some outlying sights, including the only local (legal) access to the **Gracevale caves** in Aramac, the oldest and largest single collection of Aboriginal rock art in Australia. The drawings date back 10,000-12,000 years and include an example of Nyalyod, the rainbow serpent from Kakadu's Ubirr caves. The stuff is utterly fantastic: etched-out boomerangs (only ones in Australia), a second Rainbow serpent spread 60m long, and emu tracks everywhere, similar to those found on Whitsunday's Nara Inlet. The site's custodian is represented as well—six-toed feet that grow as they walk across the rock face until suddenly splayed north-south to represent the custodian's death. At this point, emu tracks take up where the footprints left off, making a full circle back to the baby footprints and suggesting the return home of the custodian's totem. The trip out costs a bundle ($80) but includes lunch and dinner, and a few other sights along the way (creeks, pools, and Aboriginal massacres remembered). Check in with the folks at the **Central West Aboriginal Corporation** (the funky-colored building across from the shire offices) to see if they've managed to get the rights back yet, and started up any tours. As for nightlife, there's a country-style cinema, **Radio Theatre,** in an old church (look for the building with the most color in town), showing flicks on the weekends (tickets $7, students $5; occasional guest concerts $8-10).

Longreach

The relative metropolis of Longreach is nothing to be trifled with. This is the major watering hole for the outback communities, where folks come for loud gossip and louder late-night drinking, wheels turning up dust as the weekend ends and folks jump in their souped-up utes for the long, long ride back to the station. People have an edge about them, earned from years of working a hard and unforgiving earth with few modern creature comforts. The city itself is nothing flash. Most of its petrol stations close on the weekends.

Practical Information, Accommodations, and Food The **information center** (tel. 4658 3555; fax 4658 3733; open Mon.-Fri. 8:45am-5:15pm, Sat.-Sun. 8:30am-1:30pm) acts as a clearing house for all the local goings-on. Along the street is a Commonwealth **ATM** which accepts Visa, MasterCard, and Cirrus and an ANZ machine that also takes Plus. The **library** nearby has fax service and free **internet access** (tel. 4658 4104; open Tues. and Thurs., 9:30am-1pm, Wed. and Fri. 12:30-5pm, Sat. 9am-noon). For emergencies, call the **police** (tel. 4658 2200; on Galah St.) or **hospital** (tel. 4658 4700; on Jabiro St.). **McCafferty's** (tel. 4658 1155) pulls into the center of town, in front of Transwest Travelworld, while the **train station** (tel. 4658 1028) is five minutes from the center ($5 by taxi). The **post office** (tel. 4658 1887) is across the street from the info center (open Mon.-Fri. 9am-5pm; postal code 4730).

If you're stuck for the night, try the **Lyceum Hotel** (tel. 4658 1036) all the way down the main street and on the right. The manager, Peter, should drop the room price to $12 a head if you flash your copy of *Let's Go;* otherwise it's singles $20; doubles $35. Linen included, free tea and coffee, and some A/C in the summer months. The **Merino Bakery** (tel. 4658 1715; open Mon.-Fri. 4:30am-5pm, Sat. 4am-noon) sells the freshest bread in town.

Sights The only reason to visit Longreach, but a reason which attracts flocks of pensioners throughout the year, is the **Australian Stockman's Hall of Fame,** a massive, multi-media museum on the highway east of town (tel. 005 531 034; open daily 9am-5pm; admission $15, students $12). Within you'll find a brief introduction to the geological formation of the island continent astride a panel or two on the original inhabitants, then a continuation of the timeline from the hard-core adventures of the early days to a more recent **Hall of Fame Computer,** with information on the plagues, drives, and livestock of the contemporary stockman. The public library has nearly every book on the subject on the top floor, and the eerie Talking Drover's face is a projected image downstairs. The Drover reminisces aloud about the cattle tracks that hold the country together. A taxi to the Hall of Fame costs $5.50.

The other museum in town, **Qantas Founders Outback Museum** (tel. 4658 3737), on the highway east of town, is overshadowed by its competition. The museum informs on minutia (Qantas stands for Queensland and Northern Territory Aerial Service) and tries to entertain with a dizzyingly quick and sentimental look at the airline's past. Longreach and Winton have an ongoing debate over which is the true birthplace of Qantas, the world's first airline to both build and fly its own airplanes. Longreach has the first hanger and a replica of the first airplane, while Winston has the first board meeting (open daily 9am-5pm; admission $6, students $3).

Ilfracombe Half an hour to the east is Ilfracombe, Longreach's satellite suburb. There's plenty of elbow room in the shire, with about 7000 acres for each of the 350 people spread over it. The **Wellshot Hotel** (tel. 4658 2106) bears the town's original name, and is decorated with old bush hats and $5 notes that cling magically to the ceiling (singles $25; twins and doubles $40). The Wellshot is also home to a stockmanship show, complete with whip-cracking and bull-wrestling (Thurs., Sat., and Sun. afternoons; admission $8, with dinner $20). The **historical museum** across the road is a storehouse for old knick-knacks, including the "first car wash," a boxcar stored in the back bathroom (open daily 7am-3:30pm). The historical society has published a handful of free brochures on the area, with strange trivia delivered nonchalantly: for instance, the **largest flock of sheep ever to be moved** (43,000) was shepherded here back in 1886. Now you know.

Winton and Around

The long, lonely Landsborough Highway spans the outback between Longreach and Mount Isa (see p. 363). Along the way, it passes through Winton, Kynuna, and McKinlay on its way to Cloncurry, the junction of the Landsborough Hwy. and the Flinders Hwy. from Townsville and Charters Towers.

Winton is always getting the short end of the stick. By at least one method of reckoning, it's the birthplace of Qantas, which held its first board meeting in the Winton Club (now a Chinese restaurant), but Winton and Longreach have a perpetual tug-of-war over who has rights to the legacy, and Winton seems to end up giving ground. The town is also the site of Banjo Paterson's first performance of "Waltzing Matilda," Australia's unofficial national anthem, but neighboring **Kynuna** is much closer to the actual billabong in the song, and *they've* got the original music score. The result is a confused local historical museum, the **Qantilda Pioneer Place** (tel. 4657 1105; open daily 9am-4pm; admission $5, students $3), which, like its name, gracelessly incorporates both myths into an unapproachable jumble. **Kynuna's Swagman Hall of Fame** (the circus tent on the highway with begonias growing out front) has elected only one swagman thus far, the anonymous jolly one from the song. This is kitsch like nowhere else in Queensland, a roadside attraction where it's free to step into the tent but $3 to go behind the curtain and view Paterson's score. And $8 to buy the book. And $10 for the live floor show (daily 7:30-9:30pm, includes a soup and coffee dinner).

Winton does have two-up on its neighbors, though. Behind the North Gregory Hotel you'll find **Arno's Wall,** a 100 ft. long stretch of home implements and motorcycles set in concrete. The townsfolk don't really know what to do with this Arno fellow, a German immigrant and itinerant opal miner. Pick up a copy of the town's *Mud Map,* $1 at the Qantilda, for the scoop.

The second boon is the **Lark Quarry,** a bumpy, two-hour ride south from the town center. This is dinosaur country, where you'll find an immense zigzag of footprints, a preserved snapshot of an afternoon in prehistoric Australia when a hungry dinosaur tromped into a flock of small, two-legged lunchboxes. The meat-eater was not a *Tyrannosaurus rex,* despite the hype in Winton (which includes rubbish bins made to look like *T. rex* feet). Paleontologists can sniff out details of the dinosaurs involved by looking at particulars of the footprints and have concluded that the little guys were coelurosaurs and ornithopods, small and lightweight dinosaurs with hollow bones, a likely forebear to the modern bird, and that the larger tracks predate the infamous carnivore by almost 50 million years.

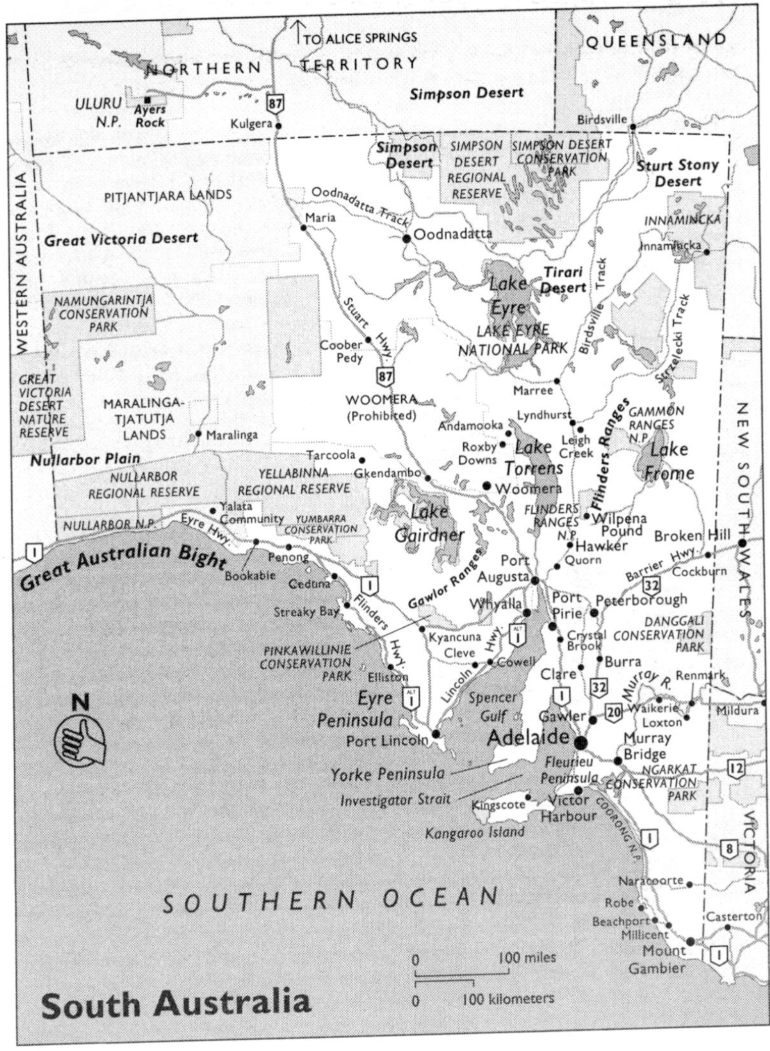

South Australia

South Australia lives in a state of sublime schizophrenia. Alongside some of the harshest, most uncompromising terrain on the continent, peaceful vineyards sleep lazily and a sophisticated city basks under a steady sun. Capital Adelaide is a stately, serene oasis in the midst of expansive desert, well-fed and well-watered by some of the best cuisine and finest wines in the country. Gracious buildings line its streets, world-class festivals crowd its boulevards, and hip cafes occupy its East End. As if in defiance, Adelaide's green parklands challenge the searing heat of the ever-encroaching desert.

This is the driest state in Australia, yet it is the most urbanized precisely because its outback is so inhospitable. In this sparsely populated region, indigenous pitjantjatjara and colonial farmers alike subsist on land which may see rain only a few times a decade, and miners at Cooper Pedy must literally extract a living from the earth. The tenacity of these pioneers is plainly evident to the determined traveler who traverses the rugged Flinders Ranges or goes "back of beyond."

But the common appeal of South Australia lies nearer its water. The majestic Murray River, Australia's largest waterway, winds through the lowlands east of Adelaide and irrigates the state's famous vineyards before emptying into the Southern Ocean. Of South Australia's seven distinct wine regions, those of the Adelaide Hills are most accessible from the capital, while the Coonawarra, southeast of Adelaide, produces Australia's finest reds. Slightly more removed, the fertile valleys of the Murray River and the grassy knolls of McLaren Vale also earn recognition from connoisseurs. North toward the outback, the famous Barossa and Clare Valleys comprise the central wine regions. The gently undulating vineyards of the Eyre Peninsula lie farther northwest.

For those less interested in wine and not drawn to the desert, the Eyre Peninsula's cliffs and sandy beaches combine with the country towns of the Yorke Peninsula to reward those travelers who venture forth from Adelaide, proving that South Australia is not entirely a land of extremes.

Phone numbers in South Australia have recently changed. Regional phone codes are now all 08, followed by eight-digit numbers. If you have trouble making a call, use the following scheme to get the old number, and try that instead. For more details, see the **appendix** (p. 574). For numbers in Kangaroo Island, see **Kangaroo Island** (p. 390).

New Number:	Old Number:	New Number:	Old Number:
(08) 84xx xxxx	(08) xx xxxx	(08) 87xx xxxx	(087) xx xxxx
(08) 8xxx xxxx	(08) xxx xxxx	(08) 88xx xxxx	(088) xx xxxx
(08) 85xx xxxx	(085) xx xxxx	(08) 89xx xxxx	(089) xx xxxx
(08) 86xx xxxx	(086) xx xxxx	*(08) 855a bxxx	*(0848) y zxxx

Adelaide

Once known only for its inordinate number of churches, Adelaide has emerged as a city with far more to offer than an uplifting Sunday sermon. The first completely planned city in Australia, in the first state not to be settled by convict labor, Adelaide was destined to a history unlike that of the other Australian capitals. The one million people who call Adelaide home take pride in the city's big leafy trees, historic buildings, and flourishing arts scene and enjoy a big-city lifestyle that belies the lower cost of living. The long list of cultural attractions, headed by the Adelaide Festival of Arts, includes a fine symphony and chamber orchestra, numerous small, experimental theaters, and world-class galleries and museums. With more restaurants per capita than any other city in Australia, Adelaide can satisfy any palate at any budget, and then wash it all down with some of the country's best wines. For those who prefer a more raucous pace, the nightclubs along Hindly St., the pubs in the city center, and the cafes on Rundle St. fit the hedonistic bill.

In the summer months, Adelaide's coastline becomes a temple of sun worship, with devotion to the deity reflected in the nut-brown skin of its followers. The beachfront suburb of Glenelg is a favorite late night haunt, since many of its pubs, clubs, and restaurants face the ocean. Home to the first colonists of South Australia, Glenelg is now one of Adelaide's most popular residences for families, fishermen, yuppies, and at least a bazillion seagulls. Be warned, however, that this is very much an urban hangout, and it can be difficult to find your own patch of beach. That said, buy some fish and chips, slop on the sunblock, and stake your claim on the golden sand. If sand and surf are not your first choice in outdoor activity, the city's 668 hectares of parkland provide plenty of room to romp. Some of the most visually stunning hikes in the country can be found in the Adelaide Hills, a short drive from the city center.

Adelaide

ACCOMMODATIONS

Adelaide Backpackers Hostel, **G**
Adelaide Backpacker's Inn, **E**
Adelaide Rucksackers, **F**
Backpack Australia, **B**
East Park Lodge, **I**
New World International Hostel, **D**
Sunny's, **A**
YHA Hostel, **H**
YMCA, **C**

SIGHTS & SERVICES

Adelaide Casino, **2**
Adelaide Gaol, **1**
Adult Deaf Society, **19**
Art Gallery of South Australia, **10**
Ayers House, **11**
Central Bus Station, **15**
Central Market, **18**
Government House, **6**
Museum, **4**
Parliament House, **5**
Performing Arts Multicultural Centre, **17**
The Playhouse Festival Theatre, **3**
South Australian Museum, **9**
State Information Centre, **12**
State Library, **8**
State Opera Theatre, **16**
Stock Exchange, **13**
Town Hall, **14**
War Memorial, **7**

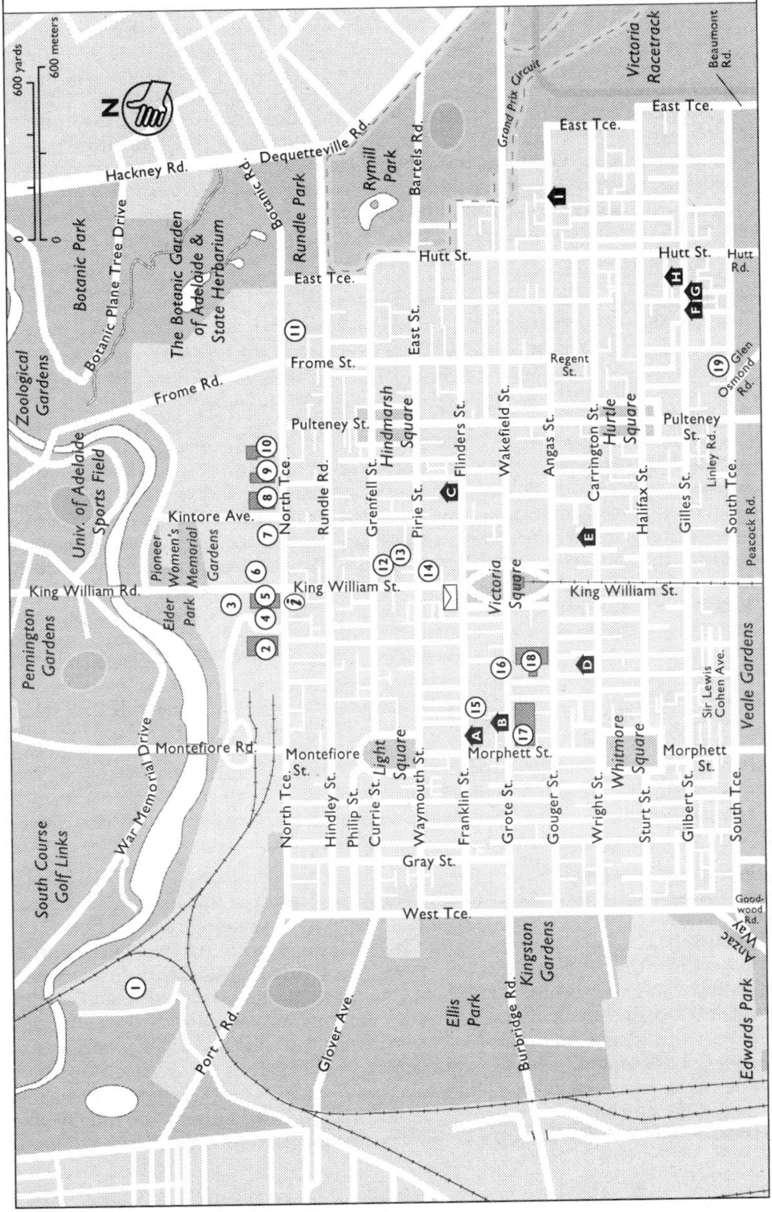

ARRIVAL AND DEPARTURE

By Plane

Most of the flights in and out of Adelaide are domestic. **Kendell Airlines** is the major local carrier; book through Ansett (tel. 13 13 00). Kendell offers flights to: Coober Pedy (return $514), Port Augusta ($230), and Mount Gambier ($290). **Students** under 26 pay 25% off the full fare; seniors enjoy a 40% discount. Smaller airlines generally service a particular area of the state. **Eyre Commuter** (tel. 1800 088 822) services the Eyre Peninsula, **O'Conner** (tel. 13 13 13 through Qantas) services Mount Gambier, and **Emu Airways** (tel. 1800 182 353) services Kangaroo Island.

The airport, located 7km west of the city center, services domestic and international carriers in separate terminals, a 15-minute walk from one another. It takes no more than 20 minutes by car to get from the airport to the city; a taxi ride runs $12-15. The cheapest way to get from the airport to Adelaide proper is on the **Airport to City Bus** (tel. 8381 5311), which makes a loop within the city itself and drops passengers at many major hostels and hotels (Mon.-Fri. every 30min. 7am-9pm, Sat.-Sun. and holidays every 1hr.; $6 one-way, $10 return good any time). **Trans Adelaide** public bus #270 will bring you to the airport entrance on Burbridge Rd. From there it is a 15-minute walk to the terminal. Bus #270 leaves the city from Currie St., just across from the Passenger Transport Information Centre.

By Bus

Adelaide's **central bus station** is at 101-111 Franklin St. Once at the station, cross the street to the bright pink **Backpacker Travel and Transit Center** (open Mon.-Fri. 9am-5:15pm, Sat. 9am-2pm) for budget tour information. National bus companies provide regular service to and from Adelaide at prices that generally beat rail travel. **Greyhound Pioneer** (tel. 13 20 30) or **McCafferty's** (tel. 13 14 99) can take you to Alice Springs (20hr., $135-150), Melbourne (10hr., $45-55), Perth (34 hr., $190-200) or Sydney (22hr., $80-95), as well as nearly anywhere else you'd like to go. **Firefly Express** (tel. 8231 1488) offers good fares to Melbourne and Sydney. In addition, a handful of bus companies give good rates to destinations within South Australia. **Premier Stateliner** (tel. 8415 5500 or 8415 5555) services routes north toward Port Augusta, the Flinders Ranges, and the outback. **Bonds** services routes south of Adelaide toward Mount Gambier. **Wayward Bus** (tel. 8232 6646) offers tour packages to Melbourne (3 days, $160) and to Alice Springs (8 days, $600). Ask about student discounts for each company.

By Train

All interstate and local trains depart from the **Adelaide Rail Passenger Terminal** (tel. 13 22 32), in Keswick. It's usually not as economical as bus travel, but student fares can make train travel a good way to see the outback. Adelaide is serviced by the *Overland Train* to Melbourne (1 per day, 12hr., $50), the *Ghan* to Alice Springs (1-2 per week, 21hr., $140), the *Indian Pacific* to Perth (2 per week, 36hr., $200), and the *Speedlink* (mixture of train and bus travel) to Sydney (1 per day; 19hr., $99). Make bookings through the Keswick terminal.

ORIENTATION

Adelaide is built on a coastal plain nestled between Gulf Vincent on the west and the Adelaide Hills to the northeast. Adelaide's grid-like plan and surrounding **parklands** make it easy to navigate on foot or by public transportation. Most of the major tourist attractions, cultural centers, and restaurants are within easy walking distance of each other. Girdling the city on all four sides are the **four terraces,** creatively named North, South, East, and West. The streets running east to west are set out in a perfect grid, but are separated by **King William St.,** a north-south thoroughfare, at which point their names change (Flinders becomes Franklin St., for example). Streets running north to south retain their names, and are divided only by the four smaller squares and by **Victoria Square** in the very center of the city.

Although Adelaide is a relatively peaceful city, it is not safe to walk through parkland areas at night, especially those near the River Torrens and along the southwest corner of the city.

GETTING AROUND

By Public Transportation

Adelaide is serviced by public buses, trains, and one lone tram (in Glenelg) that make up an integrated public transport system called **Trans Adelaide.** A unique feature of Adelaide's public transport system is the **O-Bahn busway**—a bus that runs on concrete tracks from Adelaide city through beautiful parkland areas to the Tea Tree Plaza shopping center. All suburban trains depart from the **Adelaide Railway Station** (tel. 8210 1000) on North Terrace.

For general inquiries or ticket and timetable information, stop into the **Passenger Transport Information Centre** (tel. 8210 1000) at the corner of King William and Currie St. Tickets can be purchased when boarding buses but must be purchased *prior* to getting on trains. They can also be purchased at most delis, newsagents, post offices, and at the central train station. **Daytrip tickets** ($5.10) allow unlimited travel for the day. **Single tickets** used during the off-peak hours of 9am to 3pm cost $1.60, at other times $2.70, and are good for two hours from the time of validation. You must validate your ticket each time you enter a new bus or train. An option for those staying longer is the **Multitrip ticket,** good for 10 two-hour trips, which must be purchased prior to boarding ($17, off-peak only $10.60).

The **Beeline** is a free bus service operating in the city center. Catch it outside the Adelaide railway station on North Terrace or as it makes its way down King William St. to Victoria Square, before circling back around to the train station. (Runs Mon.-Thurs. every 5min. 9am-6pm, Fri. every 15min. 9am-7pm, Sat. every 15min. 8am-5pm, Sun. no service.) Another free bus service is the **Loop,** which, true to its name, makes a loop that stops at most of the major tourist attractions. Catch it at any point along its route (it runs along the North, East, and West Terraces, but only goes south as far as Grote and Wakefield St.). The Loop buses lower to almost curb height to allow passengers to disembark. All Loop buses are wheelchair accessible.

The best way to get to **Glenelg** if you are based in Adelaide City is to take the tram from Victoria Square. The ride takes approximately 25 minutes and the trams leave about every 15 minutes. Tickets can be purchased on board and use the same system as Adelaide's trains and buses.

By Car

The **Royal Automobile Association (RAA),** 41 Hindmarsh Sq. (tel. 8202 4500), provides members with full roadside assistance, extensive road maps, a travel agency, and information on travel and the rules of the road within South Australia (open Mon.-Fri. 8:30am-5pm, Sat.-Sun. 9am-noon). Overseas travelers with autoclub membership may be able to use RAA services (see **Getting Around By Car,** p. 37).

Some of the cheaper rental companies include **Action Rent-a-Car** (tel. 8352 7044), **Delta** (tel. 13 13 90), and **Rent-a-Bug** (tel. 8234 0655). Major companies such as **Hertz** (tel. 13 30 39) and **Avis** (tel. 8410 5727) have branches at the airport. On a fine day, Maandini will obligingly give guests a ride through the Adelaide Hills in one of his two Le Mans Racing Cars.

By Taxi

Taxis are not usually a good budget option, but when trains and buses stop running around midnight, they may become the only option. Some companies include **Adelaide Independent** (tel. 8234 6000), **Des's Cabs** (tel. 13 13 23), **Suburban** (tel. 8211 8888), and **Access Cabs** (wheelchair taxis) (tel. 8234 6444).

By Bicycle

Many of the city streets are fairly flat and have designated cycling lanes. More scenic bike tracks include the **Linear Park Bike and Walking Track.** This 40km track provides the biking enthusiast with beachside breezes and river views in the beautiful Adelaide foothills. Further information can be found at bike rental establishments including **Linear Park Mountain Hire** (tel. 8223 6953), **Freewheelin** (tel. 8232 6860), and **Mountain Bike Hire** (tel. 8212 7800). Rental starts at $15 to 20 a day; weekly rental is usually discounted. Some hostels also rent bikes to guests. Much of the shore in Glenelg has bike tracks; hire bikes from **Holdfast Cycles,** 768 Anzac Hwy., Glenelg (tel. 8294 4537).

PRACTICAL INFORMATION

Tourist Offices: South Australian Tourism Commission Travel Centre, 1 King William St. (tel. 8303 2070, bookings 8303 2033; email SthAusTour@Tourism.sa.gov.au; http://www.tourism.sa.gov.au), directly across from Parliament House and a 2min. walk up North Tce. from the central railway station. Go, go, go to this office. Well-informed, multilingual staff can advise on numerous tours, sights, and activities. Bookings cannot be made on weekends or holidays. Wheelchair accessible. Open Mon. and Wed.-Fri. 8:45am-5pm, Tues. 9am-5pm, Sat.-Sun. and holidays 9am-2pm. **State Information Centre,** 77 Grenfell St. (tel. 8204 1900), is a gold mine of info on state history and government, Aboriginal history, and general tourist interests. Not a booking office for tours. The building also houses the **National Parks Information Centre** (tel. 8204 1910). **Flinders Ranges and Outback South Australia Tourism,** 56B Glen Osmond Rd., Parkside, Adelaide (tel. 8373 3432 or 1800 633 060; http://www.outback.aus.com), offers the most complete information for those headed to northern South Australia. Open Mon.-Fri. 9am-5pm. The small **Glenelg Tourist Office** can be found to the right of the jetty (as you face the water), situated within the Sandbank delicatessen and cafe.

Consulate: U.K. (tel. 8212 7280).

Money: Thomas Cook Travel Agencies, 45 Grenfell St. (tel. 8212 3354), offers **currency exchange.** The main offices of Australia's largest banks are found along King William St., between North Tce. and Victoria Sq. These include the **National Australia Bank,** 22 King William St. (tel. 13 22 65), **Commonwealth Bank,** 96 King William St. (tel. 13 22 21), **ANZ,** 81 King William St. (tel. 13 13 14), **Bank of South Australia,** 97 King William St. (tel. 13 13 76), and **Westpac,** 2 King William St. (tel. 8210 3311). Banks open Mon.-Thurs. 9:30am-4pm, Fri. 9:30am-5pm. **ATMs** are found throughout the city. Cirrus is the main network. Nearly all shops and services also offer EFTPOS (debit card) service.

American Express: (tel. 8212 7099) on Grenfell St. Open Mon.-Fri. 8:30am-5:30pm, Sat. 9am-noon. Call to report loss of cards (tel. 1800 230 100) or checks (tel. 1800 251 902). In emergencies, call 1800 644 379.

Maps: Mapland, 282 Richmond Rd., Netley (tel. 8226 4946), **The Map Shop,** 16A Peel St. (tel. 8231 2033), along with the **RAA** (see **Getting Around,** above).

Bookstores: Europa bookshop, 238 Rundle St. (tel. 8223 2289), for foreign language and travel books; **Unibooks** (tel. 8223 4366) university bookstore, on Victoria Drive just as you enter Adelaide University; **Murphy Sister's Bookshop,** 240 The Parade, Norwood (tel. 8332 7508), specializing in feminist and lesbian writing.

Library: The State Library of South Australia (tel. 8207 7200), at the corner of Kintore Ave. and North Tce.

Ticket Agencies: Bass Bookings (tel. 13 12 46). 24-hr. info line tel. 0055 3330.

Hotlines: Women's Information Switchboard (tel. 8223 1244). **Disability Information and Resource Centre,** 195 Gillies St. (tel. 8223 7522). **Gayline** (tel. 8362 3223 or 1800 182 232).

Medical Assistance: Crisis Care Service (tel. 8272 1222). **Emergency Medical Service** (tel. 8223 0230, 8445 0230, or 8275 9911). **Emergency Dental Service** (tel. 8272 8111; open nightly 5-9pm, Sat.-Sun. also 9am-9pm). **Poison Information Center** (tel. 8267 4999).

Emergency: Dial 000.

Police Station: 1 Angas St. Main switchboard (tel. 8207 5000).

Post Office: General Post Office (GPO), at the corner of King William and Franklin St. Open Mon.-Fri. 8am-6pm, Sat. 8:30am-noon. Another post office at the eastern end of Rundle Mall in Shop 18 "Citi" Centre. Open Mon.-Fri. 8am-6pm, Sat 8:30am-noon. **Postal code:** 5000.

Phone Code: 08.

ACCOMMODATIONS

If you are visiting predominantly to soak up the sun and venture along South Australia's coastline, consider basing yourself in **Glenelg,** a tram ride from the city center. Two excellent Glenelg hostels are listed after Adelaide's offerings below. If you are in Adelaide to see the city sights, sample the food and wine selection, or delve into the thriving cultural life, however, a locale in the **city center** is your best bet.

Most hostels are in the southeast corner of the city or are a short walk from the Franklin St. bus depot, and nearly all of them can be accessed from the airport (by the Airport to City Bus) or from the Keswick railway station. Those that are distant from the bus station are best reached by public transport or by arranging pick-up in advance. Book ahead, especially in summer and during the Adelaide Festival. All of the listed hostels have self-catering kitchens, free tea and coffee, and 24-hour access.

Pricier options include bed and breakfasts or motels in **North Adelaide.** This district is only a 10-minute walk from the city along Frome Rd. An additional resource is the **South Australian Short Holidays** book, available at the South Australian Tourism Commission Travel Centre. Adelaide has some beautiful heritage buildings which have been converted into B&Bs.

YHA Hostel, 290 Gillies St. (tel. 8223 6007; fax 8223 2888). Facing the street in front of the bus station, turn right and walk up Franklin St. until you reach King William St. Turn right again, walk down King William St. through Victoria Sq., and turn left onto Gillies St. (25min.). Or take bus #171 or 172 from King William St. to the corner of Hutt and Halifax St. Gillies is the next street up from Halifax. If you book in advance, pick-up from the bus station can be arranged. A lovely, clean, and affordable hostel close to the city center and a 10min. walk from Hutt St. A/C, linen. Dorms $15.50, with YHA $12.50. Try to book ahead, especially Dec.-March.

East Park Lodge, 341 Angas St. (tel. 8223 1228; fax 8223 7772; email eastpark@microtronics.com.au). Follow the YHA Hostel directions to Victoria Sq., and then turn left onto Angas St. Pick-up from the bus station can be arranged. This beautiful building is close to some of Adelaide's oldest and most coveted residences on East Terrace. The rooftop offers a fantastic 360° view of the city and in summer months doubles as a recreation area. A/C, heating, linen supplied, laundry. Dorms $13; doubles $19 per person. VIP, YHA. The owners sponsor $6 curry dinner night.

Adelaide Backpacker's Inn, 112 Carrington St. (tel. 8223 6635; fax 8232 5464; email abackinn@tne.net.au; http://www.tne.net.au/abackinn). Follow the YHA Hostel directions to Victoria Sq., and then turn left onto Carrington St. The annex across the street is newer and more comfortable than the old main building. Extremely amiable owners serve apple pie and ice cream on a nightly basis. A/C, heating, linen supplied, laundry. Dorms $15; singles $25; doubles $40. VIP, YHA.

Adelaide Backpackers Hostel, 263 Gillies St. (tel. 8223 5680, reservations only 1800 677 351). Down the street from the YHA hostel. If you book in advance, pick-up from the bus station can be arranged. This is the oldest hostel in Adelaide, and although some of the furniture bears witness to this fact, the smiling proprietor and fruit trees in the yard make this as close to home as you'll get in Adelaide. A/C, heating, no laundry (one on closest corner). Dorms $12; doubles $28.

Adelaide Rucksackers, 257 Gillies St. (tel. 8232 0823), right next door to Adelaide Backpackers. With extensive (and multilingual) biking and bike hiring information, owner Margaret sends her guests off well-prepared to cycle for days. This restored Victorian villa is clean and well-kept. Heating (in some rooms only), no laundry (one on closest corner). Dorms $10-12 in summer; $9 in winter. Showers 20¢ for 5min.

YMCA, 76 Flinders St. (tel. 8223 6007). From the bus station, head down Franklin St. toward the city. After crossing King William, Franklin becomes Flinders St. Clean and well-priced, if slightly austere. In a central location, just a 10min. walk from the East End, Rundle Mall, Victoria Sq., and the Central Markets. A/C, heating, linen supplied, laundry. No wheelchair access. Dorms $12; singles $20; doubles $32. YMCA members get a 10% discount. Gym access $2.50.

Backpack Australia, 128 Grote St. (tel. 8231 0639 or 1800 804 133; fax 8410 5881). From bus station stand facing Franklin St., turn left onto Morphett, walk down 1 street to Grote and turn left again. This is very much a partier's hostel. The sociable owner loves arranging parties for guests and conveniently owns the pub next door. All the hubbub has put some wear-and-tear on the rooms and furniture. Breakfast included, other meals cheap. A/C, heating, linen supplied, laundry, rooftop area for recreation activities. Smoking is allowed. Dorms $11; doubles $30.

Sunny's, 139 Franklin St. (tel. 8231 2430 or 1800 631 391; fax 8231 0131). Located next to the bus station. Friendly, well-run, and clean. A/C, heating, linen supplied, laundry. Dorms $12; twins $28. Breakfast included.

Princess Lodge Motel, 73 Lefevre Tce., North Adelaide (tel. 8267 2266; fax 8239 0787). You will probably need to catch a taxi from the bus station. Although more expensive than the hostels, it is a pleasant option, especially if you are savvy enough to book in advance. Situated in Adelaide's beautiful North Adelaide, the view is great and the beds comfortable. 5min. from the restaurants of Melbourne St. Singles $30; doubles $48. Continental breakfast included.

Camping: Adelaide Caravan Park (tel. 8363 1566) on Bruny St. in Hackney, 2km east of the city. Tent sites from $18. **Windsor Gardens Caravan Park,** 78 Winsdor Grove, Windsor Gardens (tel. 8261 1091). Tent sites from $12.

Glenelg

Albert Hall, 16 South Esplanade (tel. 8376 0488, for bookings 1800 060 488; fax 8295 2397). As you face the jetty, turn left and walk along the South Esplanade between the Grand Hotel and the beachfront. 5min. on, a mansion appears on your left. This, ladies and gentlemen, is your hostel. Complete with marble bathrooms, a ballroom, and an unrivaled beachside view, this is the place to live cheap and feel like a million bucks. Limited wheelchair access, kitchen facilities, safe for valuables, laundry, free pick-up and drop off at the airport, bus and train station. Dorms $13, with balcony $14 (book ahead for these—it's worth it); doubles $34. In winter, weekly rates: dorms $70; singles $90; doubles $160.

Glenelg Backpackers Resort, 1-7 Mosely St. (tel. 1800 066 422). Mosely St. is up 1 block from the shore on your right as you walk away from the beach. This is an excellent hostel with a licensed bar, pool table, cafe, spa, and games room. Kitchen facilities, laundry, mountain bikes, free breakfast, and free pick-up and drop off at airport, and bus and train stations. 105 beds available, but all are twin beds (no bunkbeds). Dorms $14; singles $20; doubles $32. VIP, YHA. During the winter, inquire about low fees for extended stays.

FOOD

Adelaide has more restaurants per capita than any other city in the country. There are two major restaurant areas in the city center, each with its own distinctive flair. **Gouger Street,** located in the center of the city, near Victoria Sq., is a haven for those who enjoy good, reasonably priced ethnic cuisine. **Rundle Street,** in the northeast section of the city, caters more to the young bohemian crowd. Here, students forgo lectures in nearby Adelaide University in favor of strong cups of espresso. Finally, if you end up hungry in the beach suburb of Glenelg, we offer a short guide to beach fare below. Barbara Santich's *Apples to Zampone,* published by Wakefield Press and found in most major bookstores in the city, is a good guide to Adelaide's restaurants.

If you want something a little less formal, the bakeries, pie carts, and fish and chip shops found around Adelaide are a great alternative. Most meat-based morsels can be found in a vegetarian form as well. For a real Aussie experience, try a late-night snack at the **"Pie Cart"** outside of the Adelaide Train Station. The various **food halls** along Rundle Mall and at Hawker's Corner (at the corner of Wright St.) are also good for cheap and filling lunches. The infamous **pie floater**—an Aussie meat pie swimming amid a thick pea soup and topped off with a generous dollop of tomato sauce—is a South Australian original and one such budget bite. If put off by the appearance, try it with your eyes closed, but you shouldn't leave Adelaide without at least giving it a go.

West Terrace provides an excellent Asian Food Court open for lunch and dinner Monday through Saturday. **Perryman's Bakery,** 54 Tyne St., North Adelaide (tel. 8267 2766), is one of the city's best. It's the home of great pasties and "penny pies," originally made in 1930 to sell to the nearby North Adelaide primary school kids (open Mon.-Fri. 8:30am-5:30pm, Sat. 8:30am-12:15pm).

Gouger Street

Gouger St., minutes from Victoria Sq. in the center of the city, houses the Central Market. During the day, Gouger St.'s restaurants and cafes fill with lawyers and businessmen on lunch, but on market days and at night the street turns into a bustling, cosmopolitan center, where a wonderful array of **ethnic cuisine** awaits. Korean, Malaysian, Japanese, Mongolian, and Chinese cuisines are all represented, along with traditional and not-so-traditional Australian fare. Daytime meals tend to be cheaper, especially at the restaurants within the market itself.

In the northeast center of the market, try **Malacca Corner** (tel. 8231 5650) for good Malaysian fare. In the southwest, **Zuma's Cafe** (tel. 8231 4410) makes a great latte and many other delicious morsels, and **The Big Table** (tel. 8212 3899) serves a generous salad for $5. If you're feeling peckish, don't forget about the market's numerous bakeries. One of the best is **Fresh and Crusty** (tel. 8231 8999) in the Market Plaza section of the market hub. More formal Gouger St. restaurants include:

Matsuri, 167 Gouger St. (tel. 8231 3494). Although Japanese is not often a first choice for budget food, if you can catch this restaurant during one of its Sushi Festivals you'll enjoy a fabulous meal at half-price. Open Mon.-Fri. 5:30-10pm, Sat.-Sun. 5:30-10:30pm.

George's Seafood Restaurant, 113-115 Gouger St. (tel. 8231 4449). Seafood is not cheap anywhere, but here prices are within reason and helpings are plentiful enough to share comfortably. By blending down-to-earth hospitality with world-class cuisine, George's has retained a family ambience that has been lost in many of Gouger St.'s classier restaurants. Open for lunch and dinner.

Noodles, 119 Gouger St. (tel. 8231 8177), serves exactly that: noodles in every shape, form, and color. Big servings of spicy noodles at lunch and dinner at very reasonable prices. A good number of vegetarian options as well.

Rundle Street

Rundle St. flows neatly on from Rundle Mall (going east, out of the city). It is *the* place to be in Adelaide, day or night, and offers an incredible range of restaurants, cafes, pubs, and holes-in-the-wall to choose from. In summer, crowds fill overflowing cafes well into the wee hours. As an opportunity for a good meal which won't break the budget, it is unparalleled.

Vego and Lovin It!, 240 Rundle St. (tel. 8223 7411). Just past Mindfield bookstore and hidden up a narrow set of stairs on the 2nd floor. Listen for strains of Bing Crosby and watch for 50s tackorama decor. A huge range of vegan and vegetarian food, large portions, and delicious concoctions make this an extremely popular daytime eating spot. All ingredients are fresh each day, from the organic vegetables to the home-baked bread. The veggieburgers, entrees, sandwiches, and desserts are original and plentiful. Main dishes $5-7. Open Mon.-Fri. 10am-5pm.

Al Fresco's, 260 Rundle St. (tel. 8223 4589). An Adelaide landmark since it opened 20 years ago, Al Fresco's is the prototype to which all other Italian cafes in Adelaide pay homage. Serves a tempting range of Italian cakes and some of the best gelato in the city. Pick up a light Italian meal in minutes or linger over a latte for hours, and nobody will trouble you. Long hours make it a good option when the rest of the city begins to snooze. Open every day, all day, and well into the night.

Scoozi, 272 Rundle St. (tel. 8232 4733). If you can put it on bread, Scoozi will put it on mouth-watering foccacia in minutes. Tempting "designer pizza" (kangaroo meat and provolone anyone?), a huge selection of antipasto, and a daunting display of cakes. Scoozi provides good food and coffee with great flair and buzzing atmosphere. Foccacia $5, pasta $8-10. Open all day and much of the night.

Glenelg

There is no shortage of food at the bay, but many of the beachside cafes are expensive. For an authentic day at the beach head for a local fish and chippery or a yiros (gyros) and falafel stand, along the shore. Since all fish and chips are not created equal, walk down Jetty Rd. toward the city to **Glenelg Seafoods,** 91 Jetty Rd. for the cream of the crop. A yummy selection of Aussie baked goods can be found at **Vanderman's Homemade Cakes,** 39 Jetty Rd. Here you can still buy authentic finger buns, lamingtons, and those hard-to-find green frog sponge cakes.

SIGHTS AND ACTIVITIES

Visitors to Adelaide are encouraged to indulge all of their sight-seeing cravings, from historical buildings and peaceful parks to summer festivals and outdoor adventures. Many of Adelaide's sights and museums are located along **North Terrace,** the city's cultural boulevard. Starting at the east end, you'll pass the Botanic Gardens, the University of Adelaide, the Art Gallery, the Museum, the Central Public Library, the War Memorial, Government House, Parliament House, and Old Parliament House before finally ending up at Adelaide's historic railway station. A two-minute walk down King William St. from its intersection with North Tce. at Parliament House will bring you to the **Festival Centre.** Situated on the Torrens River, this is the focus of Adelaide's cultural life, especially during the **Adelaide Festival,** held in even-numbered years in late February or early March. Throughout the summer it holds fairs, outdoor theater events, and concerts, the majority of which are free and open to the public. Pick up a calendar of events from inside the Festival Centre complex.

For guided exploration of the area, the **Adelaide Explorer,** a tram-replica bus, does a city-Glenelg touring run that takes two and a half hours. Books and pamphlets outlining self-guided walking tours can be found at the SA Tourism Commission Travel Centre. **Wirra Mai** (tel. 8281 3393) runs Aboriginal Cultural Tours.

If you want more water action and don't mind fighting the crowds, you may enjoy **Magic Mountain,** based in **Glenelg.** The water park is to the right of the jetty as you face the ocean. Water slides, bumper boats, and a variety of non-water parlor games are available. This place can be a zoo during school holiday periods and peak summer months. (Open in summer Mon.-Fri. 9am-9pm, Sat.-Sun. 9am-late; winter Mon.-Fri. 10am-5pm, Sat.-Sun. 9am-10pm.) During the summer, the smooth surf of Glenelg's Holdfast Bay is also a great spot to try your hand at **parasailing** (tel. 0411 191 653).

Gardens

Adelaide Botanic Gardens, (tel. 8228 2311) North Tce., include many heritage buildings, and house the oldest greenhouse in Australia. The gardens are the perfect spot for a leisurely picnic lunch of Adelaide's best cheese and wine purchased from the East End Markets, only a minute's walk away. Open Mon.-Fri. 8am-sunset, Sat.-Sun. and holidays 9am-sunset.

Zoological Gardens (tel. 8267 3255) Frome Rd. A zoo in the middle of the city, 5min. from the University and the major city shopping district. Situated in the northern Parkland area and easily incorporated into a day's excursion of the Botanic Gardens. Admission $9.50, concessions $7.50, ages 4-14 $4.50. Open daily 9:30am-5pm.

Bicentennial Conservatory (tel. 8228 2311) North Tce. (enter at the Botanic Gardens and follow the signs). This tropical glass house shaped like an overgrown garden slug has a computer-controlled atmosphere that simulates a tropical rainforest. Open daily 10am-4pm. Admission $2.50, concessions $1.25, families $6.

Heritage Buildings

Even as the elegance of times past is abandoned in favor of the avant-garde scene in Rundle St. and the all-night raves on Hindley, some people in Adelaide are dedicated to preserving the dignified demeanor of the city's past. Heritage buildings are no longer allowed to be torn down in the city center and many have been restored to their former glory. Some are open to the public, though hours can be limited.

Old Adelaide Gaol (Jail), 18 Gaol Rd., Thebarton (tel. 8231 4062). Between 1841 and 1988, 49 people were executed here. Self-guided tours (with audio tape) Mon.-Fri. Volunteer guides give detailed historical tours of the jail every half hour on Sun. Open Mon.-Fri. 11am-4pm, Sun. and selected public holidays 11am-3:30pm. Admission $5 (Sun. $6), concessions $4, children $3, families $15.

Carrick Hill, 46 Carrick Hill Dr., Springfield (tel. 8379 3886). Situated in the leafy greens of Springfield, this house is built in the style of an English country manor and is surrounded by stunning gardens on 30 hectares of land. It was bequeathed to South Australia by Sir Edward Hayward and his wife, Ursula. The house was imported in its entirety from an estate in the U.K., piece by painstaking piece, in order to satisfy Sir Hayward's bride. Tours of the house operate at 11am, noon, 2, and 3pm. Open Wed.-Sun. and holidays 10am-5pm.

Ayers House, 288 North Tce. (tel. 8223 1234). Originally built in 1846 as a simple cottage, Sir Henry Ayers (after whom Ayers' Rock is named) then leased the house and made extensions to it in 1858. Served as a government events function center during Ayers' premiership of the state, and later as a nurses' quarters for the Royal Adelaide Hospital. Each of the enormous chandeliers weighs in at close to half a ton. Open Tues.-Fri. 10am-4pm, Sat.-Sun. 1-4pm. Admission $5, concessions $3.

Beaumont House, 631 Glynburn Rd., Beaumont (tel. 8379 5301). Built around 1850, the glory of the estate is its vast grounds, complete with olive groves and gardens. Admission $4, children $2. Open the first Sun. of every month 2-4:30pm.

Cummins Historical House (tel. 8294 1939), Sheoak Ave., Novar Gardens. Home to John Morphett, a surveyor, witness to the proclamation of the state in 1836, speaker, president of the Legislative Council, and knight. Open the 1st and 3rd Sun. of each month 2-4.30pm. $2.50 to walk through, but $5 admission includes Devonshire tea and scones.

MUSEUMS

South Australian Museum, North Tce. (tel. 8207 7500). Contains a comprehensive collection of Aboriginal artifacts. Most of the exhibitions are concerned with South Australian history—both indigenous and post-white settlement. The shop regularly features the works of local artists. In summer, the lawn outside the museum is a great spot to relax and get some sun. Watch out for the schoolchildren playing in the fountain or you may end up soaked. Open daily 10am-5pm.

Art Gallery of South Australia, North Tce. (tel. 8207 7000). The gallery showcases Australian, Asian, and European prints, paintings, sculpture, and decorative arts. It boasts an especially good collection of Australian and South Australian 20th-century art, along with strong visiting exhibits. Open daily 10am-5pm.

The Jam Factory, Craft and Design Centre, 19 Morphett St. (tel. 8410 0727). The Jam Factory is part craft shop, part artist's studio, and part shop for some of the best local and interstate crafts. During opening hours, activity in the glass studio can be observed in the factory itself. The artwork is distinctly South Australian, with colors that reflect the changing hues of the local landscape. Many of the products made by local artists are available for sale. Open Mon.-Fri. 9am-5:30pm, Sat.-Sun.10am-5pm.

Tandanya-National Aboriginal Cultural Institute, 253 Grenfell St. (tel. 8223 2467). This is the first major Aboriginal multi-arts complex in Australia and a good place to begin your education in South Australian and Australian indigenous culture. Exhibitions of art by Aboriginal artists change every 6 weeks. The gift shop stocks a broad range of Aboriginal arts and crafts. Tandanya runs guided tours of the exhibitions and, by appointment, Aboriginal guides give introductory talks on various aspects of indigenous heritage and culture. It is advisable to book ahead, although the management may let you tag along with tours in progress. Open daily 10am-5pm. Admission $4, concessions $3.

South Australian Maritime Museum, 126 Lipson St., Port Adelaide (tel. 8240 0200). This museum is spread over a number of sites at Port Adelaide, including old Bond Stores (1850s), an 1869 lighthouse, museum wharf, and historic vessels. Open Tues.-Sun. 10am-5pm. Admission $8, students $5, families $18.

Migration Museum (tel. 8207 7580) on Kintore Ave. The Migration Museum combines history, biography, and oral testimony to give a multifaceted insight into the patterns of immigration that have shaped South Australian society. Free 1hr. guided tours $4.50, 6-person min. All tours must be booked. Wheelchair access. Open Mon.-Fri. 10am-5pm, Sat.-Sun. and holidays 1-5pm.

The Investigator Science and Technology Centre (tel. 8410 1115) on Rose Tce., Wayville. Interactive exhibits ensure that even the most unscientifically-inclined mind can learn something and have fun in the Investigator. Open daily 10am-5pm. Admission $7.50, concessions $6, ages 4-17 $5.

H.M.S. Buffalo (tel. 8294 7000) along the Patawalonga, near Wigley Reserve in Glenelg. This complete reconstruction of the original sailboat that brought the first colonists to South Australia's Holdfast Bay is now a free museum and seafood restaurant. Small fee for the oral history presentation.

MARKETS

Central Markets (tel. 8203 7345), between Gouger and Grote St. The largest enclosed fresh produce market in the Southern hemisphere, with more than 250 stalls. The market has a bustling, cosmopolitan atmosphere and some of the best budget cuisine in Australia. Some of the delicacies include pickled squid, taramasaltata, German breads and pastries, fresh pasta, local nuts, dried fruits, and of course, fairy floss (the Aussie version of cotton candy). The market also contains a superb variety of inexpensive cafes and restaurants. If you go near closing time, you'll find the market at its loudest and best, and you can pick up bags of veggies for a dollar and rolls, breads, and pastries at half-price. Parking available. Open Tues. 7am-5:30pm, Thurs. 11am-5:30pm, Fri. 7am-9pm, Sat. 7am-5pm.

East End Markets (tel. 8232 5606), Rundle St. East. All that is funky in Adelaide usually ends up for sale in the 200 stalls here. Clothing, ceramics, jewelry, leather goods, and plants at good prices if you shop around. There's also an extensive produce market and a cinema complex. 2hr. free parking in carpark opposite. Open Fri.-Sun. and most holidays 9am-6pm.

Orange Lane Markets (tel. 8414 1346), Orange Ln., Norwood. These markets sell everything from food to plants, books to antiques, and crystals to curry. A mecca for the New Age, Orange Ln. is a great spot to witness Adelaide's version of the spirit of the 60s. Some bargain gifts can be found, and the retro clothing calls up images of *Priscilla, Queen of the Desert* meets *Picnic at Hanging Rock.* Once there, take a stroll down Norwood Parade for its good retail shopping outlets, Italian cafes, and excellent bakeries. Open Sat.-Sun. and holidays 10am-5pm.

Brickworks, 36 South Rd., Torrensville, (tel. 8352 4822), refers to the markets centered in and around the old Brickworks kiln. A multitude of stalls and shops with pottery, new-age jewelry, clothing, bikes, ceramics, arts and crafts, and a pet shop. There is also a large fresh produce section, but the unique feature of the Brickworks are the go-carts, sideshows, and mini golf. Parking at rear off Ashwin Parade. Open Fri.-Sun. and holidays that fall on Mon. 9am-5pm.

Junction Markets (tel. 8349 4866), at the corner of Grand Junction and Prospect Rd., provide a great winter alternative, since they are in one large shed. Features mainly hardware, leather goods, and plants. There's also an international food hall and a large range of fresh produce. Live bands on Sat.-Sun. Open Fri.-Sun. and public holidays 9am-5pm.

Fisherman's Wharf Market (tel. 8341 2040) by the lighthouse, Port Adelaide. The market is contained within 5000 sq. m of a 1940s cargo shed. Linen, glass, bric-a-brac, arts and crafts, clothing, hardware, garden supplies, and old sheet music all at bargain prices. A wide range of food and refreshments. Open Sun. and holidays that fall on Mon. 8am-5pm.

Boomerang Arts and Crafts Centre, 716 Anzac Hwy., Glenelg (tel. and fax 8376 3921). Though not technically a market, this Glenelg gallery has a large selection of Aboriginal art, didgeridoos, and Australian opals.

NIGHTLIFE AND ENTERTAINMENT

Besides a thriving nightlife and gambling scene, Adelaide has some lovely old pubs for casual drinks, and new cinemas for movie buffs. To know what's on, pick up Thursday's *Advertiser,* which will include *The Guide.* Also, *Rip it Up* is free and available in cafes all along Rundle St. The *Adelaide Review* has some good nightlife information as well. *GT (Gay Times),* Adelaide's free gay newspaper, can be picked up at **BSharp Records** on Rundle St. or at the **Adelaide University Union** (in the North Tce. Uni Complex). *GT* provides information on gay and lesbian events and nightlife, lists of gay-friendly establishments, and articles on gay and lesbian issues.

Adelaide's two new alternative cinemas, both on Rundle St., are **The Palace** (tel. 8232 3434) and **NOVA** (tel. 8223 6333). The classic art house cinema is **The Track,** 375 Greenhill Rd. (tel. 8332 8020). **The Capri,** 141 Goodwood Rd. (tel. 8272 1177), and **The Piccadily,** O'Connell St. North Adelaide (tel. 8267 1500), have good offerings of both mainstream and alternative movies. The Capri also has a kitschy but wonderfully entertaining **Wurlitzer Organ recital,** complete with moving parts and a trap door (Tues., Fri., and Sat. night). Discounts apply at most theaters on Tuesdays.

Good pubs for a quiet beer include **The British,** 58 Finness St. North Adelaide (tel. 8267 2188), and **The Earl of Aberdeen,** Carrington St. at Hurtle Sq. (tel. 8223 6433). Both are woodsy, old-style pubs with a variety of beers on tap and good pub meals. Trendier pubs are **The Exeter** (tel. 8223 2623) and **The Austral** (tel. 8223 4660) (known affectionately by the locals as the "Excreter" and the "Nostril"). Both serve a colorful clientele and feature the up-and-coming pub bands on weekends. Call for cover charges. If you're feeling lucky, **The Casino,** Old Railway Building, North Tce. (tel. 8212 2811), provides gambling excitement and a place to hang out long after the rest of Adelaide is content to snooze. (Open Mon.-Fri. 10am-4am, Sat.-Sun. 24hr. Smart casual dress (collared shirt and jacket for men, no sneakers or denims) required.)

Clubs

Heaven II, at the New Market Hotel, provides a celestial vision of sorts, if your idea of an afterlife includes a hedonistic mixture of alcohol, dance music, and lycra. Filled with nubile 20-somethings, Heaven opens at 9pm on Fri. (cover $5) and Sat. (cover $8). If you want to go back for a second dose of nectar and ambrosia, become a member (you can apply at the door *and* it's free). Membership can get you great discounts on entry, drinks, and special offers.

Cargo Club, 213 Hindly St. (tel. 8231 2327). One of Adelaide's funkier clubs, the Cargo is a great spot for live music and hip decor. An interesting crowd swings between trendy and alternative with alarming regularity. Cover around $6. Doors open at 10pm.

The Big Ticket, 128 Hindly St. (tel. 8410 0109). Loud, packed, and lots of fun for a night of serious partying, dancing, and drinking.

The Planet, 77 Pine St. (tel. 8359 2797). House music and hundreds of tightly packed, writhing young bodies create all the atmosphere this hugely successful nightclub needs. An upstairs viewing area and downstairs lounge provide escape space. Cover $8.

Cue, 274 Rundle St., Level 1 (tel. 8223 6160). Directly next door to and upstairs from **Scuzzi** cafe, this club is home to Adelaide's "beautiful people." The bouncers are selective, so be warned—dress hip or don't even try. House music is usually playing, but the pinball machines and pool tables are still in use for those who don't feel confident enough to dance with the elect. No cover. Open Wed.-Sun. nights.

The Synagogue, 9 Synagogue Pl. (tel. 8223 4233), just off the Pultney St. end of Rundle St. It seems apt that a city so concerned with both the spiritual and the pleasurable should be home to a nightclub housed in the heritage-listed and once-Orthodox Jewish synagogue. When the Jewish community decided it was time for a newer, larger complex, marketers grabbed the opportunity to remodel the interior of this prime piece of real estate into a funky dance club and live music venue, complete with its own garish 10 commandments and other semitic symbols. Although the new owners tried mightily to change the name, Adeladians had known this building as "the synagogue" for far too long for it to be anything else. Open Thurs.-Sat. with varying cover.

The Mars Bar, 120 Gouger St. (tel. 8231 9636). Campy surrounds and aging queens make the Mars Bar a haven for rejects from *Priscilla: Queen of the Desert.* Drag nights on Fri. and Sat. A mix of straight and gay clientele. Good for a late night bop and a glimpse at this week's fashion *faux pas.*

Edinburgh Castle, 233 Currie St. (tel. 8410 1211). Mainly gay male clientele. Pub atmosphere, beer garden, and recently refurbished interior.

Bean's Bar, 258a Hindly St. (tel. 8231 9614). The mixed gay and lesbian clientele of this pokey little pub save it from being simply another "daggy Aussie pub." Women only Fri. 6:30-9:30pm. The pace picks up around 10:30pm on Sat. and Sun.

ADELAIDE HILLS

In a state where much of the terrain is unfriendly at best, the Adelaide Hills provide a haven of lush greenery, reminiscent of the land the settlers left behind in England. As you climb toward the Mt. Lofty summit, Adelaide's lights, coastline, and its green belts of parklands unfold below you, rendering apparent the brilliance of Colonel Light's vision. But don't just look down. Huge expanses of national parkland surround the peak, which is filled with all those crazy marsupials made famous by the Simpsons. Picturesque towns from a gentler, slower past break up the wilderness. Browse in the numerous arts and crafts stores, eat in the many family bakeries, take long, deep breaths of the fresh mountain air, and revel in the region's overwhelming sense of peace and relaxation.

GETTING THERE

Much of the Adelaide Hills is a 20- to 40-minute drive from the Adelaide city center. The main road through the Adelaide Hills is the South Eastern Freeway (Hwy. 1), and town exits are clearly marked. If you wish to take **public transportation,** bus #840 runs to Mt. Barker, #841 to Nairne, and #842 and 843 to Strathalbyn. These buses usually leave from the Adelaide Bus Terminal on Franklin St., but may switch to Currie St. Call 8210 1000 for updated departure information. Buses #163, 165, 166, and TL9 run daily from Currie St. to smaller towns in the area. Other ways to get to the hills include car hire or a day tour. The former is economical if you're traveling in a group, while the latter is generally cheaper for single travelers. **Tour Delights** (tel. 0411 470 094) has a variety of daytrip packages available. The region's main **information center** is in Hahndorf (tel. 8388 1185, see below); other tourist offices are located at Mt. Lofty's summit and in Strathylbyn.

ACCOMMODATIONS

Unfortunately, there is not a lot to be found in the way of budget accommodation in the Adelaide Hills. If you are planning on hiking in the hills, however, YHA maintains five **"limited access" hostels** along the **Heysen Trail.** They are located at Para Wirra, Norton Summit, Mt. Lofty, Mylor, and Kuitpo. Bookings must be made in advance at the YHA office, 32 Sturt St., Adelaide (tel. 8231 5583), where you will be given a key. Be warned: these hostels, though well-kept, only provide bare bones amenities (beds, kitchen, and bathrooms). Hikers must bring all bedding and food.

Fuzzies Farm, Colonial Dr., Norton Summit (tel. 8390 1111), caters to those who don't mind a few odd jobs and have always wanted to experience communal living in gorgeous, natural surroundings. A man named Fuzzy actually runs Fuzzies Farm (although its name predates him). For $10 a day (plus chores) you will be fed and lodged in lovely cabins overlooking the 3500 acres of beautiful bushland that make up **Morialta Conservation Park.** Regular backpacker accommodation (in handmade solid wood bunks) is also available for $12 a night, but this does not include food. The members of Fuzzies Farm see themselves as a service community and are actively involved in environmental and heritage issues, farming and management concerns, and the preservation of Aboriginal sacred sites. Book ahead.

SIGHTS AND ACTIVITIES

The biggest attraction in the Adelaide Hills is **Mt. Lofty (Urebilla),** visited by 500,000 people annually. Take the South Eastern Freeway out of the city, exit at Crafers, and follow the signs. The local Aboriginal people, the Kaurna, describe Mt. Lofty and Mt. Bonython as Jureidla—"the place of the two ears." According to their tradition, the mountains are the ears of Urebilla (a benevolent ancestral being slain in battle), whose body forms the Mt. Lofty Ranges. Urebilla's feet lie north toward Clare and his head points south toward Victor Harbor. His spirit gives life to all in the plains and valley below. The summit has spectacular views of the city, as well as an extensive **Information Centre** (tel. 8370 1054; http://www.denr.sa.gov.au/nrg/mtlofty) with detailed information about the surrounding bush area, and a restaurant-cafe (tel. 8339 2600). Mt. Lofty's original information center was destroyed in the 1983 Ash Wednesday Bushfires, and the new state-of-the-art center was just completed in 1997 (open Nov.-March 10am-6pm; April-Nov. 10am-4pm). The outdoor viewing plaza area is open 24 hours.

If you've ever had a penchant for a potoroo or a yen for a yellow-footed rock wallaby, but haven't wanted to go bush to see them, **Cleland Wildlife Park** (tel. 8339 2444 or 8339 2572) is the perfect compromise. Cleland is directly below the Mt. Lofty summit, and both can be experienced in an easy daytrip from Adelaide. The short walking trail can be competed in 1½ hours, and you can wander freely among kangaroos, koalas, wallabies, emus, and waterfowl along the way (open daily 9:30am-5pm; admission $7, students $6, children $4.50). **Night walks** (tel. 8339 2444) can be arranged as well, in order to view some of the rarer (and often endangered) species of wildlife. For a more intensive hiking experience, try the numerous trails through the broader Cleland conservation park area. Some, like the **Women's Pioneer Trail,** have local historical significance, while others, such as the **ETSA Spur Track,** are designed to display local flora and fauna.

For more adventurous types, **Warrawong Sanctuary** at Stock Rd., Mylor (tel. 8370 9422; fax 8370 8332), is famous for its guided dawn and sunset nature walks. Other area attractions include **Melba's Chocolate Factory,** on Henry St. in Woodside (tel. 8389 7868; fax 8389 7977). With free entry and free samples seven days per week, the factory is more popular than most industrial complexes. The **biggest rocking horse in the world** is hitched along the road in Gumeracha. The 60-ft.-high red and white wooden beast actually marks the spot for **The Toy Factory** (tel. 8389 1085), open daily. Artisans make gorgeous, hand-crafted wooden toys, and the view from the horse's head is actually worth the climb. A seven acre nature park surrounds the horse, and entrance is free.

Hahndorf A little bit of Bavaria in Adelaide's backyard, Hahndorf is proud of its German heritage and flaunts its origins. In 1839, a group of Prussian Lutherans fled the motherland to escape religious persecution and ended up here. Just 35 minutes southeast of Adelaide on the South Eastern Freeway, Hahndorf can be part of a larger day tour of the Adelaide Hills. The **Adelaide Hills Visitors Information Centre** is at 41 Main St. (tel. 8388 1185; fax 8388 1319).

The Cedars: Hans Heysen's House, Heysen Rd. (tel. 8388 7277) was the home of Australian artist Hans Heysen (1877-1963) and has been preserved in its original state. This landscape watercolor artist had the 1500km Heysen trail (and his own street, apparently) named after him. See where Hans ate, slept, and spilled paint as you tour his house, studio, and garden (open Mon.-Fri. and Sun; admission $5; tours at 11am, 1, and 3pm). Masterpieces of the future could be in progress at the **Hahndorf Academy,** 41 Main St. (tel. 8388 7250), next to the information center. The academy includes an art gallery, museum, and craft shop, and much of Heysen's own stunning collection, stolen in 1995, is now back on show (open Mon.-Sat. 10am-5pm, Sun. noon-5pm).

At **Beerenberg Strawberry Farm,** Mt. Barker Rd. (tel. 8388 7272; fax 8388 1108), half a kilometer through Hahndorf, you can pick your own strawberries in season

(Nov.-May) or let someone else do it while you view the farm kitchen. Jams, pickles, and other innovative strawberry ideas are all on sale in the farm shop (open Mon.-Fri.). For a live display of Aussie snakes, lizards, crocs, ants, scorpions, and eels, slither over to **Hoop's Reptiles,** 33 Main St. (tel./fax 8388 1477). Yeah, so ants are insects, scorpions are arachnids, and eels are fish; reptiles still reign at Hoop's (open daily 9am-5pm).

If the Hansel and Gretel atmosphere of the town has you longing for some gingerbread or hankering for a fine glass of German beer, you'll be pleased to find *gutes Essen* everywhere. Hahndorf won't let you forget where you are; almost every restaurant includes the word "German" in its name. For a budget-oriented meal, head straight for the various (German, of course) bakeries and small goods stores. One of the best is the **German Cake Shop,** 2 Pine Ave. (tel. 8388 7086). Try *Sacher Torte* for a sweet tooth, or *Sauerkraut* for something more substantial (open daily 8am-6pm).

Mt. Barker and Strathalbyn Both Mt. Barker and Strathalbyn are worth short visits, if only to browse in the local **arts and crafts shops** and view some of the lovely **heritage buildings** that lend character to these little settlements. But most importantly, Mt. Barker and Strathalbyn provide the back way into the Fleurieu Peninsula via car or the recently reconstructed *Southern Encounter* and *Cockle Train* **steam engines.** These vintage reproduction trains will spirit you away to the coastal towns of Goolwa and Victor Harbor (p. 388) or just shuttle you between Mt. Barker and Strathalbyn (bookings tel. 8391 1223; student fares available). Strathalbyn's **tourist information center** (tel. 8536 3212) is in the old railway station at 20 South Tce. (open Mon.-Fri. 9:30am-4pm, Sat. 10am-4pm, Sun. 11am-4pm).

FLEURIEU PENINSULA

The Kauma tell the story of Tjilbruke, who carried the body of his slain nephew down the coast to Cape Jervis from where the Adelaide suburb Marion now sits. Each time that Tjilbruke stopped along the way and wept for his nephew, a spring welled up from the ground. According to legend, these tears form the lush section of South Australia that stretches southeast from Adelaide, encompassing the hills and wineries of McLaren Vale. The Fleurieu Peninsula also boasts the small-town nature attractions of Victor Harbor and miles of coastline that includes some of the best beaches in South Australia.

The Fleurieu regional office for the **National Parks and Wildlife Service** (tel. 8552 3677; fax 8552 3950) is at 57 Ocean St. in Victor Harbor (open Mon.-Fri. 8:45am-5pm). If you're planning your trip in advance, the **Fleurieu Regional Booking Office** (tel. 1800 630 144) may be able to help. On dry, summer days, a complete fire ban may be in effect; call the **CFS Fire Ban Hotline** (tel. 1800 188 100). For medical trouble, dial the **Goolwa Medical Centre** (tel. 8555 2404), call an **ambulance** (tel. 8552 2111), or, as always, dial **000** in an **emergency.** For car trouble, contact the **RAA** (tel. 8555 2009). The **police** are at 8555 2018. When ringing South Australia from out of state, dial the prefix **08.**

McLaren Vale

Just 45 minutes south of Adelaide, McLaren Vale sits in the grassy inland knolls of the Fleurieu Peninsula. McLaren Vale is an idyllic, sleepy set of vineyards, where world-class wines are produced in a typically understated Australian manner. Over 45 area wineries, the majority of which are still family-owned, operate cellar door sales and grow and process their product meters from the front door. If you really love a good drop, buy a dozen, but if you're just an amateur, sip and smile in blissful ignorance, knowing full well that the best thing about wine tasting is that it's absolutely free.

ORIENTATION AND PRACTICAL INFORMATION

The best way to get to McLaren Vale is with a group of friends, a car, and a designated driver. Take the last part seriously, because the Australian police take drunk driving *extremely* seriously. It is not uncommon to find Random Breath Testing Units (commonly known as Breatho's) stationed on main roads to and from wine regions. That said, drive out of Adelaide on Main South Rd. After 20-30 minutes, follow the signs for McLaren Vale, which lead to Main Rd. After you pass a row of flags proudly proclaiming the best vineyards in the region, the **McLaren Vale and Fleurieu Visitor Centre** (tel. 8323 9455) will be directly to your left. Drop in, grab a map, and off you go. The **police station** (tel. 8323 8330) and the **post office** (no. 139) are also on Main Rd.

Geographically, McLaren Vale is just east of the coast as you head south on the Fleurieu Peninsula, between Port Stanvac and Aldinga Beach. The public transportation, **Premier Coachlines** (tel. 8415 5555), runs a daily bus service from Adelaide at 10am, 3:50, and 5:30pm ($5). If you take public transportation, though, getting around once in McLaren Vale will be a problem. A more practical way to avoid driving yourself is to take one of the numerous **tours** based in Adelaide. **Tour Delights** (tel. 0411 470 094) runs tours from Adelaide every Tuesday and Sunday. **Seat Vine Tours** (tel. 8384 5151) is another good option. Consult the South Australia tourist office in Adelaide for an extensive list. Day tours cost about $30.

ACCOMMODATIONS, FOOD, AND FESTIVALS

The majority of accommodations are old world heritage B&Bs at new world prices. Budget accommodations are limited to caravan parks, so you're best off making the region a daytrip from Adelaide. **Lakeside Caravan Park,** Field St. (tel. 8323 9255), offers basic on-site caravans with a separate block for toilets and showers. Each van sleeps two and is clean and comfortable, although it can be chilly in winter ($32).

The cheapest way to dine is to bring a picnic and buy a good drop at a picturesque winery. Most of the wineries have picnic grounds and some, like **Andrew Garrett,** offer tables as well. The other option is to try the great selection of bakeries. The folks at **McLaren Vale Bakery,** Main Rd., McLaren Vale Shopping Centre, won last year's National Pie Award for their Wine Pie. Other winners include the Lamb Piquant Pie and the Chicken Champagne Pie. If you are looking for a treat and are willing to splurge, any number of the gourmet restaurants in McLaren Vale would be happy to oblige. Try **d'Arry's Verandah Restaurant** on Osborn Rd. or **The Barn** (tel. 8323 8618) on Main Rd. Down the road, **Koffee & Snax** offers great cappuccino and honey logs with fresh cream for a mere $1.50. **Medlow Fine Gels and Chocolates,** off Kangarilla Rd. on Sand Rd. (tel. 8383 0030; fax 8383 0410), makes vegetable-based gels and chocolates and sells them directly from the factory floor. Free tastes serve to alleviate at least one of those painful decisions.

Although any time is a good time to visit the McLaren wineries, three annual festivals are particularly exciting. **McLaren Vale's Sea and Vines Festival** is held on the long holiday weekend in June (usually the first weekend), Sunday and Monday only. With seafood at $7 a plate and wine $3 a glass, this is a good deal for fine fare. The feast is complemented by live music at each of the participating wineries. On the Sunday and Monday of the long Labor Day weekend at the beginning of October, **The Continuous Picnic** comes to town. Park your car, hop on the shuttle bus that operates between the wineries, and join in an all-day feast of the best local produce and wines (food $7 a plate, wine $3 a glass). Finally, the **McLaren Vale Wine Bushing Festival** is held on the last weekend in October. Following the Elizabethan custom of placing ivy branches over wine merchants' doors to celebrate the arrival of the new season's wines, the Wine Bushing Festival marks the arrival of the region's new whites. Weekend organizers provide food, entertainment, arts and crafts, and a Sunday street fair complete with a 60-float parade.

WINERIES

Wirra Wirra Vineyards, McMurtrie Rd. (tel. 8323 8414; fax 8323 8596). When you see the fence made entirely from giant tree trunks you'll know you've arrived; once you've tasted the "Church Block Red," you may not wish to leave. Wirra Wirra has won numerous awards for both their reds and whites. If you prefer red make sure you taste their Cabernet Savignon—"The Angelus" (affectionately know as "Cab Sav"). For a dry white, try the Hand-Picked Riesling. The staff are as friendly as they are knowledgable and will make both the wine buff and the wine buffoon welcome.

Dennis of McLaren Vale, Kangarilla Rd. (tel. 8323 8665). Fancy a drop of hot spiced mead? Made with honey, scented with cloves, and warmed by the glass, this is a superb wine for those with a sweeter tooth. Make sure to fuss over Sophie, the super-friendly family dog, to ensure greater complimentary quantities of this delicious brew.

Marienberg Wines, 2 Chalk Hill Rd. (tel. 8323 9666; fax 8323 9600). The cottage that forms the nexus of this complex was built in 1854, and despite the fact that the additions now dwarf the original, the warmth and charm of the original stonework seems to permeate the whole. You can try over 40 of McLaren Vale's boutique wines at this center as well as a selection of Marienberg's own, including a classy 12-year-old Tawny Port.

Shottesbrooke Vineyards, Bagshaws Rd., off Kangarilla Rd. (tel. 8383 0002; fax 8383 0222). This is about as small and exclusive as a winery can get—1 family, 2 vineyards, and 4 wines. But what a *great* 4. Nick Holmes, the owner, aims for "big rich reds" and "luscious whites," and he gets what he aims for.

Noon's Winery, Rifle Range Rd. (tel./fax 8323 8290). Specializing in reds only, this is a great place for a BBQ (there are facilities), since the wines will compliment anything from your basic sanger (sausage) to kangaroo cutlets.

Richard Hamilton Wines, Willunga Rd., Willunga (tel. 8556 2288). A fine selection of reds and whites to choose from and a number of state and national prizes. Small, family-owned and run; the family cat loves a cuddle.

Andrew Garrett Wines, Kangarilla Rd. (tel. 8323 8853). One of the larger wineries with a broad selection of wines and an idyllic lake setting, complete with picnic tables and a flourishing troop of ducks, swans, and other varieties of bird life. **The Opal Gem Factory** is also situated on the premises.

Haselgrove Wines, off Chalk Hill Rd. (tel. 8323 8706). Haselgrove can finish off a good day's tasting with an intense Tawny Port. Strictly for port lovers—those who want a good Cab Sav should steer clear of this one.

■ Beaches West of McLaren Vale

In the summer months, the beaches west of McLaren Vale are not to be missed. To get to **Maslin Beach** (SA's only nudist beach) by car, take South Rd. out of the city. Turn onto Maslin Beach Rd. and follow that onto Gulf Pde.—parking is at the end of this road. To get to the southern end of the beach, turn left onto Eastview Rd. from Maslin Beach Rd. and right onto Tuit Rd. To get to **Moana Beach** by car, turn onto Griffiths Ave. from South Rd. For **Christie's Beach,** turn onto Beach Rd. from South Rd. and follow it until the end, or take the Esplanade from Noarlunga Beach. For **Port Noarlunga,** turn left onto Dyson Rd. from South Rd., then right onto Murray Rd. and left onto Saltfleet St. To hit the southern beaches via **public transportation,** take the **Noarlunga line train** from Adelaide Railway Station (North Tce.) to Noarlunga. Transfer to the #741 or 742 bus at the Noarlunga Interchange for Maslin Beach or Moana Beach. For Christie's Beach, transfer to bus #741 only. For Port Noarlunga, take bus #741, 742, or 745.

Victor Harbor

Sheltered from the immense Southern Ocean by the sands of Encounter Bay, the small seaside town of Victor Harbor is not totally sleepy but is hardly wide awake. After white settlement, South Australia's colonial governors chose Victor Harbor as their first summer residence. First a whaling port and later a shipping port for wool and farm produce, Victor Harbor (one of the few harbors in Australia spelled without a "u") is now a charming spot for a summer seaside frolic and the perfect place for contemplative winter weekends. Prior to white settlement, the bay, the bluff, and Granite Island had great spiritual importance for the local Ngarrindjeri.

Orientation and Practical Information Victor Harbor is 80km from Adelaide. By car, take Main South Rd. out of Adelaide and watch for signs to Victor Harbor. By bus, **Premier Roadlines** (tel. 8415 5555) provides daily service. *Southern Encounter,* the historic **steam train** running from Strathalbyn and between Goolwa and Victor Harbor is an alternative means of transport. Victor Harbor is small enough to navigate on foot, but the caves and beaches are easily accessible only by car. Most attractions are around Railway Tce., the Causeway, and Ocean St. **The Visitor Information Centre,** 10 Railway Tce. (behind the Grosvenor Hotel) is open daily from 10am to 4pm (with extended hours in Dec. and Jan.). The local **RAA** number is 8552 1033. For **police,** call 8552 2088. The **South Coast District Hospital** (tel. 8552 1066) and **Victor Harbor Medical Clinic** (tel. 8552 1444) are both right in town.

Accommodations and Food Budget accommodation in **Victor Harbor** is not easy to find. There are no hostels, but two of the hotels provide backpacker-style dorms. **Grosvenor Junction,** at the corner of Canal and Ocean St. (tel. 8552 1011; fax 8552 7274), offers lovely, clean rooms and is three blocks from the shore. The Grosvenor is primarily a hotel and pub but has some rooms set aside for backpackers. ($20 per person includes continental breakfast, linen, and hall bathroom. Book ahead, especially Dec.-Feb.) **The Anchorage,** at the corner of Coral St. and Flinders Pde. (tel. 8552 5970; fax 8552 1970), is right on the sea, and offers gorgeous views of the Southern Ocean. Also primarily a hotel and B&B, it does have a kitchen and rooms for backpackers ($15 without linen or breakfast; book ahead, especially Dec.-Feb.). **Victor Harbor Council Caravan Park** (tel. 8552 1142) on the beachfront off Victoria St., and **Adare Caravan Park** (tel. 8552 1657), off Ocean St., start at approximately $40 a night for a caravan for two people. Groups can hire a house or cottage through the **Fleurieu Booking Office** (tel. 1800 630 144).

A day at Victor Harbor is not complete without seafood of some kind. For those with less limited budgets, the hotels provide excellent seafood at reasonable prices. **The Original Fish n' Chip** shop on Ocean St. has top grade—surprise—fish and chips. The higher end of the scale is the **Hotel Victor** (tel. 8552 1288) on the seafront, by the causeway, and the lower end is the **Grosvenor** (tel. 8552 1011) on the corner of Coral and Ocean St.

Sights and Activities Little penguins win top billing on **Granite Island.** Entry onto this little island is free if you walk (a 20min. stroll from the causeway entrance) or $3 if you take the horse-drawn tram (complete with huge Clydesdales). At night, you can see the island's penguins by joining one of the **Little Penguin Sunset Walks** (tel. 8552 7555). The walks generally begin at sunset and start at the bridge entrance to the island. Call for times and bookings. Everything you could possibly want to know about whales can be learned at the **South Australian Whale Centre,** 2 Railway Tce. (open Mon.-Fri. 9am-5pm; admission $5). For smaller creatures, including koalas, nocturnal native animals, and dingoes, check out the **Urimbirra Wildlife Park** (tel. 8554 6554). The wildlife park is gorgeous and is situated across from **Nangawookka Flora Park,** creating a home for thousands of varieties of native flora and fauna. Plan to spend at least a few hours here on a nice day. (Wildlife park open 9am-5pm. Admission $6.50, children $3.50, 10% student discount.)

Fifteen thousand people come to town each year for the 700 performers and 120 events of October's **Victor Harbor Folk Festival.** The festivities go on during the October Labor Day weekend. For information call 8340 1069 or fax 8346 8506. Accommodations and ticket information is available at 1800 630 144.

KANGAROO ISLAND

A popular summertime escape from the rigors of mainland life, Kangaroo Island (pop. 4000) is located across the Backstairs Passage from the South Australian Fleurieu Peninsula. It forms Australia's third largest island, stretching 156km from the eastern Dudley Peninsula (once an island itself) across the western mainland. With 30% of its landmass contained in national park land, Kangaroo Island teems with well-protected flora and fauna. The sprawling Flinders Chase National Park occupies the island's western corner, allowing both distinctive native wildlife and endangered mainland species to thrive. Visitors enjoy strolling along the Southern Ocean coast among snoozing sea lions or past the awesome geological formations of Remarkable Rocks, Admirals Arch, and Kelly Hill Caves. A full measure of summer languor is yours for the taking on pleasant swimming beaches. Closer to the towns of Penneshaw and Kingscote, little penguins return home each night to burrows which shelter yapping, hungry chicks.

Phone numbers on Kangaroo Island have recently changed. Regional phone codes are now all 08, followed by eight-digit numbers. If you have trouble making a call, use the following "scheme" to get the old number, and try that instead.

New Number:	Old Number:	New Number:	Old Number:
(08) 8553 5xxx	(0848) 35 xxxx	(08) 8553 3xxx	(0848) 23 xxxx
(08) 8553 1xxx	(0848) 31 xxxx	(08) 8553 8xxx	(0848) 28 xxxx
(08) 8559 4xxx	(0848) 94 xxxx	(08) 8553 9xxx	(0848) 29 xxxx
(08) 8559 6xxx	(0848) 96 xxxx	(08) 8559 5xxx	(0848) 97 xxxx
(08) 8559 3xxx	(0848) 93 xxxx	(08) 8553 7xxx	(0848) 33 xxxx
(08) 8553 4xxx	(0848) 21 xxxx	(08) 8559 7xxx	(0848) 37 xxxx
(08) 8553 2xxx	(0848) 22 xxxx	(08) 8559 2xxx	(0848) 36 xxxx

GETTING THERE AND AROUND

Ferry and tour packages go to Kangaroo Island from Cape Jervis, near Adelaide, but some tend to rush visitors through the island's assortment of natural attractions. To reach the island on your own, choose between a flight into Kingscote and a ferry ride into Penneshaw.

By Air

Marked-down airfares rival the ferry's cost for those booking at least a week in advance. The **Kingscote Airport** is located 15km from the town of Kingscote and contains three airlines and two rental car agents. **Kendell Airlines** (tel. 8553 2855; fax 8553 2820) has an office at 61 Dauncey St. in downtown Kingscote in addition to their terminal space (open daily 8:30am-5pm). Kendell makes two flights per day each way between Kingscote and Adelaide (30min., $45-82; cheaper fares for evening arrival). Kendell passengers enjoy a 10% discount on **Budget** car rental. **Albatross Airlines** (tel. 8553 2296 or in Adelaide 8234 3399) provides service three times daily (30min., $60, children $40). They provide complimentary shuttle drop-off and pick-up anywhere in Kingscote. **Emu Airways** (tel. only in Adelaide 8234 3711 or 1800 182 353; fax 8234 3747) is not as earthbound as its flightless namesake (2-5 flights per day, 30min., $70, ages 3-15 $43). Both Emu and Albatross limit the luggage load to 10kg checked and 3kg carry-on, charging $1 per kg thereafter. An **airport shuttle** (tel. 8553 2390) transports passengers between the airport and Kingscote ($10 each way; reserve ahead if possible).

By Ferry and Coach

Two ferry companies operate out of Penneshaw. **Kangaroo Island Sealink,** 7 North Terrace Rd. (tel. 8553 1122; fax 8553 1207), runs two large car ferries to Cape Jervis.

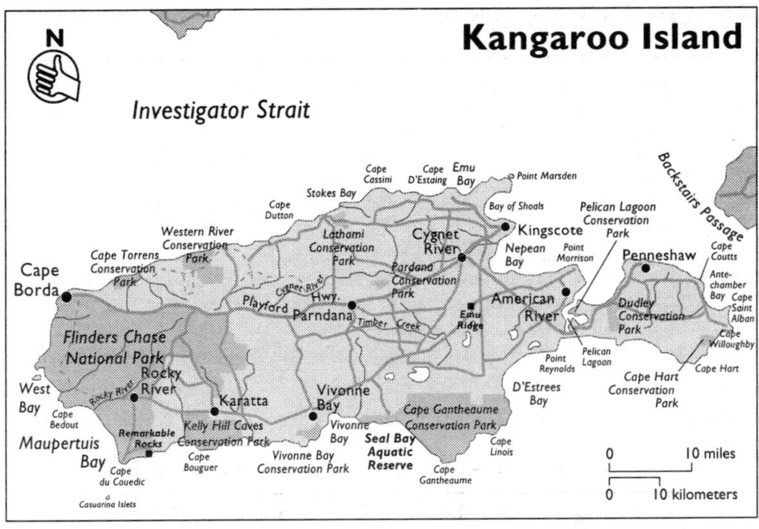

The ferry costs $30 (children $15; cars $60; bikes and surfboards additional $5). Ferries depart Cape Jervis daily at 9am and 8pm with additional service on Saturday at 10am and noon during summer school holidays. A shuttle coach connects to American River ($6.50, children $3.25) and Kingscote ($11, children $5.50).

Kangaroo Island Ferry Connections (tel. 8553 1233; fax 8553 1190) operates the *MV Valerie Jane* passenger ferry between Cape Jervis and Penneshaw twice per day. It departs Cape Jervis for Kangaroo Island at 10am and 7:30pm and leaves Penneshaw for the mainland at 9:15am and 6:45pm (30min., $30, backpackers bearing VIP, YHA, ITC, or Dreamtime cards $28, children $15). A transportation package, which includes coach service from Adelaide to Cape Jervis (daily 7:30am and 5pm, return 9:30am and 7pm; 2hr) and the ferry trip, costs $43 (backpackers $38, children $21; bikes and surfboards $5 surcharge). Kangaroo Island Ferry Connections will have resumed Adelaide-to-Kingscote service by the summer of 1998.

Coaches run from the island ferry terminal to Kingscote. They also run from Kingscote (daily 7am) through the hamlet of **American River** (7:30am) en route to the Penneshaw ferry. Unfortunately, there is no other public transportation on the island.

Vehicle Hire

A vehicle is indispensable to those who want to explore Kangaroo Island's remote sights. Hertz-affiliate **Kangaroo Island Rental Cars** (tel. 8553 2390 or 1800 088 296; fax 8553 2878) is in Kingscote on the corner of Franklin St. and Telegraph Rd., and has counters at the airport and the Kingscote Wharf. Cars at any of these locations range from manual minis ($55 per day, $336 per week) to 4WD vehicles ($120 per day; agency open 9am-5pm; V, MC, AmEx, Discover, and Bancard). **Budget** (tel. 8553 3133), on Commercial and Dauncey St., serves the airport and Penneshaw. (Vehicles start at $65 per day, $385 per week. Open 9am-5pm.)

A good option for drivers under 21 and those with ample derring-do is **scooter rental,** available at the **Country Cottage** (tel. 8553 2148) on Centenary Ave. in Kingscote. Rental begins at $10 per hour or $45 per day, although off-season and multiple-day discounts can be arranged. These scooters get good fuel efficiency but are limited to sealed roads, putting Flinders Chase National Park and isolated coasts off limits. Country Cottage is open daily from 8am to 8pm, and its EFTPOS facility accepts Visa, MC, AmEx, and Bancard. Helmets are provided.

Kingscote

Kingscote (pop. 1400) bustles by Kangaroo Island standards. Most of the island's commercial services operate in the town center, and its location 15km from the airport and on the eastern edge of the island's northern coast makes it centrally accessible. This micropolis cradles a rich array of native flora and fauna, including South Australia's oldest European tree and Little Penguin burrows all along the coast.

ORIENTATION AND PRACTICAL INFORMATION

Although the island's formal tourist office operates in Penneshaw, tourist information is available in the back of the **Kingscote Gift Shop** (tel. 8553 2165; open Mon.-Fri.), on Dauncey and Commercial St. For information and maps on the island's national parks, visit the **Department of Environmental and Natural Resources** headquarters (tel. 8553 2381; open Mon.-Fri. 9am-5pm) on Dauncey St., between Murray and Drew St. Though **banks** operate on Dauncey St., there are no ATM facilities. Both backpackers hostels have EFTPOS cash withdrawal facilities. A **Foodland supermarket** is on Commercial and Osmond St. (open Mon.-Fri. 9am-5:30pm, Sat. 9am-12:30pm). Also on Dauncey between Murray and Drew St. is the **post office** (open Mon.-Fri. 9am-5pm; postal code 5223).

ACCOMMODATIONS AND FOOD

Seaview Nomads Backpackers (tel. 8553 2030; fax 8553 2368; http://kigateway.kin.on.net/ellsons/default.htm), on Chapman Tce. and Drew St. overlooking the sea. You can watch the sunset from the shaded veranda or sample the delicious meals served nightly in the stately lounge. A roaring fire has burned through the winter here since 1928. Rooms come with fridges, handbasins, and tea and coffee. If you're not pampered enough, just order breakfast to your room for as little as $5. Dorms $18, multiple nights $16; singles $20. V, MC, AmEx.

Kangaroo Island Central Backpackers, 19 Murray St. (tel. 8553 2787; fax 8553 2694), 4 blocks west of the coast. This facility has basic dorms, a large kitchen, and a lounge. The extremely budget-conscious who don't mind sharing their pillows with six-legged guests can take advantage of bicycle rentals, cheap breakfasts, laundry facilities, and a pool table. Dorms $13. Linen hire $2. V, MC, AmEx.

Blue Gum Cafe (tel. 8553 2089), on Dauncey St. between Murray and Commercial St. Serves breakfast from 7:30am and offers inexpensive cappuccino. Hearty, delicious sandwiches are as little as $2.50. V, MC. Open Mon.-Fri. 7:30am-5:30pm, Sat.-Sun. 7:30am-12:30pm.

SIGHTS

Kingscote's primary historical attractions are clustered in the **Reeves Point Historical Area** on the north end of the Esplanade. Walking along the Esplanade from town, you'll approach **South Australia's oldest European tree,** a mulberry planted in 1836 which still bears fruit. This gnarled grande dame had a cutting planted nearby several years ago to ensure its indirect genetic survival should the original trunk die. Nearby, a marker commemorates **Kingscote's first post office,** another South Australian first. A walk to the top of the hill brings you to a **pioneer memorial** and a view of the Bay of Shoals to your left and Nepean Bay to the right. Descending the hill to the south, one will approach the old cemetery ringed in white fencing, which occupies a small wooded glen overlooking the sea. Twelve headstones, one of which is original, testify to the hardship early Kangaroo Island settlers endured.

West along Seaview Rd. is the **Hope Cottage Museum** on Centenary St. Now a National Trust facility, the site originally housed three limestone cottages, called Faith, Hope, and Charity, constructed by the Cowlan brothers, a pair of successful goldminers. Today the site is Faith-less and Charity remains in private hands. Three of Hope's rooms are preserved with elegant period furnishings and memorabilia. One room is reserved for historical documents, one for reading, and one as a regional museum with a wide assortment of local, historically significant holdings. Sheds outside house farm machinery and tractors spanning a century of agriculture. There is also an outdoor room which houses a history of sea and air transport to Kangaroo Island.

In the courtyard stands a small **lighthouse.** Actually the original Cape Willoughby Lighthouse beacon, the base was constructed with an unusually short stature because no machinery on the island could raise the beacon any higher. Climb to the top and examine the beautifully etched glass slowly rotating; spin around and take in a view of Kingscote and the surrounding bays. Farther down the front lawn sits the **eucalypt press,** which still produces eucalypt oil ($3) from the Kangaroo Island narrow-leaved mallee. The interesting boiling and vaporization process can be observed when volunteers produce the oil sold in the gift shop. A small **heritage garden** along the front of the house provides another interesting sight (open daily Sept.-June 2-4pm; also winter school holidays 10am-noon; admission $2.50, children 50¢).

A refreshing summer spot is the **John Downing Swimming Pool Reserve** located directly in front of the Nomads guesthouse. This ocean pool ringed in mortared rocks has 1m diving platforms, showers, and cabanas by the shore. At dusk, the rocky coast to the north of the pool and all the way out to the jetty awakens with **Little Penguin** activity. Though not as prominent as the Penneshaw sites, Kingscote's coastal burrows still receive a fair-sized crowd of the birds. Guided tours of the burrows depart nightly at dusk ($5) in front of the Ozone Hotel. **Pelicans** take center stage at the jetty every day at 4pm when a feeding brings them together to jostle for fish.

■ Around Kingscote

South and west of Kingscote, many of Kangaroo Island's distinctive cottage industries invite the public to tour and purchase on-site. In Cygnet River, 12km from Kingscote, you can sample cheese and dairy products, tour the dairy and cheese factory, and watch the sheep being milked at the **Island Pure Sheep Milking Dairy** (tel. 8553 9110) on Gum Creek Rd. In case you miss the milking (3-5pm) or dairy processing, there's a detailed video you can watch (open Sept.-May 10am-5pm; admission $3, under 15 $2).

South of Kingscote just off Hundred Line Rd. on Willsons Rd. is **Emu Ridge** (tel. 8553 8228; fax 8553 8272), a eucalyptus distillery. The workers offer tours of their press and distillation facilities where the Kangaroo Island Narrow Leaf Mallee becomes refined into clear eucalyptus oil. Sold on-site, the mildly toxic oil is a cleanser, lubricant, topical antibiotic, and insect repellant. The process of distillation produces 5 liters of oil from a ton of leaves (distillery open daily 9am-2pm; free admission; frequent guided tours $3). **Emu Bay,** on the other hand, is 18km northwest of Kingscote. This popular local swimming beach is accessible by sealed road. Along the foreshore the **Emu's Nest** (tel. 8553 5384) can provide food and drink.

South of Emu Ridge, along Hundred Line Rd. between Moores Rd. and Barretts Rd., **Clifford's Honey Farm** (tel. 8553 8295) produces the honey of Ligurian bees. This northern Italian breed was introduced to Kangaroo Island in 1881. Since it was declared a Bee Sanctuary in 1885, the island's docile Ligurians have remained disease-free. Today they're the only pure strain of bee in the world and they produce a rich, impeccable honey. Clifford's offers tours of the hives and a variety of honey and beeswax products (open daily 9am-5pm; free admission; tours $2, concessions $1). But bees aren't the only domesticates to see. For a closer look at the million sheep that populate the island, attend a **Jumbuck Shearing Demo** (tel. 8553 9193) on sealed Birchmore Rd., 5km south of the airport turnoff. Watch the sheepdogs earn their keep while sheep are stripped (well, sheared) before your paying eyes (tours daily 12:30 and 1:30pm; $5).

Parndana Wildlife Park (tel. 8553 6050), 3km west of Parndana on the Playford Hwy., boasts a wide variety of birds and animals for visitors to observe. Stroll through aviaries and watch Australian natives and colorful exotics soaring about. Along with the native 'roos, tamar wallabies, and feral pigs, you'll find a few freakish domesticated animals (open daily 9am-5pm).

Penneshaw

The seaside hamlet of Penneshaw (pop. 250) perches on Kangaroo Island's northeast coast, and is the primary ferry arrival point from Cape Jervis on South Australia's mainland. In 1802, British explorer Captain Matthew Flinders first sighted Kangaroo Island and obtained water along nearby Freshwater Bay. His French counterpart Captain Nicolas Baudin stopped by a year later to collect water as well, and one of his crew left the island's first graffiti—Frenchman's Rock—now on display in the **Kangaroo Island Gateway Visitors Centre** (tel. 8553 1185), just 1km down the road towards Kingscote from Penneshaw's ferry terminus (open Mon.-Fri. 9am-5pm, Sat.-Sun. 10am-4pm). The **Penneshaw Supermarket** is on Middle Tce. between Nat Thomas St. and Bay Tce. (open Mon.-Fri. 9am-5pm, Sat. 9am-noon). The **post office** is on Nat Thomas St. between Middle Tce. and North Tce. (open Mon.-Fri. 9am-5pm, Sat. 9am-11:30am; postal code 5223).

Accommodations and Food The **Penneshaw Youth Hostel,** 43 North Tce. (tel. 8553 1284 or 1800 018 258; fax 8553 1295), is behind a small cafe and takeaway. This YHA affiliate boasts comfortable accommodations and a heated, airy TV lounge connected to the kitchen facilities and bathrooms. The adjoining **cafe** offers cheap, tasty meals, a laundromat, and a souvenir shop. Dorm bunks cost $14, with YHA or VIP card $12. Bring or rent linen. Reserve several weeks in advance during summer.

One block south on the corner of Middle Tce. and Bay Tce., the **Penguin Walk Hostel** (tel. 8553 1233) has converted motel units into dorm-style accommodations. Flexible room configurations and private bathrooms are ideal for families or groups seeking a little space for themselves. The rooms are complemented by a laundry facility and adjacent pizzeria. Kangaroo Island Ferry Connections operates the hostel and coordinates package tours at the adjacent office. (Dorms $12; twins and doubles $16; linen and a light breakfast included).

Sights Penneshaw's finest attraction is its **Little Penguin colony.** Each night, with curious amateur naturalists looking on, the penguins return to their burrows lining the coastline. The **Penguin Interpretive Centre,** on the shore off Middle Terrace's east end, offers the best way to see the world's smallest penguin species. Here, an informative display center is open nightly for three hours starting at dusk. A guided tour makes the experience complete, as skilled rangers guide groups through a restricted access reserve within the colony. The tour offers insight into the preening, feeding, and mating behavior of the penguins, and the guides can answer almost any question. Penguin tours occur between 6:30 and 9:30pm (call for exact times; $5, children $3.50, families $13.50). Profits fund penguin protection efforts. There is also a specially lit viewing boardwalk adjacent to the center. If you choose to explore the coastline yourself, please step carefully to avoid damaging penguin burrows. Keep a minimum distance of 3m from the penguins, and don't shine flashlights directly in their eyes.

The **Penneshaw's Maritime and Folk Museum** (tel. 8553 1108) educates visitors about local history and culture. Displays chronicle the exploits of colorful figures since the early 1800s. The museum is 1km from Penneshaw along the main road (open Sept.-Dec. and Feb.-May Mon., Wed., and Sat. 3-5pm; Jan. daily 3-5pm).

Seal Bay Aquatic Reserve

Arguably Kangaroo Island's finest natural attraction, Seal Bay allows visitors to stroll through a colony of Australian sea lions. This is the rarest sea lion species in the world, and Kangaroo Island has 600 of the world population of 12,000. Weave your way between sunning cows and bulls flopped down on the sand after three-day hunting expeditions, or stick to the boardwalk and watch the snoozing beasts below.

A sealed road leads directly to the seals on the island's southern coast, 60km from Kingscote. Here, an award-winning, environmentally sustainable **visitors center** (tel.

8553 4207) offers general information, a gift shop, toilets, and a snack bar. Although an individual entry is available ($5, children $3.50, families $13.50), a guided tour admission is an infinitely better option ($7.50, $5, $15). These tours leave every 15 to 30 minutes while the park is open, and the park rangers provide invaluable insights. A guided tour is included in the **Island Parks Pass** ($20, children $15, families $55), which is a good value if you plan to visit numerous national park attractions (park open 9am-4:30pm).

Passage across the dunes to the beach is on an elevated boardwalk beneath which pups cavort and juveniles sun themselves. The sea lions weave an intricate maze of paths through the heathlands between the dunes and water. Don't be deceived by their seemingly labored movement. These agile creatures can actually move twice as fast as humans on land. Once on the beach you can distinguish adult males by the distinctive golden manes about their necks. The massive bulls reach lengths of up to 3m and weigh 300-350kg. Females mature three years before males, at age six, but are only about a third as large. Cows usually outlive bulls, sometimes reaching the ripe age of 25. Needless to say, approaching these glorious mammals (*never* come closer than 5m) provides an unforgettable experience and admittedly awesome photo opportunity. On their three-day hunting trips the sea lions travel up to 60km off-shore and descend up to 275m in search of octopus, squid, and crustaceans. The lions are spread out along six beaches, and many females breed and give birth in the sheltered caves on the west end of the Seal Bay Reserve.

Flinders Chase National Park

This splendid reserve occupies the entire western end of the island and, with 73,920 hectares, covers 17% of the island's total area. Its expanse teems with an extensive variety of Australian flora and fauna which are unusually accessible to visitors. Just over 105km from Kingscote (often along a dirt track), Flinders Chase headquarters is located at **Rocky River** along the South Coast Rd. (park entry $6.50 per car, $3 per motorcycle; fee covered by Island Parks Pass: $20, children $15, families $55). Rocky River was cleared by the May family for their farm in the late 19th century, and it's one of the few open spaces in the park. Near the park headquarters and toilet block, a **koala walk** lets visitors observe these marsupials. The koala population has swelled so large that they are now decimating edible eucalypt stands. The nearby hillsides, grazed by an ever-present mob of kangaroos, are covered by a thin layer of an irridescent lime green moss.

The best attractions are clustered 15-20km south of Rocky River, all along Boxer Drive. The easternmost sight, situated on Kirkpatrick Point, is **Remarkable Rocks.** The name could not be more apropos. The approach to the granite configuration is through bonsai-like forests of eucalypt shrubbery stunted by salt spray. As you approach from a distance, the rocks transform from inconspicuous to surreal, to, well, utterly remarkable. The granite has been cracked into cubes by 750 million years of erosion. Ice, wind, sea, and sun have sculpted delicate details on these monoliths so that they now resemble a cross between Dalí's sensual forms and abstract modern mega-sculpture, all flecked with orange lichen.

Five km west along Boxer Dr., **Cape du Couedic** houses Kangaroo Island's finest **lighthouse.** The red-capped, functioning beacon was painstakingly constructed of hand-cut limestone between 1907 and 1909. It still emits a beam which can be seen 100km out to sea. Just south of the lighthouse, a footpath winds to the edge of Cape du Couedic, which was named by the French explorer Nicolas Baudin when he mapped the coastline in 1803. In the distance, the two Casuarinas Islands are visibly bombarded by the vigorous Southern Ocean surf. These two reserves are uninhabited, except for colonies of New Zealand fur seals. More common than the Australian sea lions, 15,000 fur seals reside on Kangaroo Island.

Descending the steps, one approaches the **Admirals Arch** and the adjacent seal breeding area. While the seals quietly bask on the rocks, a splendorous surf crashes around them, framing the Admirals Arch. The arch is actually an eroded limestone cave whose attenuated stalactites remain, framing the setting sun.

SOUTHEAST OF THE MURRAY RIVER

The majestic Murray River winds west from the Great Dividing Range. Fed by a watershed that spans most of New South Wales and portions of Victoria, the largest waterway in Australia slices through the southeast corner of South Australia and empties into the Southern Ocean. Fruit, especially wine grapes, flourishes along the irrigated river basin, while the **Coorong,** a 145km stretch of coastal lagoons, supports over 240 species of native birdlife. The towns near the Victoria border can be associated with geographic regions within that state. The area around Naracoorte is an extension of the agricultural Wimmera district (see p. 496) and Mount Gambier continues the themes of Victoria's southwest coast (see p. 473).

Murray Bridge

Murray Bridge spans the breadth of Australia's largest river. Apart from marveling at this fact, however, there's little reason to linger on either bank. The town isn't terribly pretty or even particularly budget-friendly, but it is the gateway to the settlements that dot the Murray River to the north and east, where the watercourse becomes the border between Victoria and New South Wales.

The turn-off to Murray Bridge, approximately one hour out of Adelaide on the Southeastern Freeway, leads into **Bridge St.** and down toward the city center and river. The **Murray Bridge Community Information and Tourist Centre,** 3 South Tce. (tel. 8532 2900; fax 8532 2766), is the local tourist office and departure point for intercity buses. Book **bus** transport to Adelaide (1 per day, $10.50) through the **Murray Bridge Passenger Service** (tel. 8532 6660). If arriving by **train,** you'll land at the Manum St. depot, three blocks northwest of the center. To contact the **RAA** call 8532 2022; the **police** are at 8535 6020; **taxis** respond to 8531 0555.

The Balcony Bed and Breakfast, 12 Sixth St. (tel. 8531 1411), is centrally located near the intersection of Sixth and Bridge St., one block from the wharf. This clean, friendly B&B has rates from $20; bookings are advised. The **Cockatoo Haven Diner** (tel. 8532 3666), on Jervois Rd., will stuff you silly with a three-course lunch (daily) or dinner (Thurs.-Fri. only) for only $6. Other tasty spots include **McCues Bakery,** 60 Adelaide Rd. (tel. 8532 2111), and the **Murray Bridge Fish and Chip Shop,** 90 Swanport Rd. (tel. 8532 4248).

Near Murray Bridge

Once you've seen the bridges, the best sights in Murray Bridge are outside the town. Fortunately, the town of **Monarto,** only 11km west on the Princes Hwy., features the **Monarto Zoological Park** (tel. 8534 4100). A virtual mini-safari, the park houses exotic denizens like Scimitar oryx, elands, ostriches, and giraffes. The minibus to the park, an hour-long guided tour, and an optional guided walk costs $10 (students $8; open daily 9am-4pm; last tour at 3pm).

A quirky reconstruction of South Australia's colonial past, **Old Tailem Town-Pioneer Village** (tel. 8572 3838) is 5km from **Tailem Bend** as you head toward Adelaide on the Princes Hwy., smack in the middle of nowhere (open daily 10am-5pm; admission $5).

Naracoorte

Naracoorte is a small town roughly 125km west of Horsham, Victoria on the Wimmera Highway, cradled between two world-famous **wine regions** (Coonawarra to the south and Padthway to the north) and within striking distance of the **Naracoorte Caves Conservation Park.** The limestone caves have been attracting visitors for many years, but their recent designation as a World Heritage site (only the eleventh in

Australia) will increase the flow of tourists considerably. The **Tourist Information Centre** (tel. 1800 244 421) is located in the **Sheep's Back,** a museum dedicated to wool and things sheepish. The museum, in turn, is located on MacDonnell St., and is open daily from 10am to 4pm. The **bus depot** is on Rolland St., just off Smith St., but V/Line does not service Naracoorte. There is a **post office** at 23 Ormerod St. (open Mon.-Fri. 9am-5pm; fax 8762 2021; postal code 5271), with an **ATM** next door.

When people come to Naracoorte, they almost inevitably drive 12km south of town, to the **Naracoorte Caves Conservation Park,** off the Penola Rd. Four caves are available for touring and a fifth is rigged with television cameras for remote viewing. The **Alexandra Cave** features five chambers full of delicate calcite stalagmites, stalactites, straws, and flowstone. Bizarre cave crickets also call Alexandra home. When food grows scarce, the crickets remove their own legs to eat instead. **Blanche Cave** lacks the delicate decorations and limping crickets found in Alexandra Cave, but has immense columns and windows caused by a partial collapse of the roof. Back in the 1850s, before the days of conservation, the local landlord used the cave for lavish parties, and the wooden furniture remains inside.

Now the most famous of the caves, the **Victoria Fossil Cave,** discovered in 1969, contains the remains of nearly 100 different species of Pleistocene fauna from 2 million to 10,000 years ago. Buried under silt after dying in the cave, the fossils of these animals provide important clues as to how the Australian marsupial megafauna were affected by the arrival of humans. Now-extinct species found here include a giant boa-like snake, marsupial "lions," hippo-sized wombats, and gigantic leaf-eating kangaroos. The fossils here are of such international significance that the area has been placed on the World Heritage list, joining such stars as the Giza Pyramids and the Great Barrier Reef.

Every spring, hundreds of thousands of **bent-wing bats** descend on the Naracoorte caves to breed. **Bat Cave** provides perfect nursery conditions for the winged critters to bear and raise their darkling brood. Infrared bat-cameras have been installed to allow tourists to view the bats without disturbing the breeding grounds. **Wet Cave** gives amateur spelunkers the opportunity to wriggle in the muck on their own, without a guide to goad them.

Excellent guided **cave tours** are available from 9:30am to 4pm daily. Tours of Alexandra Cave cost $5, the Victoria Fossil Cave $7.50, Blanche Cave $6, viewings of the Bat Cave $7.50, and self-guided tours of Wet Cave $3. Day passes to all of the guided caves cost $22.50. More strenuous "adventure caving" tours are available, with guides, and must be booked ahead of time. These tours most closely approximate the joy and peril of genuine cave exploration. Pricing depends on the number of people and the tour particulars. Call 8762 2340 for information.

A few kilometers south, **Bool Lagoon** is an important stopover point for many species of migratory birds. Boardwalks and walking tracks allow the wetland to be explored in comfort.

Camping is available both at Bool Lagoon and at Naracoorte Caves Conservation Park ($15 per car, $8 per motorcycle, or $4 per person for groups of 6 or more). The Naracoorte sites feature free laundry and barbecues, showers, and toilets. The Bool Lagoon sites are more primitive, and it is advisable to bring drinking water. Permits are available from the ticket office. The **Naracoorte Caravan Park,** 81 Park Tce. (tel. 8762 2128), provides more commercial camping, campervan parks, cabins, and caravans. (Tent sites for 2 $12; office open Mon.-Sat. 8:30am-6:30pm, Sun. 9am-5pm.)

Mount Gambier

Mount Gambier's claim to fame (other than being Australia's Tidiest Town in 1991) is the deep blue lake that fills a volcanic crater above the city. Blue Lake's color is not as boring as its name implies: the water actually changes color throughout the year as the striking blue fades to gray in March and then regains its sapphire hue in November. The color changes are caused by the shifting moods of the Lake King, who dwells in an obsidian palace deep in the middle of the crater. Not really. But the real cause is unknown, so feel free to speculate. The adjacent Valley Lake and beautifully named Leg of Mutton Lake are used for aquatic recreation. The town itself (pop. 21,000) is one of the largest in the area and is more often associated with the Wimmera region of Victoria (see p. 496) than with neighboring parts of South Australia.

Practical Information, Accommodations, and Food The main commercial area is at the intersection of Bay and Commercial St. Here you will find a **post office** (6 Bay Rd., open Mon.-Fri. 9am-5pm, postal code 5290), the **telephone bureau** (adjacent to the post office, always open), and several ATM-equipped **banks** (open Mon.-Thurs. 9:30am-4pm, Fri. 9:30am-5pm). **V/Line buses** stop at the Shell Blue service station on Commercial St. West. Buses run northwest to Adelaide and east to the Victorian cities of Warnambool (via Dartmoor, Heywood, Portland, and Port Fairy, $38) and Hamilton (via Castertan and Coleraine).

There are a few budget bedding options in Mount Gambier. The **Blue Lake Motel,** 1 Kennedy Ave. (tel. 8725 5211; fax 8725 5410), off the Jubilee Hwy. East, bills itself as Mt. Gambier's Most Homely Motel in Australia's Tidiest Town." Converted motel rooms are a bit cramped but clean. The motel lobby serves as a pleasant lounge area, complete with a fireplace and TV ($12 per person; breakfast $5; linen $1.50; laundry $3.50). The **Federal Hotel Motel,** 112 Commercial St. East (tel. 8723 1099), offers recently modernized rooms in a grand old building. Hall showers are well-maintained, and the pub downstairs is available for socializing. (Singles $17; doubles $30. Pub meals $4-5.) The **Central Caravan Park,** 6 Krummel St. (tel./fax 8725 4427), just east of the central business district, is in a good location but a bit noisy. (Tent sites $8; powered sites $12; on-site caravans $25; cabins $28-38.) BBQ facilities and a laundromat sleep across the street.

Commercial St. is choked with chip shops and takeaway joints. The **Aquarium Cafe,** just south of Commercial on Wehl St., is a bit more interesting than most. In addition to standard chip shop fare, the cafe serves Mexican food with a conspicuously Australian interpretation. True to its name, there is an enormous aquarium in the back room (open Wed.-Sat. 4:30pm-1am, Sun. 4:30pm-10pm). Supermarkets and greengrocers can be found in the central business district.

Sights Bay Rd., after passing through the middle of town, circles the **lakes** outside of town and provides several scenic lookouts. The first European to sight Mount Gambier and the surrounding areas was Lieutenant James Grant, sailing the brig Lady Nelson in 1800. A replica of this historic ship now graces the **Lady Nelson Visitor and Discovery Centre** (Jubilee Highway East; tel. 8724 9750 or 1800 087 187; fax 8723 2833; open daily 9am-5pm). The center is packed with informative brochures and features a diorama portraying the perils faced by 19th-century migrants.

There are two **caves** right in the middle of town. The **Cave Gardens,** once the original water source for the town, are now developed for strolling and loafing. The flooded **Engelbrecht cave,** located on Jubilee Hwy. West between Victoria Tce. and Ehret St., is a popular spot for cave divers. Two of the cave's chambers have been opened for viewing (open daily noon-3pm, tours on the hr.; admission $4, children $2). There is a third nifty hole in the ground on Jubilee Hwy. East known as the **Umpherston Sinkhole.** This one has barbecue and picnic facilities, and is flood-lit at night, when possums emerge to scarf food offered by irresponsible tourists. Adjacent to the Sinkhole is the **Carter, Holt, Harvey Timber Mill.** Take a free two-hour tour (meets at Possums Hideaway in the Umpherston parking lot; Mon. 10am, Wed. 1:15pm) to learn about the Australian timber industry and its use of the vast pinus radiata forests around Mount Gambier. Just north of the Umpherston-Timber Mill area is the **Attamurra Cottage** (tel. 8725 3296), a cuddly little tourist trap with high quality, locally made trinkets, a greenhouse and cacti display, and a collection of cute animals and Australian characters. (Located on Attamurra Rd. 2km north of the highway. Open daily 10am-4:30pm. Character display costs $1.50, everything else is free.)

CENTRAL WINE REGIONS

Given a choice, Bacchus might have fled his ancient Mediterranean abode in favor of South Australia, where wine is a religion and the fertile valleys produce a nectar divine. Indeed, the gods have blessed SA with many sanctuaries and filled winemakers with missionary zeal. Regular worship is encouraged, with cellar door sales and tastings occurring every day (except Christmas and Easter) in most regions. For the observant, the ritual is sure to provide an unending source of spiritual nourishment. Sublime in offerings and eternal in design, the wine regions of SA bring the playground of gods within the grasp of mortals.

Tours Numerous companies offer tours of one or several days featuring South Australia's wine regions. They generally average $30 per day, but "gourmet tours" add a hefty charge for meals. Some companies run winter (June-Sept.) specials, and prices fluctuate as companies attempt to undercut their competitors. If you don't feel like comparing several companies directly, contact the **SA Travel Centre,** 1 King William St. (tel. 8212 1505), in Adelaide. Private operators include **E&K Mini Tours** (tel. 8365 3816), **Festival Tours** (tel. 8374 1270 or 1800 634 724), **Premier's** (tel. 8415 5566), **AAA Tours** (tel. 8281 0530), **Freewheelin' Cycle Tours** (tel. 8232 6860), **Mac's Winery Tours** (tel. 8362 7328), **Prime Mini Tours** (tel. 8293 4900), and **Tour Delights** (tel. 8366 0550). Car hire (with a designated driver) is strongly recommended for those bent on a serious wine tour; too many wineries are in out-of-the-way places to do a fulfilling circuit by public bus or on a whirlwind tour.

Barossa Valley

Arguably Australia's most famous wine region, the Barossa Valley offers a variety of wines to suit all palates and budgets. Taste all the wine you want at no cost whatsoever, or, if one particularly strikes your fancy, begin your own wine cellar for as little as $8 a bottle. In between sips, there is plenty of time to explore the townships, each with its own quirky attractions, hidden hamlets, and budget bakeries.

ORIENTATION AND PRACTICAL INFORMATION

The Barossa is comprised of several townships. Approaching from Adelaide via **Gawler,** the first town you will enter is **Lyndoch** (LIN-dock). Continuing through Lyndoch on the **Barossa Valley Highway,** the road enters **Tanunda** and changes its name to **Murray St.** It then continues on to **Nuriootpa** (noor-ee-OOT-pah) and proceeds east to **Angaston. Williamstown** lies south of Lyndoch. Alternately, you may choose to bypass Gawler and take the **Sturt Hwy.** from Adelaide, which enters the Barossa at Nuriootpa. The towns are small enough to navigate easily, but for individual wineries it is best to pick up a wineries map from the Tanunda tourist office.

Tourist Office: Barossa Tourist Information and Wine Centre, 66-68 Murray St., Tanunda (tel. 8563 0600 or 1800 812 662; fax 8563 0616; email bwta@dove.net.au). Open Mon.-Fri. 9am-5pm, Sat.-Sun. 10am-4pm.

Buses: Barossa Adelaide Passenger Service (tel. 8564 3022) sends buses to Barossa from Adelaide Mon.-Fri. 9am, 1 and 5:45pm, Sat. 9am and 5:45pm, Sun. 5:45pm. One-way fares to: Lyndoch $7.90, Tanunda $9.70, Nuriootpa $10.50, and Angaston $11.50. Buses leave Angaston for Adelaide Mon.-Fri. 6:25, 9am and 3:25pm, Sat. 7:05am and 3:25pm, Sun. 3:25pm.

Taxi: Barossa Valley Taxi Service, Tanunda (tel. 8563 3600).

Royal Automobile Association: Understaffed offices in Gawler (tel. 8522 2478), Tanunda (tel. 8563 2123 or 018 811 118), and Williamstown (tel. 8524 6268).

Bike Hire: Barossa Bunkhaus, Nuriootpa (tel. 8562 2260), or **Zinfandel Tea Rooms,** Tanunda (tel. 8563 2822). The Barossa Valley isn't terribly compact and the summer (Dec.-March) is the only time it can be covered by bike practically.

Hospitals: Doctors can be contacted in Angaston (tel. 8564 2266; hospital tel. 8564 2062), Gawler (hospital tel. 8521 2000), Nuriootpa (tel. 8562 2444), and Tanunda (tel. 8563 2777; hospital tel. 8563 2398).
Emergency: Dial 000.
Police: In Gawler (tel. 8522 1088); in Nuriootpa (tel. 8568 6020); in Williamstown (tel. 8524 6288).
Post Offices: In **Gawler** on Tod St., in **Lyndoch** on the Barossa Valley Hwy., and in **Williamstown** on Queens St. Murray St. is the address of 3 post offices in Barossa: one in **Tanunda,** another in **Nuriootpa,** and a third in **Angaston.**

ACCOMMODATIONS

Although the Barossa is easily covered as a daytrip from Adelaide, you won't want to make the drive back if you've tanked up on wine. Turn your visit into a leisurely stay so you can sample more of the local ambrosia.

The Bunkhaus Travelers' Hostel (tel. 8562 2260), before the turnoff to Angaston on the Barossa Valley Way from Tanunda to Nuriootpa. The best value in the Barossa, this clean, comfortable hostel overlooks gorgeous vineyards. A great location for those who wish to bike around the area (mountain bikes $8 per day). Dorms $11. Doonas (quilts) are included, but bring your own sheets. The nearby **Shiraz Cottage,** with a kitchen, BBQ, pool, laundry, and TV, can also be rented at $30 for 2 or $44 for 4.

The Angas Park Hotel, 22 Murray St., Nuriootpa (tel. 8562 1050). This bright, clean hotel is billed by the friendly owner simply as "a place to put your head." $15 will give you just that, and access to a shared bathroom.

Barossa Valley Hotel, 41 Murray St., Angaston (tel. 8564 2014). This B&B is basic, clean, and comfortable, with shared bathrooms. Beds $20.

FOOD

Food is a high priority in the Barossa, and the most sumptuous display of this obsession is the Barossa Classic Gourmet Festival. There are some fantastic (though pricey) gourmet cellars for moments of complete self-indulgence. The best budget tucker is found in the bakeries.

Die Barossa Wurst Haus and Bakery, 86A Murray St., Tanunda (tel. 8563 3598, mobile tel. 041 999 9852). Billed as the "home of genuine German Mettwurst, sausages and cheese," Wurst Haus is also home of light scones, rich strudels, fresh breads, and plump pies and pastries.

Lyndoch Bakery (tel. 8524 4422), on Barossa Valley Way, Lyndoch. Another great German bakery with many tortes and tarts. The attached restaurant has fine German cuisine but is considerably more expensive than the bakery.

Linkes Nuriootpa Bakery and Tearooms, 40 Murray St., Nuriootpa (tel. 8562 1129). In addition to its famous cheese pasty, Linkes has a huge variety of hot foods and cakes at very reasonable prices. Eat takeaway and avoid the table charge.

Angas Park Fruit Company, 3 Murray St., Angaston (tel. 8564 2052; fax 8564 2686). After dinner, treat yourself to something sweet. Angas Park markets fruits glacé, dried fruit confectionery, nuts, chocolates, honey, and other preserves. All South Australian and all delicious. Yum!

WINERIES

The complete tour of over 40 wineries requires Herculean effort and Gargantuan ability to hold your liquor. Most wineries are open daily from 10am to 4pm for free tastings and sales. Those walking or biking can head out of Tanunda, beginning at **Basedow Wines** on Murray St. Follow the loop starting at **Richmond Grove Barossa Winery,** on Para Rd., Tanunda (tel. 8563 2204), around to **Peter Lehmann Wines** (tel. 8563 2500), **Langmeil Winery** (tel. 8563 2595), and **Ventas Winery** (tel. 8563 2330). The walking and tasting will take at least a couple of hours, and on a nice day, you'll get scenic views all around.

The additional mobility afforded by a car allows you to be a little more selective. As your party drives between these excellent wineries, remember to keep a designated driver absolutely sober. Roads are not in top condition, and Barossa Valley's police are diligent and unforgiving when it comes to drunk driving.

Saltram Wine Estate (tel. 8564 3355), Nuriootpa Rd., Angaston. Saltram's Semillon is the stuff from which dreams are made—smooth, fruity, and fabulously decadent. A little plate of delicious nibbles ($1) will aid your palate as you wade your way through liters of pure joy.

Kellermeister, Barossa Valley Way, Lyndoch. Perched upon a hill with a panoramic view of the valley, this family-owned winery sells only from the cellar door. Family dedication and generations of accumulated knowledge make Kellermeister's wines distinctive. Try as many of their offerings as you like, but don't leave without a swig of the Sable—a chocolate port.

Grant Burge Wines (tel. 8563 3700), Barossa Valley Way, Tanunda. One of the larger Barossa wineries, Grant Burge has an extensive range of fine reds and whites. Linger at this lovely estate to absorb them all.

Kaesler Wines (tel. 8562 2711), Barossa Valley Way, Nuriootpa. Set in an old stable, this cozy, wooded winery has a Tawny Port that will have you reeling with visions of musty English parlors and cigar-smoking aristocrats. Perfect on a chilly winter afternoon.

SIGHTS AND FESTIVALS

The Barossa has a few other quirky attractions to round out your tour. Step in at the **Southern Australia Museum of Mechanical Music** (tel. 8524 4014), on Barossa Valley Hwy. in Lyndoch. Don't be deceived by the ramshackle exterior; inside the rickety walls you'll find musical wonders you never dreamed possible. Tom, the guide, is an eccentric old man who likes to pull visitors' legs. Take his own advice and "if you don't have a sense of humor—don't come in" (open daily 9am-5pm; admission $5). The **Story Book Cottage and Whacky Wood** (tel. 8563 2910), Oak St., Tanunda, offers animal feeding and a good dose of nostalgia.

The Barossa has plenty of festivals to maximize wine-drinking opportunities. The **Barossa Classic Gourmet Festival** is a veritable carnival and runs concurrently this year with the **Barossa Music Festival** (Aug. 20-24, 1998). The **Oom-Pah Festival,** on February 1, 1998, is a German celebration with food stalls, music, entertainment, and, of course, wine. The **Barossa Balloon Regatta** will be held on May 17 in Nuriootpa, followed on May 29-30 by the **Melodienacht** in the Tanunda Show Hall.

Clare

In limbo between Adelaide and the South Australian outback, Clare and its neighbor, Burra, constitute the last outposts of civilization. It's one more wine area with a dozen vineyards and the attendant revelry. Take advantage of this last bastion—feast on genuine Aussie fare, sip wine, snoop around heritage buildings, and embrace decadence. In short, eat, drink, and be merry, for tomorrow the desert awaits.

Clare is 136km north of Adelaide. If you're driving from Adelaide, take Main North Rd., which runs directly between the two cities, through the center of Clare, and past most of the wineries. The **Clare Valley Tourist Information Centre** (tel. 8842 2131) is on 229 Main North Rd. Commonwealth, ANZ, and Bank SA all have branches (and, more importantly, **ATMs**) along North Main Rd. If you need a **taxi** to get to that out-of-the-way winery, call 018 847 000. In late May on the Adelaide Cup Weekend, Clare celebrates the **Clare Valley Gourmet Weekend.**

Bungaree Station (tel. 8842 2677; fax 8842 3004), 12km north of Clare along Main North Rd., is an attractive spot to stay for historical reasons (it was established as a sheep station in 1841), but is otherwise quite ordinary. Kitchen facilities provided; bring your own linen. The old shearers' quarters now offer basic but clean lodging

($15). A central location and clean, standard rooms make **Taminga Hotel** (tel. 8842 2808), on Main St., a good choice for those without their own transport ($15).

Clare offers a good selection of bakeries and cafes, but for a heartier feed, you'll have to grab a counter meal in a hotel. **Bebas Coffee Lounge** (tel. 8842 2917), opposite the post office on Main St., has a mouth-watering display of cakes and pastries, plus espresso that would stand up to that served in any Adelaide cafe. Devonshire tea is generous enough to keep you going right past supper. **Price's Traditional Bakery** (tel. 8842 2473), north of the post office, has all of its specialties on display. Try the honey log with fresh cream ($1.50), or partake of the variety of pies, pastries, and sausage rolls. The **Taminga Hotel** (tel. 8842 2808), on Main St., serves the town's best counter meals. Generous portions of the freshest ingredients ensure dining pleasure for as little as $5. The pub decor is oh-so-seventies, but if you're into retro it could be just your scene.

■ Wineries of the Clare Valley

The wineries that draw travelers to Clare dot the main thoroughfare from Auburn north to central Clare. A car is required to fully sample the fruit of these vineyards. Signs to the wineries tend to be very poor and opening times change frequently; it is essential to pick up a guide to the wineries at Clare's tourist office.

Sevenhill Cellars (tel. 8843 4222) had its beginnings in sacramental wine made by and for the brothers of the adjoining St. Aloysius church. Seven Jesuit brothers have continued the tradition of wine making here for the past 145 years, branching out from purely religious endeavors to enchant connoisseurs with a fine array of red, white, and fortified wines.

Leasingham Wines, 7 Dominic St. (tel. 8842 2785). Given the quality of the reds here, it's easy to see why Leasingham is a perennial medal-winner. The appeal is rounded out by lovely surroundings and friendly service.

Taylor's Wines (tel. 8849 2008), on Mintaro Rd. in Auburn. The "Southern Gateway" to the Clare Valley, Taylor's is a family-owned-and-operated winery which produces lovely, cool whites and hearty reds.

Jim Barry Wines (tel. 8842 2261). This vineyard has one of the best views in the valley. On a nice day, take a picnic and buy a bottle of fine white wine from the cellar door for an afternoon of indulgence.

Burra

Thirty minutes north of Clare and 156km north of Adelaide, this old mining town boasts plenty of heritage buildings. Burra and Clare are often grouped together, and some people choose to stay in Burra to access the vineyards of the Clare Valley. Both towns lie amid rolling hills so sleepy that it's difficult to believe that the rocky terrain of Flinders Range begins mere hours to the north.

From Adelaide, pass through Clare and then take the right fork at the end of Main North Rd. to Burra. The route is well-marked. The southern half of Burra, starting at the intersection of Market and Commercial St., has most of the tourist services. The **Burra Tourist Information Office** (tel. 8892 2154) is in Market Square. Contact the regional **RAA** outfit at 8892 2423 (24hr. tel. 8892 2487).

The first backpacker establishment in Burra, **Old Miner's Cottages** (tel. 8892 2154), in Paxton Square, is a joint venture between Greyhound Pioneer and the Burra Tourist Information Center. It's so popular and inexpensive that bookings are essential (twins $30; triples $39). Beds in the grand old **Burra Hotel** (tel. 8892 2389), in Market Square, carry a higher price tag, but clean rooms and a cooked breakfast may justify the expense (singles $26; doubles $50).

For food, head to Market Square, at the intersection of Market and Commercial St. The **Burra Country Pantry** proffers freshly baked treats at pleasing prices. **Water's Burra Baker** has delectable Cornish pasties (fresh pies $1.50), many of them vegetarian. At the **Commercial Hotel,** $2.50 will get you soup and a fresh roll, $5 a generous counter meal. There is not always a vegetarian option on the menu, but the food is good, plentiful, and best of all, cheap.

A great way to see the town's historic structures is to buy the "Burra Passport" at the tourist office, which grants discounts to local museums and comes with the booklet *Discovering Historic Burra.* The **Mangdata Gold Mine Tours** (tel. 8892 2573 or mobile tel. 019 692 981), 23km east of Burra, offers a guided tour of the old government battery and an underground tour of the mine (admission $5; call ahead to book). The **Martindale Hall** (tel. 8843 9088), in Mintaro off the road between Burra and Clare, was featured in the film *Picnic at Hanging Rock.* This stunning mansion is worth seeing even if you haven't seen the movie or read the book. You can almost hear the laughter and see the flashes of muslin as the schoolgirls in the film glide gracefully by.

YORKE PENINSULA

Sheer cliffs into the Southern Ocean are punctuated by sandy coves and sheltered bays on this peninsula directly west of Adelaide. The inland towns of Kadina, Moonta, and Wallaroo comprise the "Copper Triangle," about a 90-minute drive from Adelaide's center, and offer some insight into SA's colonial history. The northern half of the Yorke primarily features the mining history of the Copper Triangle. Spectacular views of the sea, pleasant surfing beaches, and gorgeous camping in Innes National Park, however, draw many travelers further south. The southern tip of the peninsula is an additional two hours past the Copper Triangle from Adelaide, between the Spencer Gulf to the west and the Gulf of St. Vincent to the east.

The Copper Triangle

A trio of old mining towns, **Kadina, Wallaroo,** and **Moonta,** sprang up as a result of discoveries of large copper deposits in the 1860s. The nightlife isn't as hopping as it may have been during the heyday of miners' tenure, but these settlements retain some of the feel of SA's colonial days. They're also a convenient stop on the way to destinations farther south on the Yorke Peninsula.

ORIENTATION AND PRACTICAL INFORMATION

Each of the main towns has their own tourist office. These operate out of the **Moonta Town Hall** (tel. 8825 2622) on George St., the **Wallaroo Tourist Information Centre** (tel. 8823 2023) in Wallaroo Town Hall on Irwin St. (open Mon.-Fri.), and the **Yorke Peninsula Visitor Information Centre** (tel. 8821 2093) in Kadina Town Hall on Talor St. (open daily). Wallaroo also houses the **RAA** (tel. 8854 5138) and a **hospital** (tel. 8852 1200). The **Premier Bus Company** (tel. 8415 5555) runs daily to Kadina, Wallaroo, and Moonta, as well as the satellite coastal towns of Port Hughes and Moonta Bay (one-way $15.30, ages 5-15 $7).

ACCOMMODATIONS

Arkeringa (tel. 8821 4033), on Pine Flat Rd. in Bute, 20km northeast of Kadina. It's a piggery, but that's a good thing. For 10 years, Roslyn and Neil Paterson have had backpackers at Arkeringa mucking out the pens, feeding the chooks (chickens), harvesting the grain, and generally making a fair dinkum Aussie farm tick. Mind you, this is a working farm and guests are expected to do their share. No payment but sweat is expected in return for comfortable accommodations and meat-heavy meals. Work days can be long on the 1100-hectare property, but Roslyn and Neil are extremely personable to those willing to put in a decent day's labor. Work clothes provided. 4-day min. stay. Book ahead so transport can be arranged. Busiest in June, Sept., and Dec.

The Wombat Hotel (tel. 8821 1108), on Taylor St. in Kadina. Clean, basic hotel accommodations at $19. Breakfast of toast, cereal, juice, tea, and coffee included.

The Royal Hotel (tel. 8825 2108), on Ryan St. in Moomba. The Royal has everything a real Aussie pub hotel needs—beer, and lots of it. But it also has friendly management, clean rooms, and tasty counter meals. The beds could be firmer, but are fairly comfortable. Singles $25; doubles $40. Light breakfast included.

The Weerona Hotel (tel. 8823 2008), on John Tce. in Wallaroo. Comfortable rooms are most fiscally sound for couples. Singles $22; doubles $32.

FOOD

The Yorke Peninsula is famous for its Cornish cuisine, especially the humble Cornish pasty (about $1.50), so have two and curb your appetite without blowing your budget. Good bakeries are found throughout the peninsula, but vegetarians shouldn't miss the **Cornish Kitchen,** in Moonta, diagonally opposite the Commercial Hotel, or **Price's Bakeries,** which are found in all three of the Copper Triangle towns.

For an authentic Australian dinner you can't beat the local hotels, where the Aussie counter meal is the stuff of legends. A generous main of fish, chicken, veal "parma," prawns, calamari, or (occasionally) a vegetarian concoction of sorts is accompanied by chips and an all-you-can-eat salad bar. On special nights (generally Thurs.-Sat.) a selected number of these mains cost just $5. Most hotel kitchens close around 8pm, so don't be fashionably late. For the freshest seafood, friendliest service, and most authentic Australian decor (read: brown vinyl), go to **The Royal,** on Ryan St., Moonta.

SIGHTS

The **Moonta Museum** (tel. 8825 1988 or 8825 2588) pays tribute to the Cornish immigrants who settled here to mine copper (open Wed. and Sat.-Sun. 1:30-4pm, school and public holidays 11am-4pm). In the schoolhouse to the rear is the **Family History Resource Centre** (open Wed. and Sun. 1-4pm), the **Miner's Cottage** (open Wed. and Sat.-Sun. 1:30-4pm; school holidays daily), and the **Tourist Railway** (departs museum hourly). Across the road, the **Old Sweet Shop** (tel. 8825 1988) has enough lollies (candy) for any dentist's nightmare. The **Wallaroo Heritage and Nautical Museum** (tel. 8823 2843 or 8823 2366) is in the Old Post Office on Jetty Rd. (open Wed. 10:30am-4pm, Sat.-Sun. and school holidays 2-4pm, and public holidays 10am-4pm; admission $2.50, concessions $2, children 50¢).

The **Kadina Heritage Museum** (tel. 8821 2721 or 8821 1083), 2km south of the Kadina post office on Matta Rd., can be accessed from the Kadina-Moonta Rd. or from Russell St. (open Wed. and Sat.-Sun. 2-4:30pm; admission $4, under 5 free). For something a bit more eccentric, go to the privately owned **Banking and Currency Museum,** 3 Groves St., Kadina (tel. 8821 2906). Take Mick's free guided tour through this tribute to tender. His own collection is the basis for the entire museum. With money lining everything from the walls to the doors, only the most die-hard socialists will fail to be impressed (open Sun.-Thurs. 10am-5pm; admission $3, ages 5-17 $1).

Southern Yorke Peninsula

If surf, sand, and sun are your major reasons for visiting the Yorke Peninsula, either coast will do the aquatic trick. The road down the east coast follows the shoreline more closely than that along the west coast, but both areas offer beautiful swimming beaches, good snorkeling and diving facilities, and excellent surf. The remote Innes National Park is the most idyllic spot for any of these activities.

Orientation and Practical Information The southern half of the peninsula is served by the **Yorke Peninsula Passenger Service** (tel. 1800 625 099), which runs daily from Adelaide to **Yorketown** (one-way $25). Buses go no further than Warooka, west of Yorketown. Stenhouse Bay is more than 50km distant, requiring a car for any measure of flexibility in exploring the park. **Minlaton** qualifies as the main inland town just because it has a **tourist office** in the Harvest Corner Information and Craft Co-op, 59 Main St. (tel. 8853 2600; open Mon.-Fri. 10am-5:30pm, Sat.-Sun. 10am-4pm), the **RAA** (tel. 8853 2243), a **hospital** (tel. 8853 2200), and **police** (tel. 8853 2100). The town of **Port Vincent** lies along the east coast.

Farther south, the peninsula dog-legs west. If this protrusion were a foot, the toe of the peninsula would contain **Innes National Park,** at the southwestern extreme. The tourist office for the national park is in **Stenhouse Bay,** along the southern coast, at the **Stenhouse Bay Information Centre** (tel. 8854 4040 or 8854 4066; open daily). This hamlet has the **RAA** (tel. 8854 5138), a **hospital** (tel. 8852 1200), and **police** (tel. 8852 1100). Inside the national park, the historic mining village of **Inneston** has several accommodations.

Accommodations and Food The **Tuckerway** (tel./fax 8853 7285), in Port Vincent, provides a simple but clean place to lay your head. To get there, follow the road along the east coast of the peninsula from Port Wakefield through Port Clinton, Pine Point, and Port Julia. Take the Port Vincent turnoff down the gulf. Linen is not provided but there are kitchen facilities and the beach is 10 minutes away. Beds in barracks-like dorms cost $8 (non-YHA members $9).

Most of the beds in the southern peninsula are inside **Innes National Park.** Numerous **campsites** up and down the coast within the park are overseen by the national park office in Stenhouse Bay. To camp, self-register at the office just inside the entrance. No bookings are required for tent sites; the brochures at the office will help you choose the campground to pitch your tent. Sites at **Pondalowie Bay** are $12 per vehicle. **Casuarina** charges $15 per site per vehicle (plus a $5 key deposit). All other camping areas at Innes National Park cost $5 per night per vehicle.

Several **lodges and huts** provide shelter in Inneston, within the park. It is crucial to book ahead; call the national park office (tel. 8854 4040; fax 8854 4072). Some have solar-heated water, full kitchens, and flush toilets. Others just have four walls. The lodges usually sleep four to 12 people and cost $22-50 per night.

In most of the southern peninsula, you're destined to fish and chip shops or hotel counter meals at mealtime. But since the Yorke is completely surrounded by water, even average fish and chip shops serve fish that is anything but average. For exceptional butterfish, whiting, and garfish, don't miss **Gum Flat Deli, Fish n' Chips** on Main St. in Minlaton. Go authentic with the takeaway wrapped in paper, head for the nearest beach, and eat some of the freshest seafood in Australia with a seaview for less than $5.

Beaches and Innes National Park Beaches line both coasts of the peninsula. Most are ideal for swimming, but a few spots are dangerous; speak with the knowledgable folks at the Kadina tourist office before taking the plunge. They also distribute the free booklet *Walk the Yorke* to those interested in coastal walks. **Innes National Park** is a fantastic spot for surfing, diving, snorkeling, whale watching, and fishing. Approximately 10,000 hectares were set aside as national parkland in 1970 to encourage the repopulation of the rare Great Western Whipbird. You may not catch sight of these rather shy creatures, but there's a good chance that you'll see enough sculptured, rocky headlands and gorgeous, crashing Southern Ocean waves to make up for any disappointment. **Stenhouse Bay Information Centre** (see **Practical Information,** above) has detailed information on which areas are safe for swimming and surfing and with the number of shipwrecks scattered along this uncompromising coastline, it is best to frolic in recommended areas only.

EYRE PENINSULA

In the driest state on the driest continent on Earth, the Eyre Peninsula provides a welcome belt of lush countryside and sandy, white coves. The peninsula covers a huge area stretching nearly 1000km from Port Augusta and Whyalla in the east to the border with Western Australia. Projecting into the Southern Ocean and circumscribed to the north by the Gawler Ranges, Eyre is traversed by two main routes. The inland Eyre Highway runs 468km from Whyalla west to Ceduna. The coastal route, via the Lincoln Hwy. and Flinders Hwy. stretches 763km from Whyalla to Ceduna.

The eastern side of the Peninsula offers quirky coastal towns with sheltered bays, good swimming areas, and vast stretches of white sand. At the tip of the peninsula, Port Lincoln rests by the calm waters of Boston Bay, while farther west the rugged coastline bears the full force of the Southern Ocean's pounding surf. Eyre's charm lies in its remote inlets and expansive national parks. Even if the towns don't hold your attention themselves, they provide good bases for exploring mile after mile of spectacular, isolated coastline.

Port Augusta

"Port Augusta: Crossroads of Australia," declares a sign on the outskirts of town. There is an element of truth to this—many travelers pass through Port Augusta to carry on farther north into the outback and on to Ayers rock, to make their way along the coast of the Eyre Peninsula, or to head straight across the Nullarbor toward Perth. Port Augusta may not rate highly in excitement, but the crossroads of Australia can provide a comfortable bed, a good meal, and some modern conveniences to ease you into the next leg of your journey.

Orientation and Practical Information Port Augusta lies on the northernmost shore of **Spencer Gulf** at the eastern endpoint of the Eyre Peninsula. If you're just passing through from Adelaide, stick to the highway, which becomes **Victoria Parade.** This then becomes Hwy. 1 to the peninsula and sprouts Hwy. 87 heading north to Coober Pedy. The city center focuses around **Commercial Rd.** with the other main streets forming a surrounding grid. As any driver will soon learn, Port Augusta has a penchant for one-way streets. The **Port Augusta Tourist Information Office,** in Wadlata Outback Centre, 41 Flinders Tce. (tel. 8641 0793), is open daily from 9am to 5:30pm. The North District Office of the **National Parks and Wildlife Service** (tel. 8548 5300) is also in town.

The Ghan railway (tel. 13 22 32) stops in Port Augusta between Adelaide and Alice Springs, NT. **Stateliner** (tel. 8642 5055) runs buses to and from Adelaide (3-5 per day, 4hr.), and to Whyalla (2-5 per day, 1hr.), Port Lincoln (2 per day, 4½hr.), and Quorn (Wed. 1:10pm, Fri. 4pm, Sun. 12:15pm, 35min.; continuing to Hawker, 1½hr., and Wilpena Pound, 2¼hr.). **Greyhound Pioneer** (tel. 13 20 30) runs to Coober Pedy. **Budget,** 16 Young St. (tel. 8642 6040), rents vehicles. The **RAA** (tel. 8642 4357) and **police** (tel. 8648 5020) provide assistance.

Accommodations and Food **Port Augusta Backpackers,** 17 Trent Rd. (tel. 8641 1063), is just off the highway and before the city center coming from Adelaide. A brisk walk from the town center, this quiet, relaxing spot has rooms with four beds each, bunk style ($14, YHA non-members $15), kitchen, and bathroom facilities. **Hotel Augusta,** 1 Loudon Rd., is on the waterfront. Continue along the highway from Adelaide, cross to Westside Beach, turn left onto Caboona Rd., and then left onto Loudon. Clean, comfortable singles or doubles cost $35; linen is provided. The **Flinders Hotel Motel,** 39 Commercial Rd. (tel. 8642 2544), offers backpacker accommodation at $14 per person. Linen is provided. There is a fridge for guests, but no kitchen.

Of the numerous cafes and bakeries along Commercial Rd., **Price's Bakery** has the best array of fresh baked goods. Another good choice is the **Black Bear,** farther down Commercial Rd. Pub counter meals will have to suffice for dinners, and vegetarians may find Port Augusta a bit lacking in variety.

Sights **Wadlata Outback Center,** 41 Flinders Tce. (tel. 8642 4511), offers a hands-on outback exhibit on the geological evolution of the Flinders Range. Displays also address Aboriginal Dreaming and early colonial exploration (admission to Interpretive Centre $6, children $3.50). The **School of the Air,** 59 Power Cr. (tel. 8642 2077), provides radio-based primary education for remote communities (tours daily at 10am, $2). Isolated outback townships also rely on the **Royal Flying Doctor Service,** 4 Vincent St. (tel. 8642 2044), which provides medical service from 14 bases throughout Australia (open Mon.-Fri. 10am-3pm).

Whyalla

Gateway to the beautiful Eyre Peninsula, Whyalla is South Australia's second largest city. A commercial mining port, Whyalla doesn't have much to offer apart from modern amenities, bustling shopping areas, and a general sense of civilization that will be missed on a trek across the rugged terrain farther west.

Orientation and Practical Information The town is large enough to warrant investing in a good map. Whyalla is divided into five major suburbs, each named after an old mayor. **Whyalla** proper is to the northeast of its suburban sprawl; **Whyalla Playford** is southeast, **Whyalla Stuart** southwest, **Whyalla Jenkins** northwest, and **Whyalla Norrie** central.

The **Whyalla Tourist Centre** (tel. 8645 7900 or 1 800 088 589) is on the Lincoln Hwy. as you enter Whyalla from the north (open Mon.-Fri. 8:45am-5:10pm, Sat. 9am-4pm, Sun. 10am-4pm). There are plenty of **banks** and ATMs in town, and an **RAA** (tel. 8645 7257). **Stateliner** runs from Adelaide to Whyalla (3-5 per day) and returns to Adelaide (4 per day, 2 on Sat.) via Port Pirie and Port Augusta. To get around, catch **Whyalla City Transport** (tel. 8645 7257; timetables available at the tourist center), or call **Des's Cabs** (tel. 13 13 23). The largest shopping center of the city, **Westland Shopping Centre,** on the corner of McDouall Stuart Ave. and Nicolson Ave. in Whyalla Norrie, might be considered the city's hub and contains the **post office.**

Accommodations and Food The **Hotel Spencer,** 1 Forsyth Ave. (tel. 8645 8411), offers Aussie pub-style accommodation, with a clean bed, shared bath, and courteous management. Singles start at $25; doubles are a good deal at $30. The **Lord Gowrie Hotel,** on Gowrie Ave. (tel. 8645 8955), has singles for $25 and slightly more expensive doubles for $40. **Hillview Caravan Park** (tel. 8645 9357), is off the Lincoln Hwy. 6km south of Whyalla. Tent sites are $10, with power $13. On-site caravans will accommodate two people for $25.

Two cafes worth trying are **Hannah's Kitchen** (tel. 8645 2151) on Essington Lewis Ave., and the **Foreshore Cafeteria** at Foreshore Beach, Whyalla, which offers a lovely view of the sea. The **Westland Shopping Centre** has an extensive food court.

Sights and Attractions The Lincoln Hwy. runs by several points of interest. North of the city, the **Whyalla Maritime Museum** is housed in the mammoth *HMAS Whyalla,* the first ship built in the Whyalla Shipyard in 1941. Tours of maritime history depart at 11am, noon, 1, 2, and 3pm. Book through the tourist office. Heading west on the highway, one passes **Whyalla Wildlife and Reptile Sanctuary** (tel. 8645 7044). A diverse display of fauna, both native and imported, lies along a lush, 1km walking trail (open daily 10am-dusk; admission $5). To see the **Whyalla Steelworks,** book a coach tour through the tourist office (tours Mon., Wed., and Sat. 9:30am, 2hr., $8).

Port Lincoln

At the southern tip of the Eyre Peninsula sits breezy Port Lincoln, a bustling coastal town that spreads a metaphorical net for tourists as it once spread nets for fish. Port Lincoln is a frequent port-of-call for holiday makers, as both a stopover for those on their way to the more remote attractions of the Eyre Peninsula, and a decent vacation destination for those with an affinity for urban beach culture.

Orientation and Practical Information Nestled along **Boston Bay,** the town peers out toward the Southern Ocean. The main drag is **Tasman Tce.,** where the major hotels, pubs, cafes, and tourist shops are to be found. Farther in, **Liverpool St.** provides good grocery and department store shopping. Port Lincoln is small enough to walk around comfortably, but a car is advantageous for reaching the more secluded beaches in the vicinity.

The **Port Lincoln Visitor Information Centre,** 66 Tasman Tce. (tel. 8683 3544 or 1 800 62 9911), is open daily 9am to 5pm. There are several **banks** and ATMs in town. The **airport** is served by Kendell Airlines (tel. 8231 9567; to Adelaide $80 with 14-day advance purchase) and Lincoln Airlines (tel. 8682 5688 or 1800 018 234; to Adelaide $93, $78 advance purchase). Other services include the **RAA** (tel. 8682 3501), **Budget** (tel. 8684 3668), the **police** (tel. 8688 3020), and the **hospital** (tel. 8683 2200).

Accommodation and Food Hostel-less Port Lincoln has a handful of pubs offering accommodations. **Lincoln Hotel** (tel. 8682 1277), at the beginning of Tasman Tce. as you enter town from Whyalla, is a typical pub accommodation with clean, basic rooms and an ocean view, if you're lucky (singles $20; doubles $35; with bath $5 more). **The Pier Hotel** (tel. 8682 1322), at the center of Tasman Tce., incorporates stunning views of the ocean (if you ask) with hotel amenities, including private baths, front bar, dining room, and bar. Clean, if soft, beds grace singles ($30) and doubles ($40). **Kirtan Point Caravan Park** (tel. 8682 2537), just off Gawler Tce., resides in a lovely setting by Shelley Beach near the center of town (unpowered sites $5; cabins from $22).

For a cheap counter meal, try to find a hotel with a "special" night, where a hearty feed can be as low as $6. Seafood dishes are especially recommended in this area. **The Lighthouse Cafe,** on Tasman Tce. (tel. 8682 2499), stocks all the Aussie standards fresh daily. Go in for a lamington, custard slice, or piece of pavlova and you'll come out satisfied. **Paragon Cafe,** on Tasman Tce. (tel. 8682 1442), is a bargain if you are in the mood for a quick pick-me-up while taking in the deep blues and greens of Boston Bay, just meters away. A toasted fruit bun, butter, and a good cappuccino will set you back a mere $2.50. Service is friendly and fast.

Sights and Activities Port Lincoln is home to South Australia's bizarre "Tunarama Festival" (on the Australia Day long weekend in late Jan.), during which fish are elevated well beyond sea level in the highly competitive **tuna-throwing** events. The rest of the year, you can view these fish in Boston Bay from the safety of a platform at the **Tuna Farm** (tel. 8682 2425). To see more exciting sea life, contact **Dangerous Reef Tours,** which includes an underwater viewing platform on Dangerous Reef, a well-known breeding spot of the infamous great white shark. You'll also see some friendlier sea creatures such as sea lions and seals. Book through the tourist office ($25).

A daytrip from Lincoln affords plenty of time to take in the gorgeous sea views of **Lincoln National Park.** Cliffs and sheltered beaches surrounded by small islands make this area a haven for beach and nature-lovers alike. Camping is possible but access to grounds is sometimes difficult without 4WD. For further information, call the Eyre District Office of **National Parks and Wildlife Service (NPWS),** 75 Liverpool St. (tel. 8688 3111).

■ Toward Ceduna and Western Australia: Coffin Bay

Highway 1 heads northwest from Port Lincoln to the remote outpost of Ceduna, through this lonely settlement, and west across the Nullarbor Plain toward Western Australia. Only the most self-destructive of outlaws would drive this route by choice.

A mere 47km from Lincoln toward Ceduna, you'll find the idyllic **Coffin Bay,** where pelicans glide effortlessly across shimmering, sheltered waters. Wander along the coves of this Southern Ocean inlet, paddle in the cool, clear waters, or rent a boat for a lazy afternoon. **Camping** in the national park is your cheapest option, but you will need to arrange a permit prior to settling in (contact the NPWS office in Port Lincoln). **Port Lincoln Day Tours** (tel. 8682 2750) has a 4WD tour to Memory Cave Wilderness Area, on the Coffin Bay Peninsula.

FLINDERS RANGES AND OUTBACK

As you head north into South Australia's famed Flinders Ranges, all is engulfed in a sky that ends only at an unreachable horizon. The colors deepen with the setting sun as intense russets, blazing oranges, and soft purples emerge and darken before the burning sun reclaims the land with its unrelenting glare.

The Flinders Ranges begin at the northern end of the Gulf of St. Vincent and continue 400km into South Australia's vast northern outback. Within the Ranges, the southernmost national park is Mt. Remarkable (15,632 hectares). The **Flinders Ranges National Park** (92,746 hectares) comprises a large portion of the central Ranges, including Brachina Gorge and Wilpena Pound. The Gammon Ranges National Park (128,228 hectares) contains much of the rugged wilderness of the northern Ranges. If you're planning to hike in the southern Ranges, Quorn is the best base, while Hawker is more convenient in the north. Of course, camping is always an option. North of the Flinders, a moisture-deprived basin has created the salt flats of Lake Torrens and Lake Eyre. Much of the sparsely populated outback beyond has been incorporated into the Desert Parks nature reserve.

To travel in the outback is to rediscover the humbling measures of space and time. This formidable country yields its secrets only to the most patient and intrepid of travelers and to the accumulated wisdom of thousands of years of Aboriginal tradition,

The Wave

While cruising the road to nowhere you may notice that approaching drivers frequently make odd hand gestures as they pass. Are your lights on? Did you leave your indicator blinking when you made that right turn onto the highway some 250km ago? No, it's you they're waving at and you'd better learn to wave back—not to do so is an insult of the highest order and shows outright disregard for country driving etiquette. There are three forms of the wave:

The Lifted Finger: Hand still firmly placed on the steering wheel, slowly lift index finger as the oncoming traffic closes to a distance of approximately four car lengths. Relax index finger immediately upon passing. This is a good wave to employ for large trucks and road trains that may blow you off the highway if you release a full hand, but are liable to drive you off the shoulder if you don't wave at all.

The Four Finger Wave: Once again, wait until the oncoming traffic is about four lengths ahead. Raise four fingers but allow the thumb to remain resting gently upon the wheel. This casual, friendly greeting, demonstrates that you are a well-traveled and friendly, yet suave, road warrior.

The Full Hand: Reserved only for times when you feel most friendly or most in need of human contact, after 200km of outback nothingness. Release hand fully from the wheel. Smile as you move your hand in gay abandon and full swing. But don't wave out of the window—the lanes are quite narrow.

and its opals only to the most persistent of miners. Little wildlife has the tenacity to survive in this most uncompromising of terrains, through which the Stuart Hwy. stretches undaunted, the only feature that distinguishes the red earth from the burning sky.

A car ensures flexibility in traveling this region, but with many roads unsealed, a 4WD vehicle is essential. Keep in mind that this region, although arid, is subject to **flash flooding.** Before setting out it is always a good idea to check road conditions on the Northern Road Conditions Hotline (tel. 11 63 33). Also note that banking services are extremely limited in the Flinders Ranges and the outback. Only Cooper Pedy has an ATM, although Quorn has EFTPOS. Carry ample cash and traveler's checks.

Quorn

Quorn is the quintessential Australian small town. Charming simplicity and straightforward inhabitants create a relaxing atmosphere from which to take in the natural beauty of Flinders Ranges. Quorn boasts friendly pubs, yarn-spinning bushmen, and down-home country hospitality without the saccharine edge.

ORIENTATION AND PRACTICAL INFORMATION

Hwy. 1 from Port Augusta and Hwy. 87 from Clare converge on this gateway to the Flinders Range. Quorn is set out in a simple grid pattern with **Railway Terrace** as its main thoroughfare and the rest of the roads cooperating to form a compact, square town center. A 15-minute walk around central Quorn will familiarize you suitably. Be careful when venturing further afield, however—the Flinders are a bit more difficult to negotiate than these quiet streets.

The **Quorn Tourist Information Office,** on Seventh St. (tel. 8648 6419 or 8648 6031), is open daily from 10am to 4pm. **National Australia Bank,** on Railway Tce., is open daily from 1 to 4pm. There are no ATMs in Quorn. For road conditions, call the **Northern Roads Conditions Hotline** (tel. 11 63 33). **Stateliner** (tel. 8415 5555) runs to Quorn from Port Augusta (Sun., Wed., and Fri.,1 per day, 30min.) and continues on through Hawker to Wilpena Pound. The bus returns to Port Augusta (Thurs., Fri., and Sun. The **post office** (postal code 5433) is also on Railway Tce. and has **public phones** outside.

ACCOMMODATIONS AND FOOD

If not great budget beds, Quorn's four hotels at least serve inexpensive **counter meals.** On "special" nights, a schnitzel, chips, and salad may be just $4.50. Hotel bars are good places to meet locals, particularly the **Transcontinental** on Railway Tce.

Andu Lodge, 12 First St. (tel./fax 8648 6655). An excellent base for a Flinders Ranges holiday, the Lodge feels smaller than its 56 beds. The warm owner knows the Flinders like the back of his hand and is extremely helpful in planning walks around the area. If you just want to relax, hire a mountain bike, try your hand on his musical instruments, or play with the dog. Rooms are clean, beds are firm, the kitchen is well-equipped, and the chickens outside alleviate the need for an alarm clock. Dorms $14; doubles $35. Breakfast $3.

The Transcontinental Hotel (tel. 8648 6076), on Railway Tce. across from the Pichi Richi Railway Station. Good, clean pub-style accommodation. The bar below is a great place to chill out and meet locals. Shout the owner a beer and sit back for an entertaining tale. Singles start at $14; doubles $30.

At the **Pichi Richi Takeaway and Coffee Shoppe,** opposite the station on Railway Tce., walk in, ask one question, and be ready to hear a story or six and a bit of politics for good measure. A good, strong espresso can keep you up for a late-night chat with the owner. **Quandong Cafe and Bakery,** on first St., is cozy but costly. This place may be good for your constitution if you are experiencing travel burnout. Coffee and cake will set you back about $5, but the baked goods are tasty and Quandong is the owner of the second of Quorn's two espresso machines.

SIGHTS AND TOURS

To see the rugged ranges without scuffing your shoes, book a ride on the **Pichi Richi Railway** (tel. 8648 6598; in Adelaide tel. 13 12 46), a scenic heritage train that travels through the stark outback grandeur of the Flinders (2¾hr.). If a more manufactured aesthetic appeals to you, check out **Quornucopia,** 17 Railway Tce. (tel. 8648 6282). Loads of Aussie kitsch—from frill-necked lizard magnets to koala tissue box covers—flood this hippy-run store. What's more, Quornucopia is also home to Boots, still the second largest cat in South Australia, despite a year of strict dieting.

Aboriginal Cultural Tours (tel. 8395 0885), led by Yarluyandi Aboriginals, offer an indigenous look into the Flinders complete with culture, art, and dreaming stories (3 days $395, 4 days $499; includes 4WD travel, 3 meals per day, tents, and equipment except for sleeping bags). Tours are also offered by **Andu Backpacker Lodge** (tel. 8648 6655) and **Flinders Ranges-Adelaide Stepover Tours** (tel. 1800 658 866; based in Adelaide).

Quorn is a great base for bushwalking in the Flinders Ranges. **Devil's Peak,** 11km from town on the Richmond Valley Rd., offers a fantastic view at the top of a steep, stony climb (2-2½hr. return; closed during Nov.-April fire ban). Other recommended hikes include the **Buckaringa Sanctuary,** 32km from Quorn, and **Warren Gorge,** 22km down Arden Vale Rd. There's also **Waukerie Falls,** but don't take the name literally; the falls, 16km from Quorn on the Richmond Valley Rd., are usually dry.

Hawker

Hawker, lacking the charm of Quorn, provides little more than utilitarian proximity to Wilpena Pound. The town itself is quite impossible to get lost in: the simple grid pattern is centered around the intersection of **Wilpena Rd.** and **Graddock St.** On these two streets you'll find all you need before your trek to Wilpena. The **information booth** is on your left as you enter town from the south. Or contact **Hawker Motors** at the corner of Wilpena and Graddock St. (tel. 8648 4014; fax 8648 4283). Hawker possesses the Far North District Office for the **National Parks and Wildlife Service** (tel. 8648 4244).

The only budget accommodation in Hawker is the **Hawker Hotel** (tel. 8648 4102). It's across the road from the Old Ghan Railway Station as you enter Hawker from Quorn, with standard Aussie pub architecture. Beds are firm and facilities are clean (singles $25; doubles $35). For food, check out the **Sightseers Cafe** (tel. 8648 4101), opposite the information booth. It has friendly service, reasonably priced light meals, and Hawker's only real espresso machine.

Hawker Shopping Centre on Wilpena Rd. has all sorts of odds and sods for the weary, road-worn traveler. It's your typical country general store with everything from Mars bars to monkey wrenches, good for last-minute supplies and on-the-road snacks. **Gloede's General Store** at the corner of Graddock St. and Wilpena Rd. has an extremely well-stocked camping supplies section. As this is the last bit of civilization before Wilpena, campers are well advised to stock up here before heading out. The **Old Ghan Restaurant and Gallery** in the Old Ghan Railway Station has mediocre art and some up-market food; the historic building itself is the reason to visit. Home to the legendary Ghan train line for close to a century, rail buffs may find this piece of mechanical history intriguing (open Thurs.-Sun. 11:30am-3pm and 6pm-late).

Wilpena Pound

A highlight of the **Flinders Ranges National Park,** Wilpena is the stuff of legends. Of deep spiritual significance for local Aboriginal people, Wilpena was privy to secret ceremonial ritual and a source of a rich dreaming heritage. To the traveler it offers spectacular views, challenging hikes, and a calm serenity unmatched in the rest of the national park's 94,500 hectares. Tread carefully and spot rosellas, galahs, and even the occasional emu. You can explore Wilpena by foot, 4WD, or scenic flight. For tours, contact the **Wilpena Pound Motel** (tel. 1800 805 802), and be prepared to dole out at least $50 per person. You can drive to the Pound or take the **Stateliner** bus (tel. 8415 5555; to Adelaide: Thurs. 11am, Fri. 7:15am, Sun. 3:05pm, 7hr., $52).

A **campground** (sites $9, with power $14; showers) is the first landmark you'll encounter entering Wilpena from Hawker. A shop here sells camping permits, food, and furnishes **tourist information.** Walking trails begin nearby, and any walk in Wilpena is worth it. A short, picturesque walk runs along the **Heysen Trail** to Pound Gap, while the slightly more strenuous **Wangara Hill walk** (2hr. return) affords wonderful views of the Pound. A high-intensity climb for serious hikers is the trail to **St. Mary's Peak.** All trails are clearly marked in blue. If you plan to attempt a longer walk, advise someone of your plans, the direction you will be walking in, and your expected time of return.

A bit farther from Wilpena is the **Sacred Canyon.** In good weather, turn away from Hawker when exiting the Pound and follow the signs along an unsealed road to this superb collection of Aboriginal paintings on the canyon wall.

Coober Pedy

Road-weary travelers sigh in relief at the promise of civilization here on the unending Stuart Hwy. Coober Pedy is a peculiar subterranean outpost in South Australia's outback. The name, which means "white man's hole in the ground," alludes to the form of this settlement and to the economy which sustains it. Its inhabitants are here for what is *in* the ground, not what's on it: they mine opals by day and sleep in the relative cool of their underground city by night. Wizened within and ruddy skinned without, the people of Coober Pedy are tough because they have to be. Heat and dust grind down those too delicate to last; the land itself slowly chips at their resolve. Determination, stoicism, and stubborn willpower are the qualities which have carved out this hole in the ground.

Be advised that the outback town of Coober Pedy is a mining settlement. This means several things, not the least of which is that there are mineshafts everywhere. When signs indicate that an area is restricted or unsafe you should take them extremely literally. Coober Pedy also has a reputation for roughness. It is not a good idea for lone travelers, particularly females, to wander aimlessly late at night. As it is put in *Priscilla: Queen of the Desert,* "This is a tough little town."

ORIENTATION AND PRACTICAL INFORMATION

Coober Pedy may seem disconcertingly invisible until you realize that half of the town is underground. The town layout, however, is quite simple. The turn-off from the Stuart Hwy. (Hwy. 87) leads into **Hutchinson St.,** home to all three backpacker hostels, the **tourist office** (tel. 8672 5298), and the **post office** (tel. 8672 5062; postal code 5723). **Westpac Bank,** also on Hutchinson St., has an **ATM.** Coober Pedy has **police** (tel. 8672 5056) and the **RAA** (tel. 8672 5230). For car rental, compare **Coober Pedy Vehicle Hire,** on Hutchinson St. (tel. 8672 5688; fax 8672 5198) and **Desert Cave** (tel. 8672 5688). Despite a bad reputation, Cooper Pedy hosts a number of **gay-friendly** establishments. **Underground Books,** on Post Office Hill Rd., has a queer fiction section. The management is a mine of information on both gay and general travel information. Ask about gay accommodations, but don't expect anything budget.

ACCOMMODATIONS, CAMPING, AND FOOD

Joe's Backpacker's (tel. 8672 5613), attached to the Budget Motel on Hutchinson St. If the couple behind the counter look familiar, perhaps you saw them in *Priscilla,* carting a kangaroo carcass across the outback by jeep. In the film, Joe and Maria refused to give the stranded drag queens a lift. In real life, they're a good bit more friendly. Kitchen. Clean dorms $14. YHA.

Radeka's Backpacker's Inn (tel. 8672 5233), at the corner of Hutchinson and Oliver St. For truly underground living you can't beat Radeka's. Clean and comfortable, if a little claustrophobic, this maze of underground "caves" comes complete with its own dungeon. A great place to meet other backpackers. Dorms $13; doubles $30.

Tom's Backpacker's (tel. 8672 5333) on Hutchinson St., has basic dorms for $13.

Camping: Riba's (tel. 8672 5614), on William Creek Rd. Turn off 4km before Hutchinson St. coming from Port Augusta. Riba's has aboveground and subterranean campsites from $4. **Stuart Range Caravan Park,** on the right entering Cooper Pedy, has powered sites for $4.

The ethnic diversity of Cooper Pedy is reflected in its array of food: Greek, Chinese, Italian, and Aussie cuisines are readily available on but rarely cheap. The budget-conscious are best off cooking their own food. If you splurge, take a Greek counter meal at **Tom and Mary's Taverna** (tel. 8672 5622), on Hutchinson St. **John's Pizza Bar II,** also on Hutchinson St. (tel. 8672 5561), makes a mean pizza.

SIGHTS AND ATTRACTIONS

Organized tours are a decent way to see Coober Pedy's sights, if you're willing to pay about $25. Some of the best operators are **Rodeka's Desert Breakaway Tours** (tel. 8672 5223), **Desert Cave Tours** (tel. 8672 5688), and **Discovery Tours** (tel. 8672 5028). Another novel tour is the **Mail Run** (tel. 1800 069 911), which will take you on a 12-hour adventure to the remote outback communities of William Creek, Oodnadatta, and numerous cattle stations, lookouts, and other points of interest along the way ($60; lunch not included). If you've got wheels, drive yourself to the **Breakaways Reserve,** about 50km from Coober Pedy. Pick up the map (50¢) from Undergound Books, take ample water, make sure your car is in good condition, and explore a 70km return loop (roughly 2hr. drive) through to the Breakaways, where scenes from *Mad Max Beyond Thunderdome* and *Priscilla: Queen of the Desert* were filmed, on to the **Dog Fence** (a 2m high wire fence that stretches 5300km across 3 states), over the aptly named **Moon Plain,** and then back to town.

Tasmania

The solution to England's 18th-century convict problem seemed perfect. London prisons were overflowing, and Australia lay dormant in a far corner of the Empire, many thousands of leagues from any place that seemed important. Parliament members happily sent their rabble across the ocean, washed their hands, and went to tea. But transportation did not remove the criminal tendencies in all of these first unfortunates. Lawlessness was still a huge problem in the new prison colony, and penal officials in New South Wales decided to ship the troublemakers away once again. Australia was already at the end of the earth, but Tasmania, fortunately, was at the end of Australia. The British considered assignment to the wild little island, then known as Van Dieman's Land, to be the worst punishment available, reserved for the most determined, heartless recidivists.

Silly Poms. What was thought to be an inhospitable, weatherbeaten rock was in fact the lushest corner of the continent. Life was not easy for the convicts, but they toiled in gorgeous surroundings, far from the dessicated wasteland that covered most of the "north island" (mainland). The convicts harvested timber from the temperate rainforests and established sustainable wool and dairy operations, industries still important in Tasmania today. Isolation and convict heritage defined the state's social and economic development. Even today, tradition and conservatism are the overarching themes of Tasmanian society. Mainlanders mock the 476,000 Tasmanians for their bucolic ways and tepid temperament, but most Tassies don't seem to care what their northern comrades think. In any case, the state's criminal roots don't taint its current well-being: Tasmania has the lowest crime rate of any state.

Many visitors to Australia don't make it under down under. Mainland Australia is certainly a vast place, with a great deal to see and do, but it is well worth the time and money required to detour through Tassie. A third of the state is preserved as wilderness, protecting the last great temperate rainforest on the globe. Bushwalkers from around the planet come to Tasmania's mountainous interior to explore the Overland Track, the premier hiking trail in the southern hemsphere. Indeed, the entire western half of the island is a paradise for outdoor enthusiasts of many persuasions. The uninhabited west coast bears the brunt of the Southern Ocean's fury, but the storms rarely push past the mountains, so the east coast and midlands are quite pleasant year-round. Tiny holiday villages, filled with prosperous fishing fleets and vacationing families, speckle the shore. In the southeast, capital Hobart, Australia's second-oldest city, is pleasantly mired in its own history. Rolling farmland stretches north from Hobart to Launceston, Tasmania's second city and northern hub. The Cradle Mountain World Heritage Area and central plateau regions are easily accessible from Launceston, and any point on the island is within a day's drive. Those on a mission can see much of the island in just a few days, but those who lose themselves in the wilderness and history may never be able to get enough of Tasmania.

Phone numbers in Tasmania have recently changed. Regional phone codes are now all 03, followed by eight-digit numbers. If you have trouble making a call, use the following scheme to get the old number, and try that instead. For more details, see the **appendix** (p. 574).

New Number:	Old Number:
(03) 62xx xxxx	(002) xx xxxx
(03) 63xx xxxx	(003) xx xxxx
(03) 64xx xxxx	(004) xx xxxx

Hobart

Hobart is an old city by Australian standards, founded on February 21, 1804 by Lieutenant David Collins at Sullivan's Cove. Hobart Town saw the importation of tens of thousands of convicts, most from the urban areas of Great Britain. The convict system had a huge impact on the development of the city; today many reminders of its penal past can be found throughout the region. Hobart is built at the mouth of the Derwent River, shielded by a scatter of islands and breakwaters. Like the rest of Tasmania, Hobart is much more conservative than the mainland, and is considered a bit backward by Melburnians, Sydneysiders, and their cosmopolitan ilk. Hobart may lack the frenetic energy of other capitals, but it has also managed to avoid some of the gross commercialization and tawdry trendiness that plague many urban centers. Hobartians enjoy a slower pace of life than their mainland counterparts, and they seem to like it that way.

Driving distances are short in Tasmania, but many roads are steep and winding, and thick fog is common. At dawn and dusk, many wild animals gather on the roadside to ambush passing cars. To avoid any heartache, **slow down** in Tasmania. This allows for better views of the country anyway.

ARRIVAL AND DEPARTURE

There is no passenger rail service anywhere in Tasmania. The *Spirit of Tasmania* ferry connects Tasmania to Melbourne, Victoria, but only runs out of Devonport. Consequently, air and road are the only two means of transport in and out of the capital.

By Plane

Hobart Airport is 18km east of Hobart on Highway A3. **Ansett** (tel. 13 13 00) and **Qantas** (tel. 13 13 13) fly to Melbourne four times daily ($189-247) and to Sydney once daily ($289-358). International flights must make connections in Melbourne. Fares change frequently, but are cheaper with advance booking. International travelers can often get better deals; bring your passport and international ticket when arranging flights. Qantas and Air New Zealand (with Ansett as agent) have flights to Christchurch, New Zealand, through Melbourne or Sydney (return fares from $575). Call to book the **Airporter Bus** (tel. 0419 382 240 or 0419 383 462) for transport to and from the city for $7 (bikes $7).

By Bus

There are two main bus depots in Hobart. Timetables fluctuate seasonally in Tasmania. *Let's Go* has published those in effect during the Australian winter of 1997; summer service will be at least as frequent. The **Tigerline** depot is at 4 Liverpool St. (tel. 6234 4077). Tigerline buses go to Strahan (Wed., Fri., and Sun., 6hr., $40.40), with stops at Queenstown (5hr., $35) and the Derwent Bridge (3½hr., $23.80). Connections to Lake St. Clair are available from **Maxwell Coaches** (tel. 6289 1137). Tigerline buses to New Norfolk operate every day (Mon.-Fri. 6 per day, Sat.-Sun. 2 per day, 1hr., $1.70). The bus to Launceston leaves about three times per day (2¾hr., $17.80) with stops at Ross (1½hr., $13.30), Oatlands (1¼hr., $9.90), and Brighton (30min., $2.70). Coaches leave for the ferry terminal in Devonport to connect with the *Spirit of Tasmania* (Tues. and Thurs. 11am, Sat. 11:15am, 4¾hr., $30.30). Buses occasionally leave at 7:30am and allow a few hours in Ross before arriving at the ferry terminal ($40).

Buses head out of the **old Treasury building** on Murray St. to Taroona (Mon.-Fri. 1 per day, 15min., $2.40), Kettering, and the Bruny Island Ferry (request a connection if traveling on the ferry, Mon.-Fri. 1 per day, 1hr., $5.30). The bus to Cygnet leaves from St. David's Cathedral on Macquarie St. (Mon.-Fri. 1 per day, 1hr., $6.80). East coast buses depart from the depot for Triabunna (book for Maria Island connections, Sun.-Fri., 1½hr., $11.30), Swansea (Sun.-Fri., 2¼hr., $16), the Coles Bay turn-off (Wed., Fri., and Sun., 3hr., $19) with $5 connections to Freycinet National Park through **Bicheno Coaches** (tel. 6257 0293), and St. Helens (Wed., Fri., and Sun., 4hr., $28.50). Buses to Port Arthur also leave from the depot (Mon.-Fri., 2hr., $11.50).

Redline Coaches has a depot at 199 Collins St. (tel. 6231 3233). Daily coaches run to Launceston (2½hr., $17.80), with stops in Ross (1½hr., $14.20), Oatlands (1hr., $10.60), and Brighton (20min., $3.20). Coaches to the east coast operate Sunday through Friday to Swansea (3½hr., $20), St. Helens (4¼hr., $26.60), and the Coles Bay turn off. In the same building, **Tasmanian Wilderness Travel** (tel. 6334 4442; fax 6334 2029; email info@taswildtravel.com.au; http://www.tassie.net.au/wildtour) offers special bushwalking packages for Overland Trackers and other hikers. Regular services include Lake St. Clair (April-Nov. Tues., Thurs., and Sat., Dec.-March daily, 4¼hr., $40), Strahan (April-Nov. Sat., Dec.-March Thurs. and Sat., 8¼hr., $52), Frenchman's Cap (April-Nov. Sat., Dec.-March Thurs. and Sat., 6hr., $45), Mt. Field National Park (Dec.-March daily, April-Nov. Tues., Thurs., and Sat., 1hr., $19), and Launceston (only Dec.-March Mon.-Tues., Thurs., and Sat., 8hr. scenic tour, $50).

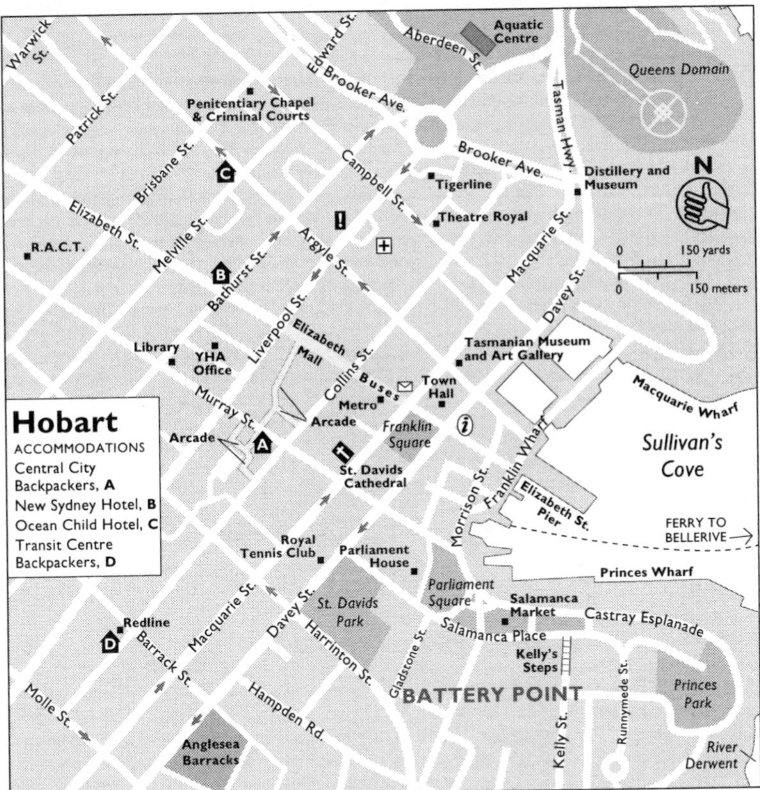

ORIENTATION

The central business district is on the western bank of the **Derwent River;** most of the city's tourist attractions and services are clustered downtown in a grid around the **Elizabeth Street Mall,** just behind Sullivan's Cove. Just south of the Cove lies **Battery Point,** one of the oldest sections of the city, choked with antique shops and cottages. The northern border of Battery Point is defined by **Salamanca Place,** a row of old Georgian warehouses that have been restored and renovated as galleries, shops, and restaurants. **Franklin Wharf,** adjacent to Salamanca Pl., is the departure point for the many cruises and tours that operate in the harbor. The Tasman Bridge spans Derwent River; just north, the Bowen crosses over from **Glenorchy,** Hobart's largest suburb.

Hobart is backed by the **Wellington Range,** which affords fine views from Mt. Nelson, to the south, or the larger Mt. Wellington, about 7km west of central Hobart. The city proper can be navigated on foot, while public buses run to the outer reaches of the suburbs. The **Tasman Peninsula** and **Huon Valley** make easy daytrips; **Bruny Island** and points along the east coast are just a few hours away by car or bus.

PRACTICAL INFORMATION

Tourist Office: Hobart Tasmanian Travel and Information Centre, 20 Davey St. (tel. 6230 8233), 200m inland on the corner of Davey and Elizabeth St. Accommodation bookings ($2), organized tours and walks, travel arrangements and itineraries. Open Mon.-Fri. 8:30am-5:15pm, Sat. 9am-4pm, Sun. 9am-1pm.

Budget Travel Office: YHA's Tasmanian Headquarters, 28 Criterion St., 2nd floor (tel. 6234 9617; fax 6234 7422), between Bathurst and Liverpool St. Travel insurance, passport photos, tickets, and travel advice, in addition to YHA memberships and hostel bookings. Open Mon.-Fri. 9am-5pm.

Currency Exchange: Mobs of banks crowd in and around the Elizabeth St. Mall. **ANZ** (tel. 13 13 14), 22 Elizabeth St., 40 Elizabeth St., and 154 Liverpool St. **Commonwealth,** 81 Elizabeth St. (tel. 6238 0400). **Westpac** has branches at 66 Murray St. (tel. 6224 8577) and 38 Elizabeth St. (tel. 6230 4142). All open Mon.-Thurs. 9:30am-4pm, Fri. 9:30am-5pm. **ATMs** are at 109 Collins St. and 85 Liverpool St.

American Express: 74a Liverpool St. (tel. 6234 3711), open Mon.-Fri. 9am-5pm.

Public Transportation: City buses are run by **Metro** (tel. 13 22 01), with a shop at 18 Elizabeth St. Service extends to the most distant suburbs and nearly all neighboring points of interest (service daily approx. 6am-midnight). Fares range from $1.20-2.80; purchase on board. "Day Tripper" tickets allow unlimited travel Mon.-Fri. 9am-4:30pm and after 6pm, all day on weekends. Timetables are available at the Metro shop.

Car Rental: Autorent Hertz, 122 Harrington St. (tel. 6237 1111), from $44 per day. **Thrifty,** 11-17 Argyle St. (tel. 6234 1341; airport tel. 6248 5678), from $57. At **Rent-A-Bug,** 105 Murray St. (tel. 6231 0300; fax 6231 5017; email rentabug@southcom.com.au), VW Beetles from $25 per day are a very popular option.

Automobile Club: RACT, at the corner of Murray and Patrick St. (tel. 6232 6300). Open Mon.-Fri. 8:45am-5pm.

Fishing Equipment: Information and equipment available at the **Compleat Angler,** 142 Elizabeth St. (tel. 6234 3791).

Public Market: There is a very popular craft and produce market in Salamanca Pl. on Sat. from early morning until about 3pm.

Library: At the corner of Bathurst and Murray St. (tel. 6233 7462). Book at the information desk for free **internet access.** Open Mon.-Thurs. 9:30am-6pm, Fri. 9:30am-8pm, Sat. 9:30am-12:30pm.

Pharmacy: Corby's Everyday Pharmacy, 170 Macquarie St. (tel. 6223 3044). Open daily 8am-10pm.

Hospital: Royal Hobart Hospital, 48 Liverpool St. (tel. 6222 8308; fax 6231 2043).

Emergency: Dial 000.

Police: 37-43 Liverpool St. (tel. 6230 2111). Lost and found tel. 6230 2277.

Post Office: At the corner of Elizabeth and Macquarie St. (tel. 6220 7351; fax 6234 9387). Open Mon.-Fri. 9am-5pm. **Postal code:** 7000.

Phone Code: 03.

ACCOMMODATIONS

The tourism industry is in decline in Hobart, and two of the three YHA hostels have recently closed. But many of the pubs downtown have rooms to let, and two backpackers remain in the middle of the city.

Transit Centre Backpackers, 199 Collins St. (tel./fax 6231 2400), above the Redline depot. A bit drab from the outside—it is a bus station, after all. Still, this hostel is extremely comfortable, and the maternal management does all it can to make guests comfortable. Huge common facilities are warmed by a large woodstove, but the bunkrooms and bathrooms can be nippy during the winter. Free storage; coin-operated laundry. Alcohol is forbidden, except by arrangement with the management; drink free tea or coffee instead. Dorms $12, bedding $4 (sleeping bags are allowed).

Central City Backpackers, 138 Collins St. (tel. 6224 2404), on the 2nd floor through the Imperial Arcade. A large hive of a hostel with a variety of rooms and industrial common areas. Efficiently run by a young couple, the atmosphere is a bit withdrawn but not entirely unfriendly. The location couldn't be better, just a few minutes' walk from any point in the city. Smoking strictly forbidden. Coin-operated laundry and internet. Reception open daily 8am-9pm. 6-bed dorms $12; 4-bed dorms $14; singles $28; twins $34; doubles $36. Sleepsheet $2, with doona $5, towels $1. Key deposit $5. Sleeping bags allowed. No credit cards.

New Sydney Hotel, 87 Bathurst St. (tel. 6234 4516), just a few blocks northwest of the central business district along Elizabeth St. Cozy, older rooms above a popular Irish pub. The facilities are being slowly modernized, but some areas remain a bit old-fashioned. The rooms are well-maintained despite their age, and the bathrooms are kept spotless. The small common area has a TV lounge and full kitchen, and the pub downstairs serves hearty meals noon-2pm and 6-8pm. The music downstairs is loud, but it shuts down by midnight at the latest. 7-night max. stay. Dorms $12; doubles $35. Key deposit $10.

Adelphi Court YHA, 17 Stoke St., New Town (tel. 6228 4829; fax 6278 2047). Take a bus from Argyle St. to stop 8A, just opposite the hostel, or take a bus from the terminus on Elizabeth St. to stop 13, and walk a few meters down Stoke St. The only YHA hostel left in Hobart, Adelphi is a sprawling complex built like a motel around a pleasant courtyard. Dorms are equipped with 2 sets of bunks and a handy wash basin. The space heaters are next to useless. There is a large kitchen and a comfy common area with a variety of games, but the lounge closes around 10pm. The kiosk stocks basic groceries. Reception can book tours, coach tickets, and other YHA accommodations (open 8am-8pm). Dorms $13; twins $36; singles with bathroom $45; doubles $47. YHA non-members pay $3 more. Breakfast: continental $5, cooked $8. Bikes $12 per half-day, $20 for 1 day, $15 per day for 2 or more days, with a $30 deposit.

Ocean Child Hotel, 86 Argyle St. (tel. 6228 4829), just a short walk from the city center. This nautical pub is being modernized to provide up-to-date amenities while retaining its wood-paneled charm. The upstairs rooms can be a bit dark, but everything is kept neat and tidy. Guests cook in the full kitchen or take a discount on pub meals. Live music on Wed.-Sat. is usually some sort of jazz or folk that isn't likely to keep people awake, even those in the audience. The pub has an above average selection of beer. Dorms $12, $15 if you want a doona and towel; doubles $30. Coin-operated laundry.

Sandy Bay Caravan Park, 1 Peel St. (tel. 6225 1264), right next to the casino off Sandy Bay Rd. This is the only caravan park near the city center, a few kilometers south near Wrest Point. The front section of this big park is paved for caravans, while the rear section consists of a series of grassy, level terraces for camping. The large cinderblock amenities complex is kept well-disinfected, and there is a reasonable camp kitchen in the rear. Unpowered sites $6 per person; powered sites for 2 $15; caravans for 2 $32; self-contained cabins for 2 $45.

FOOD

Hobart has a variety of good bargains. Pillage the central business district for take-away and chips, or head to the pubs for lunch and dinner. There are supermarkets in the northern and southern suburbs; closer to town look for **Jim's Shopping Oasis,** 190 Davey St. (tel. 6223 1090), or **Ralph's Festival,** 189 Campbell St. (tel. 6234 8077; open daily 8am-7pm). Stop for food at the 24-hour **Food Stop** on Elizabeth St., a few blocks north of Bathurst St. The Saturday **Salamanca Market** has excellent deals on local produce, honey, and cheese. Stalls sell Mutsu apples, which grow to the size of an infant's head, among other appetizing fruits. Good value restaurants cluster on Elizabeth St. a kilometer or two from the mall.

Steve's Kebab House, 127 Liverpool St. (tel. 6231 6000). Serving the best Turkish fast food in Hobart, Steve's is sprouting up around the city in various locations. International kebabs are a specialty: Yankee-doodle kebabs come with mustard and ketchup, Aussie kebabs come with a fried egg and sauce (both $4.80 for the large serving), and the vegetarian falafel is a tasty herbivorous option. Steve also serves fresh fruit and vegetable juices. Almost everything is less than $5. Open Sun.-Thurs. until 10pm.

Noah's Foods, on Constitution Dock (tel. 6231 9444). Noah's is the tastiest and least greasy fish shop on Constitution Dock—you can even get fish that hasn't been fried. For the best food, ask for something that is cooked fresh; the specials are often a good choice. Open daily 11am-7:30pm.

A Taste of Asia, 358 Elizabeth St. (tel. 6236 9191). A favorite with locals, the cuisine is "Asian inspired" rather than traditional, run o' the mill Chinese. The menu is fairly small, but many dishes are unique. The large plates ($8) are a great deal. BYO. Open Mon.-Thurs. noon-8pm, Fri. noon-9pm, Sat. 4-9pm.

Trattoria Casablanca, 213 Elizabeth St. (tel. 6234 9900). This pasta and pizza joint is staggeringly popular; bookings are recommended on weekends. Once you're seated, the meal is fairly straightforward: traditional pastas $6-9, funkier pizzas $6.50-8. A shrine to its namesake movie. Open until midnight.

The Rusty Anchor, 22 Francis St. (tel. 6224 9900), on the corner of Francis and Hampden St. in Battery Point. This tiny, well-appointed dining room has a very residential, comfortable feel. 2 separate menus: seafood takeaway is a cut above regular fish and chips, and a bit more expensive ($4-8.50). The other menu features fancy cuisine, primarily seafood but other meats as well ($10-12). Fully licensed and BYO (wine only). Open daily from 5pm.

Muffin Munchies, 138 Collins St. (tel. 6224 2520), in the Imperial Arcade. Excellent muffins, both savory and sweet. Other baked goods are available, but eat muffin instead. Particularly tasty are the spinach and cheese and the sugar-free multi-grain. From 5-5:30pm, muffins are 2 for the price of 1 ($1.50). Excellent coffee. Open daily 7:30am-5:30pm. Munchies also has a stall at the Salamanca Market on Sat.

Megasnax, 30 Criterion St. (tel./fax 6231 0225). This coffee shop provides a dose of healthy, tasty, nutritious food. Hot dishes change daily and always include a vegetarian option. The homemade soup makes a mighty fine lunch, and it's good for you, too. It's also a nice change from the usual meat pies. Open Mon.-Fri. 7am-5pm.

Liep's Restaurant, 322 Elizabeth St. (tel. 6231 1554). A converted cottage serving Thai, Vietnamese, and Indonesian cuisine. All of the food is cooked fresh to order, an uncommon feature among Aussie Asian restaurants. Most dishes ($10-12) come with a generous portion of steamed rice. Open daily until 10pm.

Kaos Kafe, 237 Elizabeth St. (tel. 6231 5699), is strewn with objets d'art and cool floor tiles. Bring your clip-on ponytail for this trendy eatery. Abundant choices include foccacia, sandwiches, nachos, and salads (all $5-10). Open Mon.-Fri. noon-midnight, Sat. 10am-midnight, Sun. 10am-10pm.

Siam Garden, 81A Bathurst St. (tel. 6234 4327), exudes a perfumed atmosphere. The lunch special ($5) can be complemented with BYO wine (corkage $3 per bottle). Traditional Thai food $10-15. Fully licensed also. Open Fri. noon-2pm and 5-10pm, Sat. 5-10pm, Sun. 5-9pm.

SIGHTS

Many of the old, convict-era buildings have survived into modern times. **Battery Point** is particularly well-preserved; a stroll through the narrow streets is very enjoyable. Obtain a Battery Point tourist map from the Travel and Information Centre for historical notes and locations of the old structures. While exploring Battery Point, make your way to the **Maritime Museum** (tel. 6223 5082), on Secheron Rd. Concentrating on local shipping and whaling, this crowded museum is filled to the gunwales with precise model boats, ancient photographs, and crusty relics of times gone by (open daily 10am-4:30pm; admission $4). **Narryna,** 103 Hampden Rd. (tel. 6234 2791), is a stately Georgian house set in a meticulous old world garden. Built in 1836 by Andrew Haig, the house today contains Australia's oldest folk museum. Household goods, furniture, clothing, and other pioneer artifacts are displayed to give an idea of what early colonial life was like for a wealthy sea merchant and his family (open Aug.-June Tues.-Fri. 10:30am-5pm, Sat.-Sun. 2-5pm).

Just behind the Esplanade on the edge of Battery Point, the pleasant green space of **Princes Park** was the site of the Mulgrave Battery, the gun emplacement after which the point is named. Look for the signal station right on the Esplanade. Built in 1818 as a guardhouse, the station is the oldest building on Battery Point. It was later converted to relay messages about shipping and criminal justice between Hobart and the surrounding country as far away as Port Arthur. There are at least a dozen craft galleries and antique shops scattered around the Point.

North of Battery Point, **Salamanca Place** is a famous row of sandstone warehouses formerly used to house jam, hops, wool, timber, and other goods waiting to be shipped to the mainland. Today the Georgian monoliths are used as galleries, restaurants, cafes, and shops. Around the bend in the cove, the Elizabeth, Brooke, and Murray Piers harbor most of Hobart's large vessels. Look for the Antarctic Research

Expedition's giant orange icebreaker, *Aurora Australis.* Constitution and Victoria Dock are thronged with fishmongers and marine restaurants. Several companies run harbor cruises from this area. **Roche O'May Ferries** sails from the Brooke St. Pier to the Wrest Point Casino on the east bank; trips are available with meals or without (tel. 6223 1914 for details and bookings). The **Lady Nelson** gives river cruises in a more historical context (tel. 6272 2823). Popular combination cruises visit the Cadbury Chocolate Factory; try contacting **Cruise Company** (tel. 6234 9294), **M.V. Emmalisa** (tel. 6223 5893), or call **Cadbury** (tel. 1800 627 367) itself.

The pleasant area just inland from the wharves features two large parks; **Parliament Square,** is the broad green in front of the Parliament House, and **St. David's Park,** featuring huge trees and a gazebo on a gently sloping hillside, is one block to the west. St. David's also has a cathedral, at the corner of Murray and Macquarie St., which is worth a gander. A bizarre, ancestral form of tennis lingers on at the **Royal Tennis Club,** 45 Davey St. (tel. 6231 1781), adjacent to the park. The club contains one of the few Royal courts in the southern hemisphere.

The **Tasmanian Museum and Art Gallery** (tel. 6235 0777), on the corner of Argyle and Macquarie St., has fine displays exploring Tasmania's early convict history, unique ecology, and artistic heritage. The modern Australian art section is particularly strong. The adjacent Bond Store houses a dynamic selection of temporary exhibits. (Free guided tours leave from the bookshop Wed.-Sun. 2:30pm. Open daily 10am-5pm. Museum and gallery free.) The **Penitentiary Chapel and Criminal Courts** (tel. 6223 5200), on the corner of Brisbane and Campbell St., is one of the oldest, best-preserved buildings in Tasmania, and an excellent example of Georgian ecclesiastical architecture. The buildings house the southern regional offices of the National Trust (guided tours available daily 10am-2pm).

The **Royal Tasmanian Botanical Gardens** (tel. 6234 6299), north of the city near the Tasman Bridge, opened to the public in 1818 to make them the second oldest in Australia. Worth a visit at any time of year, the gardens cover 13 hectares and contain 6000 species, the largest public collection of Tasmanian plants and the largest public collection of conifers in the southern hemisphere. The Chinese gardens are being developed to display flora from the Himalayan foothills. Take any service to the eastern shore and get off at stop 4 before the bridge. Or take the X3-G express to Bridgewater, which stops at the main gate. Admission is free.

Further north in Lenah Valley, the **Lady Franklin Gallery** (tel. 6228 0076), built in 1842 by Lady June Franklin, is one of the oldest galleries in the state. Take the Lenah Valley bus to the end of the line to reach the gallery (open Sat.-Sun. 1:30-5pm; free). Even further north in Glenorchy, the **Tasmanian Transport Museum,** on Anfield St. (tel. 6272 7721), has a collection of locomotives, rail cars, trams, trolleys, signal boxes, and other transport relics. Train rides are offered on the first and third Sundays of each month. (Open Sept.-April Sat.-Sun. 1-5pm; May-Aug. Sat.-Sun. 1-4:30pm. Admission $2, children $1; on train ride days $3, $1.60.)

Mt. Nelson, just south of central Hobart, offers sweeping views of Hobart and the Derwent estuary. A signal station at the top, part of the chain that connected Port Arthur to the capital, is today equipped with a tea house (open daily). The road to the top is open daily from 9am to 9pm. Take the Mt. Nelson bus to its terminus. **Mt. Wellington,** several kilometers west of Hobart, is even more impressive, reaching a height of 1270m. The mountain was named in 1824 after the Duke of Wellington, hero of the Napoleonic Wars. The top is barren, windy, and cold; gusts in excess of 150kph have been recorded, and snow lingers for much of the year. On a clear day, you can see as far as Bruny Island and the far reaches of the Wellington Range (observation shelter open 8am-4:30pm). The road to the top closes occasionally due to snow and ice. **Fern Tree,** on the lower foothills of the mountain, is a lovely picnic and BBQ area with walking tracks up the slope. For track details, get the Mt. Wellington Day Walk Map from the Travel and Information Centre. By bus, take the Fern Tree service to stop 27.

Ten kilometers to the south, in Taroona, stands the **Shot Tower** (tel. 6227 8885), built in 1870 by Joseph Mair and once used to manufacture lead shot. The freestone tower is the tallest shot tower in the southern hemisphere. The top overlooks the Derwent estuary (open daily 9am-5:30pm; admission $3, children $1.50). Take the Taroona/Proctor's Road bus to stop 45.

Risdon Cove (tel. 6243 8830), on the east bank of the Derwent at Risdon Vale, is the site of Tasmania's first settlement in 1802. The location was then deemed foolish and the colony was moved across the river to Sullivans Cove. The government returned the site to the Aboriginal community in 1995 (open daily 9:30am-4:30pm).

One of the most popular attractions in Hobart is the **Cadbury Chocolate Factory** (tel. 6249 0333 or 1800 627 367; fax 6249 0334), in Claremont. Tours examine a variety of packaging, mixing, shaping, and coating machines, and chocolate tasting features prominently. (Tours Mon.-Fri. 5 per day; tickets $10, students $7, children $5. Advanced bookings required.) Take the Claremont service right to the factory.

If you prefer death by beer rather than chocolate, visit the **Cascade Brewery** (tel. 6224 1144), built in 1824 by a Mr. Degraves, who was fleeing debt in England. His luck ran out, landing him five years in prison. While in the belly of the beast, Mr. Degraves drew up plans to make his building a brewery, and production began in 1832 on what is now the oldest brewery in Australia. Today, 800 stubbies are produced every minute. (Tours require bookings Mon.-Fri., about 1½hr.; tickets $7, students $5. Free beer at the end.) Take the Strickland Ave. bus service to stop 17.

See the fabulous beasts that roam the island's wilderness up close at the **Bonorong Wildlife Park** (tel. 6268 1184; fax 6268 1811), north of Hobart in Brighton. Devils (Tasmanian, that is), koalas, quolls, and wombats live in enclosures, while 'roos bounce where they will. Every visitor gets a bag of kangaroo feed, which the mannerless brutes will eat right out of your hand. Food for humans is also available. Devil feeding time is particularly interesting and noisy (park open daily 9am-5pm; admission $7, children $3.50). Take the Brighton bus all the way to the end.

South of Hobart in Kingston, the **Australian Antarctic Division** (tel. 6232 3205) organizes and supports the Australian National Antarctic Research Expeditions (ANARE). The Division maintains a small museum with displays on the Australian role in the exploration of the last great wilderness on earth. The exhibit is well worth the effort of getting there; take Tigerline Coaches from St. David's Cathedral on Murray St. (Sun.-Fri. 5 per day, $2.50).

NIGHTLIFE AND ENTERTAINMENT

Hobart is often mocked for its lukewarm nightlife, but with an open mind, one can find things to do. This isn't the place to find a world-class club scene on par with that of Melbourne or Sydney, however. Big name acts rarely bother to go to Tasmania, but the crowds are gigantic and wildly appreciative when they do.

Pubs, Clubs, and Music

The main dance clubs in Hobart are **Hazard Zone,** 86 Sandy Bay Rd. (tel. 6223 3655), and **'round Midnight,** 39 Salamanca Pl. (tel. 6223 2491), with ever-fluctuating standards of dress and behavior. Expect to pay a cover ($8-10). Most pubs downtown have music on weekends.

The New Sydney Hotel, 87 Bathurst St. (tel. 6234 4516), is an extremely popular Irish pub with live music Tues.-Sun., mainly cover bands. On Sat. afternoons, there are open Irish jam sessions. Margaritas, in a dubious Irish tradition, are the most popular beverage at the bar. Meals are available noon-2pm and 6-8pm ($6-15). The place closes down at midnight.

Joe's Garage, 145 Elizabeth St. (tel. 6234 3501; fax 6234 3502), is half-pub, half-auto parts store. A shrine to all things automotive, Joe's is an honest bar serving honest drinks to honest folks at honest prices. No bouncer—only good people come here. Engine block tables and license plates on the walls make you feel like you're inside a machine. The restaurant next-door has Cadillac tailfin booths and a Beatles corner equipped with a papier-maché yellow submarine. Open daily until midnight.

The Shamrock Hotel, 195 Liverpool St. (tel. 6234 3892), is the local footy pub, with posters and pictures of the game's heroes and legends. Fairly empty, with plenty of room to spread out and drink. Open Mon.-Tues. 11am-10pm, Wed.-Thurs. 11am-midnight, Fri. 10am-4am, Sat. 10:30am-4am, Sun. noon-8pm.

Cafe Who, 251 Liverpool St. (tel. 6231 2744; fax 6231 5241), is the place for both aging and youthful hipsters. The modern, abstract architecture distinguishes the place from its surroundings. Local, national, and international acts appear regularly; genres include jazz, world, and dance music. Very modern cuisine ($8-15) to go with the paintings and the interior design. Open Tues.-Thurs. 4:30pm-midnight, Fri.-Sat. 4:30pm-late.

Cinema, Theater, and the Casino

The giant **Village Cinema** complex, 181 Collins St. (tel. 6234 7288), screens Hollywood's best a few months after the flicks tour the States. For friskier fare, try the Salamanca Arts Centre's **Cinema After Dark,** 77 Salamanca Pl. (tel. 6223 4930), which shows independent, avant-garde features and documentaries (tickets $6). The other art house cinema is the **State,** 375 Elizabeth St. (tel. 6234 6318; fax 6278 1704). A similar repertoire plays in glitzier facilities (tickets $9, students $6.50; all Wed. shows $6). **The Theatre Royal,** 31 Campbell St. (tel. 6233 2299, outside Hobart 1800 650 277), is the oldest theater in Australia and can generally be counted on to have a strong season. More experimental theater is produced in the **Salamanca Theatre,** 79 Salamanca Pl. (tel. 6234 8561), with several spaces around the city. There are also puppets in Salamanca at the **Terrapin Puppet Theatre,** 77 Salamanca Pl. (tel. 6223 6834).

The **Wrest Point Hotel** in Sandy Bay, the oldest casino in Australia, caters to Hobart gamblers 24 hours a day. The emphasis is on pokies and other electronic games, but there are a few real gaming tables. The on-site nightclub, **Blackjacks Showroom,** is free, except when it books live acts.

Port Arthur and the Tasman Peninsula

The Tasman Peninsula is very nearly the Tasman Island, since it is barely connected to the mainland at Eaglehawk Neck. When the British were looking for a place to dump recidivists, this narrow access, coupled with a reasonable climate and a safe harbor, made the peninsula a natural choice. Beginning in 1830, convicts were shipped to Port Arthur, on the Tasman Peninsula, for offenses including murder, "gross filthiness," and "skulking without permission." The inmates were put to work, and Port Arthur eventually became a self-contained, sustainable settlement that exported timber, leather, and high-quality church bells. Many fine sandstone buildings were erected through the convicts' labor; the ruins of these structures are Tasmania's most popular tourist attraction, with 250,000 visitors touring the site annually.

Accommodations and Transport Port Arthur is the most convenient place to stay on the peninsula, as it's right next to the infamous prison and the sight most people come to see anyway. The **Garden Point Caravan Park** (tel. 6250 2340; fax 6250 2509) has dormitory bunkhouses ($13), cabins ($50-65), and tent sites (unpowered $11; powered $13) in a wooded setting filled with flocks of noisy birds. Prices increase after Christmas. The **Port Arthur YHA** (tel. 6250 2311) is ideally located mere yards from the historic ruins. The building is an old wooden cottage, which is pleasant to the eye but a deep freeze in winter (dorms $12; YHA non-members $15). **Tigerline** (tel. 6250 2402) has buses to Hobart that depart from the Coach House, 23 Safety Cove Rd., Port Arthur (Mon.-Fri. 6am, 2hr., $11.50), running through Eaglehawk Neck about 15 minutes later. Bookings can be made with the YHA management. Tigerline's depot in Hobart is at 4 Liverpool St. (tel. 6234 4077).

The Solitary System

The basic principles of the "reformed" Port Arthur prison of the 1840s were anonymity, isolation, and contemplation. Each prisoner was kept in a separate cell and referred to by number, on the rare occasions that guards needed to verbally communicate. Silence was strictly enforced; most communication took the form of hand signals. The floors of the prison were covered in reed mats, and the guards wore felt overshoes to deaden the sound of footfalls. The inmates were set to tasks during the day, since idleness was thought to promote violence. Activities included tailoring, shoe making, and other quiet tasks that could be pursued in a solitary cell. When not working, prisoners were expected to pray for salvation or attend chapel. Services were conducted in a specially built room that prevented the occupants from seeing anyone other than the bellowing preacher. Prisoners were exercised in solitary, individually partitioned yards, where they were commanded to walk briskly, never leaning on the walls or loafing. Whenever they were transported, inmates wore cloth masks over their entire heads. If any of the prison's regulations were broken, offenders were sent to the punishment cell, a tiny room with yard-thick stone walls that prevented any sound or light from disturbing the occupant. This complete sensory deprivation could be maintained for weeks at a time, but most prisoners repented within a matter of days. Interestingly, the lunatic asylum right next door stayed filled to capacity throughout the existence of the model prison and its "humane" tortures.

Port Arthur, Tours, and History The **Port Arthur Historic Site** (tel. 6250 2363; http://www.portarthur.org.au) is the most striking reminder of Australia's convict heritage. Penal colonies for repeat offenders were also set up at Sarah Island near Strahan and at Maria Island just northeast of Hobart, but both of these have since been razed, leaving Port Arthur as the final remnant of this troubled time. The model prison, lunatic asylum, hospital, and church are some of the best-preserved penal buildings, on display alongside some private residences. The dwellings retain some of the period furniture, giving an idea of what life was like in the 19th century. Guided **tours** of the grounds, included in the price of admission, are a good way to explore the site (meet at the visitor center; bookings not required). The **Historic Ghost Tour** runs nightly at 6:30 and 8:30pm; $10 buys nearly two hours of spooky stories and creepy shadows (pay the YHA manager). Many of the buildings are floodlit at night to spectacular effect. Allow four hours for a reasonable exploration of the site. (Open daily 8:30am-8:30pm, but most of the buildings close at 5pm. Admission is $13, after 4:30pm $6.50.) A cruise around the harbor to inspect the **Isle of the Dead,** the colony's cemetery, and **Point Puer,** the convict boys' colony, is included in the price of admission; bookings must be made at the visitor center. Cruises that land on the Isle of the Dead can also be arranged for $5.

The colony was under martial administration from its founding in 1830 until 1854, when civilian governors took over. The military period gave the colony a fearsome reputation for physical hardship and cruelty. For years, Port Arthur was feared throughout the empire as the foulest hell-hole in the British penal system. Convicts were punished for crimes with back-snapping labor and liberal use of the lash. The **cat o' nine tails** was a whip made of nine strands of nautical cord, each with nine knots, soaked in sea water to make the tails stiff and salty. Guides tell the story of Denis Doherty, an Irish man who spent 43 of his 61 years in prison. Doherty boasted that he had taken over 3000 lashes from the cat, and guards complained that he could withstand 100 without emitting any cry of pain. It was thought that physical pain would discourage the criminal element that led to anti-social behaviors. This was seldom the result, however. In most cases, hardship engendered a hatred of authority, hardened minds against change, and formed strong ties between convicts, perpetuating and strengthening the outlaw mentality. People like Doherty convinced officials that physical punishment just made matters worse, so that the whip was abandoned in favor of more subtle torments. A separate prison was built at Port Arthur in the late

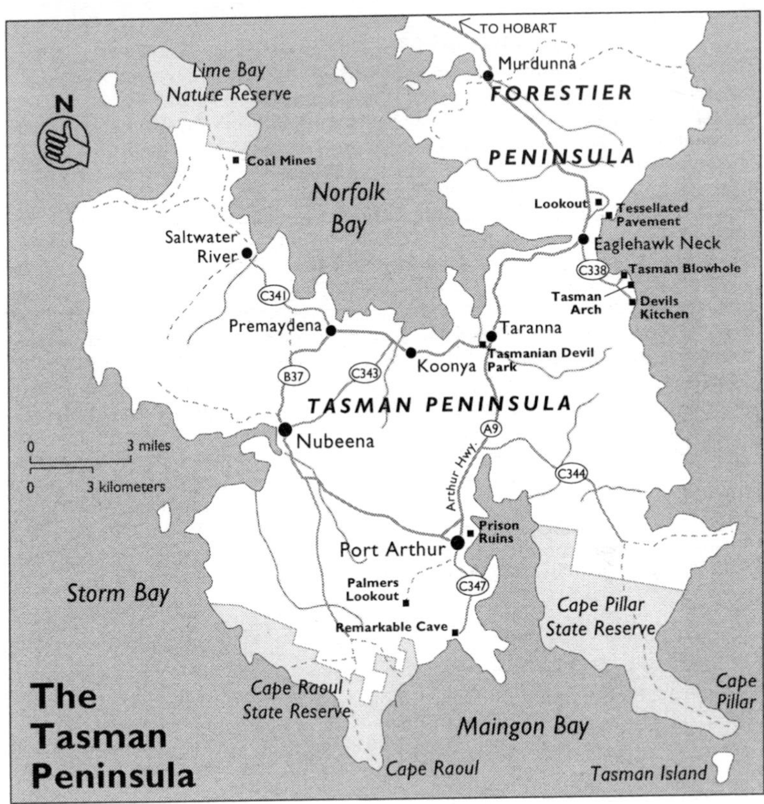

1840s. The new facility was modeled on London's Pentonville Prison, which was developed by an innovative Quaker minister who abhorred the violence in prisons.

Around the Tasman Peninsula The **Tasmanian Devil Park Wildlife Reserve Centre** (tel. 6250 3230; fax 6250 3406), in Taranna, is one of the nicest wildlife parks around. The majority of the center's critters have been injured or orphaned and would not be able to survive in the wild. Over 25 species are housed in large, unobtrusive enclosures on spacious grounds, with rambling paths connecting the displays. Many of the animals spend only a short time in the park before being returned to the wild. Others are long-term residents or have been bred in captivity. The center runs a variety of **wilderness tours,** ranging from a few hours to several days in length. This place is the best value for your animal-watching dollar, and you needn't feel guilty about supporting animal imprisonment. The Tasmanian devils feed each day at 10 and 11am (open daily 9am-5pm; admission $11, children $5.50).

Several remarkable rock formations near Eaglehawk Neck demand a detour. The **Tasman Blowhole, Tasman Arch,** and **Devils Kitchen** (a narrow gorge filled with jutting rocks) are right next to each other, just south of the Neck and Pirates Bay. You can also bike from the Neck to the **Tessellated Pavement,** a series of uniformly eroded sea stones, is on the northern side of the Bay past the Neck. Another formation meriting inspection, **Remarkable Cave,** lies south of Port Arthur on Hwy. C347. When the tide is low, you can walk down into the mouth of the cave (which would be suicide when the tide is high). **Palmers Lookout,** just north of the cave, offers wide views of the Port Arthur harbor and the southern reaches of the peninsula.

And Now for Something Completely Different

On May 17, 1832, Port Arthur escapee George "Billy" Hunt tried to cross Eaglehawk Neck, which was protected by guard stations and a line of savage dogs. He attempted to disguise himself by donning a kangaroo skin and hopping through the blockade. The guards bought the act—and started shooting at him; kangaroo meat was an important supplement to their rations. Mr. Hunt threw off the skin, crying "It's only me, Billy Hunt!"

D'ENTRECASTEAUX CHANNEL

The channels, islands, and caves south of Hobart were first charted by the Frenchman Bruni D'Entrecasteaux in 1792, more than a decade before the first English settlement in the area. Captain D'Entrecasteaux discovered the channel which separates Bruny Island from the mainland; the channel and many other features of the landscape bear the names of members of his crew. The Huon River flows gently through the valley, resulting in extremely fertile land. Berries, pears, and apples fare particularly well in the cool, misty climate. The spit of land between the Huon River and the D'Entrecasteaux Channel teems with antiques, crafts, cottages, and vineyards, all in a tranquil pastoral setting. The hamlet of Cygnet is a good base for exploring the area. A ferry crosses the channel to Bruny Island from Kettering, a tiny town just 10km northeast of Cygnet. Bruny Island itself is practically deserted and well worth a look.

Cygnet and the Huon Valley

Located near the mouth of the Nicholls Rivulet on Port Cygnet, peace and quiet are the only real selling points of Cygnet proper, but most of the Huon Valley's attractions are just a few minutes from the town. Facilities are fairly primitive, although there is a **newsagent** with limited ANZ banking capability at 74 Mary St. (tel./fax 6295 1500; open Mon.-Thurs. 7am-6pm, Fri. 7am-7pm, Sat. 8am-5pm) and a **post office,** also on Mary St. (tel. 6295 1400; postal code 7112). **Tigerline** (tel. 6234 4077) runs buses from the Green Inn cafe, 97 Mary St. (depot tel. 6295 1880), to Hobart (Mon.-Fri. 6:55am, 1hr., $6.80). The main street has a few small supermarkets and the **Red Velvet Lounge** (tel. 6295 0466), a cafe art gallery serving breakfast, vegetarian dishes, and other nibbly bits ($4-8; open Thurs.-Mon. 10:30am-late).

The **Balfes Hill YHA** (tel./fax 6295 1551; mobile tel. 018 142 982), just north of Cygnet in **Cradoc,** is the best bet for a budget bed in the valley. The hostel caters to the flocks of eager workers that come to pick fruit, train vines, and prune orchards between November and May. The manager has connections with local growers and helps guests find employment. The hostel even offers transportation to and from work for $10 per week. Workers and loafers alike enjoy the video lounge, pool and ping-pong tables, big kitchen, and twin rooms. Basic groceries and meals can be arranged. Moderately priced bus trips to Hobart, points in the valley, and the wilderness to the southwest are also available (no smoking; beds $12, weekly: $75).

TASMANIA

The **Talune Wildlife Park and Koala Garden** (tel. 6295 1775; fax 6295 0818), 6km south of Cygnet on the road to Gordon, specializes in wombats and devils, backed by roaming bands of 'roos and wallabies, and an overly friendly deer. Some of the enclosures are a bit ramshackle, but the animals look healthy and well-cared for (open daily 9:30am-5pm; admission $6, children $2.50, families $14.50). Just outside of Cygnet on Nicholls Rivulet, the **Deepings Woodturner** (tel. 6295 1398; fax 6295 0498) transforms native timbers into beautiful, practical items ranging from abalone tenderizers to nativity sets. Watch the craftsman in action seven days a week, then buy direct.

This region of Tasmania is (locally) famous for its cool-climate wines, many of which are available at the **Hartzview Vineyard and Wine Centre** (tel./fax 6295 1623), in Gardner's Bay. The center stocks Hartzview's wines, port, and mead, and also represents drops from smaller area vineyards without cellar door sales of their own (Hartzview open for tastings and sales daily 9am-5pm).

Bruny Island

Bruny Island was the first bit of land Abel Tasman glimpsed when he "discovered" Tasmania in 1642. The island has seen more than its share of famous explorers since. Captain Cook and his understudy Captain Bligh (of *Bounty* fame) both visited the island and believed it to be part of the mainland. This assumption was shattered when D'Entrecasteaux sailed through the channel that bears his name in 1792. Back in the glory days of bay whaling, the island's shores teemed with whalers, but with the end of the great creatures came the end of industry on Bruny. Half-hearted attempts to mine coal failed, so the few remaining inhabitants fell back on timber and agriculture; this pastoral lifestyle continues today. The island offers visitors dramatic coastal scenery, remnants of its exploratory past, and, above all, plenty of space.

Practical Information A **tourist information center** is across the channel in **Kettering** (tel. 6267 4494; fax 6267 4266; open Jan.-April daily 9am-5pm; April-Dec. Sun.-Fri. 9am-5pm). Bicycles and sea kayaks can be rented here (or at the YHA on the island), and brochures on the history of Bruny Island are available, including one suggesting a self-guided driving tour. The **ferry terminal** is adjacent to the information center (boats run roughly every hr., Mon.-Sat. 7am-6pm, Fri. 7am-7:30pm, Sun. 8am-6pm). The crossing takes about 15 minutes (automobiles $18, motorcycles $11, bicycles $3, pedestrians free). There is no public transportation on the island. **Buses** to Hobart leave from the Kettering General Store (tel. 6267 4413) four times per day (Mon.-Fri., 45min., $5.30).

Camping and Accommodations Camping is a feasible option on the island. The **Adventure Bay Holiday Villages** (tel. 6293 1270), in Adventure Bay, has an array of cabins and caravans that could be economical for groups of three or more, as well as excellent tent sites (unpowered $10, powered sites $13). The ablution block is decorated with bleached whalebones and holds coin-operated showers. Many of the island's state reserves also offer camping. **Cloudy Bay** (on the southern part of the island), **Neck Beach** (on the spit of land between North and South Bruny, just north of Adventure Bay), **Jetty Beach** (near the lighthouse and accessible by kayak), and **Partridge Island** (off the southern cape, accessible by boat only) all offer free primitive sites with pit toilets, no water, and unreliable firewood.

The **Bruny Island YHA** (tel. 6293 1265), in Lumeah, Adventure Bay, is a superb hostel offering comfortable beds in a friendly setting. Run by a young couple and their boisterous brood, Lumeah has spacious wooden dormitories and huge common areas, as well as a brick fireplace that is well appreciated on stormy winter nights. The managers will organize sea kayaking, camel trekking, and bushwalking, and even offer massages at reasonable rates. They're also good resources for advice on fishing, diving, and swimming spots. (Dorms $13, YHA non-members $15; doubles $40. Bike hire $12 per day, tandem bikes $15.)

Sights and Recreation **The Bligh Museum** (tel. 6293 1117), in Adventure Bay, contains marine photos and memorabilia concentrating on Captain Cook and the much-maligned Captain Bligh. The small museum could still hold your attention for a long time, if you have an interest in Pacific exploration (open daily 10am-3pm; admission $4, concessions $3, children $2). The museum is the only official tourist attraction, but the terrain itself is just as interesting. Cloudy Bay has excellent surf, while Jetty Beach has more sheltered waters suitable for youngsters. Both **fairy penguins** and **shearwaters** (muttonbirds) roost on the **Neck,** the thin strip of land that connects North and South Bruny Islands. The Neck has fine views from the top and has been fitted with a long staircase, called **Truganini's Steps** after the last full-blooded Tasmanian Aboriginal woman, who was a Bruny Islander.

A ranger stationed at the **Labillardiere State Reserve** (tel. 6298 3229) can provide information on the many coastal recreation opportunities on Bruny, including the popular daytrip destination **Cape Bruny Lighthouse.** The lighthouse was built by convict gangs between 1836 and 1838. A hike out to the light through the coastal heath of the Labillardiere Reserve and back takes about seven hours.

DERWENT VALLEY AND MIDLANDS

The Derwent River flows down into Hobart from the northwest and empties into the Tasman Sea. From the coast, the A10 highway traces the river toward its source in the heavily forested interior wilderness. North of the river, the agricultural Midlands region covers the central hinterlands. Highway 1 traverses hilly fields of grain on its way to Launceston and the north coast.

New Norfolk

A cool, misty valley enfolds the small town of New Norfolk, 25km northwest of Hobart on the Derwent River. The climate is perfect for growing hops, and regional cultivators harvest up to 45 tons per day. The well-maintained **Oast House** (tel. 6261 1030), on Hobart Rd., was once used to dry the harvest. New Norfolk's biggest tourist attraction today, Oast House contains a hop museum, hop gallery, and hophouse cafe (open Wed.-Sun. 9am-5pm). A few of the town's old 19th-century buildings have been preserved, including the church of St. Matthew and the Bush Inn. Historical walking tour maps are sold for $1 by the **Derwent Valley Council** (tel. 6261 0700), on Circle St. (open Mon.-Fri. 8:15am-5pm). The Council can also provide info on other tourist attractions in the area. **Tigerline** (tel. 6261 2055) coaches to Hobart depart from the Fairview Newsagency, 1 Station St., and from Circle St. (daily, 30min., $4.10).

The only budget accommodation in town is the substandard **New Norfolk Esplanade Caravan Park** (tel. 6261 1269), down by the river. (Coin-operated showers and laundry. Swampy unpowered sites for 2 people $8, additional adults $5; powered sites for 2 $12, additional adults $10. Use of the amenities block $3; a keycard for the gate requires a $7 deposit.)

Devil-Jet Jet Boats (tel. 6261 3460; fax 6261 1743) operate daily on the Derwent River near New Norfolk. Bookings for the 30-minute cruises ($40, students $30) can be made at the Bush Inn on the Lyell Hwy. or by phone. At top speed, the prop-less jet boats draw only four inches of water, so they can shoot through rigorous rapids without getting stuck on rocks.

Mt. Field National Park

Founded in 1916, Mt. Field is one of Tasmania's oldest national parks, just an hour from Hobart. Russell Falls has long been the favorite destination, but Mt. Field is more than just this cataract. The park can be divided into two distinct areas. The lower slopes near the park entrance have picnic and BBQ facilities, a **visitor kiosk** (tel. 6288 1477), and short, easy walks to **Russell Falls** and other rainforest attractions. On the upper slopes, alpine moorland around **Lake Dobson** features Mt. Field's primitive **ski** facilities, glassy highland lakes, and large network of extended bushwalking tracks. The **Pendani Grove** nature walk circumnavigates Lake Dobson and provides a good introduction to the unusual plant life. Swamp gum (*Eucalyptus regnans*), the tallest flowering plant in the world, and the man fern, which can live to be 800 years old, both thrive in the lower levels of Mr. Field. Brochures mapping the walk are available at the kiosk at the bottom of the hill.

The upper and lower areas are connected by a tortuous 16km-long unsealed road. A gradual change from rainforest to heath can be observed while winding up the mountain, but winter weather can make the road impassable. The ski area is a 30-minute hike from the Lake Dobson carpark. During the ski season, **buses** leave for the skifields from the kiosk at 9am and 10:15am ($8 round-trip). A discovery tour bus runs from the same spot at 10:15am (in summer daily, off season Tues.-Thurs.; $15). For bus information, call 6334 4442. **Tasmanian Wilderness Travel** (tel. 6334 4442; fax 6334 2029) runs buses to Mt. Field from Hobart (Dec.-April daily, May-Nov. Tues., Thurs., and Sat.; 1¾hr.; $19). Buses back to Hobart run daily during summer (off season Tues., Thurs., and Sun.; $19). Ski, snow, and road information is available on the **Mt. Field Information Line** (tel. 6288 1319).

The snow cover is seldom very good, and the lifts servicing the ski fields are quite ancient, but the ski kiosk rents skis and sells food and lift tickets. The National Park Office administers three very rustic **cabins** near Lake Dobson. Each six-person cabin comes with mattresses, a wood heater, firewood, and cold water ($10, concessions $8, children $5; $20 min. per night). Bookings must be made at least a week in advance (tel. 6288 1149). The visitor kiosk also runs a campground near the park entrance.The **campsites** are equipped with excellent showers and bathrooms, as well as coin-operated laundry machines. (Unpowered sites $5 per person, students $2.50. Powered sites $7, $3.) Just outside the national park on Garden River Rd., **Jack Thwaites Memorial Hostel** (tel. 6288 1269) provides basic beds within earshot of the park's falls. Some patrons wish that the bathrooms were cleaner and that the mattresses on the metal bunks were thicker, but the location can't be beat. (No smoking or drinking. Bunks $11, YHA non-members $14; sleep sheets $1.)

The Midlands

The fertile, rolling hills between Hobart and Launceston were originally settled as garrison towns to keep watch over the colony's convicts. The English settlers decided to make the midcountry of Tasmania look more like the midcountry back home, planting a wealth of English plants and built hedges and narrow lanes. The spirit of the Midlands is exemplified by the small town of **Oatlands,** a bit closer to Hobart than Launceston. There are no oats anywhere near the place, but the current theory is that Macquarie was nostalgic for Scotland when he named the place. This village has more historic sandstone buildings in a two-square-kilometer area than any other town in Australia. A walk down High St. takes you past a great number of old stone stores, cottages, and government buildings that have been recycled as antique galleries or cafes.

One of the gems of the Midlands is the **Oatlands YHA,** 9 Wellington St. (tel. 6254 1320). This tiny building is full of trinkets and curios sent back by the hordes of weary travelers who have come to regard this hostel as a second home. No amusements are provided save the company, but you will not find yourself lacking for entertainment. Beds in the tiny bunkrooms cost $10. **Blossom's Cottage,** 114-118 High St. (tel. 6254 1516), serves delightful teas and lunches ($4-8; open occasionally, try Thurs. and Sat.-Sun. 10:30am-3:30pm).

The town's showpiece building is the **Callington Mill,** opened in 1837. At peak capacity, the mill could grind up to one ton of grain every hour, but the introduction of the steam engine rendered it obsolete by the turn of the century. Even without its 25m sails, the mill is an impressive sight (open daily 9am-5pm; admission $2). If you're staying overnight in Oatlands, don't miss the **Ghost Tour,** given every night at 8pm. The guide dons period dress and knows all there is to know about the area and its potential spectral inhabitants. The tours take around two hours and cost $8. Meet at the Callington Mill, rain or stars.

Tigerline has buses to Launceston (daily, 2hr., $13) and Hobart (daily, 1¼hr., $10). **Redline** coaches run to Hobart (daily, 1½hr., $10.60) and Launceston (daily, 1½hr., $13.80). The **Oatlands post office** is on High St. (tel. 6254 1160; open Mon.-Fri. 9am-1pm and 2-5pm; postal code 7120).

WILDERNESS AND WEST COAST

At the upper end of the Derwent Valley, the road crosses the Derwent Bridge and winds past Lake St. Clair and the Franklin River toward Tasmania's west coast. Much of the interior has been set aside to preserve the dense temperate rainforest that dominates the terrain and borders the road on either side. Far to the south, Lakes Gordon and Pedder bask in the rich woodlands of the Southwest National Park.

The western coastline of Tasmania is among the most desolate, uncivilized areas in Australia. Twenty thousand kilometers of Indian Ocean separate the shore from the nearest landmass and periodically send violent storms crashing against the formidable coastline. Strahan, the only coastal settlement of any size between Hazard Bay in the northwest and Recherche Bay, south of Hobart, is hardly a sprawling metropolis.

The first communities in the area supported themselves by exploiting thick stands of old growth timber. Soon after logging began, prospectors began searching the hills and creeks for gold, hoping to strike it rich like their Victorian comrades. Alas, they never reached the end of the rainbow, and many hapless diggers departed bankrupt and frustrated. Eventually, explorers less blinded by gold lust discovered mountains of tin, silver, and copper just beneath the surface. But extractive industries like mining and logging could not continue indefinitely, and exhaustion of minerals and natural resources spelled the end for many of the ramshackle communities that had formed to service the workers.

Even with the extensive harvesting of the 19th and 20th centuries, vast tracts remain untouched, and much of the virgin forest has been permanently designated World Heritage Areas and national parks. These wilderness areas are the region's largest attraction, and virtually unlimited opportunities exist for exploring the borders of the wild coast. Access to the interior, however, is extremely difficult, since preserving the wilderness means not marring it with roads.

Franklin-Gordon Wild Rivers N. P.

The Lyell Highway connecting the Derwent Bridge to Queenstown cuts through the meat of the Tasmanian Wilderness World Heritage area, specifically the Franklin-Gordon Wild Rivers National Park. Several areas along the road have been developed to allow casual visitors to get a taste of the wildlands. The eastern side offers lookout points over the King William Saddle, the Surprise Valley, and **Frenchman's Cap.** The

Sympathy for the Sarcophilus harrisii

The remarkable Tasmanian devil *(Sarcophilus harrisii)* is the most famous of the state's critters. Once common throughout Australia, the devil is now confined to the island prison from which it takes its name. Tasmanian devils are seldom more than 45cm high and are not built for speed; they make awkward runners but climb adeptly. Their jet black coats are occasionally marked with white bands or spots across the pectoral region. The maw is the most striking feature, full of jagged teeth and usually open wide. The powerful jaws can crush bones up to 7.5cm in diameter and allow the devil to eat almost anything. Devils subsist on an entirely carnivorous diet; in addition to eating large amounts of carrion, they also hunt a variety of small mammals, including some domesticated animals. Although driven off the mainland by dingoes, devils thrive in Tasmania to the point that they are considered a pest in some areas. Although they don't attack humans, devils can claim the lives of farm animals, particularly young sheep. Devils are also extremely noisy, particularly when feeding, and can prove quite irritating when they take up residence under inhabited dwellings. Despite their healthy numbers, devils usually escape human detection in the wild, as they are primarily nocturnal and secretive by nature. Your best hope of spotting one is to visit one of the many wildlife parks featuring this odd marsupial.

Saddle is a fairly believable saddle, but the Cap seems neither *beret* nor *chapeau* to most. If you think a closer examination of Frenchman's Cap might justify the name, follow the track to the top (4-5 days round-trip). Bushwalkers can park at the lot on the southern side of the highway. **Ponaghys Hill Lookout,** accessed by a 40-minute round-trip track, boasts panoramic views of the Franklin River Valley and Frenchman's Cap. A bit to the east, the Franklin River Nature Trail is a well-maintained track through rainforest with interpretive markers that ponder the meaning of the wilderness. To the west near Queenstown, the Nelson Falls Nature Trail leads to a charming cataract (20min.). To use any of these facilities legally, purchase a National Parks Pass.

Lake Saint Clair National Park

Half of the headline act of the **Cradle Mountain-Lake Saint Clair National Park,** Lake St. Clair is Australia's deepest lake as well as the source of the Derwent River. The lake anchors the southern end of the famous **Overland Track,** with Cradle Mountain at its northern terminus. The exceptionally beautiful track requires a good deal of time, equipment, and preparation, not to mention tolerance for the region's heavy rainfall, which can exceed 2.5m annually. There are a number of shorter half-day and day hikes, and even a few nature trails suitable for families, in the vicinity of the lake.

The park's **visitors center** (tel. 6289 1172; fax 6289 1227), just a few kilometers from the Derwent Bridge at Cynthia Bay, has excellent displays on wildlife and European and Aboriginal inhabitants of the area. A spooky hologram of a group of thylacines (Tasmanian tigers) dominates the exhibit (open daily 8am-5pm). The **ranger's office** offers maps and information on local trails. It is important to register your party here for any extended walks, especially the Overland Track. The **general store** (tel. 6289 1137; fax 6289 1250), adjacent to the ranger's office, provides a variety of services. Book here for cruises on the lake. Fishing equipment rents from $15 per day, with a $15 deposit. The store also runs **campsites** (powered sites $6 per person, unpowered sites $5 per person). Hostel **bunks** are comfortable enough but overpriced at $20. The other accommodation option is the **Derwent Bridge Wilderness Hotel** (tel. 6289 1144; fax 6289 1173), on the Lyell Hwy. near where it crosses the river. Backpacker rooms are small modular units detached from the main hotel building (all singles $20, in winter $15). The hotel serves hearty, plain meals at reasonable prices.

Tigerline buses depart Wednesday, Friday, and Sunday from the **Roadhouse** (tel. 6289 1125) to Hobart (3hr., $23.80), Strahan (3hr., $18.10), and Queenstown (2hr., $12.70). Connections from the highway to Lake St. Clair are available through **Maxwell Coaches** (tel. 6289 1137). Tigerline offers a special Overland Track Walkers Fare ($59; with national park fees $69). Call the Hobart office (tel. 6234 4077) or enquire at any office for details. **Tasmanian Wilderness Travel** has buses from the lake car-park to Strahan (Sat., plus Thurs. in summer, 3hr., $40) and Hobart (April-Nov. Tues., Thurs., and Sun., Dec.-March daily; 4hr.; $40); this bus also stops at Mt. Field National Park (2¼hr., $30).

The Overland Track

Stretching 80km through untouched World Heritage Wilderness, the Overland Track connects Cradle Mountain and Lake St. Clair, in one of the most famous trails in the southern hemisphere. Every year, more than 300,000 visit Cradle Mountain National Park, and approximately 3000 attempt the track, many breaking their journeys in the 12 small huts along the path. Most people take five to eight days to complete the journey, and even in the dead of winter an average of 50 are on the track any given time. This heavy traffic can have disastrous impacts on the fragile alpine ecosystems along much of the path, so it is very important that visitors observe minimum-impact bushwalking practices. If you are planning to walk the track, write to the rangers to request an information kit at Parks and Wildlife Service, Cradle Mountain Visitor Cen-

Cold Kills

Many people come to Tasmania to hike the endless, untamed wilderness. Tourist brochures emphasize the splendor and majesty of the island's mountains and forests, showing crystal-blue skies and shining peaks, encouraging tourists with little bushwalking experience to brave the wild with little idea of what they are doing. Make no mistake, Tasmania's wilderness is still wild, and will kill the unwary given half a chance. The greatest hazard in the wilderness is the unruly weather that can shift from zephyr to gale in a heartbeat. Even in the summertime, when the weather is hot, carry warm and waterproof clothing to protect yourself from hypothermia, a lowering of the body's core temperature that can be fatal. With a little planning, you can prevent hypothermia in the first place. Do not attempt bushwalks without the proper equipment and experience. Ask the locals about what kind of weather and track conditions to expect. Wear wool or fiber pile clothing, including gloves and a hat. Wet cotton, especially jeans, will kill you. Go prepared, have a great time, and come back safe. For details on symptoms and treatment of hypothermia, see **Essentials,** p. 17.

tre, P.O. Box 20, Sheffield TAS 7306 (tel. 6492 1133; fax 6492 1120). The Track itself can be undertaken from either the Cradle Mountain end (see p. 446) or the Lake St. Clair access (see above); it costs $12 for a national park permit to the trail.

Queenstown

In 1883, Mick and Bill McDonough, also mysteriously known as the Cooney Brothers, discovered a large outcropping of copper-rich rock, later termed (for an equally mysterious reason) the **Iron Blow.** The brothers Cooney were looking for gold, so the Blow was mined for gold alone for many years, though each ton of rock yielded just two ounces of the precious metal. The Mount Lyell Gold Mining Company formed in 1888, but redirected its efforts toward copper in 1891. This was a wise decision, for millions of pounds of copper had already slipped away during the relatively poor gold mining days. The company built a smelter to process the copper ore on-site, indirectly wreaking environmental havoc. Nearly every large tree in the surrounding hills was felled to feed the smelter, young growth was killed by the thick yellow sulphur haze released during the pyritic processing, and the exposed topsoil was washed into the Queen River by heavy rainfall. This same rainfall supports incredibly lush forest in areas not ravaged by mining, so the town (pop. 3000 and falling) currently resembles a sort of lunar wasteland in the midst of otherwise dense vegetation.

Information is available from the **Queenstown Parks and Wildlife Service** (tel. 6471 2511; open Mon.-Fri. 8am-4pm). **Trust Bank** (tel. 6471 1381; fax 6471 1958; open Mon.-Fri. 9am-5pm), one of few banks in the region, stands on the corner of Orr and Sticht St. **Tigerline** (tel. 6471 1193; student discount 20%) buses leave from Gumleys News bound for Hobart (Tues. and Thurs., 8hr., $35), Devonport (Tues. and Thurs., 5hr., $29.10), Burnie (Tues. and Thurs., 6hr., $35.60), Cradle Mountain (Tues. and Thurs., 2½hr., $17), the Derwent Bridge (Wed., Fri., and Sun., 1½hr., $12.70), and Strahan (Sun.-Fri., 1hr., $5.40). The **police** station is at 2 Sticht St. (tel. 6471 3020). The **post office** is at 32 Orr St. (tel. 6471 1782; fax 6471 2381; open Mon.-Fri. 9am-5pm, postal code 7467).

The **Empire Hotel,** 2 Orr St. (tel. 6471 1699), retains some of the glory of its heyday as a miners' pub. A grand wooden staircase leads up to clean accommodations. Meals are available downstairs, while minimal kitchen facilities are upstairs, adjacent to the avocado-green lounge room (singles $15; doubles $30).

The **Mt. Lyell Mine** still churns along, as do tours that explore the working areas of the mine and the state-of-the-art equipment used by the miners. Underground tours leave from the offices at 1 Driffield St. (tel. 6471 2388; fax 6471 2222). Surface tours visit the old open-cut mines and other relics of the past daily. (Surface tours Oct.-April 9:15am, 2:30pm, and 4:30pm; May-Sept. 9:15am and 4pm; 1hr.; $11, under 16

$6.50.) Underground tours are more thorough but quite pricey (Mon.-Fri. 8:30am and 1:30pm; 3½hr; $45). Bookings are essential. The old Iron Blow open-cut mine, just off the Lyell Hwy. near Gomanston, offers broad views of the barren hills around Queenstown and of the water-filled crater that was once a mine. The **Galley Museum** (tel. 6471 1483) has artifacts from the operation's early days and an impressive collection of photographs, along with a less impressive display of ladies' underpants. (Open Oct.-March Mon.-Fri. 10am-5:30pm, Sat.-Sun. 1-5:30pm; April-Sept. 10am-12:30pm and 1:30-4:30pm. Admission $3, concessions $2.)

Strahan

Strahan is built on Macquarie Harbour, the only sheltered cove on the west coast. As such, it became an important port for the minerals and timber of the interior in the days before roads and railways. As these industries declined and overland transport routes were established, the port's main industry shifted from shipping to fishing. Strahan has a few interesting historical attractions, but is best known as a gateway to the **Franklin-Gordon Wild Rivers National Park** World Heritage Area, and the rest of the southwest wilderness. Franklin-Gordon is accessible only by bushwalk or boat.

The **Strahan World Heritage Area Visitor Centre** (tel. 6471 7122), located in the historic customs house, dispenses information on local wildlife and history (open daily 8am-5pm). This branch office of the Parks and Wildlife Service also sells passes to national parks (vehicles $9 per day; pedestrians $3). The *Strahan Foreshore Historic Walkway* pamphlet outlines a 2.5km path that visits many of Strahan's old buildings. **Tigerline** (tel. 6471 7255) runs buses from the Strahan YHA hostel to Queenstown (Sun.-Fri., 1hr., $5.40), the Derwent Bridge (Wed., Fri., and Sun., 2hr., $18.10), Hobart (Wed., Fri., and Sun., 7hr., $40.40), Burnie (Tues. and Thurs., 7hr., $41), and Devonport (Tues. and Thurs., 6½hr., $34.50). **Tasmanian Wilderness Travel** (tel. 6334 4442; fax 6334 2029) runs a Sunday bus year-round from the Macquarie Harbour Cafe to Lake St. Clair (2½hr., $40), Mt. Field National Park (4½hr., $50), and Hobart (6hr., $52). A Thursday bus supplements the Sunday service during the summer. The **police station** (tel. 6471 8000) is on Beach St. The Strahan **post office** is in the other half of the Customs House (tel. 6471 7171; postal code 7468; open Mon.-Fri. 9am-5pm).

The only good budget accommodation is the **Strahan YHA** (tel. 6471 7255) on Harvey St., one block inland. A complex of cabins, the hostel furnishes bunkbed dormitories and large communal areas. Don't miss the resident platypus. (Reception open daily 8-10am and 4-9pm. Dorms $13, YHA non-members $16.)

With any luck, walkers will encounter abundant wildlife on the pleasant track to **Hogarth Falls,** just a few kilometers from central Strahan. The path follows Botanical Creek, which is home to all manner of aquatic Tasmanian critters, including the elusive platypus. The Hogarth Track is accessed through People's Park; just follow the dirt road to the track. Just north of town, **Ocean Beach** stretches from Macquarie Head in the south to Trial Harbour, over 30km to the north. Ocean Beach is the longest beach in Tasmania and one of the wildest, with brooding surf and windy dunes. Open seas across the Indian and Atlantic Oceans all the way to South America allow massive swells to develop; swimming can be unsafe. Beginning in late September, thousands of muttonbirds descend on the beach after flying 15,000km from their Arctic summer homes.

Many Strahan visitors try a cruise up the **Gordon River.** A multitude of cruises operate from the wharf in central Strahan, offering tours of varying length. A typical tour with **Gordon River Cruises** (tel. 6471 7187 or 6471 7281; fax 6471 7317) runs across Macquarie Harbour and up the Gordon to the Heritage Landing, where tourists can inspect a 2000-year-old huon pine that has managed to survive all of the decades of intensive logging. Take flight for a more exciting, if more expensive, view of the area with **Strahan Wilderness Air** (tel. 6471 7280; fax 6471 7303) over the harbor and river; an 80-minute flight costs around $99. Note that flights are subject to the vagaries of weather. Commercial tours and private boats can provide access to **Sarah**

Island, a penal colony for secondary offenders from 1822 until 1833. Known as one of the darkest pits in the British penal system, convicts on the island were forced to wade chest-deep in the harbor's freezing water, pushing giant huon pine logs. Today, all of Sarah Island's buildings have been reduced to sign-posted ruins.

EAST COAST

If Tasmania is a huge serpent, the east coast is its soft underbelly. The weather is mild, the folks are mild-mannered, and the mild waters produce mild-tasting fish. Where Tasmania's western shoreline is wild and uninhabited, perpetually pounded by huge open water storms, a mountainous interior shelters the east coast. The docile climate, combined with decent tracts of arable land, has led to fairly thick settlement, at least by Tasmanian standards. By mainland standards, the area remains quiet year-round and grows positively hushed in the winter. Most of the settlements rely on agriculture or maintain the image of popular summer holiday spots for fresh- and saltwater fishing, swimming, and just loafing in the sunshine.

Most of the east coast towns are serviced by bus, but winter schedules are often restrictive. There are currently **no ATMs** between Sorell and St. Helens, so don't leave home without plenty of cash, even if it *is* plastic.

Triabunna This tiny town makes a good place to stock up on food before heading out to Maria Island. The **Triabunna Caravan Park,** 6 Vicary St. (tel. 6257 3575), maintains a small, homespun lot with a shady, grassy corner for tents. The toilet and shower block is small but well-scrubbed (unpowered sites $10, powered sites $12). The **Triabunna YHA** is at 12 Spencer St. (tel. 6257 3439), off Amelia St. A pack of friendly dogs patrols this rural, ramshackle domicile. A total of 20 beds are scattered through modular units and the main house, with basic but operable facilities. Water is scarce, so laundry is done by hand (fee depending on amount and filthiness of clothes). Fresh veggies and eggs are available seasonally. (Dorms $12; YHA non-members $15; doubles $26-28.)

For a restful, harmonious treat, head to the **Girraween Gardens and Tearoom,** 4 Henry St. (tel./fax 6257 3458), in "downtown" Triabunna. Light meals and snacks are served in a green, peaceful grove, and the award-winning gardens can be toured for $2. (Free with the purchase of food; most items are less than $7. Open daily 9:30am-4pm.) **Buses** to Hobart leave the Shell Roadhouse in Triabunna (tel. 6257 3251; Sun.-Fri. 1 or 2 per day, 1½hr., $11.30), with connections to the **Eastcoaster** resort on Wednesdays, Fridays, and Sundays only. Call **Tigerline** (tel. 6234 4077) to book.

Maria Island National Park Maria (muh-RYE-uh) Island used to be a penal colony with thriving industries. When the colony closed and the industries failed, only an empty, desolate rock was left. Today, the island national park is almost devoid of civilization, accessible only by boat or plane. The ruins of the settlement at **Darlington** are the main attraction, along with the abundant wildlife and isolation. There are no shops or facilities on the island save a **ranger station** (tel. 6257 1420), which has a public telephone and distributes maps and brochures. The old Darlington prison has been renovated into **dormitory** accommodation with toilets and laundry, but no showers or hot water. Bookings must be made with the ranger before arrival. There is also a large **campsite** at Darlington. National park fees apply to all visitors.

Maria can be reached via the **Eastcoaster Express** catamaran, which leaves the Eastcoaster Resort (tel. 6257 1589) daily at 10:30am, 1pm, and 3:30pm, returning from the island at 11am, 1:30pm, and 4pm (daytrip fare $17, children $10; overnight fare $20, children $13; bikes, kayaks, and other large cargo items $3). The **Eastcoaster Resort** is midway between Triabunna and Orford, a 20-minute drive from either town.

Swansea

Midway up the east coast, Swansea is a tiny village on the Great Oyster Bay just south of the Freycinet Peninsula. Douglas-Apsley and Freycinet National Parks are just minutes away, and almost any other point along the coast is within two hours' drive, making the pleasant town a good base for exploration. **Coles Bay,** the Hwy. A3 turn-off to the Freycinet Peninsula, is 30 minutes north of Swansea by road. Swansea has a **Westpac Bank** (tel. 6257 8147), on Noyes St. (open Mon.-Thurs. 9:30am-4pm, Fri. 9:30am-5pm), and a **post office** (tel. 6257 8170), on the corner of Arnoll and Franklin St. (open Mon.-Fri. 9am-5pm; postal code 7190). **Redline Coaches** (tel. 6257 8118) runs buses from Swansea north to Bicheno (Sun.-Fri., 45min., $6.40) and the Coles Bay turn-off (Sun.-Fri., 30min., $5.40). From there, connections can be made to Coles Bay with **Bicheno Coaches** (tel. 6257 0293; one-way $5). Redline also runs south to Hobart via Campbell Town (Sun.-Fri., 2¾hr., $25.80). **Tigerline** operates coaches from the Swansea Shell service station (tel. 6257 8127) to Bicheno (Sun.-Fri., 45min., $3.60), the Coles Bay turn-off (Wed., Fri., and Sun., 30min., $3), St. Helens (Wed., Fri., and Sun., 1¾hr., $13), and Hobart (Sun.-Fri., 2hr., $16).

The **Swansea-Kenmore Cabin and Tourist Park,** 2 Bridge St. (tel. 6257 8148; fax 6257 8554), is right on the beach, nicely landscaped and efficiently run. The management has set up a kiosk with basic groceries and fishing tackle, a spa-sauna ($7 for 2 people), and a swimming pool (open Nov.-April 9:30am-dusk). Laundry and BBQs are coin-operated. (Unpowered sites $10-12; powered sites $12-15; on-site caravans $30-35; cabins $42.) The other budget option is the **Swansea YHA,** 5 Franklin St. (tel. 6257 8367). This hostel boasts a well-equipped kitchen, a piano in the common room, and rude metal bunks with bedclothes in asylum green. Hand-washing tubs replace laundry machines (dorms $11, YHA non-members $14).

Swansea's most unique attraction is the **Black Wattle Bark Mill,** 96 Tasman Hwy. (tel. 6257 8382; fax 6257 8485), the only **bark crusher** in Australia. In days gone by, bark was stripped from wattle trees, dried in bundles, then ground to a powder to make "vegetable tonic," a solution of tannic acid used in the tanning of hides. The machine has been faithfully restored along with a number of tools and contraptions from the area's past. The adjacent wine and wool center has a selection of local vintages and woolen goods. (Open daily 9am-5pm. Complex admission $5, children $2.75. Wine and wool center is free.) Swansea's **beaches** are usually excellent for swimming, and there are some lovely fishing holes as well. The weather is generally fine, as the mountainous interior of Tasmania absorbs the brunt of eastbound storms.

Near Swansea: Freycinet National Park

Dominated by massive rocky peaks known as the **Hazards,** the Freycinet Peninsula is popular for bushwalking, water sports, and beachside relaxation. The spine of mountains that runs down the peninsula is flanked by some of the nicest beaches in Tasmania, including **Wineglass Bay,** featured on most of the park's postcards and a favorite destination for daytrippers. For information on many walking tracks, stop at the **visitors kiosk** (tel. 6257 0107) near the park entrance. Since it's a national park, regular park fees apply, and passes are valid. There are excellent **campsites** within the boundaries of the park. Wood, water, and basic toilets are provided. (Unpowered sites $5, concessions $4, children $2.50. Powered sites $6, concessions $5, children $3.) Fees are payable through self-registration at the visitor kiosk.

Bicheno Coaches (tel. 6257 0293) runs buses that connect to Tigerline and Redline coaches at the Coles Bay turn-off (Sun.-Fri., $5), and provide service to all points north and south. Excellent beaches just north of the park include the **Friendly Beaches** and the **Lagoon Beaches Coastal Reserve.** The coastal reserve has broad, soft sand beaches with shallow lagoons full of beautiful black swans. There are free primitive campsites, with a four-week maximum stay.

St. Helens

St. Helens is the northernmost of the vacation villages that dot the east coast. The settlement began as a land grant around Georges Bay in the 1830s, with most of its income coming from timber and fishing. Tin was discovered in the Blue Tier to the west, prompting a large influx of people during the 1870s. At first, tin was so plentiful that people could collect it by uprooting shrubs and simply shaking it off the roots. But it didn't last long. By the 1890s, the price of tin had dropped to the point that mining became unprofitable, and the town reverted to harvesting the sea. Information on the area's history can be found in the **St. Helen's History Room,** 59 Cecilia St. (tel. 6376 1744). The displays include a large collection of old photographs (open Mon.-Fri. 9am-4pm; admission $4, children $2). Almost any question about St. Helens and the surrounding region can be answered by the staff of the History Room. If they don't have the answer, try the **St. Helens Visitor Information Centre** (tel. 6376 3765), on the corner of Quail and Cecilia St. (open Mon.-Fri. 9am-5pm).

Trust Bank is at 18 Cecilia St. (tel. 6376 1111), complete with an **ATM,** a rarity on the east coast (open Mon.-Thurs. 9:30am-4pm, Fri. 9:30am-5pm). **Redline Coaches** (tel. 6376 1182) buses run to Hobart (Sun.-Fri., 4hr., $26.60) and Launceston (Sun.-Fri., 2½hr., $16.60). **Tigerline** buses run to Hobart (Wed., Fri., and Sun., 4hr., $28.50) and the Coral Bay turn-off (Wed., Fri., and Sun., 1hr., $11), from where Bicheno Coaches (tel. 6257 0293) connects to Freycinet Peninsula ($5). Get the equipment you need to experience St. Helens from **East Lines,** 28 Cecilia St. (tel. 6376 1720), which rents a huge variety of sporting goods, including golf clubs and fishing tackle. Bicycles cost $5 per hour or $20 per day, with a $50 deposit. If they don't have it, it's just not fun (open Mon.-Fri. 9am-5pm). The **post office** is at 46 Cecilia St. (tel. 6376 12 55; fax 6376 1099; open Mon.-Fri. 9am-5pm; postal code 7216).

The **St. Helens Caravan Park** (tel. 6376 1290; fax 6376 1514), on Penelope St., is just off the Tasman Hwy., on the southeast side of the bridge, about 1km from the town center. There is a campers' kitchen, and a Possums' Playroom for the kiddies, along with the standard amenities. The park caters to summer vacationers, so expect to pay more from December to March. (Unpowered sites $12-13; powered sites $14-15; sites with private bath $18. On-site caravans $30-35. Plain cabins $40-50; deluxe cabins $45-55.) The **St. Helens YHA,** 5 Cameron St. (tel. 6376 1661), stands about half a block off Quail St. The hostel has beautiful views of Georges Bay through enormous windows, but the bunks themselves are mere foam, and a little the worse for wear (dorms $12, YHA non-members $15; book ahead in summer). Cheap and healthy eats are available at the **Deli,** 22 Cecilia St. (tel. 6376 1649), essentially coffee lounge fare without the grease (open Mon.-Fri. 7:30am-5pm).

Points of interest include the state recreation areas of **Humbug Point** and **St. Helens Point.** Humbug Point offers better-than-humbug walks and views, while St. Helens Point has decent fishing and good surf at **Beerbarrel Beach** (say *that* a few times quickly). North of Humbug Point, the **Bay of Fires Coastal Reserve** rounds out the roster of peculiar place names with its long beaches and primitive campsites.

About 30 minutes north of St. Helens on the way to Launceston, **The St. Columba Falls Hotel** (tel. 6373 6121) epitomizes the Aussie pub in an Aussie location. In the middle of a pasture in **Pyengana,** the pub recalls a time before pokies, and before pubs had to be Irish or Western to attract customers. The old timber structure houses a mixed crowd, with bikies mingling happily with vacationing retirees. There's good beer, excellent counter meals (rabbit, 'roo, and beef prepared in a variety of ways $8-14), and Piggy Boo, the beer-drinking pig. Accommodation is a good deal (singles $20; doubles $30). The beautiful **St. Columba Falls,** the highest falls in Tasmania, are just down the road.

NORTHEAST

The northeastern lobe of Tasmania is a tame, settled section of the island, although not as densely populated as Hobart and its environs. The land is given over to vineyards, pastures, orchards, and commercially managed forests, including large *pinus radiata* plantations. The region is bordered to the south by the Midlands and lake country, and to the west by the foothills of Cradle Mountain and the Walls of Jerusalem National Park. Launceston, the largest city in the area, lies within reach of all points of regional interest. According to Tasmanians, the rivers and lakes of the northeast have some of the best trout fishing in the world. They also maintain that Ben Lomond National Park has the best skifields in Tasmania—which isn't necessarily saying much.

Launceston

Built where the North and South Esk rivers join to form the Tamar, Launceston (LAWN-che-stun) is Tasmania's second-largest city and Australia's third-oldest, founded in 1805. In the early days, an intense rivalry shook Hobart and Launceston. The rivalry has decreased only slightly with Hobart's emergence as the capital, manifesting itself most clearly in beer loyalty: Boags is the ale of choice in the north, Cascade in the south. Launcestonians are a friendly bunch and welcome visitors to their city, but the town's attractions are quickly exhausted, especially with globally famous wilderness right on its doorstep.

ORIENTATION

Launceston is built on a very regular grid. Downtown, most of the streets are one-way, an impediment to automobile navigation. The main pedestrian mall is on **Brisbane St.,** between Charles and St. John St. The city center is bounded on the north by the **North Esk River** and on the west by the **South Esk.** The Cataract Gorge Reserve is on the South Esk, just a few kilometers west of downtown. All of Launceston's facilities and attractions are in or near the city center, which is easy to explore on foot. Highway A8 runs north to George Town, Hwy. 1 heads south to Hobart through the Midlands and west to Deloraine and Devonport, and Hwy. A3 snakes east to St. Helens and the east coast.

PRACTICAL INFORMATION

Tourist Office: On the corner of St. John and Paterson St. (tel. 6331 3679). Offers a walking tour Mon.-Fri. 9:45am. Open Mon.-Fri. 9am-5pm, Sat. 9am-3pm.

Currency Exchange: Commonwealth Bank, 97 Brisbane St. (tel. 13 22 21). Open Mon.-Thurs. 9:30am-4pm, Fri. 9:30am-5pm. **Trust Bank,** 79 St. John (tel. 6336 6444), open Mon.-Thurs. 9:30am-4pm, Fri. 9:30am-5pm. The mall features plenty of **ATMs** of every stripe.

American Express Office: Crawford International, 66 Cameron St. (tel. 6334 1787). Open Mon.-Fri. 9am-5pm.

Airport: South of Launceston. **Airporter Bus,** 112 George St. (tel. 6331 5755), provides transportation to the airport ($7). **Ansett** (tel. 13 13 00) and **Qantas** (tel. 13 13 13) run flights to Australian capitals through Melbourne. One-way, economy fares to Melbourne $196, to Sydney $286.

Buses: Redline (tel. 6331 3233) has a depot at 112 George St. Buses run to: Burnie (3-4 per day, 2½ hr., $16.70), Deloraine (Mon.-Fri. 5 per day, 40min., $6.20), Devonport (3-4 per day, with connections to the ferry terminal Tues., Thurs., Sat., and Sun.; 1½hr.; $13.30), George Town (Sun.-Fri. 3 per day, 45min., $7), Hobart (4-5 per day, 2½hr., $19), Oatlands (2-3 per day, 1½hr., $14.80), St. Helens (Sun.-Fri., 2½hr., $16.60), Swansea (Sun.-Fri., 2hr., $17), and the Coles Bay turn-off (2½hr., $20.7), with connections to Freycinet through **Bicheno Coaches** (tel. 6257 8127; $5). **Tigerline's** depot is at 180 Brisbane St. (tel. 6334 3600), with buses to Burnie (daily, 2½hr., $16.70), Deloraine (daily, 45min., $6.30), Devonport (daily, with connections to the ferry terminal Tues., Thurs., and Sat.; 1½hr.; $12.50), and Oatlands (daily, 1½hr., $17.80). Connections to Cradle Mountain and the west coast can be made in Devonport. **Tasmanian Wilderness Travel,** 101 George St. (tel. 6334 4447; fax 6334 2029), has buses to Cradle Mountain (April-Oct. Tues., Thurs., and Sat., Nov.-March daily; 4½hr.; $40), Hobart (Dec.-April Mon., Tues., Thurs., and Sat.; 6¾hr.; $50), Lake St. Clair (April-Oct. Sat., Nov.-March Mon., Tues., Thurs., and Sat.; 2½hr.; $45), and Strahan (Tues. and Sat., 9hr., $49).

Public Transportation: Run by **Metro,** 168 Wellington St. (tel. 6336 5888; fax 6336 5899; hotline 13 22 01). Most buses run 7am-7pm, fares $1-3.

Taxis: Central Cabs (tel. 6331 3555 or 13 10 08).

Car Rental: Hertz, 58 Paterson St. (tel. 6335 1111), from $37 per day. **Advance Car Rentals,** 32 Cameron St. (tel. 6391 8000), from $39 per day. **Budget,** 138 George St. (tel. 6334 5533, airport tel. 6391 8566), from $38 per day.

Automobile Club: RACT, at the corner of York and Macquarie St. (tel. 6335 5633, 24hr. help tel. 13 11 11). Open Mon.-Fri. 8:45am-5pm.

Bicycle Rental: Rik Sloane Cycles, 10-14 Paterson St. (tel. 6331 9414 or 6331 9482; fax 6334 4476). $20 per day. Open Mon.-Fri. 8:30am-5:30pm, Sat. 8am-2pm.

Laundromat: 341a Wellington St. (tel. 6344 5418), in the district of Glen Dhu. Open daily 6am-11pm.

Library: 1 Civic Sq. (tel./fax 6336 2625).

Ticket Agencies: Centretainment (tel. 0334 3033), in the visitor center on the corner of St. John and Paterson St.

Ben Lomond Ski Info Line: Tel. 19 0229 0530.

Pharmacy: Centre Pharmacy (tel. 6331 7777), in the Brisbane St. mall, open Mon.-Sat. 8:30am-10pm, Sun. 9am-8pm.

Hospital: Launceston General (tel. 6332 7111), on Charles St.

Police: On Cimitiere St. (tel. 6336 3701). Lost and found tel. 6336 3818.

Emergency: Dial 000.

Post Office: 107 Brisbane St. (tel. 6331 9477; fax 6331 844). **Postal code:** 7250. Open Mon.-Fri. 9am-5pm.

Phone Code: 03.

ACCOMMODATIONS

Launceston Central City Backpackers, 173 George St. (tel. 6334 2327), just a few blocks south of the city center. Cleaned daily and in top condition, the whole place has a very domestic feel. The common room is equipped with a couch, deep chairs, and even a giant bean bag. The lounge is well-heated by a wood stove, but the kitchen and bunkrooms can get cold during the winter. Dorms $14; doubles $30. This place is crowded even during winter, so book ahead.

Andy's Backpack, 1 Tamar St. (tel. 6331 4513), part of the Andy's empire on the northern terminus of Tamar St. The backpackers is on the 2nd floor of a well-renovated hotel, with its beds packed together as closely as possible. The cafe, bar, and bakery downstairs are convenient, since there is no full kitchen (tea and coffee provided). Sardine dorms $12; more spacious singles $25; twins $35; doubles $35-45. All of the rooms use the shared shower and bathroom facilities. Linen rental $5. Key deposit $5.

Launceston City Youth Hostel, 36 Thistle St. (tel. 6344 9779), near the Coats Patons building off Wellington. This monstrous hostel occupies the old wool mill's canteen building, probably the most imposing hostel in Tasmania. The accommodation is geared for quantity, making it perfect for huge groups and no-frills vagabonds. A large fleet of bicycles is available for hire ($10 per day for guests), and the manager boasts that he can provide and organize everything you could need for bushwalking, except underwear. The walls are being repainted, and the facilities are kept clean. The hostel is sealed tight at midnight. Dorms $12; $30 for 3 nights.

Glen Dhu Caravan Park, 94 Glen Dhu St. (tel. 6344 2600; fax 6343 1764). The best (and only) caravan park in Launceston. The lot is spacious but convenient, bordered on 3 sides by blossoming trees. Extremely personable management offers free BBQs, clean, legitimate (not coin-op) showers with abundant hot water, a cozy campers' kitchen, and coin-operated laundry. Unpowered sites $8; powered sites $15; caravans $32; cabins $45-52.

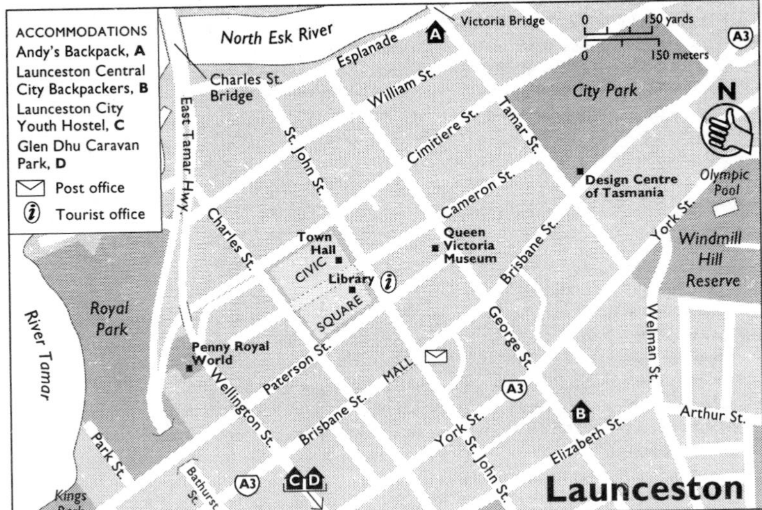

FOOD

The Happy Pumpkin, 117 Charles St. (tel. 6334 2985). More than a great name, this place serves delicious seafood, chicken, and vegetable dishes, in addition to tasty coffee and pastries. Most selections $3-5. Open Mon.-Thurs. 9am-5pm, Fri. 9am-4:30pm, Sat. 11am-3pm.

Nevroz, 195a Charles St. (tel. 6334 9833). A Greek-inspired takeaway a cut above the ubiquitous souvlaki bar. Homemade Greek pastry is a treat. Open Tues.-Thurs. 8am-9pm, Fri.-Sun. 8am-late.

The Royal Oak, corner of Tamar and Brisbane St. (tel. 6331 5346), has fancier Greek counter meals ($6.50-9). Grill and seafood are a bit more ($7-12.50). Occasional live music will keep you entertained. Open daily noon-2pm and 5:30pm-late.

O'Keefe's Hotel, 124 George St. (tel. 6331 4015). A very popular spot for lunch and dinner, the menu covers a broad spectrum of cuisine, from wallaby salad to sushi. Live music Fri.-Sun. evenings. Meals $6-16. Open daily noon-2pm and 5:30pm-late.

Grand Central Super Store, on the corner of Frederick and Wellington St. (tel. 6331 9422). A good selection of groceries. Open daily 24hr. (a big deal in Tasmania). Equipped with an ATM.

SIGHTS

The most spectacular sight in Launceston is the handiwork of the South Esk River, the **Cataract George Reserve** (tel. 6337 1288), about a 20-minute walk from York St. toward the Kings Bridge. The **Duck Reach Power Station** (open daily dawn to dusk), at the far end of the gorge, and the **Band Rotunda** (open Mon.-Fri. 9am-4pm, Sat.-Sun. 9am-4:30pm), near the far end of the Alexandra Bridge, are both gorge information centers. Walking tracks run on either side of the river; some climb to the rim of the gorge for excellent views of the river and cataracts. A circuit of the gorge can be done in two hours at a leisurely pace. If hiking doesn't do it for you, try **Cable Hang Gliding** (tel. 13 27 88) above the Trevallyn Dam Quarry. It's not as much fun as the real thing, but you're much less likely to leave a crater in the ground. (Open May-Nov. daily 10am-4pm; Dec.-April 10am-5pm; $10.) The longest single-span **chairlift** on the globe runs across the first basin (tel. 6331 5915; open Dec.-May daily 9am-4:30pm, June-Aug. Sat.-Sun. 9am-4:30pm; rides $5).

The Queen Victoria Museum and Art Gallery, at the corner of Cameron and Wellington St. (tel. 6331 6777), houses an impressive natural history display that focuses on Tasmania's wildlife and a popular science section that seeks to explain mining and other industrial phenomena. The upstairs gallery has some interesting sculptural pieces and innovative textile artwork. Guided gallery tours run Saturdays and Sundays at 2:30pm. The **Launceston Planetarium** is part of the complex (shows Tues.-Fri. 3pm, Sat. 2pm and 3pm; museum open Mon.-Sat. 10am-5pm, Sun. 2-5pm; free).

Launceston is blessed with an abundant supply of parks. **City Park,** on the corner of Tamar and Brisbane St., houses a sprawling 150-year-old wisteria as well as the **City Park Radio Station** (tel. 6334 3344), with a small radio museum on the ground floor (museum open Tues.-Thurs. and Fri. 10am-3pm; free). The City Park also has an enclosure teeming with Japanese Macaque monkeys.

The Design Centre of Tasmania, on the corner of Tamar and Brisbane St. (tel. 6331 5506; fax 6331 5662), was founded in 1976 to showcase Tasmanian crafts. While most of the superb objects on display are beyond the means of the average backpacker, it is still fun to have a gander (open Mon.-Fri. 10am-6pm, Sat. 10am-1pm, Sun. 2pm-5pm; free).

Historic walks depart from the visitor information center Monday through Friday at 9:45am (about 1hr., $10). Bookings are preferred (tel. 6331 3679). **Tamar River Cruises** (tel. 6334 9900; fax 6334 9911) have daily lunch river cruises ($46, students $40, children $23) and evening buffet cruises (Wed. and Fri.-Sun.; $55, students and seniors $49.50, children $27.50). The **Tamar Seaplane** (tel. 6334 9922) offers 20-minute ($50) and 60-minute ($100) flights.

ENTERTAINMENT

Many of the pubs downtown have live music on the weekends; the best and most popular is **Irish Murphy's,** 211 Brisbane St. (tel. 6331 4440; fax 6334 5503). True to its name, there's Gaelic decor, but it's not as overdone as many Aussie Irish bars (pints of Guinness $5; open Sun.-Wed. noon-midnight, Thurs.-Sat. noon-late). **The Royal Oak** on the corner of Tamar and Brisbane St. (tel. 6331 5346) also has live music on the weekends. **The Princess Theatre** on Brisbane St. hosts orchestral and other musical events. Get tickets and information through Centretainment at the visitor information center. Brisbane St. also has a **Village Cinema** with first-run Hollywood films.

■ Near Launceston: Ben Lomond National Park

Tasmania's premier ski resort, **Ben Lomond National Park** is about 60km from Launceston. Snow is often scarce, and the lifts are nothing to brag about, but Ben Lomond could satisfy a hard-core ski junkie in a pinch. Park entry costs $12 per car for the first day (additional days $6). **Ski rental** costs $34 per day (snowboards $40 plus deposit $100). Lift tickets run $20-28 for adults and $15-20 for students. Beginner packages include a lesson, lift pass, and equipment ($68, children $58). Spartan backpacker accommodation is available at the **Creek Inn** (tel./fax 6372 2444; Aug. to Sept. 20 $30, Sept. 21 to July $15). Bring everything you need for the night, since nothing is provided. **Tasmanian Wilderness Travel** (tel. 6334 4442) provides daily service from Launceston (round-trip $29) or from the base of the mountain (round-trip $5), in addition to package deals. If driving your own vehicle, chains can—and should—be rented at the base for $15 (fitting them is an additional $5).

George Town

The coastal port of George Town is perched on the Bass Strait 50km northeast of Launceston. The settlement was named by Lachlan Macquarie in 1811, after King George III (of American Revolution infamy). For the first few decades, shipping through George Town was restricted, in an effort to keep convicts from escaping Van Diemen's Land. When this restriction was lifted, the port thrived, and a complement of navigational aids was built to keep ships safe. A lighthouse powered by 25 whale-oil lanterns was built by the famous colonial architect John Lee Archer in 1833. A pair of leading lights, miniature lighthouses used for short-range navigation, were constructed in 1882 to combat the treacherous Hebe Reef. These measures were not

A Day in the Life: The Hunter

Aboriginals crossed over to Tasmania from mainland Australia during the last ice age, about 30,000 years ago. When the ice caps melted, the peninsula connecting Tasmania to the continent flooded with water, isolating these first colonists. For 30 millennia, Tasmanian Aboriginal culture thrived. These peoples pursued a semi-nomadic existence, following seasonal food supplies within a well-established home range. Fire was used to drive game out of the bush onto the spears of waiting hunters, and the periodic burning of vegetation shaped the terrain throughout the island. Although stones were used as tools, they used no stone-tipped weapons or implements. Instead, spears were fashioned entirely from wood, hardened in fire and sharpened with stone tools. The result was a highly effective weapon that could be thrown with deadly force and precision at a range of 60m. Analysis has revealed that these ancient Aboriginal spears had the same aerodynamics as today's Olympic javelins, with similar weight distribution.

completely effective, however. As recently as 1995, the *Iron Baron* wrecked on the reef, spilling countless liters of oil into the sea. The hulk was eventually towed away and scuttled near Flinders Island.

There is no reliable budget accommodation in George Town, but **Redline** has regular bus services to Launceston, making daytrips easy. **Buses** depart Pines Gift and Hardware, 21 Elizabeth St. (tel. 6382 1484), for Launceston (Mon.-Fri. 3 per day, Sun. 1 per day, 45min., $6). The **post office** is at 78 Macquarie St. (tel. 6382 1464; fax 6382 6547; postal code 7253), near **Trust Bank** (tel. 6382 2877; open Mon.-Thurs. 9:30am-4pm, Fri. 9:30am-5pm), and the **police** station (tel. 6382 4040).

The town's colorful seafaring history has been preserved in the **Pilot Station Maritime Museum** in **Low Head** (tel. 6382 1143; fax 6382 0143). The Pilot Station, established in 1805, is the oldest continuously operating facility of its kind in Australia. The museum contains thoughtful displays on the many facets of the marine experience, including communication, navigation, and shipbuilding (open daily 8am-late; admission $2, children and concessions $1). Fairy penguins use some of the beaches around George Town and Low Head as rookeries during the spring.

Deloraine

Set in the foothills of the western Tiens and ensconced in the Meander Valley, Deloraine functions as a perfect base for exploration of the World Heritage Wilderness to the southwest. The land around Deloraine is used for dairying, berrying, and all sorts of small-scale agriculture. Nearby **Mole Creek** has some of the most spectacular caves in Australia: **Marakoopa** and **King Solomon's Cave.** Tours of the caves run daily at regular intervals (tel. 6363 5182; fax 6363 5122). Entrance to each cave costs $6 (children and concessions $4; both caves for children and concessions $6).

The **Deloraine Visitor Information Centre,** 29 West Church St. (tel. 6362 2046; open Mon.-Fri. 9am-5:30pm, Sat. 9:30am-3:30pm, Sun. 9:30am-2:30pm), hands out pamphlets and advice. **Trust Bank** is at 24 Emu Bay Rd. (tel. 6362 2051; open Mon.-Thurs. 9:30am-4pm, Fri. 9:30am-5pm). **Redline** (tel. 6362 2046) has coaches to Launceston (daily, 1hr., $6.70) and Devonport (daily, 1hr., $9). **Tigerline** (tel. 6334 3600) has buses to Devonport (daily, 1hr., $8.50) and Launceston (daily, 45min., $6.30). **Tasmanian Wilderness Travel** (tel. 6334 4442; fax 6334 2029) has coaches to Cradle Mountain (April-Oct. Tues., Thurs., and Sat., Nov.-March daily; 4hr.; $40) and Launceston (April-Oct. Tues., Thurs., and Sat., Nov.-March daily; $40). All coaches depart from the visitors center. The **police** (tel. 6363 4004) are at Westbury Pl. The **post office,** 10 Emu Bay Rd. (tel. 6362 216; fax 6362 3244; open Mon.-Fri. 9am-5pm; postal code 7304), brings news from the outside world.

The Deloraine Highview Lodge YHA, 8 Blake St. (tel. 6362 2996), is praised by visitors above all other hostels. Perched above Deloraine, the hostel has fine mountain views. Day tours and activities can be arranged through the hostel, as many operators pick up directly at the door. The bunks are comfy and of higher quality than most ($12, YHA non-members $15). Bikes can be hired for $15 per day. **The Apex Caravan Park,** down by the river on West Pde. (tel. 6362 2345), is pleasant and green. If nothing fancy, it's at least well-maintained and tidy (unpowered sites $8, powered sites $10).

NORTHERN TASMANIA

Devonport

Many people come to Tasmania in search of untouched wildlands, unspoiled rivers, and mountains without end. Many people also arrive in Devonport, which proves a bit of a shock. While by no means an industrial hell, Devonport is not what most people expect from the smallest, wildest state in Australia. As they step off the ferry, visitors are greeted by the grim waterfront, which is dominated by a cluster of gigantic grey silos. Devonport is a port city after all, and function dictates form. The city plays gateway to the rest of the state by furnishing information outlets and a variety of transportation options. A couple of quality budget accommodations ensure that any time you spend here before moving on will be comfortable, if not aesthetically rewarding.

ORIENTATION

Devonport is situated on a promontory between two rivers. The city center lies on the west bank of the **Mersey River,** and the **Don River** bounds the city to the west. The ferry terminal is on the east bank of the Mersey, while **Fromby St.** runs along the left bank. Fromby converges with **Rooke St.** downstream from the ferry, eventually becoming **Victoria Pde.** The Parade runs to the coast by the Maritime Museum by the beach. **Bluff Rd.** runs west to Mersey Bluff along a stretch of pleasant beaches.

The Bass Hwy. bounds the city to the south and leads east to the airport. By road, Devonport is about an hour and a half from Launceston, via Bass Hwy. to the east, and three and a half hours from Hobart via Midlands Hwy. to the south.

PRACTICAL INFORMATION

Tourist Information: The official **Tasmanian Travel and Information Centre,** 5 Best St. (tel. 6424 8176; fax 6424 8476), in the Devonport Showcase next to the McDonalds off Formby Rd., can book accommodations and bus, air, and auto transport. Open daily 9am-5pm. **The Backpackers' Barn,** 10-12 Edwards St. (tel. 6424 3628; fax 6423 1119), specializes in orienting prospective bushwalkers. The Barn stocks a large selection of bush gear, maps, and trail guides for purchase or rental, and the staff provide experienced advice, all in a relaxed, warm atmosphere. A good place to meet other hikers. Open Mon.-Fri. 9am-6pm, Sat. 9am-noon.

Currency Exchange: Commonwealth Bank, 20 Rooke St. (tel. 13 22 21), and **ANZ,** 150C William St. (tel. 6423 1300), are both open Mon.-Thurs. 9:30am-4pm, Fri. 9:30-5pm.

ATMs: Machines of every stripe are in the Rooke St. mall, between Best and Steel St.

American Express: Pat Young Travel (tel. 6424 7699), in Day's Building on Best St., Rooms 7-8. Open Mon.-Fri. 9am-5pm.

Airport: The **Devonport Airport** is 6km east of the city center on the Bass Hwy. **Kendell** (tel. 6424 1411 or 13 13 00) and **Southern Australia** (Qantas affiliate; tel. 13 13 13) operate flights 3-4 times per day to Melbourne (55min., $105-185; book well ahead for cheaper rates).

Buses: Redline Coaches, 9 Edward St. (tel. 6424 5100), runs daily buses to Burnie (1hr., $7.10), Hobart (5hr., $32.30), Launceston (2hr., $13.30), Penguin (45min., $4.80), and Ulverstone (30min., $3.70). **Tasmanian Wilderness Travel** (tel. 6334 4442; fax 6334 2029) buses leave from the Redline Terminal or the Visitor Centre on Best St., bound for Cradle Mountain (April-Oct. Tues., Thurs., and Sat., Nov.-

March daily; 3hr.; $38), Lake Saint Clair (Nov.-March Mon.,Tues., and Thurs., 4hr., $49), and Strahan (daily, 7hr., $43). **Tigerline** operates from 41 Stewart St. (tel. 6424 6599), with a coach on Tues. and Thurs. to Strahan (6hr., $34.50) via Queenstown (4½hr., $29.10), Cradle Mountain (2hr., $22.70), and Zeehan (3½hr., $24.30). Tigerline also runs daily to Burnie (1hr., $6.50), Deloraine (45min., $8.50), Hobart (4½hr., $30.30), and Launceston (1½hr., $12.50). Ask about student/YHA discounts.

Ferries: The Spirit of Tasmania departs for Melbourne (Sat., Tues., and Thurs. 6pm, 14½hr.). The overnight ferry passage includes dinner, breakfast, and hostel-style accommodation on the lowest decks of the ship. (Dec.-Jan. $126; Feb.-March and Oct.-Nov. $105; April-Sept. $100. Cars Dec.-Jan. $35; Feb.-Dec. $25.) It is essential to book ahead at the info center or by calling 13 20 10.

Car Rental: Major companies with counters at the airport and ferry terminals include **Hertz** (tel. 6424 1013), **Avis** (tel. 6427 9797), **Budget** (tel. 6424 7088), and **Thrifty** (tel. 6427 9119). **Advance** (tel. 6424 8885 or 1800 030 118) and **Rent a Bug** (tel. 6427 9034) often have better prices than the bigger chains.

Automobile Club: Royal Automobile Club of Tasmania (RACT), 5 Steele St. (tel. 6421 1933), is open Mon.-Fri. 8:45am-5pm.

Bike Rental: Hire a Bicycle, 51 Raymond Ave. (tel. 6424 3889), makes deliveries and pickups daily 24hr. Bikes $15 per day.

Public Toilets: In the carpark adjacent to the Rooke St. mall. **Public showers** at the Backpackers Barn for $2.

Pharmacy: 155 William St. (tel. 6424 4233). Open 9am-9pm.

Emergency: Dial 000.

Police: 17 Oldaker St. (tel. 6421 7511).

Post Office: 88 Formby St. (tel. 6424 8282; fax 6424 7658). Open Mon.-Fri. 9am-5pm. **Postal code:** 7310.

Phone Code: 03.

ACCOMMODATIONS AND FOOD

Tasman House Backpackers, 114 Tasman St. (tel. 6423 2335; fax 6423 2340). From Formby Rd. on the river, proceed west along Steele St., turn left at William St., then right onto Tasman St. Tasman House will be on the right. Located in a sprawling former hospital, the facilities have a pronounced institutional flavor, but the family running the hostel adds a personal touch. Huge lounge, kitchen, and dining areas are kept toasty by an immense wood stove. Fresh bread and produce are provided from time to time, and special occasions are marked by potluck dinners. The dorm rooms can be chilly in the winter, and the beds themselves may prove a bit short for tall folks. The owners also operate a variety of tours and bushwalking trips. Dorms $9; 2-bed dorms $11; doubles $25, with bath $30. Free storage.

Tamahere Hotel, 34 Best St. (tel. 6424 1898), near the city center. Recently renovated for use by backpackers, this hotel still has a thriving pub downstairs. The bunkrooms are a bit cramped, but the mattresses are new, the walls have been freshly painted, and each room has a small heater. There is a small but fully stocked kitchen and an adjoining large room resembling a family den from the 1970s. Associated with the Backpackers Barn just down the street, check in with the Barn or the downstairs pub. Counter meals, pokies, pool, darts, and beer all available in the pub. Dorm beds $10.

MacWright House-Devonport YHA, 115 Middle Rd. (tel. 6424 5696), past Home Hill. Very basic, aging facilities. Alcohol is forbidden, and the dormitories are closed from 10am-5pm. The atmosphere in some of the rooms is moist and musty. Dorms $9, YHA non-members $12.

Mersey Bluff Caravan Park (tel. 6424 8655), on Bluff Rd., on the Mersey Bluff headland, about 1.5km from the city center. A well-equipped caravan park in an interesting spot on the Bluffs. Kitchen, BBQ, clean showers, and coin-operated laundry. Tent sites $6.50, powered sites $15; on-site caravans $38; cabins $48.

Abel Tasman Caravan Park, 6 Wright St. (tel. 6427 8794), on the east bank of the Mersey. Very convenient to the ferry terminal, located next to the East Devonport Beach. Tent sites $7, powered sites $10; on-site caravans $32; cabins $46.

The **Rooke St. mall** is packed with takeaways, chippies, hotel counter meals, and multinational fast food outposts. **The Kitchen Cappuccino Bar,** 2A Stewart St. (tel. 6424 1129), is one of the better coffee lounges downtown (open Mon.-Fri. 9am-4pm). **The Family Hotel** (tel. 6424 1601), on Formby St., has excellent counter fare with a rotating schedule of half-price specials on the trinity of Tasmanian tucker: schnitzel, steak, and seafood (around $6; open Mon.-Thurs.). **Renusha's Indian Restaurant,** 157 Rooke St. (tel. 6424 2293), stocks a good variety of vegetarian and carnivorous dishes ($10-12), eat-in or takeaway.

SIGHTS AND ENTERTAINMENT

Tiagarra, on the Mersey Bluff near the lighthouse (tel. 6424 8250 or 6427 9037; fax 6427 0506), is a Tasmanian Aboriginal interpretive center that highlights the achievements of a 30,000-year-old culture. Detailed displays explain Aboriginal hunting methods, tool manufacture, and the genocide that came with the arrival of the Europeans. Guided tours are given every 30 minutes (open 8:30am-5pm; admission $3, concessions $2). The bluffs around the center bear many signs of Aboriginal occupation. A short walking trail leads to many **rock engravings** left by the area's original inhabitants. Some of the carvings are inconspicuous, so keep alert.

The **Devonport Maritime Museum,** on Gloucester Ave. just off Bluff Rd., preserves a history decidedly less ancient. Mainly a collection of old photographs and model boats, the museum focuses on local lore, with a good archive of family history (open April-Sept. Tues.-Sun. 10am-4pm, Oct.-March Tues.-Sun. 10am-4:30pm; admission $2, children 40¢). Housed in an old church, the **Devonport Gallery,** 45-47 Stewart St. (tel. 6424 8296), showcases the best of Tasmanian arts and crafts, concentrating on paintings, ceramics, and glass. The gallery also hosts occasional cultural events, workshops, and performances (open Mon.-Sat. 10am-5pm, Sun. 2-5pm; free).

To the west of Devonport proper, in the small hamlet of Don, the **Don River Railway** (tel. 6424 6335) offers steam train rides to and from Coles Beach, a few kilometers away, as well as a small display of historical train equipment and memorabilia. Trains run on the hour from 10am to 4pm daily ($7, children $4; admission to the display is $4, which is refunded if you ride the train).

At night, **Spurs** and the **Warehouse,** 18-22 King St. (tel. 6424 7851), come alive with two music options. The country-western American theme, video games, and pool tables at Spurs attract a young, casual crowd (open Wed.-Sun. 4pm-1:30am; live music Fri.-Sat.). Next door, the Warehouse is a weekend dance club with big name acts (Fri. open until 3am, $5 cover; Sat. open until 4am, $6 cover). **Devonport Village Cinema,** 9 Stewart St. (tel. 6424 4622), shows first-run movies.

■ Near Devonport

Two interesting geological formations can be found in the country south of Devonport. The **Leven Canyon Reserve,** southwest of the city near Nietta, boasts a lookout with absolutely gorgeous views of the Leven Gorge. To reach the Reserve, take the Bass Hwy. west, then the B15 south to Nietta, then route 128 to the Canyon. A bit to the north, buried under nondescript farmland, lie the **Gunns Plains Caves** (tel. 6429 1388). The caves are decorated with immense limestone columns, colorful rock curtains and shawls, and a host of other strange formations. The cold creek running through the caves is home to duck-billed platypuses, while the ceiling has a few resident glowworms. Freshwater crayfish, some the size of very, very small horses (3-4kg), use the caves for breeding. The 50-minute tours are packed with informative banter and comedic stylings of dubious hilarity and political correctness (tours daily on the hr. 10am-4pm; $8, children $4).

The Northwest Coast

West of Devonport, the A2 highway traces the northern coast of Tasmania. A2 passes through **Ulverston** and Burnie before reaching the junction where A10 branches south toward Queenstown, Zeehan, and Strahan. From Burnie, A2 continues northwest past Wynyard and **Rocky Cape National Park** to **Smithton** and nearby Stanley.

Burnie Burnie is an industrial city in a state where industry is in decline. Young people go away to university or to the larger urban areas of Hobart or Launceston and don't return. For the visitor, Burnie serves more as a transportation hub than a destination. **Tigerline** (tel. 6431 1971) departs from Rivoli Cafe, 54 Cattley St., to Cradle Mountain (Tues. and Thurs., 3hr., $29.20), Devonport (daily, 1hr., $6.50), Hobart (daily, 5¼hr., $34.50), Launceston (daily, 2¼hr., $16.70), Queenstown (Tues. and Thurs., 6hr., $35.60), and Strahan (Tues. and Thurs., 8hr., $41). **Redline,** 117 Wilson St. (tel. 6431 3233), sends coaches east and west along the north coast but doesn't go down the west coast: Devonport (daily, 1hr., $7.10), Hobart (daily, 4hr., $37), Launceston (daily, 2½hr., $18), and Stanley or Smithton (Mon.-Sat., 1½hr., $10.40).

Should you happen to get stuck in Burnie, the only budget accommodation is the **Treasure Island Caravan Park,** 253 Bass Hwy. (tel. 6431 1925; fax 6431 1753), west of town. The park has an indoor pool, a coin-operated laundry, and BBQ facilities. In addition to the standard tent sites ($7), powered sites ($10), caravans ($30), and cabins ($44), there are two small bunkrooms, complete with kitchens ($10). Good counter meals can be had at the **Beach Hotel,** 1 Wilson St. (tel. 6431 2333), also a popular night spot on weekends. The **Tasmanian Travel and Information Centre** (tel. 6434 6111; open Mon.-Fri. 9am-5pm, Sat. 9am-noon) is located in the Civic Centre complex, in the same building as the **Pioneer Village Museum** (open Mon.-Fri. 9am-5pm, Sat.-Sun. and holidays 1:30-4:30pm; free). Next door, the **Burnie Gallery** keeps the same hours as the museum. An **ANZ Bank** with an ATM is on the corner of Wilson and Cattley St. (tel. 6430 4311).

Wynyard Known (to itself) as Tulip Town, Wynyard is a charming tiny town with many green areas and Tulip Festivals each spring. Southern Australia and Kendell both operate flights from the **Wynyard airport** to Melbourne (several daily $93-168, call 6431 2166 for airport information). The **Redline** Burnie-Smithton coaches stop in Wynyard at **Gales Auto Service** (tel. 6442 2205) Monday to Saturday to Stanley ($9 and Burnie ($2.50).

The **Wynyard YHA,** 36 Dodgin St. (tel. 6442 2013), is convenient to the airport, with a stained glass doorway, pleasant kitchen, and flowers from local nurseries. The one drawback is the coin-operated showers (dorms $11, YHA non-members $14). There is a **caravan park** right off the highway, which charges $10 for unpowered sites and $13 for powered sites. The caravan park also has backpacker beds, but the hostel is nicer and cheaper. The **Table Cape** is a striking volcanic promontory right outside Wynyard. Covered in a mosaic of farmland, the cape has a lighthouse and striking views of the coastline.

Stanley In the extreme northwest of the state, Stanley is one of the oldest European settlements, colonized by the Van Diemen's Land company in the 1840s as part of a 250,000-acre land grant. Stanley is built at the base of the **Nut,** a huge volcanic plateau first seen by a European, Matthew Flinders, in December 1798. Flinders described it as a "cliffy round lump in form resembling a Christmas cake." Stanley is just a small, quiet town, thick with tea rooms, craft shops, and little else. But the Nut is well worth seeing, and the townspeople couldn't be nicer. The best way to see the Nut is to make the short, sweet **climb** yourself, but there's a chairlift to cart the less-ambitious to the top (open 10am-4pm; return $6, children $4). If you can't even be bothered to walk around at the top, take a **Nut Buggy tour** (tel. 6458 1312; $5; closed in winter). The same company offers night tours of the area for $15, including a lift ticket. The top of the Nut is windy and can be bitterly cold; dress appropriately. Fine views in all directions reward those who brave the climb and the wind.

Redline leaves from Stanley Garage and Store (tel. 6458 1263) for Burnie ($10.40) and Wynyard ($9). A small **post office** and **general store** is on 11-13 Church St. (open 9am-12:30pm and 1:30-5pm). The pub serves counter meals. The **Stanley Caravan Park,** on the waterfront on Wharf Rd. (tel. 6458 1266), doubles as a **YHA hostel.** Most rooms are linoleum-tiled twins or doubles. There is a full kitchen and a lounge with a fireplace and TV. (Office open 8am-8pm. Twins or doubles $12, YHA non-members $14. Tent sites $9.50; powered sites $12.)

Cradle Mountain National Park

Cradle Mountain National Park is the most famous natural landmark in Tasmania, visited by hundreds of thousands every year. One of the last temperate wildlands on earth, the entire area is a World Heritage Wilderness, which means that it has been judged so unique and irreplaceable that its preservation is a matter of international importance.

The importance of the area was first championed by Gustav Weindorfer, an Austrian mountaineer and naturalist who built a lodge named Waldheim ("forest home"), to allow people to see the area he loved so well. "This is Waldheim," he wrote, "where there is no time and nothing matters." Such removal from temporal pressures remains popular today at the **Waldheim Cabins,** which lack electricity or conveniences ($55-75). The Visitors Centre (tel. 6492 1110; fax 6492 1120) oversees the cabins and features an informative educational display with suggestions for day hikes, as well as an excellent shop (open daily 8am-5pm). The two-hour walk around Dove Lake is a state-of-the-art, environmentally friendly track suitable for almost anyone. The national park fees (bus passengers $3, vehicles $9, bushwalkers on **Overland Track,** see p. 431, $12), paid at the gate, maintain and build facilities.

Just outside the gates to the park, the **Cradle Mountain Campground** (tel. 6492 1395; fax 6492 1438) provides bunk rooms and tent sites in an ideal location. (Tent sites in summer $6 per person; in winter $5 per person. Basic bunks in summer $18; in winter $16.) **Tigerline** (tel. 6492 1400) has a depot at the Cradle View restaurant, opposite the campground. The company runs a bus on Tuesdays and Thursdays from the campground and visitor center to Queenstown (3hr., $17), Hobart (5½hr., $53), Devonport (2hr., $22.70), and Launceston (2½hr., $29.20). **Tasmanian Wilderness Travel** (tel. 6334 4442; fax 6334 2029) has buses to Launceston (April-Oct. Tues., Thurs., and Sat., Nov.-March daily; 4¼hr.; $40) and Devonport (April-Oct. Tues., Thurs., and Sat., Nov.-March daily; 2¾hr.; $38).

Victoria

Blessed with abundant natural beauty and wealth, Victoria occupies the southeast corner of the continent. Although it is the mainland's smallest state, its environment runs the gamut from the dry and empty western plains of the Wimmera to the inviting wineries along the fertile banks of the Murray River, from the ski resorts of the Victorian Alps to the forested parks of the southern coast. The capital of the state and the cultural center of the nation, orderly Melbourne overflows with stained glass and elaborate iron latticework. Inner city suburbs link visitors to verdant gardens, a world class zoo, eclectic ethnic neighborhoods, seaside strips, and student haunts. Because Victoria is compact and has a well-developed infrastructure, its attractions lie within easy reach of one another and of Melbourne.

Victoria's most distinctive attractions are found on the coast. West of Melbourne, the breathtaking Great Ocean Road, hand-cut between 1919 and 1931 from the limestone cliffs, winds its way alongside the roaring Southern Ocean. The road passes surfing beaches, coastal getaways, temperate rainforests, and geological wonders, including the 12 Apostles rock formation, which pokes precariously from the sea like ancient fingers. East of the capital, the coastline unfolds past Phillip Island's penguin colony and the beach resorts of the Mornington Peninsula, heading into Gippsland. Crashing waves collide with granite outcroppings, forming the sandy beaches at the edge of the renowned Wilsons Promontory National Park. A riviera climate complete with resort beaches dominates East Gippsland while the Princes Hwy. stretches onward toward the Croajingolong National Park. In this stony, sandy expanse at Victoria's eastern extreme, tidal estuaries teem with birdlife and fish.

The interior of the state is visually less remarkable, but historically and economically more significant. Tremendous quantities of ore flowed from Victoria in the mid-19th century, and this gold rush wealth created a host of beautiful country towns in the central goldfields, preserved today in sleepy nostalgia. The 20th century brought extensive agricultural and commercial development, including several massive hydroelectric public works projects which continue to impact the state's ecosystems. Another burst of growth in the 1980s left Melbourne with a steely skyline and introduced eco-tourism to Victoria.

Phone numbers in Victoria have recently changed. Regional phone codes are now **almost all** 03, followed by eight-digit numbers. The last two digits of the old area code have become the first two digits of the new number. If you have trouble making a call, use the following scheme to get the old number, and try that instead. For more details, see the **appendix** (p. 574). Towns close to the New South Wales border may take that state's new area codes.

New number:	Old number:
(03) 54xx xxxx	(054) xx xxxx
(03) 58xx xxxx	(058) xx xxxx
*(02) 60xx xxxx	*(060) xx xxxx (Wodonga)

Melbourne

The second largest city in Australia and the capital of Victoria, Melbourne sometimes has trouble escaping Sydney's shadow. But life can be good in the shade; Melbourne reigns over Australia culturally and has been dubbed the planet's most liveable city. Distinctive neighborhoods, leafy streets, and the clean, efficient transport system mean that Melbourne rarely feels like a city of 3.5 million people. The exotic fauna of Melbourne Zoo, the grizzly images of Old Melbourne Gaol, and the relaxing atmosphere of well-preserved Victorian residential neighborhoods draw thousands of weekend sightseers and world travelers, while the city's multiple Mediterranean and

Asian communities enrich the city's cuisine. The 19th-century architecture has been utilized, rather than mothballed into historical museums. Consequently, central Melbourne displays ornamental Victorian structures standing proudly beside steel and glass skyscrapers.

Melbourne's history is best charted through its iconic rivalry with Sydney. Settled by Sydney ex-pats, Melbourne quickly established itself in the first year of Queen Victoria's reign (1837) and embarked on an era of growth and development that powerfully shaped the city's character. The mid-19th-century Victoria gold rush provided the wealth that built so many distinctive structures and established an extensive network of healthy, beautiful, public green spaces. Leaving Sydney in its (gold) dust, Melbourne set about building Australia's cultural institutions, including the national opera company—now housed in Sydney's distinctive structure. The city billed itself as "Marvellous Melbourne" (parodied as "Marvellous Smellbourne" because of open sewers in the 1890s) as it battled Sydney for national capital status. Ultimately, the two cities agreed on Canberra as a midpoint compromise, though Melbourne happily housed the national government until Canberra's completion. Melbourne's 20th century apex—the 1956 Summer Olympic Games—marked the settling and refinement of Melbourne's character.

Melbourne's funky suburbs—from trendy, seaside St. Kilda to uber-cool, alternative Fitzroy—lie just minutes away from the city center by tram. The Royal Botanical Gardens, just across the muddy Yarra River from downtown, strike an environmental counterpoint and support one of the world's best plant collections. Though Melbourne's weather is infamously unpredictable, its generally temperate climate enables tropical palms to dwell beside temperate oaks. With waterfronts, public parks, famous sporting events, and world-class museums, Melbourne invites visitors to relax, explore, and enjoy the attractions of a large city freed from the pressure of an international spotlight.

ARRIVAL AND DEPARTURE

By Plane

The boomerang-shaped **Tullamarine International Airport,** 22km northwest of Melbourne, has three terminals under its roof. The central terminal houses all international arrivals and departures. The international departures on the first floor serves **United Airlines** (tel. 9335 1133), **Cathay Pacific** (tel. 13 17 47), **Singapore Airlines** (tel. 9339 3344, reservations 13 10 11), **Ansett Airlines,** and **Qantas.**

Exiting from international arrivals, the **domestic** terminal to the left houses **Qantas** (tel. 13 12 11), which flies to all Australian state capitals at least once daily (standard fares to: Adelaide $182, Alice Springs $391, Brisbane $309, Cairns $460, Canberra $156, Darwin $483, Hobart $173, Perth $437, and Sydney $194). **Ansett Airlines** (tel. 9339 5290), to the right leaving international arrivals, offers backpackers' fares for three or more tickets purchased at least two weeks in advance to Adelaide ($118), Alice Springs ($299), Brisbane ($218), Cairns ($314), Canberra ($117), Hobart ($132), Perth ($258), or Sydney ($117).

Travellers Information (tel. 9297 1805; fax 9297 1051), directly in front of arriving international passengers as they exit, books same-day accommodations and provides maps and brochures. A backpacker board provides postings and valuable information. **Lockers** ($4 per day) are located on either end of the international terminal.

Skybus (tel. 9335 2811; fax 9338 5075) provides ground transport to Melbourne's city center every half-hour. It stops at the YHA Queensberry and at the Spencer Street bus and train station downtown. The bus departs from the station for the airport at a quarter past and a quarter to the hour, and from the Melbourne Transit Centre, 58 Franklin St., on the hour and half-hour. One-way tickets are $9, return is $16. **Taxis** (tel. 13 10 08) to city center cost $28 and take approximately 30 minutes. **Car rental** companies are clustered to the left when exiting international arrivals. **Thrifty** (tel. 9330 1522; fax 9335 1706), **Budget** (tel. 9241 6366; fax 9335 1760), **Hertz** (tel. 13 30 39), and **Avis** (tel. 9338 1800) rent to those over 21 (all accept V, MC, AmEx).

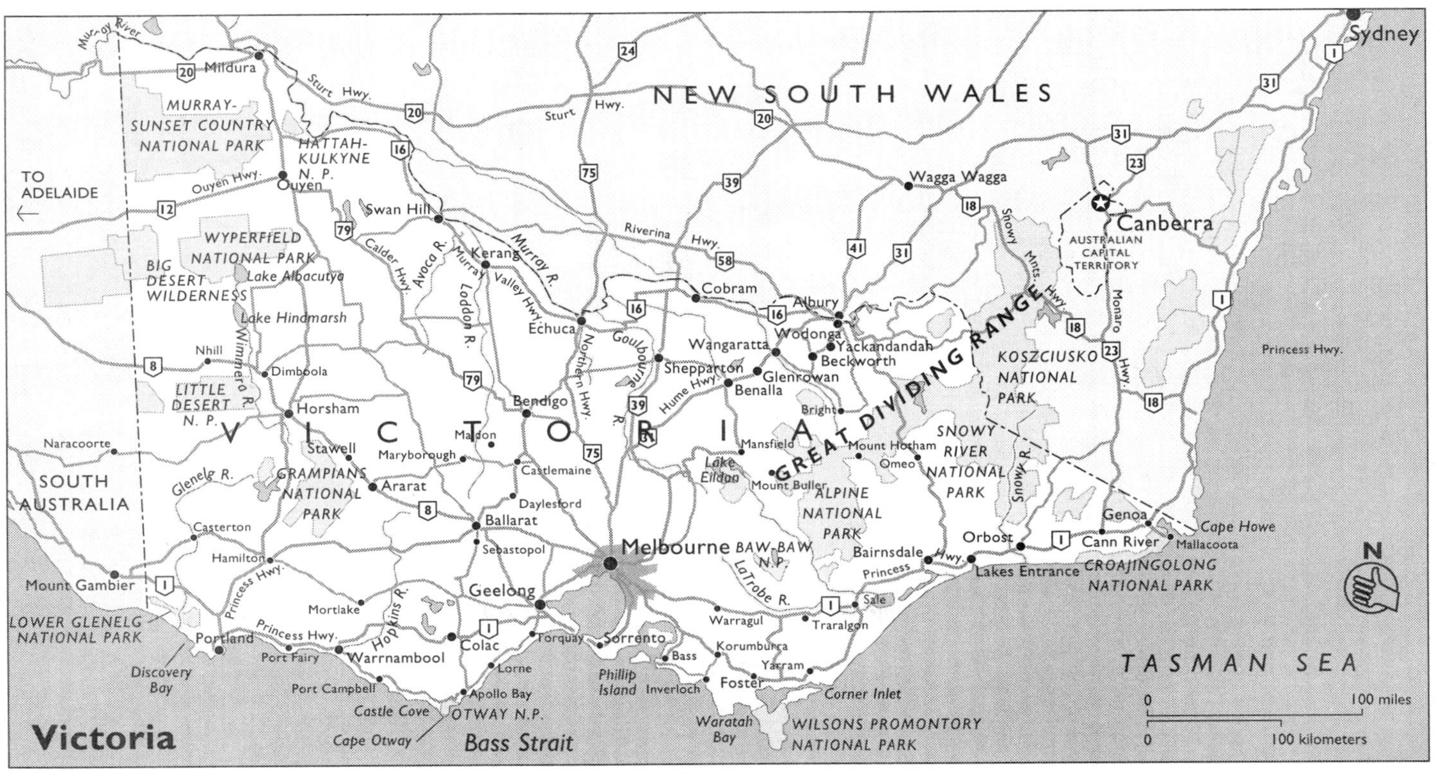
Victoria
NEW SOUTH WALES
VICTORIA
SOUTH AUSTRALIA
TASMAN SEA
Bass Strait
Sydney
Canberra
AUSTRALIAN CAPITAL TERRITORY
Wagga Wagga
Albury
Wodonga
Yackandandah
Beckworth
Glenrowan
Wangaratta
Benalla
Shepparton
Cobram
Echuca
Bendigo
Castlemaine
Daylesford
Maldon
Ballarat
Sebastopol
Geelong
Melbourne
Torquay
Sorrento
Phillip Island
Bass
Inverloch
Foster
Yarram
Korumburra
Warragul
Traralgon
Sale
Bairnsdale
Orbost
Lakes Entrance
Cann River
Genoa
Mallacoota
Cape Howe
Omeo
Mount Hotham
Bright
Mount Buller
Mansfield
Lake Eildon
Kerang
Swan Hill
Ouyen
Mildura
Horsham
Dimboola
Nhill
Stawell
Ararat
Maryborough
Hamilton
Casterton
Portland
Port Fairy
Warrnambool
Mortlake
Colac
Lorne
Apollo Bay
Port Campbell
Castle Cove
Cape Otway
OTWAY N.P.
Discovery Bay
Mount Gambier
Naracoorte
TO ADELAIDE
Corner Inlet
Waratah Bay
WILSONS PROMONTORY NATIONAL PARK
CROAJINGOLONG NATIONAL PARK
SNOWY RIVER NATIONAL PARK
ALPINE NATIONAL PARK
BAW BAW N.P.
KOSZCIUSKO NATIONAL PARK
GREAT DIVIDING RANGE
Snowy Mnts. Hwy.
Monaro Hwy.
Princess Hwy.
Hume Hwy.
Riverina Hwy.
Sturt Hwy.
Northern Hwy.
Murray Valley Hwy.
Calder Hwy.
Ouyen Hwy.
Murray R.
Goulbourne R.
Loddon R.
Avoca R.
Wimmera R.
Glenelg R.
Hopkins R.
LaTrobe R.
Snowy R.
Murray River
GRAMPIANS NATIONAL PARK
HATTAH-KULKYNE N.P.
MURRAY-SUNSET COUNTRY NATIONAL PARK
WYPERFIELD NATIONAL PARK
Lake Albacutya
Lake Hindmarsh
BIG DESERT WILDERNESS
LITTLE DESERT N.P.
LOWER GLENELG NATIONAL PARK
N
0 100 miles
0 100 kilometers

Several banks offer **currency exchange** and cash traveler's checks. National Australian Bank **ATM** machines on the first floor accept Visa, MC, Cirrus, and Plus cards. Telstra **telephones** are located throughout the airport. **Post Australia** (tel. 9338 3865; open Mon.-Fri. 9am-5pm, Sat.-Sun. 10am-4pm) has international mail, poste restante, **fax** and **photocopying** services. The address is Melbourne Airport, Vic 3045.

By Bus and Train

Spencer Street Station, on Spencer and Bourke St. (tel. 9619 2300; open daily 7am-9pm) serves as Melbourne's main intercity bus and train station. **V/Line** (tel. 13 22 32), a network of trains and buses that covers Victoria, runs service to Adelaide (1 per day, 11hr., $56), Albury (Mon.-Fri. 6 per day, 3-3½hr., $45), Ballarat (Mon.-Fri. 12 per day, Sat.-Sun. 6 per day, 2hr., $13), Bendigo (Mon.-Fri. 12 per day, 2hr., $20), Bright (Sun.-Fri., 1 per day, 4½hr., $38), Canberra (1 per day, 8½hr., $47), Echuca (Mon.-Sat. 6 per day, Sun. 3 per day, 3-4hr., $20), Geelong (12 per day, 1hr., $8.40), and Sydney via Albury (2 per day, 11hr., $90, $54). To reach Wilsons Promontory National Park, take V/Line to Foster (Mon.-Fri. 4:30pm, Sat. 6:40pm, Sun. 5:35pm, 2¾hr., $21.30). **McCafferty's,** located in the barrel-shaped coach station just north of the main station, offers limited bus service around Victoria. YHA-discounted one-way tickets are available (to Adelaide $35, Alice Springs $146, Ayers Rock $135, Brisbane $113, Cairns $215, Canberra $41, Darwin $264, and Sydney $45). McCafferty's accepts MC, Visa, Discover, and AmEx. **Melbourne Transit Centre,** 58 Franklin St., near Elizabeth St. and the brown Qantas tower, is the main terminal for Skybus, Ansett Airlines, and **Greyhound Pioneer** (tel. 9663 3299 or 13 20 30), which has daily service to Adelaide ($50), Brisbane ($67), Canberra ($26), and Sydney ($29).

By Car

The **Royal Automobile Club of Victoria (RACV),** 360 Bourke St. (tel. 13 19 55 or 9642 5566; fax 9642 5040). The excellent RACV should be your first resource for car-related problems and questions. Members of automobile clubs in other countries may already have reciprocal membership. To join in Victoria, the basic RACV Roadside Care package (including 4 free service calls each year and limited free towing) costs $47, plus a $28 first-time-joiner's fee. (See AAA in **Essentials,** p. 37, for more information). RACV also sells car insurance (accepts V, MC).

Most major **car rental** companies only hire cars to those 21 years of age and older. **Budget's** main office is at 398 Elizabeth St. on the corner of A'Beckett St. (tel. 9203 4844). **Hertz** is at 97 Franklin St. (tel. 9663 6244; nationwide 13 30 39). **National** is on Peel and Queensbury St., North Melbourne (tel. 9329 5000; fax 9329 7000). **Thrifty** is near Budget at 390 Elizabeth St. (tel. 9663 5200; toll-free 1800 652 008). **Backpacker Car Rental,** 169 Peel St., North Melbourne (tel. 9329 4411; fax 9329 4422), charges $100 per week with unlimited kilometers in the metropolitan area. Backpacker has a car re-purchase plan where cars are guaranteed to be bought back at set rates after 12 weeks; a great deal for long-term visitors or younger drivers.

By Ferry

The **Spirit of Tasmania** (tel. 13 20 10) departs for Devonport, Tasmania, from Port Phillip Bay's Station Pier (at the end of Tram 109) on Mondays, Wednesdays, and Fridays at 6pm. Walk-on passenger check-in is 3-5pm, while vehicles must board between 1:30 and 4:30pm. The 14-hour trip can be made in a variety of cabin accommodations. Fares quoted are round-trip in hostel berth, and include both dinner and breakfast. (Dec. 13-Jan. 24 $226; Sept. 28-Dec. 12 and Jan. 25-April 18 $210; April 19-Sept. 27 $200.) Cars, depending on size, cost $25-35 for transport each way. Children cannot travel in hostel berths. Return trips leave Tasmania on Tuesdays, Thursdays, and Saturdays at 6pm.

In winter of 1997, a smaller catamaran ferry made several test runs across the Bass Strait. Its performance in storms was less than satisfactory, so plans to retire the *Spirit* have been put on hold for the moment.

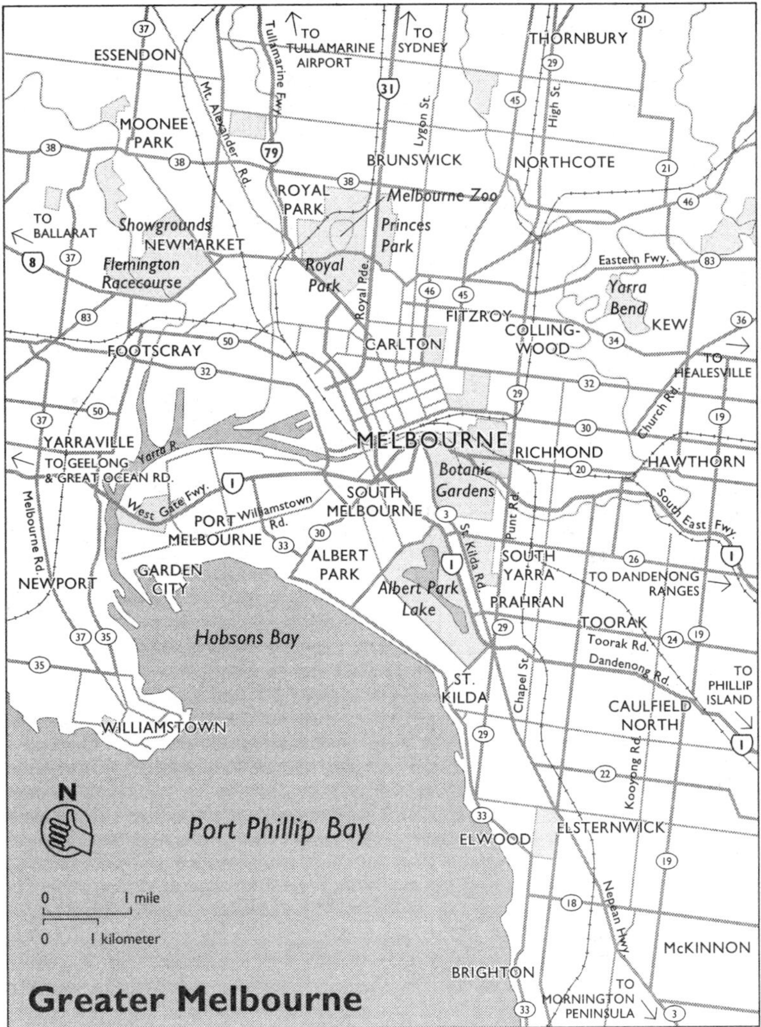

ORIENTATION

Melbourne's superb **public transportation** system makes getting around a breeze—once you've got the hang of it. The **Met** is comprised of trains, buses, and trams, the last proudly wearing their green and yellow colors as symbols of Melbourne. The network criss-crosses the metropolitan area (every 3-12min.; Mon.-Sat. 5am-midnight, Sun. 8am-11pm). **Flinders Street Station** serves as the Met's primary train depot. Zone 1 (of 3) covers most of Melbourne. Tickets within Zone 1 can be used on any of the three types of transportation, and are valid for unlimited travel for a two-hour period ($2.20), the day ($4.30), the week ($18.60), or the month ($69.50). Only two-hour tickets can be purchased on board; day tickets tend to be more economical. Ask about value packs for families and multiple zone travel. Tickets are sold at stations, on board trams (not wheelchair accessible) and buses, and at **The Met Shop,** 103 Elizabeth St. (tel. 13 16 38), 2½ blocks north of Flinders St. Station. The shop carries an all-important map showing every Met route.

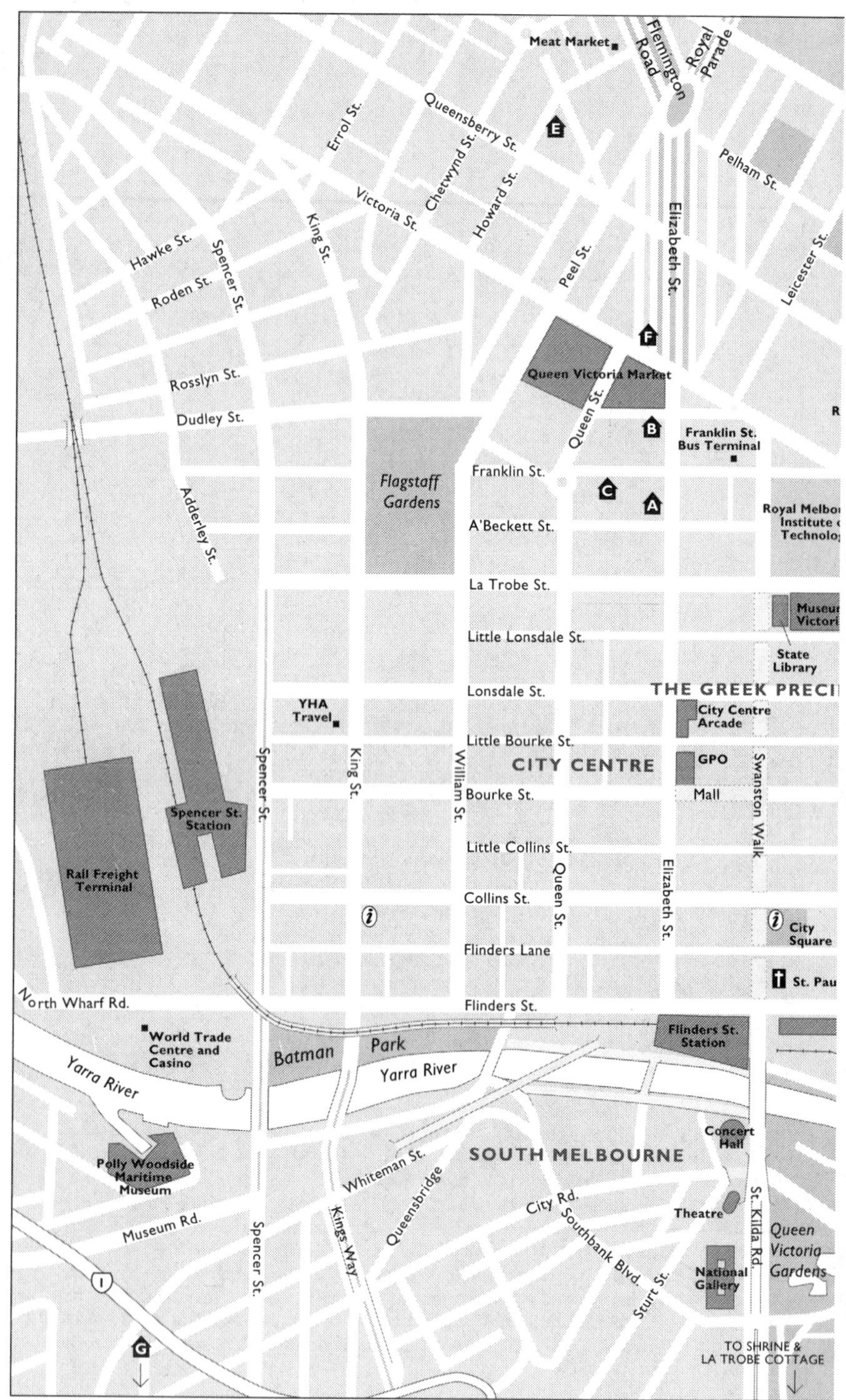
Meat Market
Flemington Road
Royal Parade
Queensberry St.
Errol St.
Chetwynd St.
Howard St.
Victoria St.
King St.
Pelham St.
Elizabeth St.
Leicester St.
Hawke St.
Spencer St.
Roden St.
Peel St.
Rosslyn St.
Dudley St.
Queen Victoria Market
Queen St.
Franklin St. Bus Terminal
Franklin St.
Flagstaff Gardens
Adderley St.
A'Beckett St.
Royal Melbo Institute Technolo
La Trobe St.
Little Lonsdale St.
Museu Victori
State Library
Lonsdale St.
THE GREEK PRECI
YHA Travel
City Centre Arcade
Little Bourke St.
CITY CENTRE
GPO
King St.
William St.
Bourke St.
Mall
Swanston Walk
Spencer St. Station
Little Collins St.
Rail Freight Terminal
Collins St.
City Square
Flinders Lane
St. Pau
North Wharf Rd.
Flinders St.
World Trade Centre and Casino
Flinders St. Station
Batman Park
Yarra River
Concert Hall
SOUTH MELBOURNE
Polly Woodside Maritime Museum
Whiteman St.
Queensbridge
City Rd.
Southbank Blvd.
Theatre
St. Kilda Rd.
Queen Victoria Gardens
Museum Rd.
Kings Way
National Gallery
Sturt St.
TO SHRINE & LA TROBE COTTAGE

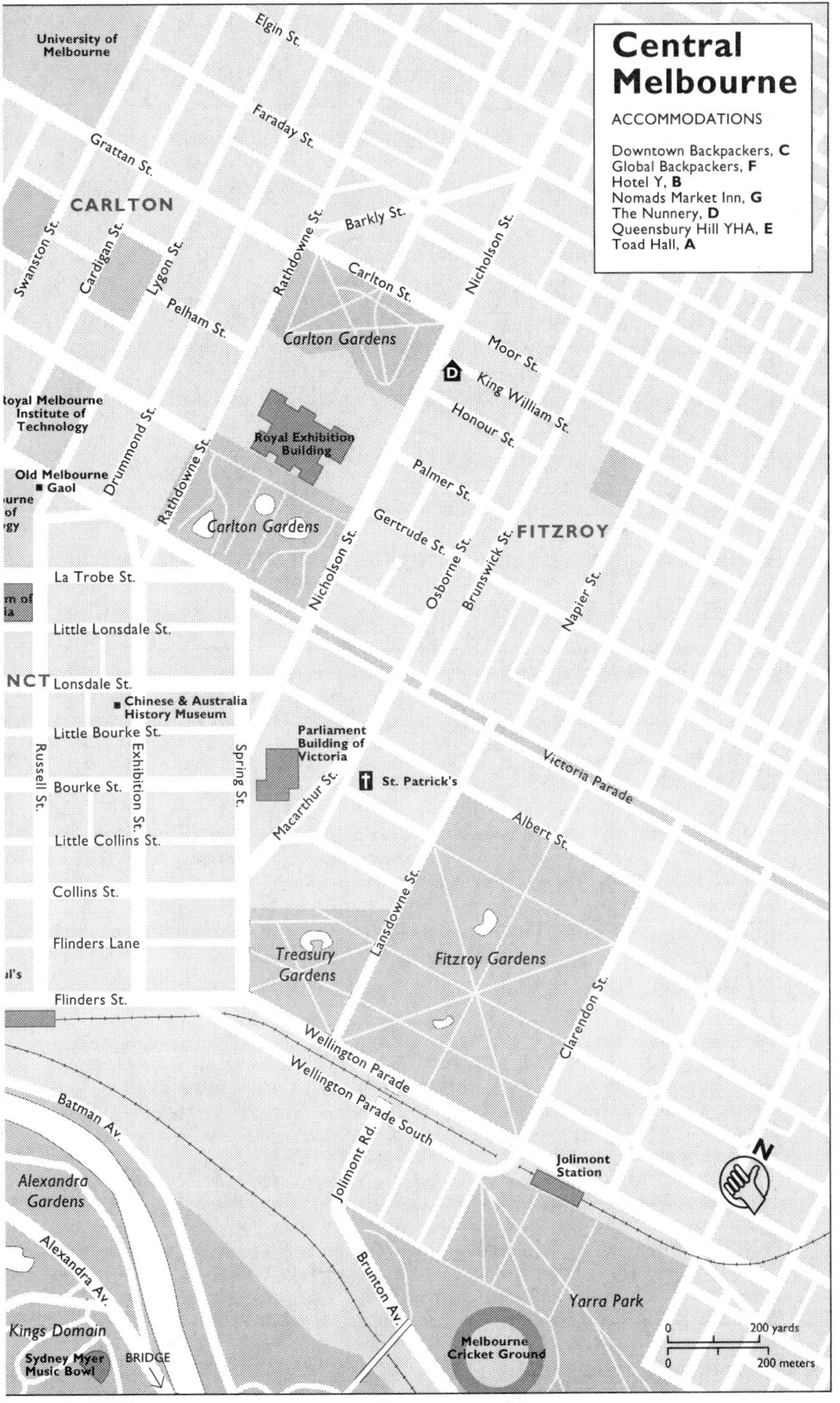
Central Melbourne
ACCOMMODATIONS
Downtown Backpackers, C
Global Backpackers, F
Hotel Y, B
Nomads Market Inn, G
The Nunnery, D
Queensbury Hill YHA, E
Toad Hall, A
University of Melbourne
Elgin St.
Faraday St.
Grattan St.
CARLTON
Swanston St.
Cardigan St.
Lygon St.
Pelham St.
Rathdowne St.
Barkly St.
Carlton St.
Nicholson St.
Carlton Gardens
Moor St.
King William St.
Honour St.
Royal Melbourne Institute of Technology
Drummond St.
Royal Exhibition Building
Old Melbourne Gaol
Palmer St.
Gertrude St.
FITZROY
Osborne St.
Brunswick St.
Napier St.
La Trobe St.
Little Lonsdale St.
Lonsdale St.
Chinese & Australia History Museum
Little Bourke St.
Parliament Building of Victoria
St. Patrick's
Russell St.
Exhibition St.
Spring St.
Bourke St.
Macarthur St.
Victoria Parade
Albert St.
Little Collins St.
Collins St.
Lansdowne St.
Flinders Lane
Treasury Gardens
Fitzroy Gardens
Clarendon St.
Flinders St.
Wellington Parade
Wellington Parade South
Batman Av.
Jolimont Rd.
Jolimont Station
Alexandra Gardens
Alexandra Av.
Brunton Av.
Yarra Park
Kings Domain
Sydney Myer Music Bowl
BRIDGE
Melbourne Cricket Ground
0
200 yards
200 meters
N

Many hostels rent **bicycles** and **Bicycle Victoria,** 19 O'Connell St. (tel. 9328 3000; see listing under **Melbourne Recreation,** p. 464) provides other services. If you'd rather not sweat, call **Silver Top Taxi** (tel. 13 10 08). A ride to the airport runs $28.

City Center

The city center is a well-arranged rectangular grid of streets bordered by **Spencer Street Station** to the west and **Flinders Street Station** to the south. Five major streets run east to west. To navigate them, remember the mnemonic "Let's Leave Behind Casual Fears" (**L**aTrobe, **L**onsdale, **B**ourke, **C**ollins, **F**linders), or choose your own. To the north of all but LaTrobe are "little" streets—roads named after their southern superior (Collins St., for example, is flanked by Little Collins St. and Flinders Ln.). Nine streets cross this grid running north to south: Spencer (the western-most), King, William, Queen, Elizabeth, Swanston, Russell, Exhibition, and Spring. Spencer St. runs by the primary bus and train depot, bridges the **Yarra River** to South Melbourne, and carries trams #48, 75, 95, and 96. On the east end, Spring St. borders Parliament and both Treasury and Carlton Gardens. Directly in the middle, Elizabeth St. carries major northbound tram lines (#19, 50, 57, 59, and 68). One block to its east, Swanston Walk is a pedestrian walk but also carries important north-south tram routes. Trams connect St. Kilda and suburbs south of Melbourne with Melbourne University, Fitzroy, Carlton, and North Melbourne. Still confused? Plop down on the free burgundy-and-gold **City Circle Tram** and follow a 45-minute city center circuit.

Fitzroy & Carlton

These northern suburbs offer easy excursions from the city center. Tram #11 runs along **Brunswick St.,** Fitzroy's main artery, where kitsch meets urban bitch in an array of wicked (if slightly overpriced) cafe bistros, clothing shops, and houseware stores. Brunswick becomes sunnier, more retail-oriented, and more gourmet as one approaches the city center. Dominated by Italiana, Carlton begins at **Nicholson St.** and extends westward to Melbourne University. Sidewalk cafes and Italian restaurants all along **Lygon St.** provide cappuccino and *gelati* for neighboring uni students and the families and older folks who congregate here on the weekends.

North Melbourne

North Melbourne is a pleasant mix of bungalows, flats, refurbished residences, and neighborhood shops and eateries. Forming its eastern edge, **Elizabeth St.** heads north from the city center and passes the **Queen Victoria Market** with its abundant, inexpensive food stocks and wares. William St. heads north from the city center past Flagstaff Gardens and becomes **Peel St.** Peel and Elizabeth intersect near the University of Melbourne with Elizabeth continuing northwest as **Flemington Rd.** (along which tram #55 continues to run), ultimately leading to the extraordinary **Melbourne Zoo.** At this intersection Peel St. becomes **Royal Parade,** which borders **Melbourne University.**

South Melbourne

This cluster of suburbs between the city center and St. Kilda is primarily residential, but its local pubs can provide a relaxing retreat from the more touristy and fast-paced parts of the city. South Melbourne lies west of **St. Kilda Rd.** and stretches south from the **West Gate Freeway** to Albert Park. From this working-class neighborhood it is a quick strike to the park, the Royal Botanical Gardens, the city center, or the beach at Port Phillip Bay.

By Port Phillip Bay

South of South Melbourne and north of St. Kilda, the suburbs of Albert Park and Middle Park border Port Phillip Bay. **Bay St.** (known as City Rd. closer to the city center) marks the division from Port Melbourne, Albert Park's neighbor to the west. Beaconsfield Parade runs along the bay and connects the two suburbs. More urbane **Albert Park,** features some of Melbourne's finest Victorian architecture in the iron lattice work that adorns its stately, well-maintained, seaside bungalows. **St. Vincent's Gar-**

dens, just east of Ferrar's St. between Park and Bridgeport St., provides a pleasant green space for relaxation. The ferry to Tasmania departs from the station pier, tram #109's terminus. **Middle Park,** just south of Albert Park and Kerferd Rd., is the quietest residential neighborhood of all. Cafes and eateries dot the streets, and wide roads provide lovely paths to cycle or stroll along while viewing well-preserved Victorian and Art Deco cottages.

St. Kilda

Though it's a bit removed to the southeast of the city center (and officially in the city of Port Phillip), St. Kilda is a budget hot spot with excellent accommodations and trendy eateries. Trams #16 and 96 bring people to St. Kilda from the city center's Flinders St. and Spencer St. Stations, respectively. **St. Kilda Rd.** passes the Royal Botanic Gardens and Albert Park—Melbourne's two largest green spaces—en route to St. Kilda. At **St. Kilda Junction,** St. Kilda Rd. intersects **Fitzroy St.,** which runs toward the beach. There, Fitzroy curves left to follow the waterfront and becomes the **Esplanade.** From St. Kilda Junction, **Barkly St.** also runs south toward the beach, completing a triangle with Fitzroy St. and the Esplanade. A block toward the beach from St. Kilda Junction, **Grey St.** links Fitzroy and Barkly St., and is the focus of St. Kilda's budget accommodations.

PRACTICAL INFORMATION

Tourist and Travel Information

Tourist Office: Victoria Visitor Information Centre, Melbourne Town Hall, Swanston St., between Collins and Lt. Collins St. (tel. 9658 9036 or 9658 9524; fax 9654 1054; email greeter@melbourne.vic.gov.au). This interactive information resource with touch screens provides information in 6 languages. The **Melbourne Greeter Service** offers personalized 3-4hr. tours led by volunteer Melburnians. Arrange a free one-on-one tour by filling out a brief application 3 days in advance. Open Mon.-Fri. 9am-7pm, Sat.-Sun. 10am-5pm.

Travellers Aid, 169 Swanston St., 2nd fl. (tel. 9654 2600; fax 9654 1926), by the corner of Bourke St. This agency specializes in assisting disabled, elderly, and non-English speaking travelers. A cafe, lounge, lockers, showers, and disability access service at Flinders St. Station lend a helping hand. Open Mon.-Fri. 8am-5pm.

Outdoors Information Centre, 8 Nicholson St., East Melbourne (tel. 9412 4745), but moving. The authoritative resource for camping, fishing, hunting, bushwalking, and coastal exploration. Information on obtaining various licenses. Scores of maps available, many free. Open Mon.-Fri. 8:30am-5:30pm, Sat. 9am-noon.

Youth Hostels Association (YHA) Victoria, 205 King St. (tel. 9670 7991; fax 9670 9840; email yha@c031.aone.net.au; http://www.yha.orga.au; postal address: GPO Box 4793, Melbourne, 3001), on the corner of Little Bourke St. Provides a full listing of YHA hostels and a booking service ($5). Attached budget travel agency. Open Mon.-Fri. 9am-5:30pm, Sat. 9am-noon.

Consulates: Canada, Level 8/1 Southbank Blvd., South Melbourne (tel. 9894 8643). **Denmark,** 7 Acacia Ave., Blackburn (tel. 9894 8643). **France,** 492 St. Kilda Rd., Melbourne (tel. 9820 0921). **Germany,** 480 Punt Rd., South Yarra (tel. 9828 6888). Open Mon.-Fri. 9am-noon. **Great Britain,** Level 17/90 Collins St., Melbourne (tel. 9650 4155). Open Mon.-Fri. 9am-4:30pm. **Japan,** 360 Elizabeth St., Melbourne (tel. 9639 3244). Open Mon.-Fri. 9:30am-12:30pm and 2-4pm. **New Zealand,** 60 Albert Rd., South Melbourne (tel. 9696 0399). Open by appointment only. Visa applications available outside the door. **United States,** 553 St. Kilda Rd., Melbourne (tel. 9526 5900). Open Mon.-Fri. 9am-12:30pm and 1-3pm.

Financial Services

Currency Exchange: Thomas Cook Foreign Exchange, 330 Collins St. (tel. 9602 3811; fax 9606 0560), at the corner of Elizabeth St. No commission when exchanging Thomas Cook traveler's checks. Other checks and cash exchange face 1% commission ($4 min.). Open Mon.-Fri. 8:45am-5:15pm, Sat. 9am-5pm.

American Express Travel Office, 233 Collins St. (tel. 9633 6322), and inside the GPO at the corner of Elizabeth and Bourke St. (tel. 9203 3001). Buys all traveler's checks commission-free and provides free mail service to holders of AmEx cards or traveler's checks. Wire transfers are available from the office. Open Mon.-Fri. 8:15am-5:30pm, Sat. 10am-1pm.

ATMs: ANZ ATMs accept more international cards (V, MC, AmEx, Cirrus, and Plus) than most other ATMs. Main ANZ bank on Bourke St. by the corner of Elizabeth St.

Emergency, Social, and Postal Services

Library: State Library of Victoria, 382 Swanston St. (tel. 9669 9888), on the corner of LaTrobe St. Plenty of computers with free **World Wide Web access.** Open Mon. 1-9pm, Tue. and Thurs.-Sun. 10am-6pm, Wed. 10am-9pm.

Ticket Agency: Ticketek (tel. 13 28 49 or 1800 062 849, Mon.-Sat. 9am-9pm, Sun. 10am-7pm; fax 9639 3499) sells tickets for events. Discounts for students and seniors. $3 charge for booking by phone. **Halftix** is in Bourke St. Walk.

Weather: Dial 1196.

Hotlines: Centre Against Sexual Assault (tel. 9344 2210 or 1800 806 292). Translating and Interpreting Service (tel. 13 14 50; TTY 9657 8130).

Hospital: Royal Melbourne Hospital (tel. 9342 7000).

Emergency: Dial 000.

Police: 637 Flinders St. (tel. 9247 6666).

Post Office: General Post Office (GPO) (tel. 13 13 18 or 9203 3044), at the corner of Elizabeth and Bourke St. Inside are wire transfers, phone books, a stationery shop, and American Express office. *Poste Restante* is at counter 19. Open Mon.-Fri. 8:15am-5:30pm, Sat. 10am-1pm. **Postal code:** 3000.

Phone Code: 03.

ACCOMMODATIONS

Central Melbourne

The city center's budget accommodations are clustered around Elizabeth St., a couple blocks north of LaTrobe St. From either Spencer St. Station or Flinders St. Station, take the City Circle Tram to Elizabeth St. and walk uphill (north). A few pubs in Chinatown rent rooms. Other budget possibilities are clustered south of Spencer St.

Toad Hall, 441 Elizabeth St. (tel. 9600 9010; fax 9600 9013), between A'Beckett and Franklin St. The best value in the city center, Toad Hall's appealing Victorian structure combines the intimacy of a B&B with the conveniences and attentive staff of a large inn. Large, newly furnished dorm rooms, airy kitchen, patio, and basement den with TV, VCR, and stereo. Toad Hall's location and perks (including central heating and electric pots in every room) are well worth the cost. Reception open 7am-10pm. Dorms $16; singles $28; twins with bath $45; doubles with bath $50. VIP. 10% discounts for stays longer than a week. Linen $3, parking $5. Laundry $4. In summer, reservations recommended a week in advance. V, MC.

Hotel Y, 489 Elizabeth St. (tel. 9329 5188 or 1800 249 124; fax 9329 1469), between Therry and Franklin St., less than a block from the transit center. Awarded the 1996 Australian Tourism Award for best budget accommodation nationwide, the Y pampers guests with stellar rooms, a swimming pool, and a budget cafe. The bathroom tiles, designed by the creator of Melbourne's Ophelia statue, have even been photographed for architectural journals. Y would one want anything more? 24hr. reception. Dorms with bath $25; singles $65; doubles $75; triples $85; quads $100. 10% discount for all YMCA or YWCA members. Reservations at least 2 weeks ahead are strongly advised and require a credit card. V, MC, AmEx.

Downtown Backpackers, 167 Franklin St. (tel. 9329 7525; fax 9326 7667), between Elizabeth and Queen St. This cavernous 6-level facility boasts 600 beds and hopes to become the pulsing nerve center for Melbourne's backpackers once renovations are complete. Plans include a travel agency, employment service, medical clinic, laundrette, rooftop pool, basketball court, small movie theater, and a kitchenette on each floor by early 1998. No smoking. 10- to 16-bed barracks $14; smaller dorms $16; doubles $40; twins $44. VIP. $1-2 discount in winter. V, MC.

Fitzroy & Carlton

The Nunnery, 116 Nicholson St. (tel. 9419 8637), at stop 13 on tram #96. Two blocks west of Brunswick St. Playfully decorated with murals and "nun puns," this small hostel tenders standard amenities. Worn carpets show their turn-of-the-century age, but creative decorating and a lounge overlooking Carlton Gardens enliven this former boarding house run by the Daughters of Mercy. The staff coordinates tons of activities. Large dorms $17; small dorms $18; twins $52; doubles $54. Weekly: $102; $108; $350; $350. VIP. V, MC.

North Melbourne

The YHA presence dominates North Melbourne accommodations. Tram #57 services the area from Elizabeth St. in the city center. Neighborhood pubs also offer beds.

Queensbury Hill YHA, 76-86 Howard St. (tel. 9329 8599; fax 9326 8427). Take tram #55 from Williams St. in the city center to stop 11 on Queensbury St., turn left and go 2 blocks west to Howard St. This YHA grand dame overflows with amenities in a nearly new, highly functional facility. 314 bunks on 3 colorful floors. Glistening communal bathrooms and in-room locker space and desks. The rooftop patio offers a sweeping panorama of Melbourne and a barbecue. Perks include free parking, free use of mountain bikes, Skybus Airport Shuttle service ($9), in-house travel agency, designated quiet reading room, huge well-equipped kitchen, in-house bistro, weekly movies, pool tables, video games, internet access, currency exchange, photocopy and fax service, and YHA phone cards (with good rates on international calls and voice-mail). 2-week max. stay. Wheelchair-accessible rooms and bathrooms. Dorms $20, with YHA $17, ages 7-17 $13, under 7 free. Reservations suggested at least 1 week in advance during summer. V, MC.

Chapman Gardens YHA Hostel, 76 Chapman St. (tel. 9328 3595; fax. 9329 7863), near stop 18 on tram #57's route north along Elizabeth St. to Abbotsford St. The hostel is on the left side. With clean, quiet, softly lit rooms (mostly twins), Chapman's landscaped estate and pleasant gazebo are situated in a tree-lined residential neighborhood. Kitchen facilities, dining area, and heated rooms. Free bike use, parking, and Skybus pick-up. No smoking. Reception open 7:30am-noon and 3-10pm. Dorms $18, with YHA $15; twins $40, $34. Weekly: $106, $91; $252, $210. Linen $2. Key deposit $10. One-week advance reservations recommended, particularly in summer. V, MC.

Global Backpackers, 238 Victoria St. (tel. 9328 3728; fax 9329 8966), across from the Victoria Market, north on Elizabeth St. Seasoned wayfarers socialize at a neighboring pub all night, then come home to this 100-year-old building, where Henry—a friendly pit bull terrier—guards 65 beds. Dimly lit, ragged rooms are under renovation by new management. Dorms $11-14; singles $25; doubles $35. Key deposit $10. V, MC.

South Melbourne

Nomads Market Inn, 115 Cecil St. (tel. 9690 2220; fax 9690 2544; email nomads@dove.mtx.net.au), adjacent to the northeast corner of the South Melbourne Market, provides an excellent pub lodging. The burnt reds and oranges of its adobe-style lounge reflect Nomads inviting feel. Upstairs, beautiful wrought-iron beds stand out against white walls and trim of primary colors. Bathrooms are clean and the small kitchen doubles as a simple eatery selling breakfast and dinner. Hosts backpacker events each week. No smoking. A free beer or cappuccino will greet you when you enter. Pick-up from the bus stations is but a phone call away. Dorms $12-15; doubles and twins $72. Weekly: $75-90; $210. V, MC, AmEx.

By Port Phillip Bay

Middle Park Hotel, 102 Canterbury Rd. (tel. 9690 1958; fax 9645 8928), directly across from the Middle Park stop on trams #95 and 96, maintains a stately pub with accommodation. 12 ft. ceilings and wide hallways lead to discrete, pleasant rooms and large terrazzo bathrooms. This 1890s building is well-preserved, and its rooms offer flexibility to families and groups. No smoking. Three public spaces downstairs: a formal restaurant, a cool bistro with billiards, and a casual neighborhood pub. Dorms $15; doubles and twins $40. V, MC.

St. Kilda

St. Kilda offers some of the best budget accommodations and supports a large backpacker community. Though removed from the city center, these listings lie no more than 10 minutes from the beach. **Fitzroy St.,** the main drag, is accessible by tram.

Olembia, 96 Barkly St. (tel. 9537 1412; fax 9537 1600). Tucked behind a small canopy just off the intersection of Barkly and Grey St., Olembia embraces budget travelers of all persuasions. Its small size (40 beds) and family atmosphere encourage guests to share meals or gather to watch films on the VCR. Extremely helpful owner and staff. The fireplace crackles through the winter and inhales cool breezes in summer. The dining lounge and kitchen are compact but equipped with modern amenities. Ornate, high-ceilinged rooms show a refined attention to detail that puts Olembia above the helter-skelter hostel milieu. 24hr. reception. No smoking. Convenient free parking. Dorms $16-17; singles $35; doubles and twins $50. Reserve a week or two in advance in the summer. V, MC, AmEx.

Enfield House Backpackers, 2 Enfield St. (tel. 9534 8159; fax 9534 5579). Take tram #16 or 96 to stop 30 by Fitzroy and Grey St. Walk half a block down Grey or Fitzroy to Jackson St., which intersects Enfield St. A sign at the end of Enfield St. beckons. The original backpackers' haunt in Melbourne, Enfield House offers a wealth of information about transportation, entertainment, and employment opportunities. Organized events include weekly pub crawls and occasional extravagant parties. The rooms have seen better days but remain elegant, clean, and on par with other hostels' facilities. Courtesy bus, train, and airport pick-up. No smoking. Dorms $16; twins $38. Weekly: $94; $188. VIP. Breakfast included. V, MC.

The Ritz for Backpackers, 169 Fitzroy St. (tel. 9525 5745; fax 9525 3863). Tram #16 stops at the front door (stop 132). The name may contrast with the minimalist aesthetic, but the Ritz's sleek, super-cool atmosphere fronts a full range of amenities. TV lounges, plush couches, and a spacious, well-supplied kitchen. Complimentary ear plugs thoughtfully provided, since the central location comes with traffic noise at night and the nightclub downstairs rattles the Ritz silly on weekends. Smoking restricted to central lounge. Reception 7am-10pm. Dorms $10-14; doubles and twins $34. Weekly: $85; $200. VIP. Doona/comforter ($2) and space heaters warm guests in winter. Reservations required in early March during the Grand Prix. V, MC, AmEx.

Coffee Palace Backpackers Hotel, 24 Grey St. (tel. 9534 5283; fax 9593 9166), a block off Fitzroy St., on tram routes #16 and 96. The Coffee Palace gang downs java by day, VB beer by night, and then sleeps it all off in decent, if eclectic, digs. The dorms are basic but sufficiently maintained. Top floor deluxe rooms recently renovated. Nightly events (70s dance, wine and cheese night, billiards tourney), ensure that the hip, young backpacker crowd has a good time. No-smoking policy loosely enforced. 24hr. reception. Dorms $13-14, deluxe dorms $16; unrenovated doubles and twins $32-36, deluxe doubles and twins $45. VIP Linen included.

FOOD

City Center

Many fine restaurants for the budget traveler are situated in the heart of Melbourne. For light snacks, cafes typically charge $2.50 for cappuccino or $5 for focaccia. They often have lunchtime menus and off-peak specials. The best in this class is the **Cafe Y**—a winner of Melbourne's prestigious Gold Medallion Award. This sleek postmodern bistro is located on Elizabeth St. between Therry and Franklin St., adjoining the Hotel Y. Delicious breakfast and lunch offerings are served daily, along with a constantly shifting menu of hot entrees. No single item exceeds $6.

Chinatown, centered around Little Bourke St. between Swanston Walk and Exhibition St. offers a wide array of Asian cuisine. For Japanese, try **Yuriya**, another Gold Medallion winner located between Swanston and Russell on Little Bourke St. The modern wood-paneled dining room features authentic architecture and costumes. Sunday lunches, served until 5pm, include a full meal of vegetables, rice, sushi, entree, and dessert served in a beautiful wooden case ($10.50-15; accepts V, MC, AmEx, Discover). A smattering of restaurants in the **Greek precinct,** centered on Lonsdale St. between Swanston and Russell St., offer Mediterranean cuisine. The baklava is to die for.

Fitzroy & Carlton

In Fitzroy, the ethnic grub available includes Thai, Turkish, Greek, Indian, and Japanese food scattered all along Brunswick St. Carlton's main drag, **Lygon St.,** specializes in Italian food served in shopping plaza-style, commercial cafes for the carbo-starved traveler. An older crowd ambles along Lygon's sidewalks taking in the more upscale atmosphere.

North Melbourne

The **Queen Victoria Market** should be the culinary focus for all visitors in North Melbourne. Terrific values on a huge array of produce, meats, and breads become shocking steals after noon, as hawkers hurry to unload their stock. The delis, bakeries, and vegetarian stalls in the eastern wing of the Queen Vic offer good ready-made meals. Saturday is the biggest day for the food market. Meat and fish are found in the northeast corner along with deli and dairy goods. See **Melbourne Shopping,** p. 465, for hours and more details on the market. If hungering for restaurant service in North Melbourne, check out the eateries which extend west along **Victoria St.**

St. Kilda

Saints alive! Restaurants saturate St. Kilda's prominent avenues, and choosing among them can be a confusing and tiring affair. Fitzroy St. cafes and bistros generally offer Mediterranean fare with a sprinkling of Asian menus. **Chichio's,** near the corner of Grey St., is a quality budget choice with a savory selection of 27 kinds of pizza and other Italian options. Not as flashy as its Fitzroy St. neighbors, the tantalizing smells from the open-air kitchen waft across the area. A special backpackers' menu offers a big pizza or pasta, salad, and wine for two, for only $14 (V, MC).

West toward the beach along Fitzroy St. lies vegetarian bliss. **Veg Out Time,** 63 Fitzroy St. (tel. 9534 0077), offers a large, inexpensive menu with vegan, ovo, and lacto selections. Asian noodles, curries, and stirfry dishes (all $6-7) go well with lush salads ($5) or fruit lassis ($2.50). **Acland St.** offers reasonable ethnic food at bistros, but its cake shops are the highlight. Sate chocoholism with these rich creations, or at the very least stroll by and drool.

SIGHTS AND MUSEUMS

Melbourne's most popular attractions—the art museums, concert halls, historical sights, and Botanical Gardens—are largely clustered south of the Yarra River. In the city center, one will find heritage and government buildings, the smaller but more accessible Fitzroy Gardens, and the city's sport complexes. The precincts north of the city center are primarily residential and social centers, but are home to lovely gardens, the infamous Queen Vic Market, and the renowned Melbourne Zoo.

The City Center and Surrounds

The **Rialto Towers** looms over the city center on Collins St. between King and William St. The Rialto is Melbourne's tallest building, and the observation deck affords spectacular views of greater Melbourne. The Rialtovision Theatre plays a 20-minute film highlighting Victoria's tourist spots every half hour (open daily 10am-late).

Four blocks east, **St. Paul's Cathedral** occupies the corner of Flinders St. and Swanston Walk. This Anglican church is a beautiful cathedral on a comfortable scale. The floor tiling is especially interesting—both the simpler patterns throughout the main space and the more intricate mosaics by the altar. The unique **Anzac Christmas** painting depicts soldiers as shepherds at the Adoration of Christ. The small HIV/AIDS prayer focus and the beautifully stenciled pipe organ are also worth a closer look. (Open daily 7am-6pm. Services posted. Enter on the Swanston Walk side.)

Heading north on Swanston Walk, one can drop into the **Melbourne Central** mega-mall and **Coop's Shot Tower,** in the mall's center. The 50m-tall shot tower was built in 1889-90 and was Melbourne's tallest structure at the time of its completion. Today it houses the Australian Geographic Shop and is amazingly enclosed by a 20-story, 490-ton glass cone—the largest glass structure of its type in the world. A huge fob watch dangles in the atrium in front of the Shot Tower and has an automated Waltzing Matilda display that drops down on the hour. A bizarre but delightful spectacle, the whole complex makes a great refuge on a rainy day.

At the intersection of Collins and Exhibition St., the Hotel Sofitel offers a fine (albeit unofficial) Melbourne sight. Ascend to the 35th floor for a free **panoramic view of Melbourne.** The bar and restaurants on this level are ringed by a walk where you can view the art exhibit that lines the wall and gaze out onto Melbourne. Step into the restrooms (to the left as you exit) for the best views.

The **Parliament of Victoria,** at the intersection of Spring St. and Bourke St., is a regal 19th-century structure that functions as Melbourne's state assembly. When Parliament is not in session, free tours leave from the vestibule every hour from 10am to 3pm and at 3:45pm. For information call 9651 8568. East of the city center, just behind Parliament, **St. Patrick's Cathedral** is a beautiful product of Gothic revival. At night, its spires are floodlit, making it an attractive landmark.

Two and a half blocks south on Spring St. is the **Old Treasury Building,** with a collection of exhibits chronicling Melbourne's settlement and development. The displays are extremely informative and beautifully arranged. (Open Mon.-Fri. 9am-5pm, Sat.-Sun. 10am-4pm. Tours of the gold vaults daily 1pm and 3pm; $5, concessions $3, young children free.) Walk through the Treasury Gardens across the street to reach the **Fitzroy Gardens.** The gardens were originally laid out in the shape of the Union Jack and provide lovely shaded canopies and spacious lawns for strolling. On the south end is **Cook's Cottage.** This small stone home was constructed by Captain James Cook's family in 1755 and was rebuilt in Fitzroy Gardens in 1934 to celebrate Melbourne's centennial. Cook never actually reached the site and may not have spent time in this house, but the cottage is a good example of a period piece (admission $3, concessions $2, ages 5-15 $1.50; open daily 9am-5pm). The **Conservatory** is on the garden's southwest side. This refreshing, colorfully stocked greenhouse displays seasonal assortments of plants and flowers, and is a wedding photo favorite (free; open daily 9am-5pm).

Southeast of the Fitzroy Gardens, across Wellington Pde., sits Yarra Park and the **Melbourne Cricket Ground (MCG).** The primary stadium for the 1956 Summer Olympics, the arena still packs in up to 90,000 people for rock concerts, Australian Rules football (footy) and, obviously, cricket. On-site, one can visit the **Australian Gallery of Sport and Olympic Museum.** Home of the Australian Cricket Hall of Fame, the museum is open daily from 10am to 4pm. MCG tours depart every hour from 10am to 3pm (admission $8, concessions $5). The MCG is accessible by trams #48 and 75 which depart from Flinders Station. Across the railroad tracks to the west sits the ultramodern **National Tennis Centre.** The stadium's retractable, domed roof, shelters tennis' Australian Open grand slam event every January. Inside the grey building, former champions' photos line the walls, and one can play on courts for a charge.

North of the City Center

Heading north on Spring St. one will intersect **Carlton Gardens** at the corner of the city center. A simple tree-lined park, the gardens frame the Exhibition Hall. The Hall may seem rundown because it is being prepared to hold the Museum of Victoria. Expected to open in a couple years, the museum—formerly situated in the state library—will hold Victoria's natural history wonders.

The Old Melbourne Gaol (Jail) (tel. 9663 7228), two blocks west on LaTrobe St. and slightly north on Russell St., is a necessary stop. This imposing prison was constructed in 1845 and housed a total of 50,000 prisoners in its 84 years. Upon entering the main structure, you'll see three levels of cells tightly packed together and linked by iron catwalks. The tiny cells each house small informative displays about everything from the history and specifications of the Gaol to fascinating stories about Ned Kelly's gang. Kelly was Australia's infamous bushranger who wore a suit of armor in a shoot-out with police. He was hanged in the gaol, and the trap door and scaffold still exist. Take a spooky evening tour of the gaol and get a sense of how horrible it must have been. Or sate your thirst with a Ned Kelly soda in the gift shop on your way out and be thankful you've escaped—no criminal ever did. (Admission $7, concessions $5, children $4, families up to 4 children $21. Open daily 9:30am-4:30pm. Night tours on Wed. and Sun. evenings. The Gaol takes 1hr. to view.)

To taste a slice of local life, don't miss the **Queen Victoria Market,** facing Victoria St. between Queen and Peel St. Reportedly the Southern Hemisphere's largest covered outdoor market, the long arcades offer a tremendous variety of fruits, vegetables, meats, and dairy goods. A collection of food stalls adjoins a flea market section where vendors hawk sheepskin wear, plastic knick-knackery, and clothes ranging from bikinis to leather jackets. Try bargaining with vendors—particularly on Sundays when the flea market section swells to its greatest size. Parking along the south margin is free for the first hour on market days (Tues. and Thurs. 6am-2pm, Fri. 6am-6pm, Sat. 6am-3pm, Sun. 9am-4pm), and costs $4 per day on non-market days.

North of the University of Melbourne, **The Melbourne Zoo,** with its winding trails and natural animal habitats, is popular with residents and tourists alike. Watch Australian natives like the little penguin or the platypus, or view exotic guests like the red panda and bison. A large aviary teems with winged life, while a Japanese garden provides a meditative space. Tours are free and can be set up for anyone at any time, but call ahead. Wheelchair accessible. Strollers/prams and wheelchairs available for hire. Take tram #55 to the zoo stop. (Open daily 9am-5pm. Admission $12.60, ages 4-15 $6.30, concessions $9.50 with I.D., families up to 4 children $34.50. V, MC, AmEx.)

South Bank of the Yarra River

Just across the river on the right side of St. Kilda Rd., the gold sombrero-shaped spire of the **Melbourne Concert Hall** (box office tel. 9645 7970) tops a red velour interior and the box office and administrative offices for the Victoria Arts Centre (for ticket info contact the box office Mon.-Fri. 9am-5pm; theater box office, located in the Smorgan Family Plaza, open Mon.-Sat. 9am-9pm). The building also houses the **Performing Arts Museum** (tel. 9281 8569). Three exhibits annually display some aspect of Australia's performing arts. Only one exhibit runs at a time. (Admission $5, students and seniors $4, children $3.50, family $15; open daily 11am-5pm. V, MC, AmEx, Discover.)

On the next block south, the **Victorian Arts Centre** houses Victoria's three primary cultural facilities. The **National Gallery of Victoria** is the slate rectangular building ringed with pools and fountains. Constructed in 1968, the National Gallery houses what is generally regarded as the finest art collection in the southern hemisphere. A mesmerizing waterfall concealing a glass wall marks the entrance, and the gallery encircles an open-air sculpture garden. The ground floor houses a large collection of Australian paintings. Complementing these works, a second floor gallery displays changing exhibitions of traditional and contemporary Aboriginal art. Other highlights include the silver and china of the 17th and 18th century decorative arts room. Don't miss the huge, ornate gold candelabra dubbed "The Centerpiece of Melbourne." European paintings span from the Renaissance to modern masters. Notable selections include an intricate 16th-century Flemish carved retable of the Passion of Christ and a few of Picasso's cubist works. An Asian gallery features a sweeping, 16th-century, six-paneled Japanese screen. Temporary exhibitions are excellent, often highlighting Australia's cutting edge contemporary artists (open 10am-5pm). Admission to the gallery is free, though temporary exhibitions may charge fees. At the end of 1998 the National Gallery will undergo a significant renovation to greatly enhance its gallery size.

Continuing south, the **Royal Botanical Gardens** (tel. 9252 2300), stretch along St. Kilda Rd. east to the Yarra and south to Domain Rd. Over 49,000 plants fill the 36 acres that make up Melbourne's finest attraction. The gardens reflect the two forces that have most strongly shaped Melbourne's identity: Victorian organization and the fortuitous hand of nature. Here, kids play footy, lovers wander aimlessly, and joggers burn calories in a verdant, peaceful atmosphere. The gardens first opened in 1845, and the extensive array of mature species reflects 150 years of care and development. Stately palms not found elsewhere in Victoria share the soil with twisting oaks, exotic rainforest natives, and even a pavilion of roses. Possums and wallabies are among the many animals that call the gardens home, so keep an eye out for fauna amidst the flora. You can step into a steamy rainforest glasshouse (open 10am-4:30 pm), feed ducks and geese, or have tea by the ornamental lake. The National Herbarium and the Garden Shop (open 10am-5pm) are located at Gate F in the southeast corner and sell souvenirs and botanical information sheets. Free guided walks depart here Tuesday through Friday at 11am and 2pm and Sunday at 11am, and the Gardens host special events, such as outdoor film screenings, on summer evenings. The gardens are fully wheelchair accessible and open daily (free admission; open Nov.-March 7:30am-8:30pm; April, Sept., and Oct. 7:30am-6pm; May-Aug. 7:30am-5pm). The small cottage by Gate F is the **LaTrobe Cottage,** Melbourne's first government building. This simple home was erected for Melbourne's first governor, Charles Joseph LaTrobe, who occupied it from 1839 to 1854 (admission $2; open Mon., Wed., Sat., and Sun. 11am-4pm).

Occupying an adjacent hill is Melbourne's **Shrine of Remembrance,** an imposing columned temple with a ziggurat roof. Initially designed as a memorial to WWI veterans, the main structure commemorates fallen soldiers from both WWI and WWII, with later veterans honored by an adjacent monument. From the entrance of the monument, one can gaze down St. Kilda Rd. to the city center. From here the eternal flame—lit by Queen Elizabeth II in 1954—and Australia's national flag are visible. The flag is lowered each evening at precisely 5pm to the sounds of a bugle call. Inside the shrine, the central space is crowned by a stepped skylight which on November 11th at 11am (the time of the WWI armistice) casts a beam of light onto the word "love" in the central inscription, "Greater Love Hath No Man." Don't worry about missing this: the effect is simulated every half hour. At the back, you can read about Anzac Day—April 25th—which commemorates the bloody battle of Gallipoli in which Australian and New Zealand troops fought, and lost, during WWI. Venture down into the crypt and view the colorful division flags and memorial statue (free; open 10am-5pm).

North of the shrine, in the Kings Domain garden, picnickers lounge on blankets at the **Sidney Myer Music Bowl** (tel. 9281 8360). This open-air concert bowl features concerts in the summer months and a small ice-skating rink during the winter. (Admission to skate $8, under 15 $7, families of four $25; prices include skate hire. Rink open April 5-Oct. 5 Mon.-Tues. 10am-4:30pm, Wed.-Sat. 10am-4:30pm and 6-10pm, Sun. 10am-6pm. Enter at the rear of the stage.)

By the Royal Botanic Gardens on Dallas Brooks Dr. the **Australian Centre for Contemporary Art** shows avant-garde, multimedia work (free admission; open Tues.-Fri. 11am-5pm, Sat.-Sun. 2-5pm). Continuing south along St. Kilda Rd., you can view a spectacular sunset over the sea, at **St. Kilda's Pier,** accessible from the city on trams #16 and 96. There is a penguin habitat at the jetty's end.

Two other sights lie along the Yarra either side of St. Kilda Rd. To the east past the Botanic Gardens you'll reach the **Como House** (tel. 9827 2500), an elegant Victorian mansion originally built in an Italian villa style. The house's five acres are open daily from 10am to 5pm. Tram #8 from Swanston St. provides access at stop 33 on Toorak Rd. To the west just past the city center lies the **Polly Woodside Maritime Museum** (tel. 9699 9760), housed aboard a re-rigged sailing ship lying in the south side of the Yarra, just west of Spencer St. A recipient of the International Heritage Medal, Polly Woodside also has an adjacent museum (open daily 10am-4pm; admission $7, concessions and children $4, families $15).

ENTERTAINMENT

Glitz, glamor, and gambling reign supreme at **The Crown Casino** (tel. 9292 8888), just west of Southgate and Clarendon St. on the south side of the river. The Crown's enormous facility, Melbourne's newest and biggest spectacle, offers hypnotizing neon and stage show extravaganzas 24 hours per day. With five-star accommodations, luxury shopping, "Red Hot Rhonda" lounge acts, and fog-filled, laser-lit jumping fountains, the Crown caters to every sense or lack thereof. To provide patrons with a maximum of opportunities to lose money, the Crown has installed more gaming tables than any casino in the world. Novices should begin at the "Learn to Play Centres," where limits are lower.

Movie Houses

Up-and-coming Aussie directors stage debuts in the independent movie houses that are Melbourne's cinematic trademark.

Carlton Movie House, 235 Faraday St., Carlton (tel. 9347 8909). Smallish screen and ancient decor make for a unique experience in this converted vaudeville house. During the day, it doubles as venue for Melbourne Uni film class screenings. Notoriously bad prints of old, well-loved cult films and newer alternative releases. Tickets $11, concessions $8, seniors and under 15 $6. Showings daily noon-9pm, special screenings of Kubrick's *Clockwork Orange* Fri.-Sat. midnight.

The Nova, 380 Lygon St. (tel. 9347 5331), in Lygon Court, Carlton. 5 well-appointed theaters showing independent and foreign language film. Tickets $11, concessions $7, under 15 $6. Privilege cards ($10) entitle bearers to $7 admission. Screenings Sun.-Thurs. 11am-9:30pm, late shows Fri.-Sat. 11:30pm.

The Kino, 45 Collins St., City (tel. 9650 2100). Quality independent and foreign language films cover 3 modern screens. Conveniently situated downstairs in the Collins Place complex, next to **Klicks Bar** ($1 beer happy hour daily 5-6pm). Tickets $11, concession $8.50, pensioners and under 16 $6.50. Yearly Kino Cinecard ($10) entitles bearer to $7 admission. Screenings daily mid-day to 9pm, late shows vary.

Performing Arts

Theater in Melbourne comes in the Broadway show-stopping and artsy, alternative varieties. For the former, try the spectacular **Regent Theatre** on Little Collins St. between Swanston and Russell St. The dazzlingly ornate facility hopes to snag **Showboat** for the 1998 season. **The Forum,** on the corner of Russell and Flinders St., looks like an Arabian palace and Florentine villa combined, and its wonderfully preserved atrium and auditorium space host big budget dance and theater shows. For information about either call 9820 0239 or book through Ticketek (tel. 9299 9030). The **Victorian Arts Centre** is another excellent place to check out large scale dance, music, and theatrical performances. For more serious fare, try the **National Theatre** (tel. 9534 0221), on the corner of Barkly and Carlisle St. in St. Kilda. For more off-beat, bohemian performances, check the Fitzroy cafes and bistros.

NIGHTLIFE

Since *Let's Go* is hopelessly cutting edge, the establishments listed below may have peaked before you arrive. For more suggestions, consult the omnipresent backpacker monthly, *TNT, The Age*'s Thursday arts section, or even the tourist office, which tries to keep an updated list of clubs, bars, theaters, and attractions for a diverse audience. *Beat* magazine and *In Press* keep the public current on Melbourne's music scene, particularly concerning venues in which to catch live performances. Both are free and available at most pubs and cafes.

The Lounge, 243 Swanston St., 1st Fl. (tel. 9663 2916). Alternative cafe by day, hip young venue by night. Balcony overlooking Swanston and pool table are put to good use around the clock. If the funky interior weren't so dark, local celebrity-spotting would be a great deal easier. DJ from 10pm every night, ranging from techno on Wed. to soul, funk, hip hop, and jungle on weekends. Gay-oriented house night Thurs.; live bands on occasion. VB stubbies and house spirits $3.50. Tucker ranges from pizza slices ($3.50) to steaks ($11), served noon-10:30pm. Cover $5-6 after 10pm. Open Sun.-Tues. 11am-midnight, Wed.-Sat. 11am-6am.

Ruby Red, 9 Drewery Ln., City (tel. 9662 1544). This upscale restaurant and bar features live bands nightly. Music varies from jazz to blues to Latin. Main courses a bit pricey at around $15, but full bar caters to non-dining clientele with $2 pots. Authentically shady-looking pool room downstairs. No cover. Open Tues.-Wed. 4pm-late, Thurs.-Fri. noon-late, Sat. 6pm-late.

Up Top Cocktail Bar, 163 Russell St., 1st Fl., City (tel. 9663 8990), has an entrance down the alleyway off Russell St. Smallish but very hip, the cocktail bar and lounge sport decor featuring a most imaginative use of lamps. Established in 1997, but already gathering a name as a top local music scene hangout, the Up Top plays live jazz daily and jungle and acid into the small hours. Mixed drinks from $4, beer from $3.50, snacks from $2. No cover. Open nightly 4pm-4am.

The city center caters to multiple audiences with more established joints concentrated along **King St.,** ethnic clubs in Chinatown, and a big club scene along Bourke St. The gigantic **Metro,** 20 Bourke St., is the **southern hemisphere's largest club** and blares everything from techno to big booty bass. Metro also occasionally hosts touring acts. Fitzroy's numerous options include a diverse array of pubs and gay clubs, particularly along Brunswick St. East on Fitzroy St. at the corner of Lakeside Dr., **Club Ritz** booms and shakes to a disco/techno groove from 10:30pm to 3am each night (cover $10). Farther up Swanston St. in Carlton, the **Clyde** and three other drinking holes catch students every night. Meet the uni crowd here over a VB or a latte. The **Dan O'Connell** is a similar establishment, on Cemetery Rd. just northeast of the Uni. The members of its "Hundred Pint Club" swill Guinness and frequently listen to a live Irish band. Also up Brunswick St. is the **Evelyn,** a happening night spot that attracts new bands (cover around $2).

St. Kilda's pubs cluster along Fitzroy and Acland St., but the daddy of them all is the **Esplanade Hotel**—on the Esplanade's edge. Here live bands of all shapes and sounds play every night. A chic, older set sips fine wines and chatters away at **Dog's Bar,** just off Acland St. behind McDonalds. Fitzroy St. boasts a wider selection, including the **Prince of Wales Hotel,** which doubles as a bar and club in a slightly rundown Deco building. Weekly bands and billiards keep the mixed crowd happy. For more upscale enjoyment on funky Fitzroy St. try the **George Hotel** on the corner of Grey St. A low-key set sits in the corner wine room while a fashionable 20-something crowd enlivens the subterranean **Public Bar & Bottle Shop.** The true backpackers' club is **77 Sunset Strip** on Grey St., one block south of Fitzroy St. Here packers party in the pub and club, surrounded by live bands spiced up by theme nights.

RECREATION

Melbourne is often best enjoyed in its open spaces and fresh air. Runners will delight in the many (and scenic) well-arranged circuits. The best is the newly refurbished, crushed gravel **tan track** which circles the Royal Botanic Gardens. Other great routes include the pedestrian paths along the Yarra, the Port Phillip/St. Kilda shore, and the Albert Park Lake. Cyclers will also delight in Melbourne's numerous well-marked bike paths—particularly in southern Melbourne. An extensive bike trail travels along the Yarra, and other paths loop through residential Albert Park and Middle Park, along the Port Phillip beaches, and around North Melbourne's gardens. **Bicycle Victoria,** 19 O'Connell St. (tel. 9328 3000; fax 9328 2288), across from the Victoria Market, just off Victoria St., is the optimal resource for cyclists. Members can procure recreation maps, theft insurance, and national park info. Cycling adventurers can join groups organized here (open Mon.-Fri. 9am-5pm). Another resource for outdoor recreation is the **Victoria Visitors Information Centre** (tel. 9658 9968).

Indoor exercisers will enjoy the **Melbourne City Baths** (tel. 9663 5888), on the corner of Franklin and Swanston St. in the city center. A restored, neo-classical, brick

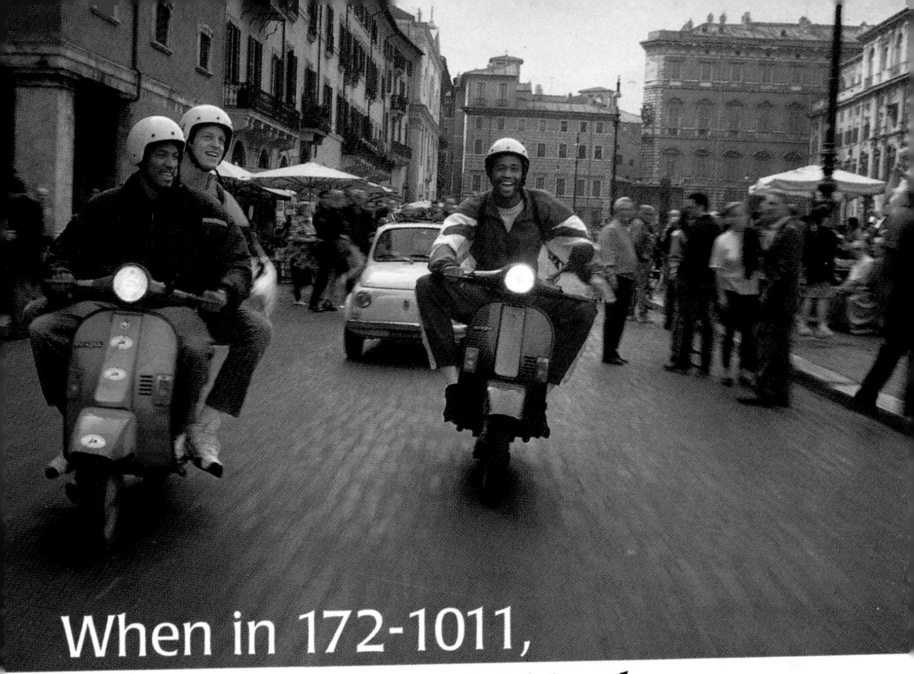

When in 172-1011, do as the 172-1011's do.

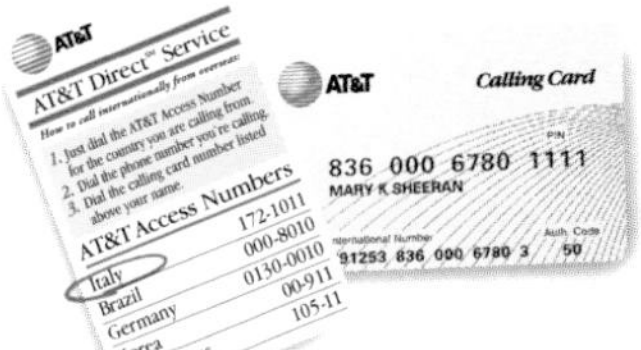

All you need for the clearest connections home.

Every country has its own AT&T Access Number which makes calling from overseas really easy. Just dial the AT&T Access Number for the country you're calling from and we'll take it from there. And be sure to charge your calls on your AT&T Calling Card. It'll help you avoid outrageous phone charges on your hotel bill and save you up to 60%.* For a free wallet card listing AT&T Access Numbers, call 1 800 446-8399.

It's all within your reach. AT&T

http://www.att.com/traveler

Clearest connections from countries with voice prompts, compared to major U.S. carriers on calls to the U.S. Clearest based on customer preference testing. *Compared to certain hotel telephone charges based on calls to the U.S. in November 1996. Actual savings may be higher or lower depending upon your billing method, time of day, length of call, fees charged by hotel and the country from which you are calling. ©1997 AT&T

Photo: R. Olken

Greetings from Let's Go Publications

The book in your hand is the work of hundreds of student researcher-writers, editors, cartographers, and designers. Each summer we brave monsoons, revolutions, and marriage proposals to bring you a fully updated, completely revised travel guide series, as we've done every year for the past 38 years.

This is a collection of our best finds, our cheapest deals, our most evocative description, and, as always, our wit, humor, and irreverence. Let's Go is filled with all the information on anything you could possibly need to know to have a successful trip, and we try to make it as much a companion as a guide.

We believe that budget travel is not the last recourse of the destitute, but rather the only way to travel; living simply and cheaply brings you closer to the people and places you've been saving up to visit. We also believe that the best adventures and discoveries are the ones you find yourself. So put us down every once in while and head out on your own. And when you find something to share, drop us a line. We're **Let's Go Publications,** 67 Mount Auburn St., Cambridge, MA 02138, USA (email: fanmail@letsgo.com; http://www.letsgo.com). And let us know if you want a free subscription to ***The Yellowjacket,*** the new Let's Go Newsletter.

structure, the colorful building has excellent pool, sauna, spa, and squash facilities. Swim for $2.80 or indulge in the sauna and spa for $6.50 (open Mon.-Fri. 6am-10pm, Sat.-Sun. 8am-6pm).

SHOPPING

Queen Victoria Market offers a wide variety of apparel, souvenirs, and more at super cheap prices. Pick up a boomerang for the old man or hunt for a bargain on sheepskins. **South Melbourne Market,** at the intersection of York and Cecil St. is a local fresh food market great for self-catering travelers (open Wed. 8am-2pm, Fri. 8am-6pm, Sat.-Sun. 8am-4pm). At **St. Kilda's Sunday Esplanade Market,** arts and crafts are on display all day long, and you can pick up anything from crystals to driftwood furniture. It's good, plain fun for a Sunday afternoon stroll. **Southgate,** across the Yarra River from Flinders St. Station on St. Kilda Rd., is a three-level shopping plaza and food court with impressive views of the city's skyline.

■ Around Melbourne

Werribee About 30 minutes west of Melbourne, the mansion at **Werribee Park** (tel. 9741 2444) presents a little piece of Australian history. The extravagant home was built between 1874 and 1877 by a Scottish immigrant who made his fortune in sheep. Determined to move beyond his working class heritage, he created an arristocratic life for himself, and the house at Werribee, with its European lawn, sculptured gardens, imposing billiard room, and expansive nursery wing, was its crowning glory. The house fell into disrepair after the death of its original owner and was taken over by a monastery. Since purchased by the Victorian government, the house and the nearby open range zoo have become attractive tourist destinations (mansion open Mon.-Fri. 10am-4pm, Sat.-Sun. 10am-5pm; admission $8; tours available). Somewhat more at home in Victoria's flat grasslands than the Werribee mansion, **Victoria's Open Range Zoo at Werribee** (tel. 9731 1311) invites you to go on safari and check out animals from the grasslands of Australia, Africa, and Asia. (Zoo open daily 9am-5pm. Mon-Fri 1st safari 10:30am, then every 30-60min. Sat-Sun 1st safari 10:00am, then every 20-30min. Last safari leaves at 3:40pm daily. 1hr. Admission $14, ages 3-14 $7, families $38.) To explore on your own, take the 30-minute walking trails; a tour of the park takes about three hours.

Healesville Sanctuary In the Yarra Valley, within the scope of the Met's Greater Melbourne service, Healesville Sanctuary offers an extraordinary, natural, and and interactive setting to view many of Australia's native animals. Set up like a minimum-security zoo, the sanctuary keeps koalas, kangaroos, dingoes, and wombats steps from visitors. The sanctuary's aviaries allow visitors to walk among kookaburra and cockatiels, while the recently constructed platypus habitat provides a walk-through enclosure to watch these peculiar monotremes swimming about and playing in waterfalls. The zookeepers oversee "close-up" encounters with the animals between 11am and 3:30pm; check signs for display times. The sanctuary also has a bistro, a snack bar, and a gift shop, with all profits supporting the sanctuary. From Melbourne, take the Met's light rail to Lilydale, then take bus #685 to Healesville Sanctuary. (Open daily 9am-5pm. Admission $12.60, students $9.50, children $6.30, families $34.50. V, MC, AmEx.)

Organ Pipes National Park The unique geological formation of the Organ Pipes lies just off the Calder Hwy. (Hwy. 79), 20km northwest of Melbourne. Although the 20-foot metamorphic landmarks look more like french fries than organ pipes, they make a great daytrip from the city or an excellent stop en route to the central Goldfields. To reach the pipes, walk 15 minutes down the gulch. In addition to the organ pipes, look for the Rosette Rock, which resembles a flowing stone frozen in time (located 10min. down the path). The park is also a laboratory for aggressive environmental restoration and has been largely repopulated with native plants and trees since the early 1970s, when weeds concealed the amazing organ pipes. The park has picnic and BBQ facilities, is wheelchair accessible, and charges no entrance fee.

Hanging Rock National Park Yes, it's more than just a movie. The unique rock formations featured in the well-known Australian film *Picnic at Hanging Rock* are nearly as curious as the protagonists' fate. Entering from Calder Hwy., follow the signs and go into the park at the south gate, on South Rock Rd. In addition to the fascinating formation, tennis, BBQ facilities, and fishing await. (Open daily dawn-dusk. Admission $2.50, $5 per car, $2 per motorcycle.)

Marysville

A precocious small town only an hour and a half from Melbourne, Marysville is best known as the closest town (20km) to cross-country ski mecca **Lake Mountain.** The resort has 31km of regularly groomed trails (entry fee $17, trail fee $5). Back in Marysville, **Lake Mountain Ski Hire** (tel. 5963 3444; open Mon.-Fri. 8am-6pm, Sat.-Sun. 7am-6:30pm; V, MC) rents skis ($16), skates ($25), and toboggans ($5). Other ski hires in town offer identical rates.

Also near Marysville, the **Stevenson Falls** are 4km down Falls Rd. These soaring, splashing cataracts are illuminated at night, which is an excellent time to visit and take a starlit stroll past huge ferns, eucalypts, and stringy-bark trees. The lush, hilly environment lends itself to bushwalking. In the town itself, stop by **Bruno's Art & Sculpture Garden,** 51 Falls Rd. (tel. 5963 3513). This extensive collection of paintings, collages, and sculptures is both whimsical and powerfully expressive. With an emphasis on portraiture in multiple moods, settings, and media, Bruno's beautiful gallery and gardens are more stimulating than the average small town museums and shops (open Fri.-Sun. and holidays 10am-5pm; admission $3).

Marysville's **Visitor Information Centre,** downtown on Murchison St., posts Lake Mountain snow reports and provides local and regional maps and accommodation information (open Mon.-Fri. 10am-4pm, Sat.-Sun. 10am-5pm). To get to Marysville, take the **V/Line** from Spencer St. Station, Melbourne. Buses depart Marysville for Melbourne (1 per day, 1½hr., $5.45) and for Eildon (1 per day, 1hr., $4.80). Tickets can be purchased in the general store across from the bus stop. By car, take the Maroondah Hwy. (Hwy. 34) to Hwy. 172, which continues to Lake Mountain. The Marysville **post office,** on Murchison St., operates a veritable boutique (open Mon.-Fri. 9am-5pm, Sat. 9am-11am).

Taggerty

The Taggerty **Australian Bush Settlement** (tel. 5774 7378; fax 5774 7442) provides a splendorous stay for a one-night guest or a several-month visitor. This 30-hectare, YHA-affiliated farm by the **Cathedral Range National Park** simulates an early pioneer village, but lies just off the Maroondah Hwy. The remarkable host, Bronwyn Rayner, has operated Taggerty for 20 years and built it into a combination B&B, hostel, campsite, working farm, classroom, museum, and youth development facility.

Rayner cultivates an organic vegetable garden and cares for a variety of unwanted, misfit, or orphaned animals ranging from sheep and horses to wombats and kangaroos. Guests and visitors have the opportunity to interact with the animals, and the working farm and bush settlement serves as a backdrop for educational programs run for special-needs and at-risk kids. Taggerty houses an extensive collection of 19th-century bush memorabilia, including costumes, carriages, and even an 1853 Norwegian slab hut, all available for guests' enjoyment.

Worlds apart from an English B&B or a European hostel, Taggerty gives guests an authentic Australian bush adventure. Rayner's work to provide and protect this experience has been cited repeatedly in the Australian media, as the subject of several TV specials. Four degrees of comfort and privacy in the accommodations allow travelers of different needs and interests to fully experience and enjoy the farm (beds $15-$30). Richly decorated with a blend of antiques and contemporary furnishings, the **homestead bungalow** was *House Beautiful*'s 1990 Home of the Year and Design of the Year. Here, one can bed down in a 250-year-old canopied wonder or simply curl up by the roaring hearth. In the **lodge,** cosy environs and hostel-style bunks offer a more familiar setting for socializing with other backpackers. The **cabins,** set a bit further uphill, are bunk-style lodgings and appeal to those interested in an authentic bush settlement—with modern conveniences. Finally, several waterproof canvas **tent sites** with mattressed beds stand ready for those wanting the most rugged bush accommodations. All lodgings come with excellent kitchen and toilet facilities in-room or nearby.

All guests are invited to range along the extensive property. For reasonable prices, guests can take advantage of a board plan or bush activities, with longer trips and more involved excursions offered for groups of six or more. Taggerty usually has vacancies, but takes reservations (V, MC). This great experience is 104km east of Melbourne on the Maroondah Hwy. (Hwy. 34), approximately 4km after Buxton. It is accessible by **V/Line** from Melbourne to Alexandra or Eildon—ask to stop at Taggerty YHA at the 104km marker. For a closer look at Taggerty, read *Don't Pet the Wombat* by Elizabeth Honey, Childrens Book Council of Australia Book of the Year 1997.

Mornington Peninsula

South of Melbourne and St. Kilda, a thick spit of land projects out and around the eastern and southern edges of Port Phillip Bay. As Melbourne suburbs give way to summer beach resort communities, the distinct atmosphere of the Mornington Peninsula becomes apparent. A wine-producing region with excellent bushwalks, the peninsula almost fuses with the Bellarine Peninsula, which flanks Port Phillip Bay to the west. It is possible to cross the strait between the peninsulas by ferry.

Sorrento From the tip of the Mornington Peninsula, sunny Sorrento beckons visitors to relax among its old sandstone buildings. Fortunately for the budget traveler, cavorting at the town's upscale resorts is not the only way to enjoy its seaside appeal. This town on the bay is just a ferry trip from Queenscliff, on the Bellarine Peninsula, and the Great Ocean Road beyond (to Queenscliff 6 ferries per day, 45min., $6 per person, $36 per vehicle for 2 people). From Melbourne take a train to Frankston, then bus #788 to stop 18. Sorrento's main services include a National Bank **ATM,** markets, and **post office** (open Mon.-Fri. 9am-5pm).

Just south of the town center down Osset St., one can follow the YHA signs to reach **Bells Environmental YHA Hostel** (tel. 5984 4323). This five-star backpackers retreat provides a tidy kitchen and inviting sofas in a wood-paneled lodge bedecked in Sorrentobilia. Wooden beams and bricks create a homey atmosphere. Dorms with bath $13 (bring linen). The hostel operators also enable you to explore the area's beautiful walking tracks by providing transport, and can help you secure discounts on everything from horse rides to swimming with dolphins. For pancakes or a late meal, try **Buckley's Chance** (open Mon.-Thurs. 8am-9pm, Fri. 8am-10pm, Sat. 8am-8pm, Sun. 8am-6pm).

Phillip Island

The picturesque setting along the Bass Strait and rolling, pastoral hills would be attractive features by themselves, but Phillip Island is truly about little penguins. These endearing birds, smallest of the world's penguins, scamper back to their burrows nightly in a "Penguin Parade." So heavily has this procession been promoted that it has become a glitzy, packaged experience which follows only Ayers Rock as Australia's most popular tourist attraction.

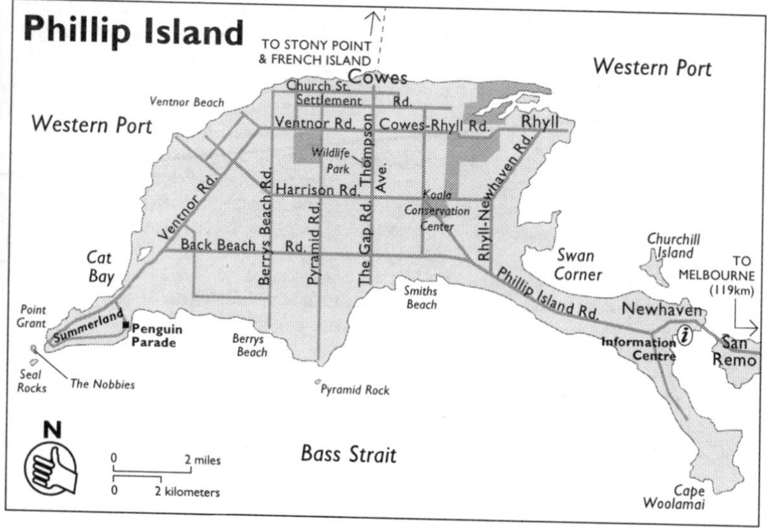

Practical Information, Accommodations, and Food Situated 120km southeast of Melbourne, Phillip Island is across a strait called "The Narrows" from San Remo, a town just off the South Gippsland Hwy. Numerous backpacker-oriented tours take groups to the island daily. An solid value, **Mac's Backpacker Bus** (tel. 5241 3180) organizes smaller group tours led by excellent guides. Their two-day tour of Phillip Island and the Great Ocean Road is a terrific bargain at $98 plus meals. For the independent traveler with access to a vehicle, Phillip Island is just 90 minutes from Melbourne via the Princes Hwy. (Hwy. 1), then the South Gippsland Hwy., and finally the Phillip Island Tourist Road (Hwy. 186). This road leads straight to **Cowes,** Phillip Island's biggest township. **V/Line** serves Cowes from Melbourne (9:10am and 6:10pm, 3¼hr., $13.40) arriving at the Cowes post office, and returns to Melbourne (6am and 3:30pm, 3¼hr., $13.40). To purchase V/Line tickets in town, head to either **Cowes Travel** or **Going Places Travel,** on the main drag, Thomson Ave.

Once on Phillip Island, you'll see the **Phillip Island Information Service** (tel. 5956 7447; open daily 9am-5pm), just over the bridge. You can also tune your dial to 87.6FM for sunny tourist radio. If you're in need of money, try the ANZ **ATM** (V, MC, AmEx, Cirrus, Plus). There's also a **Festival Supermarket** at Thomson's Ave. south end (open Mon.-Sat. 7:30am-5:30pm).

The best budget lodging on Phillip Island is the **Amaroo Park Hostel,** 97 Church St., Cowes (tel. 5952 2548), 400m west of the post office. With penguin and Wilsons Promontory National Park tours, Amaroo Park caters to eco-tourist interests. There's also a terrific free pick-up service from Melbourne each Tuesday and Friday (around 1pm) if you book for a night (dorms $12, YHA non-members $15). For tasty eats, sample the offerings of **Cafe Terrazzo,** 5 Thompson Ave. (tel. 5952 3773). The whimsically painted bistro offers a fine range of pizza and pasta. Their drink, entree, and dessert dinner special ($11) is a good meal and deal (open nightly until 9pm; V, MC, and Bancard).

Wildlife Phillip Island's tourist magnet is the **Little Penguin Parade,** on display at the Phillip Island Nature Park. Each night the penguins return to their burrows from the day's fishing expedition to attend to their hungry chicks. Most visitors come with tour bus companies, but street signs clearly direct folks to the car park and **visitors center** (tel. 5956 8300; fax 5956 8394; http://www.penguins.org.au), open daily from 10am to about 10pm (evening hours fluctuate seasonally). This facility provides extensive information about the penguins, including interactive exhibits on their life cycle and diet and windowed burrows where you can observe their behavior. (Admission to the visitors centre $3, children $2, families $10; included in group tour prices.)

An elevated boardwalk provides beach access from the visitors center and allows you to watch the penguins burrow after they arrive on shore. Two observation areas exist for viewing the penguins' beach walk. A smaller, unlit area to your right offers less touristed viewing, although fewer birds enter by this route. Most people await the penguins from the large grandstand facilities along the main boardwalk track. To grab a good seat, you need to arrive by sunset, equipped with warm clothing and something soft to pad your seat. Head straight for the sand and sit beneath the cord if space is available. Scooting towards the central tunnel area provides the best vantage point, regardless of your seating. Once seated, you'll wait 30-60 minutes for the penguins to arrive. Their parade generally lasts nearly an hour. Disarm your camera flash and pick up 1600-speed film if you want to capture Little Penguins in action, or pick up photos from the gift store. The number of penguins can vary nightly from a handful to over 1000, but at least a few score can be expected to waddle ashore in several small groups. There is full wheelchair access to the visitors center and observation sites.

Although the penguins are Phillip Island's main draw, a few other notable species make cameos. On the island's western extreme past the penguin parade, Australia's largest colony of New Zealand fur seals lives just off shore from the **Nobbies** rock formation. A boardwalk wraps around the Nobbies, enabling you to take in the beautiful eroded hills and crashing sea. The facility is open from 7:30am to dusk, and the **Seal Rocks Sea Life Centre** (scheduled to open in March, 1998) should enhance the zoological experience. The **Koala Conservation Centre** (tel. 5956 8691; fax 5956 8394) on Phillip Island Rd., en route to Cowes, is less invasive than the penguin parade. This excellent sanctuary houses 23 koalas in eucalypt canopies scattered about the park. These oft-lazy marsupials are most active when they are fed 90 minutes before dusk. An elevated platform permits closer inspection of the koalas (open daily 10am-6pm; admission $5, ages 4-13 $2, families $12; V, MC, Bancard).

Geelong

While not an attractive tourist destination itself, Geelong, just an hour southwest of Melbourne, is an important transportation hub for the Great Ocean Road and points west. The **transport station** on Brougham St. is probably Geelong's most important building. **Buses** run to Melbourne ($8.40), Ballarat ($9.60), Bendigo ($28.40), and Warrnambool ($23.80). The **National Wool Museum,** on the corner of Moorabool and Brougham St., in a historic bluestone wool store, houses the **tourist information center** (tel. 5222 2900; open daily 9am-5pm) and contains galleries explaining the agricultural, industrial, and mercantile aspects of wool production in Australia. Highlights include a huge, early 20th-century carpet loom that still produces and sells high-quality carpets (open daily 10am-5pm; admission $7, concessions $5.80, children $3.50). The **Geelong General Post Office** (tel. 5229 7687; open Mon.-Fri. 9am-5:30pm, Sat. 9am-noon; postal code 3220) is on Moorabool St. near the museum. Several **banks** and **ATMs** dot the corner of Moorabool and Malop St. (open Mon.-Thurs. 9:30am-4pm, Fri. 9:30am-5pm).

In days of yore, a YHA hostel stood in Geelong, but it has long since closed its doors, leaving few options for the budget traveler. The **Riverglen Caravan Park** (tel. 5243 6505) on Boorabool St. is the best of the lot, with sites only $8. **St. Albans Backpackers** (tel. 5248 1229), on Homestead Dr. in Whittington, is sporadically available for backpackers and their ilk. Many cheap chip shops and takeaways can be found among the ethnic cuisine on Moorabool St. A **restaurant complex** at the end of Cunningham Pier, on the waterfront, has reasonable prices, fancy cocktails, and excellent views (open Sun.-Thurs. 10am-10:30pm, Fri.-Sat. 10am-midnight).

GREAT OCEAN ROAD

The coastline of Victoria west of Melbourne and beyond Geelong (see p. 469) is one of serene wilderness beauty. The great Southern Ocean has carved the shore into spectacular, almost unearthly formations of limestone and volcanic rock. Pillars, arches, and gorges all seem as though they have been shaped by some divine will rather than by the chaotic agency of nature. Wind-scoured dunes and desolate heath form the backdrop for these marine sculptures. This stretch of coastline and its western continuation, technically not part of the Great Ocean Road, is termed the **Shipwreck Coast** because of the many vessels that foundered on the ever-changing rocks. Farther west, the heavy seas are cast in a different light; the area is known as the **Surf Coast** and is a favorite vacationing spot. Many small resort villages cater to the hosts of tourists that mob the wide, sandy beaches each summer. Even farther west, the verdant Otway Ranges reach right down to the ocean, and the misty green rainforest proves almost as great an attraction as the sunny beaches. Sections of the Shipwreck Coast near Portland and Port Fairy are developed for walkers; the **Great South West Walk** describes a 250km loop beginning and ending at the Portland Visitor Information Center. The western length of the highway leaves the coast near the Glenelg River and extends across the South Australian border to the city of **Mount Gambier** (see p. 397).

There are several options for exploring the Great Ocean Road; the most satisfactory and most expensive is to rent a car. Bicycling is also popular, but know that the eastern section of the road from Torquay to Apollo Bay is fairly hilly. Buses from Melbourne only service Lorne and Apollo Bay on Fridays and, in December and January, Mondays, making it difficult to jump from town to town using V/Line buses. Several private bus companies operate **tours from Melbourne to Adelaide** that travel along the Great Ocean Road and the southwest coast and allow participants to lay over along the way. **Oz Experience** (tel. (02) 9368 1766; fax (02) 9368 0908), based in New South Wales, runs from Melbourne to Adelaide for $110 (5% discount for YHA members). **Wayward Bus** (tel. (08) 8232 6646; fax (08) 8232 1455), based in South Australia, operates a similar tour for $160. Note that accommodation and food are usually not included.

Torquay

Torquay is the heart of the **surfing** scene in Victoria. World-famous **Bell's Beach** is just a few kilometers south, and several other excellent surf beaches are scattered about both Torquay and **Jan Juc,** also to the south. Bell's Beach is the site of the longest-running **pro surfing** competition, the **Rip Curl Pro Classic,** held every Easter. If you don't have the necessary gear, don't despair: Torquay has many specialty surf shops. The Surf Coast Plaza has everything you'd need to ride a wave (or at least look good trying) at discounted prices. Even better for die-hard fans, several big manufacturers (including Quicksilver and Rip Curl), have **factory outlet stores.** In the Surf Coast Plaza, the innovative Surfworld **surfing museum and interactive wonderland** (tel. 5261 4606) has displays explaining the physics behind wave formation, the dynamics of riding down monster swells, and the aesthetics (and high technology) behind modern board design. Extensive video exhibitions will ready you to pound the surf (open daily 10am-4pm; admission $5.50, children or concessions $3.50).

Torquay's **Nomads Bell's Beach Backpackers,** 51-53 Surfcoast Hwy. (tel. 5261 7070; fax 5261 3879), is a brand-new, state-of-the-art hostel with a pronounced surfing theme. There's an artificial beach in the front yard, surfing posters on most of the walls, and a kitchen counter fashioned from a surfboard. New mattresses and immaculate bathrooms are highlights of this brightly painted bungalow-style bunkhouse. Plenty of extras are included: free lockers, linen, bikes, tea, coffee, and good vibrations. The management offers packages for surfing, diving, and biplane tours. Transportation from Melbourne can be arranged (dorms $17; doubles $40). Fairhaven, a tiny town between Torquay and Lorne, boasts a brand-new hostel. **Surf Coast Backpackers,** 5 Covan Ave. (tel. 5289 6886), aims to please with friendly management and sunny rooms (Mon.-Fri. $12, Sat.-Sun. $15).

Lorne

A combination of forest and ocean atmosphere with much of the sophistication found in larger resort communities, Lorne is one of the most pleasing spots on the Great Ocean Road. The road is called Mountjoy Parade in town and is, not surprisingly, the main thoroughfare. Many services, shops, and restaurants line its length. Lorne started as a timber exporter, felling and shipping logs from what was to become the **Angahook-Lorne State Park.** Today, the park is a great place for bushwalking, horse riding, and fishing. Camping is permitted at several locations, although fires are allowed only at Hammonds Rd. Detailed maps and regulations, as well as info on the many small communities around Lorne, are available at the **Lorne Visitor Information Centre,** 144 Mountjoy Pde. (tel. 5289 1152; open daily 9am-5pm). The **post office** is nearby in the Cumberland Resort complex on the southwest end of Mountjoy (tel./fax 5289 1405; open Mon.-Fri. 9am-5pm). **Banks** with ATMs can also be found in the complex (open Mon.-Thurs. 9:30am-4pm, Fri. 9:30am-5pm). **Ridgeway's supermarket** (tel. 5289 1645) is just across the Erskine River on the Melbourne side of town at 1 Great Ocean Road.

The idyllic **Great Ocean Backpackers,** near the river on Erskine Ave. (tel 5289 1809), while lacking a view of the beach, boasts a wonderful hillside setting, surrounded by tall gum trees. Wooden cabins house bunkbeds and well-equipped kitchens. Sit on the patio and observe the flocks of crimson rosellas and flamboyant king parrots that guard the hostel. This YHA facility is easily the nicest hostel on the Great Ocean Road, and is therefore extremely popular year-round. (Free linen, laundry, and guided trips into the State Park. Dorms $15, YHA non-members $17. Bookings are particularly essential in Jan., when prices increase to $23-27.)

Nature serves to amuse and challenge in Lorne, and there are many adventure-style tours and programs to choose from. Pick up the *Fishing Guide: Torquay to Lorne* to plan your catch of the day, then equip yourself with bait, tackle, and a license at **Riordan's Hardware,** 57 Mountjoy Pde. **Otway Ocean Tours** (tel./fax 5232 1081), offers 4WD tours through forest and hinterland. **Otwild Adventures** (tel. 5289 1740 or 5236 2119) runs rock climbing, canoeing, and bushwalking tours of varying lengths. You could even paddle with a platypus in a rainforest. You needn't take a tour to enjoy the backcountry, though. **Teddy's Lookout,** just 30 minutes (by foot) along George St., provides sweeping views of the countryside. **Erskine Falls** is a bit farther, about 6km up the river. The way is lined with gorgeous tree ferns and the hike should take about three hours each way from the Erskine River bridge. The falls are quite beautiful and well worth the trip. Note that they can be approached by car, cutting the hiking time to about five minutes, and Erskine is but one of many falls in the area. **Buses** depart daily from the Commonwealth Bank on Mountjoy Pde. to Geelong (1½hr., $10.90) and Melbourne (2½hr., $21.30). Buses to Apollo Bay leave on Saturday and Sunday only (1hr., $4.80).

Apollo Bay

Apollo Bay is the gateway to Otway National Park and Cape Otway to the west. Lobstering is the primary industry, although many species of the sea are hauled in each day. The **Fisherman's Co-op** can tell you what's biting and how to catch it. **Apollo Bay Boat Charters,** near the co-op on the waterfront (tel. 5237 6214, mobile tel. 0419 565 812), runs snapper fishing trips (from $25 per person), diving expeditions ($20 per dive), and scenic tours (from $15 per person). Many walks lead away from the sea into the Otway forest, but one of the most popular is the **Mait's Rest boardwalk,** 17km west of Apollo Bay. Kept a secret by locals for many years, this deep forest gully has now been developed for tourists and is ready for despoiling. **Triplet Falls,** near Laver's Hill on Phillips Track, is another easy walk with a beautiful three-tiered cascade. Picnic tables and BBQ are available.

At night, **glow-worms** emerge to slither and crawl through the verdant undergrowth. To see the light, try your luck in most parts of Otway National Park, or take a tour and be led right to them. Tours leave from **Willow Bryn** (tel. 5237 6791 or 5237 6493) at the end of the Barham Valley Rd., north of Apollo Bay on the road to Paradise. Tours begin at dusk every night ($5, children $2).

The **Tourist Information Centre** is right on the Great Ocean Road (tel. 5237 6529; fax 5237 6194; open daily 9am-5pm). The staff will book accommodations and arrange tours. The town has a **post office** (open Mon.-Fri. 9am-5pm, postal code 3233), and a Rite-Way licensed **supermarket** (open Mon.-Sun. 9am-6pm), also on the highway. **Buses** leave Apollo Bay from the **Westpac bank** on Collingwood St. There are daily buses to Lorne (1hr., $4.80), Geelong (2½hr., $17.50), and Melbourne (3½hr., $20.60). Buses to other points along the Great Ocean Road operate on Friday only. The **Pisces Caravan Park** (tel. 5237 6749; fax 5237 6326), on the east side of town on the Great Ocean Road, has powered and unpowered sites, cabins, and **YHA backpacker** dorm bunks, which are amply supplied with blankets in winter. A small kitchen is available for all guests. (Free BBQ facilities, coin-operated laundry, and a playground. Dorms $12, $15 for YHA non-members; sites start at $12.) The **Apollo Bay Backpackers,** 47 Montrose St., was closed for the winter when *Let's Go* last visited, but is another budget option in the summer.

■ Around Apollo Bay: The Otways

The **Otway National Park,** 200km west of Melbourne, is home to some of the dampest yet most beautiful terrain in Victoria. Formed 150 million years ago, the temperate rainforests of the Otways have preserved some of their primeval atmosphere—giant herbivorous dinosaurs would complete the picture. The park boasts deep ravines and gullies filled with ferns, moss, and giant trees. Misty waterfalls crash and trickle down the steep hillsides to form clear creeks in the valley bottoms, sometimes diffusing into marshy bottomlands. There are many well-marked walks through the park; maps are available at the Apollo Bay Tourist Information Centre or at the **Apollo Bay National Parks Office** (tel. 5237 6889). Several companies, including **Otway Eco-Guides** (tel. 5237 7240), offer guided tours of the park. Most operators can be contacted through the Apollo Bay Tourist Information Centre. One of the highlights of the Otways is the **Cape Otway Lightstation,** built in 1848 on the terminus of Cape Otway as a beacon for ships attempting the western approach to Bass Strait, which has been dubbed the "eye of the needle." One of the many difficulties inherent in this passage was the ferocious wind of the "roaring 40s," because ship captains seldom knew their exact positions after being blown around by the stormy winds of that latitude. The lighthouse stands on the southernmost spit of land along the entire approach, and served as the only landmark disoriented captains could rely on. The lighthouse is reached by a 12km approach road off the Great Ocean Road (about 20km west of Apollo Bay), and can only be seen through a guided tour (tel. 5237 9240). The hour-long tours provide interesting historical information and magnificent views from the top of the lighthouse. They set off every half-hour beginning at 9:30am ($4, children $2).

Bimbi Park (tel. 5237 9246), right on Lighthouse Rd., is a strange haven for weary travelers. This rambling, densely wooded **caravan park** could easily be a jungle guerilla camp, and even includes a "commando course" to practice search and destroy tactics. A series of large canvas tents protects **backpacker bunks.** Old, functional showers cost $3 for non-guests (tent sites $10, with power $13; bunks $12; breakfast included). For horse-lovers, Bimbi Park is also the place for **bareback riding** in the Otways (1½hr. ride $22).

Port Campbell

Port Campbell is a sleepy, appealing fishing village on one of the nastiest yet most picturesque coastlines in the world. This most treacherous stretch of the **Shipwreck Coast** has claimed hundreds of lives and was once feared by mariners around the world. The town is an excellent overnight stop when traveling the Great Ocean Road, and provides a good base for diving, fishing, or scenic boat charters. It also holds the headquarters of the famous **Port Campbell National Park,** which preserves many of the strange and wondrous rock formations that shivered the timbers of so many ships. The town is home to one of the few **beaches** in the area that is safe for swimming, but most people are more interested in the decidedly unsafe limestone cliff formations that make the Great Ocean Road so great. The **12 Apostles** (formerly known as the Sow and Piglets, and today including just seven disciples) is perhaps the most famous of the formations, though many others are just as interesting. The **Razorback,** for example, is a long spine of rock, perforated in many places and serrated along the top. The Bay of Martyrs and Bay of Islands have many tall columns of rock which, like some of the Apostles, occasionally tumble into the sea as the rock perpetually erodes.

The **National Park Information Centre** (tel. 5598 6382), on the corner of Morris and Tregea St., one block from the Great Ocean Road, can provide information on the rock formations, wildlife, and ship corpses (open daily 9am-5pm). A Port Campbell **Discovery Walk** shows off many of the town's extraordinary natural features; obtain brochures at the Information Centre, along with a map to supplement the numerous signposts. The **post office** (postal code 3269) is in the superb **General Store,** on the Great Ocean Road. The store's hours are loose, but it is generally open into the early evening. **The Baker's Oven** (tel. 5598 6489; open daily 9am-5pm) beckons from across the street.

The small **Shipwreck Museum** (tel. 5598 6463) is next to the bakery, right on the highway. The museum has a collection of baubles, trinkets, and artifacts salvaged from the wrecks of many ships, and is mostly a gift shop (open 9am-5pm; admission $4). The museum also serves as the booking agent for **Port Campbell Boat Charters,** which offers crafts for diving, fishing, or sight-seeing expeditions. For more information, contact the skipper (tel. 5590 6411), or the agents at the museum. A **scuba** and marine center (tel. 5598 6499) is next to the General Store.

The **YHA Hostel,** just down the road from the museum at 18 Tregea St. (tel./fax 5598 6305), was recently renovated and features a marvelous, large kitchen, a lounge with a ruddy wood stove, coin-operated laundry, and small showers. Very popular with tour buses and other groups, so be sure to book ahead during the summer. Dorm accommodations are $12, $15 for YHA non-members (key deposit $5). There is a **caravan park** next to the national park information center on Morris St. (tel. 5598 6492; BBQs, showers, laundry, and shaded, grassy sites $13, with power $16).

West from Port Campbell and a few kilometers east of Warrnambool along the Great Ocean Road, **Childers Cove** is a beautiful, sheltered beach at the front of great sea-cliffs. Tour buses do not stop here, as the approach goes through several kilometers of farmland, so the beach is often completely empty. Also on the outskirts of Warrnambool on the Great Ocean Road, **Allansford Cheeseworld** (tel. 5563 2127) is, by any measure, the greatest dairy-themed attraction in southern Victoria. There's even a **Milkshake Museum** inside. Cheeseworld offers a glimpse into the cruelly beautiful world of cheese, but beware: many who dare to enter stay and gorge forever (open Mon.-Fri. 8:30am-4:30pm, Sat. 8:30am-2pm).

Warrnambool

Warrnambool is the self-proclaimed capital of the Shipwreck Coast, and life for most residents centers on the sea. Although lacking the historical charm of towns further west, such as Port Fairy and Portland, Warrnambool possesses an energy and vitality that the smaller communities lack. A popular seaside holiday destination, the city draws people for the regular marine distractions—fishing, swimming, surfing, and basking—but also entices with whale-watching and a maritime museum.

ORIENTATION AND PRACTICAL INFORMATION

The city is built around the Princes Hwy. (called **Raglan Parade** in town) and envelops Warrnambool Bay (also known as Lady Bay). The bay is bounded by the Merri River on the west and the Hopkins River on the east. The **Warrnambool Visitor Information Centre,** 600 Raglan Pde. (tel. 5564 7837; fax 5561 2133), provides excellent free maps of the district and city, marked with points of interest (open Mon.-Fri. and school and public holidays 9am-5pm, Sat.-Sun. 10am-4pm). **Bank offices** can be found at 140 Karoit St. (open Mon.-Thurs. 9:30am-4pm, Fri. 9:30am-5pm), and another **ATM** on the corner of Laura and Liebig St. The **rail station** is just north of Lake Pertrobe on Merri St. There are daily rail links with Geelong (2½hr., $23.80) and Melbourne (3½hr., $33.20). **Buses** depart from South Western Roadways on Raglan Pde. and head to: Ballarat (Mon.-Fri., 2½hr., $17.50); Mount Gambier (daily, 2½hr., $26.10); Portland (daily, 1½hr., $11.90); and Port Fairy (Mon.-Fri., 30min., $4.20). **Coast Link** to the eastern towns on the Great Ocean Road runs only on Fridays (and Mon. Dec.-Jan.) For **police** call 5562 1111. The **post office** is on the corner of Timor and Gills St. (open Mon.-Fri. 8:45am-5pm; postal code 3280).

ACCOMMODATIONS AND FOOD

During the summer months, it is important to arrange for accommodations ahead of time, as many places fill to capacity. A brand-new addition to a nationwide chain of hostels, **Nomads' Backpackers,** 17 Stanley St. (tel./fax 5562 4874), has comfortable dorm beds and excellent extras. It's located near the beach on the west side of the bay, a bit south of the town center. A courtesy bus runs to and from town every 20 minutes on weekend nights, providing relief from the hostel's own tropical-themed lounge. Each guest is supplied with a locker and linen, and the management runs a variety of free and discounted tours to Tower Hill and points on the Great Ocean Road. The front room is BYO licensed, and can get noisy on summer weekends, but the back bunkrooms are insulated by a double-thickness brick wall so that the weary might rest (free BBQ, enormous kitchen, and cable TV; dorms $15; key deposit $10). The **Stuffed Backpacker,** 52 Kepler St. (tel. 5562 2459), in the middle of town, occupies the upper floors of a large, ancient building. Bookings and reception are in Flaherty's Chocolate Shop downstairs, and there is ample parking through an alley to the rear. (Clean showers, small kitchen and lounge with a fireplace and TV, and *laissez-faire* attitude. No nonsense, no frills. Dorms $12. Toast and coffee included. Key deposit $5.)

Just down the street, the **Western Hotel Motel,** 45 Kepler St. (tel. 5562 2011; fax 5562 4324), has 30 beds spread among 15 rooms, offering more privacy than the other budget options (dorms $12; singles $15). The pub on the ground floor provides booze, a pool table, and counter meals (most $5-6; breakfast $2).

For midnight munchies, the **Coles supermarket** on Lava St. is always open. **Fishtales,** 63-65 Liebig St. (tel. 5561 2957), is open from 8am onwards every day and specializes in fish, vegetarian pasta, and Asian food. Most dishes are less than $10 (BYO, eat in or take away).

SIGHTS AND ACTIVITIES

The most popular thing to do in Warrnambool is to watch whales. This has spawned many cetacean-themed gift shops and an entire tourism sub-industry. The information center has booklets on the **southern right whales,** who are continuously tracked. Every winter in late May or June, a population of whales stops just off **Logans Beach,** to the east of Warrnambool Bay, to give birth to their calves. They stay until September or October, when they return to the Antarctic to break their five-month fast. Viewing platforms have been built above the beach to protect the delicate dune vegetation, and tourists gather to watch the beasts **roll, blow, and breach.** These right whales used to be hunted in large numbers all along the Victorian coastline, but have now been protected for several decades. Whale watching is much more fun if you have some sort of visual amplification (binoculars, telescope, or a nice telephoto lens). A common error is to look too far out to sea; the whales often swim very close to shore. A right whale is easily distinguished by its lack of a dorsal fin, the peculiar shape of its head and jaw, and its unique V-shaped spout.

Warrnambool's other great tourist attraction is the **Flagstaff Hill Maritime Museum** on Merri St. (tel. 5564 7841). The museum, a re-creation of a late 19th-century coastal village, includes a few original edifices (mostly lighthouses and gun batteries) and numerous accurate replicas. The museum houses many artifacts from wrecked ships, including the fabulous Schomberg Diamond. The **Loch Ard peacock,** taken from the wreck of the *Loch Ard* in 1878, is located in the Public Hall. Only two people survived the wreck, but this giant ceramic fowl escaped with only slight beak damage. It shouldn't take more than a few hours to wander the grounds, but the price of admission includes a second day if you need it. (Open daily 9am-5pm. The lighthouse does not open until 11am. Admission $9.50, concessions $8, children $4.50.) A series of interesting video presentations is shown in the Interpretation Centre (at the entrance complex); schedules are available from the front desk.

On the road between Warrnambool and Port Fairy, the main attraction is the **Tower Hill State Game Reserve,** situated in a volcanic crater. The reserve swarms with koalas, kangaroos, emus, possums, echidnas, and Cape Barren geese. It is possible to drive right through the crater, but to really get a good look at the wildlife, try one of the many walking paths around the reserve.

Port Fairy

In 1827, by the best reckoning, **Captain James Wishart** of the cutter *Fairy* first sailed into the mouth of the River Moyne in search of potable water. Neither wish nor art produced great water, but the commemoration of his voyage did give the 1843 port settlement a permanent Tinkerbell complex. The area was probably used as a haven by sealers and whalers throughout the early 1800s, but by the time the first government survey was made, in 1843, the whales were gone. New settlers were instead attracted by the fertility of the land and the commercial promise of the western district. Little commercial development has occurred since the late 1800s, but many of the old buildings still exist, and more than 50 buildings have been preserved by the National Trust. A booklet with historical details and a walking tour map of many of

Wanted: Sunken 16th-Century Portuguese Ship
Reward: $250,000

In 1522, **Cristovao de Mendonca,** a Portuguese adventurer, may have sailed a mahogany caravel along the east coast of Australia and mapped much of the coastline. Thus, some historians argue that the Portuguese were in fact the first Europeans to discover Australia. But thanks to 16th-century diplomatic arguments and the Lisbon earthquake of 1755, the Portuguese records are lost forever. A French map of a southern land called Java la Grande was published in Dieppe in 1547, but since many of the names appear in Portuguese, some think that the French map was actually plagiarized from de Mendonca's original charts. But de Mendonca lost more than his potential claim to the first map of Australia; his mahogany ship was wrecked on the coast somewhere between Warrnambool and Port Fairy. The wreck was first sighted in 1836, and many claim to have glimpsed it since then, but the constantly shifting coastline has prevented the discovery of the wreck and it has drifted into legend. Recent searches have used advanced chemical and physical techniques, but nothing has ever been found. So when walking this stretch of coastline, keep alert, and perhaps the legend will be verified. The ship's finder, after all, can collect the $250,000 reward still posted by authorities in Warrnambool.

these buildings is available from the **Tourist Information Centre** on Bank St. (tel. 5568 2682; open daily 9am-5pm). Occasionally, members of the Port Fairy Historical Society conduct tours of the buildings; inquire at the visitor information center.

Like most of Victoria's southwestern coast, Port Fairy can claim its share of shipwrecks. A total of 30 crafts were lost near Port Fairy, and six of them can be observed along the **Shipwreck Walk.** To mitigate future disasters, a lifeboat station and rocket house were built in 1873 and 1888, respectively. The old lifeboat (a then-state-of-the-art self-righting design with drainage valves) was recently restored. Tours of the station are available on most Sundays. It's best to book at the visitor information center.

Although it seems to have done very little in helping ships avoid a watery doom, a lighthouse still stands on **Griffith's Island,** the site of the old whaling station. The keeper's quarters have been demolished, and the light is now solar-powered. The old keeper's garden has grown wild from years of neglect, but annual blooms can still be seen in springtime. Griffith's Island is also the nesting site for a colony of migrating **mutton-birds.** Every year, thousands of birds fly back and forth over the Pacific, spending eight months of the year on the island. After the 15,000km flight to North America the birds rest briefly, then fly right back.

The best bet for **accommodation** in Port Fairy is the **YHA Hostel,** 8 Cox St. (tel. 5568 2468). The hostel is in a house built by Port Fairy's first official settler, William Rutledge (the "King of Port Fairy"), and has a full range of amenities, including a lounge with a fireplace and TV, a large communal kitchen, a coin-op laundry, and new mattresses. Sleeping bags are not permitted near these new mattresses, as the owners fear vermin from the backcountry. (Beds $13, $16 for YHA non-members.) It is essential to book well ahead for March, when the hostel fills completely. In fact, almost every bed on the Shipwreck Coast is hired out in March, for that is the time of the **Port Fairy Folk Festival.** Call 5568 2227 for festival information and order tickets many months in advance to avoid disappointment. The folksy aura lingers year-round, since many arts and crafts shops sell excellent homemade wares.

Port Fairy's whaling days are long gone, but there is still a large fishing fleet. Fresh crayfish and abalone can be bought along the Fisherman's Wharf on the Moyne. The town has recently become an artists' haven, and has therefore developed a lively cafe scene; the town center is thick with them. The **bank** at 51 Sackville St. has an **ATM,** with a **supermarket** next door. The **post office** is at 25 Sackville St. (open Mon.-Fri. 9am-5pm, postal code 3284). **Buses** connect Port Fairy to Warrnambool (3 per day, $4.20), Melbourne (daily, $35.40), Geelong (daily, $28.40), and Portland (3 per day, $8.40) and leave from Bank St. near the information center. Don't miss the **Kite-house,** 27 Cox St. (tel. 5568 2782), which sells any kind of kite or wind sock a windy day deserves, rents **bicycles,** and provides tours and tourist information. **Granny's Kitchen** on Bank St. is open late and has good bread and soups on the menu and excellent blues and jazz on the hi-fi.

■ Mt. Eccles National Park

Some 20,000 years ago, igneous activity formed Mt. Eccles, and the volcanic turbulence continued until about 7000 years ago. Because the volcano is so young, many of its topographical features are in excellent condition, and haven't been muted by the forces of weather, vegetation, and time. Although not particularly astonishing, **Lake Surprise** is pleasant for strolling around and for swimming—though if the volcano decided to erupt again, any swimmers would be quickly boiled alive, since the lake fills the three largest of Eccles's craters.

The point of entry to the park is the town of **Macarthur,** which is about 40km north of Port Fairy and 30km south of **Hamilton.** The latter township is on the Hamilton Hwy., which runs west from Geelong. Within the park, well-marked walking tracks lead to several interesting relics of the mountain's volcanic past. The **lava cave** was formed as the top skin of a lava flow hardened into rock. The liquid stone then flowed out from underneath this roof, forming the broad cavity present today. A small section of roof has collapsed, allowing visitors to explore the pitch-black interior of the cave. At the **lava canal,** the entire roof has collapsed, leaving a trench of igneous rock.

Thick **manna gum woods** cover parts of the slope, providing habitat for elusive, crabby **koalas,** who are most active in the evening. About 50 years ago, the northwest slope of the mountain was quarried for scoria (the porous volcanic rock that makes up much of the slope). Thankfully, this destructive land use was put to an end when the area was declared a national park in 1960. The **Crater Rim Nature Walk** includes all of these topographical features, and is detailed in a pamphlet available from the **tourist information center** (tel. 5576 1338). The center's rangers can also provide camping permits and information about the bushland surrounding the park.

Portland

Founded in 1834 by the Henty brothers, Portland is the oldest permanent European settlement in Victoria, and many of the town's original buildings have been preserved. Even before the first Henty sheep farm, the area was a base for whalers, sealers, escaped convicts, and other colorful characters. Whalers took hundreds of southern right whales every year, decimating the whale population. In those days, Portland was a city on par with Melbourne. Although the latter has indisputably won the contest to become Victoria's cultural capital, Portland nevertheless supports several large industries. The port bundles over $1 billion of cargo annually, as curious visitors observe the portly goings-on.

Practical Information The **Portland Visitor Information Centre** (tel. 5523 2671; fax 5521 7287), located near the waterfront on the corner of Bentinch and Cliff St., can provide maps of **historic building walking tours** and the historical information you crave. Free tours of the port leave from the information center on Saturdays at 1 and 2pm (center open daily 9am-5pm). The information center is also the trailhead for the popular Great South West Walk. **Commonwealth Bank** has offices on the corner of Henty and Percy St. (open Mon.-Thurs. 9:30am-4pm, Fri. 9:30am-5pm), and an **ATM** is at your service at 90 Percy St. Two **V/Line buses** per day connect Portland to Port Fairy ($8.40) and Warrnambool ($11.90). On Fridays (plus Mon. Dec.-Jan.), buses run to Port Campbell ($21.30), Apollo Bay ($33.20), and Lorne ($37.80). There is a **post office** at 108 Percy St. (open Mon.-Fri. 9am-5pm; postal code 3305).

Accommodation and Food **The Garden Hotel,** 63 Bentinck St. (tel. 5523 1121), provides good budget accommodation close to the information center and waterfront. There is a pub downstairs, complete with an electronic gambling den (bed and breakfast $20). Most hotels provide standard-issue counter meals for around $5 (generally "something" and chips). **Admella's Orchard,** 100 Percy St., can provide fruits and vegetables that have not yet been deep-fried. **The Phoenix Diner** (tel. 5523 7188), one block inland, near the information center on Percy St., has a variety of pasta dishes for around $4, most with heavy cream sauces. Baked potatoes with cheese and pineapple cost $3.50, and nothing is over $8.

Activities Although fairly reliable today, the port was in olden times a death trap, and many ships came to grief in or near the Portland Harbor. Many of these are memorialized along yet another **Historic Shipwreck Trail,** which begins at Moonlight Head and stretches to the South Australian border (brochures available at the information center). The many wrecked ships, forests of kelp, and delicate corals make the waters near Portland a delight for **snorkelers and divers** alike. Equipment and instruction is available at many shops. Try **Duck Dive Scuba,** 57 Bentinck St. (tel./fax 5523 5617). For a very different kind of tour, check out the **gigantic aluminum smelter,** cunningly landscaped to soften the aesthetic blow delivered by metal-processing plants. This "Smelter in the Park" is a great example of environmentally conscious design (tel. 9923 2071 to arrange a tour).

The Great South West Walk Starting and ending at Portland's information center, this 250km looping track rambles along the coast, then doubles back through the Lower Glenelg National Park. The walk encompasses a variety of terrains and provides a grand introduction to the wildlands of southwest Victoria. Sections as short as 8km can be accessed for daytrippers, and regional highlights are described here. Detailed maps and guided tours are available at the visitor information center. For safety's sake, register your travel plans with the center staff.

A few kilometers west of Portland at Cape Bridgewater, a short section of the Great South West Walk passes through some interesting terrain. A robust cliff-edge trail leads to a **seal colony.** Tourists can observe the pinnipeds without disturbing them, on a platform listening as the seals' belches and guffaws blend with the ceaseless song of the sea. A little farther along (by road, quite a walk by the path), the **"petrified forest"** looms. True petrification involves the direct replacement of vegetable matter with mineral, and this is, instead, a rock formation that formed in the cavities left behind when the trees rotted away. Nevertheless, it creates an eerie effect and is well worth a look. At the foot of the sea cliffs, pockets of stone have been weathered by the waves, forming tunnels and channels that direct the incoming swells high into the air, causing loud booming sounds. Old-timers say that they used to be audible as far away as downtown Portland. These **blowholes** can be spectacular if the tidal and meteorological conditions are right. Or they can, well...blow. The salt mist that is thrown aloft is often blown ashore, causing the plants much duress and stunting their growth. The area is currently undergoing rabbit-baiting and revegetation campaigns.

■ West of Portland: Glenelg River National Parks

Lower Glenelg National Park and Discovery Bay National Park, situated along the Glenelg River and the far southwest Victorian coastline, attract bushwalkers, canoeists, and naturalists. Covering nearly 36,000 hectares, these parks preserve a variety of terrain, including forests, heath, rivers, swamps, dunes, and cliffs. As a result, the plant and animal life is extremely diverse. Characteristically eastern species are supplanted by western ones as Victoria gives way to South Australia. **Nelson** is the most appropriate base for exploring these parks; the town is about 30km southeast of Mt. Gambier, just inside Victoria. **Portland** is much larger, and it provides easy access from the east.

The Glenelg River is usually calm, deep, and wide, making it ideal for tranquil **canoeing.** Four days of paddling can bring you all the way from Dartmoor, on the Princes Hwy., to the mouth of the river at Nelson. This 75km stretch of river supports 11 campsites along the way, most of which cannot be reached by automobile. Permits are required and can be obtained at the Department of Conservation, at the Forests and Lands Information Center on Forest Rd. in Nelson (tel. (08) 8738 4051). This office can also answer questions about river conditions and canoe rental. If you are short on time, you needn't canoe the entire 75km stretch, since there are numerous boat landings along the length of the river.

Lower Glenelg National Park

Limestone dominates the topography of the **Lower Glenelg National Park,** and for 15km near the mouth of the river, the flowing water has cut a deep gorge, with banks as high as 50m. Many caves have been formed by percolating rainwater or underground watercourses. The largest and most spectacular of these (and the only ones open to the public) are the **Princess Margaret Rose Caves,** located 2km east of the South Australian border and about 15km south of the Princes Hwy. Tours are conducted five to seven times daily (except Fri. between May 29 and Sept. 22), but the schedule is highly variable ($4.20, children $1.60). Contact the **Caves Information Centre** (tel. (08) 8738 4171) for current schedules. The caves area also features a few nature walks, a large, wooded picnicking area with BBQ, and limited camping facilities (both tent sites and on-site caravans). Camping arrangements must be made before 5pm with the ranger at the Caves Information Center.

Discovery Bay National Park

The main feature of the Discovery Bay National Park is the **Great South West Walk.** Like Lower Glenelg, Discovery Bay is extremely popular with amateur anglers. Bass, bream, and mulbuay thrive in the up-river areas, while yellow-eye mullet and Australian salmon are found in the saltier areas. A fishing license, obtainable at most bait and tackle stores, is required for all inland fishing; marine species, excluding crayfish and lobster, may be taken without a license.

GOLDFIELDS

Strange geological forces must have been operating in the middle of the last century. In 1851, just two years after the California gold rush, gold was discovered here in Clunes, prompting a massive migration for the precious metal. Thousands of people from all nations and all walks of life sold everything they had to finance the voyage to Australia. Towns sprang up almost overnight as prospectors pulled vast quantities of gold from the rich alluvial deposits throughout central Victoria. The gold rush has been over for more than a century, and people in the goldfields region today make their livings through agriculture and wool-growing rather than panning and digging. Historical buildings and presentations, however, ensure that the region's golden past is never far from the minds of tourists or locals.

Ballarat

Victoria's largest inland city (pop. 83,000), Ballarat is the self-appointed capital of the Goldfields. The most important of the boom towns during the gold rush, it clings to its gracious 1850s image. Though the gold is long gone, much of the 19th-century architecture has been preserved, and the city's golden past has been developed into a bustling tourist trade. Huge, elegant Victorian buildings line the main street, and more than 60 buildings in town have been recognized for historical architecture by the National Trust. But the main historical attraction is Sovereign Hill, a reconstructed gold town built around a mine. The town has also gained fame among gardeners for its begonias. Ballarat is a favorite for schools, churches, and other groups looking for an educational holiday.

It was here in Ballarat that Australia had its closest brush with civil war in the early morning hours of December 3, 1854. An uprising over miners' rights ended in a bloody 15-minute clash, the Eureka Rebellion, which remains an emblem of Australian populism. Ballarat retains the memory of this event by billing itself "the birthplace of the Australian spirit."

ORIENTATION

Ballarat straddles the Western Highway, which is called **Sturt Street** as it runs through town. This thoroughfare is lined with shops, restaurants, and offices, and a pleasant median with statues and pavilions stretches down its center. The **train station** is a few blocks north of Sturt on the cross street **Lydiard Street.** From the station, turn left on Lydiard and cross **Mair Street** to get to Sturt St. The **tourist center** is several blocks east of Lydiard on the corner of Sturt and Albert St. Just past the tourist office, Sturt becomes **Bridge Mall,** a pedestrian mall with shops, restaurants, and a large supermarket complex. Local buses congregate out front. To the east of the mall, the Western Highway becomes **Victoria St.** and **Main Rd.** curves off to the south. To the southeast of the city center lie the **Sovereign Hill** complex and the **Eureka Stockade. Lake Wendourree** and the adjoining **Botanical Gardens** are on the western outskirts of town, just north of Sturt St.

PRACTICAL INFORMATION

Tourist Information Centre: On the corner of Sturt and Albert St. (tel. 5332 2694 or 1800 648 450; fax 9332 7977; email tourismb@netconnect.com.au). From the V/Line station, walk south along Lydiard St. to Sturt St., turn left and walk east along Sturt to the corner of Albert St. Blue signs point the way. Open daily 9am-5pm.
Currency Exchange: There are many banks and **ATMs** along Sturt St. National is at 329 Sturt St. (tel. 5331 1700), open Mon.-Thurs. 9:30am-4pm, Fri. 9:30am-5pm.
American Express: 37 Sturt St. (tel. 5331 1144). Offers a range of travel services, but does not hold mail. Specializes in Qantas bookings. Open Mon.-Fri. 9am-5pm.
Trains and Buses: V/Line (tel. 13 22 32) operates passenger trains and coaches from Ballarat Station at 202 Lydiard St. N. (tel. 5333 4660). To Melbourne ($14.40), and Daylesford ($8.40).
Local Buses: For information, call 5331 7777. Most routes depart from the Bridge Mall at the eastern end of Sturt St. Take bus #2 to Ballarat Station. For Sovereign Hill, take bus #9 or 10. For the Botanical Gardens and Lake Wendouree, take bus #9 or 15. Services typically run every 30-35min., less frequently on weekends. Student discounts. Full bus schedules are available at the Tourist Information Centre.
Taxis: Ballarat Taxis (tel. 13 10 08) operate 24hr. Service from the city center to Sovereign Hill is about $5. Up to 5 people can share a cab.
Laundromat: 711 Sturt St. (tel. 5333 6746). Wash $2, dry $1. Open 6am-10pm.
Public Toilets: On either end of the Bridge Mall at the eastern end of Sturt St.
Hospital: St. John of God, 101 Drummond St. (tel. 5331 6677). **Ambulance:** tel. 5311 4400.
Emergency: tel. 000.
Police: (tel. 5337 7222), On Camp St., across Sturt St. from the tourist center.
Post Office: (tel. 5331 4744; fax 5331 7642), on the corner of Lydiard and Sturt St. Poste Restante and **fax** services. Open Mon.-Fri. 9am-5pm. **Postal code:** 3350.
Phone Code: 03.

ACCOMMODATIONS

Ballarat's accommodations market is aimed more at Melburnian families on weekend trips than at international backpackers. If you happen to strike it rich while in Gold Country, try one of the palatial Victorian bed and breakfasts on Lydiard St. Hapless diggers will have to make do with one of several cheaper options.

Sovereign Hill Lodge (YHA) (tel. 5331 1944; fax 5333 5861), on Magpie St. Overlooking Sovereign Hill, it's the closest accommodation to Ballarat's main attraction. Take bus #9 or 10 from Sturt St. to Sovereign Hill. The buildings retain an 1850s style, but have been recently refinished and are in excellent condition. Amenities include a full kitchen, a pool, TV lounges, ping-pong tables, and a bar with a cheery fireplace, although you're liable to be sharing a bathroom with a school or tour group. 24hr. reception. Check-out 10am. The old military barracks have been converted into dorms ($18, $16 with YHA). Breakfast $4. Book ahead for holidays or weekends, especially in the summer. V, MC, AmEx.
Goldfields Caravan Park, 108 Clayton St. (tel. 5332 7888; fax 5332 4244), 300m from Sovereign Hill. Follow the signs to Sovereign Hill from downtown. Central location lacks scenic setting. Recently purchased by a young couple, this park has undergone some serious redevelopment in the past year. Pricey new cabins, kitchens, recreation rooms, and a playground make this the most modern of the caravan parks around Ballarat. Tent sites are $9 plus a refundable $5 key deposit. V, MC.
Wandella-Ballarat B&B, 202 Dawson St., a few blocks south of Sturt St. (tel. 5333 7046; fax 5332 9339). A sprawling late 19th-century house offering plain, comfortable lodging with a bit more privacy than a hostel or campsite. All rooms have telephones, electric heaters, and complimentary tea and coffee. Large lounge and well-kept, though small, shared bathrooms. No kitchen facilities. Reception hours 8am-8pm; call ahead if arriving late. Singles $27.50; doubles $42. Multiple-day stays 10% off. Continental breakfast included. Book in advance for holidays and summer, and beware of surcharges for popular weekends. V, MC.

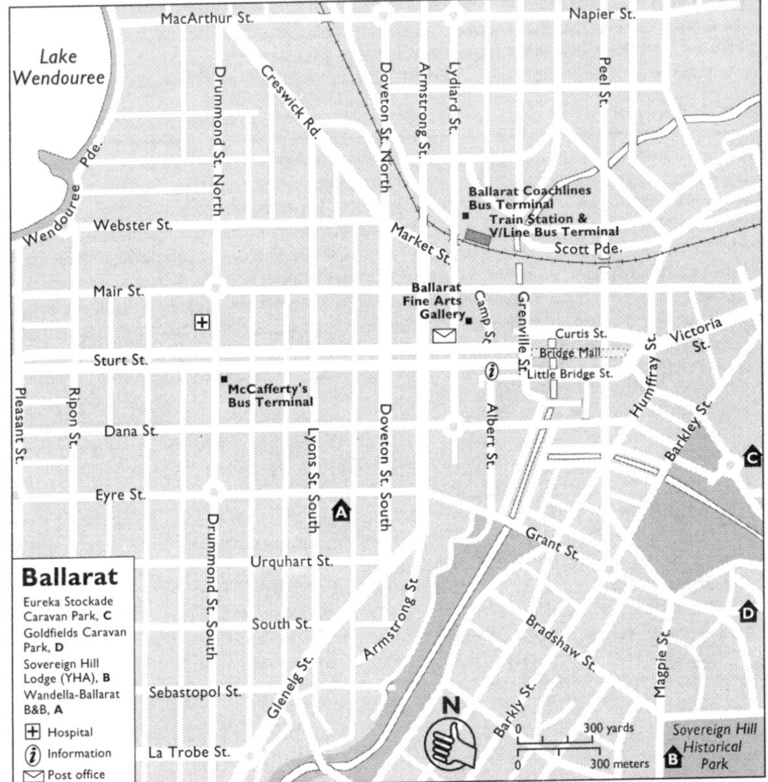

Eureka Stockade Caravan Park (tel. 5331 2281) on Stawell St., off Eureka St. Basic caravan park next to a large water slide/mini-golf compound. Facilities include barbecue, laundry, and access to an Olympic-sized pool. Reception staffed daily 9am-6pm. Tent sites $11, with power $13, on-site caravans $25-45. V, MC.

FOOD

There are many small **vineyards** in the hills around Ballarat and throughout Gold Country. The tourist information center can provide detailed information on tastings and tours. Within Ballarat, Sturt St. is lined with fish and chips shops, milk bars, and other takeaway establishments. There are two 24-hour **supermarkets,** a produce shop, and a bakery at the far eastern end of Sturt St. behind the Bridge Mall. There are also several fast-food restaurants, but you can do better than that.

Cafe Bibo, 205 Sturt St. (tel. 5331 1255). Mediterranean snack food and pasta. Excellent coffee and cakes reward those who can tolerate the campy magazine advertisements covering the walls. Takeaway is available. Entrees $4-12. BYO. Open daily 8am until late.

The Pancake Kitchen, 2 Grenville St. (tel. 5331 6555), on the corner of Lewis St. in a restored 1870s building. Bottomless coffee and pancakes in assorted incarnations ($1.50-12). The bottom floor features an open fireplace and a gigantic chess set. Fully licensed, or 80¢ corkage fee for BYO. Open Mon. 9am-midnight, Tues.-Thurs. 10am-midnight, Fri.-Sun. 7:30am-1am.

Inn of Khong, 519 Main Rd., opposite Sovereign Hill (tel. 5331 4088). The dining room features large ceramic figurines of the Buddha and a generic, all-you-can-eat

Asian buffet ($9). Chinese, Thai, and Malaysian dishes, most under $10. BYO and fully licensed. Takeaway and delivery available.

Swaggers Pasta, 107 Bridge Mall (tel. 5333 4311). Sweet and sour, barbecue, and traditional Bolognese. Lunches $5.80, dinners $7.80. Open daily 11:30am-10pm.

SIGHTS

The foremost attraction of its kind in Australia, the **Sovereign Hill** living museum (tel. 5331 1944) celebrates the region's gold rush glory. Actors playing miners mill about in period garb. Marvel as a $50,000 gold ingot is poured before your eyes. Exhibits include a 40-minute tour of the mine which reveals the harsh conditions of mining life (open daily 10am-5pm). Adjacent to Sovereign Hill is the small **Gold Museum.** Informative displays trace the function and importance of gold from the slave pits of the pharaohs to the microcircuitry of today. There are also replicas of the two largest gold nuggets ever found, the Welcome Stranger and Welcome Nugget, both unearthed near Ballarat and weighing in excess of 60kg (open 9:30am-5:20pm). Combined admission to the museum and Sovereign Hill is $17.50, students $13, children $9. Signs throughout Ballarat point the way.

A replica of the **Eureka Stockade** has been erected on Eureka St., several blocks south of Victoria St. on the east side of town. The stockade was the site of the miners' resistance in the Eureka Rebellion of 1854. State forces easily suppressed the uprising with a siege and ensuing battle, but the general discontent eventually led to important reforms in Australian government. One look at the flimsy fortifications explains how the diggers were defeated in a matter of minutes. The fallen rebels are commemorated by an impressive bluestone memorial.

The Eureka rebels fought under the Southern Cross flag, the remains of which can be seen at the **Ballarat Fine Art Gallery,** 40 Lydiard St. (tel. 5331 5622), north of Sturt St. For many years, foreign dignitaries were presented with pieces of the Eureka flag as mementos of their trips to Ballarat. Unfortunately, the tradition left this symbol of Australia's freedom-loving spirit in very poor shape. In addition to the tattered flag, the gallery houses a fine collection of Australian art, concentrating on the goldfields area. (Open daily 10:30am-5pm; guided tours available; admission $4.)

The **Ballarat Wildlife Park** (tel. 5333 5933) is located on the corner of Fussel and York St. Turn right off Victoria St. on to Fussel St. and walk two blocks south. The park's 15 hectares of open bush are home to some of Australia's diverse fauna, including flesh-rending saltwater crocodiles, fearsome Tasmanian devils, and less imposing emus, goannas, wombats, and koalas. Australia's trademark marsupial, the kangaroo, roams free. (Open daily 9am-5pm; guided tours at 11am; admission $9.50, students $7.50, under 15 $4.50.)

One for All and All for Gold

When miners first started working the Ballarat goldfields, the pickings were easy. Alluvial gold, weathered from upstream rocks, was visible to the naked eye in riverbeds and could be mined with nothing more than a shovel and pan. As the easy gold ran out, prospectors began searching for buried riverbeds that might contain gold covered by accumulated deposits. Miners formed small collectives and pooled their resources since individuals could not afford the equipment needed for this primitive underground mining. By 1854, deep lead mining had largely replaced surface methods. As mines went deeper the cost of the supportive timbers and other equipment needed for their maintenance rose, and their profitability declined. Once the majority of the deep leads had been exploited, gold-hungry miners turned to quartz reef mining, a capital-intensive method that extracted gold from quartz ore. Much of this mining occurred below the water table, so massive steam-driven pumps were required to keep the miners from drowning. As with most mining operations, this proved extremely dangerous, and roughly two miners lost their lives each week. WWI marked the end of such intensive mining.

Less wild but just as entertaining is the **Great Southern Woolshed** (tel. 5334 7887), located several kilometers east of Ballarat on the Western Highway. A shrine to the sheep industry, this gigantic shed is insulated with several inches of wool, and is thus cool in summer and warm in winter. Learn about the many varieties of sheep raised in Australia through the entertaining ram parade, and witness the speed and skill of the modern shearer as one unlucky lamb is unceremoniously stripped. Several shops and craftsmen sell wool in various forms. Don't leave before experiencing the **Waltzing Matilda 3D holographic historical diorama**. (Open daily 9:30am-5pm; admission $9, students $7, children $4.)

Portions of Ballarat retain their gold rush charm and are excellent for evening walks. **Lydiard Street** in particular is famous for its Victorian streetscape. Several companies offer guided tours of Ballarat's historic areas. Try **Timeless Tours** (tel. 5342 0652) or **Golden Heritage Walks** (tel. 5333 1632). The **Botanical Gardens** next to Lake Wendourree are also popular with joggers and cyclists. The annual **Ballarat Begonia Festival,** held in early March, is an open-air fair featuring arts and crafts.

For evening entertainment, the **Bridge Mall** at the east end of Sturt St. fills with pedestrians and street musicians on weekends. Numerous hotels and pubs serve as venues for live bands. Popular with locals, the **Provincial Hotel,** at 121 Lydiard St., features pool, video entertainment, and a breathometer to check for drunkenness. At 13 Lydiard St., the historic **Her Majesty's Theatre** presents live drama nightly. Call Majestix (tel. 5333 5888) for information and tickets. **Blood on the Southern Cross** (tel. 5333 5777), an 80-minute sound and light show telling the bitter tale of the Eureka Rebellion, dazzles visitors six nights per week (Mon.-Sat., plus Sun. during holiday periods). Bookings are essential, and reservations made less than two weeks ahead of time require credit card information. Admission $20.50, full-time Australian students $15.50, under 15 $10.50.

Other area attractions include the **Kryal Castle**, a few kilometers past the Woolshed on the Western Highway. It's not an authentic medieval castle, and the reenactments of hangings, jousts, and banquets aren't based on entirely rigorous scholarship. But who says that can't be fun? Dinner theater, magic, and mystery shows spice up this bit of imported lore.

■ Near Ballarat: Clunes

Perhaps the archetype of a Goldfields' town, Clunes enjoyed its heyday in the 1850s. In 1851, this tiny town was the site of the initial discovery that sparked the gold rush in Victoria. Clunes was home to the first profitable Victorian gold mine, established by a British company. Unfortunately, the mine peaked in 1857 and the town has been struggling since. Mines operated into the early 1930s, but far richer deposits of gold were found elsewhere. The two-story **Clunes Museum** (open Sat. 10am-4:30pm and Sun. 11am-4:30pm, admission $2) holds assorted knick-knacks, photographs, and other historical objects. The only budget accommodation option is the **Clunes Caravan Park** (tel. 5345 3278) on Pessell St. (tent sites $8). Clunes is about 30km northwest of Ballarat along the Sunraysia Highway.

Ararat

At the intersection of the Pyrenees and Western Highways, Ararat is just a few kilometers from **Grampians (Gariwerd) National Park** (see p. 497). Most visitors use the town as a base camp for trips into the Gramps. In 1857, a party of 700 Chinese miners discovered gold on the **Canton Lead,** just outside of town on the Western Highway. The discovery caused a massive influx of people—20,000 in two weeks—and spawned the settlement that would become Ararat. A Chinese pagoda is currently being built here.

Practical Information Within town, the Western Hwy. is called **Barkly St.** The **tourist information center** (tel. 5352 2096; fax 5392 1695), located in Town

Hall Square on Barkly St., can provide information on any of the town's attractions and recreational opportunities (open daily 9am-5pm). The **post office** is at 93 Barkly St. (postal code 3377; open Mon.-Fri. 9am-5pm). There are two **banks** on Barkly St. with **ATMs** (both banks open Mon.-Thurs. 9:30am-4pm, Fri. 9:30am-5pm). **V/Line buses** to and from Ararat stop at the BP Station at 10 Ingor St. Buses run to Ballarat (4 per day, $10.90), Stawell (2 per day, $3.30), Melbourne (4 per day, $26.10), and other points in western Victoria.

Accommodations and Food The **Acacia Caravan Park,** 6 Acacia Ave. (tel. 5352 2994) is right in town. A lot of noise intrudes from the nearby highway, but with $7 tent sites, the price is right. The **Grampians Hotel,** 157 Barkly St. (tel. 5352 2393), has private rooms with shared baths for $20. The three-story hotel is definitely aging, but the bathrooms are clean, renovations are on the way, and counter meals are around $5. **Robinson Foodworks,** 102 Barkly St., is a good fully-licensed grocer with decent coffee and takeaway food. For a quick bite (excellent pancakes $5) before a long bus ride, try the friendly **Mt. Langi Ghiron Roadhouse,** adjoining the BP on Ingor St.

Sights and Entertainment Built in the 1860s as a country jail, the infamous **J-Ward** (tel. 5352 3621) was taken over by the Lunacy Department soon after and made into a prison for the criminally insane. It served in this capacity until 1991, but today even sane visitors are allowed to tour (Mon.-Sat. 11am, Sun. 11am, noon, 1, 2, 3pm). The **Alexandra Gardens,** across Girdlestone from J-Ward, bloom with orchids and are an excellent place to regain sanity. The **Lani Morgala Museum** (tel. 5354 2544; from Aboriginal words meaning "home of yesterday"), on the corner of Queen and Barkly St., houses Aboriginal artifacts, old mining implements, photographs, and murals (open Sat. and Sun. 1-4pm or by arrangement; admission $2, children 50¢). More modern works are housed in the **Ararat Gallery,** on the corner of Vincent and High St. (tel. 5352 2836), which specializes in textiles, woven sculpture, and fiber arts. Rotating exhibits of local work supplement the permanent exhibits (open Mon.-Fri. 11am-4pm, Sun. noon-4pm).

There is an **indoor pool** in the YMCA on the corner of Queen and High St. (open to the public Mon.-Fri. 6am-9pm, Sat.-Sun. 8am-6pm; admission $3). The **Ararat Entertainment Center** (tel. 5352 2616) is across the street and screens mainstream Hollywood movies. For something more intellectual, try the **Ararat Municipal Library,** at the intersection of Barkly and Queen St (tel. 5352 1722; open Mon.-Wed. 10:30am-5:30pm, Thurs.-Fri. 10:30am-7pm, Sun. 10am-noon).

Daylesford and Hepburn Springs

Feeling disharmonious? Picking up negative vibrations? Energies out of alignment? If so, the twin townships of Daylesford and Hepburn Springs could be the answer. This region contains the largest concentration of mineral springs in Australia, and has dedicated itself to relaxation and rejuvenation. The springs have been in use since before European settlement, but the scores of guest cottages and B&Bs have sprung up recently, as New Age culture has infused these quiet communities with healing crystals, essences, oils, and aromatherapy. Stressed Melburnians frequent these hillside retreats and the associated gourmet and specialty shops in a steady stream year-round. The spa complex is in Hepburn Springs, while most of the restaurants and services are in Daylesford.

ORIENTATION AND PRACTICAL INFORMATION

Daylesford is 107km northwest of Melbourne, and 45km northeast of Ballarat. **V/Line buses** depart for Melbourne (4 per day, $11.90) and Ballarat (3 per day, $8.40) from **Little's Garage** at 45 Vincent St. in the heart of Daylesford. The **Tourist Information Centre** (tel. 5348 1339) is located several blocks south of the garage and has a listing of local accommodations and information on masseurs, healers, and other indulgences (open daily 9am-5pm). Next door, find the **post office** at 86 Vincent St. (tel. 5348 2101; **fax** service available; open Mon.-Fri. 9am-5pm; postal code 3460). **Public phones** are located outside the post office. ANZ and Commonwealth **banks** are both on Vincent St., and the latter has an **ATM** across from Little's Garage. Emergency (tel. 000), **police** (tel. 5348 2342), and **medical** (tel. 5348 2371).

Hepburn Springs is about 2km north of Daylesford. Buses run between the two towns throughout the week ($1.50), but it is an easy, pleasant walk.

ACCOMMODATIONS AND FOOD

Most of the area's lovely guest cottages and B&Bs will set you back $80-100 per night. The **Hepburn Springs Caravan Park** (tel. 5348 3161) is considerably cheaper, and closer to the springs (tent sites $8, with power $10). **Continental House,** 9 Lone Pine Ave. (tel. 5348 2005), described by some of its patrons as a living work of art, hides behind a dense 5m hedge just a few hundred meters from the spa. Refresh yourself at this strictly vegetarian, strictly relaxed guesthouse. Large, tranquil common areas (singles $18, doubles $40, call ahead for reservations). The Continental House's resident eatery, the **Strange Fruit Cafe,** provides biodynamically and organically sound meals for guests on Saturday nights or when the place is busy.

Other spiritually enlightened aliments are proffered at **Naturally Fine Foods,** 59-61 Vincent St. (tel. 5348 3109), which serves mountainous veggie burgers ($6), veggie pies and cakes, and bulk dried goods. **The Food Gallery,** 77 Vincent St. (tel. 5348 1077) caters to carnivores and herbivores alike. Gourmet breakfast and takeaway items cost $7-10. Of the many fish and chips shops on Vincent St., **Town Hall Takeaway,** 74 Vincent St. (delivery tel. 5313 1481) has the best selection and most reasonable prices (sandwiches and assorted fried items $2-4). The **Cosy Corner Cafe,** 3 10th St. in Hepburn Springs (tel. 5348 3825) is a little nicer, a little more expensive, and a lot more popular with locals. (Hip pasta and veggie creations $10-15, BYO. Book ahead for weekends.)

SIGHTS AND ENTERTAINMENT

Most visitors come to Hepburn Springs to take advantage of the curative properties of its waters. The **Hepburn Spa Resort** (tel. 5348 2034; fax 5348 1167), located next to the springs, provides massages, spas, facials, and even "radionically prepared electrohomeopathic baths." Services are pricey, but spring waters are free for the taking.

In Daylesford, the **Wombat Hill Botanical Gardens** offer pleasant grounds for strolling, while the **Pioneer Memorial** tower on top of the hill affords views of the rolling countryside. The excellent **Convent Gallery** (tel. 5348 3211) occupies the side of the hill and showcases many local artists' work. In the 19th century, the convent served as a reform school for girls. Today, it has been beautifully restored as a gallery and landscaped with lush, terraced gardens (open 10am-6pm; admission $3).

The **Hepburn Regional Park** surrounds much of Daylesford and Hepburn Springs and lures tourists with its excellent walking trails. Many relics of the gold rush days are visible, but others are less so—take care to avoid plunging into an abandoned shaft. Areas along the path are set aside for picnics and barbecues, and trail maps are available at the tourist information center.

Castlemaine

After hitting its peak in the gold rush era, Castlemaine did not have the sustained natural resources of neighboring Ballarat and Bendigo, and so could not share in their development. But this small town has its own history to share, and the explosion of blossoming color and fragrance in the gardens each spring draws many to town. Castlemaine is located 120km from Melbourne in the central Goldfields.

Orientation and Practical Information To get to Castlemaine, take a bus from Melbourne's Spencer St. Station (3 depart daily). From Castlemaine, **V/Line** has bus and train service to Melbourne ($14.80), Bendigo ($10.60), Maldon ($2.40), Ballarat ($6.70), and Maryborough ($8.60). By car, take Hwy. 79, the Calder Hwy., to Elphinstone, then take Hwy. 122, the Pyrenees Hwy., to Castlemaine.

V/Line originates from the **railway station,** which faces the town's center. Kennedy, Barker, Hargraves, and Urquhart St. run north to south, and Templeton, Lyttleton, Mostyn, and Forest St. run east to west. The **tourist office** is a kiosk located on the Pyrenees Hwy. just a block from where it becomes Forest St. (Open daily 10am-4pm, lists of accommodations posted outside for after-hours perusal.)

Accommodations and Food It's tough to grab a cheap bed in Castlemaine, so overnight guests may prefer less expensive Maryborough (44km west) or a return to Melbourne. Castlemaine's most unique accommodation is a cell in the **Old Castlemaine Gaol** (tel. 5470 5311; fax 5470 5097), atop the hill to the west of the railroad station. Cars coming from Melbourne can drive beneath the Forest St. railroad bridge and take the second right onto Bowden St. Built in 1861, the jail held inmates until 1990, when it was converted into a well-heated and ventilated B&B. The iron catwalks and small cells of the gaol have been preserved and the latter, now carpeted, contain 130 bunks that allow guests to slumber in the slammer. Don't fear, the subterranean wine bar, breakfast and dinner dining room, billiards table, TV room, and comfy sofas will make your "hard time" an enjoyable sentence. (Fri.-Sun. nights only, $45 for bunk and cooked breakfast, $65 with dinner. V, MC, AmEx accepted; fraud discouraged. Reservations suggested 1 month in advance.)

A simpler accommodation—clean, quiet, and generally delightful—is the **Castlemaine Gardens Caravan Park** (tel. 5472 1125), with tent sites and on-site caravans available. The park has laundry facilities, toilets, a 50m pool, picnic and BBQ facilities, and even two cabins with bathrooms. (Tent sites $10; powered caravan sites $11.50; on-site caravans $26 single, $31 double. Cabins $40 single, $45 double. Wheelchair accessible. V, MC.)

You'll find a slightly more up-market lodging at the **Bookshop Cottage B&B,** 242 Barker St. (tel. 5472 1557; fax 5470 5008), two blocks north of the city center. Behind a bookstore specializing in Australiana, this 1857 cottage is among the most spacious B&Bs available with a master bedroom, small child's room, kitchen, living room, and generous bathroom all tastefully decorated with a blend of Victorian-era antiquity and colorful modern amenities. (Doubles $70. Breakfast included, but not prepared. V, MC. Reserve 3-4 weeks in advance for weekend stays.)

Hungry? Markets run the length of Mostyn St. including the **supermarket** (open Mon.-Fri. 7:30am-9pm, Sat. 7:30am-5pm, Sun. 9am-5pm). Fish shops also dot Mostyn St., while bistros line nearby Hargraves St. For a treat, pick up a can of **Barnes' Castlemaine Rock** ($3). This golden-colored peppermint candy has been made in town since the 1850s. Sorry, no factory tours.

Sights and Activities The Castlemaine **Botanic Gardens,** six blocks north of the railway station at the end of Kennedy St., possess a rich array of cypress trees, along with rose bushes, a central pond, and even BBQ facilities for visitors to enjoy. The biennial Garden Festival celebrates the blossoming of the city in November of odd years, alternating with the Castlemaine Arts Festival, held in even years. Both festivals are Victoria-wide events, attracting spectators from all over the state.

The newly renovated **Castlemaine Market Complex,** an historic market and pleasant courtyard, offers local wares and shady resting spots (in the city's heart on Mostyn St. between Barker and Hargraves St.). A 10-minute walk north up Urquhart St. leads to the **Buda Historic House,** a period home with decorative arts and antiques dating to the 1860s. The adjacent gardens and cafe are enjoyable in all seasons but particularly rapturous in springtime. (Open Mon.-Fri. 10am-5pm, Sat.-Sun. noon-5pm. Admission $5, concessions $3.50, children $2, families $12. V, MC, AmEx.)

The **Castlemaine Art Gallery and Historic Museum**, located on Lyttleton St. between Kennedy and Barker St., displays strong collections of "Golden Period" (late 19th century) Australian art and artifacts, as well as more recent paintings, ceramics, and metalwork by local artists. A **monument** to ill-fated Australian explorers **Burke and Wills** sits perched off Lyttleton St. four blocks east of downtown.

Maldon

Named Victoria's "first notable city" by the National Trust in 1966, Maldon presents the best preserved and most extensive array of gold rush era buildings in the state. Most of these rough-and-tumble 19th-century prospector buildings are clustered around the intersection of Main and High St., their corrugated tin canopies shading strolling visitors. This collection of tea rooms, country collectible shops, blacksmiths, and small town grocers harkens back to the town's golden age, but are geared toward a somewhat up-market crowd. Many Maldon attractions are focused at the weekend tourist market and close during the week, so plan your visit accordingly.

Orientation and Practical Information The **Visitors Information Centre** (tel. 5475 2569) on High St., in the tan brick building, offers invaluable brochures including maps, walking tours with descriptions of the preserved buildings, and guides to nearby mining and park attractions (open daily 10am-4pm). Although Maldon lacks ATMs, the **bank** at 59 High St. will **exchange currency** (open Mon. and Wed.-Thurs. 11am-4pm, Fri. 11am-5pm). To get to Maldon, take the **V/Line** from Castlemaine (3 per day, $2.40). The **post office** north of the Visitors Centre on High St. has *Poste Restante* (open Mon.-Fri. 9am-5pm, Sat. 8:30-11am; postal code 3463).

Accommodation and Food Maldon's B&Bs can be pricey, but may be worth a splurge for visitors enamored with the period feel and small town atmosphere. The **Maldon Caravan and Camping Park** (tel. 5475 2344) on Hospital St., northwest along High St., offers a wide range of shelters with toilets and BBQ facilities. (Tent sites $5 per person; on-site caravans $29 for 2; cabins $43 for 2. Multiple night discounts.) Behind Main St., the **Derby Hill Accommodation Centre** (tel. 5475 2033) on Phoenix St. provides weekend lodging in a new, funky, and functional wood and concrete youth camp. Units are centrally heated and include a TV, linens, crockery, utensils, and complimentary coffee and tea in a kitchenette. (Singles $35; doubles $60. Fri.-Sun. only.) The tea shops along Main and High St. provide light lunch fare, with slightly cheaper grub served at the milk bars or fish and chip shops.

Sights and Activities Adjacent to the visitor center, amateur historians may enjoy the **Maldon Museum and Archives** (tel. 5475 1633) which displays local artifacts from the 1850s to the early 20th century. (Open Mon.-Fri. 1:30pm-4pm, Sat.-Sun. 1:30pm-5pm. Admission $2, children 50¢, families $5.) For a bird's-eye view of Maldon, follow High St. north to the signs for **Mt. Tarrangower,** which rises 570m above sea level from the geographic center of Victoria. The windblown iron **lookout tower** enables daring souls to ascend an additional 24m. On a clear day, you can see more than 50km in all directions. During Easter, the entire tower is illuminated. South of Maldon, toward Newstead off the Pyrenees Hwy., is **Carman's Tunnel Goldmine** (tel. 5475 2667), where gold-hungry tourists can view the remnants of a rich mine (open Sat.-Sun. 1:30-4pm). The **Vintage Railway steam train** (tel. 5475 1427), located off Hornsby St., north along Main St., runs the 8km trip to Muckleford (Sat.-Sun. 12:30-3:30pm; round-trip $9, ages 4-15 $5, families $25). **Seasonal highlights** in Maldon include its colorful Easter festivities and the annual influx of musicians and performers for the early November Folk Festival.

Maryborough

Zippy, modernized Maryborough contrasts pleasantly with its central goldfield neighbors' sleepiness. The town's most impressive attraction, the **Maryborough Railway Station,** is a stately Victorian structure somewhat out of place in the suburban bustle. Famous for **Mark Twain's** remark that Maryborough was a railway station with a town attached, the station now serves as the **Central Goldfields Tourist Centre** (tel. 5460 4511; open daily 10am-6pm). Inside, there's an adjoining antique emporium and cafe. **V/Line** departs for Melbourne from the car park behind the building on Clarendon St. (5 per day, 1hr., $8.60) and Castlemaine (3 per day, 1hr., $5.80). Tickets can be purchased at **Hoober's Meals/Tahiti Coffee Lounge** (tel. 5461 1527) on High St. The **post office** (open Mon.-Fri. 9am-5pm) is on Campbell St. behind the Bull and Mouth Hotel (postal code 3465).

Maryborough offers numerous inexpensive accommodations for those interested in visiting nearby Maldon (33km), Castlemaine (43km), and gold prospecting areas. The **Bull and Mouth Hotel** (tel. 5461 1002) on High and Nolan St. offers no-nonsense, practical accommodations above the pub. The clean, high-ceilinged rooms come with electric blankets and closets. Mark Twain stayed here during his Maryborough visit and chided town leaders who wanted a chiming clock tower, since Bendigo's had prevented him from his morning repose. (Singles $18, with bath $25; doubles $30, $37. V, MC.) Farther along High St., the **Albion Motel** (tel. 5461 1035) offers slightly more upscale rooms with bath, continental breakfast, fridge, electric blanket, TV, and car park in earthtone and brick surrounds. The amiable owner claims to have Victoria's second-best cricket-theme bar (singles $40; doubles $60; triples $70; V, MC). Check at the visitor center for additional listings of caravan parks and inexpensive hotels.

Bendigo

During the rush of the 1850s, Bendigo was one of the country's most lucrative goldfields. The easy surface gold was depleted a century ago, but Bendigo sits atop many fortunes of gold trapped in massive quartz reefs. Mines operated commercially in Bendigo from 1851 to 1954, and during that time 25 million ounces of gold were taken from the ground. Recent geological exploration has revealed that at least that much is still under the city. The early gold money allowed the city planners to indulge their Victorian fancy; the public buildings are grand and Gothic, the boulevards broad, and the parks full of fountains and statuary. Nostalgia prompted the adoption of English names, resulting in Pall Mall and Charing Cross in the city center. Bendigo still celebrates its history, but is by no means stuck in the past.

ORIENTATION

Bendigo is a combination of wide, well-planned streets and winding gold gullies originally packed down by the trampings of diggers' feet. Most of the points of interest are near the city center, bounded on the south and east by the railroad tracks and on the north by Rosalind Park. The **Calder Highway** (which leads eventually to Melbourne) runs through the center of town and changes names a few times along the way (from southwest to northeast it's named Calder Hwy., **High St., Pall Mall,** McRae St., Napier St., and then the Midland Hwy. to Elmore). **Rosalind Park** is to the north of this thoroughfare, while **Hargreaves St.** runs parallel to the south. Mitchell St. runs perpendicular to High and Hargreaves St., heading south toward the **transit center.** This bus and train station is in the **Market Place Discovery Centre,** which also contains a shopping mall and supermarket. Bendigo Creek, a pathetic trickle enclosed by massive concrete banks, struggles along parallel to the highway.

PRACTICAL INFORMATION

Tourist Office: (tel. 5444 4445), on Pall Mall. Located in the gigantic old post office building (no longer a post office). Interactive computer displays provide informa-

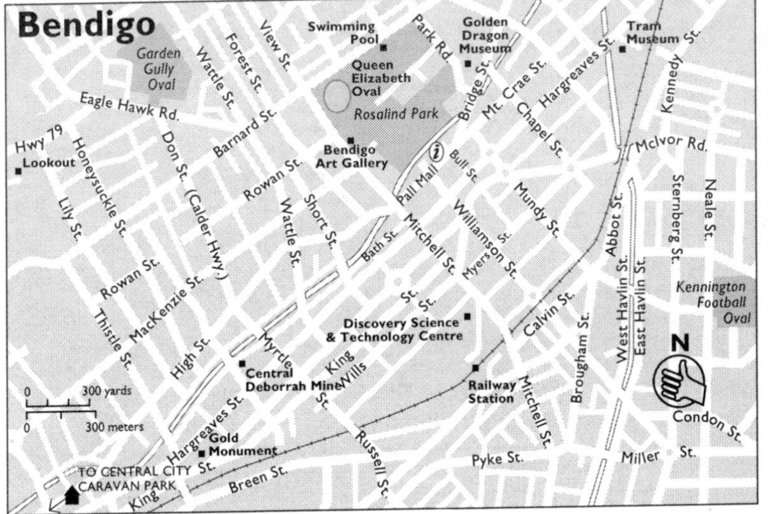

tion on history, gold production, nightlife, and local culture. From the train station, walk down Railway Pl. to Mitchell St. and turn left. Proceed along Mitchell until you reach Pall Mall, then turn right. The center is on the park side of the street in the large Gothic building. Open daily 9am-5pm.

Currency Exchange: National Bank and its ATM, on the corner of Queen and Mitchell St., are open Mon.-Thurs. 9:30am-4pm, Fri. 9:30am-5pm. Other **ATMs** can be found on Pall Mall and throughout the city center.

Trains and Buses: Transit Center is in the Market Place Discovery Centre at the south end of Mitchell St. Recorded information is available (tel. 005 539 295), and reservations can be made statewide (tel. 13 22 32), or at the Regional Center in Bendigo (tel. 5440 2765). You can purchase bus tickets on board if there are empty seats. Rail and/or coach service connects Ballarat (Sun.-Fri. 1 per day, 2½hr., $17.50), Geelong (Mon.-Fri. 1 per day, 3½hr., $28.40), Adelaide (1 per day, 8½hr., $49), Mildura (1 per day, 6hr., $45.50), and Swan Hill (1 per day, 2¼hr., $22.60). Bookings Mon.-Fri. 5:35am-8pm, Sat. 6:50am-4pm, Sun. 7:05am-2:25pm.

Car Rental: Budget, 150-152 High St. (tel. 5442 2766; fax 5441 5859). **Thrifty,** 90 Wand St. (tel. 5446 7000; fax 5446 9897).

Public Market: There is a **Safeway Supermarket,** as well as many specialized retail shops in the Bendigo Marketplace, next to the train station off Mitchell St.

Laundromat: 39 View St. (tel. 5441 8877), next to Rosalind Park. Open daily 6am-9pm.

Public Library: Hargreaves St. (tel. 5443 5100). Books, magazines, and free internet access. Inquire at the desk to book internet time. Open Mon., Wed., and Fri. 9:30am-8:30pm, Tues. and Thurs. 9:30am-6pm, Sat. 9am-noon.

Internet Access: The library and **Innet Cafe,** 66 Pall Mall (tel. 5442 3177), opposite the tourist information center. $5 per hr. Telnet, email, www, chat, games. Open daily 11am-7pm.

Police: Dial 5440 2555.

Emergency: Dial 000.

Phone Code: 03.

ACCOMMODATIONS AND FOOD

The only real budget lodging option is the **Central City Caravan Park,** 362 High St. (tel./fax 5443 6937), next to the Subaru dealership. This is the most central of the several caravan parks, and 2.5km south of the Alexandra Fountain. Formerly a YHA-associated facility, the management decided to sever the connection, but hostel beds are still available. There are two sets of bunks in each of six small rooms, but the owners allow single occupancy when possible. Showers and a small kitchen are in separate buildings. There are electric barbecues and a pool, and most of the tent sites are well-shaded. Hostel beds and sites cost $12.

Many of the first immigrants to work on the Bendigo goldfields were Chinese, and one of the many lasting reminders of the Asian presence is the variety and diversity of Chinese restaurants. There are many good ones to choose from; the **Imperial Palace Food Court** (tel. 5443 4329), on the corner of Forest and High St. is fully licensed, delivers for free, and has freshly prepared lunchboxes ($4.50; V, MC). Most main dishes cost less than $10 (open Mon.-Sat. 11am-2pm, also Sun.-Thurs. 5-10pm and Fri.-Sat. 5-11:30pm). **The Turkish Kitchen,** 289 Lyttleton Tce. (tel. 5441 1556), is too small to house diners, but serves extremely affordable dips, salads, kebabs, and Turkish pastries for takeaway. Almost everything is less than $5 (open Mon.-Sat. 11am-9pm). **Rasoyee,** 40-42 High St. (tel. 5441 1530), is a popular Indian restaurant with a good selection of vegetarian dishes, curries, and tasty breads. Main dishes run $7 to $10, and the restaurant is BYO licensed. Bendigo's own **Gillies Brothers** make a mean meat pie; their window is in the middle of the Hargreaves Mall.

SIGHTS AND ENTERTAINMENT

The **Central Deborah Mine,** 76 Violet St., was the last mine to operate commercially in Bendigo and one of the very few that continued operations right through WWII. Although no longer a commercial mine, it is still operational. Tours take visitors 61m down to the second level where mining history and techniques are explained and, in some cases, demonstrated. On the surface, much of the original processing equipment has been preserved and displayed, including a gigantic, evil-looking stamper battery (mine tours start at 9:30am daily and cost $13). The prosperous mines of the late 19th century allowed Bendigo to install a state-of-the-art **tram** system, and a portion of the original network, along with an impressive collection of trams, has been preserved. During the day, tram tours regularly pass through the center of town and feature recorded commentary (1hr., $7.50). In keeping with the efforts to establish an antipodean London, **double-decker buses** also tour the town's major attractions (1hr., $7). Combined mine/tram tickets cost $18.50. The whole Central Deborah tourist empire is open daily from 9am to 5pm.

The **Golden Dragon Museum** (tel. 5441 5044), on Bridge St., presents the history of the Chinese population in Bendigo from the early gold rush days. There has always been some discrimination and prejudice in the relationship between European and Asian gold-diggers, but one bright spot in the troubled history of race relations has been the **Bendigo Easter Fair.** Early in the history of the Fair, a Chinese imperial dragon, "Loong," became an important part of the procession on Easter Monday. Loong has been retired, but its heir Sun Loong (the **longest imperial dragon in the world**) is still a favorite part of the Easter parade, and a vibrant symbol of the contributions made by Bendigo's Chinese population. In addition to Loong and Sun Loong, the museum houses artifacts and memorabilia from the early days. Adjacent to the museum is the recently completed Chinese garden, a tranquil courtyard patterned after formal Chinese landscaping. (Museum and garden open daily 9:30am-5pm; museum and garden admission $6, children $3. Garden alone $2, children 50¢.)

The **Bendigo Art Gallery,** 42 View St. (tel. 5443 4991; fax 5443 6586), was established in 1887, but the building has been altered several times, most recently in 1962, a grim time for architectural change. Collections of Australian art dating back to the goldfields are supplemented by an assortment of European works. The gallery shop deals in locally produced handicrafts and prints (admission $2, concessions $1; free guided tours on Wed.-Thurs. and Sat.-Sun. 2:15 and 3:15pm).

MURRAY RIVER

Australia's longest river, the Murray rambles along the New South Wales-Victoria border for 2600km before meeting the sea in South Australia's Encounter Bay. The river served as an important transportation artery in the days before extensive rail and road networks, but the giant paddlesteamers that once churned these waters became obsolete by the end of the 1930s. The power of nostalgia saved many paddlesteamers from rot and disrepair, reincarnating them as tourist attractions. The river is a favorite spot for picnicking, water sports, fishing, and all manner of family fun. In addition to its recreational value, the river feeds a productive agriculture of vegetables and fruits (including wine grapes) through a complex irrigation system. Both the vineyards so watered and the glowing memories of days gone by draw romantics to the grand Murray.

Echuca

Echuca was once Australia's largest inland port, with fleets of paddlesteamers plying the Murray. The closest point to Melbourne along the river, it was a clearinghouse for the wool and agricultural products of southern New South Wales. A massive redgum wharf was built to accommodate the paddlesteamers and barges, and a lively array of hotels, brothels, and breweries was built to accommodate the men who sailed them. Many of the steamers have been preserved, even after river traffic declined in the late 1800s, and Echuca now possesses the world's largest flotilla of side-wheel paddlesteamers. The boats and the river are centerpieces of a bustling tourist industry.

ORIENTATION AND PRACTICAL INFORMATION

Echuca is about 200km north of Melbourne, on the Northern Hwy. The town straddles two rivers, with the **Campaspe River** on a north-south alignment, and the **Murray River** on an east-west. Most shops and services can be found on **Hare** and **High St.,** parallel roads that run from the Murray to the Murray Valley Hwy. The **Visitor Information Centre,** 2 Heygarth St. (tel. 5480 7555 or 1800 804 446; fax 5482 6413), is at the northern end of Hare St. right on the Murray River. The staff can assist in booking accommodation (open daily 9am-5pm). The visitor center is also the **bus depot.** V/Line has buses to Melbourne (3 per day, 3hr., $26.10), Bendigo (2 per day, 1¾hr., $6), Kerang (Mon., Wed., Thurs., and Sun., 1 per day, 1¼hr., $10.90), Swan Hill (Mon., Wed., Thurs., and Sun., 2¼hr., $17.50), and Mildura (Mon., Wed., Thurs., and Sat., 6hr., $33.20). The **post office** is on the corner of Hare and Anstruther St. (open Mon.-Fri. 9am-5pm; postal code 3564). **ANZ** and **Commonwealth banks** with **ATMs** are diagonally across from the post office on Hare St. (both banks open Mon.-Thurs. 9:30am-4pm, Fri. 9:30am-5pm).

ACCOMMODATION

The **Echuca Gardens Hostel,** 103 Mitchell St. (tel. 5480 6522), is just a few hundred meters from the wharf. The YHA-affiliated hostel is set behind a bed and breakfast, next to a pleasant garden courtyard filled with fountains and fruit trees. There is a small kitchen and a cozy, smartly appointed lounge. Dorms start at $15.

The other budget option near town is the **Echuca Caravan Park** (tel. 5482 2157) on Crofton St. This gigantic, park-like facility is run by the local government, and is often choked with campervans. Tent sites ($13) are well-shaded and grassy. Cabins sleep five and cost $55 (bathroom attached); on-site caravans sleep five or six and cost $40 (separate bathrooms).

SIGHTS AND ENTERTAINMENT

The main attraction in Echuca is the historic **port** (tel. 5482 4248; fax 5482 6951), which consists of the **redgum wharf** and several historic buildings right next to it (admission $7, students $5). The wharf itself, built in 1865 of local redgum from nearby Barmah forest, has three levels to accommodate the changing river conditions, with a steam-driven sawmill on the top level. The mill was used in its day to process redgum logs right off the river and is still fully functional. There are also blacksmith and woodturning shops, only too happy to sell you their handmade wares. Several old hotels are on display. The **Star Hotel** is equipped with a secret underground tunnel in case the festivities of old got out of hand, and the **Bridge Hotel,** Echuca's first, boasts a carefully preserved suite and gallery upstairs.

The most popular thing to do at the port is to take a cruise on a **paddlesteamer.** There are four or five operators, but only the *Pevensey* and *Alexander Arbuthnot* still use wood to power their boilers. Tickets are available at the main port ticket office ($10, students $5). Package deals are also available, combining wharf admission and an hour-long cruise ($16, students $9; port and steamers open daily 9am-5pm).

Adjacent to the port, **Sharp's Magic Movie House and Penny Arcade** (tel. 5482 2361; fax 5480 1881) houses Australia's largest collection of working penny arcade machines. Also on display is an array of antique cinematic equipment, along with continuous screenings of old newsreels, comedy shorts, and historical documentaries (open daily 9am-5pm; admission $8.50, children $5.50, which includes the movies and a modest supply of pennies for the arcade machines).

Although not particularly relevant to the history of the Murray, the **World in Wax Museum** (tel. 5482 3630) near the port on High St., can provide great fun if approached with the right attitude. Figures include dignitaries both foreign and domestic, arranged by era and disposition (Stalin, Hitler, Castro, and Churchill share a case). Other displays include Mao Tse-Tung, Count Dracula, and, of course, Dolly Parton (open daily 9am-5:30pm; admission $6, students $5).

■ Near Echuca

BARMAH STATE PARK AND STATE FOREST

The Barmah State Park and State Forest is the largest redgum forest in Victoria. The forest is located in the Murray's floodplain, so much of it is either permanently or periodically inundated. Located 27km from Echuca, the forest is well-endowed with roads and walking tracks, but rain and high water levels can render many of them impassable. The **Dharnya Centre** (tel. 5869 3302; fax 5869 3249), on Sand Ridge Rd. near the park entrance, 9km north of the township of Barmah, can provide information on road conditions and should be visited before venturing into the bottomlands. The center contains displays exploring the complex ecology of the swamp-forest and the history and culture of the Aboriginal Yorta Yorta people (open daily 10:30am-4pm; access to the interpretive portion $2, students $1). Camping is free and abundant in the park. The Barmah Lakes area has basic facilities (toilet, fireplace), and there are many likely spots on Barmah Island. Fishing is excellent in the park, and licenses are not required for angling in the Murray. When water levels are high enough, the wetlands can be explored by boat. **Kingfisher Wetland Cruises** (tel. 5869 3399; fax 5869 3388) offers two-hour trips (Mon., Wed., Thurs., and Sun. 12:30pm; $15, children $10). **Gondwana Canoe Hire** (tel. 5869 3347), on Moira Lakes Rd. on the way to the park entrance from Barmah, provides canoes for private trips. Transportation from Echuca and trip-planning can be provided, and detailed river charts come with each canoe (rental $15 per hr., half-day $25, full day $40, 2 days $70). Note that dry conditions may make canoeing the park impossible. Just up the road from the canoe shop, the **Barmah Lakes Gallery** (tel. 5869 3358; fax 5869 3387) is a tranquil little cottage that displays locally produced woodwork and gourd paintings (open Wed.-Mon. 10am-4pm).

KERANG

The tiny township of Kerang, between Echuca and Swan Hill, is surrounded by lakes teeming with waterbirds. **Middle Lake** serves as a rookery for huge flocks of ibis, and a shelter has been built to allow visitors to view the birds without disturbing them. The **Kerang Caravan Park** (tel. 5452 1161) is in the middle of town right on the Murray River on Riverwood Dr. Unpowered sites with full amenities cost $11. Cabins and on-site caravans are an option if you're traveling with a group (caravans $30, cabins $42). The **Gunbower Creek,** a few kilometers east of Kerang, is another popular area for bird-watching and swamp-rambling. To see the wetland in air-conditioned style, book a cruise on **The Wetlander** (tel. 5453 3000; fax 5453 2697), off Koondrook-Cahuna Rd. on Oris Rd. (also called Southern Rd.). Two-hour cruises leave daily, except Thursday at 2pm ($15, children $8; tours run Aug. 14-May 16).

Swan Hill

Located on the Murray River about 340km northwest of Melbourne, Swan Hill is a tranquil little rural city, a perfect spot for families, caravaners, and anybody else who values peace over energy. The area is thick with nurseries, craft shops, tea rooms, wineries, and other passive pastimes. This section of the Murray is used for fishing and water sports; many people like to cruise up and down the river on rented houseboats.

Practical Information and Accommodations **The Swan Hill Development and Information Centre,** 306 Campbell St. (tel. 5032 3033 or 1800 625 373; fax 5032 3032), on the main drag one block west of the river, provides both tourist information and development propaganda (open Mon.-Fri. 9am-5pm, Sat.-Sun. 9am-4pm). There is a **National Bank** and **ATM** just up and across the street (open Mon.-Thurs. 9:30am-4pm, Fri. 9:30am-5pm). Swan Hill is the northern terminus of **passenger rail service** to Melbourne; trains leave daily (4½hr., $42.10). The **station** is on Curlewis St., between McCrane and Rutherford St., near the Giant Murray Cod. **Coach service** is available to points along the Murray: Mildura (Mon., Wed., Thurs., and Sat., 3hr., $28.40), Echuca (Tues., Wed., Fri., and Sun., 2hr., $17.50), Shepparton (Tues., Wed., Fri., and Sun., 4¼hr., $28.40), and Albury-Wodonga (Tues., Wed., Fri., and Sun., 7¼hr., $38.50). The **Swan Hill District Hospital** (tel. 5432 1111) is on Splatt St., and the **RACV** (tel. 5433 1555) is at 7 Pritchard St. The **post office,** 164 Campbell St., is across from the bank at the intersection with McCallum (open Mon.-Fri. 9am-5pm, Sat. 9am-noon; postal code 3585).

Swan Hill is primarily a family destination, so budget accommodations are somewhat limited. The best bet is the **Swan Hill Riverside Caravan Park,** 1 Manash Dr. (tel./fax 5032 1494), on the river adjacent to the Pioneer Settlement. The office doubles as a small grocery, and bikes are available for hire. The large park features an electric BBQ pit, swimming pool, and squadrons of noisy parrots and waterbirds to awaken guests in the morning. Tent sites cost $11.

Sights The **Horseshoe Bend Pioneer Settlement** (tel. 5032 1093; fax 5032 1096) is the oldest outdoor museum in Australia, and started a wave of heritage attractions and recreations. The settlement's seven acres are carefully stocked with original buildings and equipment, transported from their original locations and reassembled in Swan Hill. A full century of history (1830-1930) is represented, giving a comprehensive if anachronistic picture of frontier agricultural settlements. Many old-fashioned shops and services are staffed by costumed personnel, who also enact uproarious street theater at regular intervals. Paddle-steamers cruise the river along the banks of the settlement, and nighttime brings the **Mallee Heritage Sound and Light Show.** (Settlement admission $12, children $6. River cruises $8, children $4. Sound and light show $8, children $4. Package tickets for all 3 sights $23, children $12. Open daily 8:30am-5pm.)

Swan Hill is proud of its excellent fishing. That pride is given rock-solid substance by the **Giant Murray Cod,** quite possibly the largest Murray Cod in the world, towering over its living brethren. The statue measures 6m by 11m by 6m, and was originally built as a prop for the movie *Eight Ball.* It now guards the northern end of the rail station on Curlewis St. The **Swan Hill Art Gallery** is housed in a mud-brick structure adjacent to the Pioneer Settlement. Exhibitions change regularly, but the emphasis is on the Australian countryside (open Mon.-Fri. 10am-5pm, Sat.-Sun. 11am-5pm).

Mildura

With wide, palm-lined streets, Mildura is an oasis in the middle of dry Mallee country in the extreme northwest corner of Victoria. The area was settled in 1887 by the brothers Chaffey, Canadians who had established irrigation communities in California and repeated their successes here. The cleverly-harnessed waters of the Murray support thriving citrus groves and make Mildura one of Australia's most productive fruit-growing areas. This is one of the sunniest parts of Australia, and were it not for the massive irrigation system, the landscape would be as arid as the outback which marches north and west to the horizon. Enjoy it while you're here; Mildura is the last bastion of green foliage for a long, long time.

ORIENTATION AND PRACTICAL INFORMATION

Mildura, as an irrigation community, was thoroughly planned before being built, and it is laid out in a regular grid pattern on the southern bank of the Murray. The **Mildura Visitor Information and Booking Centre,** 180-190 Deakin Ave. (tel. 5021 4424, booking desk tel. 1800 039 043), is housed in the brand new Alfred Deakin Centre. A strange statue resembling a brass tornado is outside this gigantic center, and inside there are more unorthodox decorations and the public library, which has **internet access** (library tel. 5023 5011; info center open Mon.-Fri. 9am-9:30pm, Sat.-Sun. 9am-5pm). There is an **ANZ bank** (tel. 5023 9200) on the corner of Eighth and Deakin St. with an **ATM** (office open Mon.-Thurs. 9:30am-4pm, Fri. 9:30am-5pm).

The **railway station** and **bus depot** is on Seventh St., near the river (from Deakin Ave. turn left onto Seventh; booking office open Mon.-Fri. 7am-5:30pm and 8pm-9pm, Sat. 9am-11am). Service to Melbourne (daily, 6½hr., $52), Echuca (Tue., Wed., Fri., and Sun., 5hr., $33.20), Swan Hill (daily, 3hr., $28.40), Bendigo (daily, 5hr., $45.50), Ballarat (Sun.-Fri., 5hr., $45.50), and Broken Hill (Wed. and Fri., $37). **Sunraysia Transit** has daily buses to Adelaide ($39) and Sydney ($77). Mildura Associated **taxis** are on call 24 hours (tel. 5023 0033).

A friendly **supermarket** is on Deakin Ave., just a few blocks north of the Visitor Information Centre. The **police station** (tel. 5023 9555) is on Madden St., between Eighth and Ninth St. The **Mildura Private Hospital** (tel. 5022 2611) is located at 220 Thirteenth St. In an **emergency,** dial 000. The Mildura **post office** is on the corner of Eighth and Deakin Ave. (open Mon.-Fri. 9am-5pm; postal code 3500). Dial **03** when ringing Mildura from outside the region.

ACCOMMODATION AND FOOD

The best place to stay in Mildura is the YHA-affiliated **Rosemont Guest House,** 154 Madden Ave. (tel./fax 5023 1935), one block east of Deakin Ave. off Eleventh St. A traditional guest house with fragrant gardens and a swimming pool, Rosemont combines hostel and B&B-style rooms. Dual kitchens and numerous showers ensure that everyone's basic needs are met. There's free coffee and tea; generous breakfasts are available for $3. Most of the hostel beds are singles or twin share ($15, weekly $90; YHA non-members $3 more per night). Fancier rooms can also be had (twin room with bath $42). The affable manager can book tours of the outback and nearby national parks (no commission, often with a YHA discount), and provides job search assistance during the fruit-picking seasons. **Mildura International Backpackers,** 5 Cedar Ave. (tel. 5021 0133), one block east of Deakin Ave. between Eleventh and

Twelfth St., is a hostel designed with the migrant worker in mind. Rooms are basic and the demeanor of the place is very proletarian. The height of fruit-picking season is February and March, but limited agricultural employment is available through most of the year. This is the place for information from experienced pickers. The place remains friendly despite its functionality, and it has a full kitchen, laundry, BBQ facilities, and cable TV. Rental bikes are available (beds $13; weekly $80).

Mildura is a typical country city when it comes to cuisine, but there are a few bright spots. The **Mildura Workingman's Club** (tel. 5023 0531), on Deakin Ave. just north of the YHA hostel, provides value family meals in a classic Aussie atmosphere. Large meals are available for less than $10, although variety is not the restaurant's strong suit (open daily). For a respite from roasted meats, try the Chinese takeaway **Jackie's Corner** (tel. 5023 7744), on the corner of Eighth and Deakin St. While far from dainty or gourmet, the joint's $5 lunch boxes get the job done (open Mon.-Sat. 11:30am-2:30pm and 5-10pm, Sun. 5-10pm). There are several more upscale options in the Langtree Avenue Mall, one block west of Deakin between Eighth and Ninth St. The **Club Langtree Cafe,** 32 Langtree Ave. (tel. 5023 2336), is open late and serves Greek-inspired pasta, souvlaki, and insanely popular foccacia. The cafe is near several nightclubs; in keeping with the neighborhood, the P.A. emits occasional eruptions of dance music that may startle unwary diners.

SIGHTS AND ENTERTAINMENT

Mildura is the base camp for a variety of tours into the outback and associated national parks. Commercial operators abound, and information on most is available at the visitor center. **Mallee Outback Experiences** (tel. 5021 1621) has a good reputation locally; it runs a daytrip to Mungo National Park (see p. 218; Wed. and Sat.; $45, families $100), another along the Chaffey Trail highlighting the early history of the Mildura Settlement (Thurs.; $35, families $90), and a third to the Hattah Kulkyne National Park lakes system (Fri.; $45, families $100). Call directly or book through Rosemont Guest House. **Junction Tours** (tel. 5027 4309, mobile tel. 018 596 438; http://www.ruralnet.net.au/junction/) runs a variety of local and regional tours. Junction goes to Mungo (Fri. and Sun., $38), leads a nature and history tour (Fri., $38) and runs a longer outback tour to Broken Hill (3 days and 2 nights, $285). Ride a bit easier with **Mildura Freedom Harley Rides** (tel. 5023 3796), also available for weddings.

Several paddlesteamers still ply the waters near Mildura. The **Mildura Wharf,** at the end of Deakin Ave. (on the river, of course) is home to several ships. The *P.S. Melbourne* departs daily at 10:50am and 1:50pm for a two-hour cruise through historic Lock 11 ($16). The *Rathbury* does longer cruises to local wineries (Thurs., $34). Call 5023 2200 for bookings.

There are a few remnants of Mildura's past available for touring. The **Old Mildura Homestead** is a reconstruction of the first 1850 station and is located on Cureton Ave., west of the railway station on the river (open daily 10am-4pm; admission $2). Right next door, the much grander **Rio Vista mansion** was built in 1889 by W. B. Chaffey, one of Mildura's founding fathers. The home has been preserved with the original furnishings (open Mon.-Fri. 9am-5pm, Sat.-Sun. 1-5pm; admission $2, children and students free). The **Psyche Bend Pumping Station,** just south of the Kings' Billabong, a few kilometers southeast of the town center, houses the restored steam pumps that kept Mildura alive and growing in the early days. The nearby **Billabong** is a wetland reserve teeming with waterbirds (station open Tues. and Thurs. 1-4:30pm, Sun. 9:15am-12:30pm, public holidays 10am-3pm; admission $2, families $5).

The area along Langtree and Deakin Ave. near the river (between Ninth and Seventh St.) is the city's nightclub area. One of the most popular is the **Sandbar** on Langtree (tel. 5021 2181). The club strives for a tropical atmosphere, which can seem a bit out of place on chilly winter nights. Live music starts at 10:30 or 11pm (open Tues.-Sat.), and the doors are open until 3am, with no cover charge. The mixed crowd adheres to the "neat and casual" dress code, as does the music.

If you've always wanted to learn how to tell good fruit from bad, **Orange World** (tel. 5023 5197) beckons you to the "land of the living orange," more commonly known as the town of **Buronga,** north of Mildura on the Silver City Hwy. Orange World offers tours of groves and processing and packaging plants; free tastings and tours at 10:30am and 2:30pm (open Sun.-Fri. 9am-4pm; $6, concessions $5, children $3).

■ National Parks near Mildura

MURRAY-SUNSET NATIONAL PARK

Murray-Sunset is Victoria's second largest national park, covering 6330 square kilometers. The most spectacular feature of the park is the **Pink Lakes** system, a series of small salt lakes on the southern edge of the park. Earlier in the century, the lakes were mined for salt, with shovels and wheelbarrows. The large bags of salt were loaded onto camels and carried through the arid Mallee plains, each camel carrying four 100-pound sacks. There is abundant evidence of long-term Aboriginal inhabitation, including shell middens, stone hearths, and trees that bear the scars of boat building. The park is accessible with a 2WD vehicle, but much of the interior requires 4WD. All of the tracks are susceptible to adverse weather; consult with the rangers before setting out. There are **park offices** in Underbool near the Pink Lakes entrance on Fasham St. (tel. 5094 6267) and in Mildura at 253 Eleventh St. (tel. 5022 3000), both staffed sporadically. **Bushwalking** is popular, and there are well-marked tracks in the Pink Lakes Region. Summer temperatures can be quite high, so walkers undertaking longer trips should be prepared with water, maps, and a compass. Remote **campsites** are located throughout the park; toilets, BBQ, fireplaces, and information are available at Pink Lakes. This entrance is just east of the town of **Linga,** on the Mallee Hwy. From Mildura, take the Calder Hwy. south to Ouyen, then take the Mallee Hwy. west.

HATTAH KULKYNE NATIONAL PARK

Lake Hattah and its many satellite lakes are popular recreational destinations, offering water sport in the middle of Mallee scrub. When water levels allow, the lakes are excellent for canoeing, fishing (yellowbelly, redfin, and the introduced European carp are common), and swimming. When water levels are low, the lakes are excellent for wallowing in slime. There is a short nature walk that begins near the main entrance east of Hattah; just to the east is a nature drive suitable for any vehicle. There are no spectacular natural rock formations or bizarre landforms, just tranquil waters and native ecosystems. The main park entrance is 4km east of Hattah, about 40km south of Mildura on the Calder Hwy. Basic **camping** facilities are available at Lake Macinpoul and Lake Hattah (toilets, tables, fireplaces, rubbish bins). Visitors should bring their own supply of drinking water. (Dial 5029 3253 to book a campsite. Fees for 1 vehicle and up to 6 people $7.90, each additional vehicle $3.50.)

THE WIMMERA

West of the Goldfields, inland Victoria rises among the rugged peaks of Grampians National Park before slowly settling into an immense plain. This flat expanse is often taken for wasteland by the uninformed observer, but the region is actually extremely productive agricultural land, full of sheep, cattle stations, and vineyards. The Wimmera's many lakes and waterways teem with fish and attract a steady stream of anglers. The region extends north and west to the Little Desert National Park, a sanctuary for threatened species of flora and fauna. To the west of the Little Desert, South Australia's Coonawarra region boasts some of Australia's most-lauded vineyards. Just over the border, the Naracoorte cave system and Bool Lagoon are of interest to naturalists the world over. These sites, as well as the South Australia towns of Naracoorte (see p. 396) and Mount Gambier (see p. 397), are traditionally considered part of the Wimmera.

The scrub plain north of the Wimmera is referred to as the Mallee, after the *mallee eucalypt,* a hardy water-hoarding tree that thrives in the semi-arid environment. Although its namesake is known for high survival rates, the entire Mallee ecosystem is in fact extremely delicate. Agricultural pressure, increasing salinity, and the introduction of alien species like goats, cats, and bees, are steadily eroding the once vast areas of mallee. Unlike the oft-lamented clearing of rainforest, the destruction of this seemingly desolate habitat has proceeded without much public outcry.

Grampians (Gariwerd) National Park

Located 260km west of Melbourne and 400km east of Adelaide, Grampians National Park covers 167,000 hectares. Millions of years ago, the region lay under a shallow sea. Through geological heat and pressure over the span of millennia, the sandy bottom of this primeval ocean solidified into 6000m-thick slabs of sandstone. Tectonic disturbances then tilted and jostled the sandstone beds to form the jagged peaks we observe today, all of which will eventually be ground back into sand by the merciless wind and rain. But don't worry, you still have plenty of time to enjoy the park's breathtaking ranges, packed with wild beasts, rare birds (nearly 200 species), and in the spring, a carpet of technicolor wildflowers. The Grampians also contain numerous Aboriginal rock art sites.

Practical Information The most convenient point of entry is on the eastern edge of the park at **Halls Gap,** 26km west of **Stawell.** This is the main entrance to the park, with a large **Visitors Centre** (tel. 5356 4381; 2.5km south of Hall's Gap, on the road to Dunkeld; open daily 9am-4:45pm) and a cultural center. **V/Line buses** leave across from the newsagent in Hall's Gap (Mon.-Fri. at 1:15pm, Sat. at 12:50pm, and Sun. at 4:20pm) for Stawell (45min., $7.30), Ararat (1hr., $10.90), Ballarat (2½hr., $23.80), and Melbourne (4½hr., $37.80). There is no general tourist information in Hall's Gap; the closest **tourist information center** is in Stawell (54 Western Hwy., tel. 5358 2314; open daily 9am-5pm). Stawell also has a **post office,** 87 Main St. (tel. 5358 4022; open Mon.-Fri. 9am-5pm; postal code 3380) and a **bank** with an ATM (Commonwealth Bank, 101 Gold Reef Mall, tel. 5358 2600). The approach from the north passes through the almost-empty town of **Horsham,** situated at the junction of the Western and Henty Hwy. Horsham is roughly 80km north of the park. From the south, the town of **Dunkeld,** on the Glenelg Hwy., right on the border of the park, provides access via Mt. Abrupt Rd.

Camping and Accommodation There are 16 major camping areas in the national park. All have toilets and fireplaces, and all but Hollow Mountain and Rosea have some sort of water, be it creeks, taps, or tanks. All sites are first-come, first-served, and campers must pay a $7.50 fee (up to six people or one vehicle, additional vehicles $3.20). The fee is payable through a self service permit system, available at

The Gift

Back in the 1850s, people from all walks of life were rushing to the Victorian goldfields to make their fortunes. Life on the goldfield was hard, as hours of spine-snapping work yielded only an occasional nugget of gold. But as hard as the diggers worked, they played even harder. Bare knuckles fighting was a popular pastime, and huge sums were wagered on the inevitably bloody battles. Eventually, foot racing, another easy vector for wagering hard-won nuggets, grew in popularity. In order to organize and more thoroughly develop these contests, a group of young men founded the Stawell Athletic Club in January of 1878. The first "official" race was run that Easter, and the first to cover 130 yards won a purse of 20 sovereigns. Since that first running (won by W.J. Millard), the prize money has increased to over $75,000, making the Stawell Easter Gift the most lucrative footrace in the world.

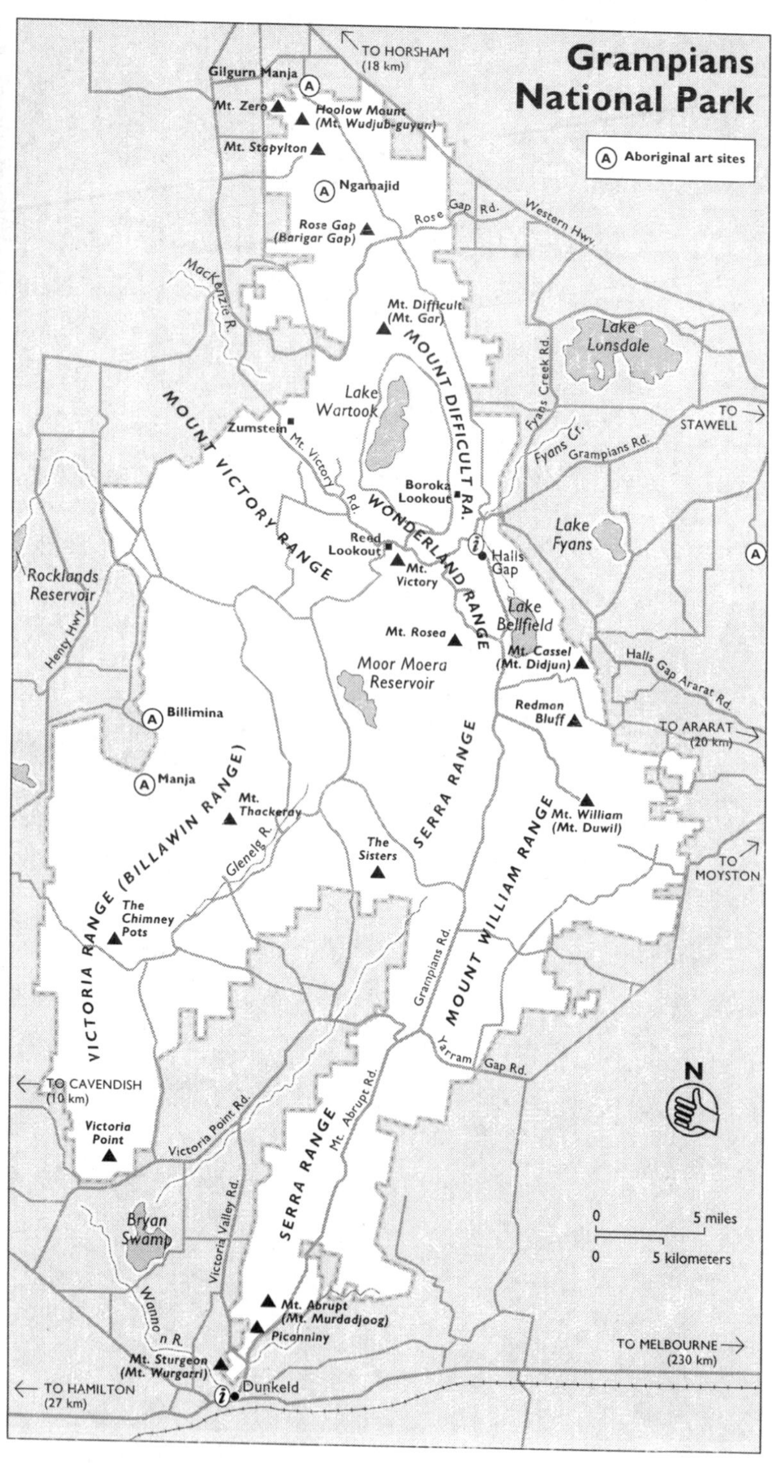
Grampians National Park
Aboriginal art sites
TO HORSHAM (18 km)
Gilgurn Manja
Mt. Zero
Hoolow Mount (Mt. Wudjub-guyun)
Mt. Stapylton
Ngamajid
Rose Gap (Barigar Gap)
Rose Gap Rd.
Western Hwy.
MacKenzie R.
Mt. Difficult (Mt. Gar)
MOUNT DIFFICULT RA.
Lake Lonsdale
Fyans Creek Rd.
Lake Wartook
TO STAWELL
Zumstein
MOUNT VICTORY RANGE
Mt. Victory Rd.
Fyans Cr.
Grampians Rd.
Boroka Lookout
WONDERLAND RANGE
Lake Fyans
Reed Lookout
Halls Gap
Mt. Victory
Rocklands Reservoir
Lake Bellfield
Henty Hwy.
Mt. Rosea
Mt. Cassel (Mt. Didjun)
Halls Gap Ararat Rd.
Moor Moera Reservoir
Redman Bluff
Billimina
TO ARARAT (20 km)
SERRA RANGE
Manja
Mt. Thackeray
Mt. William (Mt. Duwil)
VICTORIA RANGE (BILLAWIN RANGE)
Glenelg R.
The Sisters
MOUNT WILLIAM RANGE
TO MOYSTON
The Chimney Pots
Grampians Rd.
Yarram Gap Rd.
TO CAVENDISH (10 km)
N
Mt. Abrupt Rd.
Victoria Point Rd.
Victoria Point
SERRA RANGE
Victoria Valley Rd.
0 5 miles
0 5 kilometers
Bryan Swamp
Wannon R.
Mt. Abrupt (Mt. Murdadjoog)
Piccaninny
TO MELBOURNE (230 km)
Mt. Sturgeon (Mt. Wurgarri)
TO HAMILTON (27 km)
Dunkeld

the Visitors Centre and at most of the camping areas. Bush camping is free, but is forbidden in the Wonderland Range, on the Major Mitchell Plateau, in the Lake Wartook watershed, and in any other areas with no camping signs. More commercial camping is available in Stawell at the **Grampians Gate Caravan Park,** Burgh St. (tel. 5358 2376), complete with laundry, BBQs, a playground, and sparkling showers. Unpowered sites cost $8. In Halls Gap, the **Brambok Backpackers,** directly across from the visitors center, provides hostel accommodation for $15 per person. Large lounge areas and friendly staff make this a relaxing pre- or post-Gramps bivouac. **Halls Gap YHA** (tel. 5356 6221), less than 1km down Grampians Rd., has dorm beds for $13 (YHA non-members $16) and provides bedding and laundry facilities.

Sights Grampians is a very user-friendly national park. Although extremely rugged, many of the park's highlights can be reached via relatively easy walking trails, most without the need to overnight in the bush. Thus, the park is a favorite with families and those not interested in Iron-Man level exertion. The **Boroka Lookout,** 5km off Mt. Victory Rd., offers spectacular views of Fyans Valley, the Mt. William Range with the aptly-named Elephant's Hide, and the majestic, man-made Lake Bellfield. The **Wonderland Range,** in the heart of the park, is extremely popular with daytrippers. Several easy walks lead to serene waterfalls, curious rock formations, and hookah-smoking caterpillars (?). Detailed maps of the area are available from the Visitors Centre. The **Jaws of Death,** more gently known as the Balconies, are a brief jaunt from Reed Lookout, just off Mt. Victory Rd. This rock formation, consisting of parallel slabs of sandstone jutting out over the steep sides of Mt. Victory, is found on the cover of most Grampians tourist brochures. The approach is flat, but it takes nearly an hour. The **Zumstein recreation area,** west of Lake Wartook off the Mt. Victory Rd. and complete with picnic and BBQ facilities, is extremely popular with tourists because it crawls with kangaroos. The 'roos have grown accustomed to handouts and congregate here in frightening numbers. *Do not* feed the kangaroos, since refined human food can harm the little beasties both physically and psychologically. Note that kangaroos, and many other interesting critters, can be seen in all areas of the park, not just in Zumstein. One-day highlight routes are detailed in brochures available from the visitors center.

The **Brambuk Living Cultural Centre,** adjacent to the Visitors Center in Halls Gap, offers cultural education activities, tours of the rock art sites in the park, and displays of Aboriginal implements. The building itself is intriguing; the architect was inspired by the Dreaming myths of the area. The cafe in the center is reasonably priced and serves succulent emu, along with other bush tucker selections. The programs and activities offered by the center change frequently, so inquire for current information (tel. 5356 4381; fax 5356 4455; open 10am-5pm; free).

Little Desert National Park

The first tracts of Mallee were set aside as the Kiata Lowan Sanctuary in 1955. Over the years, the park size increased piecemeal as controversy over clearing the area grew. In 1986, a final expansion increased the park to 132,000 hectares. Little Desert National Park currently stretches from the Wimmera River in the east all the way to the South Australian border. Since it is such a large park, there is considerable variation in precipitation and a resultant diversity of vegetation. The park is covered predominantly by mallee scrub, but over 670 species of plants share the ecosystem.

Practical Information The Little Desert is best approached from either **Dimboola,** on the Wimmera River in the east, or from **Nhill,** north of the central block of parkland. **Ranger stations** in Wail (Nursery Rd., tel. 5389 1204), Horsham (21 McLachlan St., tel. 5381 1255), and Nhill (6 Victoria St., tel. 5391 1275) can provide information and camping permits. There is a general **tourist information center** in Dimboola (119 Lloyd St., tel. 5389 1290; open Wed.-Mon. 9am-5pm) for information on the entire region; you can also call the **Victoria Parks Hotline** (tel. 13 19 63).

There is a **post office** with fax service in Dimboola (61 Lloyd St.; tel. 5389 1542, open Mon.-Fri. 9am-5pm; postal code 3414) and another in Nhill (98 Nelson St.; open Mon.-Fri. 8:30am-5pm; postal code 3418). There is a **National Bank** office in Dimboola at the corner of Lochiel and Lloyd St. (open Mon. 10am-4pm, Tues.-Thurs. noon-4pm, and Fri. 10am-5pm.) **Buses** depart Dimboola from the station at the corner of Lochiel and Hindmarsh St. twice daily for Nhill (20min., $4.20), Horsham (30min., $4.20), Stawell (1½hr., $14.80), Ararat (2hr., $19), Ballarat (4hr., $30.70), Melbourne (5¼hr., $43), and other points. Timetables available at the station or **V/Line** (tel. 13 22 32).

Camping, Accommodations, and Food There are two camping areas in the National Park, one just south of **Kiata** (a small hamlet on the Western Hwy. between Nhill and Dimboola), and the other at **Horseshoe Bend** just south of Dimboola. Both campgrounds have fireplaces, tables, and toilets. A $7.50 fee is required of all campers at those sites, payable at any of the ranger stations. **Bush camping** is permitted in the western and central blocks only and must be vehicle-based. The **Little Desert Lodge,** 16km south of Nhill (tel. 5391 5232), is run by Malleefowl expert Whimpey Reichelt and provides both accommodations and an excellent introduction to Mallee wildlife. The Lodge has comfortable bunk beds for $15 (breakfast included) and campsites in the lush, surrounding bush for $9 (with power $11.50). The lodge is fully licensed and serves meals. The **Tuckerbag Supermarket** is on Lochiel St. in Dimboola (open Mon.-Thurs. 9am-5:30pm, Fri. 9am-6pm, Sat.-Sun. 9am-12:30pm).

Sights and Activities The unique Mallee ecology is the main attraction of the Little Desert. The park is best explored on foot, although rough, unpaved roads, suitable only for four-wheel drive vehicles (and often closed in winter) provide access to some of the more remote corners. An excellent 30-minute introductory walk leads to the **lookout** on Pomponderoo Hill, and shows off typical Little Desert terrain and biota. The trail begins at a point 1km west of the road along the Wimmera that runs south of Dimboola. Detailed brochures are available at the Little Desert Lodge, at ranger stations, and at the tourist information centers. Other **self-guided walks** begin at the campground south of Kiata and at the Gymbouen Rd. south of Nhill. A longer, 84km **Desert Discovery Walk** can be tackled all at once or in sections, and information is available from the rangers. The Little Desert Lodge runs half ($25), three-quarter ($40), and full-day ($50) **Land Rover tours** deep into the heart of the park. If the desert does not provide enough wildlife, the **Malleefowl Aviary** at the Little Desert Lodge (open daily 9:30am-4:30pm; admission $4, children $2) can guarantee up-close views of the fowl, sugar-gliders, and other scrub denizens.

No Small Feat

Most birds sit on their eggs and use the heat of their bodies to warm their unborn young. But Malleefowl, members of the family Megapodiiae, meaning "great footed," have come up with a way to save on baby-sitting and still get out of the nest. These cousins of the pheasant mate for life and then use their great feet to build a mound out of dirt, sticks, and tree litter, in which the female deposits her eggs. Each mound takes weeks or months to build, but once completed it garners its warmth from the sun and the fermentation of the litter in which the eggs are buried. Over the next few months, the parents tend and repair the natural incubators. By changing the depth of the sand and litter layers, the Malleefowl can control the temperature of the eggs. In studies of the Malleefowl hatching cycle, researchers have found that the temperature of a mound's interior varies by fewer than two degrees over a span of several months. Once the eggs hatch, the chicks dig themselves out of their nurseries and are immediately on their own, receiving no assistance from their parents. These hatchlings are nearly mature and can fly within a few hours.

HUME CORRIDOR

The Hume Highway links Melbourne and Sydney, shuttling visitors between the two urban centers through relatively unspectacular scenery. Intrepid travelers who venture an hour or two off the Hume will be rewarded with world-class wineries, dusty, unassuming hamlets, and quietly inviting country towns. Don't blink or you'll miss Glenrowan and Ned Kelly's Last Stand. Stray a bit more from the highway, and you can snowboard or schuss on Mt. Buller's powdery slopes. The culturally inclined can cruise through Wangaratta, and even catch the November Jazz Festival, arguably Australia's finest. Sun worshippers can laze away the days by toddling west along the Murray Valley Highway to fish, swim, or snooze on the Murray's banks in Yarrawonga and Cobram. Those in a hurry can simply cover the 872km in nine or ten hours. Across the Murray River, the Hume continues north into New South Wales (see Albury-Wodonga, p. 205).

Eildon

The locus of this small town is the gigantic, man-made **Lake Eildon.** Dammed in the 1950s to generate hydroelectric power, Lake Eildon wrought long-lasting environmental damage from which the region has only recently recovered. The lake is a playground for water sport enthusiasts, offering summer water-skiing and year-round fishing and boating. Houseboat rentals are popular and the cost is not entirely prohibitive for large groups. Contact **Lake Eildon Holiday Boats** (tel. 5774 2107) for details. A small, elevated station on the other side of the dam affords expansive views of the lake and surrounding countryside. To reach the lookout, proceed down Sugarloaf Rd., turn off toward the dam itself, and cross it.

Back in Eildon, activity is centered around the shopping village, off Main and Centre St., where travelers can find the butcher, the baker, or the fishing license maker. Across the street from the village on Utah and Main St. is the **Tourist Information Centre** (open daily 10am-2pm). The V/Line bus arrives at the shopping village and departs for Melbourne (Sun.-Fri. 1 per day, 3½hr., $17.50), stopping in small towns along the way.

Fraser National Park

From Eildon, a 13km drive up the Skyline Rd. brings travelers to Fraser National Park, a vast camping and bushwalking area. Kangaroo mobs, native birds, and small marsupials populate the park and can be observed at close range. Fraser's 3750 hectares offer access to Lake Eildon and marked nature and bike tracks. (Admission $6 per car. Camping sites for 4 people Oct.-May $13; June-Sept. $10.50. Cabins for 4 with shared facilities $38; off-season $35. Book ahead Dec.-Feb. and April.) To proceed northward toward Mt. Buller or the Murray River, the adventuresome, well-equipped, and brave can navigate the **Skyline Rd.** as it winds its way north toward Bonnie Doon and Mansfield. This 30km route is paved for half of its length and can be treacherous during less-than-ideal weather. A more scenic and comfortable route north follows the **Maroondah Hwy.** (Hwy. 153) through Alexandra toward Mansfield and Mt. Buller.

Mansfield

Well-situated as a base for both Mt. Buller winter skiing and Lake Eildon summer fun, Mansfield is a tourist service town through-and-through. After visitors enter on the Maroondah or Midland Highways, High St., Mansfield's main drag, provides the focus of their stays. Just west of the city center on High St. is the **Mansfield Visitors Centre** (tel. 5775 1464), where the charming staff provide oodles of brochures and maps. Heading east into town, the street is separated by a large parking median. **ATMs** are found on the south side of High St. (and accept V, MC, Cirrus, and Plus). On the north (left) side of High St. are three ski and chain hire shops. All vehicles heading to Mt. Buller must carry chains from June 8 (Queen's Birthday) until October 1. **Budget Ski Hire** (tel. 5775 2238) rents chains for $10 (a tad cheaper than its competitors) and offers a 10% discount on all chain and ski hire to folks who mention *Let's Go.* **PJ's Ski Hire** and **Ski Centre Mansfield** (tel. 1800 647 754 or 5775 2859) offer a wider range of ski paraphernalia. (All 3 shops accept V, MC, AmEx, and Discover and are open Mon.-Thurs. 6am-7pm, Fri. 6am-midnight, Sat.-Sun. 6am-at least 7pm.) Stock up on food at the **Festival Supermarket,** 47 High St., on the north side of the road (open Mon.-Wed. 8am-6pm, Thurs. 8am-7pm, Fri. 8am-8pm, Sat. 8am-5pm, Sun. 10am-5pm). The **post office,** 90 High St., is located just to the west, and offers fax and *Poste Restante.* The postal code is 3722.

The best place for budget travelers to bed down for the night is the **Mansfield Backpackers Inn,** 112-116 High St (tel. 5775 1800), on the south side. This restored building preserves a rustic atmosphere with its high cedar ceiling and brickwork, while providing spacious, well-lit dormitories. Sturdy metal bunks come with linen and doona, as well as a reading light. Spotless bathroom facilities are a quick run down the hall (dorms Sun.-Thurs. $15, Fri.-Sat. $20; weekly $84; YHA discount). Slightly more private, newly constructed triples provide an intermediate level of accommodation with shared adjoining bathrooms (Sun.-Thurs. $60, Fri.-Sat. $75). Or spring for large motel-style family rooms (Sun.-Thurs. $120, Fri.-Sat. $150). As with all ski-related services, reserve weekend spots at least two weeks in advance and week-day spots at least a week in advance during the height of the season (V, MC, and AmEx accepted).

Twenty kilometers from Mansfield, **Bonnie Doon's Lakeside Leisure Resort (YHA)** (tel. 5778 7252) sits on the north side of Lake Eildon. The resort is east of Bonnie Doon off Hutchinsons Rd. on the south side of the Maroondah Hwy. By bus, travelers should book to Mansfield and stop in Bonnie Doon, where the resort's bus can pick up guests. Despite the grandiose name, the leisure resort is just a lakeside caravan park, but it offers comfortable, well-heated bunks in six-bed dorms with bath ($13, $15 YHA non-member; weekly $65, $75). Cabins for two are also available ($50; weekly $250). A pool, game room, mini-market, sauna, and licensed restaurant are on-site. The resort charters fishing boats and ski boats with gear ($60 per hr.).

Good eats are a bit pricey, but **Buckley's Chance,** 141 High St. (tel. 5775 1277), provides reasonable pancakes and fast food. Takeaway prices are a deal (V, MC). The **Mansfield Passenger Terminal,** 137 High St. (tel. 5777 6070), is the **V/Line** agent, with service to Melbourne (2 per day, 3hr., $26.10) and to Mt. Buller (6 per day, 1hr., $18, return $29.70). Bus travelers receive a 10% discount on rentals at Ski Center Mansfield.

Mt. Buller

Victoria's largest and most popular ski resort, **Mt. Buller** (tel. 5777 6052; fax 5777 6027; http://www.skibuller.com.au) is a three-hour drive from Melbourne. Although a mecca for Aussie skiers and snowboarders, Buller's relatively tame slopes, sparse snowfall, and short season may fail to impress visitors from the northern hemisphere. Nevertheless, it's the place to ski from the Queen's Birthday (June 8) through early October, and the slopes are packed on weekends and public holidays during the height of the season, mid-July through late August.

Getting There, Orientation, and Practical Information Buses to Mt. Buller depart from Melbourne's Spencer St. Station (2 per day, 3hr., $89.80 round-trip including lodge delivery and resort entry fees) or from Mansfield. Service from Mt. Buller to Mansfield (6 per day, 1hr., $15) departs from the **Mt. Buller Village Center.** If traveling by car, bring your **snow chains** (or rent some in Mansfield) and take Hwy. 153 east to Mt. Buller. (Daily car admission $17. Free parking and shuttle service available on the side of the mountain.)

Once at the Village Center, most services and amenities lie up the mountain. Directly adjacent to the bus depot is the **skiosk** with public changing areas and an upstairs eatery, **The Pancake Parlour** (pancakes $5-10). Directly across from the skiosk is the information tower with brochures and maps of the resort. The **lift ticket office** is next to the tower. (Tickets $58 for 1 day, $106 for 2 days, $247 for 5 days. Ages 5-14 $30, $55, $128. Children under 5 free.) Full-time Mt. Buller employees enjoy free lift service, so snow bunnies should consider job hunting at the chalet or ski center.

Up Summit Rd. from the lift ticket office, **Molony's** has a small market with pricey food, a paucity of fresh produce, and a snack bar. A small **post office** down Summit Rd. has *Poste Restante* and daily mail service (open 8:30am-5pm; postal code 3723).

Accommodations For lodgings on the mountain, **Mt. Buller YHA Hostel Lodge** (tel. 5777 6181) is the least outrageous of the bunch. Located next to the lifts, the lodge has heated dorm-style bunk accommodations and still piles three blankets on each bed. A TV lounge with a stereo creates a space to unwind next to the complete kitchen. Ski lockers are available (locks $3). (Check-in 8-10am and 5-10pm. $45, YHA non-members $49; Sept.-June 29 $36, $40. Linen $3.) Reserve at least two weeks in advance for July weekdays, one month in advance for July weekends and August weekdays, and two months in advance for August weekends. Call to ask about last-minute vacancies or ski packages. (V, MC, AmEx.)

Next to the Village Center, the **Kooroora Hotel** (tel. 5777 6050; fax 5777 6202) offers similar bunk-style rooms in more intimate four-person dorms. The hotel has a bistro pub, bar, and ski shop, and offers late-night entertainment with live bands four nights per week. Video games and a restaurant round out the amenities, along with a 15% discount for guests' ski hire on-site. (Mon.-Thurs. $60, Fri.-Sun. $70, Sun.-Thurs. 5-night stay $200. Weekly: $340. Breakfast included. Reservations require a deposit and should be made months in advance.)

Ned Kelly: Outlaw and Hero

Born in Beveridge in 1855, Edward "Ned" Kelly gained a reputation as Australia's foremost outlaw and, for many, its most colorful hero. The son of a convicted thief, Kelly, along with the other boys in his clan, began claiming unbranded horses at an early age. He served his first jail time at 14, but became a serious horse thief only after teaming up with his father-in-law George King in 1874. Over the next nine years, Kelly and his small gang terrorized the countryside between Beechworth and Benalla, an area now known as Kelly Country. Constantly running from the law, they shot officers when confronted, took townspeople hostage, and robbed two banks. In Jerilderie in 1879, for example, the gang came into town, captured two policemen, dressed in their uniforms and wandered the streets. Before leaving town, they smashed equipment in the small telegraph office, and cut the wires. Two days later, they came back and robbed the bank. An autobiographical manifesto written by Kelly and handed to a teller at that heist can today be viewed at the Melbourne Public Library (see p. 456). The document, intended to give Kelly's side of his much-contested story, was never published during his lifetime nor examined during his trial. The Kelly gang made its last stand at the Glenrowan Inn on Monday, June 28, 1880. That day, Ned Kelly, wearing a 44kg suit of armor fashioned from melted (and stolen) plows and an overcoat, walked steadily toward a wave of shooting policemen. The officers, finally realizing his deceit, shot at Kelly's exposed legs. Kelly was brought to Melbourne and hanged on November 11, 1880, in the Melbourne Gaol, at the age of 25. The jail (see p. 460) displays Kelly's death mask, his famous armor, and the gallows on which he met his end. Ned Kelly's legendary status looms large in Australia, and an excellent account of his life and feats can be found at http://www.netspace.net.au/~bradwebb/.

Glenrowan

A small stop off the Hume Highway (Hwy. 31) between Benalla and Wangaratta, Glenrowan owes its fame entirely to Ned Kelly. For a few small blocks, the notorious bushranger still rules the land. Upon entering the town, visitors will be greeted by the 6m Kelly statue, a bit bulky in proportions, clad in the infamous armor mask. The primary attraction is the $2.5 million animatronic show, **Ned Kelly's Last Stand,** a corny, cultish, 40-minute narrative presentation on Ned's outlaw exploits and his shoot-out with police (every 30min. 9:30am-4:30pm; $15, ages 5-15 $8). Next door, the **Ned Kelly Memorial Museum and Homestead** offers a small shack in gold prospector style as a re-creation of Kelly's homestead. The display includes period photos, farming machinery, and artifacts of the late 19th century. A sprawling gift shop has Kelly-ware and Kelly kitsch galore (museum admission $2, kids 50¢; MC, Visa, AmEx). Beneath the Kelly statue is **Kate Kelly's Tea House,** a pretty, aromatic country tearoom that dispenses snacks and lunches ($4-7) and a fine selection of teas and coffees (open daily noon-5pm).

Wangaratta

Wangaratta's prim and pristine downtown beckons visitors with expansive brick sidewalks, sloping, curved streetlights, and perfectly preserved buildings from the Victorian era. Modern industrial storefronts also decorate this cheerful rural crossroads, which is set among fields of snow in winter. Wangaratta is a convenient stop on the Hume Hwy., which runs north through Chiltern to Wodonga (p. 205), and is a natural base for exploring Victoria's high alpine country (p. 507).

Orientation and Practical Information For information on Wangaratta and the surrounding snowfields, tune to 88 FM or spin by the **Wangaratta Visitor's Centre** (tel. 5721 3711), located on the Hume Hwy. (Tone Rd.), 1km southwest of the city center. Tone Rd. becomes **Murphy St.** downtown, and is crossed by Ford, Ely, Reid, and Faithful St. as you proceed north. **ATMs** are clustered on Reid St. northwest of Murphy St., and several camping and outdoors stores are along Murphy. The **V/Line** ticketing agent is **JetSet Travel** (tel. 5721 7677) on Murphy, just north of Reid St. V/Line runs to Bright (1 per day, 1½hr., $9.60), Melbourne (6 per day, 3½hr., $28.40), and Albury-Wodonga (6 per day, 1hr., $9.60). **Trains** depart from the railway station, which is a short walk down Docker St. (called Ford St. downtown). The **post office** is on the corner of Murphy and Ely St. (open Mon.-Fri. 9am-5pm; postal code 3677).

Accommodations and Food The **Royal Victoria Hotel Motel** (tel. 5721 5455), on Faithful St. just north of Murphy St., offers basic lodging with linens and hand basins in small rooms (singles $15; doubles $30; $4 pub meals; V, MC). A spiffier, more central hotel is the **Grand Central Hotel** (tel. 5721 3705), on Murphy just north of Reid St. Although the heated rooms are a tad dark, they each have a clean bathroom and hand basin. The hotel is above a lively sports bar, so sleepless travelers can wander down for a pint and a spin on a race car video game (rooms $20; V, MC). The best motel value is the **Billabong Motel** (tel. 5721 2353), an homage to 70s furnishings, with a well-preserved blend of earth tones and grandma's condo objets d'art. Centrally heated rooms come with bathrooms, TVs, coffee and tea service, and fridges. (Singles $27; doubles $40. V, MC. Reservations suggested for weekend stays.) Book all beds well in advance for early November's jazz festival.

One block north of Murphy St. on Ovens St. between Reid and Ford St. is **Safeway supermarket,** open daily 7am to midnight. For elevated cuisine in a jazzy, Mediterranean bistro setting, try **Vespa's Cafe** on the corner of Reid and Ovens St. The cool, crisp table settings in a frescoed, cedar-bedecked cafe enhance the excellent menu, while the bar offers a substantial selection of local wines. (Dinner $11-15, lunch $5-7.50 noon-2:30pm. Open daily noon-10pm. V, MC, AmEx, Diners Club.)

Sights and Activities Aircraft enthusiasts should jet down Greta Rd. (the street behind K-Mart) about 7km to **Air World** (tel. 5721 8788), a vintage aviation museum and hangar housing over 40 aircraft. It's an aeronautical tour through time (open daily 9am-5pm; admission $6, ages 6-15 $4, families $12.50; V, MC; wheelchair accessible). Wangaratta's **Heritage Trail** is an excellent walking tour of the city's architecturally exquisite edifices. Brochures are available at the tourist office. Highlights include **Holy Trinity Cathedral,** a granite structure with an unusual wooden tower, and the shapely **Exhibitions Gallery.** Forays into nearby **wine country** are also recommended. In Milawa, to the east, the **Brown Brothers Winery** (tel. 5720 5547) is a highlight. Wangaratta's legendary **jazz festival,** the first week of November, is considered by some to be Australia's best.

Chiltern

A sleepy, dusty gold mining town, Chiltern is 35km north of Wangaratta along the Hume Hwy. From the Hume Hwy., drivers enter town along **Main St.,** passing toilets and a parking lot on the right. The city centers around the intersection of Main St. and **Conness St.** A small **tourist information center** (tel. 5726 1395; open daily 10am-5pm) here can provide local maps and walking tour guides to Chiltern's historic buildings.

Across the street is the nation's largest grapevine. This swollen, gnarled beast hangs well-supported over a patio accessible through a small alleyway on Conness St. Planted in 1867, its longest limb extends 12m. South on Main St. to Wills St. and east one block sits the **Lakeview National Trust Building,** constructed in 1867. The building was the home of author Henry Handel (Ethel Florence) Richardson, and the setting for her novel *The Fortunes of Richard Mahoney.* Another excursion from Chiltern is an historic drive around **Chiltern Regional Park** (tel. 5726 1234). The 25km loop around this box-ironbark forest, generally considered the best-preserved in northeast Victoria, is marked with car signs. Although no facilities are available, camping in the park is permitted.

The **Telegraph Hotel** (tel. 5726 1470), just west of Main St. on Conness St., provides simple, clean rooms with linens, towels, and a communal bathroom facility. A small TV lounge with tea-making facilities enlivens the otherwise quiet place. The bistro has great $5 lunch meals (accommodation $15). A few tea rooms and milk bars can be found along Conness, and a **Goodfellows Supermarket** is open daily. **V/Line** service is available from the tourist parking center on Main and Wills St. Tickets can be purchased at the Chiltern Newsagent on Conness St. for trips to Melbourne (2 per day, 4hr., $33.20) or Albury-Wodonga (2 per day, 1hr., $4.40).

Rutherglen

Small Rutherglen is at the center of Victoria's most renowned **wine region,** and a mere mention of the town evokes images of vintages, carafes, and oak fermenting casks. Rutherglen serves as an excellent base for touring the surrounding wineries. The **tourist office** (tel. 6032 9166 or 1800 622 871), located in the Jolimont Centre on Drummon and Main St. down the hill from the city center, is the place to go for winery literature and maps. The tourist office also rents bicycles with baskets and helmets ($10 half-day, $15 full day). A Commonwealth Bank **ATM** on the corner of Murray and High St. accepts MC and Cirrus. Back down Murray St. is the **post office** (open Mon.-Fri. 9am-5pm, postal code 3685). Note that the **phone code** for the region is 02, not 03.

Rutherglen has very limited **public transport** service. The V/Line leaves Rutherglen for Melbourne (Mon., Wed., and Fri. 6:35am, 3½hr., $33.20). To make more V/Line connections while school is in session (and relive elementary school days), take the Wangaratta-bound school bus from the post office at about 8am. Pay the driver upon boarding. **Kelly's Bus Service** shuttles to Albury-Wodonga at 9:30am on weekdays from the BP station west of the city center ($3). V/Line tickets can be purchased at the hardware store (tel. 6032 9533; open Mon.-Fri. 8am-5:30pm, Sat. 8:30am-noon) across from the post office. General transport inquiries can be made here as well. For visitors who can't spare the time to see the wineries but want a souvenir, the **Walkabout Cellar** next to the Victoria Hotel sells all of the local labels (open Mon.-Fri. 9am-5pm).

The **Victoria Hotel,** 90 Main St. (tel. 6032 8610; fax 6032 8128), across from the post office, provides excellent lodging in a beautifully restored building that has been classified by the National Trust. Rooms are painted in a Victorian cottage scheme, and contain lovely period desks and beds. The paneled ceiling and preserved fixture bases are thoroughly authentic. Amenities include fans, space heaters, and electric blankets tucked beneath comfy doonas. (Singles $20; doubles $36. Reserve in advance during school holidays and major wine festivals. V, MC.) A less expensive nearby alternative is the **Star Hotel** (tel. 6032 9625; fax 6032 8081), on the corner of Main and High St. Although a bit worn and dim, these rooms are an adequate place to crash after a day of tastings. Electric blankets come in each room, and the shared bathrooms are fine (singles $15, doubles $30; V, MC). A **Riteway market,** 134 Main St. (open Mon.-Fri. 7:30am-6pm, Sat. 7:30am-1pm, Sun. 9am-noon), supplements the street's basic milk bars.

■ Rutherglen Wineries

Choosing from among these excellent wineries can be quite difficult. The **Rutherglen Touring Guide** is indispensable as a good motoring map. If you only have time to visit one, make it **All Saints Estate** (tel. 6033 1922; fax 6033 3515; email allsaints@albury.net.au), east of Rutherglen via Corowa Rd., then north on All Saints Rd. This experience matches most people's romantic visions of what wineries should look like. Towering elms line the driveway as visitors approach the striking red brick castle, and a sculptured rose garden with a central fountain borders the parking lot. All Saints proudly welcomes all visitors to its **Cellar Door,** open daily from 9am to 5:30pm for tastings, and its **Terrace Restaurant,** open daily for lunch. A marked, self-guided tour leads past immaculate gardens, huge display casks, and even a playground. A peek into the well-preserved **Chinese Dormitory and Gardens** gives a sense of the early laborers' living conditions. The path turns into the cool, dim cellar, with century-old wine-making equipment and fermentation vats, before entering the **Rutherglen Keg Factory,** a keg and wine furniture workshop. The **North East Victoria Winemakers Hall of Fame,** an informative display of the region's leading figures and wineries, is adjacent to the parking lot.

For the best in fortified wines, connoisseurs should stop by **Morris Wines** (tel. 6026 7303; fax 6026 7445), west of Rutherglen and north of the Murray Valley Hwy. on Mia Mia Rd. The muscats are among the world's finest, and Morris displays the awards to prove it. Muscats, tokays, and ports range in price from $9.50 (for 4-year aged) to $13 (for gift-boxed, 8-year aged), to $38 (for the Old Premium 20-year aged). Reds are also excellent ($14-16.50; V, MC, AmEx). To visit a lovely Victorian mansion set in a vineyard, check out the 1889 **Fairfeld Vineyard** (tel. 6032 9381) nearby. (Guided tours, during school holidays only, Mon.-Sat. at 11am, 1, and 3pm.) These three wineries are only the beginning of the riches. The **bike tours** (maps available at tourist office) are an excellent way to navigate the vineyards. The marked **tourist road** is also an excellent loop for driving the valley's sloping hills.

■ Yarrawonga

Yarrawonga's identity is deeply intertwined with its water. The Murray River flows through town and the town's Aboriginal name means "water running over rocks." Lake Mulwala, created in the 1930s as a dam project, is now the hub of the town's tourism. The stellar **tourist information center** (tel. 5744 1989 or 1800 062 260) is located at the lake's edge, beside the bridge to Mulwala (open daily 9am-5pm). The office also displays the **Old Yarra Mine Shaft,** a mock mine with a gem and fossil collection (admission $2, children 50¢).

V/Line offers service from the corner of Orr and Belmore St. Service to Mildura (Mon., Wed., Thurs., and Sat. 7:45 and 8:55am, 8hr.), Albury-Wodonga (Tues., Wed., Fri., and Sun., 1½hr.), Melbourne (2 per day, 4hr.), and Mulwala (2 per day, 5min.). Tickets can be purchased at the neighboring **Dalgerty's Travel Agency** (tel. 5713 2232) or on the bus.

Two blocks east of the tourist office along the lake, the **Paradise Queen** (tel. 5744 1843) offers 90-minute paddleboat tours. On weekends, a BBQ lunch cruise departs at 12:30pm ($15, children $7), while regular cruises leave Tuesday through Thursday, Saturday, and Sunday at 2pm ($10, children $5).

Extending south from the lake, **Belmore St.** is Yarrawonga's main street. It extends five blocks before intersecting the Murray Valley Hwy. (Telford St.). Hotel accommodations are scattered along Belmore St. The best of the bunch is the **Terminus Hotel** (tel. 5744-3025), a cheerful pub hotel. The rooms are well-painted and furnished, and come with fans and electric blankets. Communal bathrooms are spotless. (Singles $20; doubles $35. Cooked breakfast included. V, MC.) Cafes and milk bars populate the downtown, and a **Festival Supermarket** is on Belmore St. three blocks south of the lake (open Mon.-Wed. 8:30am-7pm, Thurs.-Fri. 8:30am-9pm, Sat. 8:30am-6pm, Sun. 10am-5pm).

Across the river, **Mulwala** peers back at Yarrawonga through a tangle of clubs—essentially thinly-disguised casinos. Prior to Victoria's recent legalization of gambling, people flocked to Mulwala's slots. More subdued today, these clubs can be fun for the lucky or the rich. The bridge between Mulwala and Yarrawonga dips because the New South Wales and Victoria governments began construction at different heights and had to try to fix the mistake in the middle. The chief engineer killed himself shortly after the project's completion.

■ West of Yarrawonga: Cobram and Tocumwal

A small stop along the Murray Valley Hwy., Cobram (COB-rum) is a quiet residential community that attracts a multitude of outdoor enthusiasts in the summer months. The **tourist information center** (tel. 5872 2132) is on Station St. across from the railway station and sells V/Line tickets. Buses depart from the station for Albury-Wodonga, Mildura, Melbourne, and Tocumwal. Down Mookarri St. at the river's edge is **Thompson's Beach.** A spacious, sandy park, the beach boasts BBQ, picnic, and bathroom facilities as well as a fitness track and 3.5km walking trail.

New South Wales' first or last city on the Newell Hwy, Tocumwal is an inconspicuous town with a **tourist office** (tel. 5874 2131), just east of Hwy. 39. It provides maps and information on both Victoria and New South Wales (open Tues.-Thurs. 10am-4pm, Fri.-Mon. 9am-5pm).

HIGH COUNTRY

Tourists who come to Australia expecting to see Great Whites or the Red Centre are often surprised by Victoria's high country, tucked between the Murray River and the thick forests of Gippsland. Here, old growth forests display dazzling fall colors and rambling valleys nurture spring flowers that shame Crayola. Though you may miss the waves, Mt. Buffalo's warm thermal winds support paragliders, and the area's eco-adventure opportunities include skiing in winter, hiking in summer, and abseiling off sheer cliffs all year 'round. For those who prefer tamer pleasures, the small town of Beechworth boasts a terrific concentration of gold rush era Australiana. Bed down in Bright, and you'll be centrally located in sub-Alpine Australia and supplied with forests to scour and ski slopes to tackle. All vehicles heading into the mountains in this area must carry chains from June 8 (Queen's Birthday) until October 1.

Beechworth

This robust, upscale country town preserves a large number of gold rush era stone masonry buildings amid a slew of elegant boutiques, antique shops, and galleries. The contemporary attraction for tourists can be traced to the supporting role Beechworth played in the life of the infamous criminal Ned Kelly.

Practical Information The **Visitors Information Centre** (tel. 5728 3233) is located in beautifully restored Shire Hall on Ford St., Beechworth's main north-south street (open daily 9am-5pm). Albert Rd. forms the major east-west thoroughfare.

Clustered to the south on Ford St. are a Commercial Bank **ATM** (accepts V, MC, Cirrus, and Plus), a **laundromat** (open daily 7am-9pm), a **Foodtown market** (open Mon.-Fri. 8:30am-5:30pm, Sat.-Sun. 8:30am-5pm), and the **post office** (open Mon.-Fri. 9am-5pm, postal code 3747). The V/Line **bus** stop is on Camp St., just west of Ford St., but tickets should be purchased at the pet store on Ford St. Buses run to: Melbourne (2 per day, 4hr., $33.20); Sydney via Albury (2 per day, $79); and regional hubs Albury (2 per day, 30min., $5); and Wangaratta (2 per day, 30min., $5).

Accommodations and Food Beechworth overflows with B&Bs. The visitors center can help you select one based on price (starting at $45 per double), theme, or amenities. A reasonable hotel-style accommodation with B&B charm is the **Hibernian Hotel** (tel. 5728 1070) on the corner of Loch and Camp St., one block west of the town center. Patterned doonas and rugs blend nicely with tasteful, eclectic country decor. Rooms include an electric blanket and coffee and tea service. A comfy sitting space with plush sofas and oodles of books invites guests to sit back and relax, and the garden makes an ideal breakfast nook. (Singles $25; doubles or twins $45. Breakfast $5-10. V, MC, Bancard.) A larger, similarly styled pub hotel is the **Tanswells Commercial Hotel** (tel. 5728 1480). Centrally heated rooms come decked out in Victorian-era decor, and the extensive bar and bistro service downstairs complements the atmosphere. Friday and Saturday nights are noisy until late. (Singles Sun.-Thurs. $25, Fri.-Sat. $35; doubles Sun.-Thurs. $40, Fri.-Sat. $55. V, MC.)

The award-winning **Beechworth Bakery** (tel. 5728 1132), on Albert Rd., should not be missed by those who prize anything leavened. Seating in the sunny bistro-style cafe provides a convenient niche from which to sip a chocaccino ($2.15) or devour a scone (80¢). Loaves cost $2-3 (open daily 6am-7pm).

Sights and Activities The bushranger **Ned Kelly** was first tried and jailed in Beechworth, in a cell you can still visit behind Shire Hall (admission 50¢, children 20¢). Three trials later, proceedings against Kelly for the killing of constables Lonigan and Scanlon in the infamous Glenrowan siege commenced here before moving to Melbourne in search of an impartial jury. The **Historic Court House** (tel. 5728 2721) is open to the public and restored to its original 19th-century condition. You can tour the building and view exhibits on the courthouse's colorful history (open daily 10am-4pm; admission $2, family $4).

Directly behind the information center, on Loch St., the **Burke Museum** (tel. 5728 1420) displays an extensive collection of regional natural history, gold-rush era artifacts, and exhibits of Aboriginal culture. The museum was named after another famous local, Robert O'Hara Burke, one-half of the ill-fated Burke and Wills expedition which set out to explore central Australia. Burke served as Beechworth's superintendent of police from 1854 to 1858. Behind the lovely stained glass window sits a row of 16 period shops whose lively displays and ongoing recordings simulate 1860s bustle with a Disney World feel (open daily 10:30am-3:30pm; admission $5, children $3, families $12). A Gold Ticket ($6, families $15) provides admission to the Burke Museum, Historic Court House, Powder Museum, and **Carriage Museum** (open Feb. and July-Aug. 10am-noon and 1-4pm), which is just off Albert Rd. heading south towards Myrtleford.

Beechworth **cemetery,** located north of the town center and east on Cemetery Rd., houses the **Chinese Burning Towers.** The towers, which resemble giant firecrackers, and the simple headstones are all that remain of the gold rush era Chinese presence in Beechworth. Chinese miners once outnumbered whites five to one, but their segregated, diminutive, and tightly-packed grave sites testify to the discrimination they faced.

One block north and three blocks west of the town center is the site of **M.B. Historic Cellars,** 29 Last St. (tel. 5728 1304). The 100-year-old brewery produces non-alcoholic cordials in 10 authentic turn-of-the-century flavors. These unusual beverages tickle the palate in flavors ranging from Lemon Ginger and Sarsaparilla to Chilli Punch. They're available for purchase ($6 per bottle) and free tasting. Next door, a large, dusty gem exhibit showcases a range of luminescent gems, fossils, shells, and gold, representing the best of the treasures found in the surrounding hills. Downstairs, brewery antiques and memorabilia provide visitors with another taste of the town's heyday (site open daily 9am-5pm; free to tour).

■ Near Beechworth: Yackandandah

A small, friendly gold rush town with a funny name, Yackandandah offers a less touristy and less expensive getaway in Victoria's rugged northeast country than better-known Beechworth. In town, shops and services can be found on High St. An informal **tourist office** operates from **Frankly Speaking Antiques** (tel. 6027 1931; open daily 9am-5pm). Craft shops, fragrance parlors, and historic buildings dominate the shady walk. There are no ATMs in Yackandandah. The **post office** is located on the west of High St. (open Mon.-Fri. 9am-5pm; postal code 3749).

Although a night in the nearby town of Albury-Wodonga is probably preferable, the **Yackandandah Hotel** (tel. 6027 1210) on High St. and Isaacs Ave. makes a good alternative to Beechworth's pricier digs ($20; V, MC). For excellent breakfasts or lunches, try the sandwiches, pies, and loaves from **The Yackandandah Bakery** (tel. 6027 1549).

From Beechworth or Wodonga (35km), Hwy. 154 leads to Yackandandah. Entering from the north, 3km from Yackandandah's downtown is **Schmidt's Strawberry Winery** (tel. 6027 1454) at the Allans Flat turnoff. The Schmidts made wine for generations, and began strawberry production and winemaking in 1968. They produce dry and semi-sweet wines, popular with spicy food, and sweet, tasty dessert wines ($10 each, all 3 varieties for $25). A luscious strawberry liqueur is also available for $20. (Open for sales and tastings daily 9am-5pm. V, MC, Bancard.)

With over 7000 plants and 20 varieties of lavender cultivated, **The Lavender Patch** (tel. 6027 1603), 5km west of Yackandandah on Beechworth Rd. (called High St. in the town center), soothes and delights the senses. Natural lavender products including soaps, potpourri, and lotions can be purchased in the gift shop, and the hosts encourage guests to roam the aromatic hillside, picnic at the BBQ kiosk, and enjoy complimentary tea or coffee in the gazebo. Prettiest during the summer bloom, *Landandula augustifolia* (English Lavender) can be enjoyed year-round in its living form and as a bottled salve (patch open daily 9am-5:30pm; V, MC, and Bancard). The **Bank of Victoria Museum** (tel. 6027 1308) on High St. depicts a bank and living quarters from the late 19th century (open Sun. and school holidays noon-4pm; admission $2, children 50¢).

Mt. Buffalo National Park

Rising up beside the Ovens Hwy. (Great Alpine Rd.), the impressive **Mt. Buffalo National Park** encompasses a lush, rugged area around the plateau peaks and sheer rock faces of Mt. Buffalo. The park was created 100 years ago and has expanded incrementally since. The rich sub-alpine ecosystem offers numerous walking trails, awesome panoramic lookouts, and scattered picnic areas. At the summit plateau, two chalets accommodate visitors bound for outdoor adventures. A cross-country and downhill ski resort in the winter, Mt. Buffalo blooms in the summer with a large number of water sports and outdoor activities including abseiling, rock climbing, mountain biking, hang gliding, and bushwalking.

Practical Information and Accommodations Entrance to the national park is just off the Great Alpine Rd. roundabout by Porepunkah, 5km north of Bright and 320km from Melbourne. There is a $7 entrance fee (per car) but it is waived for guests of either mountain top lodging. The **park office** (tel. 5755 1466), provides maps, posters, and information on peak-season tours (open Mon.-Fri. 8am-4:30pm).

Just up the hill, the beautifully restored **Mt. Buffalo Chalet** (tel. 5755 1500; reservations tel. 1800 037 038; fax 5755 1892), built in 1909, provides comfortable accommodations in an historic lodge. Enjoy a drink on the veranda or in the plush leather loungers lining the sitting rooms. A guest house style accommodation ($105 per person) may stab at the heart of a budget traveler, but it makes an unforgettable splurge and is actually an excellent value since three hugely satisfying meals, park admission, and use of the spa, small gym, outdoor pool, tennis courts, and games room are all included in the nightly tariff. (V, MC, AmEx, EFTPOS accepted. Book at least a month in advance July-Aug.) The majority of Mt. Buffalo's walking trails, a number of spectacular geographic formations, and the Tatra Inn are all nearby.

The clean, simple lines of the **Tatra Inn's** (tel. 5755 1988) main lounge and cafeteria overlook the slopes (meals $2.50-10). Inside, a ski shop and ski hire serve visitors for both cross-country and downhill skiing, while guests have access to laundry facilities, towels, and use of the games room and TV/VCR lounge. Dorms have basic bunks, storage, shared facilities, and coffee and tea service. (Dorms Aug. $32; July and Sept. $20; Oct.-June $16.) Motel units have bath, veranda, and cheery decor ($65 off-season, $95 during the ski season). Three meals are included for all rooms. Ask about employment opportunities.

Skiing, Sights, and Activities The Mt. Buffalo slopes cater to beginner and intermediate skiers, but some advanced runs are available. Lift passes are available for the Cresta Valley site adjacent to the Tatra Inn. (Morning $23, afternoon $27, full day $34; ages 7-16 $14, $16, $19; under 7 $5, $7, $10.) A complete introduction to skiing—lift, lesson, and hire—will cost $43, or $32 for children.

After entering the park, the winding mountain road passes through dense eucalypt forests which hold over 400 plant species and 90km of walking tracks. A left turn just before the park office leads drivers toward the Mt. Buffalo Chalet and **Bent's Lookout.** This stunning view provides a panoramic sweep across the Buckland Valley, with giant Mt. Kosciusko visible in the distance on clear days. In the carpark, brilliantly colored crimson rosellas display uncanny intelligence and will land on you to feed if you entice them with snacks. Abseilers descend and hang gliders launch from all along the rock face.

Driving south past the park office toward the Tatra Inn, you'll see numerous marked walking trails. Opposite the park office the tremendous views from the **Monolith** rock outcropping is definitely worth the short walk. A kilometer further along, **Lake Catani** serves as a hub for summer water sports and winter ice skating. Campground facilities are available beside the lake, and bookings can be made through the information office. Farther south, you'll pass **Dingo Dell,** the first ski run to have a chairlift in Australia. Past Dingo Dell, the **Cathedral**—another dramatic rock formation—provides an excellent short bushwalk.

Mt. Buffalo doesn't shut down when the skiing stops. **Abseilers** descend near Bent's lookout year-round. **Rock climbing, caving,** and rugged **mountaineering** expeditions led by certified instructors are run through the **Mt. Buffalo Chalet Activities Center** (tel. 5755 1988), and can be coordinated through Bright's two hostels (half-day $50, full day $100). Price include meals, transport, and equipment. Tamer, cheaper activities like bushwalking, fly-fishing, and mountain biking are popular in the park, and wilderness photography tours ($22 for 2hr.) and day-long art classes ($39) cater to the more artistic (V, MC, AmEx, Bancard; book ahead).

Bright

Never was there a name more apt than Bright for an alpine community whose radiant natural beauty is complemented by glowing hospitality and adventure. Outdoor activities range seasonally from snow skiing to bushwalking, paragliding, and abseiling. Excellent budget accommodations and proximity to wineries, snowfields, and larger cities impart a measure of convenience to Bright's eco-tourism opportunities.

Practical Information Situated 79km southeast of Wangaratta along the Ovens Hwy. (the Great Alpine Rd.), the **Alpine High Country Visitors Centre** (tel. 5755 2275 or 1800 500 117; fax 5750 1165) greets visitors as the Ovens Hwy. becomes Gavan St. (open daily 9am-5pm). The info center also sells **V/Line** tickets to Melbourne (1 per day, 4½hr., $37.80), Mt. Beauty (1 per day, 30min., $5), Wangaratta (1 per day, 1½hr., $9.20), and Albury-Wodonga (1 per day, 2hr., $18.20). Buses depart from the post office in the town center.

To reach the town center, marked by an Art Deco clock tower, head south of the tourist office along Camp St. Ireland St. approaches the tower before splitting left into Anderson St. and right into Barnard St., both of which continue to Gavan St., where you can locate your favorite **ATM.** ANZ's accepts MC, Visa, Plus, and Cirrus. The **post office** is on the southern end of Gavan St. (open Mon.-Fri. 9am-5pm, postal code 3741). The **Riteway** supermarket is on Ireland St. (open Mon.-Fri. 8am-7pm, Sat. 8am-5pm, Sun. 9am-2pm).

Accommodations and Food Budget travelers are doubly blessed in Bright. **Bright Hikers Backpackers Hostel,** 4 Ireland St. (tel. 5750 1244; fax 5750 1246; email gwhite@www.netc.net.au), is located across from the post office on the second floor. A model hostel, Bright Hikers overflows with amenities in a light, airy self-contained structure. The comfy common room has great lounge furniture, a video library, and Monopoly. Kitchens, dorms, and bathrooms are clean and comfortable; extras include hot water bottles, laundry facilities, safe for valuables, and email access. (Linen deposit $2.50; lockers 50¢; mountain bikes $3 per hr., $12 per day; breakfast $4-5.50. Dorms with 4-6 beds $15. Weekly: $84. VIP. V, MC, AmEx.) Bright Hikers books local adventure activities at a discount basis.

One block east of the information center, off Cherry Lane and just across a creek from the town center, is the **Bright Caravan Park and High Mountain Country Hostel** (tel. 5755 1141; fax 5750 1077). The YHA-affiliated hostel is a masterfully constructed modern lodge with four-bunk rooms adjoining shared bathrooms. Cheerily decorated with bed lamps and storage lockers, each bed has a personal window and shade which looks out on the surrounding trees and nearby creek-side caravan park. The central kitchen, dining room, and TV lounge adjoin the dorms. (Dorms $15, YHA non-members $18. Weekly: $105, $126. Wheelchair-accessible suites available. Linen deposit $2.) The **caravan park** is ideal for tents in the warm weather months, as sites are sheltered by a canopy of trees. (During school holidays, long weekends, and ski season, sites $15, with power $18. Weekly: $105, $126. Off-season sites $12, $15. Weekly: $72, $90. Cabins $50-60 per double. V, MC.) Reserve in advance during peak seasons.

To treat yourself to an excellent meal, try the **Cozy Kangaroo** (tel. 5750 1838) on Gavan St. and Star Rd. Adorable 'roos adorn the walls, and the warm, friendly atmosphere and award-winning service complement scrumptious food. Lunches ($5-7), crepes, and vegetarian specials ($7-10) dominate the menu. Try the dinner and dessert special ($12.50); the cakes and pastries are irresistible (open 8am-late; V, MC, AmEx).

Sights and Activities Undeniably the alpine region's outdoor adventure capital, Bright offers a slew of activities exist for visitors' enjoyment. The most conventional and popular activity is **skiing** in neighboring **Mt. Hotham, Falls Creek,** and **Mt. Buffalo.** The numerous walking trails in the area provide less expensive enjoyment.

At the center of town, **Adina Ski Hire,** 15 Ireland St. (tel. 5755 1177; fax 5755 2177), can equip travelers with ski gear, apparel, and snow chains. (Per day rentals: skis, boots, and poles $23, under 15 $18; snowboards and boots $45; toboggans $10; chains $20. V, MC, AmEx. Multi-day rentals discounted. Open Sat.-Thurs. 7am-7pm, Fri. 7am-2am.) Every set of rented skis comes with a ski rack.

The area's warm thermal air currents fuel glorious hang-gliding and paragliding flights throughout the surrounding valleys. The 1986 World Championships are the area's claim to fame. The **Alpine Paragliding Center** (tel. 5755 1753), next to Bright Hikers, offers tandem paraglides ($95). These flights are guaranteed to last seven to 10 minutes, and often extend longer. An $8 round-trip bus can take you to the top of the hill to watch the gliders launch and soar en masse, particularly in the summer. Ultralite plane flights offer another exhilarating experience. These duo flights are operated by **Holiday Air Adventures** (tel. 5753 5250). Pilot Don Walpole provides a wealth of local knowledge in-flight and has over 35 years of flying experience. **Adventure Guides Australia** (tel. 5728 1804) directs ground-based fun, including abseiling (half-day $42), night caving ($48), rock climbing (full day $95), and bush-walking and camping excursions. Their top-notch staff overflows with advice and encouragement. All adventure activities are year-round; group bookings are encouraged.

For a tamer local excursion, try panning for gold. Several operators can be contacted through **Morses Creek Store,** 22 Wills St. (tel. 5750 1577; open 9am-5pm). Five minutes south of Bright along the Great Alpine Rd., the **Wandiligong Maze and Garden Cafe** (tel. 5750 1311) is a delightful hedge maze, whose 3m walls and complex patterns take about a half-hour to navigate. The fragrances of the surrounding gardens and children's laughter fill the air (admission $5, children $2).

■ Near Bright: Falls Creek

Just an hour's drive uphill from Bright along a fine alpine road, **Falls Creek Ski Resort** (tel. 5754 4718, or 1800 033 079; fax 5754 4287; http://www.skifallscreek.com.au) lifts guests as high as 1780m. Over the past four years, the resort has had more snow—both natural and man-made—than any other Victorian resort. Excellent intermediate runs predominate at Falls Creek, but a 2.2km beginner run and 3km advanced run satisfy skiers of all abilities. Lift tickets allow unlimited use of both Falls Creek and Mt. Hotham resort lifts, as well as cross-country loops. (Resort entry $15 per day, $23 overnight. 1-day lift tickets $65, under 15 $30, families of 4 $152. 1-day lift and lesson package $80, under 15 $51.) Discounts are available with advance purchase.

Activity at Falls Creek is concentrated at the eastern and western edges of the village. The **ski lodge** by the base of the Halley's Comet chairlift has public toilets and eating areas. Just uphill on Slalom St. is the **Wombat Cafe** (tel. 5758 3666), which holds the **post office** (postal code 3699; open Mon.-Fri. 9am-5pm, Sat. 9am-noon) and a mini-market downstairs, and an inexpensive snack bar upstairs. At the western end of the village by the Eagle Triple Chairlift is the **Frying Pan Inn** (tel. 5758 3390; fax 5758 3695), where **dorms** cost $32-65. The bistro and associated nightlife make it a hub of evening activity after a day on the slopes. Weekdays on the margins of the season are cheapest (V, MC, AmEx, Discover). Nearby, at the Village Bowl, the **Ski School** (tel. 5758 3331) offers a wide variety of lesson and lift packages with seasonal and multi-day discounts (open 8:30am-5pm).

An active summer resort as well, Falls Creek offers bushwalking, horseback riding, tennis, and water sports. The gourmet **Food, Wine, and Wildflower Festival** encourages guests to eat, drink, and smell the wildflowers during the second week of January.

Mt. Hotham

Australia's no-nonsense intermediate and advanced skiing headquarters, Mt. Hotham is a slick power experience. Hotham's three new chairlifts offer practiced ski enthusiasts Victoria's "highest average snowfall depth" and a strong partnership with neighboring Falls Creek. Those traveling the Great Alpine Rd. should indicate length of stay to the toll booth operator (cars $17 to enter resort, $25 per night, $100 season pass). There is no cost to drive through, but travelers will nonetheless require a transport ticket nonetheless. From the north, Mt. Hotham is accessible for most of the winter on a winding sealed road. Entrance from Omeo to the south is safer and more reliable, but inconvenient for those based in Melbourne or Sydney.

To get to Mt. Hotham by bus, depart from Melbourne's Spencer St. Station (1 per day, $65), Wangaratta Railway Station (1 per day, $50), or Bright's post office (2 per day, 1½hr., $16). Contact **Trekset Tours** (tel. 9370 9055 or 1800 659 009; fax 9372 0689) to book. Drivers heading for Omeo and parts south can rent snow chains in Harrietville at **Hoy's Ski Hire** (tel. 5759 2622) for $20 with a $30 deposit. These can be returned to **Burke's** in Omeo on the south side of Mt. Hotham.

The resort has a village set-up, with lodges clustered to the south and ski lifts and services farther north. A green tractor transports folks for free around the resort. The **information center** (tel. 5759 3550 or 1800 354 555) is located on the first floor of the tourist shelter and administration building, just north of the Corral carpark. Directly across the street, **Hotham Central** houses a ski school office, helicopter and lift agent, and the **Swindlers Valley Brand Bistro.** The bistro overlooks the slopes and sells lift tickets, valid both here and at Falls Creek. (Full day ticket $59, children $30. Lift and lesson packages start at $151 for 2 days, children $96.) Student "extreme" packages (ages 15-18) provide discounts on lift and lessons. Tickets for round-trip helicopter rides to Falls Creek are $49.

On the south side of both the resort and the Big D chair lift sits **Big D,** housing **Isobar Diner and Take-Out,** and a ski boutique. This is where beginner ski lessons begin, and where night skiing (Tues., Thurs., and Sat. 6:30-10:30pm) is allowed. Next door is **The General** (tel. 5759 3532), a general store with a mini-market, simple pub, and mailbox. The excellent 11km cross-country track en route to Dinner Plain begins just beyond the store.

Lodging on Mt. Hotham is pricey, and Bright's excellent hostels offer an inexpensive alternative. Those interested in ski lodge accommodations should contact the **Mount Hotham Accommodation Service** (tel. 5759 3636 or 1800 032 061; fax 5759 3111), who can sometimes place you in a club lodge for as low as $35-50 from late July to mid-September, or $20 in the off-peak season.

In the summer, Hotham stays relatively quiet with nature trails and a few shops and lodgings open for visitors. From mid-October to Queen's Birthday in June, resort admission is free.

Near Mt. Hotham: Dinner Plain

Ten kilometers south, Dinner Plain rests quietly in Mt. Hotham's shadow. A small, unstaffed information booth sits at the village entrance. Significant because it sits at one end of a lovely **cross-country ski trail,** Dinner Plain also boasts an inexpensive **ski school** with a basic lift. There are lift, lesson, and ski hire packages available ($65, children $30) as well as snowboard packages ($65). **Horseback trail rides** are offered year-round throughout the Alpine National Park area. Contact Helen Packer (tel. 5159 6445) in Dinner Plain to book (in winter $30 per hr., in summer $25 per hr.). A **shuttle bus** runs to Mt. Hotham from Dinner Plain's Halter Lodge and Forecourt (service 7:45am-4:50pm, 30-45min.).

Omeo

Omeo (pop. 350) bills itself as the "gateway to the high country" and lives up to the name by providing the best all-weather access to the Mt. Hotham and Falls Creek ski resorts. Omeo also marks distinct environmental change for those departing the alpine region, as they enter Gippsland's sloping hills and grassy pastures. A stretch of the road between Mt. Hotham and Dinner Plain is unpaved, but the road slopes and turns less abruptly than on the northern face.

For **visitor information,** the **Mobil Gas Station** operates a small booth with maps and brochures. If you're heading north from Omeo, the station is your last chance for petrol before the mountain ascent. **Burke's** operates the only snow chain rental ($20, $30 deposit). Chains can be returned on the other side of the mountains, at **Hoy's** in Harrietville, 24km south of Bright. No public transport is available to Omeo. There is a **post office** on the Great Alpine Rd. (postal code 3898; open Mon.-Fri. 8:30am-12:30pm, 1:30-5pm).

Omeo's budget beds are at the **Holston Tourist Park,** opposite the Bairnsdale turn-off and 1.3km down the road, indicated by signs. Campsites and on-site vans sit in the shade beside a hill on the edge of a creek. Mountain bike hire, fishing, a games room, and gold panning provide recreation.

Gold mine enthusiasts should check out the remnants of the abandoned **Oriental Claims** hydraulic sluicing claim which surround Omeo. If your skiing vacation has left your wallet empty, try your own hand at panning in Livingston Creek; ore can be found within several hundred meters of Omeo township.

GIPPSLAND

South and east of Melbourne, the Princes Highway loosely follows the contours of the Victoria coast on its way through verdant, rolling wilderness interspersed with extensive lake systems and small towns to the border of New South Wales. Undeveloped and sparsely populated, this belt plays host to eco-tourists and witnesses frequent struggles among developers, loggers, and environmentalists. National parks pepper the region, yet even Croajingolong National Park, the distinguished World Biosphere Reserve, sees far fewer visitors than parks farther west. Meander off the highway to immerse yourself in this splendid ecology. A distinction is generally made between Gippsland proper, or South Gippsland, and East Gippsland, the former more populated and not as thickly forested as the latter.

Wilsons Promontory National Park

A natural reserve of almost mythic proportions, **the Prom** became Australia's first national park in 1905 and, despite ongoing efforts by special interests, remains one of the world's most unspoiled biologically rich regions. Tidal flats and marshland meet clusters of heath and towering gum forests. Rich fern gullies follow the contours of the land. This diversity of flora creates habitats for a plethora of native marsupials and bird life. Protruding like a beard to form the continent's southernmost extreme, Wilsons Prom consists of 49,000 hectares of parkland and an additional 8300 marine hectares off the mesmerizing granite coastline. Declared a UNESCO World Biosphere Reserve, the Prom is off limits to both public transportation and human settlement to preserve its environment. Although the possibility of cutting a road through the park is under consideration by the state government, environmentalists maintain that the effect would be disastrous for its delicate ecosystems. The lack of roads doesn't seem to deter thousands of vacationing Melburnian families, who spend holidays playing beach cricket by sandy coves.

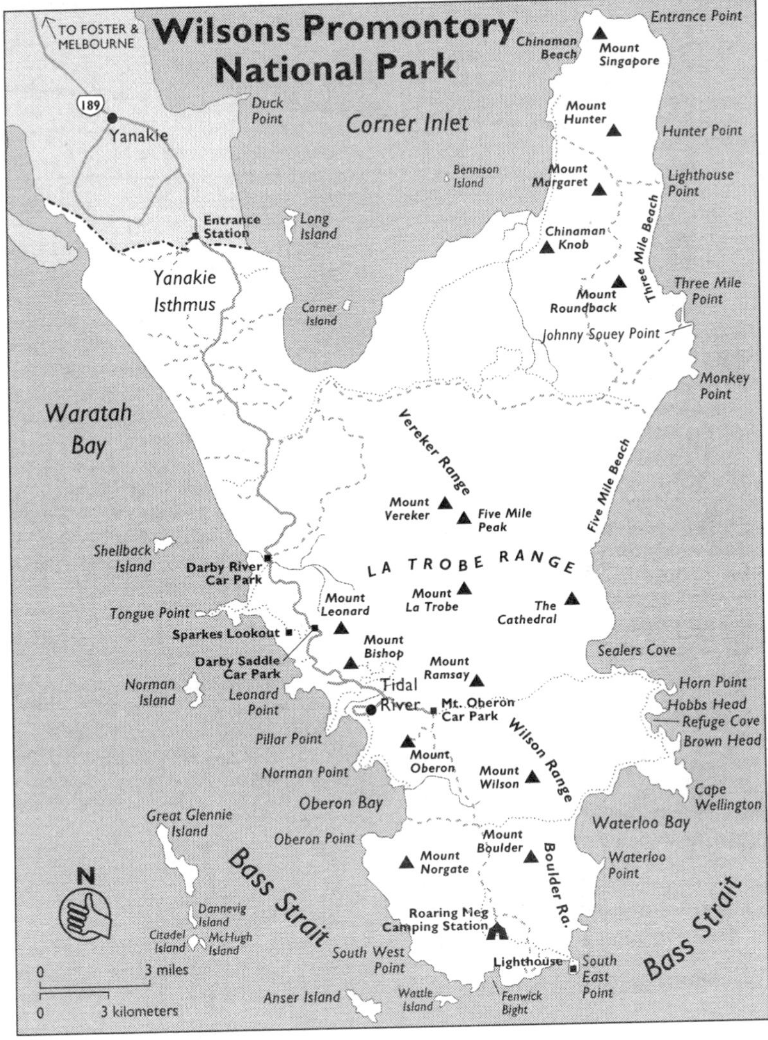

ACCESS TO WILSONS PROMONTORY: FOSTER

Don't fret, transportationally-challenged backpackers; Wilsons Prom is accessible via Foster, the closest city with public transportation. There's a small **tourist office** (tel. 5682 1125; open Thurs.-Sun. 10am-4pm) on Main St. and an ANZ **bank** opposite for last-minute cash. The Prom-bound can provision at **Tosch's Foodmarket,** also downtown. The **V/Line bus** from Melbourne's Spencer St. Station passes through Foster (Mon.-Fri. 4:30pm, Sat. 6:40pm, Sun. 5:35pm, 2¾hr., $21.30; returns Mon.-Sat. 7:49am, Sun. 3:20pm). The **post office** (open Mon.-Fri. 9am-5pm) distributes mail to Tidal River—a boon to backpackers since the **Prom Postie** (tel. 5682 2614) provides shuttle transport even if you're not metered mail (departs Mon.-Fri. 9:30am, Sun. 1:30pm; returns to Foster Mon.-Fri. 12:30pm, Sun. 2:30pm; return $20).

Unfortunately, the timing of the buses requires most travelers to spend a night in Foster. Head west from the post office toward Pearl Park and cross over the little brook by a footbridge to reach **The Little Mud Hut,** 17 Pioneer St. (tel. 5682 2614).

This YHA affiliate has tiny cabin rooms with simple, homespun amenities. Nine beds, all in heated rooms, and an outdoor stove and kitchen area complement a TV lounge where you can sip tea and coffee as you await your trip to the Prom. Beds cost $15, doubles $35. Reserve a couple days in advance during peak season

THE PARK

South of Foster, the Prom's lone access road snakes toward the national park passing through the town of Yanakie along the way. The entrance to the park is nearly 10km past **Yanakie** (entry $7 per car, free if you have arranged for accommodations in the park). Driving south, travelers begin to glimpse the gum forests, abundant bird and marsupial life, and granite cliffs whose breathtaking panoramas bear witness to the awesome beauty of rock and surf colliding. In fact, a few hours of exploration prove that these roadside views are the least spectacular in the park. To most richly experience the Prom's natural majesty, one ought to tackle a few bushwalking trails. A day is enough to sample the Prom; allow five days to savor it.

Until the Yanakie gateway visitor center opens at the park's main entrance, all visitors should continue 30km into the park to the **Tidal River Information Centre** (tel. 5680 9555 or 1800 350 552; fax 5680 9516; open Tues.-Thurs. 8am-7:30pm, Fri.-Sat. 8am-9pm) at the end of the main road. Here, visitors can obtain maps of the park, trail guides, updates on weather conditions, and information about the Prom's geology and teeming plant and animal populations. It is critical that all visitors register their intentions to bushwalk and camp so that park officials will be on the lookout should things go awry. Tidal River also has the last toilets, pay phones, snack machines, and mini-market you'll see before setting off into the bush.

WALKS AND TRAILS

The park is crisscrossed by walking trails, which are described in the information center's *Discovering the Prom on Foot* ($7). The less-visited northern reaches of the park are traversed mostly by overnight hikes which originate from the **5 Mile Road Car Park,** the first left after the Yanakie entrance. The **Southern Section** contains nearly all of the Prom's well-known sights and trails. Seven short walks (1-2km at most) depart from Tidal River, including **Whale Rock,** with a delightful view of Mt. Oberon, **Loo-ern Track,** specially designed for those with limited mobility, and the **Squeaky Beach Nature Walk.** This third track winds through dunes, coastal scrub, and beautiful granite outcroppings. Look for wombats in the scrub, and once on the beach, slide your feet to hear the remarkably uniform white-grained sand squeak. On all hikes, carry water, food, sunblock, a hat, and insect repellent.

Another eight trails take you farther afield from Tidal River (each 1-5km) and can easily be accomplished in a day. They take in the Prom's rich habitats, which range from the Picnic and Whiskey Bay beaches to the koala-laden eucalypt forests to the cool, fern-filled temperate rainforest.

For more ambitious hikers, three spectacular day hikes cover some of the most beloved spots in the Prom. In the southern half of the park, **Tongue Point Track** starts from Darby Saddle 6.7km north of Tidal River and proceeds past two sweeping lookouts to a small granite peninsula with a stunning view of the coast. The **Oberon Bay Track** (6km) follows the scenic western coastline along yellow sand beaches from Norman Bay to Norman Point, site of both Oberon Bay and Little Oberon Bay. In the opposite direction, departing from the Mt. Oberon car park east of Tidal River, the **Sealers Cove Track** (19.5km) takes you across nearly every environment in the Prom. This popular route passes through eucalypt, stringy bark, and Messmate forest before opening into a grassy area 3km from the car park. From here it descends into Sealers Swamp and through fern gullies en route to the striking **Sealers Cove.**

The two overnight hikes in the south are absolutely worth the time and extra preparation, as they allow hikers to savor the multitude of terrains and spectacular, secluded spots. The most popular two-to-three day hike sweeps 36km around the eastern coastal areas along well-maintained trails, to Sealers Cove, Refuge Cove, and

Waterloo Bay. Camping facilities and pit toilets line the trail. To slip off the beaten path for a truly invigorating experience, try the **Lighthouse Trail.** Departing the Mt. Oberon car park you'll head south past the Halfway Hut through stands of eucalypts. From here a more rugged walking trail through tea tree groves, temperate rainforest, and wind-blown plateaus proceeds past Roaring Meg before making a final steep descent along the old telegraph line. The fury of gale and surf combine with the majestic 1858 vintage lighthouse to frame an unparalleled bushwalk.

ACCOMMODATIONS

Securing a place to spend the night at the Prom during the summer months is notoriously difficult, and Victorian residents lottery for spots. Reserve a campsite, cabin, hut, lodge, or cottage space far in advance for Easter, Christmas, and summer school holidays (high season Sept.-April). Contact the **Tidal River Office** (tel. 5680 9555) for all bookings. The newest accommodation is at one of the **Lighthouse's Cottages** ($30 high season; $25 off season). Nearly 20km from Tidal River, these former residences for keepers of the lighthouse provide great kitchen facilities, bathrooms, and snug beds. Best of all, glorious sunrises reward early risers. Stick around until 10am when lighthouse tours are given. There is linen hire (sheets, doona, towel; $7.50; request when booking) and a meal plan, though you'll save by bringing your own food. **Huts** at Tidal River with four to six beds ($9.50) contain hot plates, heaters, fridges, cold water, and crockery. Bring linens, blankets, and food. **Tidal River Camping** has 480 sites with access to toilets and telephones. (high season $13.60, off season $7.10; includes 1 vehicle). You can also camp at one of 11 outstation campsites, such as **Roaring Meg,** which feature designated grounds, fresh water, shelters, and pit toilets ($3.90 per person; children $2).

Lakes Entrance

Stretching out along a long and expansive estuary system, Lakes Entrance (pop. 7000) delights numerous tourists with its mild Riviera climate. A dizzying strip of motels and stores services the sun-worshippers who descend on the seaside resort year-round.

ORIENTATION AND PRACTICAL INFORMATION

Princes Hwy., called the **Esplanade** in town, runs along the waterfront, home to most accommodations and stores. Entering from the west, beautiful vistas of the 400 square kilometer lake system greet visitors. Survey the view from the safety of your car at turn-off areas, or take the walking trail from town to the top of Mt. Barkly.

Myer St. forms the main north-south cross street. **Lakes Entrance Visitors Centre** (tel. 5155 1966) is on the corner of Marine Pde. and the Esplanade (open daily 9am-5pm) at Lakes' eastern extreme. The center has a museum upstairs and is one of three tourist offices in East Gippsland. Three very long blocks west is the **post office** (open Mon.-Fri. 9am-5pm, postal code 3909). Across the street is the **bus stop** with **V/Line** service east along the Princes Hwy. all the way to Narooma, NSW (1 per day, 12:20-2:15pm). Westbound service goes to Melbourne (3 per day, 4¾hr., $40.10) via Bairnsdale (30min., $7.30). The bus also stops near the hostels on the east end of town by request. **Greyhound** serves Lakes Entrance, albeit in the middle of the night. Four blocks east, **Tuckerbag grocery store** is on Myer and Roadknight St. (open daily 8am-7pm). **National Bank ATM,** at 299-301 the Esplanade, east of the post office, accepts Visa, MC, Cirrus, and Plus.

ACCOMMODATIONS AND FOOD

Riviera Backpackers, 5 Clarkes Rd. (tel./fax 5155 4558), 3 blocks east on the Princes Hwy. and just north. Ask the bus to stop near the hostel, although hostel staff will pick you up at the station if you call in advance. This excellent YHA earns high marks for its sparkling new, well-stocked facilities. Large lounge with TV, a solar-heated pool, and pool table. Car park. Laundry facilities. Free linen and safe storage. 24hr. reception. Heated and fan-cooled dorms with bath $13 with YHA (weekly $78). V, MC, AmEx, DC. Book in early Dec. for summer school holidays.

Lakes Main Caravan Park (tel. 5155 2365), 2 blocks north of the YHA, offers a more spartan hostel. On-site vans and bunk-style snug cabins provide basic accommodation. Small kitchen, TV room, and a shed full of video games and billiards. BBQ by the toilet block. Laundry facilities. Dorms $10, during Christmas holiday $15. Tent sites $10, peak season $17; powered sites $12, $20; on-site caravans for 2 $20, $40 ($5 each additional person, under 14 $3); mobile homes $30, $55. V, MC, Bancard.

Restaurants and takeaway shops dot the Esplanade. **Aldo's Pinocchio Inn,** 569 the Esplanade (tel. 5155 2565), offers a great all-you-can-eat pizza and pasta dinner ($10, children $5). They're open late and accept Visa, MC, DC, and Bancard. An absolute culinary must is the **Riviera Natural Farm Ice Cream and Shop** (tel. 5155 2972) on the Esplanade opposite the footbridge. A Royal Melbourne and Royal Sydney Gold Medalist, Riviera's award-winning ice cream is entirely farm produced—from the cows' milk to the final product. Generous portions ($1.80-4) come in 35 distinctive flavors (open daily 9am-5pm).

SIGHTS AND ACTIVITIES

Lake's biggest attraction is its expansive beachfront. To reach the **90-mile beach** cross the footbridge opposite Myer St. From the snack bar and toilet area, a one-hour (one-way) walking track goes west to the entrance of the natural reserve area. From here, water taxis can ferry you to the Gippsland Lakes park. Tours of the lakes operated by **Peels Tourist and Ferry Service** (tel. 5155 1246) launch from the jetty opposite the Centrepoint clock tower on the Esplanade (depart 9:30am or 2pm, $15-21, 2-2½hr.). The **Corque Winery Cruises** (tel. 5155 1508) offer a chance to tour the lakes and sample vintages from the Wyanga Park Winery. Cruises also stop to tour the old Signal Station overlooking Bass Strait (morning tea or lunch, 2-4hr., $18-28) and include free tastings, a main course, and a glass of wine at Henry's Winery Cafe. If you're more ambitious, visit **Victor Hire Boats** (tel. 5155 1888) on the north arm behind Glenara Motel and be your own skipper for the day.

Curious landlubbers can watch fishing boats unload at the **Fisherman's Cooperative Wharf,** south of the visitors center. Viewing platforms overlook trawlers dropping off fish, prawns, scallops, and oysters. Fantastically fresh creatures of the deep are sold at the adjacent **Lakes Entrance Fish Shop** (open daily 8:30am-5pm). An interesting rainy day stop is the **Griffith Sea Shell Museum** (tel. 5155 1538), just east of Centrepoint on the Esplanade. Browse an extensive collection of shell displays and shells for sale (in summer open daily 9am-noon and 2-5pm; in winter 10am-noon and 2-4pm).

Buchan

In the heart of Gippsland, Buchan (rhymes with "truckin"), immerses visitors in the region's distinctive environment. The town's spectacular caves are only the best-known of its numerous natural sights. Just 50km north of Lakes Entrance and 53km northeast of Bruthen, Buchan serves as a central point from which to explore Gippsland's coastal regions and rugged inland gorges. Since no public transport serves Buchan, most backpackers meander through on the **Oz Experience bus** (tel. 1300 300 028), bound for Melbourne or Sydney. South of the Buchan Caves, the small town center contains a **general store** (open 8:30am-5:30pm) with basic food and **tourist information.** Across the street, additional visitor information can be collected from the **post office** (postal code 3885; open Mon.-Fri. 9am-5pm).

The **Buchan Lodge** on Saleyard Rd. (tel. 5155 9421), just north of the town center, provides a stellar budget accommodation in a building beautifully constructed with natural timbers. The lodge's large dorm-style rooms teem with Oz Experience backpackers. The grand central lodge houses a dining area and a kitchen packed with condiments, appliances, and crockery. Guests are invited to swim, take tube rides, or watch for platypuses in the Buchan River out back. Beds with bath are $15, breakfast included, and dinner ($5) can be ordered as well. Book ahead.

The **Buchan Caves** is a 260-hectare reserve just across the Buchan River. These simply dazzling limestone caves draw as many visitors as omnipresent 'roos. Numerous campsites make the park an excellent stop. As you enter the park, the **visitors information center** on the left reserves campsites and sells refreshments and tickets for cave tours (open 9am-3pm in peak season; latecomers can pay in the morning). The two big caves, **Fairy Cave** and **Royal Cave,** are open for guided tours (departing each hour 10am-3pm, 1hr.; admission to each $10, children $5, families $25).

Detours Eco-Adventures (tel. 5155 9264) runs a wide range of outdoor activities from the Buchan Lodge and other locations. Try your hand at abseiling, horseback riding, or bushwalking, or place your bets on a mystery trip.

Snowy River National Park

Shrouded in mythic Australiana, Snowy River National Park surrounds the once mighty Snowy River with rugged, jagged hills dressed in green. The park is accessible only by perilous dirt tracks; most visitors will approach on the Buchan Gelantipy Rd. to MacKillop Bridge via the Little River track. From the road's turnoff it is a treacherous 45-minute drive to the unmanned information kiosk just east of the Snowy River. From this point you'll stare down at a once-roaring river (notice the bridge's span) whose damming for hydroelectric power generation has limited water flow to less than 5% of its original levels. Despite that, the rugged beauty depicted in the legendary film *The Man From Snowy River* (which was actually filmed in **Mansfield,** p. 501) can still be appreciated from campsites based at MacKillop Bridge and along walking tracks which depart from the kiosk and traverse the full range of the park. Whitewater rafting, canoeing, and kayaking are quite popular, water levels permitting. Those confident with their vehicle's ability can complete a circuit to Bonang or back to Buchan by continuing on the gravel Bonang Gelantipy Rd. as it skirts the park's eastern edge.

If you're interested in visiting the Snowy from a nearby lodging, there are two good options. The **Karoonda Park YHA** (tel. 5155 0220), on the sealed portion of the Buchan Gelantipy Rd. south of MacKillop Bridge, boasts a newly completed facility. Spacious, heated, dorm-style rooms ($14, YHA non-members $17) come equipped with linens, towels, and sparkling toilet facilities. Guests can enjoy tasty meals in the spacious, fire-lit central hall (meals $21, YHA non-members $24), and may use the large gym, ping pong and pool tables, and the swimming pool and tennis courts. This working farm also operates horseback riding tours, abseiling, and two-day rafting trips when the Snowy's rapids roar. Caravan-style cottages with slightly dated furnishings sleep up to six ($65; V, MC, AmEx, Bancard).

Farther north along the dirt track en route to Suggan Buggan and Jindabyne, NSW, one can enjoy a tranquil mountain retreat at the **Candlebark Cottage** (tel. 5155 0263) at "Springs" along the Snowy River-Jindabyne Rd. Adjacent to Alpine National Park in a picturesque country valley, the heated cottage contains a double bed and six loft bunks. It's an ideal base for bushwalking, trout fishing, or exploring the grand natural surroundings. Rob and Esme Boys can arrange activities, meals, and tours within their property and the surrounding national parks, and will generously look after troubled motorists (thanks!). The on-site Eagle Loft Gallery exhibits an excellent range of country artisanry. The cottage costs $40 for two, $15 for each additional person, or can be rented for $300 per week (V, MC, and Bancard accepted).

Croajingolong National Park

Tickling Victoria's eastern coastline from the New South Wales border to Sydenham Inlet, Croajingolong (crow-uh-ZHING-a-long) National Park provides visitors with a rich diversity of environments and the chance for secluded exploration. This rarely visited national park extends nearly 100km and covers 87,500 hectares. Despite having been recognized by UNESCO as a World Biosphere Reserve, Croajingolong remains a largely undiscovered gem.

WILDERNESS COAST ORIENTATION

East of Lakes Entrance, the coast of Victoria becomes a seemingly endless stretch of wilderness punctuated by secluded lakes and estuarine inlets. The **Princes Hwy.** surrenders the coast to this length of wild and retreats 10 to 20km inland. The highway passes through **Cann River** and **Genoa** before crossing the border into New South Wales. The park is most accessible from the east, via the town of **Mallacoota,** south of Genoa.

From Cann River, it is possible to take the Tambook Road south into the western regions of the park. Also from Cann River, the Cann Valley Highway (Hwy. 23) heads north past Mt. Coopracambra and into New South Wales toward Cooma (see p. 196) and Canberra (see p. 72).

ACCESS TO CROAJINGOLONG: MALLACOOTA

Surrounded by Croajingolong National Park and Bass Strait, Mallacoota (pop. 1200) bobs between forest and sea at Victoria's easternmost edge. The town thrives on its environmental wealth by giving eco-tours and harvesting abalone during a 60-day season. Sleepy caravan parks blossom into bustling tent towns during summer and Easter school holidays, as if mirroring the cyclical ecology of the area. The community also sustains a strong artistic community with many writers and artists in residence. Mallacoota's July Blues Festival punctuates the hamlet's cultural diversity.

Public transportation misses Mallacoota, approaching only as close as **Genoa** (jen-OH-uh), 23km north on the Princes Hwy. Visitors should arrange transport with a tour provider before arriving in Genoa if they can't find another way to get there. Once in Mallacoota, you'll approach the town center along Maurice Ave., which possesses a **Tuckerbag market** (open daily 8:30am-6:30pm) and **post office** (open Mon.-Fri. 9am-5pm, Sat. 9am-noon).

The YHA **Mallacoota Wilderness Lodge** (tel. 5158 0455), also on Maurice Ave., is part of the adjacent hotel, and boasts a few bunk rooms, a communal kitchen, and bathrooms. With laundry, BBQ, a pool, and a terrific location nearly on the water, it's an excellent place to unwind after a day of kayaking or bushwalking (dorms $13; doubles and twins $30; V, MC, AmEx, DC, and Bancard). Book in advance for peak times.

For a distinctive splurge, the **Karbeethong Lodge** (tel. 5158 0411 or 1800 035 661; fax 5158 0081), on Schnapper Point Dr. in neighboring Karbeethong, offers historic lodging and stunning views beside Mallacoota Inlet with the gently undulating Howe Ranges in the distance. The dining room's walls are adorned with leaded glass and bedecked with photos. Spacious, lovingly decorated rooms come with a loo or a view (opt for the view), a kitchen, and a fridge. Rooms for two are $60-90, depending on season. Longer stays receive discounts. Breakfast is included (V, MC, Bancard). Book in advance for peak season.

The best way to navigate Mallacoota's neighboring Croajingolong National Park is with **Journey Beyond Eco-Adventures** (tel. 5158 0166; fax 5158 0090), on Lincoln Lane opposite the YHA hostel. The staff coordinates activities from sea kayaking and bushwalking to 4WD adventures and evening spotlight walks. Their price for a full day's activity hovers around $100. This always includes the cost of equipment, transport, top-notch guides, and nourishment. They're quite flexible in tailoring activities for visitors (V, MC, Bancard).

For maps, bookings, and general information on Croajingolong National Park, visit a DCNR center either in Cann River (tel. 5158 6351) or Mallacoota (tel. 5158 0219). Campsites should be booked weeks in advance if you plan to visit during the summer school holidays. Remember to bring firewood, food, and water.

THE PARK AND VICINITY

Before exploring Croajingolong it's necessary to contact the **Department of Conservation and Natural Resources** (tel. 5158 0219), on the corner of Allan and Buckland Dr. in Mallacoota, and inform them of your plans.

Croajingolong from Mallacoota

The easternmost extreme of Croajingolong boasts a richly diverse environment. From the New South Wales border west past Lake Barracoota, the **Cape Howe Wilderness Area** is comprised of craggy red granite shores, tidal rivers, temperate rainforest, eucalypt forest, and sweeping sand dunes. They can also provide maps and general camping and bushwalking information. From the east end of Bottom Lake in the Mallacoota Inlet the **Lake View Track** heads northeast, intersects the **Barracoota Track** (which heads southeast), and terminates at Lake Barracoota. Unlike the tidal estuaries which surround it, **Lake Barracoota,** Australia's second largest freshwater lake, stores freshwater less than 1km from the edge of the sea. Pick up the brochure *Discovering Mallacoota Inlet* for more detailed information.

Although not a part of Croajingolong, **Gabo Island** juts out to the south of the Cape Howe Wilderness Area. Connected to the mainland until the isthmus eroded away at the turn of the century, Gabo Island's vibrant, exotic red granite composes Victoria's easternmost isle. Quarried from the island in a Herculean feat of 1862, the **lighthouse** (Australia's second-tallest at 47.5m) continues to steer ships clear of the coast. Gabo Island also houses the world's largest colony of Little Penguins, with over 40,000 adult birds. Access to Gabo Island can be coordinated by boat, kayak, or plane.

West from Mallacoota, the **Centre Track** provides a decent unsealed road which leads to the **Shipwreck Creek Camping Area** and its five campsites, pit toilet, fireplaces, and fresh water. The camping area is a 45-minute drive from Mallacoota, and puts you near the beachfront forest and rock outcroppings nearby. One can also sea kayak into the Creek's tidal basin. The surf beach can be quite rough in places, but the inlet by the creek is ideal for family water play. Tracks facilitate exploration of the heath from Mallacoota to Seal Creek.

Croajingolong from the Princes Highway

Heading south from Cann River along the **Tamboon Rd.** will bring you to three camping areas in Croajingolong's western half. The **Mueller River Camping Area** is 15km down Tamboon Rd. and then 24km left down Point Hicks Rd. From here a left turn on to Bald Hills Track leads to the campsite, just 1km away. Twelve walk-in and drive-in sites along the Mueller Inlet and Sandy Beach are complemented by two pit toilets. Nearby on Point Hicks Rd., 1km closer to the beach, the 47-site **Thurra River Camping Area** offers similar facilities. Swimming and canoeing are popular at both locations. A short walk to the **Point Hicks Lighthouse**, erected in 1888, is a terrific outing.

On the Princes Hwy. about 12km west of Genoa and 17km east of Cann River, West Wingan Road turns off south toward the wild coast. A drive on West Wingan leads visitors 34km south to **Wingan Inlet Camping Area.** All 24 sites have access to pit toilets, fresh water, picnic tables, and a small boat launch. The **Wingan Nature Walk** skirts the inlet and leads to the beach, Lake Elusive, Rame Head, and Easby Creek. Fishing is excellent, but don't forget to purchase a license from the Cann River DCNR, and consider provisioning there.

Western Australia

Western Australia is huge, to put it mildly. The water pipes that stretch from Perth to Kalgoorlie are the length of England. The state boundaries enclose an area three-and-a-half times the size of Texas and could contain the Netherlands 70 times over. Yet most visitors, like most Western Australians (or Westralians), never see more than a fraction of the gargantuan state. The population of WA, as the state is commonly known, is overwhelmingly urban and oriented toward the coast. Over 90% of the state's 1.7 million people live within a short drive of the Indian Ocean, whether among the vineyards of the southwest, along the surf-pounded capes of the northwest, or in the oasis of Perth itself. The economy of this coastal fringe is booming, and streams of pre-fabricated houses strapped to flatbed trailers roll down the highway. Perth, WA's capital, is a city complete with shiny skyscrapers, four universities, and a gentle climate. Brochures gleefully quote the American consulate there as saying that the city "has the kind of weather that California thinks it has."

But away from the populated western strip, WA undergoes a sobering transformation. In stark contrast to the coast's greenery, the interior contains the combined wasteland of three deserts. Unpopulated except by scattered cattle and sheep stations, this vast country is divided by long, empty stretches of red road flanked by spinifex grass and sandy plains. Even where the climate is not stone-dry, it is uncompromisingly harsh; in the far north, the monsoon-affected Kimberley region is so remote that Perth is regarded with a reverence usually reserved for the Holy Land.

Despite the importance of deserts and floods in the topography and culture of Western Australia, as a tourist destination the state is best known for its wildflowers and woods. Between August and November, 8000 species of wildflower bloom in carpets that sweep south down the coast and through the Great Southern region, inspiring pilgrimage in cults of devoted blossom-worshippers. Meanwhile, southwestern WA is the domain of old-growth forests of the huge karri and jarrah eucalypts. Among the world's largest trees, the majestic karri can reach heights of 80m and stand in defiance of the state's thriving wood-chipping industry.

Sheer geographic isolation reinforces the independent nature of the people of WA. In 1933, a state referendum revealed a two-to-one preference to separate from the Commonwealth of Australia. Secession never became a political reality, but the self-sufficient spirit that bred the movement remains a subtle undercurrent. While many proud Westralians depend on heavy industry for their livelihood, a growing minority regard as crucial the protection of their state's natural resources. Ecotourism and promotion of natural attractions have begun to edge out the fishing and animal husbandry industries, and tourists certainly prefer swimming with the dolphins at Monkey Mia to visiting the massive open-pit mines of the outback. But lucrative resource exploitation is unlikely to cease, and the ongoing debate suggests that sometimes a state just can't be large enough.

Phone numbers in Western Australia have recently changed. Regional phone codes are now all 08, followed by eight-digit numbers. If you have trouble making a call, use the following scheme to get the old number, and try that instead. For more details, see the **appendix** (p. 574). For all numbers with a three-digit phone code followed by six digits, the last two digits of the code become the first digits of the new eight-digit number.

New Number:	Old Number:
(08) 9xxx xxxx	(09) xxx xxxx (Perth)
(08) 90xx xxxx	(090) xx xxxx
(08) 99xx xxxx	(099) xx xxxx

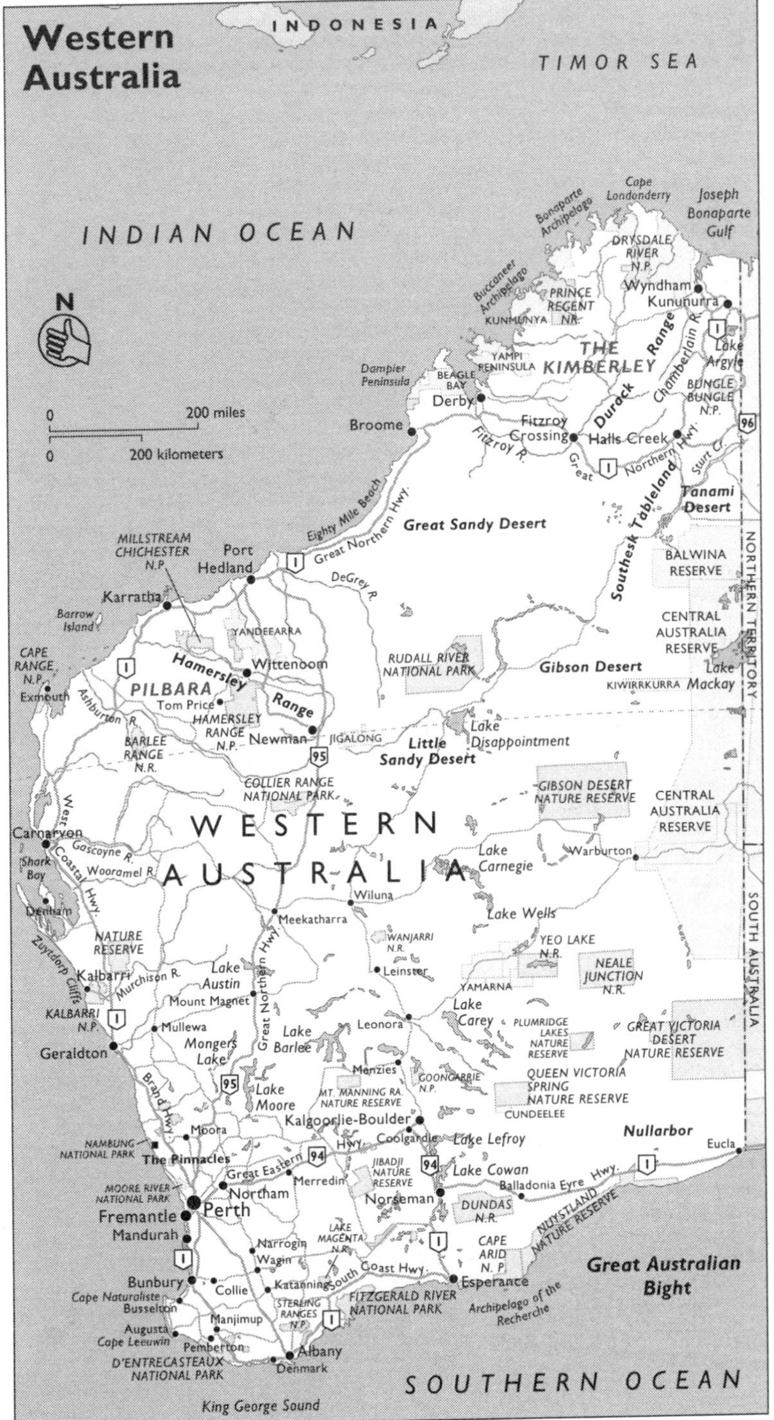
Western Australia
INDONESIA
TIMOR SEA
INDIAN OCEAN
N
0
200 miles
0
200 kilometers
Cape Londonderry
Joseph Bonaparte Gulf
Bonaparte Archipelago
DRYSDALE RIVER N.P.
Buccaneer Archipelago
PRINCE REGENT N.R.
KUNMUNYA
Wyndham
Kununurra
Lake Argyle
THE KIMBERLEY
YAMPI PENINSULA
Durack Range
Chamberlain R.
BUNGLE BUNGLE N.P.
Dampier Peninsula
BEAGLE BAY
Derby
Broome
Fitzroy Crossing
Halls Creek
Fitzroy R.
Great Northern Hwy.
Sturt Cr.
Tanami Desert
Eighty Mile Beach
Great Sandy Desert
Southesk Tableland
BALWINA RESERVE
MILLSTREAM CHICHESTER N.P.
Port Hedland
DeGrey R.
Karratha
Barrow Island
YANDEEARRA
CENTRAL AUSTRALIA RESERVE
CAPE RANGE N.P.
Exmouth
Hamersley Range
Wittenoom
RUDALL RIVER NATIONAL PARK
Gibson Desert
Lake Mackay
KIWIRRKURRA
NORTHERN TERRITORY
PILBARA
Tom Price
Ashburton R.
HAMERSLEY RANGE N.P.
Newman
JIGALONG
Little Sandy Desert
Lake Disappointment
BARLEE RANGE N.R.
COLLIER RANGE NATIONAL PARK
GIBSON DESERT NATURE RESERVE
CENTRAL AUSTRALIA RESERVE
WESTERN AUSTRALIA
Carnarvon
Gascoyne R.
Shark Bay
North West Coastal Hwy.
Wooramel R.
Lake Carnegie
Warburton
Denham
Wiluna
Meekatharra
Lake Wells
NATURE RESERVE
WANJARRI N.R.
YEO LAKE N.R.
NEALE JUNCTION N.R.
SOUTH AUSTRALIA
Zuytdorp Cliffs
Kalbarri
Murchison R.
Lake Austin
Leinster
YAMARNA
Mount Magnet
Lake Carey
KALBARRI N.P.
Mullewa
Leonora
PLUMRIDGE LAKES NATURE RESERVE
GREAT VICTORIA DESERT NATURE RESERVE
Geraldton
Mongers Lake
Lake Barlee
Great Northern Hwy.
Menzies
GOONGARRIE N.P.
QUEEN VICTORIA SPRING NATURE RESERVE
Brand Hwy.
Lake Moore
MT. MANNING RA. NATURE RESERVE
CUNDEELEE
Kalgoorlie-Boulder
Moora
Nullarbor
NAMBUNG NATIONAL PARK
The Pinnacles
Coolgardie
Lake Lefroy
Eucla
Great Eastern Hwy.
Merredin
JIBADJI NATURE RESERVE
Lake Cowan
MOORE RIVER NATIONAL PARK
Northam
Norseman
Balladonia
Eyre Hwy.
Perth
Fremantle
DUNDAS N.R.
NUYTSLAND NATURE RESERVE
Mandurah
Narrogin
LAKE MAGENTA N.R.
Wagin
CAPE ARID N.P.
Great Australian Bight
Bunbury
Collie
Katanning
South Coast Hwy.
Esperance
Cape Naturaliste
Busselton
STERLING RANGES N.P.
FITZGERALD RIVER NATIONAL PARK
Archipelago of the Recherche
Manjimup
Augusta
Cape Leeuwin
Pemberton
Albany
D'ENTRECASTEAUX NATIONAL PARK
Denmark
SOUTHERN OCEAN
King George Sound

WESTERN AUSTRALIA

GETTING AROUND WESTERN AUSTRALIA

Because of the size of Western Australia, the distances between points of interest, and the dearth of long-haul transportation, many travelers—even budget travelers—**buy a car** for long visits. It's probably the best way to see Western Australia, and the freedom is usually worth the added responsibility. A thriving gray market exists for used cars, 4WD vehicles, and campervans, perpetuated by message boards at hostels in Perth. **Used car dealerships** line Beaufort St. several kilometers north of Northbridge, outside Perth. WA is in the middle of a $1 billion **Main Roads** infrastructure project. If you plan to make a long **drive through the desert,** be sure to keep on hand plenty of water and petrol/gasoline, in addition to a spare tire and a spare fanbelt. Winter and early spring are the safest times of year to drive the Great Northern Hwy. because temperatures are lower and traffic more frequent. Either way, you'll have to share the highway with road trains, massive tractor-multiple-trailers that dominate the bitumen.

With the exception of the Kalgoorlie stop on the Indian Pacific line, passenger **rail** service is essentially non-existent. A "Rails to Trails" program has phased out rail service south of Bunbury, and the rail lines in the north are abandoned or used exclusively by the mining companies. Sometimes the **bus** is the only way, despite long rides, cramped seats, and ridiculous arrivals (3am? at a closed petrol station? 3km out of town?). **Greyhound Pioneer** (tel. 13 20 30) runs all the service north of Geraldton. The 75-page Greyhound timetable book, available at bus stations and tourist bureaus and updated seasonally, is indispensable. Try to book fares at least a day ahead; since most stops are en route, space for partial-route passengers may be limited, and the bus might not stop unless the driver knows that someone there wants to get on. If you plan to do a lot of bus traveling, the Greyhound Pioneer 11,000km pass may be a good investment. South of Perth and Kalgoorlie, Greyhound service ends and **South West Coach Lines, Westrail,** and **EasyRider** take over.

It is possible to tour portions of Western Australia by **bicycle.** But if you go without support vehicles, you won't be able to camp, since water will take up much of the bike's rack space. In the north, the dryer, cooler, winter season is the time to go. It is unwise to travel alone. Advise regional police, and in the north and outback, the Royal Flying Doctor Service, of your itinerary. Contact the **Ministry of Sport and Recreation** (tel. 9387 9700) for more information.

Let's Go does not recommend **hitchhiking,** although it is done. Particularly in the northern and eastern parts of the state, there's so little traffic that you could get genuinely stuck in the middle of nowhere. Hitchers report that roadhouses are the places to look for rides. Better still, ask at employment offices in Broome and Kalgoorlie about jobs in isolated roadhouses and get to know tour coach drivers. They may be willing to give you a lift to nearby sights, and you'll learn to size up potential rides.

Money Matters

Banks and ATMs in the northern part of WA are rare, although you'll see some in Carnarvon, and one in Exmouth. Visa and Mastercard are widely accepted, and for Australian account-holders, EFTPOS is an option. In small towns, tourist bureaus or post offices often act as bank agents. Supermarkets, bars, and service stations sometimes have "mini-tellers" for cash card withdrawal at the register, but these have $200 withdrawal limits and often do not take Cirrus or Plus cards. Don't get stuck 100km from nowhere with no cash and no plastic.

Perth

Perth is all about water and people, spread out like a picnic by the tranquil, lake-like Swan River and the eternal surf of the Indian Ocean. Everything is as easily done outdoors as in, with family as with friends, in sandals as in shoes. Rumor has it that WA spurns daylight saving time so that business executives can get in a quick surf at Cottesloe Beach before work. The unhurried lifestyle is a point of pride for many of

Perth's 1.5 million citizens, as is their city's status as the most isolated capital in the world. (Adelaide, the nearest state capital, is at least a two days' drive away.)

But isolation does not mean desolation. WA's capital, home to 88% of the state's population and welcoming more and more to its picnic blanket, is an extreme example of Australian demography. Business booms of the 80s and 90s injected fresh funds into the city, which now bristles noticeably with new skyscrapers and condominiums. The growth is easy to understand, given the clean air, accessible beaches, gorgeous sunsets, and mild climate that locals insist on calling "Mediterranean." As long as Western Australia's frontier is ripe for speculation, its capital city will continue to reap the rewards and to plant ever-larger symbols of progress near the sloping banks of the Swan River.

Yet as central Perth grows, some nostalgic residents point to Fremantle, the city's port and the other focus of Perth's energy, as the example to emulate. Funds flowing into "Freo" have been spent on historic, restorative facelifts rather than skyline lifts. Tourist maps even ask visitors to park outside Fremantle's center to help maintain its historic character. In between the port and the central business district lie parks, sails, beaches, and plenty of souls content to share with visitors the lifestyle that their city is famous for. If you've made the effort to cross the kilometers to Perth, you'll be more than welcome. Pick your pub, your sliver of Kings Park, or your patch of sand, and join the picnic.

ARRIVAL AND DEPARTURE

By Plane

Qantas (tel. 13 13 13) and **Ansett** (tel. 13 13 00) fly daily between Perth and Sydney (4½hr.). For travelers arriving from the Americas or planning to fly to Perth after seeing the east coast, it may make sense to purchase a **Qantas Boomerang Pass** (US$400) before entering Australia. The pass is a pair of tickets, the first fixed and the second open-ended. Schedule a flight on the second fare a few weeks before you plan to use it and have your flight coupon validated at a Qantas travel center. Qantas also flies a Perth-to-Sydney red-eye if you wait until the last minute to book. British and other Commonwealth travelers and those with "around-the-world" type tickets can enter Australia at Perth, flying from Hong Kong, Singapore, or Johannesburg.

Ansett, Qantas, and regional carrier **SkyWest** all fly out of Perth. Qantas' **Airlink** network offers direct flights between Perth, Karratha, Port Hedland, Tom Price, Broome, and Kalgoorlie. Local tourist flights around the Perth region fly from **Jandakot Airport,** south of the city; air traffic into and out of the region arrives and departs at **Perth Airport,** east of the city. The terminals are small and easy to navigate, but the international terminal is several kilometers away from the domestic terminals. Keep this in mind if you're planning a connection.

Getting to and from the Perth Airport is a bit vexing. **TransPerth buses** #200, 201, 202, 208, and 209 run between the domestic terminals and St. Georges Tce. in the city center (2 per hr., 35min.). The bus from Perth to the airport leaves from the north side of St. George Tce., stop 39, just west of William St. An **Airport City Shuttle** bus with more room for luggage runs frequently to a number of stops in Perth from both the domestic ($7) and international ($9) terminals. Travelers can also book trips to the airport, with pick-up from hostels or hotels. A **taxi** ride to or from the airport costs around $20. The **Fremantle Airport Shuttle** (tel. 9383 4115) goes to both Perth Airport terminals. The shuttle departs from the Fremantle Railway Station; pick-ups at Fremantle hostels and hotels can be pre-arranged (runs daily, every 2hr., 6am-10pm; $12).

By Train

Intercity trains run from the **East Perth Terminal** on West Pde., a 20-minute walk northeast from the Perth tourist center. **Westrail** (tel. 9326 2244, 9326 2813) has service to Kalgoorlie (Mon.-Sat. 8:45am, Mon., Wed., and Fri. 5:15pm, Sun. 4:15pm, 8hr., $59) and to Bunbury (Mon.-Sat. 9:30am and 5:45pm, Sun. 8:30am and 7:15pm, 2hr., $18). The **Indian Pacific** runs to Sydney (Mon. and Fri. 1:35pm, 65hr., $389).

By Bus

Westrail (tel. 9326 2244) runs buses from the East Perth Terminal to Albany (2 per day, 8hr., $35), Esperance (1-2 per day, 10hr., $53), Geraldton (1-2 per day, 6-8hr., $37), and Kalbarri (Mon., Wed., and Fri. 8:30am, 8hr., $59). **Greyhound** (tel. 13 20 30), also at the East Perth Terminal, runs to Kalgoorlie (daily 6:30am, 8hr., $78), Adelaide (daily 6:30am, 13hr., $193), and Port Hedland (daily 10:30am and Wed., Fri., and Sun. 3:30pm, 24hr., $143) via Geraldton (3¾hr., $38), Cervantes (3hr., $68, including the Pinnacles), Kalbarri (7½hr., $70), Monkey Mia (10hr., $115), Carnarvon (12hr., $103), and Exmouth (16½hr., $151) continuing to Broome (32hr., $220) and Darwin (59½hr., $393). **Southwest Coach Lines** (tel. 9324 2333) departs from the **Perth City Bus Port,** William St., and runs to Bunbury (daily 9am, 1:30, and 5:45pm, 2½hr., $16), and Margaret River (daily 9am and 1:30pm, 5hr., $23).

By Car

To the southwest coast, take the Kwinana Freeway (Hwy. 2) from the west side of Perth and follow the signs for Hwy. 1. To head east to Kalgoorlie, take Riverside Dr. (Hwy. 5) to the Great Eastern Hwy. (Hwy. 1, then National 94). To head north to Geraldton, follow the Great Eastern until Midland, change to the Great Northern Hwy. (National 95), and take the Brand Hwy. (Hwy. 1) at Muchea. To head toward Meekatharra or Newman, follow the Great Northern, and take lots of water and fuel. For more information on traveling by car, see **Essentials,** p. 37.

Car rental can augment infrequent bus service to more distant points. **Budget,** 960 Hay St. (tel. 9322 1100), starts from $25 per day for long-term (2-week) rentals with mileage limits. Budget will rent to anyone with a license but will not insure those under 21 and maintains a higher deductible (excess) for those under 25. **Avis,** 46 Hill St. (tel. 9325 7677), starts from $44 per day. Prices go up on short-term rentals. Avis rents to drivers 25 and older but will rent to people 21-24 who belong to Ansett Australia's or United Airline's Frequent-Flyer programs. Both firms offer monthly rates and caravan rentals. **Bayswater Car Hire,** 160 Adelaide Tce. (tel. 9325 1000; fax 9271 7206), offers cars and 4WDs with full insurance and unlimited mileage to people 20 and older, for prices comparable to Avis and Budget. Many automatic-transmission cars are available. Most agencies are understandably paranoid about clients driving their cars through the bush; inquire as to whether or not insurance coverage cuts off on unpaved roads or in certain areas of the state, particularly the north.

The **Royal Automobile Club (RAC)** at the corner of Adelaide Tce. and Hill St. does vehicle inspections or $90.

Ride-Sharing and Hitchhiking

Hostel message boards are a good way to find a ride or someone to share gas costs on your own drive, and almost all of Perth's hostels provide them. In Perth hitchhiking is hardly necessary, although one may be able to get a lift with a tour operator passing through the suburbs on the way back downtown in the late afternoon. Farther out, road trains cannot stop for passengers—they measure their braking distance in kilometers. Hitchers report better luck waiting at a road house and politely approaching a trucker having coffee. *Let's Go* does not recommend hitching.

ORIENTATION

Although the street grid of downtown Perth is not quite aligned north-south and east-west, it is easy to think of it as such, and locals will understand what you mean by these labels. The rail line is then the northern boundary of the city, and the **Swan River** the southern. The east-west avenues from the railroad tracks downhill to the river are **Wellington St., Murray St., Hay St., Saint Georges Tce.,** and **Riverside Dr.** As they pass **Victoria Square** heading east out of the city, Murray St. becomes Goderich St. and St. Georges Tce. becomes Adelaide Tce. The principal north-south streets, from west to east, are **William, Barrack, Pier, Victoria,** and **Hill St.** Victoria becomes Lord St. as it heads north of Wellington. Between William and Barrack St., Hay and Murray St. become **pedestrian malls.** A series of shopping arcades runs between the

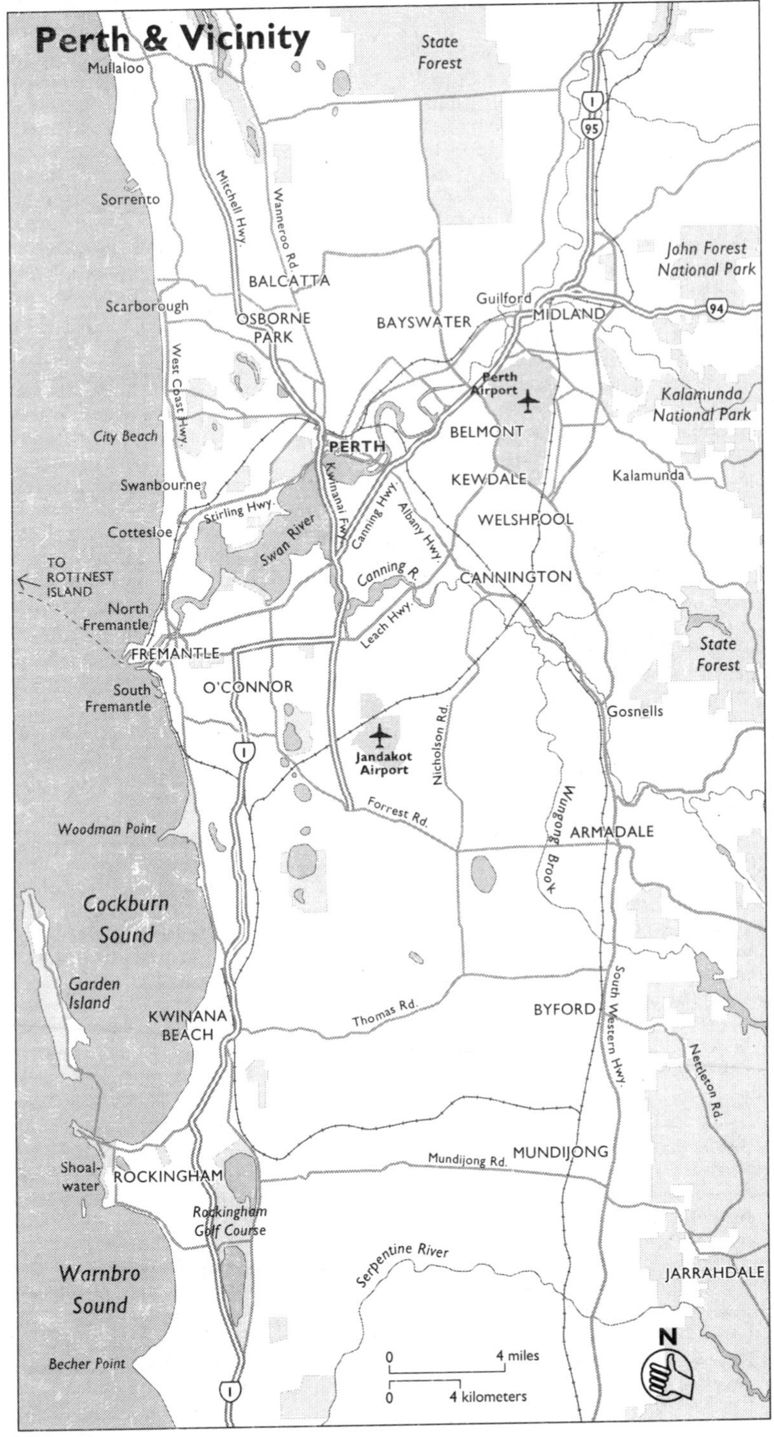

WESTERN AUSTRALIA

malls, and an overhead walkway connects downtown pedestrians to the **Perth Railway Station.** The **Wellington St. Bus Station,** one of two city bus hubs, is one block west of the railway station, across William St. Downtown Perth is relatively safe, but much of it is not well-lit. In the late evening, steer clear of Forrest Place and the railway station.

Northbridge, the city's nexus of culture and nightlife, is north of the railway station. Most activity is clustered in a square formed by Newcastle St., Roe St., Russel Square, and William St., and many budget accommodations lie north and east of this area. The most lively district of the city on weekends, hip Northbridge is generally hospitable to gay and lesbian travelers. Directly south of Perth city, the Mitchell Freeway (Hwy. 2) passes over the Narrows Bridge to the "other side" of the river—an important distinction to locals. A half-hour drive will bring you to the impressively international student population of **Murdoch University,** but everything in-between is suburbia. Great green **Kings Park** rises just southwest of downtown, overlooking the city and the great sweep of the Swan. Beyond the park, the beautiful sandstone campus of the **University of Western Australia** rises by the river. The train running west out of the city behind King's Park passes through the older Perth suburbs, each with their own bakeries and pubs. **Subiaco** in particular is a hot spot for cafes and cuisine, and offers weekend market stalls on either side of the Subiaco train stop. West of the train line are the beach suburbs, well worth a visit for a taste of the heart of Perth culture.

Although technically its own city, **Fremantle** is best thought of as the other pole in the wet-cell battery of greater Perth. Perth is the central business district, Freo is the lucrative fishing port, and everyone goes to both all the time. Because TransPerth buses and trains run frequently between Perth and Fremantle, it is easy to spend a day people-watching in Northbridge cafes, then to return to Fremantle for dinner, or vice versa. The Fremantle **Railway Station** is across the street from the Fremantle Harbour, in the northwest corner of the downtown area. To get to the **Tourist Information Centre** from the railway station, walk down Market St. and turn left to walk through the High St. pedestrian mall to King's Square. The tourist center stands next to Town Hall. At the far end of High St., a 10- to 12-minute walk from King's Square, are **Arthur Head, Bathers Beach,** and, to the south, the **Fishing Boat Harbour.**

GETTING AROUND

Downtown Perth is compact and easy to get around on foot; the walk up William St. from St. Georges Tce. to Aberdeen St. in Northbridge takes 10 minutes. The downtown grid is served by the Central Area Transit or CAT. A free service, sleek gray CAT buses run every five to 10 minutes on weekdays, 7am to 6pm. Service on Friday evenings and weekends is a little less frequent. CAT maps are available at bus stations. Essentially, the CAT with blue trim runs up Barrack St., through Northbridge, and down Lake and William St.; the CAT with red trim runs east on Murray St. and west on Hay St. The weekend CAT is a modified blue loop.

For destinations beyond the downtown area, TransPerth runs an elaborate network of green-striped buses, trains, and ferries. Schedules and information are available weekdays at the **Perth City Bus Port,** west of the Esplanade along Mounts Bay Rd. Information is also available at the **Wellington St. Bus Station** just west of William St. The system is divided into eight fare zones; a two-zone ride costs \$2.30 and will get you from the city center to the airport or to Fremantle (day pass \$6, discounts on multi-ride cards). The **Perth Railway Station** handles TransPerth's suburban train lines. Trains depart daily for **Fremantle** at least twice per hour between 7am and 11pm (30min., \$2.30).

Ongoing roadwork in the Perth area can lead to delays. The western end of the Great Eastern Hwy., as it passes through the Darling Range and down into the interchange with Hwy. 1 in Midland, is being widened. At the moment, bottlenecks are frequent near the airport and along Hwy. 1 through Redcliffe and Belmont, heading west into Perth. Much of Newcastle St. will be out of commission for a few years as construction gets underway on a subterranean freeway tunnel. Most residents say the

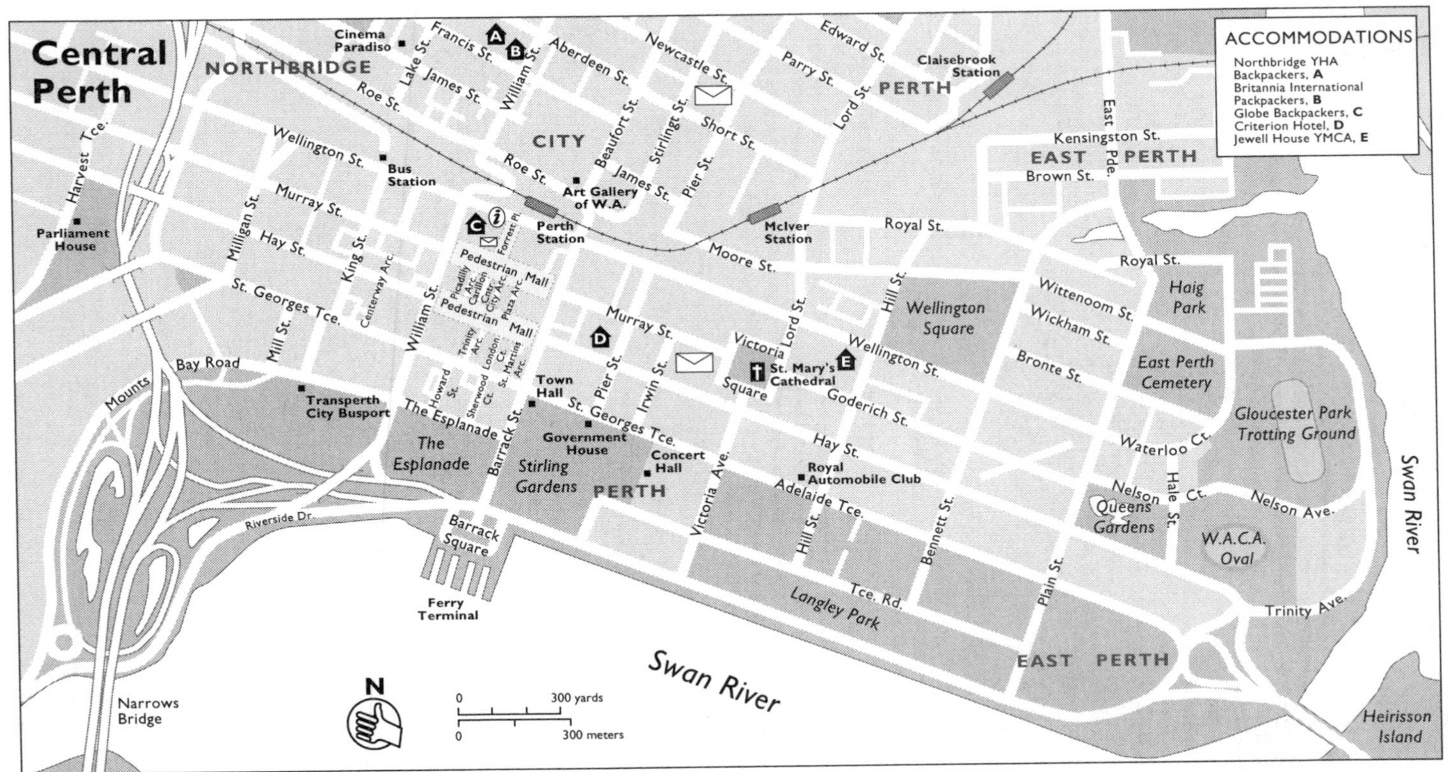
Central Perth
ACCOMMODATIONS
Northbridge YHA Backpackers, A
Britannia International Packpackers, B
Globe Backpackers, C
Criterion Hotel, D
Jewell House YMCA, E
Cinema Paradiso
NORTHBRIDGE
Francis St.
Lake St.
James St.
William St.
Aberdeen St.
Newcastle St.
Edward St.
Parry St.
Claisebrook Station
PERTH
Lord St.
Roe St.
CITY
Beaufort St.
Stirlingt St.
Short St.
East Pde.
Kensington St.
EAST PERTH
Brown St.
Harvest Tce.
Wellington St.
Bus Station
Roe St.
James St.
Pier St.
Art Gallery of W.A.
Murray St.
Perth Station
McIver Station
Royal St.
Parliament House
Milligan St.
Hay St.
King St.
Forrest Pl.
Moore St.
Royal St.
Pedestrian Mall
Piccadilly Arc.
Carillon Cntr.
City Arc.
Plaza Arc.
Centerway Arc.
Wittenoom St.
Haig Park
St. Georges Tce.
William St.
Pedestrian Mall
Hill St.
Wellington Square
Wickham St.
Mill St.
Trinity Arc.
London Ct.
St. Martins Arc.
Murray St.
Victoria
Lord St.
Wellington St.
East Perth Cemetery
Bay Road
Howard St.
Sherwood Ct.
Town Hall
Pier St.
Irwin St.
St. Mary's Cathedral
Square
Bronte St.
Mounts
Transperth City Busport
The Esplanade
Barrack St.
St. Georges Tce.
Goderich St.
Gloucester Park Trotting Ground
The Esplanade
Government House
Concert Hall
Hay St.
Waterloo Ct.
Stirling Gardens
PERTH
Royal Automobile Club
Victoria Ave.
Adelaide Tce.
Nelson Ct.
Hale St.
Nelson Ave.
Queens Gardens
Swan River
Riverside Dr.
Barrack Square
Hill St.
Bennett St.
W.A.C.A. Oval
Plain St.
Ferry Terminal
Tce. Rd.
Langley Park
Trinity Ave.
EAST PERTH
Swan River
N
0 300 yards
0 300 meters
Narrows Bridge
Heirisson Island

tunnel is necessary, but it has forced stores and parks along Newcastle St. to close, provoking controversy.

PRACTICAL INFORMATION

Most shops and services close at noon on Saturdays and open late or remain closed on Sundays. Some Cal-Tex gas (petrol) stations with convenience stores are open 24-hours—try Beaufort St., north of Northbridge.

Tourist Office: At the corner of Wellington St. and Forrest Pl. (tel. 1300 361 351). Across the street from the Railway Station. Free tour-booking service. Open Mon.-Thurs. 8:30am-6pm, Fri. 8:30am-7pm, Sat. 8:30am-5pm, Sun. 10am-5pm.
Budget Travel: STA (tel. 9227 7299), James St. between William and Lake St. Open Mon.-Fri. 9am-5pm. In Fremantle, 53 Market St., open Mon.-Fri. 9am-5pm.
Consulates: Britain, 77 St. Georges Tce. (tel. 9221 5400); **Canada,** 267 St. Georges Tce. (tel. 9322 7930); **Ireland** (tel. 9385 8247); **Japan,** 221 St. Georges Tce. (tel. 9321 7816), **United States,** 16 St. Georges Tce. (tel. 9231 9400; fax 9231 9444).
ATMs: High concentrations on William St. in Northbridge and on Hay St. in the mall area between Barrack and William St. Most machines accept both Cirrus and Plus.
American Express: At 645 Hay St. (Hay Street Mall) in London Court (tel. 9221 0777).
Library: The Alexander Library Building (tel. 9427 3111), at the north end of the Perth Cultural Centre, has limited **internet access.** Wheelchair accessible. Open Mon.-Thurs. 9am-4:45pm, Fri. 9am-5:30pm, Sat.-Sun. 10am-5:30pm.
Public Toilets and Showers: Scattered about the Hay St. Malls, generally on the top garage levels (B1).
Hotlines: Sexual Assault referral center (24hr. tel. 9340 1828). **HIV-Positive Youth Support** (tel. 9227 7978). **Fre-Info** (Fremantle info: tel. 9430 2333).
Hospital: Royal Perth Hospital (tel. 9382 7171), north side of Victoria Sq., near Lord St. **Fremantle Hospital** (tel. 9431 3333), South Tce. and Alma St.
Emergency: Dial 000.
Police: tel. 9221 1048; Fremantle tel. 9430 1222.
Post Office: General Post Office (GPO) (tel. 9237 5460; fax 9322 7862), on the west side of Forrest Pl. *Poste Restante* available Mon.-Fri. only; mail held 1 month. Open Mon.-Fri. 2-5:30pm, Sat. 9am-12.30pm, Sun. noon-4pm. Branch offices on Frances St. in Northbridge and several along Hay St. and St. George Tce. open Mon.-Fri. 8:30am-5pm. **Postal code:** 6000. **Fremantle GPO** (tel. 9335 1611), 13 Market St. Open Mon.-Sat. 8:30am-5pm.
Phone Code: 08.

ACCOMMODATIONS

The most difficult time to find a bed in Perth is in the summer, during December and January. Try to book hostel rooms, in particular, weeks to months in advance. Unfortunately, there is little middle-range accommodation: hotels billing themselves as "three-star" establishments charge nearly as much as luxury hotels, and only a few hotel rooms can be found for as little as $50 per night.

The hostels cluster in both the city center and the Northbridge quarter, just north of the central train and bus station. A few are located south of the city center, east along Hay St. Long-term hostel guests are generally looking for temporary work, and the hostels which cater to them tend to be less pristine and more homey, with dishes piling up in the kitchen sinks. Those below prefer short-term, international guests. All offer free luggage storage, laundry facilities, and kitchens with food storage space. There are no lockout times, though offices are often closed in the middle of the day. It's a good idea to call ahead with your estimated time of arrival.

North Lodge Central City Backpackers, 225 Beaufort St., Northbridge (tel. 9227 7588; fax 9386 9065). At the corner of Beaufort and Monger St. A beautiful, well-kept old house with 25 beds and self-contained flats occupied by a quiet, international crowd. Office open 8:30-11:30am, but the owner will come over if you call.

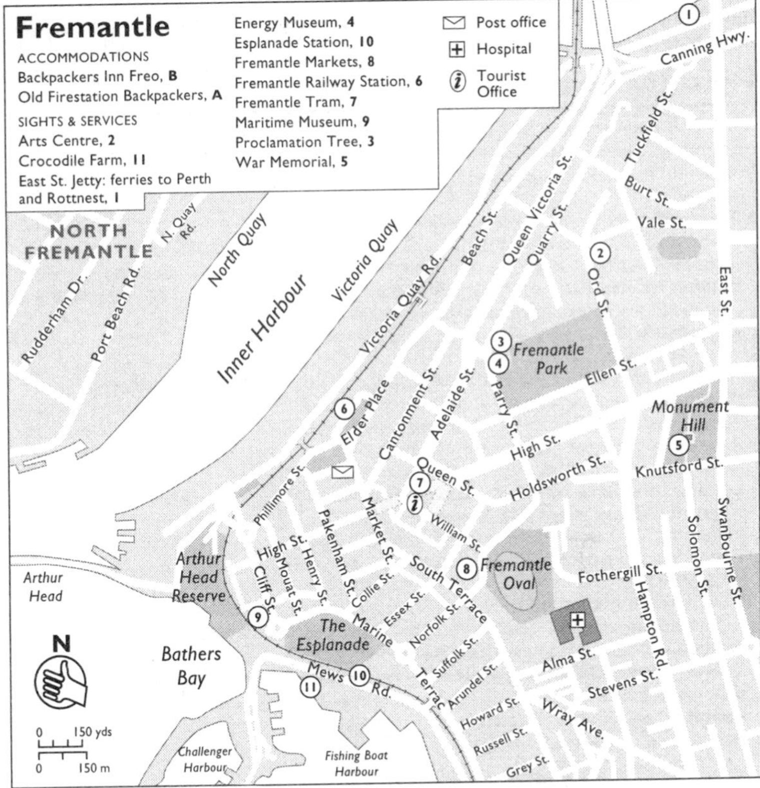

Check-out 9:30am, but feel free to stick around and use the facilities for the rest of the day. 3-bed dorms $12; singles $25; twins $30; flats $20 per person. Weekly: dorms $77, with the option to skip days.

Rainbow Lodge Backpackers, 133 Summers St., Northbridge (tel. 015 773 457). Just east of the Perth Oval, cross Lord St. to Summers St. Bright, airy, and very new; 60 beds and a friendly Canadian owner. Tidy kitchen, big patio area. A hike from the center of town but 3min. from the intercity railway station. Office open 8am-1pm and 4-10pm. 4-bed dorms $13; doubles $32. Weekly: $70; $95. Hot breakfast included. Ask for the *Let's Go* discount.

The Shiralee, 107 Brisbane St., Northbridge (tel. 9227 7448). Walk up William St., and turn right onto Brisbane. Mellow and reserved, with 63 beds and corrugated aluminum siding inside for that pioneer ambience. Patio looks out on a quiet neighborhood. Beautiful glass showers, A/C. 2-week max. stay. Office open 6am-8pm. 4- to 6-bed dorms $15; twins $18 per person. Weekly: $90; $110.

Britannia International Backpackers (YHA), 253 William St., just past Francis St. (tel. 9328 6121; fax 9227 9784). The mother of all Perth hostels, weighing in at 134 beds, with umpteen kitchens and heaps of 8-bed dorms. Well-run and clean. Partially wheelchair accessible. Office open 7am-11pm. Dorms $14; singles $18; doubles $32; family rooms $59. YHA non-members $3 more. Linen $2.50. Book far in advance for summer—despite the size, it does fill up.

Northbridge YHA Backpackers Hostel, 42-46 Frances St. (tel./fax 9328 7794), walk up William St. and then left onto Francis St. Massive renovation to this pleasant, 84-bed hostel will end the outdoor walk to the showers and, the new owner hopes, draw in a younger, livelier crowd. Bike rental, field trips to the beach, and internet access coming soon. Office open 8am-11pm. 4- to 6-bed dorms $14; twin $16 per person. Weekly $70 and up. Book ahead in summer.

Globe Backpackers, 479 Wellington St. (tel. 9321 4080), half a block west of the tourist center. Half hostel and half hotel, Globe is huge, with fresh paint, carpeting, and fridges in the rooms. The hotel part is wheelchair accessible. Aussies are not allowed to stay in the hostel part. Office open 8am-midnight. 6-bed dorms $15; singles $25; twins $19. Weekly: $90; $110; $150. Breakfast included.

Field Touring Hostel, 74 Aberdeen St., Northbridge (tel. 9328 4692), west off William St. A brand-new hostel intended for climbers and bushwalkers, with an attendant distaste for loud partying. Office open 8am-noon and 4-8pm; later check-in available. Flexible check-out. 3- to 6-bed dorms $13, weekly $70.

Jewell House YMCA, 180 Goderich St. (tel. 9325 8488; fax 9221 4694). Head east on Murray St., through Victoria Sq., to the west end of Goderich St. Humongous and institutional, but it offers private rooms with desks and shared bathrooms. Singles $32; doubles $38; triples $48; family room $58. Singles $12.50 per night for minimum 4-week stay, paid in advance.

Fremantle

Backpackers Inn Freo, 11 Pakenham St. (tel. 9431 7065; fax 9336 7106). From the train station, turn right on Phillimore St., then left on Pakenham. On the spot of the old Roo on the Roof hostel, the Inn's plush carpeting and carved woodwork create a pleasant atmosphere for the somewhat quiet crowd. No WA residents. Laundry, kitchen, cafe. 2-week max stay. Reception open daily 7:30am-10:30pm. 24hr. check-in. Check-out 10am. 2- to 4-bed dorms $14; singles $19.50; doubles $30. Weekly: 7th day free. YHA discount.

Old Firestation Backpackers, 18 Phillimore St. (tel. 041 996 6066; fax 9319 1414; email kundip@msn.com.au), turn right from the train station onto Phillimore. Hosts a lively crowd of both short and long-term guests, with a lounge reserved for women and couples. No WA residents. Laundry, luggage storage, off-street parking. Reception open daily 9am-6pm. 24hr. check-in. Check-out 10:30am. 4- to 6-bed dorms $12; doubles $30. Weekly: $72; $150-170. Book ahead for summer. Nightly curry for guests ($5) from the attached Indian restaurant.

FOOD

Perth is crammed to the rafters with coffee bars and bakeries. It's not difficult to find Italian, Thai, Japanese, Cantonese, or Malaysian food; most regional cuisine is located in Northbridge. Inexpensive supermarkets are difficult to find; try the **Supa Valu** on Beaufort St., a 10-minute walk north of Northbridge (open daily 8am-9pm). Surprisingly, the prices are pretty reasonable in the food hall in the basement of the **Myer** department store on Forrest Pl., and the selection of baked goods is excellent. For grains, nuts, and dried fruit by the kilo, head to **Kakulas Brothers Wholesale Importers,** 185 William St. (open Mon.-Fri. 8am-5:30pm, Sat. 8am-12:30pm).

Perhaps the best deal in town is the $5 all-you-can-eat lunch at the **Hare Krishna Food for Life** cafeteria, at 200 William St., with mild, vegetarian Indian food (open Mon.-Fri. noon-2:30pm). **Giuseppe Corica Pastries,** at the corner of Lake and Aberdeen St., has a 40-year history as the heart of Little Italy in Northbridge. You'll pay little more here for a tartlet or neapolitan pastry than you would for a hedgehog slice or a lamington across town (open Mon.-Fri. 8am-5:30pm, Sat. 8am-noon). **Revely's Cafe,** 139 St. Georges Tce. in the Old Perth Boys School, is a plastered-brick house with exposed rafters and an open fire. It serves unusual, vegetarian-friendly sandwiches and gooey mud cakes (lunch $5-10, coffee and cake $4; open Mon.-Fri. 7am-4pm).

Downtown **Fremantle** is riddled with restaurants, especially along Market St. and **South Tce.,** the latter known as "Cappuccino Strip" for its abundant cafes. The strip is quite popular and the mayor has considered a plan to turn part of it into a pedestrian promenade. Indian and Thai food are well represented in the Market St. area, and several bakeries spread toward the High St. mall. For groceries, try the **Coles supermarket** on Cantonment St., across from the train station. **Kakulas Sister,** like her brothers in Perth, sells dry goods on the corner of Market and Leake St. (open Mon.-Fri. 9am-5:30pm, Sat. 9am-2pm).

SIGHTS

If you do nothing else in Perth, visit **Kings Park.** To reach the park from the city center, head west up St. Georges Tce. and bear left as it becomes Malcolm St. This will bring you to the roundabout at the north end of the park. Alternatively, head down to the Swan River and turn right, following the signs for the park as the walking path passes under the freeway. On top of the Mount Eliza Escarpment, you'll find a **memorial** to Western Australian soldiers killed in battles overseas during WWI. The large granite bench will convey whispered speech from one end to the other. The park is recovering from the second of two major brushfires in the past decade, but the wildflowers are making a good comeback. One can **rent a bike** at the Fraser Ave. Information Centre just across from the memorial, but the hour-long **tram tour** ($10) of King's Park and neighboring University of WA, is a better way to learn about the park's wildlife and history. (Wheelchair-accessible nature trails. 4 tours daily 11am-2:15pm, plus a Sun. 3:15 tour.)

North of the railway station and east of Northbridge lies the **Perth Cultural Centre,** including the **Alexander Library Building,** the **Art Gallery of Western Australia,** and the **Perth Institute of the Contemporary Arts (PICA).** The Art Gallery has free admission to the permanent collection of Aboriginal and Anglo-Australian painting and 20th-century design works (open daily 10am-5pm). PICA shows contemporary and student work (open Wed.-Mon. 11am-8pm), and hosts theater and performance pieces in the evenings.

A trip on the TransPerth Soondalup Train and bus #423 from the Warwick Interchange to the Sorrento stop brings one to **Hillary's Harbour.** On a sunny day, the beach alone is worth the trip. But the bright aquarium of **Underwater World** (tel. 9447 7500), with dolphin feedings and guided marine biology tours, is impressive too. (Open daily 9am-5pm. Admission $15.50, concessions $12.50, children $7.50, families $39.) Pigeons fly throughout the area.

You probably can't afford to stay at **The Criterion Hotel,** 500 Hay St., but you can at least stop to gawk at this restored Art Deco structure in downtown Perth. If you're dressed fairly nicely, check out the **Oak and Ivy Bar** downstairs.

Fremantle

The **Fremantle Prison** (tel. 9430 7177), off of Hampton Rd. just south of the War Memorial, closed in 1991 because it lacked modern plumbing (in fact, the inmates' cells lacked plumbing altogether). Today, it offers a fascinating and grotesque look at Australia's penal history. (Open daily 10am-6pm; guided tours every 30min., candlelight tours Wed. and Fri. 7:30pm. Book ahead for tours. Admission $10.)

The **Fremantle War Memorial** on High St. is dedicated to WA soldiers killed in WWI. The spot is perfect for picnicking or reading in peace, and affords an outstanding view of the harbor, the town, and the hills to the east. At the coastal end of High St., the limestone **Roundhouse** affords excellent views of Rottnest Island and the harbor (open daily 9am-6pm). The well-designed **Western Australia Maritime Museum**

Escape from Fremantle

Although its colonial keepers regarded Fremantle Prison as escape-proof, one man managed not only to escape but to dramatically embarrass British authorities in the process. John Boyle O'Reilly and six of his comrades were sentenced to imprisonment at Fremantle for their role in the Fenian uprising in Ireland in 1868. O'Reilly broke out of the prison and hitched a ride to North America aboard a whaling ship. He moved to Boston, where the Irish-American community raised money on his behalf. With this financing, O'Reilly then outfitted a new ship, the *Catalpu,* and sailed for Australia to rescue his brethren. When British ships fired on the *Catalpu* off Fremantle, O'Reilly raised the American flag and reminded his attackers that they were in international waters, whereupon his aggressors grudgingly backed off. O'Reilly made his rendezvous with his fellow Fenians and returned to Boston.

at the corner of Cliff St. and Marine Tce., explains the history of Fremantle, port trading, and marine archaeology (open daily 10:30am-5pm; admission by donation, charges for special exhibits).

Though it feels like an indoor amusement park, the **Fremantle Crocodile Park,** on Mews Rd. in the Boat Harbour does offer the chance to see the meanest of reptiles chow down on chicken necks and kangaroo meat. (Open Mon.-Fri. 10am-4pm, Sat.-Sun. 10am-5pm. Feedings daily at 2pm. Admission $8.)

ENTERTAINMENT

Perth's nightlife, like its food scene, is centered in Northbridge. Weekend nights, James St. stays up very late, but the crowd is well-behaved. Dance clubs open Wednesday through Sunday; bars and clubs impose a no-white-sneakers, no-flannel standard on weekend nights. For drinking, try **The Brass Monkey,** at the corner of James and William St. Ignore the James Dean sacrilege and try the house brew, Seven Seas. Heineken, Guinness, and Corona are available in bottles. Down the street, take in French or artsy American films at **Cinema Paradiso,** 164 James St. Ticket prices are steep in paradise, but $3 student concessions with an ID are available.

Not all entertainment happens after dark. Browse through the cramped but well-stocked **Arcane Bookshop,** on William St. between James and Francis St. The owner is very knowledgable about books and about the local **gay scene.** The shop has a good selection of classics, and if you're hell-bent on reading some Durkheim while in WA, this is the only place you have any chance of getting your fix.

On weekends, **Fremantle** is crowded with visitors from Perth. Shopping at the markets is a popular activity, and the people-watching along the Cappuccino Strip is especially good. Check out **Creative Native,** 65 High St., for Aboriginal art and didgeridoos (open Mon.-Fri. 9am-5:30pm, Sat. 10am-5pm, Sun. 11am-5pm). Perhaps the best bookstore in WA, **New Edition Bookshop,** 50 South Tce., has strong selections of classic, art, and travel books. In-shop reading is encouraged, and there's a 10% student discount (open daily 9:30am-10:30pm).

Water Sports

The coast around Perth stretches for 80km, beach after beach, and there's something for everyone. Leighton Beach has the most consistent board surfing; Cottesloe Beach is best serviced with beach-side restaurants, pubs, and a golf course: "North Cott" has pre- and post-office hour body surfing shifts; City Beach hosts amateur and professional beach volleyball tournaments (as well as the ubiquitous beach cricket matches); and Swanbourne Beach offers separate sections for dogs, horseback-riding, and nude-bathing.

The Swan River offers freshwater fun, particularly from the south bank off of Mill Point Rd., opposite the city center. Here you'll find easy access to river activities, including catamaran and windsurfer hire. The **yachting season** opens in September, with a number of operators in the Fishing Boat Harbour offering twilight cruises. The Whitbread sailing regatta arrives in Fremantle the last week in November, cause for a 10-day festival that imbues that city with a carnival atmosphere. Call 9430 2228 for more information.

■ Near Perth

Although a car facilitates daytrips around Perth, TransPerth bus service is fairly comprehensive, if not always frequent or easy to understand. Do not be daunted: it's worthwhile figuring out the timetables to see some of the neighboring country. Much of greater Perth is even accessible by bicycle, if you have the stamina.

Guildford This quiet hamlet sits between the Perth Airport and the Swan River, and is worth an afternoon's visit. A very old community by local standards, Guildford features well-preserved architecture, such as the 19th-century **Old Gaol** and **Post Office.** Guildford was once a rather rowdy little place—the hotel had a tunnel down to the Swan for smuggling liquor. To get to Guildford, take bus #306 or 340 from the Perth City Bus Port.

The Darling Range The Darling Range, a verdant plateau peppered with small towns and forests, looms east of the city. Take the M1 train from Perth Railway Station to Midland, then TransPerth buses #317-320 or 327-330 from Midland Station.

John Forrest National Park offers miles of shaded hiking trails. The **wildflower** seasons have been better since the large 1996 bushfire, and the dearth of underbrush makes the blooms easier to see. The park also has kangaroos, parrots, and kookaburras galore. **Lake Leschenaultia,** an artificial lake designed to provide water for steam locomotives a century ago, is a popular spot for relaxation, affording peaceful freshwater swimming and a campsite with shower facilities. Come mid-week and book ahead for **camping** space (tel. 9572 4248; $5 plus $3 per person).

The **Mundaring Weir,** constructed to provide a reservoir for the Goldfields Water Scheme, is a beautiful picnic site as well as a fascinating example of engineering history and a tribute to its suicidal designer, C. Y. O'Connor. The museum is worth the $1 charge if you're not put off by the 2km walk from the bus stop.

York and the Avon Valley Rolling hills, misty dales, and wildflower-studded fields make the Avon Valley, located 100km east and somewhat north of Perth, a great place for a drive or a bicycle ride. The Avon River is a tributary of the Swan, and its valley was the first area of colonial agricultural settlement to be established outside Perth. Leaving Perth along the Great Eastern Hwy., take Riverside Drive (Hwy. 5) to National 94. From the mostly residential town of **Northam,** about an hour down the road, follow Tourist Drive 254 south to York, about 35km.

WA's first inland settlement, York is well-preserved but unpretentious, and full of parks and picnic spots. The **tourist office** (tel. 9641 4301) is in the Town Hall on Avon Tce. (open Mon.-Fri. 9:30am-5pm, Sat.-Sun. 10am-5pm). On Saturdays and Sundays between 11am and 4pm, people can visit the **1885 Railway Station Museum and Tea Gardens.** The town holds an annual **folk and jazz festival** (tel. 9641 1366) in the spring, setting up an empty paddock for musicians and visitors to camp. The **Old York Gaol and Courthouse** complex, with buildings dating from the 1840s to 1900, is also open for inspection (open Mon.-Fri. 11am-3pm, Sat.-Sun. 10am-4pm; admission $3). Stroll down Avon Tce. for a look at the 1840s **Settlers' House** (tel. 9641 1007; fax 9641 1606), which has exquisite rooms for nightly lodging. Although the rates are fairly high, four adults can share a family room with bath for approximately $30 per person, and children under 12 stay free. Book two weeks in advance.

Caversham Wildlife Park Although only accessible by car or taxi, it's worth the pain. A well-run, privately-owned park for (mostly native) wild animals, Caversham is the place to go to fulfill all of your wildest wombat-petting, kangaroo-feeding, or camel-riding fantasies. Tours are given by interns, many preparing for careers in biology or husbandry. Don't miss a chance to chat with the owner, David Thorne.

Tours The best way to see the natural and historical sights outside Perth may be on guided group tours. While it's true that you run the risk of becoming part of a herd, a good tour frees you from worrying about logistics and food. In addition, a good guide will know a lot of local history, and will be able to track 'roos by their spoor. For one-day trips, the hands-down winner is **Planet Perth Tours** (tel./fax 9276 5295), an ecologically savvy outfit ($39 with lunch, vegetarian no problem). For a one-day trip to the Pinnacles and the Yellow Desert, **Pinnacles 4WD Adventure Tours** (tel. 9359 1100) is well-regarded ($85).

■ Off the Coast of Perth: Rottnest Island

Called a "rats' nest" by Dutch settlers who mistook the local wallabies—quokka—for giant rats, Rottnest Island is a hunk of limestone off the coast near Perth. The island has served at various times as a prison, a boys' reformatory, and a coastal defense installation, but today it is purely a retreat. On a clear day, one can look out across the water from the ferry landing at Thompsons Bay and see the Perth skyline, before setting off in pursuit of less harried pleasures than Perth has to offer. A bike ride on the paved roads around the island's perimeter is many visitors' favorite experience. It takes a good day to get all the way around.

Catch a ferry to the island from the Perth **Barrack St. Jetty,** Pier 4, with **Boat Torque Cruises** (tel. 9221 5844; ferry departs Perth daily 8:45am, $40 same-day return). From Fremantle, the **Rottnest Express** ferry (tel. 9335 6406) departs from the left side of Shed C on the Victoria Quay, behind the railway station and across the footbridge (ferry departs Fremantle daily 9:30am and 3:30pm; ferry departs Rottnest daily 4:30pm; $28 same-day return). In the summer, you may have to show proof of previously arranged accommodation to purchase an extended-return ticket. Bicycles are allowed on the ferries.

The **Visitors Centre** is in Thompsons Bay, directly in front of the ferry jetty (open daily 8am-5pm). It provides information on accommodations and bus tours of the island. A courtesy bus makes a 30-minute loop of the island, departing the Visitors Centre every hour from 8:45am to 4:45pm. The **Bayseeker Bus** (day ticket $3) offers a more extensive tour of Rottnest's bays and inlets, departing from the Visitors Centre every hour between 9:30am and 4:30pm.

Rottnest Island is an ideal picnicking location, with the best spots on the dunes and beaches away from the settlements. The beaches get progressively less peopled as you head around the island from the settled areas. Go far enough, and you should find the luxury of a cove to yourself. Some southern coves reward the determined snorkeler with pockets of tropical coral and fish. A bike is essential. **Rottnest Island Bike Hire** (tel. 9292 5105) is a three-minute walk from the Visitors Centre. Facing the Visitors Centre, turn left and walk left of the tearooms and right of the hotel. (1-speed $13 for a full day; 18-speed $18. All bikes come with helmets and locks.) You may want to bring your own picnic supplies; the Thompsons Bay settlement does have a bakery and a grocery store, both in the pedestrian mall behind the tourist center, but prices are considerably higher than on the mainland.

The **Rottnest Youth Hostel** (tel. 9372 9780; fax 9292 5141) is on Bickley Point, a 15-minute walk from the Visitors Centre. Facing the center, head left and follow the YHA signs. The 54-bed hostel has kitchen, laundry, and luggage storage facilities. (7-night max. stay. Check-in 7:30am-5pm, later by arrangement. Check-out 10am. 6- to 10-bed dorms $17; family rooms $40. YHA. Linens $4. Wheelchair accessible. No WA residents. Book months in advance for Dec.- Feb.)

SOUTHWEST

The Indian Ocean coast of Southwest Australia is experiencing a boom in both tourism and year-round residency. This winery region features a mild climate of wet winters and dry summers, the world's greatest variety of wildflowers, and beautiful dunes. And it's primed for visitors. Many of the hostels, caravan parks, and even vineyards in the area are less than five years old. Land prices are rising and large commercial wine makers are moving in. By some accounts, the region is only at 10% of vineyard saturation. Meanwhile, cattle and sheep stations, the latter long profitable as a source of Merino wool, are being pushed out. The Department of Conservation and Land Management (CALM) is struggling to set limits on beachfront development, as "ecotourism" threatens to destroy the natural ecology.

The most convenient way to see the region is by car, but **South West Coachlines** has frequent bus service to most towns. Many people use the **Easy Rider Backpackers** bus (tel. 9383 7848; 24hr. notice for pick-up). A three-month pass ($129) covers bus service among most regional hostels. (Sun., Tues., and Fri. buses head south toward Pemberton; Mon., Wed., and Sat. buses run to Albany and back to Perth. During June and July, buses only run once every 2 weeks.)

Many travelers, sometimes called "rounders," **trace a circuit** south from Perth along the west coast (the Southwest), east through the Great Southern, and north into the Goldfields, before driving west back to Perth. Drivers unfamiliar with Australia's roads may prefer this direction of travel, since they'll begin with well-traveled highways around Margaret River before heading out into the interior and Goldfields.

Other tourists make the circle clockwise, however, starting with the Goldfields, while still others just want to make an excursion from Perth east to Kalgoorlie (in the Goldfields) and back again. *Let's Go* attempts to accommodate both directions by presenting the information on the regions south of Perth (the Southwest, the Great Southern, and the Goldfields) in a hub-and-spoke fashion, with Perth at the hub.

PERTH TO BUNBURY

The two-hour drive south of Perth toward Bunbury is lined with forests, cattle stations, and limestone quarries. Picnic areas abound, and service stations appear at regular intervals. From Victoria Square in Perth, drive south on Victoria Ave. to Riverside Dr. and head west. Follow the signs for Hwy. 2 southbound and stay on Hwy. 2 until the exit for Hwy. 1.

About 100km south of Perth is **Yalgorup National Park,** a right-hand turn-off marked by a sign 500m up the road. The park features tent sites, nature reserves, miles of dunes, and a forest of jarrah and tuart with peppermint undergrowth. Beach zones are popular for fishing, sailing, and power boating. A variety of water birds, including cormorants, sandpipers, and black swans, shares the water between October and February.

Bunbury

Although surrounded by commercial strips, Bunbury retains a tacit pride in being the largest of the small towns peppering the coast south of Perth. The town (pop. 30,000) is actually on a peninsula surrounded by the blue waters of the Indian Ocean, Koombana Bay, and the Leschenault Inlet. Two hours south of Perth, Bunbury is the secondary cultural center for southwest coast residents who don't want to travel all the way to the big city. Bunbury recently opened new mineral sands mines, and the eucalyptus woodchipping industry is thriving. Some say that development underway is intended to give town and bay the feel of a small village on the French Riviera. For now, however, it's more like a miniature Hamburg—with lots of dolphins.

Bunbury is 3km from **Wollaston,** the southern terminus of WA's **train** network. Transit buses will honor a train ticket stub for a free lift to Bunbury. The **bus station** is much closer to the center of Bunbury. **South West Coachlines** runs daily service to Perth (3 per day, 1½hr., $16). **Transit buses** circle the city (Mon.-Sat., $1.60). The **tourist office** (tel. 9721 7922) is conveniently located next door. A block west on Wellington St. is the intersection with **Victoria St.,** the city's main drag. Victoria St. is lined with the **post office,** many **banks,** shops, and restaurants, and the incongruous Bunbury Tower. Three blocks farther west is a ridge that overlooks Back Beach, basaltic protrusions, and the Indian Ocean. A **hospital** lies two blocks south of the tourist office, right behind the **shopping center** and disused rail station.

Bunbury has two hostels. The **Wander Inn,** 16 Clifton St. (tel. 1800 064 704), has a clean kitchen, lounges, laundry machines, and a friendly staff. Some bathrooms are inconveniently located and require going outdoors. (Dorms $14; singles and doubles $16 per person. VIP, YHA.) The **Bunbury YHA** (tel. 9791 2621), at the corner of Stirling and Moore St., is quiet and neat, with a kitchen and common area (dorm beds $13 and up with YHA; family rooms $35). December through February, try to book accommodations at least a week in advance.

The shopping center behind the tourist office features two **supermarkets.** Dewsons is slightly cheaper for staples, but Coles is bigger (both open Mon.-Sat. 9am-

6pm). **John Carey's Tasty Bread Shop,** at the east end of Clifton St., offers good, cheap breads and pastries (open daily 6am-5:30pm). Fruits and veggies are sold next door.

Locals maintain that the dolphin-viewing in Bunbury is less contrived and far superior to that in Monkey Mia and other towns along the coast. Check out the **Dolphin Discovery Center** (tel. 9791 8088; open Oct.-April daily 8am-5pm; May-Sept. 8:30am-4:30pm), on Koombana Dr. Dolphin-sighting **cruises** run daily between December and May. Inquire at the tourist office or the Discovery Center. An 815-seat **Entertainment Centre** features live dance and theater performances, while a **cinema** shows movies seven nights per week. Guided **walking tours** of town depart from the tourist office (Wed., Fri., and Sat. 10am and 1pm; tel. 9795 9261 for appointments; $8). The town's golf courses, swimming beaches, and horse-racing tracks also attract summer tourists. In addition, many bush and wildlife tours use Bunbury as a base during the summer months.

Busselton

When French explorer Nicolas Baudin mapped Geographe Bay in 1801, he named several land formations after members of his crew, but Busselton is named for a family of English settlers who landed here in 1834. Today, the sleepy coastal community of 18,000 gives no hint of the hardships and trials faced by the Bussells. Instead, it serves as the gateway to the vineyard-stocked Cape Naturaliste region.

South West Coachlines runs **buses** to the Albert St. terminus from Perth via Bunbury ($20 one-way). By car, Busselton is about an hour's drive down the Bussell Highway (Hwy. 10), from Bunbury. The transition from South St. to Queen St. marks the commercial heart of Busselton, where one will find **banks,** the **post office,** and the **police station.** The **tourist office** (tel. 9752 1288; fax 9754 1470) is located in the civic center complex on Southern Dr., just outside the city center.

Turn left onto Jane St., one block from the tourist office, to reach **Busselton Backpackers** (tel. 9754 2763), small, cozy, and the only hostel in town. Guests have use of the hostel's bikes, and the owner cooks a free vegetarian curry for guests every Wednesday night. Book ahead in the summer (dorms $13; private rooms $20). On Marine Tce. just past the jetty heading away from Queen St., the **Kookaburra Caravan Park** (tel. 9752 1516) offers sites (power optional) by the coast.

Clustered near the police station at the intersection of Queen St. and Marine Tce. are the **Old Post Office Tea Rooms** (serving good, inexpensive cakes and light lunches), the **Busselton Art Society** workshop and gallery, and a store full of exquisite but expensive jarrah furniture. Heading right on Marine Tce., you'll quickly come to the **Busselton Jetty,** once the longest timber jetty in the southern hemisphere. Construction began in 1865 to allow ships to dock and load timber, but after the closing of the port in 1973 and the cyclone of 1978, the jetty fell into disrepair. It still stretches 2km into Geographe Bay, and attracts many tourists. An all-day pass to walk on the jetty is $2; for $6, ride the timber train out to the end (daily 10am-4pm). The jetty closes at 6pm in winter but may be open as late as 10pm in summer.

Around Busselton, outlying hamlets have taken on personalities of their own. **Yallingup** is well-known for excellent surf and for the limestone Ngilgi Cave. **Dunsborough** is reputed to be a great destination for families, in part because the swimming is somewhat safer than in neighboring areas. South West Coachlines runs **buses** to Dunsborough every day.

The Coast from Busselton to Augusta

Heading south from Busselton, Hwy. 10 passes through a thicket of Margaret River area vineyards. Wine was not grown in this region until 1967, but the area is now home to more than 50 vineyards. **Vasse River Wines,** established in 1992, is emblematic of a new crop of small wineries. Taste their estate-bottled products for free (open daily 10am-5pm). A few kilometers down the road lies the much-hailed **Taunton**

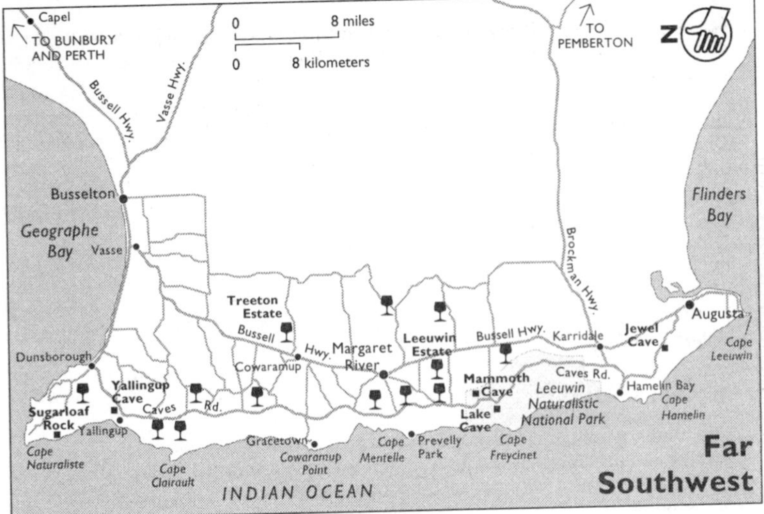

Farm Caravan Park (tel. 9755 5334), which offers powered and unpowered sites, cottages, and on-site caravans. Campers have access to a kitchen and showers. The smallest vineyard you'll ever visit, **Treeton Estate** lies 4km farther down Hwy. 10. The proprietors at Treeton first pressed grapes in 1991, and plan to keep no more than 36 acres under vine. Free tastings (try the round, peppery Shiraz) and complimentary tea and cheese. Assemble a picnic for $2.50 per item, or sit and sip before the wood stove (open daily 10am-6pm). Say hello to Ralph, the Border collie.

Margaret River Though a settlement of only 22,000, Margaret River makes a good base for exploring the vineyards and natural beauty of the southwest coast. Two hostels serve the village. **Inne Town Backpackers** (tel. 1800 244 115), on the Bussell Hwy. at the north end of town, offers dorms for $14 (YHA discount) with parking out front. Larger **Margaret River Lodge** (tel. 9757 2532) is out of town, a few kilometers west of the Bussell Hwy. along Wallcliffe Rd. Showers and toilets require an outdoor walk. (Dorms $14; singles $25; doubles $35. YHA. Bike rental $10.)

The South West Coachlines **bus stop** in Margaret River is on the Bussell Hwy., across the street from the **tourist office** (tel. 9757 2911) and the **supermarket.** A $35 half-day tour of the area's vineyards departs the tourist office at 12:30pm every Tuesday, Thursday, and Sunday. Call 1800 818 102 to book. The **post office** is one block east, up Wilmott Ave. There is a **hospital** on Wallcliffe Rd. just west of the Bussell Hwy. The **beach,** 9km east along Wallcliffe Rd., is the site of the **Margaret River Surf Classic,** held the third weekend in November. To see the limestone cliffs overlooking the ocean, pass the cemetery and head over the dunes. Take care: the cliffs have been known to collapse.

Around Margaret River Internationally respected and thoroughly pretentious **Leeuwin Estates Vineyard** (tastings daily, tours $6) lies east of town on Boodjidup Rd. During the summer, the estate hosts concerts by such luminaries as the London Philharmonic Orchestra, the Berlin State Orchestra, and Ray Charles. Even when the big-shots aren't in town, the lunch restaurant is open (daily noon-2:30pm). For a very different kind of experience, visit the **Eagles Heritage Raptor Wilderness Centre,** to the south, also on Boodjidup Rd. (open daily 10am-5pm, flight displays at 11am and 1:30pm).

A drive down Caves Rd. provides an alternative to Hwy. 10. The road runs through **Leeuwin-Naturaliste National Park** to the stunning Boranup karri regrowth forest.

In the summer, a carefully tended labyrinth of shrubs forms the **Boranup Maze** ($2); in the winter, the vegetation is not thick enough to create much of a maze.

It is extremely difficult to see the nearby **caves** without a car. At **Mammoth Cave,** 45-minute tours run every hour from 9am to 3pm ($10, children $5, family pass $30). A **taxi** from Margaret River to Mammoth Cave costs $20 each way. **Lake Cave** features a snack bar and picnic area, an information center, and a one-hour cave tour (every half-hr. 9:30am-3:30pm; in winter every hr.). The outer chamber of Mammoth Giant's Cave offers a chance for self-guided cave walks. The caves are not currently wheelchair accessible, although there are plans in the works.

At the southern tip of Caves Rd. lies **Hamelin Bay,** the site of 11 shipwrecks since 1882. Independent scuba and snorkeling outings to survey the four visible wrecks are welcome, but you'll need to hire a boat and pilot. The **Hamelin Bay Caravan Park** (tel. 9758 5540) requires bookings months in advance for the summer season (Oct.-June unpowered site $13; July-Sept. $10). Several operators run caving, bushwalking, and abseiling tours around Margaret River (around $80 for a full day). Trevor McGowan's outfit (tel. 9757 2104) is reputed to be especially good.

Augusta A small community at the southern tip of Australia's west coast, Augusta is best known for **Cape Leeuwin,** the point where the Indian and Southern Oceans meet. Other notable geographic features include **Flinders Bay** and the mouth of the **Blackwood River,** both to the east. Naturaliste Charters (tel. 9755 2276) runs daily **whale-watching** expeditions off Cape Leeuwin (June-Sept.).

Backpackers retire to the immaculate **YHA Augusta,** also known as the **Baywatch Manor Resort,** 88 Blackwood Ave. (Tel. 9758 1290. Office open 7am-9pm. 6-bed dorms $15; doubles $35; suites $45. YHA discount. Free linen. Bike rental $5 per day.) The **Augusta Bakery and Cafe** is across Blackwood Ave. (open Mon.-Thurs. 8am-5pm, Fri. 8am-8pm, Sat.-Sun. 8am-3pm). Heading south, one encounters a **newsstand** and **fruit market** (open daily 8:30am-6:30pm) on the left and a **tourist office** (closed Sun.) and **post office** on the right.

GREAT SOUTHERN

The karri forests of Pemberton, the peaks of the Stirling Range, and the vast scrubland to the east of the South-Western Hwy. (Hwy. 1) are together known as the Great Southern. As one emerges from the karri forests along the Vasse Hwy. and heads east along Hwy. 1 toward Walpole, the character of the land and its inhabitants changes. Although Albany functions as an urban hub, the area is more sparsely populated than the coast to the west, and it is less influenced by the cosmopolitan strivings of Perth. Land sales and farm subdivisions are few; farmers, ranchers, and viniculturists hang on, some of them the fourth or fifth generation on the same plot, although many have accepted offers from large wood-chipping concerns to grow blue-gum trees.

In the winter months, the weather can be quite cool, and long rainy stretches are not uncommon. The peak visiting seasons are spring (wildflower season in the Stirling Range) and summer (beach season at Denmark and Albany).

The Great Southern doesn't promote its vineyards as aggressively as the west coast does, and Margaret River's wineries are much better known. But with the Valley of the Giants Treetop Walk outside Walpole poised to overtake Monkey Mia's dolphins as WA's biggest tourist attraction, the Great Southern has begun to manifest a quiet competence in revealing itself to outsiders.

Pemberton

The eastern spur of Hwy. 10 runs from Karridale, north of Augusta, out to Pemberton, a good 90-minute drive. Watch the signs around Nannup—an easily missed right turn leads to the last 69km to Pemberton. The town lies in a nebulous zone between

Protecting Their Own

The towering karri trees of WA's southwest fear fire like any other trees, but they also once served to fight flames. Rangers the world over erect fire towers to catch signs of forest fire as early as possible, but those in WA decided to construct cabins in the tops of the trees themselves. Rather than attempt to build 60m-tall observation towers up to the lofty canopy from the forest floor, the rangers drove pegs into the karri trunks so that they could climb to these treetop dwellings. From here, the fearless (and vertigo-resistant) firefighters remained vigilant from the 1930s to 1970s, when they switched to aircraft. Today, the towers are open to visitors. Tremendous views reward those who can muster the courage to ascend a mammoth eucalypt. The highest such treehouse, at 75m, is in the **Bicentennial Tree** in Warren National Park.

the Indian Ocean coastal region of the southwest and the scrub land of the Great Southern to the east.

The lone hostel, **Pimelea Chalets** (tel. 9776 1953), is 9km out of town; call in advance if you want a pick-up from Pemberton. Each cabin has a kitchen and living room. (Dorms $14; double and family rooms available. YHA discounts. Blankets provided in winter.) Book in advance during summer. The **Karri Visitors Centre,** on Brockman St. (the main road, a slow spot in the Vasse Hwy.) will provide information about wildlife and other attractions in Pemberton and nearby Northcliffe.

The **Gloucester Tree,** one of the tallest fire lookouts in the world, is a prime attraction in Pemberton. Steel dowels wind 61m up the trunk to the lookout platform, from which the dauntless get a breathtaking view of the forest canopy, a golf course, and, in the distance, sand dunes. If you want to stay low to the ground, explore the miles of walking trails which crisscross **Gloucester National Park.** To get to the tree and the park, head up Ellis St. and follow the signs.

Outside Pemberton, stop in **Beedelup National Park** to see the **Beedelup Falls** and a drive-through karri tree. Be aware that the roads inside the park are not paved once one leaves the highway and can be rough on vehicles without 4WD. The ascent to the falls is quite dangerous after dark.

Denmark

Southeast of Pemberton along the South Coast Hwy., this town of winemakers, potters, and artisans depends largely on tourism. Summer arts festivals and clean, contrived quaintness contribute to a pleasant, if veneer-like, ambience. Founded in 1895 as a timber town, Denmark rapidly exhausted its trees. An innovative government buy-out program converted Denmark into a farming community and rescued it from premature economic doom. Later evolution brought a cattle industry to town before Denmark once again turned to timber.

To enjoy nature, picnic on beautiful Ocean Beach or turn to Wilson Inlet for excellent fishing and boating opportunities. Most find Albany a more convenient base for exploring distant points of interest. But if you have a car, Denmark is central to the Red Tingle Forest and the Valley of the Giants to the west, William Bay to the south, and Mt. Barren and the Porongurup Range to the north. Unfortunately, there is no public transport to these sights and a taxi ride to the area is a prohibitive $60 return.

Strickland St., Denmark's main thoroughfare, intersects the **South Coast Hwy.** Heading east, turn right on Strickland to reach the **tourist office** and adjacent bus stop. **Westrail buses** run to Perth (Mon., Thurs., and Sun. 9:57am; Tues.-Wed. and Fri.-Sat. 9:22am; 5-6hr.) and to Albany (Mon.-Tues., Thurs., and Sat. 5:13pm; Wed. and Fri. 4:38pm; Sun. 5:34pm; 40min.). The **post office** is across the street and the **hospital** is at the north end of Strickland. The **police station** (tel. 9848 1311) is west of Strickland St. along the south side of the highway.

The **Wilson Inlet Holiday Park** (tel. 9848 1267) is 4km down Ocean Beach Rd. right on the inlet. For $10 a night, a backpacker can get a room in an unheated cabin with a kitchen. Another structure contains toilets and showers. In town, the **Denmark Unit Hotel** (tel. 9849 2206), one block east of Strickland St. at the corner of Walker St. and Holling Rd., offers singles and doubles for $20 per person. Book ahead for the summer. Strickland St. is crowded with cafes. Enjoy a slice of cake on the terrace outside the **Denmark Bakery** (open in summer daily 7am-6pm; in winter 7am-4:30pm).

West of Denmark: Walpole

Although it's nothing more than a wide place along the South Coast Hwy. with a few blocks of houses running south toward the dunes, Walpole makes a good rest stop. Two bakery-cafes and a grocery store lie on the south side of Hwy. 1, along with a **post office,** the westbound **bus stop,** and the **tourist office** (open daily 9am-5pm). Stay at the **Tingle All Over** (tel. 9840 1041), a few hundred meters east of the tourist office, south of the highway. All rooms have heat and sinks, but showers are a short walk outdoors. (Singles $20; twins $14 per person. Family rooms available.)

Bushwalking in **Walpole-Nornalup National Park,** 11km from Walpole, is popular. In the park, the biggest mainstream attraction is the recently opened **Valley of the Giants Treetop Walk** (tel. 9840 8263). This catwalk forms a 600m loop suspended as high as 40m above ground. (Open March-Nov. daily 9am-5pm; Dec.-Feb. 8am-6pm. Admission $5, children $2, families $12. Last admission 45min. before closing. Wheelchair accessible.)

Mt. Barker

Just a few kilometers east of Denmark, road-weary travelers can make a left-hand turn and head to Mt. Barker. Though not really a tourist destination in and of itself, Mt. Barker is a popular extended detour on the route between Denmark and Albany since it is the gateway to the floral paradise of **Stirling Range National Park.**

Turn right onto the Muir Hwy. at its intersection with the Denmark Mt. Barker Rd. The Muir Hwy. becomes **Langton Rd.** as it enters town. Past the **hospital** at the corner of Langton Rd. and Marmion St., turn right onto **Lowood Rd.** The **tourist office** is on the right. The **police station** is two blocks south and one block west, on the northwest corner of Montem and Mt. Barker St. **Westrail buses** service Albany (Mon.-Fri. 2:06pm, Sat. 3:07pm, Sun. 8:06pm, 40min.) and Perth (1 per day, 5-6hr.).

For lunch and pub grub, try **Gene's Kitchen,** north of the tourist office on Lowood Rd. Bring your own liquor from the vineyards all around Mt. Barker. For inexpensive lodging in town, head west around the corner to the **Boronia Cafe and Guest House** (tel. 9851 1375). Guests share clean bathrooms, a small kitchen, and a TV room (singles $25; doubles $40; breakfast included). There's a laundromat nearby.

To get to **Porongurup National Park,** which is closer to town than Stirling Range but much smaller, follow Lowood Rd. north and turn right onto Albany Hwy. Turn off left on Tourist Drive 252, marked for the national park. The **Porongurup Shop and Tearoom** (tel. 9853 1110), 22km down this road on the right, offers rooms ($13, linen included) and fuel. **Castle Rock,** the best-known of the granite hillocks inside the park, is an easy climb. There is also a plethora of **vineyards** along Porongurup Rd.

Stirling Range National Park

The Stirling Range is an eerie green plateau ringed by massive, sedimentary knolls deposited by the sea that covered this region in the Precambrian epoch. The drive through the range from the east end of Tourist Drive 252 north toward Borden along Chester Pass Rd. is worth an excursion; plan to spend a whole day or overnight in the Stirlings to fully appreciate its beautiful dignity.

Accommodations can be found at the **Stirling Range Chalet and Caravan Park** (tel. 9827 9229). Well-heated trailers with beds and a stove are $25 (for 1) to $30 (for 2 or 3), linen included. Four to six can take a spacious cabin with a microwave for

$12 per person. Showers and toilets are in a separate ablution block. Book months in advance for the wildflower season (late Sept.-Nov.). Across the highway, the **Bluff Knoll Cafe** purveys an assortment of local wines (for on-site consumption only; open 7am-9pm). **The Lily,** an exact replica of a 16th-century Dutch windmill, stands 11km to the north. Built by Dutch expatriates Hennie and Pleun Hitzert, Lily's lower stories currently function as a cafe with a cellar of inexpensive local wines (open Tues.-Sun. 10am-5pm; lunch from $5, supper $22). Construction slated to begin summer 1997-98 will convert it into a flour mill.

There are a number of worthwhile **hikes** in the Stirling Range. The best known is that to the top of **Bluff Knoll,** the highest peak in the range. Known to local Aborigines as Bullah Meual, "Great Many Face Hill" for its mercurial climate and visage-like aspect, the knoll offers a sinuous, moderately strenuous climb. Experienced hikers can make the 3.1km ascent in a little more than an hour. Some parts of the track consist of loose stones; other parts border on bouldering. Those looking for real bouldering should head south to the second-highest peak in the range, **Toolbrunup.** Buy a $5 day pass for your car at the Bluff Knoll Cafe at the entrance to the site, register at the CALM ranger station across the road, and carry an anorak—high winds and rain are common near the top and one may see snow between May and September. Between late September and mid-November, visitors to town are likely to get better weather and see a gorgeous array of **wildflowers,** such as the red and yellow Darwinia.

For touring the mountains, pick up wheels from **Rainbow Coast Car Rentals** (tel. 9842 2456 in Albany, or through either of the hostels in town). Working through the hostel, rental runs $30 per day including insurance and 100km. Hitchhikers find that there is a well-established route from Albany, and that truck drivers are the best bets for rides. *Let's Go* does not recommend hitching.

Albany

Established in 1826, Albany was the first colonial settlement in what is now WA. Its sheltered harbor allowed the town to flourish as a port, a coaling stop for steamships, and the center of a local whaling industry which lasted until 1978. Today the shire has a population of 31,000, the majority of whom live in the city proper, and Albany is confronting problems of urban congestion. Problems caused by increased automobile traffic resulted in an innovative system of downtown traffic circles in 1991. Further growth may necessitate the use of traffic lights, though the current mayor has made it clear he'll sack the first engineer to propose such heresy. With the whaling industry dead, the beaches and harbors around Middleton Bay function largely as tourist attractions, particularly popular in the summer.

Though a conservative area, the diffusion of "alternative-living" folk (easily identified by their "Magic Happens" bumper stickers) from Denmark has granted Albany a tolerant atmosphere. The city is fairly nonchalant about its history; depictions of Albany, past and present, are mounted above the aisles in the convenience store. The key to enjoying Albany is to get out of the city and explore the coast and the Stirling Range. Rent a bike, hire a car, or go whale-watching. The York St. nightlife is mellow—you can use evenings in Albany to relax after days around Albany.

Orientation and Practical Information The **tourist office** (open Mon.-Fri. 8:30am-5:30pm, Sat.-Sun. 9am-5pm) and **bus stop** are on **Lower Stirling Tce.** just east of the southern end of **York St.,** the main thoroughfare. The tourist office is in a *model* train station; the only mass transit in and out of Albany consists of bus coaches. The Westrail "Southerner" bus departs for Perth (Mon.-Sat. 9am, Sun. 3pm, 6hr.). "The Bays" bus, route E4, heads to Esperance (Mon. and Thurs. noon, 6hr.). Hitchhikers usually wait by the "Big Roundabout" on the Albany Hwy., 2km west of the north end of York St., but road trains only stop at designated truck stops. If you are arriving by car, head southeast on the tail of the Albany Hwy. (Hwy. 3) and turn right onto York St. (Hwy. 4) at the traffic circle. The Albany Backpackers has a steady stream of travelers sharing rides. Louie's Bus Service provides **city transport** (Mon.-Sat.; tourist office has schedules), but it's not hard to get around Albany on foot. The **National Australia Bank,** north of Grey St. on York St., has **ATM** machines that take both Cirrus and Plus cards. The regional **hospital** is a few kilometers northeast of the city center, on Hardie Rd. The **police** station (24hr. tel. 9841 0555) is on Sterling Tce. one block west of York St., on the right. The **post office** (open 8:30am-5pm) is located on the northeast corner of York St. and Peels Pl.

Accommodation and Food Albany has two hostels near the center of town. The **Albany Backpackers,** on Spencer St. just around the corner from Stirling Tce. and one block east of York St., is the more appealing. The contrast between the whimsical yet sage-like owner, Anton, and his more down-to-earth managers, Adrian and Brøn, ensures a mix that is lively and friendly but not overboard. Kitchen and TV lounge are adorned with murals by the legendary Jack Davies, who, according to local folklore, jumped ship in Albany while traveling with a British merchantman at age 14. Davies' deft interpretations of early Albany and the natural bridge are not to be missed. Nor is the 6:30 evening ritual: free coffee and cake. (Reception open daily 8-10am and 5-10pm. Dorms $14; doubles $32. Linen included. VIP, YHA, ISIC discounts.) The **Albany Bayview Backpackers YHA** (tel. 9842 3300) on the South side of Duke St., two blocks west of York St., caters to a slightly older crowd. Make your own food or buy into the meal plan. (Dorms $14; twins $17 per person; doubles $32. YHA discount. Linen $2. Bike rental.)

Expensive diners and cafes can be found on York St. For **groceries,** head east on Albany Hwy. to the **Coles** supermarket, about 100m from York St. **Foodland,** at the bottom of York, is open daily until 9pm but is more expensive than Coles. **French Hot Bread** (open Mon.-Fri. 6am-6pm, Sat.-Sun. 6am-4pm), offers incredibly cheap, delicious bread, huge lamingtons, and jam doughnuts. For hiking rations, hit the **Health Nut** (open Mon.-Fri. 8am-4:30pm, Sat. 8am-12:30pm), on the northeast corner of York and Peel St.

Activities and Entertainment York St. bears right into Middleton St. as it heads away from the harbor. The **Dog Rock** on Middleton Rd. looks just like a dog's head—especially since the city has painted a collar around its base and the Dog Rock Motel across the street has thoughtfully provided a visual aid on its sign. For more rock formations, head south of town to The Gap, the Natural Bridge, and the blowholes in Torndirrup National Park. Follow Middleton Rd. to the beautiful and protected **Middleton Beach.** The **Middleton Bay Scenic Path** goes all the way out to **Emu Point** and **Oyster Harbor. Escape Tours** (tel. 018 936 541) offers a variety of area tours, and several cruise operators conduct **whale-watching** cruises for humpback and southern right whales in winter.

Albany does have two or three dance clubs, but they're weekend-only affairs. **The 1912 Club,** toward the harbor-end of York St., has a no flannel, no dirty-sneakers dress code. **Ryans Premier Hotel,** farther up York, is a local institution. To relax over Toohey's or a mulled wine, head to The **Earl of Spencer Historic Inn,** on the corner of Spencer and Earl St.

ALBANY TO ESPERANCE

Although considered part of the Great Southern, the terrain around Esperance is different from that of the rest of the region. Along the South Coast Hwy. east of Albany, karri forests give way to brush. The highway is low and straight and covers nearly 500km with red asphalt. Rest stops are few and far between—fuel up as regularly as possible. Jerramungup, Ravensthorpe, and Munglinup make convenient stops. Travelers may encounter high cross-winds and winter flooding. Do not disregard road trains; you may be approaching them at a combined speed of 240kph.

Esperance

A town of 12,000 strung out along Australia's southern coast and hemmed in by fields of oat and barley, Esperance conforms to the crescent of Esperance Bay in order to maximize its coastline. The ocean represents the town's livelihood, bringing tourists to its beach resorts, fish to its trawlers' nets, and winter rains to its thirsty crops. In summer flocks of tourists frolic on the beaches and in the surf, while winter ushers in the whale-watching season. Esperance is the easternmost town in WA that *Let's Go* covers; to make the long, lonely drive east to Adelaide, first head north to Norseman (p. 549) to access the Eyre Hwy across the Nullarbor Plain.

Orientation and Practical Information The **Esplanade** flanks the bay while **Dempster St.** snakes along parallel to it for several kilometers, without ever quite feeling like a main street. All **buses** arrive at and depart from the shelter at the intersection of Dempster and **Andrew St.,** two blocks north of the town center. **Westrail** runs to Albany (Tues. and Fri. 8am, 6hr.). The Westrail E3 "Gold Coaster" departs for Kalgoorlie (Wed. 3:15pm and Fri. 11am). **Hitchhiking** is popular; travelers report getting rides from the north end of Dempster St. and from the suburb of Castletown further north. Arriving by **car** from the west, the South Coast Hwy. (Monjingup Rd.) intersects Harbour Rd., which runs south into town.

The **post office** is located at the unmarked corner near the bus shelter, and the **tourist office** is one block north. Banks with **ATMs** accepting Cirrus and Plus cards lie along Andrew St. and the block of Dempster St. immediately to the north.

Accommodation, Camping, and Food Esperance has two inexpensive backpackers' hostels, both built fairly recently. The **Blue Waters Lodge** (YHA-affiliated; tel. 9071 1040) is located on Goldfields Rd, just across the road from Esperance Bay. Head north 1km on Dempster until it becomes Norseman Rd. and take the first right. This large establishment has a lounge, a small kitchen, and an institutional feel. Showers are outside. Six-bed dorms are $13 (YHA non-members $14); twins $34; family rooms $40. **Esperance Backpackers** (tel. 9071 4724) is south of town on Emily St. Turn left off Dempster as you head south, just before Dempster ends at Harbour Rd. Smaller, with 34 beds, clean baths, and a spacious kitchen and living room, the backpackers offers dorm beds for $14 and doubles for $30 (YHA discount), linens included. Book in advance for the summer months. The friendly European managers offers 4WD tours to Cape Le Grand National Park.

There is **camping** in Cape Le Grand National Park, 60km east of town, and on Woody Island in Esperance Bay (call 9071 5757 for info on trips out to the island). Purchase a park pass ($5 per car per day) at park entrances. For up-to-the-minute info on camping, contact CALM (tel. 9071 3733) on the east side of Dempster St. north of Andrew St.

Among the bakeries on Andrew St., the burgeoning chain **French Hot Bread** offers the best prices on lamingtons, doughnuts and, of course, french hot, er, hot french bread (open Mon.-Fri. 6am-6pm, Sat.-Sun. 6am-4pm). A **supermarket** (open Mon.-Sat.) is in the shopping center along Pink Lake Rd., one block west of Dempster St.

Activities To enjoy Esperance, get outdoors—even if it's raining. The twisting Tourist Drive 358, around Twilight Beach Rd., Eleven Mile Beach Rd., and Pink Lake Rd., affords numerous places to stop and survey the southern ocean vistas, or descend to the beaches via steep paths carved into the dunes. Start at the southern end of Dempster Rd. and turn right onto Great Ocean Dr. Check out the experimental power-generative **wind farms** at Salmon Beach and Ten Mile Lagoon (open to visitors).

Natural splendor awaits 60km west in **Cape Le Grand National Park.** Take Goldfields Rd. north to Fisheries Rd, turn right onto Marivalk Rd. and right again onto Cape Le Grand Rd. The road into the park is muddy and narrow at times but is accessible to most vehicles. Try the gentle ascent at **Frenchman Peak** (less than an hour's climb). At the top, phenomenal natural topology allows for completely sheltered views of coast and sea. Down the road at **Lucky Bay,** enjoy incredible white sands, some surf, and grey kangaroos, but beware of riptides, undertows, and quicksand. For transportation to the park, ask at Esperance Backpackers on Emily St. before 10am (tours leave by 11am). Several car rental agencies have offices in town, if you plan to drive yourself.

GOLDFIELDS

A few hundred kilometers east of Perth, a handful of goldmining towns cling tenaciously to an existence in the middle of WA's desert. Since 1903, water has been piped into the region and signs everywhere warn against wastage. People seeking employment follow this trickle toward Kalgoorlie, the center of the local mining industry. Kalgoorlie and its neighbors demand a strong work ethic and offer a hard life. Unlike the towns along the coast, their economies do not depend on tourism; many of the people one meets in hostels are there for an extended period of time, working for one of the mining companies. As a consequence, the Goldfields lack pretensions toward their visitors and expect those who stay for any length of time to settle down and earn their keep.

PERTH TO COOLGARDIE

This drive along the Great Eastern Highway is long (nearly 600km), but uneventful. The road, while not superb, is paved the whole way. There are fewer road trains and gas stations are more frequent than on other roads in the Goldfields. The first hour heading out of Perth winds through the city's suburbs and the Swan River Valley, then up a steep slope into the Darling Range. Traffic may back up near Perth even in mid-afternoon on weekdays as a result of ongoing construction and the general congestion and poor design of the interchanges near Midland and the Perth Airport. The soon-to-be-built Newcastle St. Freeway tunnel is intended to ameliorate this problem.

One feature of the Great Eastern worth a specific mention is the Pipeline. It's a pair of pipelines, actually, that carry potable water from Mundaring Weir to the Goldfields region, and run alongside National 94 for the entire stretch, usually less than 30m from the road. Each pipe is less than a meter wide; sometimes they're visible to the north of the road, sometimes to the south.

Coolgardie

Coolgardie is a residential satellite for the families of miners employed at Kalgoorlie, 40km to the northeast. In Coolgardie, a rough trace of momentary urbanity flickers in the endless pastures of dust and grass along the highway. National 94 broadens into four lanes for the 2km known as **Bayley St.** There is a **tourist office** and a police station on the north side of Bayley St., on the right driving in from Norseman or Kalgoorlie. The streets to the north are lined with trailer houses, and shade trees have been plunked in the dirt. In the winter of 1997, the tea room closed its doors and the bed and breakfast across the street went up for auction. This town may become more populated as Kalgoorlie's Super Pit recruits more labor, but for the time being, even the road trains grind by without stopping.

If you must spend the night in Coolgardie, try the **Denver City Hotel** on the south side of Bayley St. midway through town. Clean but unheated private rooms with shared bath cost $25 a night, but noise from the bar downstairs may keep you up. At the west end of town, the Cal-Tex service station rents motel rooms for $50 a night. Coolgardie has no ATMs, but there are minitellers at the bar at the Denver City and at the convenience store in the service station. The former accepts overseas Cirrus cards.

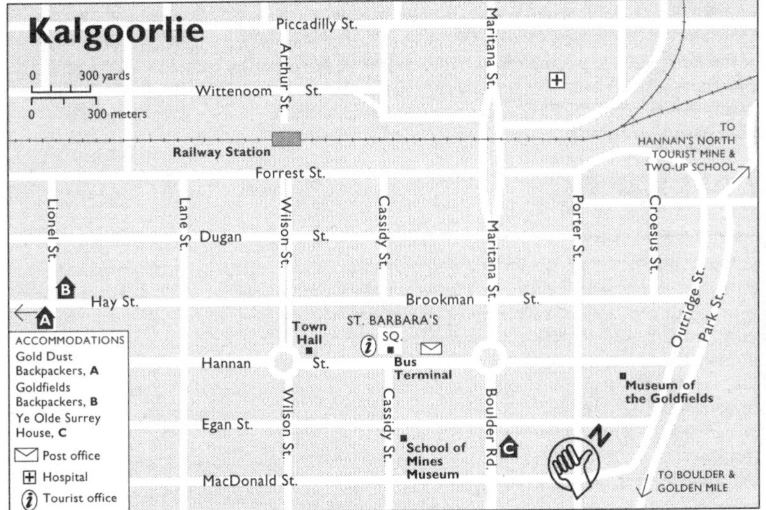

Kalgoorlie-Boulder

The twin towns of Kalgoorlie and Boulder, with their 30,000 residents, cling together as if to escape the isolation of the surrounding outback. Boulder is primarily residential and draws few sight-seers. Kalgoorlie is where people come to work. More than a century after panning began here, the gold industry in "Kal" continues to dig and blast. These days, folks don't come to town hoping to find a vein or a lode of alluvial gold a day's walk out of town, stake a claim, and strike it rich. What gold there is can only be recovered from the Super Pit at a rate of 2g per ton of earth. The work—be it mining, geological surveying, cooking, bartending, or entertaining the miners—is dirty, the hours are long, and the pay is low. Miners work shifts up to 12 hours long, 21 days on, seven days off, and fly to Perth on company-chartered planes for their week-long vacations. But they come back, and they bring friends. Even travelers come here, if only to leave when they've filled their wallet. Work and drink aren't the only pastimes in Kalgoorlie, but it's best to approach it as a working city, a gritty, golden money machine in the middle of the desert.

ORIENTATION AND PRACTICAL INFORMATION

The main commercial boulevard in Kalgoorlie is **Hannan St.,** where the Great Eastern Hwy. (the continuation of National 95 from Coolgardie) ends at the Goldfield Hwy. Hannan St. runs southwest to northeast, and forms a grid with parallel streets labeled Brookman, Egan, and MacDonald St., and perpendicular streets named Lionel St., Wilson St., and **Boulder Rd.** The residential district of Boulder lies several kilometers to the southeast. To reach Boulder from downtown Kalgoorlie, turn right on Boulder Rd. at the north end of Hannan and follow it into **Lane St.** The once gold-rich ground of the **Golden Mile** is a few kilometers east of Boulder.

Heading north on Hannan St. between Wilson St. and Boulder Rd., the **tourist office,** 250 Hannan St. (tel. 9021 1966), is on the left just south of St. Barbara's Square. The **post office** is a little further on, also on the left. The **police station** (tel. 9021 9777) is one block east, on Brookman St., through St. Barbara's Sq. from the tourist office. The police maintain that no areas of Kalgoorlie-Boulder are particularly unsafe for visitors, but much of the city is poorly lit and it's a good idea for women to exercise caution after dark. The Kalgoorlie Regional **Hospital** (tel. 9080 5888; 24hr. sexual assault tel. 9091 1922) is on Maritana St., several blocks north of Hannan St. and Boulder Rd.

The **bus station** is between the tourist office and the post office on Hannan St. **Greyhound Pioneer** departs for Perth daily at 10:15am (8hr., $86 one-way, book at tourist office). From the tourist office, **Goldfields Express** serves Perth (Wed. and Fri. 11:10pm, 8hr., $65, concession $58.50). **Westrail Prospector** trains depart for Perth from the **train station** on the corner of Forrest and Wilson St. (Mon-Sat. 1 per day at 8:15am, 8hr., $58.50, concession with Westrail card $34.15). Westrail also runs to Esperance (Mon.-Wed. and Fri. at 5pm, 5hr., $18). The **airport** is south of Boulder off Gatacre St. Automobile services are clustered along the highway several blocks southwest of the city center.

ACCOMMODATIONS

Most of the low-cost accommodation in Kalgoorlie is geared toward visitors who have come to town to work and are looking to stay several weeks or months. Some hostels will only rent rooms by the week. The two hostels on Hay St. are the most amenable to backpackers and short-term guests, but these tend to be noisy.

Goldfields Backpackers, 166 Hay St. (tel. 9091 1482, cellular 017 110 001), is 2 blocks south of the intersection of Wilson and Hay St. This backpacker-friendly hostel houses longer-term visitors as well. Shared kitchen, swimming pool, and a lounge. Friendly management staffs reception at irregular hours; call the cellular phone. 4-bed dorms $15; twins $19 per person; doubles $38. YHA discount. The attached **Hay Street Homestay,** 164 Hay St. (same phone), has homier accommodations in a former brothel. Intended for long-term guests. Singles $40; weekly dorm rates negotiable.

Gold Dust Backpackers, 192 Hay St. (tel. 9091 3737), is further down Hay. The cinderblock construction isn't pretty, but at least it's clean and neat. Kitchen and lounges. Wheelchair accessible. 4-bed dorms $15; doubles $35. YHA discount.

Ye Olde Surrey House, 9 Boulder Rd. (tel. 9021 1340). Head east on Maritana St. until it becomes Boulder Rd. Cramped, but carpeted, with a fridge in each room. Kitchen, wheelchair accessible, 24hr. check-in. Dorms $20; twins $25 per person; singles $30. Good weekly rates (singles $140). Linen included.

FOOD AND ENTERTAINMENT

There are two **supermarkets** near the center of town. **Woolworths** at the corner of Wilson and Hay St. has a better selection of fruits and breads and better prices than **Coles,** near St. Barbara's Square (both open Mon.-Sat. until about 5:30pm).

The **Kalgoorlie French Hot Bread Bakery,** on Wilson St. just around the corner from Woolworth's, has the best prices on fresh rolls and baguettes. Cafes line Hannan St.; many open early or close later to serve the miners. For a really good lunch or tea, visit **Heavenly Cakes and Patisseries,** 2 Boulder Rd., which sells salads, sandwiches, and pastries ($5-10; open Mon.-Fri. 9am-5pm, Sat. 9am-1pm). **Goldfields Health Works,** 75 Hannan St., is a little cheaper (vegetarian lunches $3-6; open Mon.-Fri. 9am-5:30pm, Sat. 9am-1pm).

Most of the **pubs** in Kalgoorlie cluster on Hannan St. Some feature striptease shows. A few do have dress codes, generally prohibiting sneakers and mandating a collared shirt on men. For an inexpensive meat-and-potatoes dinner, locals recommend the **Star and Garter,** 497 Hannan St., on the left heading south (open daily 6-9pm).

SIGHTS AND ACTIVITIES

Kalgoorlie's most unique sight is the **Super Pit,** a working open-pit goldmine run by Kalgoorlie Consolidated Gold Mines, and the largest hole in the southern hemisphere. Turn right at the end of Hannan St. on the Goldfields Hwy. (Eastern Bypass Rd.), then turn left at the pit just before Burt St. Several kilometers in circumference and hundreds of meters deep, this pit is indeed super. No one knows what will become of it when the gold runs out sometime in the next century; a mineral spa similar to the Dead Sea or the Great Salt Lake, perhaps? (Open daily 6am-6pm. Free.)

Engineering a Tragedy

Ask any WA local for the story of the Kalgoorlie pipeline, and you'll likely hear a popular Westralian legend. The tale concerns an engineer who claimed he could build a conduit which would carry water from Perth all the way to Kalgoorlie. Since Kalgoorlie is over 500km away from Perth and 400m higher in elevation, no one believed that it could be done, but he insisted, and finally someone gave him the money to try. The local yarn relates that after he designed and built this huge pipeline, the engineer went to Kalgoorlie and turned on the tap. When nothing happened, the broken man shot himself in the head. No one bothered to turn off the tap, and about an hour later, water flowed out of the pipe and into Kalgoorlie. Tragic as the myth is, only the real circumstances of his death do justice to the true extent of the engineer's despair. After proposing the project in 1898, C. Y. O'Connor, frustrated by delays in construction and plagued by faithless critics, took his own life in 1902, one year before his visionary pipeline became a successful reality.

Hannans North Tourist Mine, a right turn off the Goldfields Hwy. 2km north of Hannan St., offers demonstrations of gold panning and underground mining techniques by former miners. The gold pouring and drilling demonstrations are worthwhile, but watching gold panning is almost as boring as doing it. Take ear plugs for the underground demonstration. (Underground tour not wheelchair accessible. Open daily 9am-5pm. Admission $13, children $6, families $35.)

The **Museum of the Goldfields,** at the north end of Hannan St. on the right, has small exhibits on the history and ecology of the Goldfields region (open daily 10am-4:30pm; requested donation $2).

To explore **around Kalgoorlie,** take a drive or walk along the old railway. The woodlines mark the limits of the early century clear-cutting of marble gums and spinifex brush for mine structural timber, building material, and firewood. Regeneration is not yet complete and evidence of the timber industry is still apparent.

Many **sheep stations** allow visitors; inquire at the tourist office. Groups interested in **bush tours** should call Geoff Smith (tel./fax 9021 2669 or 018 928 409). He takes groups of any size into the bush for any length of time, and his tours have as much or as little structure as the group desires. For long trips, contact him months in advance, but if you're in town, he may be available for a daytrip. (Tours $50 per vehicle per day plus fuel; fully-catered tours $60 per day.)

Norseman

Norseman is not a destination, it's a waystation. If traveling north from Esperance, Norseman is the first encounter with the Goldfields. If heading east from Coolgardie across the desolate Nullarbor Plain, it is the last taste of civilization (except for roadhouses, which are a civilization all their own) for over 1000km. A claim was established here shortly after gold was discovered to the north and by Lake Dundas to the west. According to a popular (though perhaps apocryphal) story, a horse (named Norseman) kicked over a stone to reveal gold, and gold has been mined in Norseman ever since. South of town, Lookout Point provides a good spot from which to observe the workings of the Central Norseman Gold Corporation.

A **police station** is located at the corner of Prinsep and Ramsey St., a **hospital** at the west end of Talbot St. The **tourist office** on Robert St., one block east on the highway between Sinclair and Richardson St., is attached to a wheelchair-accessible park (open daily 8am-6pm with showers and a picnic site). Also on Robert St. is a **supermarket,** closed on Sundays. There are no ATMs in town, but the service stations permit **ATM withdrawals** at the cash register. Cirrus acceptance is more common than Plus. The BP 24-hour Travelstop offers a diner, convenience store, and **petrol.** Hitchhikers can sometimes be seen loitering here. If you've got your own wheels, keep in mind that this area has few inhabitants and no natural fresh water supply. In summer temperatures get well over 100°F. In early winter, dark falls before 6pm and the nights are cold. Keep bottled water and plenty of gas on hand. Take it easy on the road after nightfall. Radio stations are scarce, so bring along some good music—the drive between Norseman and Coolgardie can be a lonely two hours.

Coming east from Perth or west from South Australia, travelers sometimes spend the night in Norseman before starting or completing the Eyre Hwy. The charming **Lodge 101** (tel. 9039 1541) on Prince St. offers dorm beds for $15 a night, singles for $25, and doubles for $45. Private room rates include breakfast, and backpackers can use a small kitchen. Farther north on Prinsep St. is the **Gateway Caravan Park** (tel. 9039 1500), where two people can share an on-site caravan for $38 a night, but there are no hostel accommodations. Cabins with refrigerator, range, and table are $46. Space heaters are available in the office. Book ahead in summer.

The **Eyre Highway** itself, running between Norseman and Adelaide across the Nullarbor Plain, is a grueling haul across the desert, and takes 34 hours on a Greyhound bus. While the road is more heavily traveled and not as isolated as the highways up north, distances between roadhouses do approach 200km. Always carry spare gas.

MIDLANDS AND BATAVIA COASTS

The Brand Highway marches north from Perth along the Indian Ocean coastline as to the east the wheat-growing Midlands region extends inland, filling the Westralian bread basket. The main industry of the coastal strip, however, is crayfish, and the area's draws include its renowned wildflowers and intriguing caves, which the elements have fashioned into bizarre patterns. Like weathered headstones in a frontier graveyard, the sandstone columns of the Pinnacles mark the end of the western heartland and represent the gateway to the vast, northern half of WA often called the Unique North.

Well north of the Pinnacles, the Batavia Coast takes its name from the most famous of the many shipwrecks that litter its waters. Only two large towns break the continuity of towering red stone bluffs and gorges, and they have little in common. Geraldton is comfortable in summer and functions mainly as a base for exploring the wildflowers that flourish to its east. Kalbarri, far more popular in the winter, earns its livelihood by light industry. National park land and Murchison River gorges to the east of Kalbarri encompass some of Australia's most arid expanses.

ALONG THE COAST NORTH OF PERTH

The major route north from Perth toward Gascoyne River is Hwy. 1, known along this stretch as the **Brand Hwy.** and peppered with service stations. Leaving Perth, take Riverside Dr. (Hwy. 5) east and follow the signs for the Great Northern Hwy. The Brand Hwy. splits from the Great Northern almost an hour north of Perth. The Wanneroo Rd., which continues from Charles St. northwest of the Northbridge district of Perth, hugs the coast but goes only as far north as Lancelin. To see the **Pinnacles** (see p. 551) en route north or south requires a detour of more than an hour each way from the Brand Hwy., which runs well inland of Cervantes. A new road along the coast between Jurien and Leeman speeds this trip. The road is well-paved, but as of July, 1997, was unmarked except for roadside reflectors. Service stations along this route are closed at night. North of Green Head, the narrow road snakes sinuously up the coast to Geraldton and Kalbarri, rejoining the Brand Hwy. for a relatively short stretch just before Geraldton.

Lancelin

A beautiful beach 115km north of Perth, Lancelin has long been favored by French and German tourists for its excellent **windsurfing.** The windsurfing season runs from the end of October through March; at other times of year, the low surf and shallow tide in Lancelin Bay make the beach excellent for swimming, even for young children. The beach is accessible to 4WD vehicles, which can make the trip over the dunes up the coast to **Cervantes.** If you do make the drive, keep in mind that even Land Rovers can get stuck in the soft, wet sand. For a full beach experience, **Lancelin Surfsports** (tel. 9655 1441), in the shops at 127 Gingin Rd., rents scuba, snorkeling, sandboarding, and surfing equipment. A one-hour windsurfing lesson costs $30.

There is no public transportation to Lancelin. **Coastal Coachlines** (tel. 9652 1036) runs buses from Perth's Wellington St. Bus Station to nearby Regans Ford (Mon. and Fri. 4:30pm, 2hr., $16), but you've still got to get yourself the last few kilometers. The easiest way to reach Lancelin is by car; from Perth, take Bulwer St. to Charles St., which becomes Hwy. 60, the Wanneroo Rd. As you pass through Wanneroo, note the pine tree plantations. Pines are not native to the area, but they're lower-maintenance than eucalypts, since they are self-pruning and do not shed their bark. These trees are a mixed blessing: they're ideal for timber and paper, but also use much more water than indigenous species, and the presence of these plantations has significantly lowered the water table north of Perth.

The **Lancelin Lodge** (tel. 9655 2020; fax 9655 2021; email lanlodge@iinet.net.au), is absolutely pristine, and removed from the more popular, touristed areas north and south along the coast. The 54-bed hostel has spotless common areas and kitchen, laundry facilities, storage areas, and free bicycles. (Office open daily 8am-10pm, check-in 24hr. Check-out 10am, flexible in winter. 6-bed dorms $15; doubles $50, $40 in winter. Weekly: $90; $300. Family rooms available. Wheelchair accessible.)

WESTERN AUSTRALIA

Nanbung National Park: The Pinnacles

Anyone who spends even a few hours hanging around a hostel in Perth will encounter so much hype about the so-called Pinnacles Desert that when it's time to actually visit Nanbung National Park, site of the Pinnacles, travelers just want to get the sightseeing over with. This is unfortunate, because while the limestone pillars are overhyped, they do possess an eerie beauty worth seeing. Despite the moniker, the Pinnacles is not a desert, but a sand dune with wind-eroded limestone formations. The Pinnacles is perhaps best seen just before sunset, as the evening the sun slips dramatically into the Indian Ocean and cool darkness descends.

Nanbung National Park is several hours north of Perth. **Jurien Bus Lines** runs service to nearby **Cervantes,** and tourists can also choose from a plethora of one-day and overnight tour packages. If you have a car, it's possible to see the park on your way north. Allow an hour for the drive west to Cervantes from the left-hand turn off the Brand Hwy., about 20km north of the Cataby Roadhouse. Camping is not allowed in the park, but there are picnic areas and a beach at **Hangover Bay,** a few kilometers from the Pinnacles site. The last stretch of road before the Pinnacles is unsealed, and there's a $5 vehicle fee to drive the sandy loop through the site. Do not get caught out on the driving loop after dark—it's challenging enough when the jagged rocks are actually visible.

Base for Nanbung: Cervantes

The little town of Cervantes, 2km west of the turnoff for the Pinnacles, now has a hostel of its own. The **Pinnacles Beach Backpackers,** 91 Seville St. (tel. 9652 7377; fax 9652 7318; http://www.ca.com.au/pbb), is all the way at the end of Seville St., at the intersection with Barcelona St., just before the road turns to dirt and heads to Thirsty Point. The hostel has 24-hour check-in, is wheelchair accessible, and offers beds in four- or eight-bed dorms for $15. Many travelers say it's the best-run place they've seen. Besides incongruous references to Castille (are the Pinnacles supposed to resemble windmills?) Cervantes offers nothing extraordinary, except easy access to Nanbung National Park. But it's a relaxing place, comfortable in winter and with nearby ocean swimming in the summer. Buses run by **Happyday Tours** (tel. 9652 7244) shuttle daily between the Greyhound stop at the Brand Hwy. turnoff and the Cervantes **post office.**

Geraldton

In the summer, windsurfers from Europe flock to Geraldton for its strong southerly wind. But besides windsurfers, there's not much to see in this "crayfish capital of the world": the Midwest's wildflowers, mainly everlastings which appear in September and October, blossom 150km inland. The shoreline railroad carries no passengers, just mineral sands, talc, and grain. Geraldton, one of WA's northernmost population centers, is trying to become more attractive to tourists and potential residents. Expensive ocean-view property is selling just north of town at Champion Bay, and a recent battle to protect the beach area by shifting an industrial zone farther inland suggests hope of tourism to come.

Orientation and Practical Information If you're arriving by car from the south along the Brand Hwy., drive past the BP Roadhouse straight through the traffic circle and up Cathedral Ave. and turn left onto Chapman Rd. The **tourist bureau** (tel. 9921 3999; open Mon.-Fri. 8:30am-5pm, Sat. 9am-4:30pm, Sun. 9:30am-4:30pm) is about 2km north of the intersection, on the corner of Bayly St., across from the Gulf service station, in the **Bill Sewall Complex.** Coming from the north, turn left at the traffic circle onto Chapman Rd. and head south for several kilometers. The **Greyhound bus** stops at the tourist bureau; the **Westrail** bus stops across the street half a block south, at the **railway station.**

Geraldton's main commercial strip is Chapman Rd., between Cathedral Ave. and the Bill Sewall Complex. The **police station** (tel. 9964 1511) is at the corner of Chapman Rd. and Forrest St., and you can find the **Geraldton Regional Hospital** (tel. 9956 2222) at the corner of Shanton St. and Milford St. The **post office** is on Durlacher St., opposite the McDonald's (open Mon.-Fri. 8:30am-5pm).

Accommodations and Food In the Bill Sewall Complex, around the corner from the tourist bureau, you'll find 109 beds at the **Batavia Backpackers** (tel. 9964 3001; fax 9964 3611), with large dorms in former wards of the old Victoria Hospital. (Reception and check-in 8am-12:30pm, 2:30-7pm, and 8:30-10:30pm. Check-out 10am. 24hr. building access. 12-bed dorms $13; singles $17; twins $30. VIP, YHA. Wheelchair accessible.)

For a more personal experience, stay up the road at **234 Chapman Rd.** (tel. 9921 3024), with Dutch expatriate John Luk. The Luks have lived in Geraldton for 47 years and run their bed and breakfast to meet international travelers. (Check-in late afternoon; check-out relaxed. Couples $60; single rates available.)

A **supermarket** is located on the ocean side of the street, two blocks south of the tourist bureau, next to the Sunseeker Hotel (supermarket open Mon.-Wed. and Fri. 8am-6pm, Thurs. 8am-9pm, Sat. 8am-5pm). The **Batavia Bounty** bakery is at 127 Marine Tce. (open daily 6am-5pm).

Sights and Activities The Romanesque revival **cathedral** with the odd pastiche facade on Cathedral Ave., two blocks east of Chapman Rd., is worth a look. If you're just passing through town, **Spalding Park,** near Bluff Point along Chapman Rd. north of town, makes a great picnic spot, with grassy knolls rolling down to the Chapman River. But people really do come to Geraldton for just one reason: to **windsurf.** The peak season for windsurfing is October to March. Conditions can be good in winter, but wetsuits are necessary. The **Geraldton Surf Company,** 164 Chapman Rd. (tel. 9964 5533), rents, sells, and repairs sailboards and provides information on the different windsurfing spots along the Geraldton coast. It also books windsurfing vacations and gives windsurfing lessons ($25 per hr., including equipment), and surfing lessons ($20 for 2hr.; company open Mon.-Fri. 9:30am-5:30pm, Sat. 9am-2pm).

Kalbarri

A small fishing town, Kalbarri has embraced tourism wholeheartedly with the to-the-point slogan, "Kalbarri—You'll Love It!" In the late autumn, crayfishing boats populate the mouth of the Murchison River, but in the winter months, vacationers fill the warm beaches near Chinamans Rock and the Red Bluff. The season peaks during the mid-July winter school holiday.

Practical Information **Grey St.,** which intersects the access road from the North West Coastal Hwy., skirts the coast and provides access to all of the town's facilities. The **tourist bureau** (tel. 9937 1104) is south of Woods St., and open daily from 8:30am to 5pm. The Department of Conservation and Land Management **(CALM) office** is at 9937 1140. The **police station** (tel. 9937 1006) is on Porter St. The **Medical Centre Doctor** can be reached at 9937 1159. The **post office** is on the corner of Grey and Porter St. (open Mon.-Fri. 8:30am-5:30pm, Sat. 8:30am-12:30pm). There are two **supermarkets** in town, a Foodland at the Ampol station at the north end of town and the Kalbarri Supermarket near the post office. The former may be slightly cheaper; the latter opens at 6:30am every morning. **Greyhound buses** depart from the tourist bureau (Mon., Thurs., and Sat. 4:35pm) headed to Asana for connections to Perth and Carnarvon.

Accommodations Turn right from the tourist bureau, walk up Grey St., and turn left onto Woods St. to get to **Kalbarri Backpackers,** 2 Mortimer St. (tel. 9937 1430). This standard hostel with a mix of international and Australian travelers sports 85 beds and single-sex six-bed dorms. Kitchen, luggage storage, laundry facilities, and 24-hour check-in are available. (Office open 8am-8pm. 10am check-out. Dorms $14; singles $22; doubles $32. 7th night free.) If you turn left from the tourist bureau onto Grey St. and left again onto Porter St., you'll find **Kalbarri Palm Resort,** 8 Porter St. (tel. 9937 2333; fax 9937 1324), by the post office and shopping center. A nightly cinema in the resort's restaurant livens up the 50 clean, spare, no-nonsense suites. Most also have kitchens. (24hr. check-in. Check-out 10am. Family rooms suitable for 4 or 5 adults, $75 peak season (spring), $65 off-peak. Book ahead for spring.) To find **Murchison Park Caravan Park,** at the corner of Grey and Woods St. (tel. 9937 1005; fax 9937 1415). It's central and cheap, so it fills up in winter—book ahead. On-site campervans for four cost $35.

Sights The sandstone and limestone **Red Bluff,** 4km south of town, offers hours of great bouldering and rocky hiking. There are some difficult spots, but it's largely accessible even to children and dogs. North and west of town, **Kalbarri National Park** affords excellent hiking opportunities through gorges along the Murchison River. It's a 25km drive over dirt roads to the sights. The roads are accessible but not pleasant with a front-wheel-drive car. The $5 park fee is taken by a machine that doesn't accept paper money, so have $1- and $2-dollar coins ready. A full hike through the gorges ("The Loop") takes up to six hours. **Kalbarri Safari Tours** runs full-day treks in the park (Tues., Fri., and Sun., pick-up at accommodations at 8am, $35). Book at the tourist bureau or at the backpackers.

The **Abrolhos Islands,** site of the 1629 wreck of the Dutch ship *Batavia* are visible by airplane. **Kalbarri Air Charters** (tel. 9937 1130), next door to the tourist bureau, runs tours to the islands and several other locations ($29-125), including Monkey Mia.

NORTHWEST COAST

This corner of Australia—north of Geraldton and Kalbarri on the west coast, and including the dolphins of Shark Bay, the working town of Carnarvon, and the diving paradises of Coral Bay and Exmouth on the North West Cape—is primed for an explosion of tourism in the coming decade. Settlement is thick enough to support the industry, and the Gascoyne River's excellent fishing and swimming are appeal enough. For the time being, this coast maintains a more relaxed atmosphere than Queensland's resort areas (notwithstanding the circus sideshow of Monkey Mia), but the burgeoning beach culture may someday match that on the east coast.

KALBARRI TO SHARK BAY AND EXMOUTH

Of the major destinations up the coast between Perth and Exmouth, only Geraldton and Carnarvon are actually along Hwy. 1. Kalbarri, Shark Bay, and Exmouth all require significant departures from the artery. The roads from the highway to the coast are all paved, but service stops are less frequent (as much as 160km apart) and the roads tend to be hillier and narrower. Keep your eyes peeled for wandering 'roos, emus, sheep, and cattle in the roadway.

Heading north from Kalbarri or south from Carnarvon, you'll pass a roadhouse at **Overlander** (open 24hr.). The turnoff for Shark Bay is at this roadhouse. It's a 129km drive northwest along the Peron Peninsula to Denham, then another 24km to the Monkey Mia Reserve. The road to Coral Bay and Exmouth splits from the North West Coastal Hwy. at the **Minilya Roadhouse** (also open 24hr.). Exmouth lies 217km to the north and Hwy. 1 continues on toward Port Hedland.

Shark Bay

The only region in Western Australia to be declared a World Heritage Area by the Department of Conservation and Land Management thus far, Shark Bay is the site of the earliest recorded European contact with Australia. Dirk Hartog came ashore on what is now known as Cape Inscription in 1616—and even bothered to write it down. Today, Shark Bay is known largely for the dolphins at Monkey Mia, and Denham is the closest town. The term Shark Bay refers to a beautiful region between two peninsulas. The roads on the western peninsula are inaccessible and unpaved, and the peninsula itself is basically just an access to a salt mine. The towns of Denham and Monkey Mia, about three quarters of the way out on the eastern peninsula, are easy to reach by car. Bus service is inconvenient and infrequent.

Denham With around 500 permanent residents, the westernmost town in Australia is part of Shark Bay and just a speck on the Peron Peninsula, looking out across the Freycinet Reach toward Useless Inlet and Dirk Hartog Island. The main street is Knight Tce., which runs parallel to the town's narrow beach. Although a row of shiny new halogen streetlamps whispers "growth," Denham is, for now, still just a place to stay overnight on a visit to Monkey Mia.

The **bus,** a Shark Bay Tours coach contracted by Greyhound, stops at the **Shell station** (departs for the **Overlander Roadhouse** Mon., Thurs., and Sat., 5:20am and 6:15pm; returns to Denham same days, 8:45am and 11:20pm). Although Denham is warm year-round, fierce southerly winds can make it unpleasant to stand outside, and the Shell station is not open when the early bus out departs. The **tourist bureau** (tel. 9948 1253; open daily 8am-6pm), is on Knight Tce., next door to the Shell station. Its main function seems to be the selling of T-shirts, but staff will also book bus tickets to Monkey Mia ($7 each way—ask for a lift at the hostel before you spend that much). The **police station** (tel. 9948 1201) is on the corner of Hughes and Durlacher St. The **post office** is two doors down from the tourist bureau (enter through the newsagent).

Caravan parks fill up months ahead for the peak season, during the mid-July school break. If you arrive on the bus and need a place to crash, try the **Bay Lodge** (tel. 9948 1278; fax 9948 1031), on Knight Tce. nearly 100m south of the Shell station bus drop or the intersection with Hamelin Rd. (facing the water, head left). Bunks in small, co-ed rooms are $12. Late check-out is available for those catching the evening bus.

There are **supermarkets** at either end of town. **Foodland,** at the Ampol station, is less expensive, but **Tradewinds** at the BP station stays open a bit later and is more central.

Monkey Mia All along the coast, the debate rages over the Shark Bay region's Monkey Mia (pronounced as in "my, uh, special friend") and its dolphins. The Indian bottlenose dolphins really do come right up to visitors' knees, eat fish and click as obliging tourists scratch their flanks, and thousands of tourists come for the experience. Some think Monkey Mia provides an unparalleled opportunity to interact with intelligent, sociable cetaceans and to learn to better appreciate the need for marine environmental protection. Others find it a contrived, exploitative, and downright tacky tourist show. But the dolphins seem to have people trained to bring them food, not the other way around, so just who's being exploited? Mention to other travelers that you're headed to Monkey Mia and you'll get vehement arguments for both sides.

One-day access is $5; for $8, you can come as often as you like for two weeks (although it only takes half an hour to "do" Monkey Mia). Feeding times vary so the dolphins won't start to expect food at any particular time. Generally there are three feedings between 8am and 1pm. A $7 shuttle bus departs the Denham Shell station at 8am and a return run leaves Monkey Mia at noon. The reserve also features picnic space, a swimming beach, walking trails, and aggressive pelicans. If time and money are of concern to you, plan ahead so you can skip the restaurant.

Mosquito-borne Diseases

From Carnarvon north, those annoying bites from mosquitoes ("mozzies") can also be dangerous. In this region, certain species of mosquito can transmit the Ross River and Barmah Forest viruses, as well as encephalitis. The viruses cause low-level somatic problems such as joint ache and fatigue, but are self-limiting and not contagious. Symptoms usually arise within two weeks after transmission and may last intermittently for months. Less common but more serious is Australian encephalitis. Carriers breed annually north of Port Hedland between February and April. Very wet summers can produce a risk as far south as Kalbarri. The incubation time for this kind of encephalitis is at least five days. The disease can be fatal—seek diagnosis if you suffer headaches, neck stiffness, or nausea that do not seem to be caused by dehydration. The Health Department of Western Australia recommends wearing long, loose clothing and using topical DEET to fend off bites. Try to avoid long periods outdoors at dawn and at dusk.

Carnarvon

The only reason most people come to Carnarvon (pop. 7000) is to find work. The area's banana plantations and commercial fishing and shellfishing operations nearly always need cheap, unskilled labor, particularly during the winter picking season (work dries up somewhat during December and January). The town beach is less impressive than those in neighboring areas. The pedestrian footbridge across the Gascoyne River is splendid—but on the far side a muddy path is criss-crossed by bulldozer tracks and interrupted by rotted-out bridges. Even the bars are rowdy and less than inspiring. Ask guests at the hostels in Carnarvon how long they've been in town and chances are good you'll hear "too long."

But Carnarvon makes big plans: the 1 mi. jetty near the town beach may be half-closed now, but it should soon be the site of a new marine museum. In 1964, the U.S. National Air and Space Administration installed a satellite antenna just outside of town to track spacecraft during the Gemini and Apollo missions. The visitors' guide says it all: "The ownership [of the satellite base] has been transferred to the Shire of Carnarvon [which] intends to develop the area as a tourist attraction."

Orientation and Practical Information The center of Carnarvon is Robinson St., between Babbage Island Rd. and **Olivia Tce.,** which crosses the **Gascoyne**

River. The **tourist bureau,** 11 Robinson St. (tel. 9941 1146), is in the Carnarvon Civic Centre at the corner of Stuart St. (open Mon.-Fri. 8:30am-5pm, Sat.-Sun. 9am-noon and 1-4pm). **Greyhound buses** depart from the tourist bureau bound for Perth (Mon., Thurs., and Sat. 7:25pm) and for Broome and Darwin (daily 10:25pm). Several **banks** with **ATMs** are located on Robinson St. The **police station** (tel. 9941 1444) is just next door. The **regional hospital** is two blocks down Francis St.; an **ambulance** is available by calling 9941 1555. The **post office** (open Mon.-Fri. 9am-5pm) is on Stuart St., across from the Civic Centre.

Accommodations **Carnarvon Backpackers,** 50 Olivia Tce. (tel. 9941 1095), lies to the right leaving the tourist office; at the end of Robinson St., turn left onto Olivia Tce. An assortment of dorms and kitchens spreads over several buildings that have seen better days. The hostel has a well-formalized procedure for finding residents work in Carnarvon. Check out by 10am, but you can use the facilities later if you're leaving on a late bus. (Nice patio; off-street parking. Dorms $13; doubles $30; family rooms $10 per person. Weekly: $80; $185; $280. Peak season is May to November. No Australians or New Zealanders.) **Backpackers Paradise** (tel. 9941 2966; fax 9941 3662) is diagonally across the street from the tourist bureau. A mix of workers and overnight guests share this barebones 50-bed hostel that doesn't always live up to its name (dorms $13; twins $30). **Carnarvon Tourist Centre Caravan Park,** 90 Robinson St. (tel. 9941 1438), five blocks down Robinson St. to the left from the tourist office. Much closer to town than the other parks, the center has very clean ablution blocks. (Check-in 7:30am-8:30pm. Check-out 10am. Powered campsites $13. On-site cabins for 4-6 people, $45 with kitchenette.) Book ahead for winter.

Sights and Food The coast is not very impressive, but you might enjoy the walk down Babbage Island Rd., along the highway to the beach by Pelican Point. A drive through the outskirts of town is the real attraction, since the back roads are jammed with banana plantations. Usually these plantations cultivate other tropical fruit as well, including mangoes and figs. **Munro's Plantation,** out along South River Rd. and worth a cab ride, offers tours (Sun.-Fri. 11am, $2). Feel free to wander around even without a tour. The cafe at the plantation serves excellent homemade scones and jams in addition to pancakes, cakes, and, improbably, mango beef nachos. Lunch runs about $5. Otherwise, shop for food at **Woolworths** (open daily 8am-8pm), on Robinson St. two blocks from the tourist bureau.

Finding the Tunes

For lone drivers, music can be critical to staying alert and comfortable. If you run out of tapes or lack a tape deck, try 666 AM kHz. "Triple-six" may never be your favorite radio station, but it's the only one in the region (unless you like listening to the pre-recorded message on tourist radio, 88 FM). The mix is vociferously eclectic—don't be surprised to hear the Beach Boys, Midnight Oil, the Supremes, and Flock of Seagulls all in the same hour, in addition to the latest alternapop. Interruptions are frequent but fascinating; listen for the Carnarvon market report to hear how bananas, mangoes, and paw-paws are trading.

Exmouth

The scuba diving epicenter of the west coast, this is the place to go to swim with giant, easygoing whale sharks. Unlike Coral Bay or Kalbarri, the beach is not right in the center of town, so Exmouth is not a good place for lounging on the beach all day. But for diving, fishing, or hiding from one's own vacation, it's ideal.

Orientation and Practical Information Most of the action in Exmouth takes place in the vicinity of Maidstone Crescent, which intersects with Murat Rd. (the highway) at both ends. The **tourist bureau** (tel. 9949 1176) and Conservation and Land Management (CALM) office are both toward the northern end of Maidstone. The town has one **ATM. Buses** arrive at the tourist bureau and depart for Perth (Mon., Thurs., and Sat. 2:30pm). A shopping center with two **supermarkets** and a very popular bakery is behind Maidstone Cr., near Learmonth and Kennedy St. Both Foodland and Exmouth Supermarket stay open until 7pm or later; the latter is slightly less expensive. The **police station** is just to the south, on the corner of Bennett St. The **hospital** (tel. 9949 1011) is two blocks west, on Lyon St. near Fyfe St. The **post office** is around the corner from the tourist bureau.

Accommodations and Camping The best place to stay in town is the **Excape Backpackers** (tel. 9949 1201), across the street from the tourist bureau. Clean and quiet, with a mellow crowd and an enclosed pebble yard, the Excape is affiliated with both the Exmouth Diving Centre and the Potshot Resort. Guests at the hostel may use the hotel's pool and spas, and enjoy free BBQ on Friday evenings and free bicycle use. Linens are provided. (Check-in 8am-8pm. Check-out 9:30am. 4-bed coed dorms $14; twins $32. Weekly or for those doing a course with the dive center: dorms $12 per night. Walk-in space is usually available, but book ahead to be sure.)

You may **camp** independently near a number of the beaches in Cape Range National Park, but 4WD is essential (sites for 2 $5). Most sites have no shade or shelter; few have toilet facilities. The Milyering Visitor Centre near the north end of the park has detailed information on all the sites. Between April and October, they crowd up. Call CALM at 9949 1676 for more information. No pets are allowed in the park.

Diving and Sights The **Exmouth Diving Centre** (tel. 9949 1201; fax 9949 1680) bills its divemasters as the number one whale shark team in the world, and they may well be. But the Ningaloo Reef offers more than whale sharks, and the good people at the Dive Centre will show you all. A five-day **PADI certification course** costs $299, plus the cost of a medical exam. Its four dives include one near the Naval Base Pier to which the Diving Centre has exclusive rights. Several dive packages are available for those already certified; have your log book handy to indicate your experience.

A drive around the cape into **Cape Range National Park** is also worthwhile. Currently, the beaches and hiking trails are barely accessible to 2WD vehicles. Plans are underway to finish paving the main road, but for now, either get a truck or go with the highly recommended **Paul Wittwer's Reef Retreat.** For $85, Paul will take you into the park for three days of camping, swimming, hiking, and lying around in the nearly pristine bush. (Meals included. Groups are small. Inquire at the tourist bureau.)

■ Near Exmouth: Coral Bay

On the way from the Minilya Roadhouse to Exmouth, Coral Bay is tiny but has one of the most beautiful beaches on the west coast. The town offers swimming, dune hiking, and snorkeling off the inner reaches of the **Ningaloo Reef.** The **Ningaloo Reef Dive Centre** conducts three dives daily. A one-day "resort course" costs $95. Snorkelers are welcome on the boats. The shop also offers a five-day PADI certification course, but they encourage people to take the course with their sister shop in Exmouth, which has better facilities.

The Perth-Exmouth **Greyhound** stops in Coral Bay (bound for Exmouth Wed., Fri., and Sun. at noon; for Perth Mon., Thurs., and Sat. at 4:20pm). A **supermarket** and an inexpensive bakery are in the complex which includes a dive shop and nursing post, on the right as one enters town from the highway. The supermarket acts as a **tourist information center.** Perhaps 100m farther, on the left, past the Reef Cafe and set back from the road, is the **Bayview Coral Bay Backpackers** (tel. 9942 5932), an airy 50-bed hostel. (Office open 8-10am, 24hr. check-in with prior booking, or pick up a key until 10pm at the Reef Cafe. Twins $15 per person. Linens provided. Book ahead in winter.)

THE PILBARA

North of Carnarvon and as far east as Broome lies the tropical coastal plain known as the Pilbara. The Pilbara region shares the tropical seasons of the Northern Territory's Top End: wet in the summer, dry in the winter, and hot year-round. As one penetrates eastward into this sparsely-settled region, the earth turns pinker and silhouettes of bizarre geological formations appear on the horizon on the western edge of the Hamersley Ranges. The road is surrounded by prickly spinifex brush and mulga and gum trees, and the bitumen is festooned with kangaroo carcasses.

Iron and salt mining rule the economy here, and there's not much to see apart from mines and salt flats. Many people pass right through bound for Broome or Darwin. But the Pilbara is so big that passing through means spending a night (even if that night is spent on the bus), so have a look around. It's a place where people have staked a claim on the earth's resources in the face of an utterly inhospitable environment. Heat, floods, cyclones, winds, and mosquito-borne encephalitis are some of the regional impediments to settlement. If the locals seem preoccupied and the towns less tourist-oriented, there's good reason. At least no one will shove a glossy brochure in your face.

Note that ATMs with Plus system access are not to be found in the Pilbara. If you are using ATM withdrawal from an overseas account, be sure you have Cirrus access.

Heat Kills

Winter in the northwest is a season of dry heat, and you may not realize you are dehydrated until the onset of constipation or a massive headache. By the time you feel thirsty, you're a couple liters low. Drink several liters of water every day to stave off heat stroke. Take a water break every hour during a daytime drive. Undiluted fruit juice, available in 250mL bottles at roadhouses and supermarkets, will help keep sugar and vitamin C levels high.

NORTH WEST CAPE TO PORT HEDLAND

The **Burkett Road** connects the North West Cape to the North West Coastal Highway, bypassing the Minilya Roadhouse and skirting the Gulf of Exmouth. Taking the partially sealed road will save time on a drive from Exmouth northeast, but will take you through the middle of nowhere. The turnoff is 65km north of Coral Bay. Fill up the tank at Exmouth, Coral Bay, or Minilya, because it's a long haul to the 24-hour **Nanutarra Roadhouse** (110km north from where the Burkett Road meets the North West Coastal Hwy. Take a break at Nanutarra rather than Fortescue River Roadhouse an hour up the highway. Say hello to Bill Spier, and if you can take him frosted grape Pop-Tarts, you'll make him a happy man. Tell him *Let's Go* sent you.

The **Hamersley Iron** site at Seven-mile Access along the highway between Karratha and Dampier (coming from Karratha, turn left just after the rubbish tip turnoff) is happy to give drivers a pass for a month's access to their well-kept railroad service road. Ask at the security office at the gate, staffed 24-hours. The road is unpaved but in good condition, although it is extremely winding and narrow at points. To get to it, follow the rubbish tip road to the turnoff for the North West Coastal Hwy. Turn right and cross the railroad tracks. Gas up before you go, since there's no fuel at Millstream, 125km south.

The drive through the fields of ferrous hills is spectacular if tricky. After 90km, you can cross the tracks and take another road north back to the highway. Be aware that the 10km of paved but extremely winding cliffside road down into a long vale makes for difficult driving. The road passes by Python Pool and through a channel flanked by amazing monadnocks. Unfortunately, one cannot hike up them because the grass is too sharp. After passing several stock stations, the gravel road meets the North West Coastal Hwy., which becomes the Great Northern Hwy. 27km east of the ghost town of **Roebourne.** Head east toward Port Hedland, 175km away. The bar at the Whim Creek Rest Stop, 120km west of Port Hedland, is rowdy and unpleasant.

Port Hedland

Salt mines, refineries, shipping docks, and red dust rule the skyline of Port Hedland, a narrow city sandwiched between the Indian Ocean and the Great Northern Hwy. The city itself is surprisingly small and low-key, dwarfed by its own highway interchange. Everything of interest is within walking or cycling distance. Port Hedland is not a place to stay for more than a week or two, but it is well-placed for extensive forays into the Hamersley Range. There's usually less casual labor here than in Kalgoorlie or Carnarvon, but the long, shallow low tides and the placid drifting of the cargo ships make it a relaxing place.

Orientation and Practical Information The center of downtown Port Hedland is the intersection of Wedge St. and Richardson St. All of the town's facilities lie within a few blocks of this corner, and the port itself is just a stone's throw to the north, across Richardson. Be careful walking at night, as there are many stray dogs in the neighborhood.

The **tourist bureau** (tel. 9173 1711) is at 13 Wedge St., near the corner of Anderson St. (open Mon.-Fri. 8:30am-5pm, Sat. 8:30am-12:30pm and 1:30-3:30pm, Sun. noon-4pm). A **Greyhound bus** headed toward Perth stops there every afternoon at 3:10pm; one headed north toward Broome and Darwin stops every morning at 10:15am. The tourist bureau also offers public bathrooms and shower facilities.

A **shopping center,** with an Action Supermarket (open Mon.-Wed. and Fri. 8am-6pm, Thurs. 8am-9pm, Sat. 8am-5pm, Sun. 9am-4pm) and a **pharmacy,** is 3km from Wedge St. down Anderson St. The **hospital** (tel. 9158 1666) is on Sutherland St., near the corner of Howe St. The **police station** (tel. 9173 1444) is on Anderson St., around the corner from the tourist bureau. The **post office** (open Mon.-Fri. 9am-5pm) is at 16 Wedge St., across from the tourist bureau.

Accommodations and Sights There is just one hostel in town, the **Port Hedland Backpackers,** 20 Richardson St. (tel. 9173 3282). Turn right onto Richardson St. from Wedge St. and walk two blocks. You'll find 26 beds, a kitchen, laundry facilities, and a nice enclosed porch. (Limited wheelchair access. Check-in 8am-10pm. Check-out 10am. Sheets provided. Dorms $14. Book ahead May-Oct.) The hostel runs tours of Karijini National Park (departs Mon., 2 nights, $220).

If you visit Port Hedland, you must, must, must see the **Pretty Pool.** The uninspired name does no justice to this tidal mudflat, which extends for miles at low tide. Wet sand was never this cool. The walk or bike ride is approximately 7km; follow Anderson St. to McGregor St. to Athol St. Sunrise and sunset are both exquisite times to view the pool. A bus tour of the **BHP iron ore processing plant** at Nelson Point departs from the tourist bureau and goes through the whole facility, but you'll never actually get off the bus (Mon.-Fri. 10am, 1½hr., $10).

Karijini National Park

The hills and gorges of the Hamersley range comprise the highest region in Western Australia. Karijini National Park offers relatively easy access to the gorges. You can see the park on a daytrip from Port Hedland. The one-day park fee is $5, and two-person tent sites an additional $5 (all fees paid on-site). The **camping** areas, all accessible by 2WD, and **hiking** trails for both inexperienced and experienced hikers are located at **Dales, Joffre,** and **Weano Gorges.** A paved road through the park south of the gorges should have been completed by the end of 1997. The dirt roads through the gorges area are well-kept. Still, they have sharp hills and vehicles kick up a lot of dust, so exercise caution.

Hold Your Breath

About 40km west of the Auski Roadhouse, past the turnoff for the abandoned road through the Yampire Gorge, lies the erstwhile town of Wittenoom. A 1937 asbestos boom led to the 1947 incorporation of the town as a home for miners. The road from town through Wittenoom Gorge past the old asbestos mine is actually paved with blue asbestos. Eventually, however, many of the inhabitants of Wittenoom contracted mesothelioma from inhaling the local resource. Now, the government of Western Australia would like to forget Wittenoom ever existed and wants to clear the area. For 20 years, the state has been buying buildings in Wittenoom and demolishing them. Government officials ordered the shut-off of water, electricity, and telephone service to the 30 or so remaining residents on January 1, 1997. But the residents want to stay. They maintain that air sampling has found levels of airborne asbestos to be no higher in Wittenoom than in Perth, and speculate that the government is using Wittenoom to draw attention away from the asbestos contamination dangers of open-pit iron and gold mining. The town arranged a private deed with Telstra for telephone service, and its lawyers were still wrangling over power and water in July, 1997. The state premier and a local Aboriginal elder with native claim to nearby land have both expressed interest in rebuilding the Yampire Gorge road, and the 30 residents now dream of making the town Western Australia would like to forget into one tourists will always remember.

The best way to enter the park is from the Great Northern Hwy., 34km south of the Auski Roadhouse (open 6:30am-10pm; gas is expensive here). The roadhouse, located at Munjina, is 260km from Port Hedland along a fast stretch of the Great Northern. The northern entrances to the park, through Yampire Gorge and **Wittenoom,** are not recommended. The Yampire Gorge road is in extreme disrepair and was closed in February, 1997, after flooding. The Wittenoom Gorge road is paved with blue asbestos (see the graybox).

Maps of the park, updates on road conditions, and weather information are available at the Port Hedland tourist bureau. To see the park in a single day and have time for one of the longer hikes (up to 3hr.), plan to leave Port Hedland early in the morning. Gas/petrol is available at both Tom Price and Munjina, but you should carry a canister in any case. Carry enough water to last as many days as you plan to spend camping—there are water tanks in the park but they're few and far between.

■ Near Karijini: Tom Price

Just west of Karijini National Park, Tom Price, with a population of around 3500 and the highest elevation of any town in WA, is the largest of the three towns in the vicinity of the park. Currently there is no bus service into Tom Price, partly because the roads around the area are only now being paved. One can reach Tom Price by driving Hwy. 136, 287km east from the Nanutarra Roadhouse on the North West Coastal Hwy. Make sure you know where you're going; scenic but desolate, the road passes through dry creek beds and the western Hamersleys, and has no services at all, no markings, and for the 80km west of Tom Price, no pavement.

A Hamersley Iron company town until 1988, Tom Price is now governed by the Shire of Ashburton but is still closely bound to Hamersley Iron. The **Tom Price Shell station** (open Mon.-Fri. 6am-7pm, Sat.-Sun. 6am-6pm) is the nearest fuel stop to the camping sites around Weano Gorge. The **Tom Price Caravan Park** (tel. 9189 1515; reception open Mon.-Fri. 7am-7pm, Sat.-Sun. 7am-noon), 4km west of town (turn right out of the Shell station) offers on-site caravans for two people ($40), on-site tents for two people ($25), and bunkhouse beds ($15).

PORT HEDLAND TO BROOME

Six hundred kilometers of empty Great Northern Highway separate Port Hedland and Broome. It's nearly 300km between the Sandfire Roadhouse and the Roebuck Road-

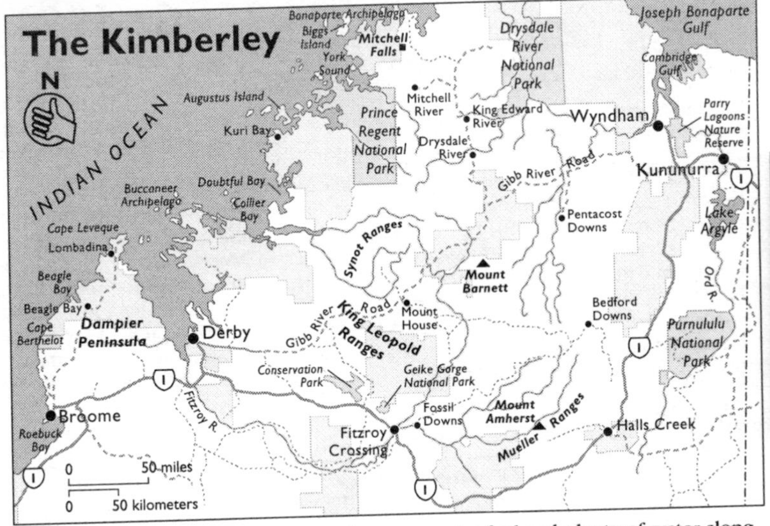

house outside Broome, so it is essential to carry extra fuel and plenty of water along this stretch. A strong headwind can cut fuel efficiency terribly. Try not to make the drive alone. Many travelers head from Port Hedland to Broome, and there's only one backpackers' hostel in Port Hedland, so it's not difficult to find traveling companions. By bus, the trip takes seven hours. The desert is full of strange driving perils. It's bad enough to hit a cow, but the potential for disaster inherent in colliding with a camel is best left to the imagination.

THE KIMBERLEY

Pressed between the Indian Ocean and the Great Sandy Desert, 320,000 square kilometers of rough, raw bush are broken only by unpredictable rivers, magnificent boulder-stacked cliffs, and tiny pockets of settlement. The notion that civilization holds claim to this tropical outback is contestable: over two-thirds of it is cattle country. Only a handful of human outposts are scattered along this route, and a large proportion of their population is Aboriginal. Rugged souls must visitors be if they intend to venture past the beach mecca of Broome. Pioneers who dare to tread this untrammeled landscape should anticipate a lesson in self-sufficiency.

THE GREAT NORTHERN HIGHWAY

The highlights of the Kimberley are isolated, and most roads, apart from the Great Northern Hwy., are for 4WD vehicles only. Flooded rivers during the monsoonal Wet from November to March often close roads altogether, although the East Kimberley is noticeably wetter than the West. Call 1800 013 314 for road conditions and register with the police before setting off.

Broome

At the base of a peninsula projecting into the Indian Ocean, Broome (pop. 8900) is the western gateway to the Kimberley. The underdeveloped resort spreads languorously between the mangrove swamps on Roebuck Bay and the enticing white sands of Cable Beach. Whereas most of Australia's population migrations were driven by gold, the ethnic diversity evident here is the consequence of a *pearl* rush in the 1880s. Broome's Chinatown remains the commercial center of this surprisingly cosmopolitan seaside settlement. In the summer, it attracts visitors like bushflies to a backpacker's back. While enjoying sunny days at the beach and nights of relaxation at local pubs, many travelers find that Broome is nothing to sweep under the carpet.

ORIENTATION

Broome sits on sheltered **Roebuck Bay,** with the Indian Ocean to its west and the Dampier Peninsula stretching to the north and east. The Great Northern Hwy., called **Broome Road** in town, curls around the bay and approaches from the north. It passes the **tourist office** and makes a slight angular adjustment, becoming **Hamersley St.,** at its intersection with **Napier Tce.** This corner is **Chinatown,** the oldest part of Broome and the closest thing it has to a center. A block south of Napier, **Frederick St.** heads west toward Cable Beach on the other side of the peninsula, where a smaller speck of civilization serves beach-goers next to the turquoise waters of the Indian Ocean. The **Great Northern Hwy.** snakes east from Broome into the Kimberley proper. The long, grueling haul leads to Kununurra and the Northern Territory beyond.

PRACTICAL INFORMATION

Tourist Office: Broome Tourist Bureau (tel. 9192 2222), well-marked on Broome Rd. at the corner of Bagot St. Open Mon.-Fri. 8am-5pm, Sat.-Sun. 9am-4pm; Nov.-March reduced hours.

Budget Travel: Harvey World Travel (tel. 9193 5599; fax 9193 5519) in Paspaley Shopping Centre, Chinatown. Exclusive broker for Qantas. Open Mon.-Fri. 8:30am-5:30pm, Sat. 9am-3pm. **Traveland** (tel. 9193 7766 or 1800 675 766) in the Boulevard Shopping Centre on Frederick St.

Currency Exchange: ANZ Bank (tel. 9193 5096) behind Paspaley Shops on Carnarvon St. **Commonwealth Bank** (tel. 9192 1103) on Hamersley a block north of Greyhound. Both have ATMs. Open Mon.-Thurs. 9:30am-4pm, Fri. 9:30am-5pm.

Airport: Broome International Airport (tel. 9193 5455) is most easily accessed by taking a right from Frederick onto Coghlan St., then a left on McPherson Rd. **Ansett** to: Derby (Mon.-Sat., $94), Kununurra ($203), Perth ($370), Darwin ($266), Alice Springs (Sat.-Sun., $253). **Qantas Airlink** to: Perth ($378), Darwin (Sun. $275), Alice Springs (Sat.-Sun., $263), Yulara (Sun., $352). The Ansett office (tel. 9193 6855; fax 9193 5184), in Paspaley Shops, is open Mon.-Fri. 8:30am-5:30pm, Sat. 8:30am-noon. Harvey World Travel handles Qantas reservations.

Buses: Greyhound Pioneer station is on Hamersley St., a few blocks south of Napier Tce. To Perth (daily 8am, $240). To Katherine (daily 7:30pm, $171), via Kununurra ($130). **Deluxe Coachline** is on Napier Tce.

Public Transportation: The **Town Bus** (tel. 9193 6000) has two shuttle lines that circle Broome hourly. Covers Chinatown, Cable Beach, Gantheaume Point, and the port. First sector $2, additional sectors $1.50 each; day ticket $8.

Taxis: There's a taxi stand in Chinatown. **Roebuck Taxis** (tel. 1800 812 441); **Broome Taxis** (tel. 9192 1133). Many hostels have free taxi phones.

Car Rental: ATC Rentacar (24hr. tel. 9193 7788, mobile 015 447 276), **Budget** (tel. 9193 5355 or 1800 649 800), and **Hertz** (tel. 9192 1428) have airport offices.

Bike Rental: Broome Cycle Centre (tel. 9192 1871), at the corner of Hamersley and Frederick St., hires bikes in good condition for $10 for 1 day, $8 each additional day. Open Mon.-Fri. 8am-5pm, Sat. 8am-noon, Sun. 9am-11am.

Markets: Thursday Night Market, at Paspaley Shopping Centre. Open 5-8pm.

Pharmacy: Chemmart (tel. 9192 1399), in Paspaley, is open Mon.-Fri. 8:30am-5:30pm, Sat. 8:30am-2pm, Sun. 10am-1pm.

Hospital: Broome District Hospital (tel. 9192 1401), on Robinson St. Turn left off Frederick St. and it's on the right. Modern facility is undergoing upgrades.

Police: At the corner of Frederick and Hamersley St. (tel. 9192 1212).

Emergency: Dial 000.

Post office: Australia Post in Paspaley Shops. *Poste Restante.* Open Mon.-Fri. 9am-5pm. **Postal code:** 6725.

Phone Code: 08.

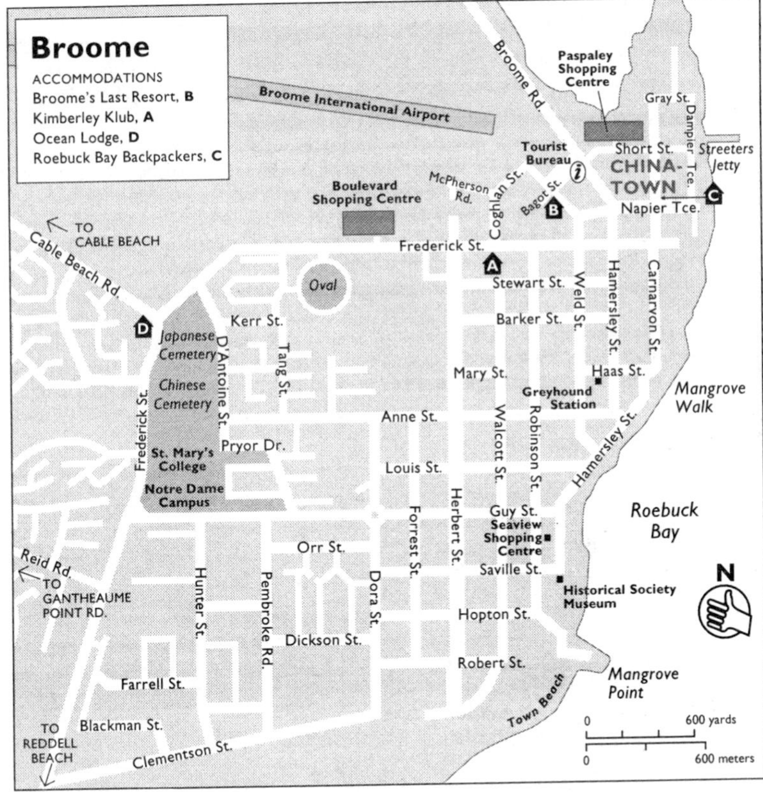

ACCOMMODATIONS

Kimberley Klub (tel. 9192 3233; fax 9192 3530), on Frederick St. opposite Coghlan St., a couple blocks from Hamersley St., claims supremacy only over the other backpacker accommodations in Broome. A social, family-friendly, young hostel with a sparkling pool, sandy volleyball court, recreation room, open-air TV den, and spacious kitchen. A veranda winds lazily through the pink corrugated steel architecture. Reception 24hr. Check-out 9:30am. Dorms $14; twins $38; doubles $45; quads $64. Key deposit $5, plates and cutlery $10. Book ahead with credit card.

Cable Beach Backpackers (tel. 9193 5511 or 1800 655 011; fax 9193 5532), on Lullfitz Dr. 400m east of main Cable Beach facilities. This backpackers is a hot pick for its proximity to the beach. Beach-goers trail orange dirt through shared baths and dorms, hence the concrete construction. The kind management maintains a pool, kitchen, laundry facilities, and a hangout area complete with air hockey and a selection of videos. A shuttle runs into town 4 times per day and makes free pick-ups and drop-offs for buses and planes. Check-out 10am. 4-bed dorms $15; twins $40. VIP, YHA. Key deposit $5, linen deposit $5. Reservations suggested.

Broome's Last Resort (tel. 9193 5000 or 1800 801 918), on Bagot St. 100m past the tourist office. This Chinatown locale caters specifically to the beer-swilling, smoke-billowing partier. The staff is distracted, and wooden-planked decks lend a tree-house feel that's pleasantly shady but a bit worn. Evening bar fuels socialites into the wee hours. Tropical waterfall pool. Laundry facilities. Free pack storage and shuttle to bus terminal. Reception 6:30am-7:30pm. Check-out 9:30am. 8-bed fan-cooled dorms $13, 6-bed $14, 4-bed $15. Cleaner twins and doubles $38. YHA.

WESTERN AUSTRALIA

Roebuck Bay Backpackers (tel. 9192 1183; fax 9192 2390), on Napier Tce. past Carnarvon St. in Chinatown. The cheapest beds in town, so don't expect it all from Roebucks. Laundry, kitchen, pool. Check-out 10am. Crowded 8-bed dorms $12. Doubles with bath $40. VIP, YHA. Key deposit $10, cutlery and plates deposit $10.

Camping: Cable Beach Caravan Park (tel. 9192 2066; fax 9192 1997), behind the Cable Beach Resort, is a short path away from the coast. Turn onto Lullfitz St. from the beach road, then left on Millington St. It's 300m on the right. Reception 8am-1pm and 4-6pm. Check-out 10am. Sites $7.50 per person, with power $10.50. **Roebuck Bay Caravan Park** (tel. 9192 1366) is on the other shore of town, and **Broome Caravan Park** (tel. 9192 1776) is nearly 5km down Broome Rd.

FOOD

Chinatown is not flooded with Chinese restaurants, but it does have a fair offering. The Paspaley Shopping Centre contains **Charlie Carters,** the biggest grocery in town (open Mon.-Wed. 8am-6pm, Thurs.-Fri. 8am-8pm, Sat. 8am-5pm, Sun. 10am-5pm). There's also **Action Food Barn,** a competitor in the Boulevard Shopping Centre on Frederick St. (same hours). Cable Beach has no supermarkets.

Blooms Cafe and Restaurant (tel. 9193 6366), on Carnarvon St. near Napier Tce. in Chinatown. In the carpark area of Carnarvon lies this favorite for locals and post-card writers alike. Colored chalkboards display the menu for this relaxed scene with some outdoor seating and a space for live music. Big Brekky (eggs, bacon, sausage, grilled tomato, and toast) $8.50, falafel baguette $9.50, plus pasta and grill delights. Open daily 7:30am-9pm.

Pango's (tel. 9192 1395), a block down Dampier Tce. near Napier Tce. A colorful atmosphere for indoor and outdoor evening dining. Elegant, yet relaxed and unconventional: roast pumpkin, sweet potato, and mixed bean salad $8, mushroom pasta in tomato sauce $13.50, and a Neanderthal-sized rib dish $23.50. Open daily 5pm until empty.

Murray's Pearler (tel. 9192 2049), upstairs from Pango's. Even if the name isn't convincing, the Asian dishes served on Murray's intimate white-clothed tables are sincere and scrumptious. Listen to movies playing at the outdoor cinema down the block while you enjoy chicken with black bean sauce or Szechuan beef ($13). Seafood is a theme; try the special whole local fish ($17). Open daily 6-10pm.

SIGHTS AND ACTIVITIES

Travelers flock to Broome for **Cable Beach.** Here, 22km of light blue waters lap against soft, creamy sand that squishes between the toes, and rolling green lawns tumble down to the edge of the beach. From town, follow Frederick St. to a right on Cable Beach Rd., take another right on Ocean Dr., and a left that hops onto another piece of Cable Beach Rd. to the end. Some folks enjoy a relaxing **camel ride** along the water's edge. Picturesque and popular, these caravan outings are run by **Ships of the Desert** for $25 per person, morning, afternoon, and evening. Book through the tourist bureau.

Broome Crocodile Park (tel. 9192 1489) basks in the sun and snarls 200m from the beach access on Cable Beach Rd. A maze of separate pens holds these modern-day dinosaurs, including 1500 aggressive salties. (Open Mon.-Fri. 10am-5pm, Sat.-Sun. 2-5pm; guided tours Mon.-Tues. 3pm; feedings Wed.-Sun. 3pm. Admission $10, backpackers $8, children $5.) The prehistoric predecessors of these crocs traipsed all over the Broome area; one set of **dinosaur footprints** is preserved in the rocks at Gantheaume Point, the western tip of the Broome Peninsula, about 4km from Cable Beach. Follow the initial directions to Cable Beach (above), but turn left onto Ocean Dr. and stay on it until it becomes Gubinge Rd., which hits Gantheaume Point Rd. south, which will take you there. The rock prints surface at low tide and may require some pointing out and explaining. A plaster cast of the prints is at the top of the cliff.

In **Chinatown,** a few rows of historic storefronts attempt to resuscitate for tourists an otherwise defunct past. The pearl outlets along the water on Dampier Tce. are persistent reminders of an industry long gone. The rest is just an outdoor mall. The Roebuck Bay side of Broome is a muddy but lovely mangrove coastline. The drive on Carnarvon St. south, where it merges with Hamersley St., steals some stellar glimpses of the Bay. Hamersley dead-ends into the parking lot of the Seaview Shopping Centre, some seven blocks south of Chinatown, where the **Broome Historical Society Museum** (tel. 9192 2075) walks you through the heritage of Broome, from the war to racial problems to the pearling industry. (Open June-Nov. Mon.-Fri. 10am-4pm, Sat.-Sun. 10am-1pm; Dec.-May daily 10am-1pm. Admission $3.) On the way to Chinatown, just south of where the Cable Beach Rd. and Frederick St. rendezvous, the **Japanese Cemetery's** impressive field of black marble and gray stone slates bears testimony to hundreds of divers who lost their lives in the pearling industry.

Town Beach is farther south on the Roebuck Bay shore. Here, for three consecutive days each month from March to October, Broome's massive 10m tide is so low that the exposed mudflats stretch for miles, reflecting shimmering moonlight. The city celebrates this phenomenon with the **Staircase to the Moon** market at the tourist office. At the lowest tides, the waters off Town Beach uncover the skeletons of **flying boats** sunk in WWII. **Reddell Beach,** the southern shore of the Broome Peninsula, is covered with rocky outcroppings and red cliffs.

Outside town, a right-hand turn 8km down Broome Rd. loops back around to Roebuck Bay and the **Broome Bird Observatory** (tel. 9193 5600), an excellent place to spy migratory birds. Head north to the **Willie Creek Pearl Farm** (tel. 9193 6000; fax 9193 6554), 38km from Broome, for the only pearling operation that welcomes public inspection. A popular but out-of-the-way attraction, the farm runs its own transport back and forth daily from its showroom on Lullfitz Dr. near Cable Beach. Take Broome Rd. 9km from town, turn left on Cape Leveque Rd., and stay on it for 14.5km. Turn left on Manari Rd, stay on it for 5km, take another left and follow the signs. (Admission $17.50, children $9; with Pearl Farm bus $39, children $20). If you're driving, check on road conditions during the wet.

ENTERTAINMENT

Like Baywatch's lifeguards, Broome's beaches and clubs seduce the weak-willed into brief affairs. A "backpackers-only" bar is run out of the Roebucks complex and borrows the name **Rattle 'n' Hum** from a semi-famous Darwin establishment (open Wed.-Sat. 6pm-late; 6-9pm meal with drink $6). About 100m away on Napier near Hamersley is the conspicuous **Tokyo Joe's** (tel. 9193 7222; open Wed.-Sat. 9pm-late). When these places close around midnight or 1am, both the patrons and the staff descend into Chinatown's **Nippon Inn,** on Dampier Tce. across from Pango's and Murray's Pearler restaurants. Cable Beachers flock to the **Divers Camp Tavern,** a bar and bistro that gets drunken and jovial on weekends.

The **Sun Pictures outdoor cinema** (tel. 9192 1077), on Carnarvon next to the car park, claims to be the oldest operating outdoor film theater in the world. It spun its first reel in 1916 and spins the newest flicks every night (admission $9, children $6).

Horse racing is big in town from June to July, but most of the other seasonal activities are on the water. Apart from simple charter fishing and reef diving, festivals color Broome throughout the year. Mid-April features the aquatic **Rotary Dragon Boat Classic.** The end of May features the even bigger **Broome Fringe Arts Festival,** when the aesthetically inclined display their stuff. Much of the art is Aboriginal. The late August **Shinju Matsuri Festival** celebrates the natural aesthetic of the pearl. In late November, the **Mango Festival** pays homage to the harvest and even includes a Mardi Gras.

■ Around Broome: The Dampier Peninsula

The Dampier, jutting into the Indian Ocean north of Broome, is Aboriginal domain. Some of the Aboriginal communities were once Catholic missions and swing their doors wide open for tourists. **Beagle Bay** (tel. 9192 4913), 120km north of Broome on the Cape Leveque Rd., proudly possesses a church with a mother-of-pearl altar. The town has gas and groceries but no accommodations, and collects a $5 entrance fee. **Lombadina** (tel. 9192 4936 or 9192 4942), another settlement 80km down the road, has its own church in the bush and lots of crafts for sale. Lombadina (entry $5) contains accommodations and leaded gas. **Cape Leveque** (tel. 9192 4970), at the northern tip of the peninsula, hides a spectacular coast for swimming, fishing, and diving. It has accommodations, camping, fuel, and restaurants. The Cape Leveque settlement lies 220km from Broome, at the end of Cape Leveque Rd. All of these Dampier destinations demand 4WD and are known to close in the wet season. It's best to notify the Broome Tourist Bureau before heading up the peninsula, in case inclement weather strikes suddenly.

Derby

The town of Derby, 220km east of Broome, is surrounded by mudflats—more at certain times of the day than at others. This phenomenon is due to the fact that Derby has the **highest fluctuating tides in the southern hemisphere.** The waters of King Sound can rise and fall as much as 10m in a few hours. This community of 5000 was established in 1883, and many of its sights are hokey historical tidbits. A portly **Prison Boab tree** served as a natural slammer, and the longest trough in the southern hemisphere (120m) was capable of quenching the thirst of 1000 cattle at once. The regional headquarters for the **Royal Flying Doctor Service** and the **School of the Air** both welcome visitors. Derby also serves as the gateway to the tropical **Buccaneer Archipelago** across the sound.

Derby has a **tourist office,** 1 Clarendon St. (tel. 9191 1426; fax 9191 1609; open dry season Mon.-Fri. 8:30am-4:30pm, Sat.-Sun. 9am-1pm; wet season Mon.-Fri. 8:30am-4:30pm, Sat. 9am-noon), a **hospital** (tel. 9193 3333; ambulance tel. 9193 1111), **police** (tel. 9191 1444), and a **post office** (tel. 9191 1350). The road to the highway is sealed. The **Greyhound Pioneer** route across the Kimberley includes a stop in town (to Broome 1 per day, $27; to Kununurra 1 per day, $103). Next to the terminal, **Derby Backpackers Lodge** (tel. 9191 1233; fax 9191 1576) does somersaults to entice budget travelers to stay, providing a kitchen, TV room, laundry facilities, and free linens and luggage storage. Dorm beds are $10; the fourth night is free.

GIBB RIVER ROAD: FROM DERBY TO KUNUNURRA

Eight kilometers south of Derby, a rugged 4WD track strikes eastward into the Kimberley. This shortcut to Kununurra provides access to some of the more remarkable sights in the region. **Windjana Gorge,** a 3.5km crevasse in the limestone landscape that looms as high as 100m over the Lennard River, is 14km from Derby (a 2hr. drive) and 150km from Fitzroy Crossing (3hr.). Inexpensive camping is available. Toward Fitzroy, **Tunnel Creek,** a 750m trench carved through a limestone range, is usually shallow enough to wade across in the dry season. The creek is 180km from Derby and 115km from Fitzroy (2½hr. driving time from either). The creek site has toilets but no camping facilities. The access road that serves these two attractions continues south to rejoin the Great Northern Hwy.

Farther east, the Gibb River meanders past a 100m chain of cascades at **Bell Creek Gorge** (camping $5) and then runs on to **Mt. Barnett.** Up to this point, all roadways are harsh but passable for sedans, but 4WD is necessary to push eastward. On the way, the unforgiving **Kalumburu Rd.** branches north toward the remote **Mitchell Falls,** a four-cataract waterfall plunging into the Indian Ocean and perhaps the most isolated sight in the Kimberley. These roads are accessible only from April to October when weather permits; don't venture onto the Gibb River Rd. without first registering with the tourist office at either end.

Fitzroy Crossing

This outpost on the Great Northern Hwy. is 256km east of Derby. Aside from its proximity to Tunnel Creek and Windjana Gorge, Fitzroy is a 20-minute drive from **Geikie Gorge,** part of the 350-million-year-old Devonian reef that once covered this region. Geikie ("geeky") Gorge has toilet and water facilities but no camping (open April-Oct.). Geikie is home to freshwater crocs and has colorful walls that can be explored on boat cruises. The few sights in Fitzroy itself pertain to its 100-year heritage. The **tourist office** (tel. 9191 5355) is at the entrance to town (open daily April-Oct.). There are **police** (tel. 9191 5000) on McLarty Rd., a **hospital** (tel. 9191 5001) on Fallon Rd., and a **post office** (tel. 9191 5060). **Greyhound Pioneer** stops once each day heading in either direction. Camping at **Crossing Inn** (tel. 9191 5080; fax 9191 5208) costs $5 per person (with power $13 for 2 people, $6 each additional).

Halls Creek

Halls Creek rushed into existence in 1885 for a short-lived gold rush but lives on as a convenient base for the Wolfe Creek Meteorite Crater and the Bungle Bungle Range. This oasis 288km east of Fitzroy Crossing lies along the Great Northern Hwy. at the edge of the Great Sandy Desert. When the **tourist center** (tel. 9168 6262; open April-Sept. Mon.-Fri. 8am-4pm) is closed, the map-and-info board in the town park suffices. Halls Creek has **police** (tel. 9168 6000), a **hospital** (tel. 9168 6003), a **post office** (tel. 9168 6111), and petrol available every day. **Greyhound Pioneer** rumbles through once each day bound in either direction. The **Shell Road House** (tel. 9168 6060; fax 9168 6018) has accommodations (dorms $15; twins $50; quads $75).

An interesting quartz formation called **China Wall** is 6km north of town, and Halls Creek is also near two of the Kimberley's most famous sights. The **Wolfe Creek Meteorite Crater,** the world's second largest, opens its gaping maw 145km (2hr.) south of town toward Alice Springs on Tanami Rd. A short walk runs along the crater lip, and camping and fuel are available at nearby Carranya Station (tel. 9168 8927). Halls Creek is also only 109km south of the turnoff to the renowned Bungle Bungles in Purnululu National Park.

The Bungle Bungles (Purnululu National Park)

Covering 45,000 hectares and poised 200m above the surrounding land, the majestic Bungle Bungles contain sheer edges, canyons, and gorges cut by seasonal rivulets and the passage of time. The name is something of a mystery. Perhaps it comes from Purnululu, an Aboriginal word for limestone; perhaps it comes from bundle bundle, the name for the local grass. Whatever its etymology, the name is quirkily appropriate for this bumpy, curvy massif that resembles an egg-carton cushion. Millions of years of rain eroded the fragile limestone of this ancient plateau, sculpting it into thousands of smooth, free-standing sandstone towers. Orange silica and black lichen create colored designs on these columns.

The 4WD-only **Spring Creek Track** (from Halls Creek, 109km north, 4hr.; from Kununurra, 250km south, 5hr.) turns eastward from the Great Northern Hwy. and runs 55km to the Bungles. The Track passes the **ranger station** (self-registered 7-day admission $11, children $1) and comes to a three-way intersection. To the left, 7km away, is the **Kurrajong camping area** (tent sites, water, toilets, and firewood; free). To the right, 13km farther, the **Walardi campground** has similar facilities. The ranger station is staffed only during the dry season. The park closes January through March.

Turkey Creek (or **Warmun**) is the last town north of the Spring Creek Track turnoff. Less than 100km from the park, it can serve as a stopover for those driving from Kununurra. The **Turkey Creek Roadhouse** (tel. 9168 7882; fax 9168 7925; reception open daily 6:30am-6:30pm) offers dorms ($17.50) and singles ($30). Tent sites are $5 per person; caravan sites are $10, with power $15.

A handful of walking tracks meander along the edge of the massif and into its colossal crevasses. The most popular hike is thorough **Cathedral Gorge,** starting from a parking lot 25km south of the ranger station (easy-to-moderate 2km return). The **Piccaninny Gorge** hike (moderate-to-difficult 30km) requires more stamina and a night in the bush. Register with the rangers before beginning the walk from the same lot. The easy-to-moderate **Echidna Chasm walk** (2km round-trip) starts 21km north of the ranger base. In the same vicinity, the more challenging **froghole** (1.4km return) and **mini palms** (3km) gorge walks leave from a second parking lot.

More extensive ground exploration requires taking a **4WD tour,** from Halls Creek or Kununurra. The other very popular way to experience the Bungle Bungles is by air. **Scenic flights** are so common that aircraft are required to fly an established one-way flight path, which skims through deep canyons and sweeps past steep walls. **Alligator Airways** (tel. 9168 1333 or 1800 632 533; fax 9168 2704) makes an excellent two-hour flight over the Bungles and passes Lake Argyle, the Argyle Diamond Mine, and the Kununurra dams along the way ($150, backpackers $140).

Kununurra

Kununurra's establishment in the cattleland of the East Kimberley was a relatively recent event, part of the 30-year-old Ord Irrigation Project, a massive rerouting of the nearby Ord River to bring water to 13,000 hectares of agricultural land. Fittingly, the settlement's name means "Big Waters." Kununurra is the eastern endpoint of the Kimberley and thus a threshold over which visitors pass on their way into the region. The main reasons travelers visit are to arrange tours of the rugged, fantastic landscape around the place or to toil in the newly irrigated land for some immediate cash.

ORIENTATION AND PRACTICAL INFORMATION

Kununurra (cun-ah-NOOR-ah) is a small town, but it is replete with parks and lawns that make strolls seem longer and spaces larger than they are. Just inside the WA border, Kununurra's checkpoint asks travelers entering from Northern Territory to surrender produce, seeds, and honey. The town has just a few main roads. **Messmate Way** turns off the Victoria Hwy. at a 24-hour fuel station and heads to the center of town, where it crosses **Konkerberry Dr.** at a traffic circle and ends at **Coolibah Dr.**

Tourist Office: Kununurra Tourist Bureau (tel. 9168 1177; fax 9168 2598), on Coolibah Dr., 100m off Messmate. Open Mon.-Fri. 8am-5pm, Sat.-Sun. 8:30am-5pm.
Budget Travel: Traveland (tel. 9168 1888) is on Papuana St. between Konkerberry Dr. and Coolibah St.
Commonwealth Bank (tel. 9169 1511), at Cotton Tree and Coolibah Dr. Open Mon.-Thurs. 9:30am-4pm, Fri. 9:30am-5pm. 24hr. **ATM.**
Buses: Greyhound Pioneer runs to: Broome (1 per day, 4:30pm, $132) and Darwin (1 per day, 9:40am, $97) via Katherine ($54). Book at tourist office; buses stop across the street.
Taxis: Spuds Taxis can be summoned by rubbing a lamp and dialing 9168 2553.
Car Rental: Handy, 653 Bandicoot Dr. (tel. 9168 2207, after hours 9168 2368; fax 9168 2208), has stand-by rates and vehicle delivery. Also **Territory** (tel. 9169 1911; fax 9169 1912), **Budget,** 947 Mango St. (tel. 9168 2033 or 1800 649 800; fax 9168 2433; mobile tel. 015 470 180), and **Avis** (tel. 9169 1258; fax 9168 2093).
Bike Rental: Kununurra Backpackers rents from $10 per day.
Kununurra Shopping Centre on Konkerberry Dr. contains **Amcal Chemist** (tel. 9168 1111) and **Ansett** (tel. 9168 1622; fax 9168 2584), which serves the airport west of town on the Victoria Hwy. The shopping center also has the best grocery in town: **Charlie Carters,** open Mon.-Fri. 7am-6pm, Sat. 7am-5pm, Sun. 8am-5pm. The smaller **Tuckerbox** is at the corner of White Gum and Coolibah Dr.
Hospital: (24hr. tel. 9168 1522), on Coolibah Dr. 100m from the end of Messmate.
Post Office: Broome Post Office (tel. 9168 1395), across the street from the tourist office. Open Mon.-Fri. 8:45am-5pm. **Postal code** 6743.
Phone Code: 08.

ACCOMMODATIONS

There are two competing backpacker lodges in Kununurra, both small enough to necessitate reservations in the dry season.

Desert Inn Oasis (tel. 9168 2702 or 1800 805 010) is closest to town. Take Konkerberry Dr. past the Shopping Centre to Trustania St., where a sign points to the lodge near that corner. A relaxing hostel with a pool patio, shaded lounge areas, spacious, moderately nice kitchen, and a purple bus for a reception office. Reception open daily 8am-noon and 4-6pm. Check-out 9am. Courtesy shuttle to Greyhound station. Comfortably spartan dorms with A/C $14; doubles $40. Plates and cutlery deposit $10. Laundry $2.

Kununurra Backpackers, 111 Nutwood Cir. (tel. 9169 1998 or 1800 641 998; fax 9168 3998), is a 15min. walk toward the imposing Kelly's Knob. From the bus station or tourist office, take the free shuttle service. The main building of this slightly disheveled lodge has bunkrooms along a carpeted hall that share a clean bath and rundown dining area. Store room. Reception has a safe. Dorms with A/C $14; twins $36; triples $55. VIP. Another building has a TV room and lower-grade digs for fruitpickers: weekly dorms $90. Key and linens deposit $10. Wash $2.

Camping: Town Caravan Park (tel. 9168 1763) is the most central campground. It's located behind the Hotel Kununurra. There's no direct path: take a left on Konkerberry and another left on Bloodwood Dr. and the entrance is 30m on your left. Outdoor communal kitchen plus new bathrooms (wheelchair accessible). Sites $7 per person; with power $16 for 2 people, $7 each additional. If Town is full, try **Kimberleyland Holiday Park** (tel. 9168 1280; fax 9168 1050), just west of Messmate Way on the Victoria Hwy.

FOOD

Cheap, greasy food is easy to come by in Kununurra. Only a few restaurants surpass this standard. The **Hot Gossip Cafe** (tel. 9169 1377), on Konkerberry Dr. in the Kununurra Shopping Centre, has a deli atmosphere with a dozen or so tables tucked into a petite mirrored room. The conventional menu is served all day (continental breakfast $5, burgers galore $5-6), and a tasty Chinese menu is added for dinner (vegetable fried rice $6.50, peppered beef $12.50). Reserve a couple of hours ahead (open Mon.-Sat. 8am-8:30pm, Sun. 5-8:30pm). **Rumours Patisserie** is an air-conditioned burger-and-milkshake counter that satiates the ravenous crowds of Kununurra Shopping Centre (patisserie open Mon.-Fri. 8am-6pm, Sat.-Sun. 9am-5pm). **Gullivers Tavern** (tel. 9168 1666), on Konkerberry Dr. at Cotton Tree, is the town's main pub and also serves counter meals (open Mon.-Thurs. 11am-11pm, Fri. 11am-1am, Sat. 11am-midnight, Sun. noon-10pm).

SIGHTS

An impressive rock peak at the north end of town offers some perspective on the stunning geography around Kununurra. **Kelly's Knob** can be reached by taking Konkerberry Dr. to the end, turning left on Ironwood, right on Speargrass, and right again at the walking path to the peak. It's a trek to the top, but that's why the view is so great. To the east, **Hidden Valley (Mirima) National Park** gives a nearby sampling of the bumpy sandstone formations in the Bungle Bungle range to the south. These "mini Bungle Bungles" are about 3km out of town and have walking tracks but no camping. Take Ironwood Dr. from the Victoria Hwy., turn right on Barringtonia Ave. and left on Hidden Valley Rd.

The **Ord River Diversion Dam** is the result of the irrigation project that gave the Kununurra region its current topography. Finished in 1963, the 335m-long dam holds back the Ord River into a plump supply of water on its south side **(Lake Kununurra).** The lake irrigates the land above and below it, and provides a sanctuary for an estimated 7000 freshwater crocodiles. The Victoria Hwy. passes by the lake and over the dam to cross the Ord River 7km west of town.

The Packsaddle Plains and the Ivanhoe Plains together are the **Ord River Irrigation Area,** the agricultural brainchild of the government to create exceptionally fertile land. Backpackers hoping to fund further sojourns find work at these farms, which grow bananas, melons, chickpeas, and dozens of other crops. Several farms invite visitors to witness, taste, and purchase the fruits of this labor.

■ Near Kununurra

Lake Argyle is the most dramatic geographical creation of the Ord River Irrigation Scheme. It came to life in 1972 with the building of a second dike, the Ord River Top Dam, 50km upstream (south) of the Diversion Dam. The Top Dam holds back the **largest freshwater body in the southern hemisphere.** At 70km long, Lake Argyle covers what was once a million-acre cattle station. Testimony to man's influence on the Australian landscape, Lake Argyle, which can hold 55 Sydney Harbours at full capacity, was created as a backup reservoir lest a drought leave too little water at Lake Kununurra. Islands—once hills—and the bony branches of dead trees rise from the shallows, still adjusting to the new waterline.

Lake Argyle Tourist Village is 35km east of Kununurra on the Victoria Hwy. and another 35km down a marked access road. Cruise tours allow closer inspection of birds, freshies, rock wallabies, and other denizens of this improvised wildlife habitat. A scenic flight can combine Lake Argyle and the Bungle Bungles; try **Alligator Airways** (tel. 9168 1333 or 1800 632 533; fax 9168 2704).

Southwest of Lake Argyle near the Bow River crossing, the **Argyle Diamond Mine** is an open-cut pit that produces eight tons of diamonds a year—34% of global output. Unfortunately, **Belray Diamond Tours** (tel. 9168 1014; fax 9168 2704) has snagged exclusive booking rights on air and coach tours.

Appendix

CLIMATE

The charts below complement **When to Go** (p. 1).

Average Temperature

Temperature in °C/°F	January		April		July		October	
	High	Low	High	Low	High	Low	High	Low
Adelaide	29/84	17/63	22/72	12/54	15/59	8/46	22/72	14/57
Alice Springs	36/97	21/70	28/82	13/55	19/66	4/39	31/88	15/59
Brisbane	29/84	21/70	26/79	17/63	20/68	10/50	26/79	16/61
Cairns	31/88	24/75	29/84	22/72	26/79	17/63	29/84	20/68
Canberra	28/82	13/55	20/68	7/45	11/52	0/32	19/66	6/43
Darwin	32/90	25/77	32/90	25/77	30/86	20/68	32/90	25/77
Hobart	22/72	12/54	17/63	9/48	12/54	4/39	17/63	8/46
Melbourne	26/79	14/57	20/68	11/52	13/55	6/43	20/68	9/48
Perth	30/86	18/64	25/77	14/57	18/64	9/48	22/72	12/54
Sydney	26/79	19/66	22/72	15/59	16/61	8/46	22/72	13/55

To convert from °C to °F, multiply by 1.8 and add 32. For a rough approximation, double the Celsius and add 25. To convert from °F to °C, subtract 32 and multiply by 0.55.

°C	-5	0	5	10	15	20	25	30	35	40
°F	23	32	41	50	59	68	77	86	95	104

Average Rainfall

Average Rainfall (mm)	Jan	Feb	Mar	Apr	May	Jun	July	Aug	Sep	Oct	Nov	Dec
Adelaide	19	6	35	52	57	70	83	74	62	45	32	21
Alice Springs	38	45	34	14	17	15	17	12	10	22	25	36
Brisbane	163	158	141	87	73	68	56	47	47	77	98	134
Cairns	424	441	449	190	94	47	28	27	34	38	87	173
Canberra	60	57	54	49	48	37	39	48	52	69	61	51
Darwin	404	430	349	63	35	8	1	2	19	73	116	313
Hobart	48	40	47	53	49	57	53	52	53	63	56	57
Melbourne	48	48	52	58	58	49	48	51	59	68	59	58
Perth	8	12	19	45	123	183	173	137	80	54	21	14
Sydney	102	113	135	124	121	131	100	80	69	78	81	78

HOLIDAYS AND FESTIVALS

Banks, museums, and other public buildings are often closed or operate with reduced hours on the following **public holidays,** which fall on weekdays. During **school holidays,** many Australians go on vacation, and accommodations fill up, often increasing prices. Public transportation may run on weekend schedules during school holidays. Cities and towns across Australia hold countless festivals and crafts fairs throughout the year, with most taking place during the summer months (Dec.-Feb.). Ask the local tourist offices for more information on these local festivals. The **Mardi Gras Parade** in Sydney, Australia's biggest gay and lesbian festival, will be held on February 28 in 1998.

Public Holidays 1998

January 1	New Year's Day
January 26	Australia Day
April 9	Maundy Thursday (Thursday before Easter)
April 10	Good Friday (Friday before Easter)
April 13	Monday after Easter
April 25	Anzac Day
October 5	The October eight-hour weekend (a.k.a. Labour Day)
December 25	Christmas
December 26	Boxing Day
December 28	Business day following Christmas

School Holidays 1998

December 21-January 23	Monday before Christmas through most of January
April 9-April 17	Thursday before Easter through Friday after Easter
June 29-July 10	Last Monday in June through second Friday in July
September 28-October 9	Last Monday in September through second Friday in October
Summer (December-January)	Seven weeks o' fun.

TELEPHONE CODES

The Australian telephone system has recently moved to a universal system, in which standard phone numbers are composed of eight digits with an associated two-digit **phone code.** There are four phone codes in total, assigned to regions that nearly, but not exactly, correspond to state boundaries. When ringing an Australian city from a different state or region within Australia, dial the proper phone code before the eight-digit local number. **You may have to dial the phone code to make a call within a region or state when distances between cities are large.**

Phone codes below are given by both state and region. Some border towns take the phone code of the neighboring state.

Central East Region	02	ACT New South Wales some Vic and Qld border areas
South East Region	03	Tasmania Victoria some NSW border areas
North East Region	07	Queensland some NSW border areas
Central and West Region	08	Northern Territory South Australia Western Australia some NSW border areas

Free Operator Calls in Australia

	Local	National	International
Operator Assisted	0176	0176	0107
Directory Assistance	013	0175	0103
Service Difficulties	1100	1100	0100

International Calls

To **call Australia from overseas,** first dial the international access prefix to get out of the country you are calling from (011 from Canada; 00 from New Zealand; 00 from the U.K.; 011 from the U.S.). Then dial 61 (Australia's country code), then the regional phone code (see above) without the initial 0, and finally the eight-digit local number. For example, to call the Sydney Opera House (in New South Wales; tel. 9250 7250) from the U.S., dial 011-61-2-9250-7250. To call from the U.K., dial: 00-61-2-9250-7250.

To **call overseas from Australia,** dial **0011** (Australia's international access prefix). Then dial the appropriate country code for the country you are trying to reach (see below), and finally the area code and local number. **Country codes** include:

Australia	61
Austria	43
Canada	1
Germany	49
Ireland	353
New Zealand	64
S. Africa	27
U.K.	44
U.S.	1

If you prefer to speak to an operator from your home country (useful when calling collect or using a calling card), use a **country direct number.** In Australia, dial:

Canada	Teleglobe: 1800 881 490
Ireland	Telecom: 1800 881 353
New Zealand	Telecom: 1800 881 640
U.K.	Telecom operator: 1800 881 440 Telecom automatic: 1800 881 440
U.S.	AT&T: 1800 881 011 MCI: 1800 881 100 or 1800 551 111 Sprint: 1800 881 877

TIME ZONES

The following table should help you convert time between different Australian states, New York City, London, and Greenwich Mean Time. Because the country is in the southern hemisphere, Australian states that observe daylight savings or summer time begin to do so just as the northern hemisphere is reverting back to standard time, so the difference between the two hemispheres can vary by as much as two hours. To use the following table, **imagine it is noon, Greenwich Mean Time (GMT),** and use the time you find below to calculate the difference in number of hours. The first column represents the difference between standard time in each city/state and GMT.

At Noon, Greenwich Mean Time (GMT)	GMT+/-	last Sunday in Oct. to last Sunday in March	last Sunday in March to first Sunday in Oct.	first Sunday in Oct. to last Sunday in Oct.
ACT	+10	11pm	10pm	10pm
New South Wales	+10	11pm	10pm	10pm
Northern Territory	+9½	9:30pm	9:30pm	9:30pm
Queensland	+10	10pm	10pm	10pm
South Australia	+9½	10:30pm	9:30pm	9:30pm
Tasmania	+10	11pm	10pm	11pm
Victoria	+10	11pm	10pm	10pm
Western Australia	+8	8pm	8pm	8pm
New York City	- 5	7am	8am	8am
London	+0	noon	1pm	1pm

MEASUREMENTS

Australians generally use the metric system, creating occasional confusion for Americans who are used to the British system of weights and measures. The following is a list of U.S. units and their metric equivalents.

1 inch = 25 millimeters (mm)	1mm = 0.04 inches (in.)
1 foot = 0.30 meters (m)	1m = 3.33 feet (ft.)
1 yard = 0.91m	1m = 1.1 yards (yd.)
1 mile = 1.61kilometers (km)	1km = 0.62 miles (mi.)
1 ounce = 25 grams (g)	1g = 0.04 ounces (oz.)
1 pound = 0.45 kilograms (kg)	1kg = 2.22 pounds (lb.)
1 quart = 0.94 liters (L)	1L = 1.06 quarts (qt.)

LANGUAGE: GLOSSARY OF STRINE

Strine is 'stralian for "Australian." You see, the first trick to good Australian slang is to abbreviate everything. It's hard to miss the trend: **Oz** for Australia, **abo** for Aboriginal, and **ute** for utility (pick-up) truck. Some words aren't as easy to guess, and nothing is sacred: **rezo** is a residential college, and **reffo** is a refugee. A **smoko** is afternoon tea or coffee (when you can step out of the office for a much-needed smoke). A **cuppa** is a cup of tea or coffee, which goes well with a **sammy** (sandwich) or with **brekkie** (breakfast). **Pommies** are Englishmen. (The origin of this term is hotly debated. One myth connects it to "pomegranate," referring to stereotypically rosy cheeks. Another leads back to the uniforms of the first convicts, which bore the acronym "POHMIE," Prisoners Of Her Majesty In Exile.)

The second trick is to rhyme whenever possible. While **Euros** are Europeans and **touros** are Australian tourists (usually surfers out of their own district), **seppos** are Americans. (Americans are Yanks, Yanks rhymes with tanks, and the worst kind of tanks are septic tanks. You could probably think of a more direct link, if you tried.) **Noahs** are sharks (shark rhymes with ark, Noah built an ark), and **"I'm on the dog,"** actually means "I'm on the phone," since bone rhymes with phone, and there's that whole dog-bone connection. Even **mate,** the quintessential 'strine word for friend or buddy, has a rhyming slang equivalent: references to **Chinas** have nothing to do with nationality. Think China. Think china plates. Think mates. You're on your way to speaking 'strine.

A

ablution block shower/toilet block at a campground

abseil rappel

ace awesome

ANZAC Australia-New Zealand Army Corps (Anzac biscuits are honey-oat cookies)

arvo afternoon

Aussie Australian (pronounced "Ozzie": thus, Australia is Oz)

B

backpackers a hostel

barbie barbecue

belt bag fanny pack (don't say "fanny" in Oz: it's a crude word for a part of the female anatomy)

billabong a watering hole

biscuit cookie

bitumen a rough black asphalt used to pave roads ("BICH-uh-min")

bluey someone with red hair (seriously)

book reserve a tour or accommodations ("you need to book 2 weeks in advance")

bottle shop liquor store

brekkie breakfast

bush wilderness (hiking is often called bushwalking)

busk play music on the street for money

BYO bring your own alcohol (at restaurants, often restricted to wine)

C

campervan mobile home, RV

caravan trailer, like a campervan without the cab

carpark parking lot

chips thick french fries or "home fries," usually served with vinegar and salt

chook chicken

concession discount; usually applies to students, seniors, or children, sometimes only to Australian students and pensioners.

cordial concentrated fruit juice

D

dag one who is daggy (usage is common, often benevolent)

daggy unfashionable, unhip, goofy, silly

damper traditionally unleavened bread

Devonshire tea and scones, often served in the late afternoon

doona, duvet comforter, feather blanket

"drier than a dead dingo's donger" very thirsty

dummy pacifier (for infants)

E

en suite with bath

entree appetizer ("main"=American entree)

esky a cooler (originally from the brand name Eskimo)

excess deductible (as in car insurance)

F

fair dinkum genuine, authentic

fairy floss cotton candy

feral wild, grunge-style (a common slang term)

flash fancy, snazzy, upscale, glamorous

"flat out like a lizard drinking" doing nothing

flat white coffee with hot milk and a touch of foam

free call toll-free call

fossicking gem-hunting and gold-sifting

G

g'day hello

glasshouse greenhouse

ground floor American first floor ("first floor" is the second floor, etc.)

H

hire to rent ("let's hire a bike for the day")

hoon a loud-mouthed show-off

I

icy-pole frozen sugared water on a stick (Popsicle)

J

jumper, jersey sweater, sweatshirt

jackaroo/ jillaroo male/female station hands in training

K

keen surprisingly popular term of respect: "a keen surfer"

Kiwi a New Zealander

L

late for restaurants, anywhere from 9pm-midnight; for pubs, anywhere from

licensed legally serves alcohol (as in a restaurant)

lollies candies

M

magic really wonderful, special: "that beach—it's magic"

mate friend, buddy (used broadly)

milk bar convenience store

moke an open-air, no-doors, "looks-like-a-golf-cart" automobile

N

nappy diaper

newsagent newstand/convenience store

"no worries" sure, fine, often substituted for "you're welcome"

O

ocker anyone you might mistake for Crocodile Dundee; a hick

"odds and sods" odds and ends

"off like a bucket of prawns in the sun" leaving like lightning

off-peak return round-trip fare at a time other than during rush hour

ordinary Bad. An "ordinary" road is full of potholes.

Oz Australia

P

pavlova a creamy meringue dessert garnished with fruit

pensioner senior citizen (someone on a pension)

petrol gasoline

piss beer (usually)

pokies gambling machines

powerpoint outlet (also electrical hookup for tents or caravans)

pram stroller (for a baby)

prawn jumbo shrimp

pub A pub. Never, never "bar." Pub.

push bike bicycle

Q

Queenslander large houses with high ceilings and verandas built in an architectural style developed in—you guess where.

R

return round-trip

'roo as in kanga-

roundabout rotary

S

sandgroper a West Australian (also Westralian)

sauce Usually tomato sauce. No such word as ketchup here. No such thing, either.

serviette napkin

sheila slang for a woman

shout (a round of x) Buy you (a round of x), as in "I'll shout you a drink." You can also participate in a shout at a pub with a small group of people. Person #1 buys the first round of drinks, #2 buys the second round, etc.

side team (in Aussie Football)

skivvie turtleneck sweater

snag or sanger sausage

spider ice cream float

squiz a look ("the huge fiberglass pineapple is worth a squiz")

stone the crows! an expression of surprise

'strine Aussie dialect (from Australian "au-STRI'NE")

suss figure out, sort out

T

ta (rhymes with la) Short for thank you–usually muttered under breath

TAB shop to place bets, sometimes in pubs

TAFE Technical and Further Education. Nationwide community education schools. For budget travelers—they're heaven. Excellent cooking schools with cheapo meals.

takeaway food to go (equivalent to the American take-out)

Tassie Tasmania ("TAZ-zie")

torch flashlight

touch wood knock on wood

track suit sweat suit, jogging suit

tucker Food. "Bush tucker" refers to traditional Aboriginal wild foods

U

uni university ("YOU-nee")

unsealed Unpaved roads (usually gravel) in rural areas. Cycling on them is asking for death (but it's even worse in New Zealand).

ute utility vehicle (pick-up)

upmarket upscale, expensive

V **Vegemite** yeast-extract spread for toast and sandwiches

W **walkabout** to spontaneously set off across the countryside

X **XXXX** pronounced "four-ex," a brand of beer

Y **yakka** hard work

yute see "ute"

Z **zed** Americans' letter "zee"

AUSTRALIAN BEER TERMINOLOGY

The frothy, liquid gold which is such a celebrated part of Australian life has spawned its own vocabulary. Because of the hot climate, Australian pubs generally eschew the standard, Imperial pint in favor of smaller portions which stay cold to the bottom of the glass. Thus, size is a major variable in this argot of ale. The following handy list should save you from leaving yourself parched with a mere Pony or drowning in a Darwin Stubbie. (If your beer-starved brain can't process this information, ordering by size, in ounces, is a shortcut recognized in most places; on the mainland, try a "5," "7," "10," or "15." In Tasmania, order using the numbers "6," "8," "10," or "20.")

Beer: 7 oz. in Qld and Vic; 15 oz. in NSW; 10 oz. elsewhere	**Middy:** 285mL (10 oz.), used in NSW and SA
Bludger: one who cannot finish a full cycle of shouts with his or her drinking mates	**Pint:** 560mL (20 oz.) in the U.K. and the U.S.; 425mL (15 oz.) in SA
Butcher: 200mL (7 oz.) in SA	**Pony:** 140mL (5 oz.)
Darwin Stubbie: 1.25L bottle in NT	**Pot:** 285mL (10 oz.) in Qld and Vic
Glass: 200mL (7 oz.) in Qld and Vic	**Real Pint:** 560mL (20 oz.); used in SA or Tas to get a proper glass of beer
Handle: 10 oz. glass with a handle	**Schooner:** 425mL (15 oz.) in NSW; 285mL (10 oz.) in SA
Jug: pitcher	**Shout:** a round; it is common practice to drink by shouts with each participant taking a turn at buying
Long neck: 750mL bottle	**Stubbie:** 375mL bottle **Tinny:** 375mL can

Index

C

G

H

M

N

Y

Z

★Let's Go 1998 Reader Questionnaire★

Please fill this out and return it to **Let's Go, St. Martin's Press,** 175 Fifth Ave., New York, NY 10010-7848. All respondents will receive a free subscription to ***The Yellowjacket*, the Let's Go Newsletter**.

Name: ______________________________

Address: ______________________________

City: ________________ **State:** ______ **Zip/Postal Code:** ________

Email: ________________ **Which book(s) did you use?**____________

How old are you? under 19 19-24 25-34 35-44 45-54 55 or over

Are you (circle one) in high school in college in graduate school employed retired between jobs

Have you used Let's Go before? yes no **Would you use it again?** yes no

How did you first hear about Let's Go? friend store clerk television bookstore display advertisement/promotion review other

Why did you choose Let's Go (circle up to two)? reputation budget focus price writing style annual updating other: ____________

Which other guides have you used, if any? Frommer's $-a-day Fodor's Rough Guides Lonely Planet Berkeley Rick Steves other: ____________

Is Let's Go the best guidebook? yes no

If not, which do you prefer? ____________

Please rank each of the following parts of Let's Go 1 to 5 (1=needs improvement, 5=perfect). packaging/cover practical information accommodations food cultural introduction sights practical introduction ("Essentials") directions entertainment gay/lesbian information maps other: ____________

How would you like to see the books improved? (continue on separate page, if necessary)______________________________

____

How long was your trip? one week two weeks three weeks one month two months or more

Which countries did you visit? ____________

What was your average daily budget, not including flights? ____________

Have you traveled extensively before? yes no

Do you buy a separate map when you visit a foreign city? yes no

Have you seen the Let's Go Map Guides? yes no

Have you used a Let's Go Map Guide? yes no

If you have, would you recommend them to others? yes no

Did you use the Internet to plan your trip? yes no

Would you use a Let's Go: recreational (e.g. skiing) guide gay/lesbian guide adventure/trekking guide phrasebook general travel information guide

Which of the following destinations do you hope to visit in the next three to five years (circle one)? South Africa China South America Russia Caribbean Scandinavia other: ____________

Where did you buy your guidebook? Internet chain bookstore independent bookstore college bookstore travel store other: ____________